The Blackwell Companion
to Paul

Blackwell Companions to Religion

The Blackwell Companions to Religion series presents a collection of the most recent scholarship and knowledge about world religions. Each volume draws together newly-commissioned essays by distinguished authors in the field, and is presented in a style which is accessible to undergraduate students, as well as scholars and the interested general reader. These volumes approach the subject in a creative and forward-thinking style, providing a forum in which leading scholars in the field can make their views and research available to a wider audience.

Published

The Blackwell Companion to Paul

Edited by

Stephen Westerholm

WILEY-BLACKWELL

A John Wiley & Sons, Ltd., Publication

Library of Congress Cataloging-in-Publication Data is available on request
ISBN 9781405188449

A catalogue record for this book is available from the British Library.

This book is published in the following electronic formats: ePDFs 9781444395754; Wiley Online Library 9781444395778; ePub 9781444395761

Set in 10/12.5 pt Photina by Toppan Best-set Premedia Limited
Printed and bound in Singapore by Markono Print Media Pte Ltd

1   2011

For Martin and Jenna

μειζοτέραν τούτων οὐκ ἔχω χαράν,
ἵνα ἀκούω τὰ ἐμὰ τέκνα ἐν τῇ ἀληθείᾳ περιπατοῦντα

Contents

Notes on Contributors

Jean-Noël Aletti is Professor of New Testament Exegesis at the Pontifical Biblical Institute in Rome. Among his fields of expertise are the Pauline epistles (on which he has published several commentaries) and Greco-Roman rhetoric and epistolography. His study *God's Justice in Romans* has been translated into English.

Lewis Ayres is Bede Chair in Catholic Theology at Durham University. His interests in the early church's Trinitarian thought and use of Scripture are reflected in his monographs *Nicaea and its Legacy: An Approach to Fourth-Century Trinitarian Theology* and *Augustine and the Trinity*.

John M. G. Barclay is Lightfoot Professor of Divinity at Durham University and editor of *New Testament Studies*. Major publications include *Jews in the Mediterranean Diaspora*, a translation and commentary on Josephus's *Against Apion*, and *Obeying the Truth: Paul's Ethics in Galatians*. A study of Paul's theology of grace is forthcoming.

Richard E. Burnett is Professor of Systematic Theology at Erskine Theological Seminary. A specialist in the study of John Calvin and Karl Barth, he has published *Karl Barth's Theological Exegesis: The Hermeneutical Principles of the* Römerbrief *Period* and is the editor of the forthcoming *Westminster Handbook to Karl Barth*.

Stephen Chester is Professor of New Testament at North Park Theological Seminary. He has published *Conversion at Corinth: Perspectives on Conversion in Paul's Theology and the Corinthian Church* as well as a number of studies on Reformation interpretations of Paul.

Ralph Del Colle is Associate Professor of Theology at Marquette University. The co-editor of the *International Journal of Systematic Theology*, he has published *Christ and the Spirit: Spirit Christology in Trinitarian Perspective* and numerous studies on Trinitarian theology, pneumatology, and the doctrine of grace.

James D. G. Dunn is Emeritus Lightfoot Professor of Divinity at Durham University. Among his major monographs may be mentioned commentaries on Romans, Galatians, Colossians, and Philemon; *The Theology of Paul the Apostle*; *Jesus Remembered*; and *Beginning from Jerusalem*.

Simon J. Gathercole is Senior Lecturer in New Testament Studies and Fellow, Fitzwilliam College, University of Cambridge. Currently the editor of the *Journal for the Study of the New Testament*, he has published monographs on the Gospel of Judas, Christology in the synoptic gospels, and Pauline soteriology.

Beverly Roberts Gaventa is Helen H. P. Manson Professor of New Testament Interpretation and Exegesis at Princeton Theological Seminary. In addition to *Our Mother Saint Paul* and *Mary: Glimpses of the Mother of Jesus*, she has published commentaries on Acts and the Thessalonian epistles, and is currently preparing a commentary on Romans.

Christopher A. Hall is Chancellor of Eastern University and Dean of Palmer Theological Seminary. The associate editor of the Ancient Christian Commentary on Scripture series, he has co-edited the volume on Mark's Gospel and published *Reading Scripture with the Church Fathers*; *Studying Theology with the Church Fathers*; and *Worshiping with the Church Fathers*.

Nicholas M. Healy is Professor of Theology and Religious Studies and Associate Dean at the College of Liberal Arts and Sciences, St. John's University. Key publications include *Thomas Aquinas: Theologian of the Christian Life* and (reflecting his interest in ecclesiology) *Church, World and the Christian Life: Practical-Prophetic Ecclesiology*.

John Paul Heil is Professor of New Testament at The Catholic University of America. He has published books on Romans, 1 Corinthians, Ephesians, Colossians, Philippians, and Hebrews, in addition to several monographs on the Gospels.

Arland J. Hultgren is Asher O. and Carrie Nasby Professor of New Testament at Luther Seminary. His published works, covering a wide range of topics in the study of Early Christianity, include *The Parables of Jesus*; *Paul's Gospel and Mission*; *Christ and His Benefits*; *The Rise of Normative Christianity*; and *Paul's Letter to the Romans: A Commentary*.

David Lyle Jeffrey is Distinguished Professor of Literature and Humanities at Baylor University and a Fellow of the Royal Society of Canada. He was general editor and co-author of *A Dictionary of Biblical Tradition in English Literature*. Other monographs include *People of the Book*; *House of the Interpreter*; and a forthcoming theological commentary on Luke.

Robin M. Jensen is Luce Chancellor's Professor of the History of Christian Art and Worship at Vanderbilt University. Key publications include *Understanding Early Christian Art*; *Face to Face: The Portrait of the Divine in Early Christianity*; and *Living Water: Images, Symbols, and Settings of Early Christian Baptism*.

Dirk Jongkind is Fellow and Graduate Tutor at St. Edmund's College, University of Cambridge, and Research Fellow at Tyndale House. He has broad interests in epigraphy, papyrology, and archaeology in the Greco-Roman world, and a special interest in the textual criticism of the Greek Bible, reflected in his monograph *Scribal Habits in Codex Sinaiticus*.

Craig S. Keener is Professor of New Testament at Palmer Theological Seminary, Eastern University. A prolific author, he has published commentaries on Matthew, John, Romans, 1 and 2 Corinthians, and Revelation. Other books include *The Historical Jesus of the Gospels* and *Paul, Women and Wives.*

P. Travis Kroeker is Professor of Philosophical Theology and Ethics in the Department of Religious Studies at McMaster University. He has published *Christian Ethics and Political Economy in North America*; *Remembering the End: Dostoevsky as Prophet to Modernity* (co-authored); and numerous articles, most recently on messianic ethics and political theology.

Anthony N. S. Lane is Professor of Historical Theology at the London School of Theology. His publications include *A Concise History of Christian Thought*; *Justification by Faith in Catholic-Protestant Dialogue*; and (on Calvin) *Calvin and Bernard of Clairvaux*; *John Calvin: Student of the Church Fathers*; and *A Reader's Guide to Calvin's Institutes.*

Daniel R. Langton is Professor of the History of Jewish-Christian Relations at the University of Manchester. His study over many years of Jewish readings of Paul has led to the publication of *The Apostle Paul in the Jewish Imagination.* Other publications include *Claude Montefiore: His Life and Thought* and *Children of Zion: Jewish and Christian Perspectives on the Holy Land.*

Grant LeMarquand is Professor of Biblical Studies and Mission at the Trinity Episcopal School for Ministry. He has contributed to *The Bible in Africa*, co-edited *Theological Education in Contemporary Africa*, and published a monograph comparing North Atlantic and African interpretations of the Gospel story of the bleeding woman.

Matthew Levering is Professor of Theology at the University of Dayton. He has co-edited the *Oxford Handbook on the Trinity* (forthcoming); *Aquinas the Augustinian*; and *Reading John with St. Thomas Aquinas.* Among his own monographs may be mentioned *Predestination*; *Participatory Biblical Exegesis*; and a theological commentary on Ezra and Nehemiah.

Margaret Y. MacDonald is Professor of Religious Studies at St. Francis Xavier University. Her interests include the Pauline epistles (*The Pauline Churches*, a commentary on Colossians and Ephesians) and women in early Christianity (*Early Christian Women and Pagan Opinion*; *A Woman's Place: House Churches in Earliest Christianity* [co-authored]).

I. Howard Marshall is Emeritus Professor of New Testament Exegesis, University of Aberdeen. His many publications include the International Critical Commentary volume on the Pastoral Epistles; commentaries on Luke, Acts, the Thessalonian and Johannine Epistles; and *New Testament Theology: Many Witnesses, One Gospel.*

Mickey L. Mattox is Associate Professor of Historical Theology at Marquette University. Specializing on the theology and biblical exegesis of Martin Luther and the

Protestant Reformation, he has co-authored *The Substance of the Faith: Luther's Doctrinal Theology for Today* and published a monograph on Luther's interpretation of the women of Genesis.

Gilbert Meilaender is Phyllis and Richard Duesenberg Professor of Christian Ethics at Valparaiso University. He has co-edited the *Oxford Handbook of Theological Ethics* and published *Faith and Faithfulness: Basic Themes in Christian Ethics*; *The Way that Leads There*; *Freedom of a Christian*; and *Neither Beast Nor God: The Dignity of the Human Person.*

Stanley E. Porter is President, Dean, and Professor of New Testament at McMaster Divinity College. The editor or co-editor of many volumes, his own monographs include *Verbal Aspect in the Greek of the New Testament*, *Paul in Acts*, *The Criteria for Authenticity in Historical Jesus Research*, and (with Wendy J. Porter) *New Testament Papyri and Parchments: New Editions.*

Heikki Räisänen is Emeritus Professor of New Testament Exegesis, University of Helsinki. His publications, reflecting a broad range of interests, include *Paul and the Law*; *Jesus, Paul and Torah*; *Beyond New Testament Theology*; *Marcion, Muhammad and the Mahatma*; and *The Rise of Christian Beliefs: The Thought World of Early Christians.*

Rainer Riesner is Professor of New Testament at the Institute for Evangelical Theology, Dortmund University. His many publications include *Paul's Early Period: Chronology, Mission Strategy, Theology*; *Jesus als Lehrer*; and *Bethanien jenseits des Jordan.*

Marguerite Shuster is Harold John Ockenga Professor of Preaching and Theology at Fuller Theological Seminary. Presently working on a study of divine providence, she has published *Power, Pathology, Paradox: The Dynamics of Evil and Good*; *Who We Are: Our Dignity as Human* (with Paul K. Jewett); and *The Fall and Sin: What We Have Become as Sinners.*

Todd D. Still is Associate Professor of Christian Scriptures at the George W. Truett Theological Seminary, Baylor University. He has edited *Jesus and Paul Reconnected*; co-edited *After The First Urban Christians*; published *Conflict at Thessalonica* and a commentary on Colossians; and has a forthcoming commentary on Philippians and Philemon.

Theodore G. Stylianopoulos is the Emeritus Archbishop Iakovos Professor of Orthodox Theology and Professor of New Testament at Holy Cross Greek Orthodox School of Theology. Among his publications may be mentioned *The Good News of Christ*; *The New Testament: An Orthodox Perspective*; and *The Way of Christ: Gospel, Spirituality, and Renewal in Orthodoxy.*

Gerd Theissen is Professor Emeritus for New Testament Theology at the University of Heidelberg. A pioneer in the sociological study of early Christianity, he has published

Sociology of Early Palestinian Christianity; *The Social Setting of Pauline Christianity*; *Psychological Aspects of Pauline Theology*; and *The Religion of the Earliest Churches*.

John R. Tyson is Professor of Theology at United Theological Seminary (Dayton). His many studies of the Wesleys and early Methodism include *Charles Wesley on Sanctification*; *Charles Wesley: A Reader*; *In the Midst of Early Methodism: Lady Huntingdon and Her Correspondence* (co-authored); and *Assist Me to Proclaim: The Life and Hymns of Charles Wesley*.

J. Ross Wagner is Associate Professor of New Testament at Princeton Theological Seminary. His interest in early Jewish and Christian interpretation of Scripture is reflected in the monograph *Heralds of the Good News: Paul and Isaiah "In Concert" in the Letter to the Romans*, as well as in ongoing studies of the Old Greek version of Isaiah.

Stephen Westerholm is Professor of Early Christianity in the Department of Religious Studies at McMaster University. He has published *Israel's Law and the Church's Faith: Paul and His Recent Interpreters*; *Understanding Paul*; and *Perspectives Old and New on Paul* in addition to studies on the Synoptic Gospels and historical Jesus.

Peter Widdicombe is Associate Professor of Patristics and Historical Theology in the Department of Religious Studies at McMaster University. He has published *The Fatherhood of God from Origen to Athanasius* and articles on the interpretation of Scripture and doctrine in the Patristic period.

N. T. Wright is Professor of New Testament and Early Christianity at the University of St. Andrews. His forthcoming *Paul and the Faithfulness of God* is the fourth volume in a series on Christian Origins and the Question of God. Among many other titles may be mentioned *Justification: God's Plan and Paul's Vision*; *Paul: Fresh Perspectives*; and *The Climax of the Covenant*.

Acknowledgments

The author and publisher gratefully acknowledge the permissions granted to reproduce copyrighted material in this book:

Figure 32.1 Paul with capsa, Catacomb of Domitilla, Rome.
Photo credit: Estelle Brettman, The International Catacomb Society.

Figure 32.2 Busts of Peter and Paul with Christ, Basilica of San Vitale, Ravenna, mid-6th century.
Photo credit: Holly Hayes, Sacred Destinations Images.

Figure 32.3 Peter and Paul, Arian Baptistery, Ravenna, early 6th century.
Photo credit: Robin Jensen.

Figure 32.4 Jesus giving the law to Peter and Paul, Mausoleum of Constanza, Rome, mid-4th century.
Photo credit: Robin M. Jensen.

Figure 32.5 Jesus enthroned with apostles, Basilica of Sta. Pudenziana, Rome, ca. 400.
Photo credit: Robin M. Jensen.

Figure 32.6 Embrace of Peter and Paul, 10th-century ivory now in the Victoria and Albert Museum, London.
Photo credit: Br. Lawrence Lew, OP.

Figure 32.7 Arrest of Paul, detail of Passion Sarcophagus, Vatican Museum, ca. 340–360.
Photo credit: Robin M. Jensen.

Figure 32.8 Alessandro Algardi, *The Beheading of St. Paul*, ca. 1650. San Paolo Maggiore, Bologna.
Photo credit: Alinari/Art Resource, NY.

Figure 32.9 Caravaggio (Michelangelo Merisi da), *The Conversion on the Way to Damascus*, ca. 1600, Cerai Chapel, Santa Maria del Popolo, Rome.
Photo credit: Scala/Art Resource, NY.

Figure 32.10 Paul disputing with the Jews and escaping from Damascus, 12th-century mosaic from the Palatine Chapel, Palermo, Sicily.
Photo credit: Alinari/Art Resource, NY.

Figure 32.11 Ivory of Paul with Thecla, Rome, ca. 430, now in the British Museum.
Photo credit: Robin M. Jensen.

Figure 32.12 Diptych with the stories of Paul on Malta and Adam in Paradise, now in the Museo Nazionale del Bargello, Florence.
Photo: George Tatge, 2000. Photo credit: Alinari/Art Resource, NY.

Figure 32.13 Slab from Paul's tomb, from the Basilica of St. Paul fuori le Mura.
Photo credit: Robin M. Jensen.

Introduction

Stephen Westerholm

Paul's primary readership is not scholarly, but among scholars he is read primarily by students of the New Testament and early Christianity, on the one hand, and of Christian theology, on the other. *The Blackwell Companion to Paul* is designed to address the interests of both and to facilitate their mutual conversation.

That students of the New Testament and of Christian theology are talking to each other is something of a recent development.[1] Any suggestion that they should do so would have made no sense in the premodern era and been programmatically opposed in the centuries that followed.[2] In the earlier period, Paul's writings were characteristically read as a vehicle of divine communication to humankind. Those who sought answers to life's most fundamental questions turned to Paul (and to the other writers of Scripture) to find them, and those who read Paul's letters (and the other writings of Scripture) did so assured that what they encountered there was true and foundational. Theology (in other words) *meant* interpreting Scripture, and Scripture was interpreted theologically. Not until the tasks were conceived of as distinct enterprises, assigned to different practitioners, could "mutual conversation" even be contemplated.

The very conditions that made such conversation possible were such as to make it unpalatable. In many ways, Spinoza set the agenda for the modern academic study of the Bible (Spinoza 1951; Latin original 1670). To read the Bible properly (it is held), one must approach the text without any of the biases of faith: to assume that its contents were divinely revealed, and hence coherent and true, is to prejudice one's understanding of the text from the outset (Spinoza 1951, 8, 99–100). The goal of biblical interpretation must be to determine the meaning rather than the truth of the text (Spinoza 1951, 101; the distinction was unthinkable earlier) as well as the (natural, not supernatural) processes that led to its composition. In short, the Bible should be

The Blackwell Companion to Paul, First Edition. Edited by Stephen Westerholm.
© 2011 Blackwell Publishing Ltd. Published 2011 by Blackwell Publishing Ltd.

read "like any other book" (Jowett 1860, 377) and studied, not for what it reveals about God, but for what it can tell us about ancient Israelite history and religion, or the history of the early followers of Jesus (Gilkey 1961). The retelling of these histories, like that of any other history, involves tracing the sequences of events to their (natural, not supernatural) causes: ancient Israelite religion had its home and origin among the many religions in the ancient Near East; early Christianity was (and must be studied as) one of many religious movements in the Greco-Roman world (Troeltsch 1991; German original 1898).

Such an approach eliminates the quest for (and, indeed, the possibility of finding) contemporary relevance in the biblical texts; but this (it is held) is hardly to be lamented, since a concern for relevance is liable to distort one's interpretation of ancient texts and reconstruction of ancient history. Their task so construed, students of the Bible have had little interest in conversation with theologians; the latter, for their part, have been wont to dismiss the modern practice of biblical studies as a trivializing antiquarianism.[3]

There is no doubt that the biblical writings, and the history of early Christianity, continue (and will continue) to be studied by many who think it important to exclude religious convictions from their work – indeed, by many in whose work *anti*-religious sentiments are very much in evidence. The attention that such readers give to hitherto overlooked aspects of the texts, and the fresh questions they raise, have led to insights that have become the common property of all interpreters of the Bible. Many of the issues much debated within this academic field are treated in the first part of this book: questions of Pauline chronology; of the apostle's continuing relations with the communities of believers that he founded; of the social stratification of those communities, and of the roles played by women within them; of Paul's stance toward the imperial powers of his day, on the one hand, and toward his Jewish heritage, on the other; of the use he made of rhetoric in his letters, and of how those letters have been transmitted over the centuries. Even topics sounding more theological – Paul's understanding of the gospel, of Scripture and (specifically) the Mosaic law, of Christology – are recognized by historians with no interest in theology to have played a crucial role in the shaping of early Christian thought and identity. In short, Part I of this book addresses topics that have always lain within the scope of biblical scholarship.

At the same time, there has always been something strange about an understanding of biblical studies that requires it to end where (as one observer put it) the history of the Bible begins (Levenson 1993, 107): are not the understandings of Paul that guided the thinking of such giants of history as Augustine, Luther, Calvin, and the Wesleys at least as important as the most recently proposed reconstruction of what the apostle *really* thought by an associate professor at a local university? Does not the insistence that Paul's writings be studied simply for what they reveal about one religious movement among many in the first-century Greco-Roman world ring hollow given that, in much of the world of the twenty-first century, one is never more than a few miles from churches in which the letters of Paul continue to find a place in lectionaries and sermons, and from private homes in which small groups, made up neither of scholars nor of clergy, meet each week to study them? That Paul's letters have been the subject of continuous and intense study for two thousand years surely merits the attention of students of the apostle. The recent explosion of interest in the history of interpretation[4] seems therefore very much in order, and it is by no means confined to scholars with theological concerns – though, to be sure, it marks a natural bridge between the disciplines of biblical studies and theology.[5] A distinctive feature of *The Blackwell Companion to Paul* is the prominence given in Part II to Paul's impact on (an inevitably select group[6] of) his interpreters.

And on certain *communities* of readers. Though only a very small sampling of such communities could be included here, their presence ought nonetheless to serve as a reminder that Paul's letters are not the preserve of the ivory tower. Of special interest, given Paul's own wrestlings with his Jewish heritage, is the way in which Jews have read his writings. It is hoped that the horizons of many readers will be expanded by an introduction to Orthodox and African readings of the apostle as well.

Part III is devoted, more broadly, to Paul's legacy. His impact on art and literature is often neglected; it is expertly introduced here. Of the many areas in which Paul's writings have shaped Christian thinking, four have been selected for inclusion. In each case, the distinctiveness and profound influence of Paul's thought are indisputable: sin and the "fall," the Spirit of God, ethics, and the church. Contributors to this section of the *Companion* were asked to say something about how Paul set the agenda for, and determined the boundaries of, Christian thinking on their topic. Their stimulating and illuminating responses make a unique contribution to this volume.

But (to repeat) Paul's primary readership is not scholarly. To fail to account for this truism is to fall short of grasping Paul's significance. In a well-known treatise, and in his own inimitable way, Søren Kierkegaard insisted that a distinction be drawn between a genius and an apostle (Kierkegaard 1962; Danish original 1847). Geniuses, however extraordinary their gifts, remain within the realm of the humanly possible, and they speak without authority. Paul was no genius: he was, after all, hardly remarkable as a literary stylist, of unknown competence as a tent-maker, and, when it comes to profundity, not to be compared with a Plato or a Shakespeare. But even to consider him in these terms, no matter how complimentary our assessment of his gifts, is to rob him of his true importance. Paul was an apostle who spoke with authority the divine message he was commissioned to deliver. As such, he commands a hearing.

Not all students of Paul will allow the reality of Kierkegaard's distinction, but it captures well Paul's own self-understanding and the point of his endeavors, and it explains why his hold on two millennia of readers exceeds that of Plato and Shakespeare. Further specification, however, is needed. An "apostle," as someone (by definition) *sent* on a mission, requires a *sender*: Paul's "calling" was that of an apostle (he could also say "servant" or "slave") *of Christ Jesus* (1 Cor 1:1; cf. Rom 1:1). It originated when (as Paul put it) "God was pleased to reveal his Son to me" (Gal 1:15–16); thereafter, both his life and his proclamation could be summed up in the single word "Christ" (Phil 1:18, 21; cf. 1 Cor 1:23; 2:2; 2 Cor 4:5), who was to be "magnified" in all he did (Phil 1:20). To be sure, Paul did not derive his idiom from Jesus: the theological abstractions and argumentation of the epistles are uniquely his own, as is the head-scratching provoked by *his* parables (Rom 7:2–3; 11:17–24). On the other hand, Paul learned from his Lord of faith that moves mountains and banishes anxiety (Matt 17:20 and 1 Cor 13:2; Matt 6:25–34 and Phil 4:6–7); of the permanence of marriage and the (secondary, but real) obligation to pay taxes (Matt 19:3–9 and 1 Cor 7:10–11; Matt 22:21 and Rom 13:6–7); of the primacy of love, even for enemies, whose evil is to be met – and overcome – with good (Matt 22:34–40 and Rom 13:8–10 [cf. 1 Cor 13]; Matt 5:43–48 and Rom 12:14–21); of the virtues of meekness and lowliness, marking a life of servanthood (Matt 5:5; 11:29 and 2 Cor 10:1; Gal 5:23; Phil 2:3; Matt 20:25–28 and 2 Cor 4:5; Gal 5:13); of a discipleship of dying in order to live (Matt 16:24–25 and 2 Cor 4:7–18). From Jesus, too, came the "good news" that, *with* Jesus, the promised day of God's salvation had dawned (Matt 4:17; 12:28; 13:16–17; cf. 2 Cor 6:2), and that the outpouring of God's love embraced "sinners" (Matt 9:10–13; Luke 15:1–32; cf. Rom 4:5; 5:8). The new age had begun, and its consummation was imminent (Matt 24:44; 1 Thess 4:13–18). In these and other ways, the life and teaching of Jesus were important to Paul.[7]

Even more foundational were Christ's death and resurrection – as, indeed, they are the climax, not merely the conclusion, of his activities in the gospels. Paul shared the common conviction of the early church that Christ "died *for our sins*" (1 Cor 15:3). But it was Paul who found peculiar significance in his death *by crucifixion*: so excruciating and shameful a death marked both the extent of Christ's humility and obedience (Phil 2:8) and the divine overturning of all human values (1 Cor 1:18–31). It was, for Paul, the ultimate proof of divine love for the weak, the sinful, the enemies of God, and it effected their reconciliation to God (Rom 5:6–10). In Christ's *resurrection*, God had decisively overcome the powers of evil and inaugurated a new age and a new creation; with Christ's resurrection came the promise of resurrection for all who are found "in Christ" (Rom 8; 1 Cor 15).

In the end, the story of Paul is the story of the power of Paul's message to create communities of faith and to transform the lives and thinking of their members. Its staying power, by any standards, has been remarkable. It invites the study of biblical scholars and the reflection of theologians, while it continues to command a hearing from those who are neither, but who find themselves addressed by the letters of Paul, the apostle of Jesus Christ.

Notes

1   Among the many forums in which this conversation is currently taking place may be mentioned the *Journal of Theological Interpretation*, the Brazos Theological Commentary series, and the Two Horizons Commentary series (Eerdmans). See also Vanhoozer (2005); O'Day and Petersen (2009).

2   See Rowe and Hays (2007).

3   Both positions were never more in evidence, or more passionately argued, than in the storm provoked by the appearance of Karl Barth's commentary on Romans. See chapter 27 of this volume.

4   It will be sufficient to mention here the launching, from the 1990s and later, of three commentary series in English devoted to the history of interpretation: the Ancient Christian Commentary on Scripture (InterVarsity Press), the Blackwell Bible Commentaries, and The Church's Bible (Eerdmans).

5   Another important bridge has been the canonical approach to scriptural texts advocated by Brevard Childs.

6   The choice of each interpreter included is easily justified. That the inclusion of others
would have been equally justifiable is not denied.

7   See the articles in Still (2007).

References

Gilkey, Langdon B. 1961. Cosmology, Ontology, and the Travail of Biblical Language. *Journal of Religion* 41: 194–205.

Jowett, Benjamin. 1860. On the Interpretation of Scripture. Pages 330–433 in Frederick Temple and others, *Essays and Reviews*. London: John W. Parker and Son.

Kierkegaard, Søren. 1962. Of the Difference between a Genius and an Apostle. Pages 87–108 in Søren Kierkegaard, *The Present Age*. Translated by Alexander Dru. New York: Harper & Row.

Levenson, Jon D. 1993. *The Hebrew Bible, the Old Testament, and Historical Criticism: Jews and Christians in Biblical Studies*. Louisville: Westminster John Knox.

O'Day, Gail R., and David L. Petersen, editors. 2009. *Theological Bible Commentary*. Louisville: Westminster John Knox.

Rowe, C. Kavin, and Richard B. Hays. 2007. Biblical Studies. Pages 435–455 in *The Oxford Handbook of Systematic Theology*. Edited by John Webster, Kathryn Tanner, and Iain Torrance. Oxford: Oxford University Press.

Spinoza, Benedict de. 1951. Theologico-Political Treatise. Pages 3–266 in *The Chief Works of Benedict de Spinoza: A Theologico-Political Treatise* and *A Political Treatise*. Translated by R. H. M. Elwes. New York: Dover.

Still, Todd D., editor. 2007. *Jesus and Paul Reconsidered: Fresh Pathways into an Old Debate*. Grand Rapids: Eerdmans.

Troeltsch, Ernst. 1991. Historical and Dogmatic Method in Theology. Pages 11–18 in Ernst Troeltsch, *Religion in History*. Minneapolis: Fortress.

Vanhoozer, Kevin J., editor. 2005. *Dictionary for Theological Interpretation of the Bible*. Grand Rapids: Baker.

PART I
Paul and Christian Origins

The Blackwell Companion to Paul, First Edition. Edited by Stephen Westerholm.
© 2011 Blackwell Publishing Ltd. Published 2011 by Blackwell Publishing Ltd.

CHAPTER 1

Pauline Chronology

Rainer Riesner

Methodological Questions

A decisive factor in any reconstruction of Pauline chronology is the evaluation of the available sources. With regard to the letters in the name of the apostle, methodological caution dictates that we begin with those letters that scholarship generally considers to be genuine: Romans, 1–2 Corinthians, Galatians, Philippians, 1 Thessalonians, and Philemon. Even here, evaluation of the letters may be influenced by the assumption that the letters to the Corinthians and Philippians, in particular, were assembled from various writings, implying that the correspondence was conducted over a protracted period of time. In the following analysis, the unity of all the letters is assumed since we lack text-critical evidence, literary parallels, and any indication in post-New Testament literature that would support breaking up the letters (cf. Carson and Moo 2005, 429–444, 509–510).

On the historical value of the Acts of the Apostles for the chronology of Paul, three positions have been taken.

(1) For historical purposes, the Acts of the Apostles is all but worthless, and a chronological reconstruction should be based exclusively on the genuine letters of Paul (Buck and Taylor 1969; Hyldahl 1986; Knox 1987). This position is problematic, however, since no statement in Paul's letters allows a clear connection to a concrete date from contemporary history, rendering the establishment of an absolute chronology effectively impossible. For this reason, reference is often made to Acts in spite of the desired methodological rigor. The isolated chronological indicators in Paul's letters leave much room for interpretation. Hence, reconstructions differ greatly from one another, and no consensus seems possible along these lines (Riesner 1998, 10–28).

The Blackwell Companion to Paul, First Edition. Edited by Stephen Westerholm.
© 2011 Blackwell Publishing Ltd. Published 2011 by Blackwell Publishing Ltd.

(2) Others, while assigning the letters basic priority, nonetheless include individual traditions deemed reliable from Acts. These traditions, however, must be tested critically before they can be added to information derived from Paul. If greater confidence is placed in Acts because, for example, the "we"-narratives (Acts 16:10–17; 20:5–15; 21:1–18; 27:1–28:16) are thought to be based on the travel diary of one of Paul's companions, then the course of events for longer narrative sequences may be judged trustworthy (Jewett 1979; Donfried 1992). If, on the other hand, all that is thought credible are a few fragments of tradition, then their arrangement becomes much more a matter of subjective judgment (Suhl 1975; Lüdemann 1984).

(3) Finally, many see in the Acts of the Apostles the work of Luke, an occasional companion of Paul (Hemer 1990; Hengel and Schwemer 1997, 6–11), and as such at least in part a primary source (Riesner 1998; Porter 2000a, 205). This does not mean, however, that the reports of Acts can be used uncritically. It is remarkable how chronological indicators appear with differing frequency and degrees of specificity in the various parts of Acts. Such indications are most striking in the "we"-narratives and segments closely related to them. On the whole, the first main section (Acts 1–15) offers only very general chronological pointers. This allows an inference to be drawn about Luke's approach: where he possessed neither personal knowledge nor traditions with specific chronological details, he clearly refused to invent them in order to lend greater authenticity to his presentation. Conversely, this increases our confidence in information that he might plausibly have acquired from first-hand experience or later inquiry. Details from the Pauline letters also require critical assessment whether, for example, they present events in a compressed fashion for rhetorical reasons. Wherever possible, the information of both sources should be further tested by correlating it with profane historical or patristic sources.

The reconstruction of a Pauline chronology should involve three steps. (1) An attempt must be made to ascertain individual chronological details by combining information from a plurality of sources. The goal of this step is to obtain as many absolute dates as possible. (2) The letters of Paul offer a few relative dates and also allow a few chains of events to be recognized. (3) Finally, the attempt is made to establish an overall picture that is as coherent as possible, combining the individual chronological details, the chains of events derived from Paul's letters, and temporal and sequential information discernible in Acts.

Individual Chronological Dates

The crucifixion of Jesus

The crucifixion of Jesus is a chronological fixed point (*terminus post quem*) after which the call of the Pharisee Saul to become the Christian apostle Paul necessarily occurred. Pontius Pilate was prefect of the "special" Roman territory of Judea from 26 to 36 (Josephus, *Jewish Antiquities* 18.89–95, 122–126; see Riesner 1998, 35–36), and was for this reason Jesus's judge in Jerusalem (Mark 15:1–15). John the Baptist appeared as a public figure "in the fifteenth year of the reign [*hēgemonia*] of Emperor Tiberius"

(Luke 3:1).[1] The Greek expression refers to the co-regency that began in 12/13; hence, the information from Luke's special source points to the year 26/27. This fits well with the fact that, in parts of the Jewish world, the year 27/28 was considered to be an apocalyptic jubilee (Wacholder 1975). The Baptist, according to the evangelists, was awaiting the imminent coming of the Son of Man/Messiah (Matt 3:7–12; Luke 3:7–9, 15–18). For the public appearance of Jesus in 27/28, we have the evidence of John 2:20, since the construction of the temple by Herod the Great (*Jewish Antiquities* 15.380), which was begun in 20/19 BC, now lay forty-six years in the past. If we then follow the narrative of John, allowing a two- to three-year period for Jesus's public activities (John 2:13; 6:4; 12:1), the Passover of his death can be placed between 29 and 31.

According to all the evangelists, the crucifixion took place on the Day of Preparation (*paraskeuē*) before a Sabbath (Matt 27:62; Mark 15:42; Luke 23:54–56; John 19:31, 42), and thus on a Friday. According to John, the Sabbath was also the start of the Passover (John 18:28; 19:14), a dating supported by Paul, who describes the crucified Jesus as a "sacrificed" Passover lamb (1 Cor 5:7). He calls the resurrected Jesus the "first fruits" (*aparchē*; 1 Cor 15:20), and speaks of the resurrection "on the third day" (1 Cor 15:4). The first fruits of the barley harvest were dedicated to God on Nisan 16 (Lev 23:10–11), and so the day on which Jesus died was Nisan 14 (Riesner 1998, 48–49; White 2007, 123–131). According to the most reliable astronomical calculation, between the years 26 and 36 it is certain that Nisan 14 fell on a Friday on April 7, 30 (Finegan 1998, 359–365); the other proposed date, April 3, 33 (Humphreys and Waddington 1989; Hoehner 1992), is very uncertain (Riesner 1998, 54–58). The date of April 7 (Clement of Alexandria, *Miscellanies* 1.21.146) and the year 30 (Tertullian, *Against the Jews* 8)[2] are also to be found in the oldest traditions of the church (Strobel 1977). Thus, there is a relatively widespread consensus that Jesus was crucified on April 7, 30 (Dunn 2003, 312).

Paul's call

For the year that Paul was called by the risen Jesus near Damascus, early Christian tradition offers two competing dates. The first places the stoning of Stephen in the "seventh year" after the resurrection and ascension of Jesus (Strobel 1977, 116). Thus, if we count from 30, we arrive at 36/37. At this point there was a vacancy in the governorship following the recall of Pilate (Josephus, *Jewish Antiquities* 18.89, 237; see Riesner 1998, 36–37), during which an unauthorized Jewish proceeding against Stephen (Acts 6:8–15; 7:54–8:1) is conceivable (Dockx 1984, 223–230). Against this tradition is the fact that it is relatively late and that it can be explained as derived from speculation about providential seven-year epochs. The second tradition can be found in relatively early (i.e., from the second century) and very diverse sources, such as the Jewish-Christian *Ascension of Isaiah* (9:16), the gnostic *Apocryphon of James* (Nag Hammadi Codex I.2.19–24), and the apocryphal *Acts of Paul* (see Gebhardt 1902, 130), which are all of the view that Paul's call occurred around one and a half years after the resurrection, or "in the second year after the ascension." That would give us the year 31/32 (Riesner 1998, 59–74; Dunn 2009, 257).

The flight from Damascus

At the time of Paul's flight from Damascus, "the ethnarch [*ethnarchēs*; NRSV "governor"] under King Aretas guarded the city" (2 Cor 11:32). The Nabatean king Aretas IV is the only person mentioned both in the undisputed letters of Paul and in other contemporary historical sources. Scholars who try to construct a chronology on the basis of the letters alone see here a fixed point on which to build (Campbell 2002). But neither a handing over of the rule of Damascus to Aretas IV by the Emperor Caligula in the years 37–39 (Welborn 1999), nor a violent occupation of the city by the Nabateans (Bunine 2006; cf. Bowersock 1983, 68–69), can be established on the basis of the literary sources (Hengel and Schwemer 1997, 129–131; Riesner 1998, 79–84) or the numismatic evidence (Knauf 1998). The "ethnarch under King Aretas" was likely the oveseer of the Nabatean quarter in Damascus (Knauf 1983; Sack 1989, 14). The same expression is used for the overseer of the Jewish quarter in Alexandria (Josephus, *Jewish Antiquities* 14.117; Strabo, *Geography* 17.798), whereas for a military governor the term *stratēgos* would be expected. The only certain chronological point (*terminus ante quem*) is the death of Aretas IV in 40, before which the flight of Paul must have occurred.

Persecution under Agrippa I and the famine under Claudius

According to Acts 12:1–2, (Herod) Agrippa I had James, the son of Zebedee, "killed with the sword." Agrippa ruled over Judea from 41 to 44 (Josephus, *Jewish Antiquities* 19.343). The demonstrative use of the *ius gladii* and the popular proceeding against a deviant religious minority such as the Jewish Christians are more likely to belong to the early part of his reign in 41/42. The persecution may have been ignited by the "Hellenists" who were driven out of Jerusalem into Syrian Antioch and had begun a mission to Gentiles (Acts 11:19–21), arousing the suspicion of the Roman authorities, who called the new group "Christians" (Acts 11:26). Evidently, there were Jewish riots against them in Antioch in 39–40 (*Chronicle of John Malalas* 244–245). Luke mentions a collection journey of Paul and Barnabas from Antioch to Jerusalem around the time of the death of Agrippa in early 44 (Acts 11:29–30; 12:25). The Jewish Christians there were suffering from "a severe famine" that struck "all the world" during the reign of Claudius (Acts 11:28). The entire reign of Claudius (41–54) was characterized by famines (Suetonius, *Claudius* 18.2), which were particularly severe in Palestine in 44/46 (Josephus, *Jewish Antiquities* 20.51–53, 101; Eusebius, *Chronicle* [Helm edition, 181]).

The Cypriot proconsul Sergius Paullus

According to Acts 13:6–12, Paul met the proconsul Sergius Paul[l]us on his first missionary voyage with Barnabas to Cyprus. Three inscriptions have been cited in order to establish the proconsul's dates. An inscription from Soloi in North Cyprus (*Inscriptiones*

Graecae ad Res Romanas III 930) should be excluded, since it belongs to the second century (Mitford 1980, 1302–1303). An inscription from Kytheria in Cyprus mentions a Quintus Sergius (*Inscriptiones Graecae ad Res Romanas* III 935) for whom dates during the reign of Claudius were long proposed, but he is now thought to have held office during the time of Gaius Caligula (Mitford 1980, 1300; cf. Christol and Drew-Bear 2002, 187) or Tiberius (Campbell 2005). These last two datings present a major problem for the framework of Acts, which puts the proconsulship of Sergius Paullus after the death of Agrippa I, and thus after 44 and within the reign of Claudius. But it is by no means evident from the fragmentary inscription that the cognomen of Quintus Sergius is to be restored as Paullus. Scholars who, in an attempt to topple the historical framework of Acts, read the cognomen Paullus into this fragmentary source are guilty of arguing in a circle. The inscription most likely to be connected to this proconsul comes from the city of Rome (*Corpus Inscriptionum Latinarum* VI 31545). It mentions an L. Sergius Paullus, who was presumably curator of the Tiber in 41/42 (Weiss 2009b). The occupancy of this office would fit well with a later career as proconsul of a senatorial province such as Cyprus.

Claudius's edict of expulsion from Rome

As Paul reached Corinth from Athens on his second missionary journey, he met "a Jew[ish Christian] named Aquila ... who had recently [*prosphatōs*] come from Italy with his wife Priscilla, because Claudius had ordered all Jews to leave Rome" (Acts 18:2). Much later than Luke, around 130, Suetonius also mentions an expulsion of Jews from Rome under the same emperor "because, incited by Christ [*impulsore Chresto*], they were constantly causing riots" (*Claudius* 25.4). Dio Cassius mentions a ban on meetings of Roman Jews (*Roman History* 60.6.6) in connection with the beginning of Claudius's reign. Scholars who see all three sources referring to the same event draw on Dio in dating it to 41/42. This assumption, too, results in an insurmountable difficulty for the framework of Acts (Murphy-O'Connor 1996, 9–15). The reconstruction of events is made more complicated by the fact that neither Josephus nor Tacitus mentions an expulsion edict of Claudius, and the work of Dio on the later period of this emperor's rule is only inadequately preserved by Byzantine excerpts. The solution least burdened with additional hypotheses and already preferred by ancient historians (Levick 1990, 121; Botermann 1996) claims that Dio referred to an early action of the emperor that was later sharpened by the banishment that Luke and Suetonius (and perhaps also a Scholion on Juvenal 4.117) jointly attest.

Suetonius's rather unclear mode of expression suggests that claims of Jesus's Messiahship made by Jewish Christians in Rome led to disturbances in synagogues, as Luke reports happened in other cities (Acts 14:1–6, 19–20; 17:1–9) and as Paul, too, presupposes (2 Cor 11:24–25). Beginning in 48, serious zealot disturbances began in Judea (Josephus, *Jewish War* 2.232–246; *Jewish Antiquities* 20.118–136), and in the same year there is evidence for a Jewish persecution of the Christian community in Antioch in Syria (*Chronicle of John Malalas* 247). Paul Orosius, a Christian writer on world history in the fourth/fifth centuries, dates the Roman edict of expulsion to "the ninth year of Claudius" (*Against the Pagans* 7.6.15–16), that is, to the year 49. Orosius relied on Josephus, who does not, however, supply any such information. It is possible, however, that just such a chronological indicator was present in the historical work of the Jewish Christian Hegesippos, who visited Rome around 180 (Eusebius, *Ecclesiastical History* 4.11; 4.22; Riesner 1998, 180–186). In any event, it is not possible for Orosius to have derived this year from Acts.

The Achaian proconsul Gallio

According to Acts 18:12–17, during Paul's first stay in Corinth, the capital of the senatorial province of Achaia, he was brought before the proconsul Gallio by a segment of the Jewish synagogue community. A turning point for the discussion of Pauline chronology came with the publication in 1905 of an inscription from Delphi, to which additional fragments were later assigned (*Sylloge Inscriptionum Graecarum* [third edition] 801; Hemer 1980, 6–8). The inscription is a rescript of Claudius on the basis of which Gallio's term as the proconsul of Achaia can be dated: its beginning can thus be assigned the date of July 1, 51 (Riesner 1998, 203–207). It seems, however, that Gallio did not serve the full year of office, but rather left Corinth earlier for reasons of health (Seneca, *Moral Epistles* 104.1), possibly even before the end of shipping on the Mediterranean in October 51.

Paul in Ephesus

According to Acts 19:23–40, during Paul's extended stay in Ephesus, the capital of the province of Asia Minor, disturbances took place, ignited by the local silversmiths. Perhaps also in the background was the discontent of the Ephesians over an edict of the governor Paullus Fabius Persicus in the year 44 (Weiss 2009a) censuring the administration of funds at the temple of Artemis (I. Ephesos 17–19). While Luke normally refers to proconsuls by name, in Acts 19:38 he uses the undefined plural *anthypatoi*. This could be an indication of the confusion that prevailed in Ephesus after the death of Claudius (October 13, 54). After his death, Agrippina, his wife and the mother of the later emperor Nero, had immediately given orders for the murder of Silanus, proconsul of Asia Minor (Tacitus, *Annals* 13.1; Dio Cassius, *Roman History* 61.6.4–5), which occurred at the latest in December 54 or January 55. While the office was vacant, administration fell into the hands of three deputies; a number of scholars see this as the reason for Luke's use of the generalizing plural (Bruce 1990, 421).

Of relevance for Pauline chronology, and especially for the order of some of the letters (Philippians, Philemon, and possibly Colossians) is the question whether or not Paul was imprisoned in Ephesus, as the Marcionite prologue to the letter to the Colossians maintains (Kümmel 1972, 14). In support of such an imprisonment is Paul's recollection of a life-threatening situation "in Asia" (2 Cor 1:8–10), which could well mean the provincial capital of Ephesus (cf. Acts 20:16). In the letter to the Romans, Paul implies an imprisonment together with Aquila and Priscilla (Rom 16:4, 7), which is perhaps best seen as occurring in Ephesus (cf. 1 Cor 16:19). For these reasons, a good number of scholars favor an imprisonment in Ephesus (Trebilco 2004, 83–87). Luke, whose report on Ephesus is both detailed and suggestive, may have passed over this imprisonment out of consideration for the Asiarchs who were "friendly" to Paul (Acts 19:30–31; Riesner 1998, 214–216). According to Acts 20:17–18, Paul avoided a later visit to Ephesus, presumably because he risked arrest there. Second Corinthians 11:23–25 show that Luke by no means reported all of the dangers faced by the apostle.

The last journey to Jerusalem

Acts 20:6–21:15 describe, partly in the form of a "we"-narrative, a seven-week trip by Paul from Philippi to Jerusalem in order to celebrate Pentecost there. Apparently, the apostle left Philippi immediately after the end of the Christian Passover celebration ("after the days of Unleavened Bread" [Acts 20:6]). The reference to the "first day of the week" in Troas (Acts 20:7) must mean a Sunday (cf. Luke 24:1). Since Luke reckons a day from sunrise to sunrise (Acts 4:3–5; 10:3–23, etc.), the Christian assembly he describes took place on Sunday, not Saturday, evening, and the subsequent departure on Monday morning (Marshall 1980, 325–326). Since Paul remained for seven days (reckoned inclusively) in Troas (Acts 20:6), he must have arrived there on Tuesday of the previous week. If we subtract the five days of travel from Philippi (Acts 20:6), we arrive at a Friday as the departure date, so that the Passover began and ended on a Thursday. Between 52 and 60, it is very probable that Nisan 14 fell on a Thursday only on April 7, 57 (Goldstine 1973, 88–89).

When Paul was arrested in the temple courtyard, the Roman tribune thought it possible that he might be a certain "Egyptian who recently stirred up a revolt and led the four thousand assassins out into the wilderness" (Acts 21:38). According to Josephus, this uprising took place after the death of Claudius in October 54 (*Jewish War* 2.261–263; *Jewish Antiquities* 20.167–172). Because the leader, an Egyptian Jew, had escaped (*Jewish Antiquities* 20.171–172), a repeat of the rebellion was feared. Since the disturbance followed a series of actions taken by Nero (20.158–164), the event can be dated no earlier than 55. It is possible that the rebellion took place during the Passover festival of 56, due to apocalyptic expectations raised by the Sabbath year 55/56 (Wacholder 1975, 216).

The change in governorship from Felix to Festus

Paul was a prisoner under both the Roman procurators Felix and Festus in Jerusalem and Caesarea. According to Acts 24:10, Felix had already occupied this office "for many years," and in reality he probably entered office first in 49, not 52 (Schwartz 1992, 223–236). After his dismissal, Felix was protected from more severe punishment by his brother Pallas (Josephus, *Jewish Antiquities* 20.182). It has been assumed that this would only have been possible prior to 55, when Pallas lost his office as the head of the imperial finance administration (Tacitus, *Annals* 13.14). But the charges against Pallas were dropped a year later (*Annals* 13.23), and until Nero ordered him to be poisoned in 62 (*Annals* 14.65), he retained great influence due to his legendary wealth (Dio Cassius, *Roman History* 62.14.3; Green 1992). The last coins that can with certainty be dated to the procuratorship of Felix are from the first year of Nero (54/55); coins from the year 56/57 are still lacking. In the fifth year of the emperor (58/59), a surprisingly large number of new coins were issued in Judea, which may well be due to the arrival of a new governor (Smallwood 1976, 269 n. 40; Kindler 1981). An earlier date has also been considered on the basis of Eusebius (Barrett 1998, 1117–1118), but his contradictory reports (*Chronicle* [Helm edition, 181–182]; *Ecclesiastical History* 2.22) can be attributed to a misinterpreted source (probably Justus of Tiberias), which gave the date of 59 (Riesner 1998, 222–223).

Intervals and Series of Events in Paul's Letters

Three series of events can be established from the letters of Paul.

(1) From the autobiographical reflections at the beginning of the letter to the Galatians, it follows that, after his calling near Damascus (implied by Gal 1:17), Paul went to "Arabia" and again to Damascus (1:17); "after three years" he went to Jerusalem (1:18); later he was in Syria and Cilicia (1:21), and "after fourteen years" again in Jerusalem (Gal 2:1). It is debated whether the conflict with Peter in Antioch (Gal 2:11–14) occurred after the second visit to Jerusalem or was placed at the end for rhetorical reasons (Lüdemann 1984, 57–59). This controversial point can only be decided as part of a complete chronological reconstruction. The letter does not tell us when the communities in Galatia were founded, or how much time had elapsed between the second visit to Jerusalem, or the incident in Antioch, and the composition of the text.

(2) A second series of events is based on 1 Thessalonians. Before the founding of the community in Thessalonica, the capital of the province of Macedonia, the apostle visited Philippi (1 Thess 2:2; cf. Phil 4:15–16); after his departure from Thessalonica, he visited Athens (1 Thess 3:1). It is probable, though not entirely certain, that the trip included Corinth as a further stop (cf. 2 Cor 11:7–9).

(3) A third series is linked to a collection, organized by Paul in communities that he had founded, to support the early church in Jerusalem. This sequence allows us to reconstruct the following order for the letters: 1 Corinthians – 2 Corinthians – Romans. Without attempting to refine the order further by adopting one of the many divergent hypotheses about the division of the letters, we have the following sequence of events: 1 Corinthians was written in Ephesus (1 Cor 16:9); 2 Corinthians looks back on a time of severe distress "in Asia" (2 Cor 1:8–10) and on a visit to Troas (2 Cor 2:12), and was evidently written in Macedonia (2 Cor 2:13). Mention is made of a forthcoming trip to Judea (2 Cor 1:16; cf. 1 Cor 16:3–4), to be preceded by a visit to Corinth (2 Cor 9:4), as well as of Paul's intention to pursue missionary work in new regions (2 Cor 10:16; cf. Rom 15:20). An intermediate visit to Corinth, widely presumed to have taken place on the basis of 2 Corinthians, is as uncertain as the presumed identification of the collection mentioned in Galatians 2:10 with the one discussed in 1 and 2 Corinthians and Romans (see below). With the sequence of events deduced from the letters to the

Corinthians, various statements in the letter to the Romans can be linked, since the latter presupposes that the collection has been completed (Rom 15:25–26) and was apparently written in Corinth (see below). A trip to Spain via Jerusalem and Rome was planned (15:23–29).

It is clear that this third sequence based on 1 and 2 Corinthians and Romans comes toward the end of Paul's career. How much time elapsed between the stay in Ephesus and the one certain earlier visit to Corinth cannot be determined from the letters alone. It is also not possible to determine in this way whether the stays in Macedonia and Achaia, which are attested by the second sequence, should – when brought into relation with the first sequence – be placed before or after the meeting of the apostles described in Galatians 2:1–10. Even John Knox admitted that an answer to this question can only be conjectural if one excludes evidence from Acts (1987, 40–52). But such an exclusion should be resorted to only if a synthesis of the evidence from Paul's letters and from Acts proves impossible. In the following attempt, possible speeds of travel and the missionary strategy of Paul are both taken into account (Riesner 1998, 235–317).

Chronological Synthesis of the Letters of Paul and the Acts of the Apostles

From Macedonia via Achaia to Jerusalem and Rome (Acts 20–28)

For this period, a particularly large number of indicators are available from Acts that can be connected to external data. The change of the governorship of Judea from Felix to Festus (Acts 24:27), and with it the sending of Paul to trial before the emperor in Rome, can be dated to 59. This agrees with the fact that in this year, the critical date for the Mediterranean voyage – that is, the Jewish Day of Atonement (Acts 27:9) – fell very late. The credibility of this piece of information enhances our confidence in the very detailed chronological indications found within the "we"-narrative covering the trip from Philippi to Jerusalem (Acts 20:6–21:17), indications that point to the year 57 for that trip (see above). If Paul came to Jerusalem for Pentecost of this year, it is understandable that he could be confused with the Jewish troublemaker from Egypt (Acts 21:38), who presumably caused an uprising at the Passover festival of 56. With this dating of the events, there are precisely two years between the apostle's arrival in Jerusalem and his transport to Rome in 59, matching the two years that Luke indicates for the imprisonment in Caesarea (Acts 24:27). We ought therefore to take seriously the reference to "two whole years" for Paul's subsequent Roman imprisonment (Acts 28:30), so that the narrative of Acts extends approximately to early 62.

It agrees with Luke's account that, according to Paul, too, the trip to Jerusalem was preceded by a stay in Macedonia and Achaia (Acts 20:1–3; 2 Cor 2:13). "Erastus, the city treasurer [oikonomos tēs poleōs]," who sends greetings in Romans 16:23, may be identified with the Corinthian Erastus (Acts 19:22), who is probably known as well from epigraphic evidence[3] (see Theissen 1982, 75–83; Gill 1989). Luke also knew that Paul wanted to travel to Rome via Jerusalem (Acts 19:21). He mentions the collection at least briefly (24:17) and seems to presuppose it in other places (cf. 20:4; 24:26). According to Luke, the apostle made his travel plans known for the first time in Ephesus (19:21), which corresponds well to the fact that the first undisputed mention of the Jerusalem collection appears in 1 Corinthians 16:1–4 and 2 Corinthians 8–9. Dating Romans to the early part of 57 also makes understandable why Paul pays special attention to the problem of paying taxes (Rom 13:1–7). An oppressive tax at that time led to a wave of complaints in 58 and to related reforms by Nero (Tacitus, *Annals* 13.50–51; Jewett 2007, 798–799).

From the meeting of the apostles in Jerusalem to Ephesus (Acts 15–18)

If there is such a thing as an "anchor" for Pauline chronology, it is the Gallio inscription. At the latest, it allows the hearing with the proconsul to have taken place between July 51 and June 52, though Gallio had probably already left Corinth in the fall of 51. The expulsion edict of Claudius that affected Roman Jews (Acts 18:2) can be dated to 49. It forced Paul to abandon his long-cherished plan (Rom 1:13; 15:22–23), which had presumably been established already during the second missionary journey (Bornkamm 1971, 51), to travel from Thessalonica along the Via Egnatia to the Adriatic in order to reach Rome (Riesner 1998, 295–296). News of the edict must have reached Paul by early 50 at the latest. The one and a half years of his stay in Corinth (Acts 18:11) point, even by a very generous calculation, to a departure at the latest at the end of 51. This calculation corresponds nicely to a probable reconstruction of the Gallio incident (Riesner 1998, 208–211). The complaint against Paul was brought forward immediately after the arrival of the governor, as the leadership of the synagogue did not yet know about his anti-Jewish sentiments (Acts 18:12–17). For the relatively short period from 49 to 51, the reports of three independent sources – the Gallio inscription, Acts, and Orosius – converge remarkably closely. If Paul left Corinth at the end of 51 to travel to Syria and Judea via Ephesus (Acts 18:18–22), it must have happened before the end of the shipping season in October. Since the Taurus mountains would then be impassable, a continuation of the journey from Jerusalem and Antioch through the Phrygian part of Galatia to Ephesus (Acts 18:22–23; 19:1) would not have been possible until the early part of 52.

Paul's chronologically well-defined first stay in Corinth makes it possible to establish dating for his (so-called) second missionary journey. Founding of the communities in Philippi and Thessalonica took place in the year 49/50. First Thessalonians was written very soon after the sudden departure of the apostle from that community, and for this reason the great majority of scholars date the letter to the beginning of his stay in Corinth in the year 50 (Carson and Moo 2005, 542–543).[4] The anti-Jewish polemic of 1 Thessalonians 2:14–16 may have been provoked by the immediate impression of the persecution in Syria in 48 (Bockmuehl 2001) and the negative effects of Claudius's edict of 49 on Paul's missionary plans (Riesner 1998, 352–354). The journey that took Paul from Jerusalem, with a stop in Antioch, over the Taurus mountains to visit the communities in the southern part of the province of Galatia, and then through the western part of Asia Minor to the Aegean (Acts 15:30–16:8), cannot have taken place entirely in the year 49. The apostolic council of Acts 15 is therefore to be dated, in agreement with many scholars, to the year 48. The order in which the communities in Philippi, Thessalonica, Athens, and Corinth were founded is also confirmed by Paul (1 Thess 2:2; Phil 4:15–16; 1 Thess 3:1; 2 Cor 11:7–9).

From Ephesus to Achaia (Acts 18–20)

Here there is, at most, one date that can be somewhat narrowly defined, but the sequence of events in Acts can be placed chronologically with the help of the previous and subsequent series. From the arrival of Paul in Ephesus in the first half of 52, the slightly less than three years of his stay (Acts 20:31) lead to a departure at the end of 54 or early 55. Yet uncertainty in the provincial capital of Asia Minor made precisely the turn of 54 to 55 a dangerous period for the apostle. According to Acts 19:23–40, he was obliged to break off his stay due to local disturbances; 2 Corinthians 1:8–10, too, presuppose a relatively recent life-threatening situation in this province. For this reason, 2 Corinthians should be dated to 55/56. With the death of Claudius in 54, the edict expelling Jews from Rome became invalid. As a result, already with 2 Corinthians 10:16 (as the point of contact with Rom 15:20–24 indicates), plans for a trip to Spain, and with it a stay in Rome, began to take shape. Paul's travels after leaving Ephesus more likely required two winters rather than one (Riesner 1998, 300–301). Some have placed missionary activity in the eastern part of the province of Macedonia and as far as Illyricum in this period (Bruce 1990, 423; Schnabel 2004, 1250–1257, cf. Rom 15:19). Acts and Paul agree that, after the stay in Ephesus, Troas was a site of Paul's activities, although, to be sure, they also mention different visits to Macedonia before and after the completion of 2 Corinthians (2 Cor 2:12; Acts 20:5–6).

First Corinthians belongs to the Ephesian period (1 Cor 16:8–9). Since, at the time it was written, there were already a number of "churches of Asia [Minor]" (16:19), this too is an indication of a longer stay. The letter should probably be placed toward the end of this stay, in 54 (before the Passover? [1 Cor 5:8]). Opposition was already evident (1 Cor 15:32; 16:5–9), but the apostle delayed a trip to Corinth because he hoped his mission would bear further results (1 Cor 16:8–9). A possible point of congruence between the letter and Acts can be seen in the sending of Timothy to Macedonia (Acts 19:22) or Corinth (1 Cor 16:10–11). It is possible that 1 Corinthians 7:26 alludes to the consequences of a famine between 52 and 54 (Winter 1989). The frequently proposed hypothesis of an intermediate visit from Ephesus to Corinth is not strictly necessary. With early church tradition (see Ambrosiaster 2009, 213, 234–235), one can identify 1 Corinthians with the "tearful letter" (2 Cor 2:3–4; 7:8–9) and think that Paul twice cancelled a planned trip (cf. 2 Cor 13:1; Hyldahl 1986, 88–106). Since, at the time Paul wrote Philippians, he expected his imminent release and planned a visit to Philippi (Phil 1:18–27; 2:24), many scholars have dated the letter to an Ephesian imprisonment (Thielman 2003), which must then be placed in 54/55. But there are also those who argue strongly that Philippians was written in Rome (Bockmuehl 1998, 25–32). The slaveowner Philemon evidently belonged to the community in Colossae (compare Col 4:9, 17 with Phlm 2, 10–12), and Paul met his escaped slave Onesimus during an imprisonment (Phlm 10), which can hardly have been in Caesarea or Rome. For this reason, and because Philemon 22 mentions a visit in Asia Minor, many scholars also put the composition of the letter to Philemon in Ephesus (Fitzmyer 2000). For Colossians, the list of greetings of which (Col 4:7–17) is similar to that in Philemon (23–24), Ephesus is explicitly claimed in one tradition as the place of composition (see above).[5]

From Paul's call near Damascus to the council of the apostles in Jerusalem (Acts 9–15)

In the autobiographical reflections of Galatians 1–2, Paul indicates that, after his call near Damascus (1:15–17), he visited Jerusalem "after three years" and again "after fourteen years" (1:18; 2:1). A number of uncertainties surround these statements. If the years mentioned are partial rather than full, the intervals amount to less than two and thirteen years respectively. Moreover, the "fourteen years" may be counted either from his original call or from his first visit to Jerusalem. The majority of scholars identify the visit to Jerusalem of Galatians 2:1–10 with the apostolic council depicted in Acts 15. On the other hand, Acts 11:28–30 and 12:25 mention an earlier collection trip to Jerusalem taken with Barnabas. At the moment, a growing number of exegetes identify this latter journey with the one mentioned in Galatians 2:1–10 (Porter 2000a, 207; de Roo 2007, 175–216; Schmidt 2007, 84–98). The result is a sequence of events that not only corresponds with Acts, but is also historically plausible (Bauckham 1995; Schäfer 2004): at the time that Paul wrote Galatians, when he wanted to cite his second visit to Jerusalem to support his claim that Gentile Christians ought not to be circumcised, he could only point to Titus as a precedent (Gal 2:3); a fundamental decision had not yet been made. After the growth of mixed communities in Syria and the emergence of largely Gentile Christian communities in southern Galatia, the threat from zealot branches of Judaism (see above) increased, as did tension between Jewish and Gentile Christians (Gal 2:12–13; 6:12; Acts 15:1–2). This explains the concerns of the early church in Jerusalem and the vacillating of Peter and even Barnabas (Gal 2:13–14).

A mission of Paul in the region of Galatia can be demonstrated neither from Acts 16:6; 18:23 nor from Galatians (Riesner 1998, 286–291); hence the letter is addressed to the communities founded during the first missionary journey in the Phrygian and Lycaonian parts of the province of Galatia (Acts 13–14; Witulski 2000). Evidently, Galatians was written soon after their founding (Gal 1:6) and in immediate reaction to the incident in Antioch (Gal 2:11–14). The letter is best dated shortly before the council of the apostles in Jerusalem (Acts 15; cf. Witherington 1998, 8–20; Carson and Moo 2005, 461–468). If Galatians appeared before 1 Corinthians rather than after, it is also clear why, in the latter letter, Paul mentions Peter, the Lord's brothers, and Barnabas without any apparent strain (1 Cor 9:1–6). Galatians 2:10 can be understood as looking back to the collection he had delivered with Barnabas (Longenecker 1990, 60–61). If twelve to thirteen years (Gal 2:1) are added to the date of Paul's call in 31/32, then this collection took place in 44/45 and thus at the time of the death of Agrippa I (Acts 12:20–23). The first visit to Jerusalem two to three years after his call (Gal 1:18; also mentioned in Acts 9:26–29) would have taken place in 33/34. Paul and Luke agree that this was followed by a stay in Syria and Cilicia (Gal 1:21) or Tarsus in Cilicia (Acts 9:30).

It is entirely possible that Paul aimed for a mission among Jews in the eastern diaspora following his call near Damascus (Bauckham 2000). A number of scholars, however, believe he started at once in the Nabatean kingdom (cf. Gal 4:25), perhaps even evangelizing Gentiles and Jews in its capital, Petra (cf. Gal 1:17; Hengel and Schwemer 1997, 106–113). For this reason, he was also persecuted by the Nabatean king Aretas (2 Cor 11:32–33). Luke, for his part, knows nothing of this; Acts 9:23–25 are not, however, by any means irreconcilable with the remarks of Paul (Harding 1993). According to Acts 22:17–21, Paul first received his call to undertake a Gentile mission through a vision in the temple during the visit to Jerusalem that followed his call. If Paul speaks of a "secret" (*mystērion*) of God's salvific plan that included Gentiles (Rom 11:25–26), then exegesis of Isaiah 6 lies in the background (Kim 2002). Acts 22:17–21, too, echo the vision of the prophet Isaiah in the temple (Riesner 2004, 150–152). Furthermore, Paul saw Jerusalem as the starting-point of his eschatologically based mission to Gentiles (Rom 15:19). Romans 15:16–28 draw on Isaiah 66:18–21; at the end of the book of Isaiah, Paul evidently found the path of his mission sketched out (Riesner 1998, 245–253). In the terms of ancient Jewish geography, the stations of that mission were Jerusalem, Tarsus, Cilicia, Lydia in Asia Minor, Mysia, Bithynia, Macedonia/Greece, and the western end of the world. That corresponds remarkably to the route of the Pauline mission according to Acts, and thus enhances the latter's credibility. Perhaps, too, the dispersal of the sons of Japhet according to the table of nations in Genesis 10 had an influence on the apostle's missionary strategy (Scott 1995).

Occasionally, scholars have connected the ecstatic experience that, according to Paul, took place "fourteen years" before the writing of 2 Corinthians (2 Cor 12:2–9) with the vision in the temple (Hyldahl 1986, 118–120). But this is problematic chronologically, since the "fourteen years" would bring us to 42/43 as the date of the temple vision, which is too late. Moreover, according to 2 Corinthians 12:4, what Paul experienced at that time could not be communicated with human words, whereas Acts 22:17–21 speak of the reception of a prophetic message. Chronologically, 42/43 was the time of Paul's transition to the Antiochene mission (Acts 11:25–26), and since he mentions the ecstatic experience as part of his apostolic defense (beginning in 2 Cor 11:5), there may well be a connection (Martin 1986, 399). Buck and Taylor (1969, 222–226) identify the ecstatic experience with the call, which they place in 32. This compels them to date 2 Corinthians 10–13 to 47, and thus even before the Gallio incident.

Paul before his call

A scribal education (Acts 22:3) and activity as a persecutor in Jerusalem (Acts 8:3) are presupposed by Paul himself (Gal 1:13–14, 22–23; cf. Hengel 1991; Haacker 2003, 20–24). Only the dating of his birth in Tarsus (Acts 22:3) is quite uncertain. According to Joachim Jeremias (1971, 14), Paul as an ordained rabbi would have been between

25 and 30 years old at the time of his call, but the value of the rabbinic evidence on which Jeremias draws is uncertain. The apostle's Roman citizenship (Acts 16:37–38, etc.)[6] may carry us a little further, since his father was probably a freed slave. According to Jerome, Paul's parents came from Giscalis in Upper Gallilee to Tarsus as slaves following a rebellion (*On Illustrious Men* 5). Especially after the death of Herod the Great in 4 BC (Josephus, *Jewish War* 2.11–13) and the assumption of direct Roman rule of Judea in AD 6 (*Jewish War* 2.117–118), zealot uprisings broke out. Thus, the date of Paul's birth may have been around the turn of the era (Dunn 2009, 510). This corresponds well to the fact that Acts 7:58 refers to him as *neanias* (one under 40) at the stoning of Stephen, and he refers to himself as an older man (*presbytēs*) in Philemon 9.

Paul from the end of Acts to his martyrdom in Rome

The value of Acts is further illustrated by the way reconstructions of events following its conclusion (Acts 28) sharply diverge. (1) Against the assumption that the apostle was executed immediately thereafter is the unanimous tradition of a martyrdom in Rome during the persecutions under Nero that began in July 64. Because of the illegal execution of the Lord's brother James in 62, the high priest Annas II was removed (Josephus, *Jewish Antiquities* 20.197–203). For this reason, the Sanhedrin may have abandoned its charges in Rome, so that the legal action against Paul ended without a verdict after two years (cf. Acts 28:30; Tajra 1994). (2) With this in mind, a number of scholars who believe that the letter to the Philippians was written from Rome assume that Paul made another journey to the east on the basis of this text and the Pastoral epistles (cf. Phil 2:24; 1 Tim 1:3; Tit 1:5, etc.). But if so, then Paul had abandoned his plan for Spain, which for him held eschatological significance (Riesner 2010). Eusebius possessed no tradition for a last journey to the east, but attempts his own reconstruction of events after Acts (*Ecclesiastical History* 2.22). The indications in 1 Timothy and Titus, whether or not these letters are genuine, can find a place within the framework of Acts 15–28 (Riesner 2006). (3) *First Clement* 5:5–7 attest to a tradition from the first century according to which Paul reached Spain, possibly as an exile (Gunther 1972, 139–150; Löhr 2001).

Proposed Chronological Synthesis

On the basis of the discussion above, the chronological reconstruction in table 1.1 is suggested for Paul:

Alternative chronological syntheses

For the sake of comparison, table 1.2 offers six other chronologies. In table 1.2, "Jerus. I–V" stand for the five journeys to Jerusalem mentioned in Acts, while "1 and 2 Miss." represent Paul's first and second missionary journeys.

Table 1.1 Proposed chronological synthesis for Paul

Contemporary history	Paul and early Christianity
26–36 Pilate prefect of Judea	30 Crucifixion of Jesus
	31/32 Stephen's martyrdom; call
	33/34 Jerusalem
	34–42 Syria and Cilicia
37 Death of Tiberius; 39/40 disturbances in Antioch	Around 37 term "Christians" used in Antioch
40 Death of Aretas IV of Nabatea	
41 Death of Caligula; Agrippa I king of Judea	41/42 Martyrdom of James, son of Zebedee
	42/44 Antioch
44 Death of Agrippa I	44/45 Antioch collection, with Barnabas, for Jerusalem
44–49 Dearth and famine in Judea	Between 45 and 47 with Barnabas in Cyprus and southern Galatia
48 Jewish disturbances in Antioch	48 Conflict with Peter in Antioch (Galatians)
	Apostolic council in Jerusalem
49 Edict of Claudius on the Jews in Rome	49/50 Macedonia: Philippi, Thessalonica
	50 Corinth (1 Thessalonians, 2 Thessalonians [?])
51 Gallio proconsul of Achaia	51 Trial before Gallio; journey to Jerusalem
54 Death of Claudius	52–55 Ephesus (54: 1 Corinthians)
54/55 Murder of the proconsul Silanus of Asia Minor	54/55 Imprisonment in Ephesus (Philippians, Philemon, Colossians [?])
	55 Troas
55/56 Sabbath year in Palestine	55/56 Macedonia (2 Corinthians)
56 Uprising of "the Egyptian"	56/57 Corinth (57: Romans)
	57 Arrest in Jerusalem
Until 59, Felix procurator in Judea	57–59 Imprisonment in Caesarea
59 Festus procurator in Judea	59 Sent to Rome
	60–62 Imprisonment in Rome
	62/63 Spain (exile?)
64 Fire in Rome, persecution under Nero	64 Martyrdom in Rome

Table 1.2 Alternative chronological syntheses for Paul

	Knox	Lüdemann	Hyldahl	Jewett	Porter	Dunn	Riesner
Crucifixion	30	27 (30)	–	33	30 (33)	30	30
Damascus	34	30 (33)	39/40	34	33/34	32	31/32
Jerus. I	37	33 (36)	41/42	37	37	34/35	33/34
Jerus. II	–	–	–	–	47	–	44/45
1 Miss.	From 40	34 (37)	–	43–45	47/48	Before 47/48	ca. 45–47
Jerus. III	51	47 (50)	52/53	49	49	47/48	48
2 Miss.	–	36 (39)	–	46–49	49–52	–	48–50
Corinth	53/54	51/52 (2nd time)	49–51	50–51	51/52	49/50–51/52	50–51
Jerus. IV	–	–	–	–	–	–	51/52
Ephesus	From 46	48–50 (51–53)	53/54	53–55	53–56	52/53–55	52–55
Macedonia	–	50 (53)	54/55	56	56	–	55/56
Jerus. V	54 (55)	52 (55)	55	57	57	57	57
Festus	–	–	–	59	59	59	59
Rome	–	–	–	60–62	60–62	60–62	60–62

It is striking how widely the three reconstructions that attempt to detach themselves entirely from the framework of Acts differ from each other. This is to be attributed to the risky emphasis each places on an uncertain date (Knox and Hyldahl: Aretas; Lüdemann: a Claudius edict in 41), which is used as foundational for the entire chronology. That this method cannot lead to a chronological consensus is apparent. By way of contrast, the three most recently proposed reconstructions are in striking agreement with each other, since each takes the framework of Acts as largely reliable. Robert Jewett has adopted an intermediate position. Because he gives a late date of 51 for the apostolic council and assumes too lengthy periods of travel for the second missionary journey (1979, 95–100), he runs into chronological difficulties and is obliged to set this trip before the council. From the Gallio incident on, however, he follows the framework of Acts and agrees with the three chronologies that take their orientation from it.

Chronology and theology

Chronological reconstructions can have implications for the understanding of Pauline theology. Gerd Lüdemann (1984) dates 1 Thessalonians to 41 and derives from it a Pauline theology that differs substantially from the later letters in its soteriology and eschatology. The reconstruction proposed here also has possible consequences. (1) Chronologically, it is not impossible that Paul encountered Jesus during Jesus's final activities in Jerusalem. (2) The proximity in time between 1 Corinthians and Philippians renders the assumption unnecessary that Paul abandoned a cosmic in favor of an individualistic eschatology. (3) If Galatians is dated prior to the apostolic council, it follows that Paul possessed a distinctive understanding of justification already at that time. (4) The sequence Galatians – 1 Corinthians suggests that there was no decisive break with Peter and the Lord's brother James. (5) After the Jewish persecutions (1 Thessalonians) and the conflict in Galatia (Galatians) in the 40s, Paul could later acknowledge Israel's abiding salvation-historic significance (Rom 9–11) and argue for the rights of Jewish Christians to live according to Torah (Rom 14–15).

Notes

1   Biblical quotations are taken from the New Revised Standard Version.
2   What Tertullian referred to as "the year of the Gemini" was AD 29. But because the calculation probably originated in Egypt, where the year began in August, here too the year 30 should be used as a starting-point.
3   *Corinth: Results of Excavations Conducted by the American School of Classical Studies at Athens,* Volume 8, Part 3: *The Inscriptions 1926–1950* (Princeton: American School of Classical Studies at Athens, 1966), inscription 232.
4   If 2 Thessalonians is genuine, then it was most likely written shortly after 1 Thessalonians in order to clear up misunderstandings created by eschatalogical statements in 1 Thessalonians 4:13–5:11 (Bruce 1982, xxxix–xliv; Röcker 2009).

5   For the composition of Colossians during an Ephesian imprisonment, see Wright (1986, 21–39).
6   That Paul was brought to Rome for trial speaks against an invention of Paul's Roman citizenship by Luke (Rapske 1994).

References

Alexander, Loveday C. A. 1993. Chronology of Paul. Pages 115–123 in *Dictionary of Paul and his Letters*. Edited by Gerald F. Hawthorne and Ralph P. Martin. Downers Grove, Ill.: InterVarsity.

Ambrosiaster. 2009. *Commentaries on Romans and 1–2 Corinthians*. Translated by Gerald L. Bray. Downers Grove, Ill.: IVP Academic.

Barrett, C. K. 1998. *A Critical and Exegetical Commentary on the Acts of the Apostles*. Volume 2. Edinburgh: T. & T. Clark.

Bauckham, Richard. 1995. James and the Jerusalem Church. Pages 415–480 in *The Book of Acts in its Palestinian Setting*. Edited by Richard Bauckham. Grand Rapids: Eerdmans.

Bauckham, Richard. 2000. What if Paul Had Travelled East rather than West? *Biblical Interpretation* 8: 171–184.

Bockmuehl, Markus. 1998. *The Epistle to the Philippians*. London: A. & C. Black.

Bockmuehl, Markus. 2001. 1 Thessalonians 2:14–16 and the Church in Jerusalem. *Tyndale Bulletin* 52: 1–31.

Bornkamm, Günther. 1971. *Paul*. London: Hodder and Stoughton.

Botermann, Helga. 1996. *Das Judenedikt des Kaisers Claudius: Römischer Staat und Christiani im 1. Jahrhundert*. Stuttgart: Steiner.

Bowersock, G. W. 1983. *Roman Arabia*. Cambridge, Mass.: Harvard University Press.

Bruce, F. F. 1982. *1 and 2 Thessalonians*. Waco, Tex.: Word.

Bruce, F. F. 1990. *The Acts of the Apostles: The Greek Text with Introduction and Commentary*. Third edition. Grand Rapids: Eerdmans.

Buck, Charles, and Greer Taylor. 1969. *Saint Paul: A Study in the Development of his Thought*. New York: Scribner.

Bunine, Alexis. 2004. Paul, Jacques, Félix, Festus et les autres: pour une révision de la chronologie des derniers procurateurs de Palestine. *Revue biblique* 111: 387–408, 531–562.

Bunine, Alexis. 2006. La date de la première visite de Paul à Jérusalem. *Revue biblique* 113: 436–456, 601–622.

Campbell, Douglas A. 2002. An Anchor for Pauline Chronology: Paul's Flight from "the Ethnarch of King Aretas" (2 Corinthians 11:32–33). *Journal of Biblical Literature* 121: 279–302.

Campbell, Douglas A. 2005. Possible Inscriptional Attestation to Sergius Paul[l]us (Acts 13:6–12), and the Implications for Pauline Chronology. *Journal of Theological Studies* 56: 1–29.

Carson, D. A., and Douglas J. Moo. 2005. *An Introduction to the New Testament*. Second edition. Grand Rapids: Zondervan.

Christol, M., and Thomas Drew-Bear. 2002. Les Sergii Paulli et Antioche. Pages 177–191 in *Actes du Ier Congrès International sur Antioche de Pisidie*. Edited by Thomas Drew-Bear, Mehmet Taşlialan, and Christine M. Thomas. Paris: Diffusion de Boccard.

De Roo, Jacqueline C. R. 2007. *"Works of the Law" at Qumran and in Paul*. Sheffield: Sheffield Phoenix.

Dockx, S. 1984. *Chronologies néotestamentaires et vie de l'Église primitive: recherches exégétiques*. Second edition. Leuven: Peeters.

Donfried, Karl P. 1992. Chronology: New Testament. *Anchor Bible Dictionary* 1: 1011–1022.

Downs, David J. 2006. Chronology of the NT. *New Interpreter's Dictionary of the Bible* 1: 633–636.

Dunn, James D. G. 2003. *Jesus Remembered.* Grand Rapids: Eerdmans.

Dunn, James D. G. 2009. *Beginning from Jerusalem.* Grand Rapids: Eerdmans.

Finegan, Jack. 1998. *Handbook of Biblical Chronology: Principles of Time Reckoning in the Ancient World and Problems of Chronology in the Bible.* Revised edition. Peabody, Mass.: Hendrickson.

Fitzmyer, Joseph A. 2000. *The Letter to Philemon.* New York: Doubleday.

Gebhardt, Oscar von. 1902. *Passio S. Theclae Virginis: die lateinischen Übersetzungen der Acta Pauli et Theclae.* Leipzig: J. C. Hinrichs.

Gill, D. W. J. 1989. Erastus the Aedile. *Tyndale Bulletin* 40: 293–301.

Goldstine, Herman H. 1973. *New and Full Moons 1001 BC to AD 1651.* Philadelphia: American Philosophical Society.

Green, Joel B. 1992. Festus, Porcius. *Anchor Bible Dictionary* 2: 794–795.

Gunther, John J. 1972. *Paul: Messenger and Exile: A Study in the Chronology of his Life and Letters.* Valley Forge: Judson.

Haacker, Klaus. 2003. Paul's Life. Pages 19–33 in *The Cambridge Companion to St. Paul.* Edited by James D. G. Dunn. Cambridge: Cambridge University Press.

Harding, Mark. 1993. On the Historicity of Acts: Comparing Acts 9.23–5 with 2 Corinthians 11.32–3. *New Testament Studies* 39: 518–538.

Hemer, Colin J. 1980. Observations on Pauline Chronology. Pages 3–18 in *Pauline Studies: Essays Presented to Professor F. F. Bruce on his 70th Birthday.* Edited by Donald A. Hagner and Murray J. Harris. Grand Rapids: Eerdmans.

Hemer, Colin J. 1990. *The Book of Acts in the Setting of Hellenistic History.* Winona Lake: Eisenbrauns.

Hengel, Martin, in collaboration with Roland Deines. 1991. *The Pre-Christian Paul.* London: SCM.

Hengel, Martin, and Anna Maria Schwemer. 1997. *Paul between Damascus and Antioch: The Unknown Years.* Louisville: Westminster John Knox.

Hoehner, H. W. 1992. Chronology. Pages 118–122 in *Dictionary of Jesus and the Gospels.* Edited by Joel B. Green, Scot McKnight, and I. Howard Marshall. Downers Grove, Ill.: InterVarsity.

Humphreys, Colin J., and W. G. Waddington. 1989. Astronomy and the Date of the Crucifixion. Pages 165–181 in *Chronos, Kairos, Christos: Nativity and Chronological Studies Presented to Jack Finegan.* Edited by Jerry Vardaman and Edwin M. Yamauchi. Winona Lake: Eisenbrauns.

Hyldahl, Niels. 1986. *Die paulinische Chronologie.* Leiden: Brill.

Jeremias, Joachim. 1971. *Der Schlüssel zur Theologie des Apostels Paulus.* Stuttgart: Calwer.

Jewett, Robert. 1979: *A Chronology of Paul's Life.* Philadelphia: Fortress.

Jewett, Robert. 2007. *Romans.* Minneapolis: Fortress.

Kim, Seyoon. 2002. The "Mystery" of Romans 11:25–26 Once More. Pages 239–257 in *Paul and the New Perspective: Second Thoughts on the Origin of Paul's Gospel.* Grand Rapids: Eerdmans.

Kindler, Arie. 1981. A Re-assessment of the Dates of Some Coins of the Roman Procurators of Judaea. *Israel Numismatic Journal* 5: 19–21.

Knauf, Ernst Axel. 1983. Zum Ethnarchen des Aretas 2 Kor 11,32. *Zeitschrift für die neutestamentliche Wissenschaft* 74: 145–147.

Knauf, Ernst Axel. 1998. Die Arabienreise des Apostels Paulus. Pages 465–471 in Martin Hengel and Anna Maria Schwemer, *Paulus zwischen Damaskus und Antiochien: die unbekannten Jahre des Apostels.* Tübingen: Mohr Siebeck.

Knox, John. 1987. *Chapters in a Life of Paul.* Revised and edited by Douglas R. A. Hare. Macon, Ga.: Mercer University Press.

Kokkinos, Nikos. 1998. *The Herodian Dynasty: Origins, Role in Society and Eclipse.* Sheffield: Sheffield Academic.

Kümmel, Werner Georg. 1972. *The New Testament: The History of the Investigation of its Problems*. Nashville: Abingdon.

Levick, Barbara. 1990. *Claudius*. London: Batsford.

Löhr, Hermut. 2001. Zur Paulus-Notiz in 1 Clem 5,5–7. Pages 197–213 in *Das Ende des Paulus: historische, theologische und literaturgeschichtliche Aspekte*. Edited by Friedrich Wilhelm Horn. Berlin: De Gruyter.

Longenecker, Richard N. 1990. *Galatians*. Dallas: Word.

Lüdemann, Gerd. 1984. *Paul, Apostle to the Gentiles: Studies in Chronology*. Philadelphia: Fortress.

Marshall, I. Howard. 1980. *The Acts of the Apostles: An Introduction and Commentary*. Grand Rapids: Eerdmans.

Martin, Ralph P. 1986. *2 Corinthians*. Waco, Tex.: Word.

Mitford, Terence Bruce. 1980. Roman Cyprus. *Aufstieg und Niedergang der römischen Welt* II 7/2: 1285–1384.

Murphy-O'Connor, Jerome. 1996. *Paul: A Critical Life*. Oxford: Clarendon.

Porter, Stanley E. 2000a. Chronology, New Testament. Pages 201–208 in *Dictionary of New Testament Background*. Edited by Craig A. Evans and Stanley E. Porter. Downers Grove, Ill.: InterVarsity.

Porter, Stanley E. 2000b. Chronology of the New Testament. Pages 248–252 in *Eerdmans Dictionary of the Bible*. Edited by David Noel Freedman. Grand Rapids: Eerdmans.

Rapske, Brian. 1994. *The Book of Acts and Paul in Roman Custody*. Grand Rapids: Eerdmans.

Riesner, Rainer. 1998. *Paul's Early Period: Chronology, Mission Strategy, Theology*. Grand Rapids: Eerdmans.

Riesner, Rainer. 2004. L'héritage juif de Paul et les débuts de sa mission. Pages 135–155 in *Paul, une théologie en construction*. Edited by Andreas Dettwiler, Jean-Daniel Kaestli, and Daniel Marguerat. Geneva: Labor et Fides.

Riesner, Rainer. 2006. Once More: Luke-Acts and the Pastoral Epistles. Pages 239–258 in *History and Exegesis: New Testament Essays in Honor of Dr. E. Earle Ellis for his 80th Birthday*. Edited by Sang-Won Son. New York: T. & T. Clark.

Riesner, Rainer. 2010. Romans 15 and Paul's Projected Journey to Spain (Hispania). Pages 93–100 in *Pau, Fructuós i el cristianisme primitiu a Tarragona*. Edited by José M. Gavaldà, A. Muñoz, and Armand Puig i Tárrech. Tarragona: Insat-Liber.

Röcker, Fritz W. 2009. *Belial und Katechon: eine Untersuchung zu 2 Thess 2,1–12 und 1 Thess 4,13–5,11*. Tübingen: Mohr Siebeck.

Sack, Dorothée. 1989. *Damaskus: Entwicklung und Struktur einer orientalisch-islamischen Stadt*. Mainz am Rhein: Von Zabern.

Schäfer, Ruth. 2004. *Paulus bis zum Apostelkonzil: ein Beitrag zur Einleitung in den Galaterbrief, zur Geschichte der Jesusbewegung und zur Pauluschronologie*. Tübingen: Mohr Siebeck.

Schmidt, Josef. 2007. *Gesetzesfreie Heilsverkündigung im Evangelium nach Matthäus: das Apostelkonzil (Apg 15) als historischer und theologischer Bezugspunkt für die Theologie des Matthäusevangeliums*. Würzburg: Echter.

Schnabel, Eckhard J. 2004. *Early Christian Mission*. Volume 2: *Paul and the Early Church*. Downers Grove, Ill.: InterVarsity.

Schwartz, Daniel R. 1992. *Studies in the Jewish Background of Christianity*. Tübingen: J. C. B. Mohr (Paul Siebeck).

Scott, James M. 1995. *Paul and the Nations: The Old Testament and Jewish Background of Paul's Mission to the Nations with Special Reference to the Destination of Galatians*. Tübingen: J. C. B. Mohr (Paul Siebeck).

Smallwood, E. Mary. 1976. *The Jews under Roman Rule: From Pompey to Diocletian*. Leiden: Brill.

Strobel, August. 1977. *Ursprung und Geschichte des frühchristlichen Osterkalenders*. Berlin: Akademie.

Suhl, Alfred. 1975. *Paulus und seine Briefe: Ein Beitrag zur paulinischen Chronologie*. Gütersloh: Gütersloher Verlagshaus Gerd Mohn.

Tajra, H. W. 1994. *The Martyrdom of St. Paul: Historical and Judicial Context, Traditions, and Legends*. Tübingen: J. C. B. Mohr.

Tatum, Gregory. 2006. *New Chapters in the Life of Paul: The Relative Chronology of his Career*. Washington: Catholic Biblical Association of America.

Taylor, Justin. 1992. The Ethnarch of King Aretas at Damascus: A Note on 2 Cor 11, 32–33. *Revue biblique* 99: 719–728.

Theissen, Gerd. 1982. *The Social Setting of Pauline Christianity: Essays on Corinth*. Philadelphia: Fortress.

Thielman, Frank S. 2003. Ephesus and the Literary Setting of Philippians. Pages 205–223 in *New Testament Greek and Exegesis: Essays in Honor of Gerald F. Hawthorne*. Edited by Amy M. Donaldson and Timothy B. Sailors. Grand Rapids: Eerdmans.

Trebilco, Paul. 2004. *The Early Christians in Ephesus from Paul to Ignatius*. Tübingen: Mohr Siebeck.

Wacholder, Ben Zion. 1975. Chronomessianism: The Timing of Messianic Movements and the Calendar of Sabbatical Cycles. *Hebrew Union College Annual* 46: 201–218.

Weiss, Alexander. 2009a. Der Aufruhr der Silberschmiede (Apg 19,23–40) und das Edikt des Paullus Fabius Persicus (I. Ephesos 17–19). *Biblische Zeitschrift* 53: 69–81.

Weiss, Alexander. 2009b. Sergius Paullus, Statthalter von Zypern. *Zeitschrift für Papyrologie und Epigraphik* 169: 188–192.

Welborn, L. L. 1999. Primum tirocinium Pauli (2 Cor 11, 32–33). *Biblische Zeitschrift* 43: 49–71.

White, Joel. 2007. *Die Erstlingsgabe im Neuen Testament*. Tübingen: Francke.

Winter, Bruce W. 1989. Secular and Christian Responses to Corinthian Famines. *Tyndale Bulletin* 40: 86–106.

Witherington III, Ben. 1998. *Grace in Galatia: A Commentary on St. Paul's Letter to the Galatians*. London: T. & T. Clark.

Witulski, Thomas. 2000. *Die Adressaten des Galaterbriefes: Untersuchungen zur Gemeinde von Antiochia ad Pisidiam*. Göttingen: Vandenhoeck & Ruprecht.

Wright, N. T. 1986. *The Epistles of Paul to the Colossians and to Philemon: An Introduction and Commentary*. Grand Rapids: Eerdmans.

CHAPTER 2

Paul and the Macedonian Believers

Todd D. Still

Although Paul seemingly spent more time founding and forming fellowships of Christ-followers in Galatia, Asia, and Achaia than he did in Macedonia, the apostle was nevertheless able to foster especially meaningful and mutual relations with the Macedonian churches. This chapter explores Paul's initial and continuing contact with his beloved congregations in Philippi and Thessalonica.

At the outset of this chapter, we will consider the arrival of the gospel in Macedonia through Paul and his co-workers. Next, we will examine Paul's subsequent communication with the Thessalonian and Philippian assemblies. A treatment of the Macedonian churches' support of the Pauline mission in general, and the Jerusalem collection in particular, then follows. Lastly, I will offer a sketch of various ecclesial developments in Thessalonica and Philippi.

The Founding of Macedonian Congregations

The beginning of the gospel in Philippi

Near the conclusion of Philippians, Paul praises the congregation for sharing in his suffering (*thlipsis*) by sending him a gift through Epaphroditus (4:14, 18; cf. 2:25–30). Although the gift is not described, and Paul's thanks are qualified, his appreciation is clear. In fact, he singles out the Philippians as the only church that partnered with him in "the matter of giving and receiving"[1] and indicates that they had done so from "the beginning of the gospel" in Macedonia (4:15; cf. Phil 1:5, where Paul expresses his thanks for the assembly's *koinōnia* ["partnership"] "from the first day until now"). Be it within or beyond provincial boundaries, the Philippian fellowship was steadfast in supporting their apostle (4:10, 16).

The Blackwell Companion to Paul, First Edition. Edited by Stephen Westerholm.
© 2011 Blackwell Publishing Ltd. Published 2011 by Blackwell Publishing Ltd.

There is a paucity of information in Philippians regarding the "beginning of the gospel" in Philippi. Indeed, the only detail the letter offers regarding the apostle's initial ministry in the city is that it was marked by conflict (*agōn*, 1:30; cf. arguably applicable general remarks in 2:22; 3:18; 4:9). This comment tallies well with 1 Thessalonians 2:2, where Paul refers to the suffering and maltreatment he experienced in Philippi before coming to Thessalonica.

One may find further corroboration and additional detail about Paul's conflict in Philippi in Acts 16. According to the Acts' account, Paul and Silas got crosswise with the owners of a slave girl when Paul exorcised a "spirit of divination" (lit. "a Pythic spirit") from her. Seeing that "their hope of gain was gone," the girl's masters dragged the missioners before the local magistrates (*stratēgoi*). They proceeded to strip, beat, and imprison them (16:16–24; cf. 2 Cor 11:25). Although these details go beyond what Paul himself reports, they are historically plausible, if not independently verifiable (see, for example, Lüdemann 1989, 183–184).

The same may be said of the other details recorded in Acts 16 regarding Paul's initial ministry in Philippi (so Marshall 1980, 264). Among other particulars, Acts reports that Paul was propelled to travel to Macedonia in the first instance as a result of a night-time vision he received, wherein he encountered a Macedonian man imploring him to come over and help (16:9). Acts also attests that Paul and his traveling companions came to Philippi, depicted in 16:12 as a leading Macedonian city and a Roman colony, via the Aegean island of Samothrace and the seaport city of Neapolis.[2] Once in Philippi, they "remained in the city for some days." While Pauline scholars continue to debate the date and duration of Paul's initial ministry in Philippi, a sizeable majority of interpreters maintains that he first visited the city ca. AD 49 for a period of time "long enough to establish a close friendship between the apostle and this community of believers" (so Fee 1995, 27).

Although Paul's first visit to Philippi was physically painful and socially shameful, it was nonetheless spiritually profitable. Acts relates the conversion and baptism of Lydia, a seller of purple goods from Thyatira, and her household (16:13–15). It also recounts the unlikely salvation and baptism of a certain Philippian jailer and his family (16:25–34). We do not know whether Epaphroditus, Euodia, Syntyche, and Clement, all of whom Paul mentions by name in Philippians, also became believers during Paul's initial visit to Philippi (Phil 2:25; 4:2–3, 18). Our literary sources suggest, however, that the Philippian fellowship was comprised primarily, if not exclusively, of Gentiles and that women were actively involved in congregational life and leadership (see further Bockmuehl 1998, 17–19).

The arrival of the gospel in Thessalonica

According to Acts, once Paul and Silas left Philippi, they journeyed (along the Via Egnatia) through Amphipolis and Apollonia before coming to and remaining in Thessalonica (17:1). These purported movements cohere with Paul's remarks in 1 Thessalonians 2:2 and Philippians 4:16. Additionally, both 1 Thessalonians and Acts report that Paul and his co-workers experienced conflict with non-Christian outsiders in Thessalonica and Philippi. In 1 Thessalonians 2:2, Paul mentions the apostles' courageous proclamation of the gospel in Thessalonica in the face of great opposition (*en pollō agōni*; cf. Phil 1:30). Arguably, Paul also alludes to his conflict in Thessalonica in 1 Thessalonians 2:15 and 2:17 (cf. 3:3–4). Furthermore, Acts 17:5–10a informs that the tension between Paul and certain Thessalonian Jews grew so acute that they sought to drag him before the city authorities (*politarchs*) in order to accuse him and his followers of sedition. We are told that when zealous Jews (who are said to have enlisted aid from some "evil" people of the agora) were unable to locate Paul and Silas at the home of Jason (their host?), they hauled Jason and some other unnamed believers before the *politarchs* instead. The charge lodged against the Christians so disturbed the people and the *politarchs* that Jason was required to post bail and the missioners were forced to leave the city under the cloak of night (see more fully Still 1999a, 61–82, 126–137).

Paul and Silas were not the only ones who experienced trouble in Thessalonica. First Thessalonians indicates that the Thessalonian believers themselves clashed with outsiders in conjunction with their conversion (1:6; 2:14; 3:3–4; cf. 2 Thess 1:4). Indeed, the letter reveals that Paul and his co-workers had instructed the Thessalonians while they were with them to expect affliction (*thlipsis*; 3:3b–4). Furthermore, the missive communicates Paul's belief that the church's reception of the gospel in the throes of *thlipsis* resulted in their imitation of the apostles as well as the Lord and served as an example (*typos*) for all Macedonian and Achaian believers (1:6–7).[3]

In addition to the church's suffering at the hands of their compatriots (*symphyletai*), 1 Thessalonians reveals other forces and factors that shaped the character of the assembly from its inception. As Paul reflects upon his ministry in Thessalonica, he highlights the Thessalonians' positive response to the gospel and their warm reception of the apostles (1:5, 9; 2:1, 13). Arguably, 1 Thessalonians 1:9b–10 functions as an all-too-brief summary of the message proclaimed and embraced in Thessalonica. There, Paul recalls how the Thessalonians "turned to God from idols, to serve a living and true God, and to wait for his Son from heaven, whom he raised from the dead, Jesus who delivers us from the coming wrath." While in their midst, Paul and his colleagues not only taught the (largely) Gentile converts in Thessalonica various aspects of theology, Christology, and eschatology, but they also offered them instructions on sexual, ecclesial, and socio-political matters (see especially 2:12; 4:2, 6, 9, 11).[4] Furthermore, Paul and his companions sought to model for the fellowship lives marked by purity, sincerity, transparency, and industry (note 1:5; 2:3–12). The missioners' evangelistic and pastoral work in Thessalonica, however, came to an abrupt end when a group of (Jewish) people none too pleased with Paul's presence and influence in the city forced the apostle to make a swift exit (2:15, 17–18; cf. Acts 17:10a).

Did Paul help to found other churches in Macedonia?

Thessalonica and Philippi are the only two Macedonian cities that Paul mentions by name in his letters. Additionally, the Thessalonians and Philippians were the only two Macedonian congregations (as far as we know) to receive letters from Paul. When the apostle refers to "the *churches* of Macedonia" in 2 Corinthians 8:1, it is possible that he had other Macedonian fellowships in view (cf. 2 Cor 11:9; Rom 15:26). The same is true when Paul states in 1 Thessalonians 4:10 that the church in Thessalonica loves all the brothers and sisters in Macedonia. Furthermore, if the "word of the Lord sounded forth from [the Thessalonian assembly] in Macedonia" (1 Thess 1:8) and if the Philippian Christians were as winsome in their witness as Paul wanted them to be (Phil 2:14–16), then it is possible that there were other Macedonian house churches begun by Pauline co-workers and converts, if not by the apostle himself. That being said, the record is silent.

Turning to Acts, we have already noted above the report that Paul and Silas traveled from Philippi to Thessalonica via Amphipolis and Apollonia (17:1). There is no indication, however, that the missioners stayed in these latter places any appreciable time, much less founded fellowships in these locales. Acts indicates that, after being forced out of Thessalonica, Paul and Silas traveled some forty miles southwesterly to the Macedonian city of Beroea. According to Acts, a goodly number of Beroean Jews, as well as a fair share of (God-fearing) Greek women and men, eagerly received Paul's message (17:10–12). When Thessalonian Jews, however, got wind of the missioners' whereabouts and activities, they came to Beroea to oppose them (17:13). This unwelcome opposition forced Paul to take leave for Athens (17:15; cf. 1 Thess 3:1). Although the Acts' account may intimate the beginnings of a Beroean congregation during Paul's abbreviated visit (see 17:12, 14), it does not explicitly indicate as much. Could it be that Sopater of Beroea (Acts 20:4), who would later travel alongside Paul, became a believer at this juncture and began to assemble with other Beroean Christ-followers for worship and fellowship?

Paul's Continued Contact with His Macedonian Congregations

The Thessalonians: Paul's "glory and joy"

"In Athens alone" Paul's forced departure from Thessalonica did not curb his desire to return to the city to continue his ministry. His repeated attempts to do so, however, were thwarted. Paul held Satan responsible for this sorry reality (note 1 Thess 2:17–18). Given his unflagging commitment to, and continuing concern for, the spiritual progress of the Thessalonians, he thought it necessary to remain in Athens alone and to send Timothy to Thessalonica so that he might "establish" and "exhort" the believers in their faith (3:1–2). Paul was particularly concerned that the Thessalonian Christians' afflictions might be used as a tool of the tempter to dissuade them from remaining steadfast in their newfound faith (3:5).

Timothy's role as a Pauline envoy to the church in Thessalonica is intriguing (see further Mitchell 1992). How can it be that Timothy was able to travel to the city if Paul (and Silas?) could not? Could it be that Timothy was not "front and center" during the founding visit and as a result would not be on the "radar screen" of non-Christian opposition? Might it be that Timothy was not with Paul and Silas (Silvanus) at the inception of the Thessalonian church? (Did he stay behind [with Luke?] in Philippi?)

Whatever the case, it was Timothy's return to Paul from Thessalonica that prompted the apostle to pen the letter we know as 1 Thessalonians.

1 Thessalonians: "Now we live, if you stand fast" When Timothy is reunited with Paul, seemingly in Corinth, he brings "glad tidings" regarding the Thessalonians' "faith and love." Additionally, he reports that the assembly has loving memories of and longs to see their missionaries (3:6). This good news comes as a comfort to Paul in the throes of his own "distress and affliction" (*anagkē kai thlipsei*; 3:7) and serves as the immediate occasion for what most Pauline scholars consider to be the apostle's earliest surviving letter.[5] Indeed, a primary reason why Paul wrote to the Thessalonians was to convey his gratitude, relief, and delight that they were standing firm in the faith and that they remained appreciative of, and affectionate toward, Paul and his companions (see especially 3:6–9).

Correlatively, Paul wants to impress upon the Thessalonians that he and his co-workers have an abiding care for and a continuing interest in them. Distance notwithstanding, they hold them in their hearts, and the assembly ought not to interpret their unanticipated, extended absence as a lack of concern. Indeed, Paul indicates in 2:19 that he views them as his "hope," "joy," and "crown of boasting" before the Lord at his coming (*parousia*). To reiterate, he refers to the fellowship in 2:20 as his "glory and joy." Although Paul had not yet managed to return to Thessalonica since he had been "orphaned" (*aporphanizein*) from them (2:17), it was not for lack of trying "again and again" (2:18). Furthermore, he was "praying night and day" that he might see them "face to face" to shore up and strengthen their faith (3:10). His "wish prayer" was that God the Father and the Lord Jesus might "direct our way to you" (3:11).

Meanwhile, not only did Paul send Timothy, "our brother and God's co-worker in the gospel of Christ" (3:2), as a surrogate for himself, but he also composed an epistle for "all the brothers and sisters" (5:27) to serve as a substitute for and extension of his presence. Throughout the letter, Paul seeks to remind the Thessalonians of, and thereby reinforce, the apostles' ministry in their midst. In addition to underscoring the Thessalonians' welcome of the gospel message and its messengers, despite considerable non-Christian opposition (for example, 1:5–6, 9; 2:1–2, 13–14), he calls upon them to recall their ministers' character, conduct, and instructions (especially 2:3–12; 4:1–2, 9–12). Whether 2:3–12 is apologetic or parenetic in intention and function (see Still 1999a, 139–148), Paul is at pains to (re-)establish the purity, integrity, and sincerity of his and his co-workers' witness in Thessalonica (note 2:3–6). He also wants the church to remember their physical labor (2:9) and exemplary behavior (2:10). Paul maintains that the Thessalonians are able to join God in bearing witness (2:5, 10) that their apostles lived among them as a nurse (2:7) and a father (2:11) with their children. The ministers' maternal and paternal care for the congregation was born out of their pastoral affection for the fellowship.[6]

In writing to the Thessalonians, Paul intends to do more than rehearse their shared spiritual past. He also wants to reiterate previous instructions and to address various communal commitments and concerns. One matter that Paul raises (again) is the believers' "sanctification" (*hagiasmos*) relative to *porneia* ("fornication, unchastity"; 4:3). In contradistinction to "Gentiles who do not know God" (v. 5), Paul declares that God has called the Thessalonians, themselves Gentiles(!), to be characterized by holiness and not uncleanness (4:7). On a practical plane, this required each one of them "to control his [or her?] own body in holiness and honor" (or, less likely to my mind, "to take for himself a wife in holiness and honor"; 4:4).[7] In addition to eschewing *porneia*, Paul urges his converts to continue to practice mutual love (*philadelphia*; 4:9–10), as well as to make it their aim "to live quietly, to mind [their] own affairs, and to work with [their] own hands," just as their ministers had commanded them (4:11).

Near the close of the letter, Paul turns to offer the congregation additional instructions. Specifically, he calls the assembly to hold in loving esteem those who labor among them and who offer them care and admonishment (5:12–13a). Further, he enjoins the fellowship to "be at peace" among themselves, while seeking to assist and to "do good" to those both within and beyond the church (5:13b–15). In rounding out his counsel to the Thessalonian believers, he charges them to be grateful and prayerful (5:16–18) as well as receptive to, if evaluative of, the presence and work of the Spirit in their midst (5:19–22).

Although none of these instructions would have been (wholly) new to the Thessalonians, the same cannot be said of 4:13–18.[8] To be sure, while in Thessalonica, Paul would have taught the assembly regarding the (proximity of the) Lord's coming and its effects (note 1:10; 2:19; 3:13; 5:1–3, 9–10, 23; cf. 2 Thess 2:5). It is also likely that he made explicit connections between eschatology and ethics in instructing the church (see especially 4:6; 5:4–10). As it happens, however, the fellowship was not (adequately) informed regarding the future of the Christian dead with special respect to the *parousia*. Whether the assembly inquired of Paul through Timothy or wrote directly to Paul "concerning the ones who are sleeping" is unclear. The manner of death and the number who had died are also unknown. What is clear is that the Thessalonians' imprecise knowledge regarding what would happen to their deceased loved ones at the time of Christ's coming was causing them to grieve in a manner that Paul deemed inappropriate for believers (4:13).

Paul begins to address their concern by appealing to a common confession. He reasons that since they "believe that Jesus died and rose again, so also God will bring with him [i.e., Jesus] those who have fallen asleep through Jesus" (4:14). Paul then turns in 4:15–17 to expound more fully upon this future reality. He declares to them "by a word of the Lord" (*en logō kyriou*) – be it a dominical saying preserved in a canonical gospel, an otherwise unknown statement of Jesus (a so-called *agraphon*), or a revelatory word from the Risen Lord to Paul or to another Christian prophet – that the believers who are living (among whom Paul includes himself [note the first-person plural personal pronoun "we"]) at the time of the Lord's coming will by no means (*ou mē*) precede those who are sleeping (4:15).[9] Accompanied by a "cry of command," "the archangel's call," and "the sound of the trumpet of God," the Lord himself will descend (4:16). At such a time, "the dead in Christ will rise first." Thereafter, the Christian living are to be caught up with the Christian dead "to meet the Lord in the air," from which point all believers "will always be with the Lord" (4:17; cf. 5:10). It was Paul's expectation that this instruction in particular, if not the letter as a whole, would comfort and console the Thessalonians (4:18; cf. 5:11).[10] Be that as it may, he wanted the church to be vigilant and sober and not to fall prey to the foolish (Roman imperial) claim that there is "peace and security" (*eirēnē kai asphaleia*), for "the day of the Lord will come like a thief in the night" (5:2–8).

2 Thessalonians: in search of a setting   While the preponderance of Pauline scholars presume that 2 Thessalonians was written after 1 Thessalonians, as the canonical order suggests, a few interpreters have posited that it was actually the first letter Paul wrote to the assembly (see especially Wanamaker 1990, 37–45). Despite robust defense by learned advocates, this proposal has found few supporters. Arguments maintaining that Paul wrote 2 Thessalonians for a segment of the Thessalonian congregation or that he intended the letter for a different assembly in another city have also failed to convince. On the contrary, an increasingly common view, if not the majority position among scholars at present, is that 2 Thessalonians is a pseudonymous letter written by a person purporting to be Paul near the end of the first century or at the beginning of the second (so, for example, Furnish 2007, 139).

Although the case against the authenticity of 2 Thessalonians is complex and the arguments are cumulative, the following points are frequently made by those who maintain the letter's pseudonymity:[11] (1) The structure, syntax, and style are similar to, yet distinct from, 1 Thessalonians. (2) Whereas the tone of 1 Thessalonians is warm and pastoral, that of its counterpart is remote and formal. (3) Consistent appeals to tradition, coupled with authenticating comments, signal another author. (4) If the eschatology of 1 Thessalonians stresses the suddenness of the *parousia*, the eschatological instruction within 2 Thessalonians is characterized by premonitory signs, and these perceptions of the *eschaton* are incompatible. Taken together, then, advocates of the letter's inauthenticity posit that Paul did not write 2 Thessalonians and are inclined to leave open for discussion the precise date and destination of this mysterious missive.

It is precisely this point, however, that those who advocate the letter's authenticity want to press. Scholars who argue for the genuineness of 2 Thessalonians, the position to which I incline (so too, for example, Malherbe 2000, 373–375), frequently build their case on the letter's *Sitz im Leben* (i.e., life-setting or occasion).[12] If advocates of pseudonymity are required to envision a situation into which a letter like 2 Thessalonians might be fitted, proponents of authenticity are able to reconstruct a plausible historical context for the epistle with relative ease. Differences in fine detail notwithstanding, scholars who espouse the Pauline authorship of 2 Thessalonians in canonical order tend to think that not too long after the apostle's first letter to the Thessalonians, significant eschatological confusion and tension arose among the congregation. Although there is disagreement as to how the "persecution" of which 2 Thessalonians 1 speaks and the "aversion to work" addressed in chapter 3 relate to this eschatological crisis,[13] almost all advocates of authenticity maintain that the apostle composed a second epistle (from Corinth ca. AD 51) to counter the erroneous claim that "the day of the Lord had come" (about which Paul had learned via the courier [Timothy?] of 1 Thessalonians?).[14]

Indeed, the second chapter of the letter is given over to the topic of "the coming of our Lord Jesus Christ and our gathering to him" (v. 1). In an effort to quell the disquiet that had arisen among the congregation because of the declaration that "the day of the Lord had come," the author, be it Paul or another, instructs the Thessalonians not to be quickly shaken in mind, excited, or deceived, whether by spirit, word, or misattributed letter (vv. 2–3a). Rather, the writer calls them to remember that "the day" will not come prior to the "apostasy" and the revelation of the "man of lawlessness, the son of perdition," who is presently being restrained (vv. 3b–7). When the lawless one does come, accompanied by power, signs, and wonders, his *parousia* will be eclipsed and eradicated by the "epiphany of the [Lord's] coming" (vv. 8–9).

This chapter, in sum and in part, is chock-full of exegetical and theological conundrums that cannot be addressed, much less resolved, here.[15] However, a few general remarks are in order. First of all, it is prudent to admit that certain particulars within this passage are lost on later readers. Exegetical industry and ingenuity notwithstanding, we cannot claim with complete confidence, for example, that we have ascertained the identity of the restraining force/restrainer (vv. 6–7). In fact, we cannot even be certain that the author had historical referents in mind for all of the eschatological events and characters that are ushered on and off the textual stage. It is also worth noting the argumentative tack that the writer takes in 2 Thessalonians 2. The author counters the assertions being made regarding the *eschaton* by reminding the audience of previous eschatological instruction (2:5) and by encouraging them to "stand firm and hold to the traditions that [they] were taught by us, either by word of mouth or by letter" (2:15). While not a few contemporary scholars regard the suddenness of the *parousia* envisioned in 1 Thessalonians as wholly incompatible with the signs that are meant to precede the day of the Lord in 2 Thessalonians, not all of the earliest Christians, including the Synoptic evangelists and John of Patmos, regarded "suddenness" and "signs" as incongruent (see further Still 1999a, 53–54).

If eschatology stands at the center of the letter, it is not the only subject addressed. In fact, the first order of epistolary business in 2 Thessalonians is a word of thankful praise to God for the assembly because of its "steadfastness and faith" in the midst of all of their "persecutions and afflictions" (1:4). It does in fact appear that the conflict that the Thessalonian believers were experiencing with outsiders had escalated between the writing of the first and second letters (cf. 1 Thess 1:6; 2:14; 3:3–5), which may have been merely a matter of months. The assembly's steadfast fidelity in the midst of external hostility is said to serve as "evidence of the righteous judgment of God" (2 Thess 1:5; cf. Phil 1:28). Although the believers were suffering and in this way being made worthy of God's kingdom and call, they are told that the time would come when the tables would be turned. When Jesus is revealed from heaven, the letter assures, those afflicting the church and rejecting God and the gospel will be subjected to divine justice and judgment. Contrariwise, God will grant the afflicted fellowship eternal rest at Christ's coming. If those who oppose the Thessalonian believers will "suffer the punishment of eternal destruction and exclusion from the presence of the Lord," the "saints" will glorify and marvel when the Lord Jesus comes (1:6–10).

The *ataktoi* ("out of step, unruly"), who are mentioned in passing in 1 Thessalonians 5:14 (cf. 4:11), are addressed more fully in 2 Thessalonians 3:6–15. Whatever the precise reason(s) (eschatological beliefs? cultural influences? ecclesial dynamics? a combination thereof?), a segment of the Thessalonian congregation had disregarded the example and jettisoned the instruction of their apostles by forgoing work, on the one hand, and by living at the expense of fellow believers, on the other. These "disorderly," "lazy" congregants were not working (*ergazomenoi*); they were meddling (*periergazomenoi*; 3:7–11). The author of 2 Thessalonians seeks to counter this deleterious influence by instructing the church to steer clear of the *ataktoi*. Meanwhile, those who are living *ataktōs* are enjoined to work quietly and to eat their own bread (3:12). Although "Paul" instructs the assembly to regard the *ataktoi* as "brothers" (*adelphoi*) and not as "enemies" (*echthroi*; 3:15), he nevertheless expects the "unruly"/"work-shy" to comply with his commands and to fall into line. In the unfortunate event that they refuse to obey what the letter requires of them, they are to be "shunned and shamed" (3:14). The directness of the address and the sharpness of the tone indicate that the writer thought this matter threatened the stability and viability of the fellowship (note Barclay 1993, 529–530).

The Philippians: Paul's "joy and crown"

Epistolary unity, Paul's captivity, and the Philippians' generosity
In the academic study of Philippians, questions abound. One query that scholars continue to consider regards the letter's unity. Is Philippians, as it has come to us, a single epistle or a composite document? Those who maintain that Philippians is comprised of two or three letters composed by Paul for the church in Philippi note the disjointed nature of the canonical work, especially between 3:1 and 3:2 and between 4:9 and 4:10. While acknowledging such "epistolary seams," interpreters who consider Philippians to be a unified whole note both the topics and the vocabulary that cut across the letter. At the present time, it appears that those who espouse the unity of Philippians are gaining and holding ground (see especially Reed 1997, 124–152).

In any case, Philippians 1:7, 13 indicate that Paul was in chains when he composed (at least a portion of) the letter. Pauline scholars seeking to pinpoint when and where Paul wrote (that part of) Philippians have tended to propose Ephesus in the mid-50s, Caesarea in the late 50s, or Rome in the early 60s (note Bockmuehl 1998, 25–32). A number of interpreters hold that Paul composed (at least some of) Philippians while imprisoned in Ephesus. Although neither Paul's letters nor Acts indicates that the apostle was in custody in that city, exegetes have inferred as much from certain remarks Paul makes in 1–2 Corinthians (see 1 Cor 15:32; 2 Cor 1:8; cf. Acts 19:23–41). Furthermore, those who advocate an Ephesian provenance for the letter maintain that Paul's expressed desire to return to Philippi (note Phil 1:26; 2:24) is more readily explained if he wrote Philippians before Romans, for in Romans, written by Paul from Corinth ca. 57, the apostle anticipates traveling to Spain (via Jerusalem and Rome), not to Macedonia (note Rom 15:24–25).

While a few scholars have suggested that Paul wrote Philippians in the late 50s from a Caesarean detainment (see Acts 23:23–26:32), commentators have most commonly held that he composed Philippians from Roman captivity in the early 60s (note especially Acts 28:30–31). If the distance between Philippi and Rome and the difference between the itinerary Paul anticipated in Romans and articulated in Philippians are great, these concerns are not regarded as definitive for exegetes who are convinced that Paul's mention of the *praetorium* (Phil 1:13) and Caesar's household (4:22) tip the scales in favor of a Roman origin for the letter. While questions regarding the unity and provenance of Philippians persist and no position is free of problems, I am presently inclined to view Philippians as a single letter written by Paul from Roman captivity in the early 60s.

Although the unity and origin of Philippians remain points of academic debate, the immediate occasion for the letter, when understood as a single epistle, is sufficiently clear. Epaphroditus, an otherwise unknown Philippian believer, delivered a monetary gift from the church in Philippi to Paul, who was seemingly being detained in Rome while awaiting trial (note Phil 1:19–26; 2:17, 23–24, 25; 4:10, 18; cf. Acts 28:16, 19). Meanwhile, Epaphroditus became gravely ill; in fact, he almost died (Phil 2:26–27a). Once restored to health, he was eager to return to Philippi, and Paul was pleased to speed him on his way. In doing so, Paul composed and sent with him the letter we now call Philippians. In this letter, among a number of other things, Paul applauds Epaphroditus for his sacrificial service to him on the church's behalf and instructs the assembly to receive him back joyfully and to honor people like him (2:28–30).

Not only does Paul commend Epaphroditus to the church but he also expresses his appreciation to the congregation for their gift. In seeking to affirm the Philippians for their protracted partnership in the gospel – not least through their repeated financial support – the apostle found himself in a precarious position. On the one hand, he desired to convey his gratitude to the church; on the other hand, he did not want to give short shrift to divine involvement and intervention in his life and ministry, nor did he desire to become a client of the assembly. If Paul's written expression of thanksgiving to the Philippians for their gift is guarded, to describe his thanks as thankless seems overstated. Perhaps it is more precise to suggest that Paul tended to construe matters of "giving and receiving" along decidedly theological lines and resultantly regarded God as the ultimate source of provision and empowerment. Furthermore, it is clear that Paul viewed a shared commitment to the gospel and grace, not an ongoing cycle of gift-exchange, as the ground of his relationship with the fellowship (see 1:3–8; 4:10–20).[16]

The progress of the gospel and the growth of the people of God   More than a letter of recommendation or friendship, Philippians is concerned with the faith and the fellowship that Paul and the Philippians shared in the gospel.[17] At the outset of the letter, Paul gives God thanks for the congregation's *koinōnia* in the gospel (1:3–8). Furthermore, he wants to assure the assembly that his fetters have not hindered the progress of the gospel; rather, irony and improbability notwithstanding, his confinement has resulted in the gospel's advancement (1:12). In order for the Philippians to perceive such unanticipated developments, however, they will need both commitment and discernment. Paul prays unto this end in 1:9–11. To support his contention that the gospel is advancing and not retreating, Paul reports that the "imperial guard" based in the *praetorium* knows that his chains are for Christ (1:13; cf. "Caesar's household" in 4:22). Furthermore, Paul informs the Philippians that his captivity had emboldened most of the (Roman) believers "to speak the word of God without fear," if not always with the noblest motivations (1:14–18).

Paul's confidence extends beyond gospel partnership and progress to encompass his very own *sōtēria* ("salvation, deliverance"). It is unclear whether Paul had in mind physical/temporal and/or spiritual/eschatological deliverance in 1:19 (cf. Job 13:16). Whatever the case, he clearly conveys his hopeful desire to honor Christ courageously in living and in dying (1:20–23). Despite his desire to "depart" and "to be with Christ," Paul was convinced that he would "remain in the flesh" for the sake of the Philippians (1:24–26). That being said, Paul enjoins the Philippians to live lives worthy of the gospel, even in the throes of external opposition, both in his presence and in his absence (1:27–30).

Part and parcel of living life as a "gospel people," Paul insists, is to stand firm with, and to strive alongside, other believers (1:27; cf. 4:3). It appears that Paul's appeal to unity in 1:27, and then again in 2:1–4, was occasioned by congregational discord.[18] That there were at least some fissures in the Philippians' fellowship is made evident by 4:2–3. There, Paul calls upon Euodia and Syntyche to "think the same thing in the Lord" and appeals to a now unknown "loyal companion" (*syzyge*) to help these women who had labored alongside him in the gospel. To promote unity in the fellowship, Paul admonishes the church to forgo "grumbling and complaining" (2:14) and to cultivate a joyful, gentle, prayerful, and honorable state of heart and mind (4:4–8).

Paul also places before the Philippians models of humility and service to embrace and examples of selfishness and divisiveness to eschew. While Paul shows no interest in developing those figures he fashions into foils and antitypes (see 1:15, 17; 2:21; 3:2, 4, 18–19), he highlights the exemplary qualities and behavior of Timothy (2:19–23), Epaphroditus (2:25–30), and himself (3:7–17; 4:9). For good measure, he also mentions Clement and unnamed others (4:3; cf. 1:15–16; 3:17).

All exemplars pale in comparison, however, to the incomparable Christ; it is Christ whom Paul enjoins the Philippians to be mindful of and obedient to (2:5, 12–13). Whether a preformed "hymn" that Paul incorporates (with [minor] modifications) or a poetic meditation on Christ that he composed (afresh for the occasion), the beauty and profundity of Philippians 2:6–11 are seldom lost on readers of the letter. Interpreters have written reams on the background, structure, and terminology of this passage.[19] Is this text best read against an Adamic or Isaianic backdrop?[20] Are there two strophes (i.e., vv. 6–8 and vv. 9–11) or more? How are, for example, *morphē* ("form," vv. 6, 7), *harpagmos* ("a thing to be grasped or clutched," v. 6), *kenoun* ("to empty," v. 7), and *schēma* ("form, appearance," v. 7) best translated and interpreted? More basic still, what is the function of this text in its context? Is its primary intent to call the Philippians to Christ-like humility, or is it meant to draw the fellowship's focus to the Christ-event? These questions illustrate the interpretive challenges that await those who are willing to struggle with this complex Christological text.

The Macedonian Believers' Support of Paul's Mission and Message

Although it is inexact, if not inaccurate, to depict the Philippians and/or the Thessalonians as Paul's favorite fellowship(s), 1 Thessalonians and Philippians bear witness to the apostle's fond affection for, and deep commitment to, these congregations. In addition to the "fictive kinship" language that recurs throughout 1 Thessalonians (Malherbe 1987, 48; Burke 2003), Paul praises the Thessalonians for being imitators of their apostles and Lord and speaks of them as an example for other Grecian believers (1:6–7; cf. 2:14). Furthermore, he refers to them as his hope, joy, crown, and glory at Christ's coming (2:19–20) and maintains that his own well-being is intertwined with their continuation and maturation in the faith (3:5, 7–8). If any doubt remained about Paul's care for the fellowship, then 2:8 would go some way toward removing it. In this verse, Paul speaks of his desire while in Thessalonica not only to share with them the gospel but also to share himself, for they had become "beloved" (*agapētoi*) to him.

Expressions of endearment also recur throughout Philippians. At the outset of the letter, Paul expresses his gratitude for the fellowship's continuing partnership in the gospel (1:5). Furthermore, Paul thinks it is fitting for him to hold them in his heart and to yearn for them with "the affection of Christ Jesus." Not only are they fellow partakers of grace, but they are also steadfast supporters of the shackled apostle and the unfettered gospel (see 1:7–8, 12–13; 4:14–16, 18). Paul's most expansive and effusive expression of praise for the Philippians is found in 4:1. In this single verse, Paul refers to the fellowship as "beloved" and "longed for" and as his "joy and crown."

If one were inclined to read Paul's language of love and affirmation for the Thessalonians and Philippians as more than "spiritual spin" and "rhetorical excess," then it would be worth asking why Paul experienced such warm relations with his Macedonian congregations. One possible reason is that the Macedonian believers in general (2 Cor 11:8–9) and the Philippian Christians in particular (Phil 2:25; 4:10, 15–16, 18) offered Paul material support in the midst of his ministry. Such tangible expressions of care and concern would understandably have endeared them to him. In addition, it appears that Paul experienced less conflict with the Thessalonian and Philippian assemblies than he did with other congregations, particularly the Corinthians and Galatians. Less controversy and acrimony between the apostle and his Macedonian assemblies would have facilitated the establishment of supportive, positive relationships between them.

A final suggestion as to why Paul's relations with the Thessalonians and Philippians were happy and healthy pertains to their initial and continual reception of Paul's proclamation and instruction, as well as their protracted, exemplary participation in the Pauline mission. Like Paul, they experienced and embraced hardship as integral to the gospel (see 1 Thess 1:6–7; 2:14; 3:3–5; 2 Thess 1:4–5; Phil 1:27–30). As with Paul, they bore witness to the gospel in their interaction with outsiders (1 Thess 1:8; Phil 2:16).[21] Jerome Murphy-O'Connor (1985, 102) maintains that Paul's "dominant impression of the Macedonian churches at Philippi and Thessalonica is that they were apostolic in the same sense as he perceived his own mission." Furthermore, Murphy-O'Connor contends, "They had so integrated the message of [Paul's] gospel that they became a living kerygma in precisely the same way that Paul himself was, insofar as he manifested 'the life of Jesus' in his comportment (2 Cor. 4.10–11)." Murphy-O'Connor continues: "The quality of life that made them exemplary communities is strongly underlined by what Paul says of their attitude towards the Collection." It is to the Macedonian believers' perception of, and participation in, the collection that we now turn.

The Macedonian Christians' Sacrificial Support of Paul's Jerusalem Collection

Paul refers to the so-called Jerusalem collection on a number of occasions in his extant letters (note 1 Cor 16:1–4; 2 Cor 8–9; Rom 15:25–28; cf. Gal 2:10; Acts 11:29–30).[22] If 2 Corinthians 8–9 constitute Paul's fullest commentary on the collection, 1 Corinthians 16:1–4 and Romans 15:25–28 provide additional details regarding the offering. It appears that, in the early to mid-50s, Paul began to lay plans for a "contribution for the poor among the saints in Jerusalem" (Rom 15:26). The apostle anticipated that (Pauline) assemblies in Galatia, Macedonia, and Achaia would participate freely in and contribute generously to this offering (see 1 Cor 16:1; 2 Cor 9:2, 7; Rom 15:26). In fact, Paul regarded it as the responsibility of his (largely) Gentile fellowships to share with their Jewish-Christian brothers and sisters in Jerusalem "material blessings," given that they were the beneficiaries of Israel's "spiritual blessings" (Rom 15:27; cf. Rom 9:4–5).

Romans 15:31 indicates that Paul was anxious about how this "service for Jerusalem" would be received by the saints in the Holy City (not to mention unbelieving Jews), and, as it would happen, with very good reason. Although Paul's later letters (assuming that Paul's extant correspondence includes letters from Rome) and Acts are silent regarding the collection, Acts narrates the Jewish opposition Paul met in Jerusalem that culminated in his arrest. Acts also reports Paul's subsequent transfer as a prisoner to Caesarea and ultimately to Rome (Acts 21:17–28:31). In spite of the potentially negative outcome of the collection, Paul was committed to seeing this service brought to fruition. He regarded the offering as an opportunity for Gentile Christians to pay a spiritual debt, and viewed it as a "gracious work" that would glorify God and demonstrate goodwill (2 Cor 8:19). In writing to the Corinthians regarding this gift, Paul encourages their participation by appealing to Christ's example of self-emptying (2 Cor 8:9), by setting forth the principles of equality, liberality, and reciprocity (8:13–15; 9:6–15), and by engaging in a fair amount of "apostolic arm-twisting" (8:1–7, 10–12, 16–24; 9:1–5).

If Paul found the Corinthian congregation to be wavering with respect to their participation in the collection (note 2 Cor 8:10–12), he discovered that the Macedonian Christians were especially eager to be involved in the "relief of the saints." Indeed, Paul reports that they regarded their involvement in this service as a "grace" (charis; 8:4). In an effort to motivate the Corinthians to follow through on their commitment to contribute to the offering, Paul praises the giving of the Macedonian churches. He informs the Corinthians that, despite a "severe test of affliction" and "extreme poverty," the Macedonian believers gave joyfully and liberally to the collection (8:2). Whereas Paul wondered if the Achaian believers would actually fulfill their promise to assist the Jerusalem saints, he was taken aback by the Macedonians' Christ-like charis (see 8:5, 9; 9:1–5). Although the apostle had great expectations for his congregations, the Thessalonians and Philippians had a knack for meeting, if not exceeding, Paul's high and holy hopes for them. While these assemblies, like their founder, were works in progress, their generous response to the collection is a clear indication that they were making spiritual strides "toward the goal for the prize of the upward call of God in Christ Jesus" (Phil 3:14).

From Paul to Polycarp to Porphyrios and Beyond

In this chapter we have seen that Paul sought to stay in consistent contact with his beloved Macedonian congregations from the time of their inception. But what happened to these fellowships after the apostle passed from the scene? One may describe subsequent (early church) history in Philippi and Thessalonica as a tale of two cities. Thessalonica has remained in continuous existence since its founding in 316 BC and appears infrequently in the annals of the early church. Although a fair number of significant ancient Christian monuments (for example, the Church of the Virgin and the Rotunda) remain in Thessalonica until now, these buildings date from the fifth century, long after Paul's engagement with the Thessalonians.

Philippi, however, which was founded in 360/359 BC, became largely depopulated between the fifth and seventh centuries AD as a result of catastrophic earthquakes. After Paul's death, we know that Polycarp, the bishop of Smyrna, wrote to the Philippians in response to a letter that he had received from the congregation (*To the Philippians* 3.1; 13.1). Polycarp's letter to the church in Philippi, which may well be a composite of two letters, was written in roughly the first third of the second century. In the centuries that followed, Philippi became "an episcopal and ecclesiastical center and perhaps also ... an important object of Christian pilgrimage" (Hendrix 1992, 314). Of the seven known churches that were built in or near Philippi, there is a direct link between the earliest one (built, or perhaps dedicated, between AD 313 and 350) and Paul.

It seems appropriate that the most ancient of the known Philippian church buildings is called the St. Paul Basilica. It is referred to as such because of an inscription on a mosaic floor that excavators discovered in 1975. The inscription reads: "Bishop Porphyrios made the embroidery of the basilica of Paul in Christ" (*Po[rphy]rios episkopos tē[n k]entēsin tēs basilikēs Paulo[u ep]oiēsen en Chr[ist]ō*). Beyond the fact that he attended the Council of Serdica in the early 340s, little is known of Bishop Porphyrios (see Abrahamsen 1989). That this bishop of some means would generously provide the funds to construct a mosaic floor in a Christian assembly hall bearing Paul's name is apropos, as generosity was a hallmark of Paul's Macedonian churches, not least the Philippian assembly. The Christian assembly hall named after Paul is the earliest known "church building" in the Balkans (Bakirtzis 1998, 42), and it hearkens back to yet an earlier time when, "in the beginning of the gospel" (Phil 4:15), Paul ministered in Macedonia to and with the Philippians and Thessalonians.

Notes

I would like to thank David L. Jeffrey, Natalie Johnston, Bruce Longenecker, and Peter Oakes for reading and commenting upon an earlier draft of this chapter.

1   Translations from biblical texts are my own.
2   Scholars differ on how best to read Acts' depiction of Philippi as a "main" or "leading" (or, less likely, "first") city of Macedonia. See Metzger (1994, 393–395).
3   In addition to Still (1999a, esp. 208–227), see also De Vos (1999, 155–170); cf. Malherbe (1987, 46–52).
4   On Paul's preaching in Thessalonica, see Barclay (1993, 516–518); cf. Still (1999a, 233–237).
5   Most commentators hold that Paul wrote 1 Thessalonians from Corinth in AD 50 or 51 (see Malherbe 2000, 71–74).
6   On familial imagery in 1 Thessalonians, see Burke (2003).
7   On 1 Thessalonians 4:4, see Still (2007, 208–209).
8   On these verses, as well as the other passages in the Thessalonian letters where eschatology features (esp. 1 Thess 5:1–11 and 2 Thess 2:1–12), see Nicholl (2004); cf. Still (1999b).
9   On 1 Thessalonians 4:15, see Pahl (2009).
10 For the argument that 1 Thessalonians is a letter of consolation, see Donfried (2002, 119–138).
11 See more fully, for example, Still (1999a, 46–60).
12 Also recognized by, for example, Donfried (2002, 49–67).
13 See the discussion in Nicholl (2004, 157–179).
14 Among others, see Bruce (1982, xxxiv–xxxv).
15 In addition to critical commentaries on 2 Thessalonians (e.g., Malherbe 2000), see the accessible, insightful, pastoral treatment by Holmes (1998, 227–250).
16 Note, especially, Peterman (1997).
17 On the genre of Philippians, see Holloway (2001).
18 This point is (over-)emphasized by Peterlin (1995).
19 Among many others, see Martin (1997), Oakes (2001), and Hellerman (2005).
20 That is, should the text be read as contrasting Christ with Adam – who, though made in the "image of God" (Gen 1:26), *did* grasp at equality with God (cf. Gen 3:5) – or as identifying Christ with the rejected but exalted servant of Isaiah 53?
21 See further Ware (2005).
22 On the Jerusalem collection, see now Downs (2008).

References

Abrahamsen, Valerie. 1989. Bishop Porphyrios and the City of Philippi in the Early Fourth Century. *Vigiliae Christianae* 43: 80–85.
Bakirtzis, Charalambos. 1998. Paul and Philippi: The Archaeological Evidence. Pages 37–48 in *Philippi at the Time of Paul and after his Death*. Edited by Charalambos Bakirtzis and Helmut Koester. Harrisburg, Pa.: Trinity Press International.
Barclay, John M. G. 1993. Conflict in Thessalonica. *Catholic Biblical Quarterly* 55: 512–530.
Bockmuehl, Markus. 1998. *The Epistle to the Philippians*. Peabody, Mass.: Hendrickson.
Bruce, F. F. 1982. *1 and 2 Thessalonians*. Waco, Tex.: Word.
Burke, Trevor J. 2003. *Family Matters: A Socio-historical Study of Kinship Metaphors in 1 Thessalonians*. London: T. & T. Clark.
De Vos, Craig Steven. 1999. *Church and Community Conflicts: The Relationships of the Thessalonian, Corinthian, and Philippian Churches with their Wider Civic Communities*. Atlanta: Scholars.

Donfried, Karl Paul. 2002. *Paul, Thessalonica, and Early Christianity*. Grand Rapids: Eerdmans.

Downs, David J. 2008. *The Offering of the Gentiles: Paul's Collection for Jerusalem in its Chronological, Cultural, and Cultic Contexts*. Tübingen: Mohr Siebeck.

Fee, Gordon D. 1995. *Paul's Letter to the Philippians*. Grand Rapids: Eerdmans.

Furnish, Victor Paul. 2007. *1 Thessalonians, 2 Thessalonians*. Nashville: Abingdon.

Hellerman, Joseph H. 2005. *Reconstructing Honor in Roman Philippi: Carmen Christi as Cursus Pudorum*. Cambridge: Cambridge University Press.

Hendrix, Holland L. 1992. Philippi. Pages 313–317 in *The Anchor Bible Dictionary*, volume 5. Edited by David Noel Freedman. Doubleday: New York.

Holloway, Paul A. 2001. *Consolation in Philippians: Philosophical Sources and Rhetorical Strategy*. Cambridge: Cambridge University Press.

Holmes, Michael W. 1998. *1 and 2 Thessalonians*. Grand Rapids: Zondervan.

Lüdemann, Gerd. 1989. *Early Christianity according to the Traditions in Acts: A Commentary*. London: SCM.

Malherbe, Abraham J. 1987. *Paul and the Thessalonians: The Philosophic Tradition of Pastoral Care*. Philadelphia: Fortress.

Malherbe, Abraham J. 2000. *The Letters to the Thessalonians*. New York: Doubleday.

Marshall, I. Howard. 1980. *The Acts of the Apostles: An Introduction and Commentary*. Grand Rapids: Eerdmans.

Martin, Ralph P. 1997. *A Hymn of Christ: Philippians 2:5–11 in Recent Interpretation and in the Setting of Early Christian Worship*. Downers Grove, Ill.: InterVarsity.

Metzger, Bruce M. 1994. *A Textual Commentary on the Greek New Testament*. Second edition. New York: United Bible Societies.

Mitchell, Margaret M. 1992. New Testament Envoys in the Context of Greco-Roman Diplomatic and Epistolary Conventions: The Example of Timothy and Titus. *Journal of Biblical Literature* 111: 641–662.

Murphy-O'Connor, Jerome. 1985. Paul and Macedonia: The Connection between 2 Corinthians 2.13 and 2.14. *Journal for the Study of the New Testament* 25: 99–103.

Nicholl, Colin R. 2004. *From Hope to Despair in Thessalonica: Situating 1 and 2 Thessalonians*. Cambridge: Cambridge University Press.

Oakes, Peter. 2001. *Philippians: From People to Letter*. Cambridge: Cambridge University Press.

Pahl, Michael W. 2009. *Discerning the "Word of the Lord": The "Word of the Lord" in 1 Thessalonians 4:15*. London: T. & T. Clark.

Peterlin, Davorin. 1995. *Paul's Letter to the Philippians in the Light of Disunity in the Church*. Leiden: Brill.

Peterman, G. W. 1997. *Paul's Gift from Philippi: Conventions of Gift-exchange and Christian Giving*. Cambridge: Cambridge University Press.

Reed, Jeffrey T. 1997. *A Discourse Analysis of Philippians: Method and Rhetoric in the Debate over Literary Integrity*. Sheffield: Sheffield Academic.

Still, Todd D. 1999a. *Conflict at Thessalonica: A Pauline Church and its Neighbours*. Sheffield: Sheffield Academic.

Still, Todd D. 1999b. Eschatology in the Thessalonian Letters. *Review and Expositor* 96: 195–210.

Still, Todd D. 2007. Interpretive Ambiguities and Scholarly Proclivities in Pauline Studies: A Treatment of Three Texts from 1 Thessalonians 4 as a Test Case. *Currents in Biblical Research* 5: 207–219.

Wanamaker, Charles A. 1990. *The Epistles to the Thessalonians*. Grand Rapids: Eerdmans.

Ware, James P. 2005. *The Mission of the Church in Paul's Letter to the Philippians in the Context of Ancient Judaism*. Leiden: Brill.

CHAPTER 3

Paul and the Corinthian Believers

Craig S. Keener

Modern readers are especially familiar with Paul's relationship with the Corinthian believers from his correspondence with them in our letters of 1 and 2 Corinthians. These letters, however, hint at other letters and interactions that have not survived, and Luke provides additional information about Paul and the Corinthians in the book of Acts. Information about ancient Corinth also helps us better understand the Corinthian believers and their struggle to comprehend and live out the teachings that Paul sought to communicate to them.

Our Sources

Neither Acts nor Paul's extant Corinthian correspondence was written primarily to help later readers reconstruct Paul's relationship with the Corinthian believers. Nevertheless, historians regularly mine whatever extant sources are available, and in this case both the primary sources (Paul's letters) and a secondary one (Acts) prove valuable and complementary (see the discussion in Porter 2001).

Acts independently complements 1–2 Corinthians. Had Luke employed Paul's letters (which most scholars count unlikely), he probably would have mentioned Stephanas (1 Cor 1:16; 16:15), Phoebe (Rom 16:1–2), and other high-status members (especially Rom 16:23), yet he does not. More importantly, although Luke likes to report miracles performed by Paul, he neglects to report any in Corinth, where Paul explicitly claims to have performed miracles (2 Cor 12:12). Luke probably collected oral reports from people rather than depending on documents such as Paul's letters; what these two sorts of sources report, therefore, appears to be independent.

The Blackwell Companion to Paul, First Edition. Edited by Stephen Westerholm.
© 2011 Blackwell Publishing Ltd. Published 2011 by Blackwell Publishing Ltd.

That the sources appear independent, however, underlines the importance of their incidental corroboration of each other, suggesting the reliability of their information. Scholars have noted many incidental correspondences, including (among others) the following:

- The Corinthian believers knew Paul's married co-workers Aquila and Priscilla (Acts 18:2, 26; 1 Cor 16:19), who also had connections with Rome (Acts 18:2; Rom 16:3) and Ephesus (Acts 18:18–19; 1 Cor 16:19).
- While in Corinth, Paul supported himself by manual labor (Acts 18:3; 1 Cor 4:12; 9:6).
- One Crispus converted and received baptism (Acts 18:8; 1 Cor 1:14).
- Timothy and Silas helped Paul (Acts 18:5; 1 Cor 4:17; 16:10–11; 2 Cor 1:19), but Paul started the work before they came (Acts 18:1–4; 1 Thess 3:1, 6).
- Both sources know a Sosthenes, possibly the same one (Acts 18:17; 1 Cor 1:1).
- Paul visited Ephesus after Corinth (Acts 18:19; 19:8–10; 1 Cor 15:32; 16:8).
- After Paul left Corinth, Apollos came (Acts 18:24–28; 1 Cor 1:12; 4:15).

Some other details that Acts records that are missing in the Corinthian correspondence match external history too well for fiction (such as Paul's appearance before Gallio, whose term of office coincides with the likely timing of Paul's stay: not the sort of information a novelist would have researched). Such corroboration encourages our use of Acts as well as 1–2 Corinthians to reconstruct Paul's relationship with the Corinthian believers.

Corinth in Paul's Day

Corinth was a strategic center for Paul's mission, the sort of place where new ideas could be given a ready hearing and disseminated. (It was said that the earlier philosopher Diogenes settled in Corinth for precisely this reason.) Corinth was a significant city by ancient standards, with city walls about six miles around. Its population has been estimated between 70,000 and over 300,000, not including a possibly even larger number of slaves. Since the theater held about 14,000, an estimate of 140,000 residents (allowing for a large margin of error) seems a reasonable guess; it was in any case one of only a small number of cities of this size.

More distinctively, Corinth was capital of the prosperous Roman province of Achaia. Its famous independent history had officially ended in 146 BCE when a Roman general destroyed the city (though some residents remained on the site afterward). In 44 BCE, however, Caesar restored it, now officially as a Roman colony. In 27 BCE, Augustus made it Achaia's capital. As a colony, it hosted many Roman freedpersons and veterans, whose descendants made up the city's actual "citizens." Such citizens of a Roman colony were citizens of Rome. Nevertheless, many non-citizens also lived in the mercantile city, including both eastern immigrants (such as Judeans) and (in larger numbers) local Greeks. Although civic architecture and inscriptions were in Latin, befitting a colony imitating Rome, a substantial number of residents spoke Greek.

Widespread use of Greek (even among intellectuals in Rome) would have facilitated Paul's ministry beyond the synagogue, just as it eventually facilitated a revival of Greek language and culture in Corinth in the early second century. An unusually high proportion of members of this church have Latin names, however (some are common names for freedpersons, which also fits the origins of much of Corinth's citizenry). While Latin names do not prove Roman citizenship, their *preponderance* in Corinth's churches suggests the inroads that Paul made into the heart of this colony. Synagogue contacts likely facilitated these inroads, as may have Paul's own Roman citizenship (according to Acts 16:37 and probably his name).

Trade made Corinth prosperous. Unlike some cities, it was not parasitic on its countryside (which was not fertile), but thrived by trade. It controlled the Isthmus of Corinth, which proved strategic in sea trade between the eastern and western empire. The isthmus's western (Rome-ward) harbor was called Lechaeum, to the city's north; its eastern harbor (to Corinth's southeast) was Cenchreae, where Paul or his associates planted a church (Rom 16:1). All attempts to build a canal through the isthmus had so far failed, but smaller ships could be transported across a four-mile stone path with smaller harbors at either end.

Manufacturing (for example, of lamps and reportedly of prized "Corinthian bronze") generated some wealth, but the city's service industry was more prominent. The Craneion was one of its wealthiest suburbs; perhaps larger house churches met there, although smaller house churches presumably existed elsewhere in Corinth for those reluctant to walk long distances. Corinth's prosperity did not extend to everyone, however. Besides its well-known underclass, many people would have lived between these extremes of wealth and poverty. Mansions and tenements presumably existed side by side (as in Rome), underlining the evident disparities between rich and poor. Such social problems could impinge on the life of Christians, and Paul is later forced to address them (1 Cor 11:21).

Corinth's involvement in trade generated large immigrant communities: impacting them would allow Paul to have an impact on peoples from around the Mediterranean world. We know of Egyptian cults in Corinth and at Cenchreae, and an inscription (of uncertain date) attests a Greek-speaking synagogue in Corinth. Corinth's wealth and trade probably also increased its negative moral reputation. Prostitution was a well-known industry in earlier, Greek Corinth, generating jokes at Corinth's expense (for example, "Corinthian lady" had sexual connotations). Despite the refounding of New Corinth as a new, Roman city, trade and prosperity helped to revive its reputation for sexual immorality. Some scholars doubt that New Corinth was more immoral than any other port city its size; if we trust ancient sources, however, this concession might not be saying much. Sexual license in Corinth also apparently affected Christians, inviting Paul's warnings (1 Cor 6:12–20).

Paul Visits Corinth

After visiting Athens (1 Thess 3:1; Acts 17:15–34), Paul visited Corinth, just 53 miles (85 km) to the west. The two cities had engaged in ancient rivalry, but Corinth had long since surpassed Athens in prosperity. That Paul's "first" convert in "Achaia" was Corinthian (1 Cor 16:15) does not demean Paul's previous mission in Athens, as some have supposed (cf. Acts 17:34); as a "free city," Athens was technically not under the province of Achaia in this period, so Paul's claim about Achaian converts does not mean that no one was converted in Athens. Nevertheless, Corinth became a center of the Pauline mission, which Athens never could have been. According to Acts, Paul had been harried from one city to the next in Macedonia (especially in Philippi and Thessalonica, where his letters show that he nevertheless established churches); in Corinth, however, he remained safely for eighteen months (Acts 18:9–11).

Probably shortly before Paul's visit to Corinth, Priscilla and Aquila had moved there from Rome. Although some scholars date Claudius's edict expelling Jews from Rome (noted in Suetonius, *Claudius* 25.4) to 41 CE, for various reasons more favor 49 CE. Scholars debate the reason for and extent of the expulsion. Would Rome's entire Jewish community (apart from Jewish Roman citizens) abandon the city, then reclaim their property several years later when Claudius died (54 CE)? (Nevertheless, a no less sweeping action occurred earlier under Tiberius.) To whatever extent Claudius's anti-Jewish edict was effective, it was sufficient to compel Priscilla and Aquila to relocate to the significant Roman colony of Corinth (Acts 18:1–2). Based on the historian Suetonius's garbled report, most scholars think that Claudius took action because of Jewish debates in Rome about Jesus as the Messiah.

Priscilla (as Luke calls her) is the informal form of the more formal "Prisca" (as she is called in Paul's letters); that Paul (once) and Luke (twice) both at times name her before her husband would suggest to an ancient audience that she was of higher status (whether socially or in the church) than her husband. Probably shared faith helps explain why Paul stayed with this couple, but Luke also mentions their shared occupation: a sort of artisan work that means either "tent-making" (possibly with linen) or (more likely) "leather-working" (Acts 18:3). People of the same trade generally lived in the same neighborhoods and participated in guild meetings; because these meetings involved a patron deity, faithful Jews and Christians (like this couple and Paul) would not participate. Such factors may have bonded these workers even closer together. People of means (including in New Corinth) often looked down on manual labor; Paul's may have eventually embarrassed some high-status people in the Corinthian church (cf. 1 Cor 4:12; 9:4–12; 2 Cor 11:7; 12:13).

When a new speaker arrived in a city, he typically announced an oration; if he impressed enough hearers to attract disciples, he could begin lectures. Paul's interest, however, was not in impressing hearers with his rhetoric, but in communicating the simple message of the gospel. The passage where Paul stresses this claim (1 Cor 2:1–5) resembles passages where orators lowered audience expectations; Paul's major letters in fact include more rhetorical devices than many rhetoricians approved in letters. But it is quite possible that many found Paul's delivery (or even accent) defective (cf. 2 Cor 11:6), at least in contrast with that of his subsequent colleague Apollos (cf. 1 Cor 1:12; 3:4–6; 4:6; 16:12) and some less agreeable competitors (2 Cor 11:5–6). Nevertheless, though by this period most philosophers used rhetoric and many orators respected philosophy, the traditional divide between the two major academic disciplines made Paul's emphasis on content over form somewhat respectable.

Given their backgrounds in idolatry and sexual vices rarely attested among Jews (1 Cor 5:11; 6:9–10), many of Paul's converts in Corinth must have been Gentiles. Nevertheless, some of the congregation was probably Jewish (1 Cor 1:22–24; 9:20; 10:32; 12:13; 2 Cor 11:22), and the synagogue remained the likeliest place to stir initial interest (including among interested Gentiles on its margins), just as Acts suggests (Acts 18:4). Apostolic "signs" attested Paul's ministry in Corinth (2 Cor 12:12). Paul's teaching emphasized the basic message of Jesus's death and resurrection for salvation (1 Cor 1:17–18; 11:23–26; 15:3–4), but also included some of Jesus's teachings (for example, 1 Cor 7:10; 9:14; especially 11:23–25). Paul's correspondence presupposes that his readers will recognize Peter's Aramaic name (1 Cor 3:22) and even an Aramaic prayer (16:22).

Paul was the Corinthian church's primary founder (1 Cor 4:15; 2 Cor 10:14), a role he would not cede to others (cf. 2 Cor 11:12–13). Silas (known in Paul's letters by the more formal Latin name Silvanus) and Timothy joined Paul in Corinth, and Paul may have sent one or both with his letter to the believers in Thessalonica (1 Thess 1:1). Silas and Timothy proved important workers in Corinth (cf. 2 Cor 1:19). Luke claims that after their arrival, Paul was able to focus on evangelism rather than manual labor (Acts 18:5). This change in Paul's activity probably suggests that they brought a gift from the Macedonian church (2 Cor 11:8–9), likely especially Philippi (cf. Phil 4:15–16). The Corinthian believers may have resented Paul's willingness to accept support from Macedonia yet not from themselves; but while Paul welcomed support for missionary endeavors (Rom 15:24; probably even from Corinthians, cf. 2 Cor 10:15–16), accepting local support would risk making him the church's dependent. In Corinth's Roman culture, this would make Paul like a client, of lower status, and could hinder Paul's influence.

Most of Corinth's synagogue eventually rejected Paul's message, but apparently a number, including some leaders, withdrew with Paul to form a house congregation next door to the synagogue (Acts 18:5–8). Since people usually lived in ethnic enclaves, and one expects synagogues in a Jewish area, one could suppose that Titius Justus (the homeowner) was a Jewish Roman citizen. Luke, however, indicates that he was a "God-fearer" (his designation for a Gentile respecter of Israel's God). Synagogues valued wealthy Gentile supporters, and perhaps Titius Justus had helped sponsor the synagogue building nearby. A residential setting is not unusual; synagogues sometimes began in houses. Some argue that this host's full Roman name was "Gaius Titius Justus," explaining the praise of Gaius as the church's host (originally, or for larger meetings) in Rom 16:23 (cf. 1 Cor 1:14).

Nor was Titius Justus the only prominent member of the new movement. Of seventeen names of Corinthian Christians, nine appear on travels, suggesting means (and possibly commercial activity; cf. Malherbe 1983, 75). Luke declares that Crispus, a leader in the synagogue, believed (his family joining him, as was usual [Acts 18:8]); both Paul and Luke attest his baptism (1 Cor 1:14). (Although we do not know where the baptism occurred, Corinth had no lack of available sites; archaeology attests Corinth's many fountains and baths.) Crispus's name is Roman, which could (but need not) identify him as a Jewish Roman citizen. (Many Jews, very possibly including Paul, were Roman citizens by virtue of their descent from Jewish slaves freed in Rome.)

Phoebe was a supporter and traveler, probably a businesswoman of means from nearby Cenchreae, as well as sponsor and perhaps leader of a house church (Rom 16:1–2). Chloe was probably another businesswoman, though we do not know whether she was based in Ephesus (so explaining Paul's freedom in naming her dependents as the church's critics) or Corinth, or whether she was a believer as presumably were her agents (thus members of her "household" in the Roman sense [1 Cor 1:11]).

Most significantly from the standpoint of public prominence, Paul mentions "Erastus, the city manager" (Rom 16:23). Erastus could be a wealthy benefactor without being a member (like some supporters of synagogues or Paul's "friends" the Asiarchs in Acts 19:31), but may well be a believer himself. An inscription, probably from roughly this period, mentions one Erastus who was an "aedile," a high civic office that required great wealth (although the holder could be a freedman). Although the matter is debated, it seems likely that this is the same Erastus that Paul mentions at a different stage in Erastus's career; the name was not a common one in Corinth. Nevertheless, it would be surprising if someone of this status would later travel with Paul, so Acts 19:22 might refer to a different Erastus (though cf. 2 Tim 4:20).

Corinth hosted the famous Isthmian Games in the spring of every other year; they undoubtedly occurred during Paul's sojourn there. Despite the games' association with Poseidon, Paul may have taken advantage of the opportunity to share the gospel (perhaps while providing leather awnings for the many visitors from outside Corinth). In any case, Paul was surely aware of these games. Like other moralists, he used athletic illustrations, referring, for example, to earthly competitions' perishable wreaths (1 Cor 9:24–27). The victory wreath in Isthmian competitions was wild celery or (later) pine.

Paul's detractors finally brought him before Lucius Junius Gallio, the Roman governor (Acts 18:12), perhaps soon after his tenure began. Most scholars believe that an inscription pinpoints Gallio's proconsulship in Corinth to within a year or two; Gallio did not finish his term of office, and probably started his term on July 1, 51 (some scholars prefer 52). The elevated tribunal where Gallio probably heard Paul's accusers is in the middle of the southern edge of Corinth's forum (illustrating also 2 Cor 5:10, though the image is not unique to Corinth; cf. Rom 14:10).

Gallio cut the case short before Paul could defend himself (given Luke's interest in Paul's speeches, Luke undoubtedly reports the event in this way for historical reasons). Scholars differ as to whether Gallio so readily dismissed the case because he recognized that the charges were baseless or out of anti-Jewish prejudice, but if, as many understand Acts 18:17, he refused to prevent a synagogue leader's beating, the explanation of anti-Jewish prejudice makes sense. (Rome, as we noted, had recently expelled or at least limited the activity of its Jewish community, setting a precedent for its colonies.) Public hearings (which were normally prejudiced in favor of the litigants with higher status) often included shouting and sometimes violence. Given the relative infrequency of the name, Sosthenes, the synagogue leader beaten in Acts 18:17, is probably (though not certainly) also the believer known to the Corinthians in 1 Corinthians 1:1. Depending on how one interprets Acts, Sosthenes may have become a believer after Paul's initial departure from Corinth.

After Paul's First Departure

Despite Paul's lengthy stay, after his departure problems arose that he could not have anticipated (cf. one learned reconstruction in Winter 2001). During his fruitful but perilous ministry in Ephesus, he maintained an affectionate but sometimes tense correspondence with the Corinthian believers. His first letter to the Corinthians, warning them against approving association with immoral persons (he meant, in the church), has not survived except in Paul's allusion to it in the letter we call 1 Corinthians (1 Cor 5:9–11).

Further information soon invited another letter, namely, 1 Corinthians. Paul depended on various sources of information for his admonitions: a letter asking him questions (1 Cor 7:1); members of Chloe's household, probably business agents traveling between Ephesus and Corinth (1:11); and the Corinthian delegation of Stephanas, Fortunatus, and Achaicus, who brought him a gift (16:17–18). That Paul does not specify these last-named, prominent members of the Corinthian churches as a source may suggest that he must be discreet – after all, his source has hardly painted a flattering picture of the church, and the delegation is returning home (perhaps with his letter in hand). Paul thus diplomatically urges unity without undercutting his own supporters who provided information.

One problem in the Corinthian church was division, perhaps facilitated partly by the diverse meeting places of the different house churches. Apollos strengthened the cause of believers in Corinth against their detractors (Acts 18:27–28) and apparently made quite an impression on the Corinthian believers (1 Cor 1:12; 3:4). (Elite Alexandrian Jews like Apollos could achieve impressive Greek educations; cf. Acts 18:24.) Unfortunately, Corinthian culture emphasized rivalry, including among partisans of different teachers. Some have envisioned as many as four parties based on 1 Corinthians 1:12, but it is Apollos to whom Paul refers most in this section. Paul may be dramatizing the Corinthian believers' partisan strife by caricaturing it in parallel slogans, rather than repeating their precise words. Such rivalry could obtain among students even when the teachers themselves were on good terms, so we learn nothing of Paul's actual relationship with Apollos here (it was apparently cordial [1 Cor 16:12; cf. Acts 18:27]). But for those who valued the world's wisdom and speech (epitomized in antiquity's two advanced disciplines, philosophy and rhetoric), Paul reminds the believers that God's true, saving wisdom involves the humiliation of the cross, which transcends the greatest human wisdom (1 Cor 1:18–2:16). Speeches urging unity were common, and Paul draws on many conventions characteristic of such exhortations (see Mitchell 1991).

Another problem in Corinth involved sexual immorality (addressed by Paul in 1 Cor 5–7). As we have noted, such behavior was (by Jewish standards) rife in Corinth (and in Greek, male, urban culture more generally). One member of the church, however, exceeded even the usual tolerance limits of Gentile culture: he had his father's wife (1 Cor 5:1; it is not clear that she belonged to the church). Greek wives were on average twelve years younger than their husbands, so a second wife (perhaps the son's stepmother) might well be close to the son's age. Whether the father was alive or deceased, such an arrangement constituted incest (Lev 18:8; 20:11). Perhaps the church supported him because of his high status or wealth; in any case, Paul demands church discipline (1 Cor 5).

The failure of the church to exercise discipline in this case highlights the inconsistency of their taking one another to secular courts, which typically favored higher-status claimants (1 Cor 6:1–8). (Some believe that Paul alludes here to a lawsuit involving the incest noted in chapter 5, but Paul may be simply digressing.) After admonishing the church (and implicitly the participating members) for such behavior, Paul denounces the use of prostitutes (6:12–20). Many scholars think that Paul, like many other ancient writers, cites and then qualifies or refutes claims used by (or potentially useful to) his audience, like "all things are lawful" or "God will destroy the body anyway" (6:12–13). Paul replies that not all things are beneficial, and God will raise the body (6:12–14). Some Greek intellectuals felt that prostitutes provided a way to relieve sexual appetites without the distractions entailed by marriage; more commonly, men simply used prostitutes for special pleasure, perhaps especially while single (Greek men often married around the age of thirty). Paul warns that those who have been joined to Christ dare not desecrate that holy connection by intercourse with prostitutes (6:15–20).

Paul must also deal with members of the church who wish to avoid intercourse within marriage (1 Cor 7:1–7). Many think that Paul again qualifies an idea held by some Corinthian believers that it is good not to touch a woman sexually (7:1); Paul insists that husbands and wives are obligated to grant each other intercourse (7:2–6). It might be relevant that a minority of thinkers considered marital duties a distraction; alternatively, if some abstained from intercourse (perhaps for spiritual reasons), this could increase the temptations to the sort of immorality Paul had just condemned in 6:12–20 (cf. 7:2, 5, 9). Paul agrees with some in the church about the advantages of (celibate) singleness, but he recognizes that some people do better to marry (1 Cor 7:8–40).

If sexual immorality was a problem, so was the other primary folly of paganism noted by Jews: association with idolatry (cf. chs. 8–10). Corinth hosted as much religious diversity as any city of comparable size; some of its more prominent cults worshiped the emperor, Poseidon (the leading sea god), Aphrodite (goddess of sexual pleasure), and Asclepius (a deified healer). Foreign cults like Isis and Serapis had also settled there.

Meat was distributed widely at festivals, after many animals had been sacrificed. Whereas the rich had regular access to meat, many scholars believe that most people had access to such meat particularly at festivals (or as clients at some banquets). Some – probably educated, elite Christians – regarded deities as nothing; hence idols and food offered to idols were religiously insignificant. Paul, however, offers a series of arguments against this perspective. First, in 1 Corinthians 8, he warns against damaging the faith of believers who do not share this "educated" perspective.

Then, in chapter 9, he offers himself as an example of someone giving up his rights on behalf of others. In this case, he uses as an example his right of support; he was "free" and independent, voluntarily "enslaving" himself to serve others (9:19), a point that may have already generated some controversy with elite believers. Paul employs accepted philosophic language to defend his behavior here.

Finally, in chapter 10, he offers a theological argument (and especially biblical analogies) against eating idol food, even affirming (along with many other Jews) that the entities worshiped by pagans were demonic beings (10:20). While the theological argument militates against eating food that one knows has been associated with idols, Paul frames it with a social argument on behalf of fellow believers (8:1–13; 10:23–33).

Paul deals with food again in 11:17–34, this time the "Lord's dinner" as opposed to food offered to idols; but first he digresses to exhort some others, probably members of the elite, to sacrifice their rights for others' good (11:2–16). Married women in traditional eastern Mediterranean cultures guarded their hair from the view of men other than their husbands (see Keener 2000). Some sources, including some Jewish sources, treat wives' publicly uncovered hair as a mark of sexual immodesty; those who shared this mentality could respond the way most traditional Western churches today might respond if visitors (of either gender) attended in bathing suits. Wealthier women, however, sported fashionable hairstyles (as their husbands sported other things), and apparently normally did not cover their heads. Issues of assumed seduction, ostentation, and class conflict demanded a response: Paul urges the wealthier women to be sensitive to the concerns of their more traditional sisters in the context of their common meetings.

Paul then addresses more serious abuses in the "Lord's supper" (11:17–34), abuses that he believes have already brought judgment on the community (perhaps by restricting gifts of healings, 11:29–32). Although there remains scholarly debate, most scholars believe that the original "last supper" Jesus held with his disciples was a Passover meal (Mark 14:12–14; cf., most fully, the older treatment of Jeremias 1966). The first participants understood the Jewish context of the meal, which commemorated God delivering his people from oppression (Exod 12:14; 13:3; Deut 16:2–3). Jesus's sacrificial death offered a new, analogous act of deliverance. Gentile Corinthians, however, naturally approached the meal in light of their own meal traditions. Ancient banquets typically seated people according to rank (cf. Luke 14:8–10); at some banquets, some received food and drink of higher quality than others, producing complaints. Such social practices may have spilled into the church (cf. Theissen 1982), but Paul reproves discrimination in Christ's body based on socioeconomic considerations (1 Cor 11:21–22).

Because the believers are further divided over special kinds of enablements by God's Spirit, probably especially tongues, Paul addresses this issue at length in chapters 12–14. Here Paul emphasizes the purpose of such giftings: ministry to one another in the diverse body of Christ. He borrows the image of a diverse body from political and philosophic discourse, which often compared the state or the cosmos with a body (although sometimes in a hierarchical manner, unlike Paul here). Each member has his or her function for building up the whole, and the whole would not be complete unless each member contributes his or her special enablement for the common good. Tongues are useful for private prayer, Paul emphasizes (offering himself as an example, 14:18), but in house church gatherings should be either interpreted or replaced with prophecy, so the church can be built up. Although Paul is correcting an abuse, we incidentally learn from his correction the radically "charismatic" character of the early house churches, probably influenced by Paul's own spiritual life (cf. 14:18; 2 Cor 12:1–4, 12).

In the midst of his exhortation to use gifts to build up the body, Paul digresses to write an encomium (praise) of love (1 Cor 13). Although one of the most celebrated passages in Scripture, Paul's comments are not simply a nice poem about love. Paul employs exalted, rhetorical prose to depict love in a manner that highlights his audience's failings: indeed, aspects of his description of love in 13:4–8 correspond with what the Corinthian believers lack (for example, 4:6, 18–19; 5:2; 8:1). Supernatural enablements without love are nothing (13:1–3), and love will remain forever even when (after Christ's return) believers no longer need these finite enablements (13:8–13).

A few lines in Paul's extended discussion, enjoining women's silence, particularly trouble modern readers (14:34–35). Because this passage starkly interrupts the flow of thought (and is relocated in a few manuscripts), many scholars think the passage was added by later scribes. This is possible, though Paul's correspondence is full of digressions, and this one, like the preceding discussion, does pertain to a point of order in the church. If, as many other scholars think, the passage is original, it should be read in the context of conflicting views about the propriety of women's public speech among Paul's contemporaries. The passage could not eliminate women speaking for God or praying (which Paul approves in 11:5), but, apparently, their interrupting teaching with questions. People often interrupted ancient lectures this way, but less-educated people (as women then tended to be) doing so was ridiculed; women doing so was unusual and probably controversial in an already divided setting.

If, like many ancient writers, Paul reserves the ultimate issue for last, he harbored one concern perhaps more urgent than the believers' disunity. Although the believers had accepted Paul's message about Jesus's resurrection, some did not accept what Paul regarded as its corollary: their own future resurrection. Jesus's resurrection was in fact the first fruits (15:20, 23) of the expected future bodily resurrection of believers (Dan 12:2). Many scholars traditionally blamed the Corinthians' perspective on an "overrealized eschatology" (i.e., treating all promised future blessings as present), but many today recognize that a Greek worldview simply predisposed them against future eschatology in general. Some affirmed and some denied afterlife, but Greeks and Romans were unfamiliar with future resurrection. Paul hinted at this issue earlier (especially 6:14), but addresses it fully in chapter 15. Anticipating objections, however, he allows that the future body is of different character than the present one (15:35–50; cf. also Phil 3:21).

Paul concludes with business in chapter 16, a common topic of ancient letters. He addresses his collection for the poor (16:1–4) and his plans to visit Corinth (16:5–7), as well as other closing matters.

More Problems with Corinth

Paul's long-range plan was to visit Macedonia (1 Cor 16:5), then Achaia (1 Cor 16:5–6; cf. 4:18–21), Judea (Rom 15:25; 2 Cor 1:16), and, finally, Rome (Rom 1:11–13; 15:23–25; cf. 2 Cor 10:16; see Acts 19:21, in the same sequence). While in Ephesus (1 Cor 16:8), Paul sent Timothy to Macedonia (Acts 19:22) and on to Corinth (1 Cor 4:17; also 16:10); we later find Timothy with Paul in Corinth (Rom 16:21; Acts 20:3–4).

At some point, whether before or after making the above plans, Paul visited Corinth again. If he voyaged across the Aegean (rather than retracing his overland journey through Macedonia), the voyage itself was time-consuming (a similar voyage in Cicero took two weeks in one direction). This visit unfortunately turned painful, and Paul again threatened discipline if matters were not put in order (2 Cor 2:1; 12:14; 13:2).

Despite the different plan in 1 Corinthians 16:5–6, at some point Paul had considered sailing to Corinth before traveling to Macedonia, and then returning to Corinth again (2 Cor 1:15–16). He was forced, however, to change these plans somehow (1:17), partly because of conflict with the Corinthian church (2:1–3). How were his plans changed? Some scholars think that Paul did visit Corinth at this time (thus making the initial visit proposed in 1:15–16a), and that this visit represents the "painful" visit just mentioned; Paul then simply refused to return to Corinth after going to Macedonia. Others suggest that the painful visit happened at some earlier point in Paul's Ephesian ministry, and that his change of plans (1:17) meant forgoing even the initial visit before Macedonia. It seems to me that this latter approach better explains Paul's movements since he planned to proceed to Judea with the collection after finishing his trips to Corinth (1:16), yet after refusing to come to Corinth we find him in Troas, not yet having entered Macedonia (2:12–13; 7:5–7), and concerned to ensure that the Corinthians' contribution to the collection is ready (chs. 8–9). In either case, his failure to carry through the promised visit, due to changed circumstances, caused offense. Paul apparently explained these matters to the believers in Corinth in a letter of reproof, written while he was in great anguish regarding them (2:4; 7:8). Some identify this letter with 2 Corinthians 10–13, but most consider it a letter that has now been lost.

Paul had already warned that he would discipline the believers as an ancient father disciplined erring children (1 Cor 4:18–21). Now, however, he avoided coming to them for a time so that he would not have to carry out the threat (2 Cor 1:23; 2:1–4). His friends in Corinth did not understand this change of plans. It was customary for friends to protest affectionately the failure of a loved one to visit, but the Corinthians' protest appears to involve a deeper level of offense: if Paul could not be trusted to keep his promise about visiting, how reliable was his message on other points (cf. 1:17–22)?

Thus, Paul sent a sorrowful letter with Titus to Corinth (2:13), expecting to meet Titus on his return in Troas. When, however, Titus failed to appear in Troas, Paul pressed into Macedonia, hoping to find him en route (2:13; 7:5; cf. 1 Cor 16:5). Apparently, Paul feared for his relationship with the Corinthian believers and for how Titus may have been received. Paul was greatly relieved to encounter Titus and learn that his firm letter had been effective in bringing repentance in the matter of a man who needed discipline (2 Cor 7:5–12). (Scholars debate the man's offense. Modern scholars most often argue that he was a vocal critic of Paul within the church; based on apparent literary connections, most church fathers contended that he was the man committing incest in 1 Cor 5.) Meanwhile, Paul was also gathering the Macedonian offerings for the impoverished believers of Jerusalem (8:1–5; 9:2).

Yet we may also gather that some or many of the Corinthian believers felt or came to feel dissatisfied with how Paul had handled their situation. They were, as we noted, unhappy that he had failed to come in person, though he would explain in his next letter that the delay was for their sake (2 Cor 1:23). Because he sent them a written reproof rather than correcting them to their faces, some were complaining that he was bold in his letters but timid in person (10:1–2, 10–11). In a culture in which rhetoric played such an important public role, such charges impugned his leadership style, requiring Paul to write a letter (part or all of 2 Corinthians) to seek to fully regain their trust.

At some point (before or after the problem with Paul's harsh letter), rival Jewish-Christian missionaries (2:17; 4:2), carrying letters of recommendation (3:1) and commending themselves (10:12–18; 11:18), came to the Corinthian churches. Apparently more appealing to local culture than Paul was, their presence and probably criticism increased the Corinthians' tension with Paul (11:4, 12–15, 19–23). Probably these newcomers, unlike Paul, accepted Corinthian financial patronage (11:7–15); they may have also criticized Paul's offering for the poor in Jerusalem, which Paul defends in great detail (chs. 8–9).

Paul then wrote some or all of the letter we call 2 Corinthians and sent it with Titus, so that the collection would be ready by the time he and the Macedonian delegation arrived (2 Cor 8:6, 16–19, 22–23; 9:3–5; cf. 1 Cor 16:2). Paul still planned to visit Corinth (2 Cor 13:1) with traveling companions from other cities (9:4–5) – once he could be assured that everything was in order. Failure of the comparatively wealthy Corinthian church to be ready would create problems with the poorer churches of Macedonia because Paul had been depending on the Corinthian believers to honor their commitments and already used their example to stir other churches. Despite his assurances of confidence in them, Paul is clearly anxious about the Corinthians' current commitment (9:4–5). Nevertheless, the letter's preservation and his later extended visit in Acts 20:2–3 (and Rom 15:26) suggest that his appeal was successful.

2 Corinthians

We must examine a question regarding 2 Corinthians before surveying the letter itself. Whereas most scholars agree that Paul sent 1 Corinthians as a single letter, scholars have long divided over the character of 2 Corinthians. This question affects how we reconstruct the situation in the letter. Some scholars believe that editors combined six letters or parts of letters (mostly from Paul) to produce 2 Corinthians. Because Paul, like many ancient writers, includes so many digressions elsewhere, many scholars find most of these divisions unpersuasive. (The hypothesis proves weakest in the supposed division between chapters 8 and 9, which might even split a single paragraph.) Paul clearly likes to use digressions (as in 1 Cor 9 and 13, noted above), so sections that shift between topics in 2 Corinthians should not surprise us.

A much larger number of scholars accept a division between chapters 1–9 and 10–13, where a shift in tone is clear. This division remained the dominant scholarly view in the twentieth century. Nevertheless, especially under the influence of current literary criticism, which is less sympathetic to speculative source reconstructions than a century ago, an increasing number of scholars today read 2 Corinthians as a whole, single letter (see arguments in, for example, Witherington 1995; Lambrecht 1999; Matera 2003; Keener 2005). Some believe that subsequent news led Paul to change his tone in the closing chapters (chs. 10–13); others believe that he simply reserved his most controversial and confrontational matters for the end. Paul offers some firm warnings in chapters 1–9 and continues loving appeals to his audience in chapters 10–13, reinforcing the possibility of the letter's unity. Our treatment here works from the simpler premise of unity (ancient letter collections normally *did* preserve greetings that would distinguish separate letters), while acknowledging that scholars who divide the letter between chapters 9 and 10 also have strong reasons for their position.

Whereas in 1 Corinthians Paul's problems were with Corinthian believers themselves, by the time Paul writes 2 Corinthians, newcomers to Corinth have exacerbated criticisms of Paul. Paul regards them as rivals undermining his apostolic work (2:17; 3:1; 5:12; 10:12; 11:4, 12–14). Because they were Jewish (11:22), some interpreters identify them with Paul's opponents in Galatia; but Paul's allies and his opponents alike were largely Jewish. Unlike the Twelve in Jerusalem, these Jews apparently have a Hellenistic education impressive to the Corinthians; their rhetorical proficiency served to highlight Paul's inadequacies in delivery (11:5–6; cf. 10:10).

Paul addresses the rivals directly in chapters 10–13, but has already been preparing his audience for that direct assault. Paul emphasizes the cruciform character of his own apostleship in chapters 3–6, and has already protested that some seek to alienate the believers from him (2:17–3:1; 5:20–6:1; 6:11–7:2). Their possible criticisms of his collection for the poor would explain his defense of the motives behind the collection in chapters 8–9 and his statements of opposition to greed (2:17; cf. 4:2) before confronting these issues toward his conclusion (12:14–18). His rivals apparently challenge his apostleship (3:1; 12:12) and his refusal to accept support (2:17; 11:7–9). Paul, by contrast, rejects their criteria for self-commendation (5:12; 10:10–18).

We are now ready to survey 2 Corinthians. Particularly in view of the new competition, Paul must resolve lesser conflicts between himself and some Corinthian believers before tackling the most serious problem. Thus, as we have noted, Paul first confronts Corinthian disappointment with his failure to come as promised; he emphasizes that it was for their sake that he had avoided coming, to afford them opportunity for repentance (1:22–2:4). Instead of coming in person, he had dispatched Titus to confirm that previous problems were resolved so that he would not need to confront the Corinthians more harshly than he desired. When Titus did not return quickly with good news of reconciliation, Paul had grown concerned about his relationship with the Corinthian believers he cared about. Titus's news had consoled him (2:12–13; 7:5–16).

In the midst of discussing this potential conflict with the Corinthians, Paul digresses at length regarding his motivation. He explains how his apostolic ministry is externally weak, marked by suffering like that of Jesus, while eyes of faith recognize the inner glory and power of Christ in it (2:14–7:1). Among the many explanations of Paul's image of the Roman triumph in 2:14, one of the most persuasive is that he and his co-workers are Christ's prisoners facing death; whether observers recognize in their suffering only death or Christ's resurrection life depends on their own spiritual state (2:15–16).

While the rivals depend on letters of recommendation (a familiar letter form in antiquity), Paul declares that the Corinthian believers are themselves sufficient evidence of his ministry (3:1–3). But God's work in them is not merely external, like the tablets of Moses' law; rather, it is internal, as in the promised new covenant (Jer 31:31–34; Ezek 36:26–27). Outward glory accompanied the law given to Moses, but it was a transient, limited glory; by contrast, the glory revealed by the experience of the Spirit provides a greater internal glory (2 Cor 3:7–18). Like divine Wisdom in Jewish tradition, Christ was the very image of God, and those looking to him would be transformed into his likeness (3:18; 4:4).

Again, however, Paul recognizes that the world cannot perceive this glory, just as Israel could not behold all the glory of the earlier covenant (3:14–16; 4:3–4). Christ's messengers carry this glory of resurrection life within, while outwardly they share the sufferings of his cross (4:7–14). Christ's agents are not crushed by the trials because their foretaste of resurrection life guarantees their future victory; this foretaste is the presence of God's Spirit within them (5:5). Thus, they are sharing death outwardly, in the sphere considered by many thinkers to be temporary, while being renewed inwardly, in the sphere recognized by many thinkers as eternal (4:16–18). Because of the Spirit, the future resurrection body was their certain possession (5:1–4), and they continued to labor for the Lord (5:6–11).

When Paul has nearly reached the end of his digression, he confronts the believers in Corinth with a decision. As in Roman partisan politics and alliances, friendship and enmity involved mutually exclusive networks (cf. Marshall 1987): if the believers wish to maintain good terms with Paul, they cannot maintain good terms with his rivals. Genuine reconciliation to God necessarily entails being reconciled with Christ's agent, Paul (2 Cor 5:20–6:2; 6:11–13), and rejecting the perverse influence of the "unbelievers" (6:14–16).

Paul's two defenses of his apostolic ministry (1:12–7:16; 10:1–13:10) frame the urgent issue of the collection for the needy – which his opponents' criticisms risk undermining. Paul had enlisted the Phrygian churches of the province of Galatia (1 Cor 16:1) as well as the Macedonian churches, but he had used the promised eagerness of the wealthier Corinthian church to help provoke the Macedonians to action. A failure in Corinth could yield trouble for the entire program. Using language familiar to us also from inscriptions honoring donors (see especially Danker 1989), Paul defends both the project and the integrity of the agents to whom he has entrusted its collection. He plays on rivalry between Corinth and Macedonia (exploiting civic competition was a familiar persuasive technique in his day), as well as the biblical model of God supplying manna equally to all in the wilderness. (Ancient philosophers often discussed the ideal of equality in good friendships.) Portraying God as the ultimate benefactor, Paul draws on ancient emphases regarding honoring donors (9:11–15).

Like some ancient orators, Paul may reserve his heaviest censure for his finale, where he directly confronts the toleration shown by the Corinthians toward rival teachers (chs. 10–13). Having defended his own ministry earlier in the letter, Paul now goes on the offensive (as those criticized were normally expected to do in ancient rhetoric). Yet even here, Paul rapidly shifts from denouncing the rival teachers to again addressing his beloved Corinthian believers (12:19–13:10).

Probably because Paul had chosen to send a warning letter rather than to confront them in person (1:23–2:4), Paul's critics complained that he was inconsistent: "bold" in his letters, but timid in person (10:10). In a culture pervaded by public speakers and hearers' evaluations of public speakers, Paul might appear inferior to more eloquent competitors (11:5–6). Paul thus emphasizes that his real power is expressed in ways that reflect Christ's model of humiliation rather than human standards (10:1–7); and he insists that his rivals are boasting in his sphere of divine authority, since God used him (and not the rivals) to win the Corinthian believers (10:12–18). The Greco-Roman world in general despised boasting unless the boaster had good justification for the boast; boasting in another's sphere was considered particularly arrogant.

Taking the posture of a father wanting to keep his daughter pure for her husband, Paul warns against these rivals as false apostles, agents of Satan who could corrupt the believers as Satan deceived Eve (and some Jewish stories recounted that Satan had corrupted Eve). One could boast if "forced" to do so, say, to set straight the claims of rivals, and Paul reluctantly enters this dispute, employing the standard rhetorical technique of an extensive comparison between himself and his rivals. But instead of boasting in his achievements (for example, churches planted), he boasts in his sufferings (11:21–33), hence identifying with the crucified Christ (cf. 13:4).

In 12:1–4 Paul notes a vision, the sort of experience many of his contemporaries respected. The pinnacle of such experiences in Jewish circles was often seeing God on his heavenly throne, but Paul narrates instead a different revelation about Christ's power being perfected in weakness (12:5–9). Such a message epitomizes the heart of the Corinthian correspondence: whereas most Corinthian believers embraced their culture's values of status and power, Paul preaches to them about the God who revealed his power in the weakness of the cross, and now continues to do so in the weakness of Christ's agents (1 Cor 1:18, 24–27; 2:3–5; 4:10; 2 Cor 4:7; 10:10; 11:30; 12:5, 10; 13:3–4, 9). (On Paul's suffering lists in 1 Cor 4:9–13; 2 Cor 4:8–11; 6:4–10; 11:23–33, see Fitzgerald 1988.)

Paul closes with a warning (12:19–13:10). Some had condemned him as "soft" for sending a letter and emissaries instead of disciplining them in person (1:23–2:4). His rivals had interpreted the delay in his coming as weakness, in contrast to their own boldness (10:1, 9–11). Now Paul again warns the believers through another letter: this time he will come, and he will be forced to discipline them if issues of division and immorality remain. Paul's later stay with them (Acts 20:2–3; Rom 15:26) suggests that his letter proved successful. At the least, the relationship between Paul and the Corinthian house churches remained deeply affectionate.

Despite moments of firmness, expected in ancient letters of correction and reproof, Paul's deep affection and concern for the Corinthian believers pervade his correspondence with them. Some of the closest literary parallels appear in ancient letters between friends expressing longing for each other and concern for the relationship. Paul's own letters model the love and concern for fellow believers that he urges in passages like 1 Corinthians 8:7–13 and 13:1–13.

The Aftermath of 2 Corinthians

The partisan, divisive culture undoubtedly continued to affect believers in Corinth; Clement later finds fault with the Corinthian church for this same issue (1 Clement 1.1;

47.1–5). Nevertheless, Paul was surely reconciled with the Corinthians, and they undoubtedly participated in his mission to aid the poor in Jerusalem. From Corinth, he writes to the believers in Rome, mentioning that the churches in both Macedonia and Achaia have contributed to it (Rom 15:26). Paul then sends this letter on to Rome by a church leader from Cenchreae (Rom 16:1).

Luke, who is not interested in Paul's past conflicts with the Corinthians (and barely interested in the collection [Acts 24:17]), simply summarizes briefly. Paul's three-month stay in Greece (20:2), presumably largely in Corinth and its environs, undoubtedly included part of winter (cf. 1 Cor 16:6), when travel was difficult. His plans for a sea voyage to Jerusalem (presumably in time for Passover) thwarted (Acts 20:3), Paul began the land journey to reach Jerusalem by Pentecost (20:16). His letters also tell us that his next planned stop was Jerusalem (Rom 15:25), though he was aware of dangers there (Rom 15:31). Whether or not the believers in Corinth saw Paul alive again, they never forgot him, and it appears that they revered him as their founder. Outsiders, at least, expected his example to move them (1 Clement 5.5–7; 47.1).

References

Belleville, Linda L. 1996. *2 Corinthians*. Downers Grove, Ill.: InterVarsity.

Danker, Frederick W. 1989. *II Corinthians*. Minneapolis: Augsburg.

Fee, Gordon D. 1987. *The First Epistle to the Corinthians*. Grand Rapids: Eerdmans.

Fitzgerald, John T. 1988. *Cracks in an Earthen Vessel: An Examination of the Catalogues of Hardships in the Corinthian Correspondence*. Atlanta: Scholars.

Garland, David E. 2003. *1 Corinthians*. Grand Rapids: Baker.

Hays, Richard B. 1997. *First Corinthians*. Louisville: John Knox.

Horsley, Richard A. 1998. *1 Corinthians*. Nashville: Abingdon.

Jeremias, Joachim. 1966. *The Eucharistic Words of Jesus*. Philadelphia: Fortress.

Keener, Craig S. 2000. Head coverings. Pages 442–447 in *Dictionary of New Testament Background*. Edited by Craig A. Evans and Stanley E. Porter. Downers Grove, Ill.: InterVarsity.

Keener, Craig S. 2005. *1 & 2 Corinthians*. Cambridge: Cambridge University Press.

Lambrecht, J. 1999. *Second Corinthians*. Sacra Pagina. Collegeville, Minn.: Liturgical.

Malherbe, Abraham J. 1983. *Social Aspects of Early Christianity*. Second edition. Philadelphia: Fortress.

Marshall, Peter. 1987. *Enmity in Corinth: Social Conventions in Paul's Relations with the Corinthians*. Tübingen: J. C. B. Mohr (Paul Siebeck).

Matera, Frank J. 2003. *II Corinthians: A Commentary*. Louisville: Westminster John Knox.

Mitchell, Margaret M. 1991. *Paul and the Rhetoric of Reconciliation: An Exegetical Investigation of the Language and Composition of 1 Corinthians*. Louisville: Westminster John Knox.

Porter, Stanley E. 2001. *Paul in Acts*. Peabody, Mass.: Hendrickson.

Talbert, Charles H. 1987. *Reading Corinthians: A Literary and Theological Commentary on 1 and 2 Corinthians*. New York: Crossroad.

Theissen, Gerd. 1982. *The Social Setting of Pauline Christianity: Essays on Corinth*. Philadelphia: Fortress.

Thiselton, Anthony C. 2000. *The First Epistle to the Corinthians: A Commentary on the Greek Text*. Grand Rapids: Eerdmans.

Thrall, Margaret E. 1994, 2000. *A Critical and Exegetical Commentary on the Second Epistle to the Corinthians*. 2 volumes. Edinburgh: T. & T. Clark.

Winter, Bruce W. 2001. *After Paul Left Corinth: The Influence of Secular Ethics and Social Change*. Grand Rapids: Eerdmans.

Witherington III, Ben. 1995. *Conflict and Community in Corinth: A Socio-rhetorical Commentary on 1 and 2 Corinthians*. Grand Rapids: Eerdmans.

CHAPTER 4

Paul and the Galatian Believers

Stephen Chester

Reconstructing the Galatian Crisis

There are few more influential texts in human history than Galatians. It has enjoyed an incendiary history of interpretation in which the letter, "like a proxy for its author, ... continues to exert a formative, often disruptive and subversive, influence on Rome and Byzantium, on Reformation and post-Reformation Europe, in a way few other books can rival. From these defining moments in human history the shock waves flow out to encompass, in the course of two millennia, the whole globe" (Riches 2008, 1). Yet, somewhat ironically, its origins are shrouded in obscurity. We do not know whether it was sent to churches in Asia Minor established by Paul in what had been the territory of the old pre-Roman ethnic kingdom of Galatia (Acts 16:6; 18:23) or if its recipients were churches further south in territory incorporated by the Romans into an expanded province of Galatia (Acts 13:14–14:23). Our answer to this question yields different dates for the founding of the Galatian churches, which in turn opens up different possibilities for the date of the letter. Galatians may have been written sometime between 53 and 57 CE, or – if written to the churches in the south – it may date from the late 40s CE and be the earliest of Paul's surviving letters. If the earlier date is correct, the crisis that prompted the writing of the letter may have been the precursor of an agreement that largely resolved within early Christianity the issues with which it is concerned (Acts 15). If the later date is correct, the crisis may instead signify the collapse of that agreement.[1]

Nor have scholars reached a consensus on the crisis in Galatia that prompted Paul to write. The dominant account, adopted by many commentators with minor variations across the centuries, focuses attention on Paul's attempts to define the relationship

The Blackwell Companion to Paul, First Edition. Edited by Stephen Westerholm.
© 2011 Blackwell Publishing Ltd. Published 2011 by Blackwell Publishing Ltd.

between the Galatian believers and Judaism. Paul has established the Galatian congregations through his preaching of the gospel (Gal 1:8; 3:1–5; 4:13). They are predominantly Gentile (1:16; 2:2, 9), and Paul has taught them that salvation does not require either circumcision or observance of the other requirements of the Mosaic law, but only faith in the saving benefits of Christ's death (2:3; 2:15–3:5). After Paul has left Galatia, others have instructed the believers differently, urging upon them circumcision and at least some wider law observance (5:2–3; 6:12–13). These teachers are clearly Jewish (even if not of Jewish origin, they cannot credibly urge others to accept circumcision without having first become Jewish by doing so themselves), and Paul's reference to their message as "another gospel" (1:6) makes it certain that they are believers. They probably question the validity of Paul's apostleship and his gospel, prompting Paul to discuss both (1:11–17), and they may have some links with the Jerusalem church, prompting Paul to recount the history of his relationship with its leaders (1:18–2:14). They probably also make extensive use of scriptural arguments, especially the Abraham narratives, which prompts Paul to offer his own interpretations (3:6–4:31). Paul's response is furious, making clear to the Galatian believers that no compromise is possible. The issues at stake concern the truth of the gospel or its perversion (1:6–9). Building on the foundation of this reconstruction, interpreters have then sought to explore more precisely the nature of Paul's critique of first-century Judaism.

However, several recent attempts have been made to challenge this traditional reconstruction of the crisis in Galatia. Mark Nanos argues that the teachers opposing Paul are not Jewish believers but non-Christ-believing representatives of local synagogues seeking to persuade the Gentile believers to become Jewish proselytes (Nanos 2002, 75–199). Paul observes the Mosaic law and regards it as obligatory for Jews, but objects to the circumcision of Gentiles because Christ's death has inaugurated a new age in which Gentiles who remain Gentiles can be included among the righteous of God. Other attempts at revision have focused not on the teachers opposing Paul but on the situation of the Galatian believers. Susan Elliott suggests that Paul's hostility to Gentile circumcision stems not from any critique of the law but from concern over the self-castration practiced by some devotees of the goddess Cybele, whose cult was prevalent across the Anatolian region of which Galatia was part. Galatian Jewish communities understand circumcision in ways shaped by the social patterns of the Cybele cult, regarding it and self-castration as comparable rites (Elliott 2003). Justin Hardin points instead to the rapid rise and spread of the imperial cult in first-century Anatolia (Hardin 2008, 23–81). Paul is concerned that the Gentile believers will accept circumcision merely as a way of avoiding persecution, claiming the privileges of Jewish identity so as to avert an angry reaction from the authorities to their refusal to participate in the cult (6:12). This is the background to Paul speaking as if to be circumcised would be equivalent to falling back into paganism (4:8–11). His anger is provoked more by the prospect of compromise with the imperial cult than by the thought of Galatian believers observing the Mosaic law as such.

These revisionist accounts attempt to open up fresh lines of interpretation, but in various ways fail to do justice to the admittedly fragmentary evidence provided by the text. For Nanos's argument, the hurdle is what Paul says or implies about the teachers opposing him. Paul's warning not to accept alternative gospels, even if the source is

Paul himself or an angel (1:8–9), is specific. It suggests concern about plausible impersonations or modifications of the gospel Paul has presented, not a very different message from synagogue representatives who are not believers in Christ and make little reference to him. Similarly, Paul's accusation that the teachers urge circumcision on the Galatians to avoid persecution for the cross of Christ (6:12) loses all rhetorical force if its target is non-Christ-believing synagogue representatives in no danger of such persecution.

For Elliott's and Hardin's arguments, the problem is rather what Paul does not say. Galatians abounds in specific, unambiguous references to circumcision, the Mosaic law, and the Abraham narratives, but lacks any to the Cybele cult or the imperial cult. Elliott fails to produce any evidence that circumcision and castration were regarded as analogous practices in terms of their social categorization. The shock value of Paul's own rhetorical linking of the two in 5:12 depends precisely upon their incommensurability. Hardin can at least demonstrate enthusiastic adoption of the imperial cult in the first century in both ethnic and provincial Galatia. Yet it is far from clear that Paul's arguments are directed against that cult. It is possible that the Galatian believers were prepared to consider circumcision partly because it would neutralize hostility toward them arising from non-participation in the imperial cult, but Paul does not engage this in his argument. Whatever their motivation, Paul's concern is with what he sees as the negative consequences of being circumcised, and this discussion he unsurprisingly frames in a Jewish context.

It is striking that in each of the revisionist accounts, a legitimate, indeed essential, awareness of the potential for Paul's argument to be misused in an anti-Jewish or antinomian manner slips over into disregard for historical plausibility. The traditional reconstruction that Paul criticizes Jewish-Christian advocates of circumcision simply makes better sense of the available evidence.

Engaging Paul's Text

Such debates over the reconstruction of the Galatian crisis illustrate both the necessity and limitations of historical criticism. The necessity is that we have no responsible alternative other than to deploy all our historical tools in an attempt to elucidate Paul's letter. To do less in the face of a challenging text is to settle for interpretation that is merely arbitrary. The limitation is that despite the sophistication of our historical tools, our ability to read as the Galatian believers heard is partial. The traditional reconstruction is not itself much more than a sketchy outline. While its acceptance certainly eliminates some possibilities, it can serve equally well mutually contradictory lines of interpretation. Thus, for example, there is a fissure in recent scholarship between those who continue to interpret the letter within trajectories established by the work of Martin Luther (1483–1546), the single most influential commentator ever on Galatians, and those who work within what is labeled the "New Perspective on Paul," which began to emerge in the late 1970s. The labels "Lutheran" and "New Perspective," with their suggestion of two homogenous opposing camps, simplify the reality of a complex web of contemporary interpretations, but it is certainly the case that many on both sides fully accept the traditional reconstruction of the Galatian crisis. In the following description of Paul's argument, its main features are outlined on the basis of that reconstruction, but there is nevertheless no shortage of debated issues and texts.

Galatians 1:1–2:21: Rebuking the Galatians and Setting the Record Straight

Paul opens his letter with a long, single-sentence salutation (1:1–5). Although it wishes the Galatian believers grace and peace, notably absent is Paul's characteristic thanksgiving to God for the recipients (Rom 1:8; 1 Cor 1:4–7; Phil 1:3–5), and he will go on angrily to suggest that they are already turning away from the truth (1:6–7). Paul instead defines himself as an apostle by divine authority, defines God the Father as the one who raised Jesus from the dead, and defines Jesus by the salvific nature of his death. Immediately apparent in the description of Christ's death "on behalf of our sins, so he might rescue us from the present evil age" (1:4)[2] is the apocalyptic nature of Paul's theology. In common with many other ancient Jewish authors, Paul believes that there is a better age to come, only to arrive through dramatic divine intervention in human history. Yet he is distinctive in regarding this intervention as already having taken place in Christ's atoning death. Jesus's sacrifice for the sins of human beings has been made so that he might liberate them from the power of evil dominating their existence. It is against the backdrop of this larger story of Christ's death and resurrection, and his own appointment as its legitimate herald, that Paul wishes the Galatians to understand their current choice whether or not to accept circumcision. Only a refusal will be consistent with God's actions in Jesus in freeing them for a new age.

To secure this understanding, Paul must demonstrate that he is a trustworthy teller of the story of divine intervention through Christ, qualified to instruct the Galatians in what it means to be obedient to its truth. This is not straightforward for Paul since he is the most junior of the apostles and has to live down his former persecution of the church (1 Cor 15:7–10). Those apostles associated with Jesus during his earthly ministry and/or who lead the original church in Jerusalem may appear to possess greater authority, and it seems that the teachers influencing the Galatians claimed to reflect their views. Paul's response is to narrate the history of his conversion and his relationship with those in Jerusalem who were apostles before him. He insists that his authority is independent of theirs, the gospel he preaches having been given to him by divine revelation (1:11–24). They have also accepted his apostleship and the gospel he preaches (2:1–10), giving to him the right hand of fellowship (2:9) and accepting without circumcision a Gentile who accompanied him (2:3). Paul is also careful not to make the validity of the gospel depend on him and his experiences, urging the Galatians to reject even him or an angel from heaven should they preach a different message (1:8). He is the servant of the gospel and not vice versa, and what is of final significance is the truth of what God has done in Jesus. Nevertheless, God has given to Paul the task of proclaiming the gospel of Christ among the Gentiles (1:15–16), and Paul's description of his conversion is soaked in the vocabulary of calling drawn from the Old Testament prophets (see Isa 49:1–6; Jer 1:5). So long as Paul adheres to the gospel, its authority and legitimacy and his own are functionally intertwined.

What Paul has to report next is an incident in which the actions of none other than Peter threatened to undermine the truth of the gospel. He and Peter have quarreled in the church at Antioch in Syria over Jewish and Gentile believers eating together (2:11–14). Peter had eaten with Gentiles but then refused to do so after the arrival of representatives from James, the brother of Jesus, leader of the Jerusalem church. Although Paul does not tell his readers precisely why Peter withdrew, it is clearly analogous for Paul to the issue of circumcision confronting the Galatians. Interpreters usually conclude that eating with Gentiles was perceived in some way to threaten the obedience to the food laws of the Old Testament of the Jewish participants in these meals. Only if the Gentile believers adopt Jewish practices can proper law observance be guaranteed and fellowship resumed; hence Paul's pointed question to Peter, "If you, though a Jew, live like a Gentile and not like a Jew, how can you compel the Gentiles to Judaize?" (2:14).

Paul leaves the end of the story untold and instead provides a tightly reasoned summary (2:15–21) of what he saw as at stake, both then in Antioch and now in Galatia. It is these statements that the rest of the letter will demonstrate to be true. What is immediately clear is that Paul's fury at the imposition of Jewish practices upon Gentile believers stems from his conviction of the sufficiency of Christ's death. If the Gentiles must be circumcised or must eat in a Jewish way, then it is implied that their belief in Jesus and the saving nature of his death must be supplemented by observance of the law: "I do not set aside the grace of God, for if righteousness comes through the law, then Christ died for nothing" (2:21). However, every aspect of Paul's explanation of why it is that he finds so objectionable supplementing the cross with the law is contested. In 2:16, in particular, there are disputed terms and phrases that have long been central to debates concerning Paul's theology.

Key Text: Galatians 2:16

This verse is a storm center of the debate between "Lutheran" and "New Perspective" interpreters. Paul begins by saying that a person is justified "not by the works of the law" (see also 3:2, 5, 10). Following Martin Luther, the traditional interpretation is that Paul here objects to the view that God's attitude toward human beings is determined by their attempts to please God by their actions: only by satisfying the divine demand for law observance can human beings be accepted by God. Paul sees rather that there is nothing humans can do to contribute to their salvation and offers a complete antithesis between faith and works, attributing everything in salvation to the divine initiative of grace. In contrast, "New Perspective" interpreters find an insistence that salvation depends on what human beings do an unlikely position for the teachers influencing the Galatians to adopt. They regard it as uncharacteristic of Judaism, which itself stresses divine grace. Paul refers by the term "works of the law" primarily to those aspects of law observance – namely, circumcision, the food laws, and Sabbath observance – that served as key markers of Jewish identity, separating Jews from Gentiles and proving their loyalty to the covenant. The need for this separation has been overcome by Christ's saving death, which makes it possible for Gentiles to become part of God's people through faith alone. The identification by Paul's opponents of righteousness with Jewish identity reveals a false ethnocentrism, and "the 'works' which Paul consistently warns against were, in his view, Israel's misunderstandings of what her covenant law required ... Furthermore, that misunderstanding meant a misunderstanding of God and of God's promised (covenanted) intention to bless also the nations" (Dunn 1998, 366). What is at stake is not so much the principle of how human beings are saved as that of how God's people is constituted.

Thus, in relation to what Paul rejects (righteousness is not by works of the law), there is straightforward opposition between what is said by "Lutheran" and "New Perspective" interpreters. In relation to what Paul affirms, however – that righteousness comes through Christ and faith – the situation is more complex. On the question of what Paul means by justification, it may at least fairly be said that in the Reformation tradition righteousness by faith involves the receiving by the believer of the alien righteousness of Christ. It is this receiving by faith of a righteousness from outside that places the individual in a right relationship with God. In "New Perspective" interpretations, the common thread is the insistence that Paul's focus here is not the question of how human beings are put right with God despite their sin, but rather the relationship between Jews and Gentiles in the church. Justification in 2:16 is "to be reckoned by God to be a true member of his family" (Wright 2009, 96). It refers specifically "to the coming together of Jews and Gentiles in faithful membership of the Christian family" (Wright 2009, 96).

Assessment of these interpretations is complex. A majority of Pauline scholars currently favor "New Perspective" positions, but some of the most widely held reasons for these decisions rest upon faulty premises. For example, it does not follow that if Judaism exhibits a strong concept of divine grace, Paul cannot be opposing those who insist that human deeds are essential to salvation. Paul's soteriology is directed not against the assumption that grace plays no part, but against the assumption that the appropriate human response to divine grace, expressed in obedience to God's law, is also essential. Paul constructs a complete antithesis between the two because he believes that this obedient response has proved impossible for human beings and that, acting in Christ, God has overcome this insurmountable obstacle by grace alone. It is this grace, expressed in the gift of the Spirit, that is the cause of the obedient lives of those who believe.

A further assumption concerns the role played by context in determining Paul's meaning. The issue that prompts Paul to write the letter to the Galatians is circumcision, a rite which indeed functions to establish a boundary between Jews and Gentiles. Further, in relation to 2:16, "the context of his talking about 'not being justified by works of the law' is that he is confronted with the question of ethnic taboos about eating together across ethnic boundaries" (Wright 2009, 96). If Paul is prompted to discuss justification by these issues, then it is natural to begin from the premise that justification itself directly concerns these issues. However, it is precisely in discerning the close relationship between issues concerning ethnic boundaries and central soteriological issues that Paul here makes a distinctive contribution. He sees, in a way that others in the early Christian movement did not, that to impose circumcision on Gentiles or deny them equal table fellowship compromises justification. It is the gift of an alien righteousness, granted not on the basis of deeds or any other dimension of human worthiness but solely by grace, that mandates a boundary-shattering communal life.

Although many interpreters in the Reformation tradition do inappropriately treat circumcision and the food laws simply as necessary pieces of staging that can simply fall into the background once their task is complete, others, most notably Calvin, pay considerable attention to the relationship between the two (Chester 2008, 323). They also introduce a contextual argument of their own, which is that in the following chapters Paul repeatedly makes mention of "works of the law" without discussing circumcision. He insists on the impossible necessity of doing all that the law requires (3:10) and offers a general contrast between law and promise (3:18). Circumcision itself does not reappear until 5:2–3, and then in the context of a further insistence on the necessity of obedience to the whole law for those who undergo it, and a general contrast between justification by law and grace. "New Perspective" interpreters do acknowledge that the phrase "works of the law" encompasses the whole law but argue that its boundary-marking aspects are particularly in view. Yet if they are particularly in view, it would be difficult to detect that fact from Galatians 3–4. The position that the phrase "works of the law" refers to any and all acts of obedience to the law makes good sense as part of an overall argument in which Paul, prompted by a crisis concerning ethnic boundaries, demonstrates its implications for understanding salvation before returning at length to apply his soteriology to the life of the church. The issue of boundaries matters profoundly for Paul because he sees the task of the church as embodying in its common life a pattern of salvation in which human actions, including those that maintain separation, are not a cause of salvation.

A final assumption is that, in speaking of an alien righteousness of Christ, interpreters in the Reformation tradition necessarily think of that righteousness as something transferred from Christ to those who believe, thus separating justification from Paul's references to participation in Christ. However, while some Protestant interpreters undoubtedly do fall into this trap, it is scarcely characteristic of Luther and Calvin in their comments on Galatians 2:15–21. Both intimately connect justification with participation in Christ, following the contours of Paul's argument as he moves from righteousness language in 2:16 to participatory language in 2:19–20 and back again to righteousness language in 2:21 (Chester 2008, 325–326). In these accounts, the righteousness of Christ is not an object or a substance transferred from him to the believer, but part of who Christ is. Faith unites those who believe with Christ, making his presence a reality; and since he is righteous, then in him they too are righteous.

In a final layer of controversy within the single verse of 2:16, there is also debate about whose faith is primarily in focus as Paul speaks of righteousness by faith. He makes one unambiguous reference to his and Peter's act of believing in Christ, but also speaks twice of *pistis Christou*, a Greek genitive phrase traditionally translated as "faith in Christ" and understood as referring to the human faith of which Christ is the *object* (the Greek *Christou* is thus read as an *objective* genitive). However, it is equally grammatically valid to translate the phrase "faith/faithfulness of Christ," a reference to Christ's own faith (i.e., that of which he is the *subject*, reading *Christou* as a *subjective* genitive), expressed in his obedience even to the cross. Here, the picture is complicated by the fact that James Dunn, one of the principal architects of the "New Perspective," holds strongly to the objective genitive view. It is nevertheless true that most "New Perspective" interpreters advocate the subjective genitive. It is often held to relieve the danger of separating Paul's righteousness language from his emphasis on participation in Christ since the justified believer participates in Christ's own saving faithfulness. It is also regarded as a safeguard of divine initiative in salvation and characterized as the Christological option in contrast to the anthropological option of the objective genitive, which is said to emphasize the salvific efficacy of the human act of faith (Hays 2002, 277). Yet this description of what is at stake is notably one-sided. Luther and Calvin both regard human faith as a divine gift and not as a human decision or disposition. Further, if the alien righteousness gifted to those who believe is received only in Christ, then the gift of faith is effective precisely because it grasps hold of Christ and not because righteousness is in some sense transferred from him to them (Luther 1963, 132).

Galatians 3:1–4:7: The Galatian Believers' Experience and Scripture (I)

The rhetorical structure of Paul's argument from this point on is much debated. The next major break in Paul's argument is identified variously as after 4:11 (Richard N. Longenecker 1990, 184–186), 4:31 (Betz 1979, 253–255), 5:12 (Matera 1992, 192–196), or 6:10 (Witherington 1998, 25–36). Galatians 4:7 is preferable since there appears to be a definite double arrangement of material in Paul's reflections from 3:1 to 5:1. He begins with the experience of the Galatian believers in receiving the gospel (3:1–5) before moving on to extended scriptural arguments (3:6–4:7). Similarly, he returns to their experience (4:8–20) before returning again to scriptural argument (4:21–5:1). As all of this forms a demonstration of 2:15–21, it is no surprise that the major disagreements in interpretation surrounding 2:16 resurface at several points.

In 3:1–5 Paul appeals to the Galatian believers' experience of the Holy Spirit. When they responded to his preaching and received the Spirit, the divine gift came not as a result of doing the works of the law, but through "the hearing of faith." The sense of this phrase is not immediately plain since the Greek noun *akoēs* (hearing) can refer either to the faculty of hearing or to the content of the message that was heard. Paul could be referring to "hearing with faith" or to "the message of faith." Advocates of "faith in Christ" as the meaning of the disputed genitive phrase in 2:16 are drawn to the first possibility. Advocates of "the faith/faithfulness of Christ," reluctant to over-emphasize the human act of faith, are often drawn to the second or to a mediating position, "the message that results in believing." Either way, Paul's main point is that if works of the law were required for righteousness, the divine gift would not have been given to those who were without them. That they received the Spirit without works demonstrates the acceptance of the Galatian believers by God as Gentiles.

A little later, in the course of arguing from Scripture, Paul includes another demonstration that righteousness does not come through works of the law (3:10–14). Using a medley of Scripture quotations, Paul speaks of a curse of the law, the power of which is broken by Christ's taking the curse upon himself in his death on the cross (3:13). The logic of Paul's argument is compressed, with at least one crucial step not made explicit, but it is traditionally taken to be that God's curse falls upon those who do not do everything commanded by the law and that this includes all human beings. If full obedience were possible, the law would save (see 3:21); but since it is not, all are under the curse from which those who receive the Spirit through faith are saved by Christ's death. If this summary of Paul's logic is correct, then it strengthens the case of "Lutheran" interpreters of Galatians: Paul speaks of deeds demanded by the law and speaks of the whole law, not especially the boundary markers of circumcision, food laws, and Sabbath observance.

Not surprisingly, alternative explanations have been developed by "New Perspective" interpreters, who argue that the ideas that obedience to the law is impossible and that any disobedience brings a curse are unlikely in the context of Second Temple Judaism, where the cult provided means of forgiveness for lapses. Yet alternative explanations of Paul's logic have proved elusive. James Dunn (1998) suggests that those who do all that the law commands according to its true intention are those who believe in Christ, while it is those who literally keep its commandments that break the law and suffer the curse. Tom Wright (2009) argues that Paul's unstated premise is that although Israel's Babylonian exile was literally long over, it continued in the sense that the promises of blessing given to post-exilic Israel were still unfulfilled. Blessing and restoration can come through Christ, but those who rely on the works of the law insist on identifying with the era of exile. The fairest evaluation of this crucial debate is that while there are significant objections to the "Lutheran" interpretation, none of the alternative explanations offered have succeeded in commanding widespread support (Bruce W. Longenecker 1998, 134–142).

The main content of Paul's arguments from Scripture, however, concerns first of all the figure of Abraham. In 3:6–14 Paul demonstrates that the patriarch shared the Galatian believers' experience of the sufficiency of faith. This is a daring move, probably made in response to the use of the patriarch by the teachers opposing Paul as their major scriptural proof that righteousness requires the works of the law. Abraham was understood in Jewish tradition as the first proselyte, and the statement that Abraham "believed God and it was credited to him as righteousness" (Gen 15:6, quoted in Gal 3:6) was taken in conjunction with the covenant of circumcision in Genesis 17:4–14 and with Abraham's readiness to sacrifice even his son Isaac in Genesis 22. As 1 Maccabees 2:52 expresses it, "Was not Abraham found faithful in temptation, and it was reckoned unto him for righteousness?" It is only by imitating Abraham in the matter of works that the Galatian believers can be children of Abraham and accounted among the righteous. In contrast, Paul exploits the fact that in Genesis 15 there is no mention of circumcision, nor in the context of Genesis 12:3 or 18:18, where God promises that all the nations will be blessed through Abraham (Gal 3:8). This promise was made to Abraham and his "seed," a collective singular noun, which Paul takes as referring to Christ (3:16) and to those who are in Christ (3:29). The promise is fulfilled precisely at the time when Gentiles such as the Galatians receive the Holy Spirit through faith (3:14).

It is at this point, having emphasized divine promise over and against obedient human response, that Paul has little alternative other than to explain the purpose of the law. For Scripture contains the law and tells of the law's giving, and if this was not in order to make possible righteousness through law, why did God give the law? Paul's answers to this question run all the way from 3:15 to 4:7. They contain a powerful temporal element. The promise to Abraham of the blessing of the nations through faith came hundreds of years before the giving of the law at Sinai and so has priority (3:17). Further, the law was intended for the period until Christ came (3:22–24). The Galatian believers are heirs of Abraham, but even the heirs of great estates go through a period of minority. Although they own everything, they are not allowed to exercise control over the property but – like slaves – remain under the authority of others. Such was the condition of humanity under the law, but with the coming of Christ and the receipt of the Spirit, the inheritance is received and the time of the law is over (4:1–7). Paul daringly terms that minority under the law a time of enslavement to the *stoicheia* or "basic principles of the world" (4:3). What exactly he means by this phrase is much debated, but it clearly refers to dominant aspects of "the present evil age" (1:4) from which Christ delivers. The association of the law with the *stoicheia* makes plain its powerlessness to bring maturity and freedom.

Yet to argue that the time of the law is past does not explain what was done through the law in that past. Paul says that the law was added because of transgressions (3:19), that it served to guard or protect and to confine or imprison (3:23), and that it functioned like a *paidagōgos*, a slave in a wealthy household granted authority over the sons of the family during childhood. Precisely what is implied by these statements is widely debated. There are at least three possible explanations, which can be held either separately or in various combinations (see Bruce W. Longenecker 1998, 122–128). Paul may mean that the law was given to increase transgression (see Rom 5:20), so that what before was implicit sinfulness becomes more concrete and serious as a violation of stated commandments (the causative view). Alternatively, it may be rather that the law reveals sin so that human beings can recognize their own sinfulness (see Rom 3:20), which would otherwise remain hidden (the cognitive view). Finally, Paul's thought may be that the law provided guidance and restraint, limiting human sinfulness, until Christ came (the corrective view). Paul's main point is plain, but his words and images leave it subject to interpretation whether the law achieves this negative preparation by concretizing and/or condemning and/or containing sin.

Galatians 4:8–5:1: The Galatian Believers' Experience and Scripture (2)

Despite Paul's assertion that law and promise ultimately complement one another in God's purposes (3:21), his arguments will have been shocking to those who reverenced the law. Yet worse is to come. When he returns to the experience of the Galatians (4:8–20), he equates their current temptation to accept circumcision and the law with turning back to their former enslavement in Greco-Roman religion (4:8). They will then again be under the control of "the basic principles of the world" (*stoicheia*, 4:9), and again be observing a sacred calendar (4:10). It will be a different calendar from that associated with the Greco-Roman gods, but a calendar nonetheless. It is much debated exactly how this scandalous equation between the law and Greco-Roman religion works, but Paul's point seems to be that the very division of existence into the spheres of Jew/Gentile and law/not law has been ended in Christ (Martyn 1997, 393–406). This organization of the cosmos, which stemmed from human sin, was nevertheless temporarily used by God, but is now abolished.

Certainly Paul has already provided one of his most powerful statements of the reconfiguring of the cosmos through the coming of Christ and the end of the time of the law. In baptism are abolished the distinctions between Jew and Greek, slave and free, male and female (3:28). Interpreters have wrestled with the implications of this for the life of the church and its relationship with wider society. Depending upon their social contexts and personal convictions, interpreters have often sought either to restrict or to maximize the potential for Paul's statement to disrupt ecclesial and social hierarchies or, in recent decades, perhaps somewhat anachronistically, either to convict or to acquit Paul of elsewhere in his letters failing fully to realize the egalitarian impact of his words here. From Paul's own immediate perspective, however, the key point is that the Galatian believers had been ready to embrace a cosmos reconfigured in Christ but are now turning back. They had shown their readiness by the way in which they received Paul when he first preached the gospel to them (4:12–20). He had appeared among them as a weak and sick person (4:13–14), incapable of presenting his message with an appropriate appearance, bearing, and manner. They might have despised Paul, but instead embraced one who embodied in his very person God's abolition in Christ of the established order in the world. Paul cannot understand why they no longer seem able to see the point. Christ needs to be formed in them so that they too might together embody the truth of the gospel (4:19). To this end, Paul is prepared to take any amount of trouble over them, and he compares himself to a mother in the pains of childbirth (4:19; see Gaventa 2007, 29–39). By contrast, the motives of the teachers enticing the Galatians away from him are characterized as self-serving (4:17). The choice the Galatians face between Paul and these people is the choice between an identity based solely on Christ and one that is not, which for Paul is also a choice between freedom and slavery.

To explain the nature of this choice, Paul returns once more to Scripture (4:21–5:1) and to the story of Abraham, this time to the matter of his sons, born of two different mothers, Sarah and Hagar (Gen 16–18, 21). In Genesis, God tarries in fulfilling his promise of a son to Abraham through his wife Sarah, and, at Sarah's prompting, Abraham fathers a son Ishmael by his slave woman Hagar. Isaac is later born to Sarah, and Abraham is divinely instructed to throw out Hagar and Ishmael. God provides for the slave and her son, but they cannot be the vehicles of divine blessing through whom God's promises to Abraham of innumerable descendants will be fulfilled (Gen 15:5). In fathering Ishmael, Abraham had refused to rely on the divine promise, wresting the initiative away from God. Paul takes this dynamic in the Genesis narratives and on its basis builds an allegory which encapsulates the choice facing the Galatians (Watson 2004, 202–208). Sarah is identified with the covenant of promise, with the heavenly Jerusalem, and with free children of the Spirit who inherit. Hagar is identified with the giving of the law in the covenant of Sinai, with the present Jerusalem, and with children of the flesh born into slavery who cannot inherit. Paul identifies himself and the Galatians as the free children who inherit through Sarah. If the Galatians were now to choose to rely on the works of the law, they would disinherit themselves and submit to slavery (5:1), foolishly preferring their own deeds to God's promises. It is debated whether by the present earthly Jerusalem Paul intends Judaism in general, or the Jerusalem church, and/or those Jewish Christians advocating a law-observant gospel to Gentiles. The latter perhaps appears more likely since this is the choice facing the Galatian believers in terms of their communal identity. What is plain is Paul's belief that, now Christ has come, it is in his law-free Gentile mission that God's promises to Abraham are fulfilled. The true meaning of the past is fully disclosed only in that eschatological present.

Key Issue: Galatians and Israel's Past

Paul's reflections on the Galatian believers' experiences and Scripture raise a major issue that cuts across the divide between "Lutheran" and "New Perspective" interpreters and provides a different axis for debate. Nearly all agree that Paul has consistently displayed an apocalyptic pattern of thought. In Christ's death and resurrection, divine intervention in human history has inaugurated the new age. Yet how is the relationship between the two ages to be characterized? In particular, how are the Galatians to think of God's actions for and among them in relation to the history of Israel? Is there continuity in which previous history leads toward the coming of a new age, or is there only a shattering moment of grace that cuts across all that has gone before? J. Louis Martyn argues that God's invasion of the world in Jesus Christ should be understood as punctiliar rather than linear (Martyn 1997, 343–352). When God enters into a covenant with Abraham, the promises given remain dormant until the advent of Christ, Abraham's singular seed (3:16). There is no history of salvation running from Abraham to Christ to be identified with the history of Israel but, at the human level, merely a void. For others, it is the essence of God's covenant with Abraham that it establishes linear movement through history. "Covenant" means God's "plan-through-Israel-for-the-world" (Wright 2009, 74). God's apocalyptic intervention in Christ is dramatic and surprising from a human perspective, but was the crucial step intended in this divine plan from the outset. Christ dies precisely as Israel's representative and, in so doing, enables both Jews and Gentiles together to form a single Abrahamic family in him.

This disagreement expresses very different senses of the nature of God's grace. Does it come from outside human traditions and disrupt them, overturning all attempts to identify the divine with human cultures or traditions? Or is it in the very nature of divine grace that it is woven into the fabric of human communities, guaranteeing continuity? Exegetical assessment of the debate is complex, not least because of the ambiguity of Paul's argument. He has both repeatedly used the language of enslavement in relation to the law and yet insisted that the law and God's promises are not opposed to each other (3:21). On the one hand, there is nothing in Galatians to suggest a denial of Israel's prior status as God's people. To this extent the case for continuity is strong. How can Israel's law play a role, albeit a negative one, in preparing for Christ's coming if Israel itself does not? On the other hand, that the law's role can only be described using terms such as "concretizing and/or condemning and/or containing sin" scarcely gives any grounds for identifying divine grace with human traditions or their achievements. The continuity that persists does so despite human beings, not because of their cooperation. Furthermore, in Galatians Paul has repeatedly identified the promises of the covenant to Abraham with the Spirit that the Galatian believers have now received. It is to that Spirit, and its power to produce obedience to divine truth where law cannot, that Paul now turns.

Key Consensus: The Place of Galatians 5 and 6

In addressing the theme of the Spirit and obedience, Paul brings his letter to a climax in chapters 5 and 6 by focusing on actions. What is it that the Galatian believers are to do in relation to circumcision and how are they to live? In much earlier interpretation, this was understood as a defensive move. Having stressed that the choice between the law and faith is also one between slavery and freedom, Paul must here guard against the danger that his insistence on freedom will be interpreted by some as permission for indulgence. He is dealing with a danger parallel to that expressed at Romans 6:15 when he rhetorically asks, "Should we sin because we are not under law but under grace? By no means!" In earlier "Lutheran" interpretations, 5:2–6:10 often form a kind of ethical appendix to the vital doctrinal and scriptural themes explored in the earlier chapters. By so treating this material, all danger of compromising Paul's polemic against works was eliminated.

One of the indisputable gains in interpretation brought by the "New Perspective" is a clear consensus that this kind of treatment of these texts is unsatisfactory, a recognition made even by those unconvinced by the "New Perspective." Just as it will not do in relation to 2:16 to treat circumcision and food laws as necessary pieces of staging that can disappear into the background once they have provided the platform for the expression of Paul's central theological themes, so it will not do here for consideration of ethical questions to be marginalized. For it is essential for Paul that the church should embody the truth of the gospel in its common life, and, far from compromising his polemic against works, an ethics based on the Spirit, the gift of which was the fulfillment of God's promises to Abraham (3:14), is in fact central to his case. Paul's "discussion of ethics in terms of faith, love and walking in the Spirit is intended to draw out the implications of justification by faith, and to describe what it means to continue, as they had begun, in the Spirit" (Barclay 1988, 217).

Galatians 5:2–6:10: The Galatian Believers' Decision and their Common Life

In 5:2–12 Paul brings all that he has said about the law and faith to bear on the immediate question facing the Galatian believers: should the men accept circumcision or not? He stresses again the mutually exclusive alternatives before them. They cannot combine their reliance upon Christ with reliance upon works of the law, for law and grace are opposites and any attempt to combine them will result in the loss of Christ (5:2, 4). It is Christ alone or Christ not at all, for those who are circumcised take on obedience to the whole law. Read in isolation, this could be construed merely as a statement that full obedience to the law will prove difficult for those of Gentile background. Taken in conjunction with 3:10, where those who rely on the law are under a curse implicitly because they fail to obey everything that the law commands (see also Jas 2:10), Paul seems here rather to place the boundary-defining issue of circumcision in the context of the issue of wider obedience to the law and its failure to justify. The irony is that, even in the matter of working, in Christ Jesus faith and love are more effective than the works of the law (5:6). Circumcision would be a fundamentally false move for the Galatian believers not because there is anything inferior about circumcision in comparison to uncircumcision, but because both are equally incidental in relation to the working of faith and love. To have confused the Galatian believers about this is a serious matter, and Paul expresses his anger at those responsible (5:7–12). If Paul was prepared to accept circumcision, then he could escape persecution; but if he did so, then the cross would be downgraded and rendered of secondary importance (5:11).

Yet if Paul stands firm, and the Galatian believers refuse circumcision, then the offense of the cross remains and both he and they live in a new cruciform world where all things are inverted by its power – even, it seems, some dimensions of Paul's own rhetoric. For having framed the choice between faith and works of the law as that between freedom and slavery, Paul reveals that the believers' freedom is for the purpose of enslavement to one another through love (5:13). Further, once the works of the law have been rejected in favor of faith, there appear a number of apparently positive references to law. True, those led by the Spirit are not subject to the law (5:18), but the law is summed up in the command to love one's neighbor (5:14), there is no law against the fruit of the Spirit in people's lives (5:23), and those who carry the burdens of others fulfill the law of Christ (6:2). Paul appears to mean that those who attempt to follow in detail all the many hundred commandments of the law will miss their way, but those guided by the Spirit will enact the intention of the law viewed as a whole. To do the works of the law is fruitless, but to fulfill the law results from the indwelling of the Spirit and is effective in promoting love of neighbor. This makes little sense from usual Jewish perspectives, and presumably inverts the moral intuition of those advocating circumcision, but it is another measure of the truly apocalyptic nature of Paul's theology. The gift of the Spirit entails ethical possibilities that Paul expects to be embodied in the life of the churches and that were simply not present prior to Christ.

Yet despite the sense of new possibilities suffusing these texts, Paul expects the lives of the Galatian believers to be marked by struggle. He speaks of opposition between the Spirit and the flesh (5:16–18), with commitment required from the believers in order to live by the Spirit. Many in the history of interpretation have regarded this struggle as one between the higher and lower parts of the human being, with the word "spirit" here understood as a reference to the human spirit. However, the contemporary consensus is that Paul here speaks of the Holy Spirit. What is still disputed is what is intended by the "flesh." Does it refer primarily to bodily desires and appetites, particularly sexual ones (Boyarin 1994, 174), or is it a reference to anything in the existence of a human being that still belongs to the present evil age and remains resistant to the Spirit (Barclay 1988, 205–207)? At stake here is the degree to which a positive account of physical human existence in general, and human sexuality in particular, might be possible for Paul. While sexual sin is certainly prominent in Paul's list of the works of the flesh (5:19–21), so too are social sins connected to disunity and strife; and while self-control is a fruit of the Spirit (5:22–23), so too are social virtues. The opposite of living in line with the Spirit is not named as sexual indulgence but as conceit and envy (5:26). It seems that Paul does speak of the entirety of human existence and of the struggle of the Galatian believers, both individually and communally, to live in the realm of Christ. They belong to him and have received the Spirit through faith but yet face day by day the backward pull of their previous existence. Their new identity is not in doubt, but to be who they now are in the Spirit requires watchfulness under temptation (6:1), care for others (6:2), honest self-evaluation (6:3–5), and unwearied effort in doing good (6:9–10).

Galatians 6:11–18: Cross and New Creation

Up until this point, Paul has been following usual practice and dictating his letter to a scribe. However, he concludes by writing the final few sentences in his own hand (6:11). He uses this more personal medium to communicate a very personal ending, comparing himself with the teachers he opposes. In his view, the advocates of circumcision are concerned above all with how they appear to human beings. They have no stomach for enduring persecution for the sake of the cross (6:12), the circumcision that should be a sign of their fidelity to the law masks only disobedience (6:13a), and they want the Galatians to be circumcised merely in order to claim them as trophies (6:13b). In contrast, all Paul cares for is to identify himself with the cross of Christ. "It was, in the Greco-Roman world, the most humiliating and degrading form of punishment, a sign of weakness and defeat. Despite this cultural aversion to the cross, Paul boasts in the cross as the sign of God's power and salvation" (Matera 1992, 231). He has suffered for this boast, enduring physical punishment for refusing to cease from preaching the gospel (6:17). Yet again, Paul recapitulates for the Galatians his burning conviction that it cannot be the cross *and* circumcision, the cross *and* law observance. It must be Christ and his cross alone that define who they are in their relationship with God.

It cannot be otherwise, for in his embrace of the cross Paul has been crucified to the world and vice versa (6:14). God's act of liberation in Christ has placed Paul in a new age. The Galatian believers must understand that those advocating circumcision are asking them to take a step backwards and embrace an impossible pining for a cosmos that no longer exists. It is not that circumcision itself is to be identified with the old age and uncircumcision with the new, but rather that, in the new age, whether or not a person is circumcised is irrelevant. To make it once again central is to behave as if the decisive event of the cross has not taken place. What matters rather is "a new creation" (6:15). It is to those who grasp this truth that Paul wishes grace and peace, and to "the Israel of God" (6:16). By "Israel" some understand Paul here to be asking a blessing upon the Jewish nation despite the rejection of Christ by a majority. Others take him to speak of the Gentile Galatian believers alone, indicating the replacement of the people of Israel in God's purposes by the church. Yet that the reference to Israel comes in the context of Paul's discussion of the irrelevance of circumcision makes it more likely that by Israel he now refers to all Jewish and Gentile believers together. To distinguish between the two now would be to go back to the language of the old age. By "new creation" itself, Paul appears to mean something wider than the other possible translation, "new creature," which would focus the strong sense of transition and transformation exclusively on the individual believer. Rather, this final theological crescendo of the letter must be read in conjunction with its first in 1:4, where Christ is said to have given himself "for our sins to set us free from the present evil age." The radical renewal of the Galatian believers, and the decision that confronts them about circumcision, matter so much from Paul's perspective precisely because they are central aspects of a divine transformation of the cosmos through Christ. Galatians is such a passionate and driven text because the stakes are so high.

Notes

1   See, further, chapters 1 and 8 in this volume.
2   Translations from biblical texts are my own.

References

Barclay, John M. G. 1988. *Obeying the Truth: A Study of Paul's Ethics in Galatians*. Edinburgh: T. & T. Clark.

Betz, Hans Dieter. 1979. *Galatians*. Philadelphia: Fortress.

Boyarin, Daniel. 1994. *A Radical Jew: Paul and the Politics of Identity*. Berkeley: University of California Press.

Chester, Stephen. 2008. When the Old Was New: Reformation Perspectives on Galatians 2:16. *Expository Times* 119: 320–329.

Dunn, James D. G. 1998. *The Theology of Paul the Apostle*. Edinburgh: T. & T. Clark.

Elliott, Susan. 2003. *Cutting Too Close for Comfort: Paul's Letter to the Galatians in its Anatolian Cultic Context*. London: T. & T. Clark.

Gaventa, Beverly Roberts. 2007. *Our Mother Saint Paul*. Louisville: Westminster John Knox.

Hardin, Justin K. 2008. *Galatians and the Imperial Cult: A Critical Analysis of the First-century Social Context of Paul's Letter*. Tübingen: Mohr Siebeck.

Hays, Richard B. 2002. *The Faith of Jesus Christ: The Narrative Substructure of Galatians 3:1–4:11*. Second edition. Grand Rapids: Eerdmans.

Longenecker, Bruce W. 1998. *The Triumph of Abraham's God: The Transformation of Identity in Galatians*. Edinburgh: T. & T. Clark.

Longenecker, Richard N. 1990. *Galatians*. Dallas: Word.

Luther, Martin. 1963. *Luther's Works*. Volume 26: *Lectures on Galatians 1535: Chapters 1–4*. St. Louis: Concordia.

Martyn, J. Louis. 1997. *Galatians*. New York: Doubleday.

Matera, Frank J. 1992. *Galatians*. Collegeville, Minn.: Liturgical.

Nanos, Mark D. 2002. *The Irony of Galatians: Paul's Letter in First-century Context*. Minneapolis: Fortress.

Riches, John. 2008. *Galatians through the Centuries*. Oxford: Blackwell.

Watson, Francis. 2004. *Paul and the Hermeneutics of Faith*. London: T. & T. Clark.

Witherington III, Ben. 1998. *Grace in Galatia: A Commentary on St. Paul's Letter to the Galatians*. Edinburgh: T. & T. Clark.

Wright, Tom. 2009. *Justification: God's Plan and Paul's Vision*. London: SPCK.

CHAPTER 5

Paul and the Believers of Western Asia

John Paul Heil

"Believers of western Asia" designates the audiences of three letters attributed to Paul: the letters to Philemon, the Colossians, and the Ephesians. These three letters were sent to various regions of western Asia, modern western Turkey. According to the Acts of the Apostles, Paul traveled as a missionary to various cities in different regions of western Asia. On his first missionary journey (Acts 13:4–14:26), Paul preached the gospel and/or founded communities in Perga, Pisidian Antioch, Iconinum, Lystra, and Derbe. His second missionary journey (15:40–18:22) included visits to such western Asian cities as Mysia and Troas. During his third missionary journey (18:23–21:17), he visited Assos, Mitylene, Miletus, and Patara, and – particularly noteworthy for the three letters under discussion – spent three years in Ephesus (Schnabel 2008).

The letter to Philemon was sent to the church that gathered at the house of Philemon, probably located in the city of Colossae, since the Onesimus mentioned as the slave of Philemon in that letter is most likely the same person described in the letter to the Colossians as "one of you"[1] (4:9; Dunn 1996, 300–301). In addition, there are several other names of individuals mentioned in both letters (cf. Phlm 2, 23–24; Col 4:10–17). The letter to the Colossians was to be read not only in Colossae, but also in nearby Laodicea (4:16). It may have been relevant to another nearby city, Hierapolis, as well (4:13). The words "in Ephesus" are lacking in some early manuscripts containing the letter to the Ephesians, but the best available evidence supports their inclusion (Hoehner 2002, 140). Although it appears to be relevant for, and may well have been read to, congregations outside Ephesus, the primary destination of the letter is all of the various

The Blackwell Companion to Paul, First Edition. Edited by Stephen Westerholm.
© 2011 Blackwell Publishing Ltd. Published 2011 by Blackwell Publishing Ltd.

local churches within the great Asia Minor metropolis of Ephesus – "the holy ones who are in Ephesus" (1:1).

But from whom and from where were these three letters sent to believers in western Asia? First, with regard to the author who sent them, opinions vary for each letter. Most scholars agree, however, that Paul was the author of the letter to Philemon. Although the letters to the Colossians and the Ephesians both present themselves as authored and sent by Paul (Eph 1:1; 3:1; Col 1:1, with Timothy as co-sender), many scholars in modern times have questioned and/or denied that the historical apostle Paul could have authored these letters because in their estimation the letters differ too greatly from the so-called main or undisputed letters of Paul. They often point to the cosmic Christology and ecclesiology of these letters (for example, Christ as "head" under which all things are summed up, and the universal church as the "body" of this cosmic Christ) as notably different from what we find in the other letters of Paul (Kiley 1986; Harding 2004). In their view, someone using "Paul" as a pseudonym authored these letters. But recently, scholars have pointed out that an appeal to pseudonymity involves problematical assumptions, making it debatable whether any of the letters in the New Testament which present Paul as their primary author are pseudonymous (Ellis 2002, 324; Wilder 2004, 265 n. 52; Carson and Moo 2005, 350).

Furthermore, recent studies of the role of co-authors, co-workers, and secretaries in the composition of the Pauline letters have indicated the complexity involved in the question of their authorship. Paul may have authored his letters in a broader sense of authorizing or directing their composition in collaboration with fellow-workers. The different audiences, situations, and times of composition could also account for many of the differences among the Pauline letters (Johnson 1999, 269, 273; Stirewalt 2003; Gorman 2004, 477–478; Richards 2004). It should be noted that the Pauline authorship of both Colossians and Ephesians, which share significant similarities in content, was not questioned until the modern era. While there are probably more scholars today who consider Paul to be the author of Colossians than consider him to be the author of Ephesians, opinions on the Pauline authorship of Ephesians are more evenly balanced than commonly thought (Hoehner 2002, 2–61).

Along with Philippians and 2 Timothy, the letters to Philemon, the Colossians, and the Ephesians are numbered among the so-called "captivity letters" of Paul, who is in prison when he sends these letters. But the question is, where? Rome, Ephesus, and Caesarea have been suggested as possible locations for Paul's imprisonment while authorizing and directing the composition of his captivity letters. Paul spent much time in Ephesus, but there is no evidence that he was ever imprisoned there long enough to compose a letter. The New Testament records imprisonments for Paul in both Caesarea and Rome. The execution of Paul, who was a Roman citizen, does not seem to be an imminent possibility in Philemon, Colossians, and Ephesians, unlike in Philippians and 2 Timothy. It thus seems more likely that the three letters to believers in western Asia were sent from his imprisonment at Caesarea rather than Rome. Although no absolute certainty is possible in this matter, it is plausible that Paul sent Tychicus with all three of these closely related letters from his Caesarean imprisonment (Reicke 2001, 75, 83; Ellis 2002, 266–275). At any rate, that the implied author "Paul" was in prison somewhere at the time of the composition and sending of these letters is significant for their interpretation.

Philemon, Colossians, and Ephesians each exhibits an overall chiastic structure. Chiastic patterns serve to organize the content to be heard and not only aid the memory of the one delivering or performing a document, but also make it easier for the audience to follow and remember the content. A chiasm works by leading its audience through introductory elements to a central, pivotal point or points, and then reaching its conclusion by recalling and developing, via the chiastic parallels, aspects of the initial elements that led to the central, pivotal point or points. Since chiasms were apparently very common in ancient oral-auricular and rhetorical cultures, the original ancient audience need not necessarily have been consciously identifying or reflecting upon any of these chiastic structures in themselves as they heard them performed within their liturgical assemblies. They unconsciously experienced the chiastic phenomenon as an organizing dynamic, which had a subtle but purposeful effect on how they perceived the content. But a discovery, delineation, and bringing to consciousness of the chiastic structures of ancient documents can greatly aid the modern audience to a more proper and precise interpretation of them.

The Letter to Philemon

The letter to Philemon centers on the change in relationship that has occurred between Philemon and his slave Onesimus, whom the imprisoned Paul converted to the Christian faith. Although Philemon is the primary recipient, the letter is a communal one, addressed to, and heard by, the entire church assembled at his house. The letter, translated literally, exhibits the following chiastic structure:

A (v. 1) Paul a prisoner of *Christ Jesus* and Timothy the brother to Philemon *our* beloved and *fellow worker* (v. 2) and Apphia the sister and Archippus our fellow soldier and the assembly at your house. (v. 3) *Grace* to *you* and peace from God our Father and the *Lord Jesus Christ*.

  B (v. 4) I *thank* my God every time I make mention of you in my *prayers*, (v. 5) hearing of your love and faith, which you have toward the *Lord* Jesus and for all the holy ones, (v. 6) that the partnership of your faith might become effective in the recognition of all the good that is among us for *Christ*. (v. 7) *For* I have had much joy and encouragement in *your love*, because *the hearts* of the holy ones have been *refreshed through* you, *brother*.

    C (v. 8) Therefore, though having much boldness in Christ to command to *you* what is proper, (v. 9) on account of love I would rather appeal, being as I am, *Paul*, an old man and now also a prisoner of Christ Jesus. (v. 10) I appeal to *you* for *my* child, whom I have begotten in prison, Onesimus,

      D (v. 11) who was once *to you* "useless" but now is indeed both *to you* and *to me* "useful," (v. 12) whom I am sending back *to you*, him, that is *my* heart, (v. 13) whom *I* wanted to *keep* for myself, so that he might serve on *your* behalf *me* in the imprisonment of the gospel,

        E (v. 14) but without your consent I resolved to do nothing, so that your good might not be as under compulsion but rather under benevolence.

D* (v. 15) For perhaps it was for this reason he was separated for awhile, so that you might have *him back* forever, (v. 16) no longer as a slave but more than a slave, a beloved brother, especially *to me*, but how much more *to you* both in the flesh and in the Lord. (v. 17) If then you have *me* as a partner, welcome *him* as *me*.

C* (v. 18) And if he has wronged *you* in any way or owes you anything, charge it *to me*. (v. 19) I, *Paul*, am writing in my own hand, I will repay; but may I not say to *you* that you more than owe me your very self!

B* (v. 20) Yes, *brother*, may I "benefit" from you in the *Lord*; *refresh* my *heart* in *Christ*. (v. 21) Confident of *your obedience* I am writing to you, knowing that you will do even more than I say. (v. 22) And at the same time also prepare for me a guest room; *for* I am hoping that *through* your *prayers I will be granted* to you.

A* (v. 23) Epaphras, my fellow captive in *Christ Jesus*, greets you, (v. 24) as well as Mark, Aristarchus, Demas, and Luke, my *fellow workers*. (v. 25) The *grace* of the *Lord Jesus Christ* be with *your* spirit.

It is sometimes maintained that precisely what Paul wants of Philemon is unclear. The chiastic structure of the letter, however, indicates not only what Paul wants from Philemon – namely, Onesimus (not necessarily as freed from slavery) to serve on his behalf in the work of the gospel (v. 13) – but also why he wants it: namely, as a further "good" that Philemon can do under benevolence (v. 14) for Paul and the holy ones based on love and in response to grace.

In the A unit (vv. 1–3) of the chiasm, Paul's greeting as a prisoner of Christ Jesus places the audience of the letter, as they listen to it within a liturgical assembly, within a framework of God's grace. In response to this grace, Paul in the B unit (vv. 4–7) thanks God in his prayers for Philemon's faithful love toward the holy ones, suggesting that as partners they can do a further "good" for Christ. On the basis of love, Paul as an old man and prisoner of Christ Jesus appeals for his "child" Onesimus in the C unit (vv. 8–10). In the D unit (vv. 11–13), Paul indicates that he would like Onesimus, his very heart, who as a Christian has become "useful" to both Philemon and Paul, to serve Paul on behalf of Philemon in the work of the gospel. The first half of the chiasm reaches its climax in the E unit (v. 14) with Paul's resolve that the "good" that Philemon can do in granting him Onesimus be under benevolence.

As the center and pivotal point of the chiasm, the E unit (v. 14) serves as the dominant motivation for the development of Paul's appeal in the second half. Through inverse parallelism with the D unit, in which Paul wants to keep Onesimus for himself, the D* unit (vv. 15–17) suggests that Philemon can have Onesimus back forever by giving him back to Paul after welcoming him as a beloved brother and as a partner like Paul himself. In the C* unit (vv. 18–19), Paul himself offers to pay any debts of his "child" Onesimus, for whom he appealed in the C unit, but reminds Philemon that he more than owes Paul his very self, thus suggesting Onesimus as payment. Paul, in the B* unit (vv. 20–22), wants his "brother" Philemon to refresh his heart (Onesimus), as he refreshed the hearts of the holy ones in the B unit; in reciprocal and complementary correspondence to Paul's prayers of thanks for grace (B unit), Paul hopes through the prayers of the assembly to be granted to them from grace as further motivation and occasion for Philemon to graciously grant Onesimus to Paul (B* unit). The greetings of grace to the entire assembly that frame the letter in the A (vv. 1–3) and A* (vv. 23–25) units provide the ultimate motivation for Philemon to grant Onesimus to Paul for service to the gospel of Christ under the benevolence of grace (Heil 2001).

The Letter to the Colossians

The letter to the Colossians centers on a potential danger for believers not only in Colossae, but also in other areas of western Asia, such as Laodicea and Hierapolis, of being captivated by a false teaching described as "a philosophy that is of empty deceit" (2:8). This "philosophy," literally "love of wisdom," refers broadly to a worldview that embraces a "wise" way of living. Although there has been much debate about the precise nature of this "philosophy," it likely refers to the erroneous viewpoints and practices of some Jews in the local synagogues in the areas around Colossae and/or of some Jewish Christians influenced by them (Dunn 1996, 29–35; Bevere 2003; Smith 2006; Sumney 2008, 10–12). It evidently advocated ascetical practices and religious observances oriented to a mystical, heavenly worship of, or with, angels (2:16–18). The letter refutes any suggestion that believers in Christ lacked an authentic and complete "wisdom." It encourages them "to walk," that is, to live, "in all wisdom" (rather than in a "philosophy of empty deceit"), as "holy ones," those specially consecrated by and for God, "who are in Christ," within a realm of existence determined by the definitive salvation God accomplished in the death and resurrection of Jesus Christ. The letter exhibits the following chiastic structure :

Colossians: Encouragement to Walk in All Wisdom as Holy Ones in Christ
A (1:1–2): Grace from Paul an apostle by the will of God
 B (1:3–14): Thanking God when praying for you to walk in wisdom
  C (1:15–23): The gospel preached to every creature under heaven
   D (1:24–2:5): We are admonishing and teaching every human in all wisdom
    E (2:6–23): Walk and live in Christ with whom you have died and been raised
    E* (3:1–7): You died and were raised with Christ from living as you once walked
   D* (3:8–16): In all wisdom teaching and admonishing one another
  C* (3:17–4:1): You have a master in heaven
 B* (4:2–6): Pray for us in thanksgiving and walk in wisdom
A* (4:7–18): Full assurance in all the will of God and grace from Paul

With 3:1–7, the E* unit within the chiastic structure embracing the entire letter, the audience hear resonances, by way of the chiastic parallelism, with the corresponding E unit (2:6–23), which, together with the E* unit, forms the pivotal center of the letter. The assertion, "*you were raised with* the Christ" (3:1), in the E* unit reverberates with "*you were raised with* him" (2:12) in the E unit. The assertion, "for *you died* and your life has been hidden with the Christ in God" (3:3), in the E* unit reiterates and develops the assertion, "if then *you have died* with Christ" (2:20), in the E unit. The assertion, "your life has been hidden *with the Christ*" (3:3), in the E* unit explicitly elaborates on the assertion, "he brought you to life along *with him*" (2:13), in the E unit. The reminder, "among whom [the sons of disobedience] you also *walked* once" (3:7), in the E* unit provides a resonating reason for the exhortation, "in him [the Christ, Jesus the Lord] *go on walking*" (2:6), in the E unit. And "when you *lived* in these [earthly things]" (3:7) in the E* unit resonates with "as if *living* in the world" (2:20) in the E unit.

With 3:8–16, the D* unit within the chiastic structure, the audience hear resonances of the corresponding D unit (1:24–2:5) in the overall chiasm. That the audience have "removed the old *human being* with its practices" (3:9) in the D* unit is a consequence of "admonishing every *human being* and teaching every *human being* in all wisdom, that we may present every *human being* complete in Christ" (1:28) in the D unit. That the audience have "put on the new which is being renewed *for knowledge* according to the image of the one who created it" (3:10) in the D* unit recalls "*for knowledge* of the mystery of God, Christ" (2:2) in the D unit. The address of the audience as "*holy ones*" (3:12) in the D* unit recalls that the mystery has now been manifested to God's "*holy ones*" (1:26) in the D unit.

With 3:17–4:1, the C* unit within the chiastic structure, the audience hear resonances, by way of the chiastic parallelism, with the corresponding C unit (1:15–23) in the overall chiasm. The exhortation, "whatever you do in word or in *work*, do all things in the name of the Lord Jesus" (3:17), in the C* unit counters the audience's past behavior regarding their "works" – "and you, once being alienated and enemies in mind in *works* that are evil" (1:21) – in the C unit. "Those who are your masters according to the *flesh*" (3:22) in the C* unit, the last occurrence of the word "flesh" in the letter, recalls that "he [God] has now reconciled [you] in the body of his [Christ's] *flesh*" (1:22) in the C unit, the first of the nine occurrences of the word "flesh" in the letter. And "knowing that you also have a Master in *heaven*" (4:1) in the C* unit resonates with "[the gospel] which was proclaimed in all creation that is under *heaven*" (1:23), God's making of peace among all things in the cosmos, "whether the things on the earth or the things in the *heavens*" (1:20), and God's creation in Christ of "all things in the *heavens* and on the earth" (1:16) in the C unit.

With 4:2–6, the B* unit within the letter's chiastic structure, the audience hear echoes of 1:3–14, the corresponding B unit in the overall chiasm. The directives regarding the audience's praying for Paul and Timothy in the B* unit – "in *prayer* persevere" (4:2a) and "*praying* at the same time also for us" (4:3a) – recall the repeated reports of Paul and Timothy's reciprocal praying for the audience in the B unit – "always when *praying* for you" (1:3b) and "we do not cease *praying* on behalf of you" (1:9a). And likewise, the audience's "being watchful in it [prayer] in *thanksgiving*" (4:2b) in the B* unit recalls and reciprocates Paul and Timothy's "*thanking* God the Father of our Lord Jesus Christ" (1:3a) and "*thanking* the Father" (1:12a) in the B unit. The prayer, "that God may open for us a door for the *word*" (4:3b), and the exhortation, "let your *word* always be in grace" (4:6a), in the B* unit recall that the audience have heard before of the hope laid up for them in the heavens "in the *word* of the truth of the gospel" (1:5b) in the B unit. And the exhortation to the audience, "in *wisdom walk* toward those outside" (4:5a), in the B* unit recalls the prayer for the audience "in all *wisdom* and Spiritual understanding, to *walk* worthy of the Lord" (1:9b–10a) in the B unit.

With 4:7–18, the closing A* unit within the letter's chiastic structure, the audience hear resonances of the corresponding A unit (1:1–2) that opens the letter. The description of Tychicus as the beloved *"brother"* and *"faithful"* minister (4:7), the description of Onesimus as the *"faithful"* and beloved *"brother"* (4:9), and the directive to greet the *"brothers"* in Laodicea (4:15) in the A* unit recall for the audience the description of Timothy as the *"brother"* (1:1) and the description of the audience themselves as *"faithful"* *"brothers"* in Christ (1:2) in the A unit. That the audience "may stand complete and fully assured in all the *will of God*" (4:12) in the A* unit echoes the statement that Paul is an "apostle of Christ Jesus through the *will of God*" (1:1) in the A unit. And the letter's closing greeting in the hand of *Paul*, *"grace* be with you" (4:18), in the A* unit resonates with its opening greeting from *Paul* and Timothy (1:1), *"grace* to you and peace from God our Father" (1:2), in the A unit.

In sum, the chiastic structure of Colossians begins by exhorting its audience of "holy ones and faithful brothers in Christ" (1:2) that they, who have love for all the "holy ones" (1:4), are to be thanking the Father who has made them fit for the share of the inheritance of the "holy ones" in the light, as they have been rescued by God from the authority of the darkness and transferred into the kingdom of the Son of God's love, in whom all of us believers have redemption, the forgiveness of sins (1:12–14). At the pivotal center of the chiastic structure the audience, who have "died with Christ," are urged not to behave as if living in the world (2:20), captivated by a "philosophy" of empty deceit (2:6), having only a reputation of wisdom (2:23). Rather, as those who were "raised with the Christ" (3:1a), they are no longer to "walk" or live in accord with the things on the earth (3:5–7), seeking instead the things above, where the Christ is, seated at the right hand of God (3:1b), so that they may be "in all wisdom teaching and admonishing each other" (3:16). Chiastically developing its opening prayer wish from Paul and Timothy of "grace to you" (1:2), the letter climactically concludes with Paul's personal greeting: "Keep on remembering my chains! Grace be with you!" (4:18).

In conclusion, listening to and experiencing the rhetorical dynamics of the intricate and intriguing chiastic patterns of Paul's letter to the Colossians encourages its audience, as "holy ones" in Christ, to "walk," that is, to behave and conduct themselves, "in all wisdom," that is, within the dynamic realm of being in all the wisdom that is hidden in Christ (1:9, 28; 2:3; 3:16; 4:5), rather than "walking" in accord with a philosophy of empty deceit (2:6), only having a false reputation of wisdom (2:23). In short, Colossians functions as a concerted encouragement for its audience to walk in all wisdom as holy ones in Christ (Heil forthcoming).

The Letter to the Ephesians

The absence of the words "in Ephesus" from some manuscripts, as well as what some consider to be the impersonal tone of the letter, which is not addressed to a single church and lacks personal greetings to individuals at Ephesus, has led to the theory that Ephesians may be an encyclical or circular letter. It should be noted, however, that Paul does not send extended personal greetings to churches he knew well in such undisputed letters as 1 and 2 Corinthians, Galatians, and Philippians. And while Ephesians may be considered "impersonal" in that it only mentions two persons by name – Paul (1:1; 3:1) and Tychicus (6:21) – Paul is very personally concerned to share with his audience the mystery with which he has been gifted by God for them (3:1–4). He earnestly prays for them (1:15–23; 3:14–21), exhorts them (4:1–6:20), requests their prayers for him (6:18–20), and sends Tychicus to them, "so that you also may know the things concerning me, what I am doing" (6:21).

It should also be noted that although Tychicus carries and presumably reads to their respective audiences both Colossians and Ephesians (cf. Col 4:7–8; Eph 6:21–22), Ephesians, unlike Colossians (see Col 4:16), lacks an explicit directive for it to be read elsewhere. In addition, there are no examples in antiquity of leaving a blank space in the prescript of letters so that they could be used as encyclical letters.

Although addressed primarily to an implied audience of believers living in the large city of Ephesus, the letter to the Ephesians, while presupposing the general influence of the social and historical environment of the metropolis of Ephesus upon the audience, makes little explicit or specific mention of its Ephesian locale. This can be taken as another indication that Ephesians may be an encyclical letter intended for a more general audience living both in the metropolis of Ephesus and its more distant environs. That wives, husbands, children, parents, slaves, and masters are directly addressed in the "household code" of Ephesians (5:21–6:9) indicates that the various households in which believers gathered for worship would have been the normal setting for the public hearing of the letter.

A major concern of Paul in Ephesians is to assure the audience, characterized as "you" who came to believe (1:13) after "we," Paul and all those who first hoped in the Christ (1:12), came to believe, that they are nevertheless united to and incorporated within those who first believed as part of the cosmic unity that is a major theme of the letter. Although the "we" are generally identified as Jewish Christians and the "you" as Gentile Christians, more nuance is needed. It is not a matter of Gentile Christians ("you") being united with Jewish Christians ("we") in general, but of those originating from a Gentile cultural environment and coming to faith more recently, be they Gentiles or Jews, being united with those originating from a Jewish cultural environment and coming to faith earlier, be they Jews or Gentiles.

Although the "we" would be predominantly Christians of a Jewish origin, including Paul, they could include some Gentiles as well; for example, those like Titus, an early Greek believer who accompanied Paul yet did not become Jewish by being circumcised (Gal 2:1–3). And although the "you" may be predominantly recent Christians of a Gentile origin, they could include those of a Jewish origin who lived in the diaspora in a Gentile environment without being circumcised, so that they would have been considered "Gentiles" by circumcised Jews (cf. Timothy in Acts 16:1–3, a Christian disciple who was an uncircumcised Jew with a Jewish mother and Greek father, before being circumcised and joining Paul). The "you," then, could include Gentile pagan converts, former Gentile proselytes and "God-fearers" who frequented Jewish synagogues, as well as diaspora Jews. At any rate, the "you," those who came to believe more recently, are the Ephesian implied audience addressed by Paul as representative of the "we," those who came to believe earlier (Eph 1:12–13; 2:11–22).

Christian love is the theme central to the overall purpose of Ephesians. Throughout the letter, the noun "love" occurs ten times (1:4, 15; 2:4; 3:17, 19; 4:2, 15, 16; 5:2; 6:23), the verb "love" also occurs ten times (1:6; 2:4; 5:2, 25[x2]; 28[x3], 33; 6:24), and the adjective "beloved" occurs twice (5:1; 6:21). Within the ten occurrences of the noun "love," of special significance are the six instances of the poignant prepositional phrase "in love" (1:4; 3:17; 4:2, 15, 16; 5:2) to designate the dynamic domain or sphere of love constituted by the complex interaction of God's love for those who are in Christ, empowering their love both for God/Christ and for one another. The key theme of love in Ephesians includes, however, not only the twenty-two occurrences of the Greek terms for love, but also the many other related expressions within the love word-field, such as "blessed," "chosen," "grace," "give", "gift," and so on. The letter exhibits the following chiastic structure:

Ephesians: Empowerment to Walk in Love for the Unity of All in Christ
A (1:1–2): Grace and peace
   B (1:3–14): To the praise of his glory in love
      C (1:15–23): The gift of Christ in love as head over all to the church
         D (2:1–10): Walking by the great love with which he loved us
            E (2:11–22): The peace that establishes unity as a gift of love
               F (3:1–13): Paul's gift to make known the mystery of Christ in love
                  G (3:14–21): To know the love of Christ that surpasses knowledge
                     H (4:1–16): Walk toward the unity of all in love
                  G* (4:17–32): Walk as the new person in the truth of Christ's love
               F* (5:1–6): Walk in love as Christ loved us
            E* (5:7–14): Walk as children of light in love
         D* (5:15–6:9): Walk in love as those who are wise
         (a) (5:15–20): Always thanking God in love
         (b) (5:21–33): Husbands and wives love one another
         (c) (6:1–4): Children and parents respect one another in love
         (d) (6:5–9): Slaves and masters respect one another in love
      C* (6:10–13): Be empowered in love to withstand evil
   B* (6:14–22): Beloved Tychicus will encourage your hearts in love
A* (6:23–24): Peace, love, and grace

The H unit (4:1–16), the beginning of the paranetic half of the letter as well as the pivotal central unit within the chiastic structure, exhorts the audience to forbear one another within the dynamic realm of being "in love" in order to preserve the unity of believers, each of whom has been given, as a gift of love, grace according to the measure of the gift of the Christ (4:1–7). The pivotal center of this unit, as well as of the entire chiastic structure, makes the audience aware that the Christ who descended to the lower parts of the earth in death and burial also ascended in resurrection from the dead far above all the heavens, that he might fill all things with gifts of love (4:8–10). The unit concludes by exhorting the audience to be truthful in sharing gifts of love within the realm of being "in love," so that "we" believers might cause all things to grow to Christ as the "head" – the destiny for the cosmic unity of all things as well as the source of the gifts of love by which the "body," the church, is building itself up within the dynamic realm of being "in love" (4:11–16).

Within the chiastic structure, Paul's assertion that his audience "have not so learned the *Christ*" (4:20) as the motivation for his exhortation that they not behave like the Gentiles (4:17–19) in the G* unit (4:17–32) undergirds his prayer that his audience may "know the love of the *Christ* that surpasses knowledge" (3:19) in the G unit (3:14–21). That the audience have put off the "*old person*" (4:22) and put on the "*new person*" (4:24) as a gift of Christ's love in the G* unit is a consequence of their being strengthened in the "*inner person*" (3:16) as a gift of God's love in the G unit. The exhortation for the audience not to grieve the Holy "*Spirit*" of God (4:30) with their behavior in the G* unit is motivated by Paul's prayer that they be strengthened with power through God's "*Spirit*" (3:16) as a gift of God's love in the G unit. And that God was gracious in giving us gifts of love within the realm of our being "*in Christ*" (4:32) in the G* unit provides a further reason for Paul's declaration of glory to God for the gifts of love we have received within the realm of our being "*in Christ*" (3:21) in the G unit.

That *Christ* loved us (5:2) in the F* unit (5:1–6) provides the motivation for Paul's being the prisoner of the *Christ Jesus* (3:1), develops the content of the mystery of the *Christ* (3:4) and the wealth of the *Christ* (3:8), and gives the reason why the Gentiles are fellow heirs and fellow members of the body and fellow sharers of the promise in *Christ Jesus* (3:6), as well as how God accomplished the purpose of the ages in *Christ Jesus* our Lord (3:11) in the F unit (3:1–13). Paul's command for the audience to imitate God as children beloved by God and Christ who share that *love* with one another by "walking" within the realm of being "in love" (5:1–2) in the F* unit finds further motivation in the example of Paul who shared with the audience the grace of God he received as a gift of God's *love* to be a minister of the gospel (3:2, 7) in the F unit. And that there is no "*inheritance*" in the kingdom of Christ and God for one who is sexually immoral, impure, or greedy (5:5) in the F* unit warns the audience not to forfeit being "*fellow heirs*" in Christ Jesus (3:6) as a gift of God's love in the F unit.

Paul's command for his audience not to become "*fellow sharers*" with "them" (5:7), that is, the "sons of disobedience" (5:6), in the E* unit (5:7–14) of the chiastic structure is bolstered by his audience's recall that instead they are "*fellow citizens*" with the holy ones (2:19) as a gift of God's love in the E unit (2:11–22). That "*you were once*" darkness, but "*now*" are light (5:8) as a gift of God's love in the E* unit develops the statement that "*once you were*" without Christ (2:12) but "*now*" you who were "*once*" far away have become near in the blood of the Christ (2:13) as a gift of God's love in the E unit. And that you are not to "*be connected with*" the unfruitful works of the darkness (5:11) as you are light "*in the Lord*" (5:8) as a gift of God's love in the E* unit further develops that it is "*in the Lord*" (2:21) that "*you are being built together*" into a dwelling place of God in the Spirit (2:22) as a gift of God's love in the E unit.

Paul's warning to his audience to watch how carefully you "*walk*" (5:15) in the D* unit (5:15–6:9) of the chiastic structure recalls that, although the "you" believers once "*walked*" according to the age of this world (2:2), all of us believers may now "*walk*" in the good works God prepared beforehand (2:10) as part of what it means to walk within the dynamic realm of being "in love" in the D unit (2:1–10). "*Doing the will*" of God (6:6) as children beloved by God and Christ in the D* unit recalls and contrasts "*doing* *the wishes"* of the flesh as children of wrath (2:3) in the D unit. And Paul's directive for husbands to *"love"* their wives as the Christ *"loved"* the church (5:25) and to *"love"* their own wives as their own bodies, as he who *"loves"* his own wife *"loves"* himself (5:28) in the D* unit is inspired and empowered by the great *"love"* with which God *"loved"* us (2:4) in our union with Christ in the D unit.

In the C* unit (6:10–13) within the chiastic structure of Ephesians, the audience may be empowered *"in the might of the strength"* of the Lord Jesus Christ (6:10) to stand against the *"rulers"* and *"authorities"* who are *"in the heavenly places"* (6:12). This is because of *"the might of the strength"* (1:19) that God worked in raising Christ from the dead and seating him *"in the heavenly places"* (1:20), far above every *"ruler"* and *"authority"* (1:21), subjecting all things under his feet and giving him as head over all things to the church as a gift of God's love (1:22) in the C unit (1:15–23).

The audience may stand in *"truth"* (6:14) prepared from the *"gospel"* of peace (6:15) to receive the helmet of *"salvation"* and the sword of the *"Spirit"* (6:17) in the B* unit (6:14–22) within the chiastic structure because they have heard the word of the *"truth,"* the *"gospel"* of their *"salvation,"* and were sealed with the Holy *"Spirit"* (1:13) as a gift of God's love in the B unit (1:3–14). Paul wants *"to make known the mystery"* of the gospel (6:19) in the B* unit as a consequence of God's gift of love in *"having made known to us the mystery"* of his will (1:9) in the B unit. And encouraged by the *"beloved"* Tychicus (6:21–22), the audience are to pray for all the *"holy ones"* (6:18) in the B* unit, so that all of us believers may be *"holy"* and blameless before God within the dynamic realm of being *"in love"* (1:4) as well as *"in the Beloved"* (1:6) in the B unit.

In the A unit (1:1–2) that introduces the chiastic structure, the apostle Paul pronounces a prayer that *grace* and *peace* be granted as implicit gifts of love from *God our Father and the Lord Jesus Christ* to his audience, the holy ones in Ephesus, the believers who are in Christ Jesus. But in the concluding A* unit (6:23–24), after presenting a concerted theme of love throughout the letter, Paul proclaims a prayer that not only *peace* and *grace* but also an explicit *love* (6:23) be granted from *God the Father and the Lord Jesus Christ* not just to his audience but to the "brothers," all fellow believers who explicitly *love* the *Lord Jesus Christ* in immortality (6:24).

In sum, the chiastic structure of Ephesians begins by assuring its audience that they have been blessed by God with every Spiritual blessing so that they may be holy and blameless before God within the dynamic realm of being *"in love"* (1:4) as well as *"in the Beloved"* (1:6). At the center of the central unit (4:1–16), the audience hear that Christ ascended far above all the heavens, that he might fill all things (4:10) with gifts of love (cf. 4:7), so that, at the climactic conclusion of the central unit, we believers, being truthful *"in love,"* might cause all things to grow to him, who is the head, the Christ (cf. 1:10), from whom the whole body, the church (cf. 1:22–23), brings about the growth of the body for the building up of itself within the dynamic realm of being *"in love"* (4:15–16). Chiastically developing its opening prayer (1:1–2), the letter concludes on a climactic note of love with Paul's prayer for continued *love* from God the Father and the Lord Jesus Christ as well as grace upon all who are *loving* the Lord Jesus Christ within the dynamic realm of being "in immortality" (6:23–24).

In conclusion, listening to the intricate and intriguing chiastic patterns of Paul's letter to the Ephesians empowers its audience to "walk," that is, behave and conduct themselves, "in love," that is, within the dynamic realm of being not only loved by God and Christ but loving God, Christ, and one another, in order to bring about the cosmic unity of all things in the heavens and on earth – including believing Jews and Gentiles as well as all evil powers – within the dynamic realm of being "in Christ." In short, Ephesians functions as the empowerment to walk in love for the unity of all in Christ (Heil 2007a).

Philemon, Colossians, and Ephesians as Epistolary Rituals of Worship

As in all of the letters attributed to Paul, those sent to the believers in western Asia center upon the ramifications of believing in the definitive salvation God accomplished in the death and resurrection of Jesus Christ, epitomized as the "grace" of God. Through each of the three letters discussed in this chapter, Paul enables and facilitates believers to join him in his ongoing worship of thanksgiving, prayer, and praise to God for this grace. Delivered as an oral performance within a liturgical assembly, each letter functions as an epistolary ritual of worship. Each begins and ends with liturgical greetings of divine grace that function as ritual speech-acts, acts which do what they say, communicating a renewed experience of the grace of God aimed at extending the worship of believers into their everyday lives.

In the letter to Philemon, Paul draws the liturgical assembly into his worship of thanking God for this grace, as he prays that Philemon recognize all the "good" that can be done for Christ as part of this grateful worship. Based on a new manifestation of the grace of God evident in his slave, Onesimus, becoming a fellow believer and thus "brother," Philemon, out of love, can do the "good" of allowing Onesimus to serve Paul in advancing the gospel of Christ. By doing this "good" in obedience to God, Philemon can deepen the liturgical assembly's experience of the grace of God as the focus of their grateful worship. And they may gain a further experience of this grace, as the imprisoned Paul hopes that God will "grant" or "grace" him to them through their prayers as a worshiping community.

In the letter to the Colossians, Paul draws their liturgical assembly into the worship of his and Timothy's grateful and constant praying for their renewed experience of God's grace in terms of being filled with the knowledge of God's will in all wisdom. They are to be joyfully thanking God for the grace they have received as believers who, through their baptism, have been "buried and raised" with Christ, "in whom are all the treasures of wisdom and knowledge hidden" (2:3). As a liturgical assembly, they, rather than being captivated by a "philosophy of empty deceit" (2:8), enticing them into a worship with or of angels, are in all wisdom to teach and admonish each other "with psalms, hymns, and Spiritual songs, in grace singing in your hearts to God" (3:16). Their liturgical worship is to extend to everything they do, so that it becomes an ethical worship. Indeed, "all, whatever you do in word or in work, do all things in the name of the Lord Jesus, thanking God the Father through him" (3:17). This ethical worship includes the mutual love and respect that is to be manifested between wives and husbands, children and parents, slaves and masters (3:18–4:1). They are to persevere in grateful prayer that God grant the imprisoned Paul the grace of continuing to proclaim the mystery of Christ (4:2–4).

In the letter to the Ephesians, Paul draws the liturgical assembly of those who have more recently become believers into his praise of the God who blessed and chose all believers in Christ "to be holy and blameless before him in love" (1:4), that is, to present sacrificial, ethical worship before him through lives of mutual love, to the praise of God's glory. Paul does not cease thanking God for these believers and praying that God grant them an experiential knowledge of the power and mystery of the risen Christ as the "head" under which all things in the universe are being united. As a ritual speech-act accomplishing what it says, the solemn prayer of Paul begins to be fulfilled in the very hearing of it by his audience. They are given a renewed experience of the grace of God, as they are interiorly strengthened to comprehend, within their unity as a liturgical assembly of holy ones, the vast expanse of this cosmic unity, which enables them to experience the love of Christ that surpasses all other experiences (3:14–19).

By their ethical worship of love, they play their part in causing all things to grow to Christ, the "head" of all things (4:15–16). They are to be gracious to each other, just as also God in Christ was gracious to all of us believers (4:17–32). Functioning as a worshiping assembly enables them to be filled with the gifts of God's grace within the realm of being in the Spirit (5:18; Heil 2007b). Their liturgical worship of "speaking to each other in psalms and hymns and Spiritual songs, singing songs and singing psalms in your hearts to the Lord, giving thanks always and for all things in the name of our Lord Jesus Christ to God the Father" (5:19–20) is to extend to their ethical worship. Noteworthy is how the marital love of husbands for their wives serves as a microcosm of ethical worship within the macrocosm of the love of Christ for the church. Husbands are to love their wives in the manner that Christ loved the church. They thereby play their role in performing the ethical worship enabled by the sacrificial love of Christ. He handed himself over to death in love that he might present to himself the church as a glorious sacrificial victim suitable for the ethical worship of God – "not having a blemish or wrinkle or any of such things, but that she might be holy and blameless" (5:27; cf. 1:4).

As an epistolary ritual, the letter to the Ephesians places all three of these letters to believers in western Asia within a context of a comprehensive worship empowered by the profound experience of God's grace in Christ. Paul enables and facilitates their thanksgiving, prayer, and praise, in accord with the climactic conclusion of his own solemn prayer: "Now to him who has the power to do far more beyond all that we ask or imagine according to the power that is working in us, to him be glory in the church and in Christ Jesus to all the generations, for ever and ever. Amen!" (3:20–21).

Note

1   Translations of biblical texts are my own.

References

Bevere, Allan R. 2003. *Sharing in the Inheritance: Identity and the Moral Life in Colossians*. London: Sheffield Academic.

Carson, D. A., and Douglas J. Moo. 2005. *An Introduction to the New Testament*. Second edition. Grand Rapids: Zondervan.

Dunn, James D. G. 1996. *The Epistles to the Colossians and to Philemon: A Commentary on the Greek Text*. Grand Rapids: Eerdmans.

Ellis, E. Earle. 2002. *The Making of the New Testament Documents*. Leiden: Brill.

Gorman, Michael J. 2004. *Apostle of the Crucified Lord: A Theological Introduction to Paul and his Letters*. Grand Rapids: Eerdmans.

Harding, Mark. 2004. Disputed and Undisputed Letters of Paul. Pages 129–168 in *The Pauline Canon*. Edited by Stanley E. Porter. Leiden: Brill.

Heil, John Paul. 2001. The Chiastic Structure and Meaning of Paul's Letter to Philemon. *Biblica* 82: 178–206.

Heil, John Paul. 2007a. *Ephesians: Empowerment to Walk in Love for the Unity of All in Christ*. Atlanta: Society of Biblical Literature.

Heil, John Paul. 2007b. Ephesians 5:18b: "But Be Filled in the Spirit." *Catholic Biblical Quarterly* 69: 506–516.

Heil, John Paul. Forthcoming. *Colossians: Encouragement to Walk in All Wisdom as Holy Ones in Christ*. Atlanta: Society of Biblical Literature.

Hoehner, Harold W. 2002. *Ephesians: An Exegetical Commentary*. Grand Rapids: Baker Academic.

Johnson, Luke Timothy. 1999. *The Writings of the New Testament: An Interpretation*. Revised edition. Minneapolis: Fortress.

Kiley, Mark. 1986. *Colossians as Pseudepigraphy*. The Biblical Seminar 4. Sheffield: JSOT.

Reicke, Bo. 2001. *Re-examining Paul's Letters: The History of the Pauline Correspondence*. Harrisburg, Pa.: Trinity.

Richards, E. Randolph. 2004. *Paul and First-century Letter Writing: Secretaries, Composition and Collection*. Downers Grove, Ill.: InterVarsity.

Schnabel, Eckhard J. 2008. *Paul the Missionary: Realities, Strategies and Methods*. Downers Grove, Ill.: IVP Academic.

Smith, Ian K. 2006. *Heavenly Perspective: A Study of the Apostle Paul's Response to a Jewish Mystical Movement at Colossae*. London: T. & T. Clark.

Stirewalt Jr., M. Luther. 2003. *Paul, the Letter Writer*. Grand Rapids: Eerdmans.

Sumney, Jerry L. 2008. *Colossians: A Commentary*. Louisville: Westminster John Knox.

Wilder, Terry L. 2004. *Pseudonymity, the New Testament and Deception: An Inquiry into Intention and Reception*. Lanham: University Press of America.

CHAPTER 6

Paul and the Roman Believers

Beverly Roberts Gaventa

Locating Paul

Romans stands first in the canonical ordering of Paul's letters because of its length, but it falls late in the chronology of his letter-writing (it was probably written in the mid- to late 50s). From the letter itself, it seems clear that Paul is writing from Corinth. Phoebe, who delivers the letter as Paul's representative, is from Cenchreae, the port of Corinth (16:1), and in 16:23 Paul refers to his host Gaius, who could be the Gaius of 1 Corinthians 1:14. (Note also that the Erastus of 16:23 is associated with Corinth through an inscription discovered in the twentieth century.) And his location in Corinth, where at least some believers appear to have thought that the gospel had already transformed them into resurrection life and immunized them against moral fault (see, for example, 1 Cor 5:1–2; 6:12), may have influenced his thinking as he considered the next stage in his work (as in, for example, Rom 6:8, where Paul carefully avoids saying that believers are *already* resurrected).

Some general sense of Paul's situation as he writes to Rome can be easily gleaned from his comments in Romans 15:14–33. He is about to undertake a journey to Jerusalem, where he will deliver a collection of funds for the "saints" in that city. References to the collection, a fund gathered from Gentile believers on behalf of their Jewish counterparts in Jerusalem, appear elsewhere in Paul's letters (see 1 Cor 16:1–4 and 2 Cor 8–9; Gal 2:10 may refer to a separate collection [Downs 2008, 33–39]), and Paul's anxiety about its reception comes into view when he asks the Romans to pray alongside him that he and his work will not be rejected in Jerusalem (Rom 15:30–32). From Jerusalem, Paul intends to travel to Rome, a city in which he has not yet labored and a Christian community (or communities) in which he is unknown and perhaps

The Blackwell Companion to Paul, First Edition. Edited by Stephen Westerholm.
© 2011 Blackwell Publishing Ltd. Published 2011 by Blackwell Publishing Ltd.

even suspect (Tobin 2004, 47–78). And then Paul envisions a new mission in Spain, an area in which the gospel has not yet been preached.

These three locations – namely, Jerusalem, Spain, and Rome – may serve as indicators of three major strands in the "Romans debate," a shorthand reference to the many competing theories about the purpose of the letter (Donfried 1991). Some have argued that the letter rehearses the speech Paul anticipates giving in Jerusalem, where he expects to be called upon to defend his work among Gentiles; in particular, his insistence that Gentiles do not have to become Jews in order to participate fully alongside Jews in emerging Christian congregations (Jervell 1991). Others regard Spain as the primary concern driving the writing of the letter, contending that Paul seeks the concrete assistance of Roman believers in the form of funding and supplies as he prepares to take the gospel into a territory unknown to him. On this reading of the letter, Phoebe goes to Rome as the leader of Paul's advance team (16:1–2; Jewett 2007, 80–91). Perhaps the majority of scholars think that Paul's major concern in writing arises out of the Roman congregations themselves: either he knows of some conflict within Christian congregations (perhaps occasioned by an enforced expulsion of some Jewish Christians during the reign of the Emperor Claudius; see Watson 2007, 163–191); or he writes to introduce and defend himself from charges raised against him (Tobin 2004, 76–78); or he writes what amounts to a proclamation of the gospel (1:15) in order to correct an inadequate understanding operative at Rome (Gaventa 2009).

Identifying these three geographical locations and their places in the Romans debate is fairly straightforward, but analyzing their relative importance in Paul's letter-writing is far more complex. For today's readers, who can barely stay afloat in a sea of personal information and public self-disclosure, understanding the reticence of ancient writers to divulge autobiographical details can be challenging. Paul did not post his daily activities or his latest challenge as updates on Facebook; he did not even include them in his letters. This silence is even more pronounced in Romans than in Paul's other letters, since he had no history of a relationship with most people in Rome, and could not appeal to his knowledge of them or theirs of him. So we do well to proceed with modesty: all three of these locations are probably at play in some sense, but it seems likely that the dominant factor behind the letter is Paul's concern about the fledgling congregations in Rome, even if that concern is necessarily related also to both Jerusalem and Spain.

Locating Roman Believers

However difficult it is to catch a glimpse of Paul's situation as he undertakes this letter, it is far more difficult to identify the people to whom the letter is addressed. There are no first-century accounts of Roman Christianity outside the New Testament to help us to understand the audience of the letter. And the only other reference to Roman Christianity in the New Testament appears in the Acts of the Apostles, which briefly mentions Paul's arrival in Rome, where he is met by a group of Christians (28:15). Yet Luke's comments simply confirm that there were already believers in Rome when Paul arrived and add nothing to our knowledge.

The bulk of Romans itself reveals little about the audience of the letter, and a number of the details in the body of the letter are ambiguous. Does 1:5–6 mean that the audience itself *consists* of Gentiles, or that they live among Gentiles? Does 2:17 address Jews, or does it speak instead to Gentiles who identify themselves as Jews (adherents of the synagogue, perhaps)? Similarly, are those who "know the law"[1] in 7:1 Jews, or are they Gentiles who have learned the Mosaic law through the synagogue? Romans 11:13 directly addresses Gentiles, but perhaps the most specific information appears at the end of the letter, where Paul greets a number of individuals by name. Other letters contain similar greetings (as in 1 Cor 16:19–20; 2 Cor 13:12; Phil 4:21–22; 1 Thess 5:26; Phlm 23–24), which were a standard feature of ancient letter-writing, but this is by far the most extensive set of greetings in any Pauline letter. Since he has not yet been to Rome, and because there are some significant differences among early manuscripts (i.e., handwritten copies) of the letter, and one later manuscript omits the greetings altogether, it has been suggested that Paul sent the letter to Rome without this section of greetings and then sent what was substantially the same letter to Ephesus with greetings attached; that is, the greetings do not belong to the Roman setting (Manson 1991). The evidence for that theory is weak, however, and most scholars agree that the more likely scenario is that the original greetings were excised at a later date in order to make the letter appropriate for a larger audience; thus, the greetings in Romans 16 do contribute to our understanding of the recipients of the letter.

The people greeted may be individuals Paul has met elsewhere, as is clearly the case with Prisca and Aquila (1 Cor 16:19; and cf. Acts 18:2, 18, 26; 2 Tim 4:19). Since Paul is unknown to most Christians in Rome, it is not surprising that he would wish to greet by name everyone whom he does know, in the same way that we sometimes make connections with new acquaintances by identifying mutual friends. Some of these people he may never even have met; the last verses include a number of names without any particular description or comment, so these may be people about whom he has heard from others rather than people he knows directly (Lampe 2003, 157).

Careful study of the names and Paul's comments about them reveal a great deal. Paul addresses, not a single community of believers, but multiple communities. He greets the gathering (*ekklēsia*) in the house of Prisca and Aquila (v. 5). Similarly, in verses 14 and 15, he lists several individuals and then adds "and the brothers and sisters who are with them" or "all the saints who are with them," suggesting that Christianity at Rome consists of multiple small communities that gather in homes. House churches may also be reflected in verses 10–11. In addition, study of the names and their use elsewhere suggests that a significant number of those greeted bear names frequently given to slaves (Lampe 2003, 164–183). Only a few of the names are of Jewish origin (Lampe 2003, 74–75).

Nine of the twenty-six individuals greeted are women, and Paul's comments about them will surprise readers schooled in George Bernard Shaw's assessment of Paul as the "eternal enemy" of women. He identifies several women who "worked" with him (Prisca, v. 3; Mary, v. 6; Tryphaena, Tryphosa, and Persis, v. 12), using language that he elsewhere employs for labor carried out by apostles on behalf of the gospel (for example, 1 Cor 3:9; 4:12; 15:10; Gal 4:11; 1 Thess 5:12). His comments about two of these women are especially revealing. He says that Prisca and her husband Aquila "risked their necks" on his behalf. He also puts Prisca's name first, as is done also in Acts 18:18, 26 and 2 Timothy 4:19 (but see Acts 18:2 and 1 Cor 16:19). While that order may be meaningless for many modern readers, in the ancient world the husband's name usually went first (as in 16:7; Acts 5:1), and the reversal of the order probably reflects Prisca's senior role in the Christian community.

Perhaps even more surprising, in verse 7 Paul greets another couple, Andronicus and Junia, whom he refers to as kinfolk and fellow prisoners "who are honored among the apostles." Although most English translations of the twentieth century treat this greeting as if it addressed a man by the name of Junias, the evidence is strong that here again Paul greets a married couple, both of whom he regards as apostles. The ancient church witnesses unanimously identify Junia as a female, and there is no evidence in antiquity of any male named Junias (Epp 2005, 25–27). Although Paul does once refer to "the twelve" (1 Cor 15:5), he apparently does not think of the number of apostles as limited (see 1 Cor 15:7 and his frequent references to himself as an apostle) and here includes a woman among them.

Whatever the previous relationships between Paul and these individuals, he clearly wants to establish a strong connection with them and with other believers in Rome. Pivotal to that relationship will be another person who appears in chapter 16, Phoebe. In verses 1–2, Paul writes a brief commendation of her, asking that the Romans provide her with hospitality (a *sine qua non* of the early Christian mission). He identifies Phoebe as a deacon of Cenchreae and as a benefactor. The Greek word *diakonos* ("deacon") Paul has already applied to Jesus himself (15:8), and he has referred to his own *diakonia* ("service" or "ministry") in 11:13 and 15:31. The term did not yet have the connotation of an official office of leadership in the community that it seems to have acquired for the author of the Pastorals (1 Tim 3:8, 12; 4:6), but neither can it be presumed that Phoebe's only role is domestic. That she is a "benefactor" of Paul and of other believers (v. 2) clearly signals that she is a person of some substance. (It is noteworthy that no husband or father is mentioned, suggesting that the patronage derives from her own resources.) The singling out of Phoebe suggests that she is the one who delivers the letter (no other candidate is mentioned), and it is likely that she also is the one who reads the letter at Rome, since she would have had occasion to talk about it with Paul. If so, then Phoebe's interpretation as she both speaks about Paul and reads his letter will be crucial to the letter's reception. In fact, it is entirely possible that she has had a hand in the letter itself, having talked through it with Paul. This letter was not dashed off in a frenzy but probably went through several drafts, and in that process it is reasonable to imagine that she and others around Paul had some role.

Listening in on the Letter

Getting underway 1:1–12

The opening lines of Romans follow the format of Paul's other letters (and letters in the Roman world as a whole), including the salutation (vv. 1–7) and thanksgiving (vv. 8–12), although here the salutation is not the brief identification found elsewhere in his letters but is far more elaborate. Despite the fact (or perhaps *because*) he is an outsider to these congregations, Paul identifies himself not in terms of what we might consider customary biographical information (his family, place of origin, education), but in terms of God's action in the gospel. As Paul summarizes it here, the gospel was promised earlier through Scripture and it concerns Jesus Christ, who is both a physical descendant of King David and is powerfully confirmed as God's son by virtue of his resurrection (vv. 2–4). This same Jesus Christ has called "us" (Paul never identifies the "we" referred to here, and he may mean only himself) as representatives charged with bringing about trusting reliance ("the obedience of faith") among all peoples. Here, for the first of many times in Romans, Paul uses the word "all" (for example, 1:5, 7, 8; 3:9, 19, 23; 4:11, 5:12; 11:26, 32), reflecting the universal scope of God's powerful action in Jesus Christ.

The thanksgiving (vv. 8–12) begins with a hyperbolic statement about the fame of the faith of the Roman Christians (cf. 1 Thess 1:8), but is followed by an elaborate statement about Paul's own desire to be in Rome (vv. 9–12) and no further comment about the Romans themselves (contrast 1 Thess 1:2–10; Phil 1:3–11). This relative silence may mean that Paul simply does not have more information about Christians at Rome, yet Paul's comments about individuals in 16:3–15 suggest otherwise. The silence could also mean that Paul has some concern(s), especially since he writes that he wants to "preach the gospel" among them (v. 15), using a verb he reserves for declaring the good news about Jesus Christ to those who have not yet heard it (for example, 1 Cor 15:1–2; Gal 1:8–9; see Gaventa 2009).

God's saving power 1:13–4:25

With verse 13, Paul ends the thanksgiving and takes up the major work of this letter, to extend his proclamation of the gospel to Rome, beginning with his declaration of God's saving power through both God's righteousness and God's wrath. Here he identifies the gospel as God's own power, power that is at work to bring about salvation. The origin and connotations of the language of righteousness (*dikaiosynē*) in Romans have generated endless debate; substantively, what Paul is concerned with is God's way of making right what has gone wrong (Martyn 1997, 249–250).

The extent of what has gone wrong comes into view in the following chapters, as Paul writes about the revelation of God's own wrath. He begins in 1:18–32 with a sharp critique of human refusal to acknowledge God, a critique that plays on traditional Jewish criticism of Gentiles. This harsh section seems to reinscribe the traditional lines between Jew and Gentile, but chapter 2 then undermines those boundaries, first by saying that God is not partial and then by destabilizing the notion that having the gift of the law means that Jews are somehow exempt from sin. By the end of chapter 2, the boundaries have been eroded, so that Romans 3 opens with the obvious question: Is there no advantage to being a Jew? Paul emphatically asserts that there is, but it becomes clear as he continues that even the advantage of having God's "oracles" has not prevented Jews from landing in sin's power alongside Gentiles (3:2, 9). Nothing whatever can humanly be done, but God has already acted in Jesus Christ to make things right, presenting Jesus Christ freely as humanity's redemption (3:21–31). And God's action in Jesus for all is prefigured in Abraham, not because he did what was right but because God rectified Abraham, even before he was circumcised (4:1–25).

God's saving power extended (5:1–8:39)

Chapters 5–8 are frequently described as a depiction of the new life in Christ, and Paul does begin by referring to the "peace," "grace," and "hope" that "we" have in Christ Jesus (5:1–2). Yet there is little emphasis here on the role of human beings, and little to suggest Paul's comments pertain only to members of the believing community. The section begins with a declaration about the peace that "we" have in Jesus Christ (5:1) and ends with a declaration that nothing can separate "us" from Christ's love (8:31–39). But 5:1–11 quickly returns to Christ's death on behalf of an ungodly, hostile humanity, and then 5:12–21 doubles back to examine what it is that produced humanity's captivity to the power of sin in the first place. Here Paul introduces a complex analogy between Adam and Christ: Adam's one act of disobedience brought sin and death as rulers over all of humanity, and Christ's one act of obedience brought God's own grace as a new ruler over humanity. The imagined objection of 6:1 ("Should we continue in sin?" see also 6:15) opens a further explanation of what the death and resurrection of Christ have brought about for human beings; namely, the transfer from sin's power to that of righteousness (i.e., God). In chapter 7, Paul shows how sin's power made use even of the good and perfect gift of the Mosaic law. And in chapter 8, he returns to the new life in the Spirit of those freed from sin and death, anticipating the completion of God's triumph.

God's saving power considered in light of Israel (9:1–11:36)

This is among the most controverted sections of the letter. For many generations, scholars tended to treat it as a digression or to see Israel as nothing more than an example of God's actions. Recent decades have produced a pendulum swing in the opposite direction, so that many scholars now treat Romans 9–11 as the singular focus of the letter. If the earlier disregard failed to do justice to 9–11, however, the current focus on 9–11 fails to do justice to the remainder of the letter. The issue at work here continues to be God's saving power, but now the question raised at 3:1 returns: What does the fact that many Jews do not recognize Jesus as the Messiah of God mean about God's saving power? Or, as Paul puts it more succinctly in 9:6, has the word of God failed?

Paul rejects that notion out of hand, but his extended response to the question (which falls into three movements) reveals how important it has become. (And this section contains the letter's most extensive and probing engagement with Scripture; see below). First, 9:6–29 serves to establish Paul's understanding of Israel and God. Israel itself is a creation of God. Israel does not belong to itself and never did. Israel comes into being as God's creature and in every generation has been re-created, not by virtue of its own merit but by virtue of God's action (Gaventa 2010). Then 9:30–10:21 turns to the present, beginning with the stunning claim that God has caused Israel to stumble (9:32–33). Their salvation (i.e., Jesus) is nearby (10:1–8); it is for everyone who calls on God's name (10:9–13). Calling on God's name comes about only through God's sending of those who preach the word (10:14–17). But God has indeed called out to Israel and still Israel has not responded (10:18–21).

Paul writes chapter 10 as if Israel were a single entity, and so he forces the question at the outset of the third movement (11:1–36): Has God rejected God's people? What follows is a complex and strident rejection of that notion. Paul insists that Israel is divided; as in the past, there is a remnant, and Israel consists of the remnant and the rest (11:2–10). But that division of Israel is not the whole of the story: God brought about this division in order that the Gentiles might be brought in and thereby provoke Israel to jealousy (11:11–16). Since this division is entirely God's doing, there is no reason for Gentiles to boast (11:17–24). God's plan (the "mystery" of v. 25) is that the whole of Israel will be saved (both the elect remnant and the rest, 11:7).

God's saving power embodied in community (12:1–15:13)

At a number of points in Romans 1–11, Paul makes it clear that he does not regard God's powerful salvation on behalf of humankind as already completed in the present time: 6:5 affirms that "we" died with Christ and are raised to a new life, but "we" will in the future also share in Christ's resurrection; 8:17–25 anticipate the redemption of the whole of creation, of which "we" already have the first taste; 11:26 looks forward to God's salvation of all of Israel. While God's final triumph lies in the future, Paul nevertheless affirms that God's power has already acted decisively, delivering his addressees from the powers of sin and death and granting them new life. In 12:1–15:6, he limns some of the features of this new life. Chapter 12, verses 1–2 are pivotal: the fitting response to the gospel, a response generated by the mercies of God, is the offering of the whole person. Chapters 12:3–13:14 then follow with various instructions (many of which are traditional), having to do with life in Christian communities. The fact that this section emphasizes the right assessment of one's own gifts and judgments (e.g., 12:3, 16), care for those within the community (e.g., 12:9–10; 13:8–10), and generosity toward opponents (e.g., 12:14, 17, 18–21) suggests that Paul is preparing for the specific problem he will take up in 14:1–15:6. The instructions of 13:1–7 regarding governing authorities have generated a bewildering array of unconvincing interpretations. The restrained character of Paul's comments is worth noting, however: the governing authorities have power only because it is given to them by God (13:1), and what is owed to them is not love or the handing over of the self, but the doing of good rather than wrong and the payment of such taxes as are due.

With 14:1–15:6, Paul takes up a question about dietary regulations and other religious practices. The careful, restrained argument might suggest that this is a theoretical problem rather than a situation at Rome, but the length of the discussion prompts many scholars to conclude that Paul is aware of an actual conflict. Whatever the ethnic make-up of the congregations, they include some people who regard it as obligatory that believers continue to conform to Jewish law, while others understand themselves as released from that law. At the shared meals, this divergence of conviction and practice would have been especially problematic (Barclay 2001). Paul deftly responds, pressing those who are "strong" to compromise their practice in order not to do harm to the "weak," while also granting their principle that all foods are clean (14:14). Yet the underlying notion here is not simply that they all have to find a way to get along with one another; instead, Paul contends that they are all alike God's creatures, and only God is the rightful judge of their conduct. In 15:1–6, Paul goes a step further: they are obliged to find a way to please one another so that together they can glorify God.

In 15:7–13 Paul recasts his comments in 15:1–6. Repeating the language of "welcome" in 14:1, Paul now brings together the whole of the letter. Christ came for Jew and Gentile alike, and he did so for God's own glory. With the biblical citations that follow in verses 9–12, Paul anticipates the eschatological praise of God by Jew and Gentile together.

Closing elements (15:14–16:23[27])

The final lines of the letter include a discussion of Paul's itinerary, including his upcoming trip to Jerusalem, after which he plans to travel to Rome and then to Spain. Paul closes with an extended list of greetings (see above). The final doxology in verses 25–27 is omitted in some ancient manuscripts and in others appears after 14:23, which may mean that it has been added by someone other than Paul. That the letter ends in doxology seems entirely appropriate, however, given the repeated elements of praise and thanksgiving throughout the letter (see below).

Characterizing Romans

As noted above, Romans is distinctive in the Pauline letter corpus in being the only letter addressed to a location in which Paul had not himself already preached the gospel and established a community of believers (on the assumption that Colossians is not written by Paul but by a later follower). But it is distinctive in other ways as well, including its style of argumentation, its engagement with questions having to do with both Israel and the Gentiles, its preoccupation with sin as a controlling power in human life, and its claims about God's cosmic triumph in Jesus Christ.

Style of argumentation

Emphasizing that Romans is a real letter addressing a specific situation does not mean that it is tossed off casually, as one zips off an email message or posts a Twitter update. Whether Paul composed the letter entirely by himself or drew on conversations with co-workers such as Phoebe, Timothy, and Tertius, the letter gives evidence of having been quite carefully thought out and composed. (Hence scholars sometimes suggest that he is using portions of some earlier work, a sermon perhaps.) Because he has not yet been to Rome and cannot draw on his history of preaching and teaching these congregations (by contrast, for example, with Galatians, where he makes frequent reference to their knowledge of one another), Paul must proceed carefully. Despite the fact that he greets a number of people by name, it is likely that he is unknown to most believers in Rome, and it may well be that the rumors that have reached them regarding Paul are not flattering. For these reasons, at the very least, he argues with care.

Complex structure   The summary of content offered above largely conforms to some standard analyses of the letter; yet anyone who studies the letter at length, lingering over the ins and outs of the argument, will know that Paul's writing does not so easily fall into the tidy sections sketched above. The transitions that set chapters 9–11 apart are clear (although see Tobin 2004, 300–301), and the greetings of 16:1–16 form a distinct unit, but on the whole the letter is far less linear in its argumentation than most analyses suggest. Rather than crafting this letter by piling one building block on top of another, Paul appears to be composing a symphony, introducing themes that then disappear and reappear in a different key later on (Wright 2002, 396). For example, although Paul introduces the notion of God's righteousness or rectification in 1:16–17, he drops that topic almost immediately and picks it up again at 3:21. At 3:1 he introduces the question of the relationship between God and Israel ("What is the benefit that belongs to the Jew?"), but he very quickly drops that question in favor of a discussion of all human beings (Jews and Gentiles, v. 9). Only in chapters 9–11 does he return again to an extended response to the question about God and Israel.

Even the transitions that appear to be clear are more complex than is often recognized. Many analyses consider 5:1 as a transition to discussion of Christian life, and understandably so, since Paul says that "we" have been justified and have peace with God. Following closely on the end of chapter 4, one might expect Paul would take up some characteristics of Christian life. But instead, he returns in 5:6 to discuss the death of Jesus and then the Adam–Christ typology follows; discussion of life in Christ returns only in chapter 6.

Rhetorical strategies   Romans is also distinguished by its use of rhetoric. Most frequently discussed is Paul's use of elements of the diatribe, a pedagogical style associated with philosophical teachers who would craft imaginary dialogues that incorporated possible objections and responses to their teaching (Stowers 1981; 1992). Such rhetorical questions are a recognized hallmark of Romans (for example, 3:1; 6:1; 7:7; 11:1). Paul also includes dialogues such as the one in 9:14–23 in which the conversation partner dares to suggest that God is unjust, allowing Paul to draw on Scripture to refute the hypothetical accusation (see also 3:1–9).

In addition to these widely recognized features of the letter, Paul also employs in Romans what might be termed an argumentative feint (Gaventa 2008). In 3:10–18, he includes a collection of biblical citations that could be expected to lead to the typical wisdom motif of the punishment of the wicked and the vindication of the righteous, but in Romans there is no such distinction between the wicked and the righteous. All alike are found guilty (3:19). A similar strategy may be at work in 9:30–10:21, where he speaks consistently as if Israel were a single unit, all of whom "pursued the law" (9:31), "tripped over the stumbling stone" (9:32), had uninformed zeal for God (10:2), and failed to understand God's righteousness (10:3). In 11:1, then, his question whether God has rejected Israel comes as an entirely understandable conclusion; but instead of drawing that conclusion, Paul makes a sharp turn, insisting that Israel is divided at present and all Israel will be saved. This use of argumentative feint makes grasping Paul's ideas all the more difficult, especially when his subtle argumentative style may be misunderstood.

Romans also includes a number of smaller rhetorical features, most of which are difficult to render into idiomatic English. In 1:31, for example, there is a striking instance of alliteration in a string of four adjectives, each of which begins with an "a" sound in the Greek, and each of which is a negation (as in the "un" prefix in English): they are "without understanding, without faithfulness, without heart, without mercy" (*asynetous asynthetous astorgous aneēmonas*). Another effective example is the wordplay in 12:3, where the Greek verb *phronein* and related words appear four times: "do not be superminded [*hyperphronein*] above what one ought to be minded [*phronein*], but set your mind [*phronein*] on being sober-minded [*sōphronein*]" (trans. Jewett 2007, 736).

To a large extent, Paul's use of a complex (symphonic) structure and his multiple rhetorical strategies reflect the fact that he writes for the ear rather than the eye. He writes anticipating that his audience will be listening to Phoebe, not curled up in their armchairs reading his text. But the intricate structure and style of Romans may also reflect the delicate situation in which Paul finds himself as he endeavors to proclaim his apocalyptic interpretation of the gospel to people who have their own views already, who may be at odds with one another, and who know little about him (and who are wary because of what they do know).

Scriptural argumentation   More extensively than in Paul's other letters, Romans is explicitly engaged with Scripture. Already in 1:2, Paul writes that the gospel was promised "in holy scriptures" (a phrase he uses nowhere else). In the course of the letter, he quotes from Scripture some fifty-one times (Koch 1986, 21–24). And at some points these quotations are extensive, as at 3:10–18; 9:25–29; 15:9–12. In addition, Romans contains Paul's most expanded discussions of central figures from Israel's history known through Scripture, including Abraham in 4:1–25 and Abraham's offspring in 9:7–13. What exactly to make of this feature of Romans has been intensely debated. Does the forceful engagement with Scripture here have implications for identifying the ethnic composition of Paul's audience? Does it reflect Paul's own searching of Scripture to understand the situation of Israel (Grieb 2002, 92)? How are intertextual echoes at work in addition to the explicit quotation of Scripture (Hays 1989)? Is Paul's hermeneutic influenced especially by his reading of Torah (Watson 2004) or perhaps by his sense of identifying with Isaiah (Wagner 2002)? These are all seriously contested questions (see chapter 10 of this volume), but on any reading of Romans, Scripture plays an important role.

Israel and the Gentiles

Yet another distinctive feature of Romans is the way in which Paul makes reference to both Jews and Gentiles. In 1:16 he writes that salvation is for all, "the Jew first and also the Greek" (the Greek language has no way to refer to a single or "one" Gentile, so "Greek" in this case means an individual who is not a Jew). Similarly, in 2:9–10 Paul observes that God's judgment and God's reward fall on the "Jew first and also the Greek." Chapter 3, verse 9 concludes that all, "Jews and Greeks," are under the power of sin; 10:12 similarly observes that "there is no distinction between Jew and Greek"; and in 15:7–13 Jews and Gentiles are depicted together in praise of God. As noted earlier, one of the recurring threads in the letter is Paul's reference to "all" human beings, whether it is the "all" who died as a result of Adam's transgression or the "all" who receive God's mercy. That does not mean, however, that Paul thinks of humanity as some overcooked stew in which all the ingredients taste the same; the letter recognizes distinct histories of Jews and Gentiles.

Paul's concern with Jews comes to expression throughout the letter, as has been emphasized in recent years (for example, Grieb 2002; Wright 2002). But it is important to attend to what Paul says and does not say about Jews. To begin with, Jesus Christ is the offspring of David; that is, he is himself a Jew (1:3; 9:5). Abraham is the recipient of God's promise, but Paul presents Abraham less as the founding father of Israel than as the uncircumcised recipient of God's unconditional promise (4:1–25). When Paul takes up the children of Abraham in 9:6b–13, the emphasis at every point lies on God's initiative rather than on Israel's response or Israel's character. Nothing suggests that Isaac or Jacob behaved in a way that warranted God's selection or continued favor. Even the fact of Israel's division into the remnant and the "rest" (11:1–10) does not mean that some have been faithful of their own volition, but that God has left a remnant through God's own gracious choosing (11:5). It is God whose promise and calling have no end, not Israel's grasp of that promise and calling. In other words, Israel belongs to God, not God to Israel. And it is perhaps not incidental that Paul never uses the expression "the God of Israel" (Gaventa 2010, 256).

Closely related to Paul's comments about Israel is what he has to say about the Mosaic law, and this too has been the locus of extended debate (Koperski 2001; Westerholm 2004). In chapter 2, Paul undermines the notion that keeping the law is a distinguishing feature of Jewish life; he does so by observing that some who do not "naturally" have the law (i.e., some Gentiles) nevertheless keep the law, and some who do receive the law and even boast in it, nevertheless do not keep it (i.e., some Jews). A little later, several comments about the law serve to cast it in a limited and sometimes a negative light. Initially, Paul claims that the law functions to bring knowledge of sin (3:19–20), that works of the law do not produce rectification for human beings (3:27–31). Here Paul insists that he is actually upholding the law, but later he reiterates that sin is not counted outside the law (5:13, an apparent restatement of 3:19–20); that the law's arrival increased transgression (5:20); that "you" no longer live under the power of the law, since sin no longer rules (6:14); even that "you" have died to the law's reign (7:1–4). Paul seems to slip these comments into the discourse, leading up to the inevitable question whether Paul himself is equating the law with sin (7:7) His response is an emphatic "no": the law is not sin, but sin's power is so great that it can take advantage even of the "holy" law. It is only by the power of the "spirit of life in Christ Jesus" that the law can free human beings from the law that has been taken captive by sin and death (8:2; Martyn 2003; Meyer 2004, 57–77). This argument may help to explain what Paul writes later in 9:31 and 10:4. Israel could not achieve its goal of fulfilling the law because of sin's pernicious influence, and Christ is the *telos* of the law; that is, the one who fulfills the law by rescuing humankind from its enslavement to sin and death.

Just as one strand in recent scholarship has emphasized the discussion of Israel in Romans, another has emphasized the letter's attention to Gentiles, even contending that Paul understands the scope of the gospel to be restricted to Gentiles, since Jews already are related to God by the covenant (Gaston 1987; Gager 2000). Even if that extreme position is not persuasive, it is important to take into account what Paul does say about Gentiles in this letter. As has been noted earlier, in 1:18–32 Paul reinforces traditional Jewish stereotypes about Gentiles, only to undermine them in chapter 2. He implicitly includes Gentiles in the promises of Abraham by arguing that Abraham was the father of believers both uncircumcised and circumcised (4:11–12). Along the same lines, he later describes the Gentiles as having achieved righteousness by faith even though they were not seeking it (9:30). By virtue of God's intervention, Gentiles even play a role – a completely unexpected role – in the ultimate salvation of Israel (11:25). Because of Christ, Gentiles and Jews join together in praise of God (15:7–13). Emphasizing either Israel's story alone or the salvation of Gentiles alone distorts Paul's insistence that God's saving action is for all humanity.

Sin as a controlling power

Another of the distinguishing features of Romans is its extended and complex discussion of sin and death (Gaventa 2007, 113–136). In the letters of Paul, *hamartia* (sin) and related terms occur eighty-one times, sixty of which are in Romans. This in itself is an impressive figure, but even more revealing than the word count is the way in which Paul's statements about sin intensify as the letter progresses. Although the word does not appear until 3:9, in 1:18–32 Paul introduces the concept when he writes of human refusal to acknowledge God as God. And he may already have sin's power in mind when he three times asserts that God "handed them over" (1:24, 26, 28). The conclusion of 3:9, that all are under sin, would seem to anticipate the conclusions in 3:21–31 as a solution: God's action in Jesus Christ brings rectification for all who are incorporated in Jesus, so that sin is now defeated and might be expected to disappear from the letter. Yet sin returns again, and more forcefully still, in 5:12–21, where the power of sin is coupled with that of death. Here assertions are made that sin extended to the whole of humankind as a result of Adam's transgression. Again, it seems that the solution has been found in the reign of sin and grace, and it seems reasonable to expect that Paul has finished with his discussion of sin. But in chapter 6, sin returns once more, as Paul addresses the possible concern that his emphasis on grace results in immorality; those who have been "baptized into Christ Jesus" (6:3) are dead to sin's enslavement and are now slaves of righteousness (6:18). The most dramatic discussion is yet to come, however, as in 7:7–25 Paul contends that sin not only captured all of humanity but made use of God's own good and holy law in order to produce disobedience (Meyer 2004, 57–77).

Especially in chapters 5–7, Paul pairs sin and its partner death with active verbs: sin "entered" (5:12), death "spread" (5:12), death "ruled" (5:14, 17; 6:9), sin "increased" (5:20), sin "ruled" (5:21; 6:12, 14), sin "seized an opportunity" (7:8, 11), sin "produced" (7:8), sin "sprang to life" (7:9), sin "deceived" and "killed" me (7:11), sin "lives in me" (7:17, 20). This may appear to be nothing more than vivid imagery intended to enliven Paul's prose, unless it is read in the context of other vocabulary of conflict that appears with some frequency in the letter. To cite only a few examples: Paul addresses the Roman congregations as "weapons" of rectification, former weapons of wrong (6:13; see also 13:12); there are "enemies" here in need of "reconciliation" and "peace" (5:1–11). At the end of chapter 8, as Paul lists things that might endeavor to separate "us" from Christ's love, he includes "persecution" and the "sword," and in 16:20 he assures the Romans that "God will crush Satan" and soon. Taken together, this range of language and texts suggests that sin is, for Paul, not simply a misdeed or an unfortunate predisposition to act against society's norms, but a power that actually enslaves humanity and whose defeat is at the heart of God's action in Jesus Christ.

God's saving power in Jesus Christ and the cosmic horizon of Romans

Pervading these other distinguishing features of Romans is Paul's preoccupation with God. For Paul, language about God is not merely decorative, a discourse employed rhetorically to underscore his real point, whether that point might be construed as ethical, social, or political. From the beginning of the letter to the end, God is the central figure. It is God's gospel Paul is called to deliver concerning God's own son, Jesus Christ (1:1). That gospel is God's own saving power, making right all that has gone wrong, and God's wrath that reveals what has gone wrong (1:18). This is the same God who made promises to Abraham (4:1–25) and who now, in Jesus Christ, rescues humanity from its enslavement to sin (5:12–21). That rescue includes Israel, the people whom God called into being (9:6b–13) and for whom God intends only mercy (11:26, 32).

The scope of God's action is cosmic. By way of correcting an earlier preoccupation with God's relationship to the individual, scholars in recent decades have emphasized the corporate character of Paul's understanding of the gospel. God is acting for Israel and the Gentiles, for "all" as the letter repeatedly insists (for example, 1:16; 3:22; 5:18; 11:32). Yet, in Romans, God's grasp extends even beyond the boundary of the human community, as chapter 8, verses 18–23 include all of creation within God's impending redemption.

Reinforcing the letter's preoccupation with God is the striking use of the language of doxology and thanksgiving. It is the human refusal to give God glory that generates humanity's captivity to sin (1:18–25), and human mouths that refuse to acknowledge God are shut as a result of the law's judgment (3:10–20). Abraham alone is said to have given glory to God (4:20), anticipating the adopted children in 8:15 who cry out to God with the help of the Spirit. The communities in Rome are urged to respect one another's practices, not simply for unity for its own sake, but so that together they will praise God (15:6). This point is reinforced in 15:7–13, with repeated statements about praising God. It is not surprising, then, that Paul punctuates the letter with the language of blessing and praise, as he invites the Roman congregations to join in the Amen (1:25; 6:17; 7:25; 9:5; 11:36; 15:33; 16:20; cf. Gaventa 2008).

Epilogue

What influence Romans may have had on its initial audience, what the impact may have been when Phoebe read it to gathered congregations in Rome, we can never know. Here the silence of the book of Acts is intriguing; had Luke known of a letter to Rome and its warm reception (as he does know of other letters, such as Acts 9:2; 15:20, 23, 30; 22:5; 23:25, 33), it seems entirely likely that he would have referred to it. Even the fact that the letter was preserved does not mean that the Roman congregations were the ones who kept it, since a copy of it could have been retained by Paul's co-workers. Yet however limited its influence may have been in the first century, its impact on subsequent generations is beyond calculating. Simply to list a few of the major interpreters of Romans – Chrysostom, Augustine, Aquinas, Luther, Calvin, Wesley, Barth – is at the same time to list some significant developments in Christian thought (Westerholm 2004; Greenman and Larsen 2005). Current theological disputes about justification by faith are inevitably also arguments about Romans. Discussions about the church's relationship to Israel return time and again to Romans. Nor is interpretation of Romans confined to ecclesial circles; in European philosophical circles, figures such as Badiou (2003) and Agamben (2005) find in Paul's letter a vital conversation partner for their own engagement with questions of history and universalism. In this venue and a host of others, the letter delivered by Phoebe makes its way.

Note

1   Translations of biblical texts are my own.

References

Agamben, Giorgio. 2005. *The Time that Remains: A Commentary on the Letter to the Romans.* Stanford: Stanford University Press.

Badiou, Alain. 2003. *Saint Paul: The Foundation of Universalism.* Stanford: Stanford University Press.

Barclay, John M. G. 2001. 'Do We Undermine the Law?' A Study of Romans 14.1–15.6. Pages 287–308 in *Paul and the Mosaic Law.* Edited by James D. G. Dunn. Grand Rapids: Eerdmans.

Donfried, Karl P., editor. 1991. *The Romans Debate.* Revised and expanded edition. Peabody, Mass.: Hendrickson.

Downs, David J. 2008. *The Offering of the Gentiles: Paul's Collection for Jerusalem in its Chronological, Cultural, and Cultic Contexts.* Tübingen: Mohr Siebeck.

Epp, Eldon Jay. 2005. *Junia: The First Woman Apostle.* Minneapolis: Fortress.

Gager, John G. 2000. *Reinventing Paul.* Oxford: Oxford University Press.

Gaston, Lloyd. 1987. *Paul and the Torah.* Vancouver: University of British Columbia.

Gaventa, Beverly Roberts. 2007. *Our Mother Saint Paul*. Louisville: Westminster John Knox.

Gaventa, Beverly Roberts. 2008. From Toxic Speech to the Redemption of Doxology in Paul's Letter to the Romans. Pages 392–408 in *The Word Leaps the Gap: Essays on Scripture and Theology in Honor of Richard B. Hays*. Edited by J. Ross Wagner, C. Kavin Rowe, and A. Katherine Grieb. Grand Rapids: Eerdmans.

Gaventa, Beverly Roberts. 2009. "To Preach the Gospel": Romans 1,15 and the Purposes of Romans. Pages 179–195 in *The Letter to the Romans*. Edited by Udo Schnelle. Leuven: Peeters.

Gaventa, Beverly Roberts. 2010. On the Calling-into-being of Israel: Romans 9:6–29. Pages 255–270 in *Between Gospel and Election: Explorations in the Interpretation of Romans 9–11*. Edited by Florian Wilk and J. Ross Wagner. Tübingen: Mohr Siebeck.

Greenman, Jeffrey P., and Timothy Larsen, editors. 2005. *Reading Romans through the Centuries: From the Early Church to Karl Barth*. Grand Rapids: Brazos.

Grieb, A. Katherine. 2002. *The Story of Romans: A Narrative Defense of God's Righteousness*. Louisville: Westminster John Knox.

Hays, Richard B. 1989. *Echoes of Scripture in the Letters of Paul*. New Haven: Yale University Press.

Jervell, Jacob. 1991. The Letter to Jerusalem. Pages 53–64 in *The Romans Debate*. Edited by Karl P. Donfried. Revised and expanded edition. Peabody, Mass.: Hendrickson.

Jewett, Robert. 2007. *Romans: A Commentary*. Minneapolis: Fortress.

Koch, Dietrich-Alex. 1986. *Die Schrift als Zeuge des Evangeliums: Untersuchungen zur Verwendung und zum Verständnis der Schrift*. Tübingen: J. C. B. Mohr (Paul Siebeck).

Koperski, Veronica. 2001. *What Are They Saying about Paul and the Law?* New York: Paulist.

Lampe, Peter. 2003. *From Paul to Valentinus: Christians at Rome in the First Two Centuries*. Minneapolis: Fortress.

Manson, T. W. 1991. St. Paul's Letter to the Romans – and Others. Pages 3–15 in *The Romans Debate*. Edited by Karl P. Donfried. Revised and expanded edition. Peabody, Mass.: Hendrickson.

Martyn, J. Louis. 1997. *Galatians*. New York: Doubleday.

Martyn, J. Louis. 2003. *Nomos* Plus Genitive Noun in Paul: The History of God's Law. Pages 575–587 in *Early Christianity and Classical Culture: Comparative Studies in Honor of Abraham J. Malherbe*. Edited by John T. Fitzgerald, Thomas H. Olbricht, and L. Michael White. Leiden: Brill.

Meyer, Paul W. 2004. *The Word in this World: Essays in New Testament Exegesis and Theology*. Louisville: Westminster John Knox.

Stowers, Stanley Kent. 1981. *The Diatribe and Paul's Letter to the Romans*. Chico, Calif.: Scholars.

Stowers, Stanley Kent. 1992. Diatribe. Pages 190–193 in *Anchor Bible Dictionary*, Volume 2. Edited by David Noel Freedman. New York: Doubleday.

Tobin, Thomas H. 2004. *Paul's Rhetoric in its Contexts: The Argument of Romans*. Peabody, Mass.: Hendrickson.

Wagner, J. Ross. 2002. *Heralds of the Good News: Isaiah and Paul "in Concert" in the Letter to the Romans*. Leiden: Brill.

Watson, Francis. 2004. *Paul and the Hermeneutics of Faith*. London: T. & T. Clark.

Watson, Francis. 2007. *Paul, Judaism, and the Gentiles: Beyond the New Perspective*. Revised and expanded edition. Grand Rapids: Eerdmans.

Westerholm, Stephen. 2004. *Perspectives Old and New on Paul: The "Lutheran" Paul and his Critics*. Grand Rapids: Eerdmans.

Wright, N. T. 2002. The Letter to the Romans. Pages 393–770 in *The New Interpreter's Bible*, Volume 10. Edited by Leander E. Keck. Nashville: Abingdon.

CHAPTER 7
The Pastoral Epistles

I. Howard Marshall

It is right and proper that a volume dealing comprehensively with Paul should include a section on the Pastoral epistles, the set of three letters known conveniently by this title since the eighteenth century. They form a group even if only in that, unlike the other letters in the Pauline corpus, they are addressed from Paul to two of his colleagues who had pastoral oversight and evangelistic roles in congregations founded during the Pauline mission, and they deal mostly with what these colleagues needed to know and do (unlike the letter to Philemon, who was the local leader of a house church but not one of Paul's missionary colleagues). If we did not have this term to enable us to refer easily to this set of letters, we should have to coin another, but this one is suitable enough, even though the letters deal with more than narrowly pastoral matters and it is disputable whether they were consciously composed as a self-contained, unified trio; recent scholarship explores and emphasizes their individuality (Towner 2006).

Such a set of letters might be thought to be comparatively uninteresting both historically and theologically alongside the major writings of Paul. This impression can be quickly dispelled by dipping into the history of their influence and interpretation from the earliest times until now; this quest is now opened up for all of us thanks to an exciting and informative survey from Chrysostom through Cotton Mather to Billy Graham, Graham Greene, and Wang Ping (Twomey 2009).

Up to the nineteenth century, the letters were regarded as what they prima facie appear to be, compositions of Paul himself addressed to his co-workers. This understanding continues to be defended by many scholars, although probably a larger number hold that they are later compositions by a writer (or perhaps more than one writer) anxious to revivify the legacy of Paul for a later generation or, more loosely, to invoke the authority of Paul for what he thought needed to be said at that time. This

The Blackwell Companion to Paul, First Edition. Edited by Stephen Westerholm.
© 2011 Blackwell Publishing Ltd. Published 2011 by Blackwell Publishing Ltd.

means that the possible time-range within which the letters have been dated extends to nearly a century, from a setting in Paul's Aegean mission period, on the one hand, to the mid-second century (if 1 Tim 6:20 is an attack on Marcion), on the other. However, a fairly firm *terminus ante quem* is set for 1 Timothy by an informal citation in Polycarp's *Epistle to the Philippians* 4.1 (probably no later than 135 CE), and Marcion is said to have *excluded* the Pastorals from his canon (rather than not knowing of their existence). Either way, the letters are part of Paul's correspondence or form part of his legacy.

At one end of the spectrum, traditional Roman Catholic scholarship has tended to view the letters as the most mature and definitive statement of Pauline teaching on ministry in the church and to welcome them as examples of early catholicism, providing a biblical basis for the church's organized, hierarchical ministry and setting trajectories that continued to develop thereafter. At the other end of the spectrum, some Protestants see in them evidence of dependence upon fossilized tradition and prefer to make Paul's earlier writings normative, with their more charismatic understanding of congregational meetings and ministry. This latter type of approach may take a more radical form in which the letters are regarded as imposing a rigid suppression of women in the meeting, coupled with a general subordination of all believers to authority both inside and outside the church (Merz 2006). Simultaneously, the church is thought to have succumbed to living in conformity with the virtues and patterns of secular Greco-Roman society; its outlook has been dubbed "bourgeois," although this word means "conventionally middle class"; "humdrum, unimaginative"; "selfishly materialistic"; "upholding the interests of the capitalist class" (*Concise Oxford Dictionary*, 8th edition) and is patently anachronistic if applied to ancient ideologies.

One line of study proposes that the effect of the Pastorals was to influence the way in which the earlier Pauline letters are read and understood. They do not replace the earlier letters, but they impose a fresh interpretation upon them, qualifying what they say; on this understanding, the effect is achieved by the author falsely and deceptively claiming to be Paul himself. It is arguable that later writings will have this effect on readers anyhow, but for some scholars the process was one intended by the pseudonymous author, who makes frequent allusions to the earlier letters and thus offers a commentary upon them (Richards 2002; Merz 2006). Certainly pseudonymity is not necessary for this to happen. Paul himself was capable of correcting false impressions picked up from his earlier writings (cf. 1 Cor 5:9–11). It is easy to see that this practice of self-correction might be imitated by later writers who wrote in the name of Paul in an attempt to modify things that he had previously said. Either way, the effect of the later writings could be to affect readers' interpretation of the earlier statements.

This raises the general question of how intertextualism (the mutual relationships of texts and their influence upon one another) functions. One school of interpretation argues that the Pastorals were intended to teach the subordination of slaves to their masters (cf. 1 Tim 6:1–2; Tit 2:9–10), thus preventing readers of Philemon from concluding that masters and slaves are equals (inasmuch as they are said to be brothers "both in the flesh and in the Lord" [Phlm 16]). Similarly, the teaching about women being silent in meetings and finding their Christian vocation in wifely submission and domesticity (for example, 1 Tim 2:11–15; Tit 2:3–5) could be intended to countermand the apparent freedom granted to women to exercise ministry in the earlier Pauline letters. The Pastorals would then be an example of taming the more egalitarian pattern of relationships found in the earlier Paul. Certainly, the Pastorals were later used to give backing for a static institutionalization of the church and a conservative pattern of social behavior.

But it is erroneous to assume that later writings necessarily "correct" earlier ones (or false readings of them). It may well be that the statements in Paul that establish the new relationships to one another enjoyed by those in Christ (for example, Gal 3:28) are fundamental. Any later qualifications of them are then to be seen as local and temporary requirements necessitated by the nature of life in the real world. The Pauline fundamental texts are pointers to life as it should be in Christ, the implications of which were not as yet fully realized. Paul himself did not take the step of pressing for the freeing of all slaves, although he was very probably insinuating that this was how Philemon should treat Onesimus. At the same time, his teaching could be interpreted as encouraging slaves and wives to claim liberties for themselves that the world was not yet ready to recognize, especially when their masters and husbands were not Christians. We should not condemn early Christians who did not reach this insight; even later Christians did not realize that slavery is fundamentally inconsistent with new life in Christ until the nineteenth century, and there are still some who do not recognize the rights of women and wives in the congregation and in marriage. We also need to recognize that radical behavior on the part of slaves and women would bring the gospel into disrepute, and that regulatory teaching was needed. Add to this mixture the high probability that some of the Christian women in Ephesus were involved in the dubious teaching that was rampant in the church, and it is not difficult to see that the voice of moderation was needed. It may be that the author of the Pastorals could not see clearly beyond the immediate horizon, but that was only natural. The dangers in the long term may appear more obvious to us only with hindsight.

The Letters as They Stand

We shall commence by reading the letters as they stand, since this is how they were meant to be read whether or not Paul himself wrote them. They are addressed to people known from Paul's other writings. Titus is a junior colleague of Paul in Galatians 2:1, 3; in 2 Corinthians he is named as the bearer of messages from Paul to the congregation during a delicate situation. In the letter to him, he is in Crete with a mandate from Paul to oversee the various congregations, appointing local leaders in them and giving teaching that will help to thwart the efforts of opponents to undermine the Pauline mission. He thus has a position to which he is apparently appointed by Paul rather than by anybody else (such as by the popular choice of the congregations), although his appointment of local leaders does raise questions about the nature and continuance of his supervisory role in the long term.

Timothy is also known from Paul's other letters (and Acts) as a missionary companion of Paul and a messenger engaged in maintaining contacts with congregations founded by Paul. In 1 Timothy, he is encouraged to continue an assignment on behalf of Paul in Ephesus, and, like Titus, his role includes the oversight of congregations that already have some forms of local leadership and pastoral care (including some kind of support for widows), the refutation of opponents of Paul, and the teaching of healthy doctrine that edifies the congregations.

These broad concerns reappear in 2 Timothy, where the main concern is again the need for sound teaching over against empty speculations and continuing immorality. But here the major focus is more on the kind of person that Timothy himself needs to be if he is to be effective in his own ministry to the congregations, showing courage and perseverance in standing up to the pressures of his task. The letter closes with an urgent summons to visit Paul in his prison where he faces another stage in his trial. Opinions differ whether Paul gives the impression that he is at the imminent end of his life and mission or expects to be released for further service.

These situations, and the instructions and mandates given in them, are certainly historically appropriate to the kind of mission reflected in Paul's earlier letters and Luke's account in Acts. The existence of strong opposition, particularly from Jewish Christians (and probably from the synagogues that had lost some of their members), and the infection of congregations with immorality of the kinds associated with Hellenistic Greco-Roman society are well documented. Equally clear is the way in which Paul exercised continuing pastoral care and oversight over young congregations, especially by means of traveling colleagues who conveyed his letters. In these three respects, then, the content of the Pastoral epistles seems historically appropriate in a Pauline context.

(1) A good deal of the content of the letters is doubtless material that must have been familiar to the named recipients as close companions of Paul over several years. (Ignatius's letter to the congregational leader Polycarp shows precisely the same phenomenon of reiterating material with which the recipient must already have been familiar.) It can also be taken for granted that Paul expected the letters to be read to the congregations and local leaders with whom Titus and Timothy were associated. It has been thought strange that the Paul whose own earlier correspondence is to congregations rather than to individuals within them or to their "superintendents" should so change his ecclesiology and outlook that he wrote to the leaders instead of directing himself to the whole congregation and making it responsible for its own affairs. But this objection is an argument from silence. Even if no earlier communications with his fellow missionaries have survived (unless fragmentarily in the material in the Pastorals), he must have instructed them in some way on their teaching and duties.

(2) What was the nature of the opposition that Paul was facing? The main opposition in his earlier letters is commonly referred to as "Judaizing," that is, forcing Jewish practices, including circumcision, on Gentile Christian believers, whether as a necessity for their salvation or as a requirement for table fellowship with Jewish believers (who themselves may have been under pressure from the synagogues). There was also denigration of Paul and questioning of his authority. Immoral practices may have been given plausible theological backing (as in the slogans that are cited in 1 Cor 6:12–13).

The problems faced in the Pastorals were not dissimilar. There are references to "the circumcision" and to "genealogies" in Titus 1:10 and 3:9, which suggest a Jewish origin in allegorical teaching but may also remind us of the later speculative naming of chains of aeons in Gnosticism. There are similar references to misuse of the law and to genealogies in 1 Timothy 1:4, 7, but also to ascetic practices (4:3) and to so-called "knowledge" (6:20–21). Some think that all this points to second-century Gnosticism, but a Jewish background seems more likely. Second Timothy refers more generally to nominal faith that was not accompanied by a Christian lifestyle, as well as to specific people who had turned against Paul personally and to teachers claiming that the resurrection had already taken place (2 Tim 2:18 – possibly a misinterpretation of Pauline teaching). Whether there was any untoward charismatic activity (Pietersen 2004) is, in my view, dubious. The tone of the rejection of such views is generally very strong (it is mitigated in 2 Tim 2:25–26), but we know that Paul could respond very bitterly to opponents (Gal 1:8–9; Phil 3:2; Rom 16:17–19).

(3) The Pauline congregations show a combination of ministries undertaken by any person inspired and empowered by the Spirit to do so, and oversight and leadership by persons spiritually equipped for the task (including some of the earliest converts). Respect and submission to such leadership were expected; inevitably, recognized positions and designations for those who performed different duties developed over time (1 Cor 12, 14; 16:15–18; Phil 1:1; 1 Thess 5:12–13). The model of eldership in the synagogue had some influence, and other terms, such as overseer and minister (servant), came into use. The earliest post-New Testament documents testify to the variety of ways in which this development was implemented. Alongside these local leaders were those exercising an itinerant missionary calling that included continuing oversight over the new congregations. There could be tensions, and some delicate diplomacy was needed.

This situation is envisaged as continuing in the Pastorals. Titus is active in Crete and Dalmatia on behalf of Paul and with authority from him. Similarly, Timothy is in charge of the congregation(s) in Ephesus. Paul himself is the ultimate teaching authority for the congregations in his mission field; for his part, he invokes the authority of "trustworthy statements" and of Scripture. The gospel is likened to a specific "deposit" (1 Tim 6:20; 2 Tim 1:14) to be committed to Christian teachers who, in turn, are to preserve it undamaged (as a banker is responsible for safe-deposits that the owners expect to get back in their original condition). The stress on the need for a trustworthy leadership, accepted by the congregations and faithful to Paul, is readily comprehensible in the light of the constraints of age and imprisonment upon him.

In the light of these general background considerations, we can now read through the three letters individually as they would appear to somebody who accepts them as authentic writings of Paul addressed to his missionary colleagues but intended to be shared with their congregations.

Titus

The letter to Titus stands apart from those to Timothy by reason of its different setting. It presumes a colleague of Paul continuing the work of sustaining congregations that have been planted in a number of towns. The congregations were the fruit of evangelism, an activity that presumably continued (cf. 2 Tim 4:5). The four main elements in the instruction to Titus are as follows:

(1) The need to appoint local congregational leaders. The task of these "elders" is one of oversight, and therefore the designation "overseer" is also in use. The profile given to these appointees includes reference to their good character, their competence to exercise oversight, and their knowledge of, and ability to give, sound, health-giving teaching for the good of the congregation (Tit 1:5–9).

(2) The need to restrain people who are giving teaching contrary to that of Paul and doing so for the sake of personal gain. The effect of their activities is to cause division and to waste time in idle speculations (1:10–16; 3:9–11).

(3) The need to remind believers of the doctrinal basis for their new lifestyle. This is done twice in statements that back up the practical instructions that they follow (2:11–14; 3:3–7) and also implicitly in the self-description of Paul as a missionary at the beginning of the letter (1:1–4). The Pauline gospel came to a world where people were living dissolute and sensual lives of disobedience to God. God manifested his grace to the world in the coming of Jesus Christ, who died to redeem people from their sin and poured out the Holy Spirit upon them to transform their lives; now they live as the people of God and look forward to the end of the present evil age when Christ will again be manifested. This language is very much that of Pauline theology with its stress on salvation and justification by faith (probably deliberately mentioned to contrast with the teaching of the circumcision party). The wording is shaped to emphasize that the purpose of God is not merely to confer benefits upon the recipients of salvation but to make them a people who are equipped to live lives of such goodness and graciousness that they will commend their God to the world.

(4) The need to encourage the Christian lifestyle that is derived from the gospel itself (2:1–10, 15–3:2, 8). It is essentially expressed in self-control that overcomes licentious living, restraint that leads to submission to the patterns of an orderly society, and the eager performing of good works that add luster to the preaching of the gospel. There is a particular stress on living in conformity with the surrounding society; that is to say, in conformity with its ideal standards of behavior as opposed to the low level of practice. Congregational life is meant to be a microcosm of the kind of life in the kingdom of God that is God's will for society as a whole. The letter has in mind a people converted from a godless way of life and still entangled in its sinful ways.

All this is meant to be heard by the congregations and their nascent leadership. The pattern of life to be embodied by Titus himself as a teacher and as an exemplary believer (2:1, 7–8) is appropriate for all leaders and for believers generally, although there are also particular qualities needed for effective leadership. It is assumed that leadership will be in the hands of men who already have wives and families, but it is not an automatic position for all older people, and the instruction that Titus is to be respected probably implies his comparative youthfulness (Tit 2:15 in the light of 1 Tim 4:12).

1 Timothy

At first sight, 1 Timothy may look like a revised and expanded version of Titus, and it has been seen as a later composition that is based on material from Titus and 2 Timothy (Herzer 2008). Like Titus, it is a set of instructions from Paul for a missionary with whom Paul has a father–son relationship; in modern idiom, Paul is Timothy's line-manager rather than an equal colleague. The instruction or mandate is couched as a repetition of orders previously given; it is wider than the immediate command in 1:3–4.

The letter begins with the same kind of problem as in Titus: the presence in the congregation in Ephesus of persons teaching doctrines other than those of Paul, and turning the activities of believers into wordy and futile debates rather than good works and other expressions of faith. Closely tied in with this was teaching about the Mosaic law, which was presumably expounded and applied in ways that did not fit in with Paul's teaching that the law finds its goal in Christ (though 1 Timothy does not tackle the problem on that level of understanding). Over against this activity, Paul makes a number of related moves.

First, he stresses the need for the church to put love, faith, and the maintenance of a good conscience in the premier position. He is concerned about believers being diverted from their main interest by what is actually empty nonsense. The proper use of the law is not to place burdens upon righteous people but to lay down the norms by which evil-doers can be recognized for what they are (1 Tim 1:3–11).

Second, Paul places his own authority over against that of his opponents. This authority is rooted in his commission from Jesus Christ (just as in Galatians). He develops the paradox of his calling despite his previous sinful past, seen especially in his persecution of believers. He goes to the heart of his gospel of salvation by grace through faith (1:1–17). Some interpreters think that Paul is placed on such a pedestal here that he becomes part of the gospel himself as the pattern convert and key person through whom God has revealed his mysteries and passed them on to the Gentiles.

Third, he gives a personal reassurance to Timothy regarding the latter's vocation and reinforces it by referring to believers who have in some way apostatized (1:18–20).

From this mixture of mandate, encouragement, and instruction, Paul turns to the main body of what the believers must do. The first of two major sections (2:1–3:13) is addressed from Paul directly to the congregation. The priority in position and importance is the need for prayer that embraces all people as potential recipients of salvation and particularly rulers as the upholders of the peaceful conditions in which believers may practice their faith (2:1–7). "Everyone" has the Gentiles primarily in view, and implies that not all accepted the obligation to go to them as well as to the Jews; but nothing in the context suggests that Christ died for a limited group who are predestined for salvation rather than for all people in general. The mission and the prayer are based on the act of Christ as mediator and the calling of Paul to evangelize specifically the Gentiles. (Claims that Paul is envisaged here as the only such missionary are unwarranted; these are instructions for Paul's mission field; cf. 2 Cor 10:12–18.)

This call to prayer is then brought down to earth with instructions to avoid behavior that renders prayer ineffective: disputatiousness on the part of the men and immodest and expensive clothing and coiffure on the part of the women (1 Tim 2:8–15). The reference is primarily to conduct in congregational meetings, but it is manifestly not restricted to this context. An associated aspect of unseemly conduct by women is their teaching and assuming a kind of authority over men that conflicted with the role of women in relation to their husbands or guardians. There was evidently a tendency among some women to avoid the obligations of bearing and caring for children, a tendency that must have had some links with the forbidding of marriage and the sexual libertarianism mentioned later; a background has been seen in the pursuit by rich Roman wives of the same material and sexual freedom claimed and exercised by men.

The need for people to exercise oversight in the congregations leads to a more elaborate version of essentially the same listing of their desired qualities as we saw in Titus (1 Tim 3:1–13). But the setup envisaged here includes also deacons, who are to show the same qualities of Christian character and leadership potential. Their duties are not explained (this is not meant to be a job description), but a teaching activity is mentioned for the overseers and is implied for the deacons. There is also brief mention of "the women" (3:11), who are probably female deacons rather than deacons' wives.

Then comes a sort of conclusion (3:14–16) in which the point is made that these instructions are being given in writing in case Paul's hope of a face-to-face visit is not fulfilled. The remarkable statement that follows forms the center of the letter (3:15). The letter concerns how people are to conduct themselves in the house of God – the church – which in its turn is the foundation and pillar of the truth. The church is thus the means by which God's truth is sustained and made known. It is the temple inhabited by God; people are to behave appropriately in his presence. The thought that God presides over the church as his household is probably also present.

Parallel to this is the statement that there is a stunning mystery, a secret revealed by God, which lies at the root of the godliness that his people must show (3:16). The mystery is the person whose story is told in six cryptic statements: Christ appeared on earth in human form ("flesh"; so a divine, incarnate being is the subject); he was vindicated as such by the power of the Spirit (or in his spiritual existence); he was seen by angels (probably at his heavenly exaltation; cf. 1 Pet 3:18–22); he was proclaimed throughout the world, no doubt as Savior and Lord; hence he was the object of faith worldwide; and he was glorified in heaven. This is as profound and majestic a statement about Christ in his earthly and heavenly significance as anything elsewhere in the New Testament, and it brings out the transcendent truth that forms the basis for the comparatively mundane instructions about how to live in the church. This is the "mystery" that God's people must acknowledge (1 Tim 3:9) and that will inspire their devotion and service. Whoever penned this confession was no petty, uninspired, nitpicking ecclesiastical manipulator!

The letter now takes a fresh start with a second major section directed to Timothy and telling him what he is to do and how he is to instruct the congregation (4:1–6:21). There have already been comments about the opposition to Pauline teaching and practice. Now this point comes out into the open, as something against which God has forewarned his people. This particular form of diabolically inspired teaching leads to an asceticism that refuses marriage and imposes dietary restrictions. A brief theological refutation, based on the doctrine of creation, is provided as the basis for Timothy's response to the proponents, but this broadens out to an appeal for godly living (*eusebeia*) and an encouragement to him to be a good servant of Christ. It is not surprising that this brief section is often used as a basis for the charges at inductions of pastors. It gathers up points also made in Titus (1 Tim 4:1–16).

Paul then moves to specific matters that are Timothy's concern. There is brief comment on the need for appropriate relationships with different age and sex groups in the congregation (5:1–2). The problematic group of widows (possibly including older spinsters) is treated (5:3–16). Families must care properly for their dependents. The widows for their part must live godly lives and not live for worldly pleasures (wasting their substance in riotous living). There is already some church provision for destitute widows, and this must be administered in an orderly manner; younger widows may be tempted to take advantage of it to live in idleness and become nuisances, so they should be encouraged to remarry where possible.

Next, there are practical matters regarding the recompensing of elders for their work and the need to follow proper procedures when discipline is required; sandwiched in here is a brief comment on the medicinal use of alcohol that assumes that abstinence was a normal practice (5:17–25).

A brief instruction in the third person (i.e., teaching to be passed on by Timothy) is concerned with the danger of Christian slaves not respecting their masters (6:1–2); they should do service from which the latter will benefit (a surprising and significant form of words which would normally refer to what patrons would do for their dependents).

There then follows a complex interweaving of encouragement to Timothy to withstand those whose teaching is not in accord with Paul's warning against the deleterious effects of love of money rather than contentment with a sufficiency of provision, a further encouragement to Timothy which compares the commitment made by Timothy with that made by Christ, and a further summary of what to say to rich people regarding the use of their wealth in generous giving. A final charge warns Timothy against the dangers of false teaching (here dubbed "so-called knowledge") and reaffirms the need for him to preserve the legacy of sound teaching that he has received (6:3–19). Without any further personalia, the letter ends rather abruptly with a grace benediction (as in Tit and 2 Tim) whose plural form indicates that the letter was meant to be shared with the congregation.

This analysis of the letter indicates its somewhat unusual construction, showing that a mixture of different styles of composition is used and materials from different sources are being combined. First Timothy is thus essentially a context-specific version of the same kind of material as Titus.

2 Timothy

Second Timothy is in a different style, generally called "parenetic," in that it is written more in terms of friendship and personal encouragement with frequent appeal to past experience. It is written from a prison setting by a man who has already undergone a preliminary trial and whose future is uncertain. Much depends on Timothy, although there is mention of a significant number of other members of the Pauline circle. The letter anticipates what Paul would say directly to Timothy if the latter were able to visit him (just as the epistle to the Romans undoubtedly rehearses what Paul would say if and when he visited Rome; cf. 1 Tim 3:14–15). Although opposition to the missionaries and the gospel, both from within and from outside the church, is the constant background, the specific character of the opposition is hardly mentioned. Matters of congregational polity are not raised, although the need for good teachers is stressed.

The letter begins more like Paul's ecclesiastical letters with a prayer-report that encourages Timothy by the knowledge that he is the subject of prayer; what Paul actually says in his prayers can be worked out to some extent from what he says about his remembrance of Timothy's faith, the joy that this gives him, and the longing he has to see Timothy soon. Paul's pastoral concern soon takes over. He is worried over a propensity to timidity that could lead to Timothy's failing to stand up to difficult people in the congregation and to stand fast against the threat of persecution, suffering, and even martyrdom. Therefore, he reminds Timothy of the latter's gifting with the Spirit (associated with his commissioning as a missionary), of his own example as a prison inmate, and of the power of God. This power arises from God's gracious plan of salvation revealed through Christ and proclaimed by Paul. It is inconceivable that God will abandon his servants or let their work come to nothing. Hence Timothy can be confidently called to guard the gospel that has been entrusted to him in the power of the Spirit (2 Tim 1:3–14). We note in passing the common Pauline (and general New Testament) paradox of believers being exhorted to do what the Spirit is doing in and through them (cf. Phil 2: 12–13). Parenthetically, Paul comments on the way in which some people have deserted him while others have been faithful to him; they serve as warnings and examples (2 Tim 1:15–18). He then gives careful instruction that, just as he is handing on the sacred treasure of the gospel to Timothy, so Timothy must also pass it on to other teachers; although some think that the thought is primarily of the next generation after Timothy, it is more likely that the provision is primarily for local leadership, as in Titus 1 and 1 Timothy 3 (2 Tim 2:1–2).

These themes now get further development. The mode of instruction resembles what we have in Proverbs: various themes get treated side by side without much logical connection between them and with some repetition as the author glides from one topic and mode of discourse to another and keeps returning to familiar themes. The main topic is the need for strength to cope with the workload, to stand up to opponents, and to bear suffering while remaining loyal to the calling. Proverbial-sounding illustrations are employed with renewed appeals to the example of Paul himself and of Christ; concern for the salvation of God's people remains the fundamental goal (2:3–13).

Then the focus returns to the need to avoid argumentative strife that leads people away from the gospel and can cause spiritual disaster. We learn almost casually that some are denying the future resurrection, a major element of Christian hope and incentive to endure suffering and martyrdom. Again, we have the paradox that God sustains his people faithfully, but they must keep themselves faithful to him. And, again, there is some very general counsel regarding godly behavior and loving pastoral care (2:14–26).

As in 1 Timothy 4, prophecy regarding the coming decadence in society becomes the basis for yet another focus on the need for sound teaching and godly living, following the example of Paul as he withstood attacks from his opponents, and based on the teaching of Scripture, which is the source of vital teaching on salvation and Christian living and ministry. This leads into a direct appeal to Timothy regarding his missionary role over against the rise of popularist avant-garde teachers who can only lead people astray. And, once again, appeal is made to the example of Paul and the need to fill the gap caused by his imprisonment and absence from active missionary work (3:1–4:8).

The letter finally turns to a mixture of personal news and requests, listing Paul's faithful helpers and his adversaries, and giving an update on his situation under trial as he evidently awaits a second hearing. Much of the personalia here and in Titus not only gives news but also contains implicit encouragement and warning by good and bad examples (as also in Rom 16 and Phil). The earlier general counsels to Timothy take on specific and personal color as we see concrete expressions of the suffering of Paul, the faithful group of followers who are active in the mission and need help and encouragement, the adversaries within the church who are subverting its message and its Christian behavior, the reminders of divine support already received and the certainty that it will continue, and the ultimate assurance of final salvation in God's heavenly kingdom. Perhaps for many of us (including myself, sitting in a comfortable, warm room in a free country), these themes may seem hackneyed with their constant repetition; but where Christians are persecuted for their faith, where living conditions are wretched and war and terrorism are rampant, and where the future looks unspeakably bleak, this letter comes startlingly to life and equips God's people for courage and hope in their continuing strife (4:9–22).

This letter, then, is hard to analyze in terms of a developing argument or story, but it picks up a half dozen key themes for the church and its workers in time of crisis and works over them again and again, casting fresh light upon them from many angles and rekindling hope, steadfastness, and love. The loose movement from one topic to another is not a sign of weakness; it was a regular feature of some ancient writing (see Ignatius, Polycarp). The themes are not peculiar to this letter but reflect a similar situation to that in Philippians with its juxtaposition of external attacks on the church and internal dissension (Aageson 2008). Whereas in Philippians, Paul addresses the congregation experiencing this situation, 2 Timothy contains the kind of things that Paul must have said to Timothy and Epaphroditus directly. The theology is obviously Pauline, though its formulation here is distinctive.

The Theology that Comes to Expression in the Letters

The *Christology* of the letters is characterized by the use of the term *epiphaneia*, which refers to the helpful manifestation of a deity. It is roughly equivalent to Paul's term *parou-*

sia, but whereas the latter refers only to the future manifestation of Christ, *epiphaneia* is used here also and distinctively of the past manifestation of God's grace in Christ and the gospel (cf. the two appearances in Heb 9:28). The term Savior is used both of God (1 Tim 1:1; 2:3; 4:10; Tit 1:3; 2:10; 3:4) and of Christ (2 Tim 1:10; Tit 1:4; 2:13[?]; 3:6). Arguably, the focus is on God as Savior through Christ, but the close juxtaposition of the references to both by the same term shows that the author places Christ very close to God; he is implicitly pre-existent (1 Tim 3:16; 2 Tim 1:9), and in one place he is probably given the designation of God (*theos*; Tit 2:13). The apparently strange absence of the title of Lord for Christ in Titus is due to the infrequency with which Christ appears in this letter at all (Tit 1:1, 4; 2:13–14; 3:6) and a preference for Savior. The language used for salvation and the death of Christ is Pauline, and the thoughts of union with Christ in dying and rising (2 Tim 2:11–12) and of God acting "in Christ" (2 Tim 1:1, 9; 2:1, 10) are present, although the full Pauline range of the latter phrase is missing. There is no indication of anything unPauline in this area, even though the terminology is different.

There is much less focus on the *Holy Spirit*, although the reality of his working in all believers is taught (2 Tim 1:7, 14; Tit 3:5–6). The charisma for leadership was conveyed to Timothy when he was commissioned by the laying on of hands. The nature of the *church* is that it is the house (temple) of God in which God is present (note the tension with his transcendence in 1 Tim 6:15–16) and served by his people, who add glory to his reputation by their good works.

Considerable attention is given to training in *Christian behavior*. The vices characteristic of unbelievers are listed (for example, 1 Tim 1:9–11; 2 Tim 3:2–5; cf. Tit 3:3) in a manner comparable with Romans 1:29–31 and 1 Corinthians 5:11; 6:9–10, and similar lists are used to describe the opponents in the congregation: their teaching is not morally edifying and fruitful (for example, 1 Tim 6:3–5). Christian character is described in similar lists (1 Tim 6:11; Tit 1:8; 2:2, etc.). The accent in the latter is placed on piety (*eusebeia*), especially in 1 Timothy (2:2; 4:7, 8, etc.), where the term refers to the kind of conduct associated with the fear of the Lord in Judaism but also found in Greek morality. Prominent also is the thought of seriousness and sobriety (*sōphrosynē* [1 Tim 2:9, 15]), a contrast to the frivolousness of the opposition to Paul and its failure to take moral teaching seriously, and there is a stress on orderly conduct in submission to the pattern of ancient society. This is a note that some modern commentators find distasteful because it appears to give women and slaves a lower status than men. But the author here is in line with ancient thinking with its dislike of disorderliness, and does not quite reach the tendency to brotherhood and sisterhood and the implications for mutuality that were beginning to surface elsewhere in Paul (or his followers; but see above on 1 Tim 6:1–2).

The Problems of the Pastorals

Difficulties with the traditional setting and authorship

The three letters make good sense in the prima facie situation of Paul and his colleagues at the close of his mission amid continuing internal dissension and attacks on his teaching and authority (cf. Gal; 1 and 2 Cor; Phil) and external pressures (cf. 1 Pet; Jas; Rev; Phil; Acts). Those who see reflected in the letters a shift from Pauline charismatic congregations responsible for their own growth and stability to a hierarchical institutionalism fail to do justice to the beginnings of local leadership evidenced in the earlier Pauline letters, to the roles of Paul and his colleagues in maintaining the network, and to the heightened threats internally and externally. The material is what it claims to be or it is a good piece of historical appropriateness. As with any other New Testament letters, the contents would be relevant at later times and can be interpreted for different situations. The time- and locality-bound nature of some of the contents can be recognized for what it is, especially when read as part of a Pauline corpus of letters, where the letters throw light upon one another. Nevertheless, this scenario is widely agreed to be problematic and other possibilities must be considered.

The problem is essentially that, despite all their individuality, these three letters do form a subgroup within the Pauline collection with some odd common characteristics. If good reasons can be found for these peculiarities, well and good. For example, if the letters belong to the last period in Paul's life, this might account for their different style and outlook. However, there are very marked differences from other writings which, if authentic, most probably come from this period (Phil; Eph; Col). And if the Pastorals were written over a longer period, beginning during the so-called third missionary journey, their oddities alongside the letters to congregations written at this time are much more difficult to account for.

Letters to co-workers and individuals could differ from those sent to congregations, particularly in the mandatory style of the former, which is wholly consistent with the *Sitz im Leben* of letters to subordinate colleagues, but this will not cover many of the differences. The individuality of the Pastoral epistles is apparent in matters of both language and content.

(1)   The language is undeniably different. The vocabulary shows a rather different choice of words from the main Pauline collection of seven authentic letters. The proportions of different types of speech differ (many more nouns and adjectives, partly due to the number of lists of virtues and vices, and a poorer set of conjunctions and other linking words).

(2)   More importantly, the pattern of argument is different. There is a pattern of backing up practice by doctrine ("Do Y because you believe X") rather than developing practice out of doctrine ("You believe X, so do Y"). This is seen especially in the appeal to the trustworthy sayings, using a unique formula not found in the main Pauline letters (1 Tim 1:15; 3:1; 4:9, etc.). Opening salutations are formulated differently as well.

(3)   Further, the doctrine itself, while generally conformable to that of Paul, is expressed in new ways for which there is no apparent motivation if the Pastorals come directly from Paul. We have already noted the unusual Christological vocabulary and a more Hellenistic type of moral language. There is the lack or minimal use of familiar Pauline expressions (for example, God as father, "in Christ/the Lord," flesh), which may be an indicator of a more deep-seated difference in the underlying theology.

(4)   Some would go further and find contradictions and incompatibilities with Paul's other writings, such as the silencing of women, the tendency toward hierarchicalism in congregational order, the shift toward faith as being concerned with right doctrine and teaching rather than personal commitment to God and Christ. And is the self-portrait of Paul his own or is it framed by an admirer?

(5)   A resulting question would be whether the material is more directly relevant to a later period and shaped by a different set of circumstances, though framed as if from the time of Paul as part of the persuasive rhetoric of the writer.

Proposed solutions

These problems (real or perceived) have led to various proposals for solution.

(1)   Taking a minimal view of the differences and stressing the compatibility of the reflected situation with that of Paul's own mission and imprisonment, some scholars argue for a different mode of composition. One solution that has been canvassed is that the Pastorals are from Paul's own hand, whereas the other letters were co-written with colleagues. But can we really suppose that the religious genius evident in 1 and 2 Corinthians and Romans is the product of collaborators rather than of Paul himself? Another solution is to posit Luke as the collaborator in the Pastorals (but why only them?), but in my view neither the theology nor the style is that of the author of Luke–Acts. Granted that there is a basic theology shared in common, this is not the way in which Luke would have expressed himself. The possibility of an unknown collaborator is less easy to disprove since we have no other texts ascribed to him for comparison.

(2)   A second type of view is that Pauline materials, including correspondence with his colleagues and other material – both doctrinal and practical – which stemmed from Paul or were inspired by him, have been put together by his colleagues and followers in order to help congregations in the period after his death. Timothy and Titus could have played a role in this operation. The term "allonymity" has been used to characterize this procedure; that is, authorship by *another writer* than the one named. The weakness of this hypothesis is the lack of parallels to it, although the ascription of texts by students to their teacher may furnish a parallel. It is feasible that the letters represent Pauline materials that have been revised and reorganized or extended.

(3)   A third type of view is that a later writer wrote to deal with the congregational problems of his own time by creating fictitious letters using the name of Paul to give authority to them. He wrote letters since that was the kind of composition used by Paul; for the same reason, he used the names of addressees from Paul's entourage. He incorporated fictitious personal details to strengthen the illusion that these were genuine Pauline letters that had come to light. The background of the letters is the church problems of the writer's own time, but these are read back into the fictional situation. The tendency of scholars taking

this route is to maximize the differences in the situations and contents of the letters and to see the author as developing a hierarchical view of the church with appointed leaders and a congregation who do little more than sit quietly and listen to authorized teachers; women in particular are silenced (over against a greater earlier freedom allowed by Paul), and slaves are subjected to their masters. The church itself has lost its mission to society and conforms to the surrounding social mores in order not to be persecuted. The theology is bland and impoverished compared with that of Paul. Some scholars, however, would argue that the comparison with Paul is inappropriate; rather than make a comparison which is inevitably to the detriment of the Pastorals, the author should be seen as a churchman doing his best to help the church through a difficult time with the rise of unorthodox beliefs (incipient Gnosticism), and to promote its consolidation for the long haul ahead of it by appropriate institutionalization.

One significant proposal of this kind (Merz 2006) emphasizes the deliberate use of pseudonymity (authorship by somebody who *falsely* – and in this case very successfully – claims to be the real Paul) so as to acquire authority to present an authoritative reinterpretation and correction of what Paul had said in his authentic letters. Another proposal (Herzer 2008; cf. Richards 2002) sees the Pastorals not as a unified corpus but as the work of more than one author (possibly including Paul himself) over a rather long period of time, with 1 Timothy being based on material from 2 Timothy and Titus.

Proponents of this kind of theory face the problems of explaining how the author produced letters with so many unPauline features in the presentation alongside his alleged skill in developing the fictitious material. Nor is it clear why a writer would take the trouble to create an ecclesiastical order with roles for Timothy and Titus that correspond to nothing known at this later time. And the use of a highly deceptive form of pseudonymity seems theologically and psychologically incompatible with the great emphasis on truth here and in the New Testament writings generally.

In the present state of scholarship, there is no explanation of the Pastorals that does not leave some loose ends. Direct Pauline authorship and pseudonymity both face substantial problems. In my view, a solution involving the use of Pauline materials by some author with a different literary and theological style does seem to be less problematic.

References

Aageson, James W. 2008. *Paul, the Pastoral Epistles, and the Early Church*. Peabody, Mass.: Hendrickson.

Collins, Raymond F. 2002. *1 & 2 Timothy and Titus: A Commentary*. Louisville: Westminster John Knox.

Fee, Gordon D. 1988. *1 and 2 Timothy, Titus*. Peabody, Mass.: Hendrickson.

Harding, Mark. 1998. *Tradition and Rhetoric in the Pastoral Epistles*. New York: Peter Lang.

Harding, Mark. 2001. *What Are They Saying about the Pastoral Epistles?* New York: Paulist.

Herzer, Jens. 2008. Rearranging the "House of God": A New Perspective on the Pastoral Epistles. Pages 547–566 in Empsychoi Logoi – *Religious Innovations in Antiquity: Studies in Honour of*

Pieter Willem van der Horst. Edited by Alberdina Houtman, Albert de Jong, and Magda Misset-van de Weg. Leiden: Brill.

Johnson, Luke Timothy. 1996. *Letters to Paul's Delegates: 1 Timothy, 2 Timothy, Titus*. Valley Forge: Trinity.

Köstenberger, Andreas J., and Terry L. Wilder. 2010. *Entrusted with the Gospel: Paul's Theology in the Pastoral Epistles*. Nashville: B. & H. Academic.

Marshall, I. Howard, in collaboration with Philip H. Towner. 1999. *A Critical and Exegetical Commentary on the Pastoral Epistles*. Edinburgh: T. & T. Clark.

Merz, Annette. 2006. The Fictitious Self-exposition of Paul: How Might Intertextual Theory Suggest a Reformulation of the Hermeneutics of Pseudepigraphy? Pages 113–132 in *The Intertextuality of the Epistles: Explorations of Theory and Practice*. Edited by Thomas L. Brodie, Dennis R. MacDonald, and Stanley E. Porter. Sheffield: Sheffield Phoenix.

Pietersen, Lloyd K. 2004. *The Polemic of the Pastorals: A Sociological Examination of the Development of Pauline Christianity*. London: T. & T. Clark.

Richards, William A. 2002. *Difference and Distance in Post-Pauline Christianity: An Epistolary Analysis of the Pastorals*. New York: Peter Lang.

Towner, Philip H. 1989. *The Goal of our Instruction: The Structure of Theology and Ethics in the Pastoral Epistles*. Sheffield: JSOT.

Towner, Philip H. 2006. *The Letters to Timothy and Titus*. Grand Rapids: Eerdmans.

Twomey, Jay. 2009. *The Pastoral Epistles through the Centuries*. Chichester: Wiley-Blackwell.

Young, Frances. 1994. *The Theology of the Pastoral Letters*. Cambridge: Cambridge University Press.

CHAPTER 8

The Portrait of Paul in Acts

Stanley E. Porter

Introduction to the Issues

Thirteen letters in the New Testament are attributed to Paul the apostle (he is sometimes credited with Hebrews as well). He is also a major figure in the book of Acts,
making an entrance at Acts 7:58 at the stoning of Stephen, and continuing off and on
until the end of the book, which leaves Paul in prison in Rome after two years (28:30–
31). Thus, Paul appears in the New Testament as the major writer of letters to early
Christian communities, in terms of both number and length, and as a major participant
in the book of Acts, the narrative account of the development of early Christianity.
Differences in the authorship, literary type (genre), and purposes of Acts and the
Pauline epistles are sufficient to raise important questions regarding possibly competing
portraits of Paul in the two corpora. However, the discussion has usually not been
conducted on a general level, but with regard to a number of more specific, even incidental, factors found in the depiction of Paul in Acts as opposed to his self-representation
in his letters (or how he is depicted by early followers in the deutero-Pauline letters, if
one accepts this hypothesis). In the ongoing debate over the portrait of Paul in Acts,
the major recurring issues revolve around several significant topics. These include basic
information about Paul and the chronology of his life, his personal traits as he
approached his missionary endeavors, and his theology. After a brief history of discussion, each of these topics will be analyzed.

The Blackwell Companion to Paul, First Edition. Edited by Stephen Westerholm.
© 2011 Blackwell Publishing Ltd. Published 2011 by Blackwell Publishing Ltd.

Brief History of Discussion

Discussion of differences between the portrait of Paul in Acts and in his letters is not as contentious as it once was. As is well illustrated in Thomas Phillips's (2009) thorough treatment of the subject, this is partly because some scholars have reached decided and firm conclusions regarding the relationship, usually choosing to see distinctive differences between the Paul of Acts and his letters, and partly because others have found means of reconciling the two to their own satisfaction.

The history of discussion begins with the work of the German theologian, church historian, and New Testament scholar Ferdinand Christian Baur. Baur (1873–1875) contended that Acts was written long after the events that it purports to represent as an apologetic argument to show the unity of Christianity. To achieve this end, the author glossed over decided differences between Pauline and Petrine Christianity; therefore, its account was not deemed an accurate depiction of the historical development of the early church or of its major protagonist, Paul. By contrast, according to Baur, Galatians 1–2 offer the most important historical information regarding Paul and his relationship to Peter. Baur's portrait of what amounts to two Pauls, with the Paul of Acts not historically but theologically grounded, gained much scholarly support in the nineteenth century. Around the turn of the nineteenth to the twentieth century, William Ramsay (1915), the Scottish scholar and archaeologist, who began as a convinced follower of Baur, countered the resultant bifurcation. His numerous scholarly travels through Turkey convinced him of the veracity of what Acts says about Paul.

As a result of the work of these two giants of New Testament scholarship, there developed essentially two schools of thought regarding the relationship of the Paul of Acts to the Paul of the epistles. Numerous scholars, particularly German scholars but some elsewhere as well, have followed Baur in his hypotheses regarding the development of the early church and his conclusions regarding the relationship between Acts and Paul. In fact, much German scholarship, especially of an earlier period, either was ignorant of or chose to ignore the challenge posed by the scholarship of Ramsay and his followers and continued to promote the disjunction between the Paul of Acts and the Paul of the letters. This approach probably reached its definitive statements in two publications of the 1950s and 1960s, the commentary on Acts of Ernst Haenchen (English translation, 1971) and an article on the "Paulinism" of Acts by Philipp Vielhauer (English translation, 1980). Much (though certainly not all) of the German commentary tradition since Haenchen has followed along this path; other representatives include Martin Dibelius (1956), Robert Jewett (1979), Gerd Lüdemann (1984), John Knox (1987), and Richard Pervo (2006). The general conclusion of such thought is that the book of Acts is not primarily an historical but a theological document, and that its depiction of Paul is at fundamental odds with that of the Pauline letters.

Those who have opposed the results of Baur's investigations have themselves divided into two groups. A significant group of scholars, especially in English-speaking circles, has followed Ramsay directly, opposing categorically both the assumptions and the conclusions of Baur. A number of these scholars shared with Ramsay a background in classical studies. Representative of this group are Ward Gasque (1975), F. F. Bruce

(1976), I. Howard Marshall (1980), Colin Hemer (1990), Rainer Riesner (1998), and Richard Wallace and Wynne Williams (1998). Their arguments often concentrate on finding further evidence to support the historical reliability of details found in the book of Acts, examining both primary and secondary sources, inscriptions as well as the biblical text. The second group of scholars, while perhaps not as overtly supportive of the historical minutiae of the book of Acts, has nevertheless opposed the Baur school by advocating an approach that sees much more continuity between the portrait of Paul in Acts and that which emerges from Paul's letters. Representative of such an approach is Phillips's (2009) treatment that compares and contrasts historical and chronological data from Paul's letters (the seven undisputed letters) and the book of Acts. Other such scholars include Jacob Jervell (1979), Luke Timothy Johnson (1986), and Joseph Fitzmyer (1989).

The Portrait of the Lukan Paul versus the Epistolary Paul

There are a number of areas where differences between the Lukan portrait of Paul and that of the Pauline letters have been noted. Many of these posited or perceived differences stem, in the eyes of those who advocate such a position, from the belief that the book of Acts is a piece of apologetic or even propagandist literature, written well after the events that it purports to present. Thus, instead of the book of Acts being written by Luke the follower or companion of Paul, and possibly even the author of the first-hand account found in the "we"-passages (Acts 16:10–17; 20:5–15; 21:1–18; 27:1–29; 28:1–16), as tradition has maintained, the book of Acts is seen as a second-century document intended to reflect and justify the triumph of Paulinism.

There have been three major dates proposed for the composition of Acts: ca. AD 60–62, ca. 80–85, and ca. 100–130. The middle date, probably the most common date among scholars, is often supported by working from a post-70 date of composition for Luke's Gospel, and seems to serve simply as a compromise between the early and late dates.

Each of these dates has implications for the portrait of Paul in Acts. The late date, promoted by Baur and his followers, explains the purported differences along three lines. First, the author could not have been an eyewitness of, or even close to, the events related. Second, the book was written after major events in the development of the early church had transpired and Paulinism had triumphed. Third, the work was written from a consciously apologetic and theological, but not distinctly historical, viewpoint. The earlier two dates provide for the possibility of first-hand witness of, or at least closeness to, the events. Those who subscribe to the early date tend to see close continuity between the Paul of Acts and of the letters. Those who hold to the middle date are divided: some disregard any connection between the narrative of Acts and what actually happened, while others contend for continuity.

There are a number of different topics that have been highlighted as illustrating the similarities and differences between the depictions of Paul in Acts and in his letters. The major areas of contention concern Paul's life and chronology, his person, and his theology.

Paul's Life and Chronology

One of the major issues raised in discussing the Paul of Acts is the apparent difference between what we learn about the chronology of events in Paul's life from his letters and from Acts.

Details of Paul's life are mentioned infrequently in his letters, with comments often being incidental to the content of the letter. The following passages with details about his life are to be noted: Rom 11:1; 15:19–32; 1 Cor 15:9; 16:1–9; 2 Cor 2:12–13; 8–9; 11:22–27, 32–33; Gal 1:11–2:21; Phil 1:14; 3:5–6; Phlm 23; and, if the full corpus of Paul's letters is considered: Eph 6:20; Col 4:10–16; 1 Tim 1:13; 2 Tim 1:8–17; 4:13, 20; and Tit 1:5; 3:12. From these passages, Paul's life has been reconstructed by a number of different scholars, with varying degrees of certainty attributed to the events. Among the scholars who provide such accounts are Hurd (1967), Jewett (1979), Lüdemann (1984), Knox (1987), and Phillips (2009). The major events include: (1) birth into a Jewish household, from the tribe of Benjamin, circumcised on the eighth day, a speaker of the Hebrew or Aramaic language; (2) association with the Pharisees; (3) rising in the ranks of Judaism as a zealous persecutor of the church, although it is not stated where he was a persecutor; (4) conversion, though not stated where; (5) time spent in Arabia before returning to Damascus, where he was persecuted; (6) three years later (dating from his conversion?), first trip to Jerusalem after conversion to become acquainted with Cephas and James; (7) return to Syria and Cilicia; (8) fourteen years later (after conversion?), visit to Jerusalem, with Barnabas and Titus; (9) opposition to Cephas over eating with Gentiles in Syrian Antioch; (10) missionary activity in churches in the areas of Galatia, Asia Minor (including Troas and Ephesus), Illyricum, Macedonia, and Greece/Achaia, including time spent in prison and other mistreatment by Jews and Gentiles; (11) raising of a collection to take to Jerusalem, associated with his missionary activity; (12) visit to Jerusalem; and, if the disputed letters are taken into account, (13) further or subsequent missionary activity in other areas, including Macedonia, Asia, Ephesus, possibly Crete, Nicopolis, Troas, and Miletus; and (14) imprisonment in Rome.

In contrast to the incidental biographical details contained in Paul's letters, the book of Acts is to a large extent – at least in the second half – a narrative of the conversion and missionary travels of Paul. The major events of his life include: (1) being a Jew, born in Tarsus, as a Roman and Tarsian citizen (Acts 16:37–38; 21:39; 22:25, 27, 28); (2) being educated (possibly in Tarsus and) in Jerusalem with Gamaliel (Acts 22:3); (3) being a persecutor of the church (Acts 8:1; 9:1–2); (4) conversion on the road to Damascus (Acts 9:3–7; 22:3–16; 26:12–18); (5) time in Damascus, ending with persecution (Acts 9:8–25); (6) a visit to Jerusalem (Acts 9:26–29); (7) time spent in Tarsus in Cilicia (Acts 9:30; 11:25) before going to Syrian Antioch; (8) a visit to Jerusalem at a time of famine (Acts 11:30); (9) a possible visit to Jerusalem after Herod's death, if this is not the same as the visit in (8) (Acts 12:25, where there is an important textual variant); (10) the first missionary journey, from Antioch and including Cyprus and Asia Minor, before returning to Syrian Antioch (Acts 13:1–14:28); (11) a visit to Jerusalem (Acts 15:1–12); (12) the second missionary journey, from Antioch to Cilicia, Galatia, Troas, the cities of Philippi, Thessalonica, and Beroea in Macedonia, Athens and

Corinth in Greece, and Ephesus, before returning (Acts 15:36–18:21); (13) a visit to Jerusalem, before returning to Syrian Antioch (Acts 18:22); (14) the third missionary journey, from Antioch to Galatia and Phrygia, Ephesus, Troas, Macedonia, Greece, returning through Macedonia, Troas, Miletus, Tyre, and Caesarea (Acts 18:23–21:14); (15) a visit to Jerusalem and arrest (Acts 21:15–23:32); (16) Roman custody, and imprisonment, finally, in Rome (Acts 23:33–28:31).

Of the many particular issues regarding these accounts of Paul's life that have been cited as indicating discrepancies between Acts and the Pauline letters, I select three as representative and often discussed.

(1)   *Paul's Tarsian and Roman citizenship.*   This first example is one where Acts provides the only information on a particular topic. In all of Paul's letters, though he makes clear that he is Jewish (as is also made clear in Acts), he never mentions the Tarsian or Roman citizenship that the Paul of Acts claims. Some (such as Lentz 1993, 23–61) see this as an indication that the book of Acts is not concerned with the historical Paul but with enhancing Paul's status so that Roman readers would see him as a noble man worthy of their attention. One might go further and posit that the letters do not depict a man who had known or enjoyed the status or privilege of such citizenship. On the other hand, there is nothing in the letters to dispute these claims directly. For many scholars, especially classicists but New Testament scholars as well, Paul's Roman citizenship and at least his birth in Tarsus constitute widely accepted details of Paul's life that are provided by Acts. There are other major events in Paul's life that Acts narrates but the letters do not mention, such as Paul's arrest and Roman imprisonment. However, these may simply reflect the fact that the events took place after the writing of Paul's letters (as Knox noted [1987, 26–27]).

(2)   *Damascus in the Pauline chronology.*   The place of Damascus in Paul's life represents a case where the material in Paul's letters and in Acts is said to be contradictory by those who wish to place emphasis upon Paul's letters over the portrait of Paul in Acts. Knox (1987, 21–22) contends that Paul was not a persecutor in Jerusalem because he states in Gal 1:22–23 that he was unknown by sight to the churches of Judea, who only knew him as a persecutor elsewhere. Knox contends that Paul was not resident in Jerusalem, had never lived in Jerusalem (hence Knox uses this as further reason to question Paul's education with Gamaliel), probably lived in Damascus, was converted near Damascus and continued to live in the area, and went to Jerusalem as a visitor, not a resident (Gal 1:17–18). However, Knox's interpretation of key verses is subject to question. Galatians 1:17 may mean Paul returned home to Damascus, but it may simply mean he returned after a previous visit, such as that related to his conversion. Further, Galatians 1:18 need not mean that Paul merely visited Jerusalem; the point may be that he visited and got to know Cephas, whom he may not have known (certainly not well) even if he had lived in Jerusalem. Finally, even though Paul says he was unknown by sight to the churches of Judea (Gal 1:22), he does note that the Judean Christians saw him as one who had persecuted them (v. 23).

(3) *Galatians 2 and the trips to Jerusalem.*   Phillips (2009, 191) contends that the interpretation of Galatians 2 and Acts 15 is "*the pivotal issue* for interpreting the relationship between the Paul of Acts and the Paul of the letters." Here, the material in Paul's letters and in Acts seems to talk about similar events, but scholars have disputed how to fit the pieces together. Knox (1987, 35–42, 44–45) contends that Paul made only three visits to Jerusalem, and that Paul's language precludes the possibility of his having journeyed to Jerusalem five times (after his education there), as mentioned in Acts. Knox thus takes the mention of a visit fourteen years after Paul's conversion (Gal 2:1) as referring only to his second visit to Jerusalem, this time to meet with the Jerusalem leaders to confer on what amounts to the collection. At this point, Paul has (according to Knox) already visited the churches in Galatia, Asia, Macedonia, and Greece (although, as Knox acknowledges, Paul only mentions Syria and Cilicia [Gal 1:21]). Romans 15:25–32 then reflect the gathering of the collection, which takes Paul on his third and final visit to Jerusalem. The author of Acts rightly equates the visit of Galatians 2:1 with the Acts 15 council, Knox believes, though the author places this meeting in a different chronological order and gives it a very different purpose.

Despite Knox's objections, however, there is nothing in Paul's writings that states that these three visits to Jerusalem were the only ones Paul made. It is true that the one anticipated in Romans 15 was his last, but this is not in dispute. In regard to Galatians 2:1, however, the verse simply says that Paul went up again to Jerusalem with Barnabas. This could mean that Barnabas accompanied him on the earlier trip mentioned in Acts 9:27 and again on this second one – the one mentioned in Acts 11:30. As Knox, too, has noted, there are problems with equating the visit of Galatians 2:1 with Acts 15. In Galatians, Paul speaks of a private meeting during which nothing was added to Paul's teaching; Acts depicts a public council involving complex negotiations regarding the Gentiles. Although he himself does so, Knox admits (1987, 44 n. 1) that one should not too quickly dismiss the equation of Galatians 2:1–10 with the visit of Acts 11:27–30 and 12:25. Common features include mention of Barnabas as present, the purpose of remembering the poor, and the chronological placement.

Phillips (2009, 194–195) has noted that one result of the equation of Galatians 2 and Acts 15 by most scholars is to create a need for Paul to be rehabilitated by Acts. The equation requires that Galatians was written after Acts 15, and hence that Paul had a falling out with the Jerusalem leaders after their council (cf. Gal 2:11–14), and that Paul remained at odds with the Jerusalem church, possibly until his delivery of the collection. Acts thereby becomes an attempt to rehabilitate Paul. However, if the Jerusalem visits of Galatians 2 and Acts 11 are equated, then the falling out between Paul and Peter occurred at the end of Paul's first missionary journey and before the Jerusalem council, which marks a reconciliation between the two, depicted throughout the rest of Acts. Phillips can, however, be questioned on his depiction of Acts 21 as indicating a favorable response to Paul by James and the others, and of Acts as rehabilitating Paul (see Porter 1999, 151–171). Nevertheless, it is apparent that the correlation of Galatians 2 with Acts 11 or 15 has serious interpretive implications for understanding the course of Paul's ministry, within Acts and his letters.

In general, when we examine the two chronological accounts, the one reconstructed on the basis of Paul's letters and the other on the basis of Acts (the "traditional view," in the terms of Hurd), we notice that there is a surprisingly large amount of overlap between the two, as Hurd has noticed (1967, 244); the overlap extends even to the issue of where one chronologically places the authorship of the letters (not treated here). I would contend that the disputed letters themselves are also in overall agreement with the chronology based upon Acts. The selected examples above have addressed some of the most pronounced problems, and presented at least plausible explanations of some of the more obvious apparent discrepancies. For his part, Hurd suggests three possible reasons for the significant agreement between the chronological accounts: (1) the traditional view (as found in Acts) is correct, and the epistle-based chronology "confirms the reliability of Acts"; (2) the traditional view is not as "blindly dependent on Acts" as advocates of the epistle-based chronology have proposed; and (3) the sequencing of letters (a concern of many chronological studies, though not treated here) by advocates of the epistle-based approach is more dependent on Acts than they realize (Hurd 1967, 244–245). There are also a number of events and chronological details mentioned in the letters for which Acts provides very little evidence, but where the material can be incorporated into the traditional view. These include the issue of the number of Corinthian letters and the timing of their sending, the lack of mention of significant imprisonments to warrant the writing of the prison epistles, and the dating of the composition of Romans.

Some scholars, to be sure, continue to dismiss the evidence of Acts at every point and to advocate exclusive dependence on the epistles for a reconstruction of Paul's life. Yet such a stance leaves unexplained the widespread agreement between the two accounts that has just been noted. Those who argue for a late date of Acts might contend that Acts represents an attempt to draw the evidence of the letters into its overall narrative. In that case, however, one might have expected the author to have done a better job at a number of points, making clear, for example, the correlation between passages such as Galatians 2 and Acts 11 or 15, and making consistent the number of visits Paul made to Jerusalem. In the case of tensions like these between the evidence of Acts and that of the epistles, the conclusions one reaches on the question of their compatibility will largely depend on the degree of one's willingness to seek and accept plausible reconstructions and to maximize evidence.

The Person of Paul

In his commentary on Acts, Haenchen (1971) rejects the view that "Luke" (i.e., the author of Acts) was a companion of Paul on the basis of five major differences between his depiction of the person of Paul and what we learn of Paul from the epistles. These objections have become widely influential in discussions of the Paul of Acts; each is worth considering.

(1) *Paul's mission and the law.*   Haenchen states (1971, 112): "For both 'Luke' and Paul, the overriding problem was that of the *mission to the Gentiles without the law*. But 'Luke' is *unaware of Paul's solution.*" Haenchen defines Paul's solution in terms of what he calls "internal evidence": "the law leads not to God but into sin" because of self-righteousness, whereas faith leads to right relationship with God (112–113). The "New Perspective" on Paul might well neutralize Haenchen's criticism of the Lukan Paul since, on its view, Paul himself does not pit law against grace and faith but insists that a covenant of grace applies to all, Gentile and Jew alike, free from the notion of obedience to the law as the means of entrance into the covenant. However, for advocates of the traditional view of Pauline soteriology, the problem noted by Haenchen remains to be addressed. There are a number of possible responses. First, Haenchen characterizes the author of Acts as understanding the notion of law from a Gentile standpoint (for example, Acts 15:10). This may well be true and even expected, as the author probably was a Gentile. Second, Haenchen overlooks several passages in Acts that seem to reflect the Pauline perspective. In Acts 13:38–39, Paul tells his Gentile audience that faith, not the law of Moses, leads to freedom. In 15:7–11, Peter makes clear that salvation is by faith, as distinct from ritual practices. In 21:21, the accusation against Paul is false, and probably confuses what he was teaching Gentiles with what he endorsed for Jews (cf. Acts 16:3). Third, Haenchen accuses Luke of not understanding Paul's rationale for a Gentile mission apart from law, justifying it rather with a "bare reference to the [ineluctable] will of God" (113). But within Acts, the same negative and positive view of the law is found as in the Pauline letters, as noted above. Further, a sense of the ineluctable "will of God" is attested in the Pauline letters as well as in Acts (for example, Rom 9–11; 1 Cor 9:16–17). Fourth, as Haenchen admits, both Acts and Paul know of the Gentile mission as one without the law. That Acts does not fully reproduce, or possibly even fully understand, the nature of Paul's solution does not mean that the author was unaware of it.

(2) *Paul a miracle worker.*   Haenchen contends that Acts portrays Paul as a great miracle worker (referring to Acts 13:6–12; 14:8–10, 19–20; 19:12; 20:7–12; 28:3–6), whereas in the letters at only one place does Paul claim to do the "signs of an apostle" (2 Cor 12:12). Three responses to this claim may be noted here. First, in comparison with a legitimate miracle worker such as Jesus, the number of miracles attributed to Paul in Acts is not particularly large when one considers how much space in Acts is given to Paul. Second, many of the episodes Haenchen cites are questionable as miracles. These include Paul's rising after being stoned, his escaping unharmed after being bitten by a snake, and the episode with Eutychus. The remaining three episodes – one of which, with the handkerchief, is only indirect – do not make a strong case for Paul as miracle worker in Acts. Third, Haenchen underestimates Paul's claims to miraculous gifts in his letters (see, for example, 1 Cor 14:18; 2 Cor 12:2–5; note that Paul distinguishes between miracles and healings in 1 Cor 12:28).

(3) *Paul as orator.*   Haenchen was not the first to notice that the Paul of Acts is what he calls an "outstanding orator" (1971, 114) who always has the right

words to say in every situation, whatever his audience or occasion. By contrast, in his own letters, Paul admits to being a "feeble" and "unimpressive" orator (114; cf. 2 Cor 10:10). Haenchen concludes that the author of Acts, writing after the fact, must have presumed that the great missionary was also a great orator. There is no doubt that, on many occasions, Paul is seen in Acts as a great orator. Not including several shorter comments that he makes, Paul delivers both missionary (Acts 13:16–41; 14:15–17; 17:22–31) and apologetic speeches (Acts 22:1–21; 24:10–21; 26:2–23; 28:17–20), besides his speech to the Ephesian church leaders at Miletus (Acts 20:18–35). However, there are three further considerations to weigh. First, Paul is far from successful in every speech that he delivers. He may be depicted as ready and able to orate, but a number of his speeches fail to persuade, the major goal of oratory. For example, his speech to the Athenians on the Areopagus is interrupted and only marginally successful in terms of converts, and none of his speeches before the Jerusalem Jews, the governor Felix, or King Agrippa results in his release. Neither the speech before the Roman Jewish leaders nor the one to the church leaders in Ephesus proves convincing to his audience. Second, the evidence from Paul's letters regarding his oratorical abilities is not universally negative. In fact, Haenchen probably misinterprets 2 Corinthians 10:10. It may be that Paul is simply (or rhetorically) being humble when he says that he is personally unimpressive. In any case, it must be noted that Paul does not explicitly state that this is what he believes about his own abilities. These comments are attributed to others, and Paul seems to disagree with them when, in 2 Corinthians 10:11, he says that he will have a firm presence when he arrives. Third, there is nothing to keep us from seeing Paul as both an epistolographer *and* an orator – the two were not incompatible in the ancient world, as evidenced by Plato, Demosthenes (to whom pseudepigraphical letters were attributed in antiquity), and Cicero.

(4) *Paul the apostle.*   Haenchen asserts that Acts, despite its positive depiction of Paul, does not *"affirm Paul's real claim,"* that of being an apostle, a claim made in Paul's letters that places him on the same level as the Twelve (1971, 114). However, there are two points to note. The first is that Haenchen himself admits that Paul and Barnabas are called apostles in Acts 14:4 and 14, though Haenchen limits the meaning in these verses to "envoys from Antioch." The second is that the situation in the Pauline letters is not as clear as Haenchen asserts. Rather than there being one class of apostles in the letters, so that Paul includes himself with the Twelve, there are two classes of apostles, the Twelve and others who are called apostles (1 Cor 15:5, 7). It is plausible that Paul is called an apostle in Acts in the second sense used in the Pauline letters.

(5) *Jewish and Christian relations.*   Haenchen (1971, 115) contends that throughout Acts the Jews were hostile to Christians because the latter proclaimed the resurrection (Acts 4:2; 28:23). The proclamation of resurrection that provokes hostility to Paul is not in fact distinctively Pauline, but one advanced by all of the Christian missionaries (here Haenchen refers to Acts 7:52, 55–56; 18:24–28). Moreover, according to Haenchen, this view of resurrection corresponds

to the Jewish hope of a resurrection at the end of the age. Acts thus leaves us with the curious picture of Christians being persecuted for holding a traditional Jewish doctrine. In reality, Haenchen notes, it was Paul's teaching regarding the law that provoked Jewish hostility. Again, three points may be made in response to these claims. The first concerns the equation of the resurrection in Acts with Jewish expectations. Of the twelve places in Acts that refer to "resurrection," six are in contexts that refer to the resurrection of Christ (Acts 1:22; 2:31; 4:2, 33; 17:18, 32), four use the phrase "resurrection of the dead" (Acts 17:32; 23:6; 24:21; 26:23), and two mention the resurrection alone (Acts 23:8; 24:15). Thus, half of the instances refer specifically to the resurrection of Christ, a resurrection different from Jewish expectations of a general resurrection at the end of the age. Second, in the Pauline letters, of the eight uses of the word "resurrection" (seven in the seven generally accepted letters), five use the phrase "resurrection of the dead" (Rom 1:4; 1 Cor 15:12, 13, 21, 42), while two refer to "his resurrection" (Rom 6:5; Phil 3:10) (the other reference is to a simple "resurrection" in 2 Tim 2:18). Thus, Paul's own terminology closely parallels that of Acts. Third, the issue of law, crucial to the message of the Paul of the letters, is also found in Acts, where Paul is frequently accused of teaching errant doctrine regarding the law (cf. Acts 18:13; 21:21, 28; 22:3; 23:29; 25:8).

Haenchen raises a number of points of detail that he concludes indicate a different conception of Paul in Acts from the Paul of the epistles. He concludes that Acts was written, not by a "collaborator" of Paul, but by a later writer, giving his own perspective while wanting to respect and honor Paul (1971, 116). However, the support for Haenchen's positions is not always convincing. When examined, it can also be interpreted to indicate widespread continuity between the portrait of Paul in Acts and evidence derived from his letters.

Pauline Theology

Vielhauer (1980, 33) asks the question "whether and to what extent the author of Acts took over and passed on theological ideas of Paul, whether and to what extent he modified them." He selects four areas of investigation, concentrating upon Paul's speeches in Acts as the most likely place for finding Pauline theology in the book.

(1) *Natural theology.* Vielhauer notes that Paul's speech on the Areopagus is his only speech to Gentiles in Acts. Following Dibelius (1956), Vielhauer claims that the address was written as an example of a sermon to Gentiles, that it amounts to a "Hellenistic speech about the true knowledge of God" (1980, 34), and that it incorporates Stoic notions, for example, in the reference in 17:26 to the boundaries of human habitation, and in verses 28–29 to humans as the offspring of God (1980, 35). The speech concludes with a mention of judgment without, however, referring to the "saving significance" of Jesus' death (1980,

36). Vielhauer admits that the Paul of the epistles also speaks of "the pagan's natural knowledge of God" in Romans 1:19–20, which is also based on Stoic natural theology (1980, 36). In Paul, however, such knowledge provides a basis for speaking of human responsibility and guilt; Acts, lacking any suggestion of sin and guilt, views pagan knowledge of God positively as a forerunner of faith. Vielhauer claims, further, that in Paul's writings there is "no parallel to the motif of man's kinship to God" found in Acts 17:28–29 (1980, 37).

In response, it may be said that, even if Paul in Romans does not develop his natural theology in the same way as it is developed in Acts, this does not prove that a clear distinction is to be made between the Paul of Acts and the Paul of the letters. That (as Vielhauer himself notes) both articulate a natural theology rooted in Stoicism is itself remarkable. And note that Paul's speech in Lystra (Acts 14:15–17) also articulates a natural theology – though, like Romans 1, without any reference to human kinship with God. Second, both Paul's Areopagus speech and the one in Lystra are depicted as being interrupted or at least incomplete; hence too much should not be made of missing topics. Third, whereas Vielhauer fails to see any suggestion of human guilt in the Areopagus address, Paul's demand for repentance (17:30) strongly implies such guilt.

(2) *Law.* Vielhauer believes that the Paul of Acts presents a positive viewpoint toward Judaism in many ways. These include his practice of beginning his ministry in each city at the synagogue, his submission to the Jerusalem authorities, his circumcising of Timothy, his endorsing the apostolic decree, his taking a vow (18:18), his participation in various Jewish festivals, his taking a Nazirite vow (21:23–26), and his description of himself as a Pharisee on trial because of his hope in the resurrection (23:6; 26:5–7). In short, Vielhauer states, "Acts portrays the Gentile missionary Paul as a Jewish Christian who is utterly loyal to the law," as a "true Jew" (1980, 38). Vielhauer grants that, since Paul's understanding of Christian freedom allowed him to live either as a Jew or as a Gentile (1 Cor 9:19–23), the apostle might well have acted as a Jew in many of the ways portrayed in Acts. But the author of Acts, he believes, misrepresents Paul in claiming that the law retains its full validity for Jewish Christians, and he misunderstands Paul's proclamation of justification by faith, seeing faith as merely supplementing what the law can do, and reducing justification to the negative act of forgiving sins (1980, 41, referring to Acts 13:38–39). Note, however, that Paul, too, can pair justification with the forgiveness of sins (for example, Rom 3:21–26; 4:1–8; Gal 3:19–24; cf. also Col 1:14; Eph 1:7, though Vielhauer dismisses these latter verses because they do not come from the "major letters" [1980, 41]). To Vielhauer's claim that Luke knew of Paul's message of justification by faith but did not grasp its "central significance and absolute importance" (1980, 42), it may simply be said that Luke may have been less a disciple of Paul than his traveling companion – with his own theological perspective on Paul and his teaching. Finally, even if Acts does not depict Paul as articulating a clear law-versus-Christ antithesis, Paul is frequently

accused of neglecting or disregarding the law (for example, Acts 18:13; 21:21, 28; 22:3; 23:29; 25:8).

(3) *Christology.* Vielhauer characterizes the content of Paul's proclamation in Acts as focused first on the "kingdom" or "the kingdom of God" (19:8; 20:25; 28:23, 31), then on Jesus (19:13; 22:18), Jesus as alive (25:19), Jesus and the resurrection (17:18), and things concerning Jesus (23:11). Furthermore, this proclamation is depicted as "the whole counsel of God" (20:27), a gospel of grace (20:24), repentance and conversion (26:20), and the resurrection of the dead (23:6; 24:14–15; 26:6–8; 28:20 [Vielhauer, 1980, 43]). In Acts, Paul only makes two substantive Christological statements, in Antioch (13:16–43) and before King Agrippa (26:22–23): Paul asserts that Jesus is the promised and expected Messiah, claims that his suffering and death were according to Scripture, and links the Christian mission to his resurrection (13:32–33). Furthermore, Vielhauer sees the Christology of Acts 13:33 as adoptionistic (1980, 44). Vielhauer admits that there are parallels to these Christological perspectives in Paul's letters, in particular in Romans 1:3–4 and 1 Corinthians 15:3–4, but notes that these statements are drawn from the tradition of the "earliest congregation," and are not typical of Paul's own thought (1980, 43–44). Vielhauer further dismisses the apparent parallels between Paul's statements in Acts 13 and 26, on the one hand, and Christological passages in Paul's writings, on the other, highlighting what he finds to be their different emphases and noting that the speech in Acts 13 differs little from Peter's speeches earlier in Acts.

In response, one may wonder whether the Christological parallels between Acts and the Pauline letters, which Vielhauer admits only to dismiss, are not of more importance than he allows. Many would dispute the claim that Romans 1:3–4 and 1 Corinthians 15:3–4 are merely traditional and unrepresentative of Paul's thought. Furthermore, Vielhauer overlooks the fact that the reference to the fulfillment of Scripture occurs already in Romans 1:2, outside what is taken to be a traditional formula. Nor are Vielhauer's attempts to dismiss other parallels between Paul's speeches in Acts 13 and 26 and passages in the epistles well grounded. He labels similar language and concepts as "apparent echoes" but not true parallels (1980, 44). He is correct that the usage is not always exactly the same, but the distinctions he draws seem subtle indeed, and the expectation that a chronicler would have been sensitive to them seems unrealistic.

(4) *Eschatology.* Vielhauer contends that, though eschatology is at the heart of Pauline teaching, it has all but disappeared from Acts, occurring only as a peripheral topic in a few instances (for example, Acts 17:30–31). Paul expected the return of Christ imminently, at the consummation of the new era that has already begun. By contrast, Luke, though he believes that the new era has begun, thinks of the ages quantitatively and in a mere temporal sequence: once there was pre-Christian time (Acts 13:16–22); the current age is that of the Holy Spirit, between Pentecost and Christ's *parousia.* In other words, Luke conceives of history "as a continuous redemptive historical process," in which the

old age of promise has given way to the new age of fulfillment; "expectation of the imminent end has disappeared and the failure of the parousia is no longer a problem" (1980, 47). The very existence of the book of Acts is thought to be evidence of this non-eschatological perspective. The book serves two purposes: edifying believers through stories about the faithful, and giving an historical report of the apostolic age, though one written after the event and in the intellectual spirit of Eusebius. Such a book would not have been written while there was an expectation of an imminent *parousia*.

Several responses are in order. First, both the Pauline and the Lukan schemes that Vielhauer proposes are subject to question, modification, or even rejection. Though Paul may have expected the imminent return of Christ and would have wished for it in his lifetime, he did not have an unqualified view of this event. Even in 1 Thessalonians, where the expectation appears to be the strongest, Paul's reference to "we who are alive and remain" may only refer (generically) to the group that is alive at Christ's return, not necessarily to Paul himself (4:15, 17); and expectation of an imminent return is far less readily apparent in Philippians (for example, 1:22–24; 2:16–17; 3:11–14). The redemptive-historical view that Vielhauer, following Hans Conzelmann, endorses for Luke is itself not without difficulty. Few now would attribute such a segmented view of history to Luke, and exclude all indications of eschatological expectation. Moreover, Vielhauer's confident assertions about what the early church would have expected of its written documents are also questionable. For all their expectation of Christ's imminent return, early Christians still had a place for edifying writings and stories of the faithfulness of early believers. When Vielhauer goes on to claim that Acts is intended to be an historical report but fails to achieve that goal, he has to dismiss the position of the classical historian Eduard Meyer, attributing Meyer's more positive appraisal to his supposed misunderstanding of the theological nature of Luke's account (Vielhauer 1980, 50 n. 37).

Assessment of Major Contentions

There is little doubt that there are a number of points at which the portrait of Paul in Acts is different from that in the Pauline letters. These areas of difference include details regarding Paul's life and chronology, Paul as a person, and his theology. As indicated above, there is much continuity on all fronts, but there remain points of diversity that have been widely discussed.

The major question revolves around how one assesses such diversity in light of the fact that there are very few formal contradictions between the two bodies of data. Once this question is raised, it becomes clear that the side one takes in the debate depends on whether one inclines toward continuity or divergence, unity or diversity, evidential maximalism or minimalism. Those who stress that there are details of Paul's life found in Acts but not in the letters, that the chronological account of Acts differs at points from the reconstruction based upon the letters, that the apostle seen in the Pauline letters is oriented differently from the Paul of Acts, and that the theology of the Acts' account is different from that of the letters, tend to be those who emphasize points of divergence, see diversity in the development of early Christianity, and minimize efforts at harmonization. By contrast, those who emphasize the compatibility of details in Paul's life found in Acts with those attested by his letters, note the common chronological framework, minimize differences in the person of Paul in the two sources, and find greater theological coherence, tend to be those who emphasize points of similarity, find fundamental unity in the development of early Christianity, and maximize efforts to find convergence in the New Testament writings. Those who date Acts to the second century tend to emphasize divergence because the author, at a significant temporal and historical remove from the author of the Pauline letters, was writing essentially an apologetic account on behalf of Pauline Christianity. If so, however, it is surprising that he was not more proficient in harmonizing his account with material in the Pauline letters and in depicting a Paul whose person and theology better correspond to the evidence of the epistles – especially since such an author would have had access to all of the Pauline letters, no matter how one parses the issues of authorship of the Pauline canon.

There are many, especially in recent discussion, who note that the differences posited between the two accounts are not as telling as has often been supposed. In that case, how does one account for the similarities and differences? A way forward in the discussion may be found in a statement by Earle Ellis concerning the relationship between Paul and the author of Acts. As Ellis has pointed out (1974, 42), "the picture of Luke as the 'disciple' of Paul is not drawn from the New Testament but from the later Fathers. In the New Testament Luke is only a sometime companion of the Apostle and, therefore, should not be required to reflect Pauline theology" or to record other details in the same way Paul would have done if he had written the account himself. Those who emphasize diversity tend to separate the author from Paul, temporally and theologically. Those who emphasize continuity usually link the two closely together, with the author, Luke, being depicted as a close traveling companion or even disciple of the apostle. However, this characterization may be drawn overly close: the author of Acts may well have been a more complex and less sycophantic figure. Indeed, the author of Acts, as has been recognized in recent research, is an author in his own right, with his own historical perspective, theology, and even opinion of Paul, and with access to a variety of sources, including the "we" source generated, if not by himself, by someone else whose travels intersected at various points with the life and mission of Paul. The differences in the accounts appear to be within the range of those that one might expect to find between any two different, accomplished authors who are writing about the same events, but doing so in two different literary genres (narrative versus letter), with different purposes (one telling the story of early Christianity, the other addressing problems in local church congregations) and audiences (Gentile Christians, perhaps in Antioch or more widely, versus a particular church or set of churches in a given location). This solution does not forestall exploration of a number of areas of abiding dispute between the two accounts – for example, whether Galatians 2 reflects Acts 11 or 15, whether Paul was really a Roman and Tarsian citizen, or whether Luke knew or shared Paul's view of the law – but it helps to put the discussion in a more plausible framework that does not predetermine the issues on the basis of a simple disjunction between unity and diversity.

References

Baur, Ferdinand Christian. 1873–1875. *Paul: His Life and Works*. 2 volumes. London: Williams & Norgate.

Bruce, F. F. 1976. Is the Paul of Acts the Real Paul? *Bulletin of the John Rylands Library* 58: 282–305.

Dibelius, Martin. 1956. *Studies in the Acts of the Apostles*. New York: Scribners.

Ellis, E. Earle. 1974. *The Gospel of Luke*. Revised edition. Grand Rapids: Eerdmans.

Fitzmyer, Joseph A. 1989. *Luke the Theologian: Aspects of his Teaching*. London: Geoffrey Chapman.

Gasque, W. Ward. 1975. *A History of the Criticism of the Acts of the Apostles*. Grand Rapids: Eerdmans.

Haenchen, Ernst. 1971. *The Acts of the Apostles: A Commentary*. Philadelphia: Westminster.

Hemer, Colin J. 1990. *The Book of Acts in the Setting of Hellenistic History*. Edited by Conrad H. Gempf. Winona Lake, Ind.: Eisenbrauns.

Hurd, J. C., Jr. 1967. Pauline Chronology and Pauline Theology. Pages 225–248 in *Christian History and Interpretation: Studies Presented to John Knox*. Edited by W. R. Farmer, C. F. D. Moule, and R. R. Niebuhr. Cambridge: Cambridge University Press.

Jervell, Jacob. 1979. Paul in the Acts of the Apostles: Tradition, History, Theology. Pages 297–306 in *Les Actes des Apôtres: traditions, rédaction, théologie*. Edited by J. Kremer. Gembloux: Duculot.

Jewett, Robert. 1979. *Dating Paul's Life*. London: SCM.

Johnson, Luke Timothy. 1986. *The Writings of the New Testament: An Interpretation*. Philadelphia: Fortress.

Knox, John. 1987. *Chapters in a Life of Paul*. Revised and edited by Douglas R. A. Hare. Macon, Ga.: Mercer University Press.

Lentz, John Clayton, Jr. 1993. *Luke's Portrait of Paul*. Cambridge: Cambridge University Press.

Lüdemann, Gerd. 1984. *Paul, Apostle to the Gentiles: Studies in Chronology*. Philadelphia: Fortress.

McDonald, Lee Martin, and Stanley E. Porter. 2000. *Early Christianity and its Sacred Literature*. Peabody, Mass.: Hendrickson.

Marshall, I. Howard. 1980. *The Acts of the Apostles: An Introduction and Commentary*. Grand Rapids: Eerdmans.

Pervo, Richard I. 2006. *Dating Acts: Between the Evangelists and the Apologists*. Santa Rosa, Calif.: Polebridge.

Phillips, Thomas A. 2009. *Paul, his Letters, and Acts*. Peabody, Mass.: Hendrickson.

Porter, Stanley E. 1999. *The Paul of Acts: Essays in Literary Criticism, Rhetoric, and Theology*. Tübingen: J. C. B. Mohr (Paul Siebeck). Reprinted as *Paul in Acts*. Peabody, Mass.: Hendrickson, 2001.

Porter, Stanley E. 2009. Was Paulinism a Thing When Luke-Acts Was Written? Pages 1–13 in *Reception of Paulinism in Acts / Réception du paulinisme dans les Actes des Apôtres*. Edited by Daniel Marguerat. Leuven: Peeters.

Ramsay, William Mitchell. 1915. *The Bearing of Recent Discovery on the Trustworthiness of the New Testament*. London: Hodder & Stoughton.

Riesner, Rainer. 1998. *Paul's Early Period: Chronology, Mission Strategy, Theology*. Grand Rapids: Eerdmans.

Vielhauer, Philipp. 1980. On the "Paulinism" of Acts. Pages 33–50 in *Studies in Luke-Acts*. Edited by Leander E. Keck and J. Louis Martyn. Philadelphia: Fortress.

Wallace, Richard, and Wynne Williams. 1998. *The Three Worlds of Paul of Tarsus*. London: Routledge.

CHAPTER 9

The Gospel According to St. Paul

James D. G. Dunn

The gospel according to Paul centers on the death and resurrection of Jesus Christ and the consequent gift of the Holy Spirit to those who believe in this Christ and in God who acted through this Christ.

The "Gospel"

Paul begins his greatest letter (to Rome) by repeatedly referring to the "gospel" to which he was committed: "Paul ... set apart for the gospel of God"; "the gospel concerning his Son"; "my eagerness to proclaim the gospel"; "I am not ashamed of the gospel; it is the power of God for salvation to everyone who has faith" (Rom 1:1, 3, 15, 16 [NRSV]). These references are sufficient to indicate the importance of the gospel for Paul. In fact, the noun "gospel, good news" (*euangelion*) is one of several terms that Christianity owes to Paul. No less than sixty of its seventy-six occurrences in the New Testament appear in the Pauline corpus. So Paul's use of the term and the content he gave to it were probably decisive in establishing the meaning of "the gospel" for Christianity.

From where did Paul derive the term? A strong body of New Testament scholarship believes that Paul borrowed the term "gospel" from its political use in relation to Caesar (for example, Horsley 1997; Stanton 2004, 25–35). And it is certainly true that the word *euangelion* (usually in the plural) was used for the good news of Caesar Augustus's achievements. So one can argue with some plausibility that Paul deliberately described his message as "gospel" (*euangelion*) in order to set his good news of Christ in opposition to the Roman Empire's good news of Caesar: the peace brought by Christ (Rom 5:1)

The Blackwell Companion to Paul, First Edition. Edited by Stephen Westerholm.

was a more profound "gospel" than the *pax Romana*. However, the word *euangelion* was in wider use than simply with reference to the good news of Caesar. So a direct challenge to the political power and authority of Caesar was not immediately obvious in Paul's usage.

The decisive factor in Paul's choice of *euangelion* to denote his message probably came from the influence of the prophecy of Isaiah on Jesus and Paul. In several passages, Isaiah speaks of the bringing of good news, especially that of God's saving deeds (Isa 40:9; 52:7; 60:6; 61:1). Two of these passages (52:7 and 61:1) were already influential in Second Temple Judaism before Paul (*Pss. Sol.* 11:1; 11QMelch II.15–24; 4Q521). So it is not surprising that Jesus is recalled as drawing from Isaiah 61:1 to inspire his own mission (explicitly in Luke 4:17–21, but implicitly also in Matt 5:3/Luke 6:20 and Matt 11:5/Luke 7:22). That is, he was remembered as the one who brought the good news prophesied by Isaiah.

Paul too drew on Isaiah 52:7 in his description of the work of evangelism to which he had dedicated himself: "How beautiful are the feet of those who bring good news!" (Rom 10:15 [NRSV]). So Paul probably used the noun "gospel" to characterize his message of good news concerning Jesus primarily because he believed that Isaiah's hope of one who would preach good news *had been realized in Jesus*, a claim that was recalled as having been made by Jesus himself.

Of Jesus's Death and Resurrection

What was this good news? It focused particularly on Jesus's death and resurrection. In several passages, Paul recalls his preaching of Christ's death: "We proclaim Christ crucified, a stumbling block to Jews and foolishness to Gentiles" (1 Cor 1:23 [NRSV]). And he reminds the Galatians that "it was before your eyes that Jesus Christ was publicly exhibited as crucified!" (Gal 3:1 [NRSV]). Again, in the opening of his letter to Rome, Paul quotes what is generally regarded as a basic statement of faith shared by the first Christians. The gospel summary centers on Jesus, "who was descended from David ... and was appointed Son of God in power ... as from the resurrection of the dead" (Rom 1:3–4).[1] And in 1 Corinthians 15:1–5 he reminds his audience of the good news by which they were being saved, provided that they held firmly to it. That was the message of Jesus's death "for our sins" and of his resurrection on the third day, all in accordance with the Scriptures. Paul's use in this passage of technical terms for the receiving and passing on of tradition indicates that this gospel summary, which he himself had received and had passed on to the Corinthians, was the firm foundation of their shared faith.

It was once a popular view that Paul had transformed the simple message *of* Jesus about loving God and one's neighbor into a message *about* Jesus. But all the New Testament gospels demonstrate that the story of Jesus's mission was told with his death and resurrection as the climax of the story. That is to say, it was neither hard nor inappropriate to integrate the account of Jesus's teaching into a message climaxing in his death and resurrection. Mark, indeed, introduced his book as "the beginning of the gospel of Jesus Christ" (Mark 1:1). And he took it for granted that the story of Jesus's anointing in Bethany would be part of "the gospel" (14:9). Likewise, from the various allusions Paul makes to Jesus's character and to the traditions of his teaching (for example, Rom 12:14; 13:9; 1 Cor 13:2; Phil 4:6; 1 Thess 5:2, 13, 15), it is fairly obvious that Paul also thought of such knowledge of Jesus as part of, or of a piece with, his gospel.

Not only so, but the good news preached about Jesus by Paul must have included some narrative explaining who Jesus was and recounting something at least of the character of what he had said and done during his mission. The gospel that converted so many Gentiles could hardly have been simply that an unidentified X had died and been raised from the dead. On the contrary, since new believers in Paul's gospel were beginning to be called "Christians" (Acts 11:26), and were baptized in the name of Christ (cf. 1 Cor 1:12–15), they would inevitably have been prompted to ask more about this "Christ." "Christ," after all, was not an obvious or self-explanatory term for non-Jews; it was the Greek translation of the distinctively Jewish term "Messiah." Inevitably, therefore, Gentile converts would have to be taught about this "Christ," not least so that they could give an answer to any questions as to why they had changed their lives and now based them on this "Christ."

Why Was This "Good News"?

There are several answers to this question. One is, as Paul reminded the Corinthian believers, that "Christ died for our sins" (1 Cor 15:3). What precisely Paul meant by these words has been the subject of controversy, often intense, for many centuries, and no extensive agreement has ever been achieved. The main part of the problem – but this too is disputed – is that Paul seems to have thought of Jesus's death (in the language used in the Old Testament and in Israel's temple cult) as a "sin offering" (see, for example, Kraus 1991). This is more or less explicit in Romans 3:25, where Paul speaks of Jesus's death as a "means" or "sacrifice of atonement" (he uses the word for the lid of the ark where the sin offering on the Day of Atonement was sprinkled). Similarly, in Romans 8:3 he speaks of God sending his Son "as a sin offering" (literally, "concerning sin," but the phrase is regularly used in the Septuagint for the Hebrew "as a sin offering"). Paul's various references to Jesus's "blood" as of saving efficacy (for example, Rom 5:9; 1 Cor 11.25; Col 1:20) presuppose the practice of the sin offering, in which the manipulation of the sacrificial blood was decisive (Jesus's death itself was not particularly bloody). And Paul's summary of his gospel in 2 Corinthians 5:21 ("For our sake [God] made him to be sin who knew no sin, so that in him we might become the righteousness of God" [NRSV]) similarly presupposes the interchange implied in the sin offering between the repenting sinner and the unblemished lamb (Hooker 1995, 20–46).

Such sacrificial imagery jars for most Westernized peoples today, an effect that diminishes the value of the imagery in expressing the significance of Jesus's death. But it should be remembered that animal sacrifice was fundamental in the practice of religion in antiquity. So the first Christians had little choice but to use that imagery to describe what Jesus's death had accomplished. Nor, of course, did they have modern misgivings about doing so. Worth noting, however, is that Paul never allowed room for any idea of Jesus's death propitiating an angry God. It was God who had "put forward" Jesus as a sacrifice of atonement (Rom 3:25). "God proves his love for us in that while we still were sinners Christ died for us" (Rom 5:8 [NRSV]). Perhaps it is enough to know that the first Christians took it as given that God had provided the sacrificial system as a means by which sin could be covered and wrongs could be put right (it is not clear how), and that they understood Jesus's death to be effective in the same way (full discussion in Dunn 1998). We may infer that as they trusted in God who had so acted through Christ, they experienced peace, grace, and forgiveness (for example, Rom 5:1–2; 1 Cor 7:15; Col 1:14, 20).

It is important to note that Paul used other metaphors to describe the transformation (conversion) experienced by those who responded to his gospel and believed in Christ. The most prominent are (1) "redemption" (Rom 3:24; 1 Cor 1:30; Col 1:14), the buying back of a slave or war captive, and particularly important as an allusion to Israel's deliverance from Egypt; similarly, (2) "liberation" or "freedom" (for example, Rom 6:18; 8:2; Gal 2:4; 5:1); and (3) "reconciliation" (particularly Rom 5:10–11; 2 Cor 5:18–20), the bringing together of two parties at enmity with each other into a new peace and cooperation (Martin 1981).

Justification by Faith

Historically, the most important of the images used by Paul for the effect produced by the gospel is "justification," by which believers are "reckoned righteous" (particularly Rom 3:20, 24–26; Gal 2:16; cf. Phil 3:8–9). The image is drawn from the law court. "Justification" or "acquittal" is the term used for the verdict of "Not guilty," a verdict that releases those accused from the grip of the law and vindicates or restores them as righteous members of the community. The image came to particular prominence in Paul's own mission. For Paul, the gospel was the good news of God's readiness to count sinners (those in the wrong before God) as righteous, as nevertheless accepted by God. And for Paul, it was axiomatic that this good news was for *all* who accepted the gospel's invitation, for *all* who believed in Christ and in God working through Christ. The key factor for Paul was evidently that so many Gentiles had responded positively to his gospel and been accepted (justified) by God without more ado. So when many of his fellow Jewish believers insisted that such believing Gentiles must also become proselytes and be circumcised, Paul dug in his heels in resistance. That God had accepted these Gentiles in their faith and trust, and without requiring them to become like Jews (to "judaize"), was sufficiently clear. It was clear from the grace manifested through his evangelism and among these Gentiles – a claim and a manifestation that the leading Jewish apostles could not, and did not, deny (Gal 2:7–9).

It was such a confrontation that resulted in one of the central statements of Paul's gospel: "nobody is justified by works of the law, but only through faith in Jesus Christ" (Gal 2:16). By "works of the law" Paul meant doing what the (Jewish) law requires. The phrase denoted the demands laid upon Israel as Israel's response to God's covenant (agreement) with Israel. The covenant itself was an act of divine initiative, the promise

made to the patriarchs, Abraham, Isaac, and Jacob. And God had remained faithful to
that promise by delivering Israel from Egypt and choosing Israel to be his special people
(Deut 6:3, 23; 7:8; 8:1; 9:5; 19:8; 29:12–13). So obedience to God's commandments
was the response demanded by God from Israel. The point is clear in a passage like
Deuteronomy 26:16–19, and in the way in which the ten commandments are introduced: "I am the Lord your God, who brought you out of the land of Egypt, out of the
house of slavery; you shall have no other gods before me" (Exod 20:2–3). This interdependence of covenant and law (*nomos*) was well caught by E. P. Sanders's phrase "covenantal nomism" (Sanders 1977), though defining the relation between the two
elements has proved controversial (Carson et al. 2001).

In the controversies in which Paul's gospel embroiled him, the requirement to obey
the law ("works of the law") was seen by Paul as undermining the gospel. The demand
by more traditionalist Jewish believers that Gentile believers should respond as Israel
had responded was seen by Paul as requiring works of the law in addition to faith in
Christ. This demand had been made explicit and exemplified by the attempt of the "false
brothers" to insist that Gentile believers should be circumcised (Gal 2:1–10), and later
by Peter's attempt, in effect, "to compel the Gentiles [i.e., Gentile believers] to live like
Jews" (2:14). This is what Paul reacted against so strongly and virulently in his sharp
rebuke of Peter (cf. Gal 2:14) – one of the most embarrassing events in early Christian
history.

Paul's statement in Galatians 2:16, however, enshrines a fundamental principle that
has several ramifications. In the controversies over Paul's theology that have often
disturbed Christianity, they have become obscured and confused, and the principle has
been narrowed or become lopsided. So it is worth restating the principle and its ramifications here.

(1)   That the relation between God and his human creatures is essentially one of
      grace on God's part and of trust and reliance on God on their part. For Paul,
      Abraham was the great example of faith as such trust and reliance on God
      (Rom 4:16–21). And for Paul, it was/is the failure of humankind to respond in
      this way that lies at the heart of humankind's own failure and degeneration
      (Rom 1:21–23). Anything that obscures this principle destroys the gospel.

(2)   In the Reformation, Martin Luther reasserted this principle, over against the
      additional requirements that church tradition had layered upon the gospel – in
      particular, the claim that sin could be remitted through the purchase of papal
      indulgences. The principle restated became the article of faith by which the
      church stands or falls: that no one can earn salvation, no one can pay his/her
      way into heaven; justification is by faith alone, and not by any (good) works
      that one can do.

(3)   The principle thus rediscovered has further ramifications that are too often
      ignored. Most Christian denominations, in effect, act as did the earliest Jewish
      believers, or as did the medieval Catholicism against which Luther reacted. In
      effect, they insist that there are elements in their tradition that are so important
      that they can be required of believers in addition to their faith: episcopacy, for
      example, or an infallible papacy, believers' baptism, or biblical inerrancy. Paul's

gospel is today as much abused by those who think they are true to it as ever it was in the past. Those who insist, on such grounds, that they cannot worship together, or share the Lord's Supper together, or mission together are adding their own traditional "works" and losing sight of Paul's gospel.

(4)   The original context and significance of Paul's first statement of the principle should not be lost to sight either: that the gospel broke down the division between Jew and Gentile. From a Jewish perspective, humanity was divided into two, between Jews and Gentiles, with the former in a favored position in relation to God (cf. Eph 2:11–12). But Christ had changed all that by breaking down "the dividing wall, that is, the hostility" between the two, "that he might create in himself one new humanity in place of the two, thus making peace, and might reconcile both groups to God in one body" (2:13–16 [NRSV]). There was a horizontal as well as a vertical dimension, a racial and social as well as an individual dimension to Paul's gospel that should never by forgotten. "To *all* who believe" and "by faith and not works of the law" are two sides of the same coin. (For further discussion on these subjects, see Westerholm 2004; Wright 2005; Bird 2007; Dunn 2008.)

Participation in Christ

The prominence given to the images of atonement and justification by the disagreement between churches and theologians over their meaning and significance has tended to obscure other aspects of Paul's gospel. This has been unfortunate, since it has tended not only to squeeze and lose the rich diversity of Paul's imagery, but also to lose sight of the different ways in which Paul could express and explain his gospel.

One of these key ways has been summed up in the term "participation in Christ." The main reference point for the term is Paul's phrase "in Christ." The phrase occurs eighty-three times in the Pauline corpus. To that figure should be added the equally distinctive Pauline phrase "in the Lord" (a further forty-seven times), not to mention the many "in him/whom" phrases in the Pauline letters that also refer to Christ. Elsewhere in the New Testament "in Christ" appears only in three passages in 1 Peter (3:16; 5:10, 14). So it is a characteristic and distinctive feature of Paul's theology. In his letters, the phrase is used in a variety of contexts, which together embrace the scope of the gospel, its center, and its outworking.

Thus, Paul uses the phrase to refer to the redemptive act that has happened "in Christ," both the event of Jesus's death and its effect when the gospel was accepted. For example: "They are justified ... through the redemption that is in Christ Jesus" (Rom 3:24); "the gracious gift of God is eternal life in Christ Jesus our Lord" (6:23); "the law of the Spirit of life in Christ Jesus has set you free" (8:2); "the grace of God given you in Christ Jesus" (1 Cor 1:4); "God was in Christ reconciling the world" (2 Cor 5:19); "seeking to be justified in Christ" (Gal 2:17).

Again, Paul thought of his new life as a Christian as lived "in Christ." Believers, almost by definition (or experience?), are "in Christ" or "in the Lord." For example: "You must reckon yourselves dead indeed to sin and alive to God in Christ Jesus" (Rom 6:11);

"there is therefore now no condemnation for those in Christ Jesus" (8:1); we are all "one body in Christ" (12:5); those "sanctified in Christ Jesus" (1 Cor 1:2); "if anyone is in Christ, there is a new creation" (2 Cor 5:17); "the freedom that we have in Christ Jesus" (Gal 2:4); Paul's imprisonment was "in Christ" (Phil 1:13); he commands and exhorts "in the Lord Jesus Christ" (2 Thess 3:12); Onesimus is a beloved brother "both in the flesh and in the Lord" (Phlm 16).

Clearly, then, this phrase summed up and encapsulated a foundational feature of Paul's life as a Christian; in some passages, indeed, "in Christ" could almost be translated "Christian." Paul assumed that this was the case for all the members of the churches to which he wrote. By responding to the gospel of Jesus Christ, they had been incorporated "in Christ." They had been baptized in the name of Christ (cf. 1 Cor 1:13–15) – a formula which probably meant that they had submitted and been transferred to Christ's lordship (the imagery may be from banking, as today a check is made "to the name of" the payee). More than that, however, they had been "baptized *into* Christ Jesus" (Rom 6:3; Gal 3:27; cf. 1 Cor 10:2). Paul is pushing language here, and what he had in mind is not entirely clear, but some things can be said with some confidence.

One is indicated by the parallel he draws between Adam and Christ. The parallel is clearest in 1 Corinthians 15:22: "As in Adam all die, so also in Christ shall all be made alive." Human createdness can be summed up by reference to Adam. Paul knew well that *adam* in Hebrew meant "man/human being." So the human state of being could be described by speaking of "Adam": "Adam" represents humankind. Not only so, but Adam represents ordinary human existence in its domination by the power of sin and its subjection to the power of death. Paul develops the point by allusion in Romans 1:19–23 and 7:7–11, and explicitly in Romans 5:12–19 and 1 Corinthians 15:21–22, 45–49. Here, the fact that he can describe this representativeness of Adam by using the phrase "in Adam" (1 Cor 15:22) indicates the relevance of this line of thought. For, presumably, at least in this instance Christ is being understood as filling an equivalent representative function. So the phrase "in Christ" has at least the significance of indicating identification with Christ. Those who were baptized "in the name of Christ" or "into Christ" identified themselves with Christ and were identified with him.

We can put the point more strongly, as the phrase "in Christ" suggests. For it is hard to escape a locative significance in the "in." To be "in Christ" is to be somehow located "in Christ," to locate oneself by reference to Christ, to understand one's place or home by reference to Christ. One lives one's life within the circle of Christ: the circle not only of his teaching and example but of his lordship, where nothing is done except as an expression of the life one owes to Christ. As a variation of the thought, Paul does not hesitate to use the analogy of marriage. As in marriage "the two shall be one flesh," so "he who is united with the Lord is one spirit" (1 Cor 6:16–17). "In Christ" denotes oneness with Christ, two hearts with one beat, two lives so closely identified as to be more or less one and the same. Reversing the imagery, Paul can even say, "It is no longer I who live, but Christ lives in me" (Gal 2:20; see also Rom 8:9–10; 2 Cor 13:5; Col 1:27).

A natural extension of this theme is the image of the church in any place as the body of Christ in that place (Rom 12:4–8; 1 Cor 12), as the Corinthian believers were the body of Christ in Corinth (1 Cor 12:27). So, to be baptized into Christ was not simply to establish an intimate relation between Christ and the individual. It was to be baptized into one body, the body of Christ (1 Cor 12:13). As in the imagery of justification, the social dimension of the gospel's appeal and effect should not be passed over. To be "in Christ" was to be "one in Christ": Jew and Greek, slave and free, male and female (Gal 3:28). The gospel had inescapable corporate dimensions. The saving process begun by the gospel included the dependency of individual members of a body on the other members of the body fulfilling their function (1 Cor 12:12–26). As the later Pauline letters emphasized, maturing as a believer was not an isolated affair, but dependent on others, on the whole body growing into Christ, "the full measure of the stature of Christ" (Eph 4:13–16; Col 2:19).

Becoming like Christ

The "in Christ" motif as an expression of the outworking of the gospel has a further dimension that deserves attention. For Paul, the commitment of faith in baptism to Jesus as Lord was a decisive act, but still only the *beginning*. The work begun had to be finished, completed (Gal 3:3; Phil 1:6). *Salvation* for Paul was not completed by conversion and baptism. "Salvation" was the complete process, or the completion of the process (Rom 5:9–10; 1 Cor 5:5; 1 Thess 5:8–9). Christians were in process of "being saved" (1 Cor 1:18; 15:2; 2 Cor 2:15). To judge by such passages, Paul would have replied to the more modern question "Are you saved?" by answering, "Not yet!"

The impact of the gospel as "the power of God for salvation to every one who has faith" (Rom 1:16) thus is not a once-for-all event (conversion, baptism). Paul describes the process in different terms. "Sanctification," being made holy, has been the traditional balance to "justification," understood as the once-for-all acceptance of the sinner by God: the process begun by the initial justification is completed by sanctification, being made holy. And Paul does use the term in this sense (Rom 6:19, 22; 1 Thess 4:3–4). But he also refers to believers as already "saints," that is, "holy ones" (for example, 2 Cor 1:1; Phil 1:1), and he uses the verb for the decisive beginning of the process (1 Cor 6:11). Alternatively, he thinks of the process as one of *transformation*, of an inward renewal that makes possible a life pleasing to God (Rom 12:2; 2 Cor 4:16).

More to the point, he thinks of the process as a transformation to become like Christ. It is a transformation, from one degree of glory to another, into the image of God embodied in Jesus (2 Cor 3:18; 4:4; Col 3:10). Here, Paul picks up once again the Adam/Christ parallel. Adam had been made in the image of God, but had fallen short of the glory God had thus bestowed on him (Rom 3:23). So salvation could be envisaged as the restoration of that glory, or the transformation of humankind back to the original intention of God the creator (Rom 8:18, 21; 1 Cor 2:7). The outcome of the process of salvation intended by God was "to be conformed to the image of his Son" (Rom 8:29).

This transformation is also an increasing identification of the one being saved with the decisive redemptive event of Christ's death and resurrection. It could even be called a re-enactment of these saving events – or, more precisely, the acting out of these events (and their significance) in the lives of believers. The experience of being baptized into Christ is also the event of being baptized into his death (Rom 6:3). The process of becoming like Christ includes becoming like Christ in his death; that is, presumably, the dying away of the old nature, of the Adamic nature (Col 3:9–10; Eph 4:22–24). Using the Greek tense (perfect) which indicates the continuing result of a past action, Paul can even depict himself as having been crucified with Christ, and, as a result, still hanging with him on the cross: "I have been crucified with Christ" (Gal 2:19; similarly 6:14); "we have become knit together with the very likeness of his death" (Rom 6:5). The Christian life, for Paul, was a process of being conformed to Christ's death (Phil 3:10). This was presumably why Paul was not dismayed by the amount of suffering he endured during his mission, even quite extreme suffering. Indeed, he encouraged his fellow Christians to rejoice in their suffering because of its character-producing effect (Rom 5:3–4). He could see such sufferings as suffering with Christ, as sharing in Christ's sufferings (Rom 8:17), even his own sufferings as "filling up what is lacking of the afflictions of Christ" (Col 1:24). This aspect of Paul's gospel has been well caught in the term "cruciformity" (Gorman 2001).

The end of the process is no less Christo-form in character. For it is a becoming like Christ in his resurrection. This is why, in the end of the day, the sufferings of the process are bearable: because the sufferings will be outweighed by the glory (Rom 8:17–18); the stripping off of the old nature, the wearing away of the outer nature, will be completed by the resurrection of the body (2 Cor 4:16–5:5; Rom 8:10–11). "As we have borne the image of the man of dust [Adam], we will also bear the image of the man of heaven [the resurrected Christ]" (1 Cor 15:49 [NRSV]). Paul wanted above all "to know Christ and the power of his resurrection and the sharing of his sufferings by becoming like him in his death, if somehow [he might] attain the resurrection from the dead" (Phil 3:10–11 [NRSV]). He was confident that Christ "will transform the body of our humiliation that it may be conformed to the body of his glory" (Phil 3:21 [NRSV]).

Alternatively, Paul can speak of the salvation process as one effected "with Christ." Romans 6:4–8 are a good example: "So then we were buried with him through baptism into death ... For if we have become knit together with the very likeness of his death, we shall certainly also be knit together with the very likeness of his resurrection. Knowing this, that our old nature has been crucified with him ... But if we have died with Christ, we believe that we shall also live with him."

All this correlated in Paul's gospel with the hope of Christ's return from heaven, his *parousia*, or (second) coming. That this was an integral feature of Paul's preaching, certainly in his early mission work, is indicated in his earliest letter, 1 Thessalonians. Paul reminds the Thessalonians "how you turned to God from idols, to serve a living and true God, and to wait for his Son from heaven" (1 Thess 1:9–10 [NRSV]). And the problem that Paul confronts in 4:13–17 seems to imply confusion on the part of the Thessalonians over the fact that some of their members had died before Christ's *parousia* – presumably arising from the expectation given them by Paul's preaching that Christ's return would be soon. How much Paul tied his gospel and the expectation of a completion for the salvation process to such a *parousia* hope is less clear, though Philippians 1:6 implies that the connection remained close. But the fact that Paul accepted the possibility of his own death before the *parousia* (Phil 1:20–24) suggests that he was far from clear in his own mind how the completion of salvation in individual cases correlated with the coming of Christ (see further Plevnik 1996).

Not to be forgotten is the belief that Christ will return as judge (2 Cor 5:10), and that an integral part of the completion of the salvation process will be final judgment (Rom 2:6–16; 14:10–12; 1 Cor 3:12–15). Paul's hope was ever that the transforming power of the gospel would result in his converts being pure, blameless, and mature/perfect on that final day (1 Cor 1:8; Phil 1:10; Col 1:22, 28; 1 Thess 3:13; 5:23). But his assurance lay in the conviction that "God is for us." The justification that his gospel promised had two phases. But the decisive factor for Paul was that "it is God who justifies," and that "it is Christ who died, rather was raised, who also is at the right hand of God, who also intercedes on our behalf" (Rom 8:31–34).

The Gift of the Spirit as the Defining Mark

Paul speaks of the outworking of the gospel not only in the imagery of atonement and justification, and not only in the language of sharing "in Christ" or "with Christ." Equally important, but also traditionally quite neglected in Christian theology, is *the gift of the Spirit*. Perhaps because evidence of the Spirit at work has often been somewhat controversial or disputed, it has been easier (safer?) to use imagery that, though it has lost its vitality, can (for that reason?) provide technical terms (atonement, salvation) whose value is rooted more in their creedal or ritual context than in their actual meaning. Technical terms can be carefully hedged around with rubrics and dogmas more easily monitored and controlled. Alternatively, focus on the ritual moments related to (or which bring to focus) the gospel and its reception (such as baptism) means that the events in view can be managed and held within safe bounds. The gift of the Spirit, however, has an unpredictable character. It cannot be controlled in either of these ways. So there is something uncomfortable, perhaps even disturbing, in giving too much attention or scope to this aspect of the gospel.

Yet it should never be forgotten that it was the manifest evidence of the Spirit "coming upon" or being "given" in unexpected ways and measure that lay very much at the heart of Paul's gospel. As already noted, it was the gift of the Spirit to Gentiles, prior to, and without any expectation of, their being circumcised or becoming proselytes, that caught Paul's predecessor Jewish evangelists and missionaries completely by surprise. But they could not deny that God was dealing with such believing Gentiles just as he had been dealing with the first Jewish believers. A classic tale of this unexpected development is given by Luke in Acts 10–11: Peter was so convinced by the evidence that the Spirit had been given freely and fully to the Gentile centurion Cornelius and his friends that he found it impossible to deny them baptism. According to Luke, the leadership of the mother church in Jerusalem was equally persuaded that, since the Spirit had been thus freely bestowed on Gentile believers, traditional and scriptural practices could and should be passed over (Acts 11:15–18; 15:7–11).

Paul is the one most closely identified with the opening of the gospel to Gentiles. And he gives an equivalent account of what persuaded the Jerusalem leadership to recognize that God had truly accepted Gentiles without requiring them to be circumcised and become proselytes. In his terms, the grace of God to Gentiles was clearly evidenced through his preaching; the grace of God was manifest through him in the gospel for the uncircumcised (Gal 2:7–9). It is clear from the beginning of Galatians 3 that this manifest grace of God was another way of speaking of the gift of the Spirit: "Did you receive the Spirit by doing the works of the law or by hearing with faith?" (3:2–5). The gift of the Spirit was an alternative way of speaking of the Gentiles' justification. The argument that follows shows that Paul regarded both being reckoned righteous and the reception of the Spirit as "the blessing of Abraham" promised to Gentiles (3:6–14). God showed that he had justified/accepted them by giving them the Spirit. This reception of the Spirit solely by faith (without requiring anything more) Paul regarded as "the truth of the gospel" (2:5, 14). We can deduce from Romans 8:1–14 that Paul attributed to the Spirit his own sense of liberation from what he now regarded as the enslaving power of the law. There is a clear note of exultant relief and affirmation in Paul's cry in 2 Corinthians 3:17: "where the Spirit of the Lord is, there is freedom."

So theological reflection on Paul's gospel should give prominence – much more prominence than has traditionally been given – to the gift of the Spirit as one of the principal foci in Paul's understanding of how the power of the gospel effected salvation in human lives. For Paul, indeed, the gift and resulting possession of the Spirit were the key defining marks of the Christian. The closest he comes to giving a definition of a Christian is in his letter to Rome: "if anyone does not have the Spirit of Christ, that person does not belong to him" (Rom 8:9). He says something similar a few verses later: "as many as are led by the Spirit of God, they are sons of God" (8:14). It was precisely because Paul gave such prominence to the reception of the Spirit as the decisive factor in the event of becoming a Christian (conversion and baptism) that the gift of the Spirit to Gentiles when they believed the gospel was in itself proof positive that God had accepted them without requiring any "works of the law."

The Spirit and the Outworking of the Gospel

The traditional neglect of this key aspect of Paul's gospel has also hidden the extent to which the Spirit is the determinative factor in the whole process of the gospel's outworking (see also Fee 1994).

Paul understood that the act of receiving and responding to the gospel was itself the work of the Spirit and evidence of the Spirit's role in the success of the gospel. He reminds the Corinthians (1 Cor 2:2–5) that what won their faith was not the attractiveness of his message ("Christ crucified"), and not the rhetorical skills he demonstrated in his proclamation ("not with the persuasiveness of wisdom"). On the contrary, he presented his gospel "in weakness and in fear and in much trembling." The decisive factor was that his words came "with a demonstration of the Spirit and of power." Similarly, he reminds his Thessalonian converts that "our gospel came to you not in word only, but also in power and in the Holy Spirit and with full conviction" (1 Thess 1:5). To be noted is the fact that Paul was thinking not so much of the Spirit inspiring his own preaching as of the impact made by his words, the convicting power that persuaded much more effectively than great rhetoric, the word that so penetrated to the heart that the will could not withhold a positive response.

Paul too knew well that both *ruach* (Hebrew) and *pneuma* (Greek) could be understood as "breath" or "wind" as well as "spirit." So it was natural for him to think of the Spirit as the breath of life (as in Gen 2:7 and Ezek 37:6–10). The Spirit was not only the "life-giver" (Rom 8:11; 1 Cor 15:45; 2 Cor 3:6), but itself constituted the life given (Rom 8:10). Without the Spirit, the gospel would have fallen on barren ground. The Spirit was the life-giving force and the new life of the new creation. The indwelling Spirit was the complement to being "in Christ," another way of envisaging the resurrected life of Christ within the believer (Rom 8:9–10).

So the gift of the Spirit is also to be understood as the *beginning* of the process of salvation. As Paul rebukes the Galatians: "Are you so foolish? Having begun with the Spirit, are you now made complete with the flesh?" (Gal 3:3). The implication obviously is that their growth to maturity as Christians was as dependent on the Spirit working in and through them as their initial conversion. In two equivalent metaphors, Paul describes the gift of the Spirit as the decisive beginning that both anticipates and ensures the complete outworking of the gospel in his converts' lives. The Spirit is the *arrabōn*, the "first installment and guarantee" of the wholeness of salvation (2 Cor 1:22; 5:5; also Eph 1:13–14). Alternatively, the Spirit is the *aparchē*, the "first fruits"; that is, the first sheaves of harvest, the beginning of the harvest (Rom 8:23). Or, if the thought is of baptism as marking the beginning, then just as Paul does not hesitate to speak of having been "baptized into Christ" and "into Christ's death" (Rom 6:3; Gal 3:27), so he does not hesitate to speak of having been "baptized in the Spirit" (1 Cor 12:13). This was a being "baptized *into one body*" – again (reception of) the Spirit is the "rite of entry." And it was a being baptized "in the *one* Spirit"; that is, it was the fact that all had experienced the same thing ("the one Spirit") that ensured the oneness of the body.

Given that many – sometimes strange and exotic (even bizarre) – experiences are attributed to the Spirit, a twenty-first-century inquirer into such phenomena might well ask what the first Christians regarded as manifestations of the Spirit. What was the proof positive that it was the Spirit of God that was at work? How was the gift of the Spirit recognized? Paul never quite addresses just that question. He was certainly well aware that experiences of Spirit inspiration were not self-authenticating and had to be tested (1 Cor 12:3, 10; 14:29; 1 Thess 5:19–22). But he had no hesitation in attributing some of the experiences of his converts to the Spirit. From 1 Corinthians 1:4–7 we can deduce that the Corinthians evidently enjoyed from the beginning of their Christian experience the sort of spiritual gifts that Paul discusses in chapters 12 and 14. But he also reminds them of the moral transformation of their lives when they were "washed, sanctified, and justified in the name of the Lord Jesus Christ and in the Spirit of our God" (1 Cor 6:9–11). Elsewhere, we read that the gift of the Spirit was marked and continued to be marked for the Galatians by the working of miracles (Gal 3:5). The Thessalonians "received the word with joy inspired by the Holy Spirit" (1 Thess 1:6). And Paul assumes that the Roman believers also experienced God's love poured out in their hearts "through the Holy Spirit given to us" (Rom 5:5). This love Paul regarded as the supreme mark of the Spirit (1 Cor 12:31–14:1; Gal 5:22).

Most striking of all, Paul attributes to the Spirit the experience of sonship. As he reminded the Galatians of how they began with the Spirit, so he reminds the Romans:

"you did not receive a spirit of slavery to fall back into fear, but you have received a spirit of adoption. When we cry, 'Abba! Father!' it is that very Spirit bearing witness with our spirit that we are children of God" (Rom 8:15–16 [NRSV]). What is so striking is that the first Christians evidently remembered that Jesus's own prayer-life had been marked by his "Abba" address to God. In consequence, they understood this "Abba" experience as a reflection of Jesus's own sonship, and so as evidence that they were sharing in Jesus's sonship, "heirs of God and joint heirs with Christ" (8:17). And this they attributed to the Spirit, "the Spirit of the Son," praying the Son's prayer and attesting their own sonship (Gal 4:5–7). This, for Paul, was an integral part of the process of becoming like Christ, of being transformed into the image of Christ by the Spirit (2 Cor 3:18), of being "conformed to the image of God's Son so that he might be the first-born of many brothers" (Rom 8:29).

The other aspects of the outworking of the gospel already noted above are also dependent on the gift of the Spirit. These include the corporate dimension of the gospel. As already noted, it was by being baptized in one Spirit that believers have become one body (1 Cor 12:13). Even more important, Paul clearly regarded the metaphor of the church as the body of Christ in terms of the Spirit. The functions of the body are the charisms inspired and enabled by the Spirit (Rom 12:4–8; 1 Cor 12:4, 7, 11). The church that is the focus of the corporate outworking of the gospel is essentially charismatic in character, essentially dependent on the Spirit inspiring and enabling the words and actions by which the body flourishes.

Equally important for Paul was the degree to which the outworking of the gospel in daily living is dependent on the Spirit. This was an important issue for the apostle, since his gospel could so easily be misinterpreted. A gospel that focused so heavily on God's free grace to sinners was obviously open to the criticism that Paul, in effect, encouraged sin so that grace might abound more fully (Rom 3:8; 6:1). That was one of the reasons why a strong appeal to the law was such an attractive alternative for many of Paul's critics and opponents. The law provided the restraints and guidance for moral living that Paul's gospel could be said to disregard. Paul's answer was the Spirit. The new converts did not need the law to direct them. In Paul's and many others' experience, life determined by the law had been counter-productive: by itself, the law provoked the very greed that it forbade. Interpreted in a too superficial way, the law had been an enslaving power. The gospel's alternative was not more law, but the life-giving Spirit (Rom 7:5–6; 2 Cor 3:6). Christian conduct could be described simply in terms of "being led by the Spirit" or "walking in accord with the Spirit" (Rom 8:12–14; Gal 5:16–18, 25). Indeed, Paul could cut the ground from under the feet of his opponents by claiming that it was those who walked in accordance with the Spirit who fulfilled what the law required (Rom 8:4). For, as Jesus had taught, the law was summed up and fulfilled in the commandment "Love your neighbor as yourself" (Rom 13:8–10; Gal 5:14) – and such love is enabled by the Spirit.

Finally, it should be recalled that the completion as well as the beginning of the process of salvation was, for Paul, pre-eminently the work of the Spirit. It is by sowing to the Spirit that eternal life will be reaped from the Spirit (Gal 6:8; Rom 8:13). The same point is implied by the passages referred to above (Gal 3:3; 2 Cor 5:5; Rom 8:23). The process of salvation, the process of becoming like Christ, will be completed by the

Spirit. The process indicated in the talk of sharing Christ's sufferings will be completed by sharing in his resurrection. The process of the old or outer nature dying and the new or inner nature being renewed will be completed by the resurrection of the body or by the transformation of this body into a body like Christ's resurrection body (1 Cor 15:45–49; 2 Cor 4:16–5:5; Phil 3:11–12, 21). And this too is the work of the Spirit, pre-eminently so: "If the Spirit of him who raised Jesus from the dead dwells in you, he who raised Christ from the dead will give life to your mortal bodies also through his Spirit that dwells in you" (Rom 8:11 [NRSV]). The resurrection body is precisely a "spiritual body," a body given life by the "life-giving Spirit" and animated by that Spirit (1 Cor 15:44–46). According to Paul's gospel, the Spirit both begins and completes the work of salvation promised by the gospel. The Spirit is the gospel's power to salvation (Rom 1:16).

In sum, it is important to grasp the full roundedness of the gospel according to Paul. It can so easily be constricted or diminished – by focusing on one aspect or image and neglecting others, by emphasizing its personal and individual dimension or its corporate and social dimension to the neglect of the other, by focusing on the beginning of the salvation process rather than the whole process, or by neglecting or sidelining its ethical corollaries and outworking. It is equally important that the diversity of these aspects and dimensions are recognized and respected, even when they do not fit easily together, and that the different aspects and metaphors are not squeezed to conform to the dimensions of the one most favored. Perhaps, then, this chapter should be re-entitled, "The Whole Gospel According to St. Paul"!

Note

1   Translations are my own except where otherwise indicated.

References

Bird, Michael F. 2007. *The Saving Righteousness of God: Studies on Paul, Justification and the New Perspective*. Milton Keynes: Paternoster.
Carson, D. A., Peter T. O'Brien, and Mark A. Seifrid, editors. 2001. *Justification and Variegated Nomism*. Volume 1: *The Complexities of Second Temple Judaism*. Tübingen: Mohr Siebeck.
Dunn, James D. G. 1998. *The Theology of Paul the Apostle*. Grand Rapids: Eerdmans.
Dunn, James D. G. 2008. *The New Perspective on Paul*. Revised edition. Grand Rapids: Eerdmans.
Fee, Gordon D. 1994. *God's Empowering Presence: The Holy Spirit in the Letters of Paul*. Peabody, Mass.: Hendrickson.
Gorman, Michael J. 2001. *Cruciformity: Paul's Narrative Spirituality of the Cross*. Grand Rapids: Eerdmans.
Hooker, Morna D. 1995. *Not Ashamed of the Gospel: New Testament Interpretations of the Death of Christ*. Grand Rapids: Eerdmans.
Horrell, David G. 2000. *An Introduction to the Study of Paul*. London: T. & T. Clark.
Horsley, Richard A., editor. 1997. *Paul and Empire: Religion and Power in Roman Imperial Society*. Harrisburg: Trinity.

Jervis, L. Ann, and Peter Richardson, editors. 1994. *Gospel in Paul: Studies on Corinthians, Galatians and Romans for Richard N. Longenecker*. Sheffield: Sheffield Academic.

Kraus, Wolfgang. 1991. *Der Tod Jesu als Heiligtumsweihe: Eine Untersuchung zum Umfeld der Sühnevorstellung in Römer 3,25–26a*. Neukirchen-Vluyn: Neukirchener Verlag.

Martin, Ralph P. 1981. *Reconciliation: A Study of Paul's Theology*. London: Marshall, Morgan and Scott.

O'Brien, Peter Thomas. 1995. *Gospel and Mission in the Writings of Paul: An Exegetical and Theological Analysis*. Grand Rapids: Baker.

Plevnik, Joseph. 1996. *Paul and the Parousia: An Exegetical and Theological Investigation*. Peabody, Mass.: Hendrickson.

Sanders, E. P. 1977. *Paul and Palestinian Judaism: A Comparison of Patterns of Religion*. London: SCM.

Seifrid, Mark A. 1992. *Justification by Faith: The Origin and Development of a Central Pauline Theme*. Leiden: Brill.

Stanton, Graham N. 2003. Paul's Gospel. Pages 173–184 in *The Cambridge Companion to St. Paul*. Edited by James D. G. Dunn. Cambridge: Cambridge University Press.

Stanton, Graham N. 2004. Jesus and Gospel. Pages 9–62 in Graham N. Stanton, *Jesus and Gospel*. Cambridge: Cambridge University Press.

Westerholm, Stephen. 2004. *Perspectives Old and New on Paul: The "Lutheran" Paul and his Critics*. Grand Rapids: Eerdmans.

Wright, N. T. 2005. *Paul: In Fresh Perspective*. London: SPCK.

CHAPTER 10
Paul and Scripture

J. Ross Wagner

Paul's writings resonate with scriptural overtones. In his extant letters, the apostle to the Gentiles explicitly cites Israel's Scriptures approximately seventy-five times (see table 10.1).[1] Frequent allusions to scriptural texts, stories, and symbols enliven and advance his arguments. Scripture not only testifies to Paul's gospel; it also enables Paul to understand that gospel more deeply and to articulate it more forcefully (Hays 1989; Wagner 2002; Watson 2004).[2] This chapter surveys a number of central and, in some cases, controversial topics in the study of Paul's interpretation of Scripture. We begin by considering a passage from 2 Corinthians that brings the issues sharply into focus.

"Now is the Day of Salvation": Paul's Apostolic Hermeneutic

Writing to defend himself to a church that has begun to question his integrity and his credentials as an apostle, Paul makes a characteristically bold claim: God, who has reconciled the world to himself in Christ, is the one who has appointed Paul an ambassador in the ministry of reconciliation. God himself speaks through the apostle, broadcasting the urgent appeal, "Be reconciled to God!" (2 Cor 5:11–21). As God's co-worker, then, Paul implores the Corinthians: "Do not receive the grace of God in vain. For he says, 'At a favorable time I heard you, and on a day of salvation I helped you.' Look – now is the well-favored time! Now is the day of salvation!" (2 Cor 6:1–2).[3] In this passage, we may observe four crucial aspects of the many-faceted relationship between Paul's letters and the Scriptures of Israel.

Scripture, tradition, social location

First, by employing the citation formula "he says," Paul explicitly signals to his hearers that the following words are quoted speech. Whether or not they can identify the precise

The Blackwell Companion to Paul, First Edition. Edited by Stephen Westerholm.
© 2011 Blackwell Publishing Ltd. Published 2011 by Blackwell Publishing Ltd.

Table 10.1 Citations of Scripture in Paul's undisputed letters

Reference	Text(s) cited
Rom 1:17	Hab 2:4b (cf. Gal 3:11)
Rom 2:24	Isa 52:5
Rom 3:4	Ps 51:4
Rom 3:10–12	Ps 14:1–3
3:13a	Ps 5:9
3:13b	Ps 140:3
3:14	Ps 10:7
3:15–17	Isa 59:7–8
3:18	Ps 36:1
Rom 4:3	Gen 15:6
Rom 4:7–8	Ps 32:1–2
Rom 4:17	Gen 17:5
Rom 4:18	Gen 15:5
Rom 4:22–23	Gen 15:6
Rom 7:7	Exod 20:17/Deut 5:21
Rom 8:36	Ps 44:22
Rom 9:7	Gen 21:12
Rom 9:9	Gen 18:14 (cf. Gen 18:10)
Rom 9:12	Gen 25:23
Rom 9:13	Mal 1:2–3
Rom 9:15	Exod 33:19
Rom 9:17	Exod 9:16
Rom 9:25	Hos 2:23
9:26	Hos 1:10b
Rom 9:27–28	Hos 1:10a + Isa 10:22–23 + Isa 28:22
Rom 9:29	Isa 1:9
Rom 9:33	Isa 28:16 + 8:14
Rom 10:5	Lev 18:5 (cf. Gal 3:12)
Rom 10:6–8	Deut 9:4 + Deut 30:12–14
Rom 10:11	Isa 28:16
Rom 10:15	Isa 52:7
Rom 10:16	Isa 53:1
Rom 10:18	Ps 19:4
Rom 10:19	Deut 32:21
Rom 10:20	Isa 65:1
Rom 10:21	Isa 65:2
Rom 11:3	1 Kings 19:10 (cf. 19:14)
Rom 11:4	1 Kings 19:18
Rom 11:8	Deut 29:4/Isa 29:10

(Continued)

Table 10.1 *(Continued)*

Reference	Text(s) cited
Rom 11:9–10	Ps 69:22–23
Rom 11:26–27	Isa 59:20–21/27:9
Rom 12:19	Deut 32:35
Rom 13:9a	Exod 20:13–17/Deut 5:17–19, 21
Rom 13:9b	Lev 19:18
Rom 14:11	Isa 45:23
Rom 15:3	Ps 69:9
Rom 15:9	Ps 18:49
Rom 15:10	Deut 32:43
Rom 15:11	Ps 117:1
Rom 15:12	Isa 11:10
Rom 15:21	Isa 52:15
1 Cor 1:19	Isa 29:14
1 Cor 1:31	1 Kgdms 2:10 b–g/Jer 9:23–24 (cf. 2 Cor 10:17)
1 Cor 2:9	Isa 64:4 ?
1 Cor 3:19	Job 5:12–13
1 Cor 3:20	Ps 94:11
1 Cor 6:16	Gen 2:24
1 Cor 9:9	Deut 25:4
1 Cor 9:10	? (cf. Isa 28:24, 28; 45:9)
1 Cor 10:7	Exod 32:6
1 Cor 14:21	Isa 28:11–12
1 Cor 15:27a	Ps 8:6
1 Cor 15:45	Gen 2:7
1 Cor 15:54	Isa 25:8
15:55	Hos 13:14
2 Cor 4:6	Gen 1:3? Isa 9:2?
2 Cor 4:13	Ps 116:10
2 Cor 6:2	Isa 49:8
2 Cor 6:16	Lev 26:11–12 + Ezek 37:27
6:17a	Isa 52:11
6:17b	Ezek 20:34
6:18a	2 Sam 7:14
6:18b	2 Sam 7:8
2 Cor 8:15	Exod 16:18
2 Cor 9:9	Ps 112:9
2 Cor 10:17	1 Kgdms 2:10 f–g/Jer 9:24 (cf. 1 Cor 1:31)
Gal 3:6	Gen 15:6
Gal 3:8	Gen 12:3 (cf. Gen 18:18; 28:14)
Gal 3:10	Deut 27:26 (+Deut 28:58? 29:19?)

Table 10.1   (*Continued*)

Reference	Text(s) cited
Gal 3:11	Hab 2:4b (cf. Rom 1:17)
Gal 3:12	Lev 18:5 (cf. Rom 10:5)
Gal 3:13	Deut 21:23 (+Deut 27:26)
Gal 3:16	Gen 13:15 (cf. Gen 17:8; 24:7)
Gal 4:27	Isa 54:1
Gal 4:30	Gen 21:10
Gal 5:14	Lev 19:18

Source: Based on Stanley (1992); verse numbering follows the NRSV.

source, the Corinthians, who by this time have known and interacted with Paul over a period of several years, will recognize that he is quoting Scripture. Frequent appeals to Scripture through citation or allusion are a notable phenomenon in the Corinthian correspondence, as in a number of Paul's other letters. First Corinthians contains thirteen quotations from Scripture, along with a lengthy, if selective, narration of the story of Israel's exodus from Egypt and rebellion in the desert (1 Cor 10:1–13). In addition to seven scriptural citations, 2 Corinthians features an elaborate comparison of Paul's ministry of the gospel with Moses' reception and promulgation of the law (2 Cor 3).

By interweaving Israel's sacred texts into his letters, Paul deliberately locates himself and the communities to which he writes within an ancient tradition of thought and life. In this respect, Paul was very much a man of his time. As Loveday Alexander observes, during the Hellenistic and Roman periods, wherever the adherents of a philosophical "school" carried on the wisdom and way of life of a founder (such as Epicurus, Zeno, or Plato), they did so by handing on and reinterpreting his teachings, whether oral or written. "The canonical texts were not simply dead monuments of the founder's thought: 'the role of scriptural authority was to provide a philosophical movement with a *raison d'être* and a framework within which it could preserve its cohesion *while* continuing to inquire and debate'" (Alexander 2001, 113; citing Sedley 1989, 101).

In the context of cosmopolitan Roman Corinth, Paul's failure to cite Greek authorities would have been notable.[4] "No Greek or Roman observer of Paul's interchanges with the Corinthian church could fail to observe (as Galen did of a later generation of Christians) that the cultural matrix in which this discourse operates is distinctively 'Jewish,' in the sense that the classic text on which it draws is the Jewish scriptures" (Alexander 2001, 117). Without diminishing the surprising and world-transforming character of the apocalypse (revelation) of God's righteousness in the death and resurrection of Jesus the Messiah (Gal 1:15–16), Paul takes great pains to situate this "good news" in relation to a broad and dynamic Jewish tradition that stubbornly recalls God's past faithfulness and steadfastly hopes for God's promised redemption of Israel and of the world.

The earliest Christians all stand within this wider Jewish frame of reference. For while Paul is the earliest follower of Jesus whose writings survive, he avows that the gospel he has passed on to the Corinthians, the tradition that he himself received and that the other apostles all proclaim, is already one that regards Jesus's death "for our sins" and his resurrection on the third day to be comprehensible only "in accordance with the Scriptures" (1 Cor 15:1–11). In order to understand Paul's reading of Scripture rightly, therefore, we must recognize that he interacts with texts that are embedded in rich traditions of interpretation – Jewish and early "Christian" – that significantly shape the meaning and significance that those foundational documents bear for him.

Divine speech and the rhetoric of Paul's citations

A second noteworthy feature of Paul's appeal to Scripture in 2 Corinthians 6:2 is the rhetorical effect this citation produces. Responding to accusations that he has been unreliable and deceptive in his dealings with the Corinthians (1:17; 2:17), the apostle maintains that his conduct has consistently been upright and transparent before God and people (4:2; 5:11). He insists that the impetus for his ministry derives only from the self-giving love of Christ, through whom God has reconciled the world to himself (5:14–21). In union with Christ, Paul and his fellow believers in Corinth now partici- pate in God's new creation (5:17). Together, in Christ, they come to embody God's own righteousness (5:21) as they are progressively transformed into Christ's image (cf. 3:18; 4:6). And yet, while he makes it clear that God is the primary agent of reconciliation, Paul also reminds his listeners in the strongest terms that he himself is God's appointed emissary. God has given to Paul "the ministry of reconciliation" (5:18) and entrusted to him "the message of reconciliation" (5:19). Paul functions as God's "ambassador" who is authorized to speak on behalf of Christ (5:20). Indeed, God speaks through him (5:20). For the Corinthians to remain estranged from God's "co-worker" Paul, and from his message, is thus to risk "receiv[ing] the grace of God in vain" (6:1).

These are astonishing claims. But Paul does not make them on his own authority. God himself steps forward, as it were, and addresses the Corinthians directly: "At a favorable time I heard you, and in a day of salvation I helped you" (6:2, quoting Isa 49:8). The citation puts the weight of holy Scripture squarely behind Paul's words. More than that, as the letter is read out in the community, God's "presence" in first-person speech actualizes Paul's claim that God speaks through him. God's pronounce- ment also propels the argument forward by introducing a note of urgency to Paul's appeal, a note that the apostle amplifies in his subsequent interpretive comment. In this way, Paul employs the common Jewish and early Christian conviction that God speaks in Scripture to great rhetorical effect.

Scripture and the mission of Paul

Third, Paul's appropriation of this ancient prophecy as a divine word spoken into his own setting reflects an "apostolic hermeneutic." That is, Paul reads Scripture as one passionately engaged in the challenging, all-consuming task of planting and nurturing communities of Christ-followers. Attention to the immediate context of these words in

Isaiah suggests that this particular passage may well have carried deep personal significance for Paul. The divine speech he quotes belongs to a pair of oracles (Isa 49:1–6,
7–13) that speak of a chosen "servant" (vv. 3, 5, 6) called by God from the womb to
regather Israel's exiles (v. 5) and to serve as "a light for the Gentiles," bringing salvation
to the ends of the earth (vv. 6, 8). At some point, Paul came to conceptualize his own
calling as apostle to the Gentiles in terms of these Isaianic prophecies. Recounting for
the Galatians the origin of his gospel in "a revelation of Jesus Christ" (Gal 1:12), he
narrates his call in terms that echo Isaiah 49 (see Ciampa 1998, 111–118, 145–146).
Just as the unnamed servant has been "called" (Isa 49:1; cf. 49:6) "from his mother's
womb" (Isa 49:1; cf. 49:5), so Paul has been set apart "from his mother's womb" and
"called" by God's grace (Gal 1:15). Moreover, Paul's commission, like that of the Lord's
servant, involves proclaiming the good news of salvation to the Gentiles (Gal 1:16;
2:6–10). When Paul's citation in 2 Corinthians 6:2 is viewed against the backdrop of
Isaiah 49:1–13, Paul himself emerges as the singular "you" to whom God speaks. It is
through this servant of God, the apostle to the Gentiles, that God proclaims the good
news to the Corinthians.

Scripture and the church

A fourth dimension of Paul's reading of Scripture relates closely to the previous one.
Through the prophetic Scriptures, the living God speaks directly not only to Paul but
also to the communities God is calling into being through the gospel. Because the
apostle introduces the divine speech in 2 Corinthians 6:2 as a confirmation of his
appeal to his listeners (v. 1), the Corinthians probably identified themselves as the "you"
(singular) addressed in the quotation, "I heard you ... I helped you." Paul phrases his
plea in a way that fosters such an interpretation, despite the mismatch in grammatical
number, for in the original Greek the word that directly precedes the citation formula
is "you" (plural). Moreover, the Corinthians have already learned to regard themselves
as the addressees of Israel's Scriptures. In 1 Corinthians, after citing a Mosaic prohibition against muzzling an ox while it treads out grain (Deut 25:4), Paul asks a rhetorical
question, "Doesn't he speak entirely for our sake?" and in the next breath answers, "It
was written for our sake" (1 Cor 9:9–10; cf. Rom 4:23–24). Shortly thereafter, Paul
appends to his lengthy narration of Israel's exodus from Egypt and rebellion in the
wilderness the didactic conclusion: "Now these things happened to them as examples,
but they were written down to admonish us" (1 Cor 10:11a; cf. Rom 15:4).

Paul's confidence that the Scriptures were written "for our sake" flows from his
conviction that he and his listeners are those "upon whom the ends of the ages have
met together" (1 Cor 10:11b). This statement reflects a widespread early Jewish view
of history as divided into two distinct ages: the present age, and the age to come. For
Paul, Jesus's resurrection betokens the unexpected in-breaking of the age to come right
into the present age. Even as "the form of this world is passing away" (1 Cor 7:31),
Christ's resurrection has already inaugurated the "new creation" (2 Cor 5:17), God's
gracious reign over a reconciled humanity – the church – that is being transformed by
the Spirit into the image of the new human, the risen Christ (2 Cor 3:18; 4:16–18). At

Christ's return, those who belong to him will share in the fullness of his resurrection life, their bodies transfigured to be like his glorious body (1 Cor 15:20–58; Phil 3:21).

From Paul's perspective, all the Scriptures have in view precisely this moment in which "the ends of the ages have met together." The interpretive comments that follow his citation of the divine oracle in 2 Corinthians 6:2 drive this point home. Arresting his listener's attention with a sudden interjection – "Look!" – Paul replicates the twin temporal references of the citation, prefacing each with the emphatic declaration "Now!" and transforming the "favorable [*dektos*] time" mentioned in the quotation into the yet more forceful "well-favored [*euprosdektos*] time." The tireless missionary activity of the apostle over several decades attests just how unshakable was his conviction that the period between Christ's resurrection and Christ's return represents God's appointed time for all people, Jews and Gentiles alike, to respond to the glad summons to be reconciled to God in Christ.

Here, at the turn of the ages, the Scriptures speak to the church words of warning, encouragement, and instruction (1 Cor 10:11; Rom 15:4). Through such "apostolic interpretations" of Scripture, Paul seeks to shape and nurture communities of faith whose common life displays Christ's own pattern of self-giving love. That such is the larger objective served by the citation in 2 Corinthians 6:2 becomes apparent as the letter continues. Paul follows up his urgent appeal for reconciliation with an eloquent, impassioned defense of his own service to God (vv. 3–10). Quite abruptly, however, he softens his tone. Like a loving and long-suffering father, he cajoles, "We have opened our hearts wide to you, Corinthians. Now in fair return – I speak as to my children – open wide your hearts also" (vv. 11–13). Following the paper trail of Paul's correspondence with the Corinthians makes it clear that the reunion of this temporarily estranged community with the apostle will lead to their renewed partnership with him in the collection of relief funds for the believers in Jerusalem (2 Cor 8, 9; cf. 1 Cor 16:1–4). Through their generous, sacrificial giving, the Corinthians will come themselves to embody Christ's own loving self-donation (2 Cor 8:9). Just so, as a living letter of Christ (2 Cor 3:3), will they incarnate the true *telos* of Scripture.

Foundational Issues, Debated Questions

The past several decades have witnessed a renewed interest in Paul's appropriation of the Scriptures of Israel, leading to new insights as well as to new questions. The remainder of this chapter considers a number of important, and frequently controverted, issues in the study of Paul's reception of Scripture.

Author, text, reader

Paul left behind no scriptural commentaries. Rather, our access to Paul's interpretation of Scripture is mediated by his extant letters, each of which addresses the exigencies of a particular situation facing his churches. Any attempt to probe "behind" the text of Paul's letters in search of his understanding of Scripture or to press forward "in front of" the text in a quest to discern how much of the apostle's scriptural argumentation his audience might have comprehended must therefore be grounded in a close reading of Paul's letters themselves. For this reason, investigation of Paul's use of Scripture necessarily raises questions about the respective roles that authors, texts, and readers play in the construction of meaning, questions that continue to be vigorously debated throughout the humanities (Eagleton 2008). A number of concepts drawn from literary theory prove important for any investigation – literary, rhetorical, or theological – that seeks to understand the apostle, his letters, and the communities he addresses in relation to their first-century contexts.

Umberto Eco argues that texts, like languages, are always deeply embedded in particular historical and social contexts.[5] Eco conceptualizes such overarching contexts through the metaphor of the encyclopedia: "The encyclopedia ... registers all pieces of cultural knowledge: codes, rules, conventions, history, literature, truth claims, discourses, all the units that culture comprises: everything" (Huizenga 2009, 27, drawing on Eco 1984, 68–86). As a communicative act, a text actualizes a limited set of the infinite possibilities afforded by the encyclopedia. By means of its linguistic features, the text guides and constrains the interpretations of its "model reader," whose knowledge of the cultural encyclopedia enables him/her, through a progressive reading of the text, to discern the *intentio operis*, the intention of the text. "The Model Reader lies at the juncture where the linear manifestation of the text connects with the cultural encyclopedia in the most coherent and economic way possible" (Huizenga 2009, 23). At times, the text may require its model reader to make connections to specific intertexts (such as Isaiah's prophecy cited in 2 Cor 6:2) or to activate particular cultural frames (such as the "true philosopher's" catalog of hardships, 2 Cor 6:3–10; see Fitzgerald 1988). Good readers, then, are "those who approximate the position of the Model Reader" (Huizenga 2009, 23).

The profile of a text's model reader emerges through our interaction both with the text and with the cultural encyclopedia in which the text was produced; consequently, interpreting Paul's letters represents an historical, and not simply a literary, enterprise. Any account of the model reader must bear a plausible relationship to the historical audience, insofar as evidence allows us to reconstruct this audience. In the case of Paul's letters, the social, cultural, and political settings of the churches to which he writes differ from one another in important respects (see the relevant chapters in this volume). In this regard, it is worth pondering the significance of the data displayed in table 10.1. Explicit citations of Scripture are completely lacking in Philemon, Philippians, and 1 Thessalonians (although scriptural allusions do figure prominently in the last two); conversely, citations occur in the highest concentrations in Galatians, where Paul confronts Judaizing teachers, and in Romans, where Paul addresses house churches that appear to have had close ties to Jewish communities in Rome.

Each of the communities Paul addressed, moreover, comprised people with varying degrees of familiarity with the Scriptures, stories, and symbols of Israel. Christopher Stanley envisions the reception of Paul's letters by postulating three different types of listeners: an "informed audience" that knows the Scriptures as well as Paul and can evaluate his interpretations critically; a "competent audience" that has just enough familiarity with Scripture to understand the main point of Paul's quotations; and a "minimal audience" that has no prior knowledge of Israel's Scriptures (Stanley 2004, 68–69). While the "informed audience" approximates the "model reader" of the text, Stanley argues that the majority of listeners in the congregations Paul addressed fell into one of the remaining two categories. Literacy was not widespread in the Roman world, and most individuals encountered scriptural texts by hearing them read rather than through personal reading (Gamble 1995). Those Gentiles with limited exposure to Jews and their Scriptures before becoming Christ-followers would owe most of their scriptural knowledge to what they heard in gatherings of the church. However, it may not always have been easy for Paul's predominantly Gentile congregations to obtain their own copies of scriptural scrolls (Stanley 2004, 41–43), necessitating their reliance on other means of accessing Israel's Scriptures (see the following section).

At the same time, consideration of the social setting of the early churches should caution us against painting too minimalist a picture of the "hearer competence" of Paul's congregations. It is not enough to envision the reception of a Pauline letter simply in terms of isolated individuals listening passively to a single reading of Paul's missive. In 1 Corinthians 5:9 and 7:1, we catch glimpses of a much more active and communal process of reception in which extended discussion and argument over the meaning of Paul's "previous letter" led the congregation to send to Paul for clarification (which he then offers in 1 Corinthians; see chapter 3 of this volume). Such extended intra-community discussion of Paul's letter would afford those with greater "hearer competence" an opportunity to elucidate for others some of Paul's more difficult scriptural references (note the reference to "teachers" in 1 Cor 12:28).

It further appears that Paul normally delegated the delivery and reading of his letters to a trusted associate (cf. Rom 16:1–2), who would be in a position to help the recipients unpack the significance of Paul's statements. Moreover, in addition to the time Paul spent with a church during its founding (some eighteen months in the case of Corinth, according to Acts 18:11) and on subsequent visits (cf. 1 Cor 16:5–7; 2 Cor 2:1; 13:1), the apostle assiduously maintained continuing contact with his congregations through his associates, who were charged with continuing to teach and to nurture the fledgling communities. (1 Corinthians speaks of an upcoming visit of Timothy; 2 Corinthians of one or more embassies of Titus.) Finally, a number of Paul's communities received visits from other traveling teachers who appear also to have appealed to Israel's Scriptures in arguing for their particular interpretations of the message about Jesus. It has plausibly been suggested that Paul's discussion of Moses' shining face in 2 Corinthians 3 and his retelling of the Abraham narratives in Galatians 3–4 presuppose his listeners' familiarity with alternative interpretations of these stories by rival missionaries. In sum, while it is likely that many – perhaps most – individuals in Paul's congregations would not themselves have had the competence of the model reader, the extended process of reflection and debate that followed the reception of a letter from the apostle may well have allowed the community to attain a fairly sophisticated understanding of Paul's scriptural citations and allusions (see further Wagner 2002, 33–39; Abasciano 2007).

As in the case of the model reader, it is through engaging with a text and its cultural encyclopedia that one also develops a portrait of the "model author" – in this case, "Paul." Once again, a credible version of this figure will represent a plausible variant of the "historical Paul" (cf. Nehamas 1986). Given what can be known of Paul's background in the diaspora, his zeal as a Pharisee for Israel's ancestral traditions, and his long years of mission among Jews and Gentiles in a variety of cultural settings around the eastern Mediterranean (see, further, chapter 1 of this volume), it is to be expected that the apostle's interpretations of Scripture will often betray the influence of exegetical techniques, interpretive traditions, and religious convictions characteristic of early Judaism and the wider Greco-Roman cultures in which he lived and labored. Because Paul's reading of Scripture, like his theological reasoning, was inextricably bound up with his apostolic vocation and his tireless labors to found and nurture Christ-shaped communities of faith, we must also be alert to the possibility that Paul's understanding of Scripture developed as he confronted the challenges and crises that arose in the course of his ministry. Hans Hübner (1984) has argued, for example, that the crisis in Galatia over Gentile observance of Israel's law (see chapters 4 and 13 of this volume) impelled Paul to engage in an intensive study of the Scriptures, particularly Isaiah, which led to his eventual insight into the "mystery" of Israel's hardening and salvation as expressed in Romans 9–11. Finally, we should remain open to the possibility that Paul's interpretations of Scripture were to a significant extent hammered out collaboratively, in the back and forth of conversation and debate with associates as well as with opponents. The more elaborate exegetical arguments in Galatians 3–4 and Romans 9–11, for instance, may represent "set pieces worked out by Paul and his co-workers in their communal midrashic study" (Johnson 1999, 271; cf. Alexander 2001).

The endeavor to understand Paul's appropriations of Scripture in relation to the communicative intent of each letter and to the larger historical circumstances and cultural encyclopedia(s) in which author and addressees were embedded calls for an historically disciplined imagination. The sheer complexity of the task guarantees that no single account will be sufficiently comprehensive to capture fully the rich meaning potential of Paul's scriptural interpretations or to describe the wide variety of their effects on his first hearers.[6]

Memory, notebook, scroll

When considering the sources for Paul's knowledge of Scripture, we must reckon with a number of (non-exclusive) possibilities. Growing up as "a Hebrew of Hebrews" with parents who carefully observed the law of Moses (Phil 3:5), Paul would likely have begun hearing and memorizing the Scriptures at an early age. As a young man, he chose to follow the way of the Pharisees, who were known for their scrupulous adherence to the law. Indeed, Paul claims to have far outstripped his peers in his zeal for the ancestral traditions (Gal 1:14; Phil 3:6). It is quite probable, then, that Paul, like many other devoted Jews of his day, knew Israel's Scriptures and interpretive traditions by heart (Wagner 2002, 19–28; Sanders 2009, 77–82).

In this heavily oral/aural culture, written texts functioned as aids to memory and oral performance rather than as substitutes for them (Jaffee 1994, 70–71). As a missionary who traveled extensively, Paul would probably have relied on local synagogues for access to scriptural scrolls. On occasions when he stayed for a considerable time in a particular location, such as Corinth or Ephesus, however, he may also have been able to obtain copies of some biblical scrolls for his own and his congregation's use. It is possible that Paul owned some scriptural texts in codex (book) form (cf. 2 Tim 4:13), which would have made them easier to carry along on his travels. More likely, the apostle kept his own notebooks of excerpts from biblical scrolls, a practice for which there exist good parallels contemporaneous to Paul (Stanley 1992, 73–78). In some cases, Paul may also have utilized traditional Jewish or Christian collections of biblical "testimonies" on a particular theme (Albl 1999).

That Paul knew scriptural texts in Greek is obvious from the citations in his letters. These citations vary from one another in textual character, reflecting the textual fluidity of Scripture in the first century. Some follow quite closely the form of the "Old Greek," the original translation (as reconstructed by modern scholars). Other citations bear evidence of the sporadic and unsystematic "corrections" that were made throughout the Second Temple period to bring Greek texts into closer alignment with forms of the Hebrew text that were gradually gaining ascendancy in Palestine (Hanhart 2002). Whether Paul himself also read the Scriptures in Hebrew remains an open question. While the book of Acts suggests that he did so (Acts 22:3), the citations in his letters give no compelling evidence of his reliance on Hebrew, rather than Greek, texts (Koch 1986; Stanley 1992).

In view of the textual pluriformity of the Scriptures in the first century and the multiple modes in which Paul interacted with these sacred writings – through memory, written texts, collections of excerpts, and "testimonies" – it is no simple matter to determine just where, and to what degree, Paul altered the wording of his sources when citing Scripture. Careful investigation suggests, however, that on the whole Paul handled his sources rather conservatively. Like other authors of his time, Jewish, Greek, and Roman, the apostle normally made only minor changes to his sources, whether to fit them more seamlessly into the context of his own argument or to enable them to say more clearly and forcefully what he believed them in fact to mean (Koch 1986; Stanley 1992).

Citation, allusion, echo

Paul interweaves Scripture into his letters using a variety of techniques. The most rhetorically prominent of these is citation, in which the author explicitly signals to the hearer that the words in question come from "outside" the present discourse. The most obvious marker is a citation formula of some sort (for example, "it is written," "it says"). Scholars differ over what other criteria to employ in identifying citations, but most recognize that an interpretive gloss or a sudden incongruity in style or syntax will alert the majority of listeners to the presence of a quotation (Stanley 1992, 37). In cases where the words cited are already familiar to the audience, perhaps as a proverbial saying or slogan, the need for an explicit marker is obviated (compare 2 Cor 10:17 with 1 Cor 1:31). Table 10.1 lists the explicit citations of Scripture in Paul's undisputed letters.

Explicit appeals to Scripture perform a number of functions in Paul's letters, as the quotation in 1 Corinthians 1:19 illustrates:

18 For the message about the cross is foolishness to those who are perishing, but to us who are being saved it is the power of God.

19 For it is written, "I will destroy the wisdom of the wise, and the discernment of the discerning I will thwart."

20 Where is the one who is wise? ... Has not God made foolish the wisdom of the world? (1 Cor 1:18–20 [NRSV])

The introductory formula, "it is written," alerts Paul's listeners that the following words are drawn from Scripture even if the precise source remains unknown to them (Isa 29:14). With this citation, Paul grounds the thematic statement (v. 18) of this section of his argument in an authoritative text. In so doing, he subtly enhances his own ethos as a speaker by presenting himself as a teacher who is competent to draw upon and interpret Israel's sacred writings. Beyond this, the citation allows God to speak in his own voice, as it were, and to assume responsibility for the paradoxical state of affairs that Paul is describing. The scriptural citation, with its violent language and its strong emphasis on divine agency, further explains the somewhat surprising appearance in verse 18 of "the power of God" as the negative counterpart to "foolishness." Paul seems to have altered the final word of the citation (substituting the more forceful "thwart" for the verb "hide" that is attested by surviving Greek manuscripts of Isaiah) in order to amplify the severity and power of God's action. It is because God himself has intervened powerfully to controvert the wisdom of this age that the proclamation of the cross only appears to be foolishness. The citation also drives the argument forward by introducing into the discussion the term "wisdom," which becomes a central theme of the discourse that follows (1:18–2:16). As Paul's subsequent exposition plays with the oppositional pairs "wisdom" and "folly," "weakness" and "strength," the paradox of the cross emerges fully into view. For it is precisely in the scandal and folly of the crucified Messiah that God's "power" and God's "wisdom" are revealed (1:21–25).

Among the citation formulas that Paul employs, approximately two-thirds are variations on "it is written"; most of the rest feature verbs of speaking. Sometimes it is "Scripture" that speaks (for example, Rom 4:3; 9:17), sometimes "the law" (for example, 1 Cor 9:8); at other times the speaker remains unidentified (for example, 1 Cor 15:27). Naming the person to whom the citation is addressed contributes to the vividness of Paul's rhetoric; it may also call to mind the larger narrative context of the citation, as in Romans 9:15 (God speaks to Moses in the wake of Israel's sin with the golden calf) and 9:17 (Scripture [!] speaks to Pharaoh regarding the ten plagues on Egypt). Strikingly, in Romans, Paul frequently summons the speaker of a citation by name: Moses (10:19), David (4:6; 11:9), Elijah (11:3), Isaiah (9:27; 10:16, 20, 21; 15:12), the Messiah (15:3, 9, 10, 11), and a personified "Righteousness-from-Faith" (10:6–8). Some of these introductions are quite colorful, as in "Isaiah cries out on behalf of Israel" (9:27) or "Isaiah even dares to say" (10:20). By means of this rhetorical conceit, Paul presents these esteemed figures from the past before the audience "in person" so that they may testify at his side concerning God's dealings with Israel and the nations. Paul's frequent clustering of mutually interpreting citations (for example, Rom 15:9–12; 1 Cor 3:19–20) and his occasional conflation of two or more separate passages to form a composite quotation (for example, Rom 9:27–28, 33) provide further evidence that he hears in

Scripture a multitude of harmonious voices speaking in concert with him as witnesses to the gospel.

Most often in Paul's citations, it is God who speaks with the voice of Scripture.[7] The device of quoting first-person divine speech plays a particularly central role both rhetorically and theologically in Romans 9–11. Here, the apostle repeatedly propels his intricate scriptural argument forward by invoking the divine voice to proclaim God's surprising mercy to the nations and God's abiding faithfulness to Israel (see Hübner 1984).

A second way in which Paul draws on Scripture is through the device of allusion. In contrast to direct citation, allusion gestures obliquely toward a precursor text. This literary trope stimulates the hearer to scan the cultural "encyclopedia" for the appropriate reference. By enlisting the listener's active cooperation in making the connection with a precursor text, allusion may evoke the competent hearer's pleasure at being "in the know" and so foster a feeling of solidarity with the author.

In 2 Corinthians 3:3, for example, a cluster of allusions sets the stage for the comparison between Moses' ministry and Paul's own that will follow in verses 4–18. The mention of writing on "tablets of stone" (v. 3) recalls the giving of the law on Sinai and anticipates the discussion of this episode beginning in verse 7. In contrast, Paul's reference to writing by the "Spirit of God" on "tablets that are hearts of flesh" evokes a series of prophetic texts. In Ezekiel 11:19–20 and 36:26–28, God promises to remove his people's "hearts of stone" and replace them with "hearts of flesh"; moreover, God will put "a new Spirit" – God's own Spirit – within them so that they will keep God's statutes and ordinances. Similarly, Jeremiah 31:31–34 speaks of a time when God will write his law on the hearts of his people. The prophet announces this as a "new covenant," a term Paul uses to describe the nature of his own ministry in verse 6. Consequently, by the time Paul begins in verse 4 to construct the formal comparison, he has already laid its foundation by allusively associating his gospel with the eschatological new covenant of the Spirit that fulfills, and so surpasses, the "old covenant" (v. 14) of the letter given through Moses.

Because allusions are not overtly marked for the hearer, detecting their presence is not a science, but rather an art requiring disciplined imagination shaped by familiarity with the cultural "encyclopedia" of the text. It is possible, however, to formulate common-sense rules of thumb to guide this endeavor (see the oft-cited criteria in Hays 1989, 29–32). For example, the purported source of the allusion must have been available to the author; the probability of an allusion rises the greater the degree of verbal correspondence with the presumed source; a citation of, or clear allusion to, a particular source makes fainter allusions to the same source more plausible. Perhaps the most crucial criterion is also the most elusive: namely, that perceiving the allusion results in a more "satisfying" reading of the text. Not surprisingly, skilled interpreters often differ in their judgments concerning the presence, strength, and function of a putative allusion.

Since the groundbreaking work of Richard Hays (1989), the notion of "intertextual echo" has assumed a prominent place alongside citation and allusion in discussions of Paul's use of Scripture. Hays employs the term "echo" to denote a particular mode of allusion that "requires the reader to interpret a citation or allusion by recalling aspects of the original context that are not explicitly quoted" (Hays 1993, 43). Where this trope occurs, "the most significant elements of intertextual correspondence between old context and new can be implicit rather than voiced, perceptible only within the silent space framed by the juncture of two texts" (Hays 1989, 155).[8]

Understood in this technical sense, echoes are most clearly heard in Paul's writings in conjunction with a citation or a relatively strong allusion. In 2 Corinthians 8, for instance, Paul grounds his appeal for relief funds for the Jerusalem church in the notion of "equality" (8:13): "At the present time, your abundance is for their shortfall, so that in turn their abundance may be for your shortfall, as it is written: 'The one who had much did not have too much and the one who had little did not have too little'" (2 Cor 8:14–15). Taken by itself, the quotation in verse 15 functions rhetorically to place the weight of scriptural authority firmly behind Paul's appeal for "equality," but it contributes little else of substance to his argument. A listener who recognizes the source of the citation (Exod 16:18), however, will hear in these words echoes of the biblical narrative recounting God's provision of manna in the wilderness. Far more than simply appealing to biblical authority, Paul's citation invites his hearers to imagine themselves as participating in the economy of generosity established and maintained by their sovereign and gracious God. Echoes have the potential to evoke delight or dismay in the reader surprised by unvoiced implications of a scriptural reference. In Romans 9:1–3, for example, Paul's allusive comparison of himself to Moses interceding for the Israelites carries a hidden sting for his kinsfolk, who find themselves tacitly likened to the worshipers of the Golden Calf (cf. Rom 9:15).

Beyond citation, allusion, and echo, Paul's letters bear constant witness to the formative influence of Israel's Scriptures – and their reception in diaspora Jewish communities – on his language and patterns of thought. Paul belongs to a culture in which "all significant speech is Scriptural or Scripturally-oriented speech" (Fishbane 1986, 34). Not surprisingly, then, "the vocabulary and cadences of Scripture ... are imprinted deeply on Paul's mind" (Hays 1989, 16).

Precept, story, gospel

It is noteworthy that although Paul draws heavily on Scripture, he does not often cite it as commandment per se.[9] But while it is certainly true, at one level, that Paul does not offer Israel's Scriptures to his Gentile congregations as their "book of edification" (Harnack 1995 [1928]), Scripture does exercise a deep and pervasive influence on the shape of Paul's ethical instruction (Rosner 1994). Paul insists that, although those in Christ no longer live "under the law" (Rom 6:14; Gal 5:18), they do "fulfill" the law through the empowering agency of the Spirit (Rom 8:1–4; see, further, chapter 13 of this volume). Revealingly, it is by means of the law's own words, "You shall love your neighbor as yourself" (Lev 19:18, cited in Rom 13:9; cf. Gal 5:14), that Paul establishes the position that "the one who loves another has fulfilled the law" (Rom 13:8).

More commonly, Paul turns to Scripture's narratives and prophetic texts (which for Paul included the Psalms) to make sense of God's acts in raising the crucified Jesus from the dead and in calling the Gentiles as God's people together with Israel. For Paul, the hermeneutical key to the Scriptures is the extra-textual apocalypse of God's righteousness in the death and resurrection of Jesus the Messiah (Rom 1:16–17), to which "the law and the prophets bear witness" (Rom 3:21). This is the good news about God's son that God himself promised long ago, through the prophets, in Israel's holy Scriptures (Rom 1:2–3). These are the good tidings that Scripture foresaw and proclaimed beforehand to Abraham in the promise that in the patriarch all nations would be blessed (Gal 3:8).

Paul retells scriptural stories at various points in his letters, but he does not narrate a straight line of "salvation history" from Adam through Abraham and Israel to the Messiah. Rather, for Paul, the crucifixion and resurrection of Christ are the focal point of God's plan for the ages, the single center from which all else derives its significance. Paul thus interprets all of reality "outward" from the cross and resurrection. Paul reads Scripture backward to creation and finds Jesus Christ to be the first human's heavenly counterpart, the eschatological Adam in whom all will be made alive (1 Cor 15:21–22, 44–49); sin and death, whose tyranny has held sway over humanity since Adam's single transgression, have been overcome by the one righteous act of Jesus Christ, through whom grace now reigns, leading to eternal life (Rom 5:12–21). Likewise, Paul reads backward from the cross and resurrection to Abraham, discovering in Jesus Christ Abraham's singular "seed," the one to whom the promises were made and in whom all of Abraham's seed, Jew and Gentile alike, receive adoption as sons (Gal 3:15–29). Or again, Paul reads Scripture backward to David and sees in Jesus, the Messiah, the promised heir (Rom 1:2–3), the servant of Israel (Rom 15:8), the root of Jesse who rises to rule the Gentiles (Rom 15:12).

From the focal point of the cross, Paul reads Scripture outward to limn the cruciform pattern that shapes the lives of those who have been crucified with Christ (Rom 15:1–3; cf. 8:36). Reading outward from the Christ event, he discovers in the exodus and wilderness trials of "our ancestors" prefigurations of the church's life in this time between Christ's resurrection and Christ's return (1 Cor 10:1–13). Similarly, Paul interprets the prophecies of Israel's exile and return in the Song of Moses (Deut 32), in Isaiah, and in Hosea from the perspective of the cross, claiming that God's promised redemption has even now overtaken those whom God has graciously called together – Jew and Gentile alike – as his people in Christ (cf. Rom 9:23–26). Read outward from the cross and resurrection, these same prophecies assure the Jewish apostle to the Gentiles that God's sovereign love for Israel remains unquenchable, even though at present many of his kinsfolk do not embrace the gospel. Accordingly, Paul emphatically declares, in concert with the prophets, that God has not forsaken his people Israel (Rom 11:1–2). Finally, Paul reads Scripture forward from the cross and resurrection to the enthroned Messiah's certain conquest of the last enemy, death (1 Cor 15:20–28, 50–58), to the salvation of "the fullness of the Gentiles" and of "all Israel" (Rom 11:25–32), and so to God's restoration of the entire cosmos (Rom 8:18–39).

Interpreting Israel's Scriptures through the lens of Christ's self-giving death and victorious resurrection, Paul hears in these sacred texts a living and enduring testimony to the goodness, faithfulness, and integrity of God. For Paul, Scripture speaks above all as a trustworthy witness to God's gracious and unrelenting determination to redeem and restore his people Israel and, with them, all of creation. For this reason, Paul avows, "whatever was written in earlier times was written for our instruction, so that through perseverance and through the encouragement of the Scriptures we would have hope" (Rom 15:4).

Notes

1   For the purposes of this chapter, I consider only the letters whose authenticity is not seriously disputed: Romans, 1–2 Corinthians, Galatians, Philippians, 1 Thessalonians, and Philemon.
2   Paul refers to "Scripture" (Rom 4:3; 9:17; 10:11; 11:2; Gal 4:30) or to "the Scriptures" (Rom 15:4; 1 Cor 15:3, 4). Most often, "law" signifies the books of Moses (e.g., Rom 2:13, 15; 7:7; elsewhere Paul can speak of the "law of Moses" [1 Cor 9:9] or simply "Moses" [2 Cor 3:15]); at least twice, "law" clearly serves as a blanket term for Scripture (Rom 3:19, citing texts from the Psalms and from Isaiah; 1 Cor 14:21, citing Isaiah). Paul's single use of the phrase "the law and the prophets" (Rom 3:21) probably denotes Israel's Scriptures as a whole. In addition, he refers to God's promise "through the prophets in holy Scriptures" (Rom 1:2), as well as to "prophetic Scriptures" (Rom 16:26) and "oracles of God" (Rom 3:2; cf. 11:4). Paul explicitly names the book of Hosea (Rom 9:25), refers in Romans 11:2–3 to a scriptural passage about Elijah (1 Kings 19), and attributes citations to Moses (Rom 10:5, 19), to David (Rom 4:6; 11:9), and to Isaiah (Rom 9:27; 10:16, 20, 21; 15:12). Although it is impossible to specify the boundaries of Paul's scriptural "canon," at its core are books widely regarded as Scripture by other Jewish and early Christian authors. The books to which he appeals most frequently are the Torah (esp. Genesis and Deuteronomy), the Psalms, Isaiah, and the Twelve (minor) Prophets. His letters also contain significant allusions to Jeremiah, Ezekiel, and Daniel, among other books.
3   Translations are mine, unless noted otherwise.
4   Paul adopts in 1 Corinthians 15:33 a saying of Menander, but without marking it as a citation. He may have known it simply as an anonymous proverb.
5   This brief discussion of Eco's theory of literary interpretation is deeply indebted to the perspicuous and insightful treatment in Huizenga (2009, 21–74).
6   Of course, reading with an eye to what Paul might have meant, or what his various early listeners might have comprehended, does not begin to exhaust the significance of Paul's use of Scripture for Christian theology and practice (see Davis and Hays 2003).
7   In the following citations, the context of Paul's argument makes it clear that God is speaking: Rom 4:17, 18; 9:7, 9, 12, 13, 15, 25–26, 33; 11:4, 26–27; 13:9; 1 Cor 1:19; 2 Cor 6:2; Gal 3:16. Only 2 Corinthians 4:6 and 6:16 explicitly name God as the speaker (but note the attribution "says the Lord" in Rom 12:19; 14:11; 1 Cor 14:21; 2 Cor 6:17, 18). In several instances where the citation identifies the speaker as Scripture (Rom 10:11), Moses (Rom 10:19), or Isaiah (Rom 10:20, 21), it is clear nonetheless that the "I" who speaks through these mediators is God.
8   Apart from this technical usage, Hays and others also use "echo" for a faint allusion.
9   Paul cites Moses' law as commandment in Rom 7:7; 13:8–10; 1 Cor 9:9; Gal 5:14 (cf. 1 Cor 14:34). Fairly strong allusions to the law include 1 Corinthians 5:13 and 2 Corinthians 13:1.

References

Abasciano, Brian J. 2007. Diamonds in the Rough: A Reply to Christopher Stanley Concerning the Reader Competency of Paul's Original Audiences. *Novum Testamentum* 49: 153–183.

Albl, Martin C. 1999. *"And Scripture Cannot Be Broken": The Form and Function of the Early Christian Testimonia Collections*. Leiden: Brill.

Alexander, Loveday. 2001. *Ipse Dixit*: Citation of Authority in Paul and in the Jewish and Hellenistic Schools. Pages 103–127 in *Paul beyond the Judaism/Hellenism Divide*. Edited by Troels Engberg-Pedersen. Louisville: Westminster John Knox.

Ciampa, Roy E. 1998. *The Presence and Function of Scripture in Galatians 1 and 2*. Tübingen: Mohr Siebeck.

Davis, Ellen F., and Richard B. Hays. 2003. *The Art of Reading Scripture*. Grand Rapids: Eerdmans.

Eagleton, Terry. 2008. *Literary Theory: An Introduction*. Anniversary Edition. Minneapolis: University of Minnesota Press.

Eco, Umberto. 1984. *Semiotics and the Philosophy of Language*. Bloomington, Ind.: Indiana University Press.

Fishbane, Michael. 1985. *Biblical Interpretation in Ancient Israel*. Oxford: Oxford University Press.

Fishbane, Michael. 1986. Inner Biblical Exegesis: Types and Strategies of Interpretation in Ancient Israel. Pages 19–37 in *Midrash and Literature*. Edited by Geoffrey H. Hartman and Sanford Budick. New Haven: Yale University Press.

Fitzgerald, John T. 1988. *Cracks in an Earthen Vessel: An Examination of the Catalogues of Hardships in the Corinthian Correspondence*. Atlanta: Scholars.

Gamble, Harry Y. 1995. *Books and Readers in the Early Church: A History of Early Christian Texts*. New Haven: Yale University Press.

Hanhart, Robert. 2002. Introduction. Pages 1–17 in Martin Hengel, *The Septuagint as Christian Scripture: Its Prehistory and the Problem of the Canon*. Edinburgh: T. & T. Clark.

Harnack, Adolf von. 1995 [1928]. The Old Testament in the Pauline Letters and in the Pauline Churches. Pages 27–49 in *Understanding Paul's Ethics: Twentieth-century Approaches*. Edited by Brian S. Rosner. Grand Rapids: Eerdmans.

Hays, Richard B. 1989. *Echoes of Scripture in the Letters of Paul*. New Haven: Yale University Press.

Hays, Richard B. 1993. On the Rebound: A Response to Critiques of *Echoes of Scripture in the Letters of Paul*. Pages 72–96 in *Paul and the Scriptures of Israel*. Edited by Craig A. Evans and James A. Sanders. Sheffield: JSOT.

Hübner, Hans. 1984. *Gottes Ich und Israel: zum Schriftgebrauch des Paulus in Römer 9–11*. Göttingen: Vandenhoeck & Ruprecht.

Huizenga, Leroy A. 2009. *The New Isaac: Tradition and Intertextuality in the Gospel of Matthew*. Leiden: Brill.

Jaffee, Martin S. 1994. Figuring Early Rabbinic Literary Culture: Thoughts Occasioned by Boomershine and J. Dewey. *Semeia* 65: 67–73.

Johnson, Luke Timothy. 1999. *The Writings of the New Testament: An Introduction*. Revised edition. Minneapolis: Fortress.

Koch, Dietrich-Alex. 1986. *Die Schrift als Zeuge des Evangeliums: Untersuchungen zur Verwendung und zum Verständnis der Schrift bei Paulus*. Tübingen: Mohr Siebeck.

Nehamas, Alexander. 1986. What an Author is. *Journal of Philosophy* 83: 685–691.

Rosner, Brian S. 1994. *Paul, Scripture and Ethics: A Study of 1 Corinthians 5–7*. Leiden: Brill.

Sanders, E. P. 2009. Paul between Judaism and Hellenism. Pages 74–90 in *St. Paul among the Philosophers*. Edited by John D. Caputo and Linda Martin Alcoff. Bloomington, Ind.: Indiana University Press.

Sedley, David. 1989. Philosophical Allegiance in the Greco-Roman World. Pages 97–119 in *Philosophia Togata: Essays on Philosophy and Roman Society*. Edited by Miriam Griffin and Jonathan Barnes. Oxford: Clarendon.

Stanley, Christopher D. 1992. *Paul and the Language of Scripture: Citation Technique in the Pauline Epistles and Contemporary Literature*. Cambridge: Cambridge University Press.

Stanley, Christopher D. 2004. *Arguing with Scripture: The Rhetoric of Quotations in the Letters of Paul*. London: T. & T. Clark.

Wagner, J. Ross. 2002. *Heralds of the Good News: Isaiah and Paul "In Concert" in the Letter to the Romans*. Leiden: Brill.

Watson, Francis. 2004. *Paul and the Hermeneutics of Faith*. London: T. & T. Clark.

CHAPTER 11

Paul's Christology

Simon J. Gathercole

"The highest Christology of the New Testament is also its earliest." This was the
opinion of Professor George Caird near the end of his (posthumously published)
discussion of Paul's view of Christ (Caird 1994, 343). It ran counter to a long tradition
of scholarship associated with the so-called "History of Religions" school and expressed
most expertly by Wilhelm Bousset. In his great work *Kyrios Christos*, first published in
German in 1913, Bousset argued that the kind of cultic veneration offered to Jesus and
the acclamation of him as *kyrios* or "Lord" were late developments that came about
when the constraints of monotheism no longer held sway (for example, Bousset 1970,
147). The earliest understanding of Jesus was that of an eschatological prophet; it was
only with the later expansion of Christianity into Hellenistic territory that speculation
about Jesus as a heavenly being could arise. This early Hellenistic mutation of
Christianity then begat the "Lord Jesus Christ" of the Pauline epistles.

A number of factors have conspired to make this picture of a gradual evolution difficult. Among them has been the growing recognition that one cannot draw hard-and-
fast distinctions between "Palestinian" and "Hellenistic" Christianity in the first place:
Palestine was already considerably Hellenized, so the idea of a pure Palestine uncon-
taminated with Greek influence is a myth. Another factor has been the difficulty of
squeezing such an extensive evolution into what must have been a very short space of
time. There were, for example, probably only about twenty-five years between the first
Easter and Paul's letters to the Romans and the Corinthians. Furthermore, the time is
cut even shorter when it is considered that Paul is not setting forth his Christology in
the epistles, but rather assumes that his congregations are already well aware of it,
presumably from his original missions. Moreover, he can even treat as familiar the
Aramaic phrase *Marana tha* ("Come, our Lord") in 1 Corinthians 16:22, implying that

The Blackwell Companion to Paul, First Edition. Edited by Stephen Westerholm.
© 2011 Blackwell Publishing Ltd. Published 2011 by Blackwell Publishing Ltd.

Jesus was regarded as a transcendent Lord already in Aramaic-speaking, and not only in Greek-speaking, congregations. Hence, the growing sympathy in modern Pauline scholarship with Caird's initially rather shocking dictum.

Discussions of Pauline Christology often revolve around the question of how "high" or "low" the portrait of Jesus is. Some have argued that Paul refers to Christ as pre-existent and divine, whereas others claim that Paul sees him rather as a "second Adam" – exalted, to be sure, but not on a par with God. This question will be addressed below, but we will also see that for Paul the person of Christ is inseparable from his saving work. As such, the topics of discussion here include not only Jesus's titles and attributes, but also the language used of him to describe his action in redemption. Finally, we will also look briefly at Paul's ever-present language of how Christ is not merely a distant, abstract figure, but a *person* who can be passionately *known*.

Titles

While all the Christological titles have the same *denotation* or referent (Jesus), not all of them have the same *connotation*: that is, each of the titles brings to the fore a particular aspect of Christ's identity. David Wenham gives a nice summary of the differences: "Whereas 'Son of God' suggests Jesus' relationship to the Father and 'Lord' his relationship to the world and to individuals, 'Christ' suggests his relationship to Israel and to the Church" (Wenham 1995, 121). Paul does not use the other important title found in the gospels and Acts, "the Son of Man."

Son of God

Paul's letter to the Romans begins, after his own brief self-reference, by speaking of "the gospel he [God] promised beforehand through his prophets in the Holy Scriptures regarding his Son, who according to the flesh was a descendant of David, and who through the Spirit of holiness was declared to be the Son of God in power by his resurrection from the dead: Jesus Christ our Lord" (Rom 1:2–4).[1] One question that has perennially arisen on the subject of Jesus's sonship is whether this should be understood in the more circumscribed sense in which it appears in the Old Testament, or whether it has more heavenly, divine connotations. Some have focused on passages, such as those in the Psalms, where God's address to his "son" might merely refer to the human king of Israel (Ps 2:7; cf. 2 Sam 7:14). Indeed, elsewhere, the whole nation of Israel is God's son (Exod 4:22–23; Hos 11:1). On the other hand, the excerpt above from Romans 1 highlights the fact that Jesus's human identity as a descendant of David is only half of the story: in the resurrection, he is seen to be "the Son of God in power." In other words, he transcends the more "earthy" Son of God language of the Old Testament.

Some have taken Paul's language here to lean in an "adoptionist" direction (that is, that Jesus only *became* the Son at the resurrection), but this does not fit very well with Paul's language elsewhere in Romans (for example, Rom 8:3), nor is it clear that Paul is using a source with which he disagrees. The focus, however, as noted, is on the relationship between Jesus and his Father. From this point of view, the Son is certainly assumed to be subordinate to the Father in function: the Son is sent by the Father (Gal 4:4), and eventually the Son is to hand everything over to the Father (1 Cor 15:24; cf. v. 28). On the other hand, it is far from clear that Paul intends these resonances on every occasion that he uses the title.

Lord (kyrios)

Similarly, the title "Lord" has become for Paul so closely bound up with Jesus that it often appears in the phrase "Lord Jesus Christ" without having any strong connotations of its own. However, there are some important nuances distinctive to this appellation as well.

As one might expect, the title "Lord" conveys a sense of Jesus's supremacy. The title occurs in some contexts where Jesus's transcendent authority over all things appears: "If we live, we live to the Lord; and if we die, we die to the Lord. So, whether we live or die, we belong to the Lord. For this very reason, Christ died and returned to life so that he might be lord [kyrieusēi] of both the dead and the living" (Rom 14:8–9). Here, the title kyrios, or Lord, is connected with the Christian's belonging to Jesus ("we belong to the Lord"; cf. 1 Cor 7:22–23): as well as referring to Christ's heavenly power, it is also simply the word for the master of a slave. The passage goes on, however, to extend this lordship to encompass everyone who has ever lived as well as everyone living.

The title is also often connected with Jesus's future coming. First Thessalonians, in particular, refers to this "coming of the Lord" (1 Thess 2:19; 3:13; 4:15–16; 5:2, 23; cf. also 1 Cor 4:5; 2 Thess 2:1–2). Paul, like other early Christians, refers to "the day of the Lord," an Old Testament phrase referring to the day of reckoning, and rephrases it as the day of the Lord Jesus Christ (1 Cor 1:8; 2 Cor 1:14).

A further connotation is connected with the important theme of Jesus's identification with God. The Greek word kyrios is used in the Greek versions of the Old Testament to render the untranslatable Hebrew tetragrammaton, YHWH. As such, the application of the title to Jesus has enormous Christological potential. Paul – again in common with other New Testament writers – talks about the name of the Lord as a central reference point for early Christians. The Israelites called on the name of the Lord God; for Paul, the means to salvation (Rom 10:13) and the mark of the Christian (1 Cor 1:2) is calling on the name of the Lord Jesus Christ. Paul also makes appeals "in the name of the Lord Jesus Christ" (1 Cor 1:10; cf. 2 Thess 3:6), and refers to the Corinthians as assembling in the name of "our Lord Jesus" (1 Cor 5:4). In some ways, the invocation Marana tha joins these latter two connotations of "Lord" together.

Christ (christos)

The word "Christ" (christos, a translation of the Hebrew meshiach, or "Messiah") appears over five hundred times in the New Testament, and Paul contributes his fair share. Just as "Son of God" and "Lord" do not always seem to have a particular connotation other than a reference to the person of Jesus, so also "Christ" is often assumed by scholars simply to be a kind of "surname" for Jesus, without any particular allusion to his Messiahship. Others, however, have stressed that Paul, ever theologically minded, would not use it so unthinkingly, and Gentiles would be struck by such a strange title. The word *christos* is only found a handful of times in classical Greek prior to the New Testament, and it does not refer to a person: the playwrights Euripides and Aeschylus use it in the sense of "ointment." As such, references to a "Lord Jesus Ointment" would certainly generate discussion of what this strange title meant.

One of its principal implications is that Jesus fulfills Jewish expectations of a coming one from the line of David. Paul refers to one of the passages in the Old Testament often taken to refer to this Messiah: "And again, Isaiah says, 'The Root of Jesse will spring up, one who will arise to rule over the nations; the Gentiles will hope in him' " (Rom 15:12, quoting Isa 11:10). One of its key connotations, then, was the fulfillment of Scripture – as elsewhere in the New Testament (cf. Luke 24:25–27, 46). Again, Paul uses the title Christ in saying that the Easter events took place "according to the Scriptures" in 1 Corinthians 15:3–4.

A further connotation is that of *kingship*. More is implied than Jesus's rule, which is conveyed with the title "Lord." Whereas the latter title emphasizes Jesus's transcendent dominion, kingship in the Old Testament also carried a sense of the close connection of the king with his people. Their destinies were intertwined, so that although kingship and kings were by no means good in and of themselves, an absence of a king, in the refrain of the book of Judges, led to moral anarchy (Judg 17:6; 18:1; 19:1; 21:25). When a king reigned wickedly, the whole nation drifted into sin in consequence (for example, the case of Manasseh, 2 Kings 21:1–11), and when a good king reigned, reformation of the whole nation became possible (so with Josiah in 2 Kings 22–23). N. T. Wright argues that this idea extends into Paul's view of the "Christ," in which an "incorporative" Messiahship involves "the Messiah as the one in whom the people of God are summed up" (Wright 1991, 41). One place where this comes to the surface is in Romans 8:17 with its reference to believers being "co-heirs with Christ, if indeed we share in his sufferings in order that we may also share in his glory." The implication here is that participation in Christ in this age is the precondition for the same in the age to come. Another is Paul's description of the whole of the Christian life as lived "in Christ," a phrase sometimes thought to imply the mystical relationship of the Christian to Christ but which can also be understood as an incorporative identification. It might also have nuances of contrast to being "in Adam" (1 Cor 15:22; cf. Rom 6) and perhaps even "in Judaism" (Gal 1:13–14).

Many of the elements implied in these titles have pre-Christian precedents. The Son of God title, for example, while in some ways assuming an earthly figure, was also in the Qumran scroll 4Q246 assumed to have taken on some of the transcendent features of the Danielic Son of Man. The title "Messiah" is a familiar, if not frequent, term in the literature of Herodian Judaism. On the other hand, these three titles do not find their unity in an abstract messianism; rather, for Paul they derive their collective meaning from the person of Jesus.

Characteristics and Attributes

It goes without saying that Paul regarded Jesus as fully participating in humanity. It is only in some of the religious innovations of the late first and early second centuries (sometimes, rather misleadingly, called "Gnostic") that this came into question. Paul clearly identifies Jesus as "born of a woman" in Galatians 4:4. Some have additionally wondered whether this description of Jesus as having come (only?) from a *woman* implies a virginal conception, but this is not sufficiently clear. It is also sometimes said that when Paul simply uses the name "Jesus," he is referring to the human, earthly Jesus, but this theory is made difficult by such references as 1 Thessalonians 1:10 (Jesus, the Son from heaven, rescuing us from the coming wrath) and Philippians 2:10 (every knee bowing to Jesus).

Paul expands this characterization in Galatians 4:4 further: "God sent his Son born of a woman, *born under the Law.*" That is, Jesus is fully a Jew – in line with the presentations of him in the gospels and elsewhere in the New Testament. This is of interest to Paul, who emphasizes that Jesus's human ancestry (*to kata sarka*) is derived from Israel (Rom 9:5), that in terms of his human ancestry (*kata sarka*) he is descended from David (Rom 1:3), and that he is the seed of Abraham (Gal 3:16). Jesus is the stumbling-stone set in Zion (Rom 9:33, quoting Isa 28:16). His name *Iēsous*, used by Paul as by the other early Christian writers in Greek, is the Hellenized form of the Hebrew name *Yeshua*.

It is debated, however, to what extent Paul was interested in the earthly life and ministry of Jesus. First Timothy 6:13 presumes that Jesus was tried before Pontius Pilate, but there is little other historical information supplied in the Pauline corpus. While there is very little about Jesus's actions in his ministry in the undisputed letters, there are references to points of his teaching. In 1 Corinthians 7, Paul distinguished between ethical norms which are derived from Jesus and those which Paul has himself formulated: "not I, but the Lord" teaches that divorce and remarriage are essentially forbidden (1 Cor 7:10, referring to the teaching in Mark 10:9, 11–12). Some have seen 1 Corinthians 9:14 as also referring to the teaching of Jesus. A more debated example is 1 Thessalonians 4:15, where Paul speaks "by a word of the Lord." This has been taken by some to suggest that Paul thought Jesus spoke to him through prophetic revelations, but by others to allude simply to the teaching also found in Matthew 24:29–31. Perhaps less controversial is the saying by which all foods are declared clean in Romans 14:14, probably referring to Mark 7:15 (cf. v. 19).

One point traditionally understood to have been a feature of Christ's earthly life is his sinlessness; Paul's assumption to this effect comes to the surface in several places. In 2 Corinthians 5:21, for example, Paul refers to "him who knew no sin." More complex is the statement in Romans 8:3, where God is said to have sent his own Son "in the likeness of the flesh of sin," language often taken by commentators to express a reserve on Paul's part: he wants to maintain that Christ is both fully human and without the taint of acting sinfully.

One attempt to see Paul as even more interested in the earthly life of Jesus is the stress by some scholars on Jesus's *faithfulness*. Traditionally, most Bible translations have rendered the central passages on righteousness as referring to Christians being "justified by *faith in* Christ" (especially Rom 3–4; Gal 2–3). More recently, however, there has been a reconsideration of these passages by some scholars who have preferred the translation "justified by *the faithfulness of* Christ" (see, especially, Hays 2002). Linguistic, exegetical, and theological reasons have been given for this, although other scholars have remained unconvinced that this new interpretation is tenable.

Overall, the Bultmann school was certainly wrong to say that Paul was simply uninterested in Jesus's earthly life. On the other hand, it is clear that Paul did not regularly appeal to this or that action or saying of Jesus to solve an ethical problem. Rather, for Paul it was the totality of the gospel of Christ's death and resurrection that were brought to bear on the particular issues about which he writes in the epistles.

Pre-existence

Less contentious in the past generation of scholarship has been Paul's understanding of the pre-existence of Christ. The general view has been that Paul does think that Christ existed in pre-incarnate glory before becoming man, although this view has received strong criticism from a few (for example, Dunn 1998, 266–293). There is nonetheless broad agreement on two of the three groups of Paul's statements about pre-existence. The first group focuses on the incarnation (for example, Phil 2:6–11; 2 Cor 8:9); the second pertains to statements about Christ's involvement (in some sense) in creation (for example, 1 Cor 8:6; Col 1:16); and the third – more controverted – is the passage in 1 Corinthians 10 about Christ's involvement in the history of Israel.

First, for many scholars, Philippians 2 constitutes the highest point of Christological reflection in the New Testament. Certainly, for a number of scholars, the so-called "Philippians hymn" is the clearest statement of pre-existence: "[Christ Jesus] who, *being in the form of God*, did not reckon equality with God as something to be exploited, but *emptied himself, taking the form of a servant, coming in human likeness*" (Phil 2:6–7). As is often noted, this "hymn" talks of Christ at the outset "being in the form of God" and then "taking the form of a servant." Thus, there is a dramatic sequence in these two parallel statements that implies a prior state, or pre-existence, "in the form of God," and then a subsequent "form of a servant." Moreover, the incarnation here is a *voluntary act*: if Christ "emptied himself," then he is not merely the passive envoy of the Father; he is a willing subject of the mission, and himself undertakes to assume the form of a servant.

It is sometimes objected that at issue here is not the pre-existence of Christ; rather, Jesus is being contrasted with Adam. As Dunn puts it: "It is the prehistorical existence of Adam as a template on which a vivid Adam christology begins to be drawn" (1998, 292). On this reading, Jesus, like Adam, is (in) the image of God (cf. Gen 1:26). Unlike Adam, however, Jesus did not try to grasp at equality with God, desiring to be "like God, knowing good and evil" (Gen 3:5), but rather emptied himself in service. However, this reading does not give due weight to Christ's act of "emptying himself" whereby, according to Paul, Jesus is found in human likeness. It should also be said that some scholars see an Adamic background as quite compatible with pre-existence Christology (cf. Wright 1991, 56–98). Another statement of Paul, clearly undergirded by the same thought found in the hymn, is 2 Corinthians 8:9: "though he was rich, he became poor, so that you through his poverty might become rich."

Second, in Paul's interpretation of the *Shema* in 1 Corinthians 8:6, he identifies Christ as co-creator with God, talking of "one Lord, Jesus Christ, *through whom all things came*, and through whom we live." In this verse, the roles of God and Christ in creation are not identical: creation is *through* Christ, and *from* the Father. What this means precisely is difficult to determine, but the uncertainty does not detract from the essential point of Christ's pre-existence and involvement in creation (see, for example, Bauckham 2008, 26–30).

Christ's action as Lord in the work of creation is seen again in Colossians 1:16: "because in him all things were created, in heaven and on earth, things seen and unseen, whether thrones or dominions, whether principalities or powers; all things were created through him and for him." Here the amazing scope of Christ's creative power is highlighted, and the prepositions "in" (at the beginning) and "through" (in the last clause) show the role that Christ plays in an act of creation which is also "for" him. As in 1 Corinthians 8:6, then, we have strong evidence for pre-existence from this passage.

Third, much discussed has been the question of what Paul meant when he wrote that, in the Israelites' experience in the wilderness, they drank water from a rock, "and that rock was Christ" (1 Cor 10:4). Various options have been considered, from typology, or indirect identification via wisdom (as can be seen in Philo), to a simple identification. It is certainly striking that Philo employs an allegorical exegesis of this rock (from Exod 17; cf. also Num 20), identifying it as wisdom (Philo, *Allegorical Interpretation* 2.86). It is, then, very likely that Paul is tapping into existing speculation about some kind of personal or personified identity behind this rock. What the interaction with this exegetical tradition should not obscure, however, is that Paul here really did think of Christ as active in Israel's wilderness experience: his argument does not work if it is not Christ who provides the water. In 1 Corinthians 10:4–5, Paul is contending that the Israelites also had Christ accompanying them in the wilderness, but that did not prevent them from being overthrown there. The point Paul goes on to make is that the Corinthians ought not to fall into the same trap: "we should not test Christ, as some of them did" (1 Cor 10:9). It is difficult to avoid the obvious implication that Paul saw Christ as not only involved in creation, but also continually involved in Old Testament history.

Wisdom Christology in Paul?

Related to the question of pre-existence is that of what place should be assigned to Paul's employment of wisdom Christology. Paul clearly does employ wisdom motifs in his Christology.[2] However, early Jewish wisdom speculation is not *decisive* for Paul's Christology, or even for his deployment of pre-existence. The Philippians "hymn," for example, is not shaped by it. The significance of pre-existence for Paul is demonstrated by its appearance in a number of different contexts, such as redemption, Israel's history, and the supremacy of Christ over all things by virtue of his role in creation. It is not the case, then, that for Paul a shadowy pre-existent entity became in a secondary sense Christological.

Divinity

To raise the Christological stakes even higher, we come to the vexed question of whether or not Paul regarded Jesus as divine. Sometimes the debate has revolved around a key proof-text (Rom 9:5), which is open to being translated in two different ways:

Theirs [i.e., the Israelites'] are the patriarchs, and from them is traced the human ancestry of *Christ, who is God over all, forever praised!* Amen. (NIV)

Theirs are the patriarchs, and from them, in natural descent, sprang *the Messiah. May God, supreme above all, be blessed forever!* Amen. (NEB)

In the NIV translation (also KJV, ESV, and NRSV), Christ is thus identified as himself the God of Israel. In the NEB (and RSV), the punctuation gives a different sense. Since there is generally no punctuation in early Greek manuscripts, there is an element of uncertainty here. Most often, however, scholars note that the syntax favors the "divine-Christology" reading. On the other hand, some argue that this should not be given decisive weight because Paul does not think of Jesus in such exalted terms (see, for example, Dunn 1998, 255–257). Others note that although Paul does think of Jesus as divine, he does not actually call Jesus *theos*, a term reserved for the Father alone (see Fee 2007, 272–277). There is clearly nothing approaching a consensus here. Another "proof-text" significant for scholars who maintain Pauline authorship of the Pastoral epistles is the reference to "the glorious appearing of our great God and savior Jesus Christ" (Tit 2:13), although here, too, the syntax is not without difficulty.

These two disputed verses, however, have by no means exhausted the discussion. Of much greater significance in the debate have been 1 Corinthians 8:5–6 and Philippians 2:6–11. The former text is noteworthy for its reformulation of the Old Testament *shema* (Hebrew "Hear!"):

Hear, O Israel: The *Lord* our *God*, the *Lord* is one. (Deut 6:4)

yet for us there is but one *God*, the Father ... and there is but one *Lord*, Jesus Christ ... (1 Cor 8:6)

It is often noted that here Paul has taken this traditional formula from Deuteronomy and split it in two: the one God of Israel in the *shema* is seen by Paul as including two persons, the Father and the Christ. The "God" language applies to the Father, and the title "Lord" to Jesus, and so both share in the identity of the one Lord God.

Philippians 2:6–11 is equally rich in exalted Christology. In the first place, we have the account of Jesus's descent to death that we have already noted in the discussion of pre-existence. Here, the pre-incarnate Christ is depicted as "being in the form of God" (Phil 2:6) which, although a disputed phrase, probably refers to Jesus's divine identity. Probably the word "form" (Greek, *morphē*) here does not so much mean form *as opposed to* reality, but rather, form *as reflective of* reality. Clearer, however, is the way the passage continues after the reference to Christ's death: "Therefore God exalted him to the highest place and gave him the name that is above every name, that *at the name of Jesus every knee should bow*, in heaven and on earth and under the earth, and *every tongue confess that Jesus Christ is Lord*, to the glory of God the Father" (Phil 2:9–11). Here, as in 1 Corinthians 8, the Christological interpretation of an important Old Testament passage (in this case from Isaiah) is notable:

> And there is no God apart from me, a righteous God and a Savior; there is none but me. Turn to me and be saved, all you ends of the earth; for I am God, and there is no other. By myself I have sworn, my mouth has uttered in all integrity a word that will not be revoked: *Before me every knee will bow; by me every tongue will confess*. They will say of me, "In the Lord alone are righteousness and strength." (Isa 45:21–24)

This short extract is densely packed with at least four references (the underlined phrases) to the exclusivity of God. The repeated monotheistic formulae create a striking impression of the uniqueness of the God of Israel. It is remarkable, then, that Paul should draw on this passage to describe the worship that is due to *Jesus*: just as, in Isaiah, the one and only God will receive the worship of every bowing knee and every confessing tongue, so, in Philippians, the same will be true of Jesus. And this is not as a second god alongside YHWH; rather, it is part of the worship of the Father ("to the glory of God the Father" [Phil 2:11]).

If 1 Corinthians 8:6 is an extraordinary Christological assertion, Philippians 2 represents an equally remarkable depiction of the worship that Jesus, according to Paul, is to receive. Richard Bauckham has described this as "christological monotheism"; that is, Paul's exalted Christology is not a departure from Judaism by which the traditional belief in the unity of God is breached. Rather, it is an interpretation of that monotheism according to which Jesus is included within the single divine identity alongside the Father.[3] David Capes has shown that there are a number of additional instances of Old Testament passages which talk of YHWH but which are employed by Paul to refer to Christ, such as the references to "calling on the name of the Lord" in Romans 10:13, "boasting in the Lord" in 1 Corinthians 1:31 and 2 Corinthians 10:17, and several others (Capes 1992).

Thus, Paul assigns to Jesus a remarkably exalted status, even seeing him as sharing with the Father in the divine identity. He describes Jesus in these terms not in ways that set out to challenge traditional Jewish monotheism, but precisely using Old Testament passages that emphasize it. Furthermore, throughout his letters, Paul appears to *assume* this divine Christology, rather than arguing for it: it seems to be a commonly accepted view in the earliest Pauline communities. Alongside the language of the exalted status of Jesus with the Father, however, he also clearly emphasizes Jesus's subordination, as we have seen in the discussion of sonship. Every knee indeed bows to the Lord Jesus, but all this is ultimately "to the glory of God the Father" (Phil 2:11).

A Narrative Jesus?

More recently, there has been a reaction against approaches to Christology that – to caricature – add up the doctrinal values of the titles and the attributes and present the sum total. Especially in studies of the gospels, there has been a great deal of emphasis on examining Jesus as a character in the gospel stories, looking at the unfolding of his role and at his interaction with locations, institutions, and other characters. It may be difficult to see how a similar approach might be applied to Paul, but recently a considerable amount of research has been devoted to this area.[4]

"Narrative Christology" in the setting of Pauline scholarship focuses especially on whether and how Jesus is situated by Paul vis-à-vis the stories of creation, Israel, and the church, and indeed on how Paul's own story (for example, in Gal 1) relates to the story of God's plan. There have been mixed reactions to the viability or usefulness of this approach to Christology. A recent volume of essays on the subject (Longenecker 2002) has one very enthusiastic endorsement of a "narrative Jesus" in Paul: one contributor constructs a narrative, principally from Romans 8, of twenty-one plot elements in the descent–ascent story, and so talks of the "powerfully integrative force of the narrative methodology" (Campbell 2002, 108, 123). On the other hand, another contributor is not opposed to the approach, but wonders whether it tells us anything we did not already know (Marshall 2002, 213–214); others are more critical, on the grounds (in the case of Francis Watson) that the gospel is non-narratable (Watson 2002, 234).

It is probably pushing the evidence too far to argue that Jesus's saving action for Paul is conceived as simply a single punctiliar intersection in time. This has been an emphasis in some "apocalyptic" readings of Paul which have resisted the idea that Jesus's (hi)story can be coordinated straightforwardly with Israel's story. This view probably under-emphasizes, however, that Paul thinks of a sequence of events – incarnation, death, resurrection three days later, future coming – as constituting the work of Christ, framed by his pre-existence, on the one hand, and future existence with his people, on the other. At the other extreme, however, it is difficult to construct from Paul an elaborate plot of the Christ-story consisting of a great many narrative elements: Paul often telescopes these events together (for example, the incarnation and the death of Christ in Rom 8:3). Moreover, there is probably a good deal of truth in Marshall's observation that, despite the changed vocabulary, there is not necessarily much new light that the narrative approach sheds, except as a corrective to approaches too narrowly focused on titles.

Salvation

One of the factors complicating the study of Paul's Christology is that it does not merely involve the collection of evidence for how "highly" Paul thought of Christ. The gospel of salvation is of primary importance to Paul, and it consists specifically of Christ's death and resurrection: "For what I received I passed on to you as of first importance: that Christ died for our sins according to the Scriptures, that he was buried, that he was raised on the third day according to the Scriptures" (1 Cor 15:3–4). Of prime significance, then, is this work of Christ at the "Easter weekend," which brings new life through his death for sins (cf. Gal 1:4).

Christ the savior

Paul, then, considered Christ principally as savior. He does not use the particular title "savior" (*sōtēr*) very frequently (Phil 3:20; 2 Tim 1:10; Tit 1:4; 2:13; 3:6), but there are numerous references to Christ's salvation. Christ will "save us" (Rom 5:9–10), or "rescue us" (1 Thess 1:10), from the wrath of God. He is the "deliverer" who comes from Zion in Romans 11:26. Similarly, God has not appointed the elect for wrath but for "salvation through our Lord Jesus Christ" (1 Thess 5:9). "Salvation" is the consequence of the gospel in Romans 1:16–17 and 1 Corinthians 15:1–2.

Christ the "sin offering"

One of Paul's preferred ways of speaking about this salvation is through Old Testament sacrificial language. To begin with the "sin offering" (the *peri hamartias*): "For with the law powerless in that it was weakened by the flesh, God sent his own Son in the likeness of the flesh and *as a sin offering*. And so he condemned sin in the flesh" (Rom 8:3). The language of "sin offering" adopts a technical phrase from the Old Testament, especially the account of the Day of Atonement in Leviticus 16. In this chapter, Aaron sacrifices a bull to atone for himself and his household, and the blood is sprinkled upon the mercy-seat in the Holy of Holies (Lev 16:6, 11–14). The other two elements that constitute the sin offering are two goats (16:5). One of these is killed like the bull, and the blood is sprinkled on the mercy-seat in the same way (16:15). The result is as follows: "In this way he will make atonement for the Most Holy Place because of the uncleanness and rebellion of the Israelites, whatever their sins have been. He is to do the same for the Tent of Meeting, which is among them in the midst of their uncleanness" (Lev 16:16).

The other goat is not killed; rather, the sins of the people are transferred to it by the priest: "He is to lay both hands on the head of the live goat and confess over it all the wickedness and rebellion of the Israelites – all their sins – and put them on the goat's head" (Lev 16:21). It is then dismissed into the wilderness. Some scholars, perhaps especially in Germany, have made the sin offering the central theme of the atonement in Paul; on the other hand, however, Paul also uses different cultic imagery, such as that "Christ our Passover lamb has been sacrificed" (1 Cor 5:7).

Christ the "mercy-seat"

Moreover, we find in the New Testament that the authors do not restrict themselves to giving Christ one role in the Old Testament sacrificial drama. In the epistle to the Hebrews, Jesus is given the role of both priest and sacrificial offering. Similarly, Paul can describe Christ in the same sentence in Romans 3:25 as both the victim, whose blood makes atonement, and as the mercy-seat of Leviticus 16, where the blood is sprinkled: "God presented him as *the mercy-seat*, through faith, *in his blood*." The imagery here collapses as Paul describes Jesus as encompassing almost the whole sacrificial system in his death for sins.

Christ as "sin" and "curse"

Perhaps the most jarring statements are those which say not merely that Christ has become a sacrificial victim, but also that he has become *tout simple* "sin" and "a curse for us":

> God made him who had no sin to be sin for us, so that in him we might become the righteousness of God. (2 Cor 5:21)
> Christ redeemed us from the curse of the law by becoming a curse for us, for it is written: "Cursed is everyone who is hung on a tree." (Gal 3:13)

It is in these statements most of all that we see that Christ's saving work involves him fully bearing human sin and divine judgment. The statement in 2 Corinthians refers to the former; Galatians 3 refers to Christ's substitutionary death as he bore the curse in place of others.

Christ as "first fruits" from the dead

In 1 Corinthians 15:20–23, Paul uses more sacrificial imagery from the Old Testament, that of the requirement to offer to God the first fruits (for example, Exod 22:29 [MT 28]; 23:19). This image, however, applies not to Christ's death, but to his resurrection, which is equally integral to Paul's conception of Jesus's saving work. This image of first fruits is helpful in two ways. First, it highlights the uniqueness of Christ's resurrection as a singular event in the past. Christ's resurrection is the fulfillment of Scripture about him (1 Cor 15:4), and means that he alone is exalted to the right hand of the Father (Rom 8:34), in power as the Son of God (Rom 1:4).

On the other hand, it is the guarantee of resurrection for those who believe in him: Jesus's solidarity with believers is such that those in Christ will inevitably be raised with him. Paul employs a syllogism to this effect about the "dead in Christ" in 1 Thessalonians 4:14:

> Jesus is risen.
> Dead Christians have fallen asleep *in him*.
> Therefore God will raise with Jesus those who are in him.

Jesus's resurrection is in this sense *not* unique. It is, in contrast to Jewish expectation about the resurrection at the end of history, the resurrection of one particular person in advance of the rest of the people of God.

Another similarly logical framework underlies Paul's thinking about baptism and new life in Romans 6:

> The baptized are baptized into Christ's death (Rom 6:3).
> Christ was raised from the dead (6:4).
> Therefore, those united with him in death will be united in resurrection (6:5).

This enjoyment of resurrection life in Romans 6 is not limited to the future, however: Paul also stresses that in some sense believers *already* participate in the risen life of Christ (Rom 6:4).

The "last Adam"

"As in Adam all die, so in Christ will all be made alive" (1 Cor 15:22). This chapter of 1 Corinthians, along with Romans 5, presents Jesus as "the last Adam" – not merely *living*, like his predecessor, but *life-giving* (1 Cor 15:45). There are two particular factors in Paul's comparisons of Adam and Christ (not only in 1 Cor 15, but also in Rom 5). The first is that both are figures whose single acts have universal consequences, Adam's for condemnation and Christ's for salvation (Rom 5:12–21). (Sometimes the universal tone of Paul's statements in Rom 5:12–21 is taken to mean that Christ ultimately saves all without exception, though this is at odds with statements elsewhere in Paul; see section below, "The judgment seat of Christ.") Second, Christ's action is the undoing of Adam's action, but it is really more than just a reversal of the consequences of the fall. It is interesting that Paul begins in Romans 5:12–14 by contrasting Adam and Christ in fairly strict parallelism, but then feels the need in verses 15–17 to stress the asymmetry: "the gift is not like the trespass" (5:15), and "the gift of God is not like the result of the one man's sin" (5:16). There is an imbalance between the sin of Adam and the saving action of Christ, in part because a torrent of transgressions is dealt with by that single act of Christ. Indeed, Paul concludes: "The law was added so that the trespass might increase. But where sin increased, grace increased all the more, so that, just as sin reigned in death, so also grace might reign through righteousness to bring eternal life through Jesus Christ our Lord" (Rom 5:20–21). The saving action of Christ does not simply undo sin, but overwhelms it.

Christ as intercessor

A little-studied and less well-known feature of Paul's teaching about Jesus is that he is at the right hand of the Father *in prayer*: "Christ Jesus, who died – more than that, who was raised to life – is at the right hand of God and is also interceding for us" (Rom 8:34). Hence, Paul visualizes Jesus's work of salvation extending into the present: here, he is neither God-before-man nor man-before-God, but rather occupies a mediating position between the church and the Father.

"The judgment seat of Christ"

According to Acts 17, Paul's sermon before the Athenians concludes that God has raised a man from the dead, and that this man is the divinely appointed judge of all. Paul's letters echo this same idea. In Romans 2:16, Paul says that according to his gospel, God will judge people's secrets "through Jesus Christ." Here we have a statement about Christ's agency in the Father's judgment. Elsewhere, Paul is less circumspect in his language, and talks straightforwardly of *Christ's* judgment: "For we must all appear before the judgment seat of Christ, that each one may receive what is due him for the things done while in the body, whether good or bad" (2 Cor 5:10; cf. Rom 14:10). Those who reject Christ and the gospel are condemned (Rom 3:8; 2 Thess 1:8–9). Those who are in Christ, however, will be saved from God's wrath (Rom 8:1; 1 Thess 1:10): Christ will return on the clouds of heaven to gather together Christians, both living and dead, so that they will be with him forever (1 Thess 4:13–17).

Christology, Church, and Ethics

Finally, we need to consider the very practical ways in which Paul employs Christology. We have already noted in the context of the titles that there are two quite different aspects to Jesus's relationship to the church and the individual Christian. On the one side, Jesus is *Lord*, and so transcends the church and gives commands to it as a master to his servant(s). On the other, however, Jesus is also *Messiah*, into whose destiny the people of God are incorporated. Both of these aspects – the latter perhaps more so – come into Paul's ecclesiology and moral theology.

In the first place, the church is chosen in Christ. This is a point made in particular in Ephesians 1, but also in the undisputed Romans 8. In the latter, God has elected the saints to bear the likeness of Christ: "those God foreknew he also predestined to be conformed to the likeness of his Son, that he might be the firstborn among many brothers" (Rom 8:29). Christ, as the perfect image of God, is the one whose likeness the saints will ultimately bear. This is behind Paul's desire to present his churches holy and blameless before God on the final day (for example, 1 Thess 3:13): holiness and blamelessness here do not refer to an abstract moral perfection, or to mere sinlessness, but rather to a perfect resemblance to the character of Christ.

God's work of thus conforming his people consists both of a general shape and of particular actions. In terms of the general shape, the conformity consists particularly in being united with Christ in his death in order to share in his life: "If we have been united with him like this in his death, we will certainly also be united with him in his resurrection" (Rom 6:5). This "death" is in some sense a completed action in that it takes place once for all in the alignment, in *baptism*, of the Christian with Christ's own once-for-all death on the cross. Life in Christ also, however, consists of God's work of changing Christians in the present: "And we, who with unveiled faces all reflect the Lord's glory, are being transformed into his likeness with ever-increasing glory, which comes from the Lord, who is the Spirit" (2 Cor 3:18). Here the focus is on the divine agency; Paul typically combines this with the Christian's agency: "if by the Spirit you put to death the misdeeds of the body, you will live" (Rom 8:13).

Christology is for Paul a (perhaps *the*) crucial shaping factor in his ethics. In the post-Easter period, *following* Jesus in the straightforwardly physical sense is no longer an option, but Paul reformulates this dominical *following* (he only uses the word once, in the quite different context of 1 Cor 10:4) into a notion of *imitation*. The language of imitation comes at key points in Paul's ethical teaching. It comes, for example, at the conclusion to the discourse in 1 Corinthians 8–10, where Paul sees himself as mediating the model: "Imitate me, as I imitate Christ" (1 Cor 11:1; cf. 4:16). Similarly, in 1 Thessalonians, Paul commends his readers for having "become imitators of us and of the Lord" (1 Thess 1:6). In Galatians, Paul gives a kind of summary of the Christian's relation to fellow believers as follows: "Carry each other's burdens, and in this way you will fulfill the law of Christ" (Gal 6:2). This unparalleled phrase "the law of Christ" is often taken to refer, at least in part, to the life of love that was modeled in the earthly life of Jesus (Dunn 1998, 657). The exposition of Christ's humiliation and exaltation in Philippians 2:5–11 is included by Paul precisely for ethical purposes: "Have that mind in you which is also in Christ Jesus" (2:5).

Finally, it should be remembered that Paul very much focuses on the need for divine "energizing" in the moral life of believers, and here, too, Christ plays a central role. Paul more commonly attributes the work of ethical "leading" to the Spirit: "those who are led by the Spirit of God are sons of God" (Rom 8:14; cf. Gal 5:18). But this very Spirit in Romans 8:14 has recently been designated "the Spirit of Christ" (Rom 8:9) as well as of the Father (Rom 8:11). As such, it is easy to see how conformity to Christ is empowered by Jesus's own Spirit.

Conclusion

A final danger in any discussion of Paul's view of Christ is that the whole enterprise is considered merely in the abstract. As has already been implied in the discussion of Jesus as savior, Paul did not merely hold a set of beliefs about Christ. He claimed to have intimate knowledge of Christ, and to have been grasped by Christ (Phil 3: 8, 12), and he maintains that this relationship is his continuing desire: "I want to know Christ and the power of his resurrection and the fellowship of sharing in his sufferings, becoming like him in his death, and so, somehow, to attain to the resurrection from the dead" (Phil 3:10–11).

Paul's principal aspiration is not merely that he should possess this private experience for himself, but that he be the instrument by which knowledge of Jesus should be revealed to the nations: "It has always been my ambition to preach the gospel where Christ was not known" (Rom 15:20).

Notes

1   Translations of biblical texts are my own.
2   *Pace* Fee (2007, esp. 595–630), who downplays them almost to the point of exclusion.
3   See, in general, Bauckham (2008).
4   The most important work on this topic is Hays (2002).

References

Bauckham, Richard. 2008. *Jesus and the God of Israel:* God Crucified *and Other Studies on the New Testament's Christology of Divine Identity*. Grand Rapids: Eerdmans.

Bousset, Wilhelm. 1970. *Kyrios Christos: A History of the Belief in Christ from the Beginnings of Christianity to Irenaeus*. Nashville: Abingdon.

Caird, G. B. 1994. *New Testament Theology*. Completed and edited by L. D. Hurst. Oxford: Clarendon.

Campbell, Douglas A. 2002. The Story of Jesus in Romans and Galatians. Pages 97–124 in *Narrative Dynamics in Paul: A Critical Assessment*. Edited by Bruce W. Longenecker. Louisville: Westminster John Knox.

Capes, David B. 1992. *Old Testament Yahweh Texts in Paul's Christology*. Tübingen: J. C. B. Mohr (Paul Siebeck).

Dunn, James D. G. 1998. *The Theology of Paul the Apostle*. Grand Rapids: Eerdmans.

Fee, Gordon D. 2007. *Pauline Christology*. Peabody, Mass.: Hendrickson.

Hays, Richard B. 2002. *The Faith of Jesus Christ: The Narrative Substructure of Galatians 3:1–4.11*. Second edition. Grand Rapids: Eerdmans.

Longenecker, Bruce W., editor. 2002. *Narrative Dynamics in Paul: A Critical Assessment*. Louisville: Westminster John Knox.

Marshall, I. Howard. 2002. Response to A. T. Lincoln: The Stories of Predecessors and Inheritors in Galatians and Romans. Pages 204–214 in *Narrative Dynamics in Paul: A Critical Assessment*. Edited by Bruce W. Longenecker. Louisville: Westminster John Knox.

Watson, Francis. 2002. Is There a Story in These Texts? Pages 231–239 in *Narrative Dynamics in Paul: A Critical Assessment*. Edited by Bruce W. Longenecker. Louisville: Westminster John Knox.

Wenham, David. 1995. *Paul: Follower of Jesus or Founder of Christianity?* Grand Rapids: Eerdmans.

Wright, N. T. 1991. *The Climax of the Covenant: Christ and the Law in Pauline Theology*. Edinburgh: T. & T. Clark.

CHAPTER 12

Paul, Judaism, and the Jewish People

John M. G. Barclay

In the course of one of his "tribulation lists" (2 Cor 11:21–29), Paul imparts an intriguing nugget of historical information: "Five times I have received at the hands of the Jews the thirty-nine lashes" (2 Cor 11:24).[1] We do not know when and where this extreme synagogue punishment took place, but we know from other sources that it was inflicted on members of the synagogue who were considered very serious transgressors of its rules (Harvey 1985). This suggests that Paul was considered a Jew, a member of the synagogue, and that he wished to be considered so; that he received this punishment *five times* indicates that he kept returning to synagogues although he knew this was risky. It also suggests, however, that he tested the tolerance of his fellow Jews beyond the limit, and that he was often considered a law-breaker, and sometimes, perhaps, an apostate (Barclay 1995). It is exactly this doubleness – of a radical Jew at the margins of his own community, all the more threatening because he claims to represent its center – that we meet everywhere in Paul's own letters. On the one hand, he can speak of his "former life in Judaism" as if he is now outside it (Gal 1:13), and can list all his Jewish privileges – of ancestry, training, Pharisaic law observance, and zeal – and then declare them all "loss," even "rubbish," compared to the surpassing value of "knowing Christ Jesus my Lord" (Phil 3:7–8). On the other hand, he can lay great weight on his identity as a "Hebrew" and an "Israelite" (2 Cor 11:22; Rom 11:1), and can declare himself devastated by the present state of his fellow Jews, his "kinsmen according to the flesh" (Rom 9:1–3). At one moment, he lashes out at Jews who hinder the spread of the gospel to the "nations," and pronounces the wrath of God upon them "at last" (or even "completely" [1 Thess 2:14–16]). At another, he insists that God's gifts and God's calling in relation to Israel are irrevocable, such that, despite her present "stumbling," "all Israel will be saved" (Rom 11:11–32). Even when we ask the simple question, "Would Paul have called himself a Jew?" we get a confusing picture: at one

The Blackwell Companion to Paul, First Edition. Edited by Stephen Westerholm.
© 2011 Blackwell Publishing Ltd. Published 2011 by Blackwell Publishing Ltd.

point he includes himself and Peter among those who are "Jews by birth" (Gal 2:15); at another, he says that he can "become a Jew" among Jews, in the sense of living under the law (1 Cor 9:19–21), as if this were an identity one could put on or off; at another again, he redefines the word and declares that a "Jew" has an inward, heart-circumcision, in the Spirit – terms that seem to apply to Jewish (and non-Jewish) Christ-believers, but *not* to non-believing Jews (Rom 2:28–29; see Dunn 1999).

Paul's relationship to Jews and Judaism thus appears confusing and complex, even contradictory, in regard to his personal identity, his social practice, and his theology, which all three intertwine. The problems here are partly terminological – Paul's use of partially overlapping terms in multiple ways – and partly rhetorical. Before extracting any "system" from Paul's letters, we have to recall that they are *letters*; that is, locally targeted communications called forth by particular and very varied situations. Paul theologizes in situational and constantly developing forms, and employs his rhetorical skills to create sharply defined antitheses, loaded narratives, and excoriating polemics. What makes good sense within one letter can therefore seem inconsistent with his expressions elsewhere, and it is unclear whether this is because his thought on these matters "developed" over time, or simply because different situations called forth different responses. And when we are trying to make sense of all this, should we discount Pauline hyperbole and *ad hominem* polemics, or are these precisely the places where "the real Paul" shines through?

Before trying to unravel this tangled set of problems, it is important to get some perspective on the issues we here discuss. The variety in Paul's statements has, of course, fostered a wide variety of interpretations over the centuries, but this interpretative task has also been burdened with a weight of wider agendas. When we have come to see what is at stake in the assessment of Paul's relationship to Judaism, we will be in a better position to pick our way through the minefield of debate.

"Paul and Judaism": What is at Stake?

Paul's understanding of the Christ-event in its relation to Israel was a matter of controversy during his own life, and has remained so ever since. His partially apologetic tone in Romans (for example, Rom 3:8; 9:1–2; 10:1) indicates that he was criticized for focusing solely on his mission to "the nations" (non-Jews), for abandoning the practice of the Jewish law, and for implying, or even proclaiming, that God had abandoned his people Israel. The synagogue accusations that elicited his beatings (2 Cor 11:24) may have been on these same grounds, or may have been due to the controversies caused by his mission in pagan society, which brought trouble on diaspora Jewish communities (Goodman 2007). Soon after Paul's death, Luke had to defend him against accusations of apostasy from Judaism (Acts 21–28), and in some circles of Jewish Christianity Paul was forever dubbed "the enemy" (Lüdemann 1989). Once Paul's authority became established, however, and after the fall of Jerusalem (70 CE) and the Second Jewish Revolt (132–135 CE), the increasingly Gentile church began to look to Paul to explain why it had parted company with the Jewish community and had become identifiably separate as "Christianity." In the second century CE, Pauline phraseology was used to dismiss Judaism as external and purely "fleshly" (Justin Martyr, Ignatius; cf. Rom 2:28–29), or, more radically, to denigrate the God of the Old Testament law as an inferior deity committed to judgment, not grace (Marcion). Where Christians had dealings with Jews, the refusal of the latter to accept the gospel of Jesus as Messiah was attributed to their blindness (cf. 2 Cor 3:15; 4:4). Had not Paul called them "enemies" (Rom 11:28), and declared against them God's wrath (1 Thess 2:16)?

Conversely, where Jews became remote from Christian experience, interpreters were inclined to take their presence in Paul's letters as symbols of something else, normally some negative trait in the human condition. Thus, for Valentinian Gnostics, "Jews" and "the nations" were code words in Paul's letters for "soul-only" ("psychical") and Spirit-enhanced ("spiritual") types of Christian (Pagels 1975, 6–7). More influentially, Augustine, who placed Paul's theology in the widest possible framework, took Paul to be diagnosing the most fundamental human sin, the sin of self-reliance (an introverted idolatry): thus, where Paul attacks "works of the law" and "boasting" in relation to Jews, he is using them as exemplars of a basic human fault. Within the same tradition, though differently applied, Luther took Paul's reaction to Judaism to be an assault on all forms of self-righteousness, which by "doing" seek to make a claim on God and thus refuse his sheer grace in Jesus Christ. In interpreting Paul's letters, this Lutheran reading tends to de-historicize Paul's statements about Jews, to focus only on their negative contents, and to turn them into abstract, general, and timeless analyses of the human plight. With F. C. Baur (mid-nineteenth century), a different kind of generalizing polarity (influenced by Enlightenment values) is introduced, whereby Paul stands for the "universal" and the spiritual, as opposed to Judaism with its "narrow" ethnic base and national "particularity" (Baur 2003, 2.123–133). In the first half of the twentieth century, with the rise of "dialectical" theology (Barth) and neo-Lutheran readings of Paul (Bultmann), Paul is taken to criticize, via Judaism, the piety and self-conceit of "the religious man": it is such piety that leads to pride in privilege or achievement, and where Paul discusses this problematic, according to Käsemann, he is attacking "the hidden Jew in all of us" (Käsemann 1969, 186).

In the past fifty years, a sea change has taken place in scholarly approaches to this topic, partly as a result of the Holocaust, Christian sensitivity to anti-Semitism, and a greater desire for Jewish–Christian dialogue. In reaction against treating "Jews" or "Israel" in Pauline theology as a cipher for some (generally negative) universal trait, it is now, properly, insisted that Paul is talking about an irreducibly particular phenomenon, the Jewish people, and that his statements are neither univocal nor solely critical. In this new context, there is a strong disinclination to view Paul as "anti-Jewish," and it is hotly disputed whether he considers the church to have "superseded" Israel in the covenant purposes of God. His critical comments are viewed as an intra-mural affair (a family row), not a criticism from outside (for example, Davies 1978), and one school of scholars has gone so far as to hold that Paul propounded a "two-covenant" theology, in which "the nations" are saved by faith in Christ, but Israel is (or will be) saved, quite apart from Christ, through the Abrahamic-Mosaic covenant (Stendahl 1976; Gaston 1987; Gager 2000). For these purposes, the most central text has become Romans 9–11, where Paul agonizes over the fate of Israel and reveals his hope that "all Israel will be saved" (Rom 11:25–26).

This new era of discussion was given a decisive impetus by the re-evaluation of Second Temple Judaism initiated by E. P. Sanders's book, *Paul and Palestinian Judaism* (1977). Contesting a long tradition of Christian misreading of ancient Judaism, Sanders argued that Judaism was unambiguously founded on covenant grace in the election of Israel; although observing the law was the necessary means to remain within the covenant (in a scheme he dubs "covenantal nomism"), it was not a mechanism by which Jews thought that they *earned* salvation. This undermined the standard interpretation of Paul: if Paul's contemporary Jews were not following a religion of "legalism" or "works-righteousness," what exactly was the target of Paul's critique? On this issue, no scholarly consensus has yet emerged. Some would dispute Sanders's interpretation of Second Temple Judaism, arguing that, amidst its diversity, there were strands of thought that in whole or in part do represent some kind of "justification by works" such as Paul has been traditionally understood to attack (for example, Gathercole 2002). Sanders himself took Paul's theology to operate by a kind of a priori deduction: if God had arranged for Christ to die, and for people to be saved by faith in Christ, then Judaism was clearly insufficient, and the covenant election of Israel ineffective (Sanders 1977, 543–556). More concretely, if Christ was installed as Lord of all, the universality of Paul's appeal, to both non-Jew and Jew on the basis of faith alone, had to extend beyond the confines of Judaism (Sanders 1983, 171–210). This latter train of thought, with its echoes of Baur's critique of "particularism," was developed in the "New Perspective on Paul," associated particularly with James D. G. Dunn (for example, Dunn 1983; cf. Dunn 2005) and N. T. Wright (for example, 1978). Here, Paul is taken to oppose particularly the restrictedness and "ethnocentrism" of Judaism, where the "works of the law" (for example, in Gal 2:16; Rom 3:20) stand not for "works" (human achievement) in general, but for the boundary marks of Jewish ethnic difference (such as circumcision, Sabbath observance, and food restrictions). Proponents of the "New Perspective" understand Paul to be rightfully reclaiming the original universality of the Abrahamic promises (Gen 12, 18), but a Jewish critic might see the same phenomenon as Paul's in-principle eradication of Jewish difference by seeking "unity in Christ" (Boyarin 1994). For others again, a large part of Paul's critique of Judaism arises from his convictions concerning the depth and universality of human sin: the Jewish way to life/salvation promised by the law is simply impossible because no one, not even Israelites, can keep it (cf. Westerholm 2004).

Mixed up in this swirl of debate are also fundamentally differing convictions about the shape of Paul's theology. Was Paul a radically apocalyptic thinker, for whom the death and resurrection of Christ constituted a new creation, thus disqualifying Judaism along with all else within "the present evil age" (Gal 1:4)? Or did he see the Christ-event as the fulfillment of Jewish history, the "climax of the covenant" (Wright 1991)? In practical terms, does his theology presuppose and legitimate an extensive overlap between Christian and Jewish communities (Nanos 1996) or does it press for a complete separation of the two, because faith in Christ is simply incompatible with commitment to the law of Moses (Watson 2007)? And is Paul's extensive use of Scripture in his argumentation merely a tactical weapon with which to overcome his Jewish (-Christian) opponents, or does it reveal a theological grounding in Israel's narrative of salvation and in her hopes for the future (Hays 1989)?

Given the ideological loadedness of these debates and the complexity of the data in Paul's letters, it is clear that no exposition of our theme will be either simple or universally accepted. What follows is an attempt to keep Paul's language on Jews and Judaism concrete and particular (not reaching "beyond" it to generalizations), and to explore the doubleness of Paul's vision (without resorting to easy accusations of self-contradiction). Since chapter 13 of this volume will consider Paul's statements on the law (one of the core components of "Judaism"), we will confine ourselves here to Paul's discussions of Israel/Jews, their relationship to Christ, and their place within God's dealings with the world.

Jews and Judaism in the Light of the New Creation in Christ

Paul's letter to the Galatians constitutes the clearest (and most polemical) depiction of the "newness" of the Christ-event, with radical implications for the status of Judaism. Early in the letter (1:13–17) Paul describes his "calling" (or "conversion").[2] After a portrayal of his progress in his "former life in Judaism," which included his persecution of the church, it is clear that his encounter with Jesus Christ was not another step along the same road. This encounter came from elsewhere (a "revelation" or "apocalypse") and represented God's decision to set him apart, and God's calling through grace before he was even born – that is, without any prior condition of ethnicity, upbringing, or faithful law observance (see Barclay 2002). In this calling, he finds his commission to take the gospel to "the nations" (the non-Jewish world), and one cannot fail to notice that he describes the "calling" of these converts in terms very like his own (for example, Gal 1:6). Thus, the impact of the Christ-event through the preaching of the gospel is not presented here as the supplement to, or completion of, some prior cultural tradition, but as a new phenomenon. Indeed, in his summary of the letter, Paul strongly relativizes the difference between circumcision (*the* mark of Jewish difference) and uncircumcision, insisting that neither counts for anything, only "new creation" (6:15; cf. 5:6). This novelty is enacted and proclaimed in the rite of baptism "into Christ": those so baptized have "put on Christ," in whom "there is neither Jew nor Greek, neither slave nor free, no male and female" (Gal 3:26–28). Elsewhere in the same letter, Paul speaks of "being crucified with Christ," a "death" which causes such a radical reconstitution of identity that "it is no longer I who live, but Christ who lives in me" (Gal 2:19–20).

This suggests that if Paul continues to identify himself as a "Jew," this ethnic label is no longer the most significant marker of his identity, and no longer salient within the community of believers, and that not because circumcision is an "external" phenomenon (so is "uncircumcision" and so, conversely, is baptism), but because his identity is wholly remade in Christ. In the same way, Paul redefines in Galatians what it means to be a "child of Abraham" by reference to Christ and faith in Christ (Gal 3:6–29): Abraham's "offspring" are those who share his faith (not his genetic descendants), and the "seed" to whom the promises were made was, in fact, Christ himself (3:16). Although this Christ was born "under the law" (4:5), the previous history of Israel under the law (i.e., since Moses) is here interpreted not as a positive period of preparation or gradual development toward its climax, but as a time of abject slavery (3:22–23;

4:3), of restriction under a "childminder" (*paidagōgos*, 3:24). Since it comes as a radical act of life-giving liberation, the Christ-event marks the divine "No" to the old cosmos (especially in the crucifixion [6:14]) and the establishment of a new reality created by promise and Spirit (3:1–5, 14–18; see Martyn 1997).

Paul's fury in his letter to the Galatians is directed against those (believing Jews) who sought to fit belonging to Christ within the category of "Judaism," who wanted non-Jewish converts to "judaize" (by circumcision and law observance, 2:14), and who therefore thought and acted as if the Christ-event was a modification and not a radical reshaping of history. Paul encountered, or feared he would encounter, such people elsewhere, and his strongly worded attack on Jews who "hindered" his preaching to non-Jews (1 Thess 2:14–16), together with his radical antithesis between his old self and his new (Phil 3:2–11), mark his fear that this "new creation" (cf. 2 Cor 5:17), which he had been called to announce and embody, could fail to take effect if it was qualified and constrained by Jewish expectations. Like Moses, Paul felt commissioned to be the minister of a "covenant," but where Moses' law led to death, Paul's ministry of the Spirit and life reflected a new emerging reality, as dramatic as creation, even if presently contained within fragile bodies and vulnerable lives (2 Cor 3–4).

Since this divinely created reality was limited by no prior conditions (of ethnicity, status, or gender), it could call people of all races and all stations in life into this new existence. In 1 Corinthians 1, Paul celebrates both the negative pole of this conviction (that the message of Christ crucified breaks the mold of both "Greek" and "Jewish" assumptions about the world [1:18–25]) and its positive corollary: that God can choose the "nobodies" (the foolish, the weak, and the low born) by the power that creates from nothing (*ex nihilo*) and from the contrary (*e contrario*; 1 Cor 1:26–31). This leveling of humankind by the message of the gospel is most fully stated in the opening chapters of Romans. Here, the gospel is announced as the power of God "to both the Jew, first, and the Greek" (Rom 1:16), the "both ... and" indicating Paul's challenge to the Jewish conviction of a categorical distinction between Israel and "the nations" (on the "first," see below). Paul follows through on that announcement by declaring the absolute impartiality of God, who judges or rewards Jews and non-Jews entirely equally (Rom 2:1–24). Woven into this discussion is the charge that all humanity is subject to the power of sin (3:9), so that "there is no distinction: all have sinned and fall short of the glory of God" (3:23).

The complexity of the weave in these chapters has led to a variety of views regarding the *basis* on which Paul places all, Jew and non-Jew, on a level. Is this because of the universality of sin, to which none is immune, and regarding which Paul is especially pessimistic (1:18–3:20)? Or is it because he reads the "oneness" of God to require, by the logic of monotheism, that God is God of Jew and non-Jew alike (3:29)? Does he operate with some prior principle of "fairness," the equal rights of all before God? Or are all these convictions the secondary impact of a more fundamental fact: the reality of the new divine action in Christ (3:21–31), as an unconditioned gift, makes all alike dependent on a single act of grace, which "gives life to the dead and calls into existence the things that do not exist" (Rom 4:17). If God acts in Christ to create "out of nothing," then Jewish ethnicity cannot make any difference to the operation of his life-creating power.

An obvious objection to this emphasis on the newly creative work of God in Christ is the fact that very much of Paul's theology is, in fact, heavily indebted to his Jewish heritage: he has hardly started afresh with a *tabula rasa*. Paul's basic convictions about God (his monotheism and his abhorrence of "idolatry") are, of course, inherited from Judaism, as is very much of his understanding of the world and its future. His ethical assumptions (for instance, regarding sexual morality) are mostly rooted in the Jewish tradition; indeed, Jesus is to be understood as the Christ ("Messiah") of Israel's promises (Rom 1:3; 9:5). Moreover, as is clear both on the surface and just beneath the surface of his theology, Paul's thought is deeply rooted in the Jewish Scriptures, from which he draws not only citations and vocabulary, but large patterns of thought. Judaism, it could be said, is the cultural matrix from which Paul's thought arises in practically every dimension.

Three things may be said in response to this objection. In the first place, a distinction should be made between *our* description of Paul's theology and *Paul's own* view of the matter. Where we might describe his monotheism or his ethics as "Jewish," Paul would decline to give them an ethnic or cultural label: they are simply, for him, true – as true for non-Jews as for Jews, and in both cases also re-thought in light of the Christ-event which redefines his monotheism (for example, 1 Cor 8:1–6) and his ethics (for example, 1 Cor 6:12–20). What we might describe as his induction of non-Jews into a Jewish way of viewing the world, he would frame as teaching "the truth of the gospel" (Gal 2:5, 14); in social terms, that makes a considerable difference, as his converts are *not* made to feel that they belong to the Jewish tradition, or the Jewish community, but to a community shaped by the gospel and by Christ. Second, to describe Paul as working from the Jewish tradition is to say very little about him: every revolutionary thinker works from *some* intellectual and cultural tradition, but the question is where the major breaks occur and how decisive they become. The Jewish tradition was certainly shaped by monotheism, abstention from "idolatry," and a strict sexual code. But it was also shaped by allegiance to Moses, honor (and monetary contribution) to the temple, commitment to observe the law, male circumcision, Sabbath observance, and a strong preference for marriage within the Jewish community. For Paul, the primary allegiance is to Christ, not to Moses, and believers are to walk by the Spirit, not under the law; they are themselves the temple, and circumcision and Sabbath observance are no longer significant. This is to reshape and remold Jewish tradition in such a revolutionary way that many Jews could no longer recognize it as "Jewish."

Third, the objection is most obviously correct in its insistence that Paul works with the same Scriptures as his fellow Jews; indeed, this is absolutely crucial to him (1 Cor 10:11; Rom 1:2–3; 15:4). Even when he describes his call and the break it caused with his "former life in Judaism," he uses phrases derived from scriptural accounts of the call of the prophets (Gal 1:13–16, echoing Jer 1:5; Isa 49:1). Thus, if Jewishness consists in the possession and use of the Scriptures (Rom 3:1–2), Paul certainly remains Jewish. But it is his striking re-reading of Scripture, and his claim to offer its sole legitimate interpretation, that made (and makes) his stance so controversial to fellow Jews (cf. 2 Cor 3:6–18): that Paul claims the very ground on which other Jews stand, but claims it as a story of Israel with (not separate from) the nations, is precisely what made him so objectionable. Nonetheless, this rootedness in Scripture does mean that we need to supplement our emphasis on the novelty of the Christ-event with reference to its scriptural meaning and antecedents. But it will emerge here that this supplement is no contradiction, but in fact the deepening of the same theme of new creation in Christ.

New Creation as Israel's Promise

Even in Galatians, the letter with the most radical statements of "newness," Paul traces the creative operation of God's grace back to the very beginning of Israel's history, in the patriarchal narratives. Drawing on the scriptural story of Abraham (Gal 3:6–9), he indicates that "Scripture pre-preached the gospel to Abraham" when it declared that "in you will all the nations be blessed" (Gal 3:8, citing Gen 12:3 and 18:18). Scripture here operates as a witness, foretelling the effects of the Christ-event; but the Abraham narrative does not lose its concrete historicity, since what is true of Christ-believers (that they are justified by faith in Christ) is true in a sense also of Abraham, who "believed God and it was reckoned to him as righteousness" (Gal 3:6, citing Gen 15:6). Thus, what Paul finds to be true in the Christ-event (faith as the response to the unconditioned gift of God in Christ) is the pattern also of the Abrahamic story (faith as the response to the unconditioned promise of God), and in both cases the story is one of divine grace (Gal 2:21; 3:18).

The theme is picked up again in the allegory of Abraham's two sons (Gal 4:21–31): one, Ishmael, born "according to the flesh" (in the normal human fashion); the other, Isaac, born "through the promise" and "according to the Spirit" (4:23, 29). The contrast is developed rhetorically in such a way as to mirror Paul's antithesis between Christ-believers (created by the work of the Spirit) and those wedded to the Mosaic law (living according to the flesh). But that Paul finds this antithesis in Scripture, and enacted in the birth of the promise-bearing patriarchs, indicates that for him the miraculous, life-creating gift of God is somehow "native" to the story of Israel from its very beginning. This makes it hard to decide to whom he is referring in his final blessing in Galatians 6:16: "for those who walk by this rule [new creation, 6:15], peace be upon them and mercy and also [or, "that is"] upon the Israel of God." There are several ways of construing the clauses of this verse, and several options in translation, but most interpreters take it to represent Paul's transference of the honorific title "Israel of God" to those who believe in Christ (both Jews and non-Jew), in line with his redefinition of the label "seed of Abraham." However, the rare occurrence of the term "mercy" (associated mostly with Israel in Rom 9–11), and the fact that Paul never elsewhere uses the title "Israel" for non-Jews, give some basis for the suggestion that here Paul offers a prayer for divine mercy even on presently unbelieving Israel, inasmuch as she belongs to God and was brought into being by God. In that case, this verse gives a hint of what will come in the extended discussion of Israel in Romans 9–11.

It is in his letter to the Romans that Paul develops most fully his conviction that what has happened in the Christ-event, and what has emerged as its results, are already integral to the being of Israel and will result in her final salvation. As we noted above, at the very moment that he puts Jews and non-Jews on a par ("to both the Jew, first, and the Greek"), Paul inserts the qualifier "first" in relation to Jews (Rom 1:16; 2:9, 10), indicating that there is something "prior" about Jews that makes them special, even if not unique. This motif receives some initial discussion at the start of Romans 3: having redefined circumcision as a matter of the heart, and the term "Jew" as a matter of the Spirit (2:25–29), Paul asks whether any Jewish advantage remains (3:1). That he replies in the positive (to the surprise of many commentators), and begins a list of Jewish privileges with their possession of the "oracles of God" (3:2), indicates that Paul does not see the gospel of Christ as the eradication of Israel's special place in God's design, even if the unbelief of most Jews in the present time (that is, their unbelief in Christ) raises huge questions about the faithfulness of God (3:1–9).

Those questions are not to receive full treatment until Romans 9–11, but in the meantime Paul returns to the Abraham story to indicate the direction of his thought. Romans 4 circles around Paul's key Abraham text: Abraham "believed God and it was reckoned to him as righteousness" (Gen 15:6). Paul draws several points from this text: (1) that it was said of Abraham *before* he was circumcised (Gen 17), so that he can be the father of both the uncircumcised (non-Jews) and the circumcised (Jews; Rom 4:9–12); (2) that his key characteristic here is faith (not working), so that he corresponds exactly to Christian believers, who have faith in Christ, irrespective of law observance (works of the law; Rom 4:1–8, 13–15; cf. 3:20, 27–30); and (3) that what he believed was the promise of God that, despite his advanced age and the barrenness of Sarah, they would have an heir, and through him multiple descendants (Rom 4:16–25). This last point is of great importance to Paul: it indicates that Abraham's faith, like faith in the crucified but raised Jesus, is faith in the power of God to give life to the "dead" and to create something (in Abraham's case, offspring) out of nothing (4:17). The story of Abraham is therefore a story of new creation. This is not just a "proof-text" from Genesis, but the founding event in Israel's story (the only means by which that story gets going); "new creation" constitutes Israel from the very beginning.

It is in Romans 9–11 that Paul comes to expound all this most fully. As recent interpreters have rightly insisted, these chapters are not a digression from the flow of argument in Romans, but integral to its message on a number of levels. We have already noted the teasing "to the Jew first" in the early chapters, and the preliminary discussion of Israel and God in Romans 3. At a practical level, as he prepares for his visit to Jerusalem with the controversial collection from his largely non-Jewish churches (Rom 15:22–33), and as he anticipates his visit to Rome, where there are tensions between believers who do, and those who do not, follow the Mosaic law in matters of food and Sabbath (Rom 14:1–15:6), Paul needs to explain how his comparatively successful mission to non-Jews relates to the Jewish roots and the Jewish members of the churches. More fundamentally, as an honest reader of Scripture (and not just as a Jew with residual national pride), he needs to explain how the divine promises to Israel, which undergird the whole scriptural story, can be affirmed at a time when, at the climax of history, most Jews are not responding to the gospel. The strong emotion of these chapters (for example, 9:1–5; 10:1–2) indicates the intensity of Paul's struggle, as he juggles two non-negotiable convictions: that God made irrevocable promises to Israel (9:1–5), and that salvation is possible only through "calling on the name of the Lord" Jesus (10:5–13).

Paul's treatment of this problem moves in three steps. First, after listing the election privileges of Israel (9:3–5), he burrows through Scripture to discern the character of that election (9:6–29). What he traces here (from the Abrahamic generation to the exile) is a pattern of "calling" that operates through divine selection, based solely on the will, the mercy, and the promise of God. Isaac is born by divine, not natural means: he is a child of promise (9:6–9). Jacob is chosen without reference to his character or work (before he was born), and against the rules of primogeniture (9:10–13). As is declared to Moses, God will have mercy on whom he has mercy (9:15, citing Exod 33:19), a mysterious promise that leaves the unknowable future wholly in the hands of God and the identification of those who will receive this mercy undetermined. Thus, the election of Israel operates without any prior conditions (of ancestry, achievement, status, or human will): this is the means by which God has chosen Israel (and excluded, hardened, or rejected others), as it is also the means by which God has chosen *within* Abraham's descendants (Jacob, not Esau; the remnant, not the rest [9:27–29]), *and* the means by which God can choose, and now has chosen, from *outside* Israel, as he calls both Jews and non-Jews to constitute his people (9:24–25). This relentless emphasis on divine choice leads Paul, logically, into equally strong statements about divine rejection (9:13, 17–18, 19–23), the foundation for later doctrines of "double predestination." But this language is necessary in order to strip away all notions of human worth or effort as a contributory factor in divine choice. It is only on this basis that Paul can eventually hold out hope for Israel's future, and, in the end, the doubleness will resolve into a single will of mercy (11:32). But it is necessary to move first through this disconcerting line of thought, because both Israel and non-Jewish believers need to understand that they are called only by the creative agency of God's mercy, the mercy that can make something from nothing, a "my people" from a "not my people" (9:25–26).

In the second step of his argument (9:30–10:21), Paul considers the present state of affairs, where Israel, in large part, has failed to respond to the gospel, but many non-Jews, surprisingly, have believed in Christ. This paradoxical state of affairs is like the runners in a race not reaching its goal, while the non-competitors win the prize (9:30–32)! In explanation, Paul draws from similarly paradoxical biblical texts that indicate the stumbling of Israel over the "stumbling stone" (Rom 9:33, drawing on Isa 8:14; 28:16; the "stone" is identified with Christ), and the easy accessibility of faith (Rom 10:6–9, where Deut 30:12–14 is reinterpreted to refer to the gospel message). Israel is zealous enough, but does not recognize in Christ the "righteousness" (saving action) of God, and in that ignorance and unbelief finds herself surpassed by outsiders (10:3–4, 14–21). This topsy-turvy situation is precisely what Scripture announced and foresaw (10:18–20), but its final image is of a God who has not turned his back on Israel, but holds out his hands to his disobedient people (10:21).

In the third step (11:1–32), Paul reaches at least an outline resolution of his dilemma. It is unthinkable that God has rejected his people (11:1), although in the present only a remnant believe (in Christ) and the rest are hardened (11:1–10). But if the remnant are saved by grace (11:5–6), they constitute a seed of hope (the first fruits, 11:16) that God may have mercy on the rest. Paul finally makes sense of the present paradox: Israel's unbelief has made possible the mission to non-Jews with its remarkable success, but that mission in turn will provoke Israel to jealousy, and so pave the way for the restoration of Israel as a whole (11:11–16). The famous image of the olive tree (11:17–24) depicts the strange, unnatural ingrafting of wild olive branches (non-Jews) into the root previously and "naturally" enjoyed by Israel; many Jewish branches have been cut off (in unbelief), but they can be grafted back in, and more easily than non-Jews. The "root" of the tree from which both draw sustenance (11:16) is never defined, but is most likely to represent either the patriarchs (cf. 11:28) or the election promises extended to them (cf. 9:6–13). Thus, Paul is confident that, despite her present unbelief and divine hardening, the mercy by which Israel was created, and by which her history has been constituted from the beginning, will be triumphant in the end, such that "all Israel will be saved" (11:25–26; see Das 2003, 96–120).

Despite Paul's initial discussion of the identity of "Israel" (9:6), clarifying that she is Israel by mercy alone, there is no reason to think that "all Israel" in 11:26 means "the church" (of Jews and non-Jews; so Wright 1991, 231–257): the "Israel" and "Israelites" under discussion throughout Romans 11 (for example, 11:1, 7, 11, 25) are Paul's ethnic kin, special before God in their "natural" relationship to the patriarchal promises. Paul envisages their whole-scale salvation (after their temporary hardening and unbelief), and it is likely that this will come about only through "faith," elsewhere defined as faith in Christ (thus, not by a separate path or second covenant). Their salvation is associated with the arrival of "the Redeemer from Zion" (11:26), probably a reference to Christ (cf. 1 Thess 1:10), but it is not spelled out either how or when this will take place. The "mystery" that Paul reveals here is the fact that, and the means by which, this salvation will take place (by means of the mission to non-Jews), in a pattern that bears the characteristic shape of his gospel: just as disobedient non-Jews have received mercy (by the unconditioned grace of God), so Israel also will be saved, not by ethnic "right," but by the promised mercy of God, despite, and out of, her own disobedience and unbelief (11:28–32).

Paradoxically, therefore, the new creation that was enacted in Christ is precisely the means by which Abraham's offspring were created, and by which Israel has been constituted throughout her history; and it is her hope for the future that she will be reconstituted by the God who "has consigned all to disobedience in order that he might have mercy on all" (11:32). It is appropriate that Paul thus completes his vision of the future with a paean of praise to God (11:33–36), whose paradoxical paths none can trace and whose creative power embraces all: "from him, and through him, and to him are all things" (11:36). Israel's place in this cosmic plan is irreducibly special, but the means by which she is saved turn out to be the very same means by which "the nations" also receive mercy: both are found to depend on the single thread of the creative power of grace (cf. 15:7–13). Paul has not abandoned his commitment to the election of Israel, but he has so redefined it (in the light of Christ) that it can include "the nations," on whom God is also and equally merciful.

The Social Context of Paul's Theologizing

Paul's theology is made not in abstraction but in the midst of social practices and social circumstances which give it sharp focus and a clear rationale. Thus, full comprehension of his views on Jews and Judaism requires some appreciation of these social dimensions, whose correlations with his theology are important to note.

The first and most immediate context for Paul's theology is his mission to non-Jews, to whom he felt himself especially commissioned as an apostle (Gal 1:16; Rom 1:5). Paul's churches were thus largely made up of *converts* who had experienced a dramatic change in their identity and their lifestyle, following their acknowledgment of Jesus as Lord. Paul's emphasis on "new creation" clearly corresponds to this sense of change in the lives of his converts and, as we have seen, the rite of baptism pronounced and enacted this novelty in the abandonment of an old identity and the adoption of a new. But baptism makes the same pronouncement of both "Greek" and "Jew" (Gal 3:28), and Paul's own dramatic experience of change in life-course and life-allegiance encouraged him to think of entry into the Christian community as a moment of "new creation" for Jew and non-Jew alike. The novel gift of the Spirit, a new sense of empowerment, a new message, and the birth of new communities – all cemented the conviction that something radically new had begun in the wake of the Christ-event.

Paul's understanding of his mission, and his doubts about the adequacy of the law (a law that had once led him to persecute the church), required him to insist that his non-Jewish converts should not be "judaized" (Gal 2:14). In practice, this meant in particular that the male converts did not have to get circumcised, and that none was required to observe Jewish food and Sabbath regulations. In social terms, these practices were significant in marking one's identification with local Jewish communities, and although there were other practices that Paul's converts *did* share with local Jews (such as refusal to participate in pagan cultic rites), the socially decisive fact was that his non-Jewish converts did not regard themselves, and were not regarded by others, as belonging even by association (as "God-fearers") to the local synagogues. Instead, they belonged to "churches" (a non-Jewish term) which met in the house of a fellow believer, and this basic social differentiation also reinforced the sense that what God was creating through Paul's mission was not another form of "Judaism," but something different and new.

However, the social division was not quite that simple. Some of the members of Paul's churches (including Paul himself) were Jewish by ethnicity, and some of these attended local synagogues (including probably Paul, who, as we saw, suffered punishment as a result [2 Cor 11:24; cf. 1 Cor 9:19–21]). Although Paul strongly relativizes the significance of ethnicity, he does not consider it necessary to abandon Jewish identity: those who are circumcised do not have to undo this operation (1 Cor 7:17–20). In the churches in Rome, where some believers put great store on continuing to observe Jewish food and Sabbath laws (Rom 14:1–15:6), Paul is sensitive to their convictions and does not wish to "dejudaize" them in these respects (see Barclay 1996). On a wider scale, Paul is very conscious that, alongside his own mission to non-Jews, there is another Christian mission being conducted to "the circumcised" (Gal 2:6–9), and although his own visits to Jerusalem were few, he is committed to collecting money from his largely non-Jewish churches to take to "the poor among the saints in Jerusalem" as a symbol of the unity, and mutual indebtedness, between his churches and the Jerusalem-based Jewish Christians (Rom 15:22–33). These local and wider political dimensions correlate well with his anxiety lest non-Jewish believers "boast" over the failure of most Jews to respond to the gospel (Rom 11:17–20): Paul's sense that "the nations" belong in God's people *with* Israel, not in place of her, reflects this practice of sensitivity and honor to Jewish Christians on a local and global level.

But Paul's sense of Israel's perpetual significance within God's purposes for the world also reflects, and arises from, another very basic social practice: the reading of Scripture. This is certainly basic to Paul's own life, and probably to that of his churches (although we do not know how, in practical terms). Unless one reads "Israel" in Scripture in a wholly allegorical fashion, one cannot avoid here the sense of divine commitment to the offspring of Abraham: even if Paul radically re-reads these Scriptures in the light of Christ, they still speak eloquently of God's loyalty to Israel, despite her repeated acts of disobedience. Paul is writing before the fall of Jerusalem and the loss of the temple, before the Christian movement began to consider the Jewish people irretrievably condemned by God. He retains a strong hope that God will intervene to save all Israel, and within a comparatively short time-span. He had seen a remarkable work of the Spirit in the non-Jewish world, and it was perfectly reasonable for him to expect that God would restore Israel to her "natural" location, recreating her by mercy in accordance with his covenant promises.

Looking back on Paul's work from a long historical distance, we may ask whether Paul, in fact, hastened or delayed the "parting of the ways" between the nascent Christian movement and its Jewish matrix. On the one hand, his strong affirmation of the non-Jewish identity of his converts, his polemical antitheses, and his emphasis on "new creation" in Christ made it easy for later Christians to read him as establishing a sharp distinction between the church and Israel. Even his defense of continuing Jewish-Christian practice of the law (Rom 14:1–15:13) so relativizes that practice that it threatens to undermine the theological seriousness with which they affirmed the law (cf. Boyarin 1994). On the other hand, his own theological commitment to Israel and his affirmation of her scriptural promises prevented the church from succumbing to Marcionism, and left open the possibility of a more positive relationship to Judaism. How that positive potential is expressed and enacted now is a significant hermeneutical challenge, made complex by the long and appalling history of Christian anti-Semitism. However Paul is "activated" now within Jewish–Christian dialogue cannot simply be a matter of repeating his statements, but there is sufficient theological weight in his treatment of this subject to make him a valuable resource for the contemporary theological and political challenge of redefining Christians' relationship to Jews and Judaism.

Notes

1   All translations are my own.
2   Since Paul typically uses the term "calling" to mean conversion (e.g., 1 Cor 7:17–24), Stendahl's insistence that Paul was "called" and not converted from Judaism (1976, 7–23) loses its force.

References

Barclay, John M. G. 1995. Paul among Diaspora Jews: Anomaly or Apostate? *Journal for the Study of the New Testament* 60: 89–120.

Barclay, John M. G. 1996. "Do We Undermine the Law?" A Study of Romans 14.1–15.6. Pages 287–308 in *Paul and the Mosaic Law*. Edited by James D. G. Dunn. Tübingen: Mohr-Siebeck.

Barclay, John M. G. 2002. Paul's Story: Theology as Testimony. Pages 133–156 in *Narrative Dynamics in Paul: A Critical Assessment*. Edited by Bruce W. Longenecker. Louisville: Westminster John Knox.

Baur, F. C. 2003. *Paul the Apostle of Jesus Christ: His Life and Works, his Epistles and Teachings*. 2 volumes in one. Peabody, Mass.: Hendrickson (reprint 1873–1875).

Boyarin, Daniel. 1994. *A Radical Jew: Paul and the Politics of Identity*. Berkeley: University of California Press.

Das, A. Andrew. 2003. *Paul and the Jews*. Peabody, Mass.: Hendrickson.

Davies, W. D. 1978. Paul and the People of Israel. *New Testament Studies* 24: 4–39.

Dunn, James D. G. 1983. The New Perspective on Paul. *Bulletin of the John Rylands Library* 65: 95–122. Reprinted as pages 183–205 in James D. G. Dunn, *Jesus, Paul, and the Law: Studies in Mark and Galatians*. London: SPCK, 1990.

Dunn, James D. G. 1999. Who Did Paul Think He Was? A Study of Jewish Christian Identity. *New Testament Studies* 45: 174–193

Dunn, James D. G. 2005. *The New Perspective on Paul: Collected Essays*. Tübingen: Mohr-Siebeck.

Gager, John G. 2000. *Reinventing Paul*. Oxford: Oxford University Press.

Gaston, Lloyd. 1987. *Paul and the Torah*. Vancouver: University of British Columbia Press.

Gathercole, Simon J. 2002. *Where is Boasting? Early Jewish Soteriology and Paul's Response in Romans 1–5*. Grand Rapids: Eerdmans.

Goodman, Martin. 2007. The Persecution of Paul by Diaspora Jews. Pages 145–152 in *Judaism in the Roman World: Collected Essays*. Leiden: Brill.

Harvey, A. E. 1985. Forty Strokes Save One: Social Aspects of Judaizing and Apostasy. Pages 79–96 in *Alternative Approaches to New Testament Study*. Edited by A. E. Harvey. London: SPCK.

Hays, Richard B. 1989. *Echoes of Scripture in the Letters of Paul*. New Haven: Yale University Press.

Käsemann, Ernst. 1969. Paul and Israel. Pages 183–187 in Ernst Käsemann, *New Testament Questions of Today*. London: SCM.

Lüdemann, Gerd. 1989. *Opposition to Paul in Jewish Christianity*. Minneapolis: Fortress.

Martyn, J. Louis. 1997. *Galatians: A New Translation with Introduction and Commentary*. New York: Doubleday.

Nanos, Mark D. 1996. *The Mystery of Romans: The Jewish Context of Paul's Letter*. Minneapolis: Fortress.

Pagels, Elaine Hiesey. 1975. *The Gnostic Paul: Gnostic Exegesis of the Pauline Letters*. Philadelphia: Fortress.

Sanders, E. P. 1977. *Paul and Palestinian Judaism: A Comparison of Patterns of Religion*. London: SCM.

Sanders, E. P. 1983. *Paul, the Law, and the Jewish People*. Philadelphia: Fortress.

Stendahl, Krister. 1976. *Paul among Jews and Gentiles*. London: SCM.

Watson, Francis. 2007. *Paul, Judaism and the Gentiles: Beyond the New Perspective*. Revised and expanded edition. Grand Rapids: Eerdmans.

Westerholm, Stephen. 2004. *Perspectives Old and New on Paul: The "Lutheran" Paul and his Critics*. Grand Rapids: Eerdmans.

Wright, N. T. 1978. The Paul of History and the Apostle of Faith. *Tyndale Bulletin* 29: 61–88.

Wright, N. T. 1991. *The Climax of the Covenant: Christ and the Law in Pauline Theology*. Edinburgh: T. & T. Clark.

CHAPTER 13
Paul and the Law

Arland J. Hultgren

Although the word "law" has a wide range of meanings, most commonly it has two. It can refer collectively to a body of rules that a state or community recognizes as binding upon those who are members of it and upon any persons who enter into its sphere of authority. So one can speak of the law of the realm, federal law, state or provincial law, municipal law, and so on. Such bodies of law are binding upon both residents and visitors.

The term can have a narrower sense as well. In that case, it refers to a particular rule (or "ordinance") within the body of laws. An example would be a law that requires motorists to drive on the right side of the road in some countries, and on the left in others. Whatever the law is in such cases, it is more than a concession to habits and convention. It is a requirement, and there are penalties for anyone who does not obey it.

In modern societies, those bodies of law by which persons are expected to live represent the standards of behavior that are considered just and appropriate for a common life; moreover, they are codified and written. At a minimum, they seek to hold behaviors in check that can be harmful to others, and they seek to protect the vulnerable and innocent. They are enacted by governing authorities, and they are enforced by security systems that are themselves established in law.

In order to discern what "the law" meant for the apostle Paul, it is helpful to keep the collective, codified understanding of law in mind when he refers to "the law" as a general concept. In addition, it is necessary to go back in time and to a world that differs in many ways from our own. Paul was heir to traditions concerning law – and attitudes toward it – from Judaism, the Greco-Roman culture, and early pre-Pauline Christianity. Moreover, when he wrote concerning the law in his letters, he was addressing issues that were live in the communities to which his letters were sent. In addition to giving attention to what he actually wrote (the words on the page), it is important to observe

The Blackwell Companion to Paul, First Edition. Edited by Stephen Westerholm.
© 2011 Blackwell Publishing Ltd. Published 2011 by Blackwell Publishing Ltd.

how he expressed himself by his use of rhetorical conventions familiar to persons of his day.

Paul's Inheritance

Paul was a citizen of the Roman Empire (Acts 21:39) and grew up within a large network and community of persons who were considered Hellenistic Jews. That is to say that, although he was a Jew, he was thoroughly familiar with a world in which Greek was the language of everyday speech, commerce, and education. There are indications that he could speak Aramaic too (the living language of Jews living in Roman Palestine), as portrayed at Acts 21:40, but his primary language was Greek. His letters were written in Greek, and when he quoted from the Old Testament, it is clear that he used a Greek version of it as his working Bible. Most of his quotations correspond exactly or close to what appears in major known versions of the Septuagint that existed in antiquity and have been preserved into modern times.

As a Hellenistic Jew, Paul's education and interests were not limited to Jewish texts and subjects. He lived in a world in which Gentile Hellenism was close at hand. Whether he was steeped in the classics of the ancient Greeks is not known. In any case, there is no evidence in his letters that he was conversant with the classics as sources of his thinking. But those same letters show that he was familiar with the rhetorical skills that were taught in the schools of his day, and he was surely aware of, and even commended to his readers, certain values commonly held by educated Gentiles (Gal 5:23; Phil 4:8–9). The degree to which he was influenced by Greco-Roman views concerning law (*nomos* in Greek) is a matter of debate. To be sure, some Stoics held views that are, at least in part, similar to those of Paul. For example, in his writings, the Stoic philosopher Epictetus (ca. 55–135 CE) affirmed what is commonly called "natural law" (the view that there are certain standards of behavior known to persons everywhere without special revelation), claiming that it has universal significance and that it is of divine origin (*Discourses* 1.29.13, 19; 2.16.28; 3.17.6). So too Paul, in keeping with Jewish tradition (Neh 10:29; Ps 78:10; Josephus, *Jewish Antiquities* 15.136), thought of the law revealed to Israel as having divine origin (Rom 7:22, 25; 8:7; Gal 3:19), and once he speaks of Gentiles, who do not have the law of Moses, as capable of doing "instinctively what the law requires" (Rom 2:14).[1] But it is not necessary to conclude that Paul derived his views concerning law from Stoicism. The similarities are more incidental than evidence of dependence. Nevertheless, it is possible that some Gentile readers and hearers of his letters would have associated the term "law" (*nomos*) with common Hellenistic views, particularly those of the Stoics.

On reading Paul's letters, it is striking how much he speaks of the law in terms of his Jewish upbringing. His discussions of the law and human life are often permeated by Jewish patterns of thought. He writes as a believer in Christ, but that does not mean that his basic understanding of what the law is and how it functions could be forgotten. It is primarily from hearing and studying the biblical books and being educated thoroughly in Jewish thought and practice (Gal 1:14) that his concept of "law" was developed and retained in his thinking as an apostle.

The Law in Ancient Judaism

Paul's Jewish heritage bequeathed to him an expansive, all-encompassing understanding of the law. The Greek term that he uses (*nomos*) almost always appears in Greek versions of the Old Testament (such as the Septuagint) as a translation for the Hebrew word *torah*. The latter term has a breadth of meaning in Jewish thought. It can mean "law" in the sense of a legal code, but it can also refer to the first five books of the Old Testament, commonly known as the Torah or Pentateuch, and it can also mean "instruction." It has to do with more than moral law, for it encompasses civil, cultic (ceremonial, ritual), and dietary regulations as well. Specific regulations within the Torah (or Pentateuch) are called "commandments." They are called *mitzvoth* in Hebrew and *entolai* in Greek. (The singular forms are *mitzvah* in Hebrew, *entolē* in Greek.)

There was in Paul's day, as always in Jewish tradition, a recognition that some commandments within the Torah are more weighty than others. Laws that protect human life, for example, override those that pertain to the cultus (as attested in *m. Yoma* 8:5–7, and reflected in Matt 12:7; 23:23; Luke 14:5). Nevertheless, the person who lives according to the law is obliged to keep all the commandments (Lev 26:14–15; Num 15:40; Deut 8:1–20; 30:8; 2 Chr 33:8). While a theoretical distinction can be made between moral, dietary, and ritual commandments, the Jew is to observe all of them in a comprehensive manner. The law, sometimes called "the law of Moses" (Ezra 3:2; 7:6; Tob 7:12–13; 1 Cor 9:9), is the basis for life within the Jewish community and, as far as possible, for Jews in the wider world. Indeed, keeping the law of Moses is the mark of Jewish identity. At some times, when the oppression of the Jewish people by political powers was at stake, persons were willing to die in order to keep it (1 Macc 1:56–64; 2:37–38, 50).

It is important to recognize that keeping the law was not typically thought of as a burden to bear. The very first psalm expresses "delight ... in the law of the LORD" and declares that whoever meditates upon it day and night is blessed (Ps 1:2; cf. Josh 1:8). Indeed, "the precepts of the LORD are right, rejoicing the heart; the commandment of the LORD is clear, enlightening the eyes" (Ps 19:8). Observing the law was considered a grateful response to God's election and redemption of Israel from bondage in Egypt. At the moment of giving the very core of the law to Israel (the Ten Commandments), God says: "I am the LORD your God, who brought you out of the land of Egypt, out of the house of slavery" (Exod 20:2). With that said – rehearsing briefly the redemptive act of God in the exodus from Egypt – the stipulations follow. Observing the law was considered the way of life for those living in a covenant relationship with God (Exod 24:7–8; Deut 7:9; Ps 25:14; 103:17–18; Sir 17:12).

The number of commandments that were to be observed is difficult to pin down. At the beginning of the third century CE, Rabbi Simlai claimed that there were 613 (*b. Makkot* 23b). That figure may or may not have been known in the first century to Paul and his contemporaries, but an awareness of the multitude of commandments would have been. In addition to the laws written in the Pentateuch, there were additional regulations and legal interpretations that were derived from the written laws and that were developed over time as Jews sought to meet new circumstances and issues. Josephus calls them "traditions of our fathers" and says that the Pharisees, in particular, considered them binding no less than the written laws (Josephus, *Jewish Antiquities* 13.297; cf. 3 Macc 1:3; Matt 15:2–6). Paul himself uses that phrase, claiming that he adhered to them prior to his call as an apostle (Gal 1:14).

Paul and the Law: General Comments

In his letter to the Philippians, Paul speaks of his origins and early years with a strong sense of Jewish identity. He says that he was "circumcised on the eighth day, a member of the people of Israel, of the tribe of Benjamin, a Hebrew born of Hebrews; as to the law, a Pharisee; as to zeal, a persecutor of the church; as to righteousness under the law, blameless" (3:5–6).

From this, one can conclude that he was raised in a home that was observant (so his circumcision on the eighth day, as commanded in Gen 17:12). Either by upbringing or by discernment and choice in his adult years, he was a Pharisee, a member of a Jewish movement that emphasized Torah observance, and he himself was observant. By stating that he was "blameless," he is not necessarily saying that he observed the law perfectly. More likely he means that, in regard to being Torah-observant, no one could find him to be lax; he was not one to dismiss the Torah at any point in his behavior. According to his own testimony about himself, he must have been held in high esteem by others. In his letter to the Galatians he writes: "I advanced in Judaism beyond many among my people of the same age, for I was far more zealous for the traditions of my ancestors" (Gal 1:14).

Paul claims that, sometime early in the decade of the 30s of the first century, he was called by God to be an apostle, specifically, an apostle to the Gentiles (Gal 1:15–16; Rom 11:13). From the beginning of his work as an apostle, it would have been clear to him that the law of Moses – with all its multitude of commandments, many of which can be considered marks of Jewish identity – could not be imposed upon his Gentile converts. In addition to that, according to Paul's own description of life "under the law" (Rom 2:12; 3:19; Gal 3:23; Phil 3:6), there was an understanding among Jews in his day that righteousness before God, and consequently before others, is obtained and maintained by observing the law (Rom 9:31; 10:5; Gal 3:21; Phil 3:6, 9). He himself had known that way of thought and life prior to his call to apostleship (Phil 3:9).

It is on this theological point that Paul departed from his contemporaries and his own past in Judaism. From the beginning of his apostleship, Paul knew that God's action in the sending of his Son for human redemption had universal significance. Righteousness before God is not something attainable by observing the law. The reason for that is that "sin" (singular) is a power that affects all people, despite their best efforts, and "through the law comes the knowledge of sin" (Rom 3:20).

As one reads the letters of Paul, it seems at times that he is confused, confusing, or contradictory in his statements concerning the law.[2] He will say in one place that "the law is holy, and the commandment is holy and just and good" (Rom 7:12). On the other hand, he will say that the law is "the power of sin" (1 Cor 15:56). On another occasion, alluding to a commandment in the Old Testament that promises life (Lev 18:5), he says that "the very commandment that promised life proved to be death to me" (Rom 7:10).

The inconsistencies, however, are less real than apparent. If one places verses concerning the law next to one another, as here, there are indeed incongruous statements. But it is important to see how those verses fit within their contexts, both literary and historical. All the passages in the undisputed letters of Paul that contain the word *nomos* are located in four of Paul's letters,[3] which were written for specific occasions. Those four are Romans, 1 Corinthians, Galatians, and Philippians. Sometimes the passages concerning the law are polemical; sometimes they are set within diatribe, a rhetorical form in which a speaker or writer confronts and debates views put forward by an imaginary opponent, which provides an opportunity for the former to oppose those views and advance his or her own. It is within those contexts, including polemics and diatribe, that Paul's use of the term *nomos* has to be discussed. There is no passage where Paul takes up the law as a subject to analyze on its own terms. The following survey demonstrates his use of the word *nomos* in the four letters.

The Law in Galatians

Paul wrote his letter to the Galatians to congregations that he had founded in Asia Minor. Although the date of the letter is not certain, it is usually considered to have been written in the mid-50s of the first century, probably from Ephesus. Paul would have founded the churches in Galatia a few years earlier. From the contents of the letter itself, it is clear that, after Paul had left that area, certain persons arrived to oppose basic teachings that the Galatians had received from him.

Paul had carried on a mission among the Gentiles of Galatia without requiring them to adopt the law of Moses on their way to becoming believers in Christ and members of the church. According to Paul, the issue concerning Gentile observance of the Mosaic law had been settled earlier in Jerusalem (probably 48 or 49 CE) prior to his arrival in Galatia. The decision was that Gentile believers need not undergo ritual circumcision (Gal 2:1–10). The requirement of circumcision would have entailed adopting the law of Moses with all its commandments (moral, ritual, and dietary) as a way of life. In other words, the act of circumcision is not simply a matter of observing one of many commandments in the law (Gen 17:12). It implies the adoption of the law in its entirety (Gal 5:3; cf. Rom 2:25).

In his letter, Paul is highly polemical, and he has good reason to be. He has certain opponents in mind, who have arrived in Galatia after his departure and have taught the believers there that they must undergo ritual circumcision and thereby adopt the law of Moses to complete their identity as believers in Christ and become members of the church. Paul declares that the opponents have a "different gospel," one that is contrary to what he had preached (1:6, 9). The opponents have "bewitched" (NIV, NRSV) or "cast a spell" (NET) on the Galatians (3:1). The believers at Galatia have become willing to listen to Paul's opponents and follow them (4:21); therefore, they have become enslaved by regulations imposed upon them (4:9–10; 5:1).

Paul's approach to the situation is twofold. First, he says on several occasions in the letter that no one can be justified before God by means of observing the law (2:21; 3:11; 5:4) or performing "the works of the law" (2:16; 3:10), for righteousness under the law is impossible to attain (2:16; 3:21–22; 6:13). Second, Paul seeks to have his readers understand the place of the law in history (3:23–26). The law of Moses, he says, served the people of Israel as the primary means of the revelation of God and his will, extending from the time of its delivery at Mount Sinai up until the arrival of faith in Christ; that is, until Christ's death and resurrection, and the consequent rise of faith in him. The law had previously had an important, even essential, disciplinary function for the people of Israel. But that does not mean that God intended it to be in force beyond the coming of the Messiah either for Israel or for the rest of humanity. Therefore, those adherents of the law (the Jewish-Christian opponents of Paul) who seek to impose the law upon others are in error. All the blessings of God, including justification, are received by faith, not by observing the law (3:24–29). In fact, the person who undergoes circumcision and lives according to the law denies, even nullifies, the benefits of Christ's death (2:21); it is a matter of falling away from grace (5:4).

Although Paul speaks so firmly in this letter about justification by faith rather than by works of the law, he does not actually portray the law itself in a negative light. Moreover, he assumes that there are moral teachings in the law that are of importance, even obligatory for those who believe in Christ and claim to be his followers. Over against the view that freedom from the law of Moses leads to self-indulgence, Paul quotes the love commandment from the Torah (Lev 19:18): "For the whole law is summed up in a single commandment, 'You shall love your neighbor as yourself'" (5:14). The commandment is in keeping with the teachings of Jesus himself (Mark 12:31).

Paul sketches out an ethic for his readers by making a contrast not between those who observe the law and those who do not, but between a life that is led by the Holy Spirit and one that is under the dominion of the flesh, which seeks only its own satisfactions (5:16–26). He describes the first with what he calls "fruit of the Spirit" (a list of attitudes and actions that serve God and other persons) and the second with what he calls "works of the flesh" (a list of vices).

Finally, an important and creative feature of Paul's use of the term "law" in Galatians appears near the end of the letter. While speaking of mutual care among his readers, he gives a new twist to the term "law," using a phrase that he does not use elsewhere in his letters. He says, "Bear one another's burdens, and in this way you will fulfill the law of Christ" (6:2). The phrase "law of Christ" is used here in a rather playful or perhaps even ironic sense. Since "law" is so important among his opponents and apparently among some of the Galatians themselves (4:21), Paul says that the way of life for those in Christ is that of following him. Christ is, so to speak, the new Torah.

The Law in Romans

In his discussion of the law in his letter to the Romans, Paul is less polemical than in Galatians, but he uses diatribe to show what he does and does not think concerning the law. He writes to a community that is made up of both Jewish and Gentile believers in Christ (probably more Gentile than Jewish), a community of house churches that he himself did not establish. It is generally thought that he wrote his letter to Rome sometime in the mid-50s from Corinth. He wrote the letter to let the believers in Rome know that he planned to arrive in their city and proceed with a mission to Spain (15:24, 28). In a not so subtle way, he appeals to the believers of Rome to provide financial and any other possible support they can for his journey to Spain (15:24). Prior to his arrival in Rome, however, he says that he will bring a monetary collection from his Gentile churches in Philippi, Thessalonica, and Corinth to the church in Jerusalem (15:25–26). He has a feeling of foreboding, and well he should. He is not certain that he will be received as an apostle by the leaders of the church in Jerusalem (15:31). If not, rejection of him as an apostle would greatly jeopardize receiving any support from the Roman Christians for his mission to Spain. Therefore, by means of his letter, he presents to the community at Rome the essentials of his gospel, hoping that, whatever his fate in Jerusalem, the believers in Rome would find his teachings compatible with their own and would therefore receive him and support his mission to Spain.

There is no clear consensus among scholars whether Paul thought he had to deal with contested issues at Rome or not.[4] The view taken here is that he did not seek to provide "apostolic intervention" among (any supposedly) quarreling factions, and that he did not have any opponents in Rome with whom to contend. Rather, in his letter, Paul takes up issues that his readers in Rome might be wondering about concerning him. That is to say, he anticipates what might be on the minds of his readers. They might wonder, for example, whether he would stir up issues that had long been settled among them. He walks through the issues to show that his own thinking coincides essentially with their own. In order to do so, he uses various forms of speech, not least of all diatribe, particularly with regard to the law.

Paul deals with the law shortly after the outset of his letter. Beginning at 1:18, and going all the way to 3:20, he carries on a lengthy diatribe to show that all of humanity, Jew and Gentile alike, is under condemnation apart from the redemptive work of God in Christ. (He mentions Christ only once in this long section, 2:16.) He declares that "God shows no partiality" (2:11). If judgment were to be on the basis of works – and apart from redemption in Christ it has to be (2:6) – all would fail. He argues that Gentiles, who do not have the law of Moses, are on an equal footing with Jews in principle, for they are every bit as capable of doing right in the eyes of God as Jews (2:14). On the other hand, Jews who have the law and circumcision fail. In order to prove that point, Paul recites a chain of passages from the Scriptures of Israel that bring charges against God's elect for not doing what the law requires (3:10–18). The conclusion Paul draws is that no human being can ever be justified by "deeds prescribed by the law, for through the law comes the knowledge of sin" (3:20).

Having made his case in 1:19–3:20 that all of humanity, left to itself, stands condemned before God, Paul is able to make a shift at 3:21 to declare that God has provided a means of redemption in the sending of his Son. God's righteousness (i.e., God's saving activity) has been manifested in Christ, and all are justified (i.e., "right-wised," set in a right relationship with God) who rely on God's grace rather than on their own efforts of achieving righteousness by observing the law. The law is set aside as a means of righteousness. In one of his most eloquent and sweeping statements, Paul declares: "For we hold that a person is justified by faith apart from works prescribed by the law" (3:28).

Paul takes up other matters concerning the law in subsequent parts of the letter. The issue of a person's righteousness (or justification) is addressed again in 9:30– 10:13, which is a portion of the letter having to do with the destiny of the Jewish people within the overall plan of God for the world (9:1–11:36). In that section, Paul repeats that one's righteousness before God cannot be based on observing the law, in spite of one's striving to fulfill it. "For Christ," says Paul, "is the end of the law so that there may be righteousness for everyone who believes" (10:4).[5] The law of Moses cannot be a vehicle for arriving at righteousness any longer. Christ has replaced the law. Faith in him, rather than faith in one's ability to observe the law of Moses, is the way of attaining righteousness.

The force of Paul's arguments concerning righteousness apart from the law raises another issue for him in this letter. From what he says, it could be concluded that, for Paul, God's giving the law to Israel was disastrous. In chapter 5, while speaking about Christ as overcoming the sin of Adam, which led to the condemnation of all persons (5:18–19), he speaks of the effects of the law's entrance into the world. The result was that "the trespass multiplied" (5:20); that is, the law exposed the level of sinfulness in the world, showing it to be pervasive. After a discussion of other matters, Paul returns to a discussion of the law in chapter 7. There he says that, apart from our new life in Christ, our "sinful passions" were aroused by the law (7:5).

In light of such statements, Paul is forced to deal further with the law. As a person of Jewish heritage, he could not for a moment think that the law of Moses itself, given by God to Israel, could be an agent that causes sin. Furthermore, he would not want to be misunderstood. Using the diatribe form of expression once again, he asks: "What then should we say? That the law is sin?" He answers his own question: "By no means! Yet, if it had not been for the law, I would not have known sin. I would not have known what it is to covet if the law had not said, 'You shall not covet.' But sin, seizing an opportunity in the commandment, produced in me all kinds of covetousness. Apart from the law sin lies dead" (7:7–8).

He says, in so many words, that the law of Moses provides an opportunity for sin to carry out its mission of dominating one's life in opposition to the will of God. As elsewhere, he uses the word "sin" in the singular, which signifies a power at work in each human being, an inclination toward self-centeredness. Using first-person speech ("I") to carry on his analysis, he illustrates this with the commandment against covetousness (Exod 20:17; Deut 5:21). The argument consists of three parts: (1) "sin" dwells within "me" (7:8, 17, 20, 23), ever seeking to rebel against God and God's will; (2) God has given a commandment against covetousness; and so (3) "sin" leaps forth and seizes upon the opportunity provided in the commandment to rebel against God.

Throughout the chapter, Paul uses first-person singular pronouns ("I") to provide one of his most important treatments of the law and sin. He is not likely to be speaking purely autobiographically; he is making a theological analysis of the human condition when one is confronted with the desire to do the will of God, on the one hand, and the reality of sin as a power in one's life, on the other. He does not simply provide information about himself for its own sake, or for introducing himself to his readers. His interest is law and sin, but he speaks in the first person, and he seems to know the situation too well not to know the experience first hand.

Never in this chapter or elsewhere in his letters does Paul for a moment give the impression that the law is itself the cause of sin. On the contrary, he says that "the law is holy, and the commandment is holy and just and good" (7:12). Paul is clear, however, that the law of Moses – as a body of moral, cultic, and dietary laws – is not the basis of conduct for believers in Christ. Believers have been incorporated into Christ through their baptism into him (6:3), and having died with him, they are now free from the law (8:2). With the aid of the indwelling Spirit (8:9), and having been brought to newness of life (6:4), believers are no longer "under law but under grace" (6:14–15), and they carry on their lives as persons who "walk not according to the flesh but according to the Spirit" (8:4).

The result of such thinking can leave a person open to the charge of antinomianism (the view that the believer is free from moral law, though usually the meaning of the word is extended to include freedom from moral restraints altogether). In his letter, Paul acknowledges that he has been accused of that (3:8; cf. 6:15). But he is steadfast in his insistence that his gospel does not lead to a life devoid of moral direction. The believer is a person "in Christ" and is one who serves Christ as Lord. To put it another way, one is not "under law" but "under Christ." Whatever coheres with the life in Christ is to be expected; whatever does not must be avoided. The latter includes those behaviors that are forbidden in the Ten Commandments; Paul quotes four of them in 13:9 (those against adultery, murder, stealing, and coveting). As in Galatians (5:14), so also in Romans, Paul says that all the commandments are summed up in the love commandment, "Love your neighbor as yourself" (13:9, quoting Lev 19:18). Indeed, "love is the fulfilling of the law" (13:10).

The Law in 1 Corinthians and Philippians

As indicated above, Paul uses the term *nomos* in four of his letters (Romans, 1 Corinthians, Galatians, and Philippians). Most of his discussion is in the two that have been surveyed. What he says in the other two letters serves only to corroborate, not modify, what he has said in the two letters that have been discussed. In 1 Corinthians 9:8–9 and 14:21, *nomos* refers to passages being cited in the Old Testament; at 9:20–21 it refers to the law of Moses in general; and at 15:56 it refers to the law as "the power of sin" (much as in Rom 7:7–8). In Philippians, Paul uses the term to speak of a contrast between his righteousness prior to his call as an apostle and that which was his after his call. In the former case, he was considered "blameless" in regard to righteousness under the law (3:5–6), but in the latter his righteousness is not from the law but through faith in Christ (3:9).

Common Themes

Paul refers to the law in various contexts over the span of several years of letter-writing to different communities of believers, each of which posed particular challenges. Moreover, what he says about the law appears in different forms of expression, covering a broad range, from measured treatments of the origin and role of the law (Gal 3:19–4:7; Rom 2:12–29; 7:7–13) to polemical engagements with his readers and remarks about certain opponents (Gal 3:5; 4:21; 6:13). But the variations in their different contexts do not mean that what he says cannot be summarized. There are some common themes that can be described.

First, when he speaks of the law, Paul almost always has a specific body of law in mind, the law that constitutes the foundations of Jewish identity. There are a few exceptions where Paul uses the term *nomos* to speak of a "principle" (Rom 3:27; 7:21) or some other standard (Rom 8:2; Gal 6:2). But aside from such exceptions, when he uses the term *nomos*, he means the law of Moses provided in the first five books of the Old Testament known as the Torah or Pentateuch (Rom 2:13; 3:21; 13:10; 1 Cor 9:8–9; Gal 3:10; 4:21). On a couple of occasions, he refers to the Scriptures in a more general sense as the law, of which the Torah is the chief part (Rom 3:19; 1 Cor 14:21). But there is nevertheless a consistency. Whenever Paul engages his readers on matters concerning "the law," he refers to the code of law to which the Jewish people were heir, the law of Moses.

Second, although Paul continued, even as a believer in Christ, to claim that the law of Moses is "holy, and the commandment is holy and just and good" (Rom 7:12), for him the law was given to a specific people for a specific time and purpose. It was given to the people of Israel as a guide for life, a means of discipline, until the coming of the Messiah (Gal 3:23–25). But as God's gift to Israel, it was not intended for Gentiles. Moreover, since the Messiah Jesus has come, no one, Jew or Gentile, who professes faith in Jesus as the Messiah is bound to the law of Moses as a pattern for life. Such persons have entered into a new sphere of living.

Third, while Paul could never have thought of the law of Moses as intrinsically bad, the problem with regard to the law is that, while it promises life to those who will observe it (Lev 18:5), it has been given to human beings, who are incurably flawed. Therefore, it is impossible for its promise of life to be fulfilled. The result is death instead of life (Rom 7:10). Moreover, "sin" seeks to cut short all human aspirations to serve God with a clear conscience, and it finds an opportunity in the commandments to lead human beings astray.

Fourth, the law is not then a means by which one can live and gain righteousness before God. To seek righteousness by means of the law is an impossibility, since no one can live up to its demands (Rom 3:9; Gal 3:10–11). Furthermore, trying to lead such a life is a delusion. The law in fact brings knowledge of sin (Rom 3:20). There has to be a different way to be regarded as righteous in the sight of God (i.e., rightly related to God). That way has been provided by God himself. By means of his redemptive work through Christ, God has exercised his righteousness (his saving activity) by sending his Son into the world and condemning sin at the cross (Rom 8:3; Gal 3:13). Since God has effectively carried out his judgment upon sin at the cross, the "just requirement of the law" is thereby fulfilled in those who are beneficiaries of it (Rom 8:4); that is, all who belong to Christ in faith and are guided by the Spirit. If the requirement has been fulfilled in the crucified Christ, it has been fulfilled in his people as well. Consequently, a person's righteousness is no longer dependent upon observing the law of Moses, but is claimed as one's own by faith in what God has done through the cross of Christ.

Righteousness is a pure, undeserved gift from God that is appropriated by faith (Rom 3:21–26).

Finally, none of this implies a lack on Paul's part of concern about ethics.[6] To be sure, the believer is not under the law for righteousness. But Paul does not say that the commandments of the Decalogue are to be ignored. On the contrary, he speaks of them in a positive way (Rom 13:9). For Paul, the life of the believer is bound up in obedience to Christ. Whatever is consistent with that life can be endorsed as a guide for living, whether it be the moral teachings of the Old Testament, the teachings of Jesus, early Christian traditions, or even certain virtues of the Hellenistic pagan world (Phil 4:8–9). The point is that the believer does not walk according to the prescriptions of the law of Moses, but in newness of life (Rom 6:4) and according to the Spirit (Rom 8:4; Gal 5:25), under the lordship of Christ. The life of the believer is one of "faith working through love" (Gal 5:6). In fact, loving your neighbor is fulfilling the law (Rom 13:8–10; Gal 5:14).

Some Contested Issues

In the study of "Paul and the law," certain issues are debated among interpreters, as one might expect. Three major issues have been raised in recent years.

First, the question has been raised as to how Paul understood the word *nomos* in Judaism. There have been interpreters who have maintained that, since Paul used the Greek word *nomos* for what had traditionally been known in Hebrew as *torah*, it is not likely that he understood the richness of the latter term, which carries a wide range of meanings, including not only "law," but also "instruction" and "guidance." According to that view, Paul had a Hellenized understanding of the term and reduced it simply to law in the narrowest ("legalistic") sense.[7] Furthermore, that explains why Paul is perceived by his critics to be so negative about the law in some places.

Such a claim, however, has been faulted on various grounds. Interpreters have dismissed it on the basis of comparative studies of Hebrew and Greek versions of the Old Testament. In addition, the claim underestimates the power of symbols and traditions to cross cultures and languages intact. If it were considered valid, the claim would mean that other Jews of Paul's time whose primary language was Greek were in the same situation. That includes some of the writers of the Old Testament apocrypha, Philo, and Josephus, to name a few. Moreover, one would have to say that many, most, or perhaps even all persons throughout time and around the world whose primary language is not Hebrew do not truly understand the meaning of *torah* in all its richness. For example, by the same criterion one would have to say that the modern Jew living in New York or London, whose primary language is English, cannot understand the meaning of *torah*. That would be denied in any Jewish community.

Second, the question has been raised concerning the interpretation of the phrase "works of the law" in Paul's letters (Rom 3:20, 28; Gal 2:16; 3:2, 5, 10) or simply the word "works," a shorthand expression for the same thing (Rom 4:2, 6; 9:32; 11:6). The traditional view has been that, by means of that word or phrase, the apostle refers to a way of life in which a conscientious Jew seeks to win God's favor by keeping the precepts of the law, a way of life called "works righteousness." Since the late 1970s, however, some interpreters of Paul have advocated what is called a "New Perspective on Paul."[8] The proponents of that view challenge the traditional view and maintain that Judaism in Paul's day was not a religion of "works righteousness." Instead, doing "works of the law" meant a life of obedience to a pattern of life, including Sabbath, ritual circumcision, and food laws, in order to provide social boundaries between Jews and Gentiles. The reason for Paul's opposition to doing "works of the law" was that, for him, the Jewish people had taken upon themselves this pattern of life too thoroughly, resulting in an exaggerated emphasis on social boundaries and ethnicity, combined with a sense of election. A mission to Gentiles, emphasizing the free grace of God for all humanity through God's redemptive act in Christ, then became impossible. To insist that Gentiles adopt "works of the law" to be a part of the covenant people would mean that Christ died to no effect (Gal 2:21). Along with this interpretation of works of the law as boundary markers, the proponents of the "New Perspective" have provided a revised picture of ancient Judaism. According to that, Judaism in antiquity was a religion of grace, and observing the law was a matter of maintaining one's participation in the covenant as well as a sign of identity in the broader society.

The revised portrayal of ancient Judaism has been extremely important for modern understanding. Traditional portrayals of Judaism have often led to inaccurate and pejorative caricatures, claiming that it was legalistic to an almost unbearable degree. Correctives and revisions have been important and overdue. Nevertheless, it has to be acknowledged that ancient Judaism had many strands of tradition. Some ancient Jewish sources do, in fact, speak of doing good works for justification or salvation. Moreover, some of them appear in writings nearly contemporary with Paul. For example, in 2 Esdras 8:33 (usually regarded as a document of the first century CE), there is the declaration that "the righteous, who have many works laid up with [God], shall receive their reward in consequence of their own deeds." Other passages can be cited as well (*Pss. Sol.* 9:4–5; *2 Bar.* 14:12–13; 51:1–6; 2 Esd 7:21, 24). And in the Dead Sea Scrolls, the phrases "works of the law" and "observing the law" appear in contexts that clearly have to do with behavior that is considered meritorious before God (4QMMT; 1QS V, 21; and 1QpHab VIII, 1). The same idea appears in rabbinic literature of a later time (*m. Abot* 2:1; 3:17; 6:7, 11). In the final analysis, regardless of the variety of strands and emphases existing in ancient Judaism, Paul's opposition to "works of the law" fits within the view of those contemporaries who held that observing the law of Moses is necessary for righteousness before God. For Paul, that way of life does not, in fact, lead to righteousness. Righteousness (a right relationship between a person and God) is a matter of accepting the grace of God by faith.

Finally, since Paul opposed vehemently the view that Gentiles should be required to adopt the law of Moses, it has been proposed that his teaching of justification by faith was crafted for a specific and limited purpose, and that was to defend the rights of Gentile converts to be full heirs of the promises of God (Stendahl 1976, 2); it had no universal applicability.

There can be no doubt that the doctrine of justification by faith could function in such a way that it made admission of Gentiles *as Gentiles* into the church possible. But to think that Paul's law-free gospel was crafted for that purpose alone (making a virtue out of a necessity) is insufficient. According to Paul, observing the law is not an adequate means of righteousness for anyone, Jew or Gentile (Rom 3:20). Moreover, he is explicit in saying that all who accept the good news, Jew or Gentile, are justified (Rom 3:30; 4:11–12; Gal 2:15–16). The good news of justification by faith is not therefore for Gentiles only. It is the *basis* for their inclusion, not simply an ex post facto reason for it.

Notes

1   Biblical quotations are taken from the New Revised Standard Version.
2   Among scholars, this point is made especially by Räisänen (1987, 10–15).
3   The "undisputed" letters are Romans, 1 and 2 Corinthians, Galatians, Philippians, 1 Thessalonians, and Philemon. These are letters concerning which there is little or no dispute concerning their authorship by Paul. The authorship of the other letters attributed to Paul is often disputed, but not in every case and not universally.
4   Many of the issues are discussed in the essays in Donfried (1991).
5   The Greek word translated as "end" in this verse is *telos*. Although some interpreters have maintained that the word should be translated "goal" (which is one of the possible meanings of the word in other contexts), generally "end" is favored, which is also the translation in major English versions (KJV, RSV, NIV, NRSV).
6   Various approaches to Paul's ethics are discussed in the essays in Rosner (1995).
7   For a discussion of the views of those scholars (particularly Solomon Schechter and C. H. Dodd) who have made such a distinction between *nomos* and *torah*, and a critical response, see Westerholm (1986).
8   The beginning date is often traced to the publication of Sanders (1977). But the term "New Perspective" is typically attributed (at least for its major development and impact) to Dunn (1983). For an in-depth survey and discussion, see Westerholm (2004). For additional essays and responses to his critics, see Dunn (2008).

References

Badenas, Robert. 1985. *Christ the End of the Law: Romans 10.4 in Pauline Perspective*. Sheffield: JSOT.
Bornkamm, Günther. 1971. *Paul*. New York: Harper & Row.
Das, A. Andrew. 2001. *Paul, the Law, and the Covenant*. Peabody, Mass.: Hendrickson.
Davies, W. D. 1962a. Law in First-century Judaism. Pages 89–95 in *The Interpreter's Dictionary of the Bible*, Volume 3. Edited by George A. Buttrick. Nashville: Abingdon.
Davies, W. D. 1962b. Law in the NT. Pages 95–102 in *The Interpreter's Dictionary of the Bible*, Volume 3. Edited by George A. Buttrick. Nashville: Abingdon.
De Roo, Jacqueline C. R. 2007. *"Works of the Law" at Qumran and in Paul*. Sheffield: Sheffield Phoenix.
Donfried, Karl P., editor. 1991. *The Romans Debate*. Revised edition. Peabody, Mass.: Hendrickson.
Dunn, James D. G. 1983. The New Perspective on Paul. *Bulletin of the John Rylands Library* 65: 95–122.
Dunn, James D. G. editor. 2001. *Paul and the Mosaic Law*. Grand Rapids: Eerdmans.
Dunn, James D. G. 2008. *The New Perspective on Paul*. Revised edition. Grand Rapids: Eerdmans.

Gaston, Lloyd. 1987. *Paul and the Torah*. Vancouver: University of British Columbia Press.

Gutbrod, W. 1967a. The Law in the Old Testament. Pages 1036–1047 in *Theological Dictionary of the New Testament*, Volume 4. Edited by Gerhard Kittel. Grand Rapids: Eerdmans.

Gutbrod, W. 1967b. The Law in Judaism. Pages 1047–1059 in *Theological Dictionary of the New Testament*, Volume 4. Edited by Gerhard Kittel. Grand Rapids: Eerdmans.

Gutbrod, W. 1967c. The Law in the New Testament. Pages 1059–1091 in *Theological Dictionary of the New Testament*, Volume 4. Edited by Gerhard Kittel. Grand Rapids: Eerdmans.

Hübner, Hans. 1984. *Law in Paul's Thought*. Edinburgh: T. & T. Clark.

Kleinknecht, H. 1967. *Nomos* in the Greek and Hellenistic World. Pages 1023–1035 in *Theological Dictionary of the New Testament*, Volume 4. Edited by Gerhard Kittel. Grand Rapids: Eerdmans.

Martin, Brice L. 1989. *Christ and the Law in Paul*. Leiden: Brill.

Räisänen, Heikki. 1987. *Paul and the Law*. Second edition. Tübingen: J. C. B. Mohr (Paul Siebeck).

Rhyne, C. Thomas. 1981. *Faith Establishes the Law*. Chico, Calif.: Scholars.

Rosner, Brian S., editor. 1995. *Understanding Paul's Ethics: Twentieth Century Approaches*. Grand Rapids: Eerdmans.

Sanders, E. P. 1977. *Paul and Palestinian Judaism: A Comparison of Patterns of Religion*. Philadelphia: Fortress.

Sanders, E. P. 1983. *Paul, the Law, and the Jewish People*. Philadelphia: Fortress.

Stendahl, Krister. 1976. *Paul among Jews and Gentiles and Other Essays*. Philadelphia: Fortress.

Thielman, Frank. 1989. *From Plight to Solution: A Jewish Framework for Understanding Paul's View of the Law in Galatians and Romans*. New York: Brill.

Thielman, Frank. 1994. *Paul and the Law: A Contextual Approach*. Downers Grove, Ill.: InterVarsity.

Tomson, Peter J. 1990. *Paul and the Jewish Law: Halakha in the Letters of the Apostle to the Gentiles*. Minneapolis: Fortress.

Westerholm, Stephen. 1986. *Torah, Nomos*, and Law: A Question of "Meaning." *Studies in Religion/Sciences Religieuses* 15: 327–336.

Westerholm, Stephen. 2004. *Perspectives Old and New on Paul: The "Lutheran" Paul and his Critics*. Grand Rapids: Eerdmans.

Westerholm, Stephen. 2008a. Law in Early Judaism. Pages 587–594 in *The New Interpreter's Dictionary of the Bible*, Volume 3. Edited by Katherine Doob Sakenfeld. Nashville: Abingdon.

Westerholm, Stephen. 2008b. Law in the NT. Pages 594–602 in *The New Interpreter's Dictionary of the Bible*, Volume 3. Edited by Katherine Doob Sakenfeld. Nashville: Abingdon.

Winger, Michael. 1992. *By What Law? The Meaning of* Nomos *in the Letters of Paul*. Atlanta: Scholars.

CHAPTER 14

The Text of the Pauline Corpus

Dirk Jongkind

The raw material for any critical study of Paul's theology and thought is found in the Greek text of his writings. These writings have a transmission history ranging from the historical act of the sending of the letter itself – or, alternatively, from the moment in which the first edition of Paul was released for copying – to the mechanized printing of the modern era. Text critics have busied themselves with the text of the New Testament and produced a substantial body of detailed studies and scholarly literature. This chapter will look at the Pauline corpus through the lens of a subdiscipline of biblical studies, namely, that of textual criticism.

Modern Editions of the Text of Paul

Since no separate edition of the Greek text of the Pauline corpus has been published, New Testament scholars usually restrict themselves to one of the two critical editions of the Greek New Testament, the Nestle–Aland twenty-seventh edition (NA27) and the fourth edition published by the United Bible Society (UBS4). Both of these are pocket editions and contain only a selection of the total variation found in the manuscript tradition and only part of the available evidence. They contain exactly the same text of the New Testament, having been produced by the same committee. The difference lies in the textual apparatus: the apparatus of UBS4 contains fewer variants but tends to give more information on the evidence for each of the variants cited, whereas NA27 has many more (but certainly not all) variants and presents the evidence more compactly. The text that these two editions share was already produced for NA26 (published

The Blackwell Companion to Paul, First Edition. Edited by Stephen Westerholm.
© 2011 Blackwell Publishing Ltd. Published 2011 by Blackwell Publishing Ltd.

in 1979) and UBS3 (published in 1975). As for the Nestle-Aland series of editions, these constituted an independent critical text only from NA26 onward. Before this, the text was that formed by a comparison of three late nineteenth-century texts, those of Westcott–Hort, Tischendorf, and Weiss (or Weymouth for the first two editions).

If one does not want to consult transcriptions of individual manuscripts, but still wants to gain access to a collection of variants besides those offered in NA27, a number of older critical editions are still very useful: (1) S. P. Tregelles, *The Greek New Testament* (1857–1872); (2) Tischendorf's eighth edition, *Editio octava critica maior* (1869–1872); and (3) H. von Soden, *Die Schriften des Neuen Testaments* (second edition, 1911–1913). None of these is without errors or flaws, and one has to get used to von Soden's rather eccentric way of presenting the evidence. A good conversion table to translate his manuscript designations to those of the now standard Gregory–Aland list can be found as an appendix to Kurt Aland's *Kurzgefasste Liste* (Kurt Aland 1994). Also useful are the line-by-line collations by Reuben Swanson (*New Testament Greek Manuscripts*). The volumes on individual New Testament books compare a fair number of manuscripts and even pay attention to minor details. However, the volumes have not all been thoroughly proofread and need to be accessed with some caution. Four volumes of Pauline materials – on Galatians, Romans, and 1 and 2 Corinthians – have so far been published (Swanson 2008a–d).

The Manuscripts of the Greek Tradition

The text of the traditional Pauline corpus does not have as many individual manuscript witnesses as the four gospels, but the quality and age of the manuscripts are by no means inferior to those of any other part of the New Testament. Papyrus manuscripts are normally designated with the Gothic letter $\mathfrak{p}$; these manuscripts date from the second to the eighth century. Manuscripts written in capital letters on parchment (hence "majuscule" manuscripts) are designated by a number starting with 0, sometimes preceded by a capital letter, such as *Codex Vaticanus*: B (03); these date from the third to the tenth century. Minuscule manuscripts, written in a cursive Greek script on parchment and later also on paper, are designated by a simple number (for example, the Leicester codex: 69) and date from the ninth century until the advance of the printing press. Kurt Aland and co-workers (1991, 138) mention 798 manuscripts containing text from the Pauline corpus, though only 742 of these could be used in his 1991 work as some were inaccessible or otherwise lost. A large number of these manuscripts contain lacunae or are fragmentary.

The two earliest papyrus manuscripts are both paleographically dated around AD 200 ($\mathfrak{p}^{32}$, $\mathfrak{p}^{46}$). The first of these is a fragment of a codex leaf containing only parts of a few verses from Titus, but the second one, the Chester Beatty codex of the Pauline epistles, contains in its present form text from all the letters belonging to the traditional Pauline corpus (including Hebrews) except 2 Thessalonians, the Pastoral epistles, and Philemon. The codex was formed by folding fifty-two papyrus sheets together to form one large quire (which had 104 folios and thus 208 pages). Parts of eighty-six folios have survived and are currently kept in Michigan and at the Chester Beatty library in Dublin. The last remaining leaf ends with 1 Thessalonians 5 (the verso of folio 97), which leaves sixteen pages for 2 Thessalonians and, possibly, the Pastoral epistles. This would clearly not be enough for all the remaining text, and the discussion whether the Pastorals were included and continued on additional leaves, or whether they were never intended to be part of this collection, is still continuing (Royse 2008, 202–203).

A further twelve fragments are all dated to the third century (eleven papyri, $\mathfrak{p}^{12}$, $\mathfrak{p}^{15}$, $\mathfrak{p}^{27}$, $\mathfrak{p}^{30}$, $\mathfrak{p}^{40}$, $\mathfrak{p}^{49}$, $\mathfrak{p}^{65}$, $\mathfrak{p}^{87}$, $\mathfrak{p}^{113}$, $\mathfrak{p}^{114}$, $\mathfrak{p}^{118}$, and one majuscule parchment manuscript, 0220). Of these, only $\mathfrak{p}^{30}$ contains text from more than one letter (1–2 Thess), and all are fragmentary. $\mathfrak{p}^{40}$ is one of the more extensive as it consists of a series of eleven fragments from Romans 1–9; not only are these fragments very hard to read, however, but there is still uncertainty regarding the manuscript's date. Aland dated it to the third century (in Junack et al. 1989, xxxix), yet the holding institution, the Papyrological Institute of Heidelberg, describes Aland's claim as "*kaum richtig*" ("hardly right") and dates it much later, to the fifth/sixth century. In total, there are five third-century manuscripts that contain only text from Romans, including the oldest fragment of the text of Paul on parchment, 0220. The limited amount of preserved material of many of these manuscripts makes it hard to assess their exact textual value or to say anything definite about the origin and context of the text. Most have text on the front and back, indicating that they formed part of a leaf, which was probably part of a larger codex; but $\mathfrak{p}^{114}$ has the beginning of a few lines of Hebrews 1 written at the bottom of a page, whereas the other side of this fragment is without any text. It is possible that we are looking at "page 2" of a Hebrews codex and that page 1 was only used as a cover or title page. In the absence of more data, however, firm conclusions cannot be drawn. Another papyrus containing text from Hebrews 1 is $\mathfrak{p}^{12}$. This manuscript is a private letter in Greek, in three columns, and written from Rome to Egypt probably in the third quarter of the third century. It has Hebrews 1:1 jotted above column two (not in the same hand) and Genesis 1:1–4 on the verso. There is a clear thematic relation between the two passages of Scripture, but there is no clear link to the text of the letter itself. Though fragments such as these provide a witness to the text of the Pauline corpus, they were clearly never intended to be a continuous text.

If we look then at the manuscripts dated third/fourth century and those within the fourth century, we see that the proportion of majuscule manuscripts on parchment increases (six parchments, ℵ[01], B [03], 0185, 0221, 0228, 0230, and seven papyri, $\mathfrak{p}^{13}$, $\mathfrak{p}^{16}$, $\mathfrak{p}^{92}$, $\mathfrak{p}^{10}$, $\mathfrak{p}^{17}$, $\mathfrak{p}^{89}$, $\mathfrak{p}^{123}$). Moreover, the total amount of text preserved on parchment outweighs by far the contribution of the papyrus manuscripts in this period. The largest of the papyri is $\mathfrak{p}^{13}$. Written on the back of a scroll containing a Latin epitome of Livy, it is the only document in our survey that is a scroll rather than a codex. Each column is numbered, and about one-third of Hebrews is present. The column numbering suggests that another work preceded Hebrews. Before the scroll was reused for the biblical text, it was repaired and strengthened with strips of papyrus. $\mathfrak{p}^{92}$ has text from Ephesians and 2 Thessalonians from two different folios. However, none of the other five papyri from the third/fourth or fourth century has text from more than one folio. $\mathfrak{p}^{10}$ has been labeled a writing exercise, and it clearly betrays an inexperienced hand. Most of the papyrus sheet, which is well preserved, is left blank. Only at the beginning of the verso is the text of Romans 1:1–7 written in what may well have been a school exercise. Though a witness to the text of Paul, $\mathfrak{p}^{10}$ does not come from a manuscript containing the Pauline corpus. Parchment 0230 (dated fourth/fifth century by the original editors) is the earliest Greek–Latin manuscript of Paul, containing text from Ephesians 6. Only four lines are preserved: on the recto we find the Latin (Eph 6:5–6), on the verso the Greek (6:11–12). The text is laid out in short sense-lines, just as in the later Codex Claromontanus D (06), though the lines are shorter in the latter. If, as is likely, a page contained only a single column, then on each opening one would have had the Greek on the left hand page and the Latin on the right.

Among all the fourth-century manuscripts, the two that stand out are the majuscules Codex Vaticanus B (03) and Codex Sinaiticus ℵ (01). Though Codex Vaticanus is not complete in the Pauline corpus (the text from Heb 9:14 onward, including that of the Pastoral epistles and Philemon, is missing), Codex Sinaiticus is complete. At an early time, still in the production stage of the manuscript, one sheet was replaced in Sinaiticus, so that 1 Thessalonians 2:14–5:28 and Hebrews 4:16–8:1 are written by a different, but contemporary, scribe. The other parchment manuscripts from this period are, again, all fragmentary and contain only text from a single folio.

From the fourth century on, the total amount of evidence becomes more extensive, but only two papyrus manuscripts merit special attention. The first, $\mathfrak{p}^{99}$ (Chester Beatty codex AC1499, dated around 400), is listed as a New Testament papyrus, but does not contain any continuous text. It is a non-systematic Greek–Latin lexicon or glossary in which terms from parts of four Pauline epistles are translated. The same manuscript also contains Greek grammatical inflections. The other papyrus to be mentioned here is at present the latest papyrus with text from Paul. $\mathfrak{p}^{61}$ consists of a number of fragments from a papyrus codex that may have contained the whole of the Pauline corpus. Text has been preserved from Romans, 1 Corinthians, Philippians, Colossians, 1 Thessalonians, Titus, and Philemon. Aland dates this manuscript to around 700.

Many of the parchment manuscripts of Paul from the fifth century or later (over sixty are listed) do not contain much text, but a number of them do. From the fifth century comes Codex Ephraemi Rescriptus C (04), a palimpsest which was overwritten in the twelfth century with sermons of the Syrian church father St. Ephrem. A considerable number of the original leaves have been deciphered and were first published by Tischendorf. Also from the fifth century comes Codex Alexandrinus A (02), which contains the complete text of Paul except for 2 Corinthians 4:14–12:6. Variously dated to the fifth or sixth century, the Freer Codex of the Pauline epistles, I (016), is a heavily damaged codex of which eighty-four incomplete folios survive. A manuscript that has been reused twice (a double palimpsest) is 048 from the fifth century, with fragmentary text from almost every letter of the Pauline corpus. Of particular importance is the Codex Claromontanus D (06), a Greek–Latin bilingual manuscript with the two languages on facing pages. The text, which is virtually complete, has a close affinity with two other bilingual manuscripts of Paul: the ninth-century manuscripts Codex Augiensis F (010) and Codex Boernerianus G (012). Another majuscule manuscript of the Pauline corpus from the sixth century is Codex Coislinianus H (015), which is dispersed over no less than six holding institutions but is not complete (forty-one folios remain). Other more or less complete majuscules that contain the text of Paul are K (018) with a hiatus in Romans and 1 Corinthians, *Codex Angelicus* L (020), the palimpsest *Codex Porphyrianus* P (025), 049, 0150, and 0151. All these date from the ninth century. In addition, there are complete majuscules from the ninth/tenth century, Ψ (044), and from the tenth, 075.

From the ninth century onward, most manuscripts were no longer written in the majuscule script but in a cursive (or minuscule) script. A number of these late manuscripts preserve an old text. That, for example, minuscule 1739 (tenth century) is a copy of a fourth-century codex has been argued on the basis of the citations from the church fathers in the margin (Metzger 1981, 112). Likewise, though the main text of minuscule 424 (eleventh century) is very similar to the standard Byzantine text of the day, it contains a series of corrections that must have been made against a manuscript with a minuscule 1739 type of text. Minuscule 1881 (fourteenth century) is also a member of the same text family and is of great importance. The earliest printed New Testaments were based on late minuscule manuscripts with a Byzantine text.

Other Testimony to the Text of Paul

The Latin tradition is the most extensive of all early translations. Here – unlike the situation in the Greek tradition – we know of an official edition commissioned and sanctioned by Pope Damasus. Around AD 383, Damasus asked Jerome to remedy the situation in which a variety of Latin versions of the Scriptures were in use by producing a definitive edition; it became known as the Vulgate. Much is known about the pre-Vulgate text from a number of manuscripts, but especially from citations by church fathers. A critical text is made available in the *Vetus Latina* series, though Romans – 2 Corinthians have yet to appear (see also Frede 1964). The text of Paul as found in most Vulgate manuscripts is first found in the work of Pelagius (early fifth century) and probably goes back to the edition made by Jerome. It is unclear whether Jerome produced a critical edition of the Pauline corpus or whether he sanctioned an already existing text; Parker (2008, 266) does not find any positive evidence that Jerome actually revised the text of Paul as he had done with the gospels. For the Vulgate text, the best edition is still that of Wordsworth–White (1913–1939). The only other early translation that is reasonably well preserved is the Syriac Peshitta, which originated probably in the fourth or early fifth century. The exact origins of this particular version remain highly uncertain, as is the question whether the Peshitta, which became the dominant text in both branches of the Syriac church, is the work of a single authority or of a number of different hands (Metzger 1977, 56–63). The Pauline corpus is available in a recent edition by Barbara Aland and Andreas Juckel (1991–2002).

The other source of information on the textual history of the Pauline corpus is citations by church fathers, including commentaries on the text and even discussions of known variant readings. Though the works of these church fathers have themselves come down to us by means of a manuscript transmission and modern editions, they provide essential information for the textual criticism of Paul (note also the discussion on Marcion below).

Organizing the Evidence

Text–types

The text of the Pauline corpus presents us with fewer problems than that of the gospels, Acts, or the Apocalypse. Though there are important variations in the text, the extent of the differences between the text-types is much less than in the gospels. Recently, the traditional concept of "text-types" has itself come under criticism, with several prominent scholars voicing reservations about the imprecision of the term (Parker 2008, 171–174); a more fluid concept of the whole textual tradition is preferred. Kurt Aland and co-workers (1991, 165) dismiss the notion of a Western text in Paul, arguing that the character of the variants attested by the so-called "Western" witnesses of Paul, D (06), F (010), and G (012), is very different from the typical Western variants in the gospels and Acts. Thus, though the unique textual character of these three manuscripts is not denied, this does not, in Aland's view, justify labeling these manuscripts as representatives of a distinct text-type. On the other hand, though organizing the manuscripts in a plot diagram on the basis of statistical methods (such as multivariate analysis) has not attracted a large following in text-critical circles, preliminary results indicate that the concept of text-types is still maintainable, but without the suggestion that such a text is the result of a single recension. Eldon Epp suggested the designation "textual cluster" or "constellation" (1995, 16). All in all, there remains some practical advantage in maintaining the traditional terminology. The three traditional text-types – "Alexandrian," "Western," and "Byzantine" – can be recognized in Paul, but there is considerable overlap between them.

A particular pitfall for New Testament scholars is that of transferring wholesale to the Pauline corpus distinctions learned in the textual criticism of the four gospels. In point of fact, some important manuscripts that contain both the gospels and Paul differ in their textual character and the quality of the text between these two major subdivisions. *Codex Alexandrinus* A (02) has clear Byzantine affinities in the gospels, but is "Alexandrian" in Paul. Similarly, *Codex Vaticanus* B (03) appears to have a higher proportion of less-reliable readings in the Pauline corpus than elsewhere. The point can be illustrated from Romans 9, a chapter for which NA27 lists seven variants where *Vaticanus* has a reading with only minimal additional support, and none of these is deemed original.

As Weiss (1896a; see below) extensively demonstrated, the Byzantine text-type is well represented in the majuscules K (018), L (020), and P (025); the Western text in D (06), F (010), and G (012); and the Alexandrian text in ℵ (01), A (02), B (03), and C (04). The early papyrus $\mathfrak{p}^{46}$ belongs to the Alexandrian group as well, though it has a considerable number of non-typical readings.

Aland's Text und Textwert

To date, the most ambitious attempt to order and classify the Greek manuscripts of the Pauline epistles is the set of four volumes published by Kurt Aland and co-workers in the series *Text und Textwert der griechischen Handschriften des Neuen Testaments* (1991).

The manuscripts are classified on the basis of 251 test passages selected from throughout the corpus. The test passages were chosen to achieve a number of goals. First, they function to separate the bulk of Byzantine manuscripts from the manuscripts that contain an older text. Second, the test passages help to establish whether a manuscript has a similar type of text throughout the Pauline corpus or whether it changes character. Third, the test passages help to illustrate the history of some early corruptions in the non-Byzantine witnesses that never entered the majority text. The variants attested in a single test passage are numbered using a fixed scheme. Variant 1 is always the majority text (which includes the Byzantine text but need not be limited to this text-type); variant 2 is the reading regarded as the original text; and variants 3 and higher list alternative readings that do not belong to either group. Readings that are both considered original and found in the Byzantine tradition are labeled 1/2. This group of readings often contains places where one or more manuscripts of the Alexandrian tradition do not preserve the original text.

The data resulting from collating all the Pauline manuscripts are presented in a number of ways. The results organized by manuscript are given in the *Gesamtübersicht*; in the introduction to each of the individual letters, each manuscript is ranked according to its percentage of old readings; and the collation of all manuscripts for each test passage is found in the *Resultate der Kollation*. Then there are two lists in which a manuscript is compared with other manuscripts, measured in a percentage of agreement. In the first list, the *Hauptliste*, a manuscript is listed together with its closest relatives in descending order on the basis of agreements in non-majority variants only (i.e., where the manuscripts share a variant reading of types 2, 1/2, and 3ff., but excluding cases where they share a reading found in the majority text [=type 1]). In the separately bound *Ergänzungsliste*, the closest relatives are again listed, but this time on the basis of a comparison of all agreements in the test passages, including those in which the majority reading is shared.

Despite their cumbersome format and the plethora of statistical data, the volumes of *Text und Textwert* on the Pauline corpus are still indispensable for any serious textual criticism of Paul. They provide information on the manuscripts that most often agree with the NA26 and NA27 text, give information on the consistency of relationships to other manuscripts over the different books of the Pauline corpus, and indicate the proneness of a manuscript to contain singular or poorly attested readings. Criticism of the method followed by Aland pointed out that these volumes presuppose knowledge of the "oldest text" before assessing the quality of a manuscript, and that the grouping of variants in the various categories presupposes a certain view of the textual development and transmission. Additionally, comparing manuscripts on the basis of a percentage of agreement (a two-dimensional comparison) does not do justice to the complexity of interrelations. However, the fact that each manuscript is compared to every other manuscript obviates much of the latter objection.

One result of the comparisons in *Text und Textwert* pointed out by Aland (1991, 147–148) is that the Byzantine text is shown to have a large influence on the whole textual tradition of Paul; there are few manuscripts with a predominantly independent and old text. Also, manuscripts frequently change in textual character; minuscule 33 (ninth century), for example, has a strongly Byzantine text in Romans, but a non-Byzantine text in 1 Corinthians.

Marcion and the Text of the Pauline Canon

According to the testimony of the early church, the heretic Marcion (expelled from the Roman church in AD 144) had perhaps a greater influence on the rise of variant readings in the Pauline corpus than anyone else. Marcion produced his own Pauline corpus, the *Apostolikon*, in which he eliminated many references to Paul's use of the Old Testament and, to a certain degree, edited and rewrote other phrases or passages. Tertullian dealt with many of the so-called textual changes introduced by Marcion in Book 5 of his *Against Marcion*. Some of the readings he notes occur sporadically in actual manuscripts, but there is not a single manuscript that has been shown to contain the text of Marcion with any measure of consistency. Indeed, some of Marcion's readings that are explicitly condemned by Tertullian are now regarded as cases in which Tertullian's own biblical text was corrupt (for example, Gal 2:5, which Tertullian read without the οὐδέ; see Tertullian *Against Marcion* 5.3; Harnack 1924 [Beilage], 70–71). Despite Harnack's assertion that Tertullian used a Latin translation of Marcion's *Apostolikon*, it seems almost certain now that this was not the case (Schmid 1995, 40–59). Besides Tertullian's discussion of Marcion's interpretation and text of Paul, the other sources for particular readings of Marcion's *Apostolikon* are the dialogues of Adamantius and Epiphanius's treatment of Marcion in the *Panarion*.

What can be said about the nature of the text with which Marcion started? Clabeaux (1989) attempted in a monograph-length study to reconstruct this text. The method Clabeaux used to filter out the pre-Marcionite readings from the attested Marcionite readings was to disregard readings that are the result of the tendentious theological agenda of Marcion, and to allow readings that can be explained as having originated in merely mechanical errors or that are also found in manuscripts that cannot possibly have been influenced by Marcion. According to Clabeaux, the eighty-two remaining readings correlate most closely to a particular type of text within the Old Latin (the I group, found in Rome and central Italy from the second half of the fourth century). Schmid (1995, 17–23) raises objections against some of Clabeaux's criteria, noting, for example, that he does not reckon with the possibility that mechanical errors could have occurred in the Marcionite texts themselves after he made his edition. Moreover, according to Schmid, both the transparency and execution of the work leave much to be desired. Therefore, Schmid offers his own reconstruction of those parts of the *Apostolikon* of Marcion for which positive evidence exists and uses it as a basis for further work. It is unlikely that Marcion is the source of the Western text; rather, Schmid concludes, Marcion derived his text from a text-form that also lies at the base of the Old Latin and Old Syriac.

The Pauline Collection

Marcion may have been the first person to be charged with deliberately altering the text of Paul, but he is also the first one about whom we know that he worked with a specific collection of Paul's letters. From Tertullian, we know that Marcion accepted only the letters to the seven churches plus that to Philemon. The order of these letters is also unique, not found in any extant manuscript: Galatians, 1 and 2 Corinthians, Romans,

1 and 2 Thessalonians, Laodiceans, Colossians, Philippians, Philemon (though Epiphanius makes mention of Philemon after Colossians). Placing Galatians at the head of the collection may have been for doctrinal reasons, though an order based on a perceived chronology is also possible. The order Galatians, 1 and 2 Corinthians, Romans is also found in the Old Syriac, but there the order of the remaining letters is substantially different. Laodiceans is the letter known as Ephesians. This order of the Pauline corpus is also reflected in the so-called Marcionite Prologues, a set of brief introductions to each letter preserved only in the Latin manuscript tradition. Whether these prologues in fact come from the hand of Marcion or from an orthodox author is still under debate (Schäfer 1970; Dahl 1978; Schmid 1995, 284–294). If these Prologues are pre-Marcionite, they may provide the earliest evidence of a fixed and organized collection of the Pauline corpus that existed very early in the second century.

Our current order of the letters is found in most Greek and Latin (Vulgate) manuscripts and is first explicitly found in Amphilochius of Iconium (d. 394; see Frede 1966–1971, 294). In this order, Hebrews appears as the last letter, but elsewhere it is placed between the letters to the seven churches and the Pastorals (Paschal letter of Athanasius [AD 367]; *Codex Sinaiticus* ℵ [01]; *Codex Vaticanus* B [03], though without the Pastoral letters), or immediately after Romans (p^{46}, with Galatians and Ephesians transposed). Other variations are found, but rarely do these represent more than an idiosyncratic or accidental order. Of these, the order in the Muratorian Canon is among the most eccentric: Corinthians, Ephesians, Philippians, Colossians, Galatians, Thessalonians, Romans.

It has been argued that the Pauline corpus was the first section of the New Testament to be brought together (Trobisch 1989; 2000). Trobisch takes issue with any model that assumes a gradual development of the collection, as suggested for the whole New Testament by Theodor Zahn. To Trobisch, there is ample evidence to suggest that a deliberate and edited edition of Paul lies at the very root of the Pauline corpus; the original edition may even go back to Paul himself. As evidence for such an edition, he cites the use of the *nomina sacra* (i.e., the practice, almost universal in the manuscript tradition, of contracting certain names and words such as Jesus, Christ, God, and so on, rather than writing them out in full) and the common use of the codex, a feature characteristic of early Christianity. Trobisch also notes that the arrangement and number of writings within the four collections that make up the New Testament (the four gospels, the praxapostolos [Acts and the Catholic Letters], the Pauline collection, and Revelation) are fairly constant. The opposite view was defended by Aland, who argued on the basis of the changing textual character between the individual letters of Paul within a single manuscript that the existence of such early collections is extremely unlikely (Kurt Aland 1979b).

Studies of the Manuscript Tradition and its Variants

In the space of this chapter, it is not possible to discuss the numerous studies on individual manuscripts or specific variants. The best sources for finding such studies are Elliott (2000; supplemented in Elliott 2004 and 2007) and literature references in good technical commentaries. An overview of the past century of scholarship should start with the German scholar Bernhard Weiss, who prepared a Greek text of the New Testament and accompanied this text with a series of detailed studies of the manuscript tradition (1896a; 1896b). His study of the Pauline corpus was published separately. All elements of the method that Weiss used are still found in current New Testament textual criticism, though the balance between the various criteria and particular judgments have shifted. His edition of the Greek text became very influential on various editions of the Nestle text. The first Nestle edition (1898) was based on the editions of Tischendorf and Westcott–Hort, with the text of Weymouth assigned the deciding vote in case of any difference. From 1901, the place of Weymouth was taken by the text of Weiss, though the actual printed text was only sparingly changed. The principle of preferring the majority reading of Tischendorf, Westcott–Hort, and Weiss was rigorously applied in Nestle's thirteenth edition from 1927 (Kurt Aland and Barbara Aland 1987, 19–20).

The main focus of Weiss lies on eleven manuscripts written in majuscule (Greek capital script) that contain most of the traditional Pauline corpus, including Hebrews. The manuscripts are divided into three groups, though Weiss avoids labeling these with a specific name. The majuscules K (018 *Codex Mosquensis*), L (020 *Codex Angelicus*), and P (025 *Codex Porphyrianus*) form a group that most would call the Byzantine text. Three Greek–Latin bilingual manuscripts – D (06 *Codex Claromontanus*), F (010 *Codex Augiensis*), and G (012 *Codex Boernerianus*) – constitute the second group (the "Western text"). The last group is formed by ℵ (01 *Codex Sinaiticus*), A (02 *Codex Alexandrinus*), B (03 *Codex Vaticanus*), and C (04 *Codex Ephraemi Rescriptus*). Weiss also mentions a manuscript E (*Codex Sangermanensis*), a ninth-century copy of D, which is listed in the second group. None of these groups provides direct access to the oldest attainable text, and in Weiss's view, none of these groups is in its entirety dependent on any of the other groups. Here Weiss differs from the reconstruction of the transmission of the text proposed by Westcott–Hort, who argued, mainly on the basis of the situation in the four gospels, that the Byzantine text was derived from both the Western and the Neutral/Alexandrian groups. Still, Weiss concludes that B (03) is a very good witness to the text of Paul, one that often, against all the others, or with support from some of the other members of its group, retains the original reading. These conclusions are based on an extensive discussion of many individual variants under the general headings of substitutions, additions/omissions, and transpositions.

Probably the most important methodological rule used to decide between variants is to choose the variant that best explains the rise of the other variant(s) in a given passage. Differences between textual critics arise over the type of explanation given of how one variant derives from the other. Weiss emphasized the importance of the influence of parallels and similar constructions elsewhere in the text. Thus, in 1 Corinthians 1:6, "testimony of God" (τὸ μαρτύριον τοῦ θεοῦ) is found in a few manuscripts (B F G) instead of "testimony of Christ" (τὸ μαρτύριον τοῦ Χριστοῦ, attested by most other witnesses). Weiss was confident that the text should read "testimony of Christ" (so also NA27) since the name "God" is likely to have been introduced through the influence of a similar expression (at least in many manuscripts) in 1 Corinthians 2:1. Likewise, the article before "Christ" (ὁ Χριστός) in 1 Corinthians 1:17 as found in B F

G (and, unknown to Weiss, also in $\mathfrak{p}^{46}$) is explained as influenced by the expression "cross of Christ" (σταυρὸς τοῦ Χριστοῦ) later in the same verse. Though Weiss did not make great contributions to the theory of textual criticism or advance his own reconstruction of the earliest transmission history, he made many fine judgments on individual readings.

The next major contribution to Pauline textual scholarship is found in the work of Hans Lietzmann (1933). In his introduction to Romans, he gives a comprehensive overview of all the available materials and of his own understanding of the earliest textual history of the Pauline corpus. He contends that all the various text-forms in existence go back to a single collection of Paul's letters, the content and (in its essentials) order of which were everywhere preserved (1933, 1–2). A rather different view of the earliest shape of the text was advanced by Günther Zuntz (1953) in his landmark lectures of 1946. Seven years passed between the delivering and the publishing of these Schweich lectures, a study that still stands as a monument of critical and reasoned scholarship (Holmes 2006). Zuntz was the first to include the Chester Beatty papyrus containing the Pauline corpus ($\mathfrak{p}^{46}$) in a comprehensive view of the history of transmission. Though he concentrates on Paul, and mainly discusses variants from 1 Corinthians and Hebrews, Zuntz holds that his reconstruction can be applied to the entire New Testament. In the very first stage, the letters of Paul were copied individually. Already very early on, around AD 100, the letters were brought together into a corpus, and an edition was issued. However, at that time a rather lax attitude to copying existed within the church and many corruptions entered the text. As these became dominant and widespread, the result was the "Western text." In Alexandria, a philological attitude existed which was concerned with preserving (or re-creating) a relatively pure text. The earliest testimony to Paul, $\mathfrak{p}^{46}$, clearly shows influence of this purer text that was being developed in Egypt. It was from this text that the Coptic versions were translated. It is important to note that these two branches, the Western and Eastern (or Alexandrian) texts, are by no means internally homogeneous; they do not go back to a single recension and cannot be reduced to a single voice. Later, in the eighth century, the Byzantine text was produced within the Eastern tradition; consequently, it too contained very ancient readings. For Zuntz, therefore, it would be dangerous to ignore any of the witnesses and textual traditions, since any one of these can contain the original reading.

The earliest period, before individual letters were brought together to form a Pauline corpus, has left very few traces. One must distinguish between the "original" (i.e., the letters as written) and the "archetype" (the version from which all known copies arise). One example of a primitive, pre-edition corruption is the phrase "to judge between his brother" in 1 Corinthians 6:5, where Zuntz assumes that Paul must have written "to judge between a brother and his brother." Another is Hebrews 11:4, where Zuntz accepts Cobet's conjecture ΗΔΕΙΟΝΑ ("more agreeable offering") instead of ΠΛΕΙΟΝΑ ("more offering").

Bruce M. Metzger published a commentary on selected variants of the UBS3 Greek text in 1971 (second edition for UBS4 in 1994), reflecting the reasons behind the decisions made by the committee responsible for the text. In the first edition, a little over 170 pages are devoted to discussing 494 variants in the Pauline corpus (250 variants from Romans to 2 Corinthians, 244 from Galatians to Hebrews); the second edition contains 162 pages and 517 variants (238 from Romans to 2 Corinthians, 279 from Galatians to Hebrews). Though many of the discussions are extremely succinct, they provide good insight into how the committee tried to balance external and internal evidence (i.e., how well a particular reading is attested in the textual tradition, on the one hand; and, on the other hand, how likely it is deemed to be original in a particular context, bearing in mind the author's style, transcriptional probabilities, and so on). David Parker (2008, 246–282) discusses the Pauline collection in the context of his study of New Testament manuscripts and their texts. He starts by investigating the testimony of the individual letters to the process of their own composition, then treats their gathering into one corpus and subsequent transmission. Parker also gives an overview and assessment of the nature of the three most important versions, the Syriac, Latin, and Coptic.

Some Selected Problems

The following are among the best known textual problems in the Pauline corpus and illustrate the various issues and types of evidence brought to bear upon text-critical questions.

The Shape of Romans

Kurt Aland labeled the issue of the original shape of Romans the most difficult problem confronting the textual critic (1979a, 284; see also Gamble 1977; Parker 2008, 270–274). The position of the doxology 16:25–27 varies among the manuscripts (after 14:23, after 15:33, and after 16:23), the inclusion of 16:24 is highly uncertain, and some Latin systems of chapter headings are evidently based on a version of Romans lacking the final two chapters. Marcion's text of Romans, too, did not contain chapters 15 and 16, and it may well be that this short form of Romans was what he received. All these factors point to a complicated textual history. Which form of Romans is original? Are chapters 15 and 16 part of the letter? Interestingly, there are no manuscripts that lack the text of chapters 15 and 16, though in minuscule 1506 chapter 16 alone is missing (Aland 1979a, 297). Various explanations have been suggested, ranging from an early accidental loss of the final chapters to a deliberate attempt to edit the letter for more general usage (a similar explanation is given for the absence of "in Ephesus" in Eph 1:1). Alternatively, chapter 16 has been explained as the greetings section of a letter sent to Ephesus that became attached to Romans.

Hebrews 2:9

Though the overwhelming majority of Greek witnesses of Hebrews 2:9 read that Jesus "might taste death *by the grace of God*" (χάριτι θεοῦ), some manuscripts read "*without God*" (χωρὶς θεοῦ). This latter reading has also been found in some Syriac and Coptic manuscripts, in the margin of a Latin manuscript, and in patristic discussions of the passage going back as far as Origen, who concluded that both readings convey the same truth (*Comm. John* 1.256). Some have argued for the originality of "without God" as being in line with the theology of Hebrews (Ehrman 1993, 146–150), attributing the alternative reading to an attempt by the orthodox church to eliminate a Christologically difficult text. Others (for example, Metzger 1994, 594), working from χάριτι θεοῦ, see the second reading as a scribal lapse or the intrusion of a marginal comment that belonged originally to the previous verse.

Romans 5:1

Is the mood of the main verb in Romans 5:1 subjunctive ("let us have peace with God") or indicative ("we have peace with God")? The subjunctive ἔχωμεν was the more popular reading in the nineteenth century (Tregelles, Tischendorf, Westcott–Hort) because of its stronger external attestation. Internal considerations, taking note of the nature of Paul's argument, have led many to adopt the indicative ἔχομεν, reading the verse as a statement of what the justified already possess. Confusion could arise easily because it is likely that already in the first centuries of the transmission of the New Testament, the difference between the Greek letters omicron and omega was no longer heard. Similar variants occur at several places (for example, 1 Cor 15:49; Heb 12:28).

Issues in 1 Corinthians

Two well-known variant readings, in which the choice is between two different lexical items, are found in 1 Corinthians. In 1 Corinthians 2:1, the options are "mystery [μυστήριον] of God" or "witness [μαρτύριον] of God." Both words are used in the near vicinity of 2:1: "mystery" in 2:7, "witness" in 1:6. The external attestation is stronger for the second reading, but many believe that the use of "mystery" fits better with the following verses. The change of a single letter makes a great difference in 13:3, where the choice is basically between καυθήσομαι and καυχήσομαι (i.e., "hand over my body to be burned" or "hand over my body so that I may boast"). Since the second reading is the more difficult one, it has been argued that it is easier to explain the rise of the first from the second than vice versa. On the other hand, the sense of the second reading may be so difficult that it actually harms the natural flow of the passage. Both readings have good support.

The verses in which women are ordered to keep silence (1 Cor 14:34–35) have attracted extensive debate. Some argue that, since these verses are transposed to a position after verse 40 in the Western text, they are not original but represent a non-Pauline interpolation (see, especially, Walker 2001, 63–90). However, the textual basis for this claim is rather slim.

1 Thessalonians 2.7

A variant in 1 Thessalonians 2:7 has spawned an impressive amount of discussion and literature (see Fee 2009, 65–71). The difference between the two readings is a single letter, ν. Either the text reads ἐγενήθημεν νήπιοι ("we were as children") or ἐγενήθημεν ἤπιοι ("we were gentle"). Based on internal grounds, many commentators have preferred the reading "gentle," but the external evidence favors "children." The transcriptional closeness between the two readings becomes even more apparent when one realizes that, as a rule, the text in the oldest manuscripts was written in *scriptio continua*; that is, without accents, breathing marks, and word divisions.

1 Timothy 3:16

In 1 Timothy 3:16, all modern translations read something like "he was revealed in flesh." However, the majority of later Greek manuscripts read "God" as the subject of this phrase. Here, the difference is even less than a full letter, ΟΣ (the relative pronoun) over against ΘΣ (with a horizontal stroke over both letters, a contracted form of Θεός). A number of words and names, such as "Jesus," "Christ," "God," "Lord," and "Spirit," were written in these contracted forms (*nomina sacra*), in which only the first and last letter(s) were represented. This practice originally arose out of reverence, but in some manuscripts *nomina sacra* are applied to any qualifying word, irrespective of whether the referent was sacral or non-sacral. In this particular variant, it appears that the relative pronoun was mistaken for, or rewritten as, a *nomen sacrum*.

References

Aland, Barbara, and A. Juckel. 1991–2002. *Das Neue Testament in syrischer Überlieferung. II Die Paulinischen Briefe*. 3 volumes. Berlin: Walter de Gruyter.

Aland, Kurt. 1979a. Der Schluss und die ursprüngliche Gestalt des Römerbriefes. Pages 284–301 in Kurt Aland, *Neutestamentliche Entwürfe*. Munich: Kaiser.

Aland, Kurt. 1979b. Die Entstehung des Corpus Paulinum. Pages 302–350 in Kurt Aland, *Neutestamentliche Entwürfe*. Munich: Kaiser.

Aland, Kurt. 1994. *Kurzgefasste Liste der griechischen Handschriften des Neuen Testaments*. Second edition. Berlin: Walter de Gruyter.

Aland, Kurt, and Barbara Aland. 1987. *The Text of the New Testament: An Introduction to the Critical Editions and to the Theory and Practice of Modern Textual Criticism*. Grand Rapids: Eerdmans.

Aland, Kurt, with Annette Benduhn-Mertz, Gerd Mink, and Horst Bachmann. 1991. *Text und Textwert der griechischen Handschriften des Neuen Testaments. II. Die Paulinischen Briefe*. Berlin: Walter de Gruyter.

Clabeaux, John James. 1989. *A Lost Edition of the Letters of Paul: A Reassessment of the Text of the Pauline Corpus Attested by Marcion*. Washington, DC: Catholic Biblical Association of America.

Dahl, Nils A. 1978. The Origin of the Earliest Prologues to the Pauline Letters. *Semeia* 12: 233–277.

Ehrman, Bart D. 1993. *The Orthodox Corruption of Scripture: The Effect of Early Christological Controversies on the Text of the New Testament*. Oxford: Oxford University Press.

Elliott, J. K. 2000. *A Bibliography of Greek New Testament Manuscripts*. Second edition. Cambridge: Cambridge University Press.

Elliott, J. K. 2004. Supplement I to J. K. Elliott, *A Bibliography of Greek New Testament Manuscripts*. *Novum Testamentum* 46: 376–400.

Elliott, J. K. 2007. Supplement II to J. K. Elliott, *A Bibliography of Greek New Testament Manuscripts*. *Novum Testamentum* 49: 370–401.

Epp, Eldon Jay. 1995. The Papyrus Manuscripts of the New Testament. Page 3–21 in *The Text of the New Testament in Contemporary Research: Essays on the* Status Quaestionis. Edited by Bart D. Ehrman and Michael W. Holmes. Grand Rapids: Eerdmans.

Fee, Gordon D. 2009. *The First and Second Letter to the Thessalonians*. Grand Rapids: Eerdmans.

Frede, Hermann Josef. 1964. *Altlateinische Paulus-Handschriften*. Freiburg: Herder.

Frede, Hermann Josef. 1966–1971. *Epistulae ad Philippenses et ad Colossenses*. Freiburg: Herder.

Gamble, Harry Y. 1977. *The Textual History of the Letter to the Romans: A Study in Textual and Literary Criticism*. Grand Rapids: Eerdmans.

Harnack, Adolf von. 1924. *Marcion: Das Evangelium vom fremden Gott*. Second edition. Leipzig: J. C. Hinrichs.

Holmes, Michael W. 2006. *The Text of the Epistles* Sixty Years After: An Assessment of Günther Zuntz's Contribution to Text-critical Methodology and History. Pages 89–113 in *Transmission and Reception: New Testament Text-critical and Exegetical Studies*. Edited by J. W. Childers and D. C. Parker. Piscataway, NJ: Gorgias.

Junack, K., E. Güting, U. Nimtz, and K. Witte. 1989. *Das Neue Testament auf Papyrus. II Die Paulinischen Briefe*. Teil 1: *Röm., 1, Kor., 2. Kor.* Berlin: Walter de Gruyter.

Lietzmann, Hans. 1933. *Einführung in die Textgeschichte der Paulusbriefe: An die Römer*. Fourth edition. Tübingen: Mohr (Siebeck).

Metzger, Bruce M. 1977. *The Early Versions of the New Testament: Their Origin, Transmission and Limitations*. Oxford: Clarendon.

Metzger, Bruce M. 1981. *Manuscripts of the Greek Bible: An Introduction to Palaeography*. New York: Oxford University Press.

Metzger, Bruce M. 1994. *A Textual Commentary on the Greek New Testament: A Companion Volume to the United Bible Societies' Greek New Testament (Fourth Revised Edition)*. Second edition. Stuttgart: Deutsche Bibelgesellschaft; United Bible Societies.

Parker, D. C. 2008. *An Introduction to the New Testament Manuscripts and their Texts*. Cambridge: Cambridge University Press.

Royse, James R. 2008. *Scribal Habits in Early Greek New Testament Papyri*. Leiden: Brill.

Schäfer, Karl Th. 1970. Marcion und die ältesten Prologe zu den Paulusbriefen. Pages 135–150 in *Kyriakon: Festschrift Johannes Quasten*. Volume 1. Edited by Patrick Granfield and Josef A. Jungmann. Münster: Aschendorff.

Schmid, Ulrich. 1995. *Marcion und sein Apostolos: Rekonstruktion und historische Einordnung der marcionitischen Paulusbriefausgabe*. Berlin: Walter de Gruyter.

Swanson, Reuben J. 2008a. *New Testament Greek Manuscripts: Romans*. Atlanta: Society of Biblical Literature.

Swanson, Reuben J. 2008b. *New Testament Greek Manuscripts: 1 Corinthians*. Atlanta: Society of Biblical Literature.

Swanson, Reuben J. 2008c. *New Testament Greek Manuscripts: 2 Corinthians*. Atlanta: Society of Biblical Literature.

Swanson, Reuben J. 2008d. *New Testament Greek Manuscripts: Galatians*. Atlanta: Society of Biblical Literature.

Trobisch, David. 1989. *Die Entstehung der Paulusbriefsammlung: Studien zu den Anfängen christlicher Publizistik*. Freiburg: Universitätsverlag; Göttingen: Vandenhoeck & Ruprecht.

Trobisch, David. 2000. *The First Edition of the New Testament*. Oxford: Oxford University Press.

Walker, William O., Jr. 2001. *Interpolations in the Pauline Letters*. London: Sheffield Academic.

Weiss, Bernhard. 1896a *Textkritik der paulinischen Briefe*. Leipzig: J. C. Hinrichs.

Weiss, Bernhard. 1896b *Die paulinischen Briefe im berichtigten Text*. Leipzig: J. C. Hinrichs.

Wordsworth, John, and Henry Julian White. 1913–1939. *Nouum Testamentum Domini Nostri Iesu Christi Latine Secundum Editionem Sancti Hieronymi*. Pars Secunda: Epistulae Paulinae. Oxford: Clarendon.

Zuntz, G. 1953. *The Text of the Epistles: A Disquisition upon the Corpus Paulinum*. London: Published for the British Academy by Oxford University Press.

CHAPTER 15

Rhetoric in the Letters of Paul

Jean-Noël Aletti

The term *rhetoric* requires definition since it is often used to designate very different things. Rhetoric was initially *the art of persuasion*, a definition that comes from Aristotle. In this sense, the study of Paul's rhetoric consists in listing the proofs (in Greek, *pisteis*) provided by the apostle to support his ideas. Also of importance is the manner in which these proofs are arranged and ordered (*dispositio* or, in Greek, *taxis*). Rhetoric is also often understood as the theory of style (*elocutio* or, in Greek, *lexis*); in this context, it is frequently assimilated to the study of rhetorical figures[1] or ornamentation (*ornatus*). For the past few decades, exegetes of the Pauline letters have studied the three components just mentioned: the arrangement, proofs, and rhetorical figures of the Pauline texts. We will review these three fields of rhetoric and show their importance for a better understanding of the apostle's letters.

Patterns of Arrangement

Since the *dispositio* has been the most discussed of the three fields in recent decades, we may begin with it. Two opposing approaches are discernible; the fact that in America they are both called "rhetorical criticism"[2] makes it all the more important not to confuse them. Initially, "rhetorical criticism" was limited to the identification of parallelisms, which occur frequently in the letters of Paul, but it came to be applied also to studies covering all aspects of rhetoric, particularly discursive or argumentative rhetoric. What matters for those pursuing the former agenda is the study of the micro- and macro-parallelisms which provide the structure of many Pauline passages. Those who pursue the latter agenda, and who adopt the categories of Greco-Roman rhetoric, attend rather to the models of persuasion used by Paul in setting forth his ideas. We will attempt to describe and compare these positions, showing that they should be regarded rather as complementing than opposing each other.

The Blackwell Companion to Paul, First Edition. Edited by Stephen Westerholm.
© 2011 Blackwell Publishing Ltd. Published 2011 by Blackwell Publishing Ltd.

Parallelisms

An example will show what is meant by parallelism. In Romans 10:19, Paul quotes Deuteronomy 32:21:[3]

> Moses says,
> *a* "I will make you <u>jealous</u>
> *b* of those who are *not a nation*;
> *b'* with a *foolish nation*
> *a'* I will make you <u>angry</u>."[4]

Sentence parts preceded by the same letters (*a* and *a'*; *b* and *b'*) are parallel in that the same terms or their synonyms are used in each. In this verse, the parallelism forms a chiasm (*abb'a'*) that one must bear in mind in interpreting the text. We are here dealing with a micro-parallelism, covering a single sentence. This same type of parallelism can also be found in larger units, or even extended to entire sections of Paul's letters. First Corinthians 12–14 provides an example:

A = 1 Cor 12   general reflection on spiritual gifts
B = 1 Cor 13   [transcending spiritual gifts] praise of love
A' = 1 Cor 14   return to two particular spiritual gifts, prophecy and glossolalia

Units *A* and *A'* are parallel, in that both use the vocabulary of spiritual gifts, vocabulary which does not occur in *B*. It is very useful to identify micro- or macro-parallels because it is then possible to distinguish the various units of a Pauline letter, from the simplest to the most complex, whether single paragraphs or entire sections. One should not forget that, in Paul's day, paragraphs did not exist and, since the apostle's letters were read aloud, listeners were able to identify the epistolary and rhetorical units thanks to repetitions of vocabulary.

Paul's letters contain a number of other oral-type compositions that are relatively brief (a chapter or less). Thus, 1 Corinthians 12:4–30 itself exhibits a composition of this type:

A   vv. 4–11   the variety of spiritual gifts, but only one Spirit
B   vv. 12–27   comparison with the body, which is one, though made up of many parts
A'   vv. 28–30   application of B to spiritual gifts

The same *ABA'* pattern of composition is found in a number of Paul's exhortations: in *A* and *A'* Paul exhorts, while in *B* he justifies his exhortation. An example is Philippians 2:1–18:

A   vv. 1–5   exhortation to be of one mind
B   vv. 6–11   Christ as model of the proper attitude
A'   vv. 12–18   return to the exhortation

Once the parallelisms have been identified, it is possible to see how the units of different length are arranged. But description by itself does not go far enough. It is also necessary to interpret these compositions; after all, one could use the pattern *ABA* or *ABBA*, and so on, to describe a candlestick or a boat, to deal with church problems or exhort, to pronounce an oracle or arrange the parts of a prayer. Because they are purely formal, such patterns as *ABA* or *ABBA* provide no key to the meaning of texts, nor do they clarify the progression of thought. In short, these parallelisms, often useful for identifying semantic units, are no interpretive panacea.

Of greater interest for grasping the make-up and progression of Pauline arguments is a particular kind of parallelism, still at the level of vocabulary. It consists of short sentences (named *partitiones* by the specialists) that serve to identify the subject matter that Paul intends to develop in what follows. We may note two significant examples (1 Cor 9; 2 Cor 5:18–21).

In 1 Corinthians 9, the first verse is made up of two questions ("Am I not free?" and "Am I not an apostle?") that announce the subject matter of the remainder of the chapter. The first (*a* = am I not free?) has its parallel in (*A*), where Paul declares that even though he is free, he nonetheless makes himself a slave of all and subjugates his own body. The second (*b* = am I not an apostle?) is taken up in (*B*), where he says that, though he has all the rights of the apostles, he chooses neither to assert nor to make use of them:

a	v. 1a	am I not free?
b		am I not an apostle?
B	vv. 1b–18	though I am an apostle, I do not exercise the rights of the apostles
A	vv. 19–27	though I am free from all, I made myself a slave to all.

We encounter the same *abBA* pattern in 2 Corinthians 5:18–21. The two parts of verse 18 (*a* = God reconciled the world to himself; *b* = God has entrusted the ministry of reconciliation to us) are taken up and developed in a chiastic way in verses 19–21 (*ABB'A'*):

a = 18a	God ... reconciled us to himself through Christ,	
b = 18b	and has given us the ministry of reconciliation;	
A = 19ab	in Christ God was reconciling the world to himself, not counting their trespasses against them,	God's action
B = 19c	and entrusting the message of reconciliation to us.	ministry assigned
B' = 20	So we are ambassadors for Christ, since God is making his appeal through us; we entreat you on behalf of Christ, be reconciled to God.	ministry performed
A' = 21	For our sake he made him to be sin who knew no sin, so that in him we might become the righteousness of God.	God's action

One finds an example of yet another pattern of oral-type arrangement (*i, ii, iii, I, II, III*) in Romans 6:4–14, where verse 4 is a *partitio*; that is, a short announcement of the ideas to be developed in verses 5–14:

i = v. 4a	*preparing the aspect "death to/with"* →	*I*	developed in vv. 5–7
ii = v. 4b	*preparing the aspect "life with"* →	*II*	developed in vv. 8–10
iii = v. 4c	*preparing the aspect "walking in newness of life"* →	*III*	developed in vv. 12–14.

It is always useful to identify a *partitio* because, through it, one can see which points Paul is going to develop and what the range or length of his argument will be. Thus, the *partitio* in Colossians 1:21–23 indicates all the subsequent developments of this letter:

partitio (Col 1:21–23) or announcement of themes to be treated:
a = the work of Christ for the holiness of believers (vv. 21–22)
b = fidelity to the gospel (v. 23a)
c = proclaimed by Paul (v. 23b).
The development of the topics, in reverse order (1:24–4:1):
C = the struggle of Paul for the proclamation of the gospel/mystery (1:24–2:5)
B = fidelity to the gospel (2:6–23)
A = the holiness of believers (3:1–4:1)

If parallelisms often serve as one of the means by which we may determine the extent of a stage in Paul's argument, they are not in themselves a sufficient guide to interpretation – let us say it again – because in themselves they cannot specify what Paul wants to show or how he shows it. On the other hand, it is this that a study of the Greco-Roman models of composition helps us to determine.

Greco–Roman patterns

What Paul wants to prove and how he proves it are respectively named *propositio* and *probatio* (or *confirmatio*) in ancient Greco-Roman rhetoric. The first scholar to use the categories of this rhetoric for the letters of Paul was H. D. Betz, in a famous article of 1975, "The Literary Composition and Function of Paul's Letter to the Galatians." Betz's hypothesis was that the composition of Galatians follows that set forth in the handbooks of Greco-Roman rhetoric. Betz never denied the epistolary framework of Galatians, clearly distinguished by the initial (1:1–5) and the final greetings (6:18), but it seemed to him that the body of the letter strongly resembled an argument, and that it had to be studied as such. Paul stated a thesis or a *propositio* (namely, that justification cannot be obtained by becoming a Jew, and that it is thus useless to be circumcised) and defended it in a *probatio*; that is, by a series of clearly identifiable proofs. For Betz, the *dispositio* (outline) of Galatians looks like this:

initial epistolary greeting 1:1–5
exordium (introduction) 1:6–11
narratio (establishing the facts) 1:12–2:14
(1:12 thesis, developed in several stages [1:13–24; 2:1–10; 2:11–14])
propositio of the letter (what Paul will prove) 2:15–21
probatio (proofs which support and explain the *propositio*) 3:1–4:31
exhortatio (exhortation) 5:1–6:10
epilogue and final epistolary greeting 6:11–18

The proposed outline effectively links the *dispositio* of Galatians with that of ancient orations. A quick look at the model provided by Quintilian to describe the *dispositio* in his *Institutio oratoria* shows indeed that the main components are by and large the same: exordium, *narratio, propositio, probatio,* and conclusion (or epilogue). The *narratio* is the account of the facts on which the argument will be based; the *propositio,* what one wants to prove; and the *probatio,* the proofs provided.

With the help of this standard *dispositio,* it became possible to follow step by step the Pauline arguments. Highlighting *propositiones* and *probationes* made it possible to see what Paul wanted to prove and how he proved it. An interpretive key was thus given, one which evidently could be applied to all the letters of the New Testament. Thanks to Betz, numerous studies on the *dispositio* of Galatians and other Pauline letters were published. The assumption on which these readings were based was that all Paul's letters could be shown to follow the *dispositio* of persuasive speeches as described by Aristotle and the treatises which (more or less) took him as a model; of these latter, the best known are Quintilian's *Institutio oratoria* and the *Rhetorica ad Herennium.*

But after Betz's seminal essay, the slavish application of the model of the ancient *dispositio* as one finds it in Quintilian has come to be seen as forced; Paul, after all, displays a good deal of originality in adopting the rhetorical rules of his time. The *dispositio* that Betz proposes for Galatians does not, in fact, do too much violence to the text, inasmuch as Galatians 1–2 displays a number of the features of a narrative, and Galatians 3–4 those of the *probationes.* Still, the application of the standard pattern of ancient forensic speeches without further ado to all the other Pauline letters proves to be something of a straitjacket. Nonetheless, that is what happened: the *dispositio* singled out by Betz came to be seen as more or less a standard pattern, particularly inasmuch as it was believed to be, for Quintilian, the arrangement *par excellence.* Each letter of the apostle was supposed to have, in addition to its epistolary framework, an exordium, *narratio, propositio, probatio* (in two stages: a *confutatio,* i.e., a refutation of opposing arguments; and a *confirmatio,* i.e., the positive presentation of Paul's case), and an epilogue. In time, however, specialists perceived the arbitrariness of an approach that reduced the body of each letter to a single argument (as in the case of Galatians). Little by little, they have come to see that many units of lesser proportions are also arguments worthy of the name, since they include the two elements that already Aristotle considered essential to an argument: a thesis and the unfolding of its substantiation; that is, a *propositio* and a *probatio.* Thus, Romans 1:18–3:20, which is only a subsection of Romans, has the principal features of an argument:

propositio (thesis on divine retribution): 1:18
probatio (proofs, set out in three series): 1:19–3:18
  – facts (of the past: human injustice and divine retribution): 1:19–32
  – principles of divine retribution, their consequences at the end of time: 2:1–29
  – reflection on the principles and final proof, based on the authority of the
    Scriptures: 3:9–18
peroratio (epilogue): 3:19–20

This passage is typical of many argumentative subsections and sections of Paul's letters in which the apostle's thinking is structured by a series of arguments that are sometimes independent of each other, sometimes hierarchical.[5] The idea that the body of each letter was composed of only one argument has thus had to be revised, and as a consequence the manner in which one conceives the rhetorical *dispositio* has evolved. Let us see how.

Rather than seek to make each Pauline letter in its entirety fit a standard *dispositio*, it is much more useful to highlight the *propositiones* of the different arguments: by identifying them individually, we can grasp what Paul wants to prove and how he proves it. Recognizing the scope or boundaries of the various rhetorical units is thus crucial to understanding the goals and dynamics of Paul's arguments. Romans 1:18 is in this respect typical of the Pauline *propositiones*: the verse is sufficiently clear to permit the reader to see the focus of the section to follow – namely, the exercise of divine retributive justice in its opposition to every human injustice – but nothing is here said of the form of this retribution or of the number of those who are, or who are destined to be, its objects. General – and thus leaving room for suspense and for the progressive unfolding of Paul's case – yet specific enough that the reader can grasp the overall goal of the argument: such is the Pauline *propositio*.

The task of the exegete or reader thus includes identifying all the arguments and determining the way they follow one another to form subsections and sections. This task, having initially been done too quickly and uniformly, needed to be taken up again and oriented differently. Such studies are now multiplying, with an ever-increasing display of critical sense and mastery.

If exegetes proceed today with more flexibility, it is also partly because they no longer consider the writings of Aristotle, Cicero, and Quintilian as manuals that students and authors of their day would have followed. They are rather *treatises* whose function was above all taxonomic, theoretical, and reflective, dealing both with the tendencies and with the ideals of the schools of rhetoric in their respective periods. And if the *dispositio* presented by Quintilian is specifically that of forensic speeches, it is because such speeches are more wide-ranging than speeches of the other two kinds (deliberative and epideictic),[6] thus enabling him to review all the components that a *dispositio* can have. The mistake made was simply to take the *dispositio* as described in Quintilian as if it were the only one in existence, and by the same token the only one to be used as a grid for reading Paul's letters. Actually, no two letters of Paul have the same structure. It is thus more interesting and helpful to begin with the Pauline materials themselves to determine the configuration of the arguments, how the arguments are linked with each other, their hierarchy, and their respective functions.

Other types of arrangement

We have already presented two types of *dispositio*, the oral and the argumentative. It should immediately be added that Paul combines the two. It is thus not enough to search for only one model; one must see whether or not the *dispositio* of a passage or a section uses both.

Nor are these two models the only ones. We find several passages that follow the model of an encomium, or speech of praise (in Greek, *enkōmion*), and, more precisely, of self-praise (periautology; in Greek, *periautologia*): Philippians 3:2–14 and 2 Corinthians 11–12 are examples. The *dispositio* of encomiums usually adopted the following sequence:

> *origin* (family, native land, city, nation) and birth
> *childhood*: training and education
> *adulthood*: exceptional or memorable deeds, behavior and type of life chosen, moral
>   character, and so on
> *virtues*, identifiable through deeds (wisdom, temperance, courage, justice, piety);
>   goods received from Fortune and type of death

Often speeches of praise treat these components through the use of comparisons (in Greek, *synkriseis*), thus underlining the similarities or differences between two people, two groups, two periods of a life, and so on.

A number of indicators mark Philippians 3:2–14 out as a *periautology*: the pronounced use of the first-person singular, the chronological development (past, present, future) of the life of Paul, the stress on his origins and actions. As for comparisons, Paul begins with a contrast between two groups, the evil workers and "us" (vv. 2–3); he continues with another contrast, that between Paul the Pharisee (vv. 5–6) and Paul the disciple of Christ (vv. 7–14). Taking into account these common features, the originality of the passage becomes clear in 3:7–11, where a reversal occurs: Paul rejects any grounds he might have for self-commendation. In a first stage, more precisely until verse 6, the *periautology* follows closely the model of an encomium:

Topoi of praise	Philippians 3:5–6
origin	circumcised on the eighth day
	a member of the people of Israel
	of the tribe of Benjamin
	a Hebrew born of Hebrews
education	as to the law, a Pharisee
actions	as to zeal, a persecutor of the church
	as to righteousness under the law, blameless

But verses 5–6 form only the first part of a periautology in two parts:[7]

v. 4b + vv. 5–6 = privileges and values *in the flesh*
v. 7 + vv. 8–14 = total change; new values in Christ

Thus, the simple fact that Philippians 3:2–14 follow the model of speeches of praise (and of self-praise) permits us to see how Paul shows originality in adopting it, and how he, as it were, subverts it by proceeding to reject all that in which he once took pride, forgetting himself totally in turning to Christ. We encounter another encomium, that of love (*agapē*), in 1 Corinthians 13, which largely follows the same model, one used, for example, by Aphthonius in the encomium of a virtue (wisdom).[8] In short, to identify the different models, their *dispositio*, and the original way in which Paul uses them is an essential – though not sufficient – condition for a good interpretation of Paul's letters.

The Art of Persuasion

It is certainly necessary to attend to the *dispositio* of Paul's arguments, but it is only a first stage; one must also examine the relevance and the cogency of the *probationes*, that is, the proofs that Paul provides in support of his *propositiones*. If the apostle argues for and defends his positions, it is necessary to see how his argumentation is shaped by the culture and world of his day, but also why it has transcended the centuries and remained valid for so many generations of readers.

Once the *dispositio* of each letter has been described, the exegete needs to show how Paul proceeds to persuade his readers: how does he develop his arguments, and what do his arguments indicate about his rhetorical and hermeneutical principles?

The unfolding proof

In the argumentative micro-units, the apostle usually proceeds by successive clarifications.[9] He starts with a statement (often the *propositio* itself) that he proceeds quickly to explain in a second short sentence (called a *ratio*), itself still elliptical, which in turn is explained, and so on. In Romans 6:1–14, a passage to which attention has already been drawn, this type of progression is apparent:

6:1	question
6:2	answer in the form of a *proposition*
6:3	*ratio*: explanation of the formula "died to sin" of 6:2: baptism is effectively a baptism into the death of Christ
6:4	resumption of 6:3 and description of the life-path of the believer in conformity with Christ, in the form of a *partitio*:
	4a → vv. 5–7 died with him to sin
	4b → vv. 8–10 Christ risen → v. 11 believers alive
	4c → vv. 12–14 ethical consequences: new life of believers
6:5–7	cf. 4a: believers died and were buried with Christ

6:8–10   cf. 4b: and just as Christ risen does not die any more
6:11   so believers died to sin and are alive for God
6:12–14   cf. 4c: ethical consequences: exhortations

Facts, principles, and authorities

But what kinds of proofs does Paul provide? In many *probationes*, he begins by grounding his case on the facts: those of actual, everyday life and/or those of believers' experience. He then passes on to the principles that govern these facts and explain them, in order to develop their implications and the horizons they open. Finally, he appeals to authorities, namely, the Scriptures and (especially) Christ's words and commands. Here, too, an exhaustive classification could be made, but I content myself with quoting examples that are (as examples should be!) representative.

In Romans 1:18–3:20 (a passage mentioned above), what sorts of proofs back up the *propositio* of Romans 1:18 ("the wrath of God is revealed from heaven against all ungodliness and wickedness of those who by their wickedness suppress the truth")? The *probatio* starts by mentioning facts without which it would be difficult to affirm that God punishes injustice. If God had never punished human injustice, and if it is true that it is past experience that provides the basis for what we say about the future, would we even be able to look for a last judgment? Romans 1:19–32 thus illustrates the administration of divine justice by events (biblical, though not identified as such), admitted by all,[10] which bear witness to God's response to those who refuse to acknowledge him. Once the facts are admitted, together with their underlying principle – if God punishes, it is because people have made themselves liable for punishment[11] – Paul can shift to the principles (Rom 2) which steer God's anger – and, more generally, his retribution: God punishes (or rewards) all according to their deeds (2:6), and with impartiality (2:11), because he looks on the heart (2:16). Reviewing the principles of God's retribution, the apostle also brings out their consequences for the Jew as well as for the non-Jew (still in Rom 2): final retribution will be the same for the Jew whose heart is uncircumcised as for the non-Jew who is unjust. It remains for Paul then to show, with the help of the Scriptures,[12] that all are due the same punishment, since all are sinners (Rom 3:9–18, a catena, or chain, of quotations).

In 1 Corinthians 9, Paul substantiates his claims along more or less the same lines: facts, principles (or examples), and authorities. He begins with a reminder that he is an apostle (vv. 1b–2), and he draws up a list of the rights of apostles (rights exercised – the facts of the matter are clear – and acknowledged by all). Advancing then to principles, he starts with ones drawn from human life that support the exercise of these rights (the worker deserves a salary, and so on), then appeals to the Scriptures (vv. 8–12), to an example from the temple cult (v. 13), and, finally, to a command of the Lord himself (v. 14). To all these arguments, arranged in a climactic order, Paul gives opposing (and equally strong) reasons why he has renounced these rights (vv. 15–18), since not only does he not exercise them, but he has gone to the opposite extreme of making himself a slave, thus sharing the status of those who have no rights. As our look at 2 Corinthians 5:18–21 has already clearly suggested, this passage too demonstrates in its own way

that Paul knows very well how to proceed in his argumentation to arrive at formulations that are both the strongest possible and the most paradoxical.

As we saw above, the first proofs adduced by the apostle are based on facts or situations. Now what is most fundamental about the situation of believers is their attach-
ment to Christ. One is not, then, astonished to see Paul begin by recalling the Christ
event (the cross and/or resurrection) or baptism, with which the Christ-conformed life-
path of the believer begins. This observation holds for Romans 6:1–14; 1 Corinthians
1–4; Galatians 3:1–5; and 1 Corinthians 6:12–20, where the first and decisive argument is Christological (vv. 14–15). The passage in which the *dispositio* shows best the
importance of the Christ-event is undoubtedly 1 Corinthians 1–4, where, as is well
known, ecclesiology (1 Cor 3–4) is built on Christology (1 Cor 1). Indeed, Paul does not
immediately deal with the question of disputes among believers, but makes a long
Christological detour whose import is that every reflection on the church and the status
of believers or their ministers (apostles and others) must begin with "the word of the
cross" and must find therein its model.

Depending on the questions dealt with, the first stage of a *probatio* can also be theological or pneumatological; still, regardless of differences in nuance, Paul returns
almost always to Christian experience. The first proof that he gives – and that every
believer must also give, because the Pauline statements remain in this regard a model
for our own – is what he has experienced of the love of God, of his gifts, including the
spiritual gifts that, for all their diversity, are nevertheless ordained to serve the purpose
of unity (cf., for example, Rom 5:1–11; 1 Cor 12:4–11). The absence of this decisive
proof would render theological discourse patently empty or purely abstract. If the
apostle proceeds in a way that is fully rhetorical, by no means does he engage in rhetoric
for its own sake; his engagement is rather at the same time a movement of faith that
carries implications for the whole person – and for the Christian community in its
entirety.

Paul's rhetorical detours

In many of the argumentative passages in his letters, Paul does not respond directly to
the questions or difficulties faced by the first communities. At the beginning of 1
Corinthians, he says he has heard of disputes between members of the Corinthian community about the apostles. But he does not take up the issue immediately and say that
the apostles are only servants of the gospel; rather, he begins with a reminder of the
reversal of values brought about by the cross. In this way, he indicates to his readers
that they are still attached to the values of the world and have not yet fully embraced
those of the gospel, which in every respect are opposed to the former. In short, *he makes
a detour*, albeit a decisive one in that it takes his readers back to the death of Jesus on
the cross, when all values were definitively reversed; at the same time, he shows that
ecclesiological questions find their primary response in Christology.

Paul proceeds in the same way in 1 Corinthians 12–14. According to the commentators, certain members of the Corinthian community regarded glossolalia as superior to
prophecy – and perhaps to the other spiritual gifts as well. Paul could have intervened

at once, stressing that in his view prophecy was the more beneficial gift for the reasons spelled out at length in 1 Corinthians 14, where the whole argumentation is devoted solely to these two gifts. But instead of stating his point of view directly and at the same level at which (if one is to believe the commentators) the question was posed, the apostle begins with a reminder that spiritual gifts are multiple and diverse; what he is in effect saying is that those who speak of these gifts should not lose sight of their unique origin, the Spirit. He then adds that this diversity is complementary, like that of members in a body; one spiritual gift cannot thus ignore or scorn the others, since the diversity of gifts is deliberate, intended to serve the continued life of the one body. Paul reminds his readers as well that there is a hierarchy of spiritual gifts – and, in this hierarchy, glossolalia is listed last! But as if all these considerations (1 Cor 12) were not enough, the apostle then situates all the spiritual gifts in relation to love (in Greek, *agapē*) and declares that without love they are nothing (1 Cor 13). This double detour (1 Cor 12 and 1 Cor 13) thus aims at broadening the perspective of his readers on the relationship between prophecy and glossolalia (1 Cor 14), and at showing that, to address spiritual gifts correctly, one must do so in a roundabout fashion, beginning with the more fundamental issues at stake.

Without proceeding exactly in the same way, in the section of the same letter that deals with meat sacrificed to idols (1 Cor 8–10), Paul again broadens the perspective of his readers. At first, he does respond directly to the problem (1 Cor 8), presenting arguments of different types, and reminding readers particularly of the demands of love (*agapē*), which attends to the needs of others. But this is not enough: in 1 Corinthians 9, he wants, by presenting himself as a model, to show how far one must go in refusing privileges and making oneself a slave of all. This first detour is, moreover, followed by another in 1 Corinthians 10, in which the example of Israel in the desert enables Paul to highlight the risks that idolatry entailed, should the Corinthians accept invitations to banquets held in the local temples. In short, Paul's way of proceeding is intended to respond to questions in a roundabout way by broadening the debate and bringing his readers to a more radical level of reflection.

Detours of this type, which bring readers to a more essential level of reflection, are more frequent in Paul's letters than is commonly realized. Bearing this in mind, we can better understand the progression of other *probationes*, such as those of 1 Corinthians 15. In this chapter, according to the most recent commentaries, a number of members of the Corinthian church refused to believe in a final resurrection because they conceived it merely as reanimation. Again, the apostle does not respond to the problem immediately – not, in fact, until verse 35. Before correcting the thinking of the Corinthians, he first deals at length with the question of resurrection itself, appealing to a Christological argument and showing that the denial of a general resurrection of the dead is actually a rejection of the gospel. By doing so, Paul clearly wants to show that the question of the nature of a risen body (vv. 35–49) must be seen in a larger and more fundamental context, namely, that of faith in the resurrection of the dead. By taking the Corinthians back to the heart of the gospel, Paul shows the implications of the discussion for their own future; that is, for their salvation. In short, the argumentation of 1 Corinthians 15 provides additional evidence of Paul's rhetorical techniques. It confirms the apostle's tendency to postpone immediate answers, and it shows that in his answers, the apostle is less inclined to recall the reasons or motivations of his correspondents than he is to draw out the consequences of their positions for the questions at issue. This is the reason why it is often difficult to reconstruct precisely the situations or the problems faced by the Christians Paul addresses: since he broadens the issues and always tries to state what is fundamental and lasting, in the absence of which the questions (and any answers) would lose their relevance, his rhetoric is less contingent on immediate circumstances than the epistolary genre might at first lead us to believe.

The arrangement of the proofs should also be systematically studied; such study in fact allows us to discern the fundamental logic of an argumentative passage. That a proof from Scripture is located at the beginning or end of a passage is not due to chance. Thus, that two successive arguments in Romans 1–4, namely, Romans 1:18–3:20 and 3:21–4:25, end by appealing to Scripture (Rom 3:10–18 and 4:1–25) invites the reader to wonder why Paul placed these appeals where he did and not earlier. In short, questions must be put to all the proofs: when and why does the apostle appeal to authority, in particular, that of Scripture? When does he provide examples? And so on.

One could mention here a number of passages showing this type of progression. Let it suffice to add that the proofs and their arrangement contribute to the construction of Paul's thought. Indeed, in the Pauline letters, rhetoric and theology are inseparable.

The proofs and their relevance

It is not enough to account for the choice and the order of the different proofs (facts, examples, principles, and authorities); it is also necessary to weigh their relevance, thus shifting from description to evaluation. Let us take the examples Paul uses to explain to the Corinthians the nature of a risen body (1 Cor 15:35–41). He wants to show them that a risen body is entirely different from the current, perishable one. To illustrate this point, he employs two examples: that of the seed and the plant; and that of terrestrial and heavenly bodies. After the seed has been buried in the earth, the plant that emerges is completely different. In the same way, our current body, like the grain, must die to become something entirely new. As to the second illustration, it is used to show that the glory of our risen body will be analogous to that of the stars and entirely different from that of terrestrial bodies.

But why does Paul move from the first example to the second? The reason is that, although the first example underlines the *temporal discontinuity*, it is not totally satisfactory: the plant may be different from the seed, but it is no less perishable. Paul needs to provide an example that will illustrate the eternal glory of the resurrected body. But the second example raises a difficulty of its own: no one has ever seen a terrestrial body become celestial. Though both examples illustrate effectively the difference between a mortal and a risen body, they do not illustrate how a transformation between them can actually take place, so that our mortal body becomes a glorious one. It is precisely this that verses 44b–49 provide: the Risen Lord is the living proof that a perishable body can be transformed into a glorious one. But, even correctly understood, the examples provided by Paul cannot be used today without further ado, since we know that there is a *continuity* rather than discontinuity between the seed and the plant, and between the earth and the stars of the sky. Students of rhetoric cannot, then, be content simply to describe the proofs; they must also say why the interpretation of an argument has changed over the centuries, and reflect on the relevance of the proofs Paul provides.

Without a rhetorical approach, a number of arguments may also be misunderstood. This can be said of Romans 7:7–25. Many readers, especially since Augustine and, after him, Luther, have thought that the passage describes the Christian, who is at the same time both righteous and a sinner (*simul justus et peccator*). But if one pays attention to the rhetoric and context of the passage, this reading cannot be sustained: Romans 7:7–25 describes, not those who are Christians, but those who are not. Many Christians, however, still captives of their passions, see themselves described in Romans 7:7–25. Which interpretation, then, are we to choose, that of the rhetorical approach or the other? As noted above, the dynamic of the passage and its literary context support the rhetorical approach; this means that, for Paul, the believing Christian is dead to sin and alive for God. But, in saying that, is Paul not simply naïve? In short, the rhetorical approach cannot rest content with being descriptive; it should also see why the interpretation of an argument has changed over the centuries, and reflect on the relevance of Paul's proofs.

Another type of proof that occurs frequently in the Pauline letters, namely, the proof from Scripture, also needs to be looked at from a rhetorical perspective, inasmuch as the most decisive arguments, in particular those of Romans 4:1–10; 9:25–29; and Galatians 3:6–14, are based on a scriptural interpretation that today seems hasty and arbitrary.[13] To sum up: rhetorical criticism should examine all of Paul's arguments to determine which ones are temporary, determined by the culture and the situation of the church at a particular point in its history, and which ones remain valid and lastingly relevant.

The Rhetorical Figures

The study of the proofs and that of the *elocutio* (the use of rhetorical figures) should not be separated. To be sure, study of the rhetorical figures used in the Bible was carried out at the end of the nineteenth century,[14] but in a merely descriptive way. The relation of the figures to other parts of Paul's rhetoric needs to be examined. The question is simple enough: what is the function of the figures in Paul's argumentation? Put differently: can the apostle do without the figures, or are these essential to his theology?

That in some of his arguments, especially when he speaks of the church, Paul cannot do without the figures is clear from a number of passages. Thus, in 1 Corinthians 12, he uses the metaphor of the body to show that the various spiritual gifts are complementary, not mutually exclusive. But is it true that the church is a body, the body of Christ? And does the metaphor of the body in 1 Corinthians 12 carry more weight than those of field and building (of God) in 1 Corinthians 3:9? Rhetorically speaking, the question of the figures directly concerns the validity and relevance of Paul's arguments, particularly in the case of *exempla* selected to explain and describe ecclesial realities.

Another brief example, 1 Corinthians 3:18–23, shows that the figures have a unique importance in Pauline discourse. This passage is the conclusion (*peroratio*) of the section that extends from 1 Corinthians 1:10 to 3:23. A number of features mark out these verses as a *peroratio*: the repetition, in verse 22a, of the exordium (i.e., introduction; cf. 1:12); the repetition, in reverse order, of the *probatio* in the form of a paradox (v. 18) and of a summary (*anakephalaiōsis*), in verses 18–19a; and the majestic unfolding of verses 21–23. In the latter verses, there are at least five figures: a merism (life/death; present/future);[15] an anaphora[16] or *repetitio* (eight times the Greek particle *eite*); an anadiplosis[17] (*yours* → *you*; *Christ's* → *Christ*) which is at the same time a polyptoton;[18] and a climax, in that the series leads up to "God": "All belong to you, and you belong to Christ, and Christ belongs to God." In this conclusion, the figures are not decorative but functional. The paradox of verse 18 indicates clearly that the function of the entire *probatio* was to highlight, not resolve, the enigma: "become fools so that you may become wise!" And to show that the paradox, which expresses the radical transformation of values, is inescapable, Paul uses another figure, the hyperbole (auxesis) conveyed by the merism, repetition, and climax. If, for him, Christian reality can only be expressed paradoxically, one sees at once why he must use figures, and why his theology must be eminently rhetorical.

Paradox seems to be the most significant Pauline figure because it influences the other ones and appears in every area of his discourse (theology, Christology, soteriology, ecclesiology, and so on). God has baffled the wisdom of the world through the folly of the cross (1 Cor 1:18–21); he gave up his own Son (Rom 8:32), a formula that combines paradox and hyperbole. Doubtless one might say that God could not truly give up his Son, and that exegesis must labor to convey the coherence or cogency of the apostle's thought. But Paul is certainly familiar with the *correctio* (i.e., the amending of a claim just made) and does not hesitate to use it when he wants to do so. He never does so, however, with these abrupt and scandalous statements. Indeed, the statements in which Paul expresses the mystery of the cross are forceful in the extreme: the one who had not known sin is the very one whom God made to be *sin* for us, so that we might become the righteousness of God (2 Cor 5:21). And the divine intention is identical to that of the Son of God, who loved people to the point of giving his life for them (Gal 1:4; 2:20), of becoming a *curse*, so that in him the blessing of Abraham might be extended to all (Gal 3:13–14); or who, though he was rich, for our sake became poor, so that by means of his poverty we might become rich (2 Cor 8:9). How is the one who renounced everything completely able to enrich others, and the one who became a curse able to grant them blessing? Paul does not say: the paradox must remain a paradox!

In refusing to counterbalance or soften assertions like these, Paul indicates clearly that God's ways are beyond our capacities: Paul's paradoxical rhetoric is a rhetoric of humility. The death of Christ on the cross alters the rules of rhetoric and, in so doing, shapes the message itself: the death of Christ definitively displays the humble choices of God. Thus, Paul cannot proclaim the death of Jesus on the cross as anything other than the supreme and final subversion of the values of this world, and his language itself must embrace the folly of God's ways. In addition to his paradoxical language, we should also note how he goes about subverting the conventions of rhetoric by composing encomiums of what is usually scorned and despised: humiliations, deficiencies, failures, and weaknesses (2 Cor 11:1–12:10). Such is the paradox of the reversed encomium of 2 Corinthians 11: in the very moment in which Paul eulogizes his weaknesses, his discourse attains an unmatched strength! Is he rhetorically mocking rhetoric? With good reason one may speak here of an irony that subverts the encomium, since what the excess of hyperbole serves to underline is precisely the kenosis (i.e., Paul's self-emptying). Paradox and hyperbole (auxesis) become thus essential means for expressing the mystery of the divine extravagance found in Christ. Theology thus becomes rhetoric and rhetoric, theology; it is this relation that the rhetorical approach to Paul's letters must also – and especially – emphasize.

Conclusion

The above presentation of Pauline rhetoric makes no claim to be exhaustive. Its first goal has been to show that taking into consideration the rhetorical dimension of Paul's discourse is useful, even necessary, if we want to know what Paul wants to demonstrate and how (with what proofs) he demonstrates it. Until now, this rhetorical dimension has not been sufficiently studied; consequently, certain major passages, like Romans 1:18–3:20, have been misinterpreted. We can only hope that Paul's readers will become better and better acquainted with this essential and fine component of his theology.

Notes

1 In rhetoric, the term "figure" is used for any expression that deviates from normal (or plain) speech; it includes, for example, metaphors, exaggerations, and wordplays.
2 This expression was coined, in a groundbreaking article, by Muilenburg (1969).
3 In the examples, the small letters *a, b, c, i, ii, iii*, etc. indicate short semantic units, and the capital letters *A, B, C, I, II, III*, etc. longer units.
4 Biblical quotations are taken from the New Revised Standard Version.
5 Thus, Romans 1–4; 5–8; 9–11; Galatians 1–2; 3:1–5:12; 1 Corinthians 1:10–3:23; 15; etc.
6 The categorization of speeches as forensic, deliberative, or epideictic goes back to Aristotle. Forensic (or judicial) speeches had their natural setting in the law court and were designed to convince judges about events in the past, thus establishing the innocence or guilt of an accused party. Deliberative speeches had their home in the legislative assembly, and were designed to persuade an audience to adopt (or to dissuade an audience from adopting) a course of action in the future. Epideictic rhetoric (e.g., a festival speech) dealt with the present, its character of praise or blame being designed to entertain spectators.
7 Verses 4 and 7 form the initial declarations of each part; they are illustrated, respectively, by vv. 5–6 and 8–14.
8 Cf. Kennedy (2003, 110–111).
9 By micro-unit, I mean the elementary argument of which Aristotle speaks in *Rhetoric* 3.13.1–3, involving the *proposition* or *prothesis,* and its proof or *pistis*; i.e., an argument made up of a *proposition* and its substantiation.
10 This explains why Paul feels no need to enlarge upon these facts. Actually, he is here taking up *topoi* found in abundance in intertestamental Jewish literature.

11 The declaration of human responsibility in Romans 1:20 is essential to the *probatio*: if people were excusable, God, by giving free rein to his anger, would be unjust.

12 Paul cannot dispense with proof from the scriptural authorities because only the word of God, who looks on the heart (one sees again why Paul retained this principle of retribution), can declare that all people without exception are sinners.

13 I have in mind the scriptural proof called *gezerah shewa*, by which a verse in Scripture containing the same word found in another text is used to illuminate that second text. (Note, e.g., how Paul links Gen 15:6 and Ps 32:1–2 in Rom 4:3–8 because they share the word "reckon.") On the problems arising with regard to its validity, see Aletti (2003).

14 See Brunot (1955); Bullinger (1968).

15 A *merism* is a figure of speech which links opposite extremes (day/night; north/south; children/the elderly; men/women, etc.) to express a totality. Thus, to praise *day and night* means to praise *always*.

16 The repetition of the same word or phrase in successive clauses.

17 The beginning of a sentence or clause with a prominent word taken from the preceding sentence or clause.

18 The repetition of a word in different cases in the same sentence.

References

Aletti, Jean-Noël. 1998. Romans. Pages 1553–1600 in *The International Bible Commentary: A Catholic and Ecumenical Commentary for the Twenty-first Century*. Edited by William R. Farmer. Collegeville, Minn.: Liturgical.

Aletti, Jean-Noël. 2003. Romains 4 et Genèse 17: Quelle énigme et quelle solution? *Biblica* 84: 305–325.

Anderson, R. Dean, Jr. 1998. *Ancient Rhetorical Theory and Paul*. Revised edition. Leuven: Peeters.

Betz, H. D. 1975. The Literary Composition and Function of Paul's Letter to the Galatians. *New Testament Studies* 21: 353–379.

Brunot, Amédée. 1955. *Le génie littéraire de Saint Paul*. Paris: Cerf.

Bullinger, E. W. 1968. *Figures of Speech Used in the Bible: Explained and Illustrated*. Reprint 1898. Grand Rapids: Baker.

Harvey, John D. 1998. *Listening to the Text: Oral Patterning in Paul's Letters*. Grand Rapids: Baker.

Kennedy, George A. 1984. *New Testament Interpretation through Rhetorical Criticism*. Chapel Hill, NC: University of North Carolina Press.

Kennedy, George A. 2003. *Progymnasmata: Greek Textbooks of Prose Composition and Rhetoric*. Leiden: Brill.

Muilenburg, James. 1969. Form Criticism and Beyond. *Journal of Biblical Literature* 88: 1–18.

Porter, Stanley E. 1997. Paul of Tarsus and his Letters. Pages 533–585 in *Handbook of Classical Rhetoric in the Hellenistic Period (330 BC – AD 400)*. Edited by Stanley E. Porter. Leiden: Brill.

Siegert, Folker. 1985. *Argumentation bei Paulus: gezeigt an Röm 9–11*. Tübingen: J. C. B. Mohr.

CHAPTER 16

The Social Setting of Pauline Communities

Gerd Theissen

The New Testament offers insight into social groups that have otherwise left few writings. Paul's correspondence gives us such vivid glimpses of their lives that we are eager to learn more – a wish that often misleads us into gathering a maximum of social data from minimal hints in the sources. The methodological problem entailed in drawing such conclusions may be illustrated by two apparent contradictions between our two most important sources, Paul's epistles and the Acts of the Apostles, whose interpretation is of some significance in determining the social status of Pauline communities.

Obviously, the genuine Pauline letters are to be regarded as the more reliable source in case of doubt, but we need to reckon with rhetorical stylizing of social matters even in Paul. He is being rhetorical when, in 1 Corinthians, he ascribes high social standing to only a few in Corinth but counts the majority as socially inferior and himself as the lowest of the low, far below even the community in Corinth (1 Cor 1:26; 4:9–13). The Acts of the Apostles offers a quite different picture, with Paul as a Roman citizen (Acts 16:37; 22:25–29). This claim explains his journey to Rome as a prisoner: as a citizen, he has invoked his civic rights in order to avoid sentencing in Judea (25:9–12). It is true that Acts has a tendency to identify Christians as people of higher social standing (17:12; 18:8; 19:31). So has Roman citizenship been attributed to Paul in Acts in order to give him social reputation (Stegemann 1987)? Or is Acts correct in this matter? In the latter case, did Paul perhaps keep quiet about his Roman citizenship after his conversion because he regarded as "rubbish"[1] all that he had once prized (Phil 3:8)? Paul was convinced that he could gain authority in his communities by showing his conformity with Christ crucified. Any claim based on his worldly reputation would have been incompatible with this. When it comes to his citizenship, more arguments support it as

The Blackwell Companion to Paul, First Edition. Edited by Stephen Westerholm.
© 2011 Blackwell Publishing Ltd. Published 2011 by Blackwell Publishing Ltd.

an historical fact than speak against it (Theissen 2003, 372–374). "Paul" is a Roman name. The readiest explanation for such a name in a consciously Jewish family (Phil 3:5) is that an ancestor who had been in slavery to a Roman master as a prisoner of war had gained Roman citizenship on being set free. Many Jews in Asia Minor and Rome gained their citizenship in this way, and on the whole they do not make much of it. Jewish inscriptions in Rome seldom reveal the Roman citizens, even though their numbers are known to have been high. Paul conforms to the Jewish mentality when he conceals his Roman citizenship, so there is no contradiction with the Acts of the Apostles.

In the second instance of tension between our sources, it is the silence of Acts that requires explanation. In all his letters except the oldest and shortest ones (1 Thess; Phlm), Paul mentions his collection for Jerusalem. He sees it as important for securing unity between Jews and Gentiles. He makes the collection obligatory for the whole community, not only for wealthier members. Each can, however, decide on their own contribution (1 Cor 16:2). Paul does not call on members to work or fast in order to contribute to the collection (as in Shepherd of Hermas, *Similitude* 56.7; Aristides, *Apology* 15). Rather, he assumes they possess a surplus that can be put aside. This is important information relating to the social standing of Christians. The communities possessed enough to be able to give of their "abundance" (2 Cor 8:14). Paul differentiates between the communities, setting up the Macedonian churches in their extreme poverty as an example to the Corinthians (2 Cor 8:1–2). His aim is rhetorical, of course, but grounded in reality. Not all the Pauline communities had the same social standing (Barclay 1992).

On the other hand, the Acts of the Apostles says nothing about the collection for Jerusalem. True, the author seems to know about it: Paul is said to journey to Jerusalem "to bring alms" to his "nation" (Acts 24:17). Actually, mentioning the collection would have fitted well with the tendency of Acts to assign Christians to the local upper class. They would then appear as benefactors assisting others at a supraregional level. Acts does indeed report on Paul and Barnabas's first collection on the occasion of a severe famine (Acts 11:27–30). Why, then, is the second collection not mentioned? It is often suggested that Acts is concerned to conceal the fact that the collection was refused in Jerusalem. More likely, however, Acts seeks to avoid the impression that Paul was attempting to "buy" the goodwill of the Jerusalem community by means of a collection. Such an action would place Paul in the company of Simon Magus, who offered the apostles money in return for the right to give the gift of the Holy Spirit (Acts 8:14–24). This would explain as well why Acts separates Paul and Barnabas's (first) collection from their journey to the Apostolic Council, with the result that Paul is said to travel to Jerusalem three times (9:26; 11:27–30; 15:4) despite his own mention, in Galatians 1–2, of only two visits: Paul's success at the Apostolic Council must not be allowed to have anything to do with his first collection. This is also why Acts (24:17) speaks of the second collection as "alms to my nation" (i.e., for all Israel and not only for the community in Jerusalem). Church diplomacy by means of gifts of money was anathema to the author of Acts. We can therefore assume the historical authenticity of the collection, and conclude from it that a significant proportion of Christians in the Pauline communities possessed more than the bare minimum.

These two problems have been introduced to exemplify the need for critical evaluation of the sources. Despite such tensions in the sources, basic features of primitive Christian social history are surprisingly uncontroversial. This can be demonstrated under the following five headings: (1) general developmental tendencies in the social history of primitive Christianity; (2) the social composition of the Pauline communities; (3) socially determined conflicts; (4) the attractiveness of the community; and (5) models for the self-understanding of early Christian churches. Only in the analysis of conflicts within the communities are the disputes among exegetes more marked, since here we are not dealing with general social structures but attempting to throw light on concrete events.

General Developmental Tendencies in the Social History of Primitive Christianity

The Pauline communities reflect four general tendencies in the social development of primitive Christianity: urbanization, universalization, upward dynamic, and spiritualization. All these are interrelated, and all led to specific conflicts.

(1)   *Urbanization*   The beginnings of Christianity may certainly be found in the countryside. Jesus was active in Galilee, where his first followers were fishermen and farmers. After his death, Christianity spread to the cities of the Hellenistic Mediterranean (Oakes 2009) – beyond its original setting. Paul's own work is part of this *urbanization* of Christianity, but even before his time Christianity had reached as far as Damascus, where he was converted. Before he became active, there was a community in Antioch, and, independent of Paul, there was one in Rome.

Paul acted strategically in focusing on the cities. He began in the important regional centers of Philippi, Thessalonica, Corinth, and Ephesus, from which Christianity spread further. In most places, there were conflicts, which varied in nature and the course they took. Paul had to flee from Philippi and Thessalonica after conflicts with the local magistrates, but he was able to stay for long periods in Corinth and Ephesus. Acts 18:12–17 throw light on one of the reasons for this in Corinth. A representative of the imperial power was called upon to deal with a local conflict with the Jewish community. The proconsul Gallio refused to entertain the case against Paul because he regarded the complaints against him as internal Jewish disputes. This meant an official recognition of Christianity in Corinth as part of the Jewish community, which was not the case in Philippi or Thessalonica. We can draw a similar conclusion for Ephesus, where locally initiated conflicts with Gentile groups resulted in a trial before the proconsul of Asia. When Paul writes to the Philippians from Ephesus, he is in prison and realizes he may face a death sentence. In 2 Corinthians 1:8–11, he looks back on the good outcome of the trial. He had fully expected a death sentence but had been returned to life. In Corinth and Ephesus, Christianity was able to limit its conflicts with the Jewish and Gentile communities with the help of the imperial authorities and could thus develop in peace. In Rome, on the other hand, Christianity soon collided with the emperor and in the year 49 CE Claudius expelled Christian troublemakers from the city.

(2) *Universalization*   As well as urbanization, universalization is recognizable in the first generation. Primitive Christianity began as a Jewish renewal movement that soon after Jesus's death opened up to Gentiles. Some Gentiles – like the centurion Cornelius – were won for Christianity without missionary intent (Acts 10). Programmatic mission to the Gentiles began among Stephen's followers who had fled from Jerusalem to Antioch. It was they who introduced Paul to mission to the Gentiles. An important part in the opening of Christianity to non-Jews was played by the "God-fearers," Gentile sympathizers with the Jewish synagogue who were attracted by Jewish monotheism and ethics but did not adopt circumcision and food laws or convert fully to Judaism. According to Acts, many of them were persuaded by the Christian message (Acts 17:4). We hear nothing of these "God-fearers" from Paul, but this does not mean they are fictitious; rather, they are a weighty argument for taking the content of Acts seriously even when it is not confirmed in Paul. An inscription in Aphrodisias attests the existence of the "God-fearers" (Reynolds and Tannenbaum 1987).

If we ask why we trust Acts here despite the necessary skepticism, the answer is that these details in Acts are compatible with the general picture of Judaism and primitive Christianity in the society of the time. It is plain to see why the Christian message would have attracted the "God-fearers." In the synagogue, they were second-class members, while in the Christian community they enjoyed equality. Paul offered them a variant of Judaism which, in admitting Gentiles, deliberately did without the requirements of circumcision and food laws. This made the "God-fearers" trendsetters in the "universalization" of Judaism taking shape in the form of primitive Christianity. Universalization also led to fierce conflict. A counter-mission against Paul attempted to persuade his communities in Galatia and Philippi to adopt the most fundamental Jewish identity-markers of circumcision and food laws. The intention was to reintegrate the communities fully within Judaism, thus allowing them to become part of a publicly recognized organization. Paul resisted this counter-mission, and the conflict gave rise to some of his finest epistles: to the Galatians, Philippians, and Romans.

(3) *Upward dynamic*   There is evidence that some of the "God-fearers" were among the wealthier groups in society. If this is so, then they were an element in the upward dynamic of primitive Christianity in the first century. The dynamic as such is undisputed. Pliny the Younger reports in his letter on Christians that in his time they were found in all *ordines* (Pliny, *Epistles* 10.96). The three *ordines* were the senators, equestrians (the cavalry, or knights), and decurions (i.e., the council members in the cities). That Christians were in fact to be found in all three orders at that time is not possible. But Pliny must have come across Christians who belonged to the decurions, the politically

dominant local aristocracy; otherwise his hyperbolic rhetoric on the immense and dangerous spread of Christianity would be inexplicable. Probably the Pauline communities represented one of these steps "in an upward direction." At the end of the first century, primitive Christianity apparently even won over a member of the emperor's household, Flavia Domitilla.

However, the extent of this upward dynamic in the Pauline communities in the middle of the first century is disputed. Possibly, the Acts of the Apostles places the Pauline communities somewhat higher socially than they actually were, perhaps back-projecting by fifty years the more progressive situation of Acts' own time. That an upward process was taking place can, however, hardly be denied. Once again, this probably led to conflicts. When people from different social strata live together, their differing patterns of behavior can lead to conflict with the egalitarian ideals of Christian fellowship. Some of the conflicts in Corinth are of this nature, in particular the conflict between the haves and the have-nots concerning the Lord's Supper (1 Cor 11).

(4)   *Spiritualization*   Finally, we can also observe a spiritualization tendency in Paul (Wong 2002). Whereas Jesus envisages the kingdom of God as a great family banquet, Paul firmly rejects the idea that God's kingdom is food and drink (Rom 14:17). He sees the Messiah as descended from David according to the flesh (Rom 1:3), but not as one who liberates Israel from its enemies; rather, he liberates all people from sin, death, and the law (to the extent that it is the "letter" that "kills" [2 Cor 3:6]). Unredeemed human nature is seen at the root of universal human problems. This spiritualization inevitably resulted in conflicts. After all, the promises of salvation – such as the promise of freedom for all – could be taken literally. All are liberated by Christ, including the slaves. Did that mean they were "merely" freed from sin and death? Israel had a tradition that Israelites should not be permanently enslaved. Should the new people of God not offer real freedom to its enslaved members? Some slaves were indeed set free at the expense of the communities (cf. Ignatius, *Letter to Polycarp* 4.3). In his letter to Philemon, Paul recommends a pragmatic solution: the slave Onesimus, who has approached Paul for help following a dispute with his master, is to be of service to Paul in future and would thus be withdrawn from his master's service (Lampe 1985). The deutero-Pauline epistles (Colossians, Ephesians, and the Pastoral epistles) already appear to be dampening the high hopes of the slaves (Merz 2004, 245–267).

The four developmental tendencies may be summarily interpreted as follows. Within Judaism, the first adherents of Jesus may be regarded as a "sect." Sects are breakaway groups within an existing religion, seeking to realize specific elements of it with more consistency. Their first adherents are often recruited from among those outside the more established groups of the religion, and sometimes from the poorer circles. Among them there is no need for conversion, but only for persuasion that they can now consistently realize what they had always sought in their religion. In their own understanding, sects begin as "renewal movements." In the Hellenistic cities, however, the new movement presented itself differently, not seeking to renew old cults but offering a new

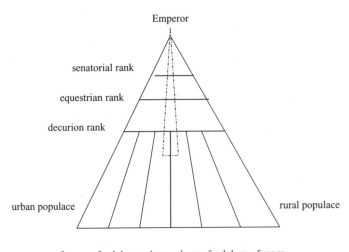

Figure 16.1   Social structure of Greco-Roman society (based on Alföldy 1985, 146).

"cult" that put forward an alternative means of salvation (Stark 1996; Theissen 2008). Joining such a movement was a far more radical act. It is quite possible that a number of intellectuals, sensitive to the impasses of their own religion and open to new ideas, found their way into the new movement.

The Social Composition of the Pauline Communities

Research into the social composition of the Pauline communities has led to a number of points of consensus, though only after protracted and heated debate. Reaching consensus was facilitated as knowledge of the social structure of Greco-Roman society grew. The structure is shown, however imperfectly, in figure 16.1.

At the head of society was a very small upper class consisting of three ranks: the senators and equestrians, who constituted the imperial elite, and the local elite of the decurions, who made up the urban councils. Altogether, these amounted to 3 percent of the population at most (which is not apparent in figure 16.1). The vast majority had their place below this level and may be divided vertically – distinguishing them from each other by differences in their dependency relationships – rather than horizontally. Slaves (*servi*), freed slaves (*liberti*), and freemen (*ingenui*) were all dependent on patrons. Dependencies in rural areas were different from those in the cities. A city slave could expect his freedom around the age of thirty as a reward for good behavior, whereas a rural slave was exploited far longer as a "living tool." Since all were concerned to improve their individual situation through their relationship with the patron, those without rights did not develop a solidarity that would have endangered the system. The top "patron" was the emperor, whose personal circle (his household, his freed slaves, and his army) was distinct from the usual distribution of power and prestige. An imperial slave was often more influential than a free citizen.

In the overall population, various "classes" may be identified by economic criteria according to their closeness to, or distance from, the poverty line. The poor were not simply a homogeneous mass (as suggested by Meggitt 1998). Some had modest property through their association with the upper class, others had only a little more than the bare minimum, many had just enough to live on, and many not even that (Friesen 2004). We can only approximately estimate which persons belonged to which of these four "classes." There is no consensus on whether the mass of the population lived below the poverty line or at the line (Longenecker 2009). The decisive point is that even below the decurion level there were significant distinctions that were perceived by the various groups themselves.

Despite the rigid boundaries between ranks and classes, social mobility did exist. For one thing, the mortality rate was high. In the upper classes, families often fell victim to political cleansing or became impoverished. In the other direction, sons of freed slaves often rose to join the decurions. Within an individual lifetime, however, the chances of moving up in society were modest. A slave could be freed, and a freed slave could become wealthy, but only his descendants had the opportunity to wield political influence. So mobility was only cross-generational, though because of lower life expectancy, the generations succeeded one another much more rapidly than today. We can thus expect to find people in the periphery of the upper class who are not members of the local elite but whose descendants might be.

This is how Paul describes the social composition of the Corinthians: "Consider your own call, brothers and sisters: not many of you were wise by human standards, not many were powerful, not many were of noble birth. But God chose what is foolish in the world to shame the wise; God chose what is weak in the world to shame the strong; God chose what is low and despised in the world, things that are not, to reduce to nothing things that are, so that no one might boast in the presence of God" (1 Cor 1:26–29). This is not irony that deliberately obscures the fact that the community included many upper-class members (Wuellner 1973). It is rather the rhetoric of chosenness, emphasizing how great a privilege it is to be chosen by focusing on the nothingness of those so privileged. Counter to this rhetorical tendency, it is conceded that there are some high-ranking members. This small minority must indeed have existed, since otherwise Paul could simply have said, as did another primitive Christian writer, "Has not God chosen the poor in the world to be rich in faith and to be heirs of the kingdom?" (Jas 2:5).

To evaluate what Paul has to say, it is helpful to draw a comparison with other voluntary associations in the ancient world (Fellmeth 1990, 53; Schmeller 1995, 46). Two types of association can be distinguished: professional and religious. An analysis of all recorded members and their "sponsoring" patrons (who supported without participating in the life of the association) shows significant diversity in their composition (table 16.1).

The professional associations had a number of high-ranking patrons, some of whom were even senators. The religious associations, on the other hand, had decurions at best as patrons, and some had to make do with freed slaves as their sponsors. This corresponds to the internal social composition of the associations. In both types, freed slaves make up the majority, accounting for about two-thirds of membership. The relatively

Table 16.1 Membership of professional and religious associations

	Professional associations (%)	Religious associations (%)
Senators	1.18	–
Equestrians	0.60	–
Decurions	0.47	0.47
Freemen	32.75	17.25
Freed Slaves	64.95	63.60
Slaves	0.05	18.68

Table 16.2 Status and role of named members of Pauline communities outside and within the church

	Status and role independent of primitive Christianity	Status and role in primitive Christianity
Offices / services	Erastus, city treasurer (*oikonomos*) (Rom 16:23)	Aquila and Priscilla (Rom 16:3)
	Crispus, official of the synagogue (Acts 18:8)	Phoebe (Rom 16:1)
		Stephanas and his household (1 Cor 16:15)
Houses	Stephanas (1 Cor 1:16; 16:15)	Aquila and Priscilla, hosts of a house church (Rom 16:5; 1 Cor 16:19)
		Gaius, host to the whole church (Rom 16:23)

high proportion of freemen is significant in the professional associations, where slaves are scarcely represented. In the religious associations, on the other hand, the proportion of freemen is much smaller, that of slaves much larger. We may assume that the social composition of the Jewish and primitive Christian communities corresponded to that of the religious associations. Many male and female slaves were among them.

What can be said of the members we encounter by name in the Pauline epistles? All the specific criteria pointing to relatively high social standing (i.e., the holding of offices, references to houses, services, and travels) are ambiguous. We can, however, distinguish between offices and functions outside and within the church community, and between the heads of profane and Christian households (table 16.2).

With regard to the much-discussed Erastus inscription, we cannot be certain whether the Aedil Erastus named there is identical with the city treasurer named in Romans 16:23. The latter is undoubtedly a prominent member of the community (Metzner 2008, 556–561). It is striking that Paul mentions a secular office here, which he never does elsewhere. He has already mentioned attributes of all the others sending greetings: co-worker, relatives, writer, host, brother. Now he needs a predicate for Erastus, who is named as last but one on the list. Paul introduces him as city treasurer. His immediate predecessor in the list of greetings is Paul's host Gaius, who will certainly have been a Christian, and his successor in the list is Quartus, a (Christian) brother. The use of "brother" suggests that someone previously named was not a brother. Possibly Erastus was not (yet) a Christian and is introduced by his secular office for that reason. Whether this Erastus ever joined the community remains an open question. This interpretation provides a solution to the problem of identifying Aedil Erastus with the Erastus of Romans 16:23, since an active male member of the community from the local aristocracy would certainly be exceptional in the pre-Constantine era.

Paul writes in 1 Corinthians 1:14 that he has personally baptized Crispus and Gaius. An official of the synagogue named Crispus is mentioned in Acts 18:8. His conversion together with that of his "household" must have been significant for the founding of the community; hence his baptism by Paul himself, which was exceptional. As a synagogue official, he will have been relatively wealthy. We have inscriptional evidence that synagogue officials acted as benefactors in Jewish communities (Theissen 2001, 80–82). Probably they were among the members of the community who had higher status. In legal terms, the synagogue official was often simply a *peregrinus* (non-citizen), but this did not exclude his corresponding to the local elite by other criteria (such as wealth and education) and being part of the upper-class periphery.

Paul is said to have baptized Crispus *with his household*. The fact that "slaves" were part of a household does not necessarily indicate prosperity. Poor people also had slaves. Here, as elsewhere, a short phrase at the end of 1 Corinthians reveals much: Paul recommends Stephanas and his household and urges the Corinthians to put themselves at their service (1 Cor 16:16). This subordination specifically includes service to the members of Stephanas's household. May we not assume that this household had high social standing, so that even the "subordinates" within it (perhaps even the slaves) commanded respect? Given these observations, Stephanas's journey to Ephesus is also an (in itself, weak) indicator of high social status.

Finally, we turn briefly to Gaius, the host of the community. It is highly unlikely that he simply hosted traveling brothers and missionaries at the request of the community; such an interpretation of Romans 16:23 requires that the two parallel genitives dependent on "host" be read in different ways: first Gaius is host *to* Paul, then host *at the request of* the community. If we take both genitives to be objective, however, we find that the whole church met at his house. For estimating the size of the community, we have some comparative materials in ancient sources. Few associations in antiquity had more than a hundred members; few had under ten. Most had a membership of between twenty and fifty (Schmeller 1995, 40). The Corinthian church will have been very large (Acts 18:10). This means that Gaius's house must also have been quite spacious, without necessarily being a stately atrium house. In Corinth there were various ways of gathering even in more modest houses (Horrell 2004).

The primitive Christian community drew its strength from the classes below decurion level and included people of varying social standing. Very few were part of the upper-class periphery; most lived around the poverty line, some above it and some below. By means of exchange, they were economically strong enough to support each other and to take collections for other communities. Their composition corresponded approximately to that of religious associations.

Table 16.3 Conflicts communicated to Paul orally and in writing

Conflict	Oral communication	Written communication
Influence and power	Apollos as representative of wisdom language (1 Cor 1–4)	Apollos as co-worker of Paul (1 Cor 16:12)
Food	Divisions over the Lord's Supper (1 Cor 11:17–34)	Conflict concerning food offered to idols (1 Cor 8:1–11:1)
Sexual behavior	Freedom to go to prostitutes (1 Cor 6:12–20)	Refraining from marriage, with asceticism (self-discipline) as the ideal (1 Cor 7:1–40)
Verbal communication	Pride in wisdom language (1 Cor 1:18–4:21)	Claims of glossolalia (gift of tongues) (1 Cor 12–14)

Socially Determined Conflicts

In such socially heterogeneous communities, conflicts could arise, even though the social factor varied in its significance from case to case. The conflicts centered on power and influence among the missionaries, common meals, sexual relations, and forms of verbal communication in the community. We gain most information about these conflicts from the epistles to the Corinthians. Paul began the first of these after receiving news by word of mouth. Not long before he wrote chapter 7, a letter with news of the community must have reached him. Beginning in 1 Corinthians 7:1, then, Paul deals in turn with the matters he has been asked about, opening each section with the words "Now concerning ..." (*peri de*). Paul has thus learned about the issues generating conflict from both oral and written communications. The conflicts themselves are various but related, and perceived somewhat differently by those who communicated with Paul orally than by those who communicated with him in writing (table 16.3).

Conflicts concerning influence and power

In 1 Corinthians 9:5–6, Paul distinguishes two types of missionaries. He and Barnabas finance their mission through their own work, whereas all the other apostles (including Peter and the Lord's brothers) are supported by donations from the community, as Jesus had directed. The same groups that were involved in negotiations between the communities in Antioch and Jerusalem at the time of the Apostolic Council are set in opposition to each other here too, with Paul and Barnabas representing the Antiochian mission to the Gentiles. This developed among the Hellenists who had fled from Jerusalem (Acts 6:1–8:4). They were not originally wandering charismatics but became missionaries as a result of being exiled. Peter and the other apostles (as well as the Lord's brother James), on the other hand, represented mission as it developed in Israel as discipleship of Jesus. These were wandering charismatics, fishermen and farmers who could not earn their own living while traveling – as Paul the craftsman could. In Corinth, these two types of missionaries met and clashed. Both the competing missionaries mentioned in 1 Corinthians (Apollos among them) and the missionaries of the counter-mission in 2 Corinthians (i.e., newly arrived missionaries) caused difficulties for Paul because, counter to Jesus's directions, he was earning his own living. Obliged to defend himself, he rightly points out that without material recompense he has better chances of winning more people for the gospel (1 Cor 9:19–23). Quite apart from the theological differences, this is a socially determined conflict arising out of different models of missionary work.

Disputes arose between representatives of these two types of missionaries. The nature of these conflicts varied. The dispute with Apollos (and with the followers of other apostles) in 1 Corinthians is rooted in rivalry, while the dispute with the counter-missionaries reflected in Galatians, Philippians, and 2 Corinthians pertains to religious issues.

Experiences of Apollos varied greatly within the Corinthian community. Some gave Paul the impression in oral reports (1 Cor 1:12) that Apollos's wisdom language fundamentally contradicted Paul's preaching of the foolishness of the cross. The group responsible for the community letter, on the other hand, saw no fundamental tension between Paul and Apollos. They asked Paul to send Apollos to Corinth (16:12). There must also have been followers of Peter in the community. Either Peter himself had been in Corinth, or missionaries linked with him had arrived there. Apollos's followers emphasized his wisdom language, while Peter's followers saw in their master the foundation of the church (cf. 3:11). Followers of Paul could only stress that it was Paul who had brought Christianity to Corinth. It was he who, as the founder of the community, had first baptized there. Possibly the rivalry between the various missionaries was reinforced by the fact that the Corinthian community met in various houses: where Apollos had stayed, he was regarded as the superior missionary; where Paul had lived, he was the favorite; where Peter had stayed, he was seen as the rock of the church.

A different view must be taken of the conflicts with missionaries with whom Paul did not cooperate, as he did with Apollos, but who initiated a counter-mission against him and sought to persuade his communities to adopt the most important Jewish identity-markers: circumcision and food laws. These missionaries were concerned to reintegrate the Christian communities within the Jewish community. In Galatia, Paul rightly observes that their aim is to avoid conflict with their environment: they want to avoid persecution (Gal 6:12). It is true that as part of Judaism the Christian groups would have belonged to a recognized and respected religion. Conflict with Jews would have been reduced, and thereby also the conflict with Gentile magistrates before whom Jews often brought complaints against Christians. In Philippi, Paul consoles the community for its lack of legal status on earth with its "citizenship" in heaven (Phil 3:20). In Corinth, on the other hand, the counter-mission (conducted by new missionaries who arrived between the writing of 1 and 2 Corinthians) did not insist on the requirements of circumcision and food laws. This is why their approach is seen by many scholars as different from that of the Galatian and Philippian missionaries. That need not be the case, however. In Corinth, the Christian groups were officially recognized by Gallio as part of Judaism – *without* adopting circumcision and food laws. Here the counter-mission found its main concern already met. For this reason, it could take a moderate line here (Theissen 2009). But in my view, it remains the same counter-mission, even if the people involved were not the same. Other exegetes, however, see different groups opposed to Paul in each city.

Conflicts concerning food

In the matter of common meals, the differences of perspective between the oral and written communications are even more marked. Paul has had oral reports that food is distributed unequally at the Lord's Supper, either because people do not wait for each other, placing slaves who are not masters of their own time at a disadvantage, or because patrons – according to well-evidenced patterns of behavior – look after their friends and their social clientele differently, depending on social status (Theissen 1982c). Paul sees this as an abuse of the Lord's Supper. Those who act in this anti-social manner are guilty once again of Christ's death. His indignation at such bad behavior adopts the perspective of those who were disadvantaged by it. Some exegetes deny that social differences between poorer and wealthier members of the church are in evidence here, but this remains the most widespread interpretation.

Written reports make Paul aware of a very different problem to do with food and eating, one that concerns meals with Gentiles rather than with other Christians. Can Christians maintain their normal social relationships if they are invited to meals at which food sacrificed to idols is eaten? Some Christians with a weak conscience had not yet realized that idols did not exist and that food sacrificed to them was therefore no different from any other. Although Paul supports this view in principle, he urges members, for the sake of the "weak" ones, not to eat food sacrificed to idols if the meal could be understood as a cultic act. This would apply to shared meals in a temple, since the setting itself gave such meals the character of cultic acts. It would apply as well to shared meals in private if the "sacrificial" nature of the food was emphasized. As poorer people ate meat mainly at the major public festivals, the connection between idolatry and meat-eating was far closer and more plausible for them than for wealthier people who often ate meat. This is why we may assume that the "weak" people Paul refers to are the poorer classes (Theissen 1982b).

But it was not *only* these who might be "weak" in their religious convictions. Paul assumes that one might be confronted with food sacrificed to idols at a private shared meal. In antiquity, invitations to meals in private homes were characteristic of the upper classes, whereas ordinary people celebrated in taverns. Paul expects that in the upper classes, too, there will be people with "weak" consciences who, as guests, are confronted with meat understood to have been sacrificed to idols. As guests of such a (wealthy) Gentile host, they cannot in good conscience eat what is declared by the host to be "holy meat" – a declaration perhaps prompted by pride in having purchased first-class (sacrificed) meat from the *macellum* (the ancient market for high-quality produce), a task of the head of the household in antiquity. So a Christian should not, in order to please a Gentile host, eat food sacrificed to idols if the host indicates that he understands this to be a cultic act. Paul concludes the discussion by summarizing that, in three directions, Christians are not to give offense by eating food sacrificed to idols: toward Jews, Greeks (=Gentiles), and the church of God (1 Cor 10:32). (My suggested interpretation of the conflict between "stronger" and "weaker" as a class-specific conflict is not, however, held universally.)

We thus encounter the topic of shared meals twice, from very different perspectives. First Corinthians 11 is concerned with the meal within the Christian community, seen from the perspective of the poorer members; 1 Corinthians 8–10 has to do with meals shared with non-Christians, in which the wealthier members will have had a greater interest.

Conflicts concerning sexual behavior

Paul has received oral reports of instances of sexual license. A man is living with his mother-in-law (probably after his father's death; 1 Cor 5:1–13). As women married very young, the man might well be about the same age as the woman. Paul urges that the man should be excluded from the church. He has also heard that some (unmarried men?) have been resorting to prostitutes and seeing this as a sign of their freedom (1 Cor 6:12–20). Adopting language that characterizes marriage in Genesis 2:24, Paul indicates that sexual intercourse with prostitutes means becoming "one body" with them and is thus a sin against oneself. This may have surprised the Corinthians because such behavior was considered normal at the time; it was only shameful for members of the upper class to associate with those below them. Paul transfers this "aristocratic" ethos to normal Christians. Their relationship with Christ makes them special, and for this reason they should not continue the libertine behavior to which they were accustomed (Kirchhoff 1994).

The written report drew Paul's attention to a problem almost the reverse. Some members of the community, particularly women, preferred to remain unmarried or wanted to exercise sexual abstinence even within marriage. They saw themselves as part of a new world, seeking to control their desires and devote themselves entirely to the Lord. For women especially, asceticism and remaining unmarried offered a means of gaining respect and reputation in an alternative role to that of housewife and mother. But some men, too, were enthusiastic about the unmarried life. For the first time, we also have allusions here to a third way of living, between marriage and celibacy, when unmarried couples renounce marriage and sexuality but remain together as a couple. Paul makes clear to all these people with ascetic tendencies that marriage is not a sin and that sexual desires may rightly be satisfied within it. On the other hand, the ascetics, both male and female, were practicing the aristocratic consciousness of the self that Paul commended and found lacking in libertine behavior.

Conflicts concerning verbal communication

A further issue in Corinth is the appropriate form of religious verbal communication. We find, on the one hand, admiration for "wisdom," articulated speech of a revelatory character in which the depths of divinity are disclosed. Apollos represents this type of religious communication, and Paul attempts not to fall short of it. He too can talk wisdom to the wise (1 Cor 2:6). But Paul's "wisdom" has the cross at its center, through which God has transformed the wisdom of the wise into foolishness (1 Cor 1:18–20). We may conclude from this that Apollos's wisdom language corresponded more closely to secular standards of rhetoric than did that of Paul, who calls himself (in 2 Cor 11:6) "untrained in speech." Note that his information about the problems associated with wisdom language came from oral communications.

The letter from the community, on the other hand, confronts Paul with the issue of unintelligible utterances (glossolalia) in which some members experienced the Holy Spirit. Such speech was interpreted as the language of angels (cf. 1 Cor 13:1), a means by which Christians could participate in the cult of heaven already in this life and be transported beyond earthly limitations. Paul recognizes spiritual gifts in a variety of verbal forms of communication. But he begins his enumeration of such gifts with "the utterance of wisdom" (1 Cor 12:8), and places "tongues" and "the interpretation of tongues" at the end (v. 10). This expresses his hierarchy of values: in the church, he would rather speak five words with his mind than ten thousand words in a tongue (1 Cor 14:19).

The four areas of conflict of which Paul learned through oral and written communications do not have a common denominator. It appears, however, that the groups responsible for the written report dominate within the community. They advocate sexual self-discipline, ritually unrestricted relations with non-Christians, and intelligible wisdom language. Paul sympathizes with them but is concerned to accommodate the other groups and urges consideration for them as well. Marriage is not a sin, he stresses; certain foods can be avoided for the sake of weaker members of the community; and glossolalia should not be rejected but, in the context of the community, must be interpreted. Class-specific factors are most apparent in the conflicts over food, whereas in other conflicts they remain in the background. Much in this regard, however, remains hidden to us. Moreover, it would be unacceptably one-sided to discuss community life with a view only for conflict.

The Attractiveness of the Community

Far greater than the potential for conflict is the internal cohesion within the community. This makes it magnetically attractive for its members. The more prosperous members could take on the role of benefactors and patrons that would be denied them in society because of their modest means. Members living below the poverty line could expect support and care of a kind that was highly unusual in antiquity. The regularly recurring Lord's Supper offered them a taste of the festival culture of the upper classes. Two theories have been developed to interpret the attractiveness of the community. At first glance these appear to contradict each other: attractiveness either because of reduced status dissonance (Meeks 1983) or because of the downward transfer of upper-class values (Theissen 2000, 123–167; 2004, 248–268).

Wayne A. Meeks (1983) has proposed the thesis that people experiencing status dissonance were especially attracted by the early Christian church and enabled to reduce the dissonance by joining it. Status dissonance occurs where there is social and local mobility. Those who are economically successful cannot automatically translate this into prestige and influence. Their prestige status is in many cases lower than their economic status. Upward and downward mobility result in status and standing being judged by different criteria. Local mobility has the same consequence. A stranger living in a city may succeed in becoming wealthy and yet, as a stranger, remain a second-class citizen. Early Christianity spread below the decurion level in the cities, where social and local mobility were far greater than in rural areas. It spread especially among people who could not be integrated into society by being bound to the interests of the Roman Empire through participation in power, either at the political level (the self-administration of the cities) or at the religious level (the cult of the emperor). As people sought to escape status dissonance, early Christianity proved attractive to them. Within the Christian community, each individual received recognition. Those who were better off could take on leadership roles; those who were needy would be cared for in a way that no other community in antiquity offered. Moreover, early Christianity provided a network of supraregional communities that could offer support. This is apparent in Paul's commending of Phoebe, who is to be helped "in whatever she may require" (Rom 16:2). The very groups that were excluded from the political *ekklēsia* – strangers, slaves, and women – had equal rights in the Christian *ekklēsia*. The "social world" within the Christian church was in harmony, though dissonance remained a factor outside the community. Reduction of dissonance was restricted to the community.

This latter consideration suggests how the above thesis can be offset by an opposing one. Membership in the Christian church exposed many Christians to *increased* status dissonance (Longenecker 2009). They found themselves in conflict with their environment. In some cases, they even had to be willing to accept self-stigmatizing, taking on roles in society in which they had no chance of public recognition – but all the more opportunity to campaign for the truth of their beliefs (Mödritzer 1994). Yet even in such subordinate roles, they could claim leadership in a way otherwise restricted to aristocratic circles. Within fallen humanity, they saw themselves "shin[ing] like stars in the world" (Phil 2:15). This claim was based on a downward transfer of upper-class values. In early Christianity, the attitudes and behavior of the upper class were reformulated in a way that made them accessible to ordinary people. This is why we find among Christians (below the decurion level) a high level of self-esteem and attitudes typically attributed to the upper class. The pneumatics in Corinth bear witness to this. Paul ascribes to them a self-esteem far above their "natural" status when he writes: "Already you have all you want! Already you have become rich! Quite apart from us you have become kings! I wish that you had become kings, so that we might be kings with you!" (1 Cor 4:8). This downward transfer of upper-class values corresponds to an upward transfer of lower-class values, such as humility and love of neighbor. These two movements actually *intensify* status dissonance: ordinary people live like kings, while privileged people confidently represent lower-class values. On this theory, such dissonance is precisely what makes the Christian churches attractive. Christians could develop a way of life that lifted them beyond the life of ordinary people.

The discrepancy between social reality and the self-understanding offered in the Christian faith is the key to the collective self-understanding of the churches. For

Christians, the internal system of relationships in the community was more important than the system of relationships in "the world" (or society). Within this internal system of relationships, status dissonances were reduced, while in the external system they were enhanced. Thus, the two theses do not contradict each other. The theory of reduction of status dissonance is just as valid as that of the downward transfer of upper-class values. The self-understanding of the Christian community was so high-minded that it increased dissonance overall, while strengthening the members to endure it.

Models for the Self-understanding of Early Christian Churches

Early Christian communities developed between the two fundamental institutions of antiquity: the *oikos* (household) and the *polis* (state). Membership in these institutions was generally by birth. Falling between these institutions, associations formed in society that consisted of persons joined together not on familial or territorial grounds but by free choice and according to norms they themselves set (Gutfeld 1998, 13–14). The self-imposed nature of these *voluntary associations* was graduated, increasing from household associations, synagogues, and professional associations to the cultic associations, where it was greatest. The initiation of Apuleius into the mysteries of Isis took place according to "the image of *voluntary* death" (Apuleius, *Metamorphoses* 11.21); Colossians 2:23 speaks of "*self-imposed* piety."

The early Christian churches were themselves formed on the basis of personal decision. When whole households took on the Christian faith (Acts 11:14; 16:15, and elsewhere), the voluntariness was less marked, but still we find that women and slaves in Gentile households held to their decision for Christianity against their social environment (1 Pet 3:1–6; 2:18–25). If we take the degree of voluntariness to be a decisive mark of ancient associations, the Christian groups were associations *par excellence*! But they did not intend to be associations, as we see from the fact that they did not use terms commonly linked with associations (for example, *thiasos*, *hetairia*, and *koinon*) of themselves. Instead, they saw themselves as a new creation in the midst of the old world (Gal 6:15; cf. 2 Cor 5:17). Scholars taking their orientation from the self-understanding of Christians find little commonality between the early Christian churches and the ancient associations (Meeks 1983, 77–80). Scholars observing the objective social structure find that the churches and associations have far more in common (Ascough 2003). Both groups of scholars are right (for the following discussion, cf. Theissen 2007).

The first Christians developed their self-understanding in imitation of familiar social forms, primarily that of the *ethnos* (nation or people), *polis* (city, city-state), and *oikos* (house, household). Christians saw themselves as the *people* of God (Rom 9:25), a unique people whose members were "no longer Greek and Jew, circumcised and uncircumcised, barbarian, Scythian, slave and free" (Col 3:11). They were an international community. At the same time, their self-understanding was modeled on the *polis*. They belonged to the heavenly city of Jerusalem (Gal 4:26) and their citizenship was in heaven (Phil 3:20). Their most important self-designation was *ekklēsia*. The term comes from the Septuagint but must have been understood in the cities as an imitation of the "people's assembly" of free citizens. The function of most associations was to instill in their members the values of the *polis* and to take on tasks within the *polis*. The majority of Christians, however, did not participate in public life. Their acceptance of martyrdom shows that they consciously turned away from the norms of the *polis*. They were prepared to be sentenced to death as law-breakers, and they honored their martyrs as saints.

Less common was their use of images of the private house (*oikos*) as terms for the church. For Paul, the church is "God's building," the model for which was found in public buildings, such as a temple (1 Cor 3:9–11). Only later, in the Pastoral epistles, does the "private" house become a model. The household, on the other hand, soon became a metaphor for early Christian groups. They formed a *familia dei* (family of God) and called each other brothers and sisters, with the result that this form of address, which was otherwise extremely rare, became an identity-marker among Christians. In general, however, terms for the church only occasionally originated with the private house. After all, the church sought public recognition! At one point especially, they were sharply opposed to the ethos of family and private house: they affirmed an ascetic lifestyle, and Paul considered refraining from marriage preferable to marrying.

So, in their self-understanding, the early Christians did not follow the pattern of associations but modeled themselves on the primary institutions into which one was born, the *ethnos* and *polis*, on the one hand, and the *oikos*, on the other. But they sought to be a quite different *polis* and found themselves in conflict with the real *polis*, even to the point of martyrdom. They wanted to be a *familia dei* (family of God) and withdrew from the earthly family to live an ascetic life. Nonetheless, they did in fact occupy the same social space in the larger community as the associations, between *polis* and *oikos*. In reality, they were closest to the associations (and thus to the related synagogue, mystery cult, and school), whereas in their self-understanding they modeled themselves least on these. Similarities and differences between churches and associations may be summarized as follows:

- The Christians established order within their communities not by means of rules but by means of a group ethos. The lack of close regulation explains the significance of charismatics.
- Shared meals were much more common among Christians than in comparable associations, and they took place in private rooms. This gave ordinary people access to elements of the lifestyle of the upper classes. It was only possible because the willingness to contribute voluntarily to these meals was considerable, and because the meals themselves were modest. Despite the proximity to what went on in other associations (and perhaps for that very reason), Christians despised the festive banquets of others for their extravagance and hedonism.
- Like all other groups, the early Christian churches achieved stability by exchanging respect and honor within the community. At the same time, they cultivated an ethos of status renunciation and humility which placed them in opposition to the ancient culture of honor and shame. On closer inspection, we find among the Christians their own subtle system of honor and respect, one in which the role of wealth and money was systematically reduced. It was not material achievements but the exchange of respect and esteem that led to an internalized system of recognition.

- Christians depended on wealthy benefactors but were careful not to lower themselves to become the social clientele of rich patrons. Rather they cultivated a fundamental criticism of wealth and (in theory at least, even if not always in practice) did not accept patrons who did not participate in church life.
- Christians wanted to be model citizens but kept their distance from the religion-pervaded life of the cities. At the same time, they formed supraregional networks, linking communities in whatever cities they were found. In ethical matters, they sought to exceed common standards and be even better citizens than others, while in religious matters they professed their dissent from the local cults.

The tension between their social self-understanding and the reality of their place in the social structure of their time is in itself part of the social reality of the early Christian churches. This tension brought a degree of unsettledness into their history from the start. Time and again it has inspired social renewal movements in church and society. The origin of this unsettledness lies in the fact that the first Christians were, in terms of their social structure, an association, while in their own self-understanding they were a new creation. As a supraregional community committed to one Lord, they came closest to being a counter-image to the social clientele of the emperor. To this extent, an anti-imperial interpretation of the Pauline communities is justified. But the Roman Empire was not a model for them either – not even a negative model from which they sought to differ. A new creation is more than a counter-society to the Roman Empire.

Note

1   Biblical quotations are taken from the New Revised Standard Version.

References

Alföldy, Geza. 1985. *The Social History of Rome*. Totowa, NJ: Barnes & Noble.

Ascough, Richard S. 2003. *Paul's Macedonian Associations: The Social Context of Philippians and 1 Thessalonians*. Tübingen: Mohr Siebeck.

Barclay, John M. G. 1992. Thessalonica and Corinth: Social Contrasts in Pauline Christianity. *Journal for the Study of the New Testament* 47: 49–74.

Fellmeth, Ulrich. 1990. Politisches Bewusstsein in den Vereinen der städtischen Massen in Rom und Italien zur Zeit der Republik und der frühen Kaiserzeit. *Eirene* 27: 49–71.

Friesen, Steven J. 2004. Poverty in Pauline Studies: Beyond the So-called New Consensus. *Journal for the Study of the New Testament* 26: 323–361.

Gutfeld, Andreas. 1998. Das Vereinigungswesen und die Städte in der römischen Kaiserzeit. Pages 13–33 in *Gesellschaften im Vergleich: Forschungen aus Sozial- und Geschichtswissenschaften*. Edited by Hartmut Kaelble and Jürgen Schriewer. Frankfurt am Main: Peter Lang.

Horrell, David G. 2004. Domestic Space and Christian Meetings at Corinth: Imagining New Contexts and the Buildings East of the Theatre. *New Testament Studies* 50: 349–369.

Kirchhoff, Renate. 1994. *Die Sünde gegen den eigenen Leib*. Göttingen: Vandenhoeck & Ruprecht.

Kloppenborg, John S. 1996. Collegia and *Thiasoi*: Issues in Function, Taxonomy and Membership. Pages 16–30 in *Voluntary Associations in the Graeco-Roman World*. Edited by John S. Kloppenborg and Stephen G. Wilson. London: Routledge.

Lampe, Peter. 1985. Keine "Sklavenflucht" des Onesimus. *Zeitschrift für die neutestamentliche Wissenschaft* 76: 135–137.

Longenecker, Bruce W. 2009. Socio-economic Profiling of the First Urban Christians. Pages 36–59 in *After the First Urban Christians: The Social-scientific Study of Pauline Christianity Twenty-five Years Later*. Edited by Todd D. Still and David G. Horrell. Edinburgh: T. & T. Clark.

Meeks, Wayne A. 1983. *The First Urban Christians: The Social World of the Apostle Paul*. New Haven: Yale University Press.

Meggitt, Justin J. 1998. *Paul, Poverty and Survival*. Edinburgh: T. & T. Clark.

Merz, Annette. 2004. *Die fiktive Selbstauslegung des Paulus: Intertextuelle Studien zur Intention und Rezeption der Pastoralbriefe*. Fribourg: Academic Press; Göttingen: Vandenhoeck & Ruprecht.

Metzner, Rainer. 2008. *Die Prominenten im Neuen Testament: Ein prosopographischer Kommentar*. Göttingen: Vandenhoeck & Ruprecht.

Mödritzer, Helmut. 1994. *Stigma und Charisma im Neuen Testament und seiner Umwelt: zur Soziologie des Urchristentums*. Freiburg: Universitätsverlag; Göttingen: Vandenhoeck & Ruprecht.

Oakes, Peter. 2009. Contours of the Urban Environment. Pages 21–35 in *After the First Urban Christians: The Social-scientific Study of Pauline Christianity Twenty-five Years Later*. Edited by Todd D. Still and David G. Horrell. Edinburgh: T. & T. Clark.

Reynolds, Joyce and Robert Tannenbaum. 1987. *Jews and God-fearers at Aphrodisias: Greek Inscriptions with Commentary*. Cambridge: Cambridge Philological Society.

Richardson, Peter. 1996. Early Synagogues as Collegia in the Diaspora and Palestine. Pages 90–109 in *Voluntary Associations in the Graeco-Roman World*. Edited by John S. Kloppenborg and Stephen G. Wilson. London: Routledge.

Schmeller, Thomas. 1995. *Hierarchie und Egalität: Eine sozialgeschichtliche Untersuchung paulinischer Gemeinden und griechisch-römischer Vereine*. Stuttgart: Katholisches Bibelwerk.

Stark, Rodney. 1996. *The Rise of Christianity: A Sociologist Reconsiders History*. Princeton: Princeton University Press.

Stegemann, Wolfgang. 1987. War der Apostel Paulus ein römischer Bürger? *Zeitschrift für die neutestamentliche Wissenschaft* 78: 200–229.

Theissen, Gerd. 1982a. Legitimation and Subsistence: An Essay on the Sociology of Early Christian Missionaries. Pages 27–67 in Gerd Theissen, *The Social Setting of Pauline Christianity: Essays on Corinth*. Philadelphia: Fortress.

Theissen, Gerd. 1982b. The Strong and the Weak in Corinth: A Sociological Analysis of a Theological Quarrel. Pages 121–143 in Gerd Theissen, *The Social Setting of Pauline Christianity: Essays on Corinth*. Philadelphia: Fortress.

Theissen, Gerd. 1982c. Social Integration and Sacramental Activity: An Analysis of 1 Cor. 11:17–34. Pages 145–174 in Gerd Theissen, *The Social Setting of Pauline Christianity: Essays on Corinth*. Philadelphia: Fortress.

Theissen, Gerd. 2000. *Die Religion der ersten Christen: Eine Theorie des Urchristentums*. Gütersloh: Gütersloher Verlagshaus.

Theissen, Gerd. 2001. The Social Structure of Pauline Communities: Some Critical Remarks on J. J. Meggitt, *Paul, Poverty and Survival*. *Journal for the Study of the New Testament* 24: 65–84.

Theissen, Gerd. 2003. Social Conflicts in the Corinthian Community: Further Remarks on J. J. Meggitt, *Paul, Poverty and Survival*. *Journal for the Study of the New Testament* 25: 371–391.

Theissen, Gerd. 2004. *Die Jesusbewegung: Sozialgeschichte einer Revolution der Werte.* Gütersloh: Gütersloher Verlagshaus.

Theissen, Gerd. 2007. Urchristliche Gemeinden und antike Vereine: Sozialdynamik im Urchristentum durch Widersprüche zwischen Selbstverständnis und Sozialstruktur. Pages 221–247 in *In Other Words: Essays on Social Science Methods and the New Testament in Honor of Jerome H. Neyrey.* Edited by Anselm C. Hagedorn, Zeba A. Crook, and Eric Stewart. Sheffield: Phoenix.

Theissen, Gerd. 2008. Kirche oder Sekte? Über Einheit und Konflikt im frühen Urchristentum. Pages 81–101 in *Einheit der Kirche im Neuen Testament: Dritte europäische orthodox-westliche Exegetenkonferenz in Sankt Petersburg 24–31 August 2005.* Edited by Anatoly A. Alexeev, Christos Karakolis, and Ulrich Luz. Tübingen: Mohr Siebeck.

Theissen, Gerd. 2009. Die Gegenmission zu Paulus in Galatien, Philippi und Korinth: Versuch einer Einheitsdeutung. Pages 277–306 in *Beiträge zur urchristlichen Theologiegeschichte.* Edited by Wolfgang Kraus. Berlin: Walter de Gruyter.

Wong, Eric. 2002. The Deradicalization of Jesus' Ethical Sayings in 1 Corinthians. *New Testament Studies* 48: 181–194.

Wuellner, W. H. 1973. The Sociological Implications of 1 Corinthians 1:26–28 Reconsidered. *Studia Evangelica* 6: 666–672.

CHAPTER 17

Women in the Pauline Churches

Margaret Y. MacDonald

Some of the most precious information we have about the importance of women to the origins of Christianity comes from Paul's letters. Over the past twenty-five years in particular, scholars have sought to untangle and resolve contradictory impressions and ambiguities in Paul's thought concerning women and gender. On the one hand, the apostle is well known for encouraging the women prophets of 1 Corinthians 11:2–16 to cover their heads and for silencing wives who persistently ask questions during church assemblies in 1 Corinthians 14:34–35. On the other hand, it is to Paul's letters that people turn for evidence of women's leadership, particularly to the description of the "deacon" Phoebe (Rom 16:1) or the "apostle" Junia (Rom 16:7). While it would be overstating the case to say that contrary impressions and ambiguities have been eradicated by New Testament scholars, it is certainly true that there have been great advances in our understanding of women in Pauline communities. These advances fall into three main categories, which will be discussed in turn: (1) women, manuscript evidence, and translation; (2) female collaborators and leaders in their Jewish and Greco-Roman settings; (3) Paul's pronouncements on women and gender.

Women, Manuscript Evidence, and Translation

Translation and Phoebe's role

Modern biblical translation has been greatly affected by research on early Christian women. As a case in point, we might consider the shift from the Revised Standard Version (RSV) to the New Revised Standard Version (NRSV) with respect to terminology used to describe Phoebe (Rom 16:1–2). While the RSV describes Phoebe as a "deaconess

The Blackwell Companion to Paul, First Edition. Edited by Stephen Westerholm.
© 2011 Blackwell Publishing Ltd. Published 2011 by Blackwell Publishing Ltd.

of the church at Cenchreae," the NRSV prefers "deacon of the church at Cenchreae." Similarly, the RSV calls Phoebe "a helper of many," but the NRSV calls Phoebe "a benefactor of many."[1] At issue here is the translation of two Greek terms.

The first term is *diakonos*. The translation of this term as "deaconess" is now generally considered incorrect for it conflates Phoebe's role with the institution of the deaconess (*diakonissa*) that emerged around the beginning of the fourth century CE and was seemingly restricted to women devoted to ministry among other women, including service to the poor and sick, assistance at baptisms, and religious instruction (see, for example, the *Didascalia Apostolorum* and the *Apostolic Constitutions*).[2] But in Romans 16:1–2, Paul uses *diakonos* (deacon) with the feminine article. This is the same term that later became used for office-holders (including men) at the beginning of the second century in some early Christian groups; the development involved a formal organizational framework with bishops, presbyters, and deacons. We cannot read this situation back into Paul's usage, but even in Paul's communities the term could refer to some type of official role. Paul can use the term to refer to general (though clearly important) ministerial/service tasks undertaken by himself and his co-workers (for example, 1 Cor 3:5; 2 Cor 3:6; 6:4; 11:23), but also in a way that suggests some type of office or function in the local community (cf. the *diakonoi* of Phil 1:1 [listed with the *episkopoi*]). The use of this plural designation in Philippians 1:1 should not be taken as a reference to an all-male group, especially in light of the reference to Phoebe's role (Madigan and Osiek 2005, 11–12). Early evidence (around the beginning of the second century CE) for the existence of female deacons comes from 1 Timothy 3:11, which may refer either to the wives of male deacons or to female deacons; early church commentators on the text favored the latter (Madigan and Osiek 2005, 11). Moreover, most commentators have taken the Roman governor of Bithynia's reference to the *ministrae*, Christian slave women whom he had interrogated and tortured, as a reference to women deacons (Pliny, *Letters* 10.96).

The second key leadership term to refer to Phoebe that has been translated in various ways is *prostatis*. Paul does not grant this title to anyone else in his correspondence, and it is clear that he holds this woman in high esteem. In translating the term as "benefactor" or "patron," scholars are drawing attention to the influence of the structures of patronage on the relationships between Phoebe, Paul, and the early church communities. The term may indicate that Phoebe is a relatively well-to-do person to whom Paul and church members (acting as clients) are indebted for social and economic support (Jewett 2007, 947). Thus, rather than the more informal "helper," the NRSV translation of "benefactor" better captures the more formal, reciprocal, cultural expectations characterizing the exchanges between Phoebe, the apostle, and other believers (see next section).

Nympha, Junia, and manuscript variation

Sometimes translation is affected directly by manuscript variation. In the past number of years, textual critics of the New Testament (those scholars who study the numerous Greek manuscripts and citations in early church writings upon which any translation is based) have increasingly been concerned with variant readings concerning gender issues (Epp 2005, 14–20). Sometimes the focus is on whether a listed individual is male or female and the possible "masculinization" of the manuscript tradition. A fairly straightforward example of this can be seen in the manuscript evidence concerning Nympha, the woman leader of the house church mentioned in Colossians 4:15. Modern translations now generally adopt the reading "*Nympha* and the church in *her* house" (following *Codex Vaticanus*) rather than the (also widely attested) reading "*Nymphas* [a man] and the church in *his* house." It is not difficult in this case to detect a motive for the masculinization attested in much of the manuscript tradition. Any uncertainty about the name would have been compounded by discomfort – in generations beyond the Pauline era, when women's leadership became more circumscribed – about a woman at the head of a house church. (A third variant reading referred to the plural, "their [*autōn*] house," apparently in an effort to include the "brothers" listed in Colossians 4:15 in house-church leadership, or perhaps to cast Nymphas as a married householder [cf. Phlm 1–2; Margaret Y. MacDonald 2000, 183].)

More controversial, if not more complicated, with respect to manuscript evidence, translation, and interpretation is the case of Junia/Junias in Romans 16:7. Are the pair mentioned in this verse and described as "prominent among the apostles" two male missionary partners, Andronicus and Junias? Or are they man and woman, most probably husband and wife, Andronicus and Junia – a pair not unlike Prisca and Aquila? A recent thorough investigation by Elden Jay Epp (2005) has settled the case quite conclusively (though debate will no doubt continue): Junia was a woman and she was an apostle (on the meaning of "apostle" here, see next section). There are some parallels with the case of Nympha described above, but the manuscript evidence is actually far more consistent. In manuscripts that lacked the Greek accents (as most did for the first seven centuries of early Christianity), the Greek name used could refer to either a woman (Junia) or a man (Junias, sometimes taken to be the shortened form of the Greek name *Junianos* or the Latin name *Iunianus* [Epp 2005, 23]), but the evidence that the name is Junia and refers to a woman is overwhelming. A very common Roman name, Junia was the reading accepted by the church authors of late antiquity without exception; in contrast, there is no evidence for the masculine forms of the name Junias from this era. Where accentuation occurs in the manuscripts, the female name Junia consistently appears (though a few manuscripts refer to Julia, also a woman). With only rare exceptions from the medieval period until the modern day, Romans 16:7 was taken to refer to a male and female pair. As Epp's careful work demonstrates, the reading of Andronicus's partner as male is largely a twentieth-century phenomenon, seemingly based on the assumption that a woman could not be an apostle. In the foreword to Epp's volume (2005, xi), Beverly Gaventa expresses the situation sharply and succinctly: "Even now ... the NRSV offers 'Junias' in the footnotes, and the NIV presents 'Junias' with no further comment, leaving Andronicus with a male partner for whom there is no ancient evidence whatsoever."

To understand Romans 16:7 as a reference to Andronicus and Junia does not settle the question of the woman's influence, for the phrase "prominent among the apostles" has been subject to two competing interpretations: either Andronicus and Junia are themselves distinguished members of the apostles, or they are well known among the apostles (but not apostles themselves). Both interpretations are strictly possible on the basis of the grammar of the phrase, and a recent thorough discussion examining Greek databases (Burer and Wallace 2001) has argued in favor of the latter. In his detailed analysis, however, Epp highlighted several problems with the examples discussed in this study and noted the meager data overall (Epp 2005, 72–78). Especially important, according to Epp, are the early church readings of the text, most notably that of John Chrysostom, who understands Andronicus and Junia as distinguished members of the apostles and draws clear attention to Junia's apostolic role: "Indeed, how great the wisdom of this woman must have been that she was even deemed worthy of the title of apostle" (*Commentary on Romans* 31.2; cited in Epp 2005, 32).[3]

1 Corinthians 14:34–35 as an interpolation

Textual criticism of the New Testament has also played a role in theories concerning interpolation within letters (i.e., theories concerning additions to original texts). This is especially true with respect to 1 Corinthians 14:34–35 (or 1 Cor 14:33b–36; see further below). At issue is the fact that some manuscripts place these verses after verse 40 (on the manuscript tradition, see Epp 2005, 15–20, who favors the interpolation theory). The uncompromising call for women to be silent in church, which is sometimes viewed as disturbing the flow of the argument, coupled with the apparent contradiction with 1 Corinthians 11:2–16, where the participation of women in prayer and prophecy (oral practices in the early church) is presumed, have led many scholars to believe that these verses were a later intrusion and most likely not written by Paul. It has often been suggested that a later scribe may have desired to bring Paul's more egalitarian position in line with the more restrictive teaching of the Pastoral epistles (for example, 1 Tim 2:12). Despite the dislocation in some manuscripts, however, the most important argument against the interpolation theory is the presence of the verses in all manuscripts. Arguably the two most important volumes on women, gender, and 1 Corinthians in the past twenty years (Wire 1990, 230–231; Økland 2004, 149–152) have supported the contention that 1 Corinthians 11:2–16 and 1 Corinthians 14:34–35 are not as contradictory as they might first appear and have favored Paul's authorship of 1 Corinthians 14:34–35. Økland has argued, for example, that what Paul says elsewhere in 1 Corinthians about the ritually constructed space of the *ekklēsia* (for example, 1 Cor 11:17–34) is congruent with 1 Corinthians 14:34–35 (see discussion below). Nevertheless, the issues remain vigorously debated among scholars.

Female Collaborators and Leaders in their Jewish and Greco-Roman Settings

Despite some scribal efforts to masculinize the texts, and persistent reluctance on the part of some translators to recognize the influence of women as on par with the influence of men (see previous section), one of the major findings of the past quarter-century is that Paul's named female collaborators are not presented as playing a lesser role than his male co-workers. Yet this statement has increasingly been tempered by an important warning not to overstate the implications of these findings. While it is true that as the church moved into later generations and centuries, leadership roles for women were restricted in certain places at varying times, the earliest era of the Pauline churches should not be presented as a golden age of Christian egalitarianism with unique opportunities for women. Scholars are increasingly convinced that women such as Phoebe or Junia, who seemingly had a good measure of social freedom, reflect advances in social freedom and public visibility that were happening already in certain places in the Empire in the first century CE (see Winter 2003). In many respects, these women were continuing in the roles they had as pagan and Jewish women before they entered believing communities. At the same time, it is important not to lose sight of the very real risks women undertook in joining these fledgling communities, which in some respects represented a counter-cultural movement.

Reports from Chloe's people

Of the named women in Paul's letters, we should begin with the one whose believing identity is in question, despite the fact that she clearly held some type of leadership role in relation to the Corinthians. The brief reference to Chloe in 1 Corinthians 1:11 introduces us to many elements that are important for understanding the lives of the women mentioned in Paul's letters. Writing from Ephesus, Paul tells us that among the factors that led him to write his letter to the Corinthians was a report made by "Chloe's people" of divisions in the community. They have evidently either written to Paul from Corinth or traveled to the apostle bearing news. At the outset, we should note the association of a woman with communication, an association we will see again in other references.

The expression "Chloe's people" literally means the "ones belonging to Chloe." This likely indicates that Chloe is at the head of a household, which in the Roman world means an extended household made up not only of immediate family, but also of varying numbers of slaves, freedpersons (slaves who continued to have obligations to their former owners after they had been manumitted), and even clients and dependent workers. In fact, historians of the Roman family have sometimes preferred the term "houseful" rather than "household" to indicate that the range of people associated with a given dwelling extended beyond kinship (for example, Wallace-Hadrill 1994). Chloe could be one of the relatively well-to-do women described in the New Testament who offered important services to the burgeoning church communities; the "ones belonging to her" would be household slaves, former slaves, or workers whom she has sent out as envoys or who for some reason (perhaps business and trade) are passing through Ephesus on the way to another destination. It is also possible that Chloe herself is not a believer, though a large number of her household are. In this case, it is also possible that Chloe's people have written to Paul – if Chloe were a believer, we would expect a written report to come from "Chloe and her people" (Osiek and MacDonald 2006, 217). It is interesting to note, however, that there is no reference to the church meeting in the house (*oikos*) of Chloe, unlike the case of Nympha (Col 4:15). Although one cannot be certain on the basis of the terminology, this could indicate that Chloe's people gather in simple and fairly cramped accommodation (see Osiek and MacDonald 2006, 9), perhaps in one or two rooms over a shop, rather than in an independent house structure of various possible proportions (a peristyled *domus*, or building with a colonnade). Increasingly, scholars are making the case for a variety of possible housing arrangements for these first believers, including very modest circumstances such as those sometimes found in ancient apartment complexes, known as *insulae* (see, for example, Jewett 1993; Horrell 2004).

Women patrons: Chloe and Phoebe

Chloe's role should also be explored with respect to the role of women patrons in Pauline communities. The phenomenon of patronage in ancient Roman society has long been of interest to historians and is now of central importance to biblical scholars. In general terms, patron–client relations involved reciprocal obligations (exchange of goods and services) between people of unequal power: the relationships were asymmetrical (though sometimes they could take place between near equals) and voluntary. Clients could expect economic and political benefits such as gifts of food, dinner invitations, hospitality, favorable recommendations, and sometimes even cash, loans, or gifts of property. In return, patrons expected loyalty and such things as votes, public praise, and support (Osiek and MacDonald 2006, 195–196). Patrons, including women patrons, could be members of the elite, but they could also be people of more modest means involved in business and trade. For example, Lydia, the merchant trader who dealt in purple, seems to have been the patron of a group of believers who met in Philippi (Acts 16:14–15, 40; Ascough 2009, 52–57).

In addition to personal patronage, the phenomenon of public patronage (or euergetism) is of particular importance for the study of the women named in Paul's letters. This involved the relationship of one dominant person to a group of social inferiors such as "a professional guild, a club, a group of the poor, the devotees of a private religion, or a city" (Osiek and MacDonald 2006, 198). Often these women are commemorated with inscriptions and public statues. Julia Severa of Acmonia in Phrygia, who held a number of distinguished priesthoods and city offices, donated property to the local synagogue; two of the synagogue's leaders (*archons*) were likely her freedmen or clients (*Corpus inscriptionum iudaicarum* 2.766; *Monumenta Asiae Minoris Antiqua* 6.264). If "Chloe's people" were her clients, it is possible that as someone who was not herself a member of the Pauline community, she sponsored their religious activities in much the same way as non-Jewish women like Julia Severa sometimes offered patronage to synagogues. Eumachia, the public priestess of Pompeii, is an especially well-known female patron from the Roman world; she was the patroness of the fullers' guild, which even erected a dedicatory statue with an inscription in her honor (*Corpus inscriptionum latinarum* 10.810, 811, 813). The efforts of Junia Theodora of first-century Corinth have often been compared to Pauline women, especially Phoebe, the female church leader from Cenchreae, the seaport of Corinth (Kearsley 1999). Originally from Lycia, she is praised for offering hospitality to traveling Lycians and facilitating their relationship with Roman authorities: "The decree of the Lycian city of Telmessos speaks of her *prostasia* (patronal leadership) in the context of hospitality and mediation. Because of her location in first-century Corinth and because of the use of the word *prostasia* for her activity, Junia Theodora is an important comparative figure for the work of Phoebe *prostatis* in Rom 16:1–2" (Osiek and MacDonald 2006, 207; see 203–219; on the translation of *prostatis*, see previous section). Phoebe's activities offer perhaps the most important evidence for women's leadership in the Pauline churches.

Despite the overlap in terminology, however, the dynamics of patronage do not seem to completely explain the relationships between Paul, Phoebe, and church members. Certain elements are maintained, but others seem to be reversed or at least qualified. On the one hand, Paul seems to acknowledge Phoebe as his patron (*prostatis*) and the patron of others as well. This suggests that Paul and others are dependent upon her in some ways. Phoebe may have acted as host to the community (though she is not explicitly named as a leader of a house church), offering hospitality to Paul and to traveling members of the Pauline churches, much as Junia Theodora did for traveling Lycians. Given that Phoebe was a woman of means, Paul would probably have been dependent upon her to expand his mission in Cenchreae or elsewhere (Margaret Y. MacDonald 1999, 209). Robert Jewett (1988) has argued that Paul may even have viewed Phoebe as a central player in his Spanish mission. Evidently traveling to Rome bearing Paul's letter (Rom 16:1–2 appears to reflect the conventional practice of ancient letters, including praise for their bearers), Phoebe, Jewett suggests, is central to Paul's plan to garner support in Rome for the next stage of his mission (Jewett 1988, 151–153). Indeed, such connotations of mediation and connection might also fit with Paul's label of Phoebe as a deacon, a leadership term about which there is very little information in the early period (see previous section), but which may point to a role in representing one church to another (cf. Ignatius, *Letter to the Philadelphians* 10.1; see Osiek and MacDonald 2006, 215). Certainly, the way that Phoebe is praised suggests that she was influential as a local church leader, but her leadership extended to the broader Pauline mission.

On the other hand, there is also a sense in which Paul seems to act as Phoebe's patron. He recommends her, and she appears to be dependent upon him for access to the Roman community, or perhaps to extend her influence in the community. The relationship seems to be more one of mutual dependence than the asymmetry that one expects with patronage; this leads Carolyn F. Whelan (one of a minority of scholars who view Romans 16 as a separate letter originally intended for Ephesus) to characterize the relationship as mutual patronage (Whelan 1993, 84–85). In any case, for Paul acting as a client to recommend his patron Phoebe would be very unusual in the ancient world (although sometimes such dynamics did exist between near equals, but almost never between men and women), unless the explanation lies in her entry into new territory: Phoebe is moving into new territory where Paul already has influence, and Paul for his part sees her role as vital to his greater plan (Osiek and MacDonald 2006, 216). Or perhaps such mutuality has something to do ultimately with the questioning of contemporary standards of power and prestige that occurs in various ways in Paul's letters, notably in 1 Corinthians, where the apostle expresses independence and clarifies a situation in which he might appear to be entangled in a relationship of personal patronage (for example, 1 Cor 1:14–17; see Murphy-O'Connor 1996, 305–307; Osiek and MacDonald 2006, 212). Elements of the dominant culture are being absorbed, reshaped, and critiqued at the same time.

Missionaries and missionary partnerships

Phoebe is one of ten women mentioned in the final chapter of Romans, where Paul sends a variety of greetings to men and women: Phoebe, Prisca, Mary, Junia, Tryphaena, Tryphosa, Persis, the unnamed mother of Rufus, Julia, and the unnamed "sister of Nereus." One is struck by the variety of possible relational contributions to the broader Pauline mission (D'Angelo 1990). Some women, like Phoebe, are singled out alone, but others are part of missionary partnerships that might involve two women, such as Tryphaena and Tryphosa (Rom 16:12; cf. Phil 4:2–3), or a man and woman, but not necessarily husband and wife; in Romans 16:13, for example, Paul greets Rufus and "his mother and mine." Three of the missionary partnerships, however, have usually been understood as husband and wife: Prisca and Aquila (v. 3); Andronicus and Junia (v. 7; on the identity of Junia, see previous section); Philogus and Julia (v. 15).

The reference to the active leadership of married couples in Paul's churches has been examined by scholars from a variety of angles, especially in light of Paul's own preference for celibacy articulated in 1 Corinthians 7 and his renunciation of the right to be accompanied by a sister as wife (*adelphēn gynaika*; *gynē* can be translated to mean either wife or woman) in 1 Corinthians 9:5. We should probably understand Paul's renunciation here as referring not merely to a wife as helpmate, but to a missionary partnership with a woman; like the term "brother," the term "sister" can be used simply to denote membership in the *ekklēsia*, but it is also one of several terms used to denote leadership, as the reference to "our sister Phoebe" in Romans 16:1 suggests and as may also be the case with Apphia (Phlm 2), a woman who has often been understood as Philemon's wife, but without enough textual evidence to justify such a claim (Margaret Y. MacDonald 1999, 206). Ultimately, Paul's language in 1 Corinthians 9:5 complicates our understanding of the references to male–female pairs, for it raises the possibility that such associations between men and women may not have been simply the natural extensions of existing marriages, but may have included arrangements made specifically for some ministerial purpose, or even partnerships shaped to provide celibate leadership. Although definitive evidence for the existence of spiritual marriages (marriages involving co-habitation with no sexual relations) comes from significantly later, some scholars have pointed to 1 Corinthians 7:36–38 as offering early evidence for the practice, and have even viewed the missionary couples in Paul's letters as living out such arrangements.[4]

On the other hand, scholars engaged in the study of families in the New Testament world have cautioned against interpretations that remove these missionary couples from the complexities of family life in the Roman world. Despite the lack of specific marital terminology (Prisca is explicitly identified as Aquila's wife only in Acts [see Acts 18:2, 18, 26, where she is called Priscilla]), on balance it seems most likely that the missionary couples were understood as married couples within the Pauline movement, and some were almost certainly already married at the time of their admission to church groups. With very few exceptions (cf. 1 Cor 7:14), references to real children are conspicuously absent from Paul's letters despite the extensive metaphorical references to children, infants, and parenting (for example, Phlm 10; Gal 4:19; 1 Thess 2:7). Nevertheless, given the almost complete lack of effectiveness of ancient birth control, it is probable that at least some of the missionary pairs conducted their work as parents of children (Osiek and MacDonald 2006, 28). We should also bear in mind, however, that when Paul addresses the married and unmarried in 1 Corinthians 7 and refers to missionary partners, he is likely not referring to legal marriages in the strict sense of the term; capacity for legal marriage in the Empire existed only between two free citizens, was subject to restrictions between certain classes and categories of people, and was ruled out for slaves altogether (Gardner 1986, 31–44). Slave funerary inscriptions indicate, however, that marital terminology was used to describe their alliances despite the legal situation, and serve as a reminder that family realities are often much more complex than legal codes and idealized textual descriptions would lead us to believe (Martin 2003).

Two married women leaders: Junia and Prisca

Whatever their precise familial circumstances may have been, Junia and Prisca have certainly attracted significant attention as two "married" women leaders in the Pauline churches. Both women were likely Jews. Paul describes both Andronicus and Junia as relatives, which could mean that they were actually members of his family or, more broadly, fellow Jews. The Jewish identity of Prisca is made explicit in Acts along with several other biographical details not supplied by Paul himself, including the expulsion of the couple from Rome (they later returned), their instruction of Apollos, and their involvement in the same leather-working/tent-making craft as Paul (cf. Acts 18:1–3, 18–19:1). Both women are leaders who took significant risks: the greetings that Paul extends to them in Romans 16 are replete with verbs that speak of labor and precarious activities for the sake of the gospel. Interest in Junia has mainly centered on her identity as an apostle (see discussion of textual and manuscript issues in the previous section). Admittedly, the term apostle (*apostolos*) had a broad range of meaning in Paul's letters, from a special identity based on witnessing resurrection appearances and receiving a commission (1 Cor 15:5–9) to simply being a messenger or emissary of the church (2 Cor 8:23). The sense of the term that fits most closely with the missionary themes shaping the greeting to Andronicus and Junia, however, is that of itinerant preachers of the gospel (2 Cor 11:4–6, 13; 12:11–12; Osiek and MacDonald 2006, 226).

In the case of Prisca, such work for the gospel is conducted in conjunction with leadership of a house church. Scholars with an interest in the study of early Christian families have highlighted the significance of house-church leadership on the part of women, either alone or as part of a couple (Margaret Y. MacDonald 2006; Osiek and MacDonald 2006, 157–159). In addition to Prisca, the Pauline epistles include the reference to Nympha, who hosts an *ekklēsia* in her house (Col 4:15); and Acts suggests that the house of Mary (12:12–17) and that of Lydia (16:14–15, 40) served as bases for the movement. Running households and hosting house churches independently (without male partners) might well also have been undertaken by Phoebe (Rom 16:1–2) and Euodia and Syntyche (Phil 4:2–3), but this must be inferred from references to resources and the use of leadership titles in these texts and is not stated explicitly. The leadership of Euodia and Syntyche seems particularly similar to that of Prisca in that these women are clearly local leaders (in fact, their membership in the group of *episkopoi* and *diakonoi* mentioned in Philippians 1:1 cannot be excluded; see previous section and Osiek 2000), and they are associated with danger and mission: these women are described as co-workers who fought (*synathleō*, a verb often translated as "to labor," but one that recalls war or the violent contests of the games) side by side with Paul in the gospel (Phil 4:3).

The merging of household and church spaces raises numerous questions, including whether the house-church base of earliest Christianity enhanced opportunities for women's leadership or, alternatively, restricted women's behavior in various ways (see next section). With respect to the house-church leadership of Prisca (and Aquila), one of the most interesting features is its transient nature. Prisca and her partner traveled between, and took up residence in, three major cities of the Roman Empire: Rome, Ephesus, and Corinth. Paul's letters indicate that they were hosts to house churches in Ephesus and Rome (1 Cor 16:19; Rom 16:3–5), and the fact that they offered hospitality to Paul in Corinth (Acts 18:2–3) suggests that they played the same role in that city. Like Paul, Prisca and Aquila were migrant craftspeople, but seemingly unlike Paul, they also sought fairly permanent domestic home bases. In studying the situation of foreigners at Rome, David Noy notes that the New Testament evidence concerning Prisca and Aquila offers one of the most complete records of migration for people of their status, indicating both the need to travel long distances and to make contacts and organize new living arrangements (Noy 2000, 259). Initially at least, the meeting place of believers might have been something as simple as a rented room in an inn; in the case of Prisca and Aquila, arrangements for accommodation may have been in place before their arrival in a given city (cf. Acts 28:15) in an establishment or house owned by a fellow Jew. In all likelihood, Prisca's influence was front and center in making these arrangements.

Prisca was a wife, artisan, missionary, and foreign immigrant. As such, she combined aspects of life traditionally associated with the male (public) sphere and female (private) sphere. Scholars drawing upon insights from cultural anthropology concerning power and gender have pointed out that even meeting traditional expectations and performing traditional duties can sometimes open up routes to power for women (Osiek and MacDonald 2006, 34–35). Although it is not explicit in the sources, Prisca may have facilitated missionary access to women, including the young women who chose to remain virgins (1 Cor 7) or the wives of non-believers who turn up in communities as early as Paul's letters (1 Cor 7:12–16; 1 Pet 3:1–2; see further in next section).

There are other explicit features of Prisca's profile that should not be neglected. Her name frequently appears before that of her husband (Acts 18:18, 26; Rom 16:3); this is usually understood as an indication of her higher social status, but may also offer testimony to her success as a missionary and teacher. One of these references unmistakably presents her as a teacher on par with her husband in taking Apollos aside and explaining "the Way of God to him more accurately" (Acts 18:26). Admittedly, recent scholarship on Acts has highlighted the complexity of drawing historical conclusions about the women of Acts given, for example, the author's propensity to stress the association of prominent women with the movement and the respectability of household arrangements (for example, Lieu 1998). Could the emphasis in Acts on the mutuality in responsibilities and partnership of Prisca and Aquila be a means of emphasizing Prisca's status as a respectable, married woman? But despite any attempt on the part of the author of Acts to shape Prisca's legacy, her impact was so great that she was celebrated as one of Paul's key fellow workers in three bodies of literature: the undisputed letters of Paul, Acts, and the Pastoral epistles. Memories of Prisca stretched forward into the decades leading into the second century as her name is included in the greetings found at the end of 2 Timothy (2 Tim 4:19).

Paul's Pronouncements on Women and Gender

When we turn to the few texts where Paul addresses the situation of women in general terms (as opposed to references to specific women), we move into material which has been of great interest not only to scholars undertaking historical studies of the New Testament, but also to those engaged in New Testament theology. In addition to highlighting the important role of female collaborators in Paul's mission and the capacity for women to exercise leadership, Elisabeth Schüssler Fiorenza's groundbreaking work *In Memory of Her: A Feminist Theological Reconstruction of Christian Origins* (1983) included an analysis of Paul's pronouncements on women and gender that set the stage for many subsequent discussions. A key theme in Fiorenza's work has been that historical reconstruction for its own sake is not enough; she has highlighted the necessity of discussing the ethical, political, and theological dimensions of texts: "I seek to work out a process and method for a feminist political reading that can empower women who, for whatever reasons, are still affected by the Bible to 'read against the grain' of its patriarchal rhetoric" (Fiorenza 1992, 7). Probably more than any other feminist scholar, Fiorenza has considered the broader implications for church and society of the interpretation of Pauline texts on women and gender. The interpretation of contentious texts on women, marriage, and sexuality in the Pauline epistles sharply raises the question of scriptural authority (Fiorenza 1992, 149; Castelli 1999, 233). Within feminist research, there is no consensus on the role of the canon of Scripture (Margaret Y. MacDonald 2006) with respect to the interpretive enterprise. Should feminist commentaries on Pauline literature, for example, include the treatment of the apocryphal *Acts of Thecla*, which offers interesting evidence concerning female initiative, and which many argue comes from the same period as the Pastoral epistles?[5] Even if we confine ourselves to the canon of the New Testament, feminist scholars have scrutinized Paul's claims of authority and have questioned the extent to which he should remain at the center of interpretation. One of the major issues of debate has been the extent to which Paul's pronouncements can offer insight into real women's lives.

I Corinthians, women, and gender

Recently, scholars have been expanding the scope of the discussion on women and gender to include not only texts that specifically refer to women, but also discourse that implicitly has a bearing on gender construction and its place within Paul's thought world. In particular, 1 Corinthians 11:2–16 has been judged to offer key insight into the shape of 1 Corinthians as a whole. Building upon earlier work employing rhetorical analysis to interpret 1 Corinthians (for example, Fiorenza 1987), in her influential 1990 study Antoinette Clark Wire sought to explore the rhetorical situation created by Paul's arguments, often coming to a more complex picture of the historical circumstances of the Corinthian correspondence. At the center of this rhetorical situation were the presence and initiative of women, including their ability to challenge Paul.

As New Testament students quickly note, Paul's argumentation in 1 Corinthians 11:2–16 is somewhat convoluted and contradictory. Drawing upon the creation account in Genesis, Paul seems to oscillate between a divinely ordained hierarchy shaping relations between man and woman and an acknowledgment of fundamental equality before God. Although it is a minority position, to some Paul's argumentation has seemed so convoluted that the passage has been deemed a non-Pauline interpolation (i.e., a later addition to the manuscript tradition). Even more popular is the view, based upon the apparent incongruity between 1 Corinthians 11:2–16 and 1 Corinthians 14:34–35 with respect to the capacity of women to speak, that 1 Corinthians 14:34–35 is a later interpolation (some argue that all of 1 Cor 14:33b–36 is an interpolation; see above). Wire, like many feminist interpreters, however, has opted for reading the text as a whole, arguing in favor of the textual integrity of the work. In essence, Wire argues that the women in Corinth who removed their head coverings (whether veils or hairstyles are in view remains debated; see Økland 2004, 190) did so as women prophets with a theology of the Spirit whereby they claimed "direct access to resurrected life in Christ through God's spirit" (Wire 1990, 185). This challenged Paul's own theological vision and authority. Of particular importance is that Wire reads all of 1 Corinthians from the perspective of the women prophets. While some have critiqued her for importing women into Paul's purview when it is not explicitly warranted by the text, her work comes as an important corrective in the history of scholarship, which has assumed that women are excluded from Paul's field of vision (see Margaret Y. MacDonald 2004).

This same tendency to analyze 1 Corinthians 11:2–16 within a broader textual unit can be seen in the recent work of Jorunn Økland, who examines 1 Corinthians 11–14 in a study of Paul's exhortations concerning women's ritual roles and ritual clothing (Økland 2004, 1). Økland has argued that the Corinthian discourse of gender functions to create sanctuary space that is potentially at odds with the aspirations and faith commitments of women of the community (though her focus is much more on Paul's own discourse than on the women themselves). She writes: "the result of Paul's outline of a mimetic hierarchy in 11.1–3 is the gendering of the *ekklesia* space as primarily a male space. What woman represents, does not have any place on the higher levels of the hierarchy, which are male places: God, Christ, Paul, Corinthian men. Woman can still be present if she keeps her place on the bottom of the hierarchy" (Økland 2004, 178). It is partly her reading of 1 Corinthians 11:2–16 within a broader textual unit that allows Økland to link the passage so firmly with sanctuary space. She finds support in 1 Corinthians 11:22 and (especially) 14:32–34 for the view that Paul distinguishes between the space of assembly, where women should keep silent, and the space of the household, where women can ask their husbands questions. Within the *ekklēsia* space, "there is a particular pattern of action and a particular place for everything following a cosmic order" (Økland 2004, 151).

For Økland, it is the ritual setting of 1 Corinthians 11–14 that is especially signifi-cant and helps to explain why Paul speaks about gender on a cosmological level in 1 Corinthians 11:2–16, establishing boundaries and hierarchies. An understanding of the ritual setting may also help explain why Paul can hold such views and continue to endorse (contradictorily, from a modern perspective) the active roles of his female fellow workers (Økland 2004, 178). Ritual has figured prominently in the interpretation of other key Pauline texts that refer to women, interpretations that at times draw connec-tions to the material in 1 Corinthians 11:2–16. The proclamation of unity in Galatians 3:28 (referring to Jew/Greek, slave/free, male/female), which is often understood as a pre-Pauline baptismal formula, has frequently been linked to the activity of the women prophets of 1 Corinthians 11:2–16; the passage is viewed as indicative of the type of theology that may have inspired them. Galatians 3:28 is one of a series of texts, some of which are associated with Jesus himself, that link salvation with the unification of opposites (especially male and female) and that are often interpreted as a call to a celi-bate lifestyle, transcending sexuality (i.e., where there is literally no "male and female"); such texts include the *Gospel of the Egyptians* as cited in Clement of Alexandria, *Miscellanies* 3.13.92; *2 Clement* 12.2; and *Gospel of Thomas* 37, 21a, 22b (see Denis Ronald MacDonald 1987; Margaret Y. MacDonald 1990; Fatum 1991). It is also fre-quently noted (and seen as not a coincidence) that Paul does not refer to the male–female distinction in 1 Corinthians 12:13, an omission that may suggest apprehension on his part about how such language would be interpreted in Corinth. Paul's treatment of the relations between Jews and Gentiles indicates that he understood baptismal proclamations of unity to have social implications, but what those implications might be for the slave–master relationship as well as the female–male relationship is far from clear and remains heavily debated among scholars. Whatever conclusions we might draw, for example, from Paul's carefully worded appeal to Philemon on behalf of the slave Onesimus, or his openness to female collaborators such as Phoebe, Paul certainly did not call for the complete abolition of patriarchal hierarchies in the social realm. Moreover, in 1 Corinthians 7 he is markedly reserved about changes to status in light of the rapidly approaching *parousia*. In this text, Paul displays a preference for celibacy for men and women, but also is concerned to avoid sexual renunciation as a permanent option for married couples or for those who do not possess this particular gift.

Paul's advice in 1 Corinthians 7 seems to have been intended to moderate some ascetic extremism in Corinth and may well be in response to the authority of the spirit-possessed – especially if, as has often been suggested, the women prophets of 1

Corinthians 11:2–16 included mainly celibate women.[6] Yet their very importance for the community and their very ability to be women of considerable power could also be related to the traditional function of virgins and monogamous brides to represent the shame (i.e., the concern for reputation) of the house or community in ancient Mediterranean culture (Margaret Y. MacDonald 1996, 144–154). Consider Paul's retort in 1 Corinthians 7:40, which was probably directed at widows who may have harbored more radical ascetical leanings than Paul himself: "I think that I too have the Spirit of God." As is highlighted by the metaphorical language used by the author of Ephesians to describe the *ekklēsia* as a church-bride, the sexual purity of women was a potent symbol of community identity (Eph 5:25–27). In 1 Corinthians 7, Paul makes several parallel statements concerning men and women, but careful reading points to a particular concern for the behavior of women (see Margaret Y. MacDonald 1990; Wire 1990, 82–90). There are several categories: unmarried women, virgins, divorcées, and widows. In particular, "virgin" (*parthenos*) seems to have been an important term for identifying ascetic women; although there is nothing to indicate sex in the first instance (1 Cor 7:25), all other uses of the term refer to women (vv. 28, 34, 36, 37). This is often masked by English translations, which sometimes render the term less literally as "unmarried," "girl," or "betrothed." Although (as in 1 Cor 7:36–38, where issues of translation are notorious) it is sometimes difficult to determine the precise scenario at issue, it remains plain that Paul seeks to circumscribe the ascetic activity of women as young women, widows, daughters, and fiancées – a tendency that becomes more clearly pronounced in 1 Timothy 5:3–16.

First Corinthian 7 brings together in a brief text several recurring aspects of Paul's pronouncements on women and gender. On the one hand, there are countercultural elements. Especially in comparison to the author of 1 Timothy's attempt to limit participation in the office of enrolled widows to older women (1 Tim 5:9–15), and the author of Ephesians' unabashed celebration of marriage as a reflection of the relationship between Christ and the church (Eph 5:22–32), Paul expresses a preference for celibacy for both men and women. In a society where political speeches and even legislation encouraged marriage, procreation, and remarriage after divorce and widowhood, Paul's teaching might be interpreted as anti-familial or at least as reinforcing the independence that women – especially well-to-do widows – were already achieving as they gained greater visibility in the Roman world.[7] Moreover, his careful treatment of marriage between believers and non-believers (1 Cor 7:12–16) masks the subversive potential of welcoming a wife into the community without the permission of her husband. On the other hand, one senses pressures of conformity and recognition of the hierarchical order of the household in Paul's teaching. Paul is cautious, and his rhetoric seems designed to remind women that they may be required to sacrifice the privileges of virginity and of a marriage-free life by marrying a partner who might otherwise lose "self-control" and fall into immorality, or by remaining married to a harsh, potentially violent, non-believing partner unless he himself decides to leave (Margaret Y. MacDonald 1990).

Very recent scholarship has complicated our understanding of this balancing act even further. Two (sometimes overlapping) approaches to the interpretation of Pauline texts should be noted. A growing recognition of the complexity of family life in the

Roman world has heightened our appreciation of the challenges and dilemmas that surface in Paul's letters. In particular, the manner in which women's lives overlap with those of children and slaves is increasing our awareness of the dynamics of house-church assemblies (Osiek and MacDonald 2006). Women in these assemblies included daughters, slaves, slave-owners, wives, and celibates, and we must be prepared to think through these overlapping categories of identity and consider the interactions between women themselves.

An interest in families is also leading to a new appreciation of the way Paul's metaphorical language and theological argumentation draw upon images of birth, mothering, and childhood (Gaventa 2007). The extent to which gender plays a role in resistance to, or compliance with, the dominant social order is also highlighted in various "political" and postcolonial readings of Paul's letters (for example, Fiorenza 2007; Lopez 2008; Marchal 2008). Such analysis may even cause us to rethink some of the most visible signs of cultural compliance: the household codes themselves (for example, Col 3:18–4:1; Eph 5:21–6:9) emerge in a new light – and even as encoding some elements of resistance – when read against a background of triumphal imperial proclamations of the unity achieved among pacified and enslaved peoples (Maier 2005).

Notes

1   Unless otherwise indicated, biblical quotations are taken from the New Revised Standard Version.
2   The issue of translation of various terms referring to female deacons is complex. Madigan and Osiek (2005) offer the following clarification: "The later term *diakonissa* appears in a datable Greek text for the first time in Canon nineteen of Nicaea. It is used in the Latin translation of the *Didascalia*, but neither the date of the translation nor the term used in the original Greek is known. It also appears in the *Apostolic Constitutions*, usually thought to date to the late fourth century (*AC* 3.11.3, a passage independent of the *Didascalia*). Book Eight, after one alternative form, *diakonē* (8.3.14), uses *diakonissa* throughout" (see Madigan and Osiek 2005, 8).
3   The translation adopted by Epp is by Brooten (1977).
4   Writing at the end of the second century CE, Clement of Alexandria interpreted 1 Corinthians 9:5 as a reference to spiritual marriage where the wives, as co-ministers, directed their leadership to other women. See *Miscellanies* 3.6.53.
5   In a work edited by Elisabeth Schüssler Fiorenza (1994), she included both canonical writings and non-canonical works such as the (so-called) apocryphal and Gnostic writings, including the *Acts of Thecla* and the *Gospel of Mary Magdalene*.
6   Although it has not gone uncontested (see Økland 2004, 10), scholars have sometimes sought to reduce the tension between 1 Corinthians 11:2–16 and 1 Corinthians 14:34–35 by arguing that the latter passage refers to married women, whereas the praying and prophesying women are virgins, widows, or celibates.
7   Although historians debate the real effects in various parts of the Empire and among people of differing social status, legislation was promulgated by Emperor Augustus and his successors making marriage and childbearing mandatory between twenty and fifty years of age, including remarriage for widows and divorcées. Penalties included restrictions on inheritance and the denial of certain privileges of legal independence for women. For details, see Margaret Y. MacDonald (1999, 212–213).

References

Ascough, Richard S. 2009. *Lydia: Paul's Cosmopolitan Hostess*. Collegeville, Minn.: Liturgical.

Brooten, Bernadette. 1977. "Junia ... Outstanding among the Apostles" (Romans 16:7). Pages 141–144 in *Women Priests: A Catholic Commentary on the Vatican Declaration*. Edited by Leonard Swidler and Arlene Swidler. New York: Paulist.

Burer, Michael H., and Daniel B. Wallace. 2001. Was Junia Really an Apostle? A Re-examination of Rom 16.7. *New Testament Studies* 47: 76–91.

Castelli, Elizabeth A. 1999. Paul on Women and Gender. Pages 221–235 in *Women and Christian Origins*. Edited by Ross Shepard Kraemer and Mary Rose D'Angelo. Oxford: Oxford University Press.

D'Angelo, Mary Rose. 1990. Women Partners in the New Testament. *Journal of Feminist Studies in Religion* 6: 65–86.

Epp, Eldon Jay. 2005. *Junia: The First Woman Apostle*. Minneapolis: Fortress.

Fatum, Lone. 1991. Image of God and Glory of Man: Women in the Pauline Congregations. Pages 56–137 in *Image of God and Gender Models in Judaeo-Christian Tradition*. Edited by Kari Elizabeth Børrensen. Oslo: Solum.

Fiorenza, Elisabeth Schüssler. 1983. *In Memory of Her: A Feminist Theological Reconstruction of Christian Origins*. New York: Crossroad.

Fiorenza, Elisabeth Schüssler. 1987. Rhetorical Situation and Historical Reconstruction in 1 Corinthians. *New Testament Studies* 33: 386–403.

Fiorenza, Elisabeth Schüssler. 1992. *But She Said: Feminist Practices of Biblical Interpretation*. Boston: Beacon.

Fiorenza, Elisabeth Schüssler, editor. 1994. *Searching the Scriptures*. Volume 2: *A Feminist Commentary*. New York: Crossroad.

Fiorenza, Elisabeth Schüssler. 2007. *The Power of the Word: Scripture and the Rhetoric of Empire*. Minneapolis: Fortress.

Gardner, Jane F. 1986. *Women in Roman Law and Society*. London: Croom Helm.

Gaventa, Beverly Roberts. 2007. *Our Mother Saint Paul*. Louisville: Westminster John Knox.

Horrell, David G. 2004. Domestic Space and Christian Meetings at Corinth: Imagining New Contexts and the Buildings East of the Theatre. *New Testament Studies* 50: 349–369.

Jewett, Robert. 1988. Paul, Phoebe, and the Spanish Mission. Pages 142–161 in *The Social World of Formative Christianity and Judaism*. Edited by Jacob Neusner, Peder Borgen, Ernest S. Frerichs, and Richard Horsley. Philadelphia: Fortress.

Jewett, Robert. 1993. Tenement Churches and Communal Meals in the Early Church: The Implications of a Form-critical Analysis of 2 Thessalonians 3:10. *Biblical Research* 38: 23–43.

Jewett, Robert. 2007. *Romans: A Commentary*. Minneapolis: Fortress.

Kearsley, R. A. 1999. Women in Public Life in the Roman East: Iunia Theodora, Claudia Metrodora and Phoebe, Benefactress of Paul. *Tyndale Bulletin* 50: 189–211.

Lieu, Judith. 1998. The "Attraction of Women" in/to Early Judaism and Christianity: Gender and the Politics of Conversion. *Journal for the Study of the New Testament* 72: 5–22.

Lopez, Davina C. 2008. *Apostle to the Conquered: Reimagining Paul's Mission*. Minneapolis: Fortress.

MacDonald, Denis Ronald. 1987. *There is no Male and Female: The Fate of a Dominical Saying in Paul and Gnosticism*. Philadelphia: Fortress.

MacDonald, Margaret Y. 1990. Women Holy in Body and Spirit: The Social Setting of 1 Corinthians 7. *New Testament Studies* 36: 161–181.

MacDonald, Margaret Y. 1996. *Early Christian Women and Pagan Opinion: The Power of the Hysterical Woman.* Cambridge: Cambridge University Press.

MacDonald, Margaret Y. 1999. Reading Real Women through the Undisputed Letters of Paul. Pages 199–220 in *Women and Christian Origins.* Edited by Ross Shepard Kraemer and Mary Rose D'Angelo. Oxford: Oxford University Press.

MacDonald, Margaret Y. 2000. *Colossians and Ephesians.* Collegeville, Minn.: Liturgical.

MacDonald, Margaret Y. 2004. The Shifting Centre: Ideology and the Interpretations of 1 Corinthians. Pages 273–294 in *Christianity at Corinth: The Quest for the Pauline Church.* Edited by Edward Adams and David G. Horrell. Louisville: Westminster John Knox.

MacDonald, Margaret Y. 2006. Women in Early Christianity: The Challenge to a New Testament Theology. Pages 135–157 in *The Nature of New Testament Theology: Essays in Honour of Robert Morgan.* Edited by Christopher Rowland and Christopher Tuckett. Oxford: Blackwell.

Madigan, Kevin, and Carolyn Osiek. 2005. *Ordained Women in the Early Church: A Documentary History.* Baltimore: Johns Hopkins University Press.

Maier, Harry O. 2005. A Sly Civility: Colossians and Empire. *Journal for the Study of the New Testament* 27: 323–349.

Marchal, Joseph A. 2008. *The Politics of Heaven: Women, Gender, and Empire in the Study of Paul.* Minneapolis: Fortress.

Martin, Dale B. 2003. Slave Families and Slaves in Families. Pages 207–230 in *Early Christian Families in Context: An Interdisciplinary Dialogue.* Edited by David L. Balch and Carolyn Osiek. Grand Rapids: Eerdmans.

Murphy-O'Connor, Jerome. 1996. *Paul: A Critical Life.* Oxford: Clarendon.

Noy, David. 2000. *Foreigners at Rome: Citizens and Strangers.* London: Duckworth.

Økland, Jorunn. 2004. *Women in their Place: Paul and the Corinthian Discourse of Gender and Sanctuary Space.* London: T. & T. Clark.

Osiek, Carolyn. 2000. *Philippians, Philemon.* Nashville: Abingdon.

Osiek, Carolyn, and Margaret Y. MacDonald, with Janet H. Tulloch. 2006. *A Woman's Place: House Churches in Earliest Christianity.* Minneapolis: Fortress.

Wallace-Hadrill, Andrew. 1994. *Houses and Society in Pompeii and Herculaneum.* Princeton: Princeton University Press.

Whelan, Caroline F. 1993. *Amica Pauli*: The Role of Phoebe in the Early Church. *Journal for the Study of the New Testament* 49: 67–85.

Winter, Bruce W. 2003. *Roman Wives, Roman Widows: The Appearance of New Women and the Pauline Communities.* Grand Rapids: Eerdmans.

Wire, Antoinette Clark. 1990. *The Corinthian Women Prophets: A Reconstruction through Paul's Rhetoric.* Minneapolis: Fortress.

CHAPTER 18

Paul and Empire

N. T. Wright

The Setting

The Roman world

When Augustus Caesar died in AD 14, he left behind him a world transformed. Previous generations of Roman leaders had extended the rule (*imperium*) of Rome around the Mediterranean world, to the point where the earlier democratic republic, full of checks and balances to stop any individual becoming too powerful, was in danger of collapsing under its own weight. This, in fact, had more or less happened fifty years earlier, when Augustus's adoptive father, Julius Caesar, had been assassinated by republican traditionalists who saw him, rightly, as a direct threat to the centuries-old Roman system. This precipitated several years of complex civil wars, played out on foreign soil, with the super-efficient Roman military machine turning on itself in support of one would-be leader or another. Augustus, the last man standing in this deadly contest, returned to Rome and declared that he had brought peace to the world. A grateful city, and system, was happy to ignore the irony. The *imperium* of Rome had become the Empire of Caesar.

Augustus extended the irony with great care: he had, he said, restored the Republic, being himself "elected" to the chief offices and outwardly deferring to the ruling body, the Senate. Under his rule, as his propaganda claimed, not only peace but also "justice" had come to the world (*Iustitia* became officially a goddess in the time of Augustus). Rome possessed "freedom" and was glad to be able to share it with the rest of the world. The "good news" of Caesar's sovereignty was hailed across his wide domains; he had instituted a new era of prosperity and plenty. The *Ara Pacis* ("Altar of Peace") in Rome

The Blackwell Companion to Paul, First Edition. Edited by Stephen Westerholm.
© 2011 Blackwell Publishing Ltd. Published 2011 by Blackwell Publishing Ltd.

solemnly celebrated a new fruitfulness for all creation. Romans as a whole, wisely, went along with this convenient fiction, hailing Augustus and then his successors as "savior" and "lord." Declaring that his adoptive father had been deified after his death, Augustus himself was styled as "son of god."

How far people actually believed all this is open to question. More pressing business was at hand, not least the running, and extending, of the huge network of government, law, administration, and infrastructure stretching from the Atlantic coasts of Europe in the west to Egypt, Syria, and "Asia" (more or less modern Turkey) in the east. The Roman army was deployed in keeping the peace and maintaining secure borders, not least to enable the safe passage of grain from Egypt to Rome. Central Italy could not produce nearly enough food to sustain the swollen population of its capital, and as more and more people poured into the city in search of money, or indeed power, grain from Egypt became for Rome what Middle Eastern oil is for the Western world today – a necessary adjunct to a way of life, to be protected in whatever way was required. The lands immediately beyond Turkey and Syria, then as now, continued (from the Western point of view) to pose problems, which Augustus's successors did their best to address.

The most obvious predecessor for Augustus was Alexander the Great in the fourth century BC, whose empire had stretched from Greece in the west to the borderlands of India in the east. Augustus, shifting the focus westwards, put the notion of a single empire on a far more stable footing, so that whereas Alexander's brief empire had broken up more or less at once after his death into different kingdoms, that of Augustus continued, and developed, for four hundred years. It survived various disasters such as the "year of the four emperors" (AD 69), when, following Nero's suicide, military commanders from the corners of the empire claimed the throne in quick, bloody succession. But the earlier achievement of Alexander, the heartland of whose empire (Greece, Turkey, and not least Egypt) became central to that of Augustus, provided more than just a rough model. For millions of inhabitants of what we now know as the Roman world, it offered far more: a way of making sense of things, a worldview, an ideology, expressed in symbol and cult.

Alexander and his successors tapped into older ideas of divine kingship, formalizing them in various ways and integrating them into the various systems of classical theology (Zeus/Jupiter and his Olympian colleagues) as well as local religions and cults. Rome already had its own eponymous goddess, *Roma*, to whom troops swore allegiance, and who was symbolized in the eagle that adorned their military standards. Now there began to appear new gods and goddesses: Augustus himself, whose adoptive father Julius Caesar had, after his death, been declared to be divine, and then various members of the imperial family. Augustus was careful not to claim divine honors in Rome itself, but in the eastern provinces there was no need for such restraint. Indeed, the locals would not have understood it. Especially in Egypt, but not only there, rulers had been divine as long as anyone could remember. Cities like Corinth in Greece and Ephesus in Asia, already major centers of Roman power and influence, became major centers also of the imperial cult – not as a strange new idea, but as the natural focal point of the massive, all-embracing presence and authority of Rome and its supreme ruler. One of the great gains in historical understanding over recent years has been the recognition that "religion" in the ancient world was not, as in post-Enlightenment modernity, set over against "politics" and other aspects of ordinary existence, but was integral to everything else. Business, taxes, art, marriage, travel, war, farming – wherever you looked, "religion" was part of it. And the cult of the emperor, stitched into the fabric of everyday life through coins, buildings, statues (including members of the imperial family carved to resemble the classic pagan deities), regular games, sacrifices, and military ideology, became the fastest growing "religion" within the Mediterranean world of the first century.

Ancient Judaism and pagan empire

Already by the first century, the Jewish people had spread far beyond their native land into the further recesses of the worlds both of Alexander and Augustus. This itself is telling, in that the main reason for this diaspora was the displacement (or "exile") they had suffered at various times at the hands of stronger nations. Ancient Judaism told its own story in terms of a perplexing struggle between the global claims of their own god and the global realities of pagan power, whether that of Assyria in the eighth century BC, Babylon in the fifth, or then the succession of other powers – Persia, Greece, Egypt, Syria, and finally Rome – that followed in quicker succession. The Jewish Scriptures presented, from many angles and in many genres, the challenge of the Jewish god to the "idols" of the nations, not simply as a "spiritual" battle involving the inner life of worshipers and their post-mortem destiny, but as a contest to be played out in the realities of the created order and the actual fortunes of the people who claimed this god, the creator, as their own. The inner dynamic of Judaism, stretching back to its earliest memories in Genesis and Exodus and bearing fruit in many different movements and subcultures, was that of a people who invoked the presence, power, and promises of the world's creator to give them hope and purpose as they were surrounded, and often overwhelmed, by the world's present human rulers. Their god had promised to rescue them from Egypt, and had done so; he would do so again. A great deal of Jewish life revolved around the festivals and other practices that symbolized and re-expressed this narrative. The well-known parties or pressure groups in the first century (Sadducees, Pharisees, Essenes, and the group Josephus refers to as the "fourth philosophy," the militant revolutionaries) can be understood as embodying different ways of telling this ancient story, different ways of being true to the ancestral traditions within a confusing and dangerous world. The Jews were known in the world of Greece and Rome as a people fiercely loyal to these traditions, keeping themselves distinct from other peoples, not least in refusing – uniquely in the world of their day – to worship either the regular pagan divinities or the newer imperial ones.

The particular traditions in which this ancient worldview was expressed and through which it was sustained were, of course, rooted in the Jewish Scriptures. The Psalms, sung and prayed day by day, were not just a handbook of personal or private piety: the second Psalm, for example, celebrates the sovereignty of Israel's god over the warring and threatening nations and their rulers, and summons those powers to humble allegiance. The prophets, likewise, were not just telling people how to behave in their private lives. The great book of Isaiah, and especially the central section (chapters

40–55), which forms one of the finest sustained poems from any language or culture, declares majestically that the gods of the nations are mere idols and that Israel's god will show himself to be king over them all, returning to his chosen city and restoring his people after their tragic exile in Babylon. The book of Daniel, shaped through the Maccabean crisis of the 160s BC (in which the Jews took on the might of Syria, and won), spoke both of the vocation of Israel to resist the blandishments of pagan idolatry and of the coming of a new divine kingdom through which the kingdoms of the world would be called to account and their power humbled.

So far as we can tell from first-century writings such as 4 Ezra and Josephus, these and other books gave shape and energy to Jewish life and expectation, generating various movements and encouraging various speculations about how and when these promises would be fulfilled. In particular, many Jews searched their Scriptures for insight as to the human leadership under which this would happen. Psalm 2 spoke of the coming king as the "son" of Israel's god; Isaiah, of a strange "servant" through whom the divine purposes would be put into effect; Daniel, of "one like a son of man" who would be vindicated by the creator god and exalted to a supreme position over the nations. The expectation, more specifically, of an anointed king (i.e., a Messiah) took many forms in the first centuries BC and AD. Some tried to calculate, on the basis of the detailed prophecies of Daniel 9, when this figure would appear, arriving at widely different results. But there was no question that, if and when a Messiah might emerge, his primary tasks would include the inflicting of divine judgment on the wicked world of paganism and the rescue and restoration of the ancient people who were loyal to the creator god and to the traditions they had received from him. The multiple other concerns of ancient Judaism – not least the development of Torah as the special way of life, especially in the diaspora where the Temple and its system of worship and sacrifice were not available – never displaced this hope, that one day Israel's god would be king of all the world, and that Israel itself would be seen to be his people. In the meantime, even the continued sufferings of the faithful could become, in some strange way, part of the eventual divine purpose of rescue and restoration.

The ancient traditions of Israel thus continued to put the Jewish people on a collision course with the all-embracing claims of human empire. During the Maccabean crisis, the Jewish people had looked to Rome as a friendly but far-off foreign power, whose help might be useful against the much closer enemy, Syria. But as Rome grew more powerful, this possibility became more ambiguous, and the political machinations of the first centuries BC and AD reflect this, creating a context for the horrible show-down which took place in the 60s AD. Rome, eager as ever to keep the Middle East quiet in order to secure the grain shipments, ruled their outlying districts through local officials, giving power both to the Sadducees as the supposed local aristocracy and then to Herod the Great as a leading local warlord, not realizing the extent to which the power of either would be resented as out of keeping with proper Jewish tradition (Herod was not even fully Jewish). Trouble flared, too, through the Roman practice of taking a census to determine tribute: those who, reading Daniel and the Psalms, believed that Israel's god alone should be their king saw this as a call to resistance. When Rome tired of indirect rule and sent "prefects" or "procurators" to govern Judea, their cynical indifference to local scruple, coupled with the threat that Jews might be compelled to worship the emperor himself, stirred up the fires of ancient devotion and loyalty. "Zeal" for Israel's god and his Torah meant, for many, zealous resistance to such pagan arrogance – and to anything that appeared to collaborate with it, to compromise the pure Jewish way of life, and so to endanger the coming of the ancient hope, the dawning of the long-awaited day of justice and peace, of rescue for Israel, of the divine kingdom.

The long, slow build-up of Roman rule, from its first beginnings to the full flowering of empire under Augustus and his successors, thus ran side by side with the long, slow build-up of Jewish aspiration and expectation. The clash between the two could not be put off forever. It came in the devastating war of 66–70 AD, in which, after early successes had given the revolutionaries the hope that a new version of the Maccabean triumph – a new version of the exodus itself – might be imminent, the Roman legions under Vespasian came on relentlessly, doing what Rome did best, crushing and crucifying the rebel forces, and finally reducing Jerusalem itself to a smoldering heap. Vespasian left the final triumph to his son Titus, since he himself had gone to Rome as the fourth of the "four emperors" of 69. Josephus, who had been a Jewish general in the early days of the war, went over to Rome, and declared afterwards that Israel's god had done so as well. As the chief priests had said in John's account of Jesus's trial before Pilate, "we have no king but Caesar" (John 19:15).[1]

Paul within the First Century

We cannot understand the early Christian movement, or Paul as part of it, unless we locate it firmly and centrally within the map of these converging and explosive forces. When we consider "Paul and empire," we are not talking about a political sideshow, a subcategory of "Pauline ethics" ("What about the state?"). We are talking about the kingdom of God and the lordship of Jesus the Messiah. Along with the already-noted great gain of contemporary scholarship, emerging from the false perspectives of modernity to recognize the all-pervasiveness of "religion" in the everyday Roman world, we have a further and consequent gain: the recognition that for Paul, too, "religion," or "salvation," was not separated off from the questions with which his contemporaries had been struggling – questions which he, too, as a zealous young Pharisee, had regarded as vital. His early loyalty to Israel's god, to the ancestral traditions and particularly the Mosaic law, and his embrace of Israel's hope of the kingdom of this god and of the resurrection of the dead through which this god, as the creator, would restore his ancient people to life in a new creation – all of this spoke directly to the issues we have been noting. When, after ten or more years of traveling around the Mediterranean world, he returned to Jerusalem to bring financial help to the struggling group of Christians there, he walked into a city where the talk of the day was not about how to go to heaven but about how Israel's god was going to become king – and about what it meant, at such a moment, to be loyal to him and to his law.

Reading Paul in this way demands, of course, a radical change of perspective for those whose own world has neatly separated out "religion" and "politics" (a modern fiction which has enormously influenced today's Western world but which was unknown before the eighteenth century and remains unknown in most of the world).

In particular, it flies in the face of the (until recently) dominant paradigm of Pauline theology, that of a Lutheran conception of "two kingdoms" which itself may have influenced the split world of Enlightenment theory. Within that world, for instance, the word *Christos* in Paul was held to be a mere name, not a title, and certainly not a reference to Jesus as the fulfillment of the world-ruling aspirations of ancient Judaism. But there are several signs, not only that *Christos* in Paul retains its full messianic significance, but that it does so as a central part of Paul's entire vision of the true god and the fulfillment of his purposes. Paul's gospel, arguably, remained firmly rooted in the soil of ancient Jewish expectation. He believed that in Jesus, and particularly in his death and resurrection, Israel's god had been true to his promises. It was therefore time for the world to be brought under the lordship of this god and of his anointed king.

But what might that mean? The attempt to explore the political meaning of Paul's letters, which has suddenly flowered within New Testament scholarship in the past couple of decades, is itself, of course, firmly contextual. In part, it relates to the demise of the existentialist interpretations which had themselves pushed into the background earlier explorations, such as those of Deissmann (1912); until recently, Georgi (1991) was something of a lone voice exploring the continuing possibility of political meaning in Paul. Earlier studies of "principalities and powers" explored the relation between what in modern terms count as "spiritual" and "temporal" powers, pointing to the conclusion that the distinction was far more fluid in Paul's world (Caird 1956; Wink 1984). In part, it relates to the increased study of Paul by those outside the world of seminaries and ministerial formation, who have brought social-scientific and other perspectives to bear. In part, it has to do with a reawakening of interest in reading Paul within his wider philosophical context, both ancient (for example, Blumenfeld 2001) and modern (for example, Taubes 2004; Agamben 2005). In part, to be sure, it relates to the sudden awareness, in North America, of what many see as a new kind of global empire, and of the multilayered challenges this poses. This, and the wider context of postcolonial discourse, relates particularly to the seminal work of Horsley (1997; 2000; 2004), as well as writers like Elliott (1995) and Cassidy (2001), and the more popular work of Borg and Crossan (2009). Frequently, these explorations have maintained the split world of the Enlightenment, perpetuating the either/or (*either* politics *or* religion/ theology), and merely shifting the focus (Paul as political activist *rather than* theologian or "spiritual writer"), and making him speak with a suspiciously direct relevance to contemporary American concerns (more nuanced and multilayered in Walsh and Keesmaat 2004). This has precipitated a reaction from those who protest that Paul was after all writing about spiritual realities (Kim 2008) and those who insist on a more nuanced reading of the Roman world and Paul in its context (Bryan 2005). The time is ripe for further mature and integrated reflection, not least on the philosophical and cultural underpinnings of imperial ideology, on the one hand, and Paul's response, on the other.

One might note, of course, that Jesus himself is hardly to be separated out from the clash of civilizations that was taking place. The phrase "king of the Jews," written up over his head on the cross, says it all: this is what Rome does to would-be rebel leaders. Jesus's vision of Israel's god and his kingdom, and his radical expression of it in deed and word, is not our present subject. But it is increasingly recognized that whatever

Jesus was about, he was not offering either a spirituality or a salvation which left the present world irrelevant and untouched. His was a message, and a mission, of cataclysmic challenge and transformation, not of detachment and abandonment. And Paul believed that Israel's god had raised Jesus from the dead, thereby retrospectively validating his kingdom-bringing mission, and declaring that he had all along been the one of whom Psalm 2 had spoken: the son of God, the true Lord of the world, the one who had defeated evil and now offered forgiveness freely to all, the one at whose name every knee shall bow. And with that we arrive at exegesis.

Counter-imperial Messages in the Letters?

Until very recently, it was possible for scholars to deal with Paul's view of politics and the Roman Empire with a quick reference to Romans 13:1–7, as though that was the only time such ideas crossed his mind (and as though his view of Caesar and all his works was that he was welcome to run the "secular" world as long as Jesus could run the "religious" one). Ironically, the very word "Romans" has become synonymous, for theologians and exegetes, not so much with the inhabitants of the ancient city of Rome and their culture, but with a nest of exciting theological and spiritual questions, debates, and possibilities. Justification, faith, sanctification, the Holy Spirit, the question of Israel, Christology, community life – all these are there, and they are important. But the question of how Paul's letter might be *heard in Rome itself*, the city that ruled the world, has until recently hardly been addressed (see now Oakes 2009).

In the same way, earlier studies of potential counter-imperial language in the letters tended to focus, as was the habit of the time, on particular words like *kyrios*, *sōtēr*, and *euangelion*. Debate then concerned questions of *derivation*: did Paul derive his ideas from the imperial cult? A negative answer was frequently driven by a concern to stress the Jewishness of Paul's thought over against a supposed Hellenizing tendency. But it is equally possible that Paul, however much he derived his key concepts and structures of thought from his native Judaism, was concerned (as was Judaism) with *confrontation*, with the challenge to express his new-found (and, he would say, still essentially Jewish) faith in Jesus as the crucified and risen Messiah within the polemical context necessitated by the new imperial reality. It is important, then, to look not only at key terms but at actual arguments, combinations of ideas, and, above all, the flow of thought in particular letters and passages.

In the light of our earlier exposition of empire, the opening "salutation" of Romans awakens echoes that, arguably, would not have been missed by its intended recipients:

> God's good news concerning his son, who was descended from the seed of David according to the flesh and was marked out as son of God with power according to the spirit of holiness by resurrection from the dead, Jesus, the Messiah, our Lord, through whom we have received grace and apostolic commission to bring about the obedience of faith for the sake of his name among all the nations, including yourselves who are called to belong to Jesus the Messiah; to all God's beloved in Rome ... (Rom 1:3–7)

Good news about the all-powerful son of God who, coming from the ancient Israelite royal family, claims universal allegiance! The echoes of Psalm 2 and similar passages are matched by the echoes of Roman imperial rhetoric. Here as elsewhere, the question presses: if Paul does not mention Caesar by name, can he be taken to be alluding to him, and to his imperial world? As with political cartoons in the modern world (and, for that matter, with the book of Revelation), it is dangerous to assume that readers would be unable to pick up allusions to the structures of power and those who embodied and enforced them. Often, in fact, such allusions are the only way, or perhaps the best way, to get the point across (see, for example, Scott 1990). But in the case of Paul, the echoes of imperial language (not necessarily explicitly "cultic" language, though as we have seen, the cult merges into, and flows out from, the wider ideology) are strong: "good news," "son of God," universal allegiance, Jesus as part of an ancient royal family and as *kyrios* ("lord"), and then, in what is generally reckoned the thematic statement of the letter (1:16–17), this "good news" as being the means of "salvation" and "justice" (*dikaiosynē*, "righteousness"). The fact that these notions have been given very different, and essentially non-political, meanings in some Christian theology ought not to make us deaf to the echoes they would almost certainly have awakened in Rome.

How does the rest of the letter relate to such a reading? Granted necessary brevity, one might suggest that the climax of the first half, in Romans 8, demonstrates that it is the god of Israelite Scripture (not, by implication, other divinities) who brings about the great renewal of creation, the outflowing of "peace" (Rom 5:1). It is the ancient Jewish story, now having reached its climax in Jesus the Messiah (10:4), that carries the universal divine purpose, rather than the not-quite-so-ancient story of Rome. And it is the Christian community of Romans 14–15 who embody the genuine universalism that Caesar had attempted. The main exposition of the letter concludes with an echo of its opening, and a direct reference to Jesus as the one foretold by psalms and prophets (especially here Isa 11:10) as the coming world ruler: "the root of Jesse ... rise[s] to rule the nations, and in him the nations shall hope" (Rom 15:12). The resurrection, in other words, constitutes Jesus as the true lord of the world, the reality of which Caesar is a mere parody.

This reading of Romans (which, of course, needs to be filled out by, and not played off against, the traditional understandings of the letter as concerned with justification, salvation, and so forth), points to a similar understanding of the "apocalyptic" exposition of resurrection in 1 Corinthians 15. Paul's argument for the future resurrection of believers is set within a global context of the kingdom of God and the sovereign lordship of Jesus the Messiah, again echoing the Psalms, this time Psalm 8 where the "son of man" has everything put in subjection under his feet:

> Then comes the end, when he hands over the kingdom to God the Father, after he has destroyed every ruler and every authority and power. For he must reign until he has put all his enemies under his feet. The last enemy to be destroyed is death. For "God has put all things in subjection under his feet." But when it says, "All things are put in subjection," it is plain that this does not include the one who put all things in subjection under him. When all things are subjected to him, then the Son himself will also be subjected to the one who put all things in subjection under him, so that God may be all in all. (1 Cor 15:24–28 [NRSV])

The delicately balanced Christology is not our concern. What matters for us is that here Paul quite explicitly evokes the whole ancient Jewish tradition of God's universal sovereignty, exercised through the Davidic king, as in several psalms (8, 72, 89, 110, and so on) and in the royal predictions from Isaiah. For Paul, the risen and ascended Jesus is *already* installed as the ruler of the world, and the present time is to be understood as the interval between his attaining that status and it having its full effect. The fact that "death" is cited as the "last enemy" should not make us imagine that the "rulers and authorities" who are brought into subjection have nothing to do with actual rulers; rather, death is the weapon by which tyrants rule, so that its abolition in the resurrection draws the sting of their power. Paul has modified the Jewish tradition of God's kingdom, not by spiritualizing it but by putting the crucified and risen Jesus into the middle of it. We now know not only the name of the universal lord but also the means of that lordship: the paradoxical power of suffering love, acted out in the cross, as expressed earlier in the letter.

It has recently been argued (Hardin 2008) that Galatians shows direct evidence of the imperial cult in the cities where Paul's first churches in Asia took root. Following Winter (1994), Hardin sketches a possible scenario in which the Gentile Christians were being seduced into claiming Jewish status by becoming circumcised so that they could then claim the Jewish privilege of being a "permitted religion" and would not have to take part in the (otherwise mandatory) festivities associated with the imperial cult. Getting circumcised would thus be a way of avoiding persecution, not from Jews anxious about earning their own salvation by good works, but from Romans anxious about maintaining imperial standards – and perhaps also from Jews who were anxious about being associated with Gentile law-breakers. This fascinating possibility remains a matter of debate, but Hardin's study of the spread of the imperial cult in central Asia demonstrates the existence of a key context that has normally been ignored.

Philippians has long been recognized as a key text for assessing Paul's relation to the world of Caesar. In particular, studies of the "hymn" in 2:6–11 have suggested that it was composed, and used by Paul in this context, with at least half an eye to the pretensions of divine rulers from Alexander onward and particularly the Caesars (Oakes 2001). It is Jesus, not Caesar, who has been a "servant," and has now been given "the name above every name," so that at his name every knee should bend and every tongue confess *Kyrios Iēsous Christos*, "Jesus Messiah is Lord." And he has come to that place of universal acclamation, not by self-aggrandizement after the manner of Hellenistic or Roman potentates, but by the self-abnegation of incarnation and cross. In this light, we might be correct to read the controversial verse 2:12 in terms of the contrast between the imperial "salvation" and the Christian version: "work out *your own salvation* in fear and trembling" may not, perhaps, refer to "salvation" in the normal Western sense but to the mode of life proper for those who hail Jesus, rather than Caesar, as *sōtēr*, "savior."

It has often been pointed out that Philippians 3 is built up rather carefully on some of the material in 2:6–11, and the climax of chapter 3 produces a further flurry of what may be read as anti-imperial polemic. Some in Philippi probably prided themselves on their Roman citizenship, and on the fact that, if the colony was in trouble, Caesar could come from the mother city to rescue them and restore their status and prestige. For us, says Paul, "our citizenship is in heaven": not, that is, a place to which we return after our present life as "colonials," but a place from which there may come the one who is already in charge, already ruling the whole world. "From there we await the Savior, the Lord, Jesus the Messiah" – the one, that is, who claims as of right titles which Caesar had usurped – and it is he who "has the power to subject all things to himself," and so will transform our bodies from their present humiliation to a glory (which includes the notion of sovereignty, not just splendor) like his own (Phil 3:20–21). Here, Paul brings together his scriptural background (Psalm 8 again) and the rhetoric of present empire: derivation on the one hand, confrontation on the other.

It is possible that this covert polemic has colored, too, the exhortation of Philippians 3:2–16. In verse 17 Paul invites the Philippians to "imitate" him, but the pattern of life he has described in verses 2–16 is the giving up of outward *Jewish* privilege in order to gain the Messiah. The Philippians, we assume, are not Jews; in what way can they then imitate him? Perhaps, he may be hinting, by at least sitting loose to their privileges in an imperial city. This kind of thing is notoriously hard to prove, but may perhaps suggest a "hidden transcript," implying more than can be said explicitly.

Other letters to northern Greece contain further possible imperial allusions. In the climax of 1 Thessalonians, Paul expounds an apocalyptic vision of the *parousia* of Jesus. The word *parousia* is not derived from the Septuagint, but carries rather the double overtones of "royal visitation" (as when Caesar might arrive at a city, or perhaps back in Rome itself) and "divine manifestation" (as when a god or goddess might suddenly appear). Obviously, if Caesar is divine, the two can be combined; but, for Paul, the real *parousia* is not that of Caesar but that of Jesus, on the day when he returns in visible power to take full control of the world, to raise the dead, and to judge the nations. This polemical context for 4:13–18 (routinely ignored, of course, by those who see here the inappropriate idea of a "rapture" away from the earth; the language is classic apocalyptic metaphor) then gives birth to one of the most direct allusions to first-century imperial rhetoric. "When they say 'Peace and Security,' then sudden destruction will come upon them" (5:3). But "peace and security," as we know from various sources, was a standard imperial slogan, with the empire posing as a kind of global protection racket (we give you peace and security, you give us money and obedience). Paul's vision of devastating future events seems to be directed not least at the Roman Empire in its power and pretension. Had he lived to see the "year of the four emperors," he might have thought that this was one manifestation at least of the "sudden destruction" in question, though of course the situation would then be complicated by the fall of Jerusalem and the rise of Vespasian.

The second letter to the Thessalonians has long been regarded with suspicion, not least (we may suppose) because the vision of Paul which inspired an earlier generation of liberal or existentialist theologians did not include apocalyptic or imperial elements. But actually 2 Thessalonians 2:1–12 is best read as a classic piece of counter-imperial rhetoric, not least for one who had fresh memories of the attempt of the emperor Gaius to erect a huge statue of himself in the Temple in Jerusalem, demanding that the Jews worship it. However we understand the rest of this difficult passage, there should be no doubt about its principal polemical target.

By the same token, scholarly study of Paul has long been content to accept the verdict of an earlier generation, motivated by quite different theological interests, that Ephesians and Colossians are not by Paul himself. Since the paradigm which produced this theory is now largely discredited, it is surely time for the theory itself to be re-examined. But however that may be, it would be a mistake to see these letters as any less counter-imperial than the others at which we have glanced (a point sometimes argued on the basis of the supposedly socially conformist "household codes" in Ephesians 5 and Colossians 3). Ephesians holds out an astonishing vision of Jesus as the lord of the whole cosmos, "far above all rule and authority and power and domin-ion, and above every name that is named, not only in this age but also in the age to come" (1:21 [NRSV]). To invite people to worship the god who has been revealed in and through this Jesus cannot but be politically subversive. In fact, the coming together of Jews and Gentiles into the single family of the Messiah (2:11–22) is to be the sign to the powers of the world that their time is up: "so that through the church the wisdom of God in its rich variety might now be made known to the rulers and authorities in the heavenly places" (3:10 [NRSV]). The cosmic battle against the spiritual forces of evil (6:10–17) does not exclude a struggle with earthly authorities (Ephesians, like Colossians, Philippians, and Philemon, claims to be written from prison), but indicates their proper context.

In the same way, Colossians offers a vision of the lordship of Jesus over all structures of human authority (1:15–20), and includes the striking note that on the cross it was not the rulers and authorities who were disarming Jesus and making a public example of him, but the other way around (2:15). This goes closely with 1 Corinthians 2:8, which suggests that the rulers of the present age would not have crucified Jesus had they realized both who he was and what would be the effect of that execution upon their own power. The counter-imperial overtones of Colossians have been suggestively and creatively explored by Walsh and Keesmaat (2004).

We return in conclusion to the famous passage of Romans 13:1–7. This is not, as used to be thought, a plea for a quietist theology in which "the state" can get on with its own business and the church simply has to do what it is told. It fits, rather, within the Jewish world in which, as part of creational monotheism, the creator god intends that the world be ordered and governed through human authorities. The risk from tyranny is great, but the risk from chaos is worse – a point often ignored by comfortable democratic Westerners, but well known elsewhere. Followers of Jesus the Lord are not exempt from the ordinary structures of human life, and part of the thrust of Romans 13 may be to curb any overexcited early Christians who might imagine that by hailing Jesus as Lord they could simply ignore the need to pay taxes and give ordinary obedi-ence to ordinary civic regulations. But the main thrust is more subtle. If Caesar is giving himself divine honors, Paul will remind the early Christians that he is not in fact divine, but that he receives his power from, and owes allegiance to, the one true god (compare the striking John 19:11). The passage constitutes a severe demotion of Caesar and his pretensions, not a charter for him to do as he pleases. This passage continues to disap-point those who want Paul to articulate their favorite form of left-wing social protest, but it continues to remind us of the basic substructures of Jewish thought which under-lie his thinking, as well as their transformation in Jesus.

Conclusion

Other passages and themes could be added, but this chapter has tried to indicate some of the ways in which Paul may be seen in the context of the imperial world of his day. It is, of course, possible to state these things excessively, and it may take some while before scholarship attains a proper historical perspective, balance, and nuance. But it is equally possible to omit such things altogether and thereby miss a key dimension of Paul's thought and strategy. Much remains to be done, not least to demonstrate the integration of these elements of his writing with the more traditional topics of his "theology" (justification, Christology, and so forth). As a start, we might note the way in which both the cross and the resurrection of Jesus, so obviously central to traditional theological analyses, are also central here: it is the cross that defeats the powers, and it is the resurrection that declares that Jesus is, and always was, the true "son of God." This suggests a much tighter integration of Paul's theology, soteriology, and spirituality with questions of (what we think of as) "politics" than has usually been attempted. The question of "Paul and empire" remains one of the most fascinating, if sometimes frustratingly elusive, of current questions about the apostle and his world.

Note

1   Translations of biblical texts are my own unless otherwise noted.

References

Agamben, Giorgio. 2005. *The Time that Remains: A Commentary on the Letter to the Romans.* Stanford: Stanford University Press.

Alexander, Loveday, editor. 1991. *Images of Empire.* Sheffield: JSOT.

Blumenfeld, Bruno. 2001. *The Political Paul: Justice, Democracy and Kingship in a Hellenistic Framework.* London: Sheffield Academic.

Borg, Marcus J., and John Dominic Crossan. 2009. *The First Paul: Reclaiming the Radical Visionary behind the Church's Conservative Icon.* New York: Harper One.

Bowman, Alan K., Hannah M. Cotton, Martin Goodman, and Simon Price, editors. 2002. *Representations of Empire: Rome and the Mediterranean World.* Oxford: Oxford University Press.

Bryan, Christopher. 2005. *Jesus, the Early Church, and the Roman Superpower.* New York: Oxford University Press.

Caird, G. B. 1956. *Principalities and Powers: A Study in Pauline Theology.* Oxford: Clarendon.

Cassidy, Richard J. 2001. *Paul in Chains: Roman Imprisonment and the Letters of St. Paul.* New York: Crossroad.

Deissmann, Adolf. 1912. *St. Paul: A Study in Social and Religious History.* London: Hodder and Stoughton.

Elliott, Neil. 1995. *Liberating Paul: The Justice of God and the Politics of the Apostle.* Sheffield: Sheffield Academic.

Garnsey, Peter, and Richard Saller. 1987. *The Roman Empire: Economy, Society, and Culture.* Berkeley: University of California Press.

Georgi, Dieter. 1991. *Theocracy in Paul's Praxis and Theology*. Minneapolis: Fortress.

Hardin, Justin K. 2008. *Galatians and the Imperial Cult: A Critical Analysis of the First-century Social Context of Paul's Letter*. Tübingen: Mohr Siebeck.

Horsley, Richard A., editor. 1997. *Paul and Empire: Religion and Power in Roman Imperial Society*. Harrisburg: Trinity Press International.

Horsley, Richard A., editor. 2000. *Paul and Politics: Ekklesia, Israel, Imperium, Interpretation: Essays in Honor of Krister Stendahl*. Harrisburg: Trinity Press International.

Horsley, Richard A., editor. 2004. *Paul and the Imperial Roman Order*. Harrisburg: Trinity Press International.

Kim, Seyoon. 2008. *Christ and Caesar: The Gospel and the Roman Empire in the Writings of Paul and Luke*. Grand Rapids: Eerdmans.

Lintott, A. W. 1993. *Imperium Romanum: Politics and Administration*. London: Routledge.

Millar, Fergus. 1992. *The Emperor in the Roman World (31 BC – AD 337)*. Second edition. Ithaca: Cornell University Press.

Millar, Fergus. 1993. *The Roman Near East, 31 BC – AD 337*. Cambridge, Mass.: Harvard University Press.

Oakes, Peter. 2001. *Philippians: From People to Letter*. Cambridge: Cambridge University Press.

Oakes, Peter. 2009. *Reading Romans in Pompeii: Paul's Letter at Ground Level*. Minneapolis: Fortress.

Price, S. R. F. 1984. *Rituals and Power: The Roman Imperial Cult in Asia Minor*. Cambridge: Cambridge University Press.

Revell, Louise. 2009. *Roman Imperialism and Local Identities*. Cambridge: Cambridge University Press.

Scott, James C. 1990. *Domination and the Arts of Resistance: Hidden Transcripts*. New Haven: Yale University Press.

Taubes, Jacob. 2004. *The Political Theology of Paul*. Stanford: Stanford University Press.

Walsh, Brian J., and Sylvia C. Keesmaat. 2004. *Colossians Remixed: Subverting the Empire*. Downers Grove, Ill.: InterVarsity.

Wink, Walter. 1984. *Naming the Powers: The Language of Power in the New Testament*. Philadelphia: Fortress.

Winter, Bruce W. 1994. *Seek the Welfare of the City: Christians as Benefactors and Citizens*. Grand Rapids: Eerdmans.

Wright, N. T. 2005. *Paul: Fresh Perspectives* (US title: *Paul in Fresh Perspective*). London: SPCK; Minneapolis: Fortress.

Zanker, Paul. 1990. *The Power of Images in the Age of Augustus*. Ann Arbor: University of Michigan Press.

PART II
Readers of Paul

CHAPTER 19

Marcion

Heikki Räisänen

Around the year 140 CE,[1] a wealthy merchant sailed to Rome. He joined the local church and donated a large sum of money to it. He was warmly welcomed. Gradually, however, the newcomer began to cause growing concern to fellow believers. Eventually, he took a momentous step by inviting the leaders of the Roman church to discuss his interpretation of the faith. This led to a scandal and to the expulsion of the self-made reformer, whose money was returned, in the year 144. The dissenter did not give in, but founded a church of his own. For a long time this was a success – a formidable rival to the emerging Catholic church. It was only suppressed through a lengthy process after the Constantinian turn when the mainstream church joined forces with the state to destroy the "heretics."

This remarkable person was Marcion of Sinope, a Greek port on the Black Sea.[2] Reliable information about his life is sparse. According to one tradition, his father was the bishop of Sinope.[3] While this is not impossible, scholars are increasingly inclined to reject as unreliable all reports on Marcion's life prior to his arrival in Rome. We know even less about his later life; it is assumed that he was active for some fifteen years after the break in Rome. But we know enough about his church to get an idea of its importance. Marcion's message found such a wide echo among Christians that, no later than a decade after his expulsion, Justin Martyr complained that his error had spread all over humankind. Half a century later, Tertullian likewise had to note that "Marcion's heretical tradition has filled the whole world."

We are better informed about Marcion's literary work – though only at second hand, through hostile sources. No genuine fragments of Marcion's writings survive; we only have references to and attacks on his work by stern opponents. The earliest extant account comes from Irenaeus (ca. 180); the most comprehensive one is the massive refutation of Marcion's and his adherents' teaching in five books by Tertullian,

The Blackwell Companion to Paul, First Edition. Edited by Stephen Westerholm.
© 2011 Blackwell Publishing Ltd. Published 2011 by Blackwell Publishing Ltd.

completed ca. 208 CE (Evans 1972). Not surprisingly, Tertullian's own argument in refuting the heretic gets the upper hand in the presentation; he does convey some key points of Marcion's thought, but "only by means of painstaking individual analysis of [Tertullian's] language and thoughts can the authentic Marcion material to some degree be filtered out" (May 2005, 23).[4]

Marcion drastically reduced the authoritative tradition of the church by rejecting the Scripture inherited from Judaism (in general in the Greek translation, the Septuagint), which had been its self-evident foundational document. Marcion submitted Scripture to rigorous moral and intellectual criticism, concluding that it could not stem from the true God, the Father of Jesus Christ; its originator must have been a lower God, who was also responsible for the creation of the world. This evaluation converged with that of some Christians known as Gnostics, whose interpretation of the faith was based on a version of Platonic philosophy. Marcion established a stark contrast between the two Gods, and no less a contrast between the law of the Creator and the gospel of the true God – a contrast that could also be expressed as a distinction between law and grace.

Marcion legitimated his attack on Scripture by a forceful appeal to Paul's letters. He sharply distinguished Paul from other apostles (such as Peter), contrasting him, the one true envoy of the true God, with them, mere minions of the Creator. The only other early Christian writing on which Marcion put value was the gospel of Luke, which he mainly used, however, as support for his understanding of Paul's theology;[5] he seems to have interpreted Paul's mention of "my gospel"[6] (Rom 2:16; cf. Gal 1:6–9) as a reference to this book.[7] Even these documents could not be used by Marcion quite in the shape in which he had received them; he had to purge them of alleged false additions, made by the false apostles. Marcion's isolating of these particular works from the stream of early Christian writings came to act as a stimulus to the establishing of a specifically Christian (as distinguished from a Jewish) canon of Scripture by the emerging "orthodox" church; no New Testament was yet in existence in Marcion's time (though most of the writings that were to form it were already in use).[8] In addition to working out a revised edition of Paul's letters and of a gospel, Marcion composed a work called *Antitheses*. In it, he demonstrated in detail the contrast he had discovered between the message of Scripture and that of the Father of Jesus Christ.

The two foci of Marcion's work, then, were criticism of Scripture and an interpretation of Paul's letters. The former was legitimated by the latter. Whether the criticism of Scripture was actually instigated by Paul's letters is hard to say. That is, we can hardly know which came first: did Marcion first become aware of the problematic sides of Scripture by studying it as such? Some other readers, including many Gnostics, did come to criticize Scripture without taking Paul's ideas as their starting-point,[9] and, according to Tertullian, the *Antitheses* were "designed to show the conflict and disagreement of the Gospel and the Law, so that from the diversity of principles between those two documents they [the Marcionites] may argue further for a diversity of gods" (*Against Marcion* 1.19). Or was Marcion inspired to a critical reading of Scripture precisely because reading Paul had first convinced him of a decisive contrast between law and grace? Conceivably, various processes were at work simultaneously. In any case, Tertullian, appealing to a letter written by Marcion himself (which, unfortunately,

Tertullian does not quote), affirms that "his faith at first agreed with ours" (*Against Marcion* 1.1). Marcion's theological innovations resulted from a process that involved intense perusal both of Scripture and of Christian writings.

An Outline of Marcion's Thought World[10]

Marcion was neither a philosopher nor a systematic theologian, but rather an expositor of texts. Basic to his thought world was a literal understanding of Scripture. Allegorical interpretation of scriptural passages was routinely practiced in most Christian circles, as well as in many Jewish ones. For mainstream expositors, Scripture was mainly important as a collection of alleged predictions and promises about Jesus that were discovered through the use of allegorical and "typological" devices. Allegorizing also helped to side-step the difficulties caused by many passages if taken literally; allegory may often be construed as implicit criticism of the text as it stands. Marcion insisted on a literal reading and was led to exercise explicit and harsh criticism of Scripture. His suspicion of allegory was "a mark of uniqueness in that age" (Blackman 1948, 116).

Marcion concluded that the God of Scripture could not be the Father of Jesus. The Scripture speaks of a Creator whose foremost quality is "righteousness" (justice) according to the principle of retaliation: an eye for an eye.[11] He is a harsh ruler with a passion for war and a thirst for blood. According to the principle of retaliation, most people face judgment and perdition in the afterlife.

But, claims Marcion, suddenly and unexpectedly (and thus in a way not anticipated by any prophecies[12]) an unknown God appeared on the earth, one who was pure goodness. He came in the form of his Son, Jesus Christ, "in the likeness of flesh." Jesus could not be a real human being of flesh and blood,[13] since the humans made by the Creator are imperfect. He taught people goodness, exhorting them to overcome the law of righteousness with love. The Creator stood for the law, the new God for the gospel. This new God did not judge anybody except "passively," allowing the godless to remain in their error. Faith meant the acceptance of his offer of goodness.

The Creator did not recognize the new God, but had him crucified and sent to Hades. There, however, Christ continued his redemptive work. He bought free from the power of death people who had belonged to the Creator. A stunning reversal of destinies – one could think of it as a truly radical version of the doctrine of the justification of the ungodly[14] – took place. The ungodly people of Scripture – Cain, the Sodomites, the Egyptians – believed and were redeemed. By contrast, Israel's pious ancestors, from Noah and Abraham onward, were too closely bound up with their Creator to be able to accept Christ's invitation.[15] They imagined that the Creator was putting them to the test by tempting them with error, as he had done so many times before; so they did not respond to Jesus (Irenaeus, *Against Heresies* 1.27.3).

Marcion pointed out one contrast after another between the two Gods.[16] The Creator is "a judge, fierce and warlike." "Joshua conquered the holy land with violence and cruelty; but Christ prohibits all violence and preaches mercy and peace." The Creator says, "Love the one who loves you and hate your enemy"; Christ says, "Love your enemies." "The prophet of the creator" (Joshua; cf. Josh 10:12–14) stopped the sun so that it would not set before the people had taken vengeance on their enemies; the Lord says, "Do not let the sun go down on your anger" (Eph 4:26). The prophet of the Creator (Moses) stretched out his arms toward God in order to kill many in war (Exod 17:11–13); the Lord stretched out his hands (on the cross) to save people. Such examples can be multiplied many times over.

Marcion also criticized the Creator for acting in a self-contradictory manner. He prohibits work on the Sabbath, but tells the Israelites to carry the ark around Jericho (to make the walls of the town collapse) even on a Sabbath. He forbids images, yet tells Moses to make a bronze serpent. He requires sacrifices and rejects them; he elects people and repents of his choices. He creates darkness and evil (Isa 45:7), sends disasters – and repents of them.

No doubt Marcion was one-sided in his scathing criticisms. He took up dark sides, contradictions, and problems in Scripture, paying no attention to the large amount of material that reflects a more profound notion of God. Tertullian, though weak in many of his answers to the criticisms just mentioned, presents a wealth of material in which the Creator shows a concern for the poor and even demands love for one's enemies (*Against Marcion* 4.14–16). Yet to Marcion goes the credit for not explaining away the moral problems of Scripture. He read it with common sense and exposed a problem that lay dormant at the roots of Christianity (and of Judaism): the emerging new religion had adopted a Scripture whose contents partly contradicted its own teachings.

For all his criticism of the contents of Scripture, Marcion regarded its *text* as reliable. Unlike the Christian documents at his disposal, it was not corrupt; no secondary additions (as the Valentinian Gnostic Ptolemy and even some later Jewish Christians were to claim) had been made to it. Scripture was a trustworthy account of the past and even of the future of the Jews; they had reason to expect the Christ (who was *not* identical with Marcion's Christ) promised to them in their Scripture.

It is much debated whether or not Marcion was a Gnostic. This is, however, largely a question of definition. Gnosticism was not a monolith; recently, doubts have been expressed regarding the usefulness of the term altogether (Williams 1996). Marcion's notion of an inferior Creator, his negative view of the world and corporeality, and his criticism of the Scripture come close to views commonly considered Gnostic. Other views of his do not. Marcion acknowledged no divine spark in man; man was not akin to the Redeemer. Salvation did not consist in the return of the divine elements in humans to the Fullness, but in freedom from the Creator's law. Faith was emphasized more than knowledge. Perhaps one can speak of "a brand of Paulinism already open to gnostic influence" (Wilson 1995, 214).

Marcion and Paul

Marcion discovered in Paul's letters two crucial contrasts: a church-political or "pragmatic" antithesis (Hoffmann 1984, 104) between Paul and other early preachers, on the one hand, and, related to it, a theological contrast between basic religious principles, on the other.

The pragmatic antithesis rested on a reading of Paul's assertions in the opening chapters of Galatians. It is likely that this epistle stood at the beginning of a collection of Paul's letters that Marcion received from the tradition of the church, so that it was not unnatural for him to read its first two chapters as a kind of historical introduction to the letters. Paul had received the true gospel that was "not of human origin" (Gal 1:11); this made him the one true apostle and the sole normative source of Christian teaching. That there were true and false apostles was clear from Galatians (Gal 1:6–9, 2:4); a similar contrast appears in 2 Corinthians (note 2 Cor 11:13–15 in particular). Marcion made this distinction "programmatic for distinguishing the truth of the gospel from the false accretions of the *pseudapostoloi* [false apostles]" (Hoffmann 1984, 105); the polemical passages in Paul led him to assume something like a conspiracy against God's truth in the early church (Harnack [1921/1924]1996, 35). There had been violent quarrels concerning Paul's gospel; Paul and Peter had been involved in a vehement conflict and Paul had severely rebuked Peter for not walking consistently according to the truth of the gospel (Gal 2:11–14). Marcion took that reproof to refer to a disagreement between the two apostles' preaching about God. The reputed pillars of the church were thus responsible for the corruption of the gospel. The only true gospel, Marcion posited, was the one that Paul had received directly from Christ.[17] The good God in his goodness had put an end to the law, and Paul, his envoy, wanted to revoke the law of the old God; the false apostles tried to impose it again.

Marcion may have exaggerated the nature and scope of the conflict between Paul and other apostles, but he certainly drew attention to a critical point in early church history, one that "orthodox" church fathers tried to explain away at any price.[18] In a sense, he anticipated the insights of the nineteenth-century Tübingen school of F. C. Baur and others, who made the internal conflicts the cornerstone of their reconstruction of early church history (cf. Harnack [1921/1924]1996, 207–208).

The theological contrast Marcion found in Paul's writings rests on his assumption of two different Gods. Marcion found in a great number of Pauline passages and phrases polemical references to the lower God, the Creator. Often his readings seem quite willful. Thus, Marcion takes Paul's critical question to allegedly self-righteous Jewish teachers in Romans 2:21 ("While you preach against stealing, do you steal?") to refer to the Creator's unacceptable way of acting in the Exodus story, when he commanded the Israelites to take the treasures of Egypt along with them when they left the country. Marcion arbitrarily assumes that the Creator, not Christ, is the subject of 1 Corinthians 15:24 (a verse that refers to Christ's return to the earth): "he hands over the kingdom to God the Father, after he has destroyed every ruler and every authority and power." Marcion takes this sentence to mean that the Creator destroys *himself* when Christ returns.[19] He takes Paul's mention of "the world" (to whom the apostle has become "a spectacle") in 1 Corinthians 4:9 to refer to "the God of the world." Ephesians 2:15 states somewhat clumsily that Christ has "abolished the law of commandments in ordinances" (NRSV: "the law with its commandments and ordinances"); Marcion makes an (artificial) distinction between "commandments" and "ordinances," ascribing the former to the Creator and the latter to the true God: the Father of Christ has abolished the commandments of the Creator through his own ordinances. In Romans 1:16–18 Paul first speaks of the gospel as "the power of God for salvation" that reveals God's righteousness (vv. 16–17), then mentions God's wrath that is revealed "against all ungodliness and wickedness" (v. 18). Marcion characteristically attributes the power for salvation to the true God and the wrath to the Creator, taking Paul to speak of two different Gods even here. In 2 Corinthians 11:14 Marcion takes Paul's mention of Satan to refer to the Creator.

At other times, however, it appears as though Marcion, while going in a novel direction, has been able to take advantage of genuine ambiguities in Paul's discourse.[20] In 2 Corinthians 4:4 Paul expresses himself in unusually dualistic terms, stating that "the God of this world" (no doubt the devil) has blinded the minds of unbelievers. Marcion exploits Paul's ad hoc rhetoric by taking "God" in a literal sense and making the sentence refer to the Creator.[21]

The statement in 1 Corinthians 8:5 that there are "so-called" Gods, even many Gods and Lords in heaven and on earth, is taken at face value by Marcion, who reckons the Creator among these apparently lower Gods. Here, too, he presses an ambiguity in Paul's text: in verse 4, Paul emphatically states that there is only one God and no idols exist, but in the very next sentence (v. 5) he concedes that there *are* other Gods (whom the Christians are to ignore).[22]

Galatians 3:13 states that Christ has "bought" believers free from the curse of the law. Marcion concludes that they had previously not belonged to the true God, for no one needs to buy what belongs to him in the first place. Here, too, Marcion avails himself of a (minor) deficiency in Paul's discussion: the comparison of Christ's work to "buying" does become problematic if one starts looking for equivalents to the seller or to the price, details probably not reflected on by Paul.

Discussing the nature of the biblical law in the famous chapter Romans 7, Paul introduces an "I" who is "sold into slavery under sin" (and under the law). This figure complains: "nothing good dwells within me, that is, in my flesh" (7:18). Marcion turns this passage against the Creator, who is responsible for producing such wretched creatures. Note that even a modern scholar can state: "The human plight, without Christ, is so hopeless in this section that one wonders what happened to the doctrine that the creation was good. Those who see here a profound analysis of why the law is not an answer to the plight of humanity may miss the criticism of God the creator and giver of the law which can easily be derived from Rom. 7:10 and 7:14–25" (Sanders 1983, 75) – though, to be sure, Paul did not do so. Marcion here took the chance to seize on an extreme, uncharacteristic discourse of Paul's[23] and to draw a conclusion that seems logical enough, if the passage is isolated from Paul's more characteristic statements on the human condition.[24]

Marcion supports his view that Jesus was not a real human being by appealing to Pauline texts. Romans 8:3 states that God sent his Son "in the likeness [*homoiōma*] of sinful flesh"; Marcion infers that Jesus was only *like* humans, not really one of them. The same conclusion is drawn from Philippians 2:7: Christ took "the *form* of a slave," being born "in human *likeness* [*homoiōma*]" and "found in human form." Marcion held that, in comparison with natural human bodies, Christ's body was a *phantasma*. Yet Christ was no ghost, just as the angels who visited Abraham were no ghosts but acted and ate like real humans. In Christ, God took a human appearance, putting himself in a position in which he could feel, act, and even suffer like a human being – even though the appearance of a humanly begotten, fleshly body was deceptive, since the substance of the flesh was missing. Harnack notes that it is therefore wrong to claim (with Marcion's opponents) that Christ had, according to Marcion, only seemingly suffered and died.[25]

The "docetism" (the view that Christ was only seemingly human) of Marcion and others has been much deplored, but one may ask whether it is indeed certain that Paul actually assumed the *full* humanity of the pre-existent Son whom the Father sent to save humans. Some scholars conclude that the statements on Christ's "likeness" with humans bring about an internal contradiction in Paul's thought, the presence of a "reservation, or misgiving, as to the full genuineness of the humanity of Jesus, which is essentially incompatible with [Paul's] basic conception of its function or role in God's saving act" (Knox 1967, 33). Paul introduced, "perhaps without intending to or even knowing that he was doing so, a hint of the flesh's unreality," apparently because he was not able to attribute anything like sin to Jesus (Knox 1967, 51).[26] The possibility is left open that Jesus did not completely identify with sinful humans. On this point, Marcion seems not to have distanced himself very far from the apostle.

The genuinely Pauline roots of Marcion's doctrine are even clearer with regard to the issue of law and grace.[27] Marcion derived the key to the contrast between the old order and the new from Galatians – the letter that probably stood first, in a leading position as it were, in the collection he used. If Marcion's picture of Paul is one-sided, this is no wonder, for Galatians *is* one-sided: "If the view of Paul that Marcion got from Galatians is exaggerated, distorted, or truncated, then so is any view that knows him only through this epistle – as is shown by the difficulty some of us have in bringing the views expressed in Galatians into line, for example, with those expressed in Romans" (Wilson 1995, 214). In Romans, Paul is at pains to find more continuity between the law and his gospel (though even there a good deal of ambiguity remains). Even in modern scholarship, one's overall picture of Paul depends on whether Galatians is read in light of Romans, or vice versa.

In Galatians, Paul speaks about the Mosaic law in a negative tone. He even claims that observant Jews are under a curse, from which "Christ [has] redeemed us" (Gal 3:10–13), and goes on to suggest (obliquely) that the law may not even stem directly from God at all: it was "added because of transgressions" and "ordained through angels by a mediator" (3:19).[28] In the next verses, Paul does make an attempt to find some positive purpose for the law (Scripture "has imprisoned all things under the power of sin, so that what was promised through faith in Jesus Christ might be given to those who believe," v. 22; "the law was our disciplinarian until Christ came," v. 24).[29] Yet no further positive theology of the law is built on these verses in the following treatment (Kuula 1999, 181). Soon enough, Paul equates the law with the "elements [NRSV: "elemental spirits"] of the world" (Gal 4:3–5), putting its observance in parallel to pagan idolatry (vv. 3–5, 9–10), and associating the holy rite of circumcision with castration (Gal 5:11–12). He here ignores the history of Israel as God's chosen people. In Galatians 4:21–31, Paul does draw an "historical" line to the present, but it is a line of slavery: the Sinaitic covenant gives birth to slaves (4:24–25)!

Not surprisingly, a Jewish scholar who reflects on Paul's talk of "the curse of the law" and the slavery of humans under it finds that Paul has "somewhat demonized the

God of Israel" (Levenson 1985, 247). Marcel Simon, an expert on Jewish–Christian relations, writes that, if Paul had been "more rigorously logical," he would perhaps have condemned the law outright; "he comes very near to doing so, as when, for example, he attempts to defend God from any compromising responsibility for the law by attributing its promulgation to angels, through the intervention of an intermediary" (Simon 1986, 74; cf. 82). Simon goes on to note that "we are not really very far here from Marcion's radical solution. Marcion, who was very much a disciple of St. Paul, did no more than push the apostle's thought to its logical conclusion" (1986, 74).[30] Harnack even argued that Marcion's radical step was *smaller* than the one taken by Paul: Paul had already, for all practical purposes, put an end to the Jewish God's order of salvation; Marcion only needed to complete a line of thought that had remained unfinished.[31]

Although Paul struggled until the end of his life to maintain some continuity between his old and new faith, and although he always wanted to remain a Jew, he did state that Christ put an end to the law (Rom 10:4) and liberated believers from its curse (Gal 3:13), and that the Mosaic order had been set aside (2 Cor 3:11, 13). Paul had gladly thrown away his Jewish privileges, listed in Philippians 3:4–6, which he now regarded as rubbish (Phil 3: 8). He even asserted that righteousness based on (God's) law is one's "own" righteousness and, as such, *opposed* to the righteousness that comes from God (v. 9). It was easy enough for Marcion to infer that the law did not come from the Father of Jesus Christ at all.

Paul even established a close connection between the law and *sin*: the law can increase or even engender sin, and, in fact, this is its very purpose (Rom 5:20; 7:7). Marcion seized on this: he seems to have asserted that the law *is* sin and that it misleads. Indeed, if the law did contribute to the increase of sin, and if this was its intention, what else can those scriptural statements be that connect the law with life and speak of the eternal character of its commandments, but false claims that lead people astray?

Hard pressed between his sacred tradition and his new faith, Paul struggled with a problem of conflicting convictions. Alongside the negative statements, he also makes a series of positive statements on the law, claiming that it is holy, just, and good (Rom 7:12), and that he himself wants to uphold rather than overthrow it (Rom 3.31; on tensions in Paul's thought, see, for example, Sanders 1983; Räisänen 1987). Marcion, on the other hand, a few generations later, coolly drew his own logical conclusion, seizing on the negative statements and bringing them to a head: an order that loses its validity can hardly have been divine to begin with (that is, cannot have been ordained by the true God). For God, of course, cannot change his mind.

It should be noted here that the problem of discontinuity is handled rather roughly in certain other writings that became part of the New Testament. The epistle to the Hebrews states brusquely that the law of the "old covenant" has been abolished – and that this law (which in this writing is crystallized as the cultic law concerning sacrifices) was "weak" and "useless" from the start (Heb 7:12, 18–19). The author does not pause to ask why God should have given such a useless law in the first place. The step from here to Marcion is not long. The gospel of John also leans toward Marcion's views in that the Jews who appeal to Moses are lumped together as children of the devil (John 8:44), even though, as we shall see, Marcion's anger is *not* directed at Jews personally.

In John's view, all "shepherds" before Jesus were "thieves and bandits" (John 10:8) – apparently even Moses. (On the similarities between the gospel of John and Marcion, see Regul 1969, 164–176.)

Marcion's Treatment of the Text of Paul's Letters

Marcion made dubious the whole tradition (oral and literary) of the church; therefore, he needed authentic documents from the earliest time. One wonders whether his radicalized Paulinism could have had the success it had, if Paul's letters had not already had an acknowledged status in many parts of the church.[32] And, indeed, it seems that a collection of ten letters, beginning with Galatians, existed prior to Marcion; he did not create it, nor was it he who elevated Galatians to a prominent position. The Pastoral epistles and Hebrews were missing in this collection (Schmid 1995, 284–296).

In Paul's letters, a good deal of continuity with the traditions of Israel is found alongside discontinuity. Marcion therefore assumed that the letters contained Judaizing additions made by the false apostles. In his mind, there was reason to think that a critical restoration of the texts was needed: as we have seen, he believed – on the basis of Galatians 1–2 – that a conspiracy against God's truth had existed in the church. Why should the early battles not have left traces in the extant letters of Paul? It was Marcion's task to purify them of such distortions.

Marcion is thought to have omitted from the texts of Paul (and Luke) much that did not suit his views, but in fact rather little is known about the texts he produced.[33] The main informants, Tertullian and Epiphanius, seldom quote Marcion's text *verbatim*. Recent research is inclined to assume that Marcion handled the texts in a more conservative way than has generally been thought. (On his treatment of the letters, see Schmid 1995.)[34] He preserved a good deal of material that one might have expected him to omit. The passages that he certainly omitted were concerned with three themes: Abraham as the father of believers (parts of Gal 3 and Rom 4); Israel and the promises given to it as the foundation of the church (sections in Rom 9–11, though the extent of the omissions is very difficult to define); and Christ as the mediator of creation (Col 1:15b–16). In addition, talk of judgment according to deeds (Rom 2:3–11) was apparently deleted.

Marcion seems to have noticed internal contradictions in the letters as they stand. In the interest of coherence, he suppressed the ambivalence of the apostle toward the legacy of Israel (cf. Hoffmann 1984, 152), making Paul speak in a consistently radical manner (favoring discontinuity instead of continuity). Unlike a Porphyry, who discovered contradictions and ascribed them to Paul's feverish mind (see Räisänen 1987, 2–3), Marcion started from the conviction that the great apostle was consistent; the pieces that did not fit must have crept in later.

Modern analogies are not lacking. John O'Neill starts his somewhat idiosyncratic analysis with the conviction that "Paul uses arguments, and expects them to hold" (O'Neill 1975, 63), but finds both Galatians and Romans to be full of obscurities and self-contradictions. He concludes: "If the choice lies between supposing that Paul was confused and contradictory and supposing that his text has been commented upon and enlarged, I have no hesitation in choosing the second" (O'Neill 1972, 86; cf. Räisänen 1987, 6). He thus shares Marcion's starting-point – and ends up by ascribing large parts of Galatians and Romans to later editors.

Whatever he did or did not omit, Marcion seems *not* to have *added* anything worth mentioning to the texts. Some slight verbal changes made by him are known to exist, but they are hardly different from those variants with which the textual history of the New Testament abounds (*all* copyists changed to some extent the text they copied, partly involuntarily, partly with intention). The lack of additions testifies to the sincerity of Marcion's intentions: he merely wanted to restore what he thought must have been the original, uncorrupted wording (cf. von Campenhausen 1984, 161–162). Such an aim is best served by limiting oneself to eliminating alleged additions; making additions of one's own would undermine the credibility of the enterprise. Marcion never composed a new gospel, though a multitude of apocryphal gospels that gave free rein to fantasy appeared in his time. Nor did he compose new "Pauline" letters – in contrast, say, to the author(s) of the Pastorals.

Some Effects

Of course, Marcion's concept of two Gods was unacceptable in a monotheistic context. But the theology of Paul implied the no less offensive idea that the one and only God had, despite his own repeated affirmations to the contrary, changed his mind. It was clear to Marcion that a true God could not display such instability. This was equally clear to Marcion's critics, though they resorted to a very different solution. Marcion put forward a radical proposal, but he did not create the problem of continuity and discontinuity. It was inherent in the roots of Christianity, not least in the letters of Paul.

While Marcion posited the existence of two different Gods, his critics resorted to reinterpreting Scripture from a Christian perspective. Moreover, the "orthodox" denied any dichotomy between law and gospel in Paul's teaching. What could not be denied was that many specifically Jewish parts of the law *had* been abolished in the church (largely as a consequence of Paul's mission). According to the "orthodox," God had not changed his plans; changes had come because the Jews had misunderstood those plans. Justin Martyr characteristically explained that certain commands of Scripture (such as the dietary regulations) were given in order to discipline the Jews who, as an exceptionally sinful people, were in need of especially strict control (*Dialogue with Trypho* 19.6–20.1). The command of circumcision had a very special purpose: it was meant to assist the Romans in identifying Jews in order to punish them (*Dialogue with Trypho* 16.2).

Marcion is often portrayed as an enemy of the Jews, sometimes even as the worst anti-Semite of antiquity (for examples, see Räisänen 1997, 64). This view needs to be thoroughly revised (cf. Hoffmann 1984, 226–234; Wilson 1995, 220–221; Räisänen 2005, 116–119). To be sure, Judaism was, for Marcion, an inferior religion. But unlike many "orthodox" church fathers, he did not blame the Jewish people for killing Jesus. At points, Marcion's criticism of "orthodox" views converged with that presented by Jews, so that Tertullian had reason to complain that the heretic had formed "an alliance with the Jewish error." Actually, Marcion's "orthodox" opponents seem more anti-

Jewish than Marcion, who was simply a catalyst who forced others to pose with new seriousness the question, triggered not least by reading Paul: If, as is agreed, parts of the law *are* to be abandoned, how can one take seriously the God who made such an inferior arrangement? Since the giver of the law cannot (by definition) be criticized, the blame, in the "orthodox" interpretation, is transferred to the people who cling to this law. In contrast with such views, Marcion's own criticism "focuses almost exclusively on the god and the scriptures of Judaism and says little of Jews as such"; it was among his "orthodox" opponents that the focus shifted to the Jews themselves (Gager 1983, 172).[35] While Catholic Christianity took the symbols and attacked the people, Marcion "attacked the symbols but left the people alone" (Wilson 1995, 221). Perhaps unexpectedly, with regard to practical consequences, Marcion's view may therefore be the less harmful of the two.

Conclusion

As an interpreter of Paul, Marcion was selective and one-sided. He took an extreme position, believing that there was no connection between Judaism and Christianity. He picked one side of Paul's ambivalent legacy and brought it to a head. The "orthodox" cultivated the other side of this legacy – and were hardly less one-sided, as they put all stress on continuity. The Pastoral epistles and the Acts of the Apostles ignored Paul's radical, negative statements on the law, seizing on his more positive statements, which they developed in unexpected directions;[36] "orthodox" church fathers followed suit. Notwithstanding the amount of arbitrariness that Marcion's interpretation undeniably contains, many of his insights deserve to be heard and pondered even today (cf. Räisänen 2005, 120–122).

Notes

1   Hoffmann (1984) dates Marcion's activity much earlier, but his attempt has been generally rejected; for a severe critique of his overall view, see May (1986). Still, Hoffmann's analysis of Marcion's thought (not least of his relation to Paul) contains many valuable insights.

2   The most important study of Marcion remains the comprehensive work by Adolf von Harnack (first edition, 1921; the enlarged second edition of 1924 was reprinted in 1996). Page numbers marked with an asterisk (*) refer to the appendices where the source material is collected . Harnack presents most of the available source material, gleaned from a number of patristic sources. Subsequent research has provided corrections on individual points (cf. Aland 1992, 89–90, 98), and Harnack's impressive overall picture has not gone unchallenged (see May and Greschat 2002; May 2005, 13–18). It is agreed that Harnack was right in emphasizing (more than anyone else had done) Marcion's historical significance, but it is also becoming clear that he drew too modern a picture, presenting Marcion as a precursor of Luther – and of Harnack himself.

3   The tradition further claims that Marcion was expelled from the congregation by his own father for having seduced a young girl. This is just an historicized allegory: Marcion corrupted the pure church through his teaching.

4   Moreover, it is often unclear whether, at a given point, Tertullian is criticizing Marcion himself or certain Marcionites of his own time.

5   Hoffmann (1984, 109, 112): "Marcion seems to have used his version of 'Luke' only as evidence for the separation of the gospel and the law"; "the epistles [of Paul] serve as a criterion by which to measure the gospel."

6   Quotations from biblical texts are taken from the New Revised Standard Version.

7   In Paul, the word "gospel" (*euangelion*) still refers to a message ("good tidings"); Marcion shows acquaintance with the later usage of the term, by which certain books containing the message came to be called gospels.

8   Paul's letters and Luke's gospel were, for Marcion, both crucial and reliable documents of the primitive church, but this did not make them inerrant Scripture in his eyes. Cf. Hoffmann (1984, 109): "it is highly doubtful that he was consciously interested in establishing a canon of scripture at all, since at no time does he appear to have attributed to his text of the gospel the high authority suggested, for example, by 2 Timothy 3.16. The editing out of offensive passages ... had improved the text. But such a procedure had not made the written text inerrant." It seems better to understand Marcion's "canon" "as having supplied not the structural principle but the *theological* stimulus for the creation of the orthodox canon" (113).

9   The Valentinian Gnostic Ptolemy criticized Scripture in light of the Sermon on the Mount, a critique which led, not to a rejection of the former, but to distinguishing within it different levels of value.

10 For general accounts, see Harnack ([1921/1924]1996); Hoffmann (1984); Aland (1992); Räisänen (2005).

11 He is not evil – not to be identified with Satan!

12 Hoffmann (1984, 103): "Christianity was not about fulfillment, but about salvation. As such, it was not based on history and prophecy, but on what in the theological idiom of another generation would be called the 'otherness' of its proclamation."

13 Marcion inferred from Luke 8:21 and 11:27–28 that Jesus was not born of a woman. He was a being similar to the angels who had visited Abraham (cf. Gen 18:1–22).

14 Cf. Hoffmann (1984, 198): "Marcion expresses in his version of the *descensus* the pauline division of law and grace (cf. Rom 6.14) in its most radical form"; also Harnack ([1921/1924]1996, 131).

15 Marcion concluded from the story of the rich man and Lazarus (Luke 16:19–31) that Abraham still dwelt in Hades (not in Heaven) during Jesus's lifetime.

16 Documentation in Harnack ([1921/1924]1996, 272*–273*, 281*–282*).

17 How Marcion conceived this happening remains unclear. Some of his pupils presuppose that Paul was given a book by the risen Christ; others think that Paul himself wrote the gospel. See Harnack ([1921/1924]1996, 39, 345*).

18 For instance, it was denied that the Cephas whom Paul rebuked in the Antiochian incident (Gal 2:11–14) was identical with Simon Peter, or asserted that Peter and Paul staged a show, pretending to oppose each other in order to teach the Antiochenes a lesson. It is interesting to note that perceiving the importance of this conflict (against apologetic interpretations of it) was a significant factor in Luther's development as well: see May (2005, 35, 39–40) with reference to a classic study by Karl Holl.

19 On his reading, the subject changes in verse 25: "For he [Christ] must reign until he has put all his enemies under his feet." For Paul, of course, Christ is the subject of both verses 24 and 25.

20 For documentation, see Harnack ([1921/1924]1996, 306*–312*).

21   In attributing to the activity of the devil the blindness of those who (relying on Moses [2 Cor 3]) reject the gospel, Paul contradicts his own treatise on *divine* hardening as the cause of Israel's unbelief in Romans 9–11. In Romans 11:7–8 he claims that "*God* gave them [the non-elect part of Israel] a sluggish spirit, eyes that would not see and ears that would not hear." Interpreting Romans in light of the 2 Corinthians passage could lead someone with Marcionite spectacles to the conclusion that the God of Scripture, who blinded the eyes of humans according to Romans 11, was identical with the God of this aeon who did the blinding according to 2 Corinthians 4 – and the latter is clearly different from the Father of Jesus Christ.

22   Wischmeyer (2002, 82) calls attention to "the lack of clarity, conscious or unconscious," with which Paul speaks of the Gods in this passage; she takes this feature to display an "anxious and defensive" attitude to Greek religion.

23   Sanders (1983, 78) notes that the "extreme presentation of human inability" in Romans 7:14–25 does not express a view that Paul consistently maintains elsewhere; it is "unique in the Pauline corpus."

24   Luther and his followers drew different but equally one-sided conclusions from Romans 7 by making this unique passage the centerpiece of Paul's supposedly thoroughly pessimistic anthropology.

25   Harnack ([1921/1924]1996, 125–126) reaches the paradoxical conclusion that Marcion's Christ really did suffer in the likeness of the human form that he had adopted – but that this likeness did not involve a "fleshly" body.

26   Cf. Weiss ([1937]1959, 489–490): "It cannot be denied that, for Paul, the human body which Christ possessed upon earth means something like a disguise, appropriate to a rôle which he played here; he avoids, even purposely, the more direct and more powerful expression 'he became man,' because he still does not dare to express the complete humanity of Christ ... He permitted himself ... to waver more or less in the balance between an actual humanity and a merely external assumption of a human body, as a result of which the inner being of the personality of Christ remains untouched by actual earthly humanity and sinfulness. In this Paul grazes the later heresy of 'Docetism.' "

27   May (2005, 7–8) belittles the impact of the *theology* of Galatians on Marcion, stating that Paul's significance for Marcion consisted in his being the only witness to the pure gospel rather than in his theology; because of his "massive dogmatic prejudice" Marcion could have discovered his doctrine even in other early Christian writings. This seems doubtful to me.

28   To be sure, this must be regarded as an ad hoc argument, not a constant conviction of Paul (Kuula 1999, 96–133).

29   According to Harnack ([1921/1924]1996, 46, 73*), Marcion omitted Galatians 3:15–25, since the passage speaks positively of Abraham as the spiritual ancestor of Christians. But the mention of Abraham is limited to verses 6–9, 14a, 15–18, and it is highly probable that only these pieces were removed by Marcion (Schmid 1995, 310, 316–317; cf. Hoffmann 1984, 201).

30   Cf. Drane (1975, 112–113): taken in isolation from his other epistles, Paul's "statements on the Law in Galatians can with a great deal of justification be called blatantly Gnostic." "The natural and logically necessary outcome" of the statement in Galatians 3:19, "whatever may have been its original justification in the face of legalistic Judaizers, was the belief that the Law was the product not of the supreme God"; "it was but a short step from Paul's statements to the assumption that the Law was the work of some evil angelic Demiurge."

31   Harnack ([1921/1924]1996, 202–203). Harnack's statement is connected with the notion, typical of his age, that Judaism was a legalistic religion composed primarily of externals. This view is now dead and buried. But Harnack's assessment of Paul's relation to Judaism seems to be on the right track, even though it can no longer be deemed a compliment to Paul.

32   Schmid (1995) even posits a broad "extremist Pauline" movement that had produced the collection; he assumes that Marcion was only the most influential representative of this movement.

33   Harnack still tried to reconstruct the wording of Marcion's new Bible; recent scholarship has not followed him.

34   Cf. the summarizing judgment of May (2005, 9): theologically based textual changes were not numerous.

35   May (2005, 4) points out that we know absolutely nothing about Marcion's attitude to contemporary Judaism; his "anti-Judaism" is of an exegetical-theoretical nature (all negative statements on Jews and their God are due to reading the Hebrew Bible) and is directed against the allegedly "Judaizing" teaching of the *church*.

36   In the Pastorals, the law is "good," for it holds sinners and criminals in check (1 Tim 1:8–11); Houlden (1976, 53) sees here "a positive travesty" of Paul's teaching. In Acts, Paul becomes a pious Jew (Acts 24:14, 26:4–5), more conservative than the Jerusalem pillars ever were; it is Peter and James who make all the critical decisions for the Gentile mission to flourish (Acts 10–11, 15). See, for example, Jervell (1972, 185–199).

References

Aland, Barbara. 1992. Marcion (ca. 85–160) / Marcioniten. *Theologische Realenzyklopädie* 22: 89–101. Berlin: Walter de Gruyter.

Blackman, E. C. 1948. *Marcion and his Influence*. London: SPCK.

Campenhausen, Hans von. 1984. *The Formation of the Christian Bible*. Second edition. Philadelphia: Fortress.

Drane, John W. 1975. *Paul, Libertine or Legalist? A Study in the Theology of the Major Pauline Epistles*. London: SPCK.

Evans, Ernest, editor and translator. 1972. *Tertullian: Adversus Marcionem: Books I–V*. 2 volumes. Oxford: Clarendon.

Gager, John G. 1983. *The Origins of Anti-Semitism: Attitudes toward Judaism in Pagan and Christian Antiquity*. New York: Oxford University Press.

Harnack, Adolf von. [1921/1924]1996. *Marcion: Das Evangelium vom fremden Gott: Eine Monographie zur Geschichte der Grundlegung der katholischen Kirche: Neue Studien zu Marcion*. Reprint of second edition (1924). Darmstadt: Wissenschaftliche Buchgesellschaft.

Hoffmann, R. Joseph. 1984. *Marcion: On the Restitution of Christianity: An Essay on the Development of Radical Paulinist Theology in the Second Century*. Chico, Calif.: Scholars.

Houlden, J. L. 1976. *The Pastoral Epistles: I and II Timothy, Titus*. Harmondsworth: Penguin.

Jervell, Jacob. 1972. *Luke and the People of God: A New Look at Luke–Acts*. Minneapolis: Augsburg.

Knox, John. 1967. *The Humanity and Divinity of Christ: A Study of Pattern in Christology*. Cambridge: Cambridge University Press.

Kuula, Kari. 1999. *Paul's Polemical Treatment of the Law in Galatians*. Volume 1: *The Law, the Covenant, and God's Plan*. Helsinki: Finnish Exegetical Society; Göttingen: Vandenhoeck & Ruprecht.

Levenson, Jon D. 1985. Is There a Counterpart in the Hebrew Bible to New Testament Antisemitism? *Journal of Ecumenical Studies* 22: 242–260.

May, Gerhard. 1986. Ein neues Markionbild? *Theologische Rundschau* 51: 404–413.

May, Gerhard. 2005. *Markion: Gesammelte Aufsätze.* Edited by Katharina Greschat and Martin Meiser. Mainz: Philipp von Zabern.

May, Gerhard, and Katharina Greschat, editors, with Martin Meiser. 2002. *Marcion und seine kirchengeschichtliche Wirkung / Marcion and his Impact on Church History.* Berlin: Walter de Gruyter.

O'Neill, J. C. 1972. *The Recovery of Paul's Letter to the Galatians.* London: SPCK.

O'Neill, J. C. 1975. *Paul's Letter to the Romans.* Harmondsworth: Penguin.

Räisänen, Heikki. 1987. *Paul and the Law.* Second edition. Tübingen: Mohr and Siebeck.

Räisänen, Heikki. 1997. *Marcion, Muhammad and the Mahatma: Exegetical Perspectives on the Encounter of Cultures and Faiths.* London: SCM.

Räisänen, Heikki. 2005. Marcion. Pages 100–124 in *A Companion to Second-century Christian "Heretics."* Edited by Antti Marjanen and Petri Luomanen. Leiden: Brill.

Regul, Jürgen. 1969. *Die antimarcionitischen Evangelienprologe.* Vetus Latina, Aus der Geschichte der lateinischen Bibel 6. Freiburg: Herder.

Sanders, E. P. 1983. *Paul, the Law, and the Jewish People.* Philadelphia: Fortress.

Schmid, Ulrich. 1995. *Marcion und sein Apostolos: Rekonstruktion und historische Einordnung der marcionitischen Paulusbriefausgabe.* Berlin: Walter de Gruyter.

Simon, Marcel. 1986. *Verus Israel: A Study of the Relations between Christians and Jews in the Roman Empire (135–425).* Translated from French by H. McKeating. Oxford: Oxford University Press.

Weiss, Johannes. [1937]1959. *Earliest Christianity: A History of the Period AD 30–150.* Volume 2. New York: Harper.

Williams, Michael Allen. 1996. *Rethinking "Gnosticism": An Argument for Dismantling a Dubious Category.* Princeton: Princeton University Press.

Wilson, Stephen G. 1995. *Related Strangers: Jews and Christians, 70–170 CE.* Minneapolis: Fortress.

Wischmeyer, Oda. 2002. Paul's Religion: A Review of the Problem. Pages 74–93 in *Paul, Luke and the Graeco-Roman World: Essays in Honour of Alexander J. M. Wedderburn.* Edited by Alf Christophersen, Carsten Claussen, Jörg Frey, and Bruce Longenecker. Sheffield: Sheffield Academic.

CHAPTER 20

Origen

Peter Widdicombe

Origen of Alexandria (ca.185–253) is the earliest Christian author to have written systematically on the Pauline corpus. He regarded Paul as a model for the Christian intellectual and spiritual life. Origen's writings on the nature of the Bible and its interpretation, on God, Christ, salvation, and the Christian life, all of which were to have a profound influence on later theology, were deeply shaped by his reading of Paul. As well as citing him frequently in his doctrinal, apologetic, and spiritual writings, Origen composed commentaries and homilies on almost all the epistles. We need to be cautious, however, if we are to refer to Origen's *Paul*. While it is certainly true that Origen had a clear sense of Paul the person and his distinctiveness over against the other New Testament authors, it cannot be said that he attributed to Paul a distinctive theology. For Origen, the writers of the New Testament, and the Old for that matter, all told one story about one subject. In practice, in both his thematic works and his commentaries, he interweaves quotations from Paul with those from a host of other biblical writings, and it is often not clear what specifically in any given discussion he has derived from Paul.

Notwithstanding his influence on subsequent Christian thought, Origen's theology was speculative and many of his teachings, especially those concerning the Trinity and Christology, were regarded as suspect both in his own lifetime and later. In 543, the Emperor Justinian decreed that his books should be proscribed and burned, and views attributed to him were condemned at the Fifth Ecumenical Council in 553. Consequently, many of his writings, including his most famous work, *On First Principles* – the first attempt at a comprehensive account of the Christian faith – survive in the original Greek only in fragmentary form, if at all. Many survive at length only in Latin translations, several of which were made by Rufinus in the late fourth and early fifth centuries. Earlier scholars of Origen were skeptical about the reliability of Rufinus's translations,

The Blackwell Companion to Paul, First Edition. Edited by Stephen Westerholm.
© 2011 Blackwell Publishing Ltd. Published 2011 by Blackwell Publishing Ltd.

but recent studies have shown that, while often free, they seldom distort Origen's meaning. With the exception of passages that deal with such subjects as the Trinity and Christology, which must be treated with caution, the translations can be taken as trustworthy (Scheck 2008, 4–5).

With regard to commentaries, Jerome reports that Origen wrote works on the epistles of Paul to the Romans, Galatians, Ephesians, Philippians, Colossians, the two epistles to the Thessalonians, and those to Titus and Philemon. He refers also to homilies of Origen on 2 Corinthians, Thessalonians – whether 1 or 2 Thessalonians he does not say – Galatians, Titus, and Hebrews (which was commonly attributed to Paul in the Patristic period). None of these has survived in the Greek. Only the commentary on Romans has survived in something close to its original length in the Latin translation of Rufinus, though he reduced it from the original fifteen books to ten. A Greek text of the *Commentary on Romans* 3:5–5:7 was discovered among the Tura papyri in 1941. There are Greek excerpts of Origen's commentary on Ephesians, his homilies on Hebrews, and his writings on 1 Corinthians in catena commentaries; and brief fragments from works on Galatians, Ephesians, Colossians, 1 Thessalonians, Titus, Philemon, and Hebrews are preserved in Latin in the works of Jerome and in Rufinus's Latin translation of the *Apology for Origen* by Pamphilus (Heine 2002, 1–2).

The Epistles and their Author

By the time of Origen, the Pauline epistles had acquired the status of Christian Scripture. Accordingly, a high view was held both of the epistles as divinely inspired and of the person of their author. Origen was the first to comment extensively on the matter. It is, he asserts, Christ who speaks through Paul's letters, for Paul had Christ within him, "according to Paul's own statement: 'Or do you seek a proof of him who speaks in me, even Christ?' [2 Cor 13:3]. And again: 'I live; yet not I, but Christ lives in me' [Gal 2:20]" (*First Principles* 4.4.2).[1] Origen is prepared to say that the apostle's writings have a lower status than the gospels, at least in those parts where Paul is writing on the basis of his own authority (*Comm. John* 1.15–16), and that we are to distinguish between the gospels and the inferior laws of the apostle (*Frag. on 1 Cor.* 35, on 7:12; cf. Wiles 1967, 15); yet since the gospel is characterized not only by narrative accounts of Christ's life, but also by "hortatory discourse to confirm the things concerning Jesus," there is no reason not to say "that the things written by the apostles are, in a certain way, gospel" (*Comm. John* 1.18). Thus, while there is nothing among Paul's writings that is "called a 'gospel' in the usual sense," by which Origen means the literary genre of gospel, "everything which he preached and said was the gospel. And the things which he preached and said he also wrote. What he wrote, therefore, was 'gospel'" (*Comm. John* 1.25).

But notwithstanding the claim that the words of Paul were really the words of Christ, Origen was also prepared to say that Paul's writings, like Scripture as a whole, were imperfect in form, their style lacking in sophistication and attractiveness, as is evidenced by Paul's use of an "ordinary vocabulary" (*Against Celsus* 3.20). Origen attributes the conflicting interpretations of Paul's writings in part to Paul's weakness of self-expression (Wiles 1967, 16). This, Origen contends, Paul himself acknowledged in his description of himself in 2 Corinthians 11:6 as "untrained in speech"[2] (Scherer 1957, 218, on Rom 4:23; Heine 2002, 120, 142, on Eph 2:1–5a; 3:1–3). Origen is not inclined, however, to dwell on Paul's lack of literary finesse. He assures us that the epistles also demonstrate a subtlety in the variety of wording, which he attributes to Paul's "profound knowledge" (*Comm. Rom.* 4.11.2); and Paul uses the principles of dialectic naturally, as is evident from the syllogisms appearing in Romans and his other letters (*Frag. on 1 Cor.* 82, on 15:14; *Comm. Rom.* 6.13.2). In keeping with his view of the text of Scripture as a whole, Origen claims that some of the problems with Paul's writings were placed in the text deliberately. Thus, for instance, Paul intentionally changed the meaning of the term "law" in Romans without giving the reader any indication that he was doing so. As in other parts of Scripture, Paul's purpose here was to conceal the divine truth from the unsophisticated and those not prepared to study the texts with intensity (*Comm. Rom.* 6.8.2; cf. Wiles 1967, 17).

Paul himself, Origen believed, was eminently qualified to be one of the writers of the gospel. As we have seen, he had Christ living within in him and speaking through him. He was pre-eminent, "the greatest of the apostles" (*Hom. Num.* 3.3.3). A "divinely inspired man" (*First Principles* 4.2.6), he is "the magnificent Paul, who knew the secrets of heaven" (*Comm. Cant.* 2.2), having seen heaven "opened" when he was caught up into the third heaven (*Against Celsus* 1.48; cf. 2 Cor 12:2). The Christian is to "listen to Paul's words as the words of God and the utterances of wisdom" (*First Principles* 4.3.8), and to cultivate "the seeds of spiritual understanding received from the blessed apostle Paul" (*Hom. Exod.* 5.1). Origen acknowledges that Paul underwent spiritual development, as evidenced by autobiographical comments in various of his letters. Origen summarizes these in the introduction to his *Commentary on Romans*, the epistle in which Paul "seems to have been more perfect" than in any other (Preface 3). Like David and Daniel elsewhere in Scripture, however, when Paul appears to speak of his own spiritual and moral weakness, as in Romans 7:14–25, it is only for heuristic reasons: he applies to himself what is, strictly speaking, true of less mature believers (*Comm. Rom.* 6.9.2–12). Wiles concludes that, while he can refer to Paul's deficiencies, "more often Origen speaks in simple and unqualified terms of Paul's perfection ... The idea of a gradual spiritual development is never really integrated into the main body of his thought about Paul's person" (Wiles 1967, 20–21). In his attribution of perfection to Paul, Origen is typical of the Eastern tradition, whereas in the Western tradition, the apostles could be allowed to fall short of perfection (Wiles 1967, 25).

But Paul, for Origen, is more than simply the conveyer of the "secrets of heaven"; he is the model for the Christian life. Had not Paul preceded him, Origen tells us, he himself would not have been able to ascend to the heavenly mysteries (*Hom. Num.* 3.3.3). Moreover, Paul exemplifies what it means to imitate Christ, at the heart of which lies the way of love. In his exegesis of Romans 9:1–5, Origen composes a paean to Paul, the devoted follower of Christ and self-sacrificing Christian leader. Commenting on Romans 9:1 ("my conscience bears witness to me in the Holy Spirit"), Origen explains that there is nothing in Paul's conscience to accuse him of wrongdoing: "But behold the greatness of the Apostle's heart. From the love of God he cannot be separated; what he speaks he speaks in Christ; what he has in his conscience is controlled by the Holy

Spirit." Paul's "great sorrow and unceasing pain" of heart because of the "lostness" of his "brothers" issue in his declaring himself "accursed" for their sake (Rom 9:2–3). This, Origen observes, should not surprise us. Origen has Paul say of himself: "I have learned from my teacher and Lord that 'whoever wants to save his soul shall lose it, and whoever loses it will find it' [Matt 16:25]." Underscoring this in the strongest possible terms, Origen draws a parallel between Paul's relation to divine love, which is the Son, and the Son's relation to the Father. As the Son, "who is by nature inseparable from the Father ... , went to death and descended into the underworld," so Paul, in imitation of "the master," declares himself accursed "even though he was incapable of being separated from love, i.e., Christ" (*Comm. Rom.* 7.13.2–5, alluding to Rom 8:38–39).

The Interpretation of Scripture

What gospel texts do, Paul's among them, is "present the sojourn of Christ and prepare for his coming and produce it in the souls of those who are willing to receive the Word of God who stands at the door and knocks and wishes to enter their souls" (*Comm. John* 1.26). Inasmuch as it is Christ living in the apostles who speaks in the apostolic epistles, Origen cautions, "not one jot or tittle" (cf. Matt 5:18) in them is to be taken as "superfluous" and every detail is to be treated as important (*Frag. on Matt.* 218; *Comm. Rom.* 2.6.1; 5.10.18). But how is Scripture to be read in such a way that Christ's presence in the text is actually perceived? Acutely aware of the complexity of the problem, Origen looks to Paul to provide the answer. He identifies three approaches to the reading of Scripture that he considers wrong-headed: that of the Jews, who read the prophecies of Scripture and conclude that Jesus did not fulfill them; that of the Marcionites and other heretics, who attribute the writings of the Old Testament to a Creator God who is just but not good, and who distinguish such a deity from the "more perfect" Father of Christ revealed in the New Testament; and that of unsophisticated Christians, who take biblical anthropomorphisms to apply literally to God (*First Principles* 4.2.1). What all three fail to appreciate is that the text of Scripture is not to be read "according to the bare letter," but for its "spiritual sense" (4.2.2).

In one of the most influential passages in the history of Christian reflection on scriptural hermeneutics, Origen contends that the text of the Bible has three levels of meaning: the literal, moral, and spiritual. The three levels correspond to the three aspects of human nature (*First Principles* 4.2.4), suggested to Origen by Paul's blessing in 1 Thessalonians 5:23, "may your spirit and soul and body be kept sound." All the writings of the Bible, including those of a patently historical nature, contain saving doctrines about Christ. The seemingly unedifying or erroneous passages – which Origen calls "stumbling blocks" – have been deliberately included by the Holy Spirit to prompt the reader to look beyond the literal level to the spiritual teaching to which it points (*First Principles* 4.2.9). Origen appeals throughout his writings to 2 Corinthians 3:6 ("The letter kills, but the Spirit [for Origen, the spiritual meaning of the text] gives life"), often in conjunction with 2 Corinthians 3:15–17 ("Indeed, to this very day whenever Moses is read, a veil lies over their minds; but when one turns to the Lord, the veil is removed. Now the Lord is the Spirit, and where the Spirit of the Lord is, there is freedom"), to justify his belief that the goal of reading the Bible is to penetrate to its spiritual meaning (*First Principles* 1.1.2).

The allegorical approach to the reading of Scripture that Origen championed, and to which he gave its classic formulation, was to dominate Christian reading of Scripture in the West until the Reformation. Again, Origen looked to Paul as his authority. Paul himself had described the story of Hagar and Sarah as allegory (*First Principles* 4.2.6; cf. Gal 4:24). As Origen demonstrates throughout *On First Principles*, allegorical reading allows problematic passages in Scripture of various sorts to be interpreted spiritually, and not simply taken in their plain sense: descriptions of God as wrathful, or as walking in the garden in the cool of the evening, or as fire; prophecies of a city of God being built, or of wolves feeding with lambs, at the coming of Messiah; laws that seem irrational or impossible to fulfill. What the reader meets when the text is read this way, under the guidance of the Holy Spirit, is the presence of the *Logos* within both testaments of Scripture. Properly read, both testaments can be perceived to give witness to one and the same God.

But given Origen's affirmation of continuity between the revelation of God in the Old Testament and the revelation of God in Christ, how was the relation between law and gospel to be construed? For Origen, there could be no tension between the two; he tends to use the distinction between the letter and the spirit to solve any problems. He does not regard parts of the law in a negative light – after all, it was inspired – nor does he argue that Christ replaced the old law with a new one. Rather, in his view, the coming of Christ removed the veil that had concealed the spiritual meaning of the law of Moses (*First Principles* 4.1.6). Not only was the gospel the historical fulfillment of the law, though Origen understood it that way too; it also enabled the hidden spiritual meaning that had been present in the law all along to be perceived. Commenting on Romans 6:14, Origen identifies the contrast it draws between law and grace with that between the letter and the spirit (*Comm. Rom.* 6.1.9), "and in his thinking as a whole the latter type of contrast tends to swallow up the former" (Wiles 1967, 65).

When we turn to Origen's treatment of the word "law" in the *Commentary on Romans*, we find him taking great care to distinguish the various senses he sees used by Paul. He lists six and illustrates them from the epistles: (1) the Mosaic law according to the letter (Gal 3:10, 19, 24; 5:4); (2) the Mosaic law according to its spiritual sense (Rom 7:12, 14); (3) the natural law (Rom 2:14); (4) the Mosaic history (Gal 4:2); (5) the prophetic books (1 Cor 14:21); and (6) the teachings of Christ (1 Cor 9:21), though this last is added tentatively (*Frag. on Rom.* 10, on 2:21–25; 36, on 7:7; see Wiles 1967, 51). Reflective of his desire always to protect the justice of God and affirm human moral responsibility, natural law is the one Origen thinks most frequently intended in Romans. Thus, Romans 3:19, which speaks of the law silencing "every mouth" and "the whole world" being "held accountable to God," refers to natural law and not the Mosaic since otherwise the universal nature of the conclusion could not be justified (*Comm. Rom.* 3.6.1). Passages where Paul says that the law makes human beings responsible for their sin Origen usually interprets as referring to natural law; the period of humankind's innocence refers not so much to a pre-Mosaic historical period as to that of children below the age of reason (*Comm. Rom.* 3.2.7–8). What Origen will not allow is any suggestion that the law is responsible for sin. That would be to commit the error of the

Marcionites, as he explains in his discussion of Romans 5:20: "But law came in, with the result that the trespass multiplied." Here again "law" must refer to natural law – or, better still, to the law in one's members (*Comm. Rom.* 5.6.2–4).

The Divine Nature

The belief that Scripture contains spiritual meaning is in harmony with Origen's conviction that the principal attribute of the divine nature is incorporeality, a conviction Origen viewed as warranted by Paul's epistles. Recognition of the attribute was for Origen the necessary precondition for the proper interpretation of biblical descriptions of God; it is the attribute that underlies all the other divine attributes, and it is central to how human beings come to the knowledge of God. Origen, of course, was not alone in maintaining that God is incorporeal. This was the common assumption of most early Christian writers, and it reflected in part the Platonist metaphysic on which they drew. But, for Origen, it was crucial that it be shown to be attested in the Bible, the definitive source for truth about God. Origen acknowledges that the *word* "incorporeal" does not appear in the Bible, but he maintains that the *idea* does. To prove his point, Origen brings forward what for him is the critical text for understanding both the nature of God and the relationship between the Father and the Son: Colossians 1:15, where Paul says of Christ that he "is the image of the invisible God, the firstborn of all creation." This verse, together with John 1:18 ("No one has ever seen God"), establishes that God is invisible by nature; but to say that God is invisible, Origen argues, is tantamount to saying that God surpasses the nature of bodies. The biblical term "invisible" and the Greek philosophical term "incorporeal" therefore are equivalent (*First Principles* 4.3.15; *Comm. John* 13.132). Accordingly, Paul proclaims that God is not a body, and Origen feels free to use the words "incorporeal" and "invisible" interchangeably throughout his writings to describe God.

Concordant with his understanding of God as incorporeal, Origen held a high doctrine of the transcendence of God. In his great work of apologetics, *Against Celsus*, written in reply to the charge of the Platonist philosopher Celsus that Christianity is crude and philosophically naïve, Origen is intent on demonstrating the superiority of the Christian conception of God to that of the Greeks. Pitting Paul against Plato, he bases his argument on the first chapter of Romans. According to Origen, Christianity puts forward a much more radical claim concerning the transcendence and unknowability of God than do the Greeks. Romans 1:20, with its references to the "eternal power" of God and to "divine nature," shows that God transcends the realm of being (*Against Celsus* 7.46). Paul's claim that, when he was caught up into heaven, he "heard things that are not to be told, that no mortal is permitted to repeat" (2 Cor 12:4), demonstrates that Christianity holds that God cannot be named, except through the grace of God (*Against Celsus* 7.42–43). Origen does not deny that Plato and the Greek philosophers were able to come to "fine ideas" about God (7.49); and he makes clear repeatedly in his *Commentary on Romans* that natural reason, unaided by divine grace, is capable of acquiring some knowledge of the truth. Nevertheless, Origen applies Paul's indictment of Romans 1:18–23 specifically to the Greek philosophers: their apprehension of divine truth was superficial and quickly abandoned. The philosophers "became vain in their reasonings; and their senseless heart wallows in darkness and ignorance where the worship of God is concerned" (*Against Celsus* 6.4; cf. 7.47).

But though these verses from Romans establish the limitations of the Greek knowledge of God, they do just the opposite with respect to the followers of Christ. Christians, regardless of their intellectual abilities, "have been inspired to a greater degree and have always remained with God and are continually being led by the divine Spirit" (7.51). The disciples of Jesus use "the invisible things of God," which "from the creation of the world are clearly seen," as stepping-stones to the apprehension of the divine being itself. "And when they have ascended from the created things of the world to the invisible things of God they do not stop there. But after exercising their minds sufficiently among them and understanding them, they ascend to the eternal power of God, and, in a word, to His Divinity" (7.46; cf. Rom 1:20). How this takes place has, for Origen, everything to do with the Son.

The Son and the Holy Spirit

In his exposition of the person of Christ, Origen employs a collage of Pauline verses to establish both the Son's eternity and divine nature, on the one hand, and his status as revealer, on the other. The most important verses are Colossians 1:15, "He is the image of the invisible God, the firstborn of all creation"; 1 Corinthians 1:24, "Christ, the power of God and the wisdom of God"; and Hebrews 1:3, "He is the reflection of God's glory and the exact imprint of God's very being." The concept he favored was that of Christ as the image of God. While it is not exclusively Pauline, it is to the Pauline verses that Origen most frequently appeals as his authority. The notion of the Son as image implied three things for Origen (cf. Wiles 1967, 76). Most fundamentally, an image participates in that of which it is the image. Colossians 1:15, with its use of both the words "image" and "invisible," served to establish that the Son, whom Origen can refer to as "the invisible image of the invisible God" (*First Principles* 1.2.6; 2.6.3), shares in what we have seen to be the most basic of divine attributes, incorporeality. Indeed, the Son as the image of God shares in all the Father's attributes, including the Father's goodness (1.2.5). That the Son is the image of the Father also implies a complete identity of will between the Son and the Father, for, as Origen notes with reference to the Son, "the will that is in him is an image of the first will" (*Comm. John* 13.234).

Secondly, an image reveals that of which it is the image. Thus, the Son images forth the God who is otherwise invisible and unknowable. As Wiles succinctly observes, the idea of the image for Origen "sums up in a phrase the whole Johannine teaching that he who has seen Christ has seen the Father" (Wiles 1967, 75), and Origen frequently cites John 14:9 together with Colossians 1:15 (*First Principles* 1.2.6; *Against Celsus* 7.43; *Comm. John.* 6.19). We see the full flavor of this in a passage from *Against Celsus*, where Origen weaves the two verses together with Hebrews 1:3 and 2 Corinthians 4:4 in a pithy summary of how the Son makes the Father manifest: "he who has seen the Son, who is an effulgence of the glory and express image of the Person of God, has seen God in him who is God's image" (8.12).

Thirdly, an image is less than that of which it is the image. Thus, while the Son participates in the Father's divinity and goodness, he does so at a lower level (an interpretation of the Son as image of the Father that subsequent orthodox Christian writers were firmly to reject). While the Son is God, the Father is divinity itself (*Comm. John* 2.17); while the Son is goodness, the Father is goodness itself (*First Principles* 1.2.13); and while the Son is truth, the Father is the father of truth (*Against Celsus* 8.12). Nevertheless, by virtue of his sharing in the divine attributes and of the identity of will between him and the Father, the Son is able to reflect the divine nature into the created order.

Origen's thinking about the Spirit was less concerted than his thinking about the Son. But his conception of God is unambiguously trinitarian. He observed that Paul had attributed an equivalence of function to the Spirit and the Son in Romans 8:9–11 (*Comm. Rom.* 6.13.2–9, if, as Wiles 1967, 92 notes, Rufinus can be trusted at this point), an interpretation followed by later Patristic writers. Origen cites 1 Corinthians 8:6 and Romans 11:36 together as attestations to the Trinity (*Comm. Rom.* 8.13.9–10); and in the Prologue to his *Commentary on the Song of Songs*, he conflates them to read "of whom are all things, and by whom are all things, and in whom are all things." It is through the Spirit that the believer can call Jesus Lord (*Comm. John* 32.128; *First Principles* 1.3.2; cf. 1 Cor 12:3). Referring to 1 Corinthians 12:4–6, Origen remarks that the Spirit supplies the saints with the "material" of the gifts of God, which are administered by the Son (*Comm. John* 2.77–78). Perhaps most important of all, following Paul, Origen assigned the Spirit a critical role in prayer, which will be taken up below.

Sin, Grace, Faith, and Works

While Origen addresses these central Pauline themes throughout his writings, he does so most thoroughly in his *Commentary on Romans*. The work is highly discursive. Origen frequently canvasses various interpretations of a phrase or passage, often at length, only then to decline to choose between them. To the post-Pelagian controversy, post-Reformation eye, his analyses may appear to be lacking in specificity, unsystematic, and inconsistent. Modern biblical commentators and theologians have tended either to ignore the *Commentary* or to mine it to support their respective positions on such issues as the relation between faith and works. (See Scheck 2008 for a history of the reception of the *Commentary*.)

Origen's view of Adam and the Fall is far from certain. Except for a few passages, his *Commentary on Genesis* is lost, and he does not address the question in anything like a systematic manner in his other writings, even in the *Commentary on Romans*. Attempts at the reconstruction of what exactly he thought have not been conclusive (but see Bammel 1989; Scheck 2008). Broadly, it can be said that Origen put forward two explanations for the Fall and its effects. On the one hand, in harmony with his concern to protect the freedom of the will, he argued that human beings are responsible for the actual sins they commit; on the other, he adhered to something like a doctrine of original sin. Both can be seen in his treatment of Romans 5:12: "Therefore, just as sin came into the world through one man, and death came through sin, and so death spread to all because all have sinned." Origen comments: "With an absolute pronouncement the Apostle has declared that the death of sin passed through to all men in this, that all sinned"; he goes on to insist that even "righteous" individuals in Scripture – his examples include Abel and Abraham – committed actual sins (*Comm. Rom.* 5.1.20). But Origen also makes comments suggesting that sin is the result of physical descent from Adam. He asks why Paul said that sin entered the world "through one man" when the woman had sinned before Adam, and the serpent before the woman. The answer he posits is that in Scripture physical descent is "reckoned to the man, as if the source, and not to the woman." He then cites Hebrews 7:9–10, where Levi is said to already have been present in the loins of Abraham when he met Melchizedek; similarly, he explains, all human beings were present in Adam when he was expelled from paradise (*Comm. Rom.* 5.1.12–14; 5.4.3). In his interpretation of Romans 6:6, Origen maintains that infants have the pollution of sin at birth, citing as proof sin offerings for newborn babies from the Mosaic law and the Christian practice of infant baptism. Origen implies that succession from Adam plays a role in the defiled condition when he remarks that it was only after his sin that Adam "knew" his wife and begat Cain, and that as a result of the virgin birth, Christ had only the "likeness" of the flesh of sin, not the flesh of sin itself (*Comm. Rom.* 5.9.10–11; cf. Rom 8:3). While Origen's treatment of the issue seems to have influenced both Pelagius's emphasis on personal sin (with Adam's role limited to that of an example for others who sin) *and* Augustine's "collective" theory of original sin (Bammel 1992; Scheck 2008, 74), Origen himself did not choose between the two explanations.

Origen had no doubt that Christ's death on the cross brought about salvation as an objective reality. Commenting on Romans 3:25–26, he observes that "through the sacrifice of himself," Christ makes God "propitious to men" in such a way that God can manifest

> his own righteousness as he forgives them their past sins ... For at the consummation of the age, at the end of time, God disclosed his own righteousness and, for the redemption price, gave him whom he made a propitiator ... For God is just, and the one who is just could not justify the unjust; for that reason he wanted there to be the mediation of a propitiator so that those who were not able to be justified through their own works might be justified through faith in him. (*Comm. Rom.* 3.8.1)

Noting the greatness of God's love for humankind shown in the death of Christ "while we still were sinners" (Rom 5:8), Origen writes that Christ is the "lamb of God," who "take[s] away the sin of the world ... and suffer[s] pain on our behalf" (cf. John 1:29). His death is unique. About none of the pagan heroes is it said that they died for the sins of the *whole* world. This is said only of Jesus, who "offered himself as a sacrifice for the whole world by handing over his own blood to the ruler of this world" (*Comm. Rom.* 4.11.4). As a rule, Origen thinks of Christ's life and death, not as a literal propitiation for sin, but as a sacrificial giving of himself to the Father (Williams 2004, 139). It cannot be said, however, that, when compared with later writers, Origen had a worked-out doctrine of the atonement.

Origen's reading of Paul's understanding of how human beings come to appropriate salvation, and its implications for their lives, is complex. We see a suggestion of this in his comments on Romans 5:9, where he reads the words "much more" closely with "justified by his blood" and contrasts them with the words "justified by faith" in verse 1. Here we see (he explains) "that neither does our faith justify us apart from the blood of Christ nor does the blood of Christ justify us apart from our faith. Of the two, however, the blood of Christ justifies us much more than our faith" (*Comm. Rom.* 4.11.5). For Origen, salvation is not to be attributed entirely either to God or to humankind; both are involved, although typically, as here, priority is given to God. Origen's both/and perspective is nowhere more in evidence than with respect to the issue of the will. In harmony with most of the early Patristic writers, especially of the Eastern tradition, Origen argued strongly for the freedom of the will against the Gnostics and others whom he accused of denying the doctrine. In the Preface to his *Commentary on Romans*, he attributes the denial of the divine gift of free will to a misreading of a few words in the letter to the Romans, and he contends that such a view contradicts the general sense of Scripture (Preface 1). To say that human beings were created with fixed natures, as Origen claims the Gnostics did (*Comm. Rom.* Preface 1; *Comm. John* 20.211–219), would be, in effect, to attribute the existence of evil to God and would render God's judgment on human actions unjust (*First Principles* 2.9.5–8; 3.3.5). Furthermore, any relationship based on love, including that between the believer and God, has to be freely chosen (cf. *First Principles* 2.6.3–5).

When Origin turns to Paul's treatment of the question of divine election, he maintains that the apostle attributes it to (fore)knowledge rather than to predetermination. Holding to a doctrine of the pre-existence of rational souls, Origen insists that God could, for instance, see the souls of Jacob and of Esau and the different degrees of virtue that they had already achieved before their birth, and could establish his will for them accordingly (*First Principles* 2.9.7; *Comm. Rom.* 7.17.7; cf. Rom 9:11–12). And if God's wonders did indeed have the effect of hardening Pharaoh's heart, it was only because that heart was already hard and impenitent (*First Principles* 3.1.10–11; *Comm. Rom.* 7.16.8). In his exegesis of Romans 9 in the *Commentary*, Origin simply sidesteps the question of the extent to which Paul emphasizes divine election by attributing the argument to an imaginary objector, referred to in verse 19, rather than to Paul himself (*Comm. Rom.* 7.16.2–4; cf. Wiles 1967, 100–101).

Faith, Origin maintains, citing 1 Corinthians 12:9, is a gift of the Holy Spirit (*Comm. Rom.* 4.5.3; *Against Celsus* 3.46; *Comm. John* 13.354; cf. Wiles 1967, 105–106). But, although he is not wholly consistent in this, Origen tends to say that the gift is not granted arbitrarily, and he cites Paul's statement in Romans 12:6 that the gifts are given "in proportion to faith" to support the claim (*Comm. Rom.* 4.5.3). There is an initial faith, which lies within our own power, and a perfect faith – the "all faith" of 1 Corinthians 13:2 – which can only come about through the addition of the God-given grace of faith (*Comm. Rom.* 4.1.10–11; 4.5.3; 9.3.7). Commenting on Romans 4:1–8, Origen is clear that only perfect faith can justify the believer (*Frag. on Rom.* 21, on 4:2–3; *Comm. Rom.* 4.1.3–11). When we turn to Origen's treatment of faith and works, we see that here, too, human agency is at play. While, on the one hand, he thinks that it is possible to be saved by faith alone – he cites the woman who was a sinner of Luke 7:36–50 and the penitent thief of Luke 23:39–43 as examples (*Comm. Rom.* 3.9.3–4) – on the other, he also maintains that good works are meritorious (*Comm. Rom.* 2.7.6). But having said that, Origen does not think that such works alone, however plentiful and virtuous they may be, can save. Entry into the kingdom of heaven requires belief in Christ and being born again of water and the Spirit (*Comm. Rom.* 2.7.6, citing John 3:5). Evil deeds are punished in proportion to their evil, but the reward for good deeds exceeds what they merit. Commenting on Romans 6:23, Origin points out that Paul describes death as the *wages* of sin, but eternal life as a *gift* of God, this:

> to establish eternal life in grace alone. According to this sense, I think we ought to interpret as referring to evil works that which is written in the Gospel, "With the same measure you use, it will be measured out to you" [Matt 7:2; Luke 6:38]. For upon his own grace God has not placed measures, since it is written, "For God does not give the Spirit according to measure" [John 3:34]. (*Comm. Rom.* 4.1.15; cf. *Frag. on Rom.* 22, on 4:4–5)

Origen's desire to honor the freedom of the human will and the value of good works, which he took the letter of James to affirm, while also honoring the Pauline emphasis on faith, meant that "at the deepest level of his thought he does not really concede the existence of such a thing as faith without works; a faith which does not issue in works is not in the real meaning of the word faith at all" (Wiles 1967, 114). As Paul makes clear in 1 Corinthians 1:30, Christ *is* his attributes, and they become the Christian's when the Christian is in Christ. One cannot put on Christ without putting on his virtues (cf. *Comm. Rom.* 5.10.18). This does not mean, however, that only the perfect are true Christians, though perfection is the ultimate goal of the Christian. While it appears that Origin did not think that one could fall out of faith (*Comm. Rom.* 4.5.6; *Frag. on Rom.* 25, on 4:15–17), being "in Christ" is something dynamic and has to be realized progressively through growth in the love and knowledge of Christ (*Comm. Rom.* 6.11.2; cf. *First Principles* 4.4.2; Wiles 1967, 117). Origen's ethics, which he thinks reflects that of Paul, while perfectionistic, is also optimistic. It is an optimism that rests finally in his confidence in the grace of God: "our perfection does not come to pass without our doing anything, and yet it is not completed as a result of our efforts, but God performs the greater part of it" (*First Principles* 3.1.19). But whatever goodness and knowledge the Christian possesses in this life, Origen regarded it as only partial (*Comm. Rom.* 10.10.2–4). We see now through a glass darkly but will see face to face (*Comm. Rom.* 1.1.4; cf. 1 Cor 13:12). Ultimate perfection lies in the eternal life lived in the resurrection with Christ (*Comm. Rom.* 5.8.11–14).

The Spiritual Life

Origen is one of the great writers on spirituality in the history of Christianity, and his understanding of it owes more to Paul than to any other biblical writer. Indeed, there are passages in his classic work *On Prayer* that largely consist of strings of quotations from the epistles. Origen's piety was Christ-centered and issued in a life of prayer. This he thought both taught and exemplified by Paul. Origen saw the relationship between the Son and the Father described in the New Testament as a personal relationship of warmth, trust, and confidence, and it was this relationship in which those who are saved come to share. The Pauline theme of adoption as "sons" of God (in conjunction with the Johannine theme of rebirth) was his primary way of depicting how this came about. Some of Origen's most beautiful and impassioned writing is to be found in his description of the movement of the believer from a relationship with God characterized by fear, like that between a slave and a master, to one characterized by love, like that between a son and a father (Widdicombe 2000, 93–118). This transformation Origen thought signaled above all by Paul in Galatians 4:1–7 and Romans 8:14–17. In a paraphrase of Romans 8:15, Origen describes the state that precedes being a child of God as one in which people are "slaves of God because they have received the spirit of servitude to fear" (*Comm. John* 20.289). Through regeneration in the Son, Christians are given the "spirit of adoption" that they may be called "children of God" (Rom 8:14–15; Gal 3:26). It is love that marks the transformation. God is not "the Lord of ignoble slaves, but of those who are ennobled, who at the beginning, because of their infancy, lived in fear, but afterwards in love serve a happier servitude than that of fear" (*Prayer* 16.1). Paul's own spiritual pilgrimage provides sterling evidence of the change that adoption brings about. Commenting on John 8:42 ("Jesus said to them, 'If God were your Father, you would love me'"), Origen writes of the apostle that there was a time when he hated Jesus; during that time, God was not his Father, for God is not the Father of those who do not love Jesus. Addressing Paul, Origen concludes: "in fact, God is your Father, Paul, therefore you love Jesus" (*Comm. John* 20.135–139).

For Origen, prayer lies at the heart of the Christian life. He regards it as the activity in which we come to our most intimate knowledge of God. His conception of the "what" and the "how" of prayer was fundamentally shaped by his reading of Paul. Prayer is not confined to times when we are actually saying our prayers; rather, it encompasses the whole of life, as Paul's injunction in 1 Thessalonians 5:17 to pray without ceasing makes clear. Origen concludes that we must think of the "whole life of the saint as one great unbroken prayer" (*Prayer* 12.2). But if the scope and promise of prayer are great, so also are the difficulties involved in doing it well. Origen regards Paul as an expert in the matter, as someone who had a comprehensive knowledge of the prayers of the law, the prophets, and the gospel, and who could draw out the spiritual lessons they taught. Yet even Paul acknowledges that "we do not know how to pray as we ought" (Rom 8:26, cited in *Prayer* 2.3). The answer to the problem, as Paul well knew, lies with the Holy Spirit. Quoting 1 Corinthians 14:15 ("I will pray with the Spirit, but I will pray with the mind also; I will sing praise with the Spirit, but I will sing praise with the mind also"), Origen maintains that our understanding can neither pray nor sing without the Holy Spirit having done both before it (*Prayer* 2.4). The Holy Spirit interprets the mind of God to us (1 Cor 2:11–13, cited in *Prayer* 1.1), and through his great love for humankind, and hearing our sighs, intercedes with God with the "unspeakable words" that it is not possible "for a man to utter" (*Prayer* 2.3; cf. Rom 8:26; 2 Cor 12:4). The Spirit "prays in the hearts of the saints," and thus their prayers are "truly spiritual" (*Prayer* 2.5).

In 1 Timothy 2:1, Origen points out, Paul specifies the four types of prayer in which Christians are to engage; namely, supplication, prayer, intercession, and thanksgiving (*Prayer* 14.2), each of which Origen goes on to discuss. The apostle also gives practical guidance about the disposition and posture one should adopt in prayer. One should pray "without anger or argument" (1 Tim 2:8). While the best bodily position for prayer generally is that of extended hands and elevated eyes, Origen advises his readers that the proper attitude for confession is humility, and – as Paul makes clear in Ephesians 3:14

("For this reason I bow my knees before the Father") and Philippians 2:10 ("at the name of Jesus every knee should bend") – the proper position is that of kneeling (*Prayer* 31.1–3).

Prayer reaches its culmination when we are able to address God as Father: "to make intercessions not only with the righteous God, but also with the Father" (*Prayer* 20.2). Once again, Origen draws on Paul. It is the Spirit "who 'cries' in 'the hearts' of the blessed ones, 'Abba, Father' [Gal 4:6]" (*Prayer* 2:3), not in "mere words," but in reality (*Against Celsus* 8.6). That reality is reflected in a life conformed in all its doings to the life of Christ. "Every deed and word and thought" of those who are led by the Holy Spirit and who "in everything" say, "Our Father who art in heaven," Origen declares, have been "formed by the only-begotten Word" after himself (*Prayer* 22.4; cf. John 1:14, 18). Origen goes on to sum up his signal vision for those who believe in Christ with a tissue of Pauline phrases.

> There is in them "the image of the heavenly" [1 Cor 15:49], who is himself "the image of God" [Col 1:15]. The saints [by which Origen simply means those sanctified by the Spirit], therefore, being "an image" of an image (that image being the Son), acquire an impression of sonship ... They become conformed to him who is in "the body of the glory" [Phil 3:21], as they are "transformed" by the "renewing of the mind" [Rom 12:2]. (*Prayer* 22.4)

Here we see how deeply imbued Origen's Pauline-shaped conception of the spiritual life was with his Pauline-shaped doctrine of Christ. Paul, for Origen, was the person who taught the church how to read the Bible, how to think about the nature of God, Christ, and salvation, and, through the leading of the Holy Spirit, how to pray and how to live. He was the "magnificent" Paul, who in his own life in his love for Christ came to know God as Father, and in his love for Christ imitated Christ in serving the church. However later Christian writers were to react to various of Origen's doctrinal formulations, the fervor of his devotion to the gospel he found in the apostle's writings, and the breadth and depth of his interpretation of those writings, had an enormous influence on subsequent Christian thinking about Paul and the significance of his writings for the Christian faith.

Notes

1 Here, as elsewhere, archaic forms in the translations used of Origen's works have been modernized without comment.
2 Biblical quotations are taken from the New Revised Standard Version, apart from instances where the text cited by Origen is simply reproduced from the translations of his work.

References

Works by Origen

Butterworth, G. W., translator. 1966. *On First Principles*. New York: Harper and Row.
Chadwick, Henry, translator. 1980. *Contra Celsum*. Cambridge: Cambridge University Press.

Heine, Ronald E., translator. 1982. *Homilies on Genesis and Exodus*. Washington: Catholic University Press of America.

Heine, Ronald E., translator. 1989. *Commentary on the Gospel According to John Books 1–10*. Washington: Catholic University Press of America.

Heine, Ronald E., translator. 1993. *Commentary on the Gospel According to John Books 13–32*. Washington: Catholic University Press of America.

Heine, Ronald E., translator. 2002. *The Commentaries of Origen and Jerome on St. Paul's Epistle to the Ephesians*. Oxford: Oxford University Press.

Jenkins, Claude, editor. 1908–1909. Origen on I Corinthians. *Journal of Theological Studies* 9 (1908): 232–247, 353–372, 500–514; and 10 (1909): 29–51.

Klostermann, E., and E. Benz, editors. 1941. *Matthäuserklärung III. Fragmente und Indices*. Origenes Werke XII/1. Die griechischen christlichen Schriftsteller der ersten drei Jahrhunderte. Leipzig: J. C. Hinrichs.

Lawson, R. P., translator. 1957. *The Song of Songs: Commentary and Homilies*. New York: Newman.

Oulton, John Ernest Leonard, and Henry Chadwick, translators. 1954. On Prayer. Pages 238–387 in *Alexandrian Christianity*. Philadelphia: Westminster.

Ramsbotham, A., editor. 1912–1913. The Commentary of Origen on the Epistle to the Romans. *Journal of Theological Studies* 13 (1912): 209–224, 357–368; and 14 (1913): 10–22.

Scheck, Thomas P., translator. 2001. *Commentary on the Epistle to the Romans Books 1–5*. Washington: Catholic University Press of America.

Scheck, Thomas P., translator. 2002. *Commentary on the Epistle to the Romans Books 6–10*. Washington: Catholic University Press of America.

Scheck, Thomas P., translator. 2009. *Homilies on Numbers*. Downers Grove, Ill.: IVP Academic.

Scherer, Jean, editor. 1957. *Le Commentaire d'Origène sur Rom. III.5–V.7*. Cairo: Institut français d'archéologie orientale.

Secondary sources

Bammel, C. P. 1989. Adam in Origen. Pages 62–93 in *The Making of Orthodoxy: Essays in Honour of Henry Chadwick*. Edited by Rowan Williams. Cambridge: Cambridge University Press.

Bammel, C. P. 1992. Augustine, Origen and the Exegesis of St. Paul. *Augustinianum* 32: 341–368.

Hanson, R. P. C. 1959. *Allegory and Event: A Study of the Sources and Significance of Origen's Interpretation of Scripture*. London: SCM.

Scheck, Thomas P. 2008. *Origen and the History of Justification: The Legacy of Origen's Commentary on Romans*. Notre Dame: University of Notre Dame Press.

Torjesen, Karen Jo. 1986. *Hermeneutical Procedure and Theological Structure in Origen's Exegesis*. Berlin: Walter de Gruyter.

Trigg, Joseph Wilson. 1983. *Origen: The Bible and Philosophy in the Third-century Church*. London: SCM.

Widdicombe, Peter. 2000. *The Fatherhood of God from Origen to Athanasius*. Revised Edition. Oxford: Oxford University Press.

Wiles, Maurice F. 1967. *The Divine Apostle: The Interpretation of St. Paul's Epistles in the Early Church*. Cambridge: Cambridge University Press.

Williams, Rowan. 2004. Origen. Pages 132–142 in *The First Christian Theologians: An Introduction to Theology in the Early Church*. Edited by G. R. Evans. Oxford: Blackwell.

CHAPTER 21

Chrysostom

Christopher A. Hall

John Chrysostom, archbishop of Constantinople in the late fourth and early fifth centuries, is recognized as one of the great expositors – indeed, great lovers – of the apostle Paul. Chrysostom's sermons on Paul have been faithfully preserved across the years; in one manner or another, they all demonstrate that Paul's mind and heart have merged with Chrysostom's on a very deep level.

Chrysostom's love for Paul is clearly evidenced in his lively and evocative descriptions of the apostle: Paul is the "spiritual trumpet" whose music delights Chrysostom's ear, a living presence so close to Chrysostom that John beholds "him conversing with me" (NPNF 11, 335).[1] To employ another favorite metaphor of Chrysostom's, Paul is the wise physician of the soul. Like all good physicians, Paul "tells the sick person what he must do. If the patient refuses to hear him, he does not write him off. Rather he continues to care for him by giving him further persuasive counsel" (Edwards 1999, 176; NPNF 13, 118).

Still, despite Chrysostom's deep love and admiration for Paul, he readily admits that the apostle was human just like other Christians, subject to the infirmities of human nature. Paul, for instance, came to the Corinthians with genuine weakness and fear:

> Was Paul really afraid of danger? Yes, he was, for even though he was Paul, he was still a man. This is not to say anything against him but rather about the infirmity of human nature. Indeed it is to the credit of his sense of determination that even when he was afraid of death and beatings, he did nothing wrong because of this fear. Therefore those who claim that Paul was not afraid of being beaten not only do not honor him, they diminish his greatness. For if he was without fear, what endurance or self-control was there in bearing dangers? (Bray 1999, 19–20; NPNF 12, 30)

The Blackwell Companion to Paul, First Edition. Edited by Stephen Westerholm.
© 2011 Blackwell Publishing Ltd. Published 2011 by Blackwell Publishing Ltd.

Paul and Christ are inseparable in Chrysostom's thinking. Paul is "the teacher of the heavenly dogmas," "the one who preached that Christ was God," "the mouth of Christ," "the voice of the gospel proclamation," "the one on whose tongue Christ sat," "the tongue which shone forth above the sun," "the spiritual rhetor," "the heavenly trumpet," "the lyre of the Spirit." "For it is not Paul who spoke, but Christ, who moved Paul's soul. So when you hear him shout and say: 'Behold, I, Paul, tell you' (Gal 5:2), consider that only the shout is Paul's; the thought and the teaching are Christ's, who is speaking to Paul from within his heart" (Mitchell 2002, 76–77; FC 68, 37).

Chrysostom's sermons are peppered with descriptions of Paul's ability as an apostle, pastor, and preacher. Frequently, he comments on the skill with which Paul approaches tangled pastoral situations with particular congregations. An example may be cited from his dealings with the Colossian church, a church Paul had never visited: "Paul rebukes without giving offense and praises without producing laziness in them, as though they were already complete" (Gorday 2000, 5; NPNF 13, 264).

In virtually every sermon on a Pauline letter, Chrysostom notices Paul's pastoral and rhetorical skills and views Paul's facility with words as a key asset in forming his readers into the image of Christ. Details in Paul's letters we might well overlook are spotted by Chrysostom and often seen as bearing unexpected importance. Sometimes Chrysostom will make a general comment: Paul "does not put everything into his epistles, but only things necessary and urgent" (Gorday 2000, 56; NPNF 13, 309). At other times, he will analyze a clause or sentence in some detail, and frequently extrude a practical implication. He observes that Paul, in responding to the Philippians, asks them to "complete my joy" rather than "give me joy" (Phil 2:2). Why? Paul wants to avoid the appearance of scolding them for failing "in their duty," thus showing a pastoral sensitivity Chrysostom often applauds in Paul. In a word, Chrysostom delights in plumbing the pastoral implications of Paul's rhetorical strategies. For Chrysostom, Paul is the impeccable, inspired wordsmith; each word, clause, and sentence of Paul's letters is to be sifted carefully, studied in its particular context, and mined for its practical implications.

Chrysostom enjoys mining the details of Paul's letters for exegetical nuggets. Why, for instance, does Paul give himself no title in his first letter to the Thessalonians? "I suppose, because the Thessalonians were newly instructed and still didn't know Paul well. His preaching ministry to this church was just beginning" (Gorday 2000, 60; NPNF 13, 323). Or consider Paul's letter to the Philippians. Why is it that "overseers and deacons"[2] are mentioned in the salutation when Paul normally greets churches more generally (cf. Phil 1:1)? "Nowhere else does Paul write specifically to the clergy – not in Rome, in Corinth, in Ephesus or anywhere. Rather he typically writes jointly to all who are holy, faithful and beloved. But in this case he addresses specifically the bishops and deacons. Why? Because it was they who had borne fruit and they who had sent Epaphroditus to him" (Edwards 1999, 218; NPNF 13, 184).

How did Chrysostom come to know Paul so well? Margaret Mitchell (2002, 43) directs us to a "suggestive comment made by Libanios (Chrysostom's teacher) that through *paideia* [Greek education, tradition, and culture] Greek gentlemen were taught to 'install Demosthenes in their souls.'" Chrysostom did much the same thing – substituting Paul and Christ for Demosthenes – during two years spent in solitude in a cave above Antioch, a learning space for immersion in Paul's letters. Mitchell comments:

> When he lived a solitary monastic life in a cave for two years, devoting most of that time to memorizing the New Testament, Chrysostom inscribed on his brain a lot of Paul, and, at that, a lot of Paul speaking in the first person, now vocalized through [Chrysostom's] own mouth. Not only did constant rereading and memorization of these texts serve to lay the foundation for a life of Scriptural exposition, but it also oriented Chrysostom's own consciousness in a Pauline direction. (Mitchell 2002, 67)

During the years in the cave, Chrysostom followed advice he would later impart to his congregation:

> The inexperienced reader when taking up a letter will consider it to be papyrus and ink; but the experienced reader will both hear a voice, and converse with one, the one who is absent ... The things their writings said, they manifested to all in their actions ... You have a most excellent portrait [of the apostle Paul]. Proportion yourself to it. (Mitchell 2002, 48–50; NPNF 12, 35; 13, 240)

In Chrysostom's thinking, to *proportion* oneself to Paul – through the use of a highly developed memory soaked in the Scripture and through concrete imitation of key aspects of Paul's life – is by definition to *proportion* one's mind and life to Christ.

For Chrysostom, even a brief title, such as "Paul the apostle," demands that readers prayerfully and imaginatively shape their minds around it, so that the reality of the title sinks into the memory and motivates holy action:

> For truly when I hear, "Paul the apostle," I have in my mind the one in afflictions, the one in tight straits, the one in blows, the one in prisons, the one who was night and day in the depth of the sea, the one snatched up into the third heaven, the one who heard inexpressible words in paradise, the vessel of election, the leader of the bridegroom of Christ, the one who prayed to be anathema from Christ for the sake of his brothers and sisters. Just like some golden cord, the chain of his good deeds comes into the head of those who attend with precision along with the remembrance of his name. (Mitchell 2002, 71)

As Chrysostom proportioned his mind to Paul, daily immersing himself in the apostle's thoughts, what emerged? To what exegetical, doctrinal, and practical conclusions did Chrysostom's mimetic or proportional hermeneutic lead?

The Grace of God

What characterizes Chrysostom's interpretation of Paul's teaching concerning the grace of God? Chrysostom clearly has a synergistic understanding of grace. On the one hand, he insists that divine grace – God's unmerited favor – is manifested in all God's overtures and actions toward human beings, enabling them to respond to God's offer of salvation and to live in a manner worthy of the kingdom of God:

Let us not let the opportunity slip, but rather let us display a zeal worthy of his grace ... The acceptable time is the time of the gift, the time of grace, when it is decreed that not only will no account of our sins be demanded from us, but that we shall also enjoy abundant blessings, righteousness, sanctification and all the rest. (Bray 1999, 255; NPNF 12, 336–337)

On the other hand, God's grace does not monergistically coerce human beings into the kingdom of God. We must willingly cooperate with God's grace, a cooperation that itself is a sign of God's grace operative – but not coercive – in bringing humans to salvation. In commenting on Paul's Philippian correspondence, Chrysostom observes that Paul "speaks of the gift of faith as if it were already granted. It is not given unilaterally from God but in a way that we can take a share in it. Even here the greater part of the share comes from God. But this gift is not given in such a way as to circumvent or overcome free will" (Edwards 1999, 232; NPNF 13, 200).

What we might call *the Chrysostomic synergism* is intimately related to Chrysostom's understanding of the human will. The core question – as Chrysostom interprets Paul – is this: what enables human beings to respond to God, choose the good, reject evil, and live a life pleasing to God? His answer: the grace of God given to believers in Christ and in their creation in the image of God.

But again, grace does not force itself upon the believer. Rather, it woos and surely can be resisted, a resistance Chrysostom explains with the help of a distinction between God's "primordial willing" and "God's actual working within history":

But let us now come to matters less sure, for example, as to the relation of the divine will and its way of working. Is God's will already immediately his working? Is it a particular type of causality? ... If to will is to work and God wills all [people] to be good and to be saved, why doesn't this come immediately to pass? There is here a subtler distinction between God's [primordial] willing and God's actual working within history. (Gorday 2000, 155; NPNF 13, 282)

Though Chrysostom finds it difficult to describe precisely the relationship between the human will and God's will, he is insistent that our choices are free, while clearly being shaped by the influences to which we open ourselves. It is *we who respond* to the grace of God, while the grace of God enables – though it does not force – our response. Other factors also strongly influence the choices we make, including the power of the Holy Spirit and our willingness to respond to his initiatives. The goal, then, of Christians (from the perspective of Chrysostom – and of Paul, as Chrysostom understood him) is to exercise, train, and cultivate the gifts God has given them (i.e., their soul, mind, body, and will – all aspects of their creation in the image of God) so that the good, true, and grace-empowered free choice can be made in the midst of the perplexities and turmoil of this present life.

For Chrysostom, the source of human evil is to be found in a perverted or disobedient choice, the choice (*proairesis*) of an evil thing in preference to a good. As we have just seen, Chrysostom views the ability to choose as a property and privilege of human nature. This ability is what distinguishes human beings from animals or inanimate objects. The Corinthians, for instance, are culpable in their failure to understand the gospel because their "inability to receive solid food was not by nature but by choice, so they were without excuse" (Bray 1999, 28; NPNF 12, 44). In Chrysostom's thinking, choice, moral actions, and moral responsibility are one piece. To be moral beings, people must be able to choose; yet their ability to choose must be empowered – but not coerced – by the grace of God.

Chrysostom is insistent that salvation is the result of God's grace. "If our peace comes from God's grace," he asks his congregation, "why are you so proud, since you are saved by grace? How can anyone find grace with God, except through humility," humility based on an awareness of our great need for the salvation only God can give us (Bray 1999, 5; NPNF 12, 4)? "You were saved by grace, not by works. And who gave you this grace? It was not Paul, or another apostle, but Jesus Christ himself" (Bray 1999, 6; NPNF 12, 6). "For no one leads a life so good as to be counted worthy of the kingdom, but the whole is his free gift" (Gorday 2000, 7; NPNF 13, 266). Indeed, in his comments on Paul's letter to the Colossians, Chrysostom strongly emphasizes the absolute necessity of God acting if human beings, whom he hyperbolically describes as "stones," are to respond to Christ and be restored to life:

> For, all of a sudden, to have brought [human beings] more senseless than stones to the dignity of angels, simply through bare words and faith alone, without any great labor or effort, shows indeed the glory and riches of mystery. It were as though one were to take a dog, quite consumed with hunger and the mange, foul and loathsome to see, and not so much as able to move but lying deserted, and were to make him all at once into a man, and to display him upon the royal throne. (Gorday 2000, 25; NPNF 13, 280)

In his analysis of Paul's letter to the Galatians, Chrysostom teaches that Paul has purposely frightened those in the Galatian church who were tempted to rely on the law rather than the grace of God alone:

> Having now multiplied their fear and shaken their minds and shown them the shipwreck that they are about to suffer, he reveals to them the haven of grace close by. This he does everywhere, showing how extremely benign and safe salvation is ... "We need none of those legal provisions," Paul says, "for grace sufficiently gives the Spirit to us, through whom we are offered righteousness and a multitude of great goods." (Edwards 1999, 75–76; NPNF 13, 37)

Indeed, the Holy Spirit never leads the believer into "the poverty of legalism," but rather into "righteousness according to the Spirit" (Edwards 1999, 105; NPNF 13, 47). God's grace is unlimited in its extent. It is offered to all persons. "For God would not have withheld this gift even from one person. He has the same love for every individual as for the whole world" (Edwards 1999, 33; NPNF 13, 23).

Chrysostom does not see the sin of Adam as fundamentally crippling or distorting human nature itself; rather, it is our choices that determine our ultimate destiny. "Moral choice rather than human nature is the determining factor and rather constitutes 'the human condition' than the natural determinants. For human nature itself does not cast one into hell, nor does it lead one into the kingdom" (Gorday 2000, 48; NPNF 13, 294). To be free to choose is to be fully human. If so, Chrysostom's insistence that human judgment and the underlying disposition that influences judgment must be trained to view and respond to life in a healthy and life-promoting manner – that is, to judge things correctly and not simply on the basis of appearances – takes on greater coherence.

Of course, many will wonder how Chrysostom interprets Paul's words in Romans 9. Chrysostom himself must have felt that his preceding exegesis would stand or fall on his ability to make sense of Paul's argument in Romans 9, and it is interesting to note that his homily on Romans 9 contains no practical exhortation, a highly unusual omission. Chrysostom provides a particularly interesting interpretation of Romans 9:11–13. "What," he asks, "was the cause then why one was loved and the other hated? Why was it that one served, the other was served?" The answer? "It was because one was wicked, and the other good" (NPNF 11, 464). God's "intent" in electing Jacob and rejecting Esau was to manifest the wonder and extent of God's foreknowledge: "Because He does not wait, as a human being does, to discern from the issue of their acts the one who is good and the one who is not, but even before these He knows who is wicked and who is not" (464–465).

Paul's principal aim at this point in the overall structure of Romans is "to show by all that he said that only God knows who are worthy, and no man whatever knows ... God only knows for a certainty who deserve a crown, and who punishment and vengeance" (NPNF 11, 465). Surprisingly, many people who by all appearances would be "esteemed good," God rejects. In like manner, God ends up justifying many people whom one would think should be rejected. How so? God understands the faith and character of people in a manner that is impossible for us to comprehend. By all appearances, one would expect it would be Esau who would receive God's approbation and blessing. After all, he was the first born. "Yet," Chrysostom comments, "this was not the only thing required, but the character too, which fact contributes no common amount of practical instruction for us" (465). God possesses a knowledge of Esau – even before his birth takes place – that forms the basis for his rejection of Esau and his election of Jacob; that is, God recognizes a "virtue of soul" in Jacob that Esau lacks. It was, then, "a sign of foreknowledge, that they were chosen from the very birth" (466).

Hence, Chrysostom insists, the importance of Paul's words in Romans 9:20: "But who are you, O man, to talk back to God?" Those who question God's election – an election based on God's foreknowledge – are guilty of "unseasonable inquisitiveness and excessive curiosity ... For our business is to obey what God does, not to be curious even if we do not know the reason of them" (NPNF 11, 467). This is the point of Paul's famous illustration of the potter and the clay. Paul, Chrysostom contends, "does not mean to do away with free-will" with this illustration. Instead, Paul is warning his readers against foolishly "calling God to account" for God's decisions.

> For in respect of calling God to account, we ought to be as little disposed to it as the clay is. For we ought to abstain not from gainsaying or questioning only, but even from speaking or thinking of it at all, and to become like that lifeless matter, which follows the potter's hands, and lets itself be drawn about anywhere he may please. (NPNF 11, 467)

Chrysostom warns against stretching Paul's illustration beyond its proper boundaries, and is particularly concerned that readers might understand Paul to be advocating a kind of monergism in which God coerces or violates the human will. "Do not suppose," Chrysostom declares, "that this is said by Paul as an account of the creation, nor as implying a necessity over the will ... for if here he were speaking about the will, and those who are good and those not so, God will be Himself the maker of these, and humankind will be free from all responsibility." No, Chrysostom insists, "there is nothing else then which he here wishes to do, save to persuade the hearer to yield entirely to God, and at no time to call Him into account for anything whatever" (NPNF 11, 468). We are to submit to the mystery of God's decisions, not because an unconditional election would be mysterious and incomprehensible, but because God's foreknowledge of the character of human beings is incomprehensible. It would be perverse to imagine that because all human beings are of the same race, God must treat them all alike. The "honor and the dishonor of the things made of the lump depends," not on the potter, but on "the use made by those that handle them"; similarly, whether God punishes or honors human beings depends on the way they exercise their own free choice (NPNF 11, 468). To derive more than this from Paul's illustration, Chrysostom believes, is to undercut fatally its fundamental meaning and purpose.

To sum up, grace has introduced a time of great gifting and opportunity for individual Christians and the church, Christ's body on earth. Chrysostom constantly points his audience toward what they have received in Christ and the possibilities that God's grace opens up, glories all based on what Jesus Christ accomplished through his ministry, death, resurrection, and ascension.

Justification by Faith and the Cross of Christ

Both Jew and Gentile are saved on the basis of their faith in Christ, the Son of God who became incarnate to save human beings from the ravaging effect of sin. Chrysostom ponders the nature of the "bond" that Christ cancelled by nailing it to his cross (cf. Col 2:14). Three possibilities come to Chrysostom's mind. The bond may represent the failure of the Jews to carry out faithfully the demands of the Mosaic law in spite of their promise to do so (Exod 24:3). Or the bond may represent more broadly the debt owed by all human beings due to their failure to obey God. Finally, the bond may be owned by Satan himself, "the bond which God made for Adam, saying, 'In the day you eat of the tree, you shall die.' This bond then the devil held in his possession" (Gorday 2000, 33; NPNF 13, 286). The glory of the cross, Chrysostom believes, shines in Christ's unwillingness to give the bond to us as our responsibility to pay. Instead, Christ "himself tore it in two, the action of one who joyfully remits what we owe" (Gorday 2000, 33; NPNF 13, 286).

> St. Paul cries out and says: "The decree of our sins which was against us, he has taken it completely away, nailing it to the cross." He did not say "erasing the decree," nor did he say "blotting it out," but "nailing it to the cross," so that no trace of it might remain. This is why he did not erase it but tore it to pieces. (Gorday 2000, 33; ACW 31, 63)

In his interpretation of Paul's comment to Timothy that the law is good (1 Tim 1:8), Chrysostom notes that Paul "seems to say" that the law is both good and "not so good."

What does Paul mean? "If anyone fulfills the law in his actions, it is good." If one "trumpets the law in words but neglects it in deeds, that is using it unlawfully." Further, Chrysostom believes, if we use the law correctly, it will send us to Christ. "For since its aim is to justify, when the law itself fails to justify, it sends you on to the One who can justify" (Gorday 2000, 137; NPNF 13, 413).

Through Christ's work on the cross, reconciliation occurs between God and human beings and between Jew and Gentile:

> He did not pass the task of reconciliation on to another. He made himself the means of combining one with the other ... He himself became their mediator. He brought them together, doing away with all that estranged them ... He became a Jew when he was circumcised. Then, being cursed, he became a Greek outside the law and one more excellent than either Greek or Jew ... What does [Paul] say? He has fully reconciled both to God in one body through the cross. He did not say "to some degree reconciled" but "fully reconciled." (Edwards 1999, 140; NPNF 13, 72–73)

In addition, Chrysostom clearly understands – and preaches – that reconciliation is the joint work of the Father and Son. The situation between God and human beings is not that of an angry Father who is somehow reconciled to sinful human beings through the actions of a loving Son. No, reconciliation is the gracious act of both the Father and the Son, an indication, as Chrysostom puts it, of "how great God's love is for us. Who was the offended party? He was. Who took the first steps toward reconciliation? He did ... Christ did not come apart from the Father who sent him. They were both involved together in the work of reconciliation" (Bray 1999, 251; NPNF 12, 333).

Reconciliation is accomplished as Christ steps into the breach on our behalf. Chrysostom recognizes that all human beings are subject to the curse of the law, since all have violated its precepts in one manner or another. Not so with Christ; hence the law itself cannot curse Christ. Yet Christ must be cursed in our place if we are to be redeemed from the curse of the law and reconciled with God. This cursing, Chrysostom believes, occurs on the cross itself. For, Moses taught, "Cursed is everyone who is hung on a tree" (Gal 3:13, quoting Deut 21:23):

> Both the one who is hanged and the one who transgresses the law are accursed. Christ, who was going to lift that curse, could not properly be made liable to it yet had to receive a curse. He received the curse instead of being liable to it and through this lifted the curse ... Just as by dying he snatched from death those who were going to die, so also when he suffered the curse he released them from the curse. (Edwards 1999, 42; NPNF 13, 27)

If Christ is to be cursed in the place of human beings – taking their sins on to himself – he must be sinless. For, Chrysostom asks, "How could Christ die for sinners if he were a sinner himself? If in fact he died for our sins, then it is clear that he himself must have been sinless. Therefore he did not die the death of sin but the death of the body. This is what the Scriptures everywhere proclaim" (Bray 1999, 149; NPNF 12, 228). Chrysostom inextricably weaves together the grace of God, the wonder of Christ, and the redemptive power of the cross.

Chrysostom delights in the Pauline motif of God sending his Son to die for his enemies (cf. Rom 5:9–11) and accentuates the "how much more" aspect of Paul's thinking:

> The wonder is not only that he gave his Son but that he did so in this way, by sacrificing the one he loved. It is astonishing that he gave the Beloved for those who hated him. See how highly he honors us. If even when we hated him and were enemies he gave the Beloved, what will he not do for us now? (Edwards 1999, 114; NPNF 13, 53)

The cross is God's great reversal of expectations and a primary illustration of a fundamental theme in Chrysostom's sermons on Paul and of his understanding of providence: *Don't judge on appearances.* In his last treatise, *On the Providence of God*, written while he was a prisoner in exile at the very end of his life, Chrysostom returns to key Pauline themes and reiterates that, though the cross appears to be foolishness and horror, it illustrates and enacts God's wisdom, power, and love.

The "stumbling block" or disturbing nature of the cross, Chrysostom argues, "does not arise from the nature of the cross," but rather from the flawed understanding of those who lack the eyes to comprehend God's work in this most unlikely place. Chrysostom turns to Paul to reinforce his point:

> This is why Paul adds: "But to those who are called, to both Jews and Greeks, Christ the power of God and the wisdom of God" (1 Cor 1:24) ... Honey seems bitter to those who are sick. What then? Should honey vanish from our lives because of this? And what about the apostles themselves? Were they not an aroma of death leading to death for some, and an aroma of life leading to life for others?" (Hall 1991, 328)

The key to seeing *reality* rather than *appearance* is *faith*: "Now indeed [the cross] appears to be a reprehensible thing, but only to the world and to unbelievers. In heaven and for believers it is the highest glory" (Edwards 1999, 102; NPNF 13, 46).

Faith

To have faith in Christ is to clothe oneself with Christ, a clothing that occurs in the waters of baptism and results in inner transformation into Christ's image. "For if Christ is the Son of God and you put him on, having the Son inside yourself and being made like him, you have been made one in kind and form" (Edwards 1999, 51; NPNF 13, 30). The language of clothing oneself with Christ appears in Chrysostom's comments on 2 Corinthians 5:17, where he compares faith in Christ and justification to taking off an old cloak and putting on a new one.

> By this [Paul] briefly showed that those who, by their faith in Christ, had put off like an old cloak the burden of their sins, those who had been set free from their error and been illumined by the light of justification, had put on this new and shining cloak, this royal robe. This is why he said: "If any man is in Christ, he is a new creature: the former things have passed away; behold, they are all made new." (Bray 1999, 250; ACW 31, 71)

Faith precedes knowledge, principally because faith provides access and understanding to realities that surpass reason's capabilities to comprehend:

> Knowledge therefore comes through faith, and without faith there is no knowledge. How so? It is only through faith that we know the power of his resurrection. For what reasoning could demonstrate the resurrection to us? None, but it is through faith. And if the resurrection of Christ in the flesh is known through faith, how can the nativity of the Word be comprehended by reason? For the resurrection is far more plausible to reason than the virgin birth. (Edwards 1999, 271; NPNF 13, 235–236)

Through faith we receive the gift of righteousness from God. "Righteousness comes from faith, which means that it too is a gift of God. For since this righteousness belongs to God, it is an unmerited gift. And the gifts of God greatly exceed any achievements of our own zeal" (Edwards 1999, 270; NPNF 13, 235).

Faith destroys fear. Chrysostom adeptly analyzes the confusion that had infiltrated the Galatian congregation. The Galatians were *afraid* that if they did not follow the law, they would be punished by God, not realizing that the attempt to follow the law as the basis of the Galatians' salvation guaranteed the loss of the very thing they desired – life with God. For many Galatians, faith was not enough. "They said also that the one who adheres to faith alone is accursed, while he shows, on the contrary, that the one who adheres to faith alone is blessed." Faith, Chrysostom writes, "is older than the law. That is obvious from Abraham, since he was justified before the appearance of the law" (Edwards 1999, 40, 39; NPNF 13, 26).

Faith must be linked to love for Christ or it is apt to place its reliance or trust on the wrong object. The Galatians, for example, lost their first love – Christ – and placed their faith in their own ability to follow the demands of the law. As Chrysostom puts it, "what is looked for is not only faith but also faith abiding in love," with love's proper object being Christ (Edwards 1999, 77; NPNF 13, 37).

What characterizes faith? Abraham's response of faith to God's promises displayed "sincere love," "the noblest soul," a "philosophic spirit" or Christian disposition, and a "lofty mind." For "to believe that it is possible for God to do things impossible requires a soul of no mean stature, and earnestly affected towards Him; for this is a sign of sincere love" (NPNF 11, 386). The ability to believe God's promises, particularly that God justifies the ungodly, highlights the glorious nature not only of Abraham's faith, but that of all believers. "For reflect how great a thing it is to be persuaded and have full confidence that God is able suddenly not only to free one who has lived in impiety from punishment, but even to make him just, and to count him worthy of those immortal honors" (NPNF 11, 386). The contribution believers make to their own salvation – their own faith exercised in response to God's acts on their behalf – is itself surrounded and supported by the grace of God. "For this is the very thing that makes the believer glorious; the fact of his enjoying so great grace, of his displaying so great faith" (NPNF 11, 386).

Healthy faith leads inevitably, Chrysostom believes, to transformation. To perceive salvation as only concerned with sin and forgiveness is shortsighted. Paul's strong words to the Corinthian congregation concerning their various transgressions are meant to lead them more deeply into the wonder of salvation itself: "He asks them to think about the great evils from which God had delivered them. But God did not limit his salvation to mere deliverance. He greatly extended the benefit by making them clean, by going on to make them holy and finally by making them righteous in his sight" (Bray 1999, 54; NPNF 12, 93).

Transformation in Christ

Chrysostom's exegesis of Romans 6 illustrates well his understanding of Paul's teaching on transformation in Christ. In the waters of baptism, believers have died to sin. "For this baptism effected once for all, it made us dead to it [i.e., sin]." What does baptism into death mean? It means that believers die a death similar to Christ's death on the cross. "For baptism is the cross. What the cross then, and burial, is to Christ, that baptism has been to us, even if not in the same respects" (NPNF 11, 405). Both Christ and the believer have died, Christ in his body on the cross, the believer in his or her death to sin. And what is the sequel to the believer's baptism and consequent death to sin? A life free from sin. "But this must of our own earnestness thenceforth continually be maintained, so that, although sin issue countless commands to us, we may never again obey it, but abide unmovable as a dead man does" (NPNF 11, 405).

If this death to sin is to be "real," believers must be diligent to contribute their own part, largely through the formation of new habits. By a "change of habits ... the fornicator becomes chaste, the covetous man merciful, the harsh subdued," demonstrating that even in this present life, a "resurrection has taken place, the prelude to the other." In fact, in our baptism, "the old life has been made to vanish, and this new and angelic one is being lived in. But when you hear of a new life, look for a great alteration, a wide change" (NPNF 11, 405–406).

Of course, the problem Chrysostom faces is the reality of post-baptismal sin in his congregation, attitudes and behavior he attributes to "listlessness" and the failure to cultivate the dispositions or habits that facilitate righteous living. The opposite of the listless soul is one that is "youthful and well-favored ... in the very prime of life ... ever ready for any fight or struggle." Think of the prodigal son, Chrysostom exhorts his congregation. Even he, "who wasted out all his share, and was reduced to the greatest wretchedness, and was in a feebler state than any imbecile or disordered person," was able to change. How so? By exercising his will. "But when he was willing, he became suddenly young by his decision alone and his change." In the same way, Christians can change. "Even if we have gotten carried beyond the boundary, let us go up to our Father's house, and not stay lingering over the length of the journey. For if we be willing, the way back again is easy and very speedy ... Do but put a beginning upon the business, and the whole is done." Again, Chrysostom emphasizes the relationship between willing and habit formation. If one avoids sinful behavior "for two days, you will keep off on the third day more easily; and after three days you will then add ten, then twenty, then a hundred, then your whole life" (NPNF 11, 406).

Love plays a special role in cultivating the will to live a holy life, Chrysostom believes. When we have "no strong feelings about a person," we will not desire his or her friendship. If we love another "warmly and really," as believers are called to love Christ, the esteem that love engenders will produce changed behavior. To lovingly respond to love received, even when our responses result in suffering, is to be "right-minded." For the right-minded, expectations are surprisingly reversed. Those very conditions and events that might seem likely to overcome the Christian – poverty, disease, calumny, and death itself – are turned to the believer's advantage. "For if we be right-minded, we are the greatest possible gainers by these things, as neither from the contrary to these shall we if not right-minded gain any advantage. But consider; does any one affront you and war against you? Does he not thereby set you upon your guard, and give you an opportunity of growing into God's likeness?" (NPNF 11, 407).

To live in the power of one's baptism requires Christians to remember, understand, and embrace their baptism, and to train themselves to live wisely after baptism has taken place. For Christ has come, Chrysostom reminds his audience, "not to destroy our nature, but to set our free choice aright. Then to show that it is not through any force or necessity that we are held down by iniquity, but willingly," Paul urges us not to allow sin to "reign" over us (NPNF 11, 410).

Yes, it is possible for one who possesses "a mortal body not to sin." How so? Because of "the abundancy of Christ's grace." Sin reigns, "not from any power of its own, but from your listlessness." The problem is not with the body itself, which Chrysostom views as "indifferent between vice and virtue," much like a weapon of war that can be wielded effectively or ineffectively. "For the fault is not laid to the suit of armor, but to those that use it to an ill end. And this one may say of the flesh too, which becomes this or that owing to the mind's decision, not owing to its own nature" (NPNF 11, 410–411).

If, for example, one's eye slips and "is curious after the beauty of another," the eye has become an instrument of a faulty mind, "the thought which commands it." A "noble spirit" must be "acquainted ... with the ways of the warfare" inherently part of life in the present time. A commander stands ready to aid the Christian soldier, but the soldier in turn must cultivate the "purpose of mind" to handle well the armor and arms that the commander supplies (NPNF 11, 411).

A dramatic change has occurred in the lives of Christians through baptism. Before baptism, they had neither the Holy Spirit to assist them, "nor any baptism of power to mortify [sin]." "But as some horse that does not answer the rein, it [i.e., our body] ran indeed, but made frequent slips, the Law meanwhile announcing what was to be done and what not, yet not conveying into those in the race anything over and above exhortation by means of words." After the coming of Christ, though, running the race well has become much easier, "in that the assistance we had given us was greater." Now, after Christ's coming, not only does the law exhort us, but the very grace that "remitted our former sins" also "secures us against future ones." Indeed, grace not only holds out the promise of crowns for faithful believers, but it has actually "crowned them first, and then led them to the contest" (NPNF 11, 411).

The Holy Spirit

Chrysostom is deeply interested in the Holy Spirit and the constellation of issues surrounding both the work and the person of the Spirit. It is the Holy Spirit who in the first place empowered Paul for his apostolic ministry. Not only does Paul do "everything in the power of the Spirit," but the Spirit dwells within Paul, and through his "indwelling presence" Paul has received the spiritual gifts necessary for ministry (Bray 1999, 257; NPNF 12, 338). The "carnal man, who is riveted to this present world … , is outside the sphere of the Spirit's influence," unlike the "servant of the Spirit," who is "led by the Spirit" (Bray 1999, 201; NPNF 12, 288).

The Spirit has been active throughout human history and particularly in the history of Israel and the church. It is the Holy Spirit who has comforted and encouraged Old Testament and New Testament saints alike in the midst of their afflictions, just as it is the Spirit who was at work in inspiring the texts the church has received as canonical: "There is a great harmony between the Old and New Testaments; it is the same Spirit at work in both" (Bray 1999, 234; NPNF 12, 322).

Chrysostom unreservedly affirms the deity of the Spirit. In his comments on Paul's teaching that we "are being transformed into his likeness with ever-increasing glory, which comes from the Lord, who is the Spirit" (2 Cor 3:18), Chrysostom writes: "The Spirit is God, and we are raised to the level of the apostles, because we shall all behold him together with uncovered faces" (Bray 1999, 225; NPNF 12, 313–314).

It is through the Spirit that the deep things of God are revealed to us, truths we could never learn if left to ourselves: "If the Spirit, who knows the secret things of God, had not revealed them to us, there is no way that we could have ever known them" (Bray 1999, 24; NPNF 12, 37). The empowering of the Holy Spirit leads believers to greater possibilities than the law could ever offer, since the law was put into place

> before the Spirit came to us … For then we were properly under the law, so that by fear we might restrain our desires, the Spirit not yet having appeared. But what need is there now of the law when the Spirit has been given? This grace does not merely bid us to abstain from the commands of the old covenant but also quenches them and leads us on to a higher rule of life. (Edwards 1999, 86; NPNF 13, 41)

The Church

Chrysostom's comments on Paul's first letter to the Corinthians contain a helpful synopsis of his understanding of the nature and purpose of the church. The fundamental aspect of the church is its unity in Christ as his body on earth. To split into factions, as the Corinthians were doing, was to violate this fundamental principle. "The building does not belong to the workman but to the master. If you are a building, you must not be split in two, since then the building will collapse. If you are a farm, you must not be divided but rather surrounded with a single fence, the fence of unanimity" (Bray 1999, 30; NPNF 12, 46).

Paul's comments on the Corinthians' warped celebration of the Eucharist are also – Chrysostom believes – founded on the principle of the unity of Christ's body. "The body of Christ is not many bodies but one body. For just as the bread, which consists of many grains, is made one to the point that the separate grains are no longer visible, even though they are still there, so we are joined to each other and to Christ" (Bray

1999, 97; NPNF 12, 140). Chrysostom is insistent: "He who formed the body is one, and the body which he formed is also one" (Bray 1999, 125; NPNF 12, 176).

The spiritual gifts distributed to different members within the body are meant to nurture the church's harmony and unity: "Even as God did not grant the greater gifts to everyone, so also did he give the lesser gifts to some and not to others. He did this in order to obtain the maximum of harmony and love, since each one would see his need of the others and therefore be brought closer to them" (Bray 1999, 129; NPNF 12, 188). In turn, the unity of the church established in Christ and nurtured by the mutual gifting of the body facilitates the broader unity between churches located in different geographical locations. Local unity nurtures universal unity. "The Corinthian church was not the whole body by itself but was part of a world-wide community of faith. Therefore the Corinthians ought to be at peace with the church in every other place, if it is a true member of the body" (Bray 1999, 129; NPNF 12, 186). "The building up of the church is Paul's touchstone in everything he says" (Bray 1999, 139–140; NPNF 12, 211).

The church is inseparable from Christ; hence, its elevated position. "Oh, how high he has raised the church! For, as if he were lifting it by some stage machine, he has led it up to a great height and installed it on that throne. For where the head is, there is the body also" (Edwards 1999, 126; NPNF 13, 62).

> The fullness of the head is the body and that of the body is the head. Observe how skillfully Paul writes and how he spares no word to express the glory of God. The *fullness* of the head, he says, is fulfilled through the body. The body consists of all its members. He shows Christ using each member individually, not merely all in common. For if we were not many – one a hand, one a foot, one another member – the body would not be full. Through all members, therefore, his body is made full. Then the head is fulfilled, then the body becomes perfect, when we are all combined and gathered into one. (Edwards 1999, 126; NPNF 13, 62)

The union between Christ and the church is wondrous: "See how he joins himself to us. Sometimes it is as if holding together and unifying the whole body from above. Sometimes it is as if joining the edifice from below, as if supporting the building with underpinnings and being its root" (Edwards 1999, 143; NPNF 13, 75).

It is the Holy Spirit that holds the various members of the church together in Christ: "In the body it is the living spirit that holds all members together, even when they are far apart. So it is here. The purpose for which the Spirit was given was to bring into unity all who remain separated by different ethnic and cultural divisions: young and old, rich and poor, women and men" (Edwards 1999, 159; NPNF 13, 97). "What is this one body? They are the faithful throughout the world – in the present, in the past and in the future ... It is a common human metaphor to say of things that are united and have coherence that they are one body. So we too take the term *body* as an expression of unity" (Edwards 1999, 159–160; NPNF 13, 99).

> But what he is saying is based on this metaphor: Just as the spirit comes down from the brain, passes through the nerves and communicates with the senses, so it makes sense of the whole body. Its communication is not to all the members equally but according to the capacity of each member to receive. It gives more to that member more able to receive and less to that member able to receive only so much. So it is with Christ. The spirit is like a

root. The souls of persons depend upon Christ as members. Each member depends on his providential distribution of gifts ... One might say that the whole body receives increase as each member partakes of the distribution of gifts proportionally. In this way ... the members, receiving the distribution in accordance with their own capacities, are thus increased. The Spirit, flowing abundantly from above, comes into contact with all the limbs and distributes according to the ability of each one to receive, thus "enabling bodily growth." (Edwards 1999, 168–169; NPNF 13, 105)

Notes

1   Where available, quotations from Chrysostom are taken from the New Testament series of the Ancient Christian Commentary on Scripture, and cited by the editor of the pertinent volume in that series (Bray 1999; Edwards 1999; Gorday 2000), as well as by the volume and page number in the first series of The Nicene and Post-Nicene Fathers (NPNF), the Fathers of the Church series (FC) of the Catholic University of America Press, or the Ancient Christian Writers series (ACW) of Newman Press. Quotations from NPNF have been modernized without comment.
2   Biblical quotations are taken from the New International Version.

References

Bray, Gerald, editor. 1999. *1–2 Corinthians*. Ancient Christian Commentary on Scripture: New Testament VII. Downers Grove, Ill.: InterVarsity.

Edwards, Mark J., editor. 1999. *Galatians, Ephesians, Philippians*. Ancient Christian Commentary on Scripture: New Testament VIII. Downers Grove, Ill.: InterVarsity.

Gorday, Peter, editor. 2000. *Colossians, 1–2 Thessalonians, 1–2 Timothy, Titus, Philemon*. Ancient Christian Commentary on Scripture: New Testament, IX. Downers Grove, Ill.: InterVarsity.

Hall, Christopher A. 1991. *Chrysostom: On the Providence of God*. Ann Arbor: UMI.

Hall, Christopher A. 2005. John Chrysostom. Pages 39–57 in *Reading Romans through the Centuries: From the Early Church to Karl Barth*. Edited by Jeffrey P. Greenman and Timothy Larsen. Grand Rapids: Brazos.

Hall, Christopher A. 2010. Reading Christ into the Heart: The Theological Foundations of *Lectio Divina*. Forthcoming in *Life in the Spirit*. Edited by Jeffrey Greenman. Downers Grove, Ill.: InterVarsity.

John Chrysostom. 1963. *Baptismal Instructions*. Translated and annotated by Paul W. Harkins. Ancient Christian Writers 31. Westminster: Newman.

John Chrysostom. 1979. *Discourses against Judaizing Christians*. Translated by Paul W. Harkins. Fathers of the Church 68. Washington, DC: Catholic University of America Press.

John Chrysostom. 1980a. *Homilies on Galatians, Ephesians, Colossians, Thessalonians, Timothy, Titus, and Philemon*. Nicene and Post-Nicene Fathers, First Series, Volume 12. Grand Rapids: Eerdmans.

John Chrysostom. 1980b. *Homilies on the Acts of the Apostles and the Epistle to the Romans*. Nicene and Post-Nicene Fathers, First Series, Volume 11. Grand Rapids: Eerdmans.

John Chrysostom. 1980c. *Homilies on the Epistles of Paul to the Corinthians*. Nicene and Post-Nicene Fathers, First Series, Volume 13. Grand Rapids: Eerdmans.

Mitchell, Margaret M. 2002. *The Heavenly Trumpet: John Chrysostom and the Art of Pauline Interpretation*. Louisville: Westminster John Knox.

CHAPTER 22

Augustine

Lewis Ayres

Paul against the Manichees

Paul was of immense importance to Augustine. Robert Markus's comment that "nothing would be more revealing for an understanding of Augustine's theology than a full study of what Paul meant for him" is certainly true; that such a study has not yet been written probably results from the sheer extent of Paul's influence on Augustine (Markus 1990, 224).[1] However, Augustine's close attention to Paul, as has often been noted, was not an isolated phenomenon, but one of the most important products of what Peter Brown famously termed "the generation of S. Paul" (Brown 2000, 144). From the second half of the fourth century and the early years of the fifth, a series of extensive commentaries on Paul survive. A number of explanations for this sudden flowering of Pauline exegesis have been offered, although none has attracted anything like broad scholarly approval, and there may be no one explanation (see Martin 2001, 4–8).

In the particular case of Augustine, the fact that Paul's texts were subject to very different and hotly contested readings by Manichees and by Catholic Christians may help to explain why he devoted such close, sustained, and early attention to those texts (Augustine himself had been a Manichee for nine years prior to his return to Catholic Christianity in 386). Paul's corpus does not seem to have been treated by Manichees as "scriptural" in the way it was by Catholic Christians; Paul was rather an authoritative source to be approached via commitments to the fundamental Manichean myths and texts. But Paul's contrasts – law versus gospel, flesh versus spirit – were easily taken up and read within a highly dualistic system which wanted to present itself as the true Christianity. (1 Cor 15:50, "flesh and blood cannot inherit the kingdom of God, nor does the perishable inherit the imperishable,"[2] is a key example of a text which the Manicheans could easily make their own.)[3]

The Blackwell Companion to Paul, First Edition. Edited by Stephen Westerholm.
© 2011 Blackwell Publishing Ltd. Published 2011 by Blackwell Publishing Ltd.

After his conversion, Augustine's many anti-Manichean works thus make use of Paul as an advocate for an intelligible universe which points to its creator, as one who preaches the unity of Old and New Testaments, and as one opposed to any food laws. His extensive refutation of a Manichean teacher called Faustus (*Against Faustus*, written ca. 408) provides many examples of Augustine arguing that the Manichean picture of Paul is one-sided (Eph 5:29, "no one ever hates his own flesh, but nourishes and cherishes it," alongside such texts as 1 Cor 3:17 and 6:19, provides good ammunition against the idea that Paul sees the body as evil), and that Paul and the gospels all see themselves as fulfilling and not rejecting the Old Testament and the history of Israel.[4] In Book 21 of *Against Faustus*, for example, Augustine places Paul's comments about the goodness of the body in the wider context of his arguments that the world is created and ordered by God: "the fullness of the universe stretches from the heavenly hosts down to the flesh and blood, beautiful with a variety of forms and arranged according to the ranks of reality" (*Against Faustus* 21.7 [Augustine 2007, 288–289]). He even quotes the entirety of 1 Corinthians 12:1–26 and uses it to argue that Paul's language about the interrelationship between members of the Christian "body" rests on an assumption about the harmonious and beautiful unity of the parts of the natural body (*Against Faustus* 21.8 [Augustine 2007, 289–290]). Augustine also uses Paul to argue that this beautiful ordering is created and sustained by the Father acting through the Son and in the Spirit without mediation (using trinitarian readings of Rom 11:36 and 1 Cor 8:6).[5]

Augustine's arguments against Manichean readings of Paul can also raise for us important questions about how Augustine reads Paul, what style of interpretation he thinks is appropriate. In Book 11 of *Against Faustus* (Augustine 2007, 114–124), we find that Augustine's opponent Faustus had argued that when Paul says that Christ was born as a descendant of David (Rom 1:3), we see only an early statement superseded by 2 Corinthians 5:16 ("even though we once knew Christ from a human point of view [literally, "according to the flesh"], we know him no longer in that way" [NRSV]). This argument enables Faustus to offer a true, mature Paul who knows the body is evil and that Christ certainly did not have one like ours. Augustine argues that this piece of literary criticism is not based on any doubt in the manuscript tradition or by reference to the original Greek, but only on personal preference, taking from Paul only verses that support Manichean beliefs. Against such a method of reading, Augustine argues that the whole of the text must be read as Paul's, and the whole of Paul taken together. Difficulty in a passage should not lead us to excise it without reason! Throughout *Against Faustus*, Augustine is keen to present a "Catholic" Paul who affirms the goodness of the material creation, the unity of the human person, and the unity of salvation history. He also wants to present a Paul who is part of a unified Scripture, and thus while the battle with Manicheism pushes Paul to center stage, the same battle leads Augustine to emphasize the unity between Paul and the other texts of the Catholic canon.

How Does Augustine Read?

These initial observations suggest the importance of a slightly closer look at how Augustine reads. Most importantly, Augustine reads Paul "grammatically"; that is, he reads Paul using the tools of grammatical and rhetorical analysis that were the posses-sion of all educated Romans of his time (and which had been at the foundation of Christian reading of Scripture since at least the end of the second century). These skills were taught initially by a figure called a *grammaticus*. The *grammaticus* taught Augustine such basic moves as identifying the overall plot of a given text in order to interpret particular passages, the importance of interpreting words and phrases by analyzing their use throughout the text being interpreted, and how to explore the meaning of terms by making use of resonant philosophical and scientific resources.[6] As with most of the more highly educated ancient exegetes, Augustine also reads Paul in the light of that discipline which was in many ways grammar's fulfillment: rhetoric. The teacher of rhetoric taught skills of analysis and speaking that built on the work of the *gram-maticus* (and for some early Christian exegetes, advanced teachers of philosophy also provided more advanced versions of these skills). With this background, Augustine was particularly attentive to Paul's structures of argument and his choice of style and effect.

Two consequences of this method of reading are important for us here. First, my statement that Augustine interprets passages within their textual context begs the question of how we identify the bounds of a text. Does one, for instance, read Romans 9 in the context of Romans as a whole, or in the context of Paul's letters as a whole, or in the context of canonical Scripture as a whole? The answer is – yes. Augustine reads in all of these ways: he is sometimes attentive to the theological emphasis of a given subtext or author, but he always also assumes that Scripture is a unit brought together and given its teaching function by the Spirit. Thus, while Augustine is attentive to the passages of the Old Testament that Paul himself engages, he also expounds Pauline teaching by means of a wide variety of Old and New Testament texts. Augustine's method of reading does not mean that he is necessarily inattentive to the particular concerns or emphases of an individual textual unit within Scripture, but it does mean that he has available a multiplicity of possible contexts within which a given text may be read. Similarly, but often most strangely to readers schooled only in modern historical-critical methods, Augustine is also able to take individual terms and phrases out of their immediate textual context and read them as part of a coherent set of terms or phrases drawn from throughout Scripture.[7]

Second, as rhetorician *and* theologian, Augustine sees Scripture as a divine rhetorical performance ultimately ordered by the Spirit. This performance is ordered to draw those who have been called and chosen toward the Father, toward a contemplation and par-ticipation that is only accomplished at the eschaton and in grace-given humility. In this context, all scriptural authors, Paul included, frequently use forms of expression that are intentionally ambiguous in order to invite our deeper reflection on the mystery of God's nature and salvific action. In some cases, this means that texts use metaphors that entice and draw us through their imagery; in other cases, it means that Scripture speaks obliquely in order that its mysteries will only open themselves to those who persevere.[8]

That Scripture is a unit thus does not simply mean that all texts may be harmonized to produce a unitary account of their supposedly "obvious" teaching. It means some-thing far more theologically interesting. Different texts draw us to reflect on the action of God in creating and redeeming in a range of different ways, and they may be combined in many ways; but all draw us to recognition of the same divine mystery. For Augustine, however much we want to treat a gospel or a Pauline (or non-Pauline) letter as a literary unit, it still remains a fact that that unit points toward the one mystery Scripture reveals. Paul is both an individual writer and always also just one voice within the scriptural fugue whose main subject is the music of God's action in the created order.

One further note about Augustine's attitude to ancient rhetoric is necessary. Augustine is highly suspicious of those who use rhetoric merely to persuade – without reference to truth – and he is highly critical of the moral values inculcated by many of the texts valued within the classical Roman educational tradition. At the same time, his work offers one of the most important examples of a Christian writer adopting and then adapting those very rhetorical traditions. A fine illustration is found in Book 4 of his *On Christian Teaching*. There Augustine argues that the Scriptures perfectly balance the use of rhetorical styles and expressions to teach and persuade, but always while putting concern for the truth front and center. Not surprisingly, Augustine turns to Paul's letters fairly extensively to illustrate the character of an appropriate Christian rhetoric (see *On Christian Teaching* 4.6.9–7.15 [Augustine 1996, 205–209]).

Paul as the Teacher of Grace

Now that we understand a little more about how Augustine read Paul, we can return to the content of his reading. There are, however, many ways in which we could explore that content. In what follows, I will focus on two themes in Augustine's thought that flow from his reading of Paul. These two themes will reveal to us a Paul who points to two complementary paradoxes at the heart of Christian existence. To understand the first, I must turn to grace; to understand the second, Augustine's account of the Holy Spirit needs to be our focus.

In 395 or 396, Augustine wrote to Simplicianus, Ambrose's successor as bishop of Milan. Simplicianus had written with a list of exegetical problems, the most famous of which concerns Romans 9:10–29. Paul speaks here of Jacob and Esau. Their mother Sarah is told (Gen 25:23, quoted at Rom 9:12) that "the elder will serve the younger" on the basis of a decision made "though they were not yet born and had done nothing either good or bad," in order to continue "God's purpose of election" (Rom 9:11). Augustine asks whether this decision on God's part is unjust. Paul is adamant that God's decision is necessarily just (Rom 9:14). The apostle further tells us that God says to Moses, "I will have mercy on whom I have mercy" (Rom 9:15, quoting Exod 33:19), and consequently, "[God] has mercy upon whomever he wills, and he hardens the heart of whomever he wills" (Rom 9:18; at v. 17, Paul gives the example of Pharaoh at Exod 9:16). This passage had first received detailed Patristic commentary in Origen's corpus (ca. 230). The great Alexandrian exegete argued that it is not actually God who "hardens" Pharaoh's heart; this is only a form of expression standing in for God giving Pharaoh the chance to make choices which, when wrongly made, result in Pharaoh hardening his own heart.

Augustine's reading is very different, and rests on two clear principles. First, God's grace is that which enables human beings to turn to God as well as that which provides them with all that they need to attain perfection. Second, God's choice of who will receive this grace is just, but this choice is not based on what a person does for themselves, or on foreknowledge of what a person will do or believe by themselves. It is a justice whose rationale is simply incomprehensible to human beings. There are then two broad themes in this reading of Paul: the character of the help that grace provides, and the nature of God's decision to save (predestination). Although I have a little to say about both themes, my focus is on the first, the character of grace. But in order to understand either, we need to step back for a moment from Paul's text and think about Augustine's anthropological assumptions.

For Augustine, human beings are desiring beings, beings in act, beings always drawn by and aiming toward what delights them. Now, the human being is by nature one who should desire God, or, more precisely, one who should be drawn by, and delighted by, the divine. Set in a world whose structure is intended to lead toward the contemplation of God, and set within this order as beings naturally loving and desiring God, all should be well: we would be truly free in exercising fully our nature's character and moving toward its end. But for whatever reason – and Augustine remains puzzled but assumes that our first parents must be understood as childlike in the fact that they could be seduced from growing into this stature – human beings are now born into a state where that contemplation is disrupted, and through habit we are drawn toward many substitutes for that which should delight us. The choices we make are thus frequently made in ignorance not only of what constitute appropriate goods or goals, but also of the very sort of beings that we are, of the most basic orientation of our existence. Two important consequences follow.

First, human beings do not control what delights them: we are drawn toward objects only by nature or by habit, and cannot just decide what will delight us without reference to our pasts or our nature. Even if the accumulated weight of habit were lifted from us, we would still not be able to determine for ourselves what would delight us. We would, rather, be able to follow freely what *should* delight us, God. In all states, fallen or restored, we move toward an object by responding either to an internal or to an external image or suggestion. We are thus desiring beings, set within and only functioning within a network of signs and stimuli. For God to draw us back to being truly human, then, God must provide *both* appropriate objects of desire *and* the force of delight in those objects – a force strong enough to overcome habit. Augustine makes the point clearly enough in the following collection of rhetorical questions:

> But who can believe without being touched by some call – that is, by the evidence of things? Who has it in his power for his mind to be touched by such a manifestation as would move his will to faith? Who embraces in his heart something that does not attract him? Who has it in his power either to come into contact with what can attract him or to be attracted once he has come into contact? (*To Simplicianus* 1.2.21 [Augustine 2008a, 205])[9]

Second (and this is only to draw out a point implied in the last paragraph), for Augustine, what we too easily think of as an expression of our freedom, the capacity for making choices that are not governed by any pre-existing forces, is simply an illusion. Thus, I might think that my choice to buy one flavor of peanut butter over another is "free," but I come to the decision with a host of preformed desires that drive me in ways I can barely comprehend. Human beings are created desiring relationship with their creator, and most able to be what they were intended to be as creative, loving, rational, and social only in that relationship. Thus, true freedom only comes when we are freed to exercise our innate desire fully and truly. But because of the force of habit, we do not control our own wills. We cannot simply decide to desire God appropriately and to love all things in relationship to God. Our re-education is not fundamentally a matter of being provided with new information, but of our wills being drawn toward what should delight them.

We can now turn back to Augustine's reading of Romans 9. Augustine begins by asking about the overall purpose of the work, following one of the techniques that he knew well from his education by the *grammaticus*. For Augustine, the point of Paul's letter to the Romans is simple: "that no one should boast of the merits of his works ... The grace of the gospel is not dependent on works; otherwise grace is no longer grace" (*To Simplicianus* 1.2.2 [Augustine 2008a, 185]). In what follows, Augustine tries to persuade Simplicianus that we cannot identify a moment that is not preceded by grace. There is no initial human decision subsequently rewarded with grace: God's call is answered because God gives grace to the one who answers.[10] In his earlier work, Augustine had struggled for some years with the possibility that we do have the power to decide that we will be drawn toward God. He had done so in his battle against the Manichees; they were only too happy to accept that our powers of choice are limited and that the battle in ourselves is partially not in our control.[11] But now, in the face of the stark claims of Romans 9, Augustine changes his mind (or perhaps returns to unformed instincts that were there all along). His anthropology of desire, examined in the last few paragraphs, is the mechanism by which he articulates Paul's hints. His new account of God drawing the human person does not deny the conflicted and dark state of human attempts to will anything (as a simple assumption that we have it within our power "freely" to decide for God might), and it draws on and expands Paul's strong emphasis on God's action.

The hardest thing for the modern reader to grasp in the account that follows is how Augustine thinks that grace and human freedom intertwine. The heart of this account appears when we note that Augustine assumes the purpose of redemption to be the reformation of the human person as a desiring being. Immediately after the passage I quoted above, Augustine writes:

> When, therefore, things attract us whereby we may advance towards God, this is inspired and furnished by the grace of God; it is not obtained by our own assent and effort or by the merits of our works because, whether it be the assent of our will or our intense effort or our works aglow with charity, it is he who gives, he who bestows it ... *It is not a matter of willing or of running, therefore, but of a merciful God* [Rom 9:16], since in fact we could neither will nor run if he did not move and rouse us. (*To Simplicianus* 1.2.21 [Augustine 2008a, 205])

And, a little earlier, commenting on Philippians 3:12–13, Augustine also states:

> Here [Paul] shows clearly that even a good will itself comes about in us through God's working ... God's mercy alone does not suffice unless our will's consent is joined to it. (*To Simplicianus* 1.2.12 [Augustine 2008a, 194])

In the first of these two quotations, Augustine emphasizes that the attraction we feel for objects that move us toward God is itself a gift of God. Whereas we saw very clearly in earlier texts that we can only move toward God if something appropriate draws us, here Augustine emphasizes that the movement toward God itself is a gift. This first text puts things in contrastive terms: we do not move toward God through our own effort, but by the gift of God. But what is it that God gives? The second text gives us the answer: God brings about in us *our* good will. Here we find what I want to highlight as one of the fundamental principles of Augustine's theology of grace: *our* willing, *our* delight in appropriate objects of desire, is given us in grace. Grace should be understood as the gift of what is most deeply our own, our own true will (as he says in his early dialogue *The Soliloquies*). All that we have we should now receive as divine gift, even what is most our own. Augustine is able to use this principle as a hermeneutical key to the whole of the Pauline corpus. Thus, his reading of Romans 9 intertwines with his frequent quotation of 1 Corinthians 4:7 ("what have you that you did not receive?") and with quotation of a host of other texts that speak of divine gift and of God's work in Christians (for example, Eph 1:4; 2:8–9; Phil 2:12–13). In the history of Christianity, Augustine has long been known as the *doctor gratiae*, "the teacher of grace." For Augustine, however, it is Paul who should be awarded this title.

Paul against Pelagius

The fundamental lines of Augustine's reading of Paul as the teacher of grace were, then, set in 395–396. Around fifteen years later, aspects of this theology became the subject of fierce controversy. A traveling monk called Pelagius had been present at a reading of Augustine's *Confessions* in Rome (remember there were no printing presses and no internet; readings to groups were a key way in which works became known). He heard, to his horror, Augustine's prayer, "Command what You will and give what You command," thinking that this strange idea could only undermine the resolve of Christians to struggle with the demands of Christian life. His own works, including a commentary on Romans, became known to Augustine. In 410, Rome itself was attacked and occupied for a time by a Germanic tribe, the Vandals. Among the refugees who made their way to North Africa were Pelagius and some of his followers. Pelagius did not stay, but headed to the eastern Mediterranean. Those he left behind taught against Augustine. This was the beginning of what is now known as "the Pelagian controversy."[12] This name is somewhat misleading as it turns a series of different conflicts between Augustine and a variety of opponents over the rest of Augustine's career into one conflict centering on Pelagius.

Throughout these conflicts, Augustine's theology of grace underwent some terminological shifts and small developments, but remained fundamentally what it had been before 411. Here I will deal briefly with two texts from this period of Augustine's career, in order to show some of the ways in which Paul remains central to Augustine's exposition. *The Spirit and the Letter* is one of the key early works of the controversies and one of the clearest. In a famous passage, Augustine writes:

Are we then doing away with free choice through grace? Heaven forbid! Rather, we make free choice stronger. After all, as the law is not done away with through faith, so free choice is not done away with, but strengthened by grace. For the law is not fulfilled without free choice. But *knowledge of sin came through the law* (Rom 3:20); through faith we obtain grace to struggle against sin; through grace the soul is healed from the wound of sin; through the good health of the soul we have freedom of choice; through free choice we have the love of righteousness; through the love of righteousness we fulfill the law. The law is not done away with, but strengthened by faith, because faith obtains the grace by which we fulfill the law. In the same way, free choice is not done away with by grace, but strengthened, because grace heals the will by which we freely love righteousness. (*The Spirit and the Letter* 30.52 [Augustine 1997, 185])

Here Augustine sets out the theological principles we have already seen with even more clarity: true freedom is the will released from its chains, not merely being presented with a knowledge that will save if followed, but given both the knowledge of what to will and the power of willing the good. Grace frees and restores the person so that she or he can be what God intended from eternity. But now Augustine suddenly changes tack, offering a gloss on this clear sequence of logical principles. He continues:

All these items which I linked together like a chain have their own expression in scripture.
    The law says, *You shall not desire* (Ex 20:17);
    faith says, *Heal my soul, for I have sinned against you* (Ps 41:5);
    grace says, *See, you have been healed; now sin no more so that nothing worse happens to you* (Jn 5:14);
    good health says, *Lord, my God, I have cried out to you, and you have healed me* (Ps 30:3);
    free choice says, *I will willingly offer you sacrifice* (Ps 54:8).
    The love of righteousness says, *Sinners described pleasures to me, but none like your law, Lord* (Ps 119:85).
    Why then do wretched human beings dare to be proud of their free choice, before they are set free ... ? They do not notice that in the very name for free choice we hear freedom; *but [only] where the Spirit of the Lord is, there is freedom* (2 Cor 3:17). (*The Spirit and the Letter* 30.52 [Augustine 1997, 177–178])

For Augustine, Scripture itself plays out for us the tensions we all feel on hearing that grace strengthens free will. However, as it plays out these tensions, Scripture also slowly teaches us that they are resolved when we see that and how God acts. Scripture thus offers a chain that leads us to recognize that true freedom comes only through accepting the Spirit. The chain that Augustine offers also shows us a great deal about how centrally Augustine locates Paul as teacher of grace. It is 2 Corinthians 3:17 that holds the pivotal position here, and it does so precisely because it is this text that, for Augustine, reveals to us the importance of recognizing that our own freedom is to be found through the presence of divine healing and the Spirit.

This technique of dramatizing Scripture for a congregation or audience is found at many places in Augustine's corpus. There survive in Augustine's corpus a number of sermons delivered on the feast of St. Peter and St. Paul. In one of the most interesting,

Augustine has both Peter and Paul come onto the "stage" and speak. When Paul speaks, we see immediately what Augustine sees as the heart of his teaching on grace:

> Let the blessed Paul too step out in front of us ... Here he is, already preaching, here he is, already showing us what he had been and what he was ... *I am*, he says, *the least of the apostles, not worthy to be called an apostle* [1 Cor 15:9]. There's what he was: *not worthy to be called an apostle.*
>
> Why not?
>
> *Because I persecuted the Church of God ...But by the grace of God I am what I am, and his grace in me has not been idle, but I worked harder than them all* [1 Cor 15:10].
>
> Pardon me, Saint Paul, but people who don't understand will think it's still Saul speaking. *I worked harder than all of them*, has the appearance of being said out of pride ... But what comes next? ... *not I, though, but the grace of God with me* [1 Cor 15:10]. Humility recognized itself, infirmity trembled, perfect charity acknowledged the gift of God ...
>
> You said, *I have fought the good fight* [2 Tim 4:7]; but it was you yourself who said, *Thanks be to God, who gives us the victory through our Lord Jesus Christ* (1 Cor 15:57). So you fought a good fight, but it was by the gift of Christ that you were victorious. You said, *I have completed the course*; but it was you yourself who said, *no thanks to the one who wills, or the one who runs, but to God who shows mercy* (Rom 9:16). You said, *I have kept the faith*; but it was you yourself who said, *I have obtained mercy, that I should be faithful* (1 Cor 7:25). So we can see that your merits are God's gifts, and that's why we rejoice over your crown. (Sermon 299B.4–5 [Augustine 1994, 246–248])

Whereas the first of the two texts considered in this section of the chapter treated a Pauline text as the hermeneutical key to a chain of texts and events in salvation history, the second text uses the voice of Paul to articulate the theological paradox of grace as providing as gift what is also our own. Augustine ends with the pithy "your merits are God's gifts," a statement found a number of times in his work to emphasize that while human beings certainly do earn rewards for good works, those good works are God's gift. This phrase is the culminating statement of *the* paradox of Christian existence: we are given what we are through divine aid and presence. Here is the heart of what Paul teaches for Augustine.

And yet, we cannot stop here. In the previous quotation, we heard Augustine quoting 2 Corinthians 3:17 to emphasize that freedom comes from the presence of the Spirit. The language of grace is now interwoven with the language of pneumatology. Elsewhere in *The Spirit and the Letter*, Augustine writes: "What then are the laws of God that are written by God himself on our hearts but the very presence of the Holy Spirit?" (21.36 [Augustine 1997, 166]). To take our discussion further, I want now to look more directly at Augustine's account of the Spirit.

"Poured into our Hearts"

Augustine's theology of the Spirit developed slowly, but along consistent lines. Early in his career, we see him speak of the Spirit's functions as the perfecter of the created order, as the one who draws us to the Father and inspires in us the love of God, as the one who is the Gift of God. But Augustine speaks only hesitantly of the Spirit's relationship to Father and Son, hinting at the Spirit as the perfect peace and concord between Father and Son. In these early works, Augustine is not at all uncertain about the separate existence and co-eternity of the Spirit, but he is very uncertain about how to describe the Spirit's place in the triune life. Things really begin to develop in his *Faith and the Creed* of 393.[13] Most famously, here Augustine explores with some hesitation the principle that the Spirit is the *deitas* or divinity shared between Father and Son. In his attempt to explain this, Augustine writes:

> This divinity, which [those who think this way about the Spirit] also interpret as the mutual love and charity of each to the other [that is, of Father to Son and *vice versa*], they say is called the Holy Spirit and that many scriptural texts exist to support their view, whether the following passage, *For the love of God has been poured into our hearts through the Holy Spirit who has been given to us* (Rom 5:5), or numerous other similar passages. They find support for their argument from the fact that it is through the Holy Spirit that we are reconciled to God. And so, whenever there is mention in scripture of the gift of God, they want to interpret it above all else as meaning that the charity of God is the Holy Spirit. For it is only through love that we are reconciled to God and through it that we are called children of God. (*Faith and the Creed* 19 [Augustine 2005, 169])

It is in this text that Augustine first offers an extended consideration of Romans 5:5, a verse that during the Pelagian controversy he will quote many times. The significance of the verse lies in the connections that Augustine suggests it offers. First, the parallel phrasing of the first and second halves of the verse identifies the Spirit and the love of God. Second, the use of the verb "given" points to the possibility of the Spirit being also the Gift of God (Augustine has in mind also the use of the title at Acts 8:17–20). Third, Augustine sees the last clause of the verse identifying the love that has been given as the Holy Spirit: to receive the love of God is nothing other than to receive the Spirit. Thus, Augustine speaks of us as being reconciled only through love, and reads this as meaning that we are reconciled to God only through God's gift of his own Spirit, his own love in our hearts. In a later sermon he puts this principle thus:

> let us love God with God. Yes indeed, since the Holy Spirit is God, let us love God with God ... Because I have said *the love of God has been poured into our hearts through the Holy Spirit which has been given to us* [Rom 5:5], it follows that since the Holy Spirit is God and we cannot love God except through the Holy Spirit, we can only love God with God. (Sermon 34.3 [Augustine 1990, 167])[14]

With this emphasis on the Spirit as the one who in us loves, or who gives us love (note the ambiguity), we see an important complement to Augustine's presentation of grace as enabling us to be what we were intended to be. In the first place, discussion of the free gift that is grace is now revealed to overlap with (and perhaps be inseparable from) discussion of the Holy Spirit's work. In the second place, we see Augustine presenting this account of the Spirit as surprising to his audience, surprising in ways similar to those in which Paul's account of grace surprised. Grace surprised because of the paradox of our merits being God's gifts; the Spirit surprises because the Spirit is the love of God in us, what we thought was our own.

What, then, is the relationship between grace and the Holy Spirit? It is easy to find constant parallels between the functions attributed to grace and those attributed to the Spirit. Grace, for example, gives us delight in God's law, through grace we love God, and grace reconciles us to God; and yet the Holy Spirit is also said to do these things. Augustine identifies the heart of the Spirit's nature and work as being and enabling love of God, and the restoration of true love constitutes the restoration of the human being. Indeed, because Augustine speaks so directly of the Spirit as Love itself, especially in discussion of Romans 5:5 and 1 John 4:8 ("God is love"), and emphasizes that when we love truly, the Spirit loves in us, this connection seems only the stronger. And yet Augustine does not say directly and consistently "grace is the presence of the Spirit."

There are two reasons for this. First, the semantic range of *gratia* in the New Testament overlaps with, but is not synonymous with *Spiritus Sanctus*. *Gratia* can mean simply "favor," describing God's gracious disposition toward, or love of, humanity. Grace is also frequently associated directly with Father, Son, and Spirit (for example, Rom 1:7; 5:15; 1 Cor 1:4; 2 Cor 8:9; Gal 1:6; 2:21; Eph 4:7). One might be able to see each of these references as a reference to the Spirit, but to do so would be to ignore Scripture's independent use of the term "grace." Second, and more theologically, although Augustine describes the Spirit bringing about in the Christian and in the Christian community the great majority of results that grace is said to accomplish, he also follows Scripture in describing the Father and Christ (and the *gratia Christi*) as accomplishing many of these results, and insists that Father, Son, and Spirit work inseparably. Clearly, separating out roles for the divine three in the mediation of grace would be an impossible and perhaps inappropriate task.[15] In the absence of a controversy that would have forced a clear articulation of the relationship between Christ, the Spirit, and grace, and in the presence of the ambiguity of Scripture's language, Augustine did not seek further definition.[16]

However, even though Augustine maintains a distinction between speaking about the presence of the Spirit and of grace, noting the parallel treatment Augustine gives is vital if we are to understand what he sees as the fundamental theme of Paul's theology. For Augustine, Paul teaches that at the heart of Christian life is the presence of God – Father, Son, and Spirit – infusing love, being love, giving grace, and transforming and restoring us into those who love God and will contemplate and share in the divine life. For yet another passage emphasizing this divine presence, we might turn to a powerful and yet rarely noted section toward the end of Augustine's *Confessions*:

> When people see these things with the help of your Spirit, it is you who are seeing in them. When, therefore, they see that things are good, you are seeing that they are good. Whatever pleases them for your sake is pleasing you in them. The things which by the help of your Spirit delight us are delighting you in us. [1 Cor 2:11–12 is then cited] ... How do we ourselves know the gifts which God has given? The answer comes to me that the statement "No one knows except the Spirit of God" [1 Cor 2:11] also applies to the things we know by the help of his Spirit ... When a man sees something which is good, God in him sees that it is good. That is, God is loved in that which he has made, and he is not loved except through the Spirit which he has given. For "the love of God is diffused in our hearts by the Holy Spirit which is given to us" (Rom. 5:5). (*Confessions* 13.31.46 [Augustine 1998, 300–301])

Once again, Paul is central; once again, the paradox of our existence in God, and of God's presence in our action, is central. In the final substantive section of this chapter, I want to consider some further developments in Augustine's mature pneumatology that round out this account.

"The Fount of Love"

In the early years of the fifth century, Augustine's pneumatology undergoes significant development when he begins to appeal to those passages, primarily Pauline, in which the Spirit is spoken of as the "Spirit of" Christ, God, Truth, "him who raised Jesus from the dead" (especially Rom 8:9–11; Gal 4:6; cf. Matt 10:20, "the Spirit of your Father"). At the simplest level, Augustine sees these texts as revealing with particular clarity the Spirit as distinct from and yet "of" both Father and Son (when Scripture speaks of "the Spirit of God," Augustine takes "God" to mean the Father). The clearest discussion of this point is to be found in Augustine's *The Trinity* and in his homilies on 1 John. The Spirit must be "distinct from" Father and Son because here one who is "of" another is also given as a gift by a giver. The Spirit is thus both the Spirit of the Father and the gift given by (and hence distinct from) the Father (*The Trinity* 5.11.12 [Augustine 1963, 189–190]).

Augustine is now able to make more progress with a question that has vexed him (and Patristic tradition) for some time. Why is the Holy Spirit known most frequently by two terms – holy and spirit – that may be predicated of Father and of Son? The Spirit is thus named, he argues, so that we will be drawn to reflect on the Spirit's status as "something common" to both Father and Son and thus come to understand more deeply the mystery of the divine life. In Book 6 of the *The Trinity* Augustine writes: "Through Him both are joined together; through Him the begotten is loved by the begetter … in Him they preserve the unity of spirit through the bond of peace, not by a participation but by their own essence, not by the gift of anyone superior to themselves but by their own gift" (*The Trinity* 6.5.7 [Augustine 1963, 206]).

Father and Son are joined because they give to each other what they are; they are not given the gift of unity (as we are), nor are they one because they share in a higher unity. They are one because they give to each other their own essence, the Spirit who is something common, who may be termed the love between them. A few years later, in Book 15 of the same work, Augustine emphasizes very clearly that when the Spirit is given, the Spirit also gives himself. Thus, for the Spirit to be understood as something common is for Augustine to assert the indwelling of Father, Son, and Spirit; the Spirit is the love of Father and of Son not as an impersonal essence, but as possessing the fullness of the divine life.

The appearance of the primarily Pauline "Spirit of" texts in Augustine complements and deepens his use of Romans 5:5. The former enable him to draw out more of the links between, on the one hand, the Spirit as that which draws us into one, and into one *with* Father and Son, and, on the other hand, the Spirit as that which is the common – though not pre-personal – love and peace between Father and Son. Turning back for the moment toward the manner in which Augustine reads Paul, throughout these two discussions we see again some of the key principles of grammatical exegesis at work. Augustine is, in both cases, highly attentive to the grammar of the verses and to the possibility that in that grammar are hidden hints of deeper meaning for those who persist. In this close attention to grammar, combined with careful comparison of passages from across the biblical text as a whole, Paul as individual writer with his "own" distinct perspective recedes; but as he does so, Paul as inspired witness to the one mystery of God's redemptive presence appears only the stronger.

Throughout his career, Augustine explores the ways in which the Spirit's function of unifying Christians reflects something of the Spirit's eternal status. The highpoint of this attempt comes in the second decade of the fifth century with Augustine's exegesis of Acts 4:31–32 ("they were all filled with the holy Spirit ... and the community of believers was of one heart and mind") and 1 Corinthians 6:17 ("whoever is joined to the Lord becomes one spirit with him"). Augustine begins for the first time to read both of these texts as suggesting an analogy: if it is the Spirit who draws together distinct and disparate human beings into one, how much more does the Spirit draw together Father and Son into one? The analogy is a difficult one for Augustine to offer: the Spirit from eternity is common to Father and Son, and from eternity the divine three are at one such that they can even be said to be one substance. And yet, the mature Augustine begins, I think, to see the possibility of saying that the Father from eternity establishes the Spirit as the one who is the Spirit of Father and Son, and thus the one who is from eternity the one who constitutes the Son as lover of the Father and himself as love of the Son. Augustine knows himself to be looking here at least toward, if not beyond, the rim of what may be seen in faith, and we find only hints. I mention this mature theme in Augustine's writing just to give a full sense of this Pauline trajectory explored by Augustine (see Ayres 2010, ch. 9). From his reflections on Romans 5:5, through his use of the Pauline "Spirit of" texts, and on to his inchoate reflections on the Spirit as the one who from eternity draws Father, Son, and Spirit into union as the one God, Augustine sees Paul as one of the great visionaries of the Christian life, understanding it as a mysterious sharing in the transforming divine presence that gives us ourselves.

Throughout my discussions of grace and of the Spirit, I have emphasized that Augustine sees Scripture's teaching on these issues as requiring meditation and careful attention from Christians. He is clear that Scripture teaches with clarity the fundamentals of Christian belief so that all may believe and so that in them hope and love may be formed; but he is also clear that Scripture speaks of some of its deepest mysteries in terms that demand attention from the spiritually mature. Scripture reveals to us an ascent in understanding and belief in which we gradually come to see with greater penetration the character of the divine love and action toward us. Indeed, it is this ascent toward understanding that Christ comes, in part, to teach and which we have seen modeled in Augustine's discussions of grace and pneumatology.[17]

One easy way of distinguishing Augustine's Paul from the Paul of earlier and contemporary Greek theologians has been to indicate the importance of Paul the "mystic" to those other traditions – the importance of the Paul who speaks allusively of his being caught up to the third heaven in 2 Corinthians 12, a theme largely absent from the Paul in Augustine, who is thought to offer only an austere teaching on predestination and grace. I hope I have shown here how much more complex the situation is. Augustine does not attend at length to 2 Corinthians 12, but he certainly makes central a Paul who is the teacher of God's mysterious gifting to us of ourselves, and of God's immediate presence through the Spirit. The paradoxes that he draws from Paul he takes to be at the heart of what Paul teaches. This view of Augustine's Paul does not answer many of the questions that readers probably wish to pose, but perhaps it suggests a new place from which to ask them.

Notes

This chapter is dedicated to the memory of my good friend Fr. Thomas Martin OSA. Tom was a scholar of Augustine's reading of Romans, but most of all he was a practitioner of the life of thankfulness that Augustine himself commends as the due response to God's gifts. Tom was supposed to have written this chapter himself.

1   I do not know of a good overall sketch in English of Paul's influence on Augustine. The best in English are probably Martin (2001, ch. 1) and Fredriksen (1999). In Italian and French, respectively, Mara (1989) and Delaroche (1996) are very helpful.
2   Except where otherwise indicated, biblical quotations are taken from the Revised Standard Version.
3   For an excellent brief introduction to Manicheism and further bibliography, see Coyle (1999).
4   *Against Faustus* 12 (Augustine 2007, 125–157) offers an excellent example.
5   For this "anti-Manichean trinitarianism," see Ayres (2010, ch. 2).
6   On the grammatical and rhetorical shaping of Augustine's exegesis, see Irvine (1994) and Young (1997).
7   One of the most useful introductions to this style of reading is provided by O'Keefe and Reno (2005, chs. 2–3).
8   In theoretical terms, these principles are most extensively discussed in Augustine's *On Christian Teaching*, Book 2 (Augustine 1996). For excellent discussion, see the collection of essays in Arnold and Bright (1995). On Augustine's attitude to allegorical reading, see also Cameron (1999).
9   For excellent examples of how Augustine later envisages the inner prompting of God, see Book 1 of *The Grace of Christ and Original Sin* (e.g., 1.13.14 and 1.45.49 [Augustine 1997, 398, 414]).
10   One consequence of this position that I have not discussed further here is that God's grace is irresistible. God's redemptive grace enables us to respond to God's call: it opens us to our most natural desires beyond the weight of sinful habit and mistaken opinion. It is therefore not something that can be resisted.
11   Wetzel (2000) offers one of the most reflective and interesting investigations of Augustine's account of grace and predestination. He reacts in part against the criticisms of Gerald Bonner (1992; 1993). On the shift that occurs in Augustine's reading of Paul after 395, see Babcock (1979).
12   A good basic account of the controversy can be found in Lancel (2002). Brown (2000, 340–410) offers a marvelous account, but Lancel is stronger on theological questions.
13   On these developments, see Ayres (2010, chs. 1–3).
14   Augustine's series of homilies on 1 John (Augustine 2008b) is also a fundamental source for his teaching on the Spirit as love. For an introduction, see Ayres (2001).

15 In a number of places, Augustine insists that the Father works always *through* the Son and *in* the Spirit, but this general statement is more a statement of principle about how the three work inseparably, and is not allowed to overrule the fluidity of scriptural language.

16 Medieval theologians will eventually develop complex theories of grace which offer divisions between uncreated grace and created grace in the human soul; they will also sustain a long debate about whether the love with which we love God is simply the Spirit within us or not. In some ways, these debates flow from Augustine, but they are alien to him. As we have seen in his talk of grace and in his account of the Spirit's presence, Augustine seems intentionally to prefer the language of paradox.

17 On this theme, see Studer (1990), Dodaro (2004, chs. 4–5), and Ayres (2005; 2010, chs. 5–6).

References

Arnold, Duane W. H., and Pamela Bright. 1995. De Doctrina Christiana: *A Classic of Western Culture.* Notre Dame, Ind.: University of Notre Dame Press.

Augustine. 1963. *The Trinity.* Translated by Stephen McKenna. Washington, DC: Catholic University of America Press.

Augustine. 1990. *Sermons.* Volume 2: *Sermons (20–50) on the Old Testament.* Translated by Edmund Hill. Brooklyn: New City Press.

Augustine. 1994. *Sermons.* Volume 8: *Sermons (273–305A) on the Saints.* Translated by Edmund Hill. Hyde Park, NY: New City Press.

Augustine. 1996. *Teaching Christianity* (De Doctrina Christiana). Translated by Edmund Hill. Hyde Park, NY: New City Press.

Augustine. 1997. *Answer to the Pelagians 1.* Translated by Roland J. Teske. Hyde Park, NY: New City Press.

Augustine. 1998. *Confessions.* Translated by Henry Chadwick. Oxford: Oxford University Press.

Augustine. 2005. *On Christian Belief.* Edited by Boniface Ramsey. Hyde Park, NY: New City Press.

Augustine. 2007. *Answer to Faustus, a Manichean* (Contra Faustum Manichaeum). Translated by Roland Teske. Hyde Park, NY: New City Press.

Augustine. 2008a. *Responses to Miscellaneous Questions.* Translated by Boniface Ramsey. Hyde Park, NY: New City Press.

Augustine. 2008b. *Homilies on the First Epistle of John.* Translated by Boniface Ramsey. Hyde Park, NY: New City Press.

Ayres, Lewis. 2001. Augustine, Christology and God as Love: An Introduction to the Homilies on 1 John. Pages 67–93 in *Nothing Greater, Nothing Better: Theological Essays on the Love of God.* Edited by Kevin J. Vanhoozer. Grand Rapids: Eerdmans.

Ayres, Lewis. 2005. Augustine on the Rule of Faith: Rhetoric, Christology, and the Foundation of Christian Thinking. *Augustinian Studies* 36: 33–49.

Ayres, Lewis. 2010. *Augustine and the Trinity.* Cambridge: Cambridge University Press.

Babcock, William S. 1979. Augustine's Interpretation of Romans (AD 394–396). *Augustinian Studies* 10: 55–74.

Bonner, Gerald. 1992. Pelagianism and Augustine. *Augustinian Studies* 23: 33–51.

Bonner, Gerald. 1993. Augustine and Pelagianism. *Augustinian Studies* 24: 27–47.

Brown, Peter. 2000. *Augustine of Hippo: A Biography.* Second edition. Berkeley: University of California Press.

Cameron, Michael. 1999. The Christological Substructure of Augustine's Figurative Exegesis. Pages 74–103 in *Augustine and the Bible*. Edited by Pamela Bright. Notre Dame, Ind.: University of Notre Dame Press.

Coyle, J. Kevin. 1999. Mani, Manicheism. Pages 520–525 in *Augustine through the Ages: An Encyclopedia*. Edited by Allan D. Fitzgerald. Grand Rapids: Eerdmans.

Delaroche, Bruno. 1996. *Saint-Augustin lecteur et interprète de Saint Paul dans le "De peccatorum meritis et remissione" (hiver 411–412)*. Paris: Institut d'études augustiniennes.

Dodaro, Robert. 2004. *Christ and the Just Society in the Thought of Augustine*. Cambridge: Cambridge University Press.

Fredriksen, Paula. 1999. Paul. Pages 621–625 in *Augustine through the Ages: An Encyclopedia*. Edited by Allan D. Fitzgerald. Grand Rapids: Eerdmans.

Irvine, Martin. 1994. *The Making of Textual Culture: "Grammatica" and Literary Theory, 350–1100*. Cambridge: Cambridge University Press.

Lancel, Serge. 2002. *Saint Augustine*. London: SCM.

Mara, Maria Grazia. 1989. L'influsso di Paolo in Agostino. Pages 125–162 in *Le Epistole Paoline nei manichei, i donatisti e il primo Agostino*. Edited by J. Ries, F. Decret, W. H. C. Frend, and M. G. Mara. Rome: Istituto Patristico Augustinianum.

Markus, R. A. 1990. Comment: Augustine's Pauline Legacies. Pages 221–225 in *Paul and the Legacies of Paul*. Edited by William S. Babcock. Dallas: Southern Methodist University Press.

Martin, Thomas F. 1999. Pauline Commentaries in Augustine's Time. Pages 625–628 in *Augustine through the Ages: An Encyclopedia*. Edited by Allan D. Fitzgerald. Grand Rapids: Eerdmans.

Martin, Thomas F. 2001. *Rhetoric and Exegesis in Augustine's Interpretation of Romans 7:24–25a*. Lewiston, NY: Edwin Mellen.

O'Keefe, John J., and R. R. Reno. 2005. *Sanctified Vision: An Introduction to Early Christian Interpretation of the Bible*. Baltimore: Johns Hopkins University Press.

Studer, Basil. 1990. Augustine and the Pauline Theme of Hope. Pages 201–221 in *Paul and the Legacies of Paul*. Edited by William S. Babcock. Dallas: Southern Methodist University Press.

Wetzel, James. 1992. *Augustine and the Limits of Virtue*. Cambridge: Cambridge University Press.

Wetzel, James. 2000. Snares of Truth: Augustine on Free Will and Predestination. Pages 124–141 in *Augustine and his Critics: Essays in Honour of Gerald Bonner*. Edited by Robert Dodaro and George Lawless. London: Routledge.

Wilken, Robert L. 1990. Free Choice and the Divine Will in Greek Christian Commentaries on Paul. Pages 123–140 in *Paul and the Legacies of Paul*. Edited by William S. Babcock. Dallas: Southern Methodist University Press.

Young, Frances M. 1997. *Biblical Exegesis and the Formation of Christian Culture*. Cambridge: Cambridge University Press.

CHAPTER 23

Aquinas

Matthew Levering

In the prologue to his massive commentary on the Pauline letters (from Romans to Hebrews), Thomas Aquinas treats the person of Paul. As Thomas Ryan points out, Aquinas interprets Paul's vocation in light of Acts 9:15, where the Lord tells Ananias that Paul "is a chosen instrument of mine to carry my name before the Gentiles and kings and the sons of Israel."[1] As an "instrument," Paul can be known in terms of his "makeup, contents, use, and fruit" (Ryan 2007, 106). Ryan summarizes Aquinas's portrait of Paul:

> Like shining gold, his wisdom shone forth. He was solid with the virtue of charity and ornate with other virtues. He was filled with the name of Christ, not only in intellect and affect but also in his whole way of life. A vessel and its contents are used for something. In this case, Paul imitated Christ bodily, by speaking of him and by communicating his grace and mercy. (2007, 106)

Aquinas, Ryan shows, reveals a sense not only for the rational argumentation used by Paul, but also for the personal and pastoral dimensions of Paul's apostolic ministry.

Lecturing on Scripture was the primary labor of a medieval *magister*. When in September 1265 his superiors in the Dominican Order directed that Aquinas move to Rome to found a new *studium* for the training of friars, he embarked upon three enormously fruitful years. Not only did he write large portions of the *Summa theologiae*, but also he commented on all the letters of Paul, although the commentary on Romans that we possess appears to be the fruit of his year in Naples (1272–1273; see Torrell 1996, 142–159, 250–257). In the *tertia pars* of the *Summa theologiae* alone, Aquinas quotes Paul 502 times, far more than he quotes any other authority.[2]

The Blackwell Companion to Paul, First Edition. Edited by Stephen Westerholm.
© 2011 Blackwell Publishing Ltd. Published 2011 by Blackwell Publishing Ltd.

So as to provide a taste of Aquinas's engagement with Paul, this chapter focuses on two brief examples: *Summa theologiae* II-II, qq. 23–25 (the first three questions of Aquinas's discussion of the virtue of charity) and his commentary on 1 Corinthians 13. Paul's rich theology of love is well known, but as Michael Sherwin observes, "One's first encounter with St. Thomas' theology of love can be disconcerting" (Sherwin 2005, xiii). Despite his profound appreciation for Aquinas's theology, Sherwin points out that Aquinas's "technical language can seem to render the rich reality of love lifeless." Sherwin praises Aquinas for possessing "the precise skills of the draftsman" (2005, xiii). Yves Congar likewise notes that Aquinas's theology gives the "impression of over-riding rationality" (Congar 1997, part 3, 116). Introducing their edited volume on Aquinas's biblical commentaries, Thomas Weinandy, Daniel Keating, and John Yocum remark in the same vein that "the commentaries admittedly make for difficult reading. Thomas follows a rather tedious method of scholastic commentary on the Bible that takes some wading through for the modern reader" (Weinandy et al. 2005, x; see also Domanyi 1979, esp. 29–38).

Yet all of these authors deeply value what Congar describes as Aquinas's "masterly knowledge and use of Scripture" (1997, part 3, 116). In what follows, therefore, I examine Aquinas's engagement with Paul as leading us into the heart of Aquinas's theology of Christian love.

Aquinas on Paul: *Summa theologiae* II-II, qq. 23–25

Romans: God's free gift and our embodied righteousness

In the second article of question 24, Aquinas asks how we obtain charity. His answer takes its bearings from Romans 5:5: "God's love has been poured into our hearts through the Holy Spirit which has been given to us." This verse concludes Paul's discussion of justification by faith, and it leads to Paul's inquiry in Romans 6 regarding what it means for believers to have received charity through the gift of the Holy Spirit. In the same article, therefore, Aquinas also quotes Romans 6:23: "the free gift of God is eternal life in Christ Jesus our Lord." Because persons are "slaves of the one whom [they] obey" (Rom 6:16), they must be "set free from sin" in order to perform actions whose "return ... is sanctification and [whose] end, eternal life" (Rom 6:22). Only God can set us free, and God does so, Aquinas notes, by the infusion of his "free gift" (Rom 6:23).

Having received God's gift, can believers lose charity? Aquinas asks this question in article 12 of question 24. In answer, he again quotes Romans 6:23, but now its first half: "For the wages of sin is death." Noting Paul's contrast between the reward of death and the free gift of eternal life, Aquinas argues that a person cannot receive both the "wages of sin" and the "free gift" at the same time. It follows that a person can renounce charitable friendship with God by committing an action that deliberately seeks a created good above God. Aquinas compares such an action to blocking the sun's light from reaching Earth: "even so charity ceases at once to be in the soul through the placing of an obstacle to the outpouring of charity by God into the soul" (II-II, q. 24, a. 12).[3]

An act is a "mortal" sin – that is, it earns the deadly "wages of sin" (Rom 6:23) – when the agent deliberately chooses a created good over "God's friendship, which requires that we should obey his will."[4]

Question 25, article 5 asks whether we should love our bodies out of charity. In his response, Aquinas rejects the Manichean view of the body by quoting Romans 6:13: "Do not yield your members to sin as instruments of wickedness, but yield yourselves to God as men who have been brought from death to life, and your members to God as instruments of righteousness." In order to understand the distinction that Paul makes here between ourselves and our "members," recall the preceding verse: "Let not sin therefore reign in your mortal bodies, to make you obey their passions" (Rom 6:12). When in the state of sin one obeys one's bodily passions rather than obeying God, one causes one's body to be an instrument of sin rather than of righteousness.

How can we love our bodies if obeying our bodily passions would lead us into slavery to sin? Paul has sometimes been thought to have a highly negative view of the body. As a case in point, Aquinas quotes another verse from Romans (7:24): "Wretched man that I am! Who will deliver me from this body of death?" This verse appears within a context where Paul seems to be drawing a sharp division between his mind and his body. In Romans 7:23, Paul contrasts his mind's inclination to obedience with his body's inclination toward disobedience: "For I delight in the law of God, in my inmost self, but I see in my members another law at war with the law of my mind and making me captive to the law of sin which dwells in my members." Similarly, Romans 7:25 concludes Paul's argument by appearing to divide spirit and body entirely, so that the Christian life consists simply in the obedience of the spirit. Paul states: "I of myself serve the law of God with my mind, but with my flesh I serve the law of sin." From these verses, it might appear that bodiliness itself is equivalent to slavery to sin and to earning the "wages of sin," death. Charity could not have one's "flesh" as an object, because one's flesh serves "the law of sin" and therefore stands against charitable friendship with God.

While the Manichees regarded the body in this fashion, Aquinas uses Romans 6:13 to help show that Paul's argument in Romans 7:24 does not favor a Manichean interpretation. If human beings can yield their bodily "members to God as instruments of righteousness" (Rom 6:13), then the human body can serve righteousness. The human body therefore is not bound intrinsically to sin. Insofar as it has the capacity to be an instrument of righteousness, to be in service to God, the human body is among the rightful objects of charity, since in charity we love God and other things as pertaining to God. What, then, of the "law of sin which dwells in my members," so as to make the body a "body of death" (Rom 7:23–24)? Aquinas explains: "Our bodies can be considered in two ways, first, in respect of their nature, secondly, in respect of the corruption of sin and its punishment" (II-II, q. 25, a. 5). Although disordered by sin and made subject to corruption, our bodies, by becoming "instruments of righteousness," participate nonetheless in the spiritual healing that Christ and his Spirit accomplish in us. The healing that we receive has both spiritual and bodily dimensions; therefore, our bodies, and not only our souls, should be loved among those things that pertain to God.

1 Corinthians 13: Charity and the life of virtue

In question 23, article 4, Aquinas quotes 1 Corinthians 13:4 so as to formulate an objection to his own position that charity is a distinct or special virtue. First Corinthians 13:4 reads, "Love is patient and kind; love is not jealous or boastful." This verse stands at the beginning of a passage in which Paul connects charity with a wide array of other virtuous qualities. The passage continues: "it [love] is not arrogant or rude. Love does not insist on its own way; it is not irritable or resentful; it does not rejoice at wrong, but rejoices in the right. Love bears all things, believes all things, hopes all things, endures all things. Love never ends" (1 Cor 13:5–8). If charity is "patient and kind," is it appropriate to distinguish charity from the virtues of patience and kindness? Perhaps charity is simply a general disposition belonging to many virtues rather than a particular virtue in its own right? The quotation of 1 Corinthians 13:4 enables Aquinas to underscore the way in which charity, while distinct in its love of the divine good, does in fact inform all other virtues: "Charity is included in the definition of every virtue, not as being essentially every virtue, but because every virtue depends on it in a way" (II-II, q. 23, a. 4, ad 1).

In question 25, article 4, on whether one should love oneself out of charity, 1 Corinthians 13:4 helps Aquinas formulate another objection. If charity is not self-centered – and 1 Corinthians 13:4 insists it is not – then how can one rightly love oneself out of charity? How would this differ from self-centered love of self? Aquinas answers by distinguishing between the love of self that desires the goods of one's *bodily* nature and the love of self that desires the goods of one's *rational* nature. The former is blameworthy, whereas the latter is praiseworthy and belongs to charity.

First Corinthians 13:4 also serves as an objection in question 25, article 8.[5] Regarding whether one should love one's enemies out of charity, Aquinas raises the objection that it would be perverse to love one's enemies, just as it would be perverse to hate one's friends. In other words, does charity require dissolving the distinction between friend and enemy? If so, how could a charitable person ever reward his or her friends for their acts of friendship? Aquinas affirms that one must love one's enemy, but he distinguishes three ways in which love of enemy might be understood. First, one might suppose that one should love one's enemy as such, that is, insofar as someone becomes an enemy by committing evil acts. First Corinthians 13:4 assists Aquinas in ruling out this position as "perverse, and contrary to charity, since it implies love of that which is evil in another."[6] The second way of loving one's enemy is to include all enemies within one's general love of neighbor. Aquinas approves of this way, but he asks how this general love is specified as regards individuals. Must we directly love all enemies all the time? He answers that human beings can only exercise particular acts of charity toward a few persons at a time. The third way of loving one's enemy consists in being "ready to love our enemies individually, if the necessity were to occur" (II-II, q. 25, a. 8). Given the inclusion of enemies within our general love of neighbor, we must be prepared to act charitably toward each enemy individually when the occasion arises.

First Corinthians 13:13 appears twice in the *sed contra* of an article in question 23; both times it provides the backbone of Aquinas's argument. Article 4 uses the first half of 1 Corinthians 13:13, "So faith, hope, love abide, these three"; article 6 uses the second half, "the greatest of these is love." The point of article 4 is that charity, like faith and hope, is a distinct virtue, as is shown by its enumeration in 1 Corinthians 13:13. The point of article 6, attested by 1 Corinthians 13:13, is that charity is the greatest virtue, "more excellent than faith or hope, and, consequently, than all the other virtues." Aquinas explains charity's excellence in terms of union with God: "among the theological virtues themselves, the first place belongs to that which attains God most" (II-II, q. 23, a. 6).

In article 7 of question 23, addressing whether "true virtue" can be possessed without charity, the *sed contra* quotes 1 Corinthians 13:3: "If I give away all I have, and if I deliver my body to be burned, but have not love, I gain nothing." As Aquinas points out, true virtue gains the true good of the person; if, then, as the Pauline text indicates, one gains nothing without charity, then no true virtue is possible without charity. Aquinas thereby distinguishes between true virtue, which gains "the enjoyment of God" as the "ultimate and principal good of man," and virtues that in a temporal way gain something but that are not ordered to attaining the true good of the human person. What about when a person seeks a true good such as "the welfare of the state"? Aquinas answers that "it will indeed be a true virtue, imperfect, however, unless it be referred to the final and perfect good" (II-II, q. 23, a. 7). Charity orders all our actions to union with God as the highest good, the desire for which should inform each of our actions.

Other texts from I Corinthians: The Holy Spirit and divine fellowship

In the first article of his first question on charity (question 23), Aquinas uses 1 Corinthians 1:9 to show the basis of friendship between human beings and God; namely, a communication of God's happiness to us. This communication (in Christ and his Spirit) establishes a friendship or fellowship: "God is faithful, by whom you were called into the fellowship of his Son, Jesus Christ our Lord" (1 Cor 1:9). Aquinas notes that this communication of spiritual good infuses charity in us, so that we can truly be in fellowship with Jesus. The quotation from 1 Corinthians is particularly apt because Paul has in view both God's faithfulness in constituting this fellowship and the fact that this fellowship can collapse, in particular persons at least. Paul tells the Corinthians that even though "you are not lacking in any spiritual gift" (1 Cor 1:7), nonetheless "it has been reported to me by Chloe's people that there is quarreling among you" (1 Cor 1:11). The understanding of charity as a friendship or fellowship based on divine communication of spiritual goods sets the tone for Aquinas's entire treatment of the virtue of charity.

First Corinthians also has a central role in Aquinas's discussion of how our charitable fellowship with God relates to our natural gifts. In asking whether our natural gifts provide the measure to which we can be transformed by charity (question 24, article 3), Aquinas quotes 1 Corinthians 12:11 in the *sed contra* to show that the infusion of charity depends solely upon the Holy Spirit. After describing the various spiritual gifts within the Body of Christ, Paul says, "All these are inspired by one and the same

Spirit, who apportions to each one individually as he wills" (1 Cor 12:11). This verse guides Aquinas's argument that "the quantity of charity depends neither on the condition of nature nor on the capacity of natural virtue, but only on the will of the Holy Spirit" (II-II, q. 24, a. 3).

Likewise, Aquinas appeals to 1 Corinthians in discussing the increase of charity in believers. At the end of his discussion of the varieties of vocations in the Body of Christ, Paul remarks, "I will show you a still more excellent way" (1 Cor 12:31). This way is charity, the subject of 1 Corinthians 13. For Aquinas, the importance of this verse consists in its affirmation that charity is a "way." As a way toward the fullness of union with God, charity in us moves from the imperfect attainment of charity that we now experience to the perfect charity of eternal life. By this "way" or path we come increasingly closer to our goal. Aquinas comments in this regard that charity must be able to increase, or else progress in the spiritual life would be impossible. As he puts it, "It is essential to the charity of a wayfarer that it can increase, for if it could not, all further advance along the way would cease" (II-II, q. 24, a. 4).

First Corinthians 16:14 twice helps Aquinas to formulate an objection to his own position, with the goal of showing that charity has to do with the ultimate end, union with God. In discussing whether charity is a distinct virtue (question 23, article 4), Aquinas raises the objection that 1 Corinthians 16:14 ("Let all that you do be done in love") indicates that the answer must be no. If every action is marked by charity, then charity describes the mode of the other virtues and is not a distinct virtue (or else charity absorbs all other virtues into itself). In response to this objection, Aquinas affirms Paul's injunction but specifies that "since charity has for its object the last end of human life, viz., everlasting happiness, it follows that it extends to the acts of a man's whole life, by commanding them, not by eliciting immediately all acts of virtue" (II-II, q. 23, a. 4, ad 2).

When he turns to examine whether charity is a habit of the will (question 24, article 1), Aquinas quotes 1 Corinthians 16:14 so as to suggest the objection that charity is not in the will (*voluntas*), but rather in the free will (*liberum arbitrium*). In reply, Aquinas emphasizes charity's focus on union with God. Even though *voluntas* and *liberum arbitrium* are the same power, they differ because "choice [which is exercised by the free will] is of things directed to the end, whereas the will is of the end itself" (II-II, q. 24, a. 1, ad 3). Charity aims at the ultimate end, union with God, and therefore it is a habit of the will (ordered to the end) rather than a habit that has primarily to do with the choice of means to an end.

2 Corinthians: Body, spirit, and participation in the Holy Spirit

In question 25, article 5, Aquinas takes up the issue of whether one should love one's body out of charity. The specific contribution made by 2 Corinthians to this issue consists in answering an objection rooted in the flight from the body. Humans experience bodiliness as a negative reality for two reasons, says Aquinas: the bodily suffering or corruption that focuses our attention on our own pain and sorrow and hinders our ability to love God and neighbor; and the concupiscence that threatens to displace charity with the movements of gluttony, greed, and lust. Corruption and concupiscence, however, characterize disordered bodiliness, not bodiliness per se – as we know when our bodies are healthy and our passions virtuously ordered. While good in itself, the human body needs healing and renewal. Aquinas finds both aspects expressed by Paul in 2 Corinthians 5:4: "not that we would be unclothed, but that we would be further clothed."

Article 6 of question 25 asks whether we should love sinners. As an objection to his own position, Aquinas quotes Paul's paraphrase of Isaiah 52:11, "Therefore come out from them, and be separate from them" (2 Cor 6:17). In his exposition of embodied holiness, Paul emphasizes the need to keep oneself holy by not entering into intimate fellowship with idolaters. This seems to imply that sinners should not be the objects of charitable love.

In reply, Aquinas points to the example of Jesus, who constantly showed sinners charitable love and intimately associated himself with them. Is Paul, then, contradicting Jesus as regards the path of embodied charity? Rather than interpreting Paul in this way, Aquinas notes that Paul has in view avoiding "the society of sinners, as regards fellowship in sin" (II-II, q. 25, a. 6, ad 5). Paul's concern is that believers will return to the practice of idolatrous rites. If Paul were commanding the avoidance of contact with sinners, then he himself would be setting a poor example, since his "ministry of reconciliation" requires constant contact with sinners. Instead, Paul is urging the Corinthians "not to accept the grace of God in vain" (2 Cor 6:1). Embodied charity does not mean isolating oneself; rather, it means not "consenting to sin." In this regard, again quoting from 2 Corinthians 6:17, Aquinas highlights the injunction to "touch nothing unclean." When we enter into sinful fellowships, we lose charity and become "unclean" in our embodied actions.

Thus, 2 Corinthians helps Aquinas to show that our bodies and sinners should be objects of charity, even though both our bodies and sinners give us trouble. In article 7 of question 25, Aquinas inquires into the love of self that sinners choose over love of God. What kind of love is this love of self? Even though it opposes union with God, does it differ significantly from the love of self possessed by charitable persons? On a natural level, Aquinas notes, both good and wicked persons "love their own preservation." What does it mean, however, to preserve oneself? Sinners think that the self consists primarily in "their sensitive and corporeal nature" (II-II, q. 25, a. 7). When sinners love themselves, therefore, they love themselves as if they were primarily corporeal. They "so desire external goods as to despise spiritual goods," and so their self-love is not charitable (II-II, q. 25, a. 7, ad 1). By contrast, charitable persons love primarily their spiritual nature. Referring to his physical afflictions and his spiritual flourishing, Paul states: "Though our outer nature is wasting away, our inner nature is being renewed every day" (2 Cor 4:16). Since in the human person the "inner nature" has primacy, Paul rightly knows his own nature and loves himself with a charity that reaches toward the fullness of union with God.

Aquinas quotes 2 Corinthians in articles 5 and 7 of question 24 as well. In both cases, he is examining how charity increases in the charitable person. In objection 3 of article 5, he quotes 2 Corinthians 9:10: "He who supplies seed to the sower and bread for food will supply and multiply your resources and increase the harvest of your righteousness." Paul is here encouraging the Corinthians to give freely, in love, to his collection of alms for the community of believers in Jerusalem. By their generosity in love, they will imitate "the grace of our Lord Jesus Christ" in that, "though he was rich, yet for your sake he became poor, so that by his poverty you might become rich" (2 Cor 8:8–9). In 2 Corinthians 9:10, Paul compares the increase of their charitable righteousness to the increase of a harvest. Aquinas uses this comparison to ask whether Paul means that charity increases "by addition," in the same way that a harvest increases by the addition of more and more produce (II-II, q. 24, a. 5, obj. 3). In reply, Aquinas shows that charity does not increase by addition, but instead increases by a deeper participation of the Holy Spirit: God causes charity "to have a greater hold on the soul, and the likeness of the Holy Spirit to be more perfectly participated by the soul" (II-II, q. 24, a. 5, ad 3). Charity deepens in the way that a friendship does rather than by addition of quantity.

Likewise in article 7, which asks whether charity increases indefinitely in this life, Aquinas quotes 2 Corinthians 6:11, "Our mouth is open to you, Corinthians; our heart is wide." Paul here is referring to his love for the Corinthians, and he asks them to increase their love for him: "You are not restricted by us, but you are restricted in your own affections. In return – I speak as to children – widen your hearts also" (2 Cor 6:12–13). What does Paul mean by saying that his "heart is wide"? Drawing upon the Vulgate's *dilatatum est*, Aquinas suggests that Paul indicates an expansive charity, a charity that "remains capable of receiving a further increase" (II-II, q. 24, a. 7, ad 2). Although the will is a finite power, by infusing charity God elevates the capacity of the will so as to enable it to attain to union with the infinite God.

Philippians: Growing toward eternal life

Aquinas does not here quote the famous verses regarding Christ's kenosis (Phil 2:5–9), but he does quote Philippians 1:23 three times, Philippians 3:12 twice, and Philippians 3:20 once. These verses all have to do with the union of the believer with God in Christ. Philippians 1:23 anticipates the fullness of this union in eternal life: "My desire is to depart and be with Christ, for that is far better." Philippians 3:12 emphasizes that this union is Christ's gift, even as we cooperate with his gifting: "Not that I have already obtained this [resurrection] or am already perfect; but I press on to make it my own, because Christ Jesus has made me his own." Philippians 3:20 makes clear that believers' union with God is not an individualistic matter, but rather constitutes believers as a communion in charity, a heavenly polity: "But our commonwealth [Latin: *conversatio*] is in heaven, and from it we await a Savior, the Lord Jesus Christ."

Not surprisingly, Aquinas cites Philippians 3:20 in his very first article on charity, where he defines charity as friendship. His point is to uphold the New Testament's insight that charity perfects human friendship by drawing human beings into spiritual union with God and fellow human beings. Friendship involves a "communication" of goodness, an exchange of gifting by which one wishes good to the friend for his or her own sake. Of their own nature, our spiritual powers do not suffice for such mutuality, even though our natural spiritual powers provide the basis for communion with spiritual beings. Although in this life God lifts our spiritual powers to himself by grace, this graced fellowship awaits its perfection in the life to come, as Aquinas confirms by recourse to Philippians 3:20, rendered "our conversation is in heaven." While we already participate in this heavenly "conversation," we do not yet do so perfectly.

For Aquinas, Philippians 3:12 shows our spiritual progress toward the fullness of this eternal "conversation." In the seventh article of question 24, Aquinas asks whether charity increases indefinitely in this life, and he grounds his affirmative answer in Philippians 3:12, where Paul describes his continuing quest for perfection in the spiritual life. Does this mean that charity cannot be "perfect" in any sense in this life? In the first objection of article 8 of question 24, Aquinas cites Philippians 3:12 to rule out any sense of "perfect" charity in this life. But Aquinas goes on to show that continuing spiritual progress does not mean that we cannot attain to a perfection of charity according to our present mode. Otherwise, one would have to imagine that every "habitus" of charity was imperfect in itself, whereas in fact we can possess a habitus that enables us to give our "whole heart to God habitually." Our need for continual spiritual progress in this life does not allow us to justify a mortal sin on the grounds that our infused charitable habitus was imperfect as a habitus.

Philippians 1:23, "My desire is to depart and be with Christ," expresses the desire of a person who has attained the perfection of charity insofar as this is possible in this life. Such a person desires the fullness of personal union with the triune God, a fullness that is possible only in the life to come; in this fullness, all the goods of this world find their true fulfillment. As the expression of "perfect" charity in this life, Philippians 1:23 provides the *sed contra* for question 24, article 8 (on whether charity can be perfect in this life) and likewise provides the capstone to Aquinas's answer in question 24, article 9 (on the three degrees of charity in this life). People who enjoy "perfect" charity in this life still grow in charity, but they no longer need to focus on avoiding sin or progressing in virtue; instead, they aim directly at union with God. Does this imply that these people seek a purely spiritual existence, away from bodiliness and other earthly goods? Aware that Philippians 1:23 can be taken in this direction, Aquinas cites it in his first objection in question 25, article 5 (on whether one should love one's body out of charity). While it is true that the fullness of union with Christ cannot be had in this life, Aquinas emphasizes that Paul desires union with the risen Christ rather than the loss of the body.

Ephesians, Galatians, Colossians, 1 and 2 Timothy: Avoiding misunderstandings

Aquinas draws upon these letters to engage central themes for the theology of charity: the relationship of faith and love, the danger of Pelagianism, charity as a general command vis-à-vis charity as a particular virtue, and the relationship of self-love to love of God. In his three quotations from Ephesians, Aquinas focuses on specifying the key aspects of charity as a virtue: it is one virtue, it is the form of all other virtues, and it is freely infused by the Holy Spirit. In article 5 of question 23, he quotes Ephesians 4:5 ("one Lord, one faith, one baptism") in order to make the point that charity, like faith, is one (rather than diversified by having uncreated and created objects). In article

8 of the same question, he makes use of Ephesians 3:17 ("rooted and grounded in love") to bring out the way in which charity is the form of the other virtues: not as a material cause, as a literal reading of "rooted" might imply, but as a formal cause supporting the other virtues' progress toward the ultimate end of union with God. In article 3 of question 24, he concludes his *respondeo* with Ephesians 4:7, "But grace was given to each of us according to the measure of Christ's gift." His point here is that we do not receive the gift of charity in proportion to our natural gifts. Rather, the virtue of charity in us depends solely upon "the will of the Holy Spirit" (II-II, q. 24, a. 3).

Aquinas's five other uses of the Pauline epistles in his first three questions on charity – Galatians 5:6, Colossians 1:12, 1 Timothy 1:5 (twice), and 2 Timothy 3:1–2 – also bear upon fundamental themes. Galatians 5:6 states that "in Christ Jesus neither circumcision nor uncircumcision is of any avail, but faith working through love." Aquinas quotes this verse in question 23, article 6 in order to suggest, in the voice of an objector, that faith is a greater virtue than charity because the latter serves as the instrument of faith. In his reply, Aquinas points out that the objector's mistake consists in supposing that love is faith's instrument rather than faith's form. Colossians 1:12 helps Aquinas avoid the Pelagian conclusion that our disposition or preparation for charity governs the degree to which we receive the gift of charity. According to Colossians 1:12, it is God the Father "who has qualified us to share in the inheritance of the saints in light." God is the one who readies us for charity, by which we share in "the inheritance of the saints" (II-II, q. 24, a. 3, ad 1).

First Timothy 1:5 reads in Aquinas's Latin "the end of the commandment is charity," whereas the RSV reads "the aim of our charge is love." Either way, the point is that the goal toward which Paul guides his flock is charity, and so charity is "a general command" as well as a particular virtue (II-II, q. 23, a. 4, ad 3). Aquinas also quotes the full text of 1 Timothy 1:5, which specifies that charity "issues from a pure heart and a good conscience and sincere faith," so as to underscore (against Pelagians) that God freely infuses charity in us. Aquinas explains that the act of charity, as differentiated from the habitus of charity, flows from our purity of heart, good conscience, and sincere faith; insofar as these attributes dispose us for charity, they too arise from God's grace (II-II, q. 24, a. 2, obj. 3 and ad 3). Lastly, in treating whether one should love oneself out of charity, Aquinas formulates an objection by means of 2 Timothy 3:1–2, which teaches that "in the last days ... men will be lovers of self." Does this passage rule out charitable love of self, so that love of self is ineluctably selfish? Aquinas argues that, on the contrary, loving God and all things in relation to God includes loving the self that God has created for spiritual relationship with him (II-II, q. 25, a. 4, obj. 3 and ad 3).

Aquinas on Paul: *Commentary on the First Epistle to the Corinthians*

When Aquinas treats 1 Corinthians 13 in his commentary on the epistle,[7] he begins by noting Paul's contrast between the charismatic graces discussed in 1 Corinthians 12 and the "more excellent way" (1 Cor 12:31), charity. The charismatic graces, Aquinas notes, are what impress the Corinthians, and so Paul's task is to emphasize that charity, not the charismatic graces, gives eternal life (see paragraph 760, p. 151). At the same time, Aquinas takes seriously the language that Paul uses, for example, regarding the speech of angels and the ability of prayer to move mountains. If prayer can move mountains, why have not saints accomplished this? While this might seem a digression, Aquinas uses it to point out that miracles, like all charismatic graces, are ordered to the end of charity rather than merely to exhibit wondrous powers. The pinnacle of charity, which merits eternal life, is martyrdom (1 Cor 13:3) rather than exhibitions of power.

In Aquinas's hands, Paul's treatment of charity's virtues in 1 Corinthians 13:4–7 resounds with echoes from all parts of Scripture: Song of Songs, James, Proverbs, 1 John, Ephesians, Wisdom of Solomon, Psalms, Isaiah, Job, Leviticus, Sirach, Colossians, Galatians, Philippians, Micah, Matthew, 2 John, Romans, Genesis, and Hebrews (paragraphs 771–785, pp. 155–158). Without needing here to quote all these texts, one can see how Aquinas, with Paul, places charity at the heart of all of Scripture's moral instruction. Voices from every corner of Scripture are drawn together in the service of the life of charity. At the same time, Aquinas follows Paul in showing in detail, through biblical texts, how charity enables us to avoid sin and to do good. As Aquinas says, charity "is the love of the supreme good, to Whom all sin is obnoxious" (paragraph 782, p. 157).

Aquinas also makes much of Paul's point that charity, unlike the charismatic graces, does not pass away but instead endures in eternal life. Addressing 1 Corinthians 13:8, "Love never ends," Aquinas notes that some misinterpret this to mean that charity, once possessed, cannot be lost. Against this view, he records the risen Christ's warning to the church in Ephesus in Revelation 2:4. Further misunderstandings arise as Paul continues: according to Aquinas, some have supposed that bodily tongues will not be present in heaven and that bodily death obliterates all acquired knowledge (1 Cor 13:8). Aquinas takes the opportunity to explore the connection between charity and eschatology, that is, "when the perfection of glory triumphs" (paragraph 793, p. 160). He asks whether it would not be more fitting for Paul to speak of charity, too, as passing away in heaven, on the grounds that "it is imperfect in the present life as compared with the life of glory" (paragraph 795, p. 161). In answer, Aquinas points out that, by contrast with knowledge, which depends upon sensible things in this life but not in heaven, charity retains its same nature in heaven. While charity endures, the charismatic graces – which Aquinas correlates with Paul's reference to "childish ways" (1 Cor 13:11) – pass away. In short, the believer should treasure charity rather than exhibitions of spiritual power, no matter how great.

How about the vision of God "face to face" (1 Cor 13:12)? Drawing upon Romans 1:20, Aquinas observes that we now see God "in a mirror dimly" (1 Cor 13:12) because we understand God through sensible things, so that "all creation is a mirror for us" (paragraph 800, p. 163). According to Aquinas, Paul uses the metaphorical expression "face to face" to describe our heavenly knowledge of God's essence. In making this claim, however, Aquinas has to account both for Jacob's assertion that he saw God's face (Gen 32:30) – Aquinas ascribes this to encountering God through the imagination in the highest way possible – and for the view of some that even our heavenly knowledge of God will be mediated by a created likeness, an interpretation that Aquinas rules out with a memorable phrase: "any created species in the soul is more distant from the divine essence than the species of a horse or whiteness from the essence of an angel" (paragraph 803, p. 164). He then explains why Paul singles out faith, hope, and charity, namely, because they unite us to God. The desire for eternal union with God, for Aquinas as for Paul, is at the center of everything.

Concluding Reflections

In the above, I have barely scratched the surface of Aquinas's theological debt to Paul and of his exegesis of Paul's letters. I hope to have shown, however, that Aquinas's theology is unthinkable without Paul. I chose to focus on Aquinas's writings on charity as a point of entry into Paul's place in Aquinas's corpus because charity is the height of the Christian life and the bond of trinitarian communion. It would have been surprising to find that Aquinas's treatment of charity lacked the powerful influence of Paul's letters. A cursory glance at the topics of Aquinas's articles on charity, however, might suggest that Paul is not strongly present: "Whether charity is friendship?" "Whether charity is something created in the soul?" "Whether charity is a virtue?" "Whether charity is a special virtue?" and so forth. These topics sound more like Aristotle than Paul. Has Aquinas's theology moved away from the spirit and letter of Paul, so that it bears witness to what Congar calls "overriding rationality" (Congar 1997, part 3, 116), or (to quote the title of an article by Otto Hermann Pesch) "Paul as Professor of Theology" (Pesch 1974)?

While Aquinas's theological argumentation does not match the rhetorical form of Paul's letters, nonetheless, far from silencing Paul's voice, Aquinas enables Paul to speak at the critical junctures of the theology of charity. By quoting Paul, Aquinas emphasizes that charity comes to us through the missions of the incarnate Son and the Holy Spirit. Charity is God's utterly free gift in us, and so charity does not arise from our preparation for charity or in accord with our natural gifts. Far from being evil, the body is an instrument of charity, although charity requires us to lead our lives according to the primacy of spiritual realities. Charity can be lost by sin. Charity strengthens all the virtues and guides them toward their proper end, union with God. Even "perfect" charity in this life continues to increase; charity is the path of spiritual progress, although the increase cannot be quantified but rather consists in a deeper participation in God. Charity unites us with God and each other, so that charity is not individualistic but rather constitutes the fellowship of the Church. Charity requires the love of enemies, and it seeks not to escape but to transform the sinful world. Charity is a distinct virtue that establishes friendship with God. Because charity unites us to the triune God, it is the goal of human existence. All of these themes are prominent in Paul, and they provide the key insights of Aquinas's teaching on charity. While speaking as a medieval professor of theology, Aquinas allows his voice to be theologically conformed to Paul's rather than vice versa – although Aquinas treats Paul's themes from within his own order of questioning.

Similarly, in his commentary on 1 Corinthians 13's encomium to charity, Aquinas draws out Paul's comparison of charismatic gifts to charity. Like Paul, Aquinas seeks to show how much greater charity is, both now and especially eschatologically. He thereby places union with God, sharing in the trinitarian communion, at the center of the spiritual life. Exhibitions of power or of knowledge through the charismatic gifts pale in light of the union with God that charity, infusing all other virtuous actions, accomplishes. Aquinas shows how the entire Scripture profoundly resonates with Paul's teachings on the Christian life. Once we see how united his theology is to Paul's, and with Paul's to the whole of Scripture's, we discover the spiritual energy, the "life and history," under the surface of Aquinas's calm prose – a spiritual energy rooted in the faith that "in all these things we are more than conquerors through him who loved us" (Rom 8:37).

Notes

1 Quotations of biblical texts are taken from the Revised Standard Version.
2 See Valkenberg (2000, 29 n. 71). The *Summa theologiae* as a whole contains 8,250 quotations from Scripture (Valkenberg 2000, 209).
3 II-II, q. 24, a. 12 = second part of the second part of the *Summa theologiae* (or *Summa Theologica*), question 24, article 12. If "obj. 3" is added to the reference, the third objection mentioned to Aquinas's own position is in view. If "ad 3" is added, the reference is to Aquinas's response to the third objection. The *sed contra* of an article ("but on the contrary") marks the transition to Aquinas's position after possible objections have been listed; the *respondeo* ("I answer") articulates his response. Note that, while quotations from the *Summa* are taken from the translation of the Fathers of the English Dominican Province (Thomas Aquinas 1948), "Holy Spirit" has been consistently substituted for the "Holy Ghost" of that translation.
4 II-II, q. 24, a. 12. Aquinas comments further: "Not every inordinate affection for things directed to the end, i.e., for created goods, constitutes a mortal sin, but only such as is directly contrary to the Divine will; and then the inordinate affection is contrary to charity" (ad 4).
5 The Vulgate text of 13:4 reads, "*Caritas patiens est, benigna est; caritas non aemulatur, non agit perperam, non inflator.*" The RSV text lacks an equivalent to "*non agit perperam*" ("does not act perversely"), although the basic point remains the same.
6 II-II, q. 25, a. 8. Aquinas observes that "their enmity should displease us." There is no reason to love enemies because of their enmity toward us. However, we should love them "as men and capable of happiness" (ad 2).
7 Citations are taken from "Commentary by Saint Thomas Aquinas on the First Epistle to the Corinthians," translated by Fabian Larcher (paragraphs 987–1046 by Daniel Keating), an unpublished translation available at the website of the Aquinas Center for Theological Renewal, Ave Maria University.

References

Congar, Yves. 1997. *I Believe in the Holy Spirit*. New York: Crossroad.
Domanyi, Thomas. 1979. *Der Römerbriefkommentar des Thomas von Aquin: Ein Beitrag zur Untersuchung seiner Auslegungsmethoden*. Bern: Peter Lang.
Pesch, Otto Hermann. 1974. Paul as Professor of Theology: The Image of the Apostle in St. Thomas's Theology. *The Thomist* 38: 584–605.

Ryan, Thomas F. 2007. The Love of Learning and the Desire for God in Thomas Aquinas's *Commentary on Romans*. Pages 101–114 in *Medieval Readings of Romans*. Edited by William S. Campbell, Peter S. Hawkins, and Brenda Deen Schildgen. New York: T. & T. Clark.

Sherwin, Michael S., OP. 2005. *By Knowledge and by Love: Charity and Knowledge in the Moral Theology of St. Thomas Aquinas*. Washington, DC: Catholic University of America Press.

Thomas Aquinas. 1948. *Summa Theologica*. 5 volumes. Translated by Fathers of the English Dominican Province. New York: Benziger.

Torrell, Jean-Pierre, OP. 1996. *Saint Thomas Aquinas*. Volume 1: *The Person and his Work*. Washington, DC: Catholic University of America Press.

Valkenberg, Wilhelmus G. B. M. 2000. *Words of the Living God: Place and Function of Holy Scripture in the Theology of St. Thomas Aquinas*. Leuven: Peeters.

Weinandy, Thomas G., OFM, Cap., Daniel A. Keating, and John P. Yocum. 2005. Preface. Pages ix–xii in *Aquinas on Scripture: An Introduction to his Biblical Commentaries*. Edited by Thomas G. Weinandy, Daniel A. Keating, and John P. Yocum. New York: T. & T. Clark.

CHAPTER 24
Luther

Mickey L. Mattox

We do well at the outset of any consideration of Luther's reading of Paul to note that the man himself was not a Pauline scholar, nor even a professor of the New Testament. As Heinrich Bornkamm insists, if we had to force Luther into the mold of a modern Scripture scholar, then we would identify his specialization as the Old Testament, on which he lectured for most of his academic career, particularly after the arrival of his gifted young colleague, the Greek scholar Philip Melanchthon, at the University of Wittenberg in 1519 (Bornkamm 1969). Given that this is so, it is not surprising to find that the bookends of Luther's academic "career" at Wittenberg are neither the letters of Paul nor, say, one of the gospels, but the Psalms and his "dear Genesis" (LW 8.333).[1]

As a young friar in the Hermits of St. Augustine, Luther was selected for the vocation of doctor of Holy Scripture (*doctor in biblia*) by his superior, Johannes von Staupitz. Installed at Wittenberg as Staupitz's own successor in 1512, Luther chose for his first lectures the Psalms, which he knew well through the spiritual disciplines of the Augustinian community. Unpublished in Luther's day, these lectures run well over a thousand pages in the modern, critical edition. Scholars interested in Luther's theology have pored over them with great care, for it was here that he first struggled to understand the relationship between the law of God and the gospel of Jesus Christ, and the simultaneity of these two within the struggle for faithfulness canonically embodied in the stories of Old Testament "saints" like David.[2] Afterwards, Luther returned frequently to the Psalms, producing in 1518–1519 a published commentary on Psalms 1–22,[3] and later a number of shorter devotional works.[4] The Psalms were

The Blackwell Companion to Paul, First Edition. Edited by Stephen Westerholm.
© 2011 Blackwell Publishing Ltd. Published 2011 by Blackwell Publishing Ltd.

not just dear but theologically central to the young Luther, and they remained so throughout his life.

Years later, he turned his attention to the text on which he would write his last and longest commentary: Genesis.[5] Never mind that he had preached at length on the book in 1523–1524, and that these sermons had been published in both Latin and German editions.[6] Taking up the text again in 1535, he was determined to navigate once more the patriarchal histories, guided this time by a lifetime's worth of hard-earned insight into the myriad ways in which the stories of the Old Testament "saints" reveal the work and the character of God. Old man Luther believed that he had learned in the Holy Spirit's school of experience to read between the lines of these narratives, alive to their revelation of the biblical saints' distinctive struggle for faith against unbelief. Luther read the stories of the patriarchs and matriarchs of Genesis as crucial witnesses to the God who not only makes promises to his saints, but who also makes their struggles the means by which he molds their faith and character, and in just that way calls them to lives of heroic faith and faithfulness. Here faith and works, obedience both to the promises and to the precepts of God, are inseparable.

Luther on Paul

It is something of an irony, then, that Luther is remembered in some circles primarily as a "Pauline" theologian, one who made his mark, for better or worse, to the extent that he was able to articulate a new, perhaps a deepened, or even, as some see the matter, a fundamentally mistaken reading of the apostle's central concerns. Typically, this new or deepened or perhaps mistaken insight is said to consist in the conviction Luther reached at the end of his "search for a gracious God," namely, that Paul teaches a doctrine of "imputed righteousness." Justification takes place by grace through faith alone apart from works of the law. Through faith the Christian is righteous, though remaining in this life a sinner (*simul iustus et peccator*). In their doctrinal elaborations of this insight, Luther's Protestant heirs have often sharpened it to create the maximum possible tension between law and gospel, even to the point where the two seem opposed to one another, specifically in the "forensic" doctrines of justification.[7] If God's final word to us is one of grace and pardon, what room for a divine command? The "righteousness of the law" is then sometimes opposed to the "righteousness of faith," with the stereotypical "self-righteous Pharisee," who tries to justify himself before God by works, standing diametrically opposed to the stereotypical "humble Christian believer," who is justified by faith alone.[8]

For some Protestants, the gospel as Luther understood it is considered the very core of Reformation faith.[9] For others, Luther's was at the very least a mistaken identification of Paul's central concern, and at worst a fundamental misunderstanding of Paul, even of the New Testament itself. My purpose in what follows is neither to adjudicate the competing claims made by contemporary New Testament scholars regarding Paul's meaning, nor even to reach in and correct this or that element in any particular scholar's understanding of Martin Luther's reading of Paul. Much work of the latter kind has already been done, a good deal of it by scholars who are otherwise sympathetic with the New Perspective. Wilfried Härle (2006), for example, easily shows that E. P. Sanders's understanding of Luther is simply wrong.[10] Contra Sanders, authentic faith and good works are, for Luther, organically related, inseparable; there is no room for antinomianism. Sanders's facile notion of the *simul* formula, moreover, ignores Luther's clear insistence that the sin that remains even in the baptized (i.e., concupiscence) must not "rule" (*peccatum regnans*) but instead be "ruled over" (*peccatum regnatum*).

Elsewhere, Risto Saarinen argues that, in the main, Luther "got Paul right" (Saarinen 2006; 2007). Saarinen's position depends on his judgment that recent Luther scholarship has given us a Luther who is not at all the inflexible forensicist who has played the role of straw man over against the New Perspective. To the contrary, Luther has a vigorous, if previously largely unrecognized, theology of Christ's presence in the Christian through faith, one that is broadly compatible with readings of Paul that stress the centrality of participation in Christ in Paul's understanding of salvation. Saarinen (1989) argues that the widespread assumption of a neo-Kantian religious epistemology rendered Luther scholars in the nineteenth and twentieth centuries unable to perceive either the realism intrinsic to Luther's talk of the "real presence of Christ in faith" or the importance of "divinization" in his vision of salvation, much less to recognize the centrality of these elements in Luther's thought.[11] This mystical notion of the real presence of Christ in the Christian, a claim still viewed with suspicion by some, radically revises our perception of Luther's notion of saving faith as well as the relationship between sanctification and justification. Given that this is so, one wonders how long Luther can continue to function as a convenient foil for the New Perspective.

For his part, Timothy George both defends Luther against the claims of some scholars representing the New Perspective and criticizes the New Perspective itself (George 2004). George takes aim at, among other things, Krister Stendahl's well-known contrast between Paul's "extroverted and robust" conscience and Luther's "introspective conscience."[12] This claim implies that Luther is guilty of a debilitating religious subjectivism. To the contrary, George insists, Luther saw the conscience itself as one of the battlefields on which the titanic struggle between God and the devil was being played out. Interiority alone can never produce confidence in God's grace and favor. Instead, the sinner must look outside (*extra nos*) in order to find the only true consolation; namely, through God's own word and promise. The difficulty, George seems to believe, is that while Luther's God (i.e., the God of Paul as *Luther* read Paul) remained the untamed lion of long Western Christian tradition, the God scholars find today in the writings of Paul (i.e., the God of Paul as *they* read Paul), has been, wrongly, "domesticated."

Building on works such as these, I introduce below Luther's work on Paul and sketch out very briefly some of his exegesis of Romans. As will become clear, the young Luther read Romans with the Psalms and Genesis very much on his mind. More importantly, he is not at all the theologically ham-handed and predictable reader of Paul that so many seem to think they know, the one who makes the law the enemy of the gospel and faith opposed to works. To the contrary, as an exegete who never ceased moving forward in his effort to understand Paul, Luther gladly sang with the Psalmist, "Oh, how I love thy law." This Luther remains a challenging and insightful conversation partner for theological exegesis today.

Reading Luther, Reading Paul

There is good reason to believe that we are in the midst of a thoroughgoing re-reading of Luther both historically and theologically, one that promises at last to release the great Reformer from his forced conscription[13] on one side or another of the theological battles that have raged between liberal, neo-orthodox, existential, and confessional Protestant theologies. Theologically sensitive research that embraces careful historical study and eschews every form of triumphalism is gradually uncovering a Luther who resists easy conscription into any of our causes, either as a hero or as a villain. As the late Heiko Oberman convincingly showed, this Luther is both more alien to our sensibilities and less theologically predictable than we may have been led to think.[14] Ironically, as Luther gradually becomes less the final bulwark of one or another version of Protestant identity, so, conversely, he becomes an engaging conversation partner with a contribution to make along a broad and rather surprising ecumenical trajectory.[15]

A caveat. It is crucial to remember that, like all of us, Luther was a creature of space and time. One must be aware of the many ways in which his theology and exegesis were shaped by such diverse elements as the Augustinian heritage in which he had been steeped as a monastic, the university setting in which the Reformation initially unfolded in Wittenberg, and Renaissance biblicism as represented by such important expositors of Paul as Desiderius Erasmus, Jacques Lefèvre d'Étaples (Faber Stapulensis), and, nearer to hand, Philip Melanchthon. At the same time, we must also remain ever vigilant to discern in Luther's work the impact of controversy. As Hinlicky (2010) points out, Luther's apocalyptic outlook on his age included a readiness to demonize his opponents. Whether he is railing against the "pig theologians" (i.e., the semi-Pelagians), the Papists, the Jews, the Turks, or the false brethren, Luther presents a figure shocking to modern sensibilities. Theology, for Luther, is not an academic discipline; it is a matter of life and death.

To understand Luther well, we should also know that he was a scholastic theologian who cut his theological teeth on the *Sentences* of Peter Lombard. His academic pedigree parallels almost exactly that of St. Thomas Aquinas, who died more than two hundred years before Luther's birth. Aware of these facts, we should be prepared to let him develop theologically. As an exegete, indeed as a Christian, Luther never rested content with what he had been given but instead strained forward to discern yet more of the truth given in Scripture. Indeed, in his last words, uttered from his death bed, he expressed his wonder at how much more the Scriptures had to give: "Let nobody suppose that he has tasted the Holy Scriptures sufficiently unless he has ruled over the churches with the prophets for a hundred years ... We are beggars. That is true" (LW 54.476). To illustrate the forward-reaching element in Luther's Pauline interpretation, and to suggest how little he can serve as straw man for anyone's perspective on Paul, we turn to his work on the writings of the apostle, examining briefly key elements in his interpretation of Romans.

Luther's Knowledge of the Bible and Familiarity with the Writings of Paul

Although he was not a professor of the New Testament, Martin Luther was, of course, thoroughly familiar with the apostle's writings. Luther reports that he read all of Paul's letters, in fact the entire Bible, through at least once each year as part of his own discipline of scriptural study. After September 1522, he could also boast that he had translated all of Paul's writings from Greek into German as part of his complete translation of the New Testament (the "September Testament"). Afterward, with the assistance of a collegium of Wittenberg scholars (whom Luther jokingly referred to as his "Sanhedrin"), he continued his translation work, which led to the publication in 1534 of the first complete German Bible based on the texts in their original languages, the so-called "Luther Bible," which is still in print today.[16]

Beginning with the "September Testament" and continuing through subsequent editions, Luther offered his readers not only a translation, but also, in continuity with the "glossed" Bibles of the Middle Ages, prefaces and marginal comments added before and alongside each of the books of Scripture. These prefaces and marginal comments provided both a précis of the book's "argument" and a brief theological commentary on its meaning. Most famously – or, perhaps, most notoriously – at Romans 3:28, Luther offered a translation that read: "Thus we now hold that one is justified apart from works of the Law, through faith *alone*" (WADB 7.39.28 [1522]). A nearby marginal annotation provided the clarification that "faith fulfills the whole Law; works fulfill no part of the Law" (WADB 7.41 [1522]). Luther's addition of "alone" here was controversial, since the term is not found in the Greek text. He argued that the addition was necessary to convey the force of the Greek text in the German language.[17] Taken on its own, this insistence is open to a wide range of misinterpretations, the most obvious being the common-sense observation that mere belief, "faith alone," changes nothing. Why, merely for the sake of one's acceptance of the gospel as true, should God "believe" what is clearly not true, namely, that the sinner is a saint?

In what amounts to a primer in Luther's soteriology, the preface to Romans offered answers to such questions, explaining such crucial Pauline terms as law and gospel, flesh and spirit, grace and the gifts of grace, faith and works. The Romans preface proved particularly influential. To take but one prominent if somewhat paradoxical example of a reader who found Luther's preface illuminating, the evangelist John Wesley had an experience of assurance at a Methodist society meeting on Aldersgate Street in London in 1738 when he felt his heart "strangely warmed" while hearing the text read aloud (Wesley 1988, 249–250). Nevertheless, Wesley later became a critic of the Luther he associated with "solifidianism," that is, a false reliance on faith alone, when the Christian life clearly calls also for good works, holiness. Misunderstanding Luther's understanding of faith, it would seem, is an old tradition.

Wesley's example makes clear that one who attempts to assess Luther's impact on the Protestant reading of Paul must take careful stock not only of his commentaries or sermons, but of his translation work as well. This raises the question whether Luther's exegetical impact was limited primarily to the German speakers to whom German printers offered the Luther Bible. In partial answer, we know that English Bible translators, particularly William Tyndale, borrowed extensively from Luther.[18] We also know that Luther and his "Sanhedrin" did not rest content with the German, but also offered a Latin version of the Luther Bible, which included the biblical prefaces. Interestingly, the Latin translation of Romans 3:28 omits the "alone," which suggests that Luther was true to his point regarding the necessity of the term specifically for the *German* translation.[19] More fundamentally, this Latin publication suggests the wide influence of Luther's Bible in the sixteenth century.

Besides his influential translation work, we also have a great many of Luther's sermons on Pauline texts. Luther typically preached several times a week. Over the years, he often preached on Paul's writings as they came up in the cycle of texts.[20] Sometimes he also offered special sermon series on Pauline texts. These were typically taken down by his students and subsequently edited for publication. So one finds today in the critical edition of Luther's writings numerous collections of sermons (i.e., Postills), as well as published "commentaries"[21] on the following Pauline or pseudo-Pauline writings: Romans, classroom lectures delivered from 1515 to 1516, unpublished until the twentieth century; Galatians, again classroom lectures, delivered from 1516 to 1517, revised and published in 1519; Hebrews, classroom lectures delivered from 1517 to 1518, unpublished until the twentieth century; 1 Corinthians 7, a treatise written in praise of marriage in 1523; Titus and Philemon, from a special sermon series delivered in 1527, followed by 1 Timothy in 1528; a new set of lectures on Galatians delivered in 1531, published in 1535, and again in revised form in 1538; and 1 Corinthians 15, based on a series of Sunday afternoon sermons preached from 1532 to 1533.[22]

Romans

This corpus is surely impressive. However, as noted above, Luther's exegeses of both Romans and Hebrews remained unpublished in the sixteenth century. Most importantly, the lectures on Romans lay unknown and virtually unread until a century ago when the text was uncovered by a Vatican librarian, Heinrich Denifle, OP, who subjected it to withering criticism.[23] Denifle's rediscovery of these all-but-forgotten lectures in the Vatican's own collection, not to mention his wince-inducing criticisms of the Wittenberger's character and scholarly abilities, produced no little consternation on the part of Protestant scholars. More importantly, however, it added the voice of Luther to the twentieth-century conversation about Romans, and about Paul.

For their part, Protestant scholars responded to Denifle's polemical blast with a frantic search, which led eventually to the discovery of a copy of Luther's text in Berlin. Soon they were able to challenge Denifle's attack on Luther, especially his reading of Paul. The Romans "commentary" itself was quickly made available in a published edition, later incorporated into the Weimar edition and, not long afterwards, translated into English.[24] That these events occurred in close proximity to the rise of dialectical theology in the early to mid twentieth century alerts us to the fact that the initial reception of Luther's work on Romans was carried out in a period of profound theological ferment that included the publication of Karl Barth's electric *Der Römerbrief* (1919; revised edition 1922). Not only the predictable struggles between Protestant theologians, but also the stresses and strains of two world wars rendered the twentieth-century reception of Luther, particularly his work on Romans, a matter of high stakes, and sometimes high drama. Thus, the assessment of Luther's understanding of Paul as reflected in the Romans lectures must take into account not only all the difficulties of late medieval exegesis and history, but also important currents and trends in twentieth-century theology, especially among German Protestants, as well as the ever-changing shape of Lutheran self-understanding in relation to the Roman Catholic Church.[25] Any attempt at a contemporary reading of Luther on Romans must be a critical, even a corrective one.

Luther's "breakthrough" at Romans 1:17

No doubt Luther believed he had learned a great deal from Paul. Perhaps most famously, in the preface he penned for the 1545 edition of his Latin writings, old man Luther reminisced about his lectures on Romans. It was a new insight into the meaning of Romans 1:17, he recollected, that had opened up for him the "gate to paradise" (LW 34.337). Luther recalled having struggled with the genitive in Paul's teaching that in the gospel "the righteousness *of God*" (Lat. *iustitia dei*) is revealed. He came to the conclusion that this verse should not be read as a reference to God's own perfection, that is, the righteousness by which God is holy in himself. How could the sheer holiness of God as God be gospel, that is, "good news" for sinners? The answer, Luther came to believe, is that the genitive case here points the reader toward the righteousness that God graciously offers to share with sinners; that is, a righteousness that God gives, to all who place their faith in him, as a gift. As a gift, moreover, this righteousness can only be received.[26] Thus, Luther often speaks of the believer's righteousness received through faith in the gospel as the "passive righteousness of God" (*iustitia dei passiva*).

Few have been willing to accept old man Luther's recollection of events at face value. This brief reminiscence about a fateful encounter with Paul, written some thirty years or so after the fact, evidently compacts a rather long and arduous period of theological development during which Luther clearly broke through to a great many theological insights. Over approximately the past century, industrious scholars, often concerned to buttress the theological self-understanding of their own tradition, have left hardly a page of the Weimar edition unturned in their effort to identify the precise date and content of what came to be called the "evangelical breakthrough." The predominant view in recent years has been that Luther reached this breakthrough well after the lectures on Romans (ca. 1518–1519), although many still believe that it happened earlier (for example, 1512–1515). As it appears, this debate is irresolvable on strictly historical grounds, but depends vitally on the researcher's own theological convictions. Since it involves matters crucial to Lutheran and, more broadly, to Protestant identity, it probably makes good sense for theologians and exegetes to continue to debate the point. Still, it now seems clear that, as noted above, there have always been competing accounts of justification at work among the theologians of the Reformation traditions.

Simul peccator et iustus

The Romans lectures take the reader back into the quintessentially medieval classroom of a pious and brilliant young Augustinian friar lecturing through what is perhaps the densest and most theologically rich text in the New Testament. These lectures present to the modern reader the ironic juxtaposition of, on the one hand, an intensely traditional exercise in spiritual and intellectual formation of the vowed religious in the Middle Ages, and, on the other hand, a theological analysis of the text that, while clearly grounded in and conversant with antecedent tradition, at the same time offers an almost bewildering series of fresh insights into Paul's text. Whether from our perspective these insights are right or wrong is for the moment unimportant. Luther himself would not rest content with what he had said or discovered in these lectures, but would press ever on toward a better understanding of Paul.

Looking briefly at Luther's remarks on Romans 1:17, the text he later cited as crucial, he says that the righteousness Paul speaks of here is that "by which we are made righteous [justified] by God ... through faith in the Gospel" (LW 25.151). Based on the autobiographical fragment from 1545, this is what one would expect. But in making this observation, Luther first quotes Augustine's *On the Spirit and the Letter* to support his point, and then mentions the views of some medieval expositors. This suggests that the young Luther thought he was reading the text in a basically traditional way, so that what we have here is hardly the fabled "reformatory insight" – unless an Augustinian reading of the *iustitia dei* could *ipso facto* be construed as such.[27] Moving on, however, Luther developed this rather traditional point in a distinctive way. The righteousness God gives, Luther says, is received through faith but admits, nevertheless, of growth, as the phrase "from faith to faith" suggests. The Christian therefore should always believe "more and more strongly so that he 'who is righteous can be justified still' (Rev. 22:11)" (Luther 1956, 19). No one should think that he or she has fully apprehended, but each should continue to grow, that is, to *increase* in righteousness. Viewed from the standpoint of the later forensic and declaratory understandings of justification found in Protestant theology, a statement like this may sound "pre-Reformational," as if one's justification before God awaits one's final achievement of complete righteousness. Be that as it may, it is clear that in Luther's understanding of Paul, justifying faith and growth in righteousness are dynamically connected, inseparable. He remained convinced of this dynamism and inseparability all his life.

Moving ahead to Luther's remarks on Romans 4, we find him working his way through Paul with one eye on Abraham and David, Genesis and the Psalms. Both Abraham and David, Luther figures, were justified by faith, since in the Old Testament itself we see that God "reckons" (*reputat*) or "imputes" (*imputat*) righteousness to them. This "reckoning" or "imputation" reverses the conventional wisdom because God "does not accept the person on account of his works, but the works on account of the person, for the person is logically prior to the works" (my translation; cf. LW 25.256). Abel,

Luther figures, amply illustrates this principle, for God had "respect" for Abel as a man of faith and so accepted his offering. David, Abraham, and Abel thus exemplify the faith of which Paul speaks. They are "saints" (*sancti*), men who know themselves as sinners who stand ever under God's mercy and grace. Their righteousness depends entirely on mercy and grace; that is, on God's forgiveness of their sin and reckoning to them of righteousness.

The text is thick here with citations from the Old Testament, particularly the Psalms: 121:2, "My help comes from the Lord"; 51:3, "My sin is ever before me"; 32:5, "you have forgiven the iniquity of my sin." "Note," Luther concludes, "that every saint is a sinner and prays for his [own] sins" (LW 25.258). Here, in the exemplars of these Old Testament saints as read through the lens of the apostle Paul, we confront the origins of the dynamic reality Luther identified at the very center of authentic Christian existence before God: pious awareness of one's own sin and unworthiness before God; abiding faith in God's forgiveness and acceptance as the foundation of the Christian life; good works as the fruit of faith that only those who are already righteous in God's sight can bring forth.

For the duration of the present life, then, the Christian is "at the same time both a sinner and a righteous man" (*simul peccator et iustus*; LW 25.260).[28] But grace has turned the believer *toward* the good and *away* from evil. God intends to perfect the faithful, to heal them completely from sin. Faith lays hold of the eschatological reality of this perfection through grace and makes it effective in the present, just as a sick man takes the medicine provided by the good physician and so begins to get better. Because the healing remains incomplete in this life, one is ever "a sinner in fact, but a just man by the reckoning and by the sure promise of God, which sets him free from sin until it heals him completely" (my translation; cf. LW 25.260). God emphatically does not, then, "believe a fiction." To the contrary, the God whose promise is sure looks ahead to and *knows* the final perfection of the faithful. God applies that very reality to believers in the here and now and in just that way sees to their becoming actually righteous through the process of healing them from sin.

Grace and gift: Romans 5:12–15

Turning now briefly to Luther's preface to Romans (first edition, 1522), we find him offering, as indicated above, a précis of his soteriology. He means to summarize the teaching of Romans as a whole, but as he does so, he utilizes a series of theological distinctions: law and gospel, faith and works, belief and unbelief, the grace and the gift of God. The last of these distinctions is drawn from Romans 5:12–15, where Paul speaks somewhat enigmatically of the "grace" and the "gift" of God. Luther's interpretation of these terms has received rather intensive analysis in the scholarly literature. Early on, in the lectures on Romans, for example, Luther took the words as synonyms: "But 'the grace of God' and 'the gift' are the same thing," he said, "namely, the very righteousness which is freely given to us through Christ" (LW 25.306).

But his view altered as the result of a series of exchanges with Philip Melanchthon.[29] According to Rolf Schäfer (1997), medieval theologians understood grace along lines laid out by Augustine; that is, as "a power that transforms an individual." Grace, on this account, is a reality *in* the human being. In 1521, based on his study of Erasmus's *Annotations* on the New Testament, Philip Melanchthon accepted a distinction between "grace" (*gratia*) and "gift" (*donum*). Grace denotes God's "favor"; that is, it refers to a reality which is itself *in God* rather than a quality of the soul (i.e., a reality in the human being). This favor is grounded in the saving work of Christ. The "gift" of God, on the other hand, denotes the renewing power of the Holy Spirit given to those whom God views with favor (i.e., with grace). The sequence is clear: the favor of God on account of the work of Christ logically and theologically precedes and is the grounds for the gift of the Spirit.

In his own work during this same period, Luther joins Melanchthon in appropriating Erasmus's distinction, but he takes it his own way. Grace means, yes, the divine favor, a quality in God. But gift denotes the faith that unites one to Christ. The one who has this gift has, just so, Christ himself, and thus becomes the recipient of grace, the divine favor. In the "Answer to Latomus" (1521), Luther put it this way:

> For although he has justified us through the *gift* of faith, and although he becomes favorable to us through his *grace*, yet he wants us to rely on Christ so that we will not waver in ourselves and in these his gifts, nor be satisfied with the righteousness which has begun in us unless it cleaves to and flows from Christ's righteousness, and so that no fool, having once accepted the gift, will think himself already contented and secure. But he does not want us to halt in what has been received, but rather to draw nearer from day to day so that we may be fully transformed into Christ. (LW 32.235; emphasis added)

Luther's understanding of grace, we might say, remains a variant of the Augustinian understanding according to which it means transformative power, while Melanchthon's departs a bit further from this conception, pointing ahead toward the classic forensic doctrine of justification where God, like a judge in a heavenly courtroom, looks at the accused sinner standing in the dock and judges him or her innocent, righteous, solely on account of Christ, who pleads his own passion and merit on his or her behalf. For Luther, on the other hand, the union with Christ effected through faith really unites the believer to Christ so that he or she may be fully transformed into his likeness. The motif here, in short, is that of the "wondrous exchange" (*commercium admirabile*), a mystical vision of the Christian's reception of the gift of Christ and the grace of God – drawn principally from Paul's letter to the Romans, and responsibly conversant with the latest exegetical findings – where salvation is effected by the union of faith; that is, through the believer's participation in Christ, and Christ's participation in him or her. At the root of Luther's notion of the simultaneity of sin and righteousness within the Christian lies the mystical union of the sinner him/herself with the righteous Christ himself. This union is effected by the means of grace in Christ's one church, and it bears the unmistakable imprint of God the Holy Trinity: through baptism the Holy Spirit forgives sin and gives the gift of faith; this faith unites the believer to Christ; Christ himself, in turn, leads the believer to know the love of the Father.[30]

Luther's Paul: A "divided self"?

Following long Catholic tradition stretching back at least to Augustine, Luther read Romans 7 as an autobiographical statement about Paul's experience as a Christian. Luther's Paul was divided against himself. This did not, however, mean that he was a man caught in the grips of a debilitating inwardness. To the contrary, Luther's Paul was an upright man, confident of the gift and grace of God. In the sermons Luther preached on the feast day of the conversion of St. Paul, for which the text was Acts 9 (Paul's Damascus road experience), he made it clear that Paul was morally blameless, a man who observed God's law.[31] Paul as Luther imagined him was no crass sinner, either before his conversion (when he was, per Luther, "the devil's hunting dog"), or afterward when he became the apostle to the Gentiles. Not surprisingly, Luther loved to cite Paul's example because he thought it demonstrated the truth of his conviction that conversion, and with it the gift of saving faith, is entirely a divine work in us. Even the good man Paul, upright in every way and extraordinarily zealous for the law of God, had to be directly confronted – bowled over and blinded! – by the risen Christ before he could be converted and made a fit instrument for the spread of the gospel. How much more so, then, someone else, someone who is not a member of the people of the promise, not raised to be zealous for the law?

In his reading of Paul, Luther also exhibited a noteworthy tendency to identify himself with the apostle. Thus, while Luther would be the first to accuse himself as a sinner, he in fact saw himself, like Paul, as a good servant of the gospel, guilty to be sure of innumerable lesser faults, but filled with faith and the Holy Spirit, not at all a man held tight in the grip of mortal sin. The introspective awareness of one's inability to do good without at the same time experiencing internal resistance means, on Luther's account, that one never does good in an utterly free and uninhibited way. It was this reality, an unnatural and contrary motion of the fallen human will, that Luther came to see at the root of Paul's complaint in Romans 7, and which he thought true to his own experience as well.[32] Paul, on Luther's reading, observed the law and lived a morally blameless life. As Luther made clear in his preface to Romans, however, even the morally blameless who observe the law cannot on that account be said to have "kept" it. Keeping the law requires, Luther argued, an utterly spontaneous movement of the heart, and this, he thought, is impossible this side of the resurrection. Clearly then, in Luther's view, the "simul status" (as it is sometimes called) of the Christian does not at all mean that one is a saint in spite of the fact that one is caught up in all manner of serious sin. To the contrary, Luther's saints – including both the apostle and Martin Luther himself! – though they are justified before God by grace and through faith alone, are virtuous, even heroic, women and men.[33]

As we observe Luther reaching forward toward a better grasp of Paul's meaning, however deficient we may judge his efforts today, it becomes clear that we cannot dismiss him as one who ignored the mystical side of Paul, or who failed to see that faith and good works were related. In his interpretation of Paul, Luther looked to the stories of the Old Testament saints, to their faith, in order both to verify and to clarify Paul's meaning. Luther was convinced that the reality Paul describes in his teaching about the grace and the gift of God, as well as faith and works, is precisely the reality the reader finds portrayed in the stories of these saints. The Christian life means nothing less than following their examples, both in faith and in works.

Notes

1 The standard biography is Brecht (1985–1993). For the abbreviations used below for Luther's writings, see the items under his name in the References. The abbreviations WA and WADB are cited with volume, page, and line numbers (e.g., WA 8.394.10). To the standard English edition (LW), a further twenty volumes are currently planned for publication (LW, New Series) by Concordia Publishing House.

2 WA 3, entire, and WA 4.1–462; English translation in LW 10–11. A revised edition may be found in WA 55.I.1, and WA 55.II.1. For Luther's reading of the Psalms in these earliest lectures, see Hendrix (1974) and Steinmetz (1980). See also Preus (1969).

3 WA 5. This commentary was cut short by Luther's involvement in the controversies following his protest over indulgences (LW 34.337–338).

4 For translations, see LW, vols. 12–14.

5 The commentary is massive, comprising approximately 2,200 folio pages. See WA 42–44. English translation in LW, vols. 1–8. On Luther's exegesis of Genesis, see Mattox (2003).

6 WA 24. See also WA 9 and 14.

7 Luther sees law and gospel not as two different words of God, but, ultimately, as one. The tension between them reflects human sin and is resolved eschatologically (Lohse 1999, 192). Cf. Hütter (2004, esp. 140).

8 This is not the place to answer the question whether Christian faith in Luther's understanding is fundamentally anti-Judaistic, perhaps even anti-Semitic, as this sadly traditional word picture seems to suggest. For my own brief assessment, see Bielfeldt et al. (2008, 28–32); more comprehensively, Kaufmann (2006).

9 There is no generally agreed Lutheran doctrine of justification. This seems to have been the case from earliest times. See Hamm (2004); as an attempted correction to Hamm, see Fink (2010). Cf. Vainio (2008).

10 Härle takes as his point of departure Sanders's pointed assertions about Luther in Sanders (1991, 48–49). In a more recent interview, Sanders appears somewhat more cautious, though he only shifts the blame from Luther himself to post-Reformation Lutheranism. See Norton (2005).

11 The seminal study is Mannermaa (2005; German original 1989). Further to divinization, see Peura (1994). A précis is offered in Braaten and Jensen (1998, 42–95).

12 George is referring, of course, to Stendahl (1963).

13 I allude here to Oberman's typically provocative essay "The Nationalist Conscription of Martin Luther" (Oberman 1994, 69–78).

14 James D. G. Dunn mentions the importance for his understanding of Luther of both Bainton (1950) and the influential Luther reader edited by John Dillenberger (1961), which includes selections from Luther's 1531 commentary on Galatians (see Dunn 2008, 18–19). Bainton's admiring biography remains an insightful and eminently readable work, but it suggests insufficiently Luther's apocalypticism. Oberman (1989) corrects this, and offers a more sophisticated reading of Luther's theological development. A more representative reader is Lull and Russell (2005).

15 For a determinedly non-triumphalistic appropriation of Luther as a theological conversation partner, see Hinlicky (2010).

16 For Luther's familiarity with the Bible generally, see Mattox (2003, 9–18). For an introduction to Luther's exegesis, see Thompson (2009); cf. Mattox (2006). For the Reformation period generally, see Pelikan (1996).

17 In his "Open Letter on Translating," Luther remarks: "Here, in Romans 3[:28], I knew very well that the word *solum* is not in the Greek or Latin text … But it is the nature of our German language that in speaking of two things, one of which is affirmed and the other denied, we use the word *solum* (*allein*) along with the word *nicht* [not] or *kein* [no]. For example, we say, 'The farmer brings *allein* grain and *kein* money'; 'No, really I have now *nicht* money, but *allein* grain'; 'I have *allein* eaten and *nicht* yet drunk'; 'Did you *allein* write it, and *nicht* read it over?' There are innumerable cases of this kind in daily use … We do not have to inquire of the literal Latin, how we are to speak German, as these asses do. Rather we must inquire about this of the mother in the home, the children on the street, the common man in the marketplace. We must be guided by their language, the way they speak, and do our translating accordingly. That way they will understand it and recognize that we are speaking German to them" (LW 35.188–189). Further to this issue, see Bluhm (1965, 125–137).

18 David Daniell notes, however, that Tyndale based his work on Erasmus's Greek New Testament (1519, 1522), and that Tyndale "was a better Greek scholar than Luther" (Daniell 1989, xvii). Concerning the Romans prologue, however, Daniell observes: "This for the most part translates Luther's prologue" (1989, 207 n. 1). Bluhm explores Luther's influence on English Bibles (Bluhm 1965, 169–232).

19 See WADB 5. The Romans preface is found at WADB 5.619–632; cf. LW 35.365–380. Romans 3:28 is translated with "*Arbitramur enim iustificari hominem per fidem sine operibus legis*" (WADB 5.636.18).

20 For a convenient sampling of Luther's sermons on Pauline texts, see vols. 6, 7, and 8 in Luther (1988).

21 For a caution against the assumption that these can be considered commentaries in the modern sense, see Hagen (1990).

22 For further detail, see Mattox (2009).

23 See Denifle (1906–1909). The story of the rediscovery of the lectures on Romans is told with verve by Wilhelm Pauck in Luther (1956, xvii–xxiv).

24 WA 56. English translation by Wilhelm Pauck in Luther (1956). Pauck's translation includes Luther's *scholia* on the text, together with some of the *glossae*. LW 25 offers a complete translation.

25 For an eye-opening study of German Luther scholarship, see Stayer (2000).

26 This is not to say that Luther sees no subjective agency in the act of faith. But, as he later said, the believer's agency in matters pertaining to salvation consists solely in the ability to "suffer" his or her justification before God. From the side of the human subject of justification, this reception requires only a "passive capacity" (*aptitudo passiva*). See LW 33.67. To this, Lohse (1999, 256–257).

27 On Luther's relationship to late medieval Augustinianism, see Saak (2002, Appendix A).

28 Luther is discussing here the healing of the sinner by Christ, "our [good] Samaritan" (LW 25.260).

29 I follow here the analysis in Schäfer (1997, here 94–101).

30 Bielfeldt et al. (2008, 16–22).

31 Mattox (2009). On the motif of the divided self in Reformation era exegesis, see Steinmetz (1995, 110–121).

32 On this issue, see Saarinen (2006, 82): "The sin of the Apostle consists of the inner aversion."
33 On "heroic virtue" in Luther, see Mattox (2003).

References

Bainton, Roland H. 1950. *Here I Stand: A Life of Martin Luther*. New York: New American Library.
Bielfeldt, Dennis, Mickey L. Mattox, and Paul R. Hinlicky. 2008. *The Substance of the Faith: Luther's Doctrinal Theology for Today*. Minneapolis: Fortress.
Bluhm, Heinz. 1965. *Martin Luther: Creative Translator*. St. Louis: Concordia.
Bornkamm, Heinrich. 1969. *Luther and the Old Testament*. Philadelphia: Fortress.
Braaten, Carl E., and Robert W. Jensen, editors. 1998. *Union with Christ: The New Finnish Interpretation of Luther*. Grand Rapids: Eerdmans.
Brecht, Martin. 1985–1993. *Martin Luther*. 3 volumes. Philadelphia/Minneapolis: Fortress.
Daniell, David. 1989. *Tyndale's New Testament*. New Haven: Yale University Press.
Denifle, Heinrich. 1906–1909. *Luther und Luthertum in der ersten Entwickelung: Quellenmässig dargesellt*. Second edition. 2 volumes. Mainz: Kirchheim.
Dillenberger, John, editor. 1961. *Martin Luther: Selections from his Writings*. New York: Anchor.
Dunn, James D. G. 2008. *The New Perspective on Paul*. Revised edition. Grand Rapids: Eerdmans.
Fink, David C. 2010. Was There a "Reformation Doctrine of Justification"? *Harvard Theological Review* 103: 205–235.
George, Timothy. 2004. Modernizing Luther, Domesticating Paul: Another Perspective. Pages 437–463 in *Justification and Variegated Nomism*. Volume 2: *The Paradoxes of Paul*. Edited by D. A. Carson, Peter T. O'Brien, and Mark A. Seifrid. Tübingen: Mohr Siebeck.
Hagen, Kenneth. 1990. What Did the Term *Commentarius* Mean to Sixteenth-century Theologians? Pages 13–38 in *Théorie et pratique de l'exégèse biblique: Actes du troisième colloque international sur l'histoire de l'exégèse biblique au XVIe siècle (Genève, 31 août – 2 septembre 1988)*. Edited by Irena Backus and Francis Higman. Geneva: Librairie Droz.
Hamm, Berndt. 2004. What Was the Reformation Doctrine of Justification? Pages 179–216 in Berndt Hamm, *The Reformation of Faith in the Context of Late Medieval Theology and Piety: Essays by Berndt Hamm*. Leiden: Brill.
Härle, Wilfried. 2006. Rethinking Paul and Luther. *Lutheran Quarterly* 20: 303–317.
Hendrix, Scott H. 1974. *Ecclesia in Via: Ecclesiological Developments in the Medieval Psalms Exegesis and the Dictata Super Psalterium (1513–1515) of Martin Luther*. Leiden: Brill.
Hinlicky, Paul R. 2010. *Luther and the Beloved Community: A Path for Christian Theology after Christendom*. Grand Rapids: Eerdmans.
Hütter, Reinhard. 2004. *Bound to Be Free: Evangelical Catholic Engagements in Ecclesiology, Ethics, and Ecumenism*. Grand Rapids: Eerdmans.
Kaufmann, Thomas. 2006. Luther and the Jews. Pages 69–104 in *Jews, Judaism, and the Reformation in Sixteenth-century Germany*. Edited by Dean Phillip Bell and Stephen G. Burnett. Leiden: Brill.
Lohrmann, Martin. 2008. A Newly Discovered Report of Luther's Reformation Breakthrough from Johannes Bugenhagen's 1550 Jonah Commentary. *Lutheran Quarterly* n.s. 22: 324–330.
Lohse, Bernhard. 1999. *Martin Luther's Theology: Its Historical and Systematic Development*. Minneapolis: Fortress.

Lull, Timothy F., and William R. Russell, editors. 2005. *Martin Luther's Basic Theological Writings.* Second edition. Minneapolis: Fortress.

Luther, Martin. 1883– . (=WA) *D. Martin Luthers Werke: Kritische Gesamtausgabe.* Weimar: Böhlau.

Luther, Martin. 1906–1961. (=WADB) *D. Martin Luthers Werke: Kritische Gesamtausgabe, Deutsche Bibel.* 12 volumes. Weimar: Böhlau.

Luther, Martin. 1955–1986. (=LW) *Luther's Works: American Edition.* 55 volumes. Edited by Jaroslav Pelikan and Helmut Lehmann. Philadelphia: Fortress; St. Louis: Concordia.

Luther, Martin. 1956. *Lectures on Romans.* Edited and translated by Wilhelm Pauck. Philadelphia: Westminster.

Luther, Martin. 1988. *Sermons of Martin Luther.* 8 volumes. Edited by John Nicholas Lenker. Grand Rapids: Baker.

Mannermaa, Tuomo. [1989]2005. *Christ Present in Faith: Luther's View of Justification.* Minneapolis: Fortress.

Mattox, Mickey Leland. 2003. *"Defender of the Most Holy Matriarchs": Martin Luther's Interpretation of the Women of Genesis in the Enarrationes in Genesin, 1535–45.* Leiden: Brill.

Mattox, Mickey Leland. 2006. Martin Luther. Pages 94–113 in *Christian Theologies of Scripture: A Comparative Introduction.* Edited by Justin S. Holcomb. New York: New York University Press.

Mattox, Mickey Leland. 2009. Martin Luther's Reception of Paul. Pages 93–128 in *A Companion to Paul in the Reformation.* Edited by R. Ward Holder. Leiden: Brill.

Norton, Michael Barnes. 2005. An Interview with E. P. Sanders: "Paul, Context and Interpretation." *Journal of Philosophy and Scripture* 2: 37–42.

Oberman, Heiko A. 1989. *Luther: Man between God and the Devil.* New Haven: Yale University Press.

Oberman, Heiko A. 1994. *The Impact of the Reformation.* Grand Rapids: Eerdmans.

Pelikan, Jaroslav. 1996. *The Reformation of the Bible: The Bible of the Reformation.* New Haven: Yale University Press.

Peura, Simo. 1994. *Mehr als ein Mensch? Die Vergöttlichung als Thema der Theologie Martin Luthers von 1513 bis 1519.* Mainz: Philipp von Zabern.

Preus, James Samuel. 1969. *From Shadow to Promise: Old Testament Interpretation from Augustine to the Young Luther.* Cambridge, Mass.: Harvard University Press.

Saak, Erik L. 2002. *High Way to Heaven: The Augustinian Platform between Reform and Reformation, 1292–1524.* Leiden: Brill.

Saarinen, Risto. 1989. *Gottes Wirken auf uns: Die transzendentale Deutung des Gegenwart-Christi-Motiv in der Lutherforschung.* Stuttgart: Franz Steiner.

Saarinen, Risto. 2006. The Pauline Luther and the Law: Lutheran Theology Re-engages the Study of Paul. *Pro Ecclesia* 15: 64–86

Saarinen, Risto. 2007. How Luther Got Paul Right. *Dialog: A Journal of Theology* 46: 170–173.

Sanders, E. P. 1991. *Paul.* New York: Oxford University Press.

Schäfer, Rolf. 1997. Melanchthon's Interpretation of Romans 5.15: His Departure from the Augustinian Concept of Grace Compared to Luther's. Pages 79–104 in *Philip Melanchthon (1497–1560) and the Commentary.* Edited by Timothy J. Wengert and M. Patrick Graham. Sheffield: Sheffield Academic.

Stayer, James M. 2000. *Martin Luther, German Saviour: German Evangelical Theological Factions and the Interpretation of Luther, 1917–1933.* Montreal: McGill-Queen's University Press.

Steinmetz, David C. 1980. *Luther and Staupitz: An Essay in the Intellectual Origins of the Protestant Reformation.* Durham, NC: Duke University Press.

Steinmetz, David C. 1995. *Calvin in Context.* Oxford: Oxford University Press.

Stendahl, Krister. 1963. The Apostle Paul and the Introspective Conscience of the West. *Harvard Theological Review* 56: 199–215.

Thompson, Mark D. 2009. Biblical Interpretation in the Works of Martin Luther. Pages 299–318 in *A History of Biblical Interpretation*. Volume 2: *The Medieval through the Reformation Periods*. Edited by Alan J. Hauser and Duane F. Watson. Grand Rapids: Eerdmans.

Vainio, Olli-Pekka. 2008. *Justification and Participation in Christ: The Development of the Lutheran Doctrine of Justification from Luther to the Formula of Concord (1580)*. Leiden: Brill.

Wesley, John. 1988. *Journals and Diaries I (1735–38)*. Edited by W. Reginald Ward and Richard P. Heitzenrater. Nashville: Abingdon.

CHAPTER 25
Calvin

Anthony N. S. Lane

Calvin holds a unique place in the history of Christian thought. He is, in my view at least, the only figure who without question belongs both in the first rank of theologians and in the first rank of exegetes. If asked to list the ten most important theologians in the history of the church, different people would come up with different lists, but Calvin would appear in most of them. Again, if people were asked to list the ten most important exegetes in the history of the church, Calvin would most likely appear in this list as well. People still read the commentaries of other leading theologians, such as Origen, Augustine, Thomas Aquinas, and Luther, but usually in order to understand better the thought of Origen, and so on, not primarily in order to understand Paul. Not all may agree with this assessment of Calvin, but I have found that it is shared by colleagues working in the area of biblical studies.

Why should this be so? There are two factors that give Calvin's exegesis value for today. The first concerns his method, his understanding of the task of the exegete, to which we will turn shortly. The second is the sheer scope of his exegetical work. His commentaries and lectures cover almost all of the New Testament and some 60 percent of the Old Testament. If his sermons are included, then roughly three-quarters of the Old Testament is covered.

In considering Calvin as a reader of Paul we will, naturally, focus especially on his commentaries,[1] but his reception of the apostle extends also to his sermons, his treatises, and the *Institutes*.

The Blackwell Companion to Paul, First Edition. Edited by Stephen Westerholm.
© 2011 Blackwell Publishing Ltd. Published 2011 by Blackwell Publishing Ltd.

Calvin's Pauline Commentaries

Calvin chose to begin his biblical exegetical work with the apostle Paul. During his first brief stay at Geneva (1536–1538) he lectured on Paul, but we have no further information about this. Since his first commentary was on Romans, it is not unlikely that his lectures also began with Romans, especially given his view of the importance of that letter. This supposition is reinforced by the fact that in Strasbourg (1538–1541) he lectured on the Corinthian letters (Parker 1993, 15), a natural progression if he had already covered Romans.

Calvin's published commentaries also begin with Paul, and with Romans in particular. His Romans commentary was first published in 1540, not long after his return to Geneva from three years of exile. It took another six years for the next to appear, on 1 Corinthians. This was followed by 2 Corinthians, but not without a major hiccup (Parker 1993, 19–22). Calvin dispatched his only copy to the publisher Rihel in Strasbourg in July 1546, only to hear that it had failed to arrive. It was not until mid-September that he heard of its safe arrival. In the meantime, he was so discouraged as to be tempted to abandon the commentary project altogether. There is also an element of mystery in that this commentary was, unusually, published first in French, in 1547, but not until the next year in Latin. Also, despite the fact that the only copy had gone to Strasbourg, both editions were published by Gerard in Geneva. Perhaps Calvin had the manuscript translated into French before it was sent to Rihel. Thereafter, Calvin restricted himself to Genevan printers for his commentaries.

After 2 Corinthians, the Pauline commentaries came thick and fast, the entire corpus (including Hebrews) being published by 1551. This is almost, but not quite, before any of Calvin's other commentaries. His commentary on James appeared in French in 1550, and in 1551 he published commentaries on the Catholic epistles – but for some reason omitting 2 and 3 John. In 1551, he also published his first Old Testament commentary, on Isaiah. It took him until 1555 to complete his New Testament commentaries (without 2 and 3 John or Revelation), and by the time of his death in 1564 he had covered a considerable proportion of the Old Testament: the Pentateuch, Joshua, Psalms, and all of the prophets except the second half of Ezekiel. While his exposition of the New Testament took the form of commentaries, for the Old Testament prophets, apart from Isaiah, what we have are transcripts of his lectures.

So Calvin's exegetical labors until 1551 were almost entirely devoted to Paul. But it should not be imagined that he forgot Paul as he turned his attention to the other parts of Scripture. In 1551, he published a volume with all of the Pauline commentaries, together with Hebrews, in which some of the earlier commentaries are substantially revised. In 1556, he again published the set with further revisions, this time together with the Catholic epistles (on these two revisions, see Parker 1993, 36–59). These were not minor corrections, and the Romans commentary, in particular, grew considerably, though the changes mostly represent expansion rather than change of mind (Holder 2006b, 231–232). Perusal of the critical editions of the other commentaries indicates that these underwent far less revision. Clearly, Calvin continued to wrestle with Paul even while he was busy writing commentaries on the rest of the New Testament and much of the Old Testament.

With Paul, Calvin's commentaries predate his sermons, so far as we know. (Until 1549 we are dependent upon scraps of information; after that date we know exactly what he preached on.) Having completed the commentaries, he went on to preach on 1 and 2 Thessalonians (1554), the Pastoral epistles (1554–1555), 1 and 2 Corinthians (1555–1557), Galatians and Ephesians (1557–1558; Parker 1992, 150–152).

Calvin started with Paul and with Romans in particular. He explains why this should be so in the *Argumentum* that precedes the commentary: "Among many other notable virtues the Epistle has one in particular which is never sufficiently appreciated. It is this – if we have gained a true understanding of this Epistle, we have an open door to all the most profound treasures of Scripture." He then argues that "the main subject of the whole Epistle ... is that we are justified by faith" (*Comm. Rom.* 5). Clearly, for Calvin, Romans is pivotal for the understanding of Scripture as a whole, and justification by faith is a key doctrine. In the *Institutes*, he maintained that justification by faith was "the main hinge on which religion turns" on the grounds that "unless you first of all grasp what your relationship to God is, and the nature of his judgment concerning you, you have neither a foundation on which to establish your salvation nor one on which to build piety toward God" (3:11:1).[2] But while he clearly regarded it as an important doctrine, the place that it occupies in the structure of the *Institutes* is not especially privileged. Various doctrines have (mistakenly) been proposed as central, controlling themes for Calvin's theology. Significantly, justification by faith has not been proposed for this role. The role that Romans plays for Calvin must not be mistaken for the Lutheran idea of a "canon within the canon," and the importance of justification must not be confused with the idea of a controlling principle or a criterion by which all other doctrines are to be tested.

Calvin commented upon Hebrews as part of the Pauline corpus, and included it when he published the collected set of Pauline commentaries, though making it clear from the title page (in which he distinguished between "all the epistles of Paul" and the Epistle to the Hebrews) that Hebrews was not by Paul. In the *Argumentum*, he discusses authorship, noting that a variety of authors have been proposed, including Paul. As far as Calvin is concerned, "we need not be greatly worried" about who wrote it. He argues that it is not in fact by Paul. "The manner of teaching and the style sufficiently show that Paul was not the author, and the writer himself confesses in the second chapter that he was one of the disciples of the apostles, which is wholly different from the way in which Paul spoke of himself" (*Comm. Heb.* 1). Calvin then proceeds to refute the theory that Paul wrote it in Hebrew and someone else translated it into Greek, pointing out that the discussion of the word testament (*diathēkē*) in chapter 9 would make no sense if written in Hebrew. But although Hebrews was not Pauline, Calvin had no doubts about its canonicity, referring to its teaching, and considered that it was only "through the craft of Satan" that this had been called into question (*Comm. Heb.* 1–2). His glowing commendation of the letter is in stark contrast with Luther's demotion of it to the end of the New Testament. Having accepted it as canonical, Calvin expounded it together with Paul, in line with its traditional place in the canon alongside the Pauline letters (Holder 2006b, 230–231).

Calvin expounded the Greek text, giving his own Latin translation. He made use of existing translations, especially the Vulgate and Erasmus, but was not bound to either

(Parker 1993, 39, 123–191). His Pauline (and other) commentaries were all translated into French by Calvin himself, with the intention of making them available to a lay audience. That Calvin took time to do this, on top of all his other commitments, shows how important he considered this task to be.

Calvin's Method

Calvin obligingly explains to us, in some key documents, what his strategy was for his biblical commentaries. In his "Letter to the Reader" at the beginning of the 1539 edition, he explains how the *Institutes* should be used. It is intended as an introduction and guide to the study of Scripture and to complement his commentaries. Because of the *Institutes*, Calvin need not digress at length on doctrinal matters in his commentaries (McNeill 1960, 4–5). This warns us against falling into the error of viewing Calvin as "a man of one book" – the *Institutes* (cf. Parker 1993, 6–7). The *Institutes* and the commentaries are designed to be used together: the *Institutes* to provide a theological undergirding for the commentaries; the latter to provide a more solid exegesis of the passages cited in the former. Thus, when he gives a biblical reference in the *Institutes*, Calvin may be pointing not just to the biblical text itself, but also to his commentary on that passage.

Calvin dedicated his first biblical commentary, on Romans, to the humanist scholar Simon Grynaeus, referring to a discussion that they had had in Basel before Calvin began his ministry in Geneva. They had agreed that lucid brevity (*perspicua brevitas*) was the goal of an exegete – to explain the text clearly yet briefly. This Calvin set out to do, and with considerable success. His Romans commentary, though of modest length, nonetheless manages to contribute to the understanding of the text in a way that still interests New Testament scholars today. This brevity is, of course, achieved in part because of the policy of relegating substantial doctrinal discussions to the *Institutes*.

Calvin goes on to state, famously, of the exegete that "it is almost his only task to unfold the mind of the writer whom he has undertaken to expound" (*Comm. Rom.* 1). It is this commitment to determine the original author's meaning that explains the abiding value of his commentaries. Those who know Calvin primarily for his theology would expect him to read the Bible in the light of his theology, or, to be more blunt, to read his theology into the Bible. Of course, he was not faultless in this respect, but it is surprising how often he rejects interpretations that are (from his perspective) doctrinally correct on the grounds that they are not what the passage is actually teaching. The other side of the quotation is that it is *almost* the only task of the exegete to unfold the mind of the author. Calvin was concerned to understand the meaning of the text not only in its original context, but also for his own time.

Calvin emphasizes the care that is required of the exegete, a care he finds lacking in many other commentators.

> If it be considered a sin to corrupt what has been dedicated to God, we assuredly cannot tolerate anyone who handles that most sacred of all things on earth with unclean or even ill-prepared hands. It is, therefore, presumptuous and almost blasphemous to turn the

meaning of Scripture around without due care, as though it were some game that we were playing. (*Comm. Rom.* 3–4)

In this dedication he names three contemporary commentators – Melanchthon, Bullinger, and Bucer – praising them all. He goes on to criticize Melanchthon for being too concise and Bucer for being too verbose, but makes no further reference to Bullinger. Does that mean that Bullinger was Calvin's model for exegesis? This has been argued by Fritz Büsser (1987). Büsser's claim is assessed by Joel Kok, whose conclusion is that he has claimed too much. "It is more accurate to see Bullinger and Calvin as sharing important exegetical standards and theological positions, with Calvin seeking to improve on the effort of his evangelical ally by offering a more doctrinally precise commentary" (Kok 1996, 254).

Hermeneutical Principles and Exegetical Practices

In an important study of Calvin's Pauline commentaries, Ward Holder distinguishes between Calvin's hermeneutical principles and his exegetical practices. Hermeneutical principles are "core conceptions which the interpreter brings to the task of interpretation, basic presuppositions which the encounter with the text is rather unlikely to change." "Exegetical practices have to do with the method of extricating meaning from a text" and take the form of tools (Holder 2006a, 14–15). The distinction is helpful and we shall review a number of Calvin's hermeneutical principles, showing how these are reflected in his exegesis of Paul in particular.[3]

(1) Foundational for Calvin is the authority of Scripture as the Word of God.

No other word is to be held as the Word of God, and given place as such in the church, than what is contained first in the Law and Prophets, then in the writings of the apostles; and the only authorized way of teaching in the church is by the prescription and standard of his Word. (*Inst.* 4:8:8)

The Scriptures' authority is properly acknowledged only when we "regard them as having sprung from heaven, as if there the living words of God were heard" (*Inst.* 1:7:1).

Because Scripture is the Word of God, it is necessary to interpret Scripture by Scripture, to expound one part in the light of the rest. So, for example, in expounding the mystery mentioned in Colossians 1:26, Calvin states that this is the gospel, as is "evident from Rom. 16.25, Eph. 3.9, and similar passages" (*Comm. Col.* 1:26). For many exegetes, this method could have the effect of flattening out the difference between different authors, of reading John into Paul, and vice versa. This is not the effect for Calvin, who is not only sensitive to peculiarities of each author, but also concerned to let each passage speak for itself. So, for example, in his commentary on Romans 7:22, he notes that "the inward man" means something different here from 2 Corinthians 4:16. Calvin views Scripture as a choir singing not in unison, each producing the same note, but in harmony, where different notes are sung but the result is a harmonious whole.

(2) At the same time, Calvin takes extremely seriously the human authorship of Scripture. While he repeatedly speaks of Scripture being "dictated" by the Holy Spirit, the purpose of that metaphor was not to reduce the human authors to mere scribes. So, for example, a major argument against the Pauline authorship of Hebrews is its style. Because Calvin takes seriously the human authorship of Scripture, he pays careful attention to the historical context of each writing, the context of specific passages, and the genre in which they are written. As we have seen, the prime task of the exegete is "to unfold the mind of the writer whom he has undertaken to expound." It is here especially that we see Calvin employing humanist ideals.

(3) Calvin made rich use of the concept of accommodation, a topic that has received considerable attention in recent years. God, in communicating his word, does so in a manner that is suited to its audience – their humanity, their sinfulness, and their position in the historical process of revelation. "God accommodates to our limited capacity every declaration which he makes of Himself" (*Comm. Rom.* 1:19).

Accommodation can be seen as a hermeneutical principle for Calvin, but it can also be seen as an exegetical practice in that it leads to a particular way of handling particular types of passage. The idea of accommodation plays less of a role in the Pauline letters than in the Old Testament because they are part of the fuller revelation that comes with the person of Christ. But since Christians remain finite and sinful human beings, accommodation still plays a significant role. So, for example, it teaches us that "only fools ... seek to know the essence of God" (*Comm. Rom.* 1:19).

(4) For Calvin, the interplay between doctrine and exegesis forms what would today be described as a hermeneutical circle or a hermeneutical spiral. The exegete comes to Scripture with a body of doctrine (as set out in the *Institutes*), and this helps him to understand the text. At the same time, it is what the theologian finds in Scripture that molds his doctrine. In his commentary on Romans 12:6, and elsewhere, Calvin refers to the "analogy of faith." Those who interpret and expound Scripture (this is what Calvin takes to be the meaning of prophecy for his time) should conform to "the first principles of religion," and "any doctrine that has been found not to correspond with these is condemned as false" (*Comm. Rom.* 12:6). So, for example, he applies this principle to argue that Lutheran teaching on the real presence of Christ conflicts with his real humanity (*Inst.* 4:17:32). Later, he interprets it to mean that all is to be tested by the Word and Spirit of God (*Comm. 1 Cor.* 14:32).[4]

The principle of the hermeneutical spiral affects Calvin's exegetical practice. It could have led him to read his doctrines into unlikely places, but generally does not. Calvin is repeatedly critical of those who seek to argue correct doctrine from passages that do not in fact teach it. But this does not mean that his exegesis is totally innocent of theological bias. While his theology may not dictate how Calvin interprets a particular passage, it can serve to *exclude* certain interpretations. So, for example, in his exegesis of 1 Corinthians 10:12, Philippians 3:11, and Colossians 1:23, he rejects the idea that Paul was teaching that true believers can lose their salvation.

(5) Scripture may be the only word of God, but this did not prevent Calvin from having a deep respect for tradition. He did not lightly depart from established interpretations:

> When, therefore, we depart from the views of our predecessors, we are not to be stimulated by any passion for innovation, impelled by any desire to slander others, aroused by any

hatred, or prompted by any ambition. Necessity alone is to compel us, and we are to have no other object than that of doing good. (*Comm. Rom.* 4)

In his exposition of Paul, Calvin paid heed to the work of his predecessors, including some 245 patristic citations in his commentaries.[5] Chrysostom (with ninety-five citations) is clearly Calvin's favorite patristic exegete. Augustine (with fifty-eight) also receives considerable attention, on dogmatic as well as exegetical issues. Jerome (with twenty-three) and Ambrose (=Ambrosiaster most or all of the time, with twenty) are also taken seriously as exegetes. That Origen receives thirteen citations is perhaps more surprising. The remaining thirty-six citations are distributed among a number of figures, with none receiving more than four.

In his dogmatic works, whether the *Institutes* or one of his treatises, Calvin's use of the church fathers is primarily the apologetic citation of authorities as witnesses to the defense of his doctrine. In his commentaries, by contrast, he is less interested in citing authorities and more interested in dialogue partners. For this reason, whereas the fathers are mostly cited with approval in the *Institutes* and the treatises, on exegetical matters they are more often cited disapprovingly (Lane 1999, 3–4). Steinmetz notes how, on Romans 8:1–11, Calvin cites thirteen exegetical opinions only to reject twelve of them (Steinmetz 1990, 111–112, 117–118). This and similar evidence should not be taken to indicate that Calvin had little respect for patristic exegesis. There was little reason to mention it when he was in agreement with it. It is when points of disagreement emerge that one engages in debate with one's dialogue partner. Holder (2006a, 219–253) shows the way in which Calvin repeatedly queried Augustine's exegetical conclusions in his Pauline commentaries.

Calvin's dependence on the fathers in his Pauline commentaries is not restricted to his citations. He limits the number of explicit references in order to keep his work uncluttered and maintain his goal of lucid brevity. Moreover, he only achieved his prodigious output by working under pressure. This means that he often cited the fathers from memory, with the inevitable consequence of inaccuracy on occasions. Many of the references to Chrysostom in the commentary on 1 Corinthians are taken from memory and are inexact (Steinmetz 1990, 113–114, 116–118).

(6) Calvin believed firmly in the unity of the two Testaments. Like all Christian theologians, he recognized both continuity and discontinuity between the Testaments. Where theologians differ is in the relative weight given to the two sides of this tension. With Calvin, the emphasis clearly lies on the continuity, as can be seen from *Institutes* 2:9–11 (cf. *Comm. 1 Cor.* 10:1–4; *Comm. 2 Cor.* 3:6–11).

(7) A point upon which Calvin repeatedly insists is that one should not speculate beyond what is revealed. Here Calvin stands clearly opposed to Augustine. What was God doing before the creation of the world? Calvin cites with approval the quip that God was preparing hell for the curious (*Inst.* 1:14:1). Augustine, by contrast, responded by developing a theory of the relation between time and eternity (Meijering 1980).

(8) Closely related to the previous point but not identical to it, Calvin held strongly to the need for all theology to be useful. In his commentary on 2 Timothy 3:16, Calvin builds upon the statement that all Scripture is "profitable": "Scripture is corrupted by sinful abuse when this profitable purpose is not sought in it ... The right use of Scripture must always lead to what is profitable."

The above should not be mistaken for an exhaustive list of Calvin's hermeneutical principles. One further example can be given to make the point. In arguing for the worthlessness of human works, even when God deigns to reward them, Calvin states that the "whole end [of Scripture] is to restrain our pride, to humble us, cast us down, and utterly crush us" (*Inst.* 3:18:4). This is not simply an occasional comment but a principle that he brings to all of his exegesis, as can be seen especially in his doctrine of justification by faith.

Pauline Themes in Calvin

As has been seen from his comments on Romans, Calvin clearly regarded the Pauline corpus as of crucial importance. This is why he chose to begin his exegetical work with Paul. The influence of the apostle is particularly marked where certain doctrines are concerned. Two examples will be examined here: his teaching on humanity's natural awareness of God and on justification by faith.

Natural awareness of God

Calvin begins his *Institutes* with a discussion of the knowledge of God and, in particular, the extent to which all people have some awareness of God. Most of this material originated with the 1539 edition, at a time when he was also working toward his Romans commentary. Parallels have been noted between the argument of this section of the *Institutes*, Romans 1:19–32, and Calvin's commentary on the latter passage. The knowledge of God is inextricably linked with that of ourselves (*Inst.* 1:1:1–2), in part because "the knowledge of God ... is that by which we not only conceive that there is a God but also grasp what befits us and is proper to his glory" (*Inst.* 1:2:1). When believers came face to face with God in Scripture, they were stricken and overcome. This is because "man is never sufficiently touched and affected by the awareness of his lowly state until he has compared himself with God's majesty" (*Inst.* 1:3:3) – a further application of the final hermeneutical principle noted above.

So what knowledge of God (if any) is found in those untouched by Judeo-Christian revelation? In answering this question, Calvin looks not to the world around him, which in Christian Europe had almost nothing to teach him on that question, but to classical antiquity and to the assessment of the pagan world found in the New Testament. He regards it as incontrovertible that "there is within the human mind, and indeed by natural instinct, an awareness of divinity," implanted by God. His judgment is that all people perceive that there is a creator God, but are condemned by their failure to honor him (*Inst.* 1:3:1). "God has put into the minds of all men the knowledge of Himself." But while his eternity, wisdom, goodness, justice, and mercy are evident, people have substituted a debased picture of God, especially through idolatry (*Comm. Rom.* 1:21–23). Religion is not a human invention but is innate to humanity (*Inst.* 1:3:2). Calvin was, of course, aware that some professed atheism, but maintained that behind this mask there lay an uneasy conscience (*Inst.* 1:3:3). While some have seen this universal awareness of God as a basis of hope for salvation, Calvin follows the argument of Romans 1 in seeing it as removing all excuse from the ungodly (*Comm. Rom.* 1:20, 24, 27–28). The innate awareness of God on its own leads not to true piety but to idolatry. "A sense of divinity is by nature engraven on human hearts," "but this seed is so corrupted that by itself it produces only the worst fruits" (*Inst.* 1:4:4).

As there is a natural awareness of God, so also God is so clearly manifest in his creation that "even unlettered and stupid folk cannot plead the excuse of ignorance." "Wherever you cast your eyes, there is no spot in the universe wherein you cannot discern at least some sparks of [God's] glory." There is no need for an education to observe this; all that is needed is eyes to see (*Inst.* 1:5:1–2). God's manifestation in creation is clear enough in itself; it is only inadequate because of human blindness (*Comm. Rom.* 1:20). Likewise, evidence for God is to be found by looking within, humans being a "micro-cosmos" (*Inst.* 1:5:3). But far from worshiping God, humanity suppresses and distorts this evidence for God, and this is true of the Greek philosophers as well as the common herd (*Inst.* 1:5:4–6). "Although the structure of the world and the most splendid ordering of the elements ought to have induced man to glorify God, yet there are none who discharge their duty. This is proof that all men are guilty of sacrilege, and of base and iniquitous ingratitude" (*Comm. Rom.* 1:18).

Calvin also sees clear evidence for God in his providence, his blessing of the godly and judging the ungodly (*Inst.* 1:5:7–10; *Comm. Rom.* 1:21). Calvin could be accused (unfairly) of teaching a form of prosperity doctrine at this point, though he does qualify such claims, especially in a quotation from Augustine: "If now every sin were to suffer open punishment, it would seem that nothing is reserved for the final judgment. Again, if God were now to punish no sin openly, one would believe that there is no providence" (*Inst.* 1:5:10).

Despite all this evidence, humanity turns away from God. We each do so in different ways, but we all "forsake the one true God for prodigious trifles," and there is scarcely a single person who does not "fashion for himself an idol or specter in place of God" (*Inst.* 1:5:11–12; cf. *Comm. Rom.* 1:21–23). Since this blindness is not for want of evidence, human ignorance is without excuse (*Inst.* 1:5:13–15).

Justification by faith

Calvin's doctrine of justification is thoroughly Pauline, and in expounding it he refers to Paul most often, but by no means exclusively. Romans is especially popular, and chapters 3 and 4 are cited almost as frequently as the other chapters of the letter combined. Much of the material on justification in the *Institutes* was introduced in the 1539 edition, at the time when Calvin was working on his Romans commentary.

Calvin understood "justification" in forensic terms: to be justified is to be accepted by God as righteous, to be declared righteous, to be acquitted. Justification is a "not guilty" verdict in a court of law. Calvin defined it as "the acceptance with which God receives us into his favor as righteous men." It consists negatively in the forgiveness or non-imputation of sins and positively in the reckoning or imputing of Christ's righteousness (2 Cor 5:19, 21; *Inst.* 3:11:2, 11).

Related to this definition of justification is his distinction between justification and sanctification. While justification refers to a person's standing in God's sight, sanctification (or regeneration; Calvin regarded the terms as more or less synonymous) refers to the lifelong process by which the believer is transformed into the likeness of Christ. Justification and sanctification must be distinguished, but cannot be separated. "We cannot be justified freely by faith alone, if we do not at the same time live in holiness. For those gifts of grace go together as if tied by an inseparable bond, so that if anyone tries to separate them, he is, in a sense, tearing Christ to pieces" (*Comm. 1 Cor. 1:30*). They are like the two legs of a pair of trousers, not like a pair of socks that may well (and, in my experience, too often do) become separated.

Central to Calvin's doctrine of salvation is the concept of union with Christ. This is seen most clearly from the structure of his *Institutes*. Having in Book Two expounded his doctrine of the person of Christ and all that he has achieved for humanity, he turns in Book Three to "The Way in which We Receive the Grace of Christ" (*Inst. 3:title*). There he starts by affirming that "as long as Christ remains outside of us, and we are separated from him, all that he has suffered and done for the salvation of the human race remains useless and of no value for us" (*Inst. 3:1:1*). Until someone is united with Christ, what Christ has achieved helps them no more than an electricity mains supply that passes their house but is not connected to it. It is the Holy Spirit that unites people with Christ, by faith, a union that brings two major benefits – justification and sanctification (*Inst. 3:3:1*). These are the themes of most of the remainder of Book Three.

In order to make it clear that forgiveness of sins cannot be separated from holiness of life (*Inst. 3:3:1*), Calvin devotes eight chapters to sanctification (*Inst. 3:3–10*) before turning to justification (*Inst. 3:11–18*). Justification and sanctification are inseparable because both flow from union with Christ, a union that Calvin once (and only once) describes as "mystical" (*Inst. 3:11:10*). Justification is not a benefit Christ confers upon someone that they then possess independently of him; a person is justified only by virtue of being in Christ. But for Calvin, union with Christ leads inevitably to sanctification as well. Calvin repeatedly appeals to 1 Corinthians 1:30 to support the point: "Therefore Christ justifies no one whom he does not at the same time sanctify" (*Inst. 3:16:1*).

How are people justified? Justification is in Christ alone and by Christ alone. "Righteousness comes to us from the mercy of God alone, is offered to us in Christ and by the Gospel, and is received by faith alone, without the merit of works" (*Comm. Eph. 2:9*). Justification is by faith alone, but faith is of value not as a virtue in its own right, but as faith *in Christ*. "Faith brings us righteousness, not because it is a meritorious virtue, but because it obtains for us the grace of God" (*Comm. Rom. 4:5*). Faith justifies because it lays hold of the righteousness of Christ (*Inst. 3:18:8*). Calvin compares faith to an empty vessel with which people come to receive Christ's grace. The power of justifying lies not in faith itself, but in the Christ who is received by faith (*Inst. 3:11:7*). Calvin gives the four (Aristotelian) causes of our justification: the efficient cause is God's mercy; the material cause is Christ and his atonement; the formal or instrumental[6] cause is faith conceived by the Word; and the final cause is the glory of God's justice and goodness (*Comm. Rom. 3:24*).

Why is justification by faith *alone*? Calvin stresses that faith is effective, not in itself, but because it unites people to Christ. Justification is by faith alone, not because of what faith merits or *achieves*, but because of what it *receives*. In response to those who maintain that justification is by love rather than by faith because love is more excellent, Calvin is happy to concede the latter point, but not the former (*Inst.* 3:11:17). "It is as if someone argued that a king is more capable of making a shoe than a shoemaker is because he is infinitely more eminent" (*Inst.* 3:18:8). Faith "justifies in no other way but in that it leads into fellowship with the righteousness of Christ" (*Inst.* 3:11:20).

Paul taught that justification was by faith apart from the works of the law (Rom 3:20, 28; Gal 2:15–16). But to what do these "works of the law" refer? Calvin was aware that some in his day, as well as some of the early fathers, limited them to the ceremonial aspects of the law. He opposed this, arguing that "Paul is here speaking of the whole law" (including the moral law) on the basis of the structure of argument in Romans (*Comm. Rom.* 3:20; cf. Rom 3:27–28, 4:9–10; Gal 2:15–16; Eph 2:9).

Roman Catholic theology distinguished between the initial free justification of the ungodly by faith (Rom 4:5) and subsequent justification, which also involves works. Calvin rejects this distinction, insisting that free justification by faith alone applies throughout the Christian life, not just at its beginning. Psalm 32:2 was written after David had served God for many years (*Comm. Rom.* 3:21, 4:6–10).

Justification is by faith alone, *sola fide*, but this faith does not stand alone, is not *nuda fides*. As Calvin put it: "It is therefore faith alone which justifies, and yet the faith which justifies is not alone: just as it is the heat alone of the sun which warms the earth, and yet in the sun it is not alone, because it is constantly conjoined with light."[7] Saving faith is not to be confused with a dead faith that does not give birth to works of love. The fact that justification is *by* faith alone does not mean that one can be justified *with* faith alone. There can be no faith without hope, nor vice versa (*Inst.* 3:2:42–43). Similarly, faith gives birth to love (*Inst.* 3:2:41) and cannot exist without it. "We confess with Paul that no other faith justifies 'but faith working through love' [Gal 5:6]" (*Inst.* 3:11:20). While works are most certainly not the ground of justification, where there is true faith, works *will* (not ought to) follow. Justification is not *by* works, but nor is it *without* works (*Inst.* 3:16:1, citing 1 Cor 1:30). In Philippians 3:8, Paul "divested himself, not of works, but of that perverted confidence in works with which he had been puffed up" (*Comm. Phil.* 3:8). It can be said that love, for example, is a *necessary* condition in that one cannot be justified without it – just as spots are a *necessary* condition of having chicken pox. This does not prejudice justification by faith alone, since love no more causes justification than having spots causes chicken pox.

The same Paul who taught justification by faith also taught judgment by works. Calvin did not have a problem with this, as should be apparent from the argument so far. Regenerate believers will not be devoid of love and good works. In his commentary on Galatians 6:8, Calvin acknowledges that eternal life is a reward but denies "that we are justified by works or that works merit salvation." Works are rewarded, but this is an undeserved reward given by grace. It is only by the grace of God, the work of the Spirit in people's lives, that they even perform any good works; such good works are themselves "the freely granted fruits of adoption." Furthermore, in themselves they are tainted and so not only unworthy of reward but worthy of condemnation. In order strictly to merit a reward, one would need to fulfill the whole law perfectly; no one manages that.

Those who are born again of the Spirit seek after holiness (*Inst.* 3:14:9–11). Conversion brings a real change and leads believers to seek from the heart to obey God. But while they aim to keep the law, they manage to do so only imperfectly (*Comm. Rom.* 3:31). Even in the best works of the godly, there remains some taint of the sinful flesh. They may indeed be motivated by love of God and neighbor, but in this life there always remain elements of sinful motivation as well. "The disciples of Christ love him with sincere and earnest affection of heart, and according to the measure of their love keep his commandments. But how small is this compared with that strict perfection in which there is no deficiency?"[8] It is not that their works are not good, but that they are less than totally good. Judged by the standard of God's holiness and purity, they fall short, they are less than perfect. "There never existed any work of a godly man which, if examined by God's stern judgment, would not deserve condemnation" (*Inst.* 3:14:11). In sum, therefore, for Calvin, "we have not a single work going forth from the saints that if it be judged in itself deserves not shame as its just reward" (*Inst.* 3:14:9).

If this were all that Calvin had to say, it would be a negatively depressing and demotivating message. What is the point of bothering to do good? Why seek to serve God if one's best works will be flung back in one's face as tainted and inadequate? Believers, however, relate to God not as a strict Judge through the law but as their gracious Father through Christ. This understanding leads to Calvin's doctrine of "double justification," as it is known.

When people approach God in faith, they are accepted as righteous – in Christ. But it is not only *they* who are accepted; God also accepts their good works in Christ, overlooking whatever defects and impurities remain in them. "When we are made partakers of Christ, we are not only ourselves righteous, but our works also are counted righteous in the sight of God, because any imperfections in them are obliterated by the blood of Christ ... God rewards our works as perfect, inasmuch as their defects are covered by free pardon" (*Comm. Rom.* 3:22). Thus, "by faith alone not only we ourselves but our works as well are justified" (*Inst.* 3:17:10).

How does this work? This is not God arbitrarily calling evil works good. These are genuinely good works in that they are done in faith from a genuine love for God and neighbor; yet (as noted above) the taint of sin remains. In Christ, then, God accepts these works by overlooking their blemishes and accepting what is genuinely good in them. "Everything imperfect in them is covered by Christ's perfection, every blemish or spot is cleansed away by his purity" (*Inst.* 3:17:8). God looks with favor both on the godly and on their good works because he embraces them "in Christ rather than in themselves" (*Inst.* 3:17:5).

This doctrine had a pastoral aim: not in vain do believers strive, imperfectly, for good works. Calvin contrasts those who approach God on the basis of law and merit, who cannot please him without perfect obedience, with those who are his adopted children in Christ, whose feeble works he approves with fatherly generosity (*Inst.* 3:19:4–5). "We ... remarkably cheer and comfort the hearts of believers by our teaching, when we tell them that they please God in their works and are without doubt acceptable to him"

(*Inst.* 3:15:7). It is worth pressing on because God is easily pleased and looks with favor even upon feeble efforts.

The doctrine also had an exegetical and apologetic aim. Calvin was forced to account for biblical passages where the writer appeals to his own righteousness or speaks of God rewarding good works. How could these be squared with other biblical teaching against human merit? Double justification was a tool to account for the whole range of biblical data, to show that "Scripture may, without quibbling, be duly brought into agreement with itself" (*Inst.* 3:17:8). Furthermore, it provided a basis for responding to Roman Catholic polemical attacks on this front. It enabled Calvin to acknowledge that believers' works do indeed have value before God, that God looks upon them with favor and rewards them – all because of his kindness to them in Christ (as in *Comm. Rom.* 4:6–8). The doctrine of double justification handles a tension found in Scripture by distinguishing between those who, advancing their merits, stand before God as a strict Judge and those who, by faith, encounter God as a loving Father.

This was not the only way in which Calvin sought to harmonize his Pauline doctrine of justification with other strands of the biblical witness, such as Acts 10:34–35 and (predictably) James 2:21, 24. He handles these two passages very differently. With the latter, he asks whether his opponents wish to "drag Paul into conflict with James." It is the same Spirit that teaches justification by faith and not works (Rom 4:3; Gal 3:6) and justification by works, not by faith alone (Jas 2:24). Since the Holy Spirit does not contradict himself, we must seek a reconciliation of these passages. This Calvin finds by arguing (as have many others, before and since) that James understands the words "faith" and "justify" differently from Paul. So, "as Paul contends that we are justified apart from the help of works, so James does not allow those who lack good works to be reckoned righteous" (*Inst.* 3:17:11–12; cf. *Comm. Rom.* 3:28).

Calvin's approach to the Acts passage is very different. Peter states, with reference to Cornelius, that anyone from any nation who fears God and does what is right is acceptable to him. Again, Calvin's concern is to "make the Scriptural passages agree," but this time he does it by referring to the "double acceptance of man before God." Initially, one is justified by faith alone, without works. Those who are justified are also born again as new creatures (2 Cor 5:17) – and Calvin regards Cornelius as already regenerate. As such, the regenerate are "approved of God also in respect of works." "For the Lord cannot fail to love and embrace the good things that he works in them through his Spirit" (*Inst.* 3:17:4–5).

So both of these passages are harmonized with Paul, but in very different ways. Why should this be so? The reason is that Calvin was a careful exegete who sought to interpret each passage in line with what it actually says.

Conclusion

Calvin's reading of the apostle Paul is manifestly that of a sixteenth-century Reformer making use of the humanist scholarly tools of his time. He was no timeless exegete, and his work at times suffers from the effects of the shortage of time at his disposal. But, despite these limitations, it has proved to have a continuing interest and value.

Notes

1 Commentaries are cited by page reference in the case of introductions, but otherwise by reference to the chapter and verse commented upon. References and quotations are taken from the translations found in Torrance and Torrance (1959–1972).
2 Passages from the *Institutes* are cited by book, chapter, and section; quotations are taken from McNeill (1960).
3 The principles and practices that I identify draw heavily on Holder's (2006a), but are not identical.
4 Ganoczy (1976, 55–58) refers to a second hermeneutical circle of Word and Spirit.
5 These figures are taken from the tables in Mooi (1965, 371, 377, 380–381), excluding references to Josephus and those found in the Hebrews commentary. They may not be exact, but give a good idea of the extent of Calvin's use of the fathers.
6 Calvin does not keep to the classical meanings and confusingly equates the formal with the instrumental cause.
7 *Acts of the Council of Trent: with the Antidote* 6th Session, can. 11 in Beveridge and Bonnet (1983, 3:152).
8 *Acts of the Council of Trent: with the Antidote* 6th Session, ch. 12 in Beveridge and Bonnet (1983, 3:132).

References

Beveridge, Henry, and Jules Bonnet, editors. 1983. *Selected Works of John Calvin*. 7 volumes. Grand Rapids: Baker.

Büsser, Fritz. 1987. Bullinger as Calvin's Model in Biblical Exposition: An Examination of Calvin's Preface to the Epistle to the Romans. Pages 64–95 in *In Honor of John Calvin, 1509–64: Papers from the 1986 International Calvin Symposium, McGill University*. Edited by E. J. Furcha. Montreal: Faculty of Religious Studies, McGill University.

Ganoczy, A. 1976. Calvin als paulinischer Theologe: Ein Forschungsansatz zur Hermeneutik Calvins. Pages 39–69 in *Calvinus Theologus*. Edited by W. H. Neuser. Neukirchen-Vluyn: Neukirchener Verlag.

Holder, R. Ward. 2006a. *John Calvin and the Grounding of Interpretation: Calvin's First Commentaries*. Leiden: Brill.

Holder, R. Ward. 2006b. Calvin as Commentator on the Pauline Epistles. Pages 224–256 in *Calvin and the Bible*. Edited by Donald K. McKim. Cambridge: Cambridge University Press.

Kok, Joel E. 1996. Heinrich Bullinger's Exegetical Method: The Model for Calvin? Pages 241–254 in *Biblical Interpretation in the Era of the Reformation: Essays Presented to David C. Steinmetz in Honor of his Sixtieth Birthday*. Edited by Richard A. Muller and John L. Thompson. Grand Rapids: Eerdmans.

Lane, Anthony N. S. 1999. *John Calvin: Student of the Church Fathers*. Edinburgh: T. & T. Clark.

McNeill, John T., editor. 1960. *Calvin: Institutes of the Christian Religion*. London: SCM.

Meijering, E. P. 1980. *Calvin wider die Neugierde: Ein Beitrag zum Vergleich zwischen reformatorischem und patristischem Denken*. Nieuwkoop: de Graaf.

Mooi, R. J. 1965. *Het Kerk – En Dogmahistorisch Element in de Werken van Johannes Calvijn*. Wageningen: Veenman.

Parker, T. H. L. 1992. *Calvin's Preaching*. Edinburgh: T. & T. Clark.

Parker, T. H. L. 1993. *Calvin's New Testament Commentaries*. Edinburgh: T. & T. Clark.

Steinmetz, David C. 1990. Calvin and the Patristic Exegesis of Paul. Pages 100–118 in *The Bible in the Sixteenth Century*. Edited by David C. Steinmetz. Durham, NC: Duke University Press.

Torrance, David W., and Thomas F. Torrance, editors. 1959–1972. *Calvin's New Testament Commentaries*. Grand Rapids: Eerdmans.

CHAPTER 26

John and Charles Wesley

John R. Tyson

John (1703–1791) and Charles (1707–1788) Wesley first encountered Pauline Scripture texts in their home, the Anglican manse of Epworth, England, where their mother, Susanna Annesley Wesley (1669–1742), operated a primary school for her growing brood of children. It was her practice to begin to teach her children to read at the age of five, and their main textbook was the Bible – in the Authorized (or King James) Version. John and Charles were so well prepared that, after winning scholarships to college preparatory schools, they were able to qualify as "King's Scholars" and gain admission to prestigious Christ Church College at Oxford University.

While the Wesley brothers were conventionally religious, at Oxford they became increasingly "serious" about religious matters as they pondered their vocational future. In an autobiographical letter, Charles recalled:

> My first year at College I lost in diversions. The next I set myself to study. Diligence led me into serious thinking. I went to the weekly sacrament, and persuaded two or three young scholars to accompany me, and to observe the method of study prescribed by the statutes of the University. This gained me the harmless nickname of Methodist. (Tyson 1989, 59)

The Oxford Methodists earned other nicknames as well, "Bible maggots" or "Bible moths," for example, which can be directly attributed to their desire to devour the New Testament and live by its precepts. But their early devotional readings, particularly those in "the mystical divines" such as William Law, sent John and Charles Wesley seeking personal holiness by imitating Christ through sheer force of their own efforts and will.

The Blackwell Companion to Paul, First Edition. Edited by Stephen Westerholm.
© 2011 Blackwell Publishing Ltd. Published 2011 by Blackwell Publishing Ltd.

The Early Sermons

John Wesley had been preparing and preaching sermons since he was ordained in 1725. One of his sermons extant from this early period was entitled – using the words of Romans 2:29[1] – "The Circumcision of the Heart." That John Wesley considered this sermon to be a quintessential exposition of holiness of heart and life (which Wesley called "Christian Perfection") is evident from the way that he consistently pointed to it as an example of his teaching (see, for example, Jackson 1872, 11:367). His exposition is a thematic one that takes into account the particular context of Romans 2:29, but then also draws upon parallel concepts, found in other biblical passages, to interpret it. After a brief discussion that describes this "circumcision" as being of the inner person (and not of the outer), and one that gains God's praise (Rom 2:29b) and acceptance, John Wesley began the more crucial process of delineating the nature of this state. "In general," he wrote,

> we may observe it is that habitual disposition of soul which in the Sacred Writings is termed "holiness", and which directly implies the being cleansed from sin, "from all filthiness both of flesh and spirit" [2 Cor 7:1], and by consequence the being endued with those virtues which were also in Christ Jesus, the being so "renewed in the image of our mind" [Eph 4:23] as to be "perfect, as our Father in heaven is perfect" [Matt 5:48]. (Outler 1984, I:402–403)

This sort of "perfection," or Christian maturity, amounted to a purification of the inner person through an infusion of God's love. John went on:

> "Love is the fulfilling of the law" [Rom 13:10], "the end of the commandment" [1 Tim 1:5] ... It is not only the first and great command, but it is all the commandments in one. Whatsoever things are just, whatsoever things are pure, whatsoever things are amiable or honourable; if there be any virtue, if there be any praise, they are all comprised in this one word – love. In this is perfection and glory and happiness. The royal law of heaven and earth is this, "Thou shalt love the Lord thy God with all thy heart, and with all thy soul, and with all thy mind, and with all thy strength" [Mark 12:30] ... The one perfect good shall be your one ultimate end. (Outler 1984, I:407–408)

Charles Wesley joined his brother in the activities of the Oxford "Holy Club" and the academic life of the university. At that time, he thought of pursing an academic life and vocation, but he got swept up in his brother's plans when John accepted an invitation to go to Georgia as an Anglican missionary. During the Atlantic crossing and the early days in America, Charles set about preparing sermons to use as a backlog, when he began his ministry; he also transcribed at least seven sermons from his brother John's notebooks (Heitzenrater 1970). Several of these sermons were published posthumously under Charles's name because they were found in his handwriting and it was clear from his sermon log that he had preached them. The fact that these sermons were used by *both* Wesleys is not completely surprising because of the depth of what they called their "partnership" in ministry; in this particular case, they could easily each use the same sermons while preaching in two different towns in Georgia.

At least one of these early sermons was based on a Pauline passage, Philippians 3:13–14: "Brethren I count not myself to have apprehended, but this one thing I do forgetting those things which are behind, and reaching forth unto those things which are before, I press towards the mark of the high calling of God in Christ Jesus." The manuscript was headed "Oct. 21, 1735, On board the Simmonds." It was a three-point sermon, about Christian perfection. Once again, the author's main concerns were clearly enunciated: he would use the Pauline passage "First to show that in this world, Christians are never absolutely certain of their crown of reward. Secondly that it is never to be attained by resting contented with any pitch of piety short of the highest. Thirdly that a constant progress toward Christian perfection is therefore the indispensable duty of all Christians" (Newport 2001, 96). "Christian Perfection" is described as "the goal of our religious race; the stand whereon our crown of reward is placed" (2001, 101). The sermon betrays its pre-conversion context both by stressing holy living ("Christian Perfection") as the absolute duty of all Christians, and by marking out the path to perfection as one of earnest striving, opting for the highest goals, and making a single-minded effort:

> it must bespeak the same ardour and diligence in working out our salvation, as the children of this world use to attain the pleasures, riches and honours of this present life. And as a man must be a master of his trade, that would get an estate by his business, so must he be a perfect Christian, who would secure to himself these invaluable riches by his Christianity. (Newport 2001, 102)

Paul, Martin Luther, and the Wesleys' Conversions

By February 1, 1738, John and Charles Wesley had returned to England from Georgia with a profound sense of failure and vocational disillusionment. These words from John's journal sum up their sentiments well:

> I went to America to convert the Indians; but Oh! who shall convert me? Who, what is he that will deliver me from this evil heart of unbelief? I have a fair summer religion. I can talk well; nay, and believe myself, while no danger is near: but let death look me in the face, and my spirit is troubled. Nor can I say, "To die is gain!" [Phil 1:21]. (Ward and Heitzenrater 1988, I:211)

During their Georgia adventure and thereafter, both Wesleys had become the focus of evangelistic endeavors by Moravian missionaries. Heirs of the continental Reformation by way of Pietism, the Moravians stressed justification by faith alone and a faith "you can feel." The Moravian missionary Peter Böhler became John's spiritual director during the spring of 1738; over the next three months, Böhler and the Scriptures gradually convinced John to give up his duty-based understanding of Christian faith in favor (as he put it in his narrative written on May 24) of "continual prayer for this very thing, justifying, saving faith, a full reliance on the blood of Christ for *me*; a trust in him as *my* Christ, as *my* sole justification, sanctification, and redemption" (Ward and Heitzenrater 1988, I:248–249).

Charles Wesley was undergoing a similar spiritual pilgrimage, amidst a lengthy bout of pleurisy. The English Moravian John Bray was Charles's witness to justification by faith in Christ alone (Kimbrough and Newport 2008, 1:101). On Wednesday, May 17, Charles "first saw Luther on the Galatians, which Mr [William] Holland had accidentally lit upon. We began [reading], and found him nobly full of faith" (2008, 103). Charles described the impact of reading Luther's *Galatians*:

> I marveled that we were so soon, and so entirely, removed from him that called us into the grace of Christ unto another gospel [Gal 1:6–7]. Who would believe our Church had been founded on this important article of justification by faith alone! I am astonished I should ever think this a new doctrine, especially while our [Standard] Articles and Homilies stand unrepealed, and the key of knowledge is not yet taken away. (2008, 103–104)

On Pentecost Sunday, May 21, 1738, Charles "waked in hope and expectation of his [Christ's] coming." Later that day, while he was in a state between waking and sleeping, one of Wesley's nurses urged him: "In the name of Jesus of Nazareth, arise, and believe, and thou shalt be healed of all thy infirmities." Though spoken by Mrs. Musgrave, Charles took these to be the words of Christ to him, and he "felt in the mean time a strange palpitation of heart, I said, yet feared to say, 'I believe, I believe!'" (2008, 106). Over the next few days, Charles's faith began to grow, and on May 23 he "began [to compose] an hymn upon my conversion" (2008, 109).

Meanwhile, in another part of London, John Wesley was in the throes of his own conversion experience. As his famous journal entry for May 24, 1738 reports:

> In the evening I went very unwillingly to a society in Aldersgate Street, where one was reading [from] Luther's Preface to the Epistle to the Romans. About a quarter before nine, while he was describing the change which God works in the heart through faith in Christ, I felt my heart strangely warmed. I felt I did trust in Christ, Christ alone for salvation, and an assurance was given me that he had taken away *my* sins, even *mine*, and saved *me* from the law of sin and death [Rom 8:2]. (Ward and Heitzenrater 1988, I:249–250)

Later that evening, John visited his brother, and Charles's journal reports: "Towards ten my brother was brought in triumph by a troop of our friends and declared, 'I believe.' We sang the hymn with great joy and parted with prayer" (Kimbrough and Newport 2008, 1:111).

Exactly *which* of Charles Wesley's early conversion hymns was written on May 23 and sung in celebration on May 24 is a matter of some debate, but it is quite clear that one of the conversion hymns that Charles wrote in those days was "And Can It Be?" which he subsequently published (in 1739) under the title "Free Grace." The "Christ for me" phraseology of Galatians 2:20, mediated to him (perhaps) through the work of Martin Luther, reverberated throughout the first verse of the hymn:

> And can it be, that I should gain
> An interest in the Saviour's blood?
> Died he *for me*, who caused his pain?
> *For me?* Who him to death pursued?
> Amazing love! How can it be
> That thou, my God, shouldst die *for me?* (*MHB* 322; emphasis added)[2]

The final verse of "And Can It Be?" celebrates the singer's redemption through faith in Jesus Christ and is a veritable mosaic of biblical phrases and allusions, many of which are drawn from the Pauline corpus.

> No condemnation now I dread, [Rom 8:1]
> Jesus, and all in him, is mine. [1 Cor 3:22]
> Alive in him, my living head, [1 Cor 15:22]
> And clothed in righteousness divine, [Phil 3:9]
> Bold I approach th'eternal throne,
> And claim the crown, through Christ my own. [2 Tim 4:8] (*MHB* 323)

Whatever we are to make of their "evangelical conversions" (and there is considerable scholarly debate about this; see Maddox 1990), it is clear that an important transition had occurred: the Wesleys had come to accept the Reformation doctrine of justification by faith alone as the foundation for their soteriology, and they distinguished more decisively between justification and sanctification. Three months after his conversion, Charles Wesley described this development to his former mentor, William Law. "I told him," Charles wrote in his journal, "he was my schoolmaster to bring me to Christ, but the reason why I did not come sooner to Him was my seeking to be sanctified before I was justified" (Kimbrough and Newport 2008, 1:184).

The Wesley brothers soon became mass evangelists who preached out of doors to multitudes of people. Their jointly published *Hymns and Sacred Poems* (1739), like the evangelism of the Wesleyan revival, was the immediate result of the Wesleys' discovery of justification by faith alone. In the "Preface" to that work, they reported that they had leaned too heavily upon the work of Christian mystics (like William Law), a reliance that had produced confusion in their earlier understanding of the role of sanctification. They wrote: "The sole cause of our acceptance with God ... is the righteousness and the death of Christ, who fulfilled God's law, and died in our stead. And even the condition of it is not (as they suppose) our holiness either of heart or life; but our faith alone" (Jackson 1872, 14:320).

Revival Sermons

Sermons of John Wesley

Four days after his "evangelical conversion," on May 28, 1738, John Wesley was preaching at Long Acre Chapel in London. His text was Romans 4:5: "To him that worketh not, but believeth on him that justifieth the ungodly, his faith is counted to him for righteousness." His topic was "Justification by Faith." Whether his published sermon (No. 5) on this text, by this same title, is an exact echo of that first proclamation is not clear, but it seems appropriate to think of the later published sermon as a fair representation (if not an exact copy) of what John Wesley preached at Long Acre and the many occasions reported in his journal thereafter.

The "ground" or foundation of the doctrine was laid, in John's view, in the creation of humans in the image of God (Gen 1:26) and the subsequent loss of that image through the disobedience and fall into sin by Adam and Eve. So deep was this fall that no human can save himself and extricate himself from the bonds of sin and death. But through the coming of God's Son, who "tasted death for every man" (Heb 2:9), God has "reconciled the world to himself, not imputing to them their former trespasses" (2 Cor 5:19). And thus, "as by the offence of one judgment came upon all men to condemnation, even so by the righteousness of one the free gift came upon all men unto justification" (Rom 5:18). Pauline texts and theology figured prominently in John Wesley's understanding and description of the plight of fallen humanity, as well as the path toward reconciliation with God.

In his second point of the sermon, John Wesley described this justification by distinguishing it from sanctification.

> What is "justification"? ... it is evident from what has been already observed that it is not the being made actually just and righteous. This is *sanctification*; which is indeed in some degree the immediate *fruit* of justification, but nevertheless is a distinct gift of God, and of a totally different nature. The one [justification] implies what God *does for us* through his Son; the other [sanctification] what he *works in us* by his Spirit. (Outler 1984, I:187)

After an extensive discussion of the various aspects and benefits of justification, John concluded: "The plain scriptural notion of justification is pardon, the forgiveness of sins. It is that act of God the Father whereby, for the sake of the propitiation made by the blood of his Son, he 'showeth forth his righteousness (or mercy) by the remission of the sins that are past' [Rom 3:25]" (Outler 1984, I:189).

In moving to his third point – "Who are they that are justified?" – Wesley returned to his Bible text: "the Apostle tells us expressly, the ungodly: he, that is, God, 'justifieth the ungodly' [Rom 4:5]; the ungodly of every kind and degree, and none but the ungodly" (Outler 1984, I:190). Wesley had several convergent concerns in this section of the sermon. He wanted to show that all people – insofar as they realize themselves to be in need of God's salvation – are appropriate candidates for justification. The sermon also mounts an onslaught upon all human schemes of self-salvation through doing good works. John concluded with an urgent plea to his hearers and readers: "Plead thou no works, no righteousness of thine own ... No. Plead thou singly the blood of the covenant, the ransom paid for thy proud, stubborn, sinful soul ... O come quickly. Believe in the Lord Jesus; and *thou*, even *thou*, art reconciled to God" (Outler 1984, I:199).

On June 11, 1738, John Wesley was once again preaching this "new" message of justification by faith alone. On that day, it was his turn to preach (again) at St. Mary's Oxford, and he spoke from Ephesians 2:8: "By grace ye are saved through faith." This sermon was subsequently published in Wesley's *Collection of Standard Sermons* (1748); the particular importance he attached to this sermon – and its message – is indicated by its location as No. 1 in that work, which was designed to summarize the main teachings of the Methodist movement. Describing the nature of saving faith, John Wesley concluded that saving faith is not only the necessary basis of our salvation, but also the means of our restoration. It is "full reliance" on the blood of Christ, as well as a trust and "recumbency" upon the living Christ.

> It acknowledges the necessity and merit of his death, and the power of his resurrection. It acknowledges his death as the only sufficient means of redeeming man from death eternal,

and his resurrection as the restoration of us all to life and immortality; inasmuch as he "was delivered for our sins, and rose again for our justification" [Rom 4:25]. Christian faith is then not only an assent to the whole gospel of Christ, but also a full reliance on the blood of Christ, a trust in the merits of his life, death, and resurrection; a recumbency upon him as our atonement and our life, as *given for us*, and *living in us*. It is a sure confidence which a man hath in God, that through the merits of Christ *his* sins are forgiven, and *he* reconciled to the favour of God; and in consequence hereof a closing with him and cleaving to him as our "wisdom, righteousness, sanctification, and redemption" [1 Cor 1:30], or, in one word, our salvation. (Outler 1984, I:121)

In the second point of this important sermon, John Wesley described what the salvation *is* that is ours through faith in Jesus Christ. In terse, outline form, Wesley marched his hearers and readers through six significant points: First, "It is a present salvation. It is something attainable, yea, actually attained on earth, by those who are partakers of this faith" (I:121). Second, "Ye are saved (to comprise all in one word) from sin" (I:121). Third, "First from the guilt of all past sin" (I:122). Fourth, "And being saved from guilt, they are saved from fear. Not indeed from a filial fear of offending, but from all servile fear, from that 'fear which hath torment' [1 John 4:18], from fear of punishment, from fear of the wrath of God, whom they now no longer regard as a severe master, but as an indulgent Father" (I:122). Fifth, "Again, through this faith they are saved from the power of sin as well as from the guilt of it" (I:123). In describing the freedom that the Christian has over sin, John Wesley moved beyond the traditional Protestant description of justification (as freedom from the guilt of sin) into sanctification (which is concerned with freedom from the power of sin). As he wrote in the same sermon:

Ye are saved (to comprise all in one word) from sin. This is the salvation which is through faith ... All his people, or as it is elsewhere expressed, all that believe in him, he will save from all their sins: from original and actual, past and present sin, of the flesh and of the spirit. Through faith that is in him they are saved both from the guilt and from the power of it. (I:121–122)

A third important sermon based on a Pauline text from this period was John Wesley's Standard Sermon No. 40, "Christian Perfection." Based on Philippians 3:12, "Not as though I had already attained, either were already perfect," the sermon was first prepared and preached in 1741 (Outler 1984, II:97–98). Taken together with his early sermon "The Circumcision of the Heart," this sermon forms a solid explanation of the Wesleys' distinctive doctrine of sanctification as Christian perfection. The intention of this sermon was to define and explain the phrase "Christian Perfection." John began by acknowledging the difficulties accompanying the use of this phrase.

There is scarce any expression in Holy Writ which has given more offence than this. The word "perfect" is what many cannot bear. The very sound of it is an abomination to them. And whosoever "preaches perfection" (as the phrase is), i.e. asserts that it is attainable in this life, runs great hazard of being accounted by them worse than a heathen man or a publican. (II:99)

Arguing that this term cannot be laid aside because "they are the words of God, not of man," Wesley went on to explain the term "Christian Perfection" so "that those who are sincere of heart may not err to the right hand or to the left from the mark of the prize of their high calling [Phil 3:14]." Hence, John reports: "I shall endeavour to show, First, in what sense Christians are *not*, and Secondly, in what sense they *are*, perfect" (II:100)

In delineating "in what sense Christians are not" perfect, Wesley focused his audience's attention on matters of human knowledge. Devout Christians are not free from ignorance or errors. Nor are they so perfect as to be free from infirmities such as slowness of speech, understanding, and "all those inward or outward imperfections which are not of a moral nature" (II:103). Finally, this sort of perfection does not imply freedom from temptations of any sort (II:104).

Explaining in what sense Christians *are* perfect seems to be the more difficult part of Wesley's agenda. He begins by describing "perfection" as another name for holiness: "They are two names for the same thing. Thus everyone that is perfect is holy, and everyone that is holy is, in the Scripture sense, perfect" (II:104). Following the meaning of the term *teleios* in Greek, Wesley likened Christian perfection to the process of maturity, and urged (as did Paul before him) that Christians ought not to continue as though they were babes in Christ (1 Cor 3:1–2). This means, in part, that those who have been justified and born again are hence freed from the power of sin, and should experience growth in Christian maturity by being victorious over sin in their lives. John's words, following those of the apostle Paul from Romans 6, stressed that

> those who are justified, who are born again ... do not "continue in sin"; that they cannot "live any longer therein" [Rom 6:1, 2]; that they are "planted together in the likeness of the death of Christ" [v. 5]; that their "old man is crucified with him, the body of sin being destroyed, so that thenceforth they do not serve sin"; that "being dead with Christ, they are freed from sin" [vv. 6,7]; that they are "dead unto sin", and "alive unto God" [v. 11]; that "sin hath not dominion over them", who are "not under the law, but under grace"; but that these, "being made free from sin, are become the servants of righteousness" [vv. 14, 15, 18]. (II:106)

From his study of these Pauline texts, Wesley concludes: "The very least which can be implied in these words is that the persons spoken of therein, namely all real Christians or believers in Christ, are made free from outward sin" (II:106).

After explaining his understanding of Christian perfection as a kind of Christian maturity that enables one to live a life of victory over outward and inward sin, Wesley urged:

> This is the glorious privilege of every Christian; yea, though he be but "a babe in Christ" [1 Cor 3:1]. But it is only of those who "are strong in the Lord" [Eph 6:10], and "have overcome the wicked one", or rather of those who "have known him that is from the beginning" [1 John 2:13, 14], that it can be affirmed they are in such a sense perfect as, secondly, to be freed from evil thoughts and evil tempers. (II:117)

This latter development, being free from evil thoughts and attitudes, is part of having the mind of Christ (Phil 2:7) and having Christ formed within. Once again, John turned to Paul for a description of Christian perfection: "Everyone of these can say with St. Paul, 'I am crucified with Christ: nevertheless I live; yet not I, but Christ liveth in me' [Gal 2:20] – words that manifestly describe a deliverance from inward as well as from outward sin" (II:118).

John Wesley's published works contain forty-six sermons based on Pauline texts (see Outler 1984, I:707–713):

On Corrupting the Word of God	2 Cor 2:17	1727
The Circumcision of the Heart	Rom 2:29	1733
Salvation by Faith	Eph 2:8	1738
Free Grace	Rom 8:32	1739
Christian Perfection	Phil 3:12	1741
Justification by Faith	Rom 4:5	1746
The Righteousness of Faith	Rom 10:5–8	1746
The First-fruits of the Spirit	Rom 8:1	1746
The Spirit of Bondage and of Adoption	Rom 8:15	1746
The Witness of the Spirit, Discourse 1	Rom 8:16	1746
The Witness of our Own Spirit	2 Cor 1:12	1746
The Original Nature, Properties, and Use of the Law	Rom 7:12	1750
The Law Established through Faith, No. 1	Rom 3:31	1750
The Law Established through Faith, No. 2	Rom 3:31	1750
Satan's Devices	2 Cor 2:11	1750
The Great Assize	Rom 14:10	1758
Wandering Thoughts	2 Cor 10:5	1762
On Sin in Believers	2 Cor 5:17	1763
The Scripture Way of Salvation	Eph 2:8	1765
The Witness of the Spirit, Discourse 2	Rom 8:16	1767
On Predestination	Rom 8:29–30	1773
The Danger of Riches	1 Tim 6:9	1781
On Zeal	Gal 4:18	1781
The Case of Reason Impartially Considered	1 Cor 14:20	1781
The General Deliverance	Rom 8:19–22	1781
On Redeeming the Time	Eph 5:16	1782
God's Love to Fallen Man	Rom 5:15	1782
Of Evil Angels	Eph 6:12	1783
The Mystery of Iniquity	2 Thess 2:7	1783
On Dissipation	1 Cor 7:35	1784
The Imperfection of Human Knowledge	1 Cor 13:9	1784
The Wisdom of God's Counsels	Rom 11:33	1784
In What Sense We are to Leave the World	2 Cor 6:17–18	1784
On Obedience to Parents	Col 3:20	1784
On Charity	1 Cor 13:1–3	1784
Of the Church	Eph 4:1–6	1785
On Working Out our Own Salvation	Phil 2:12–13	1785

On Schism	1 Cor 12:25	1786
On Temptation	1 Cor 10:13	1786
On Pleasing All Men	Rom 15:2	1787
The More Excellent Way	1 Cor 12:31	1787
On Conscience	2 Cor 1:12	1788
Walking by Sight and Walking by Faith	2 Cor 5:7	1788
On Knowing Christ After the Flesh	2 Cor 5:16	1789
Heavenly Treasure in Earthen Vessels	2 Cor 4:7	1790
On Living without God	Eph 2:12	1790

While these sermons cover the full array of Christian doctrines and practices, they typically revolve around issues of justification, new birth, and sanctification. Several of the Wesleys' distinctive doctrines – such as Christian perfection and the witness of the Spirit – are based on carefully nuanced expositions of Pauline passages. Following the text of Romans 8:16, "The Spirit itself beareth witness with our spirit, that we are the children of God," John Wesley defined the witness of the Spirit in this way: "an inward impression on the soul, whereby the Spirit of God directly 'witnesses to my spirit that I am a child of God'; that Jesus Christ hath loved me, and given himself for me; that all my sins are blotted out, and I, even I, am reconciled to God" (Outler 1984, I:274). John's characteristically Arminian emphasis was evidenced in his Sermon No. 58, "On Predestination." After working through Romans 8:29–30, from an Arminian standpoint, Wesley concluded: "What is it then that we learn from this whole account? It is this and no more: (1), God [fore] knows all believers; (2), wills that they should be saved from sin; (3), to that end justifies them; (4), sanctifies; and (5), takes them to glory" (Outler 1984, II:421).

This list of published sermons does not represent the full scale of John Wesley's proclamation of Pauline texts. For that information, we need to look at other sources. One of these is John Wesley's journal, which frequently mentions the sermon texts he was preaching in various locations. Albert Outler made a study of this resource and discovered that John Wesley's favorite New Testament sermon texts were these: Mark 1:15 (190 usages), 2 Corinthians 8:9 (167 usages), Ephesians 2:8 (133 usages), Galatians 6:14 (129 usages), and Matthew 16:26 (117 usages). A third source for chronicling John Wesley's preaching emerged in the nineteenth century; it was a sermon register which Wesley kept between January 14, 1747 and December 25, 1761 – roughly fifteen years.[3] The sermon register indicates that Wesley preached 7,149 times over those fifteen years, and 2,034 or 28.5 percent of the sermons he preached over that same period were based on Pauline passages. If one were to ask which Pauline books figure most prominently in this proclamation, the list looks like this:

Romans	455
1 Corinthians	372
2 Corinthians	313
Galatians	313
Ephesians	210

Philippians	148
1 Thessalonians	93
1 Timothy	43
2 Timothy	42
Titus	30
2 Thessalonians	15

Looking at the Pauline passages which Wesley preached from most frequently produces this list:

2 Cor 8:9	127
Gal 6:14	98
Rom 12:1	69
Rom 8:33	56
1 Cor 1:24	56
Rom 5:22	52
Gal 3:22	37
1 Cor 6:19	34
1 Cor 1:30	32
2 Cor 5:7	30
2 Cor. 5:19	30
Gal 5:22	27
Gal 5:18	25
2 Cor 5:18	21
Gal 4:18	18
Rom 10:4	16
Eph 1:13	16
Eph 2: 28	16
Col 3:11	16
Rom 3:1	15
2 Cor 4:5	15

Sermons of Charles Wesley

By June 5, 1738, Charles Wesley was well enough to abandon his sickbed and begin witnessing to his friends about his newly found doctrine, justification by faith alone. On June 6, he read Luther's *Galatians*, "as usual," to a large group of friends, one of whom was "greatly affected" by it (Kimbrough and Newport 2008, 1:115). On Sunday, June 11, the younger Wesley was preaching "the gospel" through which several received salvation by "faith in the blood of Christ" (1:120). On Saturday, June 24, he "proclaimed the glad tidings of salvation" to his friend William Delamontte, from Romans 3:28, "We are justified freely by faith alone." He continued witnessing and teaching justification by faith among his friends; by the following Wednesday, Charles rejoiced "that God had added to his living church seven more souls through my ministry" (1:127). The next Sunday morning, July 2, Charles preached "Salvation by Faith" to a "deeply attentive audience" (1:130). He preached again in the evening at a religious society, and midst tears and outcries of "I believe, I believe," one Mrs. Harper received salvation while those assembled were singing one of Charles's newly written hymns (1:130–131). This would mark the beginning of Charles Wesley's evangelistic ministry. It was a sustained and variegated ministry that spanned more than fifty years.

Charles Wesley has left us no sermon register to chronicle his pulpit ministry, but in many instances his sporadic journal is little more than an annotated sermon log. A close reading of his journal indicates that he, too, often preached from Pauline Bible passages. But only one Pauline passage appears on a "top ten" list of sermon passages derived from Charles's journal: Galatians 3:22, which Charles preached as "All under Sin" (Tyson 1989, 487). Unfortunately, this sermon has not survived as a written publication; indeed, given Wesley's penchant for extemporaneous proclamation, it may never have existed as a written sermon. Several sermons based on Pauline passages are, however, among the extant sermons that can be attributed to Charles Wesley: No. 5, on Titus 3:8; No. 6, on Romans 3:23–24; No. 7, on Romans 3:23–25; and No. 8, on Ephesians 5:14 (Newport 2001, xiii).

The sermon on Titus 3:8 is about "Faith and Good Works": "This is a faithful saying, and these things I will that thou affirm constantly, that they which have believed in God might be careful to maintain good works." It is extant only in a shorthand version. This sermon has two main concerns. The first is to show that good works are not the basis of a person's salvation; the second, that true and lively (saving) faith in Jesus Christ produces good works.

Charles's two sermons on Romans 3 are both about justification by faith. Each has survived only in Charles Wesley's shorthand version; both sermons were preached throughout 1739 and both seem to have as a sort of subtext the concern to show that the "new" doctrine (justification by faith alone) was stoutly taught by Scripture and the Anglican Articles and Homilies (from which both sermons quote directly). The second sermon, based on Romans 3:22–25, is the longer of the two and amounts to about ten thousand words; Kenneth Newport muses that it must have taken "a good hour" to deliver (Newport 2001, 183). It was preached before the University at Oxford on Sunday, July 1, 1739. It is a wide-ranging explanation of the sinfulness of all humans and the absolute necessity of their justification by faith in Jesus Christ. Once again, undercutting the theology of self-salvation, Charles urged: "St. Paul declareth here nothing upon the behalf of man concerning his justification, but only a true and lively faith, which nevertheless is the gift of God. And yet this faith doth not shut out repentance, hope, love, and the fear of God in every believer that is justified, but it shutteth them out from the office of justifying" (Newport 2001, 197–198).

Charles Wesley's most famous sermon, "Awake, Thou that Sleepest," was also based on a Pauline text: "Awake, thou that sleepest, and arise from the dead, and Christ shall give thee light" (Eph 5:14). This sermon was so popular that it circulated as a pamphlet and was subsequently published among his brother's *Standard Sermons*. The style of this sermon differs significantly from Charles's two sermons on Romans 3, which were more of the nature of textual expositions. It takes on a more evangelistic tone as Wesley told his audience that they are like those in the Pauline text who are asleep in their sins, and urged them to wake up and cry out for their own salvation:

> Awake, awake! Stand up this moment, lest thou "drink at the Lord's hand the cup of his fury" [Isa 51:17]. Stir up thyself "to lay hold on the Lord" [2 Chr 7:22], "the Lord thy righteousness, mighty to save!" [Jer 23:6; Isa 63:1]. "Shake thyself from the dust" [Isa 52:2]. At least, let the earthquake of God's threatenings shake thee. Awake and cry out with the trembling gaoler, "what must I do to be saved?" [Acts. 16:30]. And never rest till thou believest on the Lord Jesus, with a faith which is his gift, by the operation of his spirit. (Newport 2001, 216–217)

The sermon was all the more audacious for having been written to be preached "before the University at Oxford" on April 4, 1742. It would be the last time that Charles Wesley was invited to preach there. After offering a thorough exposition of the Methodist messages of "full salvation" (justification and sanctification by faith), the sermon concludes with an urgent appeal:

> My brethren, it is high time for us to awake out of sleep, before the "great trumpet of the Lord be blown", and our land become a field of blood. O may we speedily see the things that make for our peace, before they are hid from our eyes! "Turn thou us, O good Lord, and let thine anger cease from us" [Ps 85:4 Book of Common Prayer]. "O Lord, look down from heaven, behold and visit this vine" [Ps 80:14]; and cause us to know the time of our visitation. "Help us, O God of our salvation, for the glory of thy name; O deliver us, and be merciful to our sins, for thy name's sake" [Ps 79:9]. "And so we will not go back from thee: O let us live, and we shall call upon thy name. Turn us again, O Lord God of hosts, show the light of thy countenance, and we shall be whole" [Ps 80:18–19]. (Newport 2001, 224)

Charles Wesley's Hymns

The Wesleyan hymns were written in the context of the Methodist revival. They were both celebrations of God's grace and a means whereby people were intended to receive it. No less than their sermons, the Wesleys' songs were weapons of evangelism; as such, they were also faithful communicators of Christian doctrine and experience. John Wesley clearly realized the doctrinal basis of the Wesleyan hymns, and made reference to this when he described the first standard Methodist hymn book, *A Collection of Hymns for the Use of the People Called Methodists*, of 1780, as a "little body of experimental and practical divinity" (Jackson 1872, 14:340).

It is appropriate to view Charles Wesley's hymns as "biblical" in two senses: not only do they communicate a theology that is directly drawn from the Bible, but Wesley's poetical diction was profoundly shaped by the language, terms, and allusions delivered to him by the Bible.[4] Because Charles's hymns are literally constructed out of little bits of the Bible that he has fused into a whole picture of his own making, it is no surprise to find many textual allusions to Pauline passages in these hymns. In fact, the editors of the critical edition of *A Collection of Hymns for the Use of the People Called Methodists*

(*MHB*) identified 1,084 direct allusions to Pauline texts in the 525 hymns that comprise the collection; hence, one might expect to find (roughly) two direct Pauline allusions in each Charles Wesley hymn.

The entire, traditionally accepted Pauline corpus, excepting Philemon, is echoed in the 1780 *MHB*. Texts from Romans and 2 Corinthians predominate, with the former making up 20 percent of the occurrences and the latter nearly 16 percent (15.77 percent). The list of total occurrences of Pauline allusions amounts to this:

Romans	217
2 Corinthians	171
Ephesians	130
1 Corinthians	123
Philippians	105
Colossians	78
Galatians	69
2 Timothy	66
1 Thessalonians	54
1 Timothy	49
2 Thessalonians	17
Titus	5

While each and every Pauline textual allusion gave theological and poetical shape to Charles Wesley's compositions, it is possible to identify certain passages that seem to have played a prominent and recurring role for him. Examining Charles's main Pauline allusions can give us a sense of how he used Pauline theology, and to what aspects of Paul's writings Wesley found himself most often drawn. The most prevalent Pauline allusions in the *MHB*, arranged by numerical predominance, are as follows:

Phil 2:5	25
Gal 2:20	19
Rom 12:2	14
2 Cor 12:9	12
2 Cor 5:17	12
2 Cor 9:15	10
2 Cor 3:18	10
Col 3:11	10
Rom 5:5	9
Rom 8:21	9
1 Thess 5:17	9

The Pauline text to which Charles Wesley most frequently alluded is Philippians 2:5. His use of the passage revolved around the phrase "the mind of Christ," and typically referred to the transforming results that new birth and sanctification had upon the believer's inner life: he or she gained the "mind of Christ," and began to think and live in a Christ-like manner. This example, from "Primitive Christianity," is representative of many others:

> O let them all thy mind express,
> Stand forth thy chosen witnesses;
> Thy power unto salvation show
> And perfect holiness below. (*MHB* 101)

The transformation of the Christian person into "the mind of Christ," however gradual and partial it might be, was anticipated as eventually culminating in a complete and enduring Christ-likeness. Hence, Charles wrote:

> While still to thee for help I call
> Thou wilt not suffer me to fall,
> Thou canst not let me sin;
> And thou shalt give me power to pray
> Till all my sins are purged away,
> And all thy mind brought in. (*MHB* 421)

Charles knew and cherished the Pauline doctrine of justification by faith, as is clear from his use of Ephesians 2:8 and similar passages. This verse from his most famous hymn, "O for a Thousand Tongues to Sing," is a good illustration:

> Look unto him, ye nations, own
> Your God, ye fallen race; [Rom 3:23]
> Look, and be saved through faith alone,
> Be justified by grace! (*MHB* 80)

But Charles's more typical approach was to link justification with the transformation that followed it (sanctification) as the Christian gained the "mind of Christ," or was "transformed by the renewing" of his or her mind. Wesley's prominent use of the language of Romans 12:2 followed this same pattern. The transformation referred to and anticipated in the Romans passage was made real in the believer's life through faith in the work of Christ and the indwelling presence of the Holy Spirit:

> The meek and lowly heart,
> That in our Saviour was,
> To us his Spirit does impart,
> And signs us with his cross:
> Our nature's turned, our mind
> Transformed in all its powers;
> And both the witnesses are joined,
> The Spirit of God with ours. (*MHB* 197)

Second Corinthians 12:9 was frequently alluded to by Charles Wesley to stress the all-sufficient power of God's grace to actualize the process of transformation – even in the midst of human weakness. This emphasis was joined to several themes mentioned above in verses like this:

> God of all-sufficient grace,
> My God in Christ thou art;
> Bid me walk before thy face
> Till I am pure in heart;
> Till, transformed by faith divine,
> I gain that perfect love unknown,
> Bright in all thy image shine,
> By putting on thy Son. (*MHB* 526)

Galatians 2:20 ("I am crucified with Christ: nevertheless I live; yet not I, but Christ liveth in me: and the life which I now live in the flesh I live by the faith of the Son of God, who loved me, and gave himself for me") expressed the Christian's deep and transforming union with Jesus Christ. Allusions to this text in Charles Wesley's verse conveyed the concept of justification by faith ("I live by the faith of the Son of God") as well as the sanctifying effects of that faith-union. Wesley's application of this passage persistently stressed the "for me" quality of Christ's saving death:

> Jesus, thou for me hast died,
> And thou in me shalt live;
> I shall feel thy death applied,
> I shall thy life receive;
> Yet when melted in the flame
> Of love, this shall be all my plea:
> I the chief of sinners am,
> But Jesus died for me. (*MHB* 222)

The phraseology of 2 Corinthians 5:17, by which the Christian becomes "a new creation," figured prominently in Charles Wesley's description of the process of sanctification as being nothing less than the inner restoration of the image of God (*imago Dei*) in which humans were originally created (Gen 1:26). Charles's famous "Love Divine All Loves Excelling" illustrates this point well:

> Finish then thy new creation,
> Pure and spotless let us be;
> Let us see thy great salvation
> Perfectly restored in thee;
> Changed from glory into glory, [2 Cor 3:18]
> Till in heaven we take our place,
> Till we cast our crowns before thee,
> Lost in wonder, love, and praise. (*MHB* 547)

Romans 5:5 reports that the "love of God is shed abroad in our hearts by the Holy Ghost which is given unto us." This text, for Charles Wesley, was instrumental in describing *how* the process of transformation (sanctification) takes place within

Christians. By faith, Christians receive Christ, and with Christ they receive the Holy Spirit. The Holy Spirit brings the love of God into the inner person of those who have faith, and God's love transforms and makes a person whole, complete, or "perfect." Hence, this verse from "O Jesus, Let Me Bless thy Name!" is representative of many others:

> O let thy Spirit shed abroad
> The love, the perfect love of God
> In this cold heart of mine!
> O might he now descend, and rest,
> And dwell for ever in my breast,
> And make it all divine! (*MHB* 256)

Conclusion

John and Charles Wesley were deeply affected by Pauline Scripture texts. From childhood on, their lives and theology were shaped by a formative reading of the Pauline epistles. Their theology of justification by faith alone, which was mediated through Luther and the Moravians, was rooted in their Reformation understanding of passages from Galatians, Romans, and Ephesians. The distinctive Wesleyan emphasis upon the witness of the Spirit was based on their reading of Romans 8:16. The Wesleyan emphasis upon sanctification as an utter transformation of the inner person (Christian perfection) was also fueled by Pauline passages such as Romans 2:29, Galatians 2:20, and Philippians 2:5 and 3:12–13. That Pauline texts formed the heart and soul of the Wesleyan proclamation of the gospel is as evident from an examination of John and Charles Wesley's sermons as it is from a close study of the biblical expressions and allusions that shaped the phraseology of Charles Wesley's hymns.

Notes

1 Biblical quotations throughout this chapter are cited as found in the Wesleys' writings; as a rule, they are based on the King James Version.
2 Hildebrandt and Beckerlegge (1983, 322; Hymn 193). Hereafter *MHB*.
3 The sermon register was subsequently published by Nehemiah Curnock (see Curnock 1960, 8:169–252).
4 For more information on Charles Wesley's poetical diction, see Tyson (1989, 29–35), as well as the more extensive treatment in Baker (1962, ix–lxi).

References

Baker, Frank, editor. 1962. *Representative Verse of Charles Wesley*. London: Epworth.
Curnock, Nehemiah, editor. 1960. *The Journal of the Rev. John Wesley, MA*. 8 volumes. London: Epworth (reprint 1916).

Heitzenrater, Richard P. 1970. John Wesley's Early Sermons. *Proceedings of the Wesley Historical Society* 37: 110–128.

Hildebrandt, Franz, and Oliver Beckerlegge, editors, with James Dale. 1983. *A Collection of Hymns for the Use of the People Called Methodists. The Works of John Wesley,* volume 7. Nashville: Abingdon.

Jackson, Thomas, editor. 1872. *The Works of John Wesley.* 14 volumes. London: The Wesleyan Conference.

Kimbrough, S. T., Jr., and Kenneth G. C. Newport. (2007–)2008. *The Manuscript Journal of the Reverend Charles Wesley, MA.* 2 volumes. Nashville: Abingdon/Kingswood.

Maddox, Randy L., editor. 1990. *Aldersgate Reconsidered.* Nashville: Abingdon/Kingswood.

Newport, Kenneth G. C., editor. 2001. *The Sermons of Charles Wesley.* Oxford: Oxford University Press.

Outler, Albert, editor. 1984(–1987). *Sermons I–IV. The Works of John Wesley,* volumes 1–4. Nashville: Abingdon.

Tyson, John R. 1989. *Charles Wesley: A Reader.* New York: Oxford University Press.

Ward, W. Reginald, and Richard P. Heitzenrater, editors. 1988(–2003). *Journals and Diaries I–VII. The Works of John Wesley,* volumes 18–24. Nashville: Abingdon.

CHAPTER 27
Barth

Richard E. Burnett

Karl Barth's break with liberalism in the summer of 1915 is widely regarded as one of the most important events in Protestant theology in the past two hundred years, if not since the Reformation. It gave rise to Barth's commentary on *The Epistle to the Romans*, first published in German in 1919 (hereafter cited as Rom I), which Karl Adam famously described as "a bombshell which exploded on the playground of theologians." As the smoke began to clear throughout the twentieth century in the aftermath of Barth's "bombshell," it became apparent that there were many intellectual influences, movements, and figures that played a role Barth's break with liberalism. Scholars continue to analyze them. Yet the most decisive factor in Barth's theological conversion, by his own account, was his encounter with the apostle Paul.

Background to Barth's Encounter with Paul

After his university training and a two-year assistantship in Geneva, Barth became the pastor of a congregation in the small, industrial village of Safenwil, Switzerland. He served there for ten years, and his life was filled with all the joys, conflicts, challenges, and responsibilities of most village pastors. However, a significant change occurred in October 1914 when he discovered that ninety-three German intellectuals had signed a "horrible manifesto" justifying the war policy of Kaiser Wilhelm II, and that among them were almost all his former German teachers. To Barth, this constituted an enormous betrayal. Not only did it expose the hypocrisy of many liberal Protestants, together

The Blackwell Companion to Paul, First Edition. Edited by Stephen Westerholm.
© 2011 Blackwell Publishing Ltd. Published 2011 by Blackwell Publishing Ltd.

with their lofty ideals, but it also called into question an entire theological tradition that could be traced back to Schleiermacher, who until that time had been for Barth a church father for whom his enthusiasm knew no bounds. So cataclysmic was this event that Barth said: "An entire world of theological exegesis, ethics, dogmatics, and preaching, which up to that point I had accepted as basically credible, was thereby shaken to the foundations, and with it everything which flowed at that time from the pens of the German theologians" (Barth 1982, 263–264).

Yet in addition to the theological bankruptcy of Protestant liberalism in Germany, the same period exposed a crisis closer to home: that of Barth's own preaching. "The textual basis of my sermons, the Bible, which hitherto I had taken for granted, became more and more of a problem" (Barth 1981, 154). Mounting the pulpit became an increasing challenge. Having accrued great theological riches through years of study, Barth thought he had enough sermon material; but he soon discovered that such resources were not inexhaustible. Barth knew he needed to speak from the Bible; yet, given his theological orientation and training, this was easier said than done. Eduard Thurneysen, who was pastor of a neighboring congregation, had been meeting regularly with Barth to discuss their situation as pastors, their disillusionment over the current state of theology, and any possible way forward. Sometime around the summer of 1915, they decided they would turn back to the Bible. As Barth later described it:

> We made a fresh attempt to learn our theological ABCs all over again. More reflectively than ever before, we began reading and expounding the writings of the Old and New Testaments. And behold, they began to speak to us – very differently than we had supposed we were obliged to hear them speak in the school of what was then called "modern" theology. The morning after Thurneysen had whispered to me our commonly held conviction, I sat down under an apple tree and began, with all the tools at my disposal, to apply myself to the Epistle to the Romans. That was the text which as early as my own confirmation classes (1901–1902) I had heard was supposed to be concerned with something central. I began to read it as if I had never read it before ... (Barth 1982, 264)

Barth's Encounter with Paul

Barth's much-celebrated discovery of "The Strange New World within the Bible" marks a kind of Copernican revolution in the history of modern theology. Challenging the Enlightenment's "turn to the subject" inaugurated by Descartes, Barth asserted: "It is not the right human thoughts about God which form the content of the Bible, but the right divine thoughts about men" (Barth 1978a, 43). In this address, delivered on February 6, 1917, Barth repeats a single question, "What is in the Bible?" He parodies the sort of answers typically given in his day: the Bible is full of History! Morality! Religion! Piety! After discussing the inadequacy of each of these answers, he asks: What is the "highest answer"? What is really the "main subject" of the Bible, to which we are so ineluctably driven? Barth says it is God. Of course, the Bible contains history, morality, religion, and piety as well. But none of these constitutes the real "content of the contents." *God* is the content (*der Inhalt*) of the Bible (Barth 1978a, 46).

This was Barth's first public account of what he discovered in the Bible after his break with liberalism, and it is an accurate description. Yet it is still somewhat vague and abstract. He does not discuss, for example, the specific means of his discovery. Nor does he take into account, concretely, what we know was really dominating his thinking throughout this period: Paul's Romans. But this is understandable when one reads his correspondence and considers that he was still reeling from his encounter.

As a thoroughgoing liberal who had known "how to swear no higher than by the man, Daniel Ernst Friedrich Schleiermacher" (Barth 1982, 261), Barth was not prepared for what he found in reading Paul. Nothing in his theological education had prepared him for it; on the contrary, in some ways, his education had only inoculated him against it. Barth had been thoroughly inculcated into the historical-critical approach to the Bible. His first teachers at Bern were direct pupils of Wellhausen and F. C. Baur. Rudolf Steck, his first New Testament teacher, amiable though tedious in his analysis, did not think that even Galatians was authentically Pauline! Barth was not ungrateful for what he learned from such teachers. As he said in the last year of his life:

> What I owe despite everything to those Bern masters is that I learned to forget any fears I might have had. They gave me such a thorough grounding in the earlier form of the "historical-critical" school that the remarks of their later and contemporary successors could no longer get under my skin or even touch my heart – they could only get on my nerves, as is only too well known. (Barth 1982, 261–262)

Yet such an approach gave him little grist for his mill as a young pastor.

The popular answers to the question, "*Was steht in die Bibel?*" that he later parodied (viz., history, morality, religion, and piety) had been, in part, his own, especially the latter. He taught in his earliest confirmation classes that the Bible was important, and "especially the New Testament, because it is there that we find the earliest reports and thoughts about Jesus, written down by men who experienced themselves the glory of Christian certainty to the liveliest degree [*aufs Lebhafteste*]" (Barth 1987, 67). And while the New Testament is "indispensable" for this reason, Barth said that the Old Testament is also "important" because it teaches about "the religion from which Jesus emerged." In other words, the Bible is primarily about religion, about piety, about "people who *experienced* God and who now communicate these experiences" (1987, 69). This is why Paul was important. And, to be sure, there was never any doubt in Barth's mind, even as a liberal, about Paul being "inspired" or that he experienced or communicated "revelation." But prior to 1915, Barth did not hesitate to say further, as he did to his confirmation classes: "With the conclusion of the Bible, God did not close the book of revelation. Everything that is Jesus-like in people can be revelation, a message from God. People, poets, art, nature, strong impressions" (1987, 69).

Thus, for Barth prior to 1915, the only legitimate, scientific way to study the Bible was as a "document of piety." As a student of Schleiermacher, Barth thought he had been fairly well equipped to do this. He knew the importance of trying to establish an inner relationship with an author, of immersing oneself in his thought-world and piety. Schleiermacher taught that the goal of interpretation is "to understand an author better than he understands himself." Barth seems to have embraced this goal, and in

1910 he wrote an article extolling the art of empathy (*Einfühlung*) as an interpretive key and a means of overcoming the sterile historicism of many of his contemporaries (Barth 1993a). Schleiermacher's hermeneutics, his method of balancing the psychological and grammatical sides as well as the historical and divinatory sides of interpretation, are highly sophisticated and nuanced. By comparison, Barth saw the instruments of many of the historical critics of his day as barbarously blunt, crude, and reductionistic. This is why, even while he was a liberal, they could not get under his skin, much less touch his heart.

Yet, in actual practice, neither hermeneutical skills nor empathy seems to have prevented Barth himself from being somewhat crude and reductionistic in his approach, as he later admitted. For example, around 1913, Barth led a Bible study on Paul in his congregation for which he prepared the following observations about Paul:

> narrow, strict spirit in parent's household, many commands and prohibitions. Saul accepts the necessity of it, he wants to be good, but he reaches the contrary. A tendency toward the forbidden because it is forbidden. By his own choice and by parental will, he is destined to take up the profession of a rabbi … a man of will, [yet] a man of contrast: a) weakly, sick, often uncertain, yet able to accomplish, tough; b) depressive, yet self-confident, absolute, authoritarian; c) emotional softness (compassion, sympathy, love, enthusiasm), yet hard (judgmental, consistent, stiff). No saint, a man of contradiction, but also mighty in his failures. All his life he had to fight with himself and does so. (Barth 1993b, 555–557)

Drawing a psychological profile of this kind had been important to Barth prior to 1915. Cultivating such insights was part of the hermeneutical process of feeling one's way into an author. On the basis of these kinds of insights, one could begin to establish an inner relationship, immerse oneself in his thought-world and piety, and thereby begin to see what Paul saw and to experience what he experienced. Of course, Barth was not alone in discussing Paul along these lines at the time. There were many leaders of what Barth called the "dominant science of biblical exegesis" who approached Paul in this way.

Yet, given his interest in these matters throughout this period, it is striking to see the total lack of interest in such observations in Barth's writings *after* his break with liberalism. Indeed, given his hermeneutical commitments and all that he had said about the importance of empathy, of identifying with Paul, of immersing oneself in his thought-world and piety, of establishing an inner relationship, and so on, Barth's comments about Paul after 1915 are remarkable. In his preface to Rom I, he states: "The mighty voice of Paul was new to me" (Barth 1933, 2). In various preface drafts for Rom I, unpublished until 1985 (Barth 1985, 581–602) and made available in English only recently (Burnett 2004, 277–292), he describes the voice of Paul as "strange." Far from achieving a depth of familiarity with Paul, Barth describes Paul as anything but familiar. During this period he wrote to Thurneysen:

> How many there may have been before me who after a heated struggle with all these puzzling words have thought the task was "finished," until they (the words) look at the next exegete just as mysteriously. During the work it was often as though something was

blowing on me from afar, from Asia Minor or Corinth, something very ancient, early oriental, indefinably bright, wild, original, that somehow is hidden beneath these sentences and is so ready to let itself be drawn forth by ever new generations. *Paul* – what a man he must have been, and what men also those for whom he could so sketch and hint at these pithy things in a few muddled fragments! I often shudder in such company. The Reformers, even Luther, are *far* from the stature of *Paul*; only now has that become convincingly clear to me. And *behind Paul*: what realities those must have been that could set this man in motion in *such* a way! What a lot of farfetched stuff we compile then in commentary on his words, of which perhaps 99 percent of their real content eludes us! (Barth and Thurneysen 1973, 236)

Barth described his encounter with Paul as the great turning point of his life. Yet it was not Paul himself, Paul the man, or Paul as such, but the *subject matter* to which Paul's words bore witness that Barth claims was decisive: what Paul said about God, revelation, and Jesus Christ. To be sure, even in these matters what was decisive was not what Paul said *in abstracto*, but *in relationship* to man and his salvation; that is, about God and the nature of faith, grace, sin, judgment, death, life, and so on. In any case, it was not what Barth discovered *in* Paul or even *about* Paul, but what he discovered *with* Paul, in the strictest sense, that proved ultimately decisive.

Still, Paul the man, Paul the individual, Paul the religious personality, had deeply disturbed Barth and had been the instrument – or, rather, the chosen *witness* – for his theological conversion. And this experience had profound methodological implications for Barth. (For an elaboration of this topic, see Burnett 2004.) In describing some of these implications in his preface drafts to Rom I, Barth provides many insights into his encounter with Paul. For example, in one early preface draft, he writes:

The task of understanding Paul verse by verse has been enough of an assault upon my and the whole of today's thought and sensibilities. But, of course, I wanted to *understand*, not *misunderstand* Paul. Here I am forced to indicate with a few sentences the chasm which separates me from the method of today's dominant science of the biblical exegesis. To understand an author means for me mainly to *stand with him*, to take each of his words in earnest, so long as it is not proven that he does not deserve this trust, to participate with him in the subject matter ... But today's theology does not stand with the prophets and the apostles; it does not side with them but rather with the modern reader and his prejudices; it does not take the prophets and apostles in earnest, instead, while it stands smiling sympathetically beside them or above them, it takes up a cool and indifferent distance from them; it critically or merrily examines the historical-psychological surface and misses its meaning. That is what I have against it. When I speak about "standing by an author" I mean beginning with the presupposition that what once was a serious problem, is still one today and that, conversely, the problems with which we are concerned today, if they are really serious problems and not merely fads, must be the same as those with which the notable people of all times have wrestled. The decisive prerequisite for the interpretation of a text for me therefore is participation in its *subject matter*. No historical meticulousness and no art of empathy [*Einfühlungskunst*] and no trip to the Orient can offer even the slightest substitute for this participation. (Burnett 2004, 284)

Though Barth never published these remarks, they were remarkably perceptive in anticipating the sort of reception his *Römerbrief* would receive. They also tell us a great deal about his understanding of the exegetical task, especially when compared to his prior understanding. He now sees, for example, the limitations of the "art of empathy," the temptations of not standing *with an author* but "smiling sympathetically beside [him] or above" him, and the significance of what readers bring to the exegetical task. He is no longer satisfied with examining "the historical-psychological surface." He admits: "The task of understanding Paul verse by verse has been enough of an assault upon my and the whole of today's thought and sensibilities." The point here is that *after* 1915 and throughout his *Römerbrief* period, Barth says nothing whatsoever about attaining or having attained personal intimacy with Paul. Rather, he stresses how utterly "distant" and "removed" we are from Paul the man, Paul the religious personality (Burnett 2004, 287). To the extent we know anything about Paul's personality at all, Barth says one gets the impression that Paul, like other figures in the Bible, may personally have been an insufferable eccentric (Barth 1978b, 78).

The figure of Paul in some ways grew increasingly enigmatic to Barth as he wrote his *Römerbrief*. Barth made this point publicly for the first time when he was asked to give an address in 1920, which he entitled "Biblical Questions, Insights, and Vistas." Here Barth concedes that there are many similarities between the figures in the Bible and those of other ancient religions and cultures, but questions remain:

> How could any one be capable of thinking such a chapter as the fifteenth of First Corinthians and putting it down on paper? What sort of public was it of whom the devotional reading of epistles of the caliber of Romans or Hebrews was evidently once expected? What conception of God and of the world was it which made it possible for men to refuse to accept the Old and New Testaments upon the same basis, but to understand one in the light of the other? (Barth 1978b, 62)

What we encounter in the Bible is all very curious indeed. What kind of extraordinary events lie behind the texts? What could possibly have moved individuals to say and do such peculiar things?

> We all know the curiosity that comes over us when from a window we see the people in the street suddenly stop and look up – shade their eyes with their hands and look straight up into the sky toward something which is hidden from us by the roof. Our curiosity is superfluous, for what they see is doubtless an aeroplane. But as to the sudden stopping, looking up, and tense attention characteristic of the people of the Bible, our wonder will not be so lightly dismissed. (Barth 1978b, 62)

And here Barth recalls the circumstances surrounding the great turning point of his life:

> To me personally it came first with Paul: this man evidently sees and hears something which is above everything, which is absolutely beyond the range of my observation and the measure of my thought. Let me place myself as I will to ... that [which] he insists in enigmatical words that he sees and hears, I am still taken by the fact that he ... is eye and ear in a state which expressions such as inspiration, alarm, or stirring or overwhelming emotion, do not satisfactorily describe. I seem to see within so transparent a piece of literature a personality who is actually thrown out of his course and out of every ordinary

course by seeing and hearing what I for my part do not see and hear – who is, so to speak, captured, in order to be dragged as a prisoner from land to land for strange, intense, uncertain, and yet mysteriously well-planned service.

And if I ever come to fear lest mine is a case of self-hallucination, one glance at the secular events of those times, one glance at the widening circle of ripples in the pool of history, tells me of a certainty that a stone of unusual weight must have been dropped into deep water there somewhere – tells me that, among all the hundreds of peripatetic preachers and miracle-workers from the Near East who in that day must have gone along the same Appian Way into imperial Rome, it was this one Paul, seeing and hearing what he did, who was the cause, if not of all, yet of the most important developments in that city's future. (Barth 1978b, 62–63)

Barth's Conflict with the Guild over Paul

Barth knew his *Römerbrief* would not be well received by members of "the dominant science of biblical exegesis" and anticipated many of their criticisms. This is clear from his preface drafts. Here, briefly, is an example:

One should not seek in this book what is not intentionally stated there – especially all that which I would characterize as "*antiquarian.*" Whoever, for instance, wants to be informed about the little one knows and the great amount one does not know about the personality of Paul, about the composition of the Roman, Christian church, about Pauline "formulas" in the context of the history of religions, or about the questions of authenticity which become particularly acute at the end of the letter, will be disappointed here. I have dared confidently to be quiet about these matters, for as interesting in my opinion as they are, they are not really important questions for understanding the text itself, questions which can be and should be considered, but their discussion should by no means, as has occurred, replace explication itself. Whoever insists upon knowing *about* Paul and his letter, will find – according to need, direction, and taste – better things than I could ever write in B. Weiss, Godet, Lipsius, Jülicher, Lietzmann and Zahn. I think I have offered instead a few things *from* Paul which are not found in the books of these scholars. (Burnett 2004, 278)

Instead of publishing one of his early, more polemical preface drafts, Barth published a much shorter, more irenic preface that contained only a few brief remarks about his exegetical method. It began:

Paul, as a child of his age, addressed his contemporaries. It is, however, far more important that, as Prophet and Apostle of the Kingdom of God, he veritably speaks to all men of every age. The differences between then and now, there and here, no doubt require careful investigation and consideration. But ... these differences are, in fact, purely trivial. The historical-critical method of Biblical investigation has its rightful place: it is concerned with the preparation of the intelligence – and this can never be superfluous. But, were I driven to choose between it and the venerable doctrine of Inspiration, I should without hesitation adopt the latter, which has a broader, deeper, more important justification. The doctrine of Inspiration is concerned with the labour of apprehending, without which no technical equipment, however complete, is of any use whatever. Fortunately, I am not compelled to choose between the two. Nevertheless, my whole energy of interpreting has been expended in an endeavour to see through and beyond history into the spirit of the Bible, which is the Eternal Spirit ... If we rightly understand ourselves, our problems are the problems of Paul; and if we be enlightened by the brightness of his answers, those answers must be ours. (Barth 1933, 1)

Barth said he wrote his commentary with a "joyful sense of discovery" and concluded: "The mighty voice of Paul was new to me: and if to me, no doubt to many others also" (1933, 2). But this did not ameliorate the onslaught of criticism that Barth had rightly anticipated.

Several reviewers asked whether it should even be called a commentary. They could not fathom how Barth could say the things he said in the name of an "exegesis" of Paul's Romans. Adolf Jülicher, one of the most esteemed New Testament scholars of his day, called Barth a gnostic, a "pneumatic," an Alexandrian ("this is exactly the standpoint of Origen"; Jülicher 1968, 72–81). With Karl Ludwig Schmidt, he likened Barth to Marcion. Others echoed Jülicher's charges in calling Barth a "gnostic" and "Neo-Paulinist." Carl Mennicke said the commentary was the product of sheer "dogmatism"; Rudolf Steinmetz, of "impressionistic" tendencies; and Philipp Bachmann, of "enthusiasm" and "pneumatic-prophetic exegesis."

The most eminent Swiss reviewer of Rom I, Paul Wernle, Professor of New Testament and Church History at Basel, renowned liberal churchman and author of several books on Paul, charged that Barth was a "biblicist"; he simply could not understand how Barth could interpret Paul so uncritically, so sympathetically, with so much *Kongenialität* (Wernle 1919, 169). Wernle admitted, with respect to his own interpretation of Paul: "I know I do not have the whole Paul on my side, nor do I even want that. I want to hold on to that which speaks to my heart and conscience, to that which is eternal in [Paul's] message." But to do so, Wernle insisted, "I must distinguish and choose" (1919, 168). But this, he said, is precisely what Barth had refused to do. For example,

When Paul writes: "our salvation is nearer than when we first believed," Barth does not have the slightest feeling of unease that almost nineteen centuries have passed and the hoped for salvation has not yet come; on the contrary, Barth manages to carry readers – without their knowledge – happily beyond this cliff. Everything between Paul and his exegete remains in harmony ... There is absolutely no point in the thought of Paul that he finds uncomfortable ... not even the most modest remnant conditioned by the history of the times is left over. (1919, 169)

In short, the most consistent charge made against Barth was that he had not done justice to the "real," "historical" Paul. As powerful, illuminating, and insightful as his commentary was, it had been written at the expense of Paul's actual historical context. Several declared that Barth had done "violence" to Paul. Wernle said, "If Barth had not so contemptuously ignored the historical background of *Romans* he would not have gone so thoroughly wrong" (Wernle 1919, 167). Barth, it was charged, was a "bitter enemy of historical criticism" (Barth 1933, 9). Jülicher warned:

He who despises the past because only he who is alive is right cannot gain anything from the past. He who in holy egoism thinks only of his own problems and chides the dead, who can no longer answer him, can surely not demand that a product of the past – as the Letter to the Romans most surely is – should become alive for him. (Jülicher 1968, 81)

The problem, as Carl Mennicke described it, was that Barth did not make "the least attempt to deal with the difficulties of modern consciousness" (Mennicke 1920, 6). Wilhelm Loew said that the problem with Barth's approach was that one has "intensive experience without any feeling of distance" (Loew 1920, 586). The consensus among reviewers of Rom I was that it was the product of too much eisegesis, that Barth had simply read too much of the present, too much of his own situation, into the text. Many concluded that Barth's commentary said more about Barth than it did about Paul.

Barth was not happy with most of the two dozen or so reviews of Rom I. But neither was he discouraged. He knew he had struck a nerve and quickly went to work on a second edition (hereafter cited as Rom II). And because most of the reviewers had commented specifically on his preface, Barth decided he would not follow the advice of his most trusted advisers, Thurneysen and Barth's wife, Nelly, who had advised him against publishing a longer preface the first time. This time he would come out swinging.

Barth's "pugnacious preface" (Barth 1982, 265) to Rom II begins with a Greek phrase from Galatians 1:17: "not up to Jerusalem ... but away into Arabia," which reflected not only his identification with Paul but the fact that he too considered himself somewhat of an outsider who had not consulted the guild with everything he had said or was about to say. Before treating the questions about "influences" that preoccupied many reviewers of Rom I, Barth announced that his second edition reflected "First, and most important: the continued study of Paul himself" (Barth 1933, 3). He then turned his sights onto Jülicher and denied the charge that he was a "bitter enemy of historical criticism." Barth claimed:

> I have nothing whatever to say against historical criticism. I recognize it, and once more state quite definitely that it is both necessary and justified. My complaint is that recent commentators confine themselves to an interpretation of the text which seems to me to be no commentary at all, but merely the first step towards a commentary. Recent commentaries contain no more than a reconstruction of the text, a rendering of the Greek words and phrases by their precise equivalents, a number of additional notes in which archaeological and philological material is gathered together, and a more or less plausible arrangement of the subject-matter in such a manner that it may be made historically and psychologically intelligible from the standpoint of pure pragmatism. (1933, 6)

Barth said he gratefully acknowledged his indebtedness to "historians" for their "preliminary effort" to understand Paul and "never dreamed of doing anything else than sit attentively at [their] feet" (1933, 6–7). But what he found astonishing was the modesty of their claims, particularly with respect to interpreting Paul:

> For example, place the work of Jülicher side by side with that of Calvin: how energetically Calvin, having first established what stands in the text, sets himself to re-think the whole material and to wrestle with it, till the walls which separate the sixteenth century from the first become transparent! Paul speaks, and the man of the sixteenth century hears. The conversation between the original record and the reader moves round the subject-matter, until a distinction between yesterday and to-day becomes impossible. If a man persuades

himself that Calvin's method can be dismissed with the old-fashioned motto, "The Compulsion of Inspiration", he betrays himself as one who has never worked upon the interpretation of Scripture. Taking Jülicher's work as typical of much modern exegesis, we observe how closely he keeps to the mere deciphering of words as though they were runes. But, when all is done, they still remain largely unintelligible. How quick he is, without any real struggling with the raw material of the Epistle, to dismiss this or that difficult passage as simply a peculiar doctrine or opinion of Paul! How quick he is to treat a matter as explained, when it is said to belong to the religious thought, feeling, experience, conscience, or conviction, – of Paul! And, when this does not at once fit, or is manifestly impossible, how easily he leaps, like some bold William Tell, right out of the Pauline boat, and rescues himself by attributing what Paul has said, to his "personality", to the experience on the road to Damascus (an episode which seem capable of providing at any moment an explanation of every impossibility), to later Judaism, to Hellenism, or, in fact, to any exegetical semi-divinity of the ancient world! (1933, 7–8)

Barth is critiquing historicism and psychologism here, the two main tools in modernity used to reduce theological claims to matters of mere history or psychology. Barth finds it ironic that the very ones who approach Paul in this way would claim that he, Barth, had done "violence" to Paul, for if anyone was doing violence to Paul, it was them. It is also on such grounds that Barth claims: "the modern pictures of Paul are for me and a number of others no longer at all believable even historically" (Barth 1968, 95).

"In contrast to all this," Barth said, "the historical critics must be *more critical* to suit me!" He insists on "using all the crowbars and wrecking tools needed to achieve *relevant* treatment of the text" and to establish "what is there." But interpretation, if worthy of the name, cannot stop with this "first primitive attempt at paraphrase."

For how "what is there" is to be understood cannot be established by an appreciation of the words and phrases of the text, strewn in from time to time from some fortuitous standpoint of the exegete, but only through an entering, as freely and eagerly as practicable, into the inner tension of the concepts presented by the text with more or less clarity. (1968, 93)

And then Barth made the most provocative claim of his *Römerbrief* period:

Krinein [to discern] means for me, in reference to a historical document, the measuring of all the words and phrases contained in it by the matter of which it, unless everything is deceptive, is clearly speaking, and the relating to the questions it unmistakably poses all the answers given, and relating these again to the cardinal question, which contains all questions, the question of the meaning of everything that it says in the light of that which is all that *can* be said, and therefore really is all that *is* said. As little as possible should be left over of those blocks of merely historical, merely given, merely accidental concepts; as far as possible the connection of the words to the Word in the words must be disclosed. As one who would understand, I must press forward to the point where insofar as possible I confront the riddle of the *subject matter* and no longer merely the riddle of the *document* as such, where I can almost forget that I am not the author, where I have almost understood him so well that I let him speak in my name, and can myself speak in his name. (Barth 1968, 93)

What struck reviewers as most provocative was Barth's claim, "I must press forward to the point ... where I can almost forget that I am not the author, where I have almost understood him so well that I let him speak in my name, and can myself speak in his name." To some, this sounded like Schleiermacher's goal of trying "to understand an author better than he understands himself." To others, it only confirmed that Barth really was a "mystic" or "pneumatic." Barth had a habit of affirming statements of his opponents (particularly their criticisms) only to "up the ante," so to speak, and negate them. He could affirm the approach of the hermeneutical tradition of Schleiermacher as far as it went. But the sort of contemporaneity Barth sought with Paul could not be achieved by such means, that is, by any hermeneutical skill, "historical meticulousness," or "art of empathy." Nor did Barth, despite the fact that he was credited for launching it, place any stock in the methods of the "pneumatic exegesis" movement throughout the 1920s (Burnett 2004, 26–29).

Turning to Wernle's complaint that "there is absolutely no point in the thought of Paul that he finds uncomfortable ... not even the most modest remnant conditioned by the history of the times is left over," Barth lists the things Wernle thought should have been left over as "uncomfortable points" and "relics of the past": "the Pauline 'depreciation' of the earthly life of Jesus – Christ the Son of God – Redemption by the blood of Christ – Adam and Christ – Paul's use of the Old Testament – his so-called 'Baptismal-Sacramentalism' – the Double Predestination – his attitude to secular authority" (Barth 1933, 11–12). Barth then asks:

> Now, imagine a commentary on the Epistle to the Romans which left these eight points unexplained; which allowed them to "remain uncomfortable points"; and in which a maze of contemporary parallels did duty for an explanation of them. Could such a commentary really be called an interpretation? In contrast with this comfortable dismissal of uncomfortable points it has been my "Biblicism" which has compelled me to wrestle with these "scandals to modern thought" until I have found myself able to undertake the interpretation of them, because I have discovered precisely in these points the characteristic and veritable discernment of Paul. Whether I have interpreted them correctly is, of course, another matter. There are passages in the Epistle which I still find very hard to understand. But I concede much more to Wernle than this. Strictly speaking, no single verse seems to me capable of a smooth interpretation. There "remains" everywhere, more or less in the background, that which subtly escapes both understanding and interpretation, or which, at least, awaits further investigation. But this cannot be thought of as a "residuum" simply to be put on one side or disregarded. (Barth 1933, 12)

Barth denies any "privileging" of Paul, and claims he would approach Lao-Tzu or Goethe with the same " 'Biblicist' method – which means in the end no more than 'consider well' " – if it were his job to interpret Lao-Tzu or Goethe (1933, 12). But given what we have, Barth says, "it is strange how utterly harmless and unexceptionable most commentaries on the Epistle to the Romans and most books about Paul are. Why should this be so? Perhaps because the uncomfortable points are treated according to Wernle's recipe" (1933, 13).

Reviews of Rom II were as critical as those of the first, and, once again, it was the preface that drew the most attention. The two most notable reviewers were Adolf

Schlatter, Barth's former teacher in Tübingen, and Rudolf Bultmann, who had stated in an earlier review that Rom I was the product of "enthusiastic revivalism." In July 1922, Barth responded to them in the preface to the third edition, which was "an essentially unaltered reprinting" of Rom II. Barth expressed appreciation for the "friendly reception" given it by Bultmann and "its equally friendly rejection by Schlatter" (Barth 1933, 16). Though Barth said he felt more nearly related to the "positive theology" of the former, he noted Schlatter's complaint that "Barth joins the long list of exegetes of the early church and the Reformation who read the Letter to the Romans under the domination of the then-current theory of inspiration" (Schlatter 1968, 122). Barth admitted: "from the preface to the first edition onwards, I have never attempted to conceal the fact that my manner of interpretation has certain affinities with the old doctrine of Verbal Inspiration. As expounded by Calvin, the doctrine seems to me at least worthy of careful consideration" (Barth 1933, 18).

Yet Barth devoted most of his preface to Bultmann's criticism that he had not seemed to recognize that Paul did not always speak "from the subject matter itself." Rather, Bultmann said, "In [Paul] there are other spirits speaking besides the *pneuma Christou* [Spirit of Christ]" (Bultmann 1968, 120). Once again, as with Wernle, Barth was accused of sticking too closely with Paul and not being "radical" enough. Barth responded:

> I do not wish to engage in a controversy with Bultmann as to which of us is the more radical. But I must go farther than he does and say that there are in the Epistle no words at all which are not words of those "other spirits" which he calls Jewish or Popular Christian or Hellenistic or whatever else they may be. Is it really legitimate to extract a certain number of passages and claim that there the veritable Spirit of Christ has spoken? Or, to put it another way, can the Spirit of Christ be thought of as standing in the Epistle side by side with "other" spirits and in competition with them? It seems to me impossible to set the Spirit of Christ – the veritable subject-matter of the Epistle – over against other spirits, in such a manner as to deal out praise to some passages, and to depreciate others where Paul is not controlled by his true subject-matter. (Barth 1933, 16–17)

Barth is not rejecting Bultmann's claim that he discerns "a Word within the words," the divine within the human, the "Spirit of Christ" – the real subject matter of Paul's text – within the voice of "other spirits" that, no doubt, reflect what is cultural, ethnic, psychological, sociological, and so on. What Barth rejects is Bultmann's assumption that he knows, and knows clearly, at particular points the difference between the two, and that on such a basis he can "praise" certain passages and "depreciate" others. Barth wonders where Bultmann's criterion for such a *Sachkritik* comes from. He questions the standpoint from which Bultmann, who had joined the chorus of critics who said Barth had done "violence to the Letter to the Romans and to Paul" (cf. Bultmann 1968, 119), thinks he can play off the "Spirit of Christ" against "other spirits" and separate the wheat from the chaff, so to speak. Is such a standpoint possible only when taken *above* the Word rather than *under* it? Where has he gained such "pneumatic" powers of discernment? And, here again, Barth manifests his habit of "upping the ante" when he says that not just *some* of what Paul says but "everything" comes from these "other spirits." In other words, Paul is not only a man who speaks human words, but a man who speaks *only* human words that are as culturally conditioned as any others. But this is hardly the point, given the crisis to which Paul's words bear witness.

> Rather, it is for us to perceive and to make clear that the whole is placed under the KRISIS of the Spirit of Christ. The whole is litera, that is, voices of those other spirits. The problem is whether the whole must not be understood in relation to the true subject-matter which is – The Spirit of Christ. This is the problem which provides aim and purpose to our study of the litera. (Barth 1933, 17)

This leads Barth to state one of his most important hermeneutical principles:

> The question is whether or no [the exegete] is to place himself in a relation to his author of utter loyalty. Is he to read him, determined to follow him to the very last word, wholly aware of what he is doing, and assuming that the author also knew what he was doing? Loyalty surely cannot end at a particular point, and certainly cannot be exhausted by an exposure of the author's literary affinities. Anything short of utter loyalty means a commentary ON Paul's Epistle to the Romans, not a commentary so far as is possible WITH him – even to his last word. True exegesis involves, of course, much sweat and many groans. Even so, the extent to which the commentator will be able to disclose the Spirit of Christ in his reading of Paul will not be everywhere the same. But ... he will not let himself be bewildered by the voices of those other spirits, which so often render inaudible the dominant tones of the Spirit of Christ. He will, moreover, always be willing to assume that, when he fails to understand, the blame is his and not Paul's. Nor will he rest content until paradoxically he has seen the whole in the fragments, and has displayed the fragments in the context of the veritable subject-matter, so that all the other spirits are seen in some way or other to serve the Spirit of Christ. (Barth 1933, 17)

Barth does not deny the difficulty of maintaining a relationship of loyalty with Paul. Nor does he deny that such loyalty to Paul's words requires the unavoidable "criticism of the letter by the spirit," that certain ideas in the individual words of the text be "expanded" while others are "contracted" (cf. 1933, 18–19). What Barth rejects and regards as "irresponsible" is the approach of those who are willing to write *with* Paul so long as everything is clear, but to write *about* Paul when things are not. Rather, Barth insists: "I cannot, for my part, think it possible for an interpreter honestly to reproduce the meaning of any author unless he dares to accept the condition of utter loyalty. To make an oration over a man means to speak over his body, and that is to bury him finally, deeper and without hope, in his grave." Again, Barth does not underestimate the difficulty of maintaining a relationship of faithfulness with Paul: "Indeed, there are many historical personages whom it is possible only to speak ABOUT ... In any case, I am completely unable to understand Bultmann's demand that I should mingle fire and water. He asks me to think and write WITH Paul ... and then suddenly, when the whole becomes too hopelessly bizarre, I am to turn round and write 'critically' ABOUT him and against him" (1933, 18).

Conclusion

It is not possible to discuss the nuances of Barth's understanding of a "relationship of faithfulness" (*Treueverhältnis*) in the space of this chapter, but it is worth noting that maintaining such a relationship is not only one of his most important hermeneutical principles, but also one of the most important aspects of his relationship to Paul. Barth's loyalty to Paul, his determination "to stand and to fall" with Paul's words, his refusal to play Paul's "schoolmaster" (Barth 1933, 19), was one of the sources of greatest criticism of Barth throughout his *Römerbrief* period and his entire career. But despite such criticism, Barth's fidelity to Paul and his commitment to studying his letters was unwavering.

This is not to say that Barth ever presumed familiarity with Paul. In commenting on Romans 1:1 ("Paul, a servant of Jesus Christ, called to be an apostle"), Barth began both editions of his *Römerbrief* by quoting Friedrich Zündel's statement that Paul is "no genius rejoicing in his own creative ability" (Barth 1919, 1). Barth notes in both editions that Paul is "a servant, not a master," and that his task or calling is not self-chosen. In Rom II he adds: "However great and important a man Paul may have been, the essential theme of his mission is not within him but above him – unapproachably distant and utterly strange. His call to apostleship is not a familiar episode in his own personal history: 'The call to be an apostle is a paradoxical occurrence, lying always beyond his personal self-identity' (Kierkegaard)" (Barth 1933, 27). Kierkegaard proved helpful to Barth in articulating the problem of approaching Paul merely as a religious personality, genius, or hero. To Barth, what Kierkegaard said about Abraham applied equally to Paul: "I *think* myself *into* the hero; I cannot think myself into Abraham; when I reach that eminence, I sink down, for what is offered me is a paradox" (Kierkegaard 1983, 33). But Barth discovered this not by reading Kierkegaard, but by his own personal engagement with Paul. And Paul remained forever mysterious to Barth and full of surprises. While conducting a Bible study on 1 Corinthians 15 in November 1919, he remarked in a letter to Thurneysen that some of Paul's "remarkably profound disclosures ... have struck us recently like shocks from an electric eel" (Barth and Thurneysen 1973, 350). There are other examples of such surprise in Barth's correspondence.

Yet to say that Paul continued to "interest" Barth is an understatement. Indeed, it is to trivialize the relationship (cf. Barth 1933, 145–146). Barth's thought continued to be decisively shaped by Paul beyond his *Römerbrief* period. He remained the village pastor of Safenwil while writing both editions of his *Römerbrief*. Throughout this time, he studied Paul's epistles intensely, held Bible studies, and preached several sermon series on them. But in October 1921, he left Safenwil to become the first appointee to a new honorary chair in Reformed Theology at the University of Göttingen. He had neither a doctorate nor any academic credential to qualify him as a "Reformed theologian." He later admitted: "at that time I did not even possess the Reformed confessional writings, and had certainly never read them, quite apart from other horrendous gaps in my knowledge ... Fortunately my theology, such as it had been, was more Reformed and Calvinistic than I realized" (Barth 1981, 156). But he was chosen because of his commitment to biblical exegesis: Rom I had suggested he "was passionately concerned with Holy Scripture" (Barth 1963, preface).

It is not widely known that though Barth was appointed to teach Reformed doctrine, nearly half the courses he taught at Göttingen were courses in biblical exegesis. While the bulk of his teaching load was in historical or dogmatic theology (typically three or four hours per week), every semester until the summer of 1925, he taught a one-hour course in New Testament exegesis; for example, on Ephesians, Colossians, 1 Corinthians, Philippians, James, 1 John, and the Sermon on the Mount. No one asked Barth to teach these courses; he did so on his own initiative. Given the depth of study he had undertaken as a pastor, Barth probably felt that these were the courses he was most qualified to teach. Because he was an honorary professor of Reformed theology, students were not obliged to take his courses. But his exegesis courses became very popular and not only more so than his others, but more so than many of the courses of his colleagues. This did not endear Barth to his colleagues. In fact, they ridiculed his "first-rate *Bibelstunden* for the educated" and considered him more a preacher than a scholar. Yet it is obvious that Barth "did more than *just empty* their lecture halls" because of his appeal as a preacher (Barth and Thurneysen 1974, 364), for when he was invited by the University of Münster to take a teaching position on July 22, 1925, it was as Professor of Dogmatics *and* New Testament Exegesis, which he assumed until 1930.

To what may we attribute Barth's "interest" in biblical exegesis? Barth said it had to do with the central subject matter, content, and theme of the Bible, namely, God! But clearly among the penultimate reasons was Paul. Barth, who often expressed regret to Thurneysen that he had not arranged more time for his exegesis courses, wrote on May 18, 1924, only two weeks into the new semester: "What delights *me* most is the course on *The Epistle to the Philippians* on Wednesdays ... Paul! That's what it is! Next to him all dogmatics is slime, and ethics too" (Barth and Thurneysen 1974, 252–253).

References

Barth, Karl. 1919. *Der Römerbrief.* Bern: Bäschlin.
Barth, Karl. 1933. *Epistle to the Romans.* London: Oxford University Press.
Barth, Karl. 1963. *Der Romerbrief: Unveranderte Nachdruck der ersten Auflage von 1919.* Zürich: Evangelischer Verlag Zürich.
Barth, Karl. 1968. Foreword to the Second Edition. Pages 88–99 in *The Beginnings of Dialectic Theology.* Volume 1. Edited by James M. Robinson. Richmond: John Knox.
Barth, Karl. 1978a. The Strange New World within the Bible. Pages 28–50 in Karl Barth, *The Word of God and the Word of Man.* Gloucester, Mass.: Peter Smith.
Barth, Karl. 1978b. Biblical Questions, Insights, and Vistas. Pages 51–96 in Karl Barth, *The Word of God and the Word of Man.* Gloucester, Mass.: Peter Smith.
Barth, Karl. 1981. Autobiographical Sketches of Karl Barth from the Faculty Albums of the Faculties of Evangelical Theology at Münster (1927) and Bonn (1935 and 1946). Pages 150–157 in *Karl Barth–Rudolf Bultmann Letters 1922–1966.* Grand Rapids: Eerdmans.
Barth, Karl. 1982. Concluding Unscientific Postscript on Schleiermacher. Pages 261–279 in *The Theology of Schleiermacher: Lectures at Göttingen, Winter Semester of 1923/24.* Grand Rapids: Eerdmans.

Barth, Karl. 1985. *Der Römerbrief (Erste Fassung) 1919*. Edited by Hermann Schmidt. Zürich: Theologischer Verlag Zürich.

Barth, Karl. 1987. *Konfirmandenunterricht, 1909–1921*. Edited by Jürgen Fangmeier. Zürich: Theologischer Verlag Zürich.

Barth, Karl. 1993a. Der christliche Glaube und die Geschichte (1910). Pages 155–212 in *Vorträge und kleinere Arbeiten, 1909–1914*. Edited by Hans-Anton Drewes and Hinrich Stoevesandt. Zürich: Theologischer Verlag Zürich.

Barth, Karl. 1993b. Paulus. Pages 555–557 in *Vorträge und kleinere Arbeiten, 1909–1914*. Edited by Hans-Anton Drewes and Hinrich Stoevesandt. Zürich: Theologischer Verlag Zürich.

Barth, Karl, and Eduard Thurneysen. 1973. *Briefwechsel*, Volume 1: *1913–1921*; 1974. Volume 2: *1921–1930*. Edited by Eduard Thurneysen. Zürich: Theologischer Verlag Zürich.

Bultmann, Rudolf. 1968. Karl Barth's *Epistle to the Romans* in its Second Edition. Pages 100–120 in *The Beginnings of Dialectic Theology*. Volume 1. Edited by James M. Robinson. Richmond: John Knox.

Burnett, Richard E. 2004. *Karl Barth's Theological Exegesis: The Hermeneutical Principles of the Römerbrief Period*. Grand Rapids: Eerdmans.

Jülicher, Adolf. 1968. A Modern Interpreter of Paul. Pages 72–81 in *The Beginnings of Dialectic Theology*. Volume 1. Edited by James M. Robinson. Richmond: John Knox.

Kierkegaard, Søren. 1983. *Fear and Trembling. Repetition*. Princeton: Princeton University Press.

Loew, Wilhelm. 1920. Noch einmal Barths Römerbrief. *Die christliche Welt* 34: 585–587.

Mennicke, Carl. 1920. Auseinandersetzung mit Karl Barth. *Blätter für religiösen Sozialismus* 2: 5–8.

Schlatter, Adolf. 1968. Karl Barth's Epistle to the Romans. Pages 121–125 in *The Beginnings of Dialectic Theology*. Volume 1. Edited by James M. Robinson. Richmond: John Knox.

Wernle, Paul. 1919. Der Römerbrief in neuer Beleuchtung. *Kirchenblatt für die reformierte Schweiz* 34: 163–164, 167–169.

CHAPTER 28

Recent Continental Philosophers

P. Travis Kroeker

Where is the one who is wise? Where is the scribe? Where is the debater of this age? Has not God made foolish the wisdom of the world? ... But God chose what is foolish in the world to shame the wise; God chose what is weak in the world to shame the strong; God chose what is low and despised in the world, things that are not, to reduce to nothing things that are ... (1 Cor 1:20, 27–28)[1]

What might this confounding messianic wisdom have to say to contemporary political philosophy? In *The Antichrist*, Nietzsche cites this passage at length to show how completely out of touch with reality the "dysangelist"[2] Paul really was. He calls Paul the greatest of all apostles of revenge, an insolent windbag who tried to confound worldly wisdom – but to no effect (1968, 624–626). Nietzsche notwithstanding, certain recent continental philosophers have been reading Paul the apostle's confounding letters to great effect, allowing his messianic message to disrupt certain modern conventions, political ontologies, and habits of mind; to challenge the technological globalizing wisdom and rulers of this age; and to suggest a hidden messianic counter-sovereignty not conceived in any human heart. Modern political theory has often regarded messianic political theology in particular as a dangerous threat to secular liberal democracy – and not without reason. Yet it is also the case that the first theory of the *saeculum* (i.e., the world of social and political life in which we live) in the West, Augustine's *City of God*, was developed precisely within a Pauline apocalyptic messianic understanding of history and the political. It is also the case that notions of neutral technology and juridical state sovereignty that underlie current conceptions

The Blackwell Companion to Paul, First Edition. Edited by Stephen Westerholm.
© 2011 Blackwell Publishing Ltd. Published 2011 by Blackwell Publishing Ltd.

and embodiments of the secular are themselves dangerously totalitarian, exclusivist, and violent, though often hidden beneath the veneer of progressivist liberal assumptions.

This is the position articulated in the apocalyptic messianism of Walter Benjamin, whose political theology is closely related to the Paul of the New Testament on the question of sovereignty, which is also the central focus of the philosophers I shall consider in this chapter. The political theological concept at the heart of modern secular politics and political theory was given its classical formulation by Carl Schmitt: "Sovereign is he who decides on the exception," a definition which requires that sovereignty be seen not in strictly juridical terms but as a limit concept: the sovereign is the agential power behind the law who decides on the "state of emergency" that suspends the normal rule of law (Schmitt 1985, 5–15).

Walter Benjamin had precisely this definition of sovereignty in mind when he wrote his Eighth Thesis on the philosophy of history:

> The tradition of the oppressed teaches us that the "state of emergency" in which we live is not the exception but the rule. We must attain to a conception of history that is in keeping with this insight. Then we shall clearly realize that it is our task to bring about a real state of emergency, and this will improve our position in the struggle against Fascism. One reason why Fascism has a chance is that in the name of progress its opponents treat it as a historical norm. The current amazement that the things we are experiencing are "still" possible in the twentieth century is *not* philosophical. This amazement is not the beginning of knowledge ... (Benjamin 1968, 257)

Benjamin sets himself against this secular progressivist politics to which all seeming political options are conformed, and he does so in the name of a "*weak* Messianic power": each day is to be lived as the day of judgment on which the Messiah comes, "not only as the redeemer" but also "as the subduer of Antichrist" (1968, 254–255 [theses II and VI]). Such a "Messianic time" may not be thought within the categories of historicism but only from the perspective of a "*Jetztzeit*" ("time of the now" [1968, 263; thesis XVIII]), a "real state of emergency" that calls into fundamental question the normal state of emergency – that is, the politics of modern secular state sovereignty – in which we live. It will bring into view the violent and destructive foundation of this sovereignty with its homogeneous and totalitarian order by remembering another sovereignty, a messianic counter-sovereignty that reorders the secular on completely different terms: terms compatible, argue certain recent continental philosophers, with Paul's gospel.

The apostle Paul stands in the messianic tradition of biblical political theology, where the central overriding claim is "Yahweh is sovereign," a claim that subverts any merely human claim to sovereignty and political authority. This includes, as Jacob Taubes points out, any claims for the sovereignty of law – whether that law be the Torah mediated by Moses, the *nomos* mediated by Greco-Roman philosophy, or the Christendom tradition of secular juridical state sovereignty and its many modern liberal copies. "We proclaim Christ [Messiah] crucified," says Paul, "a stumbling block to Jews and foolishness to Gentiles" (1 Cor 1:23). Paul's messianism will not accommodate conventional discourses of human mastery – which is to say, all conventional political discourses. In

contrast to the Weberian "secularization thesis" (influenced by Nietzsche) that interprets Paul's apocalyptic messianism as one of indifference to worldly conditions, recent
continental thinkers such as Alain Badiou, Stanislas Breton, Jacob Taubes, and Giorgio
Agamben interpret it as radically political, a challenge to the politics of conventional
human and especially national sovereignty.

Badiou and Breton

In 1994, Daniel Boyarin's *A Radical Jew* created a stir with his provocative analysis of
Paul in terms of "identity politics." Paul, claims Boyarin, challenges first-century
Judaism from within and offers an important radical critique of Jewish culture and
identity. Jews must therefore continue to wrestle with Paul's critique in Galatians 3:
"There is no longer Jew or Greek, there is no longer slave or free, there is no longer male
and female; for all of you are one in Christ Jesus" (Gal 3:28). Boyarin calls this "the
baptismal declaration of the new humanity of no difference" (1994, 5), of a messianic
universalism. This universalism is rooted in a Hellenized Judaism that seeks "an ideal
of a universal human essence, beyond difference and hierarchy" (1994, 7), predicated
upon a Platonic dualism of flesh and spirit in which flesh is particular (Jew/Greek,
male/female) and spirit is universal. This anthropological dualism is matched by a
hermeneutical dualism between fleshly Israel/law and the universal spiritual identity
of Christ and the church, leading to a spiritualized, allegorical reading of Scripture and
Torah. While Boyarin lauds Paul's impulse toward the founding of a universal, non-
hierarchical humanity, he laments many of its cultural-political effects, especially the
eradication of carnal particularities and the merging of all differences into a dominant
normative culture – namely, "Christendom." Paul's passion for equality and oneness
has led to the cultural essentialism of coercive sameness that denies all difference –
Jewish, female, and all "others."

The reading of Paul by the French philosopher Alain Badiou in his influential *Saint
Paul: The Foundation of Universalism* takes exactly the opposite view to that of Boyarin.
For Badiou, Paul's relevance for our contemporary political situation is precisely to
counter the relativism of postmodern identity politics, the multicultural consensus of
neo-liberal progressivism that has become conscripted to the globalized logic of capital
(2003, 9). In a context of relativized particular identities, the only common currency
is the abstract imperialist count (or calculus) of commercial and economic homogene-
ity – an empty universality that cashes out all communitarianisms. The beneficence of
contemporary French cosmopolitanism that gets worked up at the sight of a young
veiled woman (2003, 11) nicely displays this problem.

Into this political context, Badiou proposes the radical disruption of Paul's messianic
proclamation concerning the conditions for a "universal singularity" that defies the
globalizing logic of the count, with its prevailing juridical and economic abstractions.
It does so by an appeal to what Badiou calls an "evental truth" that reconfigures the
universal messianically. For Badiou, Paul is a "poet-thinker of the event," a militant
apostle of the truth procedure that neither constitutes nor claims authority from an
identity or a law.

What then is the founding event of Paul's gospel? It is, says Badiou, the resurrection – the resurrection as an incalculable rupturing event that founds a completely new subjectivity. In contrast to Boyarin's Paul, for Badiou, Paul's disposition is truly "diasporic" by being neither Jewish nor Greek (2003, 40–41). Both these terms belong to discourses of *mastery*: mastery either of the totality (Greek wisdom) or of a literal tradition and the deciphering of revealed signs (Jewish prophetism). As such, they are both "discourses of the Father" that bind communities in obedience (to cosmos, empire, God, or law). For Paul, by contrast, the messianic subject is founded by the messianic event as such, which, argues Badiou, "is a-cosmic and illegal, refusing integration into any totality and signaling nothing" (2003, 42). It cannot, therefore, be a logic of mastery. Rather it is a discourse of rupture, a discourse of the sending of the Son that is detached from every particularism and every form of mastery, including a synthesis or dialectic of the two (Jew-Greek or Greek-Jew). It is a discourse of "pure fidelity to the possibility opened by the event" (2003, 45), not a discourse of knowledge. It presumes utter dependence upon evental grace, a rupture that "properly speaking knows nothing" (cf. 1 Cor 8:2; 13:8).

The diasporic identity opened up by the resurrection event, then, is a non-identity that is indifferent to customary marks of traditional or community membership (Badiou 2003, 29), that abandons Jerusalem-centeredness (pp. 19, 34), and is therefore singularly universalizing in orientation. Paul's apostolic calling is characterized by "militant peregrinations" (p. 19), a "nomadic" leadership (p. 67) that is equally out of place everywhere, a "nomadism of gratuitousness" (p. 78) that exceeds every law and therefore disrupts every established identity and difference. Evental grace has a particular site, of course; but the "becoming subject"[3] that it founds is one that must "displace the experience historically, geographically, ontologically" (p. 99). It can do this, not by escaping the embodied particularity of customs and differences, but rather by "pass[ing] through them, within them" (p. 99). As Paul puts it: "I am free with respect to all ... I have become all things to all people" (1 Cor 9:19, 22).

For Badiou, then, Paul's messianic logic offers a critique of all onto-theologies, all discourses of mastery rooted in appeals to wisdom and power as divine attributes. It does this by making possible an advent of subjectivity as "becoming son," a process of messianic filiation rooted in the foolish and scandalous power of weakness (1 Cor 1:17–29). This means that, contra Nietzsche, such a messianic becoming may not become a subject discourse of glorification that builds a new economy of power and wisdom on the strength of the ineffable. Paul will not glory in his mystical visions or try to tell "things that cannot be told"; he will glory only in his weakness. "Paul firmly holds to the militant discourse of weakness ... It is not the singularity of the subject that validates what the subject says; it is what he says that founds the singularity of the subject" (2003, 53). But what is the "real content" of this "naked declaration" that is borne in militant weakness by messianic earthen vessels (p. 54)?

Here the continental clouds of fabulation begin to obscure the figure of the real, of the truth procedure that is in question. Badiou is deeply suspicious of any Christian appeal to the way of the cross. While he wants to insist on a Pauline "subjectivity of refuse" (cf. 1 Cor 4:13: "we have become, and are now, as the refuse of the world, the offscouring of all things" [RSV]), of abasement (2003, 56), this must be detached from any historical particularity that would make of Christ a "master" or an "example" (p. 60). The truth that founds the Christian subject is not a matter of historical content; it is a birth, a filiation in which subjects are founded equally and universally as "sons" insofar as they take up the work of filiation. For Badiou's Paul, it is the law that organizes life according to the dictates of death; messianic filiation, by contrast, dwells only in life: this is the meaning of the Resurrection (p. 62).

There are two worries here for Badiou. One is the danger of a "glorying in the cross" that stands for another form of Christian triumphalism – the coercive cross-bearing of Constantine and the crusades. Badiou also wants to de-mythologize evental grace, ironically, by removing the focus on the cross, which might lead to a morbid glorying in suffering and death (à la Mel Gibson). Suffering, he argues, cannot be redemptive, but is rather the law of the world that must be transfigured (pp. 66–67). Of course there is the cross, but for Badiou's Paul, there can be no "path of the Cross" (p. 67). The cross is but the evental site – namely, death – that must be left behind in the Christ-event itself, which is the resurrection. For Badiou, the significance of Christ's death is only to show that he is mortal – the evental message of grace is that a mortal can truly live. "Death here names a renunciation of transcendence. Let us say that Christ's death *sets up an immanentization of the spirit*" and "thereby constructs the site of our divine equality within humanity itself" (p. 69; emphasis in original). The resurrection, then, is the invention of a new life by humanity itself as a dynamic process of intersubjective self-realization. Like Nietzsche, Paul is militantly committed to the *"ja-sagende Frohlichkeit"* of human self-creation that affirms life in all its excessive multiplicity as a universal, gratuitous "yes." From the constrictive subjectivity of law, evental grace releases the "becoming subject" for creative, life-affirming action. Transcending without abandoning opinions, customs, and differences, it liberates humankind for the agency rooted in the universal address of love in all its superabundant particularity. The "benevolence" it shows "with regard to customs and opinions presents itself as *an indifference that tolerates differences*" (p. 99; emphasis in original).

Badiou finally proposes, not so much a Nietzschean Paul as a Feuerbachian-Marxist Paul (in his Prologue, he calls Paul the Lenin to Marx's Christ). That is, Badiou proposes a revolutionary materialist "becoming subject" in which the universal "species being" does not reside abstractly or transcendentally in every individual but becomes visible in the revolutionary praxis of human becoming in the "ensemble of the social relations" (cf. Marx 1978, 145). From a "contemplative materialism" of civil society made up of particular individualizing identities, Badiou's Paul helps articulate and bring into practice a "socialized humanity" in which all subjects are free and equal, creating the conditions for life beyond the alienations of suffering and death represented in modern state sovereignty and the globalizing abstractions of capital that individualize in order to colonize their subjects. By contrast, the oneness of Paul's messianic universalism is an ongoing historical truth process in which the sign of the One is the *"for all"* without exception (Badiou 2003, 76): in the messianic event, "all will be made alive" (1 Cor 15:22) in a revolution in which all differences are traversed indifferently (2003, 100) in such a manner that they themselves contribute to the melody of the true (p. 106).

While there is much to learn from this Leninist Paul, it remains trapped within an idealist humanism that is not material enough precisely because it sees the resurrection as the dissolution of the incarnation (Badiou 2003, 74); it leaves the cross behind as an unnecessary "downer" – hardly in keeping with the Pauline messianism of the New Testament! This is a new gnostic politics of fabulation that divides what Paul's messianism unites, namely, the cross and the resurrection. To show this, I turn to another contemporary French philosopher, singled out for special attention by Badiou in his ego-punctuated Prologue as one with whom his reading of Paul is triangulated: the Catholic Stanislas Breton. Like Badiou, Breton believes that Pauline messianism and authentic Marxism "share a common call to dispossession and a critical detachment from the prevailing order."[4] For Pauline messianism, however, this dispossession cannot bypass the path of the cross. Indeed, Paul's distinctive messianic language of weakness and abasement in 1 Corinthians 1, so crucial for Badiou, is premised entirely on "the *logos* of the *stauros* [word of the cross]" (1 Cor 1:18) as the very power of God. It is precisely the scandal of the cross that ruptures the humanist appeals of the wise and the strong, and requires a completely different disposition.

Badiou's portrait of Paul is clearly indebted to Breton. The messianic subject is constituted by a rupturing grace, as Paul experiences it on the road to Damascus (Breton 1988, 16–17), and what is revealed in this event is not a teaching but a mission, a "sending" that completely reconfigures identity: not only Paul's identity as Jew, but the whole cosmos, insofar as in Jesus the Messiah the lordship of history and of all creation is disclosed in the form of a servant (1988, ch. 3). This "sending," furthermore, is not tied to a particular teaching about the universal that will now educate the nations. It is tied to a "mystery" (cf. 1 Cor 2:7; Rom 11:33–34) that cannot be possessed, but that calls human beings to journey with the passage of the eternal in time. The diasporic identity thus founded is as much a hermeneutic that is fully historical even while attuned to hidden spiritual mystery, as it is a mode of mission as "servant" in a "filiation" of suffering that overcomes sin and death (1988, 52–53, 89–90). Here, of course, the differences between Badiou and Breton begin to open up into a chasm, the chasm between cross and resurrection whose tension Badiou resolves into resurrection, but in which Breton will insist on dwelling as the "sign of contradiction" (1988, 111), the "crossing of the logos" (cf. 2002, 1) that constitutes the center of Paul's identity and gospel: "I have been crucified with Christ; and it is no longer I who live; but it is Christ who lives in me" (Gal 2:20).

In order to display this messianic filiation of suffering in the light of the cross, Breton pays close attention to two Pauline texts, 1 Corinthians 1:17–31 and Philippians 2:5–11. First Corinthians 1 brings into focus three staurological elements: *logos* (word), *mōria* (foolishness), and *dynamis* (power). With regard to the *logos* of the cross, Breton offers a creative reading of the Thomistic *via eminentia*, proposing the analogical participation of human reason in divine wisdom so as to articulate a "Christian humanism." With this, he contrasts a Bultmannian existential emphasis on the sovereign hidden God that ruptures every analogy and radically critiques all humanism. Each of these alternatives, he observes, privileges one of the terms (*logos* [word] or *stauros* [cross]), and thus remains stuck in the division of Greek and Jew.[5] If the cross is to unite "those whom an apparent wisdom divides" (Breton 2002, 3), we must attend to another space, an "elsewhere" that goes beyond either language: "We are invited to a new exodus whose severity excludes both the reconciliation of opposites and the unilateral decision that privileges one of them" (2002, 26). Here, the God of the cross joins the God of the mystics in a "sublime poverty" (pp. 29, 68) and nakedness (pp. 29, 81, 97, 128) that dispossesses all who believe they have found a secure dwelling place or fitting clothing for the divine. Only those who empty themselves of possessive desires that cling graspingly to the eternal form, who take on the form of the servant willing to journey elsewhere to "what is low and despised ... [even] things that are not (*ta mē onta*)" (1 Cor 1:28) – only those exilic pilgrims participate in the staurological transformation that journeys back to the dwelling place of divine glory.

Here we may be reminded of Badiou's worry about a morbid and *ressentiment*-laden glorying in the suffering of the cross. Does not this "path of the cross" simply constitute a reversal of worldly values in which obedient Christians build up heavenly treasures by trading on a divine spiritual economy that denigrates *this* world only to gain pre-eminence in the other? We know how that works. Breton is fully aware of this danger:

> poverty risks ... exalting into a *summum* those "grandeurs of the flesh" that provisionally elude our striving. The Apostle's warning is aimed precisely at mortifying this natural inclination. It goes directly to the appetite. The God of the Cross is not the God of desire. And that is why this God does not know how to be a God of the superlative. (2002, 9)

There is no avoiding the danger, and indeed Breton's response to Badiou would be that in the latter's desire to claim God's creative evental grace in all its superabundant multiplicity as a *human* invention, he has himself by no means avoided the problem and its hubristic horror. What is scandalously revealed in the resurrection event is precisely that the superlative God has died on the cross (2002, 40). Resurrection cannot be divided from the cross: "if the folly of the Cross has a meaning that is more than our desire, it probably cannot be reduced in the way we would like it to be" (p. 10). The power of the cross is to confound every "what is" by the weakness of "what is not," and this "meontological mission" is the focus of Paul's gospel.[6]

The power of the cross is therefore not an intellectual power. Nor is it a semeiological act of representational speech (or a "theory of universality"). It is rather a performative act that expresses the "form" of the foolish Lord whom it serves (Breton 2002, 37–38). This form Breton calls the "Christic exodus" (2002, 39) that continually moves outside itself in quotidian service to the least, the low, the despised, even those who are not – and that thus becomes a foolish spectacle as the refuse of the world, the offscouring of all things (1 Cor 4:9–13). It is precisely the Messiah of the cross who provides the example of what the dispossessive love of God requires, though each filiated "fool" who follows will find his or her own wandering way of "being no longer themselves" (2002, 44). Such an eccentric, exilic love seeks service in "what is not," not out of resentment or impotence but because God creates *ex nihilo* (pp. 44, 99).[7] Faithfulness to the cross is the form that the passage of the creating God takes in the world; it is a singularly universal slavery of love that is endlessly kenotic and dispossessive rather than acquisitive and accumulative.

Of course, we may well ask what all this has to do with a political ethics. Is Breton speaking merely of the exodus of the soul or the postmodern diaspora self? He insists that the word of the cross cannot be so understood: it is very much related to an *ekklēsia* that is an "ensemble of social relations" (cf. Breton 2002, 55), a body politic that cannot be reduced to an experience of the individual soul or to a church that lives unto itself (either in a liturgy of adoration or in a separatist, isolationist sect). The dispossession displayed in Acts, represented in the sharing of the fractured eucharistic body, must be continued in the diaspora messianic body (Breton 1988, 100): "Instead of persisting as establishment, the Church must in the final analysis be forgotten in the service of the poor ... in unconditional devotion to 'those who do not exist' " (2002, 56). Whatever else this may mean, it cannot mean anything like a "Christian nation," or any other self-enclosed sociopolitical entity. Breton suggests that it will be a politics of *hōs mē* – "to make use of the world as if we used it not" (2002, 60, referring here to 1 Cor 7:29–31).

Taubes and Agamben

In order to explore further the nature of such a political form, we turn from Breton to two other European philosophers who attend more explicitly to Paul's *hōs mē* political theology: the German Jewish philosopher Jacob Taubes and the Italian philosopher Giorgio Agamben.

Like Boyarin, Jacob Taubes is interested in recovering Paul, the "messianic Jew," in his significance for Judaism. Like Boyarin and Badiou, Taubes believes that Paul is a universalist; he interprets 1 Corinthians as "one great fugue around the single word *pan* [all]."[8] And yet, says Taubes, this is neither a noetic universalism nor a liberal *nomos* (law) universalism: "Sure, Paul is also universal, but by virtue of the 'eye of the needle' of the crucified one, which means: transvaluation of all the values of this world ... This is why this carries a political charge" (2004, 24). Paul's messianism of the crucified carries a charge against the *nomos* of Greco-Roman empire, but also against the *nomos* of Mosaic Judaism, and especially against the *nomos* consensus between these two. It is, in this regard, certainly a singular universalism, and one that signifies above all, claims Taubes, the election of Israel – an Israel now being transfigured as *all Israel* (Rom 9–11) – in its diasporic vocation as "light to the nations." This is in keeping with Paul's own calling, cast in Jeremian terms, to proclaim the newly revealed Messiah to the nations. The message that Paul is called to proclaim universally is a "founding" of the "new people of God," not on the basis of law, but on the basis of the one nailed to the cross by law.

At the center of Paul's messianic logic is his declaration of faith in the crucified Messiah as the enactment of divine atonement by which "all Israel" shall be saved. This entails also a political "founding" of peoplehood that calls into question all other foundings, a critical principle above all directed against all forms of "law" as the principle of salvation. For Taubes, Paul faces the same problem that Moses faced: the people have sinned and their guilt must be atoned in order for the people to be saved or made righteous. While the sacrificial logic of Yom Kippur is no less paradoxical in its logic of judgment and mercy than is Paul's messianic logic, the implications for how the people of God, the elect of God, are called to display God's judgment and mercy to the nations are completely altered. For Paul, the death of the Messiah as a scapegoat, a criminal, signals nothing less than the end of righteousness based upon the law.

Paul's political theology proclaims the new people of God, made up of both Jew and Gentile, and founded upon the absolute sovereignty of the crucified Messiah, a sovereignty that calls into question all immanent sovereignties. Paul thus seeks to "outbid Moses" (2004, 39). He believes that the Messiah, condemned according to the law, accomplishes what the law cannot – namely, the healing of the nations. Hence, the place of Moses and the law is transfigured messianically in the direction of "all Israel," an Israel whose definition can no longer be restricted to Jews.

It is important to note a difference here between Boyarin and Taubes on how to understand Paul's language of "flesh" and "spirit." Boyarin sees Paul's "takeover bid" in terms of identity politics, as a replacement of Jewish particularity with a universalist spiritual identity – a politics reliant upon a hermeneutic of spiritualization that relativizes all literal differences and abandons all material identities. One can read this either as a Hellenizing move in which Christianity transcends a narrow literalist culture for a cosmopolitan ecumenical empire, or, in modern terms, as a Hegelianizing move in which the world-spirit is historically actualized. In either case, we are left with an onto-theology of political violence and coercive essentialism, discredited in modern times by the great hermeneuticians of suspicion: Marx, Nietzsche, and Freud.

Taubes frames things quite differently. First of all, the "spirit" Paul mentions is precisely not the spirit of the world but the spirit of God, connected to the Messiah, that transforms the world and forms a new people. Second, for Paul this cannot be understood as a replacement of Israel or the law, but rather a transfiguration that takes the election of Israel seriously in a manner that is perhaps all the more embarrassing for modern Christianity (2004, 47). The key for Paul is that the "all" according to the flesh is not the "all" according to the promise, and this has, furthermore, not to do with ethics or human actions but with the transformative agency of the divine spirit. This is why, in Romans 9–11, Paul proceeds with constant reference to the Torah and election, not to leave them behind or to replace them with a different identity, but to see how peoplehood and memory are reconfigured by the messianic incursion. The Messiah redeems Israel, and does so by extending divine mercy to the enemy, even calling "my people" those who were not a people and "beloved" those who were not beloved (Rom 9:25–26; cf. Hos 2:23). In Paul, this is linked to a "drama of jealousy," as Taubes calls it (2004, 50), that runs as a thread throughout Scripture (Rom 10:19–20; 11:11–14; cf. Deut 32:21; Isa 65:1).

There is a mystery of election and of salvation centered on this messianic drama of jealousy that for Paul is highly paradoxical (Rom 11): "all" will be saved, but only by the messianic "remnant" who proclaim mercy to those who are not a people. Here the central importance of enemy-love in Paul's political theology comes into view – and in paradoxical fashion. As regards the gospel, the Jews who reject Jesus as Messiah are enemies (of God! Taubes insists) for the sake of the Gentiles (Rom 11:28). There is nothing moralistic here. The sovereign Messiah, by suffering death, bears witness to the breakdown of every human moral claim to self-sufficiency. It is God who elects a people for the sake of redeeming all. There is no ground in Messiah for anyone, Jew or Gentile, slave or free, to make a claim to represent divine election and purpose in anything other than the martyrdom and powerless "I" of faith that lives in the world as the sacrificial messianic body. For Taubes, Romans 9–11 cannot be separated from

Romans 12–13, which describe sociologically the embodiment of the messianic sovereignty in the world in terms of neighbor-love and enemy-love. Whatever allegorizing
goes on in Paul, then, cannot be understood without reference to a very particular,
embodied form of life – the *pneumatic* life of the messianic body.

The Messiah, in other words, is not indifferent to the world, nor does he merely
interpret it. As Walter Benjamin puts it in his "Theologico-political Fragment," the
Messiah and only the Messiah transforms the world. Benjamin, suggests Taubes, has a
Pauline notion of creation as articulated in Romans 8, which speaks of "the labor pains
of creation, the futility of creation" (2004, 72). At the heart of the messianic political
ethic of both Benjamin and Paul is nihilism, the "meontology" and *hōs mē* of 1
Corinthians. In a creation that groans under the burden of decay and judgment, the
messianic can appear only in the form of suffering service, as a theological politics of
martyrdom where neither neutrality nor worldly conformity is possible. The dramatic
movement of all creation is passing through the suffering of judgment and can only
find its liberation from beyond itself in divine mercy. Messianic happiness, in Benjamin,
is identified with passing away and *Untergang* (downfall); it has nothing to do with the
liberation of the eternal soul, and everything to do with the agonistic worldly transformation of messianic reconciliation as suffering.

Giorgio Agamben, in his published seminar on Paul's messianism, which he dedicates
to the memory of Taubes (Agamben 2005), helps us pursue further these reflections
on Benjamin, Taubes, and Paul. Agamben, like Taubes, emphasizes that Paul is a diaspora Jew whose Greek is neither properly Jewish (Hebrew) nor Greek. He cites Taubes's
wonderful story of his student days in Zurich when his teacher in classical Greek, Emil
Staiger, confided: " 'You know, Taubes, yesterday I was reading the Letters of the Apostle
Paul.' To which he added, with great bitterness: 'But that isn't Greek, it's Yiddish!' Upon
which I said: 'Yes, Professor, and that's why I understand it!' " (Agamben 2005, 4).

Paul speaks the language of Jews in exile in a manner that works over the host language from within and confounds its identity. In order to understand how this diaspora
linguistic situation relates to the politics of a messianic community, Agamben reflects
first on what he calls the structure of messianic time, expressed in Paul's words in 1
Corinthians 7:29: "time contracted itself, the rest is, that even those having wives may
be as not [*hōs mē*] having" (Agamben's rendering [2005, 23]). Such time is what
Benjamin (in theses XIV and XVIII of his "Theses on the Philosophy of History"
[Benjamin 1968, 261, 263]) calls "*Die Jetztzeit*" – the time of the "now" in which the
accumulative flow of *chronos* is interrupted, burst open, or "contracted" into cogni-
zance of a messianic event that coincides with the very "*Figur*" that is human history
in the universe.

Such an understanding opens up a host of significant insights into Paul's messianic
politics. Paul refers to himself frequently as *doulos* ("slave") of the Messiah. This is a
juridical term ("slave" as opposed to "free" [Agamben 2005, 12–13]), and Paul now
confounds it from within, since the sovereign Lord whom the *doulos* serves is a crucified
Messiah. As a result, the condition of the *doulos* is itself transformed, and comes to
represent a general transformation of worldly political-social conditions that are here
blasted out of the continuum of history. A similar transformation takes place with the
language of "calling" – Paul's calling as *doulos* of the Messiah, but also the calling

(*klēsis*) of the *ekklēsia* further described in 1 Corinthians 7:17–21 in confounding relation to worldly "callings": "let every man abide in the same calling wherein he was
called" (Agamben's rendering [2005, 19]) – even if that "calling" is the life of a slave.
Contrary to Weber's secularization thesis where "calling" indicates an eschatological
indifference to the worldly, Agamben shows that for Paul "calling" is the language of
messianic transformation (2005, 22). Above all, it stands for the nullification and
revocation of every vocation (pp. 23–24).

The nullification of worldly vocation does not mean abandoning it for an "elsewhere," but dwelling within it as in exile, in dispossession. This is precisely what allows
the power of God to transform it in keeping with its true condition or "figure," its
"passing away" toward an "end" that lies beyond it (cf. 1 Cor 7:31). This transforming
power enables a kind of messianic "use" of the world that stands in opposition to
"dominion" and possessiveness (Agamben 2005, 26). In other words, the messianic is
not a new *identity* with its own set of rights, but a power to use without possessing.
Worldly vocations and identities are never "replaced" by something new; rather a
"making new" occurs within them, transforming and opening them up to their true
use, in keeping with their true condition (2005, 28–29).

For Agamben, as for Benjamin, this weak messianic power accomplishes what
Marx's proletariat revolution cannot. It hollows out the progressivist alienating,
abstracting grip of the capitalist count from within, and yet does so through the very
sovereign power of creation, namely, redeeming love. This "as if not" (*hōs mē*) messianic
ethic also stands in contrast to Kant's moral "as if" (*als ob*). It is rooted in a kenotic
movement of dispossession that cannot become yet another act of (self-)legislation. It
relinquishes its moral striving and its hold – whether of the technological means of
progressive liberation from the decay and bondage of nature and natural necessity, or
of the political means of liberating particular identities from the burdens of their
oppressive traditions. The point is rather to open up, through slavery to the sovereign
crucified Messiah, all worldly callings and conditions to the transformative passage of
God. It is through such a "weak messianic power" that the present becomes opened up
to *kairotic* redemption, in which it is also possible to become properly related to the past.
Here it is necessary to get beyond the possessive identities of traditions so as to open up
our shared human memories to the transformation of messianic healing, to pass
through (and not merely leave behind or "replace") the groaning weight of past cycles
of victimization, violence, and retribution.

For Paul, the messianic calling dispossesses the entire self in all its relations; the *hōs
mē* is no mere ideal (cf. 1 Cor 4:9–13). With Barth and Kafka, the Pauline messianic
subject "knows that in messianic time, the saved world coincides exactly with the world
that is irretrievably lost" (Agamben 2005, 42) – there is no path to salvation except by
way of self-losing service to what cannot be saved. For this reason, both Kafka and
Barth emphasized the secular language of parable as the proper discourse for ethics:
the parabolic as the reversal of the conventional criteria by which we measure success
and failure.[9] It does this by discerning the passing action of God, not from above in a
position of world-historical dominance, but rather from below, in exile, in a manner
that emphasizes failure and thus "sees" differently. Only thus is the world hollowed out
for its reconciliation, its redemptive hope in the divine passage through it.

With this in mind, we may return to Paul's discussion of the law and the Messiah and their relation to election. The principle of the law is division (Agamben 2005, 47). But, of course, Paul is also "divided" – "set apart" for the gospel (Rom 1:1), which has its own principle of "division," namely, that between flesh and spirit. How is this related to the messianic gospel which Paul believes breaks down the divisions of the law (for example, the division between Jew and Greek)? How is this related to Paul's critique of the law as unable to "make just," indeed, as causing divisions within the self (Rom 7:19, 23)? How does the law of the Spirit of life, the messianic law (Rom 8:2), set one free from the law of sin and death, and thus "fulfill" the law of God?

The crucial cut – effected by the gospel, and effective in dividing the divisions brought about by the law – is that of flesh and spirit. The division of flesh and spirit does not result in a new universalism that replaces the old particular divisions and identities; rather, it hollows out, and renders inoperative, those divisions. To be "in the messianic law" (cf. 1 Cor 9:20–21), for example, is to be no longer either "under" or "outside" the law (thus the old division brought about by the law is no longer applicable); it is to be "not not-in the law. The division of the law into Jew/non-Jew, in the law/without the law, now leaves a remnant on either side, which cannot be defined either as a Jew, or as a non-Jew. He who dwells in the law of the Messiah is the non-non-Jew" (Agamben 2005, 51). Therefore, one must rethink the question of particular and universal in a completely new way – in logic, ontology, and politics (2005, 51). This is not, as Badiou has it, "indifference that tolerates differences" (Badiou 2003, 99); such indifference is the mark of the "benevolent" sovereignty of ecumenical empire which establishes a policy of religious and ethnic tolerance in order to govern more effectively as a universal authority. For Paul, on the contrary,

> no universal man, no Christian can be found in the depths of the Jew or the Greek, neither as a principle nor as an end; all that is left is a remnant and the impossibility of the Jew or the Greek to coincide with himself. The messianic vocation separates every *klēsis* [calling] from itself, engendering a tension within itself, without ever providing it with some other identity. (Agamben 2005, 52–53)

There is therefore a *remnant* or remainder, which means that the "all" that will be saved is represented by the "not all" that is now rendered messianically present as "elected by grace" (Rom 11:5).

Agamben nicely connects this relation of "all Israel" and the "remnant" with the language of "all" and "in part" in 1 Corinthians. In the secular present, all knowledge and prophecy are "in part" (*ek merous*, 13:9–10), but the messianic community looks forward in hope to the "all in all" (15:28). The only way to relate "in part" to the "all," in Paul's view, is through a self-sacrificing love. It is the patient, non-possessive, self-giving "waiting" of love that characterizes the messianic time in which the messianic body is called to live. The remnant, therefore, is not the possessive object of salvation so much as its instrument in the ministry of reconciliation, and it is precisely the kenotic movement toward the "unsavable" that effects salvation. The political implications of Paul's messianic remnant are spelled out by Agamben in the following terms: "The people is neither the all nor the part, neither the majority nor the minority.

Instead, it is that which can never coincide with itself, as all or as part, that which infinitely remains or resists in each division, and ... never allows us to be reduced to a majority or a minority" (2005, 57).

In the time that remains, then, the messianic time of the *hōs mē* is the time in which time and eternity coincide transformatively: "Time explodes here, or rather, it implodes into the other eon, into eternity" (2005, 63). It is therefore a time of judgment, "*the time that time takes to come to an end*" (p. 67; emphasis in original), the only time we have as creatures (in Breton's words, borrowed from Meister Eckhardt) to exercise our calling as "adverbs of the Verb," the divine speech that is the hidden life of each created being (Breton 1988, 29–30). And so Paul urges to "mak[e] the most of the time [*kairos*]" (Eph 5:16) – seizing it not as a proprietary possession but as a loving "bringing to fulfilment" (the "fullness [*plērōma*] of time" [Eph 1:9–10]) in keeping with the messianic agency of the *hōs mē*. It is also here that the ethical importance of Paul's typological approach to Scripture becomes clear as "figural" rather than "allegorical."[10] There is a relation between the ages that is messianically configured for Paul – it is a parabolic configuration, not a noetic one. Paul insists, "If anyone imagines that he knows something, he does not yet know as he ought to know. But if one loves God, one is known by him" (1 Cor 8:2–3 [RSV]). To be known by God is to participate in the messianic motion of kenotic love, bringing about a "fullness of time" that unites (literally, "recapitulates") all things in heaven and on earth (Eph 1:10; cf. Col 1:17–18). Such a process is not a hermeneutics that seeks to "replace" one meaning with another in a supersessionist dualism, a movement from particular to universal possession of meaning. It is rather the dispossessive process of "becoming parabolic" (Kafka 1979) in a manner that allows the redemptive aim of the law to come to fulfillment – for Paul, above all, each commandment is recapitulated in the "love your neighbor as yourself" (Rom 13:8–10).

Conclusion

The interpretations of Paul's apocalyptic political theology by recent continental philosophers show the implications of Paul's messianism as a politics of "counter-sovereignty," based upon the sovereignty of weakness displayed in the crucified Messiah. I have argued that this is not best understood as a form of identity politics or a theory of universalism, but is in fact radically non-identitarian, "meontological," and dispossessive in ways that challenge the political ontologies of our age. It is a participation "in Messiah" that seeks the perfection of love not in the domination or possession of any part, but in the apocalyptic transfiguration of all partial things to their completion in divine love. This transformation occurs in the messianic body conformed to the "mind of Messiah" that willingly empties itself to serve the other, even the enemy, in a pattern of radical humility and suffering servanthood. This pattern may only be spiritually discerned, even though it is being enacted in the bodily realm that is "passing away," and therefore appears as failure. Paul emphatically insists on this in 1 Corinthians 1, scandalously relating the calling of the *ekklēsia* to the foolish power of the cross, which is mysteriously related to divine power and wisdom depicted not as ontological plenitude but as emptiness. It is, finally, a pattern that may be described as parabolic in which the excess of the whole (the "all") may be discerned within the particular part that is, selflessly and in loving use of the world, bearing witness to its hidden divine life. This would be to restore the created secular world order to its truest meaning – its full but not self-sufficient significance as the site where God is becoming "in Messiah" *ta panta en pasin* ("all in all").

Notes

1 Unless otherwise indicated, biblical quotations are taken from the New Revised Standard Version.

2 With this play on words, Nietzsche declared Paul a "proclaimer of ill tidings."

3 Badiou's language here recalls that of Heidegger, for whom (as for Badiou) Paul's central concern is with the *how* of subjective enactment, not the *what* of a theoretical teaching, and is therefore characterized by proclamation and not a theorization of objective content (Heidegger 2004, 83–84). Behind Heidegger, of course, lies Kierkegaard's (Pauline) emphasis on subjective enactment, though Kierkegaard radically integrates rather than divides the Christic "how" and "what" of messianic becoming.

4 From an interview with Richard Kearney (Breton 2002, 136).

5 Breton points out (1988, 111–112; 2002, 4–5) that Paul's language of Jew and Greek is intended, not as an historical summary of two peoples, but as a summary of dominant human destinies or identities in a simple typology: Greeks are those who *search* for wisdom, a *logos* of the cosmos that offers a rational account of "what"; Jews are those who proclaim/interpret *signs* of the irrupting sovereign power, identifying the "who." Both are languages of representation and manners of life that Paul must use (they are his destiny), and both are equally inadequate and so must be "crossed" by the foolishness and weakness of dispossessive divine power.

6 It is important to note, here again, that Breton does not understand this as "the apotheosis of the negative ... What the Apostle insists upon [in 1 Cor 1] is the impossibility of uttering, in any language-object (of Jew or Greek, for example), that which we cannot put at our disposition, the 'Thing' to which his heart clings. He does not, by a sort of inversion, mean to substitute, for the consecrated excellences of wisdom and power, their contrary correlatives" (2002, 73).

7 Breton states: " 'To obey the Cross' is first to be attuned to it, not to receive assignments but to let ourselves be carried by the offshore wind that will lead we know not where" (2002, 76). And further: "Unlike the despot who would reign only by reducing his 'subjects' to the condition of defective modes of his excellence or docile instruments of his power, the reign of Agape imposes on its faithful no likeness of repetition. The god of the Cross has no other action than his presence, which prescribes no pre-established model but which allows each, on the ground of non-being, to become itself" (2002, 70).

8 Taubes (2004, 1; cf. 25–26, 47). The text of this work was originally given by Taubes, near his death, as a seminar on Romans in Heidelberg in January 1987.

9 For Barth, the language of parable is tied explicitly to 1 Corinthians 7:31 ("the present form of this world is passing away"), and therefore the only ethical form that bears testimony to divine action is one that is "offered up" sacrificially in self-dissolution, worldly failure, or brokenness (Barth 1968, 433–434, 445, 462–463). Kafka's discussion of parables, of course, is parabolically mediated in his inimitable "On Parables" (Kafka 1979).

10   Here Breton (1988, ch. 2), Taubes (2004, 38–54), and Agamben (2005, 73–87) all display sympathetic and illuminating accounts of Paul's typological hermeneutic that stand in stark contrast to Boyarin's account of Pauline allegory. For "figural interpretation," see the important work of Erich Auerbach (1953; 1984). It involves perceiving a connection between two historical events in their spiritual relation to divine providence, a relation that therefore cannot be reduced either to historical causality or semeiotic representations of meaning. Figural interpretation relies upon a mimetic comprehension understood as a spiritual act that deals with historical events experientially rather than in conceptual abstraction. That is, the temporal participates in and points toward the eternal for its meaning, a meaning that requires spiritual attentiveness and imitation if it is to be apprehended.

References

Agamben, Giorgio. 2005. *The Time that Remains: A Commentary on the Letter to the Romans*. Stanford: Stanford University Press.

Auerbach, Erich. 1953. *Mimesis: The Representation of Reality in Western Literature*. Princeton: Princeton University Press.

Auerbach, Erich. 1984. Figura. Pages 11–76 in Erich Auerbach, *Scenes from the Drama of European Literature*. Minneapolis: University of Minnesota Press.

Badiou, Alain. 2003. *Saint Paul: The Foundation of Universalism*. Stanford: Stanford University Press.

Barth, Karl. 1968. *The Epistle to the Romans*. Oxford: Oxford University Press.

Benjamin, Walter. 1968. Theses on the Philosophy of History. Pages 253–264 in Walter Benjamin, *Illuminations*. New York: Schocken.

Boyarin, Daniel. 1994. *A Radical Jew: Paul and the Politics of Identity*. Berkeley: University of California Press.

Breton, Stanislas. 1988. *Saint Paul*. Paris: Presses universitaires de France.

Breton, Stanislas. 2002. *The Word and the Cross*. New York: Fordham University Press.

Heidegger, Martin. 2004. *The Phenomenology of Religious Life*. Bloomington, Ind.: Indiana University Press.

Kafka, Franz. 1979. On Parables. Page 158 in *The Basic Kafka*. New York: Simon & Shuster.

Marx, Karl. 1978. Theses on Feuerbach. Pages 143–145 in *The Marx–Engels Reader*. Edited by Robert C. Tucker. Second edition. New York: W. W. Norton.

Nietzsche, Friedrich. 1968. The Antichrist. Pages 565–656 in *The Portable Nietzsche*. Edited by Walter Kaufmann. New York: Viking Penguin.

Schmitt, Carl. 1985. *Political Theology: Four Chapters on the Concept of Sovereignty*. Cambridge, Mass.: MIT Press.

Taubes, Jacob. 2004. *The Political Theology of Paul*. Stanford: Stanford University Press.

CHAPTER 29

Jewish Readings of Paul

Daniel R. Langton

Premodern Jewish Views of Paul

If the medieval *Toledot Yeshu*, or Story of Jesus, is to be believed, the apostle Paul was not only responsible for the establishment of Christianity, but actually did so at the instigation of the rabbis. Found in a variety of languages throughout Christian Europe, many versions of this notorious, anonymous, anti-Christian romance (dating to around the thirteenth century, although including much older traditions) reveal that Paul had been an agent of the Jewish sages who had sought to end the conflict between the followers of Jesus and the people of Israel by creating permanent religious divisions. The narrative explains how, in their desire to separate from Israel those who continued to claim Yeshu as the Messiah, Jewish religious leaders had called upon a learned man, Simeon Kepha, for help. This Kepha was able to heal a lame man (as was Simon Peter [or Simon *Cephas*; cf. John 1:42] in the book of Acts) and to convince the followers of Yeshu that he was one of them. Claiming to speak on behalf of Yeshu, he then introduced new festivals and rejected circumcision and the dietary laws. Such sensational claims are unhistorical, of course, as illustrated by the way in which Simon Peter and Paul were conflated in the text: "All these new ordinances which Simeon Kepha (or Paul, as he was known to the Nazarenes) taught them were really meant to separate these Nazarenes from the people of Israel and to bring the internal strife to an end" (Goldstein 1950, 153–154). Other versions of this account of a secret mole confuse Paul with another figure called Eliyahu rather than with Simon Peter. In any case, the *Toledot Yeshu* is the nearest thing we have to a widespread, popular, Jewish treatment of the apostle to the Gentiles.

The Blackwell Companion to Paul, First Edition. Edited by Stephen Westerholm.
© 2011 Blackwell Publishing Ltd. Published 2011 by Blackwell Publishing Ltd.

Arguably, the idea that Paul had introduced innovations with regard to festivals and the law can be traced back to earlier Jewish writings. For example, it has been suggested that it was Paul who was described in the second-century Mishnah as one who "profanes the Hallowed Things and despises the set feasts and puts his fellow to shame publicly and makes void the covenant of Abraham our father, and discloses meanings in the law which are not according to the Halakhah" (*Avot* 3:11 [3:12 in Danby 1933]). Likewise, a later rabbinic commentary on Proverbs 21:8 has a familiar ring: "This man ... made himself strange to the circumcision and the commandments" (*Ruth Rabba* 3). But the difficulties in establishing the date and provenance of such fragments mean that there can be little confidence that they have any connection to Paul. Even in Jewish refutations of Christianity during the Middle Ages, Paul was very rarely referred to explicitly. Those few authors who did make brief mention tended to be Karaites (Jews who rejected rabbinic authority) or minor figures living in the relative safety of Muslim lands. The composite picture that emerges from such medieval sources is of a troublemaker who introduced the trinitarian conception of God, the atoning death of Christ, and celibacy, who had modified the calendar, and whose antinomian (anti-*Torah*) misreading of Scripture had led him to set aside practices that had traditionally separated the Jews from the other nations. But the rarity of such references means that all this falls far short of any kind of Jewish tradition regarding this central figure of Christian history.

While one might regard religious Jews as anti-Pauline in their traditional Torah-centricity and devotion to the commandments, this is not the same as saying that there was a true engagement with, or even a general awareness of, the apostle's teachings. Apart from the confused account of the *Toledot Yeshu* and a few scattered, unauthoritative comments, there is no tangible evidence of Jewish interest in Paul in the premodern period. This historical silence might reflect simple ignorance, a deliberate policy to ignore a dangerous opponent, or an awareness of the political danger of engaging with such an authoritative figure in Christendom. Whatever the reason, Jews have had little or nothing to say about Paul until very recently.

The Awakening of Jewish Interest in Paul in the Modern Period

Serious Jewish interest in Paul seems to have its origins in the nineteenth-century emergence of Jewish historicism (i.e., the recognition that one's understanding of the past is profoundly shaped by one's location in a specific historical, social, and intellectual setting). Increasingly, naturalistic, rational explanations of the history of the Jews and their religion were privileged over supernatural, providential explanations. Inevitably, the new assumptions led to a reappraisal of Christianity, with which Judaism had struggled for so many centuries. If the Jewish comprehension of Christianity and its relations to the Jews shifted at this point from an essentially traditional, providential perspective to an increasingly historicist, rationalist one, then it would make good sense that Jewish curiosity in Paul became apparent at around the same time. This was because German biblical critics' revisionist histories of the New Testament period, which appeared to undermine the religious unity of the early church and to emphasize the influence of pagan thought within it, and which generated considerable enthusi-asm among many Jewish observers, placed Paul at the center of this revolution. Paul was associated by both Gentile and Jew with many of the innovations that had led Christianity to break loose from its Jewish roots. So it was that when the apostle first captured the attention of Jewish writers, he was immediately located within an account of the parting of the ways (and Jewish history) that gave great weight to human thought and action. Insofar as its emphasis upon historicism characterizes modern Jewish thought, the study of Paul represents one important area in which the transition to modernity can be observed. Without an appreciation of this phenomenon, the nineteenth-century Jewish interest in Paul seems to come out of nowhere.

While there have been a number of factors at work on Jewish commentators on Paul, including the influence of Christian Pauline studies, much of what has been written has undoubtedly been shaped by specific concerns raised by Jewish political and social emancipation in the nineteenth and twentieth centuries. Since that time, Jews every-where have debated hotly where the boundaries between Jew and Gentile should be drawn. To what extent should one maintain one's barriers? How much of the non-Jewish world should be embraced and how much guarded against? Which of Judaism's traditions were tenable in this brave new world? What, if anything, did Christianity and Judaism share in common? The basic strategies adopted by Jews committed to modernity have been either to hold Christian society at arm's length or to embrace it. Understanding this is useful in beginning to account, in broad outline, for the variety of Jewish attitudes toward Paul.

Paul and Jewish Criticism of Christianity

The most common response has been to utilize Paul as part of a wider program to stress the differences between Judaism and Christianity. Perhaps the best-known example of this was the German theologian and philosopher, Martin Buber (1878–1965). In 1923, Buber published (in German) *I and Thou*, which famously outlined his philosophy of dialogue and identified two types of interpersonal categories, namely, I-Thou and I-It. The first he described as a dialogue of two respectful partners, characterized by mutuality, openness, presentness, and directness. The second was something less, a monologue, a necessary and common form of relationship, but one without the poten-tial for generating the radical development offered by the first. In *Two Types of Faith* (1950; English translation 1951), Buber brought his dialogical philosophy to bear directly on the two central figures of Christianity, Jesus and Paul. While he could reclaim his "great brother" Jesus as the embodiment of authentic Judaism, Paul was a "gigantic figure ... whom we must regard as the real originator of the Christian concep-tion of faith" (1951, 44) and who therefore represented a quite distinct set of values.

Strictly speaking, Buber's treatment was focused more on the faith systems of these two figures than on any historical reconstruction of the men themselves. He contrasted the Hellenistic or Greek *pistis* (faith or belief in the truth of a proposition), which he argued was embodied in Paul, with the Jewish *emunah* (faith as trust), which was embod-ied in Jesus. Jesus's Jewish *emunah* reflected an intimate, trusting relationship with God, and was paradigmatic of the I-Thou relationship. In this way, Buber "reversed the theological gaze" by turning on its head the traditional Christian interpretation of the antagonistic relationship between Jesus and the Pharisees, and emphasizing instead their similarities. In contrast to their spontaneous spirituality, Paul's Hellenistic *pistis* was predicated on the I-It relationship. Paul's doctrine of justification – the teaching that faith in Christ made one righteous and the denial that "works" (the fulfillment of the law) could bring about this transformation – had been a laudable attempt to replace the legalism of Hellenistic Judaism, which was characterized by judicial concerns with guilt and innocence (1951, 46–47). But, in fact, all he had done was replace the simple, biblical, face-to-face relationship between God and man with a relationship based on "faith and faith alone"; that is, he had replaced true dialogue with a kind of mysticism (1951, 47). Paul's mystical solution of faith-in-Christ had generated an intermediary between man and God, and thus it typified the I-It relationship. In contrast with Jesus (and the Pharisees), Paul had turned away from a biblical conception of the kingdom of God which emphasized the immediacy between God and man. And Paul's pessimistic worldview, described as "Paulinism," also indicated his movement away from the authentically Jewish, intimate, direct encounter with the Eternal Thou. As Buber saw it,

> The Gnostic nature of the essential features of [Paul's] conception is obvious – the derivative powers, which, ruling the world, work against the primal divine power and waylay the human soul, the enslavement of the cosmos, the problematic character of the law, the overcoming of the "rulers" and the setting free of man ... None of this concerns the Godhead, but the intermediate being set up or permitted by Him. (1951, 83)

Thus, Buber concluded, "I no longer recognize the God of Jesus, nor his world in this world of Paul's" (1951, 89). While Jesus could be recovered as a good Jew, Paul had clearly stepped over the line.

A number of writers both before and after Buber reflected this impulse to demarcate the limits of Jewish compromise with the non-Jewish world, including Elijah Benamozegh (1823–1900) in Italy, and Heinrich Graetz (1817–1891), the younger Leo Baeck (1873–1956), Kaufmann Kohler (1843–1926) in Germany, joined later by Hyam Maccoby (1924–2004) in Britain. While fully engaged with Christian thought, they did not want to identify with it too closely; they were suspicious of the damaging inroads of assimilation and/or concerned to protect their own conceptions of Judaism from its disorientating influence. They instinctively realized that to undermine Paul, regarded as the moral and intellectual founder of the Gentile church, was to undermine its ubiquitous power, or at least to demonstrate that it did not have a monopoly on the truth. Consequently, Paul's Jewish credentials were only reluctantly acknowledged; while some attributed Paul's teachings to profound misunderstandings of Judaism, others (like Buber) pointed to the non-Jewish sources that they saw saturating the apostle's theology. By these means, the apostle's credibility as the critic *par excellence* of the Jewish law and religion was undercut, and a space for the legitimacy of the Jewish way of life carved out. Arguably, these barrier-builders are the scholars whose writings are responsible for the power and longevity of the negative Jewish image of Paul; their discrediting of Paul remains central to the Jewish critique of Christianity today.

Paul and Jewish Interest in Improving Interfaith Relations

The other way to locate oneself as a Jew within a wider Christian society, and to maintain a legitimate space for Jewish life within it, is to emphasize what is shared in common between Jews and Christians. Perhaps the earliest example of the use of Paul to this end was the North American Reform rabbi, Isaac Mayer Wise (1819–1900). In a series of public lectures published in 1883 as *Three Lectures on the Origin of Christianity*, Wise set out to encourage his congregants to engage with the non-Jewish world around them. The apostle to the Gentiles was a case in point, earning him a dedicated lecture entitled "Paul and the Mystics." Paul could easily be contrasted negatively with Jesus in terms of the law (and the comparison was made), but this was not as important to Wise as was the presentation of Paul as a "master machinist ... one of those brilliant stars in the horizon of history" whose contribution to world history could be attributed to his Jewishness (Wise 1883, 53). Wise's main source of information for Paul was not the New Testament or early Christian writings, but the rabbinic literature. Identifying Paul with a heretic referred to in the Talmud, Wise explained:

> The rabbis called him *Acher*, "another," i.e., one who passes under another or assumed name. They [the rabbis] maintain that his name was Elisha ben Abujah. But this name must be fictitious, because it is a direct and express reference to Paul's theology. It signifies "the saving deity, son of the father god," and Paul was the author of the "son of God" doctrine. The fact is, he was known to the world under his assumed name only. (1883, 55–56)

Wise's hypothesis and almost exclusive dependence upon the Talmud is unique among the Jewish writers on Paul. It enabled him to argue (anachronistically) for a Pharisaic-kabbalistic background for Paul. For Wise, Paul's vision of Paradise in 2 Corinthians 12 ("I know a man in Christ who fourteen years ago was caught up to the third heaven ...")[1] correlated with Acher's experience of Paradise as mentioned in the Talmud (*b. Hagigah* 14b), and he argued that at the time of Paul–Acher there had been a growth of superstition and mysticism among the Jews. When one also took into account the similarity of Paul's conception of Christ with the mystical semi-divine figure of the "Saar Haolam" (Prince of the World), it seemed only sensible to conclude that Paul's background had been one of Jewish mysticism (1883, 57–59). Not only was this central figure of Christianity recognizably Jewish, but Paul's motivations were entirely comprehensible to modern Reform Jews. According to Wise, Paul's particular greatness rested in his attempt to extend the knowledge of God to all the nations (53–54). In addition to his universalism, his rejection of Jewish nationalism and his preparedness to compromise regarding the law to promote progress were also admirable. While Wise echoed others in attributing originality to Paul for paganizing the gospels – the apostle was responsible for the Christian idea of the Son of God, for vicarious atonement, for abrogation of the law, and for beginning a new covenant (62–64) – he did not do this in order to attack Christianity. Wise anticipated later Jewish commentators in claiming that Paul was the author of Gentile Christianity, but this did not prevent him from partly reclaiming Paul as a Jewish hero, explaining (if not justifying)

Paul's teachings as a result of a Jewish mystic's attempt to offer the Gentiles something of the gift God had granted Israel.

Close contemporaries who emulated Wise's efforts at bridge-building included Joseph Krauskopf (1858–1923) in the United States and Claude Montefiore (1858–1938) in Britain. They, too, offered historical accounts that praised Paul's universalism, ethics, and religious sincerity, and were generally prepared to confirm his Jewish education and background (although neither followed Wise's eccentric emphasis on *kabbalah*). Their goodwill toward Paul was in part an expression of their confidence in religious progress and political emancipation. Their quickness in distancing themselves from the classic, negative view of Paul was a signal of their commitment to the modern non-Jewish world. In their optimism, they believed that by contributing to the historical reconstruction of Paul's Jewishness, and by demonstrating their appreciation for him, they could inoculate the Gentile world against an anti-Jewish reading of the apostle. Theirs remain among the most sympathetic portrayals of Paul, although later scholars, including Pinchas Lapide (1922–1997) in Israel and Mark Nanos (1954–) in the United States, have been committed to bridge-building within a specifically modern interfaith context. For these, Paul's attitude toward observance of the Torah could be recast to become authentically Jewish. Lapide argued that the apostle's abrogation of the law was relevant only to Gentile Christians while it retained its full validity for Jews; and Nanos has gone so far as to argue that not only was Paul himself a fully Torah-observant Pharisee who expected Jewish believers to follow suit, but that he even required the Gentile Christians to keep the (Jewish) Noachide laws. Thus, an attempt was made to transform the law into an instrument of Jewish–Christian rapprochement.

In a way, the older Leo Baeck (1873–1956) had pre-empted them when he interpreted Paul's view as valid from the perspective of one who believed that the messianic age had come. In his 1952 article "The Faith of Paul," the German Reform rabbi had suggested that, like many of his contemporaries, Paul had expected the law to be transcended (not abrogated) when the messianic age began; the only difference was that, for Paul, this new age had arrived with Jesus. Consequently, it had not been un-Jewish for him to exclaim, "All things are lawful for me" (1 Cor 6:12), since this closely paralleled the rabbinic teaching that in the "Days of the Messiah ... there will be no merit or guilt" (*b. Shabbat* 151b).

Paul and Modern Jewish Identity: Intra-Jewish Debate and Zionism

Almost by definition, modern Jewish identity has been constructed in a world where the idea of a normative Judaism can no longer be taken for granted, and the various approaches to Paul mirror this reality. It has been suggested that the three most important factors acting upon and shaping modern Jewry have been *anti-Semitism*, which both strengthened and weakened Jewish ties, the *Enlightenment*, which encouraged Jews to identify with a larger world beyond the boundaries of Judaism, and *Zionism*, which offered the hope of a shared national identity. The remarkable figure of the apostle resonates in each of these contexts. For those who attributed Gentile hostility and Jew-hatred to Christianity itself, and who sought to protect themselves from it or to draw its sting, Paul's relevance lies in his role in the emergence and success of the new religion. This we have already noted in the work of the barrier-builders and bridge-builders. The two other factors, the Enlightenment and Zionism, provide the essential backdrops for the way in which Paul featured in what might be described as intra-Jewish ideological debate.

For those who sought to define Judaism in terms of Enlightenment values or other-wise to reconcile the best thought and attitudes of their own day with the truths of Judaism, there has been a fascination with the apostle's endeavors in the centuries-old pursuit of synthesis between the Hellenism dominant in his day and Jewish tradition. One example of such a reformer was the founder of Anglo-Liberal Judaism, the afore-mentioned Claude Montefiore (1858–1938). A clear indication of this English scholar's position can be seen in his warning about directly comparing Paul's writings with those of the rabbis. While recognizing the "contradictions and antinomies" in Paul's theology, he felt that there was an overall coherence which made Paul far more systematic than the rabbis, and thus superior to them (Montefiore 1901, 170). In the context of the theological debates raging between progressive and traditionalist apologists, such an observation would have been provocative. As a liberal, Montefiore maintained that inspiration and wisdom could be drawn from sources outside the corpus of traditional Jewish religious writings. In seeking to introduce Paul to a Jewish audience, Montefiore had been well aware of the obstacles in his path, not least those teachings that could only be regarded as fatally flawed, including the apostle's pessimism, his Christology, much in his conception of sin and of the law, his demonology, and his view of human destiny (Montefiore 1914, 141). Even so, there were fragments of Pauline theology that attracted him. At the top of this list was Paul's introduction of a practical (although imperfect) universalism. He himself had come to the same conclusion as Paul, namely, that "Judaism could not become a universal religion together with its inviolate Law" (1914, 145). He believed that Paul's knowledge of the Hellenistic mystery cults had influenced his pre-Christian thinking and made him ready and eager to discover a universal method of salvation, suited and predestined for all humankind. But while he commended Paul for preaching universalism and solving the "puzzle of the universal God and the national cult" (1918, 119), he could not accept the new form of religious particularism that Paul had forged "in Christ." Neither could he credit Paul for originat-ing the idea. Recalling Old Testament universalist passages, he felt that "one has to acknowledge that Paul has only smoothed more completely, more definitely, what these others had begun to smooth before him" (1923, 287). To his mind, liberal Judaism and its teachings of ethical monotheism polished off the job, and presented the clearest expression of this important Jewish tradition. Another valuable element of Paul's thought was the apostle's rationale for the incorporation of the vernacular in worship, useful for justifying contemporary progressive synagogue practice. There was even one aspect of Paul's objection to justification by works that was worth salvaging. According to Montefiore, the apostle had taught that one failed to win righteousness by fulfilling the law because one could never fulfill it; worse still, one failed to win righteousness even if one did fulfill the law. In spite of his recognition that "no Jew ever looked at the

Law from this point of view," Montefiore admitted that he felt there was, indeed, a danger that "works righteousness" could lead to self-righteousness and self-delusion (1894, 443–444). Thus, Montefiore approached Paul as a source of inspiration and religious insight. More significantly, Pauline studies provided him with an opportunity to articulate progressive, liberal Jewish ideas.

It is not difficult to find other progressive theologians in Montefiore's day, such as Emil Hirsch (1851–1923) in the United States, who were just as likely to use their engagement with Paul to upbraid their Orthodox opponents, especially with regard to the *halakhah* or religious law. (More traditional Jewish Pauline commentators have also made the connection between Paul's view of the law and that of Progressive Judaism, although they have attributed a negative value judgment to such liberal attitudes, of course.) Likewise, whether consciously intended or not, the Pauline studies of later North American progressive Jewish New Testament scholars, with their casual presumptions of the apostle's Jewishness, also contributed to the undermining of traditionalist conceptions of Jewish history. Samuel Sandmel (1911–1979) is a case in point. While his book *The Genius of Paul: A Study in History* (1958) emphasized the difference between Palestinian Judaism and Hellenistic Judaism, and identified Paul with the latter category, he did not do so to undermine Paul's Jewishness.

> To call Paul a Hellenistic Jew is not to put a value judgment on the nature of his Jewish fidelity, but is only to state a fact. The Hellenistic world into which Paul was born, we know now, was one of many religious expressions and of earnest philosophical disputations ... There is no reason to be sceptical of his statement that in his study of Judaism he had surpassed his fellow students of his own age. Nor should we doubt that he had achieved a skillful knowledge of Judaism. His statement that he had learned the traditions of his fathers is to be accepted – but the content of those Graeco-Jewish "traditions" is not to be confused with that which later centuries recorded as the product of the Jewish schools in Palestine and Babylonia. (Sandmel 1958, 16–17)

Despite this emphasis on Hellenistic Judaism, Sandmel went on to place Paul in the Jewish prophetic tradition. In so doing, he offered a very different perspective on Paul's view of the law. In order to understand any prophet, Sandmel argued that one needed to take into account the historical situation, for this determined his message. He proceeded to compare Paul with the eighth-century prophets.

> Paul confronts a situation different from that of Amos, Isaiah, and Jeremiah. These pre-exilic prophets denied the validity of ritual ceremony or of a written code at a time previous to the existence of the Pentateuch ... But by Paul's time the Pentateuch had become the very center of his religious heritage. Amos could ignore it, for it did not exist; Paul (and Philo) must deal with it and account for it. Paul's denial of the validity of the Pentateuchal legislation is akin to Amos' denial of ritual sacrifice (5.21–22) and to Jeremiah's denial of the existence of any valid written code (7.21–22). The impetus in all the cases was identical; the end result was the same: Communion is the only essential, and ritual is useless. What is different is only the environment and the particulars confronted. (1958, 77–78)

As a result, the common charge that Paul had abrogated the law was, in Sandmel's opinion, a misunderstanding. Any negative remarks Paul had made about the law had been provoked by the negative reception of his message and possibly as a result of psychological trauma (1958, 56). It was a kind of critique of institutionalized religion (1958, 218). In reality, Paul had simply sought to emphasize internal over external worship, as had the prophets before him, and had done so in terms of the law, living as he had in an age of law. Despite any reservations he harbored concerning the apostle to the Gentiles, the liberal Jewish scholar was prepared to give Paul the benefit of the doubt. He was reluctant to condemn Paul as an inauthentic kind of Jew or as an enemy of the Jewish people, to the extent that he criticized the use of the term "Christian" in connection with him (1958, 21). More recently, Alan Segal (1945–) has claimed that Paul's letters represent the best evidence extant for Jewish mysticism in the first century. Such interpretations are framed in a way that simply dismisses out of hand the assumptions on which many conservative, traditional Jewish attitudes and claims rest, especially with regard to marginal Jewish figures.

For those consumed by the nationalist dream of Zionism, the third factor shaping modern Jewry, Paul could be credited with the invention of Gentile Christianity, an essentially *diaspora* enterprise, which would be forever hostile to the authentic Judaism of *eretz Yisrael* (the Land of Israel). While some liberals might have doubted this, such as Hans Joachim Schoeps (1909–1980) in Germany, who argued vehemently in his own treatment of Paul that authentic Judaism *could* be detached from Jewish nationalism, others could not help but interpret history through this ideological lens. For Joseph Klausner (1874–1958) in Palestine, Paul was at once a member of the Jewish nation who had shaped world history and, as a universalist visionary, a betrayer of the Zionist soul of the Jewish people. The revisionist history offered by his compatriot, Micah Berdichevsky (1865–1921), went even further. In an uncompleted work probably composed in Berlin shortly before his death, Berdichevsky suggested that Saul and Paul had been two different individuals whose distinct traditions had been amalgamated by the early Christians into the familiar New Testament narrative. Uniquely, he identified the earliest version of Paul's blinding and conversion as the mysterious Hebrew legend of Abba Gulish, which, although regarded by others as medieval, Berdichevsky believed to be of ancient pedigree. This story tells of a pagan who served as a priest in "an idolatrous temple" in Damascus and who used to pilfer the donations. Habitually calling upon his idol for healing and receiving none, he one day called upon "the Sovereign of the Universe," who promptly cured him. Moving to Tiberias, he converted to Judaism where "he ran after the *mitzvot* [commandments]" and began a new life as an administrator for the poor. Eventually he was overcome by temptation and began embezzling money again – with the consequence that he went blind. Returning to Damascus, he stood before the Gentiles (who believed that he had lost his sight because he had scorned the idol) and delivered a public speech. Pointing out that in all the time he had stolen from the temple donations the idol had never punished him, he went on to confess that he had resumed his criminal activities in Tiberias until struck down. He therefore attributed his condition not to the idol but to the One "whose eyes roam the whole world and no misdeed is beyond Him to see [and punish]"; whereupon, having witnessed to God's power and judgment, his sight was miraculously restored. The account concludes: "from the nations thousands and tens of thousands ... [found] shelter under the wings of the shekhinah," that is, converted to Judaism (Berdichevsky 1971, 13).

Later, Berdichevsky suggested, the Gentile followers of Paul and the Jewish followers of Jesus merged this figure with another, a Jew called Saul, to create the composite, fictitious figure of Saul–Paul, who functioned as a unifying figure between the two groups and as a bridge between the Hellenistic and the Jewish elements of Christian thought. Berdichevsky highlighted the importance placed in both accounts upon Damascus, noting that both Paul and Abba Gulish had been treasurers (1971, 126) associated with accusations of embezzlement of funds meant for the poor (18). (Berdichevsky infers this from 2 Cor 8:20–21, where Paul writes of taking precaution so that "no one should blame us about this liberal gift which we are administering.") Both men were described as zealous against idolatry (1971, 126), both became fully convinced of the new faith's power and truth having had their blindness miraculously healed (34), and both were responsible for the conversion of many Gentiles (149). In the end, of course, Berdichevsky's reconstruction must be regarded as entirely fanciful. It is clear that the underlying motive was his concern to preserve the Jewish land, religion, and people from the charge that they had given birth to Christianity; he could not tolerate the idea of Israel tainted by the link to the diaspora religion *par excellence*. In his determination to lay bare the essentially non-Jewish origins of Christianity, he went so far as to deny Paul Jewish origins whatsoever. Berdichevsky can thus be seen as a somewhat extreme example of how, in the context of debates about the impact of anti-Semitism, the Enlightenment, or Zionism upon Judaism, the apostle to the Gentiles has been interpreted in such a way as to facilitate and reinforce a wide variety of perspectives within the modern Jewish ideological landscape.

Paul as a Dialogical Partner for Jewish Self-understanding

Doubtless, the classic, negative Jewish view of Paul is alive and well, and there is every reason to believe that Paul will continue to function as a figure of abuse in public discourse, in Jewish-Christian religious polemic, and in intra-Jewish debate for a long time to come. But at the same time, others will join with those who see in the first-century apostle a pioneer in the quest to find a meaningful sense of historical continuity between the Jewish past and the Jewish future. At a time when the chasm between the modern and pre-Enlightenment Jewish worlds appears so daunting and unbreachable, the figure of Paul, who himself traversed far-flung cultures and was acutely aware of the challenges facing Judaism, looks beguilingly familiar. The study *My Brother Paul* (1972) by the anti-establishment conservative rabbi and academic Richard Rubenstein (1924–) is an excellent example of how Paul can be presented as a fellow-traveler, in that the issues that most concerned "one of the most influential Christian theologians of all time" closely paralleled his own (Rubenstein 1972, 5).

Paul's chief concern, according to Rubenstein, was the question of how to defeat death (1972, 41). Rubenstein maintained that Paul had initially persecuted the church in order to reduce the tension arising from internal conflict between his hopes that the Messiah had come and his worldly realism. His attraction to the new movement was ultimately due to a fixation with his own mortality, a fixation with which, as Rubenstein suggested, one could readily empathize.

Like the rest of us, Paul did not want to die. Until Paul learned of the Resurrection, it is likely that he was convinced that death was inevitable for all men. There may have been a time when he harbored the secret hope that, were he to fulfill the Law perfectly, God might save him from death. Some rabbis maintained that were a person to lead a sinless life of complete obedience to God's will, he might not die ... Eventually he must have concluded that no matter how scrupulously he kept God's commandments, he too was going to die. One can safely guess that Paul's first response to the reports of Jesus' Resurrection was intense scepticism if not derisive rejection. Still, some part of Paul must have wanted the report to be true, for *if Jesus had been victorious over death, there was also hope for Paul.* (1972, 42–43, emphasis in original)

Again, one of the most powerful themes dominating the apostle's thought, according to Rubenstein, was Jewish messianism. Citing Freud, he presented a psychoanalytical account of Judaism, arguing that, unlike other religious systems that allowed periodical infringements of the rules, Judaism did not. The psychological release was instead relegated to the future, namely, to the messianic age when the inhibitions and frustrations of the day-to-day world would finally be annulled. This was why "Jewish messianists from the time of Paul to Sabbatai Zvi and even some of the early reform rabbis have seen the 'end of the Law' as one of the most important consequences of the Messianic Age" (1972, 36). From this perspective, the traditional view of Paul and the law appeared unworthy. As Baeck and others had done, Rubenstein argued that it had been a mistake to view Paul as antinomian. Rather, Paul had believed that the Messiah had abolished the authority of the law (39). In Rubenstein's reading, Paul's frustration in failing to observe the law is empathetically portrayed as a natural and not uncommon reaction to the *halakhah*, and the fault is laid at the door of institutional Judaism, which had failed to provide a religious outlet for such psychological tension. At the root of Rubenstein's psychoanalytically orientated appreciation was his belief that Paul had had the profound insight that our common perception of reality was only a part of the story. This recognition of *"the deeper and truer meaning of the human world"* was a Jewish revolution that would be echoed in the writings of later Jewish mystics and, ultimately, "anticipates the work of the twentieth-century's most important secularised Jewish mystic, Sigmund Freud" (22, emphasis in original).

While not sharing his interest in psychology, one can point to Nancy Fuchs-Kreimer (1952–) and Daniel Boyarin (1946–) in the United States as other Jewish thinkers for whom Paul has inspired far-reaching personal reflections, which have bound him to each as a fellow-traveler on the path to religious self-understanding. They, too, were convinced that contemporary Jews could benefit from thinking about the questions Paul asked (if not always his answers), whether the issue be, respectively, how to retrieve as a Jewish theological truth the idea of God's grace and to find a theological space for the non-Jew; or how to begin to counter the gender biases and ethnic bigotry of a traditional system to which one is committed without threatening its foundations. Such individuals are not ashamed to articulate such concerns in the language of the apostle precisely because he is perceived to be a serious partner in a perennial dialogue concerning the very nature of Judaism itself.

Paul and Jewish Treatments from Non-religious Perspectives

In addition to the contributions of Jewish theologians, religious leaders, and scholars of religion who tend to dominate interfaith dialogue, important and distinctive Jewish perspectives on the dramatic events of the ancient "parting of the ways," and on the controversial figure of Paul, can be found elsewhere. Among those offering artistic, literary, philosophical, or psychoanalytical interpretations of the apostle are a number whose idiosyncratic self-identities and complicated backgrounds often frustrate easy categorization. For obvious reasons, they have been uncomfortable championing the Jewish community's received traditions and dialoguing with representative members of the Christian fraternity. But there are many ways to define Jewishness, and exploration of the intellectual worlds of those who regard themselves as Jewish in some sense, even if they are not committed to any kind of Judaism, is a very worthwhile endeavor. The fact that, along with so many other Jews in the modern world, they cannot easily be fitted into religious or national pigeonholes is precisely what makes them so interesting when studying their empathetic interpretations of the similarly complex character of the apostle. Their works are especially useful for illustrating two themes that are common to the majority of Jewish studies of Paul.

One recurrent theme is the attempt of Jewish intellectuals to map out the relationship between Jews and Gentiles in a context where the centuries-old rules no longer seem to apply. The difficulty for those who inhabit the cultural borderlands is how to achieve a coherent, satisfactory personal narrative. The common intellectual conundrum is whether or not there exists a common religious essence between Judaism and Christianity. Arguably, this goes back as far as Felix Mendelssohn's oratorio *Paulus* (1836), but it certainly dominates the work of an artist such as Ludwig Meidner (1884–1966) and the novels of Sholem Asch (1880–1957) and Samuel Sandmel.

Perhaps the most positive affirmation in response to the question came from the Austrian playwright Franz Werfel (1890–1945), whose play *Paul among the Jews: A Tragedy* (1926; English translation 1928) is the only example of a theatrical treatment of the subject by a Jewish playwright. The key moments of this play, which is essentially a series of debates between Paul and various first-century figures, are the discussions between Paul and his former teacher, Rabbi Gamaliel the Elder, who is portrayed as the wisest Jewish mind of his day, and who sits in judgment over him. At first, the only thing that seems to separate the two men, whose respect for each other is profound, is the classic distinction between the Jew and Christian: one believes that the Messiah has come, the other that he will come. But the original cause of Paul's dissatisfaction with his former life is soon revealed to have been frustration at his inability to observe the law. Sympathetic to this torment, which Paul claims was only assuaged by his discovery of the Messiah, the old sage Gamaliel offers support and encouragement before hinting that he is prepared to call for a rapprochement between the Jewish people and Jesus, whom he describes as "a holy man of God" (Werfel 1928, 136–137). When Paul insists that the Messiah has brought about the end of the law, Gamaliel counters by reminding Paul that Jesus, Messiah or not, would have disagreed. Paul justifies his distinctive teaching by setting aside the limited knowledge of the man Jesus, merely a rabbi from

Nazareth, in favor of his own understanding of "the Messiah, the incarnate Shekina, God's Son, [existent] before the world came into being" (1928, 139). In the face of such presumption, Gamaliel retracts his offer. Perhaps, he agonizes, it would be better to sacrifice one soul for the sake of the purity of God's Torah. In the end, however, he spares Paul, despite being prophetically aware of the fatal consequences for the world of his failure. He prays:

> Can I let Thine enemy go, my God? Let him go to a strange land, him, who wishes to destroy thy inexhaustible Torah and our holy responsibility toward men, in order that he may preach his phantom gospel? Oh, they will listen to him, and the phantom will become their Law, for a shadow lies but lightly, but Thy Law lies heavily! (1928, 143)

At this moment of the parting of the ways, Werfel refuses to condemn Paul for his beliefs or for the establishment of a religion that will triumph at the expense of the Jewish people. The apostle's raw passion and spiritual sincerity exonerate him, just as the wisdom and patience of his teacher support the moral claim of the stance adopted by the Pharisees. That these two "men possessed by religion," these equally admirable representatives of Christianity and Judaism, fail to reconcile is, for Werfel, *the* tragedy of Jewish history (preface, ii, iv). At the same time, there is no doubt that in the playwright's mind, Israel's loss is world religious civilization's gain. The play certainly did not call for a religious synthesis, for its author did not believe that one could logically reconcile Jewish and Christian theologies; this is made clear in the extensive debates between Paul and Gamaliel. But Werfel did hint at their complementary roles: Christianity going on to conquer the pagan world in demonstration of its spiritual potency; Judaism going on to suffer centuries of degradation with a dignity that expressed just as powerfully its own spiritual purity. Both witnessed to the reality of the presence of the Spirit of God. From Werfel's unsystematic, mystical perspective, the tragedy that the story of Paul symbolized was (as he put it in personal correspondence) the failure of the two "conscious manifestations" of the split "Jewish being," that is, Judaism and Christianity, to recognize in each other the mystery of true faith.

Another running theme within modern Jewish thought has been the gnawing tension between the need to criticize Christian thought and authority, on the one hand, and the desire to demonstrate one's commitment to Western society, on the other. Paul's revolutionary zeal and iconic status attracted the attention of some who saw him as an ally for their own countercultural endeavors. Again, while this adoption of Paul as an ideological supporter could be said to apply to many, it was a particularly potent dimension of the work of so-called "non-Jewish Jews," including the German and North American psychoanalysts, Sigmund Freud (1856–1939) and Hanns Sachs (1881–1947), for whom Paul's power lay in his psychological insights into the human condition, especially with regard to guilt and the fear of mortality. Sachs was effusive in his appreciation of Paul's attempt to free the individual from the unnatural constraints of civilized life and his resolution of existential anxiety, couched as it was in the theological language of love. Freud was more cautious; while he certainly acknowledged the power of the apostle's image of the sacrifice of the Son in making restitution for the ancestral murder of the Father, he never forgot that it represented a truly formidable obstacle in his mission to rid the world of the illusion of religion. Similarly, the Dutch and Russian philosophers, Baruch Spinoza (1632–1677) and Lev Shestov (1866–1938), approached Paul as a counterpoint around which they could debate the rationality of Western civilization's political and intellectual foundations, and he was called into service as an opponent of superstition and dogma, respectively.

Although he explicitly defined himself in Jewish terms, the Austrian philosopher of religion Jacob Taubes (1923–1987) might also be discussed in this context, having added politico-legal authority to the list. In *The Political Theology of Paul* (1993; English translation 2004), Paul is represented as an exciting opportunity to return to a time when what was "Jewish" and what was "Christian" had not yet been decided (2004, 20–21). If the apostle had believed that he was a Jew with a very special mission, Taubes could see no compelling reason to regard it as anything other than a Jewish mission. What precisely had this mission entailed? Taubes read Romans 9–11 as Paul's declaration that, like Moses, he was nothing less than the founder of a new people and the representative of a new law (2004, 40–41). What most interested Taubes in Paul's opening up of the covenant to the Gentiles was the authority he claimed for the consequent creation of a new community. In Paul's day, he observed, there had been only two models of human relations: the ethnic community, such as the people of Israel, and the imperial order of the Roman Empire. Paul was understood to have offered a third option, which he had defined against both. Thus, the epistle to the Romans relativized Rome's world imperialism with the Messiah's claim to world dominance, and at the same time challenges Israel's self-understanding by asserting the New Israel's independence of law (*nomos*) and peoplehood (*ethnos*). His image of Paul was of a revolutionary thinker who, having rejected all political and ethnic conceptions of identity, went on to disregard any authority that defined itself in these terms.

This was, moreover, the context in which the Jewish philosopher offered a corrective to the traditional Christian understanding of Paul and the law. For Taubes, it was important to jettison the traditional dichotomy of law and works righteousness and to acknowledge the error of regarding Pauline theology as, essentially, a critique of the Torah or Jewish religious law. Instead, he believed that the "nomos" or "law" that Paul had condemned should actually be understood as referring to the "Hellenistic theology of the sovereign" (2004, 116). Taubes maintained that Paul's critique of the law represents a negation of the use of law *per se* – whether imperial or theocratic – as a force of political order: for the apostle, legitimacy was denied to *all* sovereigns of the world. Taubes's Paul offered, then, a "negative political theology" in that he offered no *political* alternative in his program to undermine the law as a power to dominate; and this, said Taubes, had important implications for those interested in using Paul for their political theologies, for while many oppressed groups might identify with his revolutionary objectives, they could not claim the authority of Paul for the new political orders for which they called.

In offering this interpretation of Paul's view of the law, Taubes not only tried to develop a political-theological critique of the foundations of legal authority, but also to build a case for the categorization of anti-nomism as a legitimately *Jewish* enterprise. He accomplished this by challenging the traditional stereotypes of Judaism and

Christianity as two different approaches to religion, with Judaism exemplifying "reconciliation by ritualization" or ritualistic religiosity, whereby obedience to the law is prized above all else, and Christianity exemplifying "redemption by liberation" or spiritual religiosity, whereby freedom from the law is regarded as the key. And yet, historically, both approaches have had proponents within each of the two religious systems. Taubes's original contribution was to focus on "redemption by liberation" in the *Jewish* context, for which he held up Paul as his Jewish champion. (Traditionally, of course, Paul had been regarded as the *Christian* exemplar of "liberation" from the law.) For Taubes, Paul's critique of the law had *not* been a Christian polemic against Judaism or Jewish law or Torah, but rather one of a series of Jewish attempts to find freedom from the law itself (2004, 116–117); another famous example was Nathan of Gaza, apostle to the seventeenth-century self-proclaimed messiah Sabbatai Zvi (2004, 124–125). Thus, Taubes found Paul most useful in criticizing the Christian community for having missed the political import of the apostle's language of "faith" and "law," and chiding the Jewish community for having regarded anti-nomism as entirely alien to Judaism and Jewish thought.

Conclusion: Paul as an Intersection of Jewish and Christian Cultures

As has been well observed, no culture is an island unto itself and, consequently, there are no identity boundaries that are truly impermeable. For a long time now, thoughtful observers have acknowledged the symbiotic relationship between Judaism and Christianity; that is, between Jewish and Christian religious cultures. They have noted the interdependence of ritual practices, the shared vocabularies, the common fascination with "the other," the antagonistic counter-histories, and the blurred theological boundaries. It has been suggested that it is through the process of engaging with Christian culture, of exploring the intersecting boundaries, that Jewish identity is formed (and vice versa), for one is repeatedly obliged to adopt a stance in response to the challenge posed by "the other." One might agree, disagree, or compromise, but for self-reflective Jews living in a (historically) Christian society, it is simply not possible to ignore the ever-present challenges. From this point of view, Saul–Paul could be thought of as an important point of overlap between Jewish and Christian cultural boundaries. Arguably, it is precisely because the apostle *is* located at an intersection between Jewish and Christian cultural boundaries that he has proved so attractive to the Jewish commentators discussed and has facilitated so powerfully their exploration of questions concerning Jewish authenticity. For those Jewish inhabitants of modernity who have been both attracted to and critical of the non-Jewish world, there are powerful resonances with the state of mind of the first-century apostle who sought to be "all things to all men" (1 Cor 9:19–22), and yet who also refused to "be conformed to this world" (Rom 12:2). In working out their relation to Paul, there is unquestionably a sense of profound consequence in their deliberations and an awareness that their views about him are important for how they understand their own Jewishness, and for how others will perceive them.

Note

1   Biblical quotations are taken from the Revised Standard Version.

References

Asch, Sholem. 1943. *The Apostle*. New York: G. P. Putnam's Sons.

Baeck, Leo. 1952. The Faith of Paul. *Journal of Jewish Studies* 3: 93–110.

Benamozegh, Elijah. 1873. *Jewish and Christian Ethics with a Criticism on Mahomedism*. San Francisco: Emanuel Blochman.

Berdichevsky, Micah. 1971. *Shaul ve-Paul*. Edited by Immanuel Bin-Gorion. Tel Aviv: Moreshet Micha Yosef.

Boyarin, Daniel. 1994. *A Radical Jew: Paul and the Politics of Identity*. Berkeley: University of California Press.

Buber, Martin. 1951. *Two Types of Faith*. London: Routledge & Kegan Paul.

Buber, Martin. 1970. *I and Thou*. New York: Touchstone.

Danby, Herbert, translator. 1933. *The Mishnah*. Oxford: Oxford University Press.

Freud, Sigmund. 1939. *Moses and Monotheism*. London: Hogarth.

Fuchs-Kreimer, Nancy. 1990. The Essential Heresy: Paul's View of the Law according to Jewish Writers, 1886–1986. Unpublished PhD dissertation, Temple University.

Goldstein, Morris. 1950. *Jesus in the Jewish Tradition*. New York: Macmillan.

Graetz, Heinrich. 1901. *History of the Jews from the Earliest Times to the Present Day*. Edited by Bella Löwy. London: Jewish Chronicle.

Hirsch, Emil. 1885. Paul, the Apostle of Heathen Judaism, or Christianity. Pages 1–26 in *The Jewish Life of Christ, Being the Sepher Toldoth Jeshu or Book of the Generation of Jesus*. Edited by G. W. Foote. London: Progressive.

Klausner, Joseph. 1942. *From Jesus to Paul*. London: Allen & Unwin.

Kohler, Kaufmann. 1901. Saul of Tarsus. *Jewish Encyclopedia* 11: 79–87.

Kohler, Kaufmann. 1929. *The Origins of the Synagogue and the Church*. New York: Macmillan.

Krauskopf, Joseph. 1901. *A Rabbi's Impressions of the Oberammergau Passion Play*. Philadelphia: Edward Stern.

Langton, Daniel. 2010. *The Apostle Paul in the Jewish Imagination*. New York: Cambridge University Press.

Lapide, Pinchas, and Peter Stuhlmacher. 1984. *Paul: Rabbi and Apostle*. Minneapolis: Augsburg.

Maccoby, Hyam. 1986. *The Mythmaker: Paul and the Invention of Christianity*. London: Weidenfeld and Nicolson.

Meidner, Ludwig. 1919. *Pauluspredigt* (Paul's Sermon). Watercolor, 68 × 49 cm. Buller Collection, Duisberg.

Montefiore, C. G. 1894. First Impressions of Paul. *Jewish Quarterly Review* 6: 428–474.

Montefiore, C. G. 1901. Rabbinic Judaism and the Epistles of St. Paul. *Jewish Quarterly Review* 13: 161–217.

Montefiore, C. G. 1914. *Judaism and St. Paul: Two Essays*. London: Max Goschen.

Montefiore, C. G. 1918. *Liberal Judaism and Hellenism and Other Essays*. London: Macmillan.

Montefiore, C. G. 1923. *The Old Testament and After*. London: Macmillan.

Nanos, Mark. 1996. *The Mystery of Romans: The Jewish Context of Paul's Letter*. Minneapolis: Fortress.

Nanos, Mark. 2002. *The Irony of Galatians: Paul's Letter in First-century Context*. Minneapolis: Fortress.

Rubenstein, Richard L. 1972. *My Brother Paul*. New York: Harper & Row.

Sachs, Hanns. 1948. *Masks of Love and Life: The Philosophical Basis of Psychoanalysis*. Cambridge, Mass.: Sci-Art.

Sandmel, Samuel. 1958. *The Genius of Paul: A Study in History*. New York: Farrar, Straus & Cudahy.

Sandmel, Samuel. 1965. *We Jews and Jesus*. New York: Oxford University Press.

Sandmel, Samuel. n.d. The Apostle Paul: A Novel (unpublished), 472 pages, in Samuel Sandmel Papers, Manuscript Collection No. 101, Series C/1/17.7 and 18.1 at the American Jewish Archives, Cincinnati, USA.

Schoeps, Hans Joachim. 1961. *Paul: The Theology of the Apostle in the Light of Jewish Religious History*. London: Lutterworth.

Schonfield, Hugh Joseph. 1946. *The Jew of Tarsus: An Unorthodox Portrait of Paul*. London: Macdonald.

Segal, Alan. 1990. *Paul the Convert: The Apostolate and Apostasy of Saul the Pharisee*. New Haven: Yale University Press.

[Shestov] Chestov, Leo. 1932. *In Job's Balances: On the Sources of the Eternal Truths*. London: Dent.

[Shestov] Chestov, Leo. 1966. *Athens and Jerusalem*. Athens, Ohio: Ohio University Press, 1966.

Spinoza, Benedict de. 2007. *Theological-political Treatise*. Cambridge: Cambridge University Press.

Taubes, Jacob. 2004. *The Political Theology of Paul*. Stanford: Stanford University Press.

Werfel, Franz. 1928. *Paul among the Jews: A Tragedy*. London: Mowbray.

Wise, Isaac Mayer. 1883. Paul and the Mystics. Pages 53–75 in Isaac Mayer Wise, *Three Lectures on the Origin of Christianity*. Cincinnati: Bloch.

CHAPTER 30
Orthodox Readings of Paul

Theodore G. Stylianopoulos

In 1953, Panagiotes Bratsiotes, Professor of Old Testament at Athens University, published an article in English under the title "Apostle Paul and the Orthodox Church." His objective was to refute a widely known claim by German liberal scholars that the Orthodox Church had from early times all but forgotten Paul or entirely distorted his thought. What Bratsiotes actually succeeded in doing was to provide a rich array of references from the Orthodox legacy generally related to Paul. As a further step to Bratsiotes's contribution, I propose to explore the substance of some of those references, using a paradigm to organize the discussion. The paradigm is based on the apostolic confession of faith "Jesus is Lord" and on four interpenetrating aspects of the Orthodox tradition that grow from it: the formation of the Christian biblical canon, the creed, the worship, and the understanding of salvation in the light of the good news that "Jesus is Lord." The chapter will conclude with a review of "readings of Paul" by selected Orthodox scholars writing in modern Greek. My overall task is to provide, at the risk of oversimplification, a comprehensive picture of Paul in the Orthodox world from a perspective most familiar to me.

Paul, Canon, and the Rule of Faith

Once Paul's letters were taken up into the biblical canon, according to Bratsiotes, they received wide attention in theological debates, commentaries, ascetical literature, sacramental practice, as well as in the Orthodox lectionary, which features Paul's letters for ten months of the year (Bratsiotes 1953, 416–420). But we must ask further: what

The Blackwell Companion to Paul, First Edition. Edited by Stephen Westerholm.
© 2011 Blackwell Publishing Ltd. Published 2011 by Blackwell Publishing Ltd.

is the theological significance of the inclusion of Paul's letters in the canon, a primary part of the Orthodox tradition? The long process of formation of the Christian Bible was not primarily a legal procedure defined by official councils but an expression of the living tradition of the church guided by the Holy Spirit in its enormous struggle for consolidation and unity. A decisive criterion for inclusion in the canon was the church's discernment about which writings adequately proclaimed the gospel centered on the key confession "Jesus is Lord," the bedrock of the unity of the Scriptures, both new and old. Jesus is Lord because, sent by the only true God and empowered by the Holy Spirit, he has defeated the powers of sin and death through his death and resurrection and has ushered in the new creation for the whole world; he now shares the throne of God and will come as eschatological judge to complete his victory – and all this in fulfillment of God's plan foretold in the law and the prophets.

During the second century, as is well known, the many Gnostic sects and especially Marcion advocated radical revisions of Christianity. Although Marcion exalted Paul, he abridged and distorted Paul's letters, and used Paul's authority to reject the Old Testament. He drastically separated Paul from both the Jewish and Christian traditions (Pelikan 1971, 78, 113). The collection of Paul's letters into the canon, and thus Paul's "rehabilitation" within the broader apostolic tradition, as evidenced in Tertullian and Irenaeus (late second century), proved to be an indisputable corroboration of the apostolic gospel by which the church turned the tables on Marcion and the Gnostics. In particular, Irenaeus is acclaimed a foundational theologian of the Orthodox Church. He is a pre-eminent example of the "organic interdependence" (Gamble 1992, 859) between the canonization process and the creedal sensibilities of the Christian tradition called the "rule of faith." Although still fluid, the basic content of the "rule of faith" pertaining to the gospel and its integral connection with the Old Testament – whatever the theological chaos of the second century claimed by modern radical scholars who seem to favor Gnostic versions of Christianity – were clearly taught and confessed by a networking group of faithful communities (Antioch, Smyrna, Philippi, Corinth, Rome, and others) in essential consistency with the rich treasure of Paul's thought viewed in its wholeness. It matters little if, over against the totality of diverse Gnostic sects and Marcionites, those communities constituted an actual majority during the second century, although they certainly outnumbered any single opposing group. The Arians of the fourth century too were the majority, but the advocates of the classic Christian tradition adamantly and successfully fought off their thinking as incompatible with the gospel.

It was, above all, the content of Paul's teaching, then, together with the church's tradition of creed and prayer, that provided the biblical basis for the refutation of Gnostics and Marcionites. In Paul's letters, Irenaeus, Tertullian, and later others found authoritative material to affirm that the Father of Jesus Christ was indeed the God of the Old Testament (Rom 1:2–3; 15:4–6, etc.), not some other supreme and unknown deity of Marcion and the Gnostics. Jesus the Christ, God's incarnate Son whom the prophets predicted (Rom 1:1–4; Gal 4:4–5), truly died and was bodily raised (1 Cor 15:3–5); it was not the case that some phantasm entered and exited the human Jesus. Salvation was for all who responded by faith (Rom 1:16; 10:8–13), not only for the predestined elite possessing an inner divine spark. The human body was the temple of

the Holy Spirit, and conjugal intimacy a gift of God (1 Cor 6:13–20; 7:1–7), not elements intrinsically evil or the means of the transmission of evil. The Mosaic law and
the Jewish heritage were all part of God's revelation, part of the richness of the good
"olive tree" (Rom 9:4–5; 11:17–18), not a mere foil to God's true plans, something
wicked and unworthy of God. The basic error of Marcion and the Gnostics was that
they either distorted or completely rejected the "overarching story" (Young 2005, 569)
of the Bible – creation, fall, prophetic promise, redemption, and eschatological glorification – which was the non-negotiable historical narrative of the apostolic gospel attested
in Paul (Rom 4; 5:12–21; 9–11; 1 Cor 15; Gal 3). Paul's teaching of the renewal and
recapitulation of all things in Christ (Eph 1:10; cf. Rom 5:12–21; 8; 1 Cor 15) was "the
center of Irenaeus's theology" (Clark 1997, 588): like Paul, Irenaeus saw Christ, the
new Adam, uniting all things in himself, vanquishing the powers of sin and death, and
leading humanity and all creation toward resurrection and sharing in the incorruptible
glory of God (cf. Rom 3:23; 5:2; 8:18; 1 Cor 2:7–8; 15:50–55; 2 Cor 3:18; 4:4–7; Phil
3:21; 1 Thess 2:12).

Bratsiotes, in passing, also mentions the fact that the four gospels are a notable part
of the canon (Bratsiotes 1953, 416), a reference of no little theological import. The
canonical gospels, the most secure part of the canon attested by Irenaeus in the late
second century, and which Origen later called the "first fruits" of all Scripture, constitute the pre-eminent sacred books of the Orthodox tradition. The obvious reason is that
they bear testimony to the life, teachings, and saving work of the Lord himself. Although
Paul, according to the church fathers, possessed the "mind" of Christ and therefore
spoke the "words" of Christ, it would have been incomprehensible to them to put the
authority of Paul's letters above that of the gospels. However, this by no means implies
that Paul should not be given his full due as a major witness in the New Testament,
especially as historical-critical biblical studies can today judiciously recover that witness
in far more precise terms. Nonetheless, biblical students have to contend with the
authority of the Lord himself as recorded in the gospels, including the view of salvation
taught therein, and not rely one-sidedly on Paul. Together with the gospels, the canonical contextualization of Paul is an intrinsic aspect of the living and continuing apostolic
tradition that established the theological unity of Scripture. An undue "elevation of
Paul" amounts to a form of "de-contextualization" of Paul, severing him from both his
Christian and Jewish roots. Such a move would unwittingly compromise the historical
communal character of revelation, as well as biblical authority, and end up repeating
aspects of the battles of the second century.

Paul, Worship, and Doctrine

In Orthodoxy, faith, prayer, creed, proclamation, teaching, and practice form a seamless
whole. Mindful Orthodox Christians, striving to be informed and transformed, pray
what they believe, believe what they pray, and teach and live what they believe and
pray. It is no surprise, therefore, that throughout his article Bratsiotes makes innumerable references to baptism, the Eucharist, Orthodox hymnology, the use of Paul in the
lectionary, the language of Scripture, actual citations, and the character of Orthodox

liturgical texts, as well as to the ascetical practice and spirituality of the Orthodox Church. While Bratsiotes comments neither on the coherence of all these things nor on how they are related to Paul in substantive terms, his instincts are absolutely on target. For one thing, Paul's letters often read like prayer. Paul's deep sense of prayer, the centrality of Christ in his thought, his personal union with Christ, what he writes about baptism, Eucharist, and church in key texts of his letters, as well as his exhortations on vigilance and relentless war against carnality and evil in order to live worthily of Christ and the gospel – all these elements find abundant attestation in Orthodox theology, worship, and life. One will not grasp the Orthodox soul apart from its focus on the person of Christ, incarnate, crucified, and risen, "the Lord of glory" (1 Cor 2:8), in whom believers have access to and communion with the Father and live out the new creation by the power of the Spirit. The eagerly desired subject of the quest of the Orthodox soul is not merely precision in doctrinal definitions, but existential intimacy with the living God in his awesome holiness, love, mercy, transforming power, and light. What Evagrius (fourth century) declared about personal knowledge of God through prayer applies to the community as well as to the individual believer: "If you are a theologian, you will pray truly; and if you pray truly, you are a theologian" (Evagrius 1979, 62).

In his magisterial work *Lord Jesus Christ: Devotion to Jesus in Earliest Christianity* (2003), Larry Hurtado has demonstrated the unity of Christian religious belief and practice in the first two centuries. Hurtado argues that it is the study of "Christ-devotion" rather than of "Christology" that is the preferred approach to the true understanding of the character of early Christianity in its claims about the identity of Christ and the role of his ethical ideals in interpersonal and social spheres (Hurtado 2003, 3–4). According to Hurtado, this worshipful focus on Jesus in religious belief and practice is found not only in the Pauline congregations but even earlier, within the circles of Judean believers. Moreover, this pattern constitutes a fundamental tradition carried on in all subsequent forms of Christianity (2003, 152–153, 215–216). He cites Pliny's striking report to Emperor Trajan (early second century) that Christians in their regular weekly meetings chanted a hymn "to Christ as to a god" and took an oath not to steal, commit adultery, or break their word (2003, 606). Hurtado examines Justin Martyr (mid-second century) as a "proto-orthodox" example of devotion to Jesus. Whatever may be said about Justin's concept of the *logos* and Greek philosophy, Hurtado emphasizes that "for Justin the Logos is first and foremost *Jesus*, whom Christians worship ... through whose death and resurrection believers are purified of their sins ... and through whom now all nations can come to the light of the true God" (648, emphasis in original). In his conclusion, Hurtado declares that this tradition of devotion to Jesus, which "erupted suddenly and quickly, not gradually and late," became the dominant classical form of the Christian faith. He opines that even today "the continuing vitality of Christianity" depends on "how fully Christians engage the question of Jesus, and how radically they are willing to consider what devotion to him means for them" (2003, 650, 653).

Needless to say, Hurtado's words are music to Orthodox ears. Orthodox scholars ordinarily see profound continuities between Paul and patristic theology particularly to the extent that Christian thought and practice are linked to worship, especially the mysteries of baptism and Eucharist. For example, the unity of theology and conduct based on Paul's letters is underscored by John Chrysostom (fourth century) in his third baptismal instruction. Chrysostom addresses newly baptized adults:

> Before yesterday you were captives, but now you are free and citizens of the Church; lately you lived in the shame of your sins, but now you live in freedom and justice [righteousness]. You are not only free, but also holy; not only holy, but also just [righteous]; not only just, but also sons [and daughters]; not only sons, but also ... brothers [and sisters] of Christ; not only brothers of Christ, but also joint heirs; not only joint heirs, but also members; not only members, but also the temple; not only the temple, but also instruments of the Spirit. (John Chrysostom 1963, 57)

In the authentic Orthodox tradition, worship, and especially the Eucharist, along with the centrality of the gospel and a life worthy of it, shape the character and mission of the church as (to use Pauline terms) the body of Christ and the temple of the Spirit (Rom 6:3–11; 1 Cor 3:16; 6:11; 10:16–21; 11:23–31; 12:4–7). Worship is the confession and adoration of Jesus as Lord, together with the Father and the Spirit, one undivided Trinity as attested by Scripture. Baptism and Eucharist are grounded in the saving events of the cross and resurrection of Christ. They are neither sacred "things" to be mindlessly performed, nor do they merely provide data for theological systems. They are "prayer events," that is, events of the invocation and outpouring of the Holy Spirit in the context of communal faith and personal prayer by which believers share in the death and resurrection of Christ, and are summoned as new beings to carry out God's work of forgiveness and renewal for the whole world. The liturgical texts of baptism and Eucharist, just as the Pauline texts proclaiming the gospel (Rom 1–4; 5; 6; 9–11; 1 Cor 15; Gal 3–4), recite key aspects of the biblical narrative of salvation centering on God's saving work in Christ and the Spirit. They celebrate Christ's death and resurrection as the victory over the powers of sin and death, the abiding source of forgiveness, and the inauguration of the new creation. And they beckon believers to the task of world renewal in eager anticipation of the eschatological completion of God's work in glory. While the gospel is orally proclaimed and heard, the sacraments enact and celebrate the gospel through solemn acts. In Orthodox perspective, both baptism and Eucharist function as nothing less than the gospel in liturgical action, the chief priest and celebrant being Christ himself.

Moreover, the dogmatic tradition itself, understood as the intellectual contour of normative Christian thought, is integrated with worship and life. Jaroslav Pelikan has defined doctrine as that which is believed, taught, and confessed on the basis of the word of God – the content of the saving knowledge that serves for Christian instruction and conduct (Pelikan 1971, 1–2). Salvation is, of course, not to be identified with mere intellectual grasp of the "saving knowledge" itself, a Gnostic notion, but with faith in what the gospel proclaims and requires, a "faith working through love" (Gal 5:6). More than anyone in our generation, Pelikan has explored the ways of doctrinal development in East and West in his multi-volume work. He has explicated the doctrinal controversies that resulted in the dogmas on Christology and Trinity through the great councils of the fourth and fifth centuries, summed up in the Nicene Creed. The basis of these controversies was chiefly the exegesis of key biblical texts, including Pauline texts (Rom

1:1–4; 9:5; 1 Cor 2:8–11; 8:6; 15:24–28; 2 Cor 13:13; Phil 2:6–11; Col 1:15–18). We cannot here pursue these incomparable patristic achievements on Christology and Trinity except to note that they issue forth from the early Christian confession of faith that Jesus is Lord, sharing in and revealing the mystery of the one true God of the Scriptures. Contrary to the claims of Harnack and others about the "Hellenization" of dogma, strangely heard among some biblical scholars still today, Pelikan and virtually all students of the Greek patristic tradition underscore its pre-eminent biblical base. About the long and hard-fought controversies of Christian antiquity, the final assessment must be that the church's dogma essentially served just the opposite goal, that of rejecting and defending against "Hellenization," the latter being more characteristic of heresies from Gnosticism to Arianism that creeds and councils opposed (Pelikan 1971, 55).

This is not to deny that Greek words and concepts from contemporary culture were used, such as the terms *ousia* (essence) and *homoousios* (of the same essence). But the decisive criterion was biblical: to confirm and explicate the truth of the gospel that the incarnate Son of God, the true and only Savior, was not a secondary divine being but a person who fully belonged to the uncreated being of God. David S. Yeago (1997) incisively demonstrated the material theological unity between "Paul and Nicea," arguing that the Nicean *homoousios* and Philippians 2:6–11 affirm the same teaching when assessed by theological substance, rather than by time-caught words and concepts (Yeago 1997, 93–97). Richard Bauckham's extensive work moves in the same direction, advocating that the category of "divine identity" or "being" (who God is and who Jesus is in relation to God) is the key to the Christology of the New Testament, with significant continuities in the patristic tradition (Bauckham 2008, 127–139, 146–151). Bauckham cogently and thoroughly rejects the "misleading contrast between 'functional' and 'ontic' [or 'ontological'] Christology as categories for reading the New Testament texts" that have plagued so much of biblical scholarship (2008, 30–31). The critical question for the entire New Testament within its Jewish context is not "what" (a question about divine "nature") but "who" God is (a question of divine "identity"). For Bauckham, the equally critical answer is that Jesus unequivocally and uniquely is Lord! He belongs to the side of the uncreated mystery of God, and within the tradition of strong Jewish monotheism based on the worship of God that now includes Jesus.

In my view, the same fundamental concern, not a philosophical one about "nature" (what) but a biblical one about "identity" (who), drove the thinking of Athanasius and the Cappadocian fathers whose biblical theology is largely the driving force behind the promulgation of the Nicene Creed (Stylianopoulos 1991, 168–195). This creed, the bedrock of Orthodox theology, is but a normative interpretive summary of biblical teaching on God as Father, Son, and Holy Spirit; it is confessed in liturgical contexts not as "doctrinal definitions" but as a joyful "song of faith." The burning concern behind the Nicene Creed and the patristic theology it presupposes is precisely the security of salvation accomplished by an historically revealed true Savior and active Spirit of God, both belonging to the side of the uncreated and unique mystery of God. For centuries, Orthodox Christians have confessed in chant the communion hymn known even to the smallest children (and derived from Phil 2:11): "One is holy, One is Lord, Jesus Christ, to the glory of God the Father, Amen." Another liturgical confession of faith, recalling the words of Isaiah 63:8–9, reads: "For it was neither an angel, nor a man, but the Lord himself who has saved us."

Paul, the Church Fathers, and the Meaning of Salvation

Given the unity of worship, doctrine, and biblical material centering on the proclamation "Jesus is Lord," we may ask further how this integrated content is spelled out, in teaching and spirituality, in terms of the meaning of salvation. In his great work on the history of doctrine, Jaroslav Pelikan makes the point that, while the person of Christ (who Christ is in relation to God) received thorough doctrinal attention, the "meaning" of the saving work of Christ (how we are saved in specific terms) never received similar doctrinal focus in the patristic period (Pelikan 1971, 141). One will not find an Eastern parallel to the discussion about justification in the West. The Greek church fathers wrote about the meaning of salvation in a variety of ways, using multiple biblical and particularly Pauline terminology: new covenant, redemption, justification, forgiveness, reconciliation, sanctification, new creation, transformation, and glorification. No significant controversy in the East ever necessitated concentrated debate on any particular aspect of the meaning of salvation. Everywhere it was assumed that the work of salvation was wholly God's and yet entailed a life-long process until judgment day, based on the primacy of grace and faith, as well as the demonstration of that faith by deeds. Faith and works were never seen as alternative but as unitive ways to salvation. Grace was absolutely primary.

A few examples will suffice. In his Letter 22, Basil the Great (fourth century), drawing entirely from countless injunctions of Scripture, sums up the ideal Christian life as living "worthily of the Gospel of Christ" (Basil the Great 1926, 129–131). Similarly but thematically, Dorotheos of Gaza (sixth century) offers keen pedagogical reflections on the faithful practice of the evangelical virtues such as self-renunciation, humility, fear of God, refusal to judge one's neighbor, and so on, accenting absolute reliance on God together with ascetical vigilance and disciplines (Dorotheos of Gaza 1977, 77–181). Probably in indirect response to the Pelagian controversy in the West, and one thousand years before Luther, Mark the Ascetic (fifth century) authored a collection of sayings without discursive analysis entitled "On Those who Think that They Are Made Righteous by Works." The self-standing sayings advocate that "the kingdom of heaven is not a reward for works, but a gift of grace," and that "sonship is a gift." Commandments are to be fulfilled, not as meriting the kingdom, but as the mere duty of "useless servants" (cf. Luke 17:10). "A slave ... gives satisfaction as one who is in debt, and he receives freedom as a gift." Also, "do not imagine that works in themselves merit either hell or the kingdom. On the contrary, Christ rewards each man according to whether his works are done with faith or without faith in Himself" (Mark the Ascetic 1979, 125, 127). A deep charismatic stream of spirituality exemplified by Symeon the New Theologian (tenth century) stressed the radical transformation of the believer through the indwelling of Christ and the Spirit, and by means of grace and "faith alone" (*ek monēs tēs pisteōs*), and yet with the urgent necessity to practice all Christ's commandments (Symeon the New Theologian 1980, 181–185, 199–200, 249, 261–266).

It is impossible to assess this material on the "meaning" of salvation without detailed study of specific Eastern fathers in comparison with biblical texts. The same is true of the commentaries on Paul's letters in the Byzantine period mentioned by Bratsiotes (1953, 418), notably those by Oekoumenios (sixth century), Zigabenos, and Theophylaktos (both eleventh–twelfth centuries), all of whom are heavily dependent on John Chrysostom. These commentaries are of a homiletical and practical nature, written for the edification of the faithful. They make no attempt to discuss theological topics in a systematic way. They certainly presuppose and promote the doctrine of the church, while they seek to reinforce in various degrees and accents the ways of salvation described above. Generally, they share the traditional vision of the blessings of salvation – such as forgiveness, sanctification, and renewal – issuing from God's saving work in Christ and the Spirit, announced by the gospel, and received through personal faith, genuine repentance, an ongoing life of fervent prayer, and whole-hearted obedience to God's commandments. At the core of this assumed vision is a deeply personal union and communion with Christ experienced as "holy love," a true sharing in the "resurrectional" life of Christ (Symeon the New Theologian 1980, 43–44, 181–185). Christ as living Lord and by action of the Spirit continues his work of forgiveness, cleansing, illumination, and transformation of the believer, rendering him or her a vessel of grace and a sign of the kingdom in the midst of this sinful world. This intimate understanding of salvation is derived both from the witness of the gospel of John and from Paul's view of the Christian life as gift and task. Paul's concepts and language about "putting off" the old Adam and being "clothed with" and "formed in Christ" by means of faith, baptism, and unremitting Spirit-filled warfare against sinful passions (Rom 5–6; 8:5–16; 10:9–13; 1 Cor 6:9–11; 2 Cor 3:17–18; 4:6–5:10; Gal 2:19–20; 4:19; 5:16–24; Col 3:1–17) find incalculable resonance in the tradition of Orthodox spirituality. A singular example is a grace-filled life centered on the "Jesus Prayer" – "Lord Jesus Christ, Son of God, have mercy on me, a sinner" – which has been built on Paul's call for ceaseless prayer (1 Thess 5:17). The "Jesus Prayer," with its beginnings in the fourth century, was prominent in the monastic tradition, but is now ordinarily taught to all alert seekers as a way of respite and quiet communion with God amidst the hectic pace of the modern world.

Jaroslav Pelikan gives us another perspective on the above material. With considerable caution, he gleans a coherent view of the "meaning of salvation" in the Greek fathers in terms of three themes: (1) salvation as the revelation of truth, especially connected with the life and teachings of Christ; (2) salvation as forgiveness and justification based on the centrality of the cross of Christ; and (3) salvation as sharing in the incorruptible divine life through the resurrection of Christ, a theme that enjoys precedence in the tradition (Pelikan 1971, 141–155). Pelikan's proposal can be demonstrated by reference to Athanasius's *On the Incarnation*, a treatise C. S. Lewis called "a masterpiece" (Athanasius of Alexandria 1953, 9). In this treatise, the great Alexandrian father (fourth century) expounded the thesis that the whole of salvation is grounded in the incarnation, life, death, and resurrection of Christ, all prompted by the love and goodness of the Father (cf. Rom 5:8; 8:32, 37–39). Because humans did not attain true knowledge from creation but wallowed in self-inflicted error, idolatry, and degrading evils (Rom 1:18–32), the eternal Word of God necessarily took on a true body to be seen and touched, and also to act and teach (*On the Incarnation*, sections 13–18 [Athanasius 1953, 40–47]). It is the end of Christ's life, however, his true death, that constitutes the sum or center of the faith (*kephalaion tēs pisteōs*), the liberation of humanity from the power of death conceived as a dynamic personified force corrupting and destroying humanity. In sections 6–10 and 19–22 of his work (and this may actually come as a surprise to Orthodox Christians), Athanasius speaks of the death of Christ not only as a beneficent and representative death "for us" (*hyper hēmōn*) but also as a vicarious and substitutionary death "in our stead" (*anti hēmōn*), as if both belonged together. The Adamic transgression incurred the penalty of death according to God's decree. All humanity became accountable and subject to death. Only the eternal Word of God could – and for this very reason the Word became incarnate – "repay what was owed" (*apodothēnai to ōpheilomenon*); that is, the debt of having to die according to God's decree. Thus, Christ died not only for the benefit of all but also in the stead of all (*On the Incarnation* 20 [Athanasius 1953, 49]).

Nevertheless, unlike Tertullian and Hilary who, in connection with church penitential disciplines, first seem to have used the term "satisfaction" in the West, understanding Christ's sacrifice as reparation to God on behalf of sinners (Pelikan 1971, 147), Athanasius thinks in quite different categories. For Athanasius, the debt owed by desperately sinful and corrupt humanity, bereft of the original grace, was to be paid neither to God, nor (certainly not!) to the devil (as some ancient fathers speculated), but rather to death itself as a universally corruptive force caused by human transgression of God's command and hence necessarily in force by God's decree. Because the problem was corruption and death, and not merely the offense of transgression (for which divine forgiveness upon repentance would have sufficed), the only solution was the incarnation of the incorruptible and immortal Word. Christ therefore offered his own bodily temple as "substitute" for all (*antipsychon*, literally "life for life"; cf. 4 Macc 6:28–29); being united to human nature, he vanquished death and clothed humanity with incorruptible life. Athanasius celebrates with Paul by citing 1 Corinthians 15:53–55 (*On the Incarnation* 9 [Athanasius 1953, 35]). Thus, for Athanasius – and here the Alexandrian father seems to follow the line of tradition going back to Irenaeus and to Paul – the supreme goal of Christ's coming to earth was to overcome the condemnation (*katadikē*) of death by his own death and resurrection, which together form the "trophy" or "monument" (*tropaion*) of his victory over death (*On the Incarnation* 22 [Athanasius 1953, 52]). Athanasius seems to do justice to Paul's concerns about human corruption and death, but says nothing about the wrath of God or justification of the sinner as forensic acquittal, even though (drawing on Scripture) he uses the language of debt and substitution.

Another interesting example of the patristic meaning of salvation is found in the work *The Life in Christ* by Nickolas Cabasilas (fourteenth century), which builds on the Pauline understanding of the Christian life as gift and task. Its distinctive mark is the integration of patristic theology with Orthodox worship, chiefly baptism and the Eucharist, but also all the sacred rites of the church. The theological weight of the book is essentially anchored on the eschatological perspective of salvation as present and future, as well as gift and task. The biblical influence comes especially from Paul and John, who are often quoted by Cabasilas. Thus, the work of salvation is "entirely the work of God" and God "has already done so [i.e., benefited the race]" (Cabasilas 1974, 78). Now we are united to God by "faith and grace and all that depends on them"; what is required is "only to believe ... [and be] justified" as Paul wrote in Romans 10:10, though such faith is to be "shown forth in our deeds" (1974, 56, 75). But what is salvation? It is the double gift, on the one hand, of being rescued from the penalty of condemnation, suffering, sickness, corruption, and death incurred by sin, and, on the other, of being united with the living Christ in his incorruptible life, both now and perfectly in the future age. We were "justified" because Christ "paid the penalty" for our sins, paid the "ransom" by his humiliation ("sold to his murderers for a trifling sum"), pain, and death – a penalty that "more than outweighed the evils committed by men," and so "cancelled the indictment" but also added an "abundance of benefits" (1974, 53–54, 58–59). The benefits are summed up in living now "the same life He does"; and "in the world to come we shall be gods with God ... reigning with Him in the same kingdom" (1974, 63). Cabasilas, in silent conversation with Roman Catholic theology of his time, clearly moves beyond the language of justification in Athanasius. He anchors his teaching on justification on the idea of God's restorative justice, including the attributes of divine goodness and love, by which God overcomes the "injustice" of human sin and depravity, and draws all things to himself (Nellas 1975, 169). Cabasilas presents an interesting case that needs further exploration.

From a Western perspective, German theologian and ecumenist Ernst Benz (1951) sums up the comparative significance of Paul in the Western and Eastern churches. The main themes of Orthodox theology and piety, according to Benz, revolve not around justification, but around the incarnation of God and deification through new creation, rebirth, and transfiguration (1951, 297–300). The legal concept of merit and the notion of a treasury of merits are entirely missing from the Orthodox tradition, where the distinct ideal is the charismatic holy man as a manifestation of the kingdom. Because sin is not viewed in juridical terms – that is, as primarily an offense against the honor and justice of God, but as shrinkage, a wound, an infection of humanity – the main understanding of salvation is concerned with the healing of a sickness, with the renewal of being, and not at all with the satisfaction of divine justice through the merits of Christ. Correspondingly, redemption signifies not merely a righting of the relationship between God and man, but transfiguration and deification in mystical communion with God. Not the idea of righteousness but that of love, Benz declares, dominates the East theologically and ethically (1951, 300–301). Benz concludes that the Reformation was a typically Western reaction to developments in the Western tradition. This does not mean that a reformation was not necessary in the East, but only that the Protestant Reformation in its specifically Western form, based on the centrality of justification, had no presuppositions in the East (1951, 303–305). And this was the reason why, in the correspondence between Lutheran theologians and Patriarch Jeremias II (sixteenth century), the two sides found each other mutually incomprehensible, refuting each other while using the same authority – Paul! Benz's ecumenical proposal is that the one-sidedness in both the Western and Eastern traditions ought to be overcome. The gospel cannot be reduced to justification nor should justification be of minimal significance to the understanding of the gospel. The way to proceed is to listen for the original melody in the "polyphony" of Paul and the "full symphony" of the New Testament itself (Benz 1951, 304–308). It would be extremely useful to analyze the correspondence between Jeremias II and the Lutheran theologians in the light of contemporary biblical studies.

Paul in Modern Greek Biblical Studies

After the four-century long Ottoman rule, academic studies of Scripture claiming a "scientific" basis began in Greece with the establishment of the University of Athens (1837) and later the University of Thessaloniki (1960), and with tiny steps in the theological departments. A handful of mostly German-trained scholars gradually laid the first foundations from which an impressive academic tradition of biblical studies has arisen. They were concerned, on the one hand, to connect with Western biblical criticism, and, on the other hand, to secure their work within Orthodox doctrinal parameters. Bratsiotes in his article (1953, 419) cites, among others, the "excellent" commentary on Galatians by E. Zolotas, published in 1904. This is indeed a magnificent piece of scholarship, offering a wealth of historical information and commentary based on the church fathers, the main Reformers, and the leading figures in contemporary German scholarship. Of the twenty-one names listed as his primary sources, nineteen are German, one is English, and one is French (Zolotas 1904, 9–10). Clearly, his work exhibits the high standards of scholarship in which Zolotas was trained, along with his unwavering commitment to the Orthodox Church. Zolotas has embraced the methods of Western scholarship but declares that the anchors of truth are the church fathers, who were more "sensitive" to the language and "closer" to the facts of the New Testament. While he concedes that the exegesis of the church fathers was aimed chiefly at pastoral edification and is therefore "insufficient" for the needs of "scientific" interpretation (1904, 6–7), he does not explicate what those needs are and why "scientific" exegesis is helpful to Eastern Orthodoxy. He assumes the usefulness of the available vast scholarly knowledge and seems to feel secure that its radical aspects will be kept far away in Germany. But the problem of bridging, on the one hand, modern biblical criticism, its value being undermined by its chaotic character, and, on the other hand, traditional Orthodox theology and spirituality continues to be a significant alienating factor to this day (Stylianopoulos 1997, 73–77, 138–145).

Most telling is the centrality that Zolotas attributes to the teaching of justification in Paul (1904, 14–17). Justification is said to be the "governing" theme not only of Galatians and Romans but also of 1–2 Corinthians, an opinion hardly sustainable. Galatians is Paul's most important letter, even above Romans, since it clarifies the "greatest question" of Christianity, namely, justification by faith. Zolotas specifies that Paul dealt with other important subjects as well, many even in Galatians, such as the death of Christ, union with Christ, adoption, freedom, flesh and spirit, new creation, and so on, but all those were derived from and entirely dependent upon the "truth of justification," which is the "essence of the gospel" (1904, 15–16, 174). He could not yet have read the works on Paul by W. Wrede and A. Schweitzer, still to come, which moved in the opposite direction, diminishing the significance of justification as the key to Paul. However, a lively discussion over two distinct notions of salvation in Paul, one based on justification by faith ("juridical" and "ethical") and the other on baptism ("sacramental" and "mystical"), had been going on in German circles since 1872 with the publication of Hermann Lüdemann's book on Pauline anthropology (Meeks 1972, 218).

Zolotas maintains his Orthodox grounding by qualifying his exaltation of justification in distinctive ways (1904, 14, 17, 19, 28–30). It is Christ who "actualizes" justification through his "union with the Church." Galatians develops the truth of justification by speaking of a faith active through deeds of love, thereby securing the unity of the church. The church fathers did not concentrate on justification because the issue had been "forever resolved" in the apostolic period with the liberation of Christianity from the risk of "dissolution in Judaism." Consequently, Marcion and later Luther and others wrongly revisited and subverted "the dogma concerning justification unshakably established in the Church of old from the apostles." But is not the teaching on justification of permanent relevance? Zolotas never discusses this question beyond the idea of Christianity's freedom from Judaism. When the exegesis requires him to analyze the verb "justify" (Gal 2:16–17), he mentions the nuances of the related Hebrew verb – to judge, make, proclaim, acquit, or save someone as righteous – and chooses, without due explanation, the meaning "to judge righteous" not by works of the law but by faith. Faith is faith in Christ. What are the works of the law? They are found not in the moral law, which is also required by Christianity and manifest in the fruit of the Spirit, but rather in the ritual law – the Jewish festivals, sacrifices, purity injunctions, and circumcision, all matters of indifference after Christ. The eleventh-century commentator Zigabenos is then quoted at length, providing the alternative interpretation of an inclusive view of the law, a law that no one can fulfill with the result that all stand condemned; but without comment, Zolotas chooses the former option, which he applies even to Romans, a move palpably wrong for Romans 1:18–3:20 (1904, 405–406). Later, he quotes Oekoumenios on Galatians 3:10 that "the path of justification is one, that is, by faith," and it is secured by the irrefutable scriptural authority of Habakkuk 2:4 (433). Nevertheless, Zolotas neither departs from nor explains the traditional insistence on good works and ends up with a sharp rebuke of Protestants who claim that "good works are not necessary for justification" (528–529). While Zolotas's scholarship may be applauded, it can be fairly said that his commentary left many gaps to be filled and many qualifications to be made.

The pre-eminent Orthodox biblical scholar of the twentieth century was Savas Agourides (PhD from Duke University, 1950), who taught New Testament first at Thessaloniki and later at Athens. An energetic personality and prolific author, Agourides (or Agouridis) was until his death (in 2008) an intellectual force in the Greek world of religion, politics, and culture. His achievements are chronicled in a volume published in his honor in America (Stylianopoulos 2006, 1–6). Among his writings is a treatise on Paul published in a Greek encyclopedia and separately as a compact book (Agourides 1966). Although now somewhat dated, this book reflects the growth in Greek studies on Paul by that date. Agourides's Western sources included the writings of Wrede, Bultmann, Caird, Cullmann, Kümmel, Dodd, and Taylor. In his sketch of Paul's thought, Agourides rejects the single-central-issue approach in favor of the "wholeness" of Paul's theology within the context of the early church and its "general soteriological schema" (Agourides 1966, 40–41). In Paul, according to Agourides, this schema (which he curiously calls the "foundation" of Paul's thought and the "key" to Paul's understanding of the past and the future) is none other than the actualization of God's overarching salvation plan in the life, death, and resurrection of Christ, and the creation of the "new human family" promised to Abraham, the church. From this thesis, and somewhat reminiscent of Bultmann's classic work on Paul, Agourides goes on to present Paul's thought in terms of an understanding of humanity first apart from Christ and then "in Christ." He analyzes first the terms "world," "Adam," "flesh," "sin," and so on, then "redemption," "justification," "reconciliation," "victory," and "sacrifice" (1966, 45– 73); justification is no longer central but one of many topics. He concludes with distinct sections on the Spirit, the church, and eschatology in its integrated present and future aspects (1966, 73–82).

Compared to Zolotas, Agourides shows a far deeper and more nuanced engagement with the historical-critical study of Scripture. On the one hand, the obligation to cite patristic interpretations is no longer in evidence. The advanced analysis of texts in modern biblical studies seems to leave little room for meaningful contributions through citation of random patristic references. The assumed working principle is that each case must be exegetically decided not by appeal to authority but by careful critical analysis of a text in its own context – the defining mark of biblical criticism. On the other hand, Agourides well knows that that principle, far from having produced a consensus, has regularly yielded diverse and often contradictory results, noting, for example, Wrede's and Schweitzer's views that justification by faith is a "polemical" and "subsidiary" teaching in Paul (Agourides 1966, 40–41, 59–60). Nor is Agourides unaware that scholarly views are not always the pure result of objective study. His understanding of justification (1966, 68–70) as an act before the divine court, acquitting and declaring the believer innocent on the grounds of faith, is clear. He also knows of the debate whether, in the act of justification, God's righteousness is imparted (the Roman Catholic view) or only forensic (the Protestant view). However, he chooses a third scholarly option, citing Isaiah 56:1 to the effect that God's righteousness is not merely a divine attribute but also a specific saving act, closely related to sanctification (1 Cor 6:11), with largely corporate rather than individualistic meaning. It is part of the larger exodus theme as redemption from the forces of evil, sin, death, and the principalities, through Christ's death and resurrection and the gift of the Spirit (1966, 66). Exemplified by the case of the Prodigal Son, the acquittal is God's definitive but not final act; an act based not on the counting of deeds and virtues but on a radical surrender of the will to God that by no means cancels out the ethical demand for a transformed life and that presumes future judgment (pp. 68–69). The glorious result is a new eschatological reality in the midst of this world, actualized through baptism and entailing a new obedience, all signified by the church as the one people of God and the body of Christ in its eschatological status and mission (pp. 70, 76–80). By means of modern biblical scholarship, Agourides works out a comfortable understanding of Paul within an Orthodox perspective. He notes that international Pauline studies are headed toward the ancient church's understanding of Paul – his only general reference to the patristic tradition (p. 60) – a remark that arguably rings even more true today in the light of N. T. Wright's version of the "New Perspective" on Paul.

Not for some forty years was another and much longer comprehensive work on Paul authored by another Greek scholar, Petros Vasiliadis (2004), professor at the University of Thessaloniki, a former student of Agourides, and a personal friend of mine. The contents of this challenging volume, a reworking of the author's published work over twenty years, is divided into roughly three equal parts: "soteriology," "ecclesiology," and the "collection" for the Jerusalem church. Space constraints limit me to the most fleeting comments on the topic of soteriology. Vasiliadis laments the "exclusivity" and "monopoly" of dogmatic theology as the theology of the Orthodox Church, a church that hardly pays attention to the rich development of Greek biblical studies looking to contribute to an "historically grounded theology of the New Testament" (Vasiliadis 2004, 14). As my collegial and respectful critique, I may be allowed to say that the gap between the two fields will not be bridged unless we ourselves as Orthodox biblical scholars, soliciting the help of Orthodox dogmatic theologians, convincingly begin to demonstrate the theological coherence between Scripture and the patristic tradition in concrete and substantive terms. I sincerely regret to note that my friend's volume seems to accomplish little for this purpose. His erudite review of the history of Western developments on the thought of Paul draws no conclusions meaningful to Orthodox readers. If we understand the reference to the "cross" as a reference to the saving death of Christ, the idea that it was Luther who for the first time really connected "cross" and "salvation" is incomprehensible (Vasiliadis 2004, 41–42). Most astonishingly, Vasiliadis devotes not a single paragraph to the saving significance of Jesus's resurrection. Drawn by his sources, he instead talks about the "word of the cross" as the "quintessence" of Paul's gospel and *"the center of Pauline soteriology"* (2004, 131–132; emphasis added). Is not the Pauline gospel centered on both the death and resurrection of the Lord as an inseparable cosmic event (1 Cor 15:1–19)? And is not the incarnation, death, and resurrection of God's Son at the core of the Christian proclamation from Paul, to Irenaeus, to Athanasius, and so on? Petros and some of us as his friends may need to go into a room, lock the door, and respectfully have it out.

The last selected work directly pertinent to our topic is a substantial doctoral dissertation on "Pauline soteriology" composed in modern Greek by Jack G. Khalil (2004), a Lebanese Orthodox biblical scholar who studied in Greece and Germany. This work, an exegetical overview of Romans 2:1–8; 3:21–26; 5:1–11, and 8:1–17, is determined to show the coherence of Paul's thought concerning God's righteousness, justification, reconciliation, and the last judgment, and in full agreement with patristic teaching. God's righteousness is primarily not a passive attribute (*iustitia passiva*) but God's outgoing saving activity, specified as justification, an act actualized at the moment of faith and belonging entirely to the past (Khalil 2004, 84–90, 108, 147, 270). God's righteousness, justification, and reconciliation are all centered on "redemption" (Rom 3:24–25), understood as "acquittal" and "removal" of "sins," and resulting in imparted new life by God's power (2004, 82, 84–87, 93–96). The new order of "spiritual life" is absolutely dependent on active, not passive, faith (Rom 10:9) – an active personal decision attested in Christian obedience and summed up in love (2004, 23, 80–81, 88, 149, 271). Final salvation is in the future (Rom 5:10) and linked to the last judgment (Rom 2:1–8), when believers are held accountable for the obedience they have shown in response to the gift of new life (2004, 269–273). Khalil could strengthen his Orthodox positions by showing that Jesus's resurrection plays a role in justification (Rom 4:25) and that justification itself is also a future reality, an intrinsic part of God's final judgment (Rom 2:13, 16; cf. Gal 5:5). The chief weakness of his work involves "telescoping" the meaning of Paul's key words by focusing on the "forgiveness of sins" to an extent that Paul's diverse key terms lose their distinct nuances and specific theological implications (cf. Wright 2009, 71). Similarly, the expressions "law of faith," "law of Christ," "law of God," the "essence" of the Mosaic law, and "the law of the spirit [not Spirit!]" (Rom 8:2) are all said to signify the same reality of the "spiritual life" referred to by Paul as "his ways" (1 Cor 4:17) and expressed in the specifics of his various warnings and exhortations (Khalil 2004, 289–290, 310–316, 346). A comparative critical review of this work along with Wright's (2009) book on justification would be exceedingly illuminating.

References

Agourides, S. 1966. *Pavlos: Skiagraphēma tēs zōēs, tou ergou kai tēs didaskalias tou Apostolou* [Paul: Sketch of the Life, Work, and Teaching of the Apostle]. Athens: no publisher given. Reprint from pages 169–210 of the *Thrēskeutikē kai Ēthikē Encyclopaideia, Tomos 10* [Religious and Ethical Encyclopedia, Vol. 10]. Edited by A. Panotis. Athens: A. Martinos.

Athanasius of Alexandria. 1953. *St. Athanasius on the Incarnation: The Treatise* De Incarnatione verbi dei. Translated and edited by a religious of CSMV with an introduction by C. S. Lewis. London: Mowbray.

Basil the Great. 1926. Letter XXII. Pages 129–145 in *St. Basil: The Letters*. Volume 1. Loeb Classical Library. Translated by Roy J. Deferrari. London: Heinemann.

Bauckham Richard. 2008. *Jesus and the God of Israel: God Crucified and Other Studies on the New Testament's Christology of Divine Identity*. Grand Rapids: Eerdmans.

Benz, Ernst. 1951. Das Paulus-Verständnis in der morgenländischen und abendländischen Kirche. *Zeitschrift für Religions- und Geistesgeschichte* 3: 289–309.

Bratsiotes, Panagiotes. 1953. Apostle Paul and the Orthodox Church. Pages 414–423 in *Saint Paul's Mission to the Church: Nineteenth Centenary: A Volume of Commemoration*. Edited by H. S. Alivisatos. Athens: Apostolike Diakonia.

Cabasilas, Nicholas. 1974. *The Life in Christ*. Translated by Carmino J. deCatanzaro. Crestwood, NY: St. Vladimir's Seminary.

Clark, Mary T. 1997. Irenaeus (ca. 115–ca. 202). Pages 587–588 in *Encyclopedia of Early Christianity*, Volume 1. Second Edition. Edited by Everett Ferguson. New York: Garland.

Dorotheos of Gaza. 1977. *Dorotheos of Gaza: Discourses and Sayings*. Edited by E. Rozanne Elder. Kalamazoo: Cistercian.

Evagrius the Solitary. 1979. On Prayer: One Hundred and Fifty-three Texts. Pages 55–71 in *The Philokalia*, Volume 1. Edited by G. E. H. Palmer, Philip Sherrard, and Kallistos Ware. London: Faber and Faber.

Gamble, Harry Y. 1992. Canon: New Testament. Pages 852–861 in *The Anchor Bible Dictionary*. Volume 1. Edited by David Noel Freedman. New York: Doubleday.

Hurtado, Larry W. 2003. *Lord Jesus Christ: Devotion to Jesus in Earliest Christianity*. Grand Rapids: Eerdmans.

John Chrysostom. 1963. The Third Instruction. Pages 56–65 in *St. John Chrysostom: Baptismal Instructions*. Translated and annotated by Paul W. Harkins. Westminster: Newman.

Khalil, Jack G. 2004. *Dikaiōsē–Katallagē–Telikē Krisē stēn pros Rōmaious Epistolē: Symbolē stēn Pavleia Sōtēriologia* [Justification–Reconciliation–Last Judgment in the Epistle to the Romans: A Contribution to Pauline Soteriology]. Thessaloniki: Pournaras.

Mark the Ascetic. 1979. On Those who Think that They Are Made Righteous by Works: Two Hundred and Twenty-six Texts. Pages 125–146 in *The Philokalia*, Volume 1. Edited by G. E. H. Palmer, Philip Sherrard, and Kallistos Ware. London: Faber and Faber.

Meeks, Wayne A., editor. 1972. *The Writings of St. Paul*. New York: Norton.

Nellas, Panagiotes. 1975. *Hē Peri Dikaiōseōs Didaskalia Nikolaou tou Cabasila* [The Teaching of Nicolas Cabasilas concerning Justification]. Peiraeus: Karaberopoulos.

Pelikan, Jaroslav. 1971. *The Christian Tradition: A History of the Development of Doctrine*. Volume 1: *The Emergence of the Catholic Tradition (100–600)*. Chicago: University of Chicago Press.

Stylianopoulos, Theodore G. 1991. The Biblical Background of the Article on the Holy Spirit in the Constantinopolitan Creed. Pages 168–195 in *The Good News of Christ: Essays on the Gospel, Sacraments and Spirit*. By Theodore G. Stylianopoulos. Brookline: Holy Cross Orthodox.

Stylianopoulos, Theodore G. 1997. *The New Testament: An Orthodox Perspective*. Volume 1: *Scripture, Tradition, Hermeneutics*. Brookline: Holy Cross Orthodox.

Stylianopoulos, Theodore G., editor. 2006. *Sacred Text and Interpretation: Perspectives in Orthodox Biblical Studies: Papers in Honor of Professor Savas Agourides*. Brookline: Holy Cross Orthodox.

Symeon the New Theologian. 1980. *The Discourses*. New York: Paulist.

Vasiliadis, Petros. 2004. *Pavlos: Tomes stē Theologia tou* [Paul: Trajectories into his Thought]. Thessaloniki: Pournaras Editions.

Wright, N. T. 2009. *Justification: God's Plan and Paul's Vision*. Downers Grove, Ill.: IVP Academic.

Yeago, David S. 1997. The New Testament and the Nicene Dogma: A Contribution to the Recovery of Theological Exegesis. Pages 87–100 in *The Theological Interpretation of Scripture: Classic and Contemporary Readings*. Edited by Stephen E. Fowl. Oxford: Blackwell.

Young, Frances M. 2005. Patristic Biblical Interpretation. Pages 566–571 in *Dictionary for Theological Interpretation of the Bible*. Edited by Kevin J. Vanhoozer. Grand Rapids: Baker Academic.

Zolotas, Emmanouel I. 1904. *Hympomnēma eis tēn pros galatas epistolēn tou Apostolou Paulou* [Commentary on the Epistle to the Galatians of the Apostle Paul]. Athens: P. D. Sakellariou.

CHAPTER 31
African Readings of Paul

Grant LeMarquand

Until recently, Paul's letters have been the least explored section of the Christian canon in Africa. African preachers tend to lean more heavily than their Western counterparts on Old Testament texts, and when the New Testament is being preached, the gospels receive more attention than the epistles. Even within the gospels themselves, if the bulk of African scholarship is a true indicator, Africans have tended to spend more time with narrative materials than with the sayings of Jesus. Paul's letters, perhaps due to their character as extended arguments, have been less attractive to African preachers, and to African biblical scholars, than much of the rest of the canon.

This first superficial observation may be unfair, however. The past decade or so has seen a surge of interest in Paul in Africa. Numerous books and articles have appeared, some dealing with topics that have been of keen interest to scholars in the Western world, others dealing with aspects of Paul's life and writings that may seem more exotic to a non-African audience.

This chapter will not attempt to be comprehensive, but will rather take soundings that explore how African readers from different periods of time and from a diversity of African cultures have encountered the letters and the person of Paul. We must begin, however, by acknowledging that the word "Africa" itself is a multivalent and controverted term. To say that something or someone is, or is not, African raises a multitude of questions. For example, is modern Egypt a part of Africa or a part of the Middle East? Is ancient Egypt better described as African, or as a part of the Mediterranean world? In what ways is South Africa "African," and in what ways has it been so influenced by the West that its African identity is questionable or compromised? For the purposes of this chapter, we will throw the net rather wide by exploring how the entire continent

The Blackwell Companion to Paul, First Edition. Edited by Stephen Westerholm.
© 2011 Blackwell Publishing Ltd. Published 2011 by Blackwell Publishing Ltd.

has been and is home to a number of different and yet overlapping reading communities, from Patristic writers such as Origen and Augustine, through the ancient churches of North Africa, Egypt, Ethiopia, and Nubia, to those Western missionary writers whose exegesis was shaped by the places of their birth as well as their new homes in Africa, to those modern African writers, readers, and preachers whose social location includes the living traditional religions of Africa, a variety of colonial experiences, as well as the triumphs and disappointments of the postcolonial African world, with its poverty, disease, and corruption, on the one hand, and its energy, joy, and communal solidarity, on the other.

African Patristic Readings of Paul

Thomas Oden (2007) has argued that Western Christianity from late antiquity through to the modern period was shaped in very large part by the experience and thinking of the ancient African churches. Oden does not deny that Europe and Asia contributed to the formation of Christian identity in the ancient world, but it was in Africa that much of what came to be considered normative Christian dogma and experience was formed.

> This point must be savored unhurriedly to sink in deeply: The Christians to the south of the Mediterranean were teaching the Christians to the north. Africans were informing and instructing and educating the very best of Syriac, Cappodocian and Greco-Roman teachers. This flow of intellectual leadership in time matured into the ecumenical consensus on how to interpret sacred Scripture and hence into the core of Christian dogma. (Oden 2007, 28)

Oden points out that the monastic movement, which spread to such diverse contexts as Syria and Ireland, has its roots in such figures as Anthony and Pachomius, living in the deserts of Egypt; that many of the battles between orthodox and heretical (as these terms came to be defined) took place between Africans on African soil (Arius was Libyan; the views of Gnostics like Valentinus and Basilides are known to us largely from African sources); that basic Christological and trinitarian understandings later adopted by ecumenical councils were set forth and shaped decades earlier by African thinkers such as Tertullian (a Libyan), Cyprian of Carthage, Athanasius of Alexandria, Augustine of Hippo, and Cyril of Alexandria. It will not do simply to assert that since these Africans lived near the Mediterranean, they were more a part of the Greco-Roman than the African world. True, these early Christians spoke and wrote in Greek and Latin (although Coptic became a major Christian language, as did Paleo-Nubian and Arabic somewhat later) and interacted with European and Asian Christianity; but, as Oden argues, they were not merely "Europeans in disguise," and the assumption that they were betrays a modern intellectual bias (2007, 62).

In biblical exegesis as well, African thinkers were great contributors to the ecumenical discussion that developed during the Patristic period. Africa contributed to the development of translations of the Bible, first with the translation of the Septuagint in the Jewish community in Egypt, then with the African Old Latin versions, precursors to Jerome's translation, and various Coptic versions. Techniques for biblical interpretation were developed not only by Didymus the Blind and Augustine in the fourth and fifth centuries, but especially (and earlier) by the great biblical scholar Origen, working in Egypt in the late second and early third centuries.

In addition to producing many volumes of commentary on Paul's letters, ancient African readers of the Bible, especially Origen, took Paul's letters as a model for how to do biblical interpretation. It is well known that Alexandrian exegesis viewed Scripture as multi-tiered or multi-layered. For Origen, the Bible was something like the human body, which has (as Origen learned from Paul: 1 Thess 5:23) body, soul, and spirit.[1] The first tier of reading the Bible, that which is the clearest, is the "bodily" part of Scripture, the obvious sense, and the most accessible to any enquirer. The second tier, having to do with wisdom and knowledge, is somewhat less obvious and, therefore, accessible only to the wise. The third tier, the level of the spirit, is usually referred to as the allegorical sense. For this way of reading Scripture, Origen once again turns to Paul as his guide.

> In the third tier, the Bible speaks to those who are "perfect" or "mature," as Paul puts it in 1 Cor. 2:6–7: "Yet among the mature we do speak wisdom, though it is not a wisdom of this age or of the rulers of this age, who are doomed to perish. But we speak God's wisdom, secret and hidden, which God decreed before the ages for our glory." (Hall 1998, 144–145)

As with many other important figures in the history of the church, it was a passage from Paul that was instrumental in the conversion of Augustine:

> As I was ... weeping in the bitter agony of my heart, suddenly I heard a voice from the nearby house chanting as if it might be a boy or a girl (I do not know which), saying and repeating over and over again "Pick up and read, pick up and read." ... I checked the flood of tears and stood up. I interpreted it solely as a divine command to me to open the book and read the first chapter I might find ... So I hurried back to the place where Alypius was sitting. There I had put down the book of the apostle when I got up. I seized it, opened it and in silence read the first passage on which my eyes lit: "Not in riots and drunken parties, not in eroticism and indecencies, not in strife and rivalry, but put on the Lord Jesus Christ, and make no provision for the flesh in its lusts" (Rom. 13:13–14). I neither wished nor needed to read further. At once, with the last words of this sentence, it was as if a light of relief from all anxiety flooded into my heart. All the shadows of doubt were dispelled. (Augustine, *Confessions* 8.12)

For Augustine, and for the other African writers of the early church period, Paul's letters (in this case, the letter to the Romans) were not merely a source of Christian doctrine and ethics (which they certainly were), but the word of God, which conveyed the message of salvation.

The rise of Islam in the seventh century devastated North African Christianity. The church west of Egypt was Latin-speaking and as such was very much a colonial church attached to the Roman Empire, not rooted in the Berber language and culture of North African village life. The church was also divided between the "orthodox," Donatists, and Vandal Arians. When the Muslims invaded, the Latin Christians fled. The Berbers were quickly Islamized. On the other hand, the Coptic church, which had taken root in the

Coptic language and culture of Egypt, was able to resist conversion to Islam, although it had to endure centuries of accommodation and persecution. The Ethiopian church, a product of both Egyptian and Syrian evangelization, also indigenized and, because of its unique geography, remained relatively isolated, both from Western Christianity and from Islam. The Nubian orthodox church (in what we now call north Sudan) thrived for a thousand years from the sixth to the sixteenth centuries, but eventually assimilated to Islam. Much of the rich theology of these churches is lost (especially in the case of Nubia) or remains untranslated. Until the Portuguese began exploration in the late medieval period, Africa had little contact with Christianity outside these orthodox conclaves in the north-eastern corner of the continent.

Missionary Readings of Paul in African Contexts

The modern missionary movement in Africa is a complex phenomenon combining a myriad of personalities, nations, cultures, and motives. Exploration, colonialism, imperialism, the slave trade (and European Christian guilt for "Christian" nations' participation in the slave trade) all play roles in the period of history from the eighteenth to the early twentieth centuries in which Western powers scrambled to divide and dominate the less industrialized parts of the globe. Missionaries, sometimes preceding and sometimes following the traders and colonists, lived in an uneasy and shifting tension between their own national allegiances and cultural proclivities and their desire to bring the gospel to those who had not heard it. In the midst of this tension, missionaries often supported colonial regimes that attempted to bring a Western sense of civilization to non-Western cultures. In the struggle against the slave trade (both on the Atlantic and the Indian Ocean coasts), missionaries and colonial powers seemed in agreement and could work together. On the other hand, missionaries often also opposed heavy-handed and unjust structures that colonial powers frequently imposed on the indigenous population.

One result not to be overlooked is that, whereas before the colonial period Christianity was predominantly a Western phenomenon, by its end Christianity was truly international.[2] The center of global Christian life has clearly moved south, and especially to Africa. The Western missionaries who brought the Christian faith to Africa also came as readers and interpreters of the Bible. Much historical work needs to be done examining the ways in which these missionaries interpreted Scripture, including Paul, in their new, foreign contexts. A few studies are beginning to emerge.

An examination of readings of Romans 1 provides a telling example of the different ways in which Paul was read by the missionary community in Africa.

> For the wrath of God is revealed from heaven against all ungodliness and wickedness of those who by their wickedness suppress the truth. For what can be known about God is plain to them, because God has shown it to them. Ever since the creation of the world his eternal power and divine nature, invisible though they are, have been understood and seen through the things he has made. So they are without excuse; for though they knew God, they did not honor him as God or give thanks to him, but they became futile in their thinking, and their senseless minds were darkened. Claiming to be wise, they became fools; and

they exchanged the glory of the immortal God for images resembling a mortal human being or birds or four-footed animals or reptiles ... Since they did not see fit to acknowledge God, God gave them up to a debased mind and to things that should not be done. They were filled with every kind of wickedness, evil, covetousness, malice. Full of envy, murder, strife, deceit, craftiness, they are gossips, slanderers, God-haters, insolent, haughty, boastful, inventors of evil, rebellious toward parents, foolish, faithless, heartless, ruthless. (Rom 1:18–23, 28–31)[3]

Andrew Walls (1996) has produced a valuable study of missionary interpretation of this text. His investigation of nineteenth- and early twentieth-century missionary sermons and reports reveals a lack of uniformity in the use of Romans 1 by missionaries in their encounter with "foreign" cultures. For some missionaries, Paul's words self-evidently condemn non-Christian religion.

David Jonathan East, one of a small host of writers on West Africa in the 1840s, produces an imposing account (based on travellers' tales) of African slavery, drunkenness, immorality, and lack of commercial probity. He then quotes Romans 1:28–31. "What an awful comment upon this affecting portion of Holy Writ are the humiliating facts which these and the preceding chapters record." In another place, however, East recognizes that African paganism, though reprehensible, is in one respect different from that of Romans 1. Though African people have images, they do not make images of the Supreme God: they simply ignore him for the subordinate divinities and spirits. "Thus it appears, that if they have not 'changed the glory of the incorruptible God into an image, made like to corruptible man, and to birds, and four-footed beasts and creeping things' – they have, in their view, excluded him from the government of his world, and substituted in his room the wild creatures of their own imaginations, identifying these professedly spiritual existences with what is material, and oft times grossly absurd." (Walls 1996, 62)

As far as East is concerned, the truth of Romans 1 is confirmed by the self-evident depravity of African people. Their idolatry has led them to immorality. Having excluded God "from the government of his world," Africans have been "given up" to absurd spiritual and moral behavior. Such assertions about the indigenous peoples of Africa, Asia, and the Americas are made repeatedly in the nineteenth century by missionaries, travelers, and chroniclers. The corollary was that, if such religions and cultures were so obviously debased, the truth and beauty of the Christian religion shine forth all the more clearly.

Although Romans 1 (and Romans 2, as Walls points out) condemns *people* for their sinfulness and idolatry, the missionary rhetoric tended to condemn *systems* of belief. Walls's comments are apt:

As systems, and ultimately the collective labels for systems which we call the world religions, have slipped into the place of ungodly people in the interpretation of Romans 1, so Christianity, also conceived as a system, has sometimes slipped into the place of the righteousness of God. The true system has been opposed to false systems condemned there. It has sometimes, but not always, been realized that "Christianity" is a term formally identical with the other labels; that it certainly covers as wide a range of phenomena as most of them; that, if the principalities and powers work within human systems, they can and do work within this one. Man-in-Christianity lies under the wrath of God just as much, and for the same reasons, as Man-in-Hinduism ... It [is] not Christianity that saves, but Christ. (1996, 66)

In other words, if Paul's letter to the Romans has implications for the African tradition-alist, its message is addressed equally to the Western Christian: "all have sinned and fall short of the glory of God" (Rom 3:23). Romans 1 addresses the human situation, not just the *non-Western* human condition.

A missionary reading of Paul that stands in contrast to the example quoted by Walls can be found in the writings of the controversial Anglican missionary Bishop of Natal, John William Colenso (1814–1883).[4] Colenso is best known for his championing of German source critical theory on the Hexateuch through the publication of successive editions of *The Pentateuch and Book of Joshua Critically Examined* through the 1860s and into the following decade. Colenso's liberal views eventually led to his being excom-municated and removed from his see as Bishop of Natal by Bishop Grey of Cape Town, precipitating the first international gathering of Anglican bishops at Lambeth Palace. But what led to Colenso's troubles was not so much his liberal views on the sources of the Hexateuch as his work on Paul and the theological assertions that grew out of his study of Paul's letter to the Romans.

Published in 1861, Colenso's commentary had a telling title: *St. Paul's Epistle to the Romans: Newly Translated and Explained from a Missionary Point of View.*[5] When Colenso arrived in South Africa in 1854, there were already translations of the Bible available in the Zulu language. Colenso's pastoral work, however, created in him dissatisfaction with these versions, and especially for the way the word "God" had been translated. American Congregationalists working among the Zulu had followed the lead of Wesleyan Methodists translating into Xhosa in using the word *uTixo*. This word had been borrowed from another South African language, Khoi, in an attempt to avoid using an indigenous word for God. Colenso recognized that before the coming of the missionaries, the Zulu had believed that the creator of the universe was *umKulunkulu* (the Great-Great One) or *umVelinqange* (the One who Appeared First). Since this second word might imply that there was something before the "appearance" of the creator God, Colenso settled on *umKulunkulu* as the preferred translation of the word God (see Hermanson 2003, 7).

This example of Colenso's belief that Zulu culture itself ought to determine how the Bible was translated into Zulu is an early example of how reading the Bible through an African cultural lens led Colenso to his unique reading of Romans. The Colenso who came to South Africa as a missionary bishop was already influenced by the Enlightenment thinking of his day: by the universalist theology of F. D. Maurice, which rejected the doc-trine of hell, by Darwin's theory of evolution, and by German critical scholarship. "He was already predisposed to find that the Zulu people had an experience and understand-ing of God through nature and excited to listen to what they had to say about it. He understood the essence of the Christian life to consist of ethical behavior towards one's fellow human beings in general and his Zulu charges in particular" (Draper 2003b, xv).

This Enlightenment disposition, combined with Colenso's growing appreciation of Zulu culture, produced a fascinating reading of Romans. Colenso notes the tension reflected in the text of Romans between Jews and Gentiles. Unlike most interpreters, however, Colenso believes that the letter was written to Jews rather than Christians. His theory is that there was no Christian church at Rome, only Jews and Gentiles worshiping at synagogue who had some information about Jesus. Paul's purpose in setting forth his gospel is to convince the Jews in Rome that their reliance on election provides them with no basis for pride because salvation is a free gift of God given to all. Of course, Colenso's purpose in writing is much closer to his own pastoral setting: "He wishes to show that the English Christian settlers [in South Africa] have no grounds of racial pride over against the Zulus" (Draper 2003b, xxiii). Colenso says his commentary is "*from a Missionary Point of View*" because his missionary encounter with the Zulu has led him to believe that the Zulu's own religion is worthy of praise and appreciation. The message of the cross is less about Jesus's death providing a sacrifice for sin (Colenso rejected penal substitutionary atonement) and more about a revelation of God's justification of all. On Romans 3:24 ("[Christ Jesus] whom God set forth, a propitiation through faith in His blood, unto the showing forth of His righteousness" [Colenso 2003, 75–76; Colenso's translation]), Colenso writes:

> As before, the fact that such as these, who are able consciously to believe in the Gospel, are justified, – have the blessedness of *knowing* that they are justified, and so have peace with God, – does not exclude the case of baptized or other infants, nor, in fact, the mass of human kind, who are not yet privileged to know this, but of whom, in chap. v and in other parts of this epistle, the Apostle distinctly speaks as sharers in this gift of righteousness. (2003, 86; emphasis in original)

In other words, all are saved: some have the privilege of knowing this consciously; others await the good news, but are saved nonetheless.

Indigenous Readings of Paul in Postcolonial Africa

It was noted in the previous section that the center of Christian life in the modern world began to shift to the south during the colonial period. Although Western readings of Paul still have much influence in postcolonial Africa, Africans no longer depend on Western readers for their understanding of the text. In the past few decades, dissatisfaction with Western biblical scholarship has been a contributing factor in the growth of a self-consciously African biblical scholarship. Although more attention has been focused on the gospels (see LeMarquand 1997; 2000) in the emerging corpus of African New Testament scholarship, still many significant readings of Paul have been produced. Some scholarly work has treated subjects that are widely discussed in the Western world, such as Paul and his relationship to Judaism and the law;[6] but many of the readings noted below have special hermeneutical significance for the African church. The following is a sampling of what has become a flood of scholarship from Africa on Paul in recent years.

Paul in Athens: Acts 17:16–34

One of the New Testament passages related to Paul most discussed by African interpreters is the story of Paul preaching in Athens in Acts 17:16–34. In Western scholarship, this passage has sometimes been interpreted as a Pauline failure, which led the apostle to assert (1 Cor 1) that from that point on he would never preach in such an apologetic way, but would only preach the cross (Baur 1873–1875, ch. 7). For African readers, this story makes the opposite point. African readers are conscious that the missionaries who came to the continent brought a gospel wrapped in Western cultural garb. African postcolonial scholarship is filled with stories of missionaries who misunderstood African religion and culture, sometimes denigrating them not merely as "pagan," but as "demonic." The story of Paul at the Areopagus stands as a counter-narrative to stories of the ugly missionary.

An example is found in a short essay by a Nigerian Roman Catholic lay scholar, Chris Ukachukwu Manus: "The Athenians are said to be very religious, a *crux creditum* for Euro-American exegetes. For many of these authors, Luke's audience is rather 'super-stitious'. This is a judgment which is not dissimilar to early European missionaries' estimation of the Africans when they first landed on our shores" (Manus 1990, 207). The conclusion of a post-missionary reading of this text, according to Manus, is to learn from the missionaries' mistakes and engage in mission in the African context in a very different way:

> They came and castigated African religions as worship of demons and our whole societal framework as demonic ... They insisted on a total break from our past ... [The] Christian message is not supposed to remove Christians from their cultural setting in life. In the address at Athens, Luke seems to suggest that the Gospel is quite at home with everything that is *wholesome* in every culture. (1990, 214; emphasis in original)

Manus's estimation of Acts 17:16–34 is no lone voice in African biblical scholarship. In fact, this text is one of the most discussed in African published works on the New Testament (Martin 1962; Igenoza 1984; Onwu 1988; de Meester 1990; Osei-Bonsu 1994; Apochi 1995; Geraghty 1996; Isizoh 1997; Reed 2003). Quotations similar to those of Manus above could be multiplied. Clearly, one characteristic of biblical scholar-ship in Africa is that it pays explicit attention to the cultural context in which the text is being read. African readers of the story of Paul on the Areopagus are less interested in reconstructing the Pauline (or Lukan) cultural context than they are about speaking to their own contemporaries – and they do not hide this hermeneutical intention. It should also be noted that Manus is typical in that his biblical scholarship is seen to be in service of the church and its mission. This is not scholarship primarily for the academy (although Manus himself teaches in a secular university), but for the Christian community.

Paul and ethnicity: Galatians 3:28

In a continent in which over two thousand languages are spoken, in a world in which Africa is often perceived to be on the bottom rung of the ladder, in a postcolonial situ-ation in which the pain of oppression, slavery, and exploitation are still very fresh, issues of "tribe," ethnicity, and race are fundamental theological concerns. The questions they pose are not new for the Christian church. It might be argued that these issues vexed the apostle Paul more than any other: he spoke of how being in Christ relativizes gender ("no longer male and female") and class ("no longer slave or free"), but he spent most of his time arguing that in Christ there was "no longer Jew or Greek" (Gal 3:28). In an article on Galatians 3:1–29, Justin Ukpong argues that the Christian faith cannot be reduced to a tribal religion. Rather than advocating a mission practice that would have made Gentiles into converts to Judaism,

> [Paul] allowed Gentiles to preserve their cultural identity while accepting Christianity. In other words, Paul had now put a stamp on Christianity as a universal religion different from a tribal religion. Whether or not Paul knew the full implications of his decision and action is another thing. But the fact remains that he had introduced into Christianity the ideal of one Christianity with a multiplicity of cultural practice. (Ukpong 1993b, 17)[7]

Paul and spiritual gifts: 1 Corinthians 12–14

Numerous African theologians and exegetes have complained that Christian theology and exegesis came to Africa clothed in Western Enlightenment assumptions and categories. Nigerian theologian Osadolar Imasogie, for example, notes that "while the quasi-scientific world view [of Western theology] desacralized the universe, the typical African world view sees the universe as a multi-dimensional entity inhabited by hierarchical cadres of spiritual beings and forces" (1993, 66). Faced with the skepticism of much Western scholarship, which seems at best to question the reality of the spiritual forces and experiences narrated in the Bible, African exegetes find Western exegetical work inadequate to answer the questions of most Africans.

The New Testament figure of Paul is, of course, no stranger to religious experience. His encounter with the risen Christ on the Damascus road (Acts 9; 1 Cor 15:8–10; Gal 1:15–17), his subsequent visionary experiences (2 Cor 12:1–10), and his firsthand reports of his own use of charismatic gifts (1 Cor 14:13–19; Gal 3:1–5) all leave the impression that Paul would have a message for those grappling with the spiritual realities of Africa. Samuel Abogunrin likens African religious experience to the situation of the church in Corinth:

> Spirit possession and ecstatic experiences are common occurrences during acts of worship or festivals in African indigenous religion. Pneumatic experiences during worship in most of the Africa indigenous churches today are reminiscent of the ecstatic experiences in African traditional religion which often include trances, ecstatic dances and speaking in tongues, esoteric language and prophecy ... Paul's exposition on the spiritual gifts [therefore] is very important for the Church in Africa today. (1988, 126)[8]

Abogunrin's exposition of 1 Corinthians 12–14 finds numerous lessons for the churches of Africa. Some of these lessons encourage African charismatic practices: Abogunrin's discussion of Paul's mention of gifts of healing in 1 Corinthians 12:9, for example, encourages the churches to pray for healing, since God is interested in the physical as well as the soul – although Abogunrin does caution against excesses and "fake healings" that stem from some disreputable leaders (1988, 131). His discussion of tongues and prophecy both encourages and warns: these are real gifts from God, but also "the most abused spiritual gifts today" (1988, 132).

Similarly, two Roman Catholic scholars have published doctoral theses on Paul's discussion of spiritual gifts in 1 Corinthians. Donatus Udoette's *Prophecy and Tongues: A Pauline Theology of Charismata for Service in the Church [1 Cor 14]* makes no mention of Africa except for an indirect reference in the first paragraph of the introduction, where he states: "Scholarly interest in these phenomena [tongues and prophecy] has gathered in momentum, especially since the upsurge of Pentecostal and charismatic movements both in the established and independent churches" (1993a, xvii). After this, no mention is made of the hermeneutical implications of his subject for the churches in Africa. In the same year as the thesis was published, however, Udoette published an article in which he explicitly raises the issue of the use of charismatic gifts in the African church (1993b). In a private conversation with Udoette in 1994, I asked why the hermeneutical reflections had not found their way into the text of his thesis. His answer was that his supervisor in Rome insisted that he keep his exegesis and any possible implications separate – an approach he found strange, since it was pastoral concern that moved him to study that particular text in the first place. The division between exegetical and pastoral tasks may seem to make sense in the modernist Western context, but it is not perceived as helpful in most of the non-Western world.

A second published doctoral thesis, this one by Luke Ndubuisi on 1 Corinthians 12, appeared in 2003.[9] In contrast to Udoette's earlier work, Ndubuisi's book includes two full chapters (out of nine) analyzing the African ecclesial context that provided the motivation for his scholarly project. The thesis should certainly be classified as exegetical: the first seven chapters investigate the first-century situation in Corinth and produce a close reading of the text of Paul's letter; but Paul's words are not left in the first century.

Paul and spiritual power: Romans 1:3–4

Closely related to the question of spiritual gifts, in 1 Corinthians and in Africa, is the issue of how Paul's concept of "power" relates to the popular use of power language in the modern African church context. In recent years, there has been a rapid increase in neo-Pentecostal churches throughout sub-Saharan Africa. These churches, many related to American ministry organizations that make widespread use of television and other media, emphasize healing and prosperity ("health and wealth"), an attractive message for a continent that has had more than its share of disease and poverty.

Anthony Iffen Umoren's research (2008) juxtaposes this popular teaching of Christ as "power" with the "power Christology" found in Romans 1:3–4. The first part of Umoren's book focuses on a sociological analysis, based on fieldwork, of the popular conception of Christ as "power" in various church contexts. Umoren then turns to exegesis, producing a close reading of the first paragraph of Paul's letter to the Romans, and finding *en dynamei* ("with power") the center of the chiastic structure of the paragraph, and therefore the central affirmation of Paul's thinking about Christ in this section (2008, 108–109). Paul's "power Christology" is not the same as the popular conception, however, since Paul does not see Christ as the magical answer to all of life's problems, but rather "Jesus Christ is the power of God for salvation" (2008, 144). Salvation may include healings and other miraculous manifestations, but these are only "temporary manifestations or signs of God's salvific power, intended as pointers to a more powerful and enduring saving act accomplished by [Christ's] cross and resurrection" (2008, 160).

Paul and political power: Romans 13:1–5

Exegetes in some parts of the African continent, especially but not exclusively in South Africa, have struggled with another Pauline text that speaks of "power": Romans 13:1–5, with its message about submission to political authorities. During the years of apartheid in South Africa, it was widely known that the authorities would often quote Romans 13 against those struggling for an end to the racist regime in that country. Incidents similar to the following, which is related by Allan Boesak, could be repeated by many South African Christians:

> On 19 October 1977, I was visited for the first time by the South African Security Police. They stayed from 3:30 A.M. till 7:00 A.M. At one point I was challenged by the Security Police captain (who assured me that he was a Christian and, in fact, an elder of the white Dutch Reformed Church) on my persistent resistance to the government. "How can you do what you are doing," he asked, "while you know what Romans Thirteen says?" ... For him, as for millions of other Christians in South Africa and across the world, Romans 13 is an unequivocal, unrelenting call for blind, unquestioning obedience to the state. (1986, 138)

And, of course, Boesak is not the only South African who has suffered from the long history of the oppressive use of this text.

On the other hand, South African exegetes have often pointed out that Romans 13 is not a call to blind obedience and that Paul's words contain limits on the power of the state: since all authority is "from God" (v.1), all powers should recognize and reflect God's authority; government is to be "God's servant for good" (v.4) – not for evil; the word "submit" (NRSV: "be subject") does not imply force or coercion, it is argued, but rather the obligation to love one's neighbor (vv.8–10). It is further noted that Romans 13 must be read in the context of other biblical passages in which it is clear that primary obedience is to be given to God rather than human beings (Acts 4:19), and that the state itself (Rev 13) is capable of radical disobedience and evil (Moulder 1977; Vonck 1984; Kairos Theologians 1985; Maimela 1985; South African Council of Churches 1985; Nopece 1986; Nürnberger 1987; Draper 1988; Wanamaker 1988; Munro 1990; Botha 1992; 1994; Hale 1992).

Paul and holiness: 2 Corinthians 6:14–7:1

J. Ayodeji Adewuya's (2001) study of 2 Corinthians 6:14–7:1 is a meticulous and judicious study of a controverted Pauline text (so controverted that some think it to be a non-Pauline, or even an anti-Pauline, interpolation). Adewuya's critical judgments about the passage are conservative: he argues that it was written by Paul and, contrary to the opinion of many, that it fits into its context in 2 Corinthians. But the most important contributions Adewuya makes stem from the perspective he brings to his study. First, Adewuya makes clear that a neglected aspect of this passage among scholars is its emphasis on holiness: "the holiness message embedded in that passage has neither been sufficiently taken into account nor adequately articulated by exegetes" (2001, 1). His antidote to that exegetical lapse is to study the text against the background of the Holiness Code in Leviticus. He finds verbal links to Leviticus, suggesting that Paul had Old Testament holiness ideas in mind when composing this passage.

Also interesting is the suggestion made by Adewuya that his own background as a part of the holiness tradition (he is a member of a church called the Deeper Christian Life Ministry) stemming from Wesleyanism was a factor in leading him to notice this lacuna in Pauline scholarship. This fits a general (although not universal) pattern found in African biblical studies of scholars being quite open about the confessional tradition from which they come and how it has helped them to read the text.

Although not mentioned frequently in his study, Adewuya is also clearly influenced by his African background. Footnotes, for example, mention contributions to understanding the biblical text that stem from an African perspective. In one place, Adewuya mentions that the Yoruba language contains two word groups that can be translated "unbeliever"; this suggests to him that Paul may use the term in more than one sense, depending on the context (2001, 103–104 n. 49). In another place, Adewuya uses a Yoruba proverb ("'a sheep that keeps company of a dog will inevitably feed on excreta,' excreta being known as the special delicacy of the dog in Africa") to illustrate Paul's contention that believers should not be unequally yoked with unbelievers (2001, 119 n. 102). These passages and others point to the role Adewuya's African background plays in his work as an exegete.

Conclusion

It is a sign of the ever-increasing fruitfulness of scholarship in Africa that it is now impossible to produce a comprehensive review of all the exegetical work done on Paul from that continent. This review has demonstrated first of all that there has been a long history of interaction with Pauline texts by African readers through the centuries. Contemporary scholarship in Africa is not unaware of the trends in scholarship in the Western world, but is more concerned to address issues in Paul that are of interest to the churches in Africa itself. This confessional-based hermeneutics is especially interested in matters of ethnicity, spiritual and political power, holiness, and issues related to mission, past and present.

Notes

1   "For just as man consists of body, soul and spirit, so in the same way does the scripture, which has been prepared by God to be given for man's salvation" (Origen, *On First Principles* 4.2.4).

2   This is not to assert that Christianity was originally a Western religion, or that it did not have a long and largely untold history outside Europe. See now, among the many works attempting to reclaim the history of non-Western Christianity, Irvin and Sunquist (2001); Shenk (2002); Jenkins (2008).

3   Unless otherwise indicated, biblical quotations are taken from the New Revised Standard Version.

4   For a comprehensive bibliography of works by and about Colenso, see Bell (2003).

5   The volume was published in the same year both in South Africa and in England.

6   In recent years, Pauline scholarship in the Western world has expended an enormous amount of energy investigating issues related to Paul and Judaism, especially the question of Paul's understanding of the Torah. Few African scholars have ventured into this territory, perhaps because the theological and social forces motivating this discussion in the Western world are not so strong in Africa. In the West, the aftermath of the Holocaust has led to a rethinking of the relationship between Judaism and Christianity. Two monographs written by Africans have made a contribution to this discussion, however. Mary Sylvia Nwachukwu (2002) investigates Romans 9–11 against the background of the Abrahamic covenant in the book of Genesis. In doing so, she takes full account of the recent literature on Paul, especially that which has emerged since E. P. Sanders opened up what has been called the "New Perspective on Paul." Especially helpful is that Nwachukwu reads Paul's theology not as abstract theological ideas but as emerging from a narrative about God's concern for the world. Her reading of Paul is therefore profoundly missiological: God's love for humankind flows from his concern for the whole world, and God's salvation of humanity in Christ is a part of God's eschatological plan to save not just humanity but the whole creation. Fẹmi Adeyẹmi completed his doctoral studies at Dallas Theological Seminary in the USA. His dissertation (2006) is a thorough study of the influence of the promise of a new covenant in Jeremiah 31 on Paul's thought from a dispensationalist point of view.

7   The issue of African ethnic identity has been an important topic for exegetes in Africa for some decades now (see especially Atal sa Angang et al. 1980).

8   The African indigenous churches mentioned by Abogunrin (1988) are those churches that have sprung up in Africa over the past century or so either by breaking away from mission-founded churches or by following a charismatic leader who founded his or her own church. There are thousands of such denominations all over the continent, some of them with membership in the millions.

9   For further African reflections on Paul's teaching on charismatic gifts, see Owan (1993), especially the essays by Ukpong, Manus, and Obi.

References

Abogunrin, Samuel O. 1988. *The First Letter of Paul to the Corinthians*. Nairobi: Uzima.

Adewuya, J. Ayodeji. 2001. *Holiness and Community in 2 Cor 6:14–7:1: Paul's View of Communal Holiness in the Corinthian Correspondence*. New York: Peter Lang.

Adeyẹmi, Fẹmi. 2006. *The New Covenant Torah in Jeremiah and the Law of Christ in Paul*. New York: Peter Lang.

Apochi, Michael. 1995. In Search for Effective Evangelization Methodology: Lessons from Acts 13:16–41; 14:15–18 and 17:22–31. *Jos Studies* 5(1): 28–41.

Atal sa Angang, D., P. Buetubela Balembo, L. Monsengwo-Pasinya, et al. editors. 1980. *Christianisme et identité africaine: point de vue exégétique: actes du 1er Congrès des biblistes africains, Kinshasa, 26–30 décembre 1978*. Kinshasa: Faculté de théologie catholique de Kinshasa.

Augustine. 1992. *Confessions*. Translated by Henry Chadwick. Oxford: Oxford University Press.

Baur, F. C. 1873–1875. *Paul the Apostle of Jesus Christ: His Life and Works, his Epistles and Teachings*. 2 volumes. London: Williams and Norgate.

Bell, Fiona. 2003. Colenso Bibliography. Pages 365–391 in *The Eye of the Storm: Bishop John William Colenso and the Crisis of Biblical Interpretation*. London: T. & T. Clark.

Boesak, Allan A. 1986. What Belongs to Caesar? Once Again Romans 13. Pages 138–156 in *When Prayer Makes News*. Edited by Allan A. Boesak and Charles Villa-Vicencio. Philadelphia: Westminster.

Botha, Jan. 1992. Creation of New Meaning: Rhetorical Situations and the Reception of Romans 13:1–7. *Journal of Theology for Southern Africa* 79: 24–37.

Botha, Jan. 1994. *Subject to Whose Authority? Multiple Readings of Romans 13*. Atlanta: Scholars.

Colenso, John William. 1861. *St. Paul's Epistle to the Romans: Newly Translated and Explained from a Missionary Point of View*. Ekukanyeni: Mission Press; Cambridge: Macmillan.

Colenso, John William. 1871. *The Pentateuch and Book of Joshua Critically Examined*. 6 volumes. London: Longmans and Green.

Colenso, John William. 2003. *Commentary on Romans*. Edited with an introduction by Jonathan A. Draper. Pietermaritzburg: Cluster.

Draper, Jonathan A. 1988. "Humble Submission to Almighty God" and its Biblical Foundation: Contextual Exegesis of Romans 13:1–7. *Journal of Theology for Southern Africa* 63: 30–38.

Draper, Jonathan A. editor. 2003a. *The Eye of the Storm: Bishop John William Colenso and the Crisis of Biblical Interpretation*. London: T. & T. Clark.

Draper, Jonathan A. editor. 2003b. Introduction. Pages ix–xxxix in John William Colenso, *Commentary on Romans*. Edited with an introduction by Jonathan A. Draper. Pietermaritzburg: Cluster.

Geraghty, Gerard. 1996. Paul before the Areopagus: A New Approach to Priestly Formation in the Light of *Ecclesia in Africa*. *African Christian Studies* 12(3): 32–41.

Hale, Frederick. 1992. Romans 13:1–7 in South African Baptist Social Ethics. *South African Baptist Journal of Theology* 1: 66–83.

Hall, Christopher A. 1998. *Reading Scripture with the Church Fathers*. Downers Grove, Ill.: InterVarsity.

Hermanson, Eric A. 2003. Colenso's First Attempt at Bible Translation in Zulu. Pages 5–28 in *The Eye of the Storm: Bishop John William Colenso and the Crisis of Biblical Interpretation*. London: T. & T. Clark.

Igenoza, Andrew Olu. 1984. St. Paul in Athens: Acts 17:19–34: A Study in the Encounter of Christianity with Philosophical Intellectualism and other Religions: How Relevant to Africa? Unpublished seminar paper, Department of Religious Studies, University of Ife-Ife, Nigeria.

Imasogie, Osadolor. 1993. *Guidelines for Christian Theology in Africa*. Second edition. Achimota: Africa Christian.

Irvin, Dale T., and Scott W. Sunquist. 2001. *History of the World Christian Movement*. Volume 1: *Earliest Christianity to 1453*. Maryknoll, NY: Orbis.

Isizoh, Chidi Denis. 1997. *The Resurrected Jesus Preached in Athens: The Areopagus Speech (Acts 17, 16–34) – An Inquiry into the Reasons for the Greek Reaction to the Speech and a Reading of the Text from the African Traditional Religious Perspective*. Lagos: Ceedee.

Jenkins, Philip. 2008. *The Lost History of Christianity: The Thousand-year Golden Age of the Church in the Middle East, Africa, and Asia – and How It Died*. New York: HarperOne.

Kairos Theologians. 1985. The Kairos Document – Challenge to the Church: A Theological Comment on the Political Crisis in South Africa. *Journal of Theology for Southern Africa* 53: 61–81.

LeMarquand, Grant. 1997. The Historical Jesus and African New Testament Scholarship. Pages 161–180 in *Whose Historical Jesus?* Edited by William E. Arnal and Michel Desjardins. Waterloo, Ontario: Wilfrid Laurier University Press.

LeMarquand, Grant. 2000. New Testament Exegesis in (Modern) Africa. Pages 72–102 in *The Bible in Africa: Transactions, Trajectories, and Trends.* Edited by Gerald O. West and Musa W. Dube. Leiden: Brill.

Maimela, Simon S. 1985. The Implications for Theology of the Contemporary South African Understanding of War and Peace. *Africa Theological Journal* 14: 194–201.

Manus, Chris Ukachukwu. 1990. The Areopagus Speech (Acts 17/16–34): A Study on Luke's Approach to Evangelism and its Significance in the African Context. Pages 197–218 in *Les Actes des Apôtres et les jeunes Eglises: actes du deuxième Congrès des biblistes africains. Ibadan: 31 juillet – 3 août 1984.* Edited by W. Amewowo, P. J. Arowele, and P. Buetubela Balembo. Kinshasa: Faculté de théologie catholique de Kinshasa.

Manus, Chris Ukachukwu. 1993. Authority and Charism: New Testament Notes and Pastoral Implications in the Nigerian Church. Pages 45–60 in *Authority and Charism in the Nigerian Church.* Edited by Kris Owan et al. Abuja: Catholic Theological Association of Nigeria.

Martin, Marie-Louise. 1962. Acts 17:16–34: Paul's Approach to Greek Intellectuals. *Ministry* 3(1): 20–24.

Meester, Paul de. 1990. Inculturation de la foi et salut des cultures: Paul de Tarse à l'aréopage d'Athènes (Ac 17,22–32). *Telema* 62: 59–80.

Moulder, James. 1977. Romans 13 and Conscientious Disobedience. *Journal of Theology for Southern Africa* 21: 13–23.

Munro, Winsome. 1990. Romans 13:1–7: Apartheid's Last Biblical Refuge. *Biblical Theology Bulletin* 20: 161–168.

Ndubuisi, Luke. 2003. *Paul's Concept of Charisma in 1 Corinthians 12: With Emphasis on Nigerian Charismatic Movement.* Frankfurt am Main: Peter Lang.

Nopece, Bethlehem N. 1986. Romans 13 and Apartheid: A Study of Romans 13:1–7 in Relation to the Modern Political Situation in South Africa. Unpublished MTh thesis, Glasgow University.

Nürnberger, Klaus. 1987. Theses on Romans 13. *Scriptura* 22: 40–47.

Nwachukwu, Mary Sylvia Chinyere. 2002. *Creation-Covenant Scheme and Justification by Faith: A Canonical Study of the God–Human Drama in the Pentateuch and the Letter to the Romans.* Rome: Editrice Pontificia Università Gregoriana.

Obi, Chris. 1993. Charismata and Authority: A Pauline Viewpoint. Pages 10–24 in *Authority and Charism in the Nigerian Church.* Edited by Kris Owan et al. Abuja: Catholic Theological Association of Nigeria.

Oden, Thomas C. 2007. *How Africa Shaped the Christian Mind: Rediscovering the African Seedbed of Western Christianity.* Downers Grove, Ill.: InterVarsity.

Onwu, Nlenanya. 1988. Ministry to the Educated: Reinterpreting Acts 17:16–34 in Africa. *African Christian Studies* 4(4): 61–71.

Origen. 1966. *On First Principles.* Translated by G. W. Butterworth. New York: Harper.

Osei-Bonsu, Joseph. 1994. A Reflection on Paul's Speech at the Areopagus (Acts 17: 22–32). Unpublished paper presented to the Bible in Africa Project Glasgow Consultation held on 13–17 August 1994 at Scotus College, Bearsden, Glasgow, Scotland.

Owan, Kris, et al., editors. 1993. *Authority and Charism in the Nigerian Church.* Abuja: Catholic Theological Association of Nigeria.

Reed, David A. 2003. Acts 17:16–34 in an Africa Context (An Assessment from a N. Atlantic/Western Perspective). *Africa Journal of Evangelical Theology* 22(1): 87–101.

Shenk, Wilbert R., editor. 2002. *Enlarging the Story: Perspectives on Writing World Christian History*. Maryknoll, NY: Orbis.

South African Council of Churches. 1985. A Theological Rationale and a Call to Prayer for the End to Unjust Rule. *Journal of Theology for Southern Africa* 52: 57–61.

Udoette, Donatus. 1993a. *Prophecy and Tongues: A Pauline Theology of Charismata for Service in the Church [1 Cor 14]*. Rome: Pontifical Urban University.

Udoette, Donatus. 1993b. Towards a Theology of Charismata for the Nigerian Church. *Encounter: A Journal of African Life and Religion* 2: 16–28.

Ukpong, Justin S. 1993a. Charism and Church Authority: A New Testament Perspective. Pages 26–38 in *Authority and Charism in the Nigerian Church*. Edited by Kris Owan et al. Abuja: Catholic Theological Association of Nigeria.

Ukpong, Justin S. 1993b. The Letter to the Galatians and the Problem of Cultural Pluralism in Christianity. Pages 16–27 in *Proclaiming the Kingdom: Essays in Contextual New Testament Studies*. Port Harcourt: CIWA.

Umoren, Anthony Iffen. 2008. *Paul and Power Christology: Exegesis and Theology of Romans 1:3–4 in Relation to Popular Power Christology in an African Context*. Frankfurt am Main: Peter Lang.

Vonck, Pol. 1984. All Authority Comes from God: Romans 13:1–7: A Tricky Text about Obedience to Political Power. *African Ecclesial Review* 26: 338–347.

Walls, Andrew F. 1996. Romans One and the Modern Missionary Movement. Pages 55–67 in Andrew F. Walls, *The Missionary Movement in Christian History: Studies in the Transmission of Faith*. Maryknoll, NY: Orbis.

Wanamaker, C. A. 1988. Romans 13: A Hermeneutic for Church and State. Pages 91–104 in *On Reading Karl Barth in South Africa*. Edited by Charles Villa-Vicencio. Grand Rapids: Eerdmans.

PART III

The Legacy of Paul

The Blackwell Companion to Paul, First Edition. Edited by Stephen Westerholm.
© 2011 Blackwell Publishing Ltd. Published 2011 by Blackwell Publishing Ltd.

CHAPTER 32

Art

Robin M. Jensen

In his treatise *The Trinity*, Augustine asserted that one could love that which could not be seen or grasped – God, in particular. But, he conceded, human beings naturally tend to fabricate appearances for unknown things or beings, even though these appearances are essentially untrue. For example, he explains:

> Anyone, surely, who has read or heard what the apostle Paul wrote or what was written about him, will fabricate a face for the apostle in his imagination, and for everybody else whose name is mentioned in these texts. And every one of the vast number of people to whom these writings are known will think of their physical features and lineaments in a different way, and it will be quite impossible to tell whose thoughts are nearest the mark in this respect. Nor is our faith bothered with what physical features those men had, but only with the fact that they lived like that by the grace of God and did the things which those scriptures bear witness to. (8.3.7)

Thus Augustine was aware of portraits that depicted Paul, Christ, and the Virgin Mary, even though no one could know how those persons actually appeared in life. Elsewhere, Augustine complained about the false claim that Christ had written books to the apostles Peter and Paul – a deceit prompted by pictures depicting these apostles in Christ's company (Augustine, *Harmony of the Gospels* 1.10.16).

According to documentary evidence of varied reliability, Augustine's encounters with portraits of Christ, Paul, and other saints and apostles might not have been anomalous and the faithful frequently may have procured, prayed to, and accorded special honors to saints' likenesses. Irenaeus, a second-century bishop of Lyons, reported that certain Gnostic sects claimed to possess and venerate holy images, including a portrait

The Blackwell Companion to Paul, First Edition. Edited by Stephen Westerholm.
© 2011 Blackwell Publishing Ltd. Published 2011 by Blackwell Publishing Ltd.

of Christ said to have been made by Pontius Pilate, along with images of Pythagoras, Plato, and Aristotle, which they set up and crowned with flowers (Irenaeus, *Against Heresies* 1.25.6). This practice was mentioned also in the second-century *Acts of John*, which relates the story of a grateful Lycomedes (whose wife had been healed by the apostle) offering reverence to a likeness of John, which he placed upon an altar and adorned with lights and garlands (27–29). The fourth-century historian Eusebius reported that Gentile converts had, from ancient times, been inclined to express their gratitude to the Savior and his apostles (especially Paul and Peter) by making and circulating colored portraits of them (*Ecclesiastical History* 7.18). A manuscript fragment, purportedly from Epiphanius of Salamis and so dated to around his lifetime (ca. 320–403), complains that former pagans had put colored pictures of Peter, John, and Paul on church walls – a practice that the fragment acknowledges was meant to honor them, but was ultimately vain and even idolatrous.[1]

A later – almost certainly legendary – reference to an early portrait of Paul comes from a seventh-century biography of John Chrysostom authored by George of Alexandria. According to this work, the renowned fourth-century preacher kept Paul's portrait in his bedroom so that he could gaze upon it and imagine holding a conversation with the apostle, particularly while he composed his homilies on Paul's letters. On three successive nights, a servant named Proclus happened to pass his master's study and observed a figure whispering into John's ear. He mentioned this to John, who had been so intent upon his imagined conversation that he was unaware of the real visitor. Asked to identify the nocturnal guest, Proclus pointed to Paul's image. This legend not only reflects an early practice of meditating before a saint's icon; it demonstrates the image's ability to mediate its model's presence.[2]

Augustine, unaware of any eyewitness descriptions of Paul – or of any other gospel figures – had claimed that when different people read Paul's letters, they would imagine his physical appearance differently. Nevertheless, the second-century apocryphal *Acts of Paul and Thecla* (a document likely known to Tertullian, an earlier North African father) had included a brief verbal depiction of Paul.[3] In its opening narrative of Paul's journey to Iconium, the text recounts that a certain Onesiphorus went out with his children and wife to greet Paul on the road. Because he had not met him in person, Onesiphorus had sought a description, so that he would recognize Paul when he came near. As Onesiphorus carefully watched all the passers-by, he finally identified his subject: "A man small in size, bald-headed, bandy-legged, of noble mien, with eyebrows meeting, rather hooked-nosed, full of grace." However, this rather incongruous description of a short, ungainly, and balding man who yet bore a "noble mien" goes on to suggest that there might be some ambiguity about Paul's appearance: "Sometimes he seemed like a man, and sometimes he had the face of an angel" (*Acts of Paul and Thecla* 3.3).

Portraits of Paul and Peter Together

Few aspects of Onesiphorus's description show up in the oldest surviving visual representations of Paul, which date from the early fourth century. Among these early portraits are several catacomb paintings that represent Peter and Paul with Christ, either alone or with other saints or apostles. One of these, from the Catacomb of Peter and Marcellinus, presents Christ between Peter and Paul, above a scene of four martyrs (Peter, Marcellinus, Tuburius, and Gorgonis) flanking a lamb standing upon a rocky mound. Here, the only specific physical feature that Paul has in common with that unique textual depiction is his high, balding forehead. In this and other visual portraits, Paul is normally portrayed as tall and slender, with a receding hairline, a long and narrow face, a full but pointed beard, and an elegant, aquiline nose.

In these images Paul wears a tunic under a draped *pallium* (a rectangular mantle) and sandals on his feet – the everyday garb of an upper-class Roman citizen of the third or fourth century and specifically identified with teachers or philosophers.[4] He usually also holds a scroll – another mark of a learned man. In a fourth-century painting in the Catacomb of Domitilla, he stands next to a basket (*capsa*) filled with scrolls, perhaps intended to represent his epistles (fig. 32.1). A related image, from the Catacomb of the

Figure 32.1   Paul with capsa, Catacomb of Domitilla, Rome.
Photo credit: Estelle Brettman, The International Catacomb Society.

Jordani, shows Paul with a tall case of book rolls. In both representations, Paul's physiognomy projects the traditional appearance of a philosopher, as in portraits of Plato, Socrates, or Plotinus. The scrolls identify him as an intellectual, teacher, and writer. According to several scholars, such a visual presentation of Paul as a philosopher parallels his verbal portrait in the book of Acts, which arguably modeled Paul's missionary work, trial, and death on Socrates' biography.[5]

In comparison, Peter's portrait, frequently juxtaposed with Paul's, shows that apostle with thick white hair capping a low forehead, a square jaw, and a full, curly beard. Peter's facial features depict a "man of action" rather than a "man of learning." As Roman portraits of the era were constructed to delineate an idealized character and to reflect certain personal attributes, the portraits of Paul emphasize his roles as teacher, theologian, and writer. Peter's, on the other hand, portray him as a decisive figure, activist church builder, and strong leader. The two contrasting portraits thus represent Rome's traditional founding apostles as having contrasting personalities, discrete charismatic gifts, and complementary (but separate) spheres of ecclesial work.

These distinctive representations of Peter and Paul are strikingly consistent through time. Often shown together, sometimes with their names inscribed nearby against any doubt, they are easily recognizable. The two appear together in early wall paintings, relief carvings, mosaics, bronzes, ivories, ceramic ware, and gold glasses. A fourth-century epitaph for a deceased child named Asellus (now in the Vatican Museum) includes the faces of Peter and Paul, named and set off by a christogram. Other paired portraits of Peter and Paul, on gold glasses, lamps, and gems, show them receiving a single crown of victory. Such images not only asserted Peter's apostolic presence in Rome; they also represented his relationship with Paul as harmonious. Thus the iconography emphasized the Roman church's claim to a double apostolic foundation.

In one example – a late fourth-century bronze lamp most likely designed to hang in a church – Peter and Paul are shown guiding a ship at full sail. Peter holds the rudder and Paul stands at the prow.[6] In an earlier sarcophagus fragment, now in the Vatican Museum, a figure labeled "Paulus" holds the rudder of a ship named "Thecla." Another figure, possibly Peter, appears to the left.[7] Eventually, Paul takes his place as one of the twelve original apostles. In most representations of the twelve with Christ, Peter and Paul generally are shown immediately to Jesus' right and left (fig. 32.2). Paul's membership in the twelve is assured in the church's visual tradition, even though, according to Acts (1:26), Matthias was chosen as the twelfth apostle, replacing Judas.

Two outstanding examples of this inclusion of Paul among the twelve apostles appear in Ravenna's two early Christian baptisteries: the earlier building, commonly known as the Baptistery of the Orthodox (built ca. 450), and the Baptistery of the Arians (built ca. 525). In both monuments, dome mosaics depict two groups of six processing apostles. At the center (and meeting one another) are Peter and Paul. In the Orthodox baptistery, both Peter and Paul bear wreaths like the other apostles. In the Arian baptistery, however, Peter and Paul face one another across an empty throne, surmounted by a jeweled cross. Paul carries a scroll and Peter holds a large key (fig. 32.3).

Whether painted, mosaic, icons, or in other media, through the ages Paul and Peter retain the facial features that were established during the early Christian period, making them almost instantly recognizable – especially if they are shown together, as in El

Figure 32.2 Busts of Peter and Paul with Christ, Basilica of San Vitale, Ravenna, mid-6th century.
Photo credit: Holly Hayes, Sacred Destinations Images.

Figure 32.3 Peter and Paul, Arian Baptistery, Ravenna, early 6th century.
Photo credit: Robin M. Jensen.

Greco's monumental painting (ca. 1587–1592), now in St. Petersburg's Hermitage Museum. Whether he is represented in traditional Orthodox icons or later Western oil paintings on canvas, Paul usually appears as gaunt and dark, with hollow cheeks, a high forehead, and a piercing gaze. In other, later representations of Paul, an additional detail – a small curl at his crown – regularly appears.

Narrative Scenes of Paul with Peter

Certain standard depictions of Peter and Paul also occur in early Christian art. Not precisely portraits, they are based on narratives, but their formulaic pattern and their popularity set them apart from other, more specialized themes. These scenes include Paul with Peter receiving the new law from Christ, the two men meeting in Rome, and their shared martyrdom in that city.

The traditio legis

The first of these types shows Christ giving the new law to the two apostles. In most, especially those found in or near Rome, Paul stands on Christ's right. Peter, to his left, receives a scroll from Christ's left hand. These images appear painted in the Roman catacombs as well as in sarcophagus reliefs, gold glasses, mosaics, and a variety of liturgical objects made from silver and ivory. Possibly the earliest surviving example of this composition is a mid-fourth-century mosaic in Rome's mausoleum of Santa Constanza (fig. 32.4). Here an ascended Christ stands on the rock of Paradise with Paul to his right and Peter to his left. Christ makes a gesture of salutation with his right hand while Peter grasps the unfurled scroll that Christ holds in his left. The scroll is inscribed with the legend *Dominus pacem dat* ("the Lord gives peace"), probably an incorrect reconstruction of the original, *Dominus legem dat* ("the Lord gives the law").

The standard iconography of this scene varies in certain details. As in the Santa Constanza mosaic, palm trees, lambs, and small buildings (representations of Jerusalem and Bethlehem) may be included. Other compositions present additional apostles as witnesses or a phoenix as a testimony to Christ's resurrection and ascension. In the earliest examples, Christ might be sitting (enthroned) rather than standing, in either case sometimes upon a rocky mount from which the four rivers of Paradise spring, sometimes on an orb of the world. In a minority of instances, particularly in sarcophagus reliefs from Ravenna, Paul is the one who receives the scroll or book of the law.

Traditional interpretations view the scene as showing Christ granting the "power of the keys" to Peter, making him the foundation of the church and the prince of apostles (cf. Matt 16:18–19).[8] Other historians argue that the composition was strongly influenced by imperial iconography, particularly portrayals of the emperor delegating power or authority to a governor or vicar.[9] Alternative approaches focus on the eschatological or apocalyptic dimensions of the scene, and emphasize its presentation of Christ as ascended and enthroned – the Christ of the Second Coming. Such interpretations point

Figure 32.4   Jesus giving the law to Peter and Paul, Mausoleum of Constanza, Rome, mid-4th century.
Photo credit: Robin M. Jensen.

to the rock of Paradise, the palms of victory, and the phoenix as key symbolic details.[10] Still other analyses of the *traditio legis* motif claim the scroll as the central component – an iconographic element that emphasizes Christ's teachings, given to the church through its apostolic representatives.[11]

Paul's inclusion in the composition, however, suggests a slightly different option. His placement on Christ's right (with Peter on the left) could indicate their different spheres of apostolic work – Paul's to the Gentiles, Peter's to the Jews. This is the clear meaning of a related image decorating the apse of Rome's early fifth-century basilica of Santa Pudenziana (fig. 32.5). Two women, personifying the churches of the Gentiles and the Jews, hold wreaths above Paul and Peter, who are seated to Christ's right and left respectively. If the *traditio legis* scene was intended to convey a similar differentiation, the two apostles could symbolize the (old) law's distinct significance for those two different communities. According to Acts 15, the dissenting parties reached a compromise regarding Mosaic law through the leadership of Peter and Paul, both present at the Jerusalem council. Such an interpretation is strengthened by the inclusion of two buildings in the Santa Constanza apse as well as in the Vatican gold glass. As in other early Christian

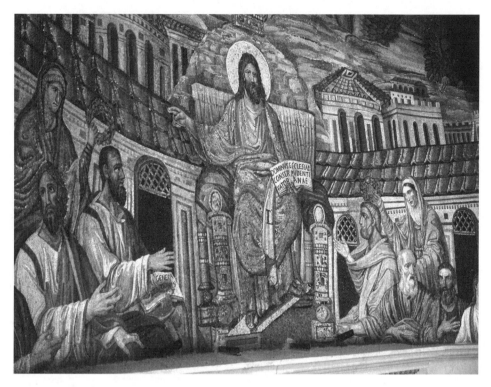

Figure 32.5 Jesus enthroned with apostles, Basilica of Sta. Pudenziana, Rome, ca. 400.
Photo credit: Robin M. Jensen.

iconography (e.g., the arch mosaic of Santa Maria Maggiore), these structures are sometimes labeled as Bethlehem and Jerusalem, perhaps to identify them with the Church of the Gentiles, on the one hand, and the Church of the Circumcised, on the other.

The concordia apostolorum

Along with Christ giving the new law to his apostles, the inclusion of Paul with Peter in the scene known as the *traditio legis* may have been meant to depict the unity and concord of the two in their shared apostolic work – a collegiality that accords better with their relationship's presentation in Acts than in Galatians (see, e.g., Gal 2:11–21). According to later apocryphal literature, their friendship was especially evident during their time in Rome. Based on a longstanding tradition (perhaps beginning in the second century) that Peter and Paul had both been martyred in Rome, stories began to circulate about their joint ministry in that city. These stories supported the Roman church's claim to have had a double foundation, a tradition particularly central to that see's assertion of juridical primacy in the fourth and fifth centuries.[12] In the *Acts of Peter and*

Paul (a revision of earlier apocryphal accounts, purportedly written by a certain Marcellus), when Paul arrived in Rome, he appealed to the Jews (who had objected to Peter's teachings about the law) to be obedient to Peter. When Peter and Paul finally met in person, they exchanged the kiss of peace.[13]

Art historians, noting the apostles' frequent pairing, have suggested possible iconographic prototypes, including Rome's other founding duo, Romulus and Remus. Another possible model is the imperial Tetrachs, represented with their arms around one another in sculptural groups from Venice and Rome.[14] Iconographic references to Paul's and Peter's mutual regard appear in numerous other Christian images, especially in the Latin West from the eighth through the sixteenth century. The motif, usually referred to as the *concordia apostolorum*, shows them embracing (like the tetrarchs), presumably at their first Roman reunion.

An early (fourth-century) version of this motif was discovered in the recent excavations of the catacomb of the "ex-vigna Chiaraviglio," near the Basilica of San Sebastiano, possibly associated with the memoria to the apostles at that site (see below). Two palm trees, standing on either side of the apostles, attest to their coming martyrdom as they lock arms in greeting.[15] Another early example of this theme, on an early fifth-century ivory belt buckle discovered beneath the cathedral of Castellammare di Stabia (30 km southeast of Naples), shows the two leaning in toward one another, their cheeks touching and their arms entwined.[16] This particular composition may have been influenced by a painting in Rome's fourth-century basilica of San Paolo fuori le Mura (destroyed by fire in 1823). Here, Paul and Peter's meeting was the final fresco on the north wall, ending a series of forty episodes on the life of Paul and concluding a biblical cycle that made brotherhood one of its unifying themes by depicting Cain and Abel, Isaac and Ishmael, Jacob and Esau, Joseph and his brothers, and Moses and Aaron.[17] One of the scenes of Moses and Aaron portrayed the two brothers embracing – perhaps an intentional allusion to the *concordia apostolorum*.

Because early Christian art regularly paralleled Peter with Moses (especially in Rome), Paul naturally came to be aligned with Aaron.[18] In the late fourth century, Gaudentius of Brescia (ca. 390) emphasized the analogous, fraternal relationships, citing the line of Psalm 133:1, "Behold how good and pleasant it is when brothers dwell in unity."[19] Gaudentius even called them "twins," born from one womb, and "blood brothers," siblings by a communion of blood.[20]

Two of the most famous of the *concordia* images appear in the mosaic programs of twelfth-century Sicilian churches, the Cappella Palatina in Palermo (begun by Roger II in 1132) and the slightly later cathedral of Monreale (built by William II a half century later). In Monreale (in the south chapel), the mosaic bears the legend: HIC PAUL[US] VENIT ROMAM ET PACEM FECIT CUM PETRO ("Here is Paul who came to Rome and made peace with Peter"). Their greeting also appears on a number of artifacts from both East and West, including a tenth-century Byzantine ivory now in the Victoria and Albert Museum (fig. 32.6), and an eleventh-century fresco on the south transept wall of the church of St. Peter in Tuscania (Italy).

Although not set in Rome, a related image of Filippino Lippi in Florence's Brancacci Chapel (ca. 1481–1482) portrays Paul visiting Peter in prison in Antioch. The image is based on a story from the Golden Legend, which tells how Paul intervened with the

Figure 32.6   Embrace of Peter and Paul, 10th-century ivory now in the Victoria and Albert Museum, London.
Photo credit: Br. Lawrence Lew, OP.

prefect of the city, Theophilus, to have Peter released so that he could resuscitate the prefect's long-dead son.[21]

Arrest and martyrdom

Although the New Testament says nothing about the deaths of Paul and Peter, the canonical Acts of the Apostles closes with Paul living under house arrest in Rome. According to later Christian documents, among them the apocryphal *Acts of Peter and Paul*, both apostles were martyred in Rome on the order of Emperor Nero around 65 CE (Peter by crucifixion and Paul by beheading), and even on the same day (June 29).[22] At the beginning of the fifth century, the Spanish poet Prudentius composed a hymn for the feast that commemorated Peter's and Paul's martyrdoms. Its verses describe the two apostles meeting their deaths on the same day, but one year apart. Peter died (first) by being crucified head downward, and Paul (a year later) by beheading. Both, it says, were killed on the marshy banks of the Tiber – a "rain of blood flowing two times and soaking the same grass." However, it adds, the Tiber now separates these two apostles, as it flows between their tombs and divides their bones. On the right bank is Peter's "golden dwelling" in the midst of an olive grove, and on the left bank, along the Ostian Road, is Paul's memorial (Prudentius, *Crowns of Martyrdom* 12).

Peter's and Paul's actual deaths are not depicted until quite late in visual art (perhaps significantly like images of Christ crucified, which appear only infrequently before the sixth or seventh century). Nevertheless, the arrests of Peter and Paul appear on a number of so-called "Passion sarcophagi" dated to the later fourth century. These depictions are sculpted in relief, generally along with scenes of Jesus' arrest, and are usually placed to either side of an empty cross, surmounted by a chi-rho within a wreath of victory.

For example, the front frieze of a fourth-century sarcophagus, now in the Vatican museum, portrays five distinct scenes, defined by trees whose branches form a canopy over them.[23] In the center, the christogram upon the empty cross alludes to Christ's victory over death. To the far left, Cain and Abel present their offerings to God, and on the far right is a scene usually identified as Job with his wife. In the niche immediately to the left of the central cross, two soldiers arrest Peter; to the right, a soldier prepares to draw his sword in order to decapitate Paul. Behind Paul are some water plants and the prow of a ship, perhaps indicating the marshy area near the Tiber where early tradition believed him to have been executed (fig. 32.7).[24]

Figure 32.7   Arrest of Paul, detail of Passion Sarcophagus, Vatican Museum, ca. 340–360.
Photo credit: Robin M. Jensen.

A similar pairing appears on the well-known sarcophagus of Junius Bassus (ca. 359). Here the arrests of Peter, Paul, and Jesus occupy three of the ten niches, complemented by scenes of Jesus giving the law to Peter and Paul (the *traditio legis*), Jesus before Pilate, Jesus entering Jerusalem, Abraham sacrificing Isaac, Job, Adam and Eve, and Daniel. The image of Paul's arrest appears in the lower right niche; Paul is shown in profile, being led away by two Roman soldiers. Again, behind him tall marshy plants indicate the place of his martyrdom. Another fourth-century sarcophagus, found in Spain (and presently in the National Museum of Madrid) but probably of Roman origin, shows Peter and Paul standing together before the Emperor Nero, who condemns them both to death.

A depiction of this same episode appears in mosaic in the twelfth-century Palatine Chapel in Palermo. In Monreale, the martyrdoms of both apostles are depicted above their seated portraits, on the façades of the chapels at the eastern ends of the north and south aisles. Both saints' deaths also appear on an early fourteenth-century triptych produced by Giotto di Bondone (or his workshop, ca. 1315–1320). Now in the Vatican Museum, the work was originally commissioned by Cardinal Stefaneschi for St. Peter's basilica. The front central panel shows Christ enthroned with angels and the Cardinal. The left panel depicts the head-down crucifixion of Peter and the right contains the beheading of Paul.

In the scene of Paul's beheading, three springs appear and a woman, Plautilla, stands upon a hill to receive a veil posthumously dropped by the saint from heaven. According to a fourth-century legend, Plautilla gave Paul her own veil to cover his eyes while being executed. Paul promised to return it and, at least according to the iconography, he kept his promise.[25] A related scene appears on bronze doors sculpted for St. Peter's Basilica in Rome by Antonio Averuline (known as Filarte) around 1445. In one panel, we see a multi-episode scene of Paul condemned by Nero, being led off to martyrdom, and beheaded. Above, Paul bequeaths his bloodstained veil to Plautilla.[26]

A seventeenth-century oil painting on canvas (ca. 1625), executed by Giovanni Serodine, depicts the parting of Peter and Paul as they are led off to martyrdom. Now in the Galleria Nazionale de'Arte Antica in Rome, it depicts an intensely emotional night scene with the two apostles facing one another wearing expressions of grim determination. Soldiers raise cudgels and brandish swords, while in the background a young man blows a bugle. Another dramatic image is the sculpture depicting Paul's beheading by Alessandro Algardi in San Paolo Maggiore, Bologna (ca. 1645), commissioned to adorn Bernini's high altar in that church. Here Paul kneels and turns his head to receive the blow from the executioner's blade. The powerful figures reflect the vigor and passion of high baroque sculpture (fig. 32.8).

Portraits of Paul without Peter

Fewer early Christian images show Paul by himself, without Peter or other saints or apostles. He appears alone on at least one gold glass, a bronze medallion, a red ware flask from North Africa, and a small bronze statuette that portrays him preaching, his right hand outstretched and his left holding a book roll.[27] A fifth-century ivory plaque,

Figure 32.8   Alessandro Algardi, *The Beheading of St. Paul*, ca. 1650. San Paolo Maggiore, Bologna.
Photo credit: Alinari/Art Resource, NY.

now in the Louvre Museum, shows Paul in profile, similarly with his right hand making a gesture of speech or greeting, his left grasping a scroll.[28]

A unique image depicting Paul as a nude, victorious athlete (wearing his crown) decorates a fourth-century silver spoon, now in the Cleveland Museum. Although the name may be a later addition, the unusual composition may have been alluding to the lines attributed to Paul in 2 Timothy 4:7–8: "I have fought the good fight, I have finished the race, I have kept the faith. Henceforth there is laid up for me the crown of righteousness, which the Lord, the righteous judge, will award to me on that day."

Later Eastern Christian icons of Paul represent him in the ancient manner, with a high forehead, receding hairline, long narrow face, and beard. Among the most famous of these is one by Andrei Rublev, painted around 1410–1420 and now in Moscow's Tretyakov Gallery. In this image, Paul holds a book and his face is in three-fourths profile; his eyes are turned away from the viewer, as if he is in deep thought. About the same time, the Italian artist Masaccio depicted Paul as part of an altarpiece for the Church of the Carmine in Pisa (ca. 1426). Paul stands in a simple iconic fashion, standing and looking over his left shoulder. In this image a book is tucked into his left arm while he holds a sword in his right.

Later Western portraits of Paul include some especially well-known images, among them some by Rembrandt, also produced in the seventeenth century. One depicts Paul writing in his prison cell (1657), another represents him as an elderly man standing at his writing table (1629–1630), and yet another is based upon a self-portrait of the artist himself (1661). Although many later images of Paul continue to show him holding a book or scroll, he is also frequently depicted with a sword, alluding to his martyrdom by beheading. Valentin de Boulogne, however, showed Paul as a writer (ca. 1620) composing his epistles at a desk, using a quill pen and surrounded by books, notes, and inkwell, which demonstrates the tenacity of Paul's reputation as a scholar. A similarly pedantic image of Paul by Georges de la Tour (ca. 1615–1620) portrays him as an elderly man reading a set of papers, glasses perched at the end of his nose. By contrast, a dramatic portrait by the French painter Nicolas Tournier depicts a younger, intently staring Paul holding both sword and scroll (ca. 1625–1626, now in the Musée des Augustins, Toulouse).

Other Pauline Narrative Scenes

Other narrative art depicts Paul without Peter. These include scenes of his vision and conversion on the Damascus road; his baptism; his preaching, healing, and ecstasy; his relationship with the woman Thecla; and his adventures on Malta.

Paul's conversion

Depictions of Paul prior to his conversion are rare. The cathedrals of Notre Dame and of St. Stephen (Saint-Etienne-du-Mont) in Paris both have reliefs depicting Paul present at the stoning of Stephen. Most narrative-based representations of Paul, however, begin with his vision on the road to Damascus (Acts 9:3–7).

One of the earliest depictions of Paul's conversion is a miniature in the ninth-century Bible of Charles the Bald, produced at Rheims and given to Pope John VIII at Charles's coronation in 875. Presented as a continuous narrative in three parts, this miniature also depicts Paul meeting Ananias, being healed, disputing with the Jews, and escaping from Damascus.[29] In the twelfth century, a miniature in the illuminated encyclopedia *Hortus Deliciarum* (Garden of Delights) shows Christ appearing to Paul, who has fallen to his knees between a wolf and a sheep (identified as such in the illumination). Christ holds a drawn sword over Paul's head.

In fourteenth- and fifteenth-century manuscripts, most notably a choir book dated to the 1430s and illuminated by the Dominican friar Fra Angelico, Paul wears the garb of a Roman soldier. Struck down by his vision, he lies on his back and gazes upward at the appearance of Christ, who is surrounded by rays of light. Around a century later, the master illuminator Jean Fouquet portrayed the scene for the *Livre d'Heures d'Étienne Chevalier* (ca. 1450–1460). In this image Paul sits astride a horse that has fallen to its knees. Above, a representation of the Trinity, rather than only of Jesus, speaks to Paul in a burst of divine light emanating from the clouds.

From the sixteenth century on, the subject of Paul's conversion was a popular artistic theme. However, in nearly all the subsequent iconography, Paul is shown as a rider fallen off his horse and prostrate on the ground, despite the fact that the book of Acts says nothing about how Paul traveled to Damascus. Among the sixteenth-century representations is a fresco by Michelangelo for the Cappella Paolina (1540s), Pope Paul III's private chapel. Juxtaposed with a painting of Peter's crucifixion, Paul here is presented as an elderly man, already blinded by the sight of Christ, who reaches down to him from heaven. Other paintings of the scene dated to the same general era were produced by Lucas Cranach the Younger (1545), Parmigianino (1552), Tintoretto (1545), and Pieter Bruegel the Elder (1567). It also appears among the colored woodblock prints in the late fifteenth-century Nuremburg Chronicle, a world history and one of the earliest printed books.

Two famous paintings by Caravaggio were painted around 1600 (approximately one year apart). The earlier is now housed in the Odescalchi Balbi Collection in Rome, although it was originally intended for the Cerasi Chapel of Santa Maria Popolo. After Tiberio Cerasi rejected his first effort, Caravaggio produced the second, which still resides in that church. Both paintings reflect the artist's distinctive use of light to create dramatic effects. The earlier composition was more complex: a tangle of horse, fallen and dazzled rider, soldier with spear defensively poised, and Jesus reaching out to Paul, supported by a young angel. The second painting's more simplified composition portrays Paul sprawled on the ground beneath his horse, his red cloak spread out on the ground, his arms stretched upwards toward the light, and his eyes already closed in blindness. In this instance, contrary to previous convention, Caravaggio omitted Jesus' appearance, allowing the observer's gaze to be drawn directly to the figure of Paul (fig. 32.9).[30]

Paul's baptism by Ananias

The story of Paul having his sight restored and being baptized by Ananias (Acts 9:10–19) rarely appears in Christian art, although it is included in the above-mentioned ninth-century manuscript of Charles the Bald as well as in the twelfth-century *Hortus Deliciarum*. The most detailed visual depiction of the scene is among the twelfth-century mosaics that adorn the Sicilian churches mentioned above: the Cappella Palatina (Palatine Chapel) and the Cathedral of Monreale. The elaborate decoration of both buildings includes images of Paul's baptism along with other scenes from Paul's life, including his disputing with Damascene Jews and escaping from Damascus by being lowered over the city walls in a basket (Acts 9:23–25; fig. 32.10).

Paul preaching, healing, and in ecstasy

Possibly the most famous image of Paul preaching is Raphael's cartoon for a tapestry (intended for the Sistine Chapel, ca. 1515). Currently in the Victoria and Albert Museum

Figure 32.9 Caravaggio (Michelangelo Merisi da), *The Conversion on the Way to Damascus*, ca. 1600, Cerai Chapel, Santa Maria del Popolo, Rome.
Photo credit: Scala/Art Resource, NY.

in London, the large cartoon (390 × 440 cm), now mounted on canvas, shows the scene from Acts of Paul preaching at the Areopagus in Athens. The artist incorporated classical architecture into this painting, and presents Paul in profile, his arms raised, speaking to a rapt audience. Another painting with a similarly classical setting is Giovanni Paolo Pannini's 1774 canvas, "The Apostle Paul Preaching on the Ruins," now in St. Petersburg's Hermitage Museum.

One of Raphael's tapestry designs also depicted Paul trying to stop the people of Lystra from making a sacrifice to himself (Acts 14:11–18). The event that triggered this near-blasphemy, Paul's healing of a cripple (Acts 14:8–10), was the subject of a painting by Karel Dujardin (ca. 1663), now in Amsterdam's Rijksmuseum. Here Paul stands among a crowd of suppliants; the crippled man placed in the foreground draws the viewer's eye most directly. Another depiction of this story, by Nicolaes Berchem (1650), is now in the Musée d'Art, Saint Etienne (France).

Figure 32.10   Paul disputing with the Jews and escaping from Damascus, 12th-century mosaic from the Palatine Chapel, Palermo, Sicily.
Photo credit: Alinari/Art Resource, NY.

Relatively rare depictions of Paul in ecstasy (cf. 2 Cor 12:1–4) include one by Johann Liss (ca. 1628), which shows an elderly Paul among his books, suddenly visited by angels playing instruments and pulling back the curtain of the heavens. Paul appears to shrink back in some fear from the vision being revealed – a golden sky in which the Trinity appears. Another, *The Ecstasy of St. Paul* by Nicolas Poussin (1649–50), has Paul being born aloft by three angels. His abandoned book and sword rest among classical columns.

Paul and Thecla

A rare fifth-century ivory plaque, once part of a small reliquary and now on display in the British Museum, reproduces a scene from the *Acts of Paul and Thecla*. Paul is shown reading to Thecla, who listens to him from her tower window. The right portion of the ivory depicts either Paul being driven from the town of Iconium (*Acts of Paul and Thecla* 21) or stoned at Lystra (Acts 14:19), a man hurling a rock at him while he flees (fig. 32.11).[31]

Figure 32.11   Ivory of Paul with Thecla, Rome, ca. 430, now in the British Museum. Photo credit: Robin M. Jensen.

Paul on Malta

A highly articulated and also unique series of scenes of Paul preaching and working miracles is found on the right leaf of a fifth-century ivory diptych, now in the Museo Nazionale del Bargello in Florence (fig. 32.12). The upper section of the panel shows Paul seated in three-quarters profile and either teaching or arguing with two men, one facing him and the other leaning over the back of his chair. This scene may portray Paul's debate with the Roman magistrate Festus and King Agrippa (Acts 25–26), or it could have been meant to show his dispute with the philosophers in Athens (Acts 17:18–19).

The center of the panel depicts Paul confronting Publius, the governor of the Island of Malta where he has been shipwrecked. Paul is about to shake the poisonous viper off his arm and into the fire at his feet (Acts 28:3–6). The two men on the right make gestures of fear, recalling their lines in the story: "No doubt this man is a murderer. Though he has escaped from the sea, justice has not allowed him to live." In the lower panel, three Maltese bring a sick man to Paul to be healed, just as Paul had healed Publius's father (Acts 28:7–9). The figure on the far left points to Paul in the center, a reminder of his miraculous survival of the viper's bite – which was to them a sign of his god-like power.

A painting of this episode also appeared in Rome's basilica of San Paolo fuori le Mura, just to the right of the scene in which Peter and Paul embrace (*concordia apostolorum*). According to a watercolor copy of the painting made in the early seventeenth century, the viper rises from the fire to bite Paul's finger. On the other side of the fire, three men observe the miracle. In the background are the sails of the beached ships.[32]

A cult of Paul was well established in Malta by the Middle Ages. Evidence of earlier Pauline veneration is lacking, although early Christian catacombs indicate the exis-

Figure 32.12   Diptych with the stories of Paul on Malta and Adam in Paradise, now in the Museo Nazionale del Bargello, Florence.
Photo: George Tatge, 2000. Photo credit: Alinari/Art Resource, NY.

tence of a sizable Christian community on the island. While the Maltese iconography maintained the traditional Pauline portrait type in most respects, certain distinct features are apparent: he is nearly always depicted as seated, holding a book in his left hand (resting on his left knee) and a sword in his right (a reference to his martyrdom). Frontal and static, the image reflects the influence of Byzantine iconography.[33]

A later depiction of Paul on Malta was produced by Adam Elsheimer (ca. 1600). Today in the National Gallery in London, the painting depicts the episode with the viper as taking place at night, giving the scene an eerie quality. Another famous image of this episode, also depicted at night and equally dramatic, was painted in 1786 by Benjamin West for the Royal Naval College Chapel in Greenwich.

The Cult of Paul in Rome and the Basilica of San Paolo fuori le Mura

According to the *Liber Pontificalis*, the first basilica dedicated to Paul was built by Constantine I.[34] The site – along the Via Ostiense where, according to tradition, the apostle was buried – was first attested to by a certain Gaius who lived at the end of the second century, according to Eusebius of Caesarea's *Ecclesiastical History* (2.25). Here, Gaius identifies the shrines of both Peter and Paul, the first at the Vatican and the other on the Ostian Road. Eusebius added that cemeteries at these sites were still associated with the names of Peter and Paul in his day. Elsewhere he noted that the sepulcher erected over Paul's tomb was a place of great veneration (*Divine Manifestation* 4.7). An additional source for the tradition that Paul's remains were buried in a tomb on the Ostian Road comes from a third- or fourth-century Roman liturgical calendar, the *Depositio Martyrum*, which gives the feast as June 29 and notes that Peter was celebrated in the Vatican catacombs, Paul along the Ostian Road.[35]

Later in the fourth century, the emperors Theodosius, Valentinian II, and Arcadius had the basilica rebuilt in order to accommodate the throngs of pilgrims arriving to venerate the relics of the saint. The newer building was modeled after the church of St. Peter on the Vatican, but surpassed it in size, splendor, and the beauty of its proportions and materials. It consisted of a nave with four side aisles, a colonnaded atrium, and a transept.[36] One of the most important artifacts possibly surviving from the Theodosian basilica is a sarcophagus located beneath the high altar, which supposedly still contains the relics of Paul. Two other objects, marble slabs with the inscription *Paolo apostolo martyr(yri)* ("to Paul, apostle and martyr") were discovered during the rebuilding of the basilica after a major fire in 1823 (fig. 32.13). These two slabs probably date to the

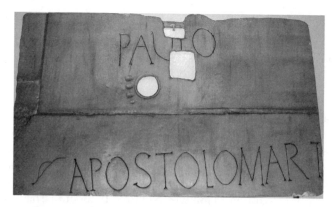

Figure 32.13   Slab from Paul's tomb, from the Basilica of St. Paul fuori le Mura. Photo credit: Robin M. Jensen.

late fourth or early fifth century; both have holes to accommodate pouring of libations or gathering of secondary relics by dipping strips of cloth (*brandea*) into the tomb.

The building had been embellished with glass mosaics in the apse and on the triumphal arch, and a painted pictorial cycle along the long nave walls.[37] These decorations were replaced or repaired in the thirteenth century, but many of the fifth-century donations of Pope Leo I survived more or less intact until the nineteenth-century and are known from pre-fire drawings or watercolors. The southern wall portrayed scenes of Aaron, as precursor to Paul. The northern cycle showed scenes from stories about Paul taken from the Acts of the Apostles, including an image of Paul's shaking off the poisonous serpent in Malta (discussed above), which was preserved in a seventeenth-century copy.

The basilica continues to be a pilgrimage destination, although it has been extensively rebuilt and renovated over the centuries, especially after its nearly complete destruction by fire in 1823. Recent excavations begun in 2002 and culminated during the Vatican's Pauline Year (2008–2009, a celebration of the two thousandth anniversary of Paul's birth) identified a white marble sarcophagus, buried beneath the basilica's high altar, as a likely repository for Paul's relics. In an announcement made by Pope Benedict XVI, on the vespers for the Feast of Peter and Paul (June 28), 2009, tiny holes were drilled into the sarcophagus to allow a small probe to inspect the interior. According to the Pope's announcement, small traces of purple-dyed linen cloth, incense, and bone fragments were picked up. According to the Pope, the discovery confirmed the "unanimous and undisputed tradition that these are the mortal remains of the Apostle Paul."[38]

Around the same time, a second discovery, of a portrait of Paul in the nearby catacomb of St. Thecla, was announced by the Vatican's official news organ, *L'Osservatore Romano*. Proclaimed "the oldest known depiction of the apostle Paul," and dated to the early fourth century, Paul's features in this image conform to the standard likeness from elsewhere in early Christian art.[39]

A second major shrine to Paul was also known from at least the sixth century, and is usually identified as the place of his martyrdom. This is cited in the Greek version of the *Acts of Peter and Paul*, and identifies the place as a pine tree on the estate called Aquae Salvias.[40] Today this shrine is within the Abbey of the Three Fountains, about 2.5 kilometers from the basilica of San Paolo fuori le Mura along the Laurentian Road. According to legends that appear to date to the Middle Ages, when Roman soldiers decapitated Paul here, his head bounced three times, causing three fountains to spring up, thus giving the church and monastery its present name. Inside the church are altars at each of the springs, and a fresco that depicts the miracle.[41]

In addition to these two main pilgrimage destinations are other sites associated with the cult of Paul in Rome, but which have less historical data to confirm their associations with the apostle. They include the church of San Paulo alla Regola, built at the place where Paul reportedly lived while under house arrest. Built in the late seventeenth century, the church's apse contains paintings by Luigi Garzi (1638–1721) that depict Paul's conversion, preaching, and martyrdom. Among the more firmly attested sites, however, is the Memoria Apostolorum, an ancient martyrium and funeral banqueting hall on the site of the cemetery basilica and catacomb complex dedicated to San

Sebastiano. The existence of graffiti addressed to both Peter and Paul at this site has led historians to believe that the remains of both apostles were transferred here during the Valerian persecution, ca. 258.

Notes

1   See Mango (1972, 41). Mango notes that the authenticity of this fragment has been questioned.

2   George of Alexandria, *Vita Chrysostomi* 26–27; translated in Mitchell (2002, 35 n.7). See also Holloway (2007).

3   Tertullian seems aware of the *Acts of Paul and Thecla*; see *Baptism* 17.

4   See Justin Martyr, *Dialogue with Trypho* 1; Eusebius, *Ecclesiastical History* 4.11; and (on the tunic, *pallium*, and sandals as a practical and worthy dress for Christian men) Tertullian, *The Pallium* 5–6.

5   See McDonald (2006).

6   See Spier (2007, 249, cat. 72).

7   This is illustrated in Utro (2009, 194–195, cat. 65).

8   See, e.g., Franke (1972, 263–271); Kollwitz (1936, 45–66).

9   See MacCormack (1981, 130–131); Schumacher (1959, 1–39); Deckers (2001, 8–10).

10   E.g., Hellemo (1989, 87–88); Herrmann and van den Hoek (2009, 33–80).

11   For this interpretation, see Styger (1913, 17–74).

12   See Huskinson (1982, 87–88).

13   *Acts of Peter and Paul* 22–29, which, unlike the earlier *Acts of Paul* and *Acts of Peter,* links the two together when in Rome. In several reworkings of these documents attributed to Pseudo-Marcellus, Paul and Peter are joined in common ministry and martyrdom in Rome, even though other ancient chronographers do not have them there at the same time. See Tajra (1994, 143–151).

14   See Kessler (1987, 265–275). This is illustrated in Donati (2000, 135, cat. 56).

15   On this image (in the Vigna Chiaraviglio), see Bisconti (2009, 170, fig. 8).

16   This is discussed and illustrated in Spier (2007, 247, cat. 70).

17   Kessler (1987, 266–268).

18   On Peter as Moses, see Brandenburg (2005, 98).

19   Biblical quotations are taken from the Revised Standard Version.

20   Gaudentius of Brescia, *Sermon* 20.10, cited also by Kessler (1987, 268), where he adds a text from the Roman poet Arator on the same theme.

21   For a long time this painting was attributed to Masaccio.

22   The earliest documentary evidence for Peter's and Paul's joint martyrdoms comes from *1 Clement* 5. Ignatius of Antioch alludes to Paul's death in *Letter to the Ephesians* 12.2, and in *Letter to the Romans* 4 he implies that both apostles died in Rome. Tertullian in two places (*Prescription against Heretics* 36 and *Antidote for the Scorpion's Sting* 15) specifically mentions Peter's death by crucifixion and Paul's by beheading. In the fourth century, Peter of Alexandria, *Canonical Epistle* 9 continues this tradition, as does Lactantius, *The Death of the Persecutors* 2; and Eusebius, *Ecclesiastical History* 2.25. In the latter source, Eusebius refers to a letter of Dionysius of Corinth to the Roman church (ca. 171), which explicitly stated that the two died at the same time. Paulinus of Nola records a pilgrimage to Rome in the late fourth or early fifth century to celebrate the feast of the two apostles (*Epistle* 17.1), a feast also mentioned by Prudentius, *Crowns of Martyrdom* 12.

23 Museo Pio Cristiano, inv. #28591. This sarcophagus was found below the confessio of San Paolo fuori le Mura after the devastating fire of 1823

24 See Eastman (2009, 48–52).

25 This comes from a fourth-century source, the *Martyrdom of Paul*, mistakenly attributed to Pope Linus.

26 On the Stefaneschi altarpiece and the bronze doors, see Utro (2009, 249–252, cat. 89; 254–256, cat. 92).

27 This object is discussed in Spier (2007, 240, cat. 62).

28 Illustrated and discussed in Donati (2000, 142, 214–215).

29 See Utro (2009, 326–328, cat. 97).

30 Another well-known painting of this scene was produced in 1662 by Karel Dujardin and is now in London's National Gallery.

31 See Spier (2007, 237–238, cat. 60).

32 See the image in Donati (2000, 135, cat. 56, discussed 211–212).

33 See Lindsey (2002, 140–155).

34 *Liber Pontificalis* 34 (Sylvester). Although this section of the *Liber Pontificalis* is almost certainly a later interpolation, the archaeological record reflects an early fourth-century date for the building, which was destroyed in the later fourth century.

35 *Monumenta Germaniae Historica: Auctorum Antiqvissimorum* 9.71, a text attached to the Roman *Filocalian Calendar* of 354. See Eastman (2009, 20–21).

36 See Docci (2006); and Brandenburg (2005, 114–130).

37 Mentioned by Prudentius, *Crowns of Martyrdom* 12.45–54.

38 Reported in multiple news sources; e.g., *Times Online*, June 29, 2009.

39 *L'Osservatore Romano*, June 28, 2009.

40 See Eastman (2009, 76, n. 101), for a discussion of the differences between the Latin and Greek versions of the Acts of Peter and Paul.

41 The Stefaneschi Triptych (discussed above) also shows these three springs.

References

Augustine. 1991. *The Trinity*. Translated by Edmund Hill. Brooklyn: New City Press.

Bisconti, Fabrizio. 2009. La sapienza, la concordia, il martirio: La figura di Paolo nell'immaginario iconografico della tarda antichità. Pages 163–176 in *San Paolo in Vaticano: La figura e la parola dell'Apostolo delle Genti nelle raccolte pontificie*. Edited by Umberto Utro. Perugia: Tau.

Brandenburg, Hugo. 2005. *Ancient Churches of Rome from the Fourth to the Seventh Century: The Dawn of Christian Architecture in the West*. Turnhout: Brepols.

Deckers, Johannes. 2001. Gottlicher Kaiser und kaiserlicher Gott. Pages 8–10 in *Epochenwandel? Kunst und Kultur zwischen Antike und Mittelalter*. Edited by Franz Alto Bauer and Norbert Zimmerman. Mainz am Rhein: P. von Zabern.

Docci, Marina. 2006. *San Paolo fuori le mura: dalle origini alla basilica delle "origini."* Rome: Gangemi.

Donati, Angela. 2000. *Pietro e Paolo: La storia, il culto, la memoria nei primi secoli*. Milan: Electra.

Eastman, David L. 2009. The Cult of the Apostle Paul the Martyr in the Latin West. Unpublished dissertation, Yale University.

Elliott, J. K. 1993. *The Apocryphal New Testament: A Collection of Apocryphal Christian Literature in an English Translation*. Oxford: Clarendon.

Franke, Peter. 1972. Traditio legis und Petrusprimat: Eine Entgegnung auf Franz Nikolasch. *Vigiliae Christianae* 26: 263–271.

Hellemo, Geir. 1989. *Adventus Domini: Eschatological Thought in 4th-Century Apses and Catecheses.* Leiden: Brill.

Herrmann, John, and Annewies van den Hoek. 2009. Apocalyptic Themes in the Monumental and Minor Art of Early Christianity. Pages 33–80 in *Apocalyptic Thought in Early Christianity.* Edited by Robert J. Daly. Grand Rapids: Baker Academic.

Holloway, Paul A. 2007. Portrait and Presence: A Note on the *Visio Procli* (George of Alexandria, Vita Chrysostomi 27). *Byzantinische Zeitschrift* 100: 71–83.

Huskinson, J. M. 1982. *Concordia Apostolorum: Christian Propaganda at Rome in the Fourth and Fifth Centuries: A Study in Early Christian Iconography and Iconology.* Oxford: B.A.R.

Kessler, Herbert L. 1987. The Meeting of Peter and Paul in Rome: An Emblematic Narrative of Spiritual Brotherhood. *Dumbarton Oaks Papers* 41: 265–275.

Kollwitz, Johannes. 1936. Christus als Lehrer und die Gesetzesübergabe an Petrus in der konstantinischen Kunst Roms. *Römische Quartalschrift* 44: 45–66.

Lindsey, Margaret. 2002. The Iconography of Paul in Medieval Malta. Pages 140–155 in *Insights and Interpretations: Studies in Celebration of the Eighty-fifth Anniversary of the Index of Christian Art.* Edited by Colum Hourihane. Princeton: Princeton University Press.

MacCormack, Sabine G. 1981. *Art and Ceremony in Late Antiquity.* Berkeley: University of California Press.

McDonald, Dennis R. 2006. Categorization of Antetextuality in the Gospels and Acts: A Case for Luke's Imitation of Plato and Xenophon to Depict Paul as a Christian Socrates. Pages 211–225 in *The Intertextuality of the Epistles: Explorations of Theory and Practice.* Edited by Thomas L. Brodie, Dennis R. MacDonald, and Stanley E. Porter. Sheffield: Sheffield Phoenix Press.

Mango, Cyril. 1972. *The Art of the Byzantine Empire 312–1453: Sources and Documents.* Englewood Cliffs, NJ: Prentice-Hall.

Mitchell, Margaret M. 2002. *The Heavenly Trumpet: John Chrysostom and the Art of Pauline Interpretation.* Louisville: Westminster John Knox.

Schumacher, Walter Nikolaus. 1959. Dominus legem dat. *Römische Quartalschrift* 54: 1–39.

Sotomayor, Manuel. 1983. Petrus und Paulus in der frühchristlichen Ikonographie. Pages 199–210 in *Spätantike und frühes Christentum: Ausstellung im Liebieghaus Museum alter Plastik Frankfurt am Main 16. Dezember 1983 bis 11. März 1984.* Frankfurt am Main: Liebieghaus, Museum alter Plastik.

Spier, Jeffrey, editor. 2007. *Picturing the Bible: The Earliest Christian Art.* New Haven: Yale University Press.

Styger, Paul. 1913. Neue Untersuchungen über die altchristlichen Petrusdarstellungen. *Römische Quartalschrift* 27: 17–74.

Tajra, H. W. 1994. *The Martyrdom of St. Paul: Historical and Judicial Context, Traditions, and Legends.* Tübingen: J. C. B. Mohr (Paul Siebeck).

Utro, Umberto, editor. 2009. *San Paolo in Vaticano: La figura e la parola dell'Apostolo delle Genti nelle raccolte pontificie.* Perugia: Tau.

CHAPTER 33

Literature

David Lyle Jeffrey

In Sholem Asch's novel *The Apostle* (1943), Paul is sympathetically portrayed from the time of the first Christian Pentecost (in which Paul did not figure) to the moment of his execution in Rome. Though Asch (1880–1957) was Jewish, comparatively conservative theologically, and wrote in Yiddish, this carefully researched, finely written, and judiciously balanced historical novel is to date the most distinguished literary treatment of Paul in Western literature. Asch is remarkably faithful both to the canonical biblical texts and to many of the early Christian traditions about the apostle; his book remains the fullest as well as the best novelistic treatment of Paul's conversion and his tumultuous life and ministry. No work by a Christian literary writer has approached its combination of fidelity to sources with literary excellence. It would seem that, among Christians, those most attracted to Paul and his letters are among those least likely to find justification for a hypothetical or literary treatment of his personality and human character.

The uneven history of Paul's influence in literature is marked by other such ironies and paradoxes. Among these one must include the fact that out of all proportion to their number and post-patristic circulation, non-canonical and evidently apocryphal works came to provide some of the better-known features of the Pauline character and his literary iconography among Christians of late antiquity and the Middle Ages. Further, despite tacit and explicit tributes by Augustine, Paul's distinctive hermeneutical formulation of biblical tradition, namely, the manner in which he proclaimed the kerygma for Mediterranean communities by anchoring it in a typological interpretation of the Hebrew Scriptures (easily his most monumental literary achievement) is scarcely noted by the authors of early narratives about him.

The Blackwell Companion to Paul, First Edition. Edited by Stephen Westerholm.
© 2011 Blackwell Publishing Ltd. Published 2011 by Blackwell Publishing Ltd.

Literary Sources

In the West the principal sources of Paul's life have been the account given in the Acts of the Apostles and autobiographical glimpses scattered throughout the thirteen letters traditionally ascribed to him (nine general letters to various churches and four pastoral/personal letters [1–2 Tim, Tit, and Phlm]). Although the early church widely credited him with the Epistle to the Hebrews, by the later Middle Ages occasional early doubts about this attribution again resurfaced; Hugh of St. Victor (twelfth century), an important source for medieval writers because of his book on the liberal arts and right reading, is typical in speculating that the author of Hebrews might rather have been Barnabas or even Clement (*Didascalicon* 4.6). While Jerome apparently knew an *Acts of Paul and Thecla* (*On Illustrious Men* 7), this apocryphal text and two other fragments of an apocryphal *Acts of Paul* have in themselves only re-emerged in modern times (Schmidt 1904). Allusions to these works, however, enter popular literature much earlier. In the Middle Ages a collection of fourteen doubtless spurious *Letters of Paul and Seneca*, first referred to in the fourth century, was also widely popular (the most copies of any of "Seneca's" works in the Middle Ages), and certainly known to Augustine and Jerome. Letters 7 and 13 are notable in that they represent Seneca as praising the high substance of Paul's letter to the Galatians and 1 Corinthians, but reproaching Paul for a Greek style inadequate to his subject matter. An echo of the influence of this pseudepigraphal text occurs as recently as Lutheran pastor and novelist Walter Wangerin's *Paul* (2000), in which the apostle is characterized through the various points of view of friends and acquaintances such as Priscilla, Barnabas, Timothy, and Titus, as well as Seneca.

Among the biographical elements recorded in the New Testament, those which, with the writings themselves, do most to characterize Paul for literary accounts include (1) his presence at the martyrdom of Stephen (Acts 8:1; 22:20); (2) his early persecution of the Christians (Acts 9:1–2); (3) his dramatic Damascus road conversion and temporary blinding (Acts 9:3–8); (4) his escape from Damascus in a basket let down from the walls (Acts 9:23–25); (5) his preaching in the agora of Athens (Acts 17:16–34); (6) his shipwreck (Acts 27); and (7) his notable confrontation with adverse political forces and his several imprisonments on his missionary travels. That he was martyred at the gates of Rome by decapitation with a sword is not recorded in the New Testament itself, but along with the canonically attested events yields a persistent aspect of Pauline iconography. Among these, in artistic representation in the Middle Ages, the most frequently occurring identifiers have been the sword (for his martyrdom and his proclamation as a *miles Christi* [soldier of Christ]; e.g., Dürer, van Dyck, Quartararo, Rembrandt) and the book (for his role as writer and expositor; e.g., Lorenzetti, Dürer, Van Leyden, Rembrandt, Lievens). These two dominant features of Pauline pictorial iconography correspond respectively to the courage and wisdom (*fortitudo* and *sapientia*) for which he is typically remembered in later literature. Throughout the history of Western art, Paul is usually represented as short (pseudo-Chrysostom calls him "the man of three cubits" [4'6"]), bald, bearded, and in Roman dress; he is occasionally shown in prison encumbered with chains.

Because of his trade as a tentmaker (Acts 18:3) and principal apostolic vocation, Catholic tradition has made him the patron saint of tent-makers, weavers, saddlers, and basket-makers, as well as of journalists, theologians, and labor unions. These associations often provide a context for allusions to Paul in vernacular literature. Other attributes include his self-acknowledged lack of eloquence (2 Cor 11:6) and his persistent "thorn in the flesh" (2 Cor 12:7),[1] identified as anything from congenitally bowed legs (cf. the second-century *Acts of Paul*) to epilepsy (Findlay 1900, 701; also effectively related to his visionary experiences by Sholem Asch). More recently, Larry Woiwode's breezy, personal, and somewhat iconoclastic rambling commentary, *Acts* (1993), ferrets out for speculation the possibility of kidney stones, but as a poet and novelist, Woiwode does not specify a source.

Ancient and Medieval Literary Characterizations

For literary authors of late antiquity and the Middle Ages, there was more interesting material to explore. Perhaps the most controversial of Paul's legacies for both the early and modern church – his counsels on marriage and virginity (1 Cor 7; Eph 5) – called forth an extensive debate among major fourth-century theologians. Notable are Jerome's *Epistle* 48.7–8 and *Against Jovinianus*, which was so hotly resented by Chaucer's Wife of Bath (*Canterbury Tales* 3.674–675), and Augustine's *Holy Virginity*, *The Good of Marriage*, and *The Good of Widowhood*. Paul's Epistle to the Romans was the book Augustine found before him in the garden at the moment of his conversion (*Confessions*, Book 8), and the passage to which his attention was drawn ("make not provision for the flesh, to fulfil the lusts thereof" [Rom 13:14]) was frequently alluded to in medieval sermons and saints' lives. Subsequently, other writings of Paul demonstrated to the once proud teacher of rhetoric that wisdom was of more value than eloquence in a Christian teacher. Paul avoids the "eloquent nonsense" of the rhetoricians, Augustine argues, offering instead an example of "true eloquence" which, for the sake of wisdom, employs select devices of rhetoric (e.g., periodic sentences) as a natural effect of the progression of thought, not merely for the sake of style or ornament (*Christian Teaching* 4.7.11). In these and important philosophical respects, such as the view of reality embodied in his doctrine of the Incarnation, Paul comes to supersede Plato for the sometime Platonist (*Confessions* 7.21.27).

Augustine's enormous influence on the poets made these points of great weight in their own search for vernacular style (e.g., Dante). Almost as importantly for literature, Augustine, perhaps in part defending Paul against the charges attributed to Seneca, comes to characterize Paul as a man of plain speech, resisting the imaginations of those like Jerome who construe, for example, his debate with Peter about "Judaizing" (Gal 2) as rhetorical "stagecraft" to clarify doctrine (cf. Jerome, *Epistle* 56 and the preface to his commentary on Galatians). In this, Augustine may have been a more sensitive reader than Jerome from a stylistic point of view, for while Paul certainly uses parallelism and rhetorical rhythm, his letters are loosely organized, informally parenthetical, analogous to the classical diatribe (indeed, not to Stoic Roman ears a suitable genre for moral philosophy). More than one later medieval commentator has noticed this feature of his prose.

The Paul of John Chrysostom is, as noted elsewhere in this volume, a heroic example of simple Christian life, an exemplar of voluntary poverty, gentleness, and magnanimity (*Hom. on 1 Corinthians* 15.13), and, despite his great zeal, of humility and self-effacement (*On the Priesthood* 3.7). Commenting on his "poverty of speech" and the relative paucity of miracles in his ministry, Chrysostom says about Paul that it is in his life and conversation rather than his miracles that the reader will find "this Christian athlete a conqueror" (*On the Priesthood* 4.6; cf. *Hom. on 1 Corinthians* 6.1; *Hom. on 2 Corinthians* 1.3–5). In an interesting development of the accounts of Paul's execution, Chrysostom also relates (*Against the Opponents of the Monastic Life* 1.3; *Hom. on Acts of the Apostles* 46) that the apostle had enraged Nero by converting both his favorite concubine and his cupbearer, aptly named in some medieval accounts of Nero's demise as Narcissus (cf. Rom 16:11). This product of a wonderfully novelistic imagination, despite analogies in Caldwell and Sienkiewicz (see below), was largely ignored in later fiction.

Partly because of his own sudden and spectacular conversion and partly because of his travels converting others, Paul became a prototype for missionary stories among the hagiographers; numerous saints' lives imitate features of both his biblical and legendary biography. Among the more colorful extraneous contributions to the legendary lore, the *Visio Sancti Pauli* (*Vision of Saint Paul*) is a Latin translation of a third-century Greek text that, despite the fact that Aldhelm and (three centuries later) Aelfric both called it a "fevered fantasy," by the eleventh century had been translated also into Old English and seems to have been widely read for more than three centuries as historical, before becoming gradually understood as pious fiction. Opening with a quotation from 2 Corinthians 12:2–4, in which Paul describes his rapture into the third heaven, the narrator describes how the "text" was found in a marble box under the foundation of Paul's house in Tarsus. The account is divided into four parts, concerning respectively (1) a cosmic tour by angel-guide (similar to the "spirits of Christmas" in Dickens's *A Christmas Carol*), (2) a Dantesque tour of the "places of the righteous" and (3) the dwellings of the wicked, an inferno with familiar Vergilian features, and (4) a visit to the paradise of Eden. An interesting feature of his third stop is that Paul's visit is said to prompt a suspension of the torments of sinners, weekly, on Sundays.

Relating the biblical story that, when on Malta, Paul was bitten by a viper without effect (Acts 28:3–6), Hilary tells that no descendant of the Maltese man who gave the apostle hospitality was ever after susceptible to snakebite. Another story passed down in the legenda clearly has its basis in Acts 20:7–12, but in it the sleeper who falls from the window to his death is not Eutychus but one Patrochlus, an intimate of Nero. When resurrected, he goes to Nero to report, and Nero, having heard of his death, is first astonished and then enraged at the young man's decision henceforth to serve Christ, the true King of Kings. It is this threat to Nero's pride and security that is said to prompt his beheading of Paul and burning of hundreds of Christians (so the *Golden Legend* of Jacopo da Varagine, later translated by William Caxton). Later elements of the legenda include the nighttime disinterral of the bodies of Paul and Peter from the catacombs and the reburial of the former, according to Bede's *Greater Chronicle* (=*De Temporum Ratione*, chapter 66), on the road to Ostia where he had been beheaded.

High Middle Ages

Later medieval spiritual writers develop the image of Paul as a "hero of faith." Among the Cistercians, for example, he is above all the "clarion voice of the New Testament" (William of St. Thierry, *Meditations* 3.5), "whose faith is not grasped by a worldly person, nor his meaning explained better by the words of another than his own" (*The Enigma of Faith* 1; cf. Hilary, *Trinity* 9.10). William understands Paul to be answering the neo-Platonists in Romans 1:20–24 (*Exposition on the Epistle to the Romans*), even as in Acts he had addressed the unformed religious intuitions of their predecessors on the Areopagus. William, who believed Paul to have self-consciously eschewed the ornaments of Greek rhetoric (see his comments on Rom 5:12; elsewhere he notes 1 Cor 2:1; 2 Cor 11:6), thinks with Augustine that literarily Paul should be regarded as an exemplar of plain speech, and this is the character Chaucer adopts for his Parson, who, quoting Paul to Timothy openly in his prologue, avers that he will avoid old fables and "drasty" speech as well as poetic and rhetorical niceties such as alliteration in favor of a direct, clear prose. But the Parson is not one who confuses "plain" with "literalistic." In this, he grasps perhaps the chief principle of Pauline biblical hermeneutic for medieval writers such as Chaucer, Petrarch, Boccaccio, and Dante: "*littera occidit, spiritus autem vivificat*" ("the letter killeth, but the spirit giveth life" [2 Cor 3:6]), a principle adduced by medieval Christian writers everywhere with reference to interpretation of their own work (e.g., Boccaccio, *De genealoga deorum gentilum* [*On the Genealogy of the Gods of the Gentiles*] 15.8; Dante, *Letter to Can Grande della Scala* 7–11 and *Convivio* [*Banquet*] 2.1.2–15), and one that William of St. Thierry finds already at work in Romans 7–8. Romans 15:4 is cited almost as widely, for example, in the last decade of the fourteenth century by Chaucer in *The Canterbury Tales* (Retractions) to indicate that whatever is written in Scripture is instructive and generates hope. This is a theme picked up often in the High Middle Ages among spiritual writers: for Aelred of Rievaulx (*De Jesu puero duodenni* [*On Jesus as a Boy of Twelve*] 19), Paul is the "vessel of election" (cf. Acts 9:15), yet most intensely *simpatico*, able to be "weak with the weak, on fire with the scandalized" (*De amicitia spirituali* [*On Spiritual Friendship*] 2.50). Bernard of Clairvaux sees him as not merely a model of Christian wisdom but, in his writings, a superb ironist (*De consideratione ad Eugenium Papam* [*On Consideration: Advice to Pope Eugenius*] 1.3.4), highlighting thus another literary feature of Paul's epistles to which writers in the later Middle Ages were on the whole more alert than those of subsequent periods.

Pre-eminently among ecclesiasts in the thirteenth and fourteenth centuries, the events of Paul's life begin to be less frequently highlighted than his influence upon hermeneutics. Paul becomes increasingly recognized, following the twelfth-century Augustinian revival, as providing the key that unlocks neglected books in the Old Testament, integrating them with the gospels. Abbot Suger in his *De administratione* (*On What Was Done During His Administration*) describes how Paul is depicted in the "anagogical" window of Saint-Denis, turning a mill toward which the prophets carry sacks of grain. The inscription reads: "By working the mill, Paul, you draw the flour out of the bran; you make known the innermost meaning of the Law of Moses." In the same window, Paul is shown removing a veil that covers Moses' face (Panofsky 1979, 74–75).

Appearances of Paul as an actual character in Old and Middle English literature are nonetheless remarkably rare. Part of the reason may be the omission of the Acts of the Apostles and Pauline epistles from the earliest programs of vernacular biblical translation: while surviving materials in Old English include psalters, gospels, and a variety of Old Testament paraphrase, the earliest systematic translation of Pauline material into English vernacular comes only in the fourteenth century, in the Wycliffite Bible. There are, however, early Old English examples of comic misuse of Paul's literary figures: his comparison of the body to a grain of wheat (1 Cor 15:37) yields Riddle 28 in the Exeter Book, which describes the brewing process as the "death" of barley followed by its "resurrection" in the bodies of inebriates. Even in the late Middle English period, perhaps because preaching was focused on the gospels rather than lections from the epistles, Paul remains a somewhat undefined character. In *The Castle of Perseverance*, "Confescio" says of Paul that, like Peter, he has "powere to lese and bynde" (1496–1497). For all that he has no role in the major biblical cycles of Corpus Christi plays (the disciples are everywhere), doubtless because the biblical material expanded upon by the cycle plays is tied fairly closely to the liturgical year. And although the Fleury Playbook has a modest trope "*conversio Beati Pauli apostoli* [*conversion of the blessed Paul the apostle*]" for his feast day (January 25), it is not until the time of Chaucer that he emerges, albeit briefly, as a major figure in the literary imagination.

Chaucer's extensive use of quotation from Paul in *The Canterbury Tales* reflects, however, a shift toward a renewal of appreciation of the epistles as texts of clear and practical Christian instruction. We have seen elsewhere in this volume that this interest is already apparent in Thomas Aquinas, who is said to have once had a vision of Paul while praying to be enlightened about a difficult passage in his writings. Aquinas apparently valued only the gospels more highly, and expresses a deep commitment to the Pauline doctrine of justification by faith and the gratuity of grace, as well as to his expectation that individuals will be finally judged by the works they have done (see his commentaries on Rom 2:6–9; 2 Cor 5:10; 11:15; 2 Tim 4:14). But reflection on Paul's doctrine of grace began in the fourteenth century to take a more characteristically Augustinian direction. Archbishop Thomas Bradwardine (d. 1348), whom Chaucer mentions in The Nun's Priest's Tale, had observed in a personal comment (*De causa Dei contra Pelagium* [*In Defense of God Against the Pelagians*] 1.35.308C) that at one point, whenever he heard Romans 9:16 read in church, with its emphasis on grace and reservation concerning free will, he felt Paul must have been in error. Yet when he read Paul carefully, the verse ("So then, it is not of him that willeth, nor of him that runneth, but of God that sheweth mercy") finally provided the insight he says was fundamental to his own *conversio* and afterward became the central text of his theological work. This emphasis on God's grace as the means of salvation takes on, following Bradwardine and Fitzralph as well as Augustine, a still larger importance in the writings of Wyclif and the Wycliffites. It tends to be coupled with a critique of "self-help" merit-peddling in some of the friars, against whom, in general terms, Paul is seen as having proleptically "prechede to þe peuple ofte" (*Piers Plowman*, C.16.72–75). In one tract, *The Leaven of the Pharisees*, the Wycliffite author charges friars with destroying the spirit of the text by burdensome legalisms, unlike the converted Pharisees Nicodemus and Paul, in whom a recognition of grace brought them "out of her ordris to fredom of þe gospel" (Wyclif 1880, 2). In a more traditional vein, John Mirk's celebrated sermon *De conuercione Sancti Pauli* (*On the Conversion of Saint Paul*), after paraphrasing the account in Acts 9, an "ensampull in amendyng," offers a cautionary tale that "Saynt Austyn lykeneþe him unto an unycorne," and the pure virgin maiden who tames his fierceness is "þe faythe of holy chyrch." Yet, he adds, "anon he fell don of his pryde, and was sympull, and meke, and soget to Crystys seruantys" (Erbe 1905, 53, 55) – the last phrase probably a reference to controversy over the resistance of some of the mendicant friars and Wycliffite preachers to Episcopal jurisdiction.

The penchant for doctrinal disputation in later scholastic theology may itself have increased Paul's stature in medieval eyes. If for Wyclif, as for Bradwardine, Paul became a hero of faith – "grettost clerk of þe apostles echone" (*South English Legendary*, Paul, 93) – for his championing of God's grace against reliance on human effort, he was prototypically "Godes champion" in dispute against those who opposed or misread Scripture. The ideas of "reformation in sensibility" and "reformation through faith," appearing notably in the Augustinian canon Walter Hilton's *Ladder of Perfection*, are, when echoed at the conclusion of the fifteenth-century morality play *Wisdom*, firmly associated with Paul:

> Now wyth Sent Powle we may sey thus
> Þat be reformyde thorow feythe in Jhesum:
> We haue peas and acorde betwyx Gode and ws,
> *Justificati ex fide pacem habemus ad Deum.* (1148–1151)

Paul is more frequently cited in the late C-text of *Piers Plowman* (ca. 1390) than in its predecessors ("A" [1362]; "B" [1383]); the apostle is much admired by the author of "C" for his willingness to support himself in his apostolic labors rather than appeal to the support of others: "Paul after his prechynge panyeres he made / And wan with hus hondes al þat hym neodyde" (C.18.17–18).

At the very end of the Middle Ages, in the Digby saints' play *The Conversion of Saint Paul* (ca. 1502), we have the first full characterization of the apostle in English literature since the apocryphal Old English *Vision of Saint Paul*. One of only two surviving full texts of medieval saints' plays, this play, like its counterpart in the Digby manuscript *Mary Magdalen*, probably owes its unusual preservation to the fact that its protagonist is a biblical saint. The text makes repeated direct references to the Acts of the Apostles, encouraging its readers to "vnderstande þis matter wo lyst to rede / the holy bybyll for the better spede" (158–159; cf. 10–11, 352–359, 652). By this point in the increasingly contestative English ecclesiastical landscape, it seems to be imperative for the playwright to give assurance from the outset that he has *not* drawn on those non-canonical sources so frequently used in earlier medieval literature: "whoo lyst to rede the booke *Actum Appostolorum*," says the *poeta* figure, "ther shall he haue the very notycyon" (11–12). The play deals primarily with the Damascus Road conversion and the three days following. Yet, despite his protest, there is some inventiveness: fictional dialogue from high priests Anna and Caypha and an entirely spurious sermon by Paul on "the Seven Deadly

Sins," along with a wailing of devils in hell at Saul's conversion, round out the play. The particular interest in this text for historians of exegesis and for theologians is the playwright's focus on the psychology of conversion, the bringing of the human will into conformity with the will of God in response to an intervention of God's grace.

Renaissance and Reformation

These themes, controversial in the fourteenth century, were to gain much strength by the sixteenth century. John Colet, before he was made Dean of St. Paul's, lectured on the Pauline epistles at Oxford to large audiences (including those with Lollard sympathies), who were attracted to his refreshingly direct textual study of the apostle. Among Colet's hearers was Erasmus, for whom the lectures were also a turning point. Erasmus's *Enchiridion Militis Christiani* (*Manual of a Christian Knight*; 1504) takes its title from the arming of the Christian soldier (Eph 6:14–17), and in his own commentary on Romans (*In epistolam Pauli Apostoli ad Romanos paraphrasis*, inspired by Colet), the Dutch humanist recommends intensive direct reading of Paul (Erasmus 1984, 3–4). Renaissance English use and characterization of Paul tends to alternate between the views of Erasmus and Colet – in which Paul is, next to Christ, placed first in the *ad fontes* call to engage the larger scriptural tradition – and the more extreme views represented by Luther, in which Paul, as champion of *sola scriptura*, is virtually set over against that tradition. Although he was trained in scholastic theology, Luther claims that from the scholastics he nonetheless learned "ignorance of ... the entire Christian life" and that, indeed, he had "lost Christ there, but now found him again in St. Paul" (Luther 1884, WA 2.414.22–28) – referring to his own pivotal lecture course (1515–1516) on the text of Paul to the Romans.

English literary responses to Paul in the Renaissance are inclined, if not exclusively so, to the Erasmian perspective. Shakespeare, who makes most of his references to the apostle in *Richard III* (1597), elsewhere creates in Paulina of *The Winter's Tale* (1611) a Pauline teacher for Leontes on the undeservedness of grace, the effect of which upon a repentant heart is a resurrection to new life. In *Measure for Measure* (1604), he satirizes the Puritans in the figure of the wicked magistrate Angelo, notably by having "the Duke, your grace" deploy some of the Puritans' favorite texts from Romans against them. Among the references which demonstrate that Shakespeare could count upon a fair degree of familiarity with the Pauline epistles on the part of his audience are the page's description of Falstaff's companions as "Ephesians, my lord, of the old church" [i.e., reprobates] (*Henry IV*, pt 2, 2.2.150), and Prince Hal's earlier commentary on Falstaff himself: "This oily rascal is known as well as Paul's" (*Henry IV*, pt 1, 2.4.526). Shakespeare develops throughout these two plays a sharp contrast between Falstaff and Prince Hal, dependent for its deeper moral force on Paul's encouragement in Ephesians to "put off ... the old man, which is corrupt according to the deceitful lusts; and ... put on the new man, which after God is created in righteousness and true holiness" (Eph 4:22–24); when, at the end of the second play, Hal at last rejects Falstaff for the responsibilities of kingship, he says to him, "I know thee not, old man" (*Henry IV*, pt 2, 5.5.47), thus indicating that he has undergone an effective conversion. Ben

Jonson's *Bartholomew Fair* (1614) is replete with lively allusions to Paul, and systematic references to Romans 7 in particular effectively structure the play.

In *A Priest to the Temple* (1652), George Herbert finds an indispensable guide to priestly vocation in Paul, whose life and letters demonstrate that "there is no greater sign of holinesse, then the procuring, and rejoycing in anothers good" (ch. 7); Paul is thus a model for Herbert's Parson in that "hee first preacheth to himselfe, and then to others" (ch. 33). Paul stands in a somewhat different fashion behind the character Interpreter in Bunyan's *Pilgrim's Progress* (1678), and it is clearly stated in his *Grace Abounding to the Chief of Sinners* (1666) that Luther's commentary on Galatians is for Bunyan the decisive influence both on his reading of Paul generally and on his own personal spiritual formation. The Puritans were committed to the emphasis of Luther and Calvin on Paul's teaching about election and grace, and made more use of Paul as typologist and perseverant *miles Christi* (soldier of Christ) than as exemplar of conversion (cf. John Owen's *Of the Mortification of Sin in Believers* [1656]; *The Nature, Power, Deceit, and Prevalency of Indwelling Sin* [1667]; and *The Grace and Duty of Being Spiritually Minded* [1681], all of which take their central texts from Romans). Yet despite the heavy dependence of their doctrine upon Paul, writers of a Calvinistic persuasion typically eschewed representation of biblical characters in fiction (Milton is an outlier in all senses), perhaps for a reason to which the contemporary Calvinist novelist Woiwode alludes in his *Acts*: the narratively astonishing lack of any description of Christ in the gospel accounts finds its parallel with the apostles, "not one of them is anywhere physically described" (101). Fiction writers and poets need physiological and personality depiction to effect their craft, and for a writer like Woiwode and most of his Reformation and Renaissance era predecessors of a traditionally Calvinist character, to provide such inventive elaborations may well seem transgressive.

Writers after the Restoration of the monarchy under nominally Anglican Charles II emphasized, for their divergent purposes, an apostle of resignation and humility. Isaac Barrow's (1630–1677) notable Pauline sermons are *Of Quietness, and Doing Our Own Business* (1 Thess 4:11), *Of a Peaceable Temper and Carriage* (Rom 12:18), and two on Philippians 4:11, "I have learned, in whatsoever state I am, therewith to be content" – ironically enough, the very passage the politically unquiet Puritan Cromwell had read to him on his deathbed. For Jeremy Taylor, as for Isaac Barrow, Paul is also the apostle of industry and charity (cf. Barrow 1849, Sermons 10 and 18); in a meditation on grace, Taylor elevates love over knowledge, saying "as was rarely well observed by St. Paul, *knowledge puffeth up, but Charity edifieth*; that is, Charity makes the best Scholars" (*Via Intelligentiae* [*Way of Understanding*] 1662, 33). Reflecting on the vision or rapture of Paul, Taylor came to the conclusion that "after all the fine things that he saw, we only know what we knew before" (1686, 395); Paul is accordingly less to be admired as a visionary or mystic than as a practical rationalist of sublunary experience. John Dryden's *Religio Laici* (*A Layman's Religion*) celebrates the "great Apostle" for his comments (Rom 2:14–15) on the efficacy of natural revelation and, by extension, reason, concluding, in a curiously un-Pauline fashion:

> Then those who follow'd *Reasons* Dictates right;
> Liv'd up, and lifted high their *Natural Light*;

With *Socrates* may see their Maker's Face,
While Thousand *Rubrick-Martyrs* want a place. (208–211)

Enlightenment and Nineteenth-century Fashioning

However sharply at variance concerning the wisdom they claim to discover in Paul, writers of the Enlightenment era tend to agree in seeing him as an exemplary teacher and sage, on occasion comparing him to Seneca. "The great Christian convert and learned apostle," Shaftesbury writes in *Characteristics*, shows that the safest attitude is "the skeptical and modest" (6.2.2) (Shaftesbury 1963, 2.202–203). Lord George Lyttleton, in his *Observations on the Conversion and Apostleship of St. Paul* (1747), takes great care to show that the apostle was a rationalist and not an "enthusiast." According to Jonathan Edwards, the apostle to the Gentiles is the first teacher of the typological interpretation fitted to all of God's works. In "Trees," from his *Images of Divine Things* (no. 78), Edwards hails Paul as the most thirsty and fruitful of the apostolic "branches" to shoot forth from the trunk of the risen Christ, "so that the bigger part of the future tree came from this branch" (Edwards 1993, 80).

Back in Enlightenment England, Paul's writings tended increasingly to be viewed by poets through the lenses afforded by classical Roman prose, in particular that of the Stoics. The Pauline practice of paradox as a logical response to the hidden unity of being is likewise compellingly attractive to Alexander Pope. His "The Dying Christian to His Soul," an ode in imitation of Hadrian's verses to his departing spirit, speaks of "the bliss of dying," of "languish[ing] into life," and ends with 1 Corinthians 15:55: "O Grave! where is thy Victory? / O Death! where is thy Sting?" For Samuel Johnson, the reasonableness of Paul's humility is not difficult to distinguish from the unreason of garrulous mystics. He responds with this irony to Jakob Boehme's claim of kinship with Paul in having seen "unutterable things": "[He] would have resembled St. Paul still more, by not attempting to utter them" (Boswell 1934, 2.123). In the retrospective "Conclusion" of *Biographia Literaria, or, Biographical Sketches of My Literary Life and Opinions* (1817), Samuel Taylor Coleridge still takes pains to locate his reading of Paul in the context of the Enlightenment. Having abridged the history of his mental life in the motto "*Credidi ideoque intellexi* [*I believed and therefore I understand*]," Coleridge associates his own last thoughts in his *Biographia* with a reflection on sentences from the conclusion of Spinoza's *Ethics*, observing that they are "thoroughly *Pauline* ... compleatly accordant with the doctrines of the established Church." "The Scheme of Christianity ... though not discoverable by human Reason, is yet in accordance with it," Coleridge avers (1983, 245, 247). William Blake is of quite another mind, his heterodoxy almost complete. While he does follow "his master St. Paul" in distinguishing the "body-garment" from the "self" (cf. 2 Cor 5:4), as Damrosch argues (1980, 170), Blake's abiding conviction that poetic vision, cleansed of natural reason, "can attain a direct apprehension of truth" (23) seems as un-Pauline as it is anti-Newtonian. Late in his life William Wordsworth, by contrast, is surely unspeculative in his recollection of traditional Pauline iconography: "and lo! with upright sword / Prefiguring his own impendent doom, / The Apostle of the Gentiles" ("Musings near Aquapendente," 310–312).

It is difficult to be certain of the effect of pictorial art or heroic music, such as Felix Mendelssohn's oratorio *St. Paul* (1836), on poets, playwrights, and novelists. Yet, given the ideological temper of most Victorian literature, the widely various and often conflicting responses to Paul in the protracted mêlée over the competing authority of faith and reason during that period are not surprising. On the one hand, poet Christina Rossetti inscribes a substantially canonical Paul in her late work, *Called to be Saints: The Minor Festivals Devotionally Studied* (1881), and John Keble devotes one of his poems in *The Christian Year* (1827) to "The Conversion of St. Paul," making of the interrogation of Saul by Christ the occasion of a call to examination for the reader in which citations of Matthew 25 play a governing role. On the other hand, for Jeremy Bentham, the Pauline epistles simply lack a sound empirical foundation: "Whatever is in Paul, and is not to be found in any one of the four Gospels, is not Christianity, but Paulism" (1823, 367). This view grew, as historians of theology well recognize, to become a more or less universal prejudice among the learned. While J. S. Mill agrees with Bentham in philosophical principle, he finds Paul's the least uncongenial of the writings in the New Testament: "St. Paul, the only known exception to the ignorance and want of education of the first generation of Christians, attests no miracle but that of his conversion, which of all the miracles of the New Testament is the one which admits of the easiest explanation from natural causes" (1874, 239).

According to Thomas Hardy in *Tess of the D'Urbervilles* (1891), the New Testament of the evangelical Mr Clare "was less a Christiad than a Pauliad ... less an argument than an intoxication" (1998, 157). Unlike the disapproving Hardy, Ralph Waldo Emerson revels in the inebriating effect of his mystical Paul: "the conversion of Paul, the aurora of Behmen, the convulsions of George Fox and his Quakers" – all illustrate that "the opening of the religious sense" is often attended by "a certain tendency to insanity" (1990, 159). Sir Alfred Lord Tennyson, in one of the moments of undoubting faith which *In Memoriam* records, likens himself to Paul in his struggle with "death" or a "science" that reckons man merely a "greater ape" (canto 120). Herman Melville, a refugee from the Reformed Church in America, is altogether independent, taking Paul for a subverter not only of reason but also of faith. "St. Paul ... argues the doubts of Montaigne," he writes in *Mardi* (1970, 367). Yet for Matthew Arnold in *St. Paul and Protestantism* (1870), Paul is an apostle of both culture and science. He is a cultivated writer who "Orientalises," while his Puritan commentators mistake his vivid, poetic speech for formal theological propositions (pt. 1). Unlike Arnold's Paul, who comes to his religion "psychologically and from experience" that can be "verified by science," these philistines come to theirs "theologically and from authority" (Arnold 1883, 43).

Søren Kierkegaard thought that aesthetic evaluations of Paul effectively disqualified him from being considered as an apostle:

> They talk in exalted terms of St. Paul's brilliance and profundity, of his beautiful similes and so on – that is mere aestheticism ... As an Apostle St. Paul has no connexion whatsoever with Plato or Shakespeare, with stylists or upholsterers, and none of them (Plato no more than Shakespeare or Harrison the upholsterer) can possibly be compared with him. (Kierkegaard 1962, 89–90)

Robert Browning shows a more refined historical sense and surer rhetorical touch in "Cleon." A nostalgic old pagan answering a letter from his king regrets that Zeus has not yet revealed some future state of felicity after death. But the accomplished Cleon is disturbed by the thought that his correspondent would for a moment consider that "one called Paulus," a "mere barbarian Jew" to whom King Protus has also written, could have "access to a secret shut" from the wisest and most cultivated of mortals (340, 343–345). At the popular level of domestic Victorian spiritual literature, John Hall's *A Christian Home: How to Make and How to Maintain It* (1884) simply ignores the cultured debate altogether, emphasizing instead such features as the un-aristocratic character of Paul's work: "Paul was a tent-maker, and not ashamed of it" (87). In reaction to just that Victorian order of Christian sentiment championed by Hall, Thomas Hardy includes a cryptic epigraph from Paul on the title page of his *Jude the Obscure*, "The letter killeth." One can readily appreciate that in a wide range of Victorian writings, religious and secularizing, Paul had become "a man for all seasons" in a way unprecedented in earlier periods; his image had become protean, a kind of cultural wax nose.

Modern

On the verge of the twentieth century, Henryk Sienkiewicz's *Quo Vadis: A Narrative of the Time of Nero* (1896) enjoyed a considerable vogue, but while Paul figures in the story and is indeed decapitated immediately following Peter's upside-down crucifixion at the end of the novel, the author is more concerned with the hideous character of Nero's reign than with the life of either apostle, and Paul plays in any case a distinct second fiddle to Peter in the plot. (The novel was translated from Polish into English by Jeremiah Curtin and dedicated to Auguste Comte.) Another novel by a Polish writer, Conrad's *Victory: An Island Tale*, though its title and theme refer to 1 Corinthians 15:51–57, is anything but uplifting in its reflection of the apostle's teaching.[2] The parody is "savage" in this novel (Purdy 1984, 125), the action of which ends in bloody mayhem, fire, and suicide, and the last word of which is "Nothing." If the book's title may be accepted as an "omen" to an English public in the trammels of war, as Conrad suggests in his note to the first edition (1915), the augury *Victory* provides is clearly ambiguous. John Buchan's *Mr. Standfast*, published four years later, is free of comparable doubt. Peter Piennar, the humble pilot who gives up his life to stop the Boche in that spy-thriller, reckons in a letter that "the head man" at the job of "the big courage ... the cold-blooded kind ... 'Fortitude'" is "the Apostle Paul" (1988, 358).

R. S. Thomas's poem "Covenanters" is shrewd, angular, and probatively acerbic, yet presents Paul as "the mountain / the teaching of the carpenter of Nazareth / congealed into." George Bowering's poem "Grandfather" pays tribute to a longsuffering and much-traveled laborer, church builder, and preacher who takes for his ruling text "Saul on the road to Damascus" (9). The same text was used by 13-year-old Ernest Hemingway, in his first and only formal sermon, at a Chicago missionary convention. If Paul was to have little impact on the later fiction of Hemingway, the apostle's notable attribute of raw courage seems perhaps to have had enduring appeal. It is certainly heroism that ultimately governs the fictional treatment of Taylor Caldwell in *Great Lion of God* (1970), although initially she characterizes Saul as ridden with guilt and a deep sense of personal anxiety. It appealed in a somewhat different way to the Canadian poet Margaret Avison in "As a Comment on Romans 1:10," where she says, speaking of Paul's full knowledge of the mortal risk he ran in going to Rome:

> Yet he urged it. He was
> glad these new Romans existed.
> His wisdom was enlisted as
> their ally, to find them his.
>
> It did not save his neck
> or probably theirs:
> he knew beforehand that when light appears
> it must night split   and earth quake.
>
> (*sunblue*, 54)

Avison's poetic characterization brings us full circle back to *The Apostle* by Sholem Asch. His Paul is above all a hero of faith, zealous for the Torah, and an observant of great perseverance and character such that, at the very moment of his execution, he feels neither fear nor remorse. His last words, a split-second before the blow of the sword strikes his neck, are the *shema*: "Hear, O Israel, the Lord our God, the Lord is One." Here, then, is the distinctive unity in the life of Paul that earlier Christian writers perhaps failed so readily to grasp, and that prevented them from what Asch has so masterfully achieved, or what Franz Werfel, the Austrian expressionist poet, in his play *Paul Among the Jews* (1926; English translation 1928) and, it seems, the American biblical scholar Samuel Sandmel, in his as yet unpublished *The Apostle Paul: A Novel* (ca. 1956), have more fully appreciated. Paul was the "apostle to the Gentiles," but his Christian apostolate is in their view substantially incomprehensible apart from his passionate and Pharisaic Jewish commitment to the fulfillment of Torah in the Messiah.

Curiously, this is almost precisely opposite to the characterization of recent Marxist-materialist cultural theorists such as Alain Badiou and Slavoj Žižek, in which Paul is seen not merely as the creator of Christianity, but essentially as the creator of Christ: for Badiou, without Paul "the Christian message would remain ambiguous" (2003, 33), while for Žižek, more starkly, "there is no Christ outside Saint Paul" (2000, 2; emphasis removed). The witness of literature itself in several European languages hardly supports this claim with respect to the imaginative life of Christian culture: there are many times more appearances of Jesus himself in literary contexts. Perhaps it might be better to think of Paul as the apostle less to the poets than to the critics.

Notes

1   Biblical quotations in this chapter are taken from the King James Version – *the* Bible for the overwhelming majority of writers in English over the past four centuries.

2   For the references to Conrad and several in Canadian literature, I am indebted to my friend and colleague the late Camille R. LaBossiere. I have drawn liberally on an earlier article that, with his gracious assistance in this respect, I wrote as an entry for Jeffrey (1992).

References

Arnold, Matthew. 1883. *St. Paul and Protestantism, with an Essay on Puritanism and the Church of England, and Last Essays on Church and Religion*. New York: Macmillan.
Asch, Sholem. 1943. *The Apostle*. New York: G. P. Putnam's Sons.
Avison, Margaret. 1978. *sunblue*. Handsport, Nova Scotia: Lancelot.
Badiou, Alain. 2003. *St. Paul: The Foundation of Universalism*. Stanford: Stanford University Press.
Barrow, Isaac. 1849. *Eighteen Sermons on Various Subjects*. London: SPCK.
Bede, the Venerable. 1955. De opere sex dierum primordialium et de sex aetatibus mundi. Pages 407–411 in *Opera homiletica. Opera rhythmica*. Edited by D. Hurst. Corpus Christianorum Series Latina 122. Brepolis: Turnholt.
Bentham, Jeremy. 1823. *Not Paul, but Jesus*. Published pseudonymously under the name Gamaliel Smith. London: John Hunt.
Boswell, James. 1934. *Boswell's Life of Johnson*. Volumes 1–6. Edited by George Birkbeck Hill, revised and enlarged by L. F. Powell. Oxford: Clarendon.
Boudreau, Gordon V. 2003. Herman Melville, Immortality, St. Paul, and Resurrection: from Rose-Bud to Billy Budd. *Christianity and Literature* 52: 343–364.
Bowering, George. 1971. *Touch: Selected Poems 1960–1970*. Toronto: McCelland and Stewart.
Buchan, John. 1988. *The Four Adventures of Richard Hannay*. Boston: David R. Godine.
Caldwell, Taylor. 1970. *Great Lion of God*. New York: Doubleday.
Coleridge, Samuel Taylor. 1983. *Bibliographia Literaria, or Biographical Sketches of my Literary Life and Opinions*. Volume 2. *The Collected Works of Samuel Taylor Coleridge 7*. Edited by James Engell and W. Jackson Bate. Princeton: Princeton University Press.
Damrosch, Leopold, Jr. 1980. *Symbol and Truth in Blake's Myth*. Princeton: Princeton University Press.
Eccles, Mark, editor. 1969. *The Macro Plays: The Castle of Perseverance, Wisdom, Mankind*. London: Oxford University Press.
Edwards, Jonathan. 1993. *Typological Writings. The Works of Jonathan Edwards*. Volume 11. New Haven: Yale University Press.
Emerson, Ralph Waldo. 1990. The Over-soul. Pages 152–165 in *Ralph Waldo Emerson*. Oxford Authors. Oxford: Oxford University Press.
Erasmus, Desiderius. 1984. *Paraphrases on Romans and Galatians. The Collected Works of Erasmus*. Volume 42. Edited by Robert D. Sider. Toronto: University of Toronto Press.
Erbe, Theodor (ed.) 1905. *Mirk's Festial: A Collection of Homilies by Johannes Mirkus (John Mirk)*. London: Kegan Paul, Trench, Trübner & Co.
Fass, Barbara. 1971. Shelley and St. Paul. *Concerning Poetry* 4: 23–24.
Findlay, George G. 1900. Paul the Apostle. Pages 696–731 in *A Dictionary of the Bible*. Volume 3. Edited by James Hastings. Edinburgh: T. & T. Clark.
Hall, John. 1884. *A Christian Home: How to Make and How to Maintain It*. Philadelphia: American Sunday School Union.
Hardy, Thomas. 1998. *Tess of the D'Urbervilles*. Harmondsworth: Penguin.
Hassel, R. Chris, Jr. 1971. Saint Paul and Shakespeare's Romantic Comedies. *Thought* 46: 371–388.

Jeffrey, David Lyle, editor. 1992. *A Dictionary of Biblical Tradition in English Literature*. Grand Rapids: Eerdmans.

Kierkegaard, Søren. 1962. Of the Difference between a Genius and an Apostle. Pages 87–108 in *The Present Age* and *Of the Difference between a Genius and an Apostle*. Translated by Alexander Dru. New York: Harper Torchback.

Langton, Daniel R. 2005. The Myth of the "Traditional View of Paul" and the Role of the Apostle in Modern Jewish-Christian Polemics. *Journal for the Study of the New Testament* 28: 69–104.

Langton, Daniel R. 2008. Jewish Literary Treatments of the Apostle Paul: The Novels of Shalom Asch and Samuel Sandmel. *Modern Judaism* 27: 284–309.

Luther, Martin. 1884. *D. Martin Luthers Werke*. Weimar edition (=*WA*). Volume 2. Weimar: Hermann Böhlau.

Madden, Deborah and David Towsey. 2002. Derrida, Faith and St. Paul. *Literature and Theology* 16: 396–409.

Melville, Herman. 1970. *Mardi. The Writings of Herman Melville*. Volume 3. Evanston: Northwestern University Press; Chicago: The Newberry Library.

Mill, John Stuart. 1874. *Three Essays on Religion*. London: Longmans, Green, Reader, and Dyer.

Osgood, Charles G. 1956. *Boccaccio on Poetry*. Second edition. New York: Liberal Arts Press.

Panofsky, Erwin. 1979. *Abbot Suger on the Abbey Church of St.-Denis and its Art Treasures*. Revised edition. Princeton: Princeton University Press.

Peck, Russell A. 1981. St. Paul and the Canterbury Tales. *Mediaevalia* 7: 91–131.

Purdy, Dwight H. 1984. *Joseph Conrad's Bible*. Norman: University of Oklahoma Press.

Rees, Joan. 1987. Falstaff, St. Paul, and the Hangman. *Review of English Studies* 38: 14–22.

Schmidt, Carl. 1904. *Acta Pauli, aus der Heidelberger koptischen Papyrushandschrift Nr. 1*. Leipzig: Hinrichs.

Shaftesbury, Anthony Earl of. 1963. *Characteristics of Men, Manners, Opinions, Times, etc.* Volumes 1 and 2. Gloucester, Mass.: Peter Smith.

Shakespeare, William. 1974. *The Riverside Shakespeare*. Edited by G. Blakemore Evans. Boston: Houghton Mifflin.

Thomas, R. S. 1983. *Later Poems: A Selection*. London: Macmillan.

Wangerin, Walter. 2000. *Paul: A Novel*. Grand Rapids: Zondervan.

Woiwode, Larry. 1993. *Acts*. San Francisco: HarperSanFrancisco.

Wyclif, John. 1880. *The English Works of Wyclif*. Edited by F. D. Matthew. London: Trübner.

Žižek, Slavoj. 2000. *The Fragile Absolute: Or, Why is the Christian Legacy Worth Fighting For?* London: Verso.

CHAPTER 34

Christian Theology: Sin and the Fall

Marguerite Shuster

Stern, sober, but finally triumphant, a classic Pauline view of sin provides a bracing alternative to all the superficially more optimistic views of the human condition that leave us finally baffled about the utter recalcitrance of moral evil, not just as manifested in the monstrous crimes committed by wicked people and corrupt institutions, but as lurking in our own hearts.[1] The heart of Paul's thought is Jesus Christ, become incarnate to deal with sin (Rom 8:3), crucified and risen for the salvation of humankind; and no conception of sin that does not require so radical a remedy can be sufficient. Thus, in his major discussions of sin Paul emphasizes its root ("Sin") rather than its fruit ("sins"); insists upon its universality as evidenced in the universality of its wage, death; and depicts human beings as having within themselves no Archimedean point by which they can get leverage against it. While he does not speculate philosophically upon its origin, he traces the beginning of Sin's fatal sway to the story of the disobedience of Adam and Eve in the ancient garden, to which Christ's obedience is the counterpoint. And in surprising moves, he speaks both of abandonment to Sin as part of God's judgment upon guilty humankind, and of Sin as a kind of personified power to which human beings become enslaved. Against this dark picture of a doomed humanity, the work of Jesus Christ shines as the sole solution God has provided.

Sin and Sins

When thinking of "sin," contemporary men and women commonly suppose that what is at issue is the violating of some boundary that has been set, perhaps quite arbitrarily

---

The Blackwell Companion to Paul, First Edition. Edited by Stephen Westerholm.
© 2011 Blackwell Publishing Ltd. Published 2011 by Blackwell Publishing Ltd.

and unreasonably, by a spoilsport deity. They tend to think of bodily pleasures they wish to indulge; and if they feel some unease about the indulgence, they resent the source of this discomfort as an unjust stricture against natural and harmless impulses. "Sin" is the green grass on the other side of a fence that should never have been erected at all. Or they think of an "adult" breaking away from an oppressive authority, enabling human development; or they note that what makes people interesting is not so much their virtues as their foibles. After all, we are "only human." In each case, particular acts violating some rule or precept are generally in view.

Paul would not deny the explicit teaching of Scripture (e.g., 1 John 3:4) that sin is a violation of the law of God, manifesting itself in particular transgressions. In his writings we find not only examples of the vice lists common among Greek moralists (e.g., Rom 1:29–31; 1 Cor 6:9–10; Gal 5:19–21; 1 Tim 1:9–10), but also particular emphasis on idolatry and sexual immorality (linked together as source and outcome in Rom 1:21–25). Nor does he ignore the dangers of money (1 Tim 3:3, 8; 6:9–10; Tit 1:7). Paul, after all, was a pastor and had to be concerned about specific misbehaviors in his churches, from seemingly petty matters like gossip, to self-serving competitiveness, to incest.[2] He addressed such matters in his letters regularly, firmly, and practically, allowing no convictions about grace, freedom from the law, or the overwhelming power of Sin to provide an excuse for bad behavior. There was to be no thought of sinning that grace might abound (Rom 6.1). Paul was no libertine.

Nonetheless, when we look more closely, we see that Paul does not suppose that the sin problem can be adequately addressed by efforts to curb particular faults, though curbed they must be if the community is not to be destroyed (1 Cor 5). Even the obvious faults listed in Gal 5:19–21 are understood not simply in themselves, but as "the works of the flesh." They express, that is, a deeper reality of the human being as he or she is fundamentally driven by self-centeredness and worldly, ungodly impulses. They are to be countered not by practice or willpower or improved moral instruction, but only by the altogether new possibilities provided by the Holy Spirit (Gal 5:22–23). We see something similar in Paul's emphasis on the evils of "boasting" (e.g., Rom 3:27; 1 Cor 1:28–29; 4:7; Eph 2:8–9) and "desire" (e.g., Rom 1:24; 6:12; 7:7–8; 13:14; Gal 5:16, 24; Eph 2:3; Col 3:5).[3] These latter may carry echoes of the story of the primal transgression of Adam and Eve in Genesis 3 – of the pride and reliance on self that constitute an alternative to humility and reliance upon God, and of the urges to experience or possess something that are especially exacerbated by a prohibition. In any case, they exemplify a deep root of Sin, of a self gone fundamentally wrong, of which particular sins are simply an expression. We are, Paul says, "by nature children of wrath" (Eph 2:3 – which should be construed not of our nature as created, but rather of our nature as fallen, since true humanity as seen in Jesus is sinless [2 Cor 5:21]).[4]

For Paul, then, not sins as specific transgressions of a clearly defined mandate, but Sin as condition (a condition that can be spoken of as a power, as we shall see below) is the fundamental problem. Indeed, one may sin through an act that is in itself morally indifferent if one thereby violates a neighbor's conscience (Rom 14:20, 23; 1 Cor 8:7–13). Hence we have the striking phenomenon that in Paul, the most common term for sin (*hamartia*) appears overwhelmingly not in the plural but in the singular – most dramatically so in his most extended treatment of sin, Romans 1–8. Furthermore, we find no emphasis on a less or more among sins, no hierarchy of wickedness, not, surely, because Paul is unconcerned about moral peccadilloes (*pace* Beker 1980, 220), but because the "small" fault as surely as the large one betrays its corrupt source.[5] Thus, Paul could at the end, remembering his past, still proclaim himself chief of sinners (1 Tim 1:15; cf. I Cor 15:9), and Protestants have commonly asserted that the ground is level at the foot of the Cross: *all* sin shows a fundamental turning away from God; "big" and "small" sinners alike are equally dependent upon God's grace. Those who doubt that they themselves exemplify any such radically compromising condition might be advised to observe certain impulses in themselves that arise unbidden, certain spontaneous pleasures in the misfortune of others, and the content of certain dreams, from which no action at all may stem but that nonetheless point to something wrong with the heart.

The Extent of Sin

To recognize the true seriousness of Sin from Paul's perspective, one must understand both the way it affects every aspect of the person, and that its humanly unavoidable result is death. Indeed, the universal sway of Sin's wage shows the universality of Sin itself. Humans' inability in their own strength to defeat death is a sort of parable of their helplessness against Sin.

In individual persons

While the idea of radical (or "total") depravity is a hallmark of the Reformed (Calvinist) tradition,[6] and though the idea itself does not rely simply upon Paul's letters, but can be found widely in both Old and New Testaments, its substance is nonetheless a significant aspect of Paul's thought. It does not mean that humans are as wicked as they could possibly be, but rather that they have in them no "pure," sinless faculty on which they can rely; they are corrupt at the very root of their actions and impulses. Paul speaks as readily of darkened understanding and hardened hearts (Eph 4:18), enslaved wills (Rom 6:17, 19), futile and debased minds (Rom 1:21, 28; Col 2:18), and seared consciences (1 Tim 4:2), as of vile affections and passions (Rom 1:26). Once, he even speaks of the possibility of a defiled spirit (2 Cor 7:1). When Paul uses the term "flesh" in its ethical sense, he is not accusing the body over against the mind or spirit, but speaking of an orientation of the person as a whole. So it is not as if there were a "lower," sensual part of the person that overcomes a "higher," willing and reasonable part; rather, the (sinful) self as a whole masters rather than serves reason (Niebuhr 1955, 17–18) – as one may see in the endless parade of human rationalizations, self-deceptions, and self-justifications.

   All such ploys show that persons have not lost their rational powers, but have corrupted them. In fact, the impulsive wickedness stemming from the passions may often do less harm in the end than that resulting from the vicious calculations of the mind. Superior culture is no protection, as the Holocaust – product of an "advanced" civilization – demonstrates. That this almost inconceivable moral disaster was not an anomaly has been demonstrated not only in the famous post-World War II Milgram experiments in the United States, which confirmed that most people will obey orders to do what they believe is potentially fatal harm to innocent others; not only in Zimbardo's "prison experiments" at Stanford University in the mid-1970s; but yet again in real life at Abu Ghraib, with all of its shocking parallels to Zimbardo's study. As Zimbardo put it, "most people can be made to do almost anything if you put them in psychologically compelling situations, regardless of their morals, ethics, values, attitudes, beliefs, or personal convictions" (quoted in Hamilton 1990, 30). The springs of moral evil in the "ordinary person" are far deeper than we want to believe, and the barriers against their eruption prove again and again to be fragile. We humans have an enemy within us. Thus, when we see Paul bemoaning the recalcitrance of sinful impulses in Romans 7, it is surely correct to see the split between what "he" approves and what "he" nonetheless does as occurring *within* the "I" itself (Dunn 1988, 389, 409), not, say, in Platonic fashion, between rational and irrational faculties of the person (as, recently, Wasserman 2008, passim). Paul finds that he has no solid ground within himself on which to stand.

Understanding human beings in this way helps to illumine why dreams of moral progress continually disappoint us, and why we live in an ever more dangerous world. Our scientific achievements are incontrovertible and give us far more power than humans once had, but it would be hard to argue that we produce nobler people today than 2,000 years ago. Humans living in earlier ages did not have the capacity to destroy life on earth, as we do, but we have no greater ability than they to use our powers well. Our corrupt reason and wills cannot save us. As a cartoon showing two extraterrestrials, conversing while observing an exploding earth, ironically puts it, "They must be very intelligent to be able to do that."

Across all persons

The situation is made yet more serious in that Sin corrupts all faculties not just of some persons, but of all persons. "There is no one who is righteous, not even one" (Rom 3:10, quoting Ps 14:3; see also Rom 3:23). Male and female, educated and illiterate, infant and elderly person, saint and criminal – all alike are sinners. Though this assessment offends many, most especially when small children are included – for whose utterly self-centered predilections many arguments from biological necessity are sometimes offered – it is hard to deny the dictum that "the wicked man is but a child grown strong" (Hobbes). Augustine thought it was not the state of the child's will but its lack of power that constituted its so-called innocence (*Confessions* 1.7.11). Fail to curb the "natural" impulses, and the full-blown adult sinner will reliably emerge. And by the time persons reach the age of accountability for their actions, they seem quite universally to manifest what might be called an uneasy sense of self: no matter what culture they have been reared within, no matter whether the strictures they have faced have been mild or severe, they seem to recognize that they break the laws of their own culture, fall short of the good that they know, do not themselves behave as they think others ought surely to behave (Shuster 2004, 167–170). We can see, then, that even if Paul was thinking specifically of the Jewish law when he spoke of the law's ineffectiveness against Sin, the applicability of his words extends just as surely to the dictates of cultures with quite different codes.

Paul's own argument about the universality of Sin, though, is not based on cultural or developmental analysis but is closely linked to the universality of death, which he understands not as a merely natural phenomenon, but as punishment for Sin (Rom 5:12–14; 6:23). While it is not entirely certain whether he thinks people would not die at all apart from Sin, or only that death would lack its terrible quality ("the sting of death is sin" [1 Cor 15:56]), it is clear that under the actual circumstances of earthly existence, death comes to all. It eventually will be defeated, but only at the End (1 Cor 15:26). Let those, then, who think they will escape death claim that they are free of Sin.

As related to the Fall

Paul does not offer a theoretical explanation for the mysterious fact that all human beings are, from their very first breath, sinners – the doctrine called "original sin,"[7] which Reinhold Niebuhr often called the one doctrine of the Christian church that can be empirically verified. Instead, Paul simply tells the story of how it came to be, referring back to the fault of Adam and Eve in the Garden of Eden: to say that, "just as sin came into the world through one man, and death came through sin, and so death spread to all because all have sinned" (Rom 5:12; see also 1 Cor 15:21–22), comes about as close to affirming original sin as one possibly could without actually using the words.

Along with the idea of original sin, the closely related and even more fundamental doctrine of the Fall – that Sin not only marks all individuals, but does so because they are somehow implicated in the primal disobedience of Adam and Eve – has been scored by many biblical scholars as being longer on theological consequences than on biblical support. They note that the rest of the Old Testament does not typically go back to Genesis 3 when referring to the fount of human sinfulness; indeed, outside of Paul himself, we must rely primarily upon intertestamental literature for such an idea.[8] But Paul clearly does make this connection in both Romans 5 and 1 Corinthians 15. Furthermore, in both places he makes it a direct counterpoint to the work of Christ, contrasting the First Adam with the Second, the source of humankind's downfall with the source of their redemption. Thus, it cannot be seen as merely incidental to his thought, and it gains the firm foothold it has long had in Christian theology. The doctrine of the Fall protects belief in the original goodness of God's creation: God must not be made the Author of sin, as if God rather than humans themselves were to blame for this disordered world; as if, say, given evolutionary realities, human beings could hardly be expected to be other than they are. Indeed, Brunner claimed that loss of the idea of the Fall produces disastrous effects for Christian doctrine in its entirety: "Only a *fallen* humanity needs a Redeemer"; every other conception of sin "makes sin either a fact of nature, or merely the moral concern of the individual" (1952, 90). Something went terribly wrong for the whole race when, tempted by the serpent,[9] Adam and Eve chose their own way instead of God's and were thus constituted sinners.

Still, the precise "how" of the transmission of Sin from the first pair to their progeny is no clearer than the precise "how" of the atoning work of Christ. The idea that all humankind were seminally present in Adam and thus sinned "in" him or were produced by a corrupt seed, prominent in the thought of Augustine, rests upon what is now generally conceded to be a mistranslation of Romans 5:12 (as, namely, "*in whom all sinned*"); though the best way to construe the prepositional phrase continues to be contested. The Augustinian understanding brought with it a stigma upon procreation, for by procreation a sinful progeny enters the world. Sin, that is, is in this view seen as in some sense inherited. But modern genetics is no more help than ancient theories in seeing how a *moral* corruption could be passed from one generation to another.[10] An environmental explanation – that persons follow bad examples and succumb to environmental pressures – is little improvement, for one may ask how, if there is no negative bent of the human will, bad examples came so to predominate that none, no matter how isolated, escapes their influence. In any case, Paul seems more interested in asserting the "that" than the "how" of the impact of the first sin. Thus, it may be best to conclude that all are connected to Adam and constituted sinners simply because God determined that such should be the case – as Paul in Romans 11:32 in any case implies (Barth 1956, 510–511).[11]

Solidarity in sin – and guilt?

The idea that all humans might suffer the consequences of another's fault is an unpopular one in a highly individualistic culture, one that many are prone to protest as altogether unfair; though consistency would entail that they should be equally ready to protest the unfairness of persons' receiving the benefit of the work of Christ – an example of Sin if there ever was one, that we should feel so keenly the wrongness of experiencing disadvantage, but not of receiving advantage, because of what another has done. Of course, the extreme individualism of our culture is the exception rather than the norm. And if we were honest, we would recognize that all the particular circumstances of our birth, at what we might construe as the simply natural level, involve us in both gifts and obstacles that are in no way of our own choosing. Even those who live in democratic societies are at war when their President declares it to be so, and so on. We are far less independent and self-made people than we might suppose.

We should also note that Paul extends the idea of solidarity in Sin very broadly. It is not just human beings who are affected by the primal sin, but the whole created order – which was obviously not itself guilty, in that the lower orders of creation are incapable of sinning. Clearly picking up on the Genesis account, where the ground is cursed because of Adam and Eve's sin, Paul in Romans 8:19–23 argues that the whole creation has been subjected to futility and is in bondage to decay, not to be freed until human redemption is complete – an eschatological vision. Until then, nature itself groans and is in disarray. Paul seems to be implying that the very aspects of the creation that might make an observer doubt the goodness of the Creator should, like death itself, be laid firmly at the door of sinners. What we see even in the natural world reflects God's judgment on Sin. Sin ruins everything.

However, unlike the lower orders of creation, human beings not only are affected by Sin but also sin for themselves all too soon and all too willingly, confirming the fault of Adam and Eve in their own persons, by their own choice (as Rom 5:12, as usually translated today, suggests). If their dispositions come to them bent toward the wrong, they nonetheless are glad enough to go where those dispositions incline them. Given that a person's own freely indulged sins are quite sufficient for him or her to stand condemned as guilty before God, the controverted question of whether everyone also bears a so-called alien guilt – the guilt as well as the corruption stemming from Adam and Eve's transgression – becomes less pressing. Indeed, Protestant traditions that affirm that all people do bear such guilt also tend to deny that infants dying before the age of accountability are held responsible for it, and so its most critical point of application turns out to be not so critical after all.[12] One might well argue that small children and persons of severely limited intellectual capacity are in a position comparable to that of those who lived after Adam and Eve but before the law was given through Moses (Whiteley 1964, 52): they sin and die, but the sin is not reckoned to them when there is no law that they deliberately violate (Rom 5:13–14); societies that treat them as fully responsible adults are widely considered to be brutal.

Sin and the Law

This is not the place to discuss the vast significance of the law generally in Pauline thought, or to engage contemporary controversies about its specific role in Jewish-Gentile relations.[13] Here, we are concerned only to examine briefly its relationship to Sin. In one sense, its role is obvious, for, as we have just seen, Paul specifies that apart from a commandment of God, including the initial prohibition given to Adam and Eve against eating of the Tree of Knowledge of Good and Evil, and the later giving of the Mosaic law, Sin has a somewhat different character. It continues as the condition marking all humans, for all die; but it does not have quite the quality of rebellion against a specific divine word. We might use the example of children given freedom to play as they will: they will surely manifest all the self-interested, self-willed behaviors anyone might care to observe, as a fruit of their sinful condition, even if no rule has been imposed for which they may specifically be called to account. On a school playground, however, where there are rules about taking turns, against hitting one another, and so on, selfish and violent behaviors gain new definition. One might say that the heart of the sinner is no different, but the head is, in a way that highlights and exacerbates the fault.

The law, then, may "multiply" the trespass (Rom 5:20), make it worse in quality, by giving it the character of specific transgression; or (to give a characteristically Lutheran interpretation) it may make it worse in both quantity and quality by tempting persons to pride and self-sufficiency when they think they can satisfy its demands, leading them to rely on themselves instead of on the sheer grace of God. Or, worse yet, its very existence may arouse precisely the impulses it is intended to curb, as Paul argues at length in Romans 7. As a cartoonist depicts it, a sign on a street corner prohibiting the juggling of machetes engenders the comment from a well-dressed businessman to his colleague,

"Suddenly I feel the urge to juggle machetes." Prohibitions, no matter how proper they may be, no matter how obviously aimed at the wellbeing of all concerned, by their very existence provoke desire (Rom 7:5, 7–8). We may be so accustomed to this reaction in ourselves that we overlook its mysterious character, for surely there is no logical or biological necessity that we should respond in this way. Thus, Paul's observation is not merely a matter of his psychological astuteness; rather, it provides devastating evidence of the deeply perverse character of the human will. The fault does lies not with the law (which Paul affirms is holy and just and good [Rom 7:12]), but with the effect of Sin within the person, that leaves the person baffled by his or her own behavior.

Pendulum swings in the interpretation of Romans 7, involving whether or not it is the specifically *Christian* Paul who is speaking of his divided self (not to mention other possible ways of construing his language), will be unlikely to alter the flash of recognition most people feel in reading his words, whether they are Christians or not. In fact, it has often been observed that it is less often the criminal than the saint who is tormented by a conviction that he or she is deeply sinful. The criminal becomes hardened by sin; the saint sees ever more clearly how far short he or she falls of what God requires. So the promised triumph over sin, by the power of the Holy Spirit, of which Paul speaks so strongly elsewhere, is a deliverance of which persons have only a foretaste in this life (Rom 7:24–25). Meanwhile, the law, so far from being able effectually to curb Sin or deliver people from it, both condemns Sin and provokes what it prohibits – a role it plays precisely because of the radically corrupting nature of Sin that leads all people to act even against what is obviously right and good. As Dunn puts it, the law "informs the willing but does not enable the doing" (1988, 393). And so our behavior baffles as surely as it defeats us.

Sin as Punishment and as Power

Two somewhat different – though perhaps related – ways Paul speaks of Sin may give us further insight into his views on human helplessness against it. One is that God uses sin to punish Sin. He "gives up" or "hands over" the sinner to every kind of wickedness of body and mind (Rom 1:24, 26, 28; note also similar phrases such as being sold, locked up, or subjected to futility [Napier 2002, 27]; and, further, Gal 3:22, on Scripture imprisoning all things under the power of sin):[14] the word used is the same used by Paul when referring to Jesus being handed over to death on account of our sins (Rom 4:25; 8:32; used also, repeatedly, by the gospel writers). The common observation that sinning – and especially the "high-handed" sinning that persons pursue and defend – is a downward spiral into increasing degradation may therefore be due not only to various acts and addictions generating their own consequences, or to the psychologically deadening effect of gratifications that do not truly satisfy, so that more and more extreme indulgence becomes necessary to get the same effect. More importantly, it has to do with the judgment of God (though a judgment finally intended for good [Rom 11:32]).

Furthermore, Paul will have none of the healthy-minded view that people sin out of ignorance, or that it is because they are mistaken about where the good lies that they do evil. No; the reverse is true. Ignorance results from sin: the senseless minds of those who do not rightly honor God are darkened (Rom 1:21–22). And first, these sinners deliberately go against the good that they know (Rom 1:18–21). As Augustine observed in reflecting on the famous pear tree incident, there is something in human beings that stoops to do evil for its own sake:

> Such was my heart, O God, such was my heart. You had pity on it when it was at the bottom of the abyss. Now let my heart tell you what it was seeking there in that I became evil for no reason. I had no motive for my wickedness except wickedness itself. It was foul, and I loved it. I loved the self-destruction, I loved my fall, not the object for which I had fallen but my fall itself. (*Confessions* 2.4.9)[15]

If hell is, as has been suggested, God saying at last to the sinner, "Have it your way," this temporal giving up of the sinner to Sin may be seen as its more provisional precursor.

The seriousness of being given over to Sin is increased when we recognize that Paul tends, especially in Romans, to speak of Sin as a power (e.g., Rom 3:9) and makes it an actor, the subject of verbs (Gaventa 2004, 230). While it is possible that Paul's language should be understood in the weaker sense of a personification of recalcitrant impulses, the frequency with which he speaks of spiritual powers opposed to God should give one pause about affirming this milder interpretation.[16] Even if Paul does not elaborate how he understands the various powers to which he refers, he clearly denies that we are dealing merely with flesh and blood (Eph 6:12). Furthermore, his language about Sin "deceiving" him (Rom 7:11) carries a clear echo of the deception of Adam and Eve by the serpent (see 2 Cor 11:3; 1 Tim 2:14; Dunn 1988, 384; Watson 2007, 283).[17] We need not conceive the sinner as somehow "possessed" by Sin; it is enough to see the sinful and thus traitorous will as aligned with larger powers of evil. Indeed, to consider the will as traitorous is not to deny but to affirm that there is an enemy with which it ought not to be allied.

The further point is that the battle against Sin is not a simply individual matter, as if only one's own wicked inclinations were the problem. We have already seen that the whole created order is marked by Sin; and now we are led to suspect that anti-God forces are at work as well, forces that actively oppose godly behavior. When we think of Sin as a power at work in the individual that is allied with these larger, pervasive, anti-God forces, we see that a quite proper "redemption-historical" view of the Sin problem that refuses to limit it to the individual and what the individual can control (Ridderbos 1975, 91–93) cannot be separated from the depth of individual engagement and responsibility. Even when Paul speaks so strongly as to say that it is not he but Sin within him that acts (Rom 7:17, 20), he is not really denying his own agency but rather expressing bafflement at behavior admittedly his own (Rom 7:15). But at the same time, he is making clear that his enslavement to Sin is not a bondage that it is within his power to break. The larger context is an eschatological one in which the evil that is the enemy of God himself has been in principle defeated in the death and resurrection of Christ, and will finally be completely overcome (Rom 16:20; 1 Cor 15:24–26; Gal 1:4; 1 Thess 4:16–18; 5:2; see Gaventa 2004, 240). That victory – not human capacities, fatally compromised as they are – is what gives Paul confidence.

Bondage to Sin and Human Freedom

The very nature of Sin, according to Paul, is to make humans unfree; that is what the language of slavery means. The strength of the Pauline affirmations about this bondage (e.g., Rom 6:16–19; 8:8 – a slavery and fundamental moral incapacity [1 Cor 2:14] that, as we have seen, affects all humankind from birth) and the impossibility of victory apart from a "new creation" in Christ (2 Cor 5:17; Gal 6:15; altogether similar to John's insistence upon the necessity of a "new birth" or "birth from above," John 3:3) has been scored by many as inimical both to human freedom and responsibility, and to a proper view of the dignity of human beings made in God's image. Liberal theology in particular has supposed that seeing people as universally and fundamentally corrupted by Sin works against their motivation to follow the example of Jesus and in general to strive to realize their full potential, leaving them with no purchase on progress. But such protestations beg the real question. It is no help to act on the assumption that we are solvent if we are actually bankrupt, morally or otherwise; nor does our inability to pay our debts when we are bankrupt automatically absolve us of responsibility for our condition. We can freely get ourselves into jams we cannot by any exercise of will power get ourselves out of, jams that disable not just us but others. And the horrors of the last century and the beginning of this one should surely instruct any who are capable of instruction at all that Liberal theology vastly underestimates the human potential for evil (Shuster 2004, 182; see also, for this whole section, all of ch. 9). The question, then, has to do with the accuracy of Paul's depiction of the human condition.

What, for instance, of people's experience of themselves as free to choose, if they are such slaves as he says? The Augustinian tradition, in a way altogether in harmony with Paul's dark view of human potential taken in itself, has understood human freedom to be a matter of persons' freedom to do as they will, in a way that is to be distinguished sharply from an ability to will aright.[18] That is to say, when people sin, they sin perfectly freely in the sense that no one is holding a gun to their heads to force them to do something wrong; they do as they have chosen to do. The trouble is that they do not want what they ought to want, they do not love God with heart and soul and mind and strength, or their neighbor as themselves. What they freely desire and choose is grounded in a sinful will, a will turned in on itself. It cannot perform the bootstrap operation of putting itself right. People know this defeat most surely when, looking in dismay at something they have done that they judge to be wrong, they not only recognize that they could have done differently (that is, there was no external barrier to doing differently, nor were they ignorant of the right), but also know deep within themselves the really terrible truth that faced with just the same circumstances, they would make the same wrong choice again. They have chosen in accord with who they are, and who they are is sinful.

Disconcerting as such a conclusion is, one might ask if a conception of the human will that depicts it as equally able to choose good or evil gives any basis for choice at all, apart from the most absolutely arbitrary, like flipping a coin. Real choices require motives – some sort of impulse or desire or vision of what is desirable. It is not *more* choices that we need, any more than we need a list of alternative people we might marry when we are deeply in love. What we need is a choice we deeply affirm. Similarly, to be lost in the woods, perfectly able to move in any direction, is not a meaningful freedom if one has no idea in which direction home lies. In the sense that what one wants drives his or her decisions, a secular person might say that one is a slave to one's own character, whereas Paul would say that one is a slave either to Sin or to Christ. "Freedom" is meaningless apart from content and direction.

Practical Implications

Persistent sin and the pursuit of sanctification

How one conceives the human predicament obviously has everything to do with the approach one takes in confronting it; and it may be that persons of different back-grounds and different emotional constitutions may be drawn to widely different inter-pretations and practices. One may be struck that Liberal Protestantism and the Social Gospel movement (and its surprising offspring,[19] the "What Would Jesus Do?" move-ment among many evangelical youth groups); Anabaptists of both the right and the left, with their emphasis on the witness of their community life; and Ignatian spiritual-ity streams in Roman Catholic theology all make heavy use of the gospels. Augustinians and those most greatly influenced by the magisterial Reformation (followers of Luther and Calvin and their heirs) put contrastingly heavy emphasis on the Pauline epistles, which will predictably give a somewhat different, though not less morally serious, style to their religious life – granting, of course, that all these groups surely wish to affirm the necessity of the use of the whole of Scripture.[20] But even among those who give considerable attention to Paul, one finds a division between those who emphasize the "already" of the gift of the Spirit, who gives new life and hence new potential for righ-teousness to the sinner, and those who emphasize the eschatological "not yet" – the reality that death still reigns over earthly lives, and that the holiest people tend to be those most conscious of their continuing defeats by sin.

How shocked should we be when those alleging Christian motives promote warfare or align themselves with evil powers of the state and of privilege, as they have again and again? How should we construe our dismay that the greatest religious leaders so regularly manifest great faults? If we are Christians ourselves, how surprised should we feel when our own attempts to do the best that we know fail, become distorted, lead to unintended bad consequences, or make us self-righteous and obnoxious? Should these terrible failures lead us to suppose that Christian faith as Paul understands it is useless or worse as far as its moral impact is concerned? Those who believe Paul to be saying plainly enough that the victory, though won in principle through Christ's resur-rection, is not yet fully manifest, and that enemies of God's purposes continue to be at work within and without (1 Cor 15:25–26), may perhaps find the world in which they live, and themselves, less puzzling than they otherwise would; and perhaps they may find engaging in the battle itself to be an outworking of the grace of God in their lives, a sign of the mysterious life of the Spirit within, in spite of everything (Dunn 1988, 411–412). The shape of the pursuit of righteousness, then, will be different for such

Christians than for those with a more sanguine view of human potential, but the path will not be less strenuous.

Civil righteousness

While some Christians assume that persons will assuredly grow in grace by relying confidently on the power of God's Spirit to bring ever-increasing victory in this life, and others more pessimistically suppose that the power of Sin will continue to surprise them in the midst of their struggles, candor calls for acknowledgment that the behavior of many who are not Christians exhibits a virtue that far surpasses what may be observed in those who are. This is the problem of so-called civil righteousness, a problem sharpened by Paul's perfectly clear affirmation, Romans 14:23, that "whatever does not proceed from faith is sin." Note that it is not sincerity that validates a behavior, as we so often suppose today, but faith: Paul entirely consistently rejects his whole portfolio of successful achievements as a practicing Pharisee as rubbish in the light of the gospel (Phil 3:2–11).

Surely, though, it would be unjust as well as dishonest for Christians of whatever stripe to contend that it is all the same to them whether their non-Christian neighbor belongs to the Mafia or is a kindly, peaceful, self-sacrificing Buddhist who seeks in every way to be a good citizen. Surely it is right that members of any group that aspires to blameless behavior should be ashamed when others who hold quite different beliefs surpass them in their own goals. Surely all ought to be grateful for every good gift God gives to anyone, not try to find a way to dismiss virtues manifested by those whose convictions are not like their own.

Even so, the crucial point remains that differences we observe in degrees of righteous behavior are differences among sinners, not differences between those who are not sinners and those who are (Brunner 1952, 110–112). We perhaps see the point most clearly when we look at the behaviors of our own about which we feel best and note the mixed motive, the covert self-interest ... Even an impulsive, unpremeditated act of self-sacrifice will surely be followed by a hint of pride, an expectation of gratitude, a hope for praise. Sin arises unbidden. From this deep corruption, no one, Paul has said, can deliver him- or herself. And that is why Paul will put no confidence in any human achievement. Civil righteousness is far better than civil unrighteousness, except insofar as it may betray people into thinking that they can, after all, save themselves.

The centrality of the need for redemption

Human beings cannot save themselves but are completely dependent upon the salvation God has provided in Christ: that is Paul's fundamental message. His purpose in painting in what he believes to be their true colors the depths of the human dilemma is not gratuitously to tear people down, but to exalt Christ, to show both the greatness and the necessity of his work on behalf of humankind. Christ is the Second Adam, the truly new beginning, the One who undoes, and more than undoes, the ruin brought by the First Adam (Rom 5:15–19; 1 Cor 15:21–22).

If humankind could by trying harder save itself, it does not, really, need a Redeemer: pep talks and punishment, instruction and self-discipline, concentration upon good examples and careful cultivation of virtues should suffice, at least for the moral athletes among them. And what is enough for the moral athletes should in principle be enough for all who are serious about their goal.

If providing commands or instruction were sufficient to get people to change their ways, the sending of Moses would have been all that was really required; there would have been no need to send the Son. Paul even goes so far as to say that "if a law had been given that could make alive, then righteousness would indeed come through the law" (Gal 3:21).

If the last enemy, death, were amenable to defeat by the march of scientific progress, and if the overcrowding and overheating and wanton use of resources that is sending our planet into its own death spiral could be remedied or escaped by a bit of intergalactic exploration, then the Resurrection and the promise of a new heavens and new earth would finally be superfluous.

But Paul is perfectly clear that the highest of human achievements fall short of what God requires (Phil. 3:2–11), that there is no law that can raise those dead in sin (Gal 3:21–22), that death will reign until the consummation of all things (1 Cor 15:24–28). As sinners, humans have a choice of despair or faith in Christ. Paul points with supreme confidence to Christ, victor over Sin and death (2 Tim 1:10), and over every conceivable enemy with which they may by allied, from whose saving love nothing whatever can separate us (Rom 8:31–39).

Notes

1 Because the purpose is to consider "Pauline" thought, I shall not seek to distinguish here between letters of undisputed and disputed authorship: even the disputed letters are "Pauline"; and making a distinction would not in any case significantly influence the exposition. For economy's sake, I shall simply say "Paul," even when "the Pauline writer" might be more precise. Further, I shall emphasize the classic perspective rooted in Augustinian thought and taken up by the magisterial Protestant Reformers Luther and Calvin, not least because of its crucial influence, but also because understanding this perspective is an essential foundation for considering "new views" of Paul. Much of the material I shall treat is more fully elaborated in my book *The Fall and Sin* (Shuster 2004).

2 It may be that 1 Cor 6:12–20 resulted from Paul's need to combat a prevailing opinion that intention was all that counted, not actions (see Smith 2008) – a principle of behavior that would obviously be disastrous for the community.

3 "Desire" (*epithymia*; NRSV also "covetousness," and, in the plural, "lusts," "passions"), like "flesh" (*sarx*), does not always have a negative connotation in Paul; both can be neutral or innocent (and indeed, "flesh" has a very large number of nuanced senses – see Marshall 2002). But a negative ethical meaning predominates in both cases. "Boasting" is negative when it is in one's own achievements rather than in Christ (2 Cor 10:17; Gal 6:14).

4 Biblical quotations are taken from the New Revised Standard Version.

5   A single instance of ignorance as a mitigating factor may be found in 1 Tim 1:13. Of course the gospels report Jesus, too, as speaking of the importance of the source of one's actions, e.g., Matt 15:11, 18–20; Mark 7:14–23; John 2:24–25; the difference is a matter of emphasis.

6   But see the equally adamant Lutheran Formula of Concord, Art. 1, neg. 6, on this point.

7   The term "original sin" is sometimes applied to the first sin, meaning that of Adam and Eve; but it is normally used to mean that all human beings are sinners from their birth.

8   In particular, 2 Esd 3:21; 4:30; 7:116–118; 2 Bar. 23:4; 48:42–43. That both sources are generally understood to be later than Paul is not a significant problem, but rather an indication that such ideas were current in the environment.

9   Most will, of course, see the serpent as a symbol; but that the temptation had an external source and is not presented as self-originating is important to the putative "original righteousness" of the primal couple. (That there should be a source of temptation at all raises another set of questions that it is not the purpose of this article to address.)

10 The Augustinian notion also rests upon strict monogenism: that all humankind derives biologically from a single first pair. True, current scientific theory favors monogenism (generally construed as referring to a small population rather than to a single couple) over polygenism; but scientific theories change; and those who do not take Gen 1–11 as referring to some sort of events occurring in time and space will be doubly disinclined to see universal human sinfulness as rooted in biological realities.

11 Such a view is consistent with the theological idea of *imputation* of sin (and, similarly, of Christ's righteousness), which rests on biblical Greek and Hebrew terms for the "reckoning" of something to another's account, usually in a commercial or legal setting (see Shuster 2004, 203–205).

12 For a single example on the Reformed side, see the answer to Q. 18 of the Westminster Shorter Catechism with respect to guilt, and the Westminster Confession 10.3 with respect to infant salvation (while this latter reference is to *elect* infants, the principle is commonly extended). On the Roman Catholic side, the *limbus infantum*, traditionally understood as the final abode of small children dying without benefit of baptism that washes away original sin, has silently disappeared from the catechism.

13 See the chapter by Hultgren in this volume.

14 Gathercole (2006, 164–165) notes the parallel with Num 11 and 1 Sam 8, where God judges the people precisely by and in giving them what they ask for; so this principle is not an exclusively Pauline one.

15 Contrast Pannenberg (1985, 118) for a sophisticated form of the argument that we do not really choose evil *as evil*, but only seeking some good.

16 See, for a variety of possible powers, Rom 8:38–39; 1 Cor 8:5; 10:20; 15:24; 2 Cor 4:4; Gal 4:8–9; Eph 1:21; 2:2; 6:12; Col 1:13, 16; 2:20. See also Dunn 1998, 104–114. For reference specifically to Satan, see Rom 16:20; 1 Cor 5:5; 7:5; 2 Cor 2:11; 11:14; 12:7; 1 Thess 2:18; 2 Thess 2:9 (Whiteley 1964, 29–30).

17 The serpent is identified with Satan not in Genesis, but in the later biblical witness (Rev 12:9; 20:2; see also John 8:44); and pursuit of the identification by the church comes as early as Justin Martyr.

18 The classic distinction is between will as *voluntas*, meaning a sort of primal volition or disposition of the heart that is not itself chosen, and *liberum arbitrium indifferentiae*, or the power of contrary choice, particularly the power freely to choose good and reject evil. The latter is affirmed by Eastern Orthodox and Arminian traditions, but not by Augustinian ones.

19   The historical link is Charles Sheldon, whose novel *In His Steps*, first published in 1897 and continuously in print since, popularized the phrase and idea.
20   It would be fair to observe that genre issues may bear here, as narrative themes are often particularly important to those groups relying heavily on the gospels; though obviously the content of the gospels themselves still shapes the resultant theological leanings. One should also note that *imitatio Christi* notes may be found in Paul – 1 Cor 11:1; 1 Thess 1:6; and, many but not all would insist, Phil 2:5–8.

References

Augustine. 1991. *Confessions*. Translated by Henry Chadwick. Oxford: Oxford University Press.
Barth, Karl. 1956. *Church Dogmatics*. Volume 4: *The Doctrine of Reconciliation*. Part 1. Edinburgh: T. & T. Clark.
Beker, J. Christiaan. 1980. *Paul the Apostle: The Triumph of God in Life and Thought*. Philadelphia: Fortress.
Brunner, Emil. 1952. *The Christian Doctrine of Creation and Redemption*. London: Lutterworth.
Dunn, James D. G. 1988. *Romans 1–8*. Dallas: Word.
Dunn, James D. G. 1998. *The Theology of Paul the Apostle*. Grand Rapids: Eerdmans.
Gathercole, Simon J. 2006. Sin in God's Economy: Agencies in Romans 1 and 7. Pages 158–172 in *Divine and Human Agency in Paul and his Cultural Environment*. Edited by J. M. G. Barclay and Simon J. Gathercole. London: T. & T. Clark.
Gaventa, Beverly Roberts. 2004. The Cosmic Power of Sin in Paul's Letter to the Romans: Toward a Widescreen Edition. *Interpretation* 58: 229–240.
Hamilton, Joan O'C. 1990. Zimbardo. *Stanford* 18: 30–35.
Marshall, I. Howard. 2002. Living in the "Flesh." *Bibliotheca Sacra* 159 (636): 387–403.
Napier, Daniel. 2002. Paul's Analysis of Sin and Torah in Romans 7:7–25. *Restoration Quarterly* 44: 15–32.
Niebuhr, Reinhold. 1955. *The Self and the Dramas of History*. New York: Charles Scribner's Sons.
Pannenberg, Wolfhart. 1985. *Anthropology in Theological Perspective*. Philadelphia: Westminster.
Ridderbos, Herman. 1975. *Paul: An Outline of his Theology*. Grand Rapids: Eerdmans.
Shuster, Marguerite. 2004. *The Fall and Sin: What We Have Become as Sinners*. Grand Rapids: Eerdmans.
Smith, Jay E. 2008. The Roots of a "Libertine" Slogan in 1 Corinthians 6:18. *Journal of Theological Studies* 59: 63–95.
Wasserman, Emma. 2008. *The Death of the Soul in Romans 7: Sin, Death, and the Law in Light of Hellenistic Moral Psychology*. Tübingen: Mohr Siebeck.
Watson, Francis. 2007. *Paul, Judaism, and the Gentiles: Beyond the New Perspective*. Grand Rapids: Eerdmans.
Whiteley, D. E. H. 1964. *The Theology of St. Paul*. Oxford: Basil Blackwell.

CHAPTER 35

Christian Theology:
The Spirit

Ralph Del Colle

Pneumatology (theology of the Spirit) may be approached in either of two ways. An analogy with Christology is helpful. Christology has traditionally focused on the person of Jesus Christ, how Christ is both human and divine. The work of Jesus Christ was usually taken up by the tractate on soteriology (the study of salvation). In similar fashion, pneumatology concentrates on the person of the Holy Spirit. However, it may also examine the pneumatological dimensions of various Christian doctrines and of the economy of God as a whole, in other words, the work of the Holy Spirit. That the Spirit is unobtrusively at work in all that God does is intimated by Jesus himself when speaking of the coming of the Spirit as the Paraclete: for "he will not speak on his own authority, but whatever he hears he will speak" (John 16:13).[1] The Spirit's mission thus concerns the entire economy of God: "But the Counselor, the Holy Spirit, whom the Father will send in my name, he will teach you all things, and bring to your remembrance all that I have said to you" (John 14:28). As a result, a study of pneumatology in Paul's writings must consider a host of pneumatological themes in addition to the explicit references to the Spirit.

The Person of the Holy Spirit

Although we cannot impose on Paul the later Trinitarian terminology that distinguishes between person (or hypostasis) and nature (essence or substance) in order to speak credibly of how God is one and yet three, it is appropriate to inquire whether Paul's view of the Spirit is consistent with later doctrinal developments. Can we discover

The Blackwell Companion to Paul, First Edition. Edited by Stephen Westerholm.
© 2011 Blackwell Publishing Ltd. Published 2011 by Blackwell Publishing Ltd.

in Paul, for example, a distinction between the agency of the Spirit and that of God the Father and the exalted and risen Christ? Is the Spirit simply a power in Paul, perhaps a way of speaking of the presence of Christ within the believer? Or does the Spirit bear an integrity that is its own, so that it would be proper for the church (when it did) to identify the Holy Spirit as the third person in the Trinity? And, if so, might a fresh reading of Paul assist our efforts to think the triune God?

In answer to these questions, it is clear that for Paul the relationship between Christ and the Spirit is an integral one. Two passages in particular demonstrate this, neither one without its problems for the systematic theologian: Romans 8:1–13 and 2 Corinthians 3:17–18 both seem to use Christ and the Spirit interchangeably. Such is the assessment of the Dutch Reformed theologian Hendrikus Berkhof, who argues for more than just a functional identity between the risen Christ and the Holy Spirit.

> How do we have to conceive of this identity of the Spirit with the exalted Lord? Traditional theology would avoid the word "identity" or merely speak of an identity in functions of the Son and the Spirit. This position is untenable, however, if we face the fact that the Spirit in Scriptures is not an autonomous substance, but a predicate to the substance God and to the substance Christ. It describes the fact and the way of functioning of both. (Berkhof 1964, 28)

This interpretation effectively undermines the doctrine of the Trinity as traditionally construed even if it proposes a robust theology of the Holy Spirit as integral to the triunity of God.

For Christian doctrine several issues intersect that affect both pneumatology and Trinitarian theology. The argument can be made that Paul (if Berkhof is correct) may still possess a robust pneumatology even if it does not warrant later Trinitarian developments. Or, the Tradition, in its efforts to recognize the full divinity of the Holy Spirit, was consistent with trajectories originating with Paul, whose language for the Holy Spirit may still enrich Trinitarian theology and praxis (as, e.g., in the church's liturgy). In other words, disagreements among systematic theologians about Paul's pneumatology bear directly on the Christian doctrine of God. As might also be expected, New Testament exegetes and theologians dispute this very same issue. Two, in particular, are worth our review: James D. G. Dunn and Gordon D. Fee. I start with the former, whose exegesis lends itself (with qualifications) to Berkhof's critique of traditional Trinitarian theology.

Dunn's work on the particular Pauline passages that seem to imply identification of Christ and the Spirit are in fact more nuanced, linking the identification specifically to Christian experience. This indeed seems to be the nub of the matter, and for the moment I let Dunn speak for himself.

> It was by receiving the Spirit that Paul entered into the dispensation of the Spirit, and through the Spirit that he experienced the life and liberty of the new covenant. He experienced God by the Spirit. He experienced the exalted Christ through the Spirit. This does not mean that they are identical in all their functions (far less their "beings"), as though, for example, the Spirit had been crucified and raised from the dead. It only means that they are identical in experience. (Dunn 1998a, 124–125)

The key here is the experiential matrix and how Dunn's conclusion bears on the doctrine of the Trinity. Is there perhaps a tendency toward a denial of any distinction between the second and third persons of the Trinity, as implied by Berkhof?

Dunn has engaged in an ongoing conversation with Gordon Fee on this matter, the specifics of which are significant for systematic theology. It is important to be as precise as we can be. The question is not so much whether the doctrine of the Trinity is a legitimate development of Pauline theology – Dunn allows as much in the above quotation, and in a later work he acknowledges that Paul's way of speaking of the relationships between God, the risen Christ, and the Spirit finds "its most lasting expression in a Trinitarian understanding of God" (Dunn 1998b, 264) – but what the lack of explicit Trinitarian distinctions in Paul (up front, so to speak) means for Christology and pneumatology. For Dunn, "Paul's somewhat puzzling talk of the risen Lord's relationship to God (closely correlated, but distinct) and Paul's similarly puzzling conception of the risen Christ's relationship with the Spirit (closely identified, but not completely)" bespeaks a dynamic "conceptuality in worship" which must not be missed, eventually (one can argue) justifying the Trinitarian structure of Christian liturgy (Dunn 1998b, 264). Yet later distinctions drawn between the divine persons, Dunn argues, must be weighed in light of New Testament and pre-Nicene concerns lest the control of Jewish-Christian monotheism be so loosened as to allow for bitheism or tritheism (Dunn 1989, xxxi–xxxii). Fee challenges Dunn on this score and argues for a more explicit Trinitarian theology in Paul (as opposed to a binitarianism of the Father and the Son) with a high Christology in tow: in Fee's view, Paul should be understood as a proto-Trinitarian (Fee 2007, 586–593). At stake is the proper understanding of God, Christ, and the Spirit.

I raise this issue of contention in order to negotiate properly the robust pneumatology that is evident (to all) in Paul. Is the Spirit the "medium of Christ's union with his own" (Dunn 1998b, 264)? Or is it that the Spirit only forges a "'uniting' relationship between the believer and the Lord" (Fee 1994a, 322)? The difference may appear subtle, but it reveals the different experiential frameworks by which both exegetes interpret Paul's pneumatology. No doubt, apart from the Spirit there is for Paul no Christian confession of faith – "no one can say 'Jesus is Lord' except by the Holy Spirit" (1 Cor 12: 3) – but there has been some consternation over how to interpret Pauline statements on the relationship between Christ and the Spirit.

The identification of Christ with the Spirit has a long history, hearkening back to Wilhelm Bousset, who argued that for Paul the "two entities" Kyrios and Pneuma "begin to merge," although "not everywhere and not completely" (Bousset 1970, 163). Larry Hurtado, as early as 1979, critiqued the continuing influence of Bousset on scholarly representations of New Testament Christologies, especially his thesis that Paul's use of the Kyrios title with its associated cult is primarily of a Hellenistic provenance (Hurtado 1979, 306–317). While this critique is widely accepted in more recent Pauline scholarship, a more interesting theme associated with Bousset and other German scholars in Pauline studies in the early twentieth century is their conception of the relationship between Christ and the Spirit, a conception that exhibits a tendency close to what Dunn advocates and Fee resists. Much of this had to do with their proposed experiential matrix for the supposed "Christ-mysticism" of Paul.

Adolf Deissmann, who agreed with Boussett that Christ-mysticism was the center of Paul's thought, argued that Paul was utilizing both Jewish and Hellenistic thought forms (Deissmann 1972, 137–138). For Deissmann, Paul's Christo-centricity was something deeper than a Christology; Paul himself lived out of a "Christ-intimacy." He "lives 'in' Christ," and the "present spiritual Christ, who is about him on all sides, who fills him, who speaks to him, and [who] speaks in and through him ... is ... not a person of the past ... not a 'historical' personage, but a reality and power of the present, an 'energy,' whose life-giving powers are daily expressing themselves in him" (135–136). This "Christ-experience" may be expressed more doctrinally as "the experience of the immanence of Christ; [but] it is more Pauline and therefore also historically more correct to speak of the experience of the Spirit-Christ" (139–140). Deissmann is explicit: "the living Christ is the Pneuma" (138).

Another strong proponent of the centrality of Christ-mysticism for Paul during this period was Albert Schweitzer. Not only did he differ from Deissmann on the provenance of this mysticism (not from Hellenistic sources but from "late-Jewish" eschatology [Schweitzer 1931, 26–40, 52–100]), but also on its association with other non-mystical elements of Paul's theology. Schweitzer argued for eschatological and juridical dimensions in Paul's doctrine of redemption as well as the mystical, the latter of which he identified as "being in Christ" (25). Being in Christ also evokes the pneumatological emphasis in Paul, and in a manner that maintains both the inseparability and the distinction between Christ and the Spirit. Pauline language of being in the Spirit "is only a form of manifestation of the being-in-Christ ... [and both] ... are descriptions of one and the same state" (167). As "the life-principle common to the Messiah and the members of his Kingdom," the "Spirit is the form of the manifestation of the powers of the resurrection"; in fact, Christ is the "vehicle of the resurrection-Spirit which is bestowed upon the Elect" (166). The Christ-mysticism of Paul is as intimate for the Christian in Schweitzer's view as it is in Deissmann's, since it sees dying and rising with Christ as more integral to the Christian life than the ecstatic manifestations of the Spirit. By such union, a union with Christ's corporeity, Christians become vehicles of the Spirit as the Spirit of Christ (165).

This early period in Pauline studies, while dated in many ways, still lends itself to the systematic concerns of the present debate over Christological and pneumatological identity and distinction. Formally, the issue is whether the apparent identification of Christ and the Spirit, in various Pauline statements about their missions and their presence in Christian experience, warrants a new theological conceptuality in Trinitarian theology. If the *Christus praesens* (the self-presentation of Christ) and the *Spiritus praesens* (the self-presentation of the Holy Spirit) are virtually identical for Paul, ought we not to reconsider the traditional distinction of persons in the divine economy? Is not some sort of systematic revision of the Christian doctrine of God necessary? Before we proceed, one other glance back to this fertile period in German New Testament scholarship is required, followed by some words about a particular systematic account of the related issue of the divine indwelling in the justified. Then we will return to our contemporary protagonists, Dunn and Fee.

Johannes Weiss (from that same period in German exegesis and theology) was not as convinced about the centrality of Christ-mysticism in Paul. However, he posed an interesting question with regard to God and Christ (i.e., the first and second persons of the later developed doctrine of the Trinity), claiming that Paul presents them as "side by side, the dispensers of Salvation": "We ask now whether we cannot find, in explanation of this apparently simple juxtaposition, with its naive and not always clarified modalism, a clearly thought-out conviction of Paul as to the relationship of God and Christ, and their meaning for Salvation" (Weiss 1959, 471). We have been posing a similar query in reference to the second and third persons.

To answer, we must attend first to the matter of "modalism," ancient and modern. The question whether Paul may be justly accused of any sort of modalism (the charge is anachronistic, to say the least) involves the systematic task (more accurately, a speculative one) of conceptualizing how the Father, Christ, and the Spirit are identified or distinguished in Paul and later Christian theology. The definition of modalism itself requires some precision if we are not to compound Weiss's characterization of Paul's naivety.

It is clear that for Paul we are not yet at the point of speaking about how God exists in Godself (*in se*), that is, the issue of the "immanent" trinity. However, Paul's understanding of the operation – and therefore the agency – of God, Christ, and the Spirit (all within a post-Easter framework) is in need of some clarification. Are there distinctions of agency and presence, or do they all amount to the same thing in Christian experience, as Boussett, Deissmann, and Dunn have argued? Ancient modalism, the type against which Tertullian fought in the third century in his treatise *Against Praxeas*, and as developed by Sabellius, was not yet on the theological landscape of Pauline Christianity or his opponents. As Bertrand de Margerie has summarized, monarchical modalism posited "an only God, Father and Legislator in the Old Testament, who became flesh and Son in the New and sanctified the Church as Holy Spirit after Pentecost" (1982, 73). This type of successive modalism, or (from a slightly different angle) mono-personalism (Son and Spirit as expressions of the person of the Father), is clearly not within the purview of Pauline theology (*pace* Weiss on the Father and Son). However, a more modern version of modalism is relevant to the interpretation of Paul's Christology and pneumatology. One such definition from the early twentieth century is as follows:

> Christian theology must conclude to the moral divinity of Jesus on earth, to the present divinity of Christ, while discarding the prehistoric divinity of Jesus and the eternal divinity of the Spirit. Thus it does not lead to a real trinity but to the unity of God, to the paternity of one God, to a sonship of Jesus that is not metaphysical but moral, to a communion of Jesus with his Father on earth, to the duality of God and of Christ in heavenly power, to the action of God or of Christ under the form of the Spirit. (Margerie 1982, 74, citing Georges Fulliquet)

This form of modalism maintains a triadic structure to divine revelation (as did Sabellius), but prefers to speak of the operation of divine agency in the human Jesus as the inspiration of the Spirit; and after Easter, Christ and the Spirit are identified. God as Spirit is present and active in the earthly life of Jesus and, following the resurrection, as the Spirit of Christ in the lives of believers and the communion of the church. No doubt, this is a serious departure from traditional Trinitarian predication that distinguishes three eternal hypostases or persons in one divine nature.

The issue may be illuminated by comparison with a later discussion of a different but connected theme. For scholastic and neo-scholastic theologians in the Catholic tradition, Christian knowledge of the Father, Son, and Holy Spirit was associated with the indwelling of the divine persons in the justified. Debate revolved around two major options. Both are indebted to the long held axiom of Latin Trinitarian theology that the operation of God relative to the world is always one; in Trinitarian terms, the external works of the Trinity are undivided (*opera Trinitatis ad extra sunt indivisa*) – one divine nature is at work, though it is inseparable from the (three) divine persons. This does not mean that the distinction of persons is not evident in the experience of grace, nor is it to deny that each divine person possesses his own distinct properties within the Godhead and his proper mission to the world. For example, all three divine persons are involved in the incarnation, but only the Son becomes incarnate – the Son sent by the Father and assuming a human nature by the Holy Spirit in the womb of the Virgin Mary.

How, then, do Christians know God as Father, Son, and Holy Spirit? At the very least, grace must elevate the human faculties of intellect and will to know and love God specifically as Father, Son, and Holy Spirit. The divine persons are the object of these operations of the soul's faculties. In the axiom of Thomas Aquinas, "God is said to be present as the object known is in the knower and the beloved in the lover" (*Summa Theologica* Ia, q.43, a.3). Precisely how the soul's faculties are enabled to know and love God may be debated: are they simply elevated by grace, or is the soul given a certain form when indwelled by the trinity (or by the Holy Spirit in particular, and by the other two persons through their *perichoresis*, viz., the indwelling of the divine persons in one another)? What is significant for our purposes is that the trinity and each of the persons distinctly can be known as a consequence of the supernatural working of divine grace. I emphasize "supernatural" to mean that this manifestation of divine agency and its effects in human beings are the fruit of the Christian dispensation of divine revelation and redemption. The Christian, therefore, encounters God as Father, Son, and Holy Spirit. Again, we turn to Aquinas on this matter, who links the missions of Son and Holy Spirit in God's dealings with humanity with their intra-trinitarian processions (or relations within the Godhead itself):

> Since mission implies the origin of the person Who is sent, and His indwelling by grace ... if we speak of mission according to origin, in this sense the Son's mission is distinguished from the mission of the Holy Ghost, as generation is distinguished from procession [i.e., whereas the Son is said to be "begotten" by the Father, the Spirit is said to "proceed" from the Father (John 15:26)]. If we consider mission as regards the effect of grace, in this sense the two missions are united in the root which is grace, but are distinguished in the effects of grace, which consist in the illumination of the intellect [=the effect of the coming of the Son to indwell the Christian] and the kindling of the affection [=the effect of the coming of the Spirit]. Thus it is manifest that one mission cannot be without the other, because neither takes place without sanctifying grace, nor is one person separated from the other. (Ia, q.43, a.5)

Aquinas is discussing the invisible missions of the Son and Holy Spirit as contrasted with their visible missions. The latter designate the Son's assumption of a human nature into the unity of his divine person in the incarnation and the Holy Spirit's appearance under various physical signs, for example, a dove at Jesus' baptism (Matt 3:16), tongues of fire at Pentecost (Acts 2:3). These differ from the *invisible* missions of the second and third persons of the Trinity, which are their indwelling in the believer by grace – in Thomistic and Catholic parlance, sanctifying grace by which one is made holy. The consequence of these invisible missions is that the soul is made like the divine person indwelling it, be it the Son who illumines the intellect or the Spirit who kindles the affections of the will. The point is that the tradition found a way to distinguish the persons in their invisible missions, though both belong to the Christian experience of grace. Within this experiential matrix of grace, however, the divine persons are not the same (*contra* Dunn).

Admittedly, medieval Latin Trinitarian theology involved a speculative Trinitarian metaphysics that is not the stuff of the Pauline correspondence even at its most theological. All I am suggesting is that if one of the more speculative traditions in Christian theology is conscious of the distinction but inseparability of the divine persons in the Christian experience of grace and was able to articulate both their distinction and their inseparability in a cogent manner, this may be of assistance in evaluating the Dunn–Fee debate over Pauline Christology and pneumatology. Essentially, there is equivalence between the Thomistic invisible missions of Son and Spirit and the Pauline experiential matrix of the risen Christ and the Spirit. Both entail distinct designations of divine agency through Christ and the Spirit, though such passages as the "Lord is the Spirit" (2 Cor 3:18) have raised questions of the extent and modality of their identification and distinction.

The basic difference between Dunn and Fee is that the latter emphasizes the agency of the Holy Spirit in Paul in a way that demonstrates the Spirit's distinction from Christ and, therefore, Paul's proto-Trinitarian credentials. The Holy Spirit is the Spirit of God as well as of Christ. This contributes to his own personal identity and counters the frequent claim (of Dunn, among others) that Christ and the Spirit are identified in Paul (Fee 1994b, 834–842). Dunn, on the other hand, denies this identification in reference to the Godward relation of Christ to the Father, but not in the relation of Christ to the believer. In the latter sphere, Christ is not differentiated from the Spirit, but acts through the Spirit and as the Spirit.

> *If the exalted Christ is to the believer as life-giving Spirit, he is to God as firstborn Son.* It is presumably in this indeterminate intermediate role of the exalted Christ between man and God as Son and between God and man as Spirit that we find the uncomfortable dynamic which was an important factor in pushing Christian thought in a Trinitarian direction. (Dunn 1989, 149; emphasis in original)

Without attempting to resolve this exegetical dispute, it is important from a systematic perspective to underscore two issues, one from each of our exegetes, and how fidelity to Paul might contribute to contemporary Christian pneumatology. First, Fee is correct when he presses for the distinct identity of the Holy Spirit based upon numerous references to the agency of the Spirit. One example will suffice. In Romans 8, the heavenly intercession of Christ ("Is it Christ Jesus, who died, yes, who was raised from the dead, who is at the right hand of God, who indeed intercedes for us?" [v. 34]) is not identical with the interior intercession of the Spirit ("Likewise the Spirit helps us in our weakness; for we do not know how to pray as we ought, but the Spirit himself intercedes for us with sighs too deep for words. And he who searches the hearts of men knows what is the mind of the Spirit, because the Spirit intercedes for the saints according to the will of God" [vv. 26–27]) (Fee 1994b, 836). One does not predicate of the Spirit the salvation-history works of Christ (e.g., death, resurrection, and session). Nor is it an exaggeration to suggest that believers are both aware of Christ's intercession for them and conscious of the Spirit groaning within them. This does not mean we are positing two separate agencies. Within the horizon of graced faith, Christians may witness the Spirit within (Rom 8:16), Christ exalted and coming (1 Cor 1:7–9), and the God from whom, through whom, and for whom all things exist (Rom 11:36) – all as a matter of present experience (2 Cor 13:14).

Whether it is a matter of degree or kind, the distinction between Christ and the Spirit in Paul does not obviate their near identity as well. The disagreement focuses on whether a form of Spirit-Christology is also at work in Paul. Fee rejects such a notion if this means that the Spirit is "identified with the risen Christ, either ontologically or functionally" (Fee 1994b, 838). Dunn agrees that the exalted Christ is neither synonymous with nor absorbed by the Spirit, but claims that within the believer's experience, there is no distinction between the two (Dunn 1989, 146–147). With regard to Jesus himself, Dunn speaks of a two-stage Spirit-Christology. Jesus of Nazareth can only be understood as inspired and empowered by the Spirit; after the resurrection, the presence of Christ is known only as he acts in, through, and as the Spirit. Dunn departs from the Tradition in two respects. He denies the pre-existence of Christ in Paul, and the Spirit-Christology that he argues is present in Paul sees the divine element in the earthly Jesus as a matter of inspiration rather than incarnation. However, Jesus' post-resurrection presence in the Spirit is strongly affirmed (Dunn 1989, 160–161). What might we draw from Dunn without denying the distinct identity of the Holy Spirit that we have gleaned from Fee?

Yves Congar, the twentieth century French Dominican theologian and ecumenist, in one of his later works set down the axiom, "No Christology without pneumatology and no pneumatology without Christology" (Congar 1986, 1). Congar was one of the most influential theologians of the conciliar period (Second Vatican Council, 1962–1965); it is noteworthy that the *Catechism of the Catholic Church*, promulgated by Pope John Paul II with the inspiration of the Council in mind, echoes the thought of Congar when it teaches that, "in their joint mission, the Son and the Holy Spirit are distinct but inseparable" (no. 689 in *Catechism of the Catholic Church* [1995, 198]). "Joint Mission," rather than separate missions (whether simultaneous or sequential), underscores the integral relationship between the work of the Son and that of the Spirit. Therefore, any Christology must have a strong pneumatological component, one that diminishes neither the divine sonship of Jesus nor the distinct identity of the Holy Spirit.

The question is whether we find this in Paul. Thus far we have seen that the close association between Christ and the Spirit in Paul has led to two views of this relationship, one emphasizing the identity between the two, the other their distinction, neither denying their interrelationship. Perhaps, following George Montague, it is better to speak of their identification rather than their identity. Commenting on 2 Corinthians 3:17–18 and 1 Corinthians 15:44–45, two of the key passages in the debate, Montague puts it thus: "This means a dynamic identification (but not a personal identity) of the Lord Jesus with the Spirit, inasmuch as the Spirit proceeds from Jesus risen" (1976, 190). Or, as Max Turner has proffered (as an alternative to Dunn's "Christ-stamped Spirit"): "*[T]he Spirit is now also thought to act as the dynamic extension of the risen Christ's personality, and activity, as formerly he had been thought to act as God's*" (1994, 432; emphasis in original)

No matter the extent of the disagreement, Paul registers for the systematic theologian an integral Christology and pneumatology. The alterations in Romans 8:1–13 between the indwelling of the Spirit ("the Spirit of God dwells in you" [v. 9]) and the indwelling of Christ ("if Christ is in you" [v. 10]) bespeak the intimate relationship between the risen and exalted Christ and the gift of the Spirit. According to Paul, it is through the Holy Spirit given that the love of God is poured into believers' hearts (Rom 5:5), a notion fully enunciated in his Trinitarian benediction: "The grace of the Lord Jesus Christ and the love of God and the fellowship (*koinōnia*) of the Holy Spirit be with you all" (2 Cor 13:14).

This *koinōnia* of the Holy Spirit (also a *koinōnia* with Christ [1 Cor 1:9]) is rooted in the Spirit-oriented Christology of Paul. In his contrasting parallels of Adam and Christ, Paul asserts in 1 Corinthians 15:45 that as the former (the first Adam) became a living soul (*psychēn zōsan*), so Christ (the last Adam) became a life-giving spirit (*pneuma zōopoioun*). The contrast is between the protological Adam and the eschatological Adam, the key being that Christ by virtue of the resurrection possesses a spiritual body (*sōma pneumatikon* [v. 44]). It is in this sense that Paul can say that the "Lord is the Spirit" (2 Cor 3:17–18). The Spirit is given through the risen and glorified humanity of Christ, and by this same Spirit Christians participate in his ecclesial corporeity (1 Cor 12:12–13), in a relationship that reproduces by adoption Christ's own filial relation to the Father (Gal 4:5). The pneumatological basis of this relation is for Paul a matter of exclamatory prayer – "Abba! Father!" – inspired by the "Spirit of his Son" (Gal 4:6; cf. Rom 8:15), and is oriented to eschatological fulfillment by virtue of the Christian's apocalyptic suffering with their crucified and glorified Lord (Rom 8:17).

The recent turn to Spirit-christologies in contemporary systematic theology has much to learn from Paul and the disputes in Pauline scholarship that we have reviewed. In fact, there is more to consider in the scholarship than in Paul's writings themselves, since the disputed passages are relatively few. Noteworthy, however, is that the two sides in the systematic arena do not necessarily coincide with the dispute between Dunn and Fee. The systematic discussion may be broken down between those who advocate a Unitarian Spirit-Christology with a triadic structure and those who adhere to a more thoroughgoing Trinitarian Spirit-Christology. The former advocate that God as Spirit is present in Jesus and then, following the resurrection, as the Holy Spirit, or even Spirit of Christ, with the character of Jesus. Certainly there are similarities to language often employed by Dunn. The latter group maintains the classical Trinitarian distinction of divine persons and would argue that Spirit-Christology does not displace but complements Logos-Christology. The divine Son still becomes incarnate, but this is understood to have taken place by the agency and power of the Spirit. Then Jesus, the Spirit-*bearer* during his earthly life, becomes – with the Father – the Spirit-*sender* as the exalted and risen one. Needless to say, Fee's position is very hospitable to this perspective. However, what we find present in Paul, and upheld by both sides in the New Testament debate, is the centrality not just of the resurrection as a past event but also of the risen Christ in the graced now of the divine economy. This latter is often absent in the Unitarian version of systematic Spirit-Christology.

The presence of the risen Christ, the *Christus praesens*, is too decisive for Paul to be ignored. The query raised above had to do with the possible modalism of Christ and the Spirit, and while I suggested that the identification, rather than identity, of Christ and the Spirit is the best way of representing Paul's theology on the issue, both Dunn and Fee are responding to the dominating motif of the *Christus praesens* in Paul. At the same time, there is no doubt that the modality or medium of Christ's presence in Paul is profoundly pneumatological. Therefore, despite my own agreement with Fee on some of the key issues, Dunn has consistently underscored the pneumatological element of Paul's Christology; and, at least for this theologian, one must appreciate the compelling attraction of that early stage in Pauline scholarship that touted Paul's Christ-mysticism as central to his theology. An American church historian of the same period, A. C. McGiffert of Union Theological Seminary (New York), characterized Paul's understanding of the Christian life as one in which the indwelling of the Spirit of God makes it possible that "Christ may dwell in [Christians] richly, that they may be not their own, but Christ's, that they may live in the Spirit and walk in the Spirit, that they may not lose their hold on Christ, but that his Spirit may fill them and abound" (McGiffert 1906, 137–138).

This poetical account of Paul bespeaks his integral theology of Christ and the Spirit. Interestingly evocative in my judgment is that Paul has managed to elicit such prose from the liberal wing of Protestantism represented by McGiffert and the German exegetes. On the very same score, their more conservative and evangelical contemporaries were likewise taken by Paul. A parallel to the intimacy of Christ-mysticism in Deissmann and Schweitzer can be found in the late nineteenth- and early twentieth-century preacher and theologian A. B. Simpson, founder of the Christian and Missionary Alliance evangelical denomination. Commenting on Paul's pneumatology he states:

> the Holy Spirit comes and takes possession of us and breathes into us the life of the Lord Jesus Christ ... Bringing Christ as a living presence into my heart and life, [the Spirit] establishes a new law of feeling, thinking, choosing, and acting, and ... makes it natural to me to be holy, obedient, and Christ-like. (Simpson [1896?], 100)

It is a testimony to Paul's concentration on the Spirit that, in regard to the essence of his thought, these modern interpreters, although far apart on many issues of biblical authority and scholarship, echoed similar themes.

The Work of the Holy Spirit

The Spirit's presence and operation are pervasive themes throughout Paul's writings. The integration with Christology is also evident. Pneumatological themes inform the beginning of Christian life and the ongoing discipleship of the mature, the nature of the Church, and the eschatological hope that the gospel nurtures. The life of prayer and the corporate worship of the church are inconceivable without the Spirit. Graces and gifts, divine power amid human weakness, the sovereignty of the Spirit and the possibility of rejecting the Spirit's work are all included in Paul's pneumatological arena.

The gospel, Christian initiation, and the knowledge of God

Although Paul makes no direct reference to the Holy Spirit in his own conversion account (Gal 1:12–24), one assumes the Spirit's work since it involved a revelation of Jesus Christ (vv. 12, 16). As it is, for Paul the divine economy is made known by "a spirit of wisdom and of revelation" (Eph 1:17), and his own preaching is governed by the demonstration of the Spirit and power (1 Cor 2:4). After all, Jesus himself is designated Son of God with power according to the Spirit of holiness at his resurrection (Rom 1:4), and the new covenant is inscribed by the Spirit on the hearts of those who believe (2 Cor 3:3). In other words, the act of God's salvation in Christ transpires in the event of the cross/resurrection, its proclamation, and its reception in faith (2 Cor 5:18–20).

Paul's theological epistemology is evangelical and pneumatological. This does not deny that the reality and power of God are accessible to human perception in the works of creation (Rom 1:19–20) or that the moral imperative is inscribed in conscience (Rom 2:14–15). It is to say that sinfulness – ungodliness and injustice – delivers human beings over to spiritual darkness and moral obduracy (Rom 1:20–32), a situation that can only be rectified by the Savior giving himself "for our sins to deliver us from the present evil age" (Gal 1:4). Salvation entails an apocalyptic handing over of Jesus "for our trespasses" (Rom 4:25), his being subjected to the rulers of this age (1 Cor 2:8), and even becoming sin "for our sake" (2 Cor 5:21), or – in terms of the law – bearing its curse "for us" (Gal 3:13). Only on this Christological and staurological basis can we understand why the proclamation of the gospel must be a demonstration of Spirit and power.

Paul reminds the church that the power of the Spirit overturns the wisdom and powers of the present age, renewing the mind to apprehend the paradoxical working of divine power and wisdom in the "weakness" and "foolishness" of a crucified Christ (1 Cor 1:18–25). Accompanying the public display of Jesus Christ crucified, the Spirit is given in increasing measure to the point of the miraculous (Gal 3:1–5). It dissembles sociological status and manifests to faith the singular glory of God. "God chose what is low and despised in the world, even things that are not, to bring to nothing things that are, so that no human being might boast in the presence of God" (1 Cor 1:28–29). For Paul, as for the writer of the Epistle to the Hebrews, the word of God penetrates to the existential and ontological depths of the human being (Heb 4:12), effecting a revelatory transformation and an apocalyptic reckoning that divide the psychical from the spiritual. The natural person (*psychikos*) and the spiritual person (*pneumatikos*) operate on different epistemological levels. "Now the natural man does not receive the things of the Spirit of God" (1 Cor 2:14, literal rendering). The knowledge enjoyed by the spiritual person is not a matter of inward possession of the spiritual self, nor is it the knowledge of different spiritual planes as in Gnosticism; it is rather the product of the public proclamation of the gospel and the outpouring of the Spirit. It is kerygmatic not esoteric, and pneumatological not astral. The receptivity of faith leads to such spiritual knowledge, an essentially relational reality because one has received not the spirit of the world but the Spirit of God and the gifts graciously given by God (1 Cor 2:12). Indeed, it follows from the integral relationship between Christ and the Spirit that Paul identifies what the Spirit reveals (even the "depths of God" [2:10]) with the mind of Christ (2:16).

Christian life and apostolic ministry

If Christian life begins in the Spirit, life in the Spirit is the hallmark of spiritual maturity. As already reviewed under the rubric of "Christ mysticism," Paul integrates life in the Spirit and life in Christ to such an extent that the Christological and pneumatological dimensions of the Christian life are identified. Paul's gospel of redemption translates into a vibrant Christian life, one in which pneumatological awareness increases conformity to Christ. In his testament to salvation and the Christian life in Romans 5–8, Paul moves from the Adam/Christ parallel (Rom 5) to baptism and its implications for holiness as freedom from sin (Rom 6). Following his exposition of the Christian's relation to the law and freedom from it (Rom 7), Paul introduces the pneumatological dimensions of the Christian life (Rom 8):

> For the law of the Spirit of life in Christ Jesus has set me free from the law of sin and death. For God has done what the law, weakened by the flesh, could not do: sending his own Son in the likeness of sinful flesh and for sin, he condemned sin in the flesh, in order that the just requirement of the law might be fulfilled in us, who walk not according to the flesh but according to the Spirit. (Rom 8:2–4)

The efficaciousness of the Spirit's work connects Christology and anthropology. Through Christ, God delivers the Christian from the captivity to sin that even the law could not rectify but, in fact, only intensified (Rom 7:21–23). The Spirit brings new life, even a law of life that counters the "law of sin," which otherwise rules our embodied existence (Rom 7:23). The new pneumatological reality cannot be separated from its Christological tether: it is only by Christ taking on sinful flesh that sin is condemned, while the law's fulfillment becomes possible by a life in the Spirit. So there is an important insight in the "Christ mysticism" tradition of interpretation, perhaps not in terms of its provenance, but in regard to the manner in which soteriology is understood by Paul and its implications for a renewal of Christian life in the church today.

Often debated in contemporary theology is the relationship in soteriology between atonement and life in the Spirit. Does the juridical and sacrificial language of Christ's expiatory death on the cross lend itself to God's transformative work in the believer? Some prefer to dispense with any notion of vicarious satisfaction or substitutionary atonement in accounting for the efficacy of Christ's death for our salvation. Their arguments range from the immorality of the image of God represented in such atonement models (e.g., God having to punish his Son to save us) to the claim that the atonement is depicted as an external transaction that does not affect the interior dispositions of fallen humanity. Related to this discussion are different views of the doctrines of justification and sanctification, both between Catholics and Protestants and within Protestantism itself. What might Paul contribute?

First off, one must be receptive to Paul. As with other conflicts in theology, Paul is represented by some as the source of what is wrong with Christian doctrine, his influence as itself needing correction. Needless to say, that is not the position offered here. However, in regard to the *quaestio disputata* of atonement and pneumatology, Paul does not even envision the problem. On the one hand, God is the one who accomplishes salvation in Christ, a salvation for which Paul utilizes metaphors of substitution, vicariousness, sacrifice, expiation, and juridical declaration (Rom 3:20–26; 5:19; 2 Cor 5:21). On the other hand, Paul understands that transformation proceeds from a process of renewal (Rom 12:2; 2 Cor 5:17) and contemplation (2 Cor 3:18) of the risen Lord. Through baptism one is incorporated into Christ's death (Rom 6:3–4); Paul himself confesses an existential Christomorphic transformation: "I have been crucified with Christ; it is no longer I who live, but Christ who lives in me; and the life I now live in the flesh I live by faith in the Son of God, who loved me and gave himself for me" (Gal 2:20). The same transformation is enunciated in pneumatological and anthropological terms (Rom 8:9–14). Note that because the Spirit of Christ indwells believers, they are already identified with the paschal Christ in death and resurrection – the body dead under the rule of sin, the spirit alive in the righteousness of justification. Only when this point has been established does Paul exhort Christians to live by the Spirit in opposition to the flesh; in effect, to enact in life their own paschal identity (Gal 5:24). For Paul, this becomes a way of life in apostolic mission (2 Cor 4:8–12) and in eschatological hope (Phil 3:7–11).

The Christian life is formed and shaped by Christ's paschal identity in the power of the Spirit. It embraces the imitation of Christ (1 Cor 11:1) and a process of maturation in which Christ's identity is reproduced in the Christian (Gal 4:19) – a process that distinguishes "babes in Christ" from the mature (1 Cor 3:1–3; Phil 3:15), those who do not transcend the opposition of the flesh from those who understand and live out their dependency on the power of God's Spirit (2 Cor 3:4–5; 4:7). Pneumatological agency and eschatological expectation coalesce to situate Paul's doctrine of sanctification and theological anthropology. The Holy Spirit is the guarantee of the inner renewal that perpetuates the Christian life (2 Cor 4:16–5:5) and enables the new creation in Christ (2 Cor 5:17) to exhibit the theological virtues of faith, hope, and love (1 Cor 13) along with the full panoply of the Spirit's fruit (Gal 5:22–23).

Conclusion

Paul's pneumatology never stands on its own. Indeed, he can speak of the Spirit directly and with the confidence of one who knew the Spirit's guidance and agency in his life (Acts 16:6–10). The saving mystery of the Spirit is the mystery of God in Christ and, with that, the mystery of the church as well. It was therefore very Pauline to link the two as emblematic of his gospel and his ministry.

Through him we both have access in one Spirit to the Father. So then you are no longer strangers and sojourners, but you are fellow citizens with the saints and members of the household of God, built upon the foundation of the apostles and prophets, Christ Jesus himself being the cornerstone, in whom the whole structure is joined together and grows into a holy temple in the Lord; in whom you also are built into it for a dwelling place of God in the Spirit. (Eph 2:18–22)

The relationship between ecclesiology and pneumatology is also integrated for Paul. The Spirit constitutes the life of the church and manifests various gifts and ministries in its mission and assemblies. Spiritual gifts and ordered ministries are both representative of the work of the Spirit. If by the agency of the Spirit all are baptized into one body (1 Cor 12:13), then the manifestations of the Spirit from each member serve the common good and instantiate the essential variety that the Body of Christ requires for its own maturation (1 Cor 12:4–11, 14–26; Rom 12:3–8; Eph 4:15–16). Paul therefore integrates the way of love (1 Cor 13) with openness to the Spirit's work and hierarchical order (1 Cor 12:27–31). Since the Holy Spirit is given to pour forth divine love in the heart (Rom 5:5), Paul's efforts to maintain the integrity of tradition (1 Cor 11:23–26) and charismatic spontaneity (1 Cor 14:26–32) along with caritative praxis bespeak the profundity of the gospel he preached. The same efforts serve as a pointer for how churches today might discover the unity they seek.

If Paul, of all the New Testament writers, can be said to be the father of systematic theology, he would never bequeath a legacy that separates understanding of dogma from the reality that it signifies in the transformative work of grace. Paul could boast that he did not receive the grace of God in vain (1 Cor 15:10). But he spoke as one who knew intimately that the experience of grace meant entering into the weakness of the cross as no mere external imitation but as the inner authenticity of apostolic ministry. "For he was crucified in weakness, but lives by the power of God. For we are weak in him, but in dealing with you we shall live with him by the power of God" (2 Cor 13:4). It was the depths of such experience that he sought to impart to his churches (2 Cor 13:14) and for which he labored in sacrificial fashion (Phil 2:17) in order to make of his charge a presentable offering to God, sanctified by the Holy Spirit (Rom 15:16; cf. Col 1:24–29). In this same priestly spirit, doxology is no stranger to this apostle and teacher of the Gentiles (1 Tim 2:7; 2 Tim 1:11; Gal 2:7–9).

For this reason I bow my knees before the Father, from whom every family in heaven and on earth is named, that according to the riches of his glory he may grant you to be strengthened with might through his Spirit in the inner man, and that Christ may dwell in your hearts through faith; that you, being rooted and grounded in love, may have power to comprehend with all the saints what is the breadth and length and height and depth, and to know the love of Christ which surpasses knowledge, that you may be filled with all the fulness of God. Now to him who by the power at work within us is able to do far more abundantly than all that we ask or think, to him be glory in the church and in Christ Jesus to all generations, for ever and ever. Amen. (Eph 3:14–21)

Note

1   Unless otherwise indicated, biblical quotations are taken from the Revised Standard Version.

References

Berkhof, Hendrikus. 1964. *The Doctrine of the Holy Spirit*. Richmond: John Knox.

Bousset, Wilhelm. 1970. *Kyrios Christos: A History of the Belief in Christ from the Beginnings of Christianity to Irenaeus*. Nashville: Abingdon.

Catechism of the Catholic Church. 1995. New York: Doubleday.

Congar, Yves M. J. 1986. *The Word and the Spirit*. London: Geoffrey Chapman.

Deissmann, Adolf. 1972. *Paul: A Study in Social and Religious History*. Gloucester, Mass.: Peter Smith.

Dunn, James D. G. 1989. *Christology in the Making: A New Testament Inquiry into the Origins of the Doctrine of the Incarnation*. Second edition. Grand Rapids: Eerdmans.

Dunn, James D. G. 1998a. *The Christ and the Spirit: Collected Essays of James D. G. Dunn*. Volume 1: *Christology*. Grand Rapids: Eerdmans.

Dunn, James D. G. 1998b. *The Theology of Paul the Apostle*. Grand Rapids: Eerdmans.

Fee, Gordon D. 1994a. Christology and Pneumatology in Romans 8:9–11 – and Elsewhere: Some Reflections on Paul as a Trinitarian. Pages 312–331 in *Jesus of Nazareth: Lord and Christ: Essays on the Historical Jesus and New Testament Christology*. Edited by Joel B. Green and Max Turner. Grand Rapids: Eerdmans.

Fee, Gordon D. 1994b *God's Empowering Presence: The Holy Spirit in the Letters of Paul*. Peabody: Mass.: Hendrickson.

Fee, Gordon D. 2007. *Pauline Christology: An Exegetical-Theological Study*. Peabody, Mass.: Hendrickson.

Hurtado, Larry W. 1979. New Testament Christology: A Critique of Bousset's Influence. *Theological Studies* 40: 306–317.

McGiffert, Arthur Cushman. 1906. *A History of Christianity in the Apostolic Age*. Revised edition. New York: Scribner.

Margerie, Bertrand de. 1982. *The Christian Trinity in History*. Still River, Mass.: St. Bede's.

Montague, George T. 1976. *The Holy Spirit: Growth of a Biblical Tradition*. New York: Paulist.

Schweitzer, Albert. 1931. *The Mysticism of Paul the Apostle*. New York: Henry Holt.

Simpson, A. B. [1896?] *The Holy Spirit or Power from on High: An Unfolding of the Doctrine of the Holy Spirit in the Old and New Testaments*. Part II: *The New Testament*. Harrisburg: Christian.

Thomas Aquinas. 1981. *Summa Theologica*. Volume 1. Translated by Fathers of the English Dominican Province. Notre Dame, Ind.: Christian Classics.

Turner, Max. 1994. The Spirit of Christ and "Divine" Christology. Pages 413–436 in *Jesus of Nazareth: Lord and Christ: Essays on the Historical Jesus and New Testament Christology*. Edited by Joel B. Green and Max Turner. Grand Rapids: Eerdmans.

Weiss, Johannes. 1959. *Earliest Christianity: A History of the Period AD 30–150*. Volume 2. New York: Harper.

CHAPTER 36

Christian Theology: Ethics

Gilbert Meilaender

To examine ways in which the writings of Paul have influenced our understanding of ethics requires that we have at least a provisional understanding of what we mean by ethics. It must be provisional, of course, for we may conclude that taking Paul seriously will reshape what we thought we knew about ethics. Still, we need a structure to guide our thought.

Imagine human beings, C. S. Lewis once wrote, as "a fleet of ships sailing in formation." What will be needed for the voyage to be a success? First, the ships must not collide with each other. Second, each ship must be "seaworthy," in good mechanical condition. And, third, the fleet must have a goal, a destination it aims to reach. "Morality, then, seems to be concerned with three things. Firstly, with fair play and harmony between individuals. Secondly, with what might be called tidying up or harmonizing the things inside each individual. Thirdly, with the general purpose of human life as a whole" (Lewis 1960, 70–71).

Lewis's engaging, if homely, example can be dressed up in the more sophisticated language of theological (and philosophical) ethics. Thus, James Gustafson suggests that the questions important for ethical reflection deal with the good (What powers and beings are good for human beings and are the source of human flourishing?), with criteria for judgment and action (To what principles do I look for guidance about what I ought to do?), and with the moral self (How is my judgment about what I ought to do shaped by the person I am?) (Gustafson 1968, 1–4). Gustafson's categories were themselves influenced by H. Richard Niebuhr's (1963) threefold characterization of (1) man-the-maker (who aims in action at what is good and asks, What is the goal or telos?); (2) man-the-citizen (who aims in action at what is right and asks, What is the

The Blackwell Companion to Paul, First Edition. Edited by Stephen Westerholm.
© 2011 Blackwell Publishing Ltd. Published 2011 by Blackwell Publishing Ltd.

law that governs my life?); and (3) man-the-answerer (who aims in action at what is fitting and asks, What is going on and to what am I responsible?).

We may say, then, that ethical reflection focuses on both our doing and our being. It probes what is good for human beings, what we must do to flourish and be fulfilled. It inquires after what constitutes right action, seeking to clarify our duties and obligations. And, concerned not only with what we should do but also with the sort of persons we should be, it seeks to depict the traits that make a person good (or bad). Hence, the basic shape of an ethic may be teleological (focused on the good to be realized in action), deontological (focused on the right action we ought to do), or agent-centered (focused on the virtues we seek to cultivate and the vices we want to discourage). If, then, we think about the legacy of Paul for ethical reflection, it may be useful to think in these terms.

Teleological Ethics

When, in the opening chapters of Book 19 of the *City of God*, Augustine outlines the schema of Marcus Varro, according to which there are 288 possible theories of the good life – and rejects them all – it marks, Peter Brown writes, "the end of classical thought" (Brown 1995, 26). Classical ethics had been teleological in character, searching for the good life – Aristotle's *eudaimonia* – that all human beings seek. Augustine by no means renounces the quest for happiness; he simply notes that "all these philosophers have wished, with amazing folly, to be happy here on earth and to achieve bliss by their own efforts" (*City of God* 19.4). Who would dare, Augustine wonders, to call this mortal life, marked by ills of various kinds and ruled seemingly by chance, the good or happy life? We can seek happiness in the good things that attract us here and now, but they will never satisfy the heart's longing for goodness. Alternatively, and preferably, we can redirect our longing to the God who can actually satisfy it, but our heart cannot rest fully in him here and now. Thus, as Augustine puts it unforgettably in the *Confessions*, "Here I have the power but not the wish to stay; there I wish to be but cannot; both ways, miserable" (10.40).

Therefore, however true it may be to say that believers live in Christ, they also live in hope, awaiting a future salvation. "As, therefore, we are saved in hope," Augustine writes, "it is in hope that we have been made happy; and as we do not yet possess a present salvation, but await salvation in the future, so we do not enjoy a present happiness, but look forward to happiness in the future, and we look forward 'with steadfast endurance'" (*City of God* 19.4). We see here the fruits of Augustine's prolonged study of the writings of Paul. In the same immediate context in Book 19.4 of *City of God*, he cites Romans 8:24–25. He might equally well have cited Romans 5. There, Paul writes that even the justified who have peace with God through Christ live for now in hope – in the "hope of sharing the glory of God" (Rom 5:2).[1] To be justified by the blood of Christ and reconciled to God by his death is not to be saved. That remains for Paul – and for Augustine, who learned it from him – the future God promises. "For if while we were enemies we were reconciled to God by the death of his Son, much more, now that we are reconciled, shall we be saved by his life" (Rom 5:10).

This reservation of salvation to the future, though by no means uncomplicated, is a consistent feature of Paul's teaching. It is "the hope of salvation" that the believer puts on as a helmet (1 Thess 5:8). Being united now with Christ in his death means that one will in the future share in a resurrection like his (Rom 6:5). To be sure, if the risen Christ is the power of salvation, that salvation must also be somehow present (2 Cor 5:17); yet it is present "in hope" (Rom 8:24). The two ages touch – and intermingle? – in the lives of believers "who are being saved" by the power of God (1 Cor 1:18).

Whatever the complexities of Paul's view, the picture of a creation subjected to futility, groaning in travail, and waiting with eager longing for a fulfillment never fully given in this life had a decisive effect on Christian ethics, with Augustine as the first case in point. That "end of classical thought" discerned by Peter Brown meant, in effect, that Christian ethics could not be simply or even primarily teleological. "There are," as Paul Ramsey put it, "two chief questions in ethics: *What* is the good? and *Whose* good shall it be when choice must be made between mine and thine?" (1950, 114). The second of these, Ramsey wrote, in what may be an overstatement but nonetheless captures an important emphasis, "is the main, perhaps the only, concern of Christian ethics" (114–115).

This is true even for a Christian who, like Augustine, continues to place teleological categories (such as the longing to rest in God) at the center of his theological reflection. As strongly as he felt the pull of desire and was steeped in the classical tradition that emphasized it, he knew just as strongly the claims of duty (or, to put it less impersonally and more biblically, of God as giver of the moral law).

The resulting tension between desire and duty can be resolved – or, at least, understood – with a scheme Alasdair MacIntyre offered in *After Virtue* for making sense of our moral principles. The scheme involves what we might call the descriptive, the attractive, and the imperative. Between a *description* of our human nature as it is in its "untutored" state and the good that *attracts* us (our nature perfected) there is a gap filled by the *imperative*. "The precepts which enjoin the various virtues and prohibit the vices which are their counterparts instruct us ... how to realize our true nature and to reach our true end" (MacIntyre 1981, 50). Thus, a teleological framework is still needed to make sense of our duties, for the imperative describes what is needed to begin to move from the persons we are to the good which, though we may in some ways resist, draws us.

Instructive as MacIntyre's threefold scheme is, and helpful as it is for seeing the continuing place of teleological considerations in Christian ethics, it does not fully capture the significance of duty in a world in which any full realization of the good is present only "in hope." As MacIntyre himself once wrote in a different context, "Any account of morality which does not allow for the fact that my death may be required of me at any moment is thereby an inadequate account" (1977, 26–27). Drawing a conclusion about ethical theory from the same possibility, Pope John Paul II wrote that the "unacceptability" of teleological ethical theories "is confirmed in a particularly eloquent way by Christian martyrdom" (1993, 112, §90).

None of this means that Christians are not to desire and long for God, the only end of human life that can truly fulfill and perfect our created nature. Paul himself expresses the desire "to depart and be with Christ" (Phil 1:23). Along the way to that end, however, believers must "fight the good fight of the faith" (1 Tim 6:12), trusting that on the day of the Lord's appearing – though not before that day – they will receive the "crown of righteousness" (2 Tim 4:8). The full realization of the promised good comes when the God who "began a good work" in those who are in Christ brings it "to completion at the day of Jesus Christ" (Phil 1:6). The classical quest for the good life can no longer be the organizing principle of the moral life.

Deontological Ethics

Life in Christ is, therefore, more a matter of what one does than what one accomplishes, more a matter of acting rightly than realizing goals. When we think about what constitutes right action, we generally look for laws or rules as action-guides, and this draws us immediately into some of the most complicated issues in Paul's writings. Paul was, of course, a Jew – indeed, "a Hebrew born of Hebrews; as to the law a Pharisee" (Phil 3:5) – and it would be surprising if he did not at all think about the moral life in categories of law and obligation. Nevertheless, the new thing God had done in Jesus forced Paul to re-examine and reshape the idea of obligation in ways that have seemed, at least to some, to eliminate entirely such a notion from the Christian life.

How difficult it is really to carry out that elimination may be demonstrated, however, if we look briefly at Luther's famous treatise on "The Freedom of a Christian." The apparent outline of the argument is given by Luther at the outset in two succinct propositions, which surely grow from his reading of Paul: (1) A Christian is a perfectly free lord of all, subject to none. (2) A Christian is a perfectly dutiful servant of all, subject to all.

Among those lords to whom the Christian is no longer subject is the "law," and Paul can sometimes characterize that freedom in very strong terms – for example, "Christ is the end of the law, that every one who has faith may be justified" (Rom 10:4). When Paul writes thus of the law, he may – indeed, probably does – have in mind the set of obligations laid upon Israel in the Torah. (So, e.g., Paul writes in Romans 2:14 that the Gentiles do not have the "law," though they evidently do, according to v. 15, have at least some requirements of the "law" written on their hearts.) By contrast, when Luther thinks of Christians as free from the law's governance, he seems to mean by "law" any divine requirement, any obligation that must be met before a person can be right with God. "It is clear, then, that a Christian has all that he needs in faith and needs no works to justify him; and if he has no need of works, he has no need of the law; and if he has no need of the law, surely he is free from the law" (Luther 1957, 349). The faith that justifies "cannot exist in connection with works," for an attempt to stand before God on that basis is incompatible with a faith that simply hears and believes the divine promise of grace (346.).

There is, however, a new kind of obligation that is laid upon the believer: "Now you are light in the Lord; walk as children of light" (Eph 5:8). Or, more directly still, Paul writes in Galatians 5:13–14: "For you were called to freedom, brethren; only do not use your freedom as an opportunity for the flesh, but through love be servants of one another. For the whole law is fulfilled in one word, 'You shall love your neighbor as yourself.'" Indeed, the aim of Paul's gospel is "to bring about the obedience of faith" among all peoples (Rom 1:5; 16:26). Hence, Luther is certainly picking up a characteristically Pauline theme when he asserts that the Christian who has been set free of all lords is a dutiful servant of each neighbor set before him, obligated to serve that neighbor in love.

Still, that service to neighbors, though supposedly a matter of obedience and even obligation, often seems in Luther's depiction to flow automatically and spontaneously from one who in faith has been set free from all attempts to please God through "works of law." "From faith thus flow forth love and joy in the Lord, and from love a joyful, willing, and free mind that serves one's neighbor willingly" (Luther 1957, 367). This, of course, is no longer the language of obedience or obligation, but of freedom – a freedom that "makes our hearts free from all sins, laws and commands, as Paul says, I Tim. 1 [:9], 'The law is not laid down for the just'" (371).

What is most striking and instructive about Luther's attempt to make sense of the Pauline language of faith, freedom, and indebtedness to the neighbor is this: Luther cannot consistently adhere to the seemingly straightforward outline of his treatise. After Luther has expounded at length the Christian's freedom from all lords who would claim an obedience based on works of law, his readers naturally expect him to turn at once to the second half of his claim – to describe how Christians, who have been set free, hasten with glad and willing hearts to serve the needs of their neighbors.

But he does not. Instead, Luther begins the second half of the treatise with a discussion that seems, at best, unnecessary and, at worst, antithetical to his argument – a discussion for which the simplicity of the outline has in no way prepared his readers. In this life, Luther says, a person must learn to control himself, hoping to attain what Paul (in Rom 8:23) calls "the first fruits of the Spirit." The believer must "take care to discipline his body by fastings, watchings, labors, and other reasonable discipline and to subject it to the Spirit so that it will obey" (358). With " joyful zeal" he attempts to get the sinful passions under control. Thus, instead of a spontaneous leap to the neighbor's side by one set free from the law's requirements, we are given first what must be said – or so Luther apparently thinks – even if it breaks the simplicity of the treatise's declared structure: namely, a call to discipline the sinful self.

Before the treatise is finished, Luther does return to the simplicity of his original outline. "We conclude, therefore, that a Christian lives not in himself, but in Christ and in his neighbor ... He lives in Christ through faith, in his neighbor through love" (371). But the complications that compel Luther at places to go beyond his outline have marked the course of Christian ethical reflection. At times, Christians have moved away from the language of rules (and attempts to characterize the kind of actions that ought or ought not be done) to the language of character, a move we will consider later. But there are at least two other ways in which these complications, and the need to make place for moral law, have been significant for Christian ethics. If neither can be treated fully here, they must at least be noted.

In the well-known words of Romans 2:14–15, Paul writes that the Gentiles, to whom the Torah has not been given, often do what the moral law requires, showing thereby that this law "is written on their hearts." Whatever exactly Paul may mean by this, it does seem to express a knowledge of at least some basic tier of moral requirements – a knowledge that has not been given by means of a special revelation (such as that through Moses to Israel). And, in the most general sense, that sort of knowledge is what has been meant by the concept of natural law. It refers to moral knowledge available to us through the use of our powers of reason and which articulates standards of behavior or conditions of association that apply to all human beings and societies (past, present, and future). To the degree that these standards and conditions are met and adhered to, human beings and their societies will flourish.

Christian theories of natural law have often been thought to be the special concern of Roman Catholic moral theology, and there is no doubt that Catholics have given detailed attention to the idea. Indeed, questions 90–97 of the *Prima Secundae* of Thomas Aquinas's *Summa theologiae* have often circulated and been read as a separate "Treatise on Law" (Kossel 2002, 169). This may be unfortunate, however, especially for theological ethics, because it easily loses sight of the fact that for Thomas the natural law is not free-standing but participates in the eternal law in the mind of God. From that perspective, the "nature" that is normative for moral reasoning will be understood in a richer theological context, though the price of doing so will be diminished confidence in the power of reason to discern the requirements of natural law.

If this concept of natural law is not entirely in harmony with Paul's normal use of *nomos* to refer to the Torah given Israel (a law including prescriptions of different sorts that we would likely characterize in various ways as moral, political, and cultic), we should not make too much of that lexicographical point. At the conceptual rather than the lexicographical level, Paul does seem to think both that the "law" has been given to Israel *and* that aspects of that law (the sort we would call moral) are binding on all human beings, who are, therefore, "without excuse" (Rom 1:20). Seeing this, we should not be surprised if other Christians besides Roman Catholics use concepts that are at least kin to notions of natural law – such as the Reformers' notions of a "political" use of the law, or of common grace. Indeed, in Calvin's carefully worked-out system of Christian teaching, it is possible to discern the outlines of what may fairly be called a Christian theory of natural law (Little 1968, 175–197).

The larger problem for theories of natural law is that, as I noted above, they attempt to give content to the meaning of human flourishing. If that is done in the way that detaches Thomas's "Treatise on Law" from the larger context of the *Summa*, it may invite us to think of human flourishing in a way that is less than a perfect fit with Pauline theology. Christians are "to grow up in every way ... into Christ" (Eph 4:15), whose fullness is the measure of human maturity and flourishing (Eph 4:13; Col 1:28). They are to be "rooted and built up" in Christ (Col 2:7). Passages such as these help us understand why Christian ethics has always struggled to do justice both to continuity between the grace revealed in Christ and the nature that grace redeems and perfects, and to discontinuity between that grace and any merely natural understanding of human flourishing.

A second angle from which Paul's treatment of law has been important, but also problematic, for Christian ethics involves the question of the continuing significance of the law in the lives of the baptized. Christians, Paul writes in Romans 6:14, "are not under law but under grace." Nevertheless, "the unrighteous [and here this certainly means those who violate the moral law] will not inherit the kingdom of God" (I Cor 6:9). Christians are to lead lives "worthy of the Lord, fully pleasing to him, bearing fruit in every good work" and being "zealous for good deeds" (Col 1:10; Tit 2:14).

The complications of Paul's thoughts on this tangled question may be better explored through consideration of a larger portion of one of his letters than through setting a few passages side by side. If we examine Galatians 2:16–4:31, in which Paul sets forth his understanding of law and faith, it is apparent that two somewhat different understandings are at work.

In 2:16–3:12, where "gospel" is the overarching category, Paul refers almost always not to "law" but to "works of law," and to "faith" as an individual person's subjective trust. In these verses, in fact, works of law and faith, treated almost ahistorically, are two (different) possible bases for an individual's relation to God. At any moment in history a person stands before God either in faith or relying on works of law. Thus, Paul does not say that God "promised" something to Abraham, but that the gospel was preached beforehand to him. The time of faith and the time of law take place not within history but existentially, within the individual who stands in every moment before God. Thus, it is "works of law" rather than the "law" itself that is here antithetical to faith. It is not the law, but reliance on works of law, that has no place in the life of the believer.

By contrast, in 3:13–4:31, "promise" becomes the overarching category – a category which divides the time of law from the time of faith. The emphasis now is upon (not "works of law," but) "law" as a power whose domain is, chronologically, a strictly limited one. And in these verses faith, or the time of faith, is less subjective trust than an objective fact – the time when faith came (3:23) being equated with the time when Christ came (3:24). On this view, we should note, the time of law and the time of faith/Christ cannot coincide in a person's life – a quite striking difference from the first way of thinking, according to which reliance on works of law (not the law itself) is incompatible with faith.

Moreover, there are hints in Galatians that the simple binary opposites established in each of these ways of thinking cannot be allowed to have the last word. Thus, a reader who has imbibed the tension between faith and works of law must be struck to read in 5:6 that what avails before God is "faith *working* through love." Faith and "working" are brought together. Likewise, a reader who has set the time of law and the time of faith/Christ over against each other must be taken aback when urged in 6:2 to "fulfill the law of Christ." The two times are not simply opposed.

No wonder, then, that Christians have often been puzzled and have disagreed about the continuing significance of the moral law in the life of believers – or, to be more precise, its continuing pedagogical significance. The Reformers, coming to terms with their reading of Paul, distinguished several different "uses" of the law. Relatively uncontroversial was the "political" use, according to which the law's basic requirements served, through the instrument of civil government, to make possible the cooperation needed for social life. Also generally accepted was a "theological" use, which served to work in hearts a consciousness of sin and guilt. But the third use – a pedagogical use, whereby the law was said to provide continuing guidance to believers for how they ought to live – was more controversial and harder to characterize precisely.

Complications and difficulties are not surprising, given the ambiguities I have noted in Paul's various formulations. We can use Helmut Thielicke's richly Lutheran theological ethic to illustrate them. Despite reading Paul's teaching of freedom from the law as meaning that "in the obedience of faith we may follow paths that are contrary to the letter of the Law" (1966, 88), Thielicke cannot deny the law's teaching a place – a continuing pedagogical significance – in the lives of Christians. The Christian life has a "quantitative" aspect, marked by advance or growth in spiritual maturity (126). This requires a complex understanding of the *simul justus et peccator* formula. As one who is *justus*, a Christian looks away from himself to the God who justifies in Christ. As one who is *peccator*, a Christian looks at himself as he is in himself, abstracted from union with Christ. But there is also, Thielicke writes, a "third perspective" from which one looks back at oneself, but now at oneself "as standing before the justifying God ... in constant relationship to him" (128). From the angle of this believing look back at oneself, the law can provide guidance without driving one to despair. "The Christian life is a pilgrimage," and to do justice to the nature of that journey – and justice to the writings of Paul – Thielicke, for all his emphasis on Christian freedom, is forced to make place for the law's continuing pedagogical significance (132).

In doing so, he keeps faith with the basic thrust of Paul's writings. Romans begins (1:5) and ends (16:26) with "the obedience of faith." Although neither circumcision nor uncircumcision counts for anything, Paul writes in I Corinthians, what does count is "keeping the commandments of God" (7:19). The Philippians, who are to work out their salvation with fear and trembling, are to seek to be "blameless and innocent, children of God without blemish" (2:15; cf. v.12), as the Colossians are to "lead a life worthy of the Lord ... bearing fruit in every good work" (1:10). The grace of God has appeared, as the letter to Titus puts it, to teach us "to live sober, upright, and godly lives in this world" (2:12). There can be no doubt that the gospel arrives accompanied by obligations (Rom 10:16; 2 Thess 1:8; Gal 6:2; I Cor 9:21), the content of which cannot be unrelated to the law that enunciates the will of God as it is embedded in the structure of the creation.

Because of the complexities and ambiguities in Paul's use of the language of law, we may prefer to speak of evangelical imperatives rather than a pedagogical use of the law, or we may follow Paul Althaus in distinguishing the original life-giving *command* of God from the life-restricting law of God that presupposes always the context of human sin (Althaus 1966, 14). These are ways of seeking to do justice to Paul's most characteristic language about divine law while also honoring the countless ways in which his writings assume and teach that the Christian life will have a structure and form governed by the will of God. Perhaps even better, we might say, with Karl Barth, that the law cannot be the law of the gracious God revealed in Christ unless it is "hidden and enclosed in the ark of the *covenant*" – unless, that is, we hear a promise embedded in the command, "You shall be holy" (Barth 1968, 71). Hence Augustine's prayer in Book 10 of the *Confessions* that God give what he commands – and then command what he will (10.29). And that is, after all, what Titus 2:11–12 says: "The grace of God has appeared ... training us ... to live sober, upright, and godly lives in this world."

Agent-centered (Virtue) Ethics

Life in Christ is more than doing, however. It is also a way of being that is focused as much on the person as the deed. Thus, Paul tells the Corinthians that they are his "letter of recommendation ... written not with ink but with the Spirit of the living God, not on tablets of stone but on tablets of human hearts" (2 Cor 3:2–3). Believers are "to grow up in every way into him who is the head, into Christ" (Eph 4:15). The three virtues that came in the tradition to be designated as the greatest "theological virtues" – faith, hope, and love – already form a triad in Paul's writing (I Cor 13:13; I Thess 1:3; 5:8).

An ethic centered on characteristics of agents rather than actions has most often used the language of virtue and vice (rather than the language of right and wrong). This approach to ethics experienced a strong resurgence among both philosophers and theologians in the last quarter of the twentieth century. The publication in 1981 of Alasdair MacIntyre's *After Virtue* was perhaps the strongest influence on this renewed attention, and the work of Stanley Hauerwas in theological ethics has been equally influential in shaping interest in virtue ethics. An ethic that focuses on the person rather than the work is likely to be of interest to Christian thinkers for several obvious reasons. Less likely to focus largely on the hard cases life presents, a virtue ethic will attend to the continuities of life – traits of character developed over time and (relatively) stable over time. It is also likely to focus on spiritual disciplines – prayer, confession, ascetic practices, praise, and adoration – that help us make us the persons we are.

Although the focus on virtue in late twentieth-century Christian ethics in the West seemed like something new, and was new in that setting, it is not a new motif in Christian thinking about the moral life. Indeed, it "emerged early in Christian ethics, and has flourished more or less continuously ever since" (Porter 2005, 206). Augustine depicted traits of character as determined by the final object of our love. Thus, to those for whom pleasure was the highest good (he had in mind Epicureans), a virtue such as prudence would take whatever steps were needed to ensure the enjoyment of pleasure. Likewise, courage would help one bear present sufferings by recalling earlier delights (*City of God* 5.20). Christian ethics did not, in his mind, cease to think in terms of the cardinal virtues; it simply redefined them in service of love for God. Prudence determines what will help and what will hinder one's progress toward God. Courage helps one to bear all difficulties and risk all dangers for the sake of faithfulness to God. Thus, the virtues are drawn into life in Christ and are reshaped and transformed, becoming Christian virtues. They remain imperfectly developed in this life, of course, but they set believers on a path that will one day eventuate in a life of perfect praise of God. Such virtue is not simply a human achievement, however, but is the work of grace. "The reward of virtue will be God himself, who gave the virtue" (*City of God* 22.30). "There we shall be still and see; we shall see and we shall love; we shall love and we shall praise" (*City of God* 22.30).

In greater detail Thomas Aquinas develops both a general theory of virtues and vices in the *Summa theologiae* (especially I–II, qq.49–89) – and then, in lavish detail, a discussion of the cardinal and theological virtues in *Summa theologiae* II–II. Thomas might seem less indebted than Augustine to Pauline theology. It is true, after all, that his work is deeply influenced by and appropriates in many respects Aristotle's ethic of virtue. Nonetheless, Thomas knows that the natural virtues must for Christians be brought into the new life empowered and shaped by grace. How precisely he accomplishes this is likely to remain a matter for discussion and argument among scholars. H. Richard Niebuhr influentially depicted Thomas's solution as a "Christ above culture" (or grace above nature) system (1951, 116–148). The natural virtues develop some aspect of what is good for human beings, as reason discerns that good. But even the highest pos-sible development of natural virtue remains inadequate, for it is the theological virtues that direct us toward God. If one thinks, as Niebuhr did, of these two kinds or levels of virtue as somewhat separate from each other, a person who lacked the theological virtues of faith, hope, and love toward God could still manifest the natural virtues at their best. Failure to direct one's love toward God would mean that the moral life was incomplete, but not that, at the purely natural level, it was distorted or less than virtu-ous. Although this has been a common way of reading Thomas, it may not do justice to the complexities of his thought, complexities which, taken seriously, may lead to a more holistic – more Augustinian, and perhaps we may add, more Pauline – vision, for which moral and spiritual life interpenetrate and no part of the moral life can be sepa-rated from the person's relation to God (Herdt 2008, 76).

Despite this long history, we should not think of virtue ethics as the preserve of Roman Catholic moral theology alone. It has played a substantial role in many streams of Protestant ethics, though the language of holiness may be more prominent there than that of virtue. Thus, among John Wesley's Sermons is one on "The Circumcision of the Heart," taking as its text Romans 2:29: "Circumcision is that of the heart, in the spirit, and not in the letter." Circumcision of the heart is "that habitual disposition of soul which, in the sacred writings, is termed holiness." It "implies humility, faith, hope and charity" (Wesley 1872). Likewise, his sermon on "The Marks of the New Birth" discusses in detail faith, hope, and love. If the language is not precisely that of virtue theory, the moral outlook is nonetheless deeply agent-centered and grows in consider-able measure out of Wesley's reading of Paul.

Charles Wesley expressed that desire for a new birth that would culminate in holi-ness in hymns such as "Love Divine, All Loves Excelling." Its thought and imagery grow out of Paul's contrast in 2 Corinthians 3 between the dispensation of Moses and that of the Spirit of Christ. Moses, having entered into God's presence, veiled his face, which shone with the divine glory, whenever he went back among the Israelites. Even so, Paul says, a veil still lies over the mind when the old covenant given to Moses is read. But for one drawn into the life of the Spirit, that veil is lifted: "And we all, with unveiled face, beholding the glory of the Lord, are being changed into his likeness from one degree of glory to another" (2 Cor 3:18). That this might happen is the prayer of Charles Wesley's hymn: "Finish then thy new creation, / Pure and spotless let us be; / Let us see thy great salvation / Perfectly restored in thee; / Changed from glory into glory." If, as Josef Pieper put it, the virtues are those excellences that enable a human being "to attain the fur-thest potentialities of his nature," then Charles Wesley has given here a powerful expression of such a virtue ethic (Pieper 1966, xii).

Thus, a focus on development of Christian character – "grow[ing] up in every way" into "the stature of the fullness of Christ" (Eph 4:15, 13) – may come quite readily to those influenced by the Pauline writings. Nevertheless, those writings also present chal-lenges to any agent-centered ethics, two of which can be briefly noted here.

Virtuous habits of behavior, when truly habitual, point to reliable continuities in a person's character. Thus, we can depend on the just person to act justly, at least most of the time. The development of such character traits generally requires a discipline of the self; hence, we say that one "cultivates" the virtues. This suggests, however, an attention to the self and, at some point, a kind of confidence in the virtues as one's possession – all of which fits rather uneasily with the thought of Paul, who, though he claims to have as much reason as anyone else for "confidence in the flesh," places his confidence instead in Christ, desiring to be "found in him" (Phil 3:4, 9). To the degree that Christians speak of virtue developed and possessed as theirs, it must be possessed in hope, by those who know themselves to be still on the way. Thus Paul: "Not that I have already obtained this or am already perfect; but I press on to make it my own, because Christ Jesus has made me his own" (Phil 3:12). It is "Christ in you" who is "the hope of glory" (Col 1:27).

This points to the still deeper issue, in some ways the chief legacy of Paul for Christian ethics, and one which has been especially prominent at least since the Reformation of the sixteenth century. From one angle, the life of the believer involves growth, becoming "more and more" (I Thess 4:10) conformed to the image of Christ, growing up "in every way into him who is the head, into Christ" (Eph 4:15). The new nature given by the Spirit of Christ is regularly "being renewed" (Col 3:10) as faith grows and love increases (2 Thess 1:3).

But from another equally Pauline angle, the life of the believer is less one of progress ("more and more") than of constant return ("again and again") to the promise of the gospel. For the new life that has been given is "hid with Christ in God" (Col 3:3). For Paul's theology of exchange believers are virtuous simply because, even while still sinful, they are covered with Christ's virtue. "For you know the grace of our Lord Jesus Christ, that though he was rich, yet for your sake he became poor, so that by his poverty you might become rich" (2 Cor 8:9). "Who then," Luther writes, "can fully appreciate what this royal marriage means? ... Here this rich and divine bridegroom Christ marries this poor, wicked harlot, redeems her from all her evil, and adorns her with all his goodness. Her sins cannot now destroy her, since they are laid upon Christ and swallowed up by him. And she has that righteousness in Christ, her husband, of which she may boast as of her own and which she can confidently display alongside her sins" (Luther 1957, 352).

"It is not easy," Niebuhr wrote, "to express both these two aspects of the life of grace" (1943, 124). In Paul's writings, grace is both pardon for sin and power to grow toward maturity in Christ. If we emphasize the pardon, the need to return "again and again" to the promise of forgiveness, we must also find a way to make clear that something genuinely new has happened, that "sin will have no dominion" (Rom 6:14) over those who are in Christ. If we emphasize the power to live "more and more" as the Spirit of Christ leads, we must also find a way to join in Paul's renunciation of "boasting" (Rom 3:27) and to say that "forgiveness is as necessary at the end as at the beginning of the Christian life" (Niebuhr 1943, 105). Karl Barth's doctrine of reconciliation in volume IV of his *Church Dogmatics* – for which justification and sanctification provide two angles from which to describe the one gracious work of God in Christ reconciling the world to himself – seeks quite persuasively to give full expression to both aspects of grace.

Life "in Christ"

A good bit of the legacy of Paul for Christian ethics can be captured by looking from these three theoretical angles – what is good, what is right, and what is virtuous – that give shape to ethics. Nevertheless, we should be cautious about interposing any theory between believers and their Lord, as if getting the theory right could in itself offer assurance. Life in Christ is moved by and is answerable to a person, not a theory. With good reason, therefore, Paul could urge the Philippians to "work out your own salvation with fear and trembling; for God is at work in you" (Phil 2:12–13).

"Faith is just this paradox," Kierkegaard writes, "that the single individual ... is higher than the universal" (1985, 84). Kierkegaard's famous "teleological suspension of the ethical" captures something quite Pauline: that our standing before God cannot be mediated through any universal moral requirement. In this sense, "the single individual" *is* "higher than the universal." It is no accident that Abraham, who figures so prominently in Romans, is, for Kierkegaard, the knight of faith. This faith embodies grace as both pardon and power. It is "the highest passion in a human being," to which one must constantly return and "further" than which one cannot go. And yet, it is also true that "anyone who comes to faith ... won't remain at a standstill there" (Kierkegaard 1985, 146).

Note

1   Biblical quotations are taken from the Revised Standard Version.

References

Althaus, Paul. 1966. *The Divine Command: A New Perspective on Law and Gospel*. Philadelphia: Fortress.

Augustine. 1963. *The Confessions of St. Augustine*. Translated by Rex Warner. New York: Mentor-Omega.

Augustine. 1984. *Concerning the City of God Against the Pagans*. Translated by Henry Bettenson. New York: Penguin.

Barth, Karl. 1956. *Church Dogmatics*. Volume 4: *The Doctrine of Reconciliation*. Part 1. Edinburgh: T. & T. Clark.

Barth, Karl. 1968. *Community, State, and Church: Three Essays*. Gloucester, Mass.: Peter Smith.

Brown, P. R. L. 1995. Saint Augustine and Political Society. Pages 17–35 in *The City of God: A Collection of Critical Essays*. Edited by Dorothy F. Donnelly. New York: Peter Lang.

Gustafson, James M. 1968. *Christ and the Moral Life*. New York: Harper & Row.

Herdt, Jennifer. 2008. *Putting on Virtue: The Legacy of the Splendid Vices*. Chicago: University of Chicago Press.

John Paul II. 1993. *The Splendor of Truth [Veritatis Splendor]*. Boston: St. Paul Books & Media.

Kierkegaard, Søren. 1985. *Fear and Trembling: Dialectical Lyric by Johannes de Silentio*. New York: Penguin.

Kossel, Clifford G. 2002. Natural Law and Human Law (Ia IIae, qq.90–97). Pages 169–193 in *The Ethics of Aquinas*. Edited by Stephen J. Pope. Washington, DC: Georgetown University Press.

Lewis, C. S. 1960. *Mere Christianity*. New York: Macmillan.

Little, David. 1968. Calvin and the Prospects for a Christian Theory of Natural Law. Pages 175–197 in *Norm and Context in Christian Ethics*. Edited by Gene H. Outka and Paul Ramsey. New York: Charles Scribner's Sons.

Luther, Martin. 1957. The Freedom of a Christian. Pages 327–377 in *Luther's Works*, volume 31, *Career of the Reformer: I*. Edited by Harold J. Grimm. Philadelphia: Muhlenberg.

MacIntyre, Alasdair. 1977. Can Medicine Dispense with a Theological Perspective on Human Nature? Pages 25–43 in *Knowledge, Value, and Belief*. Edited by H. Tristram Engelhardt, Jr. and Daniel Callahan. Hastings-on-Hudson: Institute of Society, Ethics and the Life Sciences.

MacIntyre, Alasdair. 1981. *After Virtue: A Study in Moral Theory*. Notre Dame, Ind.: University of Notre Dame Press.

Niebuhr, H. Richard. 1951. *Christ and Culture*. New York: Harper & Row.

Niebuhr, H. Richard. 1963. *The Responsible Self: An Essay in Christian Moral Philosophy*. New York: Harper & Row.

Niebuhr, Reinhold. 1943. *The Nature and Destiny of Man*. Vol. II: *Human Destiny*. New York: Charles Scribner's Sons.

Pieper, Josef. 1966. *The Four Cardinal Virtues: Prudence, Justice, Fortitude, Temperance*. Notre Dame, Ind.: University of Notre Dame Press.

Porter, Jean. 2005. Virtue. Pages 205–219 in *The Oxford Handbook of Theological Ethics*. Edited by Gilbert Meilaender and William Werpehowski. Oxford: Oxford University Press.

Ramsey, Paul. 1950. *Basic Christian Ethics*. New York: Charles Scribner's Sons.

Thielicke, Helmut. 1966. *Theological Ethics*. Volume 1: *Foundations*. Edited by William H. Lazareth. Philadelphia: Fortress.

Wesley, John. 1872. *The Standard Sermons*. Edited by Thomas Jackson (available at http://wesley.nnu.edu/john_wesley/sermons/standards.htm).

CHAPTER 37

Christian Theology: The Church

Nicholas M. Healy

While the gospels and other non-Pauline writings of the New Testament have obviously contributed much to the church's theological self-understanding, the tradition of ecclesiological inquiry has drawn upon the letters of Paul at least as much,[1] perhaps considerably more, both directly and as hermeneutical keys to other parts of Scripture. Paul's remarks about the Christian community and its relation to God – everything from a brief comment to more extended discussions – have guided ecclesiological inquiry in all branches of Christianity, and continue to do so. Whether or not Paul himself had a clear and well-rounded understanding of the nature and function of the church, or the Pauline tradition reflected in the letters displays a more or less consistent line of development, the churches of the second and subsequent centuries have generally been clear in their desire to align their ecclesiologies with Paul's texts. Yet these ecclesiologies are not simply Pauline, whatever we might take that to mean. While they are informed, often deeply, by what they take to be Paul's understanding of Christianity and his ecclesiological principles and insights, they have modified these to a greater or lesser degree so as to address the issues and concerns of their time and place. As a consequence, the Pauline texts have been used to support a wide range of ecclesiologies, some of which are far from how we might think those texts were originally understood.

We can distinguish two ways in which Paul influenced subsequent ecclesiological inquiry. One is through his broader conception of Christianity, found in his teaching about Jesus Christ, the Holy Spirit, justification, grace, election, Israel, and so on. The other is through the more specific remarks about the church, particularly the images,

The Blackwell Companion to Paul, First Edition. Edited by Stephen Westerholm.

concepts, practices, and cultural assumptions that can be found throughout the letters. Since the first way has been covered by earlier chapters, and would anyway take far too much space to treat properly in reference to ecclesiology, the focus here is on the second. It should be noted well that the aim cannot be to give a complete account of any particular ecclesiology, still less a complete account of the ecclesiological tradition in reference to Paul. Rather, this chapter indicates some of the more significant ways Paul has influenced those theologians who themselves have been particularly influential for the later tradition.

Paul's Ecclesiological Motifs

Ecclesiology has drawn upon at least five motifs that can be found in Paul's writings about the church. (There are others, to be sure, but we can note how they are used in specific cases.) The first and perhaps most significant is Paul's metaphor – or, for some later theologians, something more than a metaphor – of the church as the Body of Christ (e.g., 1 Cor 12:27; Eph 4:4, 12; Col 1:18). The head-and-body metaphor is expanded in Paul and often in later use by the corollary notion of the "many members" of the "one body" (e.g., Rom 12:4, 5). A not dissimilar parallel metaphor describes the relation of Christ and the church as a married couple, notably in Eph 5:23–25, whereby Paul draws upon an image customarily used to symbolize the unity of the Roman people, applying the notion of the husband as "head" of his wife to the unity and order of the church in its close relation to Christ.

A second motif in Paul is his emphasis upon the Holy Spirit as constitutive of the church. A relatively individualistic ecclesiology may dwell upon the personal relation to Christ brought about by the Holy Spirit, or upon the primacy of spiritual experience over institutionally sanctioned practices. On the other hand, the Spirit can be identified in some way with the church's leadership, for example, through Peter's confession and Jesus's declaration that Peter is the rock upon which the church is to be built in Matthew 16:18–19, or by reference to the story of the gift of the Spirit to the apostles in John 20:22–23. Another possibility has been to understand the Holy Spirit as active primarily within the tradition and the liturgy, as in the Eastern churches and some forms of modern Catholic and Anglican ecclesiology. What is common in every case is the acceptance of the Pauline belief that the presence of the Holy Spirit differentiates the church from all other communities, religious or otherwise.

A third motif, one often linked in the tradition with the second, is that of koinōnia, a word that can be variously translated. In 1 Corinthians 10:16, Paul uses koinōnia to refer to a "sharing" (or "participation") in Christ's body and blood; in 1 Corinthians 1:9, he writes of how the Corinthian believers had been drawn by God into the "fellowship" of his Son; in the final blessing of 2 Corinthians, he prays that they will experience the "communion" of the Holy Spirit; in Galatians 2:9, he and the church leadership mutually extend the right hand of "fellowship"; in Philippians 3:10, Paul asks that he may have a "sharing" in the sufferings of Christ. The common element, then, is union, both with God and among the members of the church, and in action, too. This motif has pervaded the Eastern Orthodox tradition and has recently become an important ecclesiological model in the West, especially among those seeking an ecclesiological ground for ecumenism (see Dulles 1991).

A rather different motif, though by no means necessarily inconsistent with any of the others, is favored especially among the churches of the Reformation, namely, the association of the church with the Word. This may draw upon either Paul's Hebraic understanding of the divine word as creative power (e.g., Col 3:16), or his often cited dictum that faith comes by hearing the preached word (Rom 10:17), or both. Here the church is conceived as the product or creation of the Word, with a concomitant emphasis upon preaching and Scripture.

Finally, the ordered ministry found in the Pastorals – deacon, presbyter and/or bishop – has been very influential. A significant early example can be found in the letters of Ignatius, a bishop of Antioch who died around the beginning of the second century. His concern to maintain unity within the churches and protect them from heresy leads him to develop a markedly hierarchical understanding of the church that reflects a threefold ministry, without which, he says, "the name of 'Church' is not given" (*To the Trallians* 3.1).[2] The church is centered upon the bishop, total obedience to whom unites all its members in the one true faith. The bishop is appointed by Jesus Christ, and represents his will (*To the Ephesians* 3.2). So "do nothing without the bishop" is Ignatius's constant refrain, complemented at times by "do nothing without the bishop and the presbyters" (e.g., *To the Magnesians* 7.1).

Augustine

In its form, if not in its substance, Ignatius's work is fairly typical of early theological reflection on the church. Like him, theologians writing in the pre-modern period presented their understanding of the church in piecemeal fashion, unsystematically, as they discussed other matters or some particular aspect of the church – in Ignatius's case, the episcopacy and church unity. Ecclesiologies in the form of free-standing, well-rounded treatises on the church are a modern phenomenon. Augustine is perhaps the great exception to this rule to the extent that his *City of God* is a kind of ecclesiology. But even in his case it is necessary to draw upon his other writings, especially his sermons and exegetical works, for a good understanding of his theology of the church.

Augustine (354–430), a bishop of Hippo in North Africa, has had an enormous influence on the Western ecclesiological tradition. He largely determined the main lines of the way Paul would be read and set out many of the issues and principles for ecclesiological inquiry for the pre-modern period and on into contemporary ecclesiology. His influence within ecclesiology is due in part to his complex and nuanced response to the situation in which his own church found itself, one very different from the Pauline communities. After years of persecution by the Roman authorities, the church had gone through heady days following the conversion of the Roman emperor Constantine in 312 and the subsequent establishment of Christianity as the religion of the Empire. While the Pauline churches had to grapple with the delayed parousia, the church now had to consider what recent events meant for the church's place and role within history.

In the East, Eusebius, a bishop of Caesarea who died around 340, wrote an *Ecclesiastical History*. This began with the New Testament period and concluded by celebrating the end of the persecutions and the triumph of the church as the work of providence, and lauding the "pious" emperor as the agent of God. In the West (and at the request of Augustine), Paulus Osorius drew up a similar, though rather less sophisticated history entitled *Seven Books Against the Pagans*, completed in 418. Osorius sought to show that God is on the side of the church, which he called the Body of Christ, over against those who do not believe. By his seventh book, Osorius makes clear that God works directly in history for the success of the church and for the success of those, such as the emperor Theodosius, who put down attempts to revive paganism. By contrast, God acts against those who do not believe, dashing them to pieces against the Rock that is Christ (1 Cor 10:4). The basic idea, then, is a quid pro quo: if we are faithful members of the church, all will be well for us; if not, not. Both these works would remain influential.

Augustine's far more nuanced understanding of history is derived from his theology, the subtlety of which is due in part to his careful reading and more extensive use of Paul, the author most cited in Augustine's discussions of ecclesiology. Augustine's basic doctrine of the church is the "whole Christ" (*Christus totus*). The church is united to Christ, the second person of the Trinity, as a body is united to its head, so as to form a single person: "*the Word was made flesh, and dwelled among us*. The Church is joined to that flesh, and Christ becomes the whole, head and body" (*Homilies on the First Epistle of John* 1.2; cf. Sermon 341.19). Thus "the whole Christ [exists] in the fullness of the Church, that is, as head and body, according to the completeness of a certain *perfect man* (Eph 4:13)" (Sermon 341.2).

If Christ is the head of the church, and together with his body forms, as it were, a complete person, it follows that the church must everywhere be one and the same, always the one body. It is one through time, from "Abel the just" till the end of time. It is also one spatially, catholic in the sense of universal, spread "throughout the whole world" (Sermon 341.19; also 198.55). This move helped Augustine challenge the ecclesiology of the Donatist sectarians. Donatism was a rigorist movement, prevalent especially in North Africa, that insisted upon the purity of the post-baptismal life of their clergy. They believed that bishops who had betrayed the faith in time of persecution in order to save themselves could no longer be bishops nor perform the sacraments validly. Consequently, the Donatists set up their own bishops in competition with those of the "Catholics," the group to which Augustine belonged. Augustine argued that if a church community is not joined with the one church, it cannot be in Christ and therefore cannot be a church. Those who separate themselves from the one church have separated themselves from the one body of Christ.

For Augustine, the church encompasses the saints in heaven. However, the heavenly and the earthly church have distinct attributes. The latter is in a state of "pilgrimage," and is to complete the sufferings of Christ (Sermon 341.20, citing Col 1:24). The church in heaven is pure; the church on earth is evidently not. The distinction between two loves – love for God or love for something this-worldly – is the primary theme of Augustine's *City of God*. It is their love of God that defines the membership of the City of God. (This "city" seems to be identical with the Body of Christ for Augustine.) Since the members of the church on earth may have the one or the other love, the pilgrim church, even though it is one, is a mixed group, not all of whom are members of the Body of Christ. Thus Augustine maintains an eschatological element in his ecclesiology, rejecting Eusebian and Orosian contentment with the establishment of the church within the empire ruled by a Christian emperor. Consistent with Romans 13, Augustine believes it is indeed a blessing to be ruled by a Christian prince. But true blessings come only in the state of glory, in heaven (*City of God*, book 5).

It is thus arguable that Augustine and the tradition he influenced tend to portray the church as rather more complex in its membership than it is for Paul – even though they account for the complexity in largely Pauline terms. Paul seems unconcerned to distinguish among the "saints" he addresses even in his letters to the less-than-saintly Corinthians. To be sure, Augustine acknowledges that saints cannot be firmly distinguished from those who do not belong in the Body of Christ, for judgment is God's alone. But in developing the notion of the mixed body, he seems less optimistic than Paul. This is further indicated by the way Augustine treats some Pauline distinctions in a way that had become fairly commonplace by his time, and which would be taken for granted until the Reformation. In 1 Corinthians 7, Paul contends that it is better to remain unmarried. He offers two reasons. First, "the impending crisis" (v. 26) (the parousia) suggests it is not an appropriate time to get married and bear children. Second, he contends that those who are married are concerned for their spouse and worldly matters, while the unmarried are more able to focus on "the affairs of the Lord" (v. 34). Augustine takes this a step further to speak of the unmarried as those "who profess a more perfect life" (*City of God* 1.9). He admits that the unmarried can still be sinful, of course. But he reads Paul's text as supporting the notion of two distinct ways of being Christian, one of which, celibacy, is better than the other. Certainly, Augustine regards marriage as a good, and his preference for celibacy is not based on sex as itself something sinful. Rather, the problem with marriage is the couple's love for one another, for something this-worldly, rather than solely for God. With this move – found elsewhere among the Fathers, and based on Paul there, too – arose the arguably non-Pauline (1 Cor) notion of two groups within the church: those, the superior, who are on a spiritual path; and the inferior remainder, who are concerned with worldly matters.

John of Damascus

John of Damascus (John Damascene), the last of the Greek Fathers, who died about 749, wrote a treatise the third part of which, *On the Orthodox Faith* (*OF*), achieved wide circulation in the West as well as the East and is, in effect, a summary of Eastern patristic theology. Living in Damascus, a Muslim city, before retiring to a monastery, John had a thorough knowledge of Islam and the Koran, and was involved in the iconoclast controversy. In spite of this, his work contains little theological reflection directly on the church as such. This may well be due to his Orthodox view that the church is not something usefully seen as a distinct entity over against others. Rather, what is distinctive about Christianity is its tradition, the Christian way of life embodied in the faith, practices, and spirituality of its members. The tradition includes unwritten elements

(*OF* 4.16, citing 2 Thess 2:14; 1 Cor 11:2). Where John writes of the church, the Pauline *koinōnia* motif is evident, especially in relation to baptism and the Eucharist. Thus the eucharistic elements, when received worthily, purify us so that "we become one with the body of the Lord and with His spirit, and we become the body of Christ" (*OF* 4.13). We participate in the divinity of Jesus through the eucharist, which is rightly called communion (*koinōnia*) "because of our having communion through it with Christ and partaking both of His flesh and His divinity, and because through it we have communion with and are united to one another. For, since we partake of one bread, we all become one body of Christ and one blood and members of one another and are accounted of the same body with Christ" (*OF* 4.13).

John also reflects the tradition mentioned above in valuing celibacy over married life. He agrees with Paul and Augustine that marriage is good, for it raises up children and helps to do away with fornication (1 Cor 7:2). But "virginity is as much more honorable than marriage as the angel is superior to man." Indeed, "Christ himself is the glory of virginity" (*OF* 4.24). In this, John arguably moves a little beyond Augustine's position and perhaps further yet from Paul. For he seems to suggest that sex itself, rather than the object of one's love, is that which differentiates between the two states of life, making the distinction firmer and more visible.

Thomas Aquinas

While Thomas Aquinas (d. 1274) drew heavily upon Augustine and Augustine's reading of Paul, he, too, had to address a new situation that included the formation of a substantial body of canon law, the Western rediscovery of Aristotle, and, perhaps most significant, the development of Christendom. With regard to Christendom: in his *Chronicon*, Otto of Freising (d. ca. 1158) had drawn upon Orosius and Augustine to give an account of history using the image of the two cities. For Otto, however, these are differentiated as Christianity and paganism rather than love of God and love of created things. As Otto describes the rise of the Holy Roman Empire, the relatively complete dominance of Christianity in all areas of life makes him think – he tells us – that he has in fact written the history of only one city, namely, the church, for the church as an institution and a way of life had encompassed all other institutions and ways of life within it: the idea, that is, of Christendom. At the same time, and in marked contrast, Aquinas faced a highly speculative, eschatological theory developed by Joachim of Fiore (d. ca. 1202). According to Joachim, a third, final age, the age of the Holy Spirit and love, is due very soon. The new age would transcend the age of the Son and the New Testament, which had in turn moved beyond the age of the Father and the Old Testament.

The guidance of Paul is evident as Thomas Aquinas addresses these and other issues in relation to the Church. The biblical orientation of his theology and the significance of his biblical commentaries for a proper understanding of Thomas's work are now generally recognized after centuries of misunderstanding by various schools of Thomism. As Francesca A. Murphy notes, Thomas's "commentary on Paul's letters can be seen to fashion a thorough survey of his ecclesiology" (2005, 167), which can help guide the reading of his more systematic works. While Thomas did not write a systematic ecclesiology, a relatively extended treatment of the church can be found in the *Summa theologiae*, in the third part, question 8, which is devoted to the "Grace of Christ" as the "Head of the Church." Here the cited scriptural texts are unusually numerous and are drawn from the full range of Pauline texts.

In scholastic fashion, Thomas treats this question by dividing it up into separate articles in what is a particularly dense treatment even for him. In the first article, he notes that the church is constituted by its relation to the Trinity: Christ is the head of the church (citing Eph 1:22 ["And he ... has made him the head over all things for the Church"] and related texts), while the Holy Spirit "is likened to the heart" since "He invisibly quickens and unifies the Church," most especially through the gift of love (cf. Rom 8:11). While Thomas explicitly acknowledges the metaphorical nature of the notion of Christ's "headship" and the church as "body," he stresses its visibility: "Christ is likened to the Head in His visible nature in which man is set over man." At the same time, Christ is head because he is divine. He is not head simply in his humanity, as if, for example, he were its founder, for Christ's humanity is but the personal instrument of his divinity. Christ is the head of the church in that he is the sole source and cause of any and all grace, both in his divinity and in his humanity as the firstborn who bestows the fruits of his salvation (Rom 8:29).

Christ is head of the church in three ways and two modes. Visibly, he is head in terms of order (rank), perfection (superiority over the church), and power, in the way a ruler is called head of his people. This threefold headship is also spiritual. Christ is higher in order because nearer God; he is superior in having the fullness of grace; and he has the power to bestow grace on others. In other words, as Thomas says in the second article, Christ works upon us in every way, upon our bodies as well as our souls – here citing Philippians 3:21: "he will transform the body of our humiliation that it may be conformed to the body of his glory." The church, then, cannot be merely spiritual (here Thomas may be thinking of Joachim of Fiore), but neither can it be merely an institution (against any simple-minded Christendom thinking). We are members of the church in both body and soul, and constituted as such by being united with Christ as both human and divine.

The third article addresses the question whether Christ is the head of all humanity – in other words, whether the church is universal in extent. The answer is: yes, but "diversely." Thomas is guided here by a number of Pauline texts. Ephesians 5:25 and 27 indicate a distinction between the heavenly and the earthly church, for while the former may be without spot or wrinkle, the latter clearly is not. Thomas cites 1 Timothy 4:10 and 1 John 2:2 in favor of the universality of salvation in Jesus Christ, and since the church is the locus of salvation, Christ's headship of his body must be universal. In the Timothy passage, Paul adds the qualifying "especially of those who believe," which prompts Thomas's "diversely." Modifying Augustine in light of these texts, he notes that the church, as the "mystical body" of Christ, consists of absolutely everyone, from the "beginning of the world until its end." However, some are more united with Christ than others. Those who are already in heaven are united to Christ in glory. Those on earth who have charity – the love for others given by the Holy Spirit, whom Thomas calls "Love" – are united to Christ in the fullest way on earth. Those who have faith but are sinners or who have no charity are not actually but only potentially united. Finally, some of those who are not baptized are not yet united but are predestined to be, while others are not so predestined and so will never be. Thomas also affirms Israel's membership, addressing Romans 9–11 by arguing the "ancient Fathers" (of the Old Testament) had the same love and faith as "we" do, and so belong to the same church. He then (in the fourth article) draws upon Colossians 2:10 (Christ is head over all principalities and powers) to confirm that angels are also members of the church.

Aquinas also defines the church as the congregation of the faithful, *congregatio fidelium*, the body of people who are set apart by their faith. They are set apart by God, that is, as a "communion of saints" rather than a mere association of the like-minded, since faith is a theological virtue, infused by God, and cannot be acquired through natural means. The members of the church on earth are further distinguished from the saints in heaven by the fact that they "walk by faith, not by sight" (2 Cor 5:7). Following 1 Corinthians 13:12 ("For now we see in a mirror, dimly, but then we will see face to face"), he contrasts those in heaven as the *comprehensores*, those who see ("comprehend" or "know") God directly, with ourselves, who know God only in faith.

In the sixth article, Thomas distinguishes between Christ, who is head of the church, and the church leadership, the bishops and the pope. Citing 2 Corinthians 2:10, in which Paul writes of his forgiving people "in the person [presence] of Christ,"[3] and v. 20, in which God is said to make his appeal "through us," Thomas argues the authority of the leaders is not their own. They are unlike Christ, who alone can move us inwardly by his Spirit, but like him in that they can provide "exterior guidance." Bishops do so for a particular place, their diocese; the pope does so for a particular time, during his reign. Neither may do so on their own authority.

Pope Boniface

Pope Boniface VIII's bull, *Unam Sanctam*, written in 1302 to justify his authority over King Phillip the Fair of France, is a good example of a rather different kind of medieval ecclesiology, the aim of which was to centralize all power in the papacy. Boniface sought to secure acceptance of the notion of the "plenitude of power" asserted by popes earlier in the thirteenth century – notably, Innocent III – according to whom all authority and final judgment lie with the pope. Interestingly, Boniface's text draws heavily upon Paul to make the argument.[4] Citing Romans 13:1 ("for there is no authority except from God, and those authorities that exist have been instituted by God"), Boniface argues that the two "swords," that is, the two kinds of authority, spiritual and secular, both derive from God. Both powers, however, have been given by God to the church, since (here Boniface follows the view of Christendom noted earlier) the church encompasses all society and thus is the source of both powers: "There had been at the time of the deluge only one ark of Noah, prefiguring the one Church, which ark, having been finished to a single cubit, had only one pilot and guide, i.e., Noah, and we read that, outside of this ark, all that subsisted on the earth was destroyed." Boniface cites the hierarchical structure of 1 Corinthians 11:3, arguing the Church "represents one sole mystical body whose Head is Christ and the head of Christ is God." Encompassing all society, the Church has one Lord, one faith, one baptism (Eph 4:5).

The secular authority must be subordinated to the ecclesiastical because it is the naturally inferior power and needs the latter's guidance. Thus, "if the terrestrial power err, it will be judged by the spiritual power; but if a minor spiritual power [i.e., a member of the lower clergy] err, it will be judged by a superior spiritual power; but if the highest power of all [the papacy] err, it can be judged only by God, and not by man, according to the testimony of the Apostle: 'Those who are spiritual discern all things, and they are themselves subject to no one else's scrutiny' (1 Cor 2:15)." And thus it follows that "it is absolutely necessary for salvation that every human creature be subject to the Roman Pontiff."

Martin Luther

The ecclesiology of Martin Luther (1483–1546) recovers many elements of Paul's theology of the church – or, perhaps better, many *other* elements, or elements inter- preted differently and often explicitly over against those appropriated by the Roman hierarchical institutionalism of his day, since the controversy with Rome clearly informs Luther's reading of Paul. Here we can look briefly at Lutheran ecclesiology in its devel- oped form in *The Book of Concord*, especially the Augsburg Confession (*AC*, 1530) and its Apology (*Ap*, 1531), the Large Confession (*LC*, 1529, written by Luther),[5] and the work of the Lutheran scholastics in the Schmid collection (Schmid 1899), since these together set out the basic position for subsequent generations of Lutherans.

Lutheran ecclesiology rejects the Roman identification of the Holy Spirit's work with the established practices of the church and the institutions and offices of the leadership – that is, with what was called the "visible" church. Against the counter-Reformation ecclesiology of Cardinal Belharmine, the church is "not merely an association of outward ties and rites," but "an association of faith and of the Holy Spirit in men's hearts" (*Ap* 169), and in that sense is invisible (Schmid 1899, 593). The church, then, is the community formed by the active presence of the Holy Spirit (*Ap* 172). At the same time, Luther and his followers faced what they considered to be the excessive enthusi- asm of the spiritualizing sectarians (the *Schwärmerei*), who supported their own posi- tion on the basis of many of the same Pauline texts. Accordingly, the Lutherans argued that, while "the church is a spiritual people, separated from the heathen not by civil rites but by being God's true people, reborn by the Holy Spirit," it is also not a "Platonic republic" (*Ap* 170–171). The church really exists, and visibly so. Furthermore, the true church can be known and pointed to by its marks, which are "the pure teaching of the Gospel and the sacraments" (*Ap* 171). To be sure, the visible signs are not of themselves constitutive of the church, yet it is necessary for everyone to belong to the visible com- munity (Schmid 1899, 595). In this way, the Lutheran reformers attempt to steer a course between Roman Catholicism and the radical reformation.[6]

In this effort, they are guided throughout by Pauline ecclesiological motifs. The defi- nition of the church is the Body of Christ (citing Eph 1:22, 23), though Luther generally preferred "community" to the word "church." He also thought "community" is a better translation of *communio* than "communion." Thus one should say "community of saints" rather than the usual creedal formula (*LC* 416–417). Luther believed there is "on earth a little holy flock or community of pure saints under one head, Christ. It is called together by the Holy Spirit," who makes us "participant[s] and co-partner[s]" and "creates and increases [our] sanctification" (*LC* 417). The church is thus the locus and means of our sanctification by the power of the Holy Spirit. However, although this community is indeed the "living body of Christ," there are within it those who are "not ruled by the Spirit of Christ" (*Ap* 170–171). Thus the church on earth is a mixed body.

Lutheran ecclesiology emphasizes the active presence of God in constituting the Christian community. As a result, it more clearly separates the Holy Spirit from the tradition and its normative practices and institutions. The authority of bishops is derived not from their office but from their role in teaching and administering the sacraments of faith. Their authority has therefore nothing to do with temporal power; the two powers and functions should be kept clearly separate (*AC* 82–83, citing Rom 1:16; Phil 3:20; 2 Cor 10:4, 5; etc.). Human traditions may be useful, but they are not "necessary for righteousness before God" (*Ap* 175, citing Rom 14:17). Yet preaching the Word and administering the sacraments are vital, for "where Christ is not preached, there is no Holy Spirit to create, call, and gather the Christian Church, and outside it no one can come to the Lord Christ" (*LC* 416). Indeed, "the chief worship of God is the preaching of the Gospel" (*Ap* 221), for it is by the church's preaching that the Word of God comes to us and makes himself heard.

With the relativizing of church traditions and the emphasis on the active presence of the Holy Spirit, Lutheran ecclesiology established the principle that the church should undertake continual self-reform (*ecclesia semper reformanda*). One of the key reforms of the Reformation churches was to dissolve the distinction between two states of life, clerical and lay, thus rejecting the notion that adopting a clerical or religious life renders one more likely to be holy than ordinary folk (see, e.g., *Ap* 268–281). This reform was based on two main doctrines: baptism (as a work of the Spirit) and baptismal faith are sufficient for justification; and sanctification is not ours to achieve but, again, is the work of the Holy Spirit – both doctrines, of course, drawn from Paul.

Friedrich Schleiermacher

The Reformed theologian Friedrich Schleiermacher (1768–1834) has been called "the father of modern theology" because he developed a new theological method that addressed Kant's critique of the possibility and limits of religious knowledge. His method draws in part upon the romantic philosophy then current in Germany, with its focus upon the inner life of the imagination and the organic nature of communities and cultures. This informs the ecclesiology of his mature work, *The Christian Faith*, in which Pauline influence is also evident to some degree, particularly in an emphasis upon the Spirit as constitutive of the church in the lived experience of the Christian community.

According to Schleiermacher, the "new life" of the Christian individual is essentially communal because it necessarily springs from within the life of the church, which in turn is dependent upon the experience of the apostles, and they in turn on the life of Jesus, the Redeemer (1928, 525). Believers may be quite different from one another, but the Holy Spirit works within the church to bring about a palpable movement toward unity. The unity is fundamentally less in externals – doctrines and practices – than in their source, the Christian "God-Consciousness," which distinguishes the church from the world – its "antithesis" – until the world's consummation. Schleiermacher seems at times to characterize the Holy Spirit as virtually identical to the spirit of the community, defining it at one point as "the vital unity of the Christian fellowship as a moral personality" (535). Thus not only is the Spirit the source of faith, but it also "comes through faith" (577). It is the Spirit that makes the church visible as an "image" of the Redeemer and justifies the metaphor of the church as the Body of Christ (580).

Johann Adam Möhler

Some aspects of Schleiermacher's pneumatological ecclesiology had a significant though somewhat delayed impact on Roman Catholic ecclesiology through their influence on a younger Catholic contemporary, Johann Adam Möhler (1796–1838). Möhler's seminal work, *Unity in the Church or The Principle of Catholicism* (UC, 1825)[7] is in effect an extended exposition of Paul's *koinōnia* motif and the church-constituting presence of the Holy Spirit. Paul is read through the Fathers, since Möhler intended UC to recover forgotten aspects of the patristic tradition rather than, as Schleiermacher, to be a new approach responding to Kant.

According to Möhler, Paul's ecclesiology stressed the underlying unity of the church within its visible diversity. Perhaps the most basic text for him is Eph 4:4: "There is one body and one Spirit." Möhler defines the church as the Body of Christ, but he dwells upon the pneumatological aspect of this motif. Christ is "the life-giving and life-forming principle to which his true disciples are related, as the spirit in a person is to the body, its image, its impression and expression" (82). Each person comes to be a Christian by "the influence of the Church community enlivened by the Holy Spirit" (92), which generates a "new life principle" (98). With 1 Corinthians 2:11–12, then, it is the Spirit of Christ who enables us to know God truly in Christ (170).

Möhler develops the *koinōnia* principle in terms of an inner-to-outer dynamic. The Spirit is not something visible as such, nor is it the principle of unity of an association of the like-minded. Rather, it is the life force of an organic community informed by love: "The Church is the external, visible structure of a holy, living power, of love, the body of the spirit of believers forming itself from the interior externally" (209). The visible aspects of the church are vital, to be sure; to think of the church as primarily invisible would be to mistake the nature of Christianity (211). Furthermore, the historical development of the hierarchy represents a genuine insight into the essential aspect of the church, for a "determined, ordered and continual teaching office" is evidently vital for the continuing tradition (214). Indeed, the bishop is an "image" of the organic unity that pertains among believers (218). Expressions of the faith are necessary for faith to communicate itself (96, citing Rom 10:17). Yet because the inner life is finally prior to its expression, the church is not based upon Scripture, but rather Scripture reflects the inner experience of the Spirit the apostles had and that believers too now have as they participate in the *koinōnia* of the Holy Spirit that is the church. It follows, then, that those outside the church cannot understand Scripture since they lack the Spirit. However, expressing and discussing their faith is also necessary for believers to understand it better, a point Möhler makes in commenting on Romans 1:10–12, where Paul seeks to come to Rome to have mutual encouragement and strengthening in the Spirit (101).

There is, then, a fundamental unity within diversity: church unity lies in its inner depths. The expressions of that unity grow in both complexity and clarity as the church is guided through its history by the Spirit. Each individual member may be different, yet all share the basic unity in communion. On this view, the Protestant Reformation appears largely misconceived because it was overly concerned with externals as such, rather than upon their organic relation to the inner spirit (201, 264). But equally mistaken were those Catholics who countered the Reformation by appealing to the Middle Ages, as if the external condition of the church at that time was always necessary. Both groups missed "the forming principle, the inner character of the constitution of the Church": the Holy Spirit (266).

Karl Barth

The ecclesiology of Karl Barth (1886–1968) is thoroughly informed by Pauline texts. Barth rejected the liberal Protestantism of his teachers in part because they actively supported German militarism in the lead-up to World War I. He saw this as more than a moral failure; it displayed the bankruptcy of theological premises that could provide little or no critical leverage against the domestication of the churches by the nation-state. In response, he sought to recover a more robust sense of the "god-ness" of God. Writing two rather different commentaries on Roman early in his career, Barth asserted the "infinite qualitative distinction" between God and humanity. God is "wholly other," and as such is the crisis (judgment) of all human projects and efforts at transcendence, including the church.

Though his ecclesiology was to remain critical and eschatological, by 1930 or so Barth had founded his theology on the self-communication of God in Jesus Christ, which is made known to the church by the witness of Scripture and the active presence of the Holy Spirit. Thus his mature ecclesiology, much of which is laid out in the fourth volume of the *Church Dogmatics*, builds on the principle that it "is grounded, critically limited, but also positively determined by Christology" (*CD* 4.3.786). This principle he owes primarily to Paul, as the small-print exegetical passages indicate, especially a detailed analysis of "the remarkable New Testament expression *sōma Christou* [body of Christ]" that is centered on 1 Corinthians 12:19 (4.1.662–668). It is only as Christ's body that the church is truly the church; it has no alternative basis, form, or *telos* (goal). Nonetheless, the church really *is* the body of Christ, not merely metaphorically but actually, for it is, in Barth's often-used phrase, the "earthly-historical form of [Christ's] existence" (e.g., 4.2.654). This does not mean, against (Barth's understanding of) Roman Catholic teaching, that the church is, as it were, another Christ or in Christ's place. It is Christ as such in this human communal form. Christ thus exists both visibly, against both a purely inward and private Christianity, and invisibly, against overly institutional ecclesiologies.

For Barth, it follows from this firmly realistic understanding of the Body of Christ that one cannot be a member of the church on the basis of some human action, such as baptism or a holy way of life. We are members of the church (or, as Barth prefers, the Christian "community") because "thereto elected by the Lord, called by His Word, and constituted by His Spirit" (4.1.696), not because some required action is performed by us. He notes, further, that there are no human standards by which we can judge whether or not our fellow-Christians are among the true members of the Body of Christ and thus among the saints. So we can remain hopeful in spite of what seems evidence for limited membership (4.1.698). Following his detailed exegesis of Romans 9–11, Barth insists that Israel is also within the body of Christ. Indeed, it is only together *with* Israel that the Christian community is the church (4.1.671, citing Gal 6:16; Rom 11:26). The scandal is that they are not together, a scandal exacerbated by the incomprehensible disunity within the Christian community.

The Christian community is the church insofar as it is in relation to Christ, as it hears and is enabled to hear the Word of God. It is truly the mystery of Christ: "according to the familiar Pauline formula, the community exists *en Christō* [in Christ]" (4.3.757). It cannot be, then, as if Jesus simply founded the church, nor even as if Christ *supports* the church's efforts by his grace. The church is *solely* the body of Christ, without remainder. It is Christ's existence encompassing and informing our own existence and activity, which thereby becomes through grace a "correspondence" to what has been already achieved in Christ. Certainly our action is vital, but it is the Holy Spirit that gathers, builds up, and maintains the church (4.2.641). Christ is in the midst of "the earthly-historical *communio sanctorum* [communion of saints]" by his Spirit (4.1.671). The Spirit, however, does not belong to the church. Nor is it attached to some part of it, such as an office or a liturgical practice. The Holy Spirit is not "a property of one or many exalted members of the community which, without further ado, can be transferred by them into the power of others – simply because it has been institutionally arranged in this way, and simply because it takes place with due legality and ritual" – here Barth is reading Matthew 16:18–20 in light of 1 Corinthians 12 and Romans 12 (4.1.717). As one might expect, then, Barth denies that Paul supports a notion of someone in authority as a representative of Christ or as having the power to bring about what only Christ can. Rather, Paul's leadership role simply "makes the authority of Jesus Christ visible and audible in the Churches" and only in that limited way is in Christ's place (4.1.673; cf. 2 Cor 5:20).

Barth emphasizes this by writing of the "event" of the "real presence" of the Spirit that constitutes the church. He does not deny continuity – the church is not episodic or punctilio. He is concerned to counter the complacent assumption that the Spirit's presence is simply there, settled in, to be "cherished" (4.1.682). The church is the "true Church" that "arises and is only when the Holy Spirit works – the quickening power of the living Lord Jesus Christ" (4.2.617; the small-print discussion of Eph 4:12–15 on pp. 623–626 supplies the ground for this).

Vatican II (1962–1965)

By the mid-twentieth century, it became clear – at least to Pope John XXIII – that the Roman Catholic Church faced new social developments that needed a thoughtful and substantive response. The pope called together the Second Vatican Council in part to complete the work of the First Vatican Council (1869–1870) and to address matters arising from its reception. The earlier council was held in the midst of political and social challenges to papal power (in its secular as well as spiritual form), and its documents are concerned to defend the faith against attack. It defines some ecclesiologically significant doctrines, not least the infallibility of the pope when speaking *ex cathedra*, as head of the church. By contrast, the Second Vatican Council reflects a far more hopeful view of the relation between church and world, while also recovering elements of the theological tradition that had been eclipsed in the previous three or four centuries. Some of these elements are clearly Pauline in origin, including a modified eschatological understanding of the church and various Pauline motifs reaffirmed during the Reformation.

The Council's primary ecclesiological texts are *Lumen Gentium (LG)*, the Dogmatic Constitution on the Church, and *Gaudium et Spes (GS)*, the Pastoral Constitution on the Church in the World of Today. In both, Pauline texts are frequently cited. In the first chapter of *LG*, on the mystery of the church, the election of those to the church is firmly set within Christology (drawing on Col 1:15 and Rom 8:29). The elect have been chosen in Christ, in whom the Father restores all things (Eph 1:4, 5, 10). Their redemption is effected by the liturgy (1 Cor 5:7; 10:17), through which their communion with Christ and unity with one another (Rom 12:5) are "expressed and brought about." Their sanctification is brought about by the Holy Spirit (Eph 2:18), who dwells in the church and in the hearts of its members "as in a temple" (1 Cor 3:16; 6:19). It is the Spirit that renews the church and leads "her to perfect union with her spouse." Here on earth, though, the church is like an "exile," her life in Christ hidden until "she appears in glory with her spouse" (Col 3:1–4).

The second chapter of *LG* discusses the church under the rubric of the People of God. All people are members of the People of God, including those who have not accepted the gospel. The third chapter discusses and affirms the hierarchical ordering of the church, but this is complemented by a fourth chapter on the laity. There we read that it is the Spirit who apportions gifts to each Christian (1 Cor 12:11), and always for the common good (1 Cor 12:7). The church is one body with many members, having "true equality" of dignity and action, because everyone is inspired by the one Spirit (1 Cor 12:11). The work of the laity is vital because they are the children of God (Rom 8:21). Chapter 5 insists that all members of the church, not just the clergy, are called to holiness (1 Thess.4:3; Eph 1:4) and to lead lives as befits the "saints" (Eph 5:3). Indeed, "all the faithful, of whatever rank or status, are called to the fullness of the Christian life and to the perfection of charity" (Rom 5:5; 13:10; Col 3:14). In and through their love for one another and their children, and their work within their communities, married couples may perform the valuable task of evangelizing the world. Here the Council relativizes the earlier understanding of the church as divided between higher and lower states of life, and it does so on the basis of Pauline texts.

Conclusion

A few conclusions are suggested by this necessarily brief and fragmentary survey. It is evident that Paul's texts are susceptible to readings that support a fairly wide variety of ecclesiologies, many of which conflict in various ways. Despite what some church people have asserted, the tradition has not achieved consensus in accepting a single ecclesiology, nor has anyone ever shown that a single ecclesiology necessarily follows from the Pauline text (nor, by extension, from Scripture more generally). This may well be a very good thing. For if it is possible that Paul can be interpreted diversely yet faithfully, it is likely that his texts are rich enough to inform the range of theological understandings of the church needed for Christians to live the gospel together in diverse contexts. Furthermore, his texts can inform a variety of ways of being church within more or less similar contexts, different ways that constitute "experiments," as it were, in Christian communal living.

It may be possible to argue that ecclesiologies that have proved their significance and adaptability by their longevity tend to display a greater willingness to listen to and be truly guided by Paul's texts rather than distorting or ignoring them. As the church faces new situations and challenges, it should continue to turn to Paul in order to discern its nature, function, and shape. And it would seem more than likely that one necessary – though not sufficient – condition of the success of any future ecclesiology is that it draw upon more than one of the Pauline motifs, preferably all of them.

Notes

1   I use the name "Paul" to refer to whoever wrote the New Testament texts attributed to Paul without making any judgment as to who in fact wrote them. Biblical quotations are taken from the New Revised Standard Version.
2   Translations from Ignatius are taken from the Loeb edition of *The Apostolic Fathers*, edited by Kirsopp Lake (Cambridge, Mass.: Harvard University Press, 1970).
3   The Vulgate – used by Thomas – has "in persona Christi," the Greek *en prosōpō Christou*, the latter translated by the NRSV as "in the presence of Christ."
4   *Unam Sanctam* can be found at: http://www.fordham.edu/halsall/source/b8-unam.html, which also reproduces a rather defensive article about the bull from the 1913 edition of the Catholic Encyclopaedia. I have replaced the site's translation of Scripture by that of the NRSV.
5   Numbers in this section refer to the pages in *The Book of Concord* edited by Tappert (1959).
6   There is, of course, something like a formal parallel here (but no more) with the Pauline tradition facing the "Judaizers," on the one hand, and the spiritual elites, on the other.
7   *UC* numbers in this section refer to Erb's 1996 translation (see Möhler 1996). Möhler's work became influential only in the twentieth century, beginning with the *Ressourcement* movement and the shift away from neo-Scholastic methods. See Doyle 2000.

References

Augustine. 1950. *The City of God: Books I–VII.* Translated by Demetrius B. Zema and Gerald G. Walsh. New York: Fathers of the Church.

Augustine. 1979–1997. *The Works of Saint Augustine*. Part III, Volumes 1–11: *Sermons*. Translated by Edmund Hill. Hyde Park, NY: New City.

Augustine. 2008. *The Works of Saint Augustine*. Part III, Volume 14: *Homilies on the First Epistle of John*. Translated by Boniface Ramsey. Hyde Park, NY: New City.

Barth, Karl. 1936–1977. *Church Dogmatics*. Edinburgh: T. & T. Clark.

Doyle, Dennis M. 2000. *Communion Ecclesiology: Visions and Versions*. Maryknoll, NY: Orbis.

Dulles, Avery. 1991. Communion. Pages 206–209 in *Dictionary of the Ecumenical Movement*. Edited by Nicholas Lossky, José Míguez Bonino, John Pobee, et al. Geneva: WCC; Grand Rapids: Eerdmans.

John of Damascus. 1958. *Writings*. Translated by Frederic H. Chase. New York: Fathers of the Church.

Möhler, Johann Adam. 1996. *Unity in the Church or The Principle of Catholicism Presented in the Spirit of the Church Fathers of the First Three Centuries*. Edited and translated by Peter C. Erb. Washington, DC: Catholic University of America Press.

Murphy, Francesca Aran. 2005. Thomas' Commentaries on Philemon, 1 and 2 Thessalonians and Philippians. Pages 167–196 in *Aquinas on Scripture: An Introduction to his Biblical Commentaries*. Edited by Thomas G. Weinandy, Daniel A. Keating, and John P. Yocum. New York: T. & T. Clark.

Schleiermacher, Friedrich. 1928. *The Christian Faith*. Edinburgh: T. & T. Clark.

Schmid, Heinrich. 1899. *The Doctrinal Theology of the Evangelical Lutheran Church*. Minneapolis: Augsburg.

Second Vatican Council. 1966. *The Teachings of the Second Vatican Council: Complete Texts of the Constitutions, Decrees, and Declarations*. Introduced by Gregory Baum. Westminster, Md.: Newman.

Tappert, Theodore G., editor. 1959. *The Book of Concord: The Confessions of the Evangelical Lutheran Church*. Philadelphia: Fortress.

Thomas Aquinas. 1948. *Summa Theologica*. 5 volumes. Translated by Fathers of the English Dominican Province. New York: Benziger.

Index

The Blackwell Companion to Paul, First Edition. Edited by Stephen Westerholm.
© 2011 Blackwell Publishing Ltd. Published 2011 by Blackwell Publishing Ltd.